Economics

SECOND EDITION

Economics

JOSEPH E. STIGLITZ

SECOND EDITION

STANFORD UNIVERSITY

W · W · NORTON & COMPANY · NEW YORK · LONDON

To Jane,
my harshest critic and best friend,
from whom I have learned the strengths and limits of economics;

and to
Julia, Jed, Michael, and Siobhan
in the hope, and belief, that a better understanding of economics
will lead to a better world for them to inherit.

Copyright © 1997, 1993 by W. W. Norton & Company, Inc.
All rights reserved.
Printed in the United States of America.

The text of this book is composed in Zapf Book
with the display set in Kabel
Composition by TSI
Manufacturing by Quebecor Hawkins
Book design by Antonina Krass
Cover painting: Laszlo Moholy-Nagy, *LIS*, 1922
Oil on canvas, 131 × 100 centimeters
Courtesy of the Kunsthaus, Zurich
Special thanks to Hattula Moholy-Nagy

Library of Congress Cataloging-in-Publication Data

Stiglitz, Joseph E.
    Economics / Joseph Stiglitz.—2nd ed.
        p.   cm.
    Includes index.
    1. Economics.   I. Title.
    HB171.5.S884   1996
    330—dc20   95-15370

ISBN 0-393-96895-2

W. W. Norton & Company, Inc., 500 Fifth Avenue, New York, N.Y. 10110
    http://www.wwnorton.com
W. W. Norton & Company Ltd., 10 Coptic Street, London WCIA IPU

2 3 4 5 6 7 8 9 0

ABOUT THE AUTHOR:

Internationally recognized as one of the leading economists of his generation, Joseph Stiglitz has made important contributions to virtually all of the major subdisciplines of economics: macroeconomics, monetary economics, public and corporate finance, trade, development, and industrial organization. After teaching at Yale, Princeton, and Oxford, in 1988 he accepted a position at Stanford University, where he has taught a wide variety of courses reflecting his broad interests, including Economics 1, one of the most popular courses on campus. In 1995, President Clinton asked him to serve as his chief economic adviser, appointing him Chairman of the Council of Economic Advisers and a member of the cabinet. In early 1997, Joseph Stiglitz will become the chief economist at the World Bank. Professor Stiglitz is the author and editor of hundreds of scholarly articles and books, including the best-selling undergraduate text *Economics of the Public Sector* (Norton) and, with Anthony Atkinson, *Lectures in Public Economics*. He is founding editor of the *Journal of Economic Perspectives,* established in 1987 to lower the barriers of specialization erected by other major economic journals, and a former vice president of the American Economic Association. Among his many prizes and awards, Professor Stiglitz has received the American Economic Association's John Bates Clark Award, given to the economist under forty who has made the most significant contributions to economics. Joe Stiglitz lives in Washington, D.C. with his wife and four children.

CONTENTS IN BRIEF

CONTENTS

CHAPTER **2**   THINKING LIKE AN ECONOMIST • 27

CHAPTER **3**   TRADE • 52

CHAPTER **4**   DEMAND, SUPPLY, AND PRICE • 71

CHAPTER **5** USING DEMAND AND SUPPLY • 96

CHAPTER **6** TIME AND RISK • 122

CHAPTER 7 THE PUBLIC SECTOR • 143

PART TWO

PERFECT MARKETS

CHAPTER 8 THE CONSUMPTION DECISION • 171

CHAPTER **9** LABOR SUPPLY AND
SAVINGS • 199

CHAPTER **10** A STUDENT'S GUIDE TO
INVESTING • 226

CHAPTER **11** THE FIRM'S COSTS • 250

CHAPTER **12** PRODUCTION • 281

CHAPTER **13** COMPETITIVE EQUILIBRIUM • 309

PART THREE

IMPERFECT MARKETS

CHAPTER **19** IMPERFECTIONS IN THE LABOR MARKET ● 454

CHAPTER **20** FINANCING, CONTROLLING, AND MANAGING THE FIRM ● 475

PART FOUR

POLICY ISSUES

PART FIVE

FULL-EMPLOYMENT MACROECONOMICS

CHAPTER **24** MACROECONOMIC GOALS AND MEASURES • 563

CHAPTER **25** THE FULL-EMPLOYMENT MODEL • 590

CHAPTER **26**   USING THE FULL-EMPLOYMENT MODEL • 617

PART SIX

UNEMPLOYMENT MACROECONOMICS

CHAPTER **27**   OVERVIEW OF UNEMPLOYMENT MACROECONOMICS • 639

CHAPTER **28** AGGREGATE DEMAND • 662

CHAPTER **29** CONSUMPTION AND
INVESTMENT • 690

CHAPTER **30** MONEY, BANKING, AND CREDIT • 717

CHAPTER **31** MONETARY THEORY • 746

CHAPTER **32**
FISCAL AND MONETARY
POLICY • 772

PART SEVEN

DYNAMICS AND MACRO POLICY

CHAPTER **33**
INFLATION: WAGE AND PRICE
DYNAMICS • 791

PART EIGHT

ISSUES IN MACROECONOMIC POLICY

CHAPTER **36** GROWTH AND PRODUCTIVITY • 873

CHAPTER **37** DEFICITS AND DEFICIT REDUCTION • 903

CHAPTER **38** TRADE POLICY • 924

CHAPTER **39**   ALTERNATIVE ECONOMIC SYSTEMS • 947

CHAPTER **40**   DEVELOPMENT • 971

P REFACE

Introductory students should know the vitality of modern economics, and this book is intended to show it to them. When I set out to write the First Edition, I felt that none of the available texts provided an adequate understanding of the principles of *modern* economics—both the principles that are necessary to understanding how modern economists think about the world, and the principles that are required to understand current economic issues. Apparently, my feelings were shared by many, as indicated by the resounding success of the First Edition. Not only was the book widely adopted in colleges and universities throughout the world, it was also rapidly translated into many languages—from major editions in Spanish, German, Italian, Japanese, and Chinese, to small editions in countries such as Latvia. This Second Edition builds on the initiatives of its predecessor. With the benefit of a wealth of feedback from the market, I have made a painstaking effort to improve the book from cover to cover. I believe both students and their instructors will be pleased with the result.

This Second Edition is also informed by my recent professional activities. During the last two years I have enjoyed a direct role in U.S. policy making as Chairman of the President's Council of Economic Advisers and as a member of the cabinet. This experience reinforced my conviction that the traditional principles course is too far removed from our national policy concerns and the modern advances in economics that can illuminate them. Moreover, my service on the council afforded me the opportunity to discuss key economic problems with leaders throughout the world, both in the major industrialized countries, and in India, China, Russia, and elsewhere. It was thus with a unique perspective that I set to work on the revision during the last two years, carving out time on weekends and during countless hours before dawn.

Economics is the science of choice and writing a textbook involves many choices. As I began work on the Second Edition, I was convinced that the choices I had made in the First Edition—for instance, the attention to new topics such as technological change and finance, and the increased emphasis on international concerns—were moves in the right direction. However, I had become even more convinced that an understanding of these new topics had to be based on solid foundations in established fundamentals, such as the law of supply and demand, the theory of the firm, and traditional perspectives on unemployment, inflation, and economic growth. Thus, in the revision I simultaneously faced several challenges, not the least of which was to reinforce the exposition of the fundamentals at the same time as I strengthened the discussion of new topics.

As I began the revision, several of the dramatic changes that had loomed so large in the early 1990s seemed still to occupy center stage, but new issues and new perspectives had emerged. The Cold War has ended, with the political and economic system of Communism the clear loser. The economies of the former Soviet Union and Eastern Europe are making a slow and painful transition to market economies. The countries of East Asia have experienced unprecedented growth, in some cases at rates in excess of 10 percent, year after year; they have shown that development is indeed possible. Japan became an economic powerhouse, while Korea, Taiwan, and the other Asian "tigers" went from being poor, backward countries to major players in the international arena. Their growth was based on international trade; and trade throughout the world, including the United States, became increasingly important. Huge private capital flows helped finance the development of many countries as well as the huge deficits that the United States and other countries began to mount. When investors lost confidence in a country, as they did in Mexico in 1995, these same capital flows precipitated an economic crisis that quickly spread, and was only arrested through strong international cooperation.

The success of East Asia during the 1970s and 1980s stands out as an exception in a world economy facing disappointment; the countries of Africa saw their desperate economic conditions worsen. Beginning around 1973, growth in the industrialized countries, including the United States, slowed markedly. Europe, where unemployment rates in the 1960s had fallen to extremely low rates, saw them soar, often to double-digit levels, and stubbornly remain there; while in the United States, where growth had been benefiting all groups, but especially the poor, inequality increased, with those at the bottom actually seeing their living standards deteriorate.

Within the United States, the mid-1990s brought signs of a reversal of some of these trends. Unemployment and inflation rates fell to low levels that had not been seen for a quarter of a century. The poverty rate began to decline, and incomes of all groups, especially those at the bottom, began to rise. American manufacturing experienced rapid productivity growth, with matching success in the international arena—U.S. car production again became the largest in the world. But among many workers, anxiety remained high; while their real wages and incomes had begun to rise, they still had not recovered to their earlier peaks, and no one was sure these trends would continue. Overall productivity growth also remained below its previous levels. Though the soaring deficit was brought under control—it had been the largest experienced in the United States during peacetime, with the national debt quadrupling between 1981 and 1992—the long-run prospects appeared daunting; the aging of the baby boomers would put unprecedented strains on the Social Security and health care systems.

As the world has changed, expectations have changed as well. While there has been enormous improvement in the quality of air in cities like Pittsburgh and Gary, Indiana, and while Lake Erie has been rescued from becoming polluted to the point where life could not survive, our expectations about the environment have grown even faster; we have become increasingly aware of environmental costs. Longevity has increased, but our knowledge of how to prolong life has grown more rapidly, and rising medical costs have become a major political issue. The economic role of women has changed: not only have they taken a more active part in the labor force, there has been a revolution in expectations concerning the kinds of jobs women can hold.

And in virtually every one of the major issues facing the economy, there is a debate about the role of government. Government in the United States has grown enormously. Before World War II, government took less than one out of every five dollars; today it takes one out of three. Still, government in the United States is proportionately smaller than in most other industrialized countries. At one level, there is remarkable agreement about what the government should do: it has, for instance, a responsibility to help the economy remain at full employment with stable prices, to protect the environment, to support education, and to provide for the national defense. But how the government should fulfill its responsibilities in each of these areas is highly contentious. Issues concerning the responsibility, capability, and strategies of government in economics have come to the center of the political debate.

These are exciting issues and events, and they fill the front pages of our newspapers and the evening television news shows. Yet in the past, as a teacher of the introductory course in economics, I felt frustrated: none of the textbooks really conveyed this sense of excitement. Try as they might, none seemed to prepare students adequately for interpreting and understanding these important economic events.

As I thought about it more, one of the reasons for this became clear: the principles expounded in the classic textbook of Alfred Marshall of a hundred years ago, or that of Paul Samuelson, now almost fifty years old, were not the principles for today. The way we economists understand our discipline had changed to reflect the changing world, but the textbooks had not kept pace. Our professional discourse was built on a *modern* economics, but these new developments simply were not adequately reflected in any of the vast array of textbooks that were available to me as a teacher.

Indeed, changes in the economics discipline over the past half century have been as significant as the changes in world events. The basic competitive model of the economy was perfected in the 1950s. Since then, economists have gone beyond that model in several directions as they have come to better understand its limitations. Earlier researchers had paid lip service to the importance of incentives and to problems posed by limited information. However, it was only in the last two decades that real progress was made in understanding these issues. The 1996 Nobel Prize was awarded to two economists who pioneered our understanding of the role of information and incentives in the economy. Their work, and the work of others in this field, have found immediate applications. Both the collapse of the former Soviet bloc economies and the failure of the American S & L's can be viewed as consequences of the failure to provide appropriate incentives. A central question in the debate over growth and productivity has been, how can an economy provide stronger incentives for innovation? The debate over pollution and the environment centers around the relative merits of regulation and providing incentives not to pollute and to conserve resources.

The past fifty years have also seen a reexamination of the boundary between economics and business. Subjects like finance and management used to be relegated to business schools, where they were taught without reference to economic principles. Today we know that to understand how market economies actually work, we have to understand how firms finance and manage themselves. Tremendous insights can be gleaned through the application of basic economic principles, particularly those grounded in an understanding of incentives. Stories of corporate takeovers have been replaced on the front page by stories of bankruptcies as acquiring corporations have found themselves overextended. The 1990 Nobel Prize was awarded to three economists who had contributed most to the endeavor to integrate finance and economics. Yet the introductory textbooks had not yet built in the basic economics of finance and management.

We have also come to better appreciate the virtues of competition. We now understand, for instance, how the benefits of competition extend beyond price to competition for technological innovation. At the same time, we have come to see better why, in so many circumstances, competition appears limited. Again, as I looked over the available textbooks, none seemed to provide my students with a sense of this new understanding.

Samuelson's path-breaking textbook is credited with being the first to integrate successfully the (then) new insights of Keynesian economics with traditional microeconomics. Samuelson employed the concept of the neoclassical synthesis—the view that once the economy was restored to full employment, the old classical principles applied. In effect, there were two distinct regimes to the economy. In one, when the economy's resources were underemployed, macroeconomic principles applied; in the other, when the economy's resources were fully employed, microeconomic principles were relevant. That these were distinct and hardly related regimes was reflected in how texts were written and courses were taught; it made no difference whether micro was taught before macro, or vice versa. In the last few decades, economists came to question the split that had developed between microeconomics and macroeconomics. The profession as a whole came to believe that macroeconomic behavior had to be related to underlying microeconomic principles; there was one set of economic principles, not two. But this view simply was not reflected in any of the available texts.

This book differs from most other texts in several ways. Let me highlight some of the most prominent distinctions.

- Reflecting my recent involvement in policy making, throughout the text I have introduced examples to relate economic theory to recent policy discussions. In each chapter, there is a policy perspective box providing a vignette on one particular issue. These policy discussions both enliven the course and enrich the student's command over the basic material.

- Economists are a contentious lot, yet on most issues differences between economists pale in comparison to differences between noneconomists. Indeed, there is a high degree of consensus among economists, and I have drawn attention to this throughout the book with 20 points of consensus in economics.

- Rather than the traditional approach of stretching out the competitive model to fill the entire microeconomics course, I teach it in a compact format in the first two parts of the book. This allows students to develop a complete picture of the basic model, before looking systematically at the role of imperfect markets.

- Economic incentives and the problems of incomplete information are given prominence. To take two of many examples, Chapter 19 discusses the role that reputation plays in providing firms with incentives to maintain the quality of their products and Chapter 20 discusses how firms try to motivate their managers and how managers try to motivate their workers.

- Key issues which have been given short shrift in other texts are explained concisely and clearly, and related to economic fundamentals. For instance, I recognize finance as an important part of economics, and give serious attention to the role of innovation—both its microeconomic foundations and its macroeconomic consequences.

- The presentation of macroeconomics has been reorganized to reflect closely microeconomic foundations. Thus, I begin the discussion in Part Five with an aggregate, full-employment, competitive model with perfectly flexible wages and prices. From there I move on to discuss the other extreme—and the focus of traditional macroeconomics—an unemployment model with rigid wages and prices in Part Six. This leads, in Part Seven, to a discussion of the dynamics of adjustment, an economy in which wages and prices are neither perfectly flexible, nor perfectly rigid, and in which a principal concern is the rate of inflation. I rely on the aggregate supply and aggregate demand framework throughout the macroeconomic presentation. Moreover, a virtue of the new organization is that I can turn to the important topic of economic growth early in the course, in Chapter 26.

- International economics features prominently and is integrated thoroughly into the analysis. For instance, trade is taken up at the outset in Chapter 3. On the macroeconomic side, after I set forth the full-employment model in Chapter 25, I use it to explain international capital flows and the determinations of exchange rates in Chapter 26. Then, in presenting the models of unemployment (Part Six) and the dynamics of adjustment (Part Seven), international dimensions are carefully addressed, especially in relation to monetary theory and policy. There is also a discussion of international trade policy in Chapter 38.

I emphasize in this book that most economic tasks are beyond the scope of any one individual. This lesson certainly applies to the writing and revision of a textbook. In writing the First Edition, I benefited greatly from the reactions of my students in the introductory courses at Princeton and Stanford who class-tested early drafts. Their enthusiastic response to the manuscript provided much-needed boosts to motivate me at several critical stages. The reception of the First Edition showed that the venture was well worth the effort. Similarly, the revision has benefited from the experience of the thousands of students who have used the book and their teachers who offered invaluable feedback.

This edition, and the previous, have benefited from numerous reviewers. The book has been improved immeasurably by their advice—some of which, quite naturally, was conflicting. In particular, I would like to thank Robert T. Averitt, Smith College; Mohsen Bahmani-Oskooee, University of Wisconsin, Milwaukee; H. Scott Bierman, Carleton College; John Payne Bigelow, University of Missouri; Bruce R. Bolnick, Northeastern University; Adhip Chaudhuri, Georgetown University; Michael D. Curley, Kennesaw State College; John Devereux, University of Miami; K. K. Fung, Memphis State; Christopher Georges, Hamilton College; Ronald D. Gilbert, Texas Tech University; Robert E. Graf, Jr., United States Military Academy; Glenn W. Harrison, University of South Carolina; Marc Hayford, Loyola University; Yutaka Horiba, Tulane University; Charles Howe, University of Colorado; Sheng Cheng Hu, Purdue University; Glenn Hubbard, Columbia University; Allen C. Kelley, Duke University; Michael M. Knetter, Dartmouth College; Stefan Lutz, Purdue University; Mark J. Machina, University of California, San Diego; Burton G. Malkiel, Princeton University; Lawrence Martin, Michigan State University; Thomas Mayer, University of California, Davis; Craig J. McCann, University of South Carolina; Henry N. McCarl, University of Alabama, Birmingham; John McDermott, University of South Carolina; Marshall H. Medoff, University of California, Irvine; Peter Mieszkowski, Rice University; W. Douglas Morgan, University of California, Santa Barbara; John S. Murphy, Canisius College; William Nielson, Texas A&M University; Neil B. Niman, University of New Hampshire; David H. Papell, University of Houston; James E. Price, Syracuse University; Daniel M. G. Raff, Harvard Business School; Christina D. Romer, University of California, Berkeley; Richard Rosenberg, Pennsylvania State University; Christopher J. Ruhm, Boston University; Suzanne A. Scotchmer, University of California, Berkeley; Richard Selden, University of Virginia; Andrei Shleifer, Harvard University; John L. Solow, University of Iowa; George Spiva, University of Tennessee; Mark Sproul, University of California at Los Angeles; Frank P. Stafford, University of Michigan; Raghu Sundaram, University of Rochester; Hal R. Varian, University of Michigan; Franklin V. Walker, State University of New York at Albany; James M. Walker, Indiana University; Andrew Weiss, Boston University; Gilbert R. Yochum, Old Dominion University.

It is a pleasure also to acknowledge the help of a number of research assistants. Many of them went well beyond the assigned tasks of looking up, assembling, and graphing data to providing helpful criticism of the manuscript. These include Edwin Lai, now at Vanderbilt University; Chulsoo Kim, now at

Rutgers University; Alexander Dyck, now at Harvard University; Patricia Nabti and Andres Rodriguez, now at University of Chicago; Marcie Smith; and Kevin Woodruff. I am particularly indebted to John Williams, who supervised and coordinated the final stages of preparation of the manuscript for the First Edition, and who assisted me on the entire preparation of the second. But John did more than this: he has been a sounding board for new ideas, new organizational structures, and new expositions.

I have been indeed fortunate in both editions of enlisting the help of individuals who combined a deep understanding of economics with an editor's fine honed pen: Timothy Taylor in the first edition and Felicity Skidmore in the second. Both have remarkable editorial skills; both have long been committed to the notion that it is important that modern economic ideas be communicated widely and that they *can* be, in a way that is both enlightening and enjoyable. Timothy, John, and Felicity all gave their energy and creativity to the enterprise, and the book is immeasurably better as a result.

This is the second book I have published with Norton, a company that reflects many of the aspects of organizational design that I discuss in the text. This book would not be nearly the one it is without the care, attention, and most important, deep thought devoted to my work by so many there. A few deserve special mention. Donald Lamm, chairman of the board at Norton, managed not only to keep the incentives straight within his firm, but also found time to read early drafts of the First Edition at several critical stages and offered his usual insightful suggestions. I cannot sufficiently acknowledge my indebtedness to Drake McFeely, who served as my editor on the First Edition (and succeeded Don Lamm as president of Norton) and Ed Parsons, who served as my editor on the Second Edition. Both have been concerned about the ideas *and* their presentation, and both have been tough, but constructive, critics. The work of Kate Barry, the manuscript editor, was as energetic as it was cheerful. All four made my work harder, so that readers of this book would have an easier time. Several others at Norton also deserve mention: Rosanne Fox for her outstanding proofreading, Ashley Deeks and Claire Acher, for their work on the photographs, Antonina Krass for the splendid design of the book, and Roy Tedoff and Jane Carter for coordinating its production. Finally, Stephen King, Steve Hoge, and Linda Puckette have contributed their unique talents in the creation of innovative electronic ancillaries for the text.

I owe a special thanks to those who prepared the ancillary materials that accompany the text. Given the fact that this book represents a departure from the standard mold of the past, the tasks they faced were both more important and more difficult. Their enthusiasm, insight, and hard work have produced a set of truly superb ancillaries: Lawrence Martin of Michigan State University prepared the print Study Guide and oversaw its transformation into an electronic counterpart, Ward Hanson of Stanford has developed an on-line version of the Instructor's Manual, and Alan Harrison of McMaster University prepared the test bank for the Second Edition.

It is common practice at this point in the preface to thank one's spouse and children, who have had to sacrifice so much (presumably time that the author would otherwise have spent with them). My debt goes beyond these commonplaces. My wife and children have motivated me, partly by the thirst for economic understanding they have evidenced by their questions about the rapidly changing economic scene, and partly by their challenging spirit—easy explanations, making heavy use of standard economics jargon, would not satisfy them. Moreover, in their perspective, the only justification for diverting my attention away from them and from my principal job as a teacher and researcher was the production of a textbook that would succeed in communicating the basic ideas of modern economics more effectively than those already available. I hope that what I—together with all of those who have helped me so much—have produced will please them.

OUTLINE FOR A ONE-SEMESTER COURSE

This book may be used either in a one or two-semester course. Below I offer a provisional outline for a one-semester course covering both microeconomics and macroeconomics. The outline includes most of the fundamentals, but of necessity it must leave out some of the exciting new topics. Naturally, to a large extent, *which* topics get omitted is a matter of taste. The following is my selection for a short course using twenty chapters.

Chapter Number	Chapter Title
2	Thinking Like an Economist
3	Trade
4	Demand, Supply, and Price
5	Using Demand and Supply
7	The Public Sector
8	The Consumption Decision
9	Labor Supply and Savings
11	The Firm's Costs
12	Production
14	Monopolies and Imperfect Competition
18	Imperfect Information in the Product Market
24	Macroeconomic Goals and Measures
25	The Full-Employment Model
27	Overview of Unemployment Macroeconomics
28	Aggregate Demand
30	Money, Banking, and Credit
31	Monetary Theory
33	Inflation: Wage and Price Dynamics
36	Growth and Productivity
37	Deficits and Deficit Reduction

PART ONE

INTRODUCTION

These days economics is big news. If we pick up a newspaper or turn on the television for the prime-time news report, we are likely to be bombarded with statistics on unemployment rates, inflation rates, exports, and imports. How well are we doing in competition with other countries, such as Japan? Everyone seems to want to know. Political fortunes as well as the fortunes of countries, firms, and individuals depend on how well the economy does.

What is economics all about? That is the subject of Part One. Chapter 1 uses the story of the automobile industry to illustrate many of the fundamental issues with which economics is concerned. The chapter describes the four basic questions at the heart of economics, and how economists attempt to answer these questions.

Chapter 2 introduces the economists' basic model and explains why notions of property, profits, prices, and cost play such a central role in economists' thinking.

A fact of life in the modern world is that individuals and countries are interdependent. Even a wealthy country like the United States is dependent on foreign countries for vital imports. Chapter 3 discusses the gains that result from trade; why trade, for instance, allows greater specialization, and why greater specialization results in increased productivity. It also explains the patterns of trade—why each country imports and exports the particular goods it does.

Prices play a central role in enabling economies to function. Chapters 4 and 5 take up the question of what determines prices. Also, what causes prices to change over time? Why is water, without which we cannot live, normally so inexpensive, while diamonds, which we surely can do without, are very expensive? What happens to the prices of beer and cigarettes if the government imposes a tax on these goods? Sometimes the government passes laws requiring firms to pay wages of at least so much, or forbidding landlords to charge rents that exceed a certain level. What are the consequences of these government interventions?

Chapter 6 introduces two important realities: economic life takes place not in a single moment of time but over long periods, and life is fraught with risk. Decisions today have effects on the future, and there is usually much uncertainty about what those effects will be. How do economists deal with problems posed by time and risk?

Finally, Chapter 7 turns to the pervasive role of the government in modern economies. Its focus is on why the government undertakes the economic roles it does and on the economic rationale for government actions. It also describes the various forms that government actions might take and the changing roles of the government over time.

1

The Automobile and Economics

I magine the world 100 years ago: no cars, airplanes, computers (and computer games!), movies—to say nothing of atomic energy, lasers, and transistors. The list of inventions since then seems almost endless.

Of all the inventions that have shaped the world during the past century, perhaps none has had so profound an effect as the automobile. It has changed how and where people work, live, and play. But like any major innovation, it has been a mixed blessing: traffic jams on the one hand, access to wilderness on the other. And the new opportunities it created for some were accompanied by havoc for others. Some occupations—such as black-smiths—virtually disappeared. Others—such as carriage makers—had to transform themselves (into car body manufacturers) or go out of business. But the gains of the many who benefited from the new industry far out-weighed the losses of those who were hurt.

The story of the automobile is familiar. But looking at it from the per-spective of economics can teach us a great deal about the economic way of thinking.

THE AUTOMOBILE: A BRIEF HISTORY

The idea of a motorized carriage occurred to many, in the United States and Europe, at roughly the same time. But ideas by themselves are not enough. Translating ideas into marketable products requires solving technical problems and persuading investors to finance the venture.

If you visit a museum of early cars, you will see that the technical problems were resolved in a variety of ways, by many people working independently. At the turn of the century, the area around Detroit was full of innovators developing cars—Ransom E. Olds, the Dodge brothers, and Henry Ford. The spirit must have been much like that of "Silicon Valley" (the area in California between San Francisco and San Jose) in the past quarter century, which has been at the center of computer technology development: a spirit of excitement, breakthroughs made, and new milestones reached. The various automobile innovators could draw upon a stock of ideas "floating in the air." They also had the help of specialized firms that had developed a variety of new technologies and skills: for example, new alloys that enabled lighter motors to be constructed and new techniques for machining that allowed for greater power, precision, and durability.

Henry Ford is generally given credit for having recognized the potential value of a vehicle that could be made and sold at a reasonable price. Before Ford, automobiles were luxuries, affordable only by the very rich. He saw the potential benefit from providing inexpensive transportation. After he introduced the Model T in 1909 at a "bargain" price of $900, he continued to cut the price—to $440 in 1914 and $360 in 1916. Sales skyrocketed from 58,000 in 1909 to 730,000 in 1916. Ford's prediction of a mass market for inexpensive cars had proved correct.

But success was neither sudden nor easy. To translate his idea into action

Ford had to put together a company to produce cars, figure out how to produce them cheaply, and raise the capital required to make all this possible.

Raising capital was particularly difficult, since the venture was extremely risky. Would Ford be successful in developing his automobile? Would someone else beat him to it? Would the price of a car be low enough for many people to buy it? If he was successful, would imitators copy his invention, robbing him of the mass market he needed to make money?

Ford formed a partnership to develop his first car. He was to supply the ideas and the work, while his partners supplied the funds. It took three partnerships before Ford produced a single car. The first two went bankrupt, with the financial partners in each case accusing Ford of spending all of his time developing ideas instead of acting on them.

But were the first two sets of partners treated unfairly? After all, they knew the risks. Ford could have entered each partnership in good faith and simply been unable to deliver.

But even in the third case, his partners were unhappy: They claimed he managed to garner for himself the lion's share of the profits. Ford may have argued that his ideas were far more important than the mere dollars that the financiers provided to carry them out.

Whatever the truth in Ford's case, the general problem of who contributes more in a partnership and who should get what share of any profits occurs often.

Ford's success was due as much to his ability to come up with innovative ways of providing incentives and organizing production as to his skill in solving technical problems. He demonstrated this ability with his original labor policies. He offered more than double the going wage and paid his workers the then princely sum of $5 a day. In exchange, Ford worked his employees hard; the moving assembly line he invented enabled him to set his workers a fast pace and push them to keep up. The amount produced per worker increased enormously. Still, it was clear that the high wages were ample compensation for the extra effort. Riots almost broke out as workers clamored for the jobs he offered. Ford had rediscovered an old truth: in some cases, higher wages for employees can repay the employer in higher productivity, through greater loyalty, harder work, and less absenteeism.

Ford's success in increasing productivity meant that he could sell his cars far more cheaply than his rivals could. The lower prices and the high level of sales that accompanied them made it possible for him to take full advantage of the mass production techniques he had developed. At one point, however, Ford's plans were almost thwarted when a lawyer-inventor named George Baldwin Selden claimed that Ford had infringed on his patent.

The U.S. government grants patents to enable inventors to reap the rewards of their innovative activity. These are generally for specific inventions, like a new type of braking system or transmission mechanism, not for general ideas. Ford's idea of an assembly line, for example, was not an invention that could be patented, and it was imitated by other car manufacturers. A patent gives the inventor the exclusive right to produce his invention for a limited time, thus helping to assure that inventors will be able to make some money from their successful inventions. Patents may lead to higher prices for these new products, since there is no competition from others making the same product. But the presumption is that the gains to society from the innovative activity more than compensate for the losses to consumers from the temporarily higher prices.

Selden had applied for, and been granted, a patent for a horseless, self-propelled carriage. He demanded that other car manufacturers pay him a royalty, which is a payment for the right to use a patented innovation. Ford challenged Selden's patent in court on the grounds that the concept of a "horseless, self-propelled carriage" was too vague to be patentable. Ford won. Providing cars to the masses at low prices made Ford millions of dollars and many millions of Americans better off, by enabling them to go where they wanted to go more easily, cheaply, and speedily.

CRISIS IN THE AMERICAN AUTOMOBILE INDUSTRY

Today people think of computers and gene-splicing, not automobiles, as the new technologies. The story of the automobile is no longer emblematic of the latest technological breakthroughs. The changing fortunes of the American automobile industry during the past two decades are similar to those of many other parts of U.S. industry.

There were more than a hundred U.S. automobile manufacturers in the fall of 1903, twenty-seven of which accounted for more than 70 percent of the total sales of the industry. By the early 1960s, however, only three companies were responsible for 88 percent of U.S. auto sales. Of the car manufacturers that existed at the beginning of the century, many had gone bankrupt or given up on the automobile business, and the remainder had been agglomerated into or taken over by the dominant firms.

The most serious problems faced by the auto industry in the 1960s involved air pollution and automobile safety. To reduce pollution, the government regulated the amount of exhaust fumes a car could produce, and design changes followed. On the safety front, automobile companies quickly responded to demands for increased safety by providing seat belts.

This relatively rosy picture changed dramatically in 1973. That year, the Organization of Petroleum Exporting Countries (OPEC)—mainly countries in the Middle East—combined forces to hold down the supply of oil, create a scarcity, and thus push up its price. OPEC actually cut off all oil exports for a few tense weeks late in 1973. Its power was a surprise to many, including the American automobile industry. American cars then tended to be bigger and heavier than those in Japan and Europe. This was easily explained: incomes in the United States were higher; Americans could afford larger cars and the gasoline they guzzled. Also, Japan and Europe imposed much heavier taxes on gasoline than did the United States, encouraging consumers in those countries to buy smaller, more fuel-efficient cars.

The U.S. auto industry, thus, was ill-prepared for the higher gas prices caused by OPEC's move. But other countries, especially Japan, stood ready to

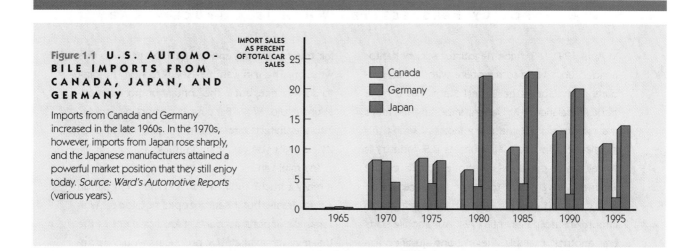

Figure 1.1 U.S. AUTOMO-BILE IMPORTS FROM CANADA, JAPAN, AND GERMANY

Imports from Canada and Germany increased in the late 1960s. In the 1970s, however, imports from Japan rose sharply, and the Japanese manufacturers attained a powerful market position that they still enjoy today. *Source: Ward's Automotive Reports* (various years).

gain, with smaller, cheaper, and more fuel-efficient cars. Auto imports as a whole nearly doubled in the 1970s, from 15 percent of the total cars sold in the United States in 1970 to 27 percent by 1980, and they remained at a high level throughout the 1980s and into the 1990s. Figure 1.1 shows the dramatic increase in imports of new passenger cars from Canada, Germany, and especially Japan over the last thirty years.

It was clear that the Japanese firms were supplying what American consumers wanted, but the effect on the American automobile industry was devastating. Profits fell and workers were laid off.

CHRYSLER: GOVERNMENT TO THE RESCUE

In the late 1970s, one firm, Chrysler, was on the verge of bankruptcy. The company did not have and could not borrow the cash to pay off loans that were due, so it asked for help from the government. In the ensuing debate about whether the government should save Chrysler, advocates of a bailout (rescue from financial ruin) painted a picture of unemployed workers and empty, wasted factories.

Critics of the bailout pointed out that the workers, machines, and buildings of a bankrupt company do not disappear. Instead, they can be hired by or sold to new companies under new management. Redeployment of resources was appropriate, critics argued, because the impending bankruptcy demonstrated that Chrysler management had failed to manage its resources well.

In the end, the government guaranteed some new loans for Chrysler. If Chrysler failed to pay back its loans, the government would do so with tax money. Because of this guarantee, Chrysler was able to obtain loans from private investors and banks, and at a relatively low rate of interest. Its subsequent

In April 1994 U.S. trade negotiator Mickey Kantor headed up a team to negotiate with its counterparts from Japan. The United States has a huge trade imbalance with Japan, importing far more than it exports. Of the many factors causing this imbalance, the one that infuriates U.S. industry is "unfair trade practices" or subtle actions by the Japanese government to restrict American sales. Rice is a good example. The Japanese refused to import American rice until 1994. Automobile parts are another example. Regulations—justified on safety grounds—restricted sales of replacement parts produced by firms other than the car's manufacturer. Only Toyota could make replacement parts for Toyota cars. But since almost all cars sold in Japan are made in Japan, this effectively kept out non-Japanese parts producers.

Part of Kantor's mission was to reduce such unfair trade practices, and he used the mini-van as a weapon. The mini-van may seem to have nothing to do with rice, but in the context of those negotiations it did. Why? Because importers of vehicles into the United States must pay a tariff (tax)—a tax that is higher on cars than on trucks.

The mini-van is currently taxed as a truck. But, is it really a truck? The mini-van is commonly built on a truck frame, but it hauls people, not goods. With Japanese imports accounting for 7 percent of the U.S. mini-van market, U.S. producers would be delighted to reduce their Japanese competition by getting the mini-van reclassified as a car and taxed as such. The higher tariff, of course, would raise the price of Japanese mini-vans to U.S. consumers and reduce their attractiveness in the U.S. market. The unspoken threat of such a reclassification was not lost on the Japanese.

success is an often-told tale, with the president of Chrysler, Lee Iacocca, claiming a large share of the credit for himself.

It turns out that the government had strong incentives to step in and help Chrysler. Not only was there concern about losing one of the three major firms in the automobile industry, but the government stood to lose money through an insurance program for workers' pensions set up several years before. This program guaranteed that even if a company went bankrupt, workers would still receive their pensions. Had Chrysler gone bankrupt, the government might have had to pay Chrysler workers hundreds of millions of dollars in pensions.

The government even ended up making money in bailing out Chrysler. In return for guaranteeing the loans, the government insisted that, in effect, it be granted some share of ownership in the firm. With the company's subsequent success, these shares turned out to be quite valuable.

PROTECTION FROM FOREIGN COMPETITION

The problems at Chrysler also existed in reduced form at General Motors and Ford. But in the early 1980s, all three began to make a recovery from the hard times of the 1970s, for several reasons. Unions dramatically reduced their wage demands. Smaller and more fuel-efficient cars were developed. And the government again stepped in, this time to help protect the industry from foreign competition. Again the concern was layoffs: in 1980, unemployment in Michigan, a major auto-producing state, had reached 12.6 percent (as contrasted with the total U.S. unemployment rate of 7.1 percent). Rather than imposing a tariff (tax) on car imports, the American government negotiated with the Japanese government to restrain Japan's automobile exports. Although the export limits were called voluntary, they were actually negotiated under pressure. If the Japanese had not taken the "voluntary" step of limiting exports, Congress probably would have passed a law forcing them to do so.

The reduced supply of Japanese cars led not only to increased sales of American cars, but to higher prices, both for Japanese and American cars. The American industry was subsidized not by the taxpayers in general but by those who bought cars, through these higher prices. The Japanese car manufacturers had little to complain about, since they too benefited from the higher prices. Had Japanese manufacturers gotten together and agreed to reduce their sales and raise prices, the action would have been viewed as a violation of U.S. antitrust laws, which were designed to enforce competition. But here the American government itself was encouraging less competition!

The Japanese responded in still another way to these restrictions. They decided to circumvent the limitations on their exports by manufacturing cars here in the United States. As shown in Figure 1.2, in 1995 more than one out of three cars produced in the United States is produced by foreign-owned firms. These are referred to as **transplants.** Honda, Mazda, Nissan, and Toyota could all claim that at least some of their cars were made in America.

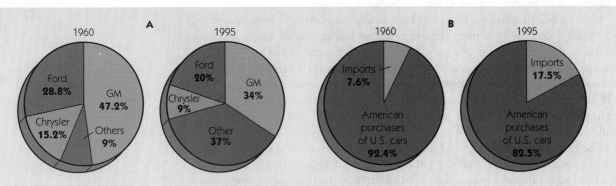

Figure 1.2 SHARES OF THE U.S. AUTOMOBILE MARKET

These pie charts show some of the changes in the U.S. auto market in recent decades. Panel A focuses on production, panel B on purchases. The charts in panel A show that production has remained concentrated. In 1960, the "other" firms were small American firms such as Studebaker and American Motors; in 1990, they were foreign-owned firms like Honda. The charts in panel B show the dramatic increase in imports. *Source: Ward's Automotive Reports* (various years).

THE REBIRTH OF THE AMERICAN AUTOMOBILE INDUSTRY

What would have happened had the automobile companies not been given the breather that the Japanese export restraints provided? We cannot tell. Perhaps they would have been forced to transform themselves more quickly. Perhaps one or more would have gone out of business. What we do know is that during the 1980s, the industry worked hard to compete effectively with its Japanese rivals. The different firms pursued different strategies.

General Motors, for instance, focused on automation, investing heavily in robots and other new equipment. Much of this turned out to be wasted. But GM did undertake a successful, major new venture—the Saturn project. In addition to innovations in product design and manufacturing, labor relations and marketing were improved. Worker participation in decision making was increased. And instead of the haggling that is typical of car purchases, Saturns were bought just like most other goods—at the prices on their stickers. The car generated so much customer loyalty that when the company invited owners to come to the factory in June 1994 to celebrate what was billed as its "homecoming," 44,000 people showed up.

THE HISTORY OF THE AUTOMOBILE IN STATISTICS

Figure 1.3 illustrates the history of U.S. car production. The ups and downs of the curve reflect the rise, fall, and recovery of the industry. Car production has

Figure 1.3 **ANNUAL U.S. AUTOMOBILE PRODUC-TION, 1900 TO THE PRESENT**

Changes in U.S. automobile production have both reflected and influenced events in the U.S. economy and the world during the twentieth century. *Source: Ward's Automotive Reports* (various years).

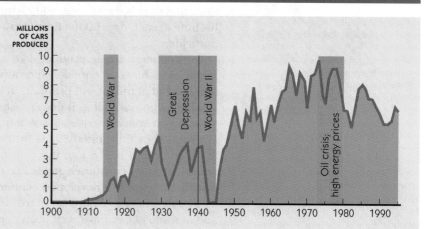

been set against a backdrop of the major events affecting the economy as a whole. Different years are listed on the horizontal axis, while the number of cars built is provided on the vertical axis. Improvements in techniques of mass production led to the boom in sales early in this century. During the Great Depression of the 1930s, sales declined sharply, and civilian automobile production halted entirely during World War II. Production then rose during the boom of the 1950s and 1960s. In the 1970s, sharp increases in the price of gasoline helped trigger two worldwide recessions, reducing car sales. The U.S. economy recovered to a pattern of steady growth in the mid-1980s, halting, at least temporarily, the decline in automobile sales.

Heading into the economic downturn that began in 1990, the industry again showed its sensitivity to the health of the overall economy. Reduced confidence in the economy and lower incomes led consumers to put off purchasing cars. The reduced sales of cars, in turn, contributed to the slowdown of the economy. It was not until interest rates fell and the economy began to recover, in 1993, that automobile sales again began to recover; profits once again soared, reaching record levels.

WHAT IS ECONOMICS?

This narrative illustrates many facets of economics, but now a definition of our subject is in order. **Economics** studies how individuals, firms, governments, and other organizations within our society make **choices,** and how those choices determine the way the resources of society are used. **Scarcity** figures prominently in economics: choices matter because resources are scarce. Imagine an enormously wealthy individual who can have everything he wants. We might think that scarcity is not in his vocabulary—until we consider that time is a resource, and he must decide what expensive toy to devote his time to each day. Taking time into account, then, scarcity is a fact in everyone's life.

To produce a single product, like an automobile, thousands of decisions and choices have to be made. Since any economy is made up not only of automobiles but of millions of products, it is a marvel that the economy functions at all, let alone as well as it does most of the time. This marvel is particularly clear if you consider instances when things do not work so well: the Great Depression in the United States in the 1930s, when 25 percent of the work force could not find a job; the countries of the former Soviet Union today, where ordinary consumer goods like carrots or toilet paper are often simply unavailable; the less developed economies of many countries in Africa, Asia, and Latin America, where standards of living have remained stubbornly low, and in some places have even been declining.

The fact that choices must be made applies as well to the economy as a whole as it does to each individual. Somehow, decisions are made—by individuals, households, firms, and government—that together determine how the economy's limited resources, including its land, labor, machines, oil, and other natural resources, are used. Why is it that land used at one time for growing crops may, at another time, be used for an automobile plant? How was it that over the space of a couple of decades, resources were transferred from making horse carriages to making automobile bodies? that blacksmiths were replaced by auto mechanics? How do the decisions of millions of consumers, workers, investors, managers, and government officials all interact to determine the use of the scarce resources available to society? Economists reduce such matters to four basic questions concerning how economies function:

1. What is produced, and in what quantities? There have been important changes in consumption over the past fifty years. Spending for medical care, for example, was only 3.5 percent of total personal consumption in 1950. By 1995, more than one out of every seven dollars was spent on medical care. What can account for changes like these? The economy seems to spew out new products like videocassette recorders and new services like automated bank tellers. What causes this process of innovation? The overall level of production has also shifted from year to year, often accompanied by large changes in the levels of employment and unemployment. How can economists explain these changes?

In the United States, the question of what is produced, and in what quantities, is answered largely by the private interaction of firms and consumers, but government also plays a role. Prices are critical in determining what goods are produced. When the price of some good rises, firms are induced to produce more of that good, to increase their profits. Thus, a central question for economists is, why are some goods more expensive than others? And why have the prices of some goods increased or decreased?

2. How are these goods produced? There are often many ways of making something. Textiles can be made with hand looms. Modern machines enable fewer workers to produce more cloth. Very modern machines may be highly computerized, allowing one worker to monitor many more machines than was possible earlier. The better machines generally cost more, but they require less labor. Which technique will be used, the advanced technology or the labor-intensive one? Henry Ford introduced the assembly line. More recently, car manufacturers have begun using robots. What determines how rapidly technology changes?

In the U.S. economy, firms answer the question of how goods are produced, again with input from the government, which sets regulations and enacts laws that affect everything from the overall organization of firms to the ways they interact with their employees and customers.

3. For whom are these goods produced?   In the United States, individuals who have higher incomes can consume more goods. But that answer only pushes the question back one step: What determines the differences in income and wages? What is the role of luck? of education? of inheritance? of savings? of experience and hard work? These questions are difficult to answer. For now, suffice it to say that while incomes are primarily determined by the private interaction of firms and households in the United States, government also plays a strong role, with taxes as well as programs that redistribute income.

Figure 1.4 shows the relative pay in a variety of different occupations. To judge by income, each physician receives five times as much of the economy's output as a firefighter, and seven times as much as a butcher.

4. Who makes economic decisions, and by what process?   In a **centrally planned economy,** as the Soviet Union was, the government takes responsibility for virtually every aspect of economic activity. The government provides the answers to the first three questions. A central economic planning agency works through a bureaucracy to say what will be produced and by what method, and who shall consume it. At the other end of the spectrum are economies that rely primarily on the free interchange of producers and their customers

Figure 1.4 **WHO TAKES HOME AMERICA'S OUTPUT?**

This chart measures the earnings of a variety of professions relative to the wages of an average worker. Firefighters make 25 percent more than an average worker, while physicians make over six times as much.

to determine what, how, and for whom. The United States, which lies near this latter end, has a **mixed economy;** that is, a mix between public (governmental) and private decision making. Within limits, producers make what they want; they use whatever method of production seems appropriate to them; and the output is distributed to consumers according to their income.

When economists examine an economy, they want to know to what extent economic decisions are made by the government, and to what extent they are made by private individuals. In the United States, while individuals for the most part make their own decisions about what kind of car to purchase, the government has inserted itself in a number of ways: it has taken actions that affect the import of Japanese cars, that restrict the amount of pollutants a car can produce, and that promote fuel efficiency and automobile safety.

A related question is whether economic decisions are made by individuals for their own interests or for the interest of an employer such as a business firm or government agency. This is an important distinction. We can expect people acting on their own behalf to make decisions that benefit themselves. When they act on behalf of organizations, however, a conflict of interest may arise. Observers often refer to corporations and governments as if they were a single individual. Economists point out that organizations consist, by definition, of a multitude of individuals and that the interests of these individuals do not necessarily coincide with one another or, for that matter, with the interests of the organization itself. Organizations bring a number of distinctive problems to the analysis of choice.

As you can see by their concern with decision making, economists are concerned not only with *how* the economy answers the four basic questions, but also *how well*. They ask, is the economy efficient? Could it produce more of some goods without producing fewer of others? Could it make some individuals better off without making some other individuals worse off?

MARKETS AND GOVERNMENT IN THE MIXED ECONOMY

The primary reliance on private decision making in the United States reflects economists' beliefs that this reliance is appropriate and necessary for economic efficiency; however, economists also believe that certain interventions by government are desirable. Finding the appropriate balance between the public and the private sectors of the economy is a central issue of economic analysis.

MARKETS

The economic concept of markets is used to include any situation where exchange takes place, though this exchange may not necessarily resemble the traditional village markets. In department stores and shopping malls, customers rarely haggle over the price. When manufacturers purchase the materials they need for production, they exchange money for them, not other goods. Most goods, from cameras to clothes, are not sold directly from producers to consumers. They are sold from producers to distributors, from distributors to retailers, from retailers to consumers. All of these transactions are embraced by the concepts of **market** and **market economy.**

In market economies with competition, individuals make choices that reflect their own desires. And firms make choices that maximize their profits; to do so, they must produce the goods consumers want, and they must produce them at lower cost than other firms. As firms compete in the quest for profits, consumers benefit, both from the kinds of goods produced and the prices at which they are supplied. The market economy thus provides answers to the four basic economic questions—what is produced, how it is produced, for whom it is produced, and how these decisions are made. And on the whole, the answers the market gives ensure the efficiency of the economy.

But the answer the market provides to the question of for whom goods are produced is one that not everyone finds acceptable. Like bidders at an auction, what market participants are willing and able to pay depends on their income. Some groups of individuals—including those without skills that are valued by the market—may receive such a low income that they could not feed and educate their children without outside assistance. Government provides the assistance by taking steps to increase income equality. These steps, however, often blunt economic incentives. While welfare payments provide an important safety net for the poor, the taxation required to finance them may discourage work and savings. If the government takes one out of three or even two dollars that an individual earns, that individual may not be inclined to work so much. And if the government takes one out of two or three dollars a person earns from interest on savings, the person may decide to spend more and save less. Like the appropriate balance between the public and private sectors, the appropriate balance between concerns about equality (often referred to as **equity concerns**) and efficiency is a central issue of modern economics.

THE ROLE OF GOVERNMENT

The answers to the basic economic questions that the market provides on the whole ensure efficiency. But in certain areas the solutions appear inadequate to many. There may be too much pollution, too much inequality, and too little concern about education, health, and safety. When the market is not perceived to be working well, people often turn to government.

The government plays a major role in modern economies. We need to understand both what that role is and why government undertakes the activities that it does. The story of the automobile provides several instances. Early on, George Baldwin Selden was almost able to use government-created patent laws to change the course of the industry. In the late 1970s, government loan guarantees enabled Chrysler to survive. The automobile industry was helped by government restrictions on Japanese imports but probably hurt by government regulations concerning pollution. The strength of the auto unions, reflected in their success in raising wages to high levels, was partly a result of the rights that federal legislation had granted to them. Later on we will see more ways in which government policy has affected industry.

The U.S. government sets the legal structure under which private firms and individuals operate. It regulates businesses to ensure that they do not discriminate by race or sex, do not mislead customers, are careful about the safety of their employees, and do not pollute air and water. In some industries, the government operates like a private business: the government-owned Tennessee Valley Authority (TVA) is one of the nation's largest producers of electricity; most children attend government-owned public schools; and most mail is still delivered by the government-owned post office. In other cases, the government supplies goods and services that the private sector does not, such as providing for the national defense, building roads, and printing money. Government programs provide for the elderly through Social Security (which pays income to retired individuals) and Medicare (which funds medical needs of the aged). The government helps those who have suffered economic dislocation, through unemployment insurance for those temporarily unemployed and disability insurance for those who are no longer able to work. The government also provides a safety net of support for the poor, particularly children, through various welfare programs.

One can easily imagine a government controlling the economy more directly. In countries where decision-making authority is centralized and concentrated in the government, government bureaucrats might decide what and how much a factory should produce and set the level of wages that should be paid. Various European governments run steel companies, coal mines, and the telephone system. At least until recently, governments in countries like the former Soviet Union and China attempted to control practically all major decisions regarding resource allocation.

THE THREE MAJOR MARKETS

The market economy revolves around exchange between individuals (or households), who buy goods and services from firms, and firms, which take **inputs,** the various materials of production, and produce **outputs,** the goods and services that they sell. In thinking about a market economy, economists focus their attention on three broad categories of markets in which individu-

CLOSE-UP: A FAILED ALTERNATIVE TO THE MIXED ECONOMY

While the mixed economy now is the dominant form of economic organization, it is not the only possible way of answering the basic economic questions. Beginning in 1917, an experiment in almost complete government control was begun in what became the Soviet Union.

What was produced in such an economy, and in what quantities? Government planners set the targets, which workers and firms then struggled to fulfill.

How were these goods produced? Again, since government planners decided what supplies would be delivered to each factory, they effectively chose how production occurred.

For whom were these goods produced? The government made decisions about what each job was paid, which affected how much people could consume. In principle, individuals could choose what to buy at government-operated stores, at

prices set by the government. But in practice, many goods were unavailable at these stores.

Who made economic decisions, and by what process? The government planners decided, basing the decisions on their view of national economic goals.

At one time, all this planning sounded very sensible, but as former Soviet premier Nikita Khrushchev once said, "Economics is a subject that does not greatly respect one's wishes." Many examples of Soviet economic woes could be cited, but two will suffice. In the shoe market, the Soviet Union was the largest national producer in the world. However, the average shoe was of such low quality that it fell apart in a few weeks, and inventories of unwanted shoes rotted in warehouses. In agriculture, the Soviet government had traditionally allowed small private plots. Although the government limited the time farmers could spend on these plots,

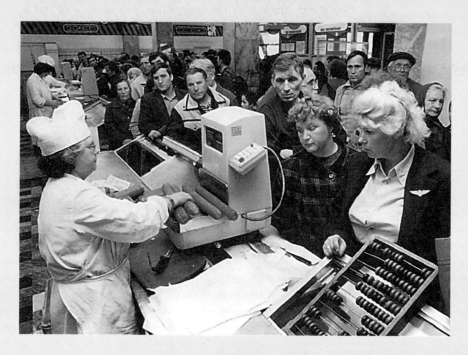

publicly run farming was so unproductive that the 3 percent of Soviet land that was privately run produced about 25 percent of the total farm output.

Today the standard of living in the former Soviet Union is not only below that in industrialized nations like the United States and those of Western Europe, but it is barely ahead of developing nations like Brazil and Mexico. Workers in the Soviet Union shared a grim one-liner: "We pretend to work and they pretend to pay us."

The collapse of the Soviet Union was, to a large extent, the result of the failure of its economic system. Much of this text is concerned with explaining why mixed economies work as well as they do.

als and firms interact. The markets in which firms sell their outputs to households are referred to collectively as the **product market.** Many firms also sell goods to other firms; the outputs of the first firm become the inputs of the second. These transactions too are said to occur in the product market.

On the input side, firms need (besides the materials that they buy in the product market) some combination of labor and machinery with which their goods can be produced. They purchase the services of workers in the **labor market.** They raise funds, with which to buy inputs, in the **capital market.** Traditionally, economists have also highlighted the importance of a third input, land, but in modern industrial economies, land is of secondary importance. For most purposes, it suffices to focus attention on the three major markets listed here, and this text will follow this pattern.

As Figure 1.5 shows, individuals participate in all three markets. When individuals buy goods or services, they act as **consumers** in the product market. When people act as **workers,** economists say they "sell their labor services" in the labor market. When individuals buy shares of stock in a firm or lend money to a business, economists note that they are participating in the capital market, and refer to them as **investors.**

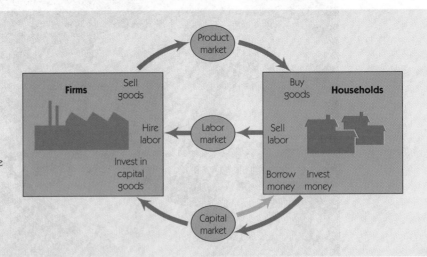

Figure 1.5 THE THREE MARKETS

To economists, people wear different hats: they are usually consumers in the product market, workers in the labor market, and borrowers and lenders in the capital market.

TWO CAVEATS

Terms in economics often are similar to terms in ordinary usage, but they can have special meanings. The terms **markets** and **capital** illustrate the problem.

Though the term "market" is used to conjure an image of a busy **marketplace,** there is no formal marketplace for most goods and services. There are buyers and sellers, and economists analyze the outcome *as if* there were a single marketplace in which all the transactions occurred.

Moreover, economists often talk about the "market for labor" as if all workers were identical. But workers obviously differ in countless ways. In some cases, these differences are important. We might then talk about the "market for skilled workers," or "the market for plumbers." But in other cases—such as when we are talking about the overall state of the economy and focusing on the unemployment rate (the fraction of workers who would like jobs but cannot get them)—these differences can be ignored.

When newspapers refer to the capital market, they mean the bond traders and stockbrokers and the companies they work for on Wall Street and other financial districts. When economists use the term capital market they have in mind a broader concept. It includes all the institutions concerned with raising funds (and, as we will see later, sharing and insuring risks), including banks and insurance companies.

The term "capital" is used in still another way—to refer to the machines and buildings used in production. To distinguish this particular usage, in this book we refer to machines and buildings as **capital goods.** Capital markets thus refers to the markets in which funds are raised, borrowed, and lent. **Capital goods markets** refers to the markets in which capital goods are bought and sold.

MICROECONOMICS AND MACROECONOMICS: THE TWO BRANCHES OF ECONOMICS

The detailed study of product, labor, and capital markets is called **microeconomics.** Microeconomics ("micro" is derived from the Greek word meaning "small") focuses on the behavior of the units—the firms, households, and individuals—that make up the economy. It is concerned with how the individual units make decisions and what affects those decisions. By contrast, **macroeconomics** ("macro" comes from the Greek word meaning "large") looks at the behavior of the economy as a whole, in particular the behavior of such aggregate measures as overall rates of unemployment, inflation, economic growth, and the balance of trade. The aggregate numbers do not tell us what any firm or household is doing. They tell us what is happening in total, or on average.

It is important to remember that these perspectives are simply two ways of looking at the same thing. Microeconomics is the bottom-up view of the economy; macroeconomics is the top-down view. The behavior of the economy as a whole is dependent on the behavior of the units that make it up.

The automobile industry is a story of both micro- and macroeconomics. It is a story of microeconomic interactions of individual companies, investors, and labor unions. It is also a story of global macroeconomic forces like oil shortages and economic fluctuations. When auto companies laid off workers in the late 1970s, their problems boosted the overall unemployment rate. The recession of the early 1990s brought heavy reductions in car sales. When the recovery occurred, auto sales grew rapidly.

THE SCIENCE OF ECONOMICS

Economics is a **social science.** It studies the social problem of choice from a scientific viewpoint, which means that it is built on a systematic exploration of the problem of choice. This systematic exploration involves both the formulation of theories and the examination of data.

A **theory** consists of a set of assumptions (or hypotheses) and conclusions derived from those assumptions. Theories are logical exercises: *if* the assumptions are correct, *then* the results follow. If all college graduates have a better chance of getting jobs and Ellen is a college graduate, then Ellen has a better chance of getting a job than a nongraduate. Economists make predictions with their theories. They might use a theory to predict what will happen if a tax is increased or if imports of foreign cars are limited. The predictions of a theory are of the form "If a tax is increased and if the market is competitive, then output will decrease and prices will increase."

In developing their theories, economists use models. To understand how economists use models, consider a modern car manufacturer trying to design a new automobile. It is extremely expensive to construct a new car. Rather than creating a separate, fully developed car for every engineer's or designer's conception of what she would like to see the new car be, the company uses models. The designers might use a plastic model to study the general shape of the vehicle and to assess reactions to the car's aesthetics. The engineers might use a computer model to study the air resistance, from which they can calculate fuel consumption and a separate model for judging the car's comfort.

Just as engineers construct different models to study particular features of a car, so too economists construct models of the economy—in words or equations—to depict particular features of the economy. An economic model might describe a general relationship ("When incomes rise, the number of cars purchased increases"), describe a quantitative relationship ("When incomes rise by 10 percent, the number of cars purchased rises, on average, by 12 percent"), or make a general prediction ("An increase in the tax on gasoline will decrease the demand for cars").

DISCOVERING AND INTERPRETING RELATIONSHIPS

A **variable** is any item that can be measured and that changes. Prices, wages, interest rates, quantities bought and sold, are all variables. What interests economists is the connection between variables. When economists see what appears to be a systematic relationship among variables, they ask, could it have arisen by chance, or is there indeed a relationship? This is the question of **correlation.**

Economists use statistical tests to measure and test correlations. Consider the problem of deciding whether a coin is biased. If you flip a coin 10 times and get 6 heads and 4 tails, is the coin a fair one? Or is it weighted to heads? Statistical tests will say that the result of 6 heads and 4 tails could easily happen by chance, so the evidence does not prove that the coin is weighted. This does not prove that it is *not* slightly weighted. The evidence is just not strong enough for either conclusion. But if you flip a coin 100 times and get 80 heads, statistical tests will tell you that the possibility of this happening by blind chance with a fair coin is extremely small. The evidence supports the assertion that the coin is weighted.

A similar logic can be used on correlations in economic data. People with more education tend to earn higher wages. Is the connection merely chance? Statistical tests show whether the evidence is too weak for a conclusion, or whether it supports the existence of a systematic relationship between education and wages.

CAUSATION VERSUS CORRELATION

Economists would like to accomplish more than just asserting that different variables are indeed correlated. They would like to conclude that changes in one variable *cause* the changes in the other variable. The distinction between correlation and **causation** is important. If one variable "causes" the other, then changing one variable necessarily will change the other. If the relationship is just a correlation, this may not be true.

Earlier, we saw that Japanese imports increased for more than a decade after 1973 and sales of U.S. cars decreased. The two variables were negatively correlated. But did that prove that increased Japanese sales caused the decreased American sales? If the decline in U.S. car production during this period was because American companies were producing large gas guzzlers that people no longer wanted, reducing Japanese car sales might not increase the sales of U.S.-made cars. In short, if there was a common cause to both changes—increased oil prices leading to increased sales of Japanese cars and decreased sales of U.S. cars—then these trends would be reversed only when American companies started to produce fuel-efficient cars.

In some cases, the *direction* of causation is not clear: did high Japanese sales cause low U.S. sales, or vice versa? For instance, it might have turned out, upon closer investigation, that the true explanation of decreased sales of U.S. cars was strikes that caused production shortages; when U.S. cars were not available, consumers turned to Japanese cars. To tell which explanation is valid—whether high Japanese sales cause low U.S. sales, whether low U.S. sales cause high Japanese sales, or whether both are caused by a third factor—requires closer examination of, for example, the circumstances in which the two variables moved in directions different from those normally observed.

EXPERIMENTS IN ECONOMICS

Many sciences use laboratory experiments to test alternative explanations, since experiments allow the scientist to change one factor at a time and see what happens. But the economy is not a chemistry lab. Instead, economics is like astronomy, in that both sciences must use the experiments that nature provides. Economists look for situations in which only one factor changes, and study the consequences of changing that factor. A change in the income tax system is an example of a natural experiment. But nature is usually not kind to economists; the world does not hold still. As the tax system changes, so do other features of the economy, and economists often have a difficult time deciding whether changes are the result of the new tax system or of some other economic change. Sometimes they can use what is called **econometrics,** the branch of statistics developed to analyze the particular measurement problems that arise in economics.

In a few cases, economists have engaged in social experiments. For example, they have given a selected group of individuals a different income tax schedule or welfare program from that faced by another, otherwise similar, group. In recent years, a major new branch of economics, called **experimental economics,** has analyzed certain aspects of economic behavior in a controlled, laboratory setting. One way of seeing how individuals respond to risk, for example, is to construct a risky situation in such a setting and force individuals to make decisions and act on them. By varying the nature of the risk and the rewards, one can learn about how individuals will respond to different risks in real life situations. Similarly, different kinds of auctions can be simulated in a controlled laboratory setting to see how buyers respond. Lessons learned from such auctions have already been used by government in designing some of the auctions it conducts. Both social and laboratory experiments have provided economists with valuable insights concerning economic behavior.

But even with all available tools, the problem of finding a variety of correlations between several different types of data and having to discern which connections are real and which are only apparent is a difficult one. Economists' interest in these questions is motivated by more than just curiosity. Often important policy questions depend on what one believes is really going on. Whether a country thinks it worthwhile to pour more resources into higher education may depend on whether it believes that the differences in wages observed between those with and without a college education are largely due to the skills and knowledge acquired during college, or whether they are mainly related to differences in ability between those who make it through college and those who do not.

The important lessons to remember here are (1) the fact of a correlation does not prove a causation; (2) the way to test different explanations of causation is to hold all of the factors constant except for one, and then allow that one to vary; (3) data do not always speak clearly, and sometimes do not allow any conclusions to be drawn.

WHY ECONOMISTS DISAGREE

Economists are frequently called upon to make judgments on matters of public policy. Should the government reduce the deficit? Should inflation be reduced? If so, how? In these public policy discussions, economists often disagree. They differ in their views of how the world works, in their *description* of the economy, in their predictions of the consequences of certain actions. And they differ in their values, in how they evaluate these consequences.

When they describe the economy, and construct models that predict either how the economy will change or the effects of different policies, they are engaged in what is called **positive economics.** When they evaluate alternative policies, weighing up the various benefits and costs, they are engaged in what is called **normative economics.** Positive economics is concerned with what "is," with describing how the economy functions. Normative economics deals with what "should be," with making judgments about the desirability of various courses of action. Normative economics makes use of positive economics. We cannot make judgments about whether a policy is desirable unless we have a clear picture of its consequences. Good normative economics also tries to be explicit about precisely what values or objectives it is incorporating. It tries to couch its statements in the form "If these are your objectives . . . , then this is the best possible policy."

Consider the normative and positive aspects of the proposal to restrict imports of Japanese cars. Positive economics would describe the consequences: the increased prices consumers have to pay; the increased sales of American cars; the increased employment and increased profits; the increased pollution and oil imports, because American cars on average are less fuel efficient than Japanese cars. In the end, the question is, *should there be restraints on imports of Japanese cars?* This is a normative question: Normative economics would weigh these various effects—the losses of the consumers, the gains to workers, the increased profits, the increased pollution, the increased oil imports—to reach an overall judgment. Normative economics develops systematic frameworks within which these complicated judgments can be conducted in a systematic way.

CLOSE-UP: ECONOMISTS AGREE!

Try the following six statements out on your class-mates or your family to see whether they, like the economists surveyed, disagree, agree with provisos, or agree:

| | **Percentage of economists who** | | |
	Disagree	**Agree with provisos**	**Agree**
1. Tariffs and import quotas usually reduce general economic welfare.	6.5%	21.3%	71.3%
2. A ceiling on rents reduces the quantity and quality of housing available.	6.5%	16.6%	76.3%
3. The cause of the rise in gasoline prices that occurred in the wake of the Iraqi invasion of Kuwait is the monopoly power of large oil companies.	67.5%	20.3%	11.4%
4. The trade deficit is primarily a consequence of the inability of U.S. firms to compete.	51.5%	29.7%	18.1%
5. Cash payments increase the welfare of recipients to a greater degree than do transfers-in-kind of equal cash value.	15.1%	25.9%	58.0%

Among the general population, these are controversial questions. You will find many people who believe that restricting foreign imports is a good thing; that government regulation of rents has few ill effects; that the trade deficit is mainly caused by the inability of U.S. companies to compete; that government should avoid giving cash to poor people (because they are likely to waste it); and that oil companies are the cause of higher oil prices.

But when professional economists are surveyed, there is broad agreement that many of those popular answers are misguided. The percentages listed above are from a survey carried out by economists at Weber State University and Brigham Young University in 1990. Notice that healthy percentages of economists apparently believe that most import quotas are economically harmful; that government control of rents does lead to adverse consequences; that oil companies are not to blame for higher oil prices; that the trade deficit is not caused by the competitive problems of individual companies; that cash payments benefit the poor more than direct (in-kind) transfers of food, shelter, and medical care.

Sources: Richard M. Alston, J. R. Kearl, and Michael B. Vaughan, "Is There a Consensus Among Economists in the 1990s?" *American Economic Review* (May 1992).

DISAGREEMENTS WITHIN POSITIVE ECONOMICS

Even when they describe how the economy works, economists may differ for two main reasons. First, economists differ over what is the appropriate model of the economy. They may disagree about how well people and firms are able to perceive and calculate their self-interest, and whether their interactions take place in a competitive or a noncompetitive market. Different models will produce different results. Often the data do not allow us to say which of two competing models provides a better description of some market.

Second, even when they agree about the appropriate theoretical model, economists may disagree about quantitative magnitudes, which will cause their predictions to differ. They may agree, for instance, that reducing the tax on interest income will encourage individuals to save more, but they may produce different estimates about the amount of the savings increase. Again, many of these disagreements arise because of inadequate data. We may have considerable data concerning savings in the United States over the past century. But institutions and economic conditions today are markedly different from those of fifty or even ten years ago.

DISAGREEMENTS WITHIN NORMATIVE ECONOMICS

There are generally many consequences of any policy, some beneficial, some harmful. In comparing two policies, one may benefit some people more, another may benefit others. One policy is not unambiguously better than another. It depends on what you care more about. A cut in the tax on the profits from the sale of stocks might encourage savings, but at the same time, most of the benefits accrue to the very wealthy; hence, it increases inequality. A reduction in taxes to stimulate the economy may reduce unemployment, but it may also increase inflation. Even though two economists agree about the model, they may make different recommendations. In assessing the effect of a tax cut on unemployment and inflation, for instance, an economist who is worried more about unemployment may recommend in favor of the tax cut, while the other, concerned about inflation, may recommend against it. In this case, the source of the disagreement is a difference in values.

But while economists may often seem to differ greatly among themselves, in fact they agree more than they disagree: their disagreements get more attention than their agreements. Most importantly, when they do disagree, they seek to be clear about the source of their disagreement: 1) to what extent does it arise out of differences in models, 2) to what extent does it arise out of differences in estimates of quantitative relations, and 3) to what extent does it arise out of differences in values? Clarifying the sources of and reasons for disagreement can be a very productive way of learning more.

CONSENSUS ON THE IMPORTANCE OF SCARCITY

Most of what we have discussed in this chapter fits within the areas on which there is broad consensus among economists. This includes the observation that the U.S. economy is a mixed economy and that there are certain basic questions that all economic systems must address. We highlight the most important points of consensus throughout the book. Our first consensus point concerns scarcity. It is the most important point of consensus in this chapter.

1 Scarcity

There is no free lunch. Having more of one thing requires giving up something else. Scarcity is a basic fact of life.

REVIEW AND PRACTICE

SUMMARY

1. Economics is the study of how individuals, firms, and governments within our society make choices. Choices are unavoidable because desired goods, services, and resources are inevitably scarce.

2. There are four basic questions that economists ask about any economy. (1) What is produced, and in what quantities? (2) How are these goods produced? (3) For whom are these goods produced? (4) Who makes economic decisions, and by what process?

3. The United States has a mixed economy; there is a mix between public and private decision making. The economy relies primarily on the private interaction of individuals and firms to answer the four basic questions, but government plays a large role as well. A central question for any mixed economy is the balance between the public and private sectors.

4. The term "market" is used to describe any situation where exchange takes place. In America's market economy, individuals, firms, and government interact in product markets, labor markets, and capital markets.

5. Economists use models to study how the economy works and to make predictions about what will happen if something is changed. A model can be expressed in words or equations, and is designed to mirror the essential characteristics of the particular phenomena under study.

6. A correlation exists when two variables tend to change together in a predictable way. However, the simple existence of a correlation does not

prove that one factor causes the other to change. Additional outside factors may be influencing both.

7. Positive economics is the study of how the economy works. Disagreements within positive economics center on the appropriate model of the economy or market and the quantitative magnitudes characterizing the models. Normative economics deals with the desirability of various actions. Disagreements within normative economics center on differences in the values placed on the various costs and benefits of different actions.

KEY TERMS

centrally planned economy	labor market	theory
mixed economy	capital market	correlation
market economy	capital goods	causation
product market	microeconomics	positive economics
	macroeconomics	normative economics

REVIEW QUESTIONS

1. Why are choices unavoidable?

2. How are the four basic economic questions answered in the U.S. economy?

3. What is a mixed economy? Describe some of the roles government might play, or not play, in a mixed economy.

4. Name the three main economic markets, and describe how an individual might participate in each one as a buyer and seller.

5. Give two examples of economic issues that are primarily microeconomic, and two examples that are primarily macroeconomic. What is the general difference between microeconomics and macroeconomics?

6. What is a model? Why do economists use models?

7. When causation exists, would you also expect a correlation to exist? When a correlation exists, would you also expect causation to exist? Explain.

8. "All disagreements between economists are purely subjective." Comment.

PROBLEMS

1. Characterize the following events as microeconomic, macroeconomic, or both.
    (a) Unemployment increases this month.

(b) A drug company invents and begins to market a new medicine.

(c) A bank loans money to a large company but turns down a small business.

(d) Interest rates decline for all borrowers.

(e) A union negotiates for higher pay and better health insurance.

(f) The price of oil increases.

2. Characterize the following events as part of the labor market, the capital market, or the product market.

(a) An investor tries to decide which company to invest in.

(b) With practice, the workers on an assembly line become more efficient.

(c) The opening up of the economies in Eastern Europe offers new markets for American products.

(d) A big company that is losing money decides to offer its workers a special set of incentives to retire early, hoping to reduce its costs.

(e) A consumer roams around a shopping mall, looking for birthday gifts.

(f) The federal government needs to borrow more money to finance its level of spending.

3. Discuss the incentive issues that might arise in each of the following situations. (Hint: Remember the history of the automobile industry at the start of this chapter.)

(a) You have some money to invest, and your financial adviser introduces you to a couple of software executives who want to start their own company. What should you worry about as you decide whether to invest?

(b) You are running a small company, and your workers promise that if you increase their pay, they will work harder.

(c) A large industry is going bankrupt and appeals for government assistance.

4. Name ways in which government intervention has helped the automobile industry in the last two decades, and ways in which it has injured the industry.

5. The back of a bag of cat litter claims, "Cats that use cat litter live three years longer than cats that don't." Do you think that cat litter actually causes an increased life expectancy of cats, or can you think of some other factors to explain this correlation? What evidence might you try to collect to test your explanation?

6. Life expectancy in Sweden is 78 years; life expectancy in India is 61 years. Does this prove that if an Indian moved to Sweden he would live longer? That is, does this prove that living in Sweden causes an increase in life expectancy, or can you think of some other factors to explain these facts? What evidence might you try to collect to test your explanation?

CHAPTER 2

THINKING LIKE AN ECONOMIST

E veryone thinks about economics, at least some of the time. We think about money (we wish we had more of it) and about work (we wish we had less of it). But there is a distinctive way that economists approach economic issues, and one of the purposes of this course is to introduce you to that way of thinking. This chapter begins with a basic model of the economy. We follow this with a closer look at how the basic units that comprise the economy—individuals, firms, and governments—make choices in situations where they are faced with scarcity. In Chapters 3 through 5, we study ways in which these units interact with one another, and how those interactions "add up" to determine how society's resources are allocated.

THE BASIC COMPETITIVE MODEL

Though different economists employ different models of the economy they all use a basic set of assumptions as a point of departure. The economist's basic competitive model has three components: assumptions about how consumers behave, assumptions about how firms behave, and assumptions about the markets in which these consumers and firms interact. The model ignores government, because we need to see how an economy without a government might function before we can understand the role of government.

RATIONAL CONSUMERS AND PROFIT-MAXIMIZING FIRMS

Scarcity, which we encountered in Chapter 1, implies that individuals and firms must make choices. Underlying much of economic analysis is the basic assumption of **rational choice,** that people weigh the costs and benefits of each possibility. This assumption is based on the expectation that individuals and firms will act in a consistent manner, with a reasonably well-defined notion of what they like and what their objectives are, and with a reasonable understanding of how to attain those objectives.

In the case of an individual, the rationality assumption is taken to mean that he makes choices and decisions in pursuit of his own self-interest. Different people will, of course, have different goals and desires. Sally may want to drive a Porsche, own a yacht, and have a large house; to attain those objectives, she knows she needs to work long hours and sacrifice time with her family. Andrew is willing to accept a lower income to get longer vacations and more leisure throughout the year.

Economists make no judgments about whether Sally's preferences are "better" or "worse" than Andrew's. They do not even spend much time asking why different individuals have different views on these matters, or why tastes change over time. These are important questions, but they are more the province of psychology and sociology. What economists are concerned about are the consequences of these different preferences. What decisions can they expect Sally and Andrew, rationally pursuing their respective interests, to make?

In the case of firms, the rationality assumption is taken to mean that firms operate to maximize their profits.

COMPETITIVE MARKETS

To complete the model, economists make assumptions about the places where self-interested consumers and profit-maximizing firms meet: markets. Economists begin by focusing on the case where there are many buyers and sellers, all buying and selling the same thing. You might picture a crowded farmers' market to get a sense of the number of buyers and sellers—except that you have to picture everyone buying and selling just one good. Let's say we are in Florida, and the booths are all full of oranges.

Each of the farmers would like to raise his prices. That way, if he can still sell his oranges, his profits go up. Yet with a large number of sellers, each is forced to charge close to the same price, since if any farmer charged much more, he would lose business to the farmer next door. Profit-maximizing firms are in the same position. In an extreme case, if a firm charged any more than the going price, it would lose *all* its sales. Economists label this case **perfect competition.** In perfect competition, each firm is a **price taker,** which simply means that because it cannot influence the market price, it must accept that price. The firm takes the market price as given because it cannot raise its price without losing all sales, and at the market price it can sell as much as it wishes. Even if it sold ten times as much, this would have a negligible effect on the total quantity marketed or the price prevailing in the market. Markets for agricultural goods would be, in the absence of government intervention, perfectly competitive. There are so many wheat farmers, for instance, that each farmer believes he can grow and sell as much wheat as he wishes and have no effect on the price of wheat. (Later in the book, we will encounter markets with limited or no competition, like monopolies, where firms can raise prices without losing all their sales.)

On the other side of our farmers' market are rational individuals, each of whom would like to pay as little as possible for her oranges. Why can't she pay less than the going price? Because the seller sees another buyer in the crowd who will pay the going price. Thus, the consumers also take the market price as given, and focus their attention on other factors—their taste for oranges, primarily—in deciding how many to buy.

This model of consumers, firms, and markets—rational, self-interested consumers interacting with rational, profit-maximizing firms, in competitive markets where firms and consumers are both price takers—is the **basic competitive model.** The model has one very strong implication: if actual markets are well described by the competitive market, then the economy will be efficient: resources are not wasted, it is not possible to produce more of one good without producing less of another, and it is not even possible to make anyone better off without making someone else worse off. These results are obtained without government.

Virtually all economists recognize that actual economies are not *perfectly* described by the competitive model, but most still use it as a convenient benchmark—as we will throughout this book. We will also point out important differences between the predictions of the competitive model and observed outcomes, which will guide us to other models which provide a better description of particular markets and situations. Economists recognize too that, while the competitive market may not provide a *perfect* description of some markets, it may provide a good description—with its predictions matching actual outcomes well, though not perfectly. As we shall see, economists differ in their views about how many such markets there are, how good the "match" is, and how well alternative models do in rectifying the deficiencies of the competitive model in particular cases.

INGREDIENTS IN THE BASIC COMPETITIVE MODEL

1. Rational, self-interested consumers

2. Rational, profit-maximizing firms

3. Competitive markets with price-taking behavior

PRICES, PROPERTY RIGHTS, AND PROFITS: INCENTIVES AND INFORMATION

For market economies to work efficiently, firms and individuals must be informed and have incentives to act on available information. Indeed, incentives can be viewed as at the heart of economics. Without incentives, why would individuals go to work in the morning? Who would undertake the risks of bringing out new products? Who would put aside savings for a rainy day? There is an old expression about the importance of having someone "mind the store." But without incentives, why would anyone bother?

Market economies provide information and incentives through *prices*, *profits*, and *property rights*. Prices provide information about the relative scarcity of different goods. The **price system** ensures that goods go to those individuals and firms who are most willing and able to pay for them. Prices convey information to firms about how individuals value different goods.

The desire for profits motivates firms to respond to the information provided by prices. By producing what consumers want in the most efficient way, in ways that least use scarce resources, they increase their profits. Similarly, rational individuals' pursuit of self-interest induces them to respond to prices: they buy goods which are more expensive—in a sense relatively more scarce—only if they provide commensurately greater benefits.

For the profit motive to be effective, firms need to be able to keep at least some of their profits. Households, in turn, need to be able to keep at least some of what they earn or receive as a return on their investments. (The return on their investments is simply what they receive back in excess of what they invested. If they receive back less than they invested, the return is negative.) There must, in short, be **private property,** with its attendant **property rights.** Property rights include both the right of the owner to use the property as she sees fit and the right to sell it.

These two attributes of property rights give individuals the incentive to use property under their control efficiently. The owner of a piece of land tries to figure out the most profitable use of the land; for example, whether to build a store or a restaurant. If he makes a mistake and opens a restaurant when he should have opened a store, he bears the consequences: the loss in income. The profits he earns if he makes the right decisions—and the losses he bears if he makes the wrong ones—give him an incentive to think carefully about the decision and do the requisite research. The owner of a store tries to make sure that her customers get the kind of merchandise and the quality of service they want. She has an incentive to establish a good reputation, because if she does so, she will do more business and earn more profits.

The store owner will also want to maintain her property—which is not just the land anymore, but includes the store as well—because she will get more for it when the time comes to sell her business to someone else. Similarly, the owner of a house has an incentive to maintain *his* property, so that he can sell it for more when he wishes to move. Again, the profit motive combines with private property to provide incentives.

How the Profit Motive Drives the Market System

In market economies, incentives are supplied to individuals and firms by prices, profits, and property rights.

INCENTIVES VERSUS EQUALITY

While incentives are at the heart of market economies, they come with a cost: inequality. Any system of incentives must tie compensation with performance. Whether through differences in luck or ability, performance of different individuals will differ. In many cases, it will not be possible to identify why performance is high. The salesperson may claim that the reason his sales are high is superior skill and effort, while his colleague may argue that it is dumb luck.

If pay is tied to performance, there will inevitably be some inequality. And the more closely compensation is tied to performance the greater the inequality. The fact that the greater the incentives, the greater the resulting inequality is called the **incentive-equality trade-off.** If society provides greater incentives, total output is likely to be higher, but there will also probably be greater inequality.

One of the basic questions facing society in the choice of tax rates and welfare systems is how much would incentives be diminished by an increase in tax rates to finance a better welfare system and thus reduce inequality? What would be the results of those reduced incentives?

WHEN PROPERTY RIGHTS FAIL

Prices, profits, and property rights are the three essential ingredients of market economies. We can learn a lot about why they are so important by examining a few cases where property rights and prices are interfered with. Each example highlights a general point. Any time society fails to define the owner of its resources and does not allow the highest bidder to use them, inefficiencies result. Resources will be wasted or not used in the most productive way.

Ill-Defined Property Rights: The Grand Banks Fish are a valuable resource. Not long ago, the area between Newfoundland and Maine, called the Grand Banks, was teeming with fish. Not surprisingly, it was also teeming with fishermen, who saw an easy livelihood scooping out the fish from the sea. Since there were no property rights, everyone tried to catch as many fish as he could. A self-interested fisherman would rationally reason that if he did not catch the fish, someone else would. The result was a tragedy: the Grand Banks was overfished, to the point where not only was it not teeming with fish, but commercial fishing became unprofitable. Today Canada and the United States have a treaty limiting the amount of fish that fishermen from each country can take from the Grand Banks, and gradually, over the years, the fish population has been restored.

Restricted Property Rights In California the government allocates water rights among various groups. Water is scarce. Hence these rights to water are extremely valuable. But they come with a restriction. They are not transferable; they cannot be sold. Cattle ranchers currently have the right to about 10 percent of the state's water, slightly less than the fraction consumed by residences. Government charges ranchers as little as $50 per acre-foot for their water, in contrast to $256 per acre-foot charged to residences in San Francisco and much more in some towns. The value of water to thirsty urban consumers—what they would be willing to pay for the additional water—exceeds the profits from raising cattle. If the water rights could be sold, those in the cattle industry would have a strong incentive to sell their rights to the towns. If cattle owners could get out of the cattle business and sell their water rights to urban residents instead, everyone would be better off.[1] In this case, restrictions on property rights have led to inefficiencies.

Entitlements as Property Rights   Property rights do not always mean that you have full ownership or control. A **legal entitlement,** such as the right to occupy an apartment for life at a rent that is controlled, common in some large cities, is viewed by economists as a property right. Individuals do not own the apartment and thus cannot sell it, but they cannot be thrown out, either.

These partial and restricted property rights result in many inefficiencies. Because the individual in a rent-controlled apartment cannot (legally) sell the right to live in her apartment, as she gets older she may have limited incentives to maintain its condition, let alone improve it.

CONSENSUS ON INCENTIVES

Incentives, prices, profits, and property rights are central features of any economy, and highlight an important area of consensus among economists. This brings us to our second point of consensus:

2   Incentives

> *Providing appropriate incentives is a fundamental economic problem. In modern market economies, profits provide incentives for firms to produce the goods individuals want, and wages provide incentives for individuals to work. Property rights also provide people with important incentives, not only to invest and to save, but to put their assets to the best possible use.*

RATIONING

The price system is only one way of allocating resources, and a comparison with other systems will help to clarify the advantages of markets. When individuals get less of a good than they would like at the terms being offered, the good is said to be **rationed.** Different rationing schemes are different ways of deciding who gets society's scarce resources.

Rationing by Queues   Rather than supplying goods to those willing and able to pay the most for them, a society could give them instead to those most willing to wait in line. This system is called **rationing by queues,** after the British term for lines. Tickets are often allocated by queues, whether they are for

---

[1] The calculation of benefits and losses does not take into account the feelings of the cattle.

movies, sporting events, or rock concerts. A price is set, and it will not change no matter how many people line up to buy at that price. (The high price that scalpers can get for "hot" tickets is a good indication of how much more than the ticket price people would have been willing to pay.)

Rationing by queues is thought by many to be a more desirable way of supplying medical services than the price system. Why, it is argued, should the rich—who are most able to pay for medical services—be the ones to get better or more medical care? Using this reasoning, Britain provides free medical care to everyone on its soil. To see a doctor there, all you have to do is wait in line. Rationing medicine by queues turns the allocation problem around: since the value of time for low-wage workers is lower, they are more willing to wait, and therefore they get a disproportionate share of (government-supplied) medical services.

In general, rationing by queues is an inefficient way of distributing resources because the time spent in line is a wasted resource. There are usually ways of achieving the same goal within a price system that can make everyone better off. Returning to the medical example, if some individuals were allowed to pay for doctors' services instead of waiting in line, more doctors could be hired with the proceeds, and the lines for those unable or unwilling to pay could actually be reduced.

Rationing by Lotteries   **Lotteries** allocate goods by a random process, like picking a name from a hat. University dormitory rooms are usually assigned by lottery. So are seats in popular courses; when more students want to enroll in a section of a principles of economics course than the size of the section allows, there may be a lottery to determine who gets to enroll. The United States used to allocate certain mining rights and licenses to radio airwaves by lottery. Like queue systems, lotteries are thought to be fair because everyone has an equal chance. However, they are also inefficient, because the scarce resources do not go to the individual or firm who is willing and able to pay (and therefore values them) the most.

Rationing by Coupons   Most governments in wartime use **coupon rationing.** People are allowed so many gallons of gasoline, so many pounds of sugar, and so much flour each month. To get the good, you have to pay the market price *and* produce a coupon. The reason for coupon rationing is that without coupons prices might soar, inflicting a hardship on poorer members of society.

Coupon systems take two forms depending on whether coupons are tradable or not. Coupons that are not tradable give rise to the same inefficiency that occurs with most of the other nonprice systems—goods do not in general go to the individuals who are willing and able to pay the most. There is generally room for a trade that will make all parties better off. For instance, I might be willing to trade some of my flour ration for some of your sugar ration. But in a nontradable coupon system, the law prohibits such transactions. When coupons cannot be legally traded, there are strong incentives for the establishment of a **black market,** an illegal market in which the goods or the coupons for goods are traded.

OPPORTUNITY SETS

We have covered a lot of ground so far in this chapter. We have seen the economist's basic model, which relies on competitive markets. We have seen how prices, the profit motive, and private property supply the incentives that drive a market economy. And we have gotten our first glimpse at why economists believe that market systems, which supply goods to those who are willing and able to pay the most, provide the most efficient means of allocating what the economy produces. They are far better than the nonprice rationing schemes that have been employed. It is time now to return to the question of choice. Market systems leave to individuals and firms the question of what to consume. How are these decisions made?

For a rational individual or firm, the first step in the economic analysis of any choice is to identify what is possible—what economists call the **opportunity set,** which is simply the group of available options. If you want a sandwich and you have only roast beef and tuna fish in the refrigerator, then your opportunity set consists of a roast beef sandwich, a tuna fish sandwich, a strange sandwich combining roast beef and tuna fish, or no sandwich. A ham sandwich is out of the question. Defining the limitations facing an individual or firm is a critical step in economic analysis. One can spend time yearning after the ham sandwich, or anything else outside the opportunity set, but when it comes to making choices and facing decisions, only what is within the opportunity set is relevant.

BUDGET AND TIME CONSTRAINTS

Constraints limit choices and define the opportunity set. In most economic situations, the constraints that limit a person's choices—that is, those constraints that actually are relevant—are not sandwich fixings, but time and money. Opportunity sets whose constraints are imposed by money are referred to as **budget constraints;** opportunity sets whose constraints are prescribed by time are called **time constraints.** A billionaire may feel that his choices are limited not by money but by time; while for an unemployed worker, time hangs heavy—lack of money rather than time limits his choices.

The budget constraint defines a typical opportunity set. Consider the budget constraint of Alfred, who has decided to spend $100 on either cassette recordings or compact discs. A CD costs $10, a cassette $5. So Alfred can buy 10 CDs or 20 cassettes; or 9 CDs and 2 cassettes; or 8 CDs and 4 cassettes. The various possibilities are set forth in Table 2.1. And they are depicted graphically in Figure 2.1:[2] along the vertical axis, we measure the number of cassettes purchased, and along the horizontal axis, we measure the number of CDs. The line marked B_1B_2 is Alfred's budget constraint. The extreme cases,

Table 2.1 **ALFRED'S OPPORTUNITY SET**

Cassettes	CDs
0	10
2	9
4	8
6	7
8	6
10	5
12	4
14	3
16	2
18	1
20	0

[2] See the Chapter appendix for help in reading graphs.

Figure 2.1 ALFRED'S BUD-GET CONSTRAINT

The budget constraint identifies the limits of an individual's opportunity set between CDs and cassettes. Points B_1 and B_2 are the extreme options, where he chooses all of one and none of the other. His actual choice is point E. Choices from the shaded area are possible, but less attractive than choices actually on the budget constraint.

where Alfred buys only CDs or cassettes, are represented by the points B_1 and B_2 in the figure. The dots between these two points, along the budget constraint, represent the other possible combinations. The cost of each combination of CDs and cassettes must add up to $100. The point actually chosen by Alfred is labeled E, where he purchases 4 CDs (for $40) and 12 cassettes (for $60).

Alfred's budget constraint is the line that defines the outer limits of his opportunity set. But the whole opportunity set is larger. It also includes all points below the budget constraint. This is the shaded area in the figure. The budget constraint shows the maximum number of cassettes Alfred can buy for each number of CDs purchased, and vice versa. Alfred is always happiest when he chooses a point on his budget constraint rather than below it. To see why, compare the points E and D. At point E, he has more of both goods than at point D. He would be even happier at point F, where he has still more cassettes and CDs, but that point, by definition, is unattainable.

Figure 2.2 depicts a time constraint. The most common time constraint simply says that the sum of what an individual spends her time on each day—including sleeping—must add up to 24 hours. The figure plots the hours spent watching television on the horizontal axis and the hours spent on all other activities on the vertical axis. People—no matter how rich or how poor—have only 24 hours a day to spend on different activities. The time constraint is quite like the budget constraint. A person cannot spend more than 24 hours or fewer than zero hours a day watching TV. The more time she spends watching television the less time she has available for all other activities. Point D (for dazed) has been added to the diagram at 5 hours a day—this is the amount of time the typical American chooses to spend watching TV.

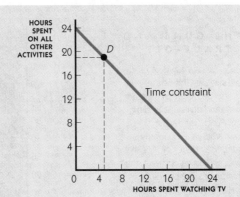

Figure 2.2 AN OPPORTUNITY SET FOR WATCHING TV AND OTHER ACTIVITIES

This opportunity set is limited by a time constraint, which shows the trade-off a person faces between spending time watching television and spending it on other activities. At 5 hours of TV time per day, point *D* represents a typical choice for an American.

THE PRODUCTION POSSIBILITIES CURVE

Business firms and whole societies face constraints. They too must make choices limited to opportunity sets. The amounts of goods a firm or society could produce, given a fixed amount of land, labor, and other inputs, are referred to as its **production possibilities.**

As one commonly discussed example, consider a simple description of a society in which all economic production is divided into two categories, military spending and civilian spending. Of course, each of these two kinds of spending has many different elements, but for the moment, let's discuss the choice between the two broad categories. For simplicity, Figure 2.3 refers to military spending as "guns" and civilian spending as "butter." The production of guns is given along the vertical axis, the production of butter along the horizontal. The possible combinations of military and civilian spending—of guns and butter—is the opportunity set. Table 2.2 sets out some of the possible combinations: 90 million guns and 40 million tons of butter, or 40 million guns and 90 million tons of butter. These possibilities are depicted in the figure. In the case of a choice involving production decisions, the boundary of the opportunity set—giving the maximum amount of guns that can be produced for each amount of butter and vice versa—is called the **production possibilities curve.**

The importance of the guns-butter trade-off can be seen dramatically by looking back at Figure 1.3, which shows that during World War II, car production plummeted almost to zero as the automobile factories were diverted to the production of tanks and other military vehicles.

When we compare the individual's opportunity set and that of society, reflected in its production possibilities curve, we notice one major difference. The individual's budget constraint is a straight line, while the production

Table 2.2 PRODUCTION POSSIBILITIES FOR THE ECONOMY

Guns (millions)	Butter (millions of tons)
100	0
90	40
70	70
40	90
0	100

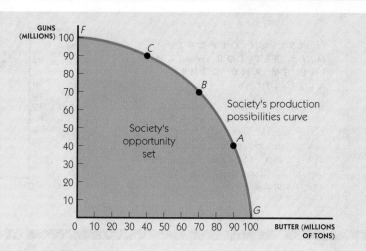

Figure 2.3 THE GUNS AND BUTTER TRADE-OFF

A production possibilities curve can show society's opportunity set. This one describes the trade-off between military spending ("guns") and civilian spending ("butter"). Points *F* and *G* show the extreme choices, where the economy produces all guns or all butter. Notice that unlike the budget and time constraint, the production possibilities line curves, reflecting diminishing returns.

possibilities curve bows outward. There is a good reason for this. An individual typically faces fixed **trade-offs:** if Alfred spends $10 more on CDs (that is, he buys one more CD), he has $10 less to spend on cassettes (he can buy two fewer cassettes).

On the other hand, the trade-offs faced by society are not fixed. If a society produces only a few guns, it will use those resources—the men and machines—that are best equipped for gun making. But as society tries to produce more and more guns, doing so becomes more difficult; it will increasingly depend on those resources that are less good at producing guns. It will be drawing these resources out of the production of other goods, in this case, butter. Thus, when the economy increases its production of guns from 40 million a year (point *A*) to 70 million (*B*), butter production falls by 20 million tons, from 90 million tons to 70 million tons. But if production of guns is increased further, to 90 million (*C*), an increase of only 20 million, butter production has to decrease by 30 million tons, to only 40 million tons. For each increase in the number of guns, the reduction in the number of tons of butter produced gets larger. That is why the production possibilities curve is curved.

In another example, assume that a firm owns land that can be used for growing wheat but not corn, and land that can grow corn but not wheat. In this case, the only way to increase wheat production is to move workers from the cornfields to the wheat fields. As more and more workers are put into the wheat fields, production of wheat goes up, but each successive worker increases production less. The first workers might pick the largest and most destructive weeds. Additional workers lead to better weeding, and better weeding leads to higher output. But the additional weeds rooted up are smaller and less destructive, so output is increased by a correspondingly smaller amount. This is an example of the general principle of **diminishing returns.**

Table 2.3 **DIMINISHING RETURNS**

Labor in cornfield (no. of workers)	Corn output (bushels)	Labor in wheat field (no. of workers)	Wheat output (bushels)
1,000	60,000	5,000	200,000
2,000	110,000	4,000	180,000
3,000	150,000	3,000	150,000
4,000	180,000	2,000	110,000
5,000	200,000	1,000	60,000

Adding successive units of any input such as fertilizer, labor, or machines to a fixed amount of other inputs—seeds or land—increases the output, or amount produced, but by less and less.

Table 2.3 shows the output of the corn and wheat fields as labor is increased in each field. Assume the firm has 6,000 workers to divide between wheat production and corn production. Thus, the second and fourth columns together give the firm's production possibilities, which are depicted in Figure 2.4.

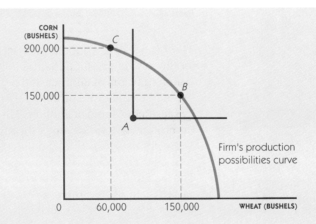

Figure 2.4 THE WHEAT AND CORN TRADE-OFF

This production possibilities curve shows that as wheat production increases, it becomes necessary to give up larger and larger amounts of corn. Or to put the same point a different way, as corn production falls, the resulting increase in wheat production gets smaller and smaller. Point A illustrates an inefficient outcome, falling inside the opportunity set.

INEFFICIENCIES: BEING OFF THE PRODUCTION POSSIBILITIES CURVE

There is no reason to assume that a firm or an economy will always be on its production possibilities curve. Any inefficiency in the economy will result in a point such as *A* in Figure 2.4, below the production possibilities curve. One of the major quests of economists is to look for instances in which the economy is inefficient in this way.

Whenever the economy is operating below the production possibilities curve, it is possible for us to have more of every good—more wheat and more corn, more guns and more butter. No matter what goods we like, we can have more of them. That is why we can unambiguously say that points below the production possibilities curve are undesirable. But this does not mean that every point on the production possibilities curve is better than any point below it. Compare points *A* and *C* in Figure 2.4. Corn production is higher at *C*, but wheat production is lower. If people do not like corn very much, the increased corn production may not adequately compensate them for the decreased wheat production.

There are many reasons why the economy may be below the production possibilities curve. If land better suited for the production of corn is mistakenly devoted to the production of wheat, the economy will operate below its production possibilities curve. If some of society's resources—its land, labor, and capital goods—are simply left idle, as happens when there is a depression, the economy operates below the production possibilities curve. The kinds of inefficiencies discussed earlier in the chapter with inadequately or improperly defined property rights also result in operating below the production possibilities curve.

COST

The beauty of an opportunity set like the budget constraint, the time constraint, or the production possibilities curve is that it specifies the cost of one option in terms of another. If the individual, the firm, or the society is operating on the constraint or curve, then it is possible to get more of one thing only by sacrificing some of another. The "cost" of one more unit of one good is how much you have to give up of the other.

Economists thus think about cost in terms of trade-offs within opportunity sets. Let's go back to Alfred choosing between CDs and cassettes in Figure 2.1. The trade-off is given by the **relative price,** the ratio of the prices of CDs and cassettes. In our example, a CD cost $10, a cassette $5. The relative price is $10 ÷ $5 = 2; for every CD Alfred gives up, he can get two cassettes. Likewise, societies and firms face trade-offs along the production possibilities curve, like the one shown in Figure 2.3. There, point *A* is the choice where 40 million guns and 90 million tons of butter are produced. The trade-off can be calculated by comparing points *A* and *B*. Society can have 30 million more guns by giving up 20 million tons of butter.

Trade-offs are necessary because resources are scarce. If you want something, you have to pay for it; you have to give up something. If you want to go to the library tomorrow night, you have to give up going to the movies. If a sawmill wants to make more two-by-four beams from its stock of wood, it will not be able to make as many one-by-four boards.

OPPORTUNITY COSTS

If someone were to ask you right now what it costs to go to a movie, you would probably answer, "Seven dollars," or whatever you paid the last time you went to the movies. But with the concept of trade-offs, you can see that a *full* answer is not that simple. To begin with, the cost is not the $7 but what that $7 could otherwise buy. Furthermore, your time is a scarce resource that must be figured into the calculation. Both the money and the time represent opportunities forgone in favor of going to the movie, or what economists refer to as the **opportunity cost** of the movie. To apply a resource to one use means that it cannot be put to any other use. Thus, we should consider the next-best, alternative use of any resource when we think about putting it to any particular use. This next-best use is the formal measurement of opportunity cost.

Some examples will help to clarify the idea of opportunity cost. Consider a student, Sarah, who enrolls in college. She thinks that the check for tuition and room and board represents the costs of her education. But the economist's mind immediately turns to the job she might have had if she had not enrolled in college. If Sarah could have earned $15,000 from September to June, this is the opportunity cost of her time, and this forgone income must be added to the college bills in calculating the total economic cost of the school year.

Now consider a business firm that has bought a building for its headquarters that is bigger than necessary. If the firm could receive $3 per month in rent for each square foot of space that is not needed, then this is the opportunity cost of leaving the space idle.

The analysis can be applied to the government as well. The federal government owns a vast amount of wilderness. In deciding whether it is worthwhile to convert some of that land into a national park, the government needs to take into account the opportunity cost of the land. The land might be used for growing timber or for grazing sheep. Whatever the value of the land in its next-best use, this is the economic cost of the national park. The fact that the government does not have to buy the land does not mean that the land should be treated as a free good.

Thus, in the economist's view, when rational firms and individuals make decisions—whether to undertake one investment project rather than another, whether to buy one product rather than another—they take into account *all* of the costs, the full opportunity costs, not just the direct expenditures.

Businesses often neglect one of the most important opportunity costs of all: the time of their top employees. The personnel agency Accountemps tried to measure some of that wasted time by surveying 200 executives from the 1,000 largest U.S. companies. The executives estimated that they spent an average of 15 minutes a day on hold on the telephone; an average of 32 minutes a day reading or writing unnecessary memos; and an average of 72 minutes a day at unnecessary meetings. Now multiply those numbers by 48 weeks (assuming that the executives take four weeks of vacation each year). The average executive would be spending 60 hours per year on telephone hold; 128 hours per year on unnecessary memos; and 288 hours a year in unnecessary meetings!

Of course, estimates like these are more for illustration than precision. Moreover, it may be impossible to tell in advance whether a meeting will be useful; the only way to have a productive meeting, after all, may be to risk having an unproductive one. But even taking the particular numbers with a grain of salt, it seems likely that many businesses schedule meetings believing that since they do not have to pay extra for people to attend, the cost of the meetings is zero. They ignore the opportunity cost, the fact that their highly paid managers could be doing something else with their time.

One semi-serious proposal is that businesses should measure and display the opportunity cost of their meetings with a scoreboard placed discreetly in the corner of their meeting rooms. As everyone entered the meeting room, she would enter her hourly salary, and the scoreboard would then start adding up the cost of everyone's time. For example, if there were twenty executives in a meeting who earned an average of $45 per hour, then the scoreboard would ring up $900 for every hour of meeting time. We could also include an opportunity cost of using the meeting room, of needing to return calls from other people who called during the meeting, and so on. Surely, as the scoreboard showed the opportunity cost of the regular afternoon meeting climbing into four figures, there would be strong incentive to finish quickly and let everyone return to her other tasks.

Source: "Executives on Hold 60 Hours a Year," *San Jose Mercury News,* July 10, 1990, p. 7A.

SUNK COSTS

Economic cost includes costs, as we have just seen, that noneconomists often exclude, but it also ignores costs that noneconomists include. If an expenditure has already been made and cannot be recovered no matter what choice is made, a rational person would ignore it. Such expenditures are called **sunk costs.**

To understand sunk costs, let's go back to the movies, assuming now that you have spent $7 to buy a movie ticket. You were skeptical about whether the movie was worth $7. Half an hour into the movie, your worst suspicions are realized: the movie is a disaster. Should you leave the movie theater? In making that decision, the $7 should be ignored. It is a sunk cost; your money is gone whether you stay or leave. The only relevant choice now is how to spend the next 90 minutes of your time: watch a terrible movie or go do something else.

Or assume you have just purchased a fancy laptop computer for $2,000. But the next week, the manufacturer announces a new computer with twice the power for $1,000; you can trade in your old computer for the new one by paying an additional $400. You are angry. You feel you have just paid $2,000 for a computer that is now almost worthless, and you have gotten hardly any use out of it. You decide not to buy the new computer for another year, until you have gotten at least some return for your investment. Again, an economist would say that you are not approaching the question rationally. The past decision is a sunk cost. The only question you should ask yourself is whether the extra power of the fancier computer is worth the additional $400. If it is, buy it. If not, don't.

MARGINAL COSTS

The third aspect of cost that economists emphasize is the extra costs of doing something, what economists call the **marginal costs.** These are weighed against the (additional) **marginal benefits** of doing it. The most difficult decisions we make are not whether to do something or not. They are whether to do a little more or a little less of something. Few of us waste much time deciding whether or not to work. We have to work; the decision is whether to work a few more or a few less hours. A country does not consider whether or not to have an army; it decides whether to have a larger or smaller army.

Jim has just obtained a job for which he needs a car. He must decide how much to spend on the car. By spending more, he can get a bigger and more luxurious car. But he has to decide whether it is worth a few hundred (or thousand) marginal dollars for a larger car or for extra items like fancy hubcaps, power windows, and so on.

Polly is considering flying to Colorado for a ski weekend. She has three days off from work. The air fare is $200, the hotel room costs $100 a night, and the ski ticket costs $35 a day. Food costs the same as at home. She is trying to decide whether to go for two or three days. The *marginal* cost of the third day is $135, the hotel cost plus the cost of the ski ticket. There are no additional transportation costs involved in staying the third day. She needs to compare the marginal cost with the additional enjoyment she will have from the third day.

People, consciously or not, think about the trade-offs at the margin in most of their decisions. Economists, however, bring them into the foreground. Like opportunity costs and sunk costs, marginal analysis is one of the critical concepts that enable economists to think systematically about the costs of alternative choices.

Investment tax credits have been a popular tool of policymakers. With a 10 percent investment tax credit, a firm that invests $100 million—say, in the construction of a new factory—gets a credit against its taxes of $10 million. The government is in effect paying 10 percent of the investment. In 1993, the Clinton administration proposed a new form of tax credit, one that would have rewarded businesses for increasing the amount they spent on new investment over what they had spent the previous year. This proposal differs from the usual investment tax credit, which rewards all new investment equally (including the vast amount that would have been invested anyway). The Clinton proposal, which Congress failed to pass, makes good economic sense. Since it focuses on the additional (marginal) dollar, which is the focus of a business's investment decision, it gets more bang for the tax buck.

Here is the logic. As we have seen, an investment tax credit that allows firms to reduce their tax bill by 10 percent of their investment expenditures effectively reduces the cost of investment by 10 percent. This is a strong incentive to invest. But it comes at a high cost, because most of the investment would have been undertaken anyway. If, for example, the economy would have undertaken $750 billion of investment, and the tax credit increases this to $810 billion, the cost of the $60 billion in increased investment is $81 billion in lost federal revenue.

The proposal that lost in the 1993 Congress, in contrast, was a net investment tax credit. The intent of this, as noted, is to reward only investment that would not have happened without the credit. How do we know what that is? We don't. But an acceptable if imperfect substitute is to provide the credit on investment increases over the previous

year. In terms of the previous example, suppose that last year's investment was in fact $700 billion—an imperfect estimate of the $750 billion that would have occurred without the tax credit. Since it is only the marginal cost that is relevant to investment decision makers, a 10 percent net investment tax credit will increase investment to $810 billion, as before. But because the credit is only paid on $110 billion ($810 billion minus $700 billion), the Treasury loses only $11 billion ($110 billion × 10 percent)—$70 billion less than the revenues lost from the regular investment tax credit.

The 1993 Congress may have dropped the ball on the investment tax credit. But it did focus on policy at the margin when it renewed a provision that makes increases in research and development (R & D) expenditures eligible for a 20 percent tax credit.

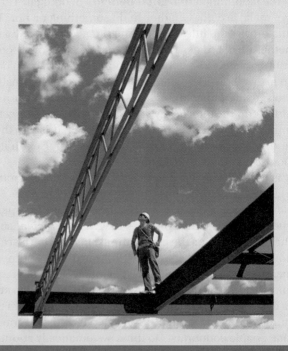

BASIC STEPS OF RATIONAL CHOICE

Identify the opportunity sets.

Define the trade-offs.

Calculate the costs correctly, taking into account opportunity costs, sunk costs, and marginal costs.

USING ECONOMICS: USING MARGINAL ANALYSIS TO SET SAFETY STANDARDS

For the past two decades, the government has taken an active role in ensuring auto safety. It sets standards that all automobiles must meet. For instance, an automobile must be able to withstand a side collision of a particular velocity. One of the most difficult problems the government faces is deciding what those standards should be. It recently considered tightening standards for withstanding side collisions on trucks. The government calculated that the higher standards would result on average in 79 fewer deaths per year. It calculated that to meet the higher standards would increase the cost of an automobile by $81. (In addition, the heavier trucks would use more fuel.) In deciding whether to impose the higher standard, it used marginal analysis. It looked at the *additional* lives saved and at the *additional* costs.

REVIEW AND PRACTICE

SUMMARY

1. The basic competitive model consists of rational, self-interested individuals and profit-maximizing firms, interacting in competitive markets.

2. The profit motive and private property provide incentives for rational individuals and firms to work hard and efficiently. Ill-defined or restricted property rights can lead to inefficient behavior.

3. Society often faces choices between efficiency, which requires incentives that enable people or firms to receive different benefits depending on their performance, and equality, which entails people receiving more or less equal benefits.

4. The price system in a market economy is one way of allocating goods and services. Other methods include rationing by queue, by lottery, and by coupon.

5. An opportunity set illustrates what choices are possible. Budget constraints and time constraints define individuals' opportunity sets. Both show the trade-offs of how much of one thing a person must give up to get more of another.

6. A production possibilities curve defines a firm or society's opportunity set, representing the possible combinations of goods that the firm or society can produce. If a firm or society is producing below its production possibilities curve, it is said to be inefficient, since it could produce more of either good without producing less of the other.

7. The opportunity cost is the cost of using any resource. It is measured by looking at the next-best, alternative use to which that resource could be put.

8. A sunk cost is a past expenditure that cannot be recovered, no matter what choice is made in the present. Thus, rational decision makers ignore them.

9. Most economic decisions concentrate on choices at the margin, where the marginal (or extra) cost of a course of action is compared with its extra benefits.

KEY TERMS

perfect competition	budget constraints	opportunity cost
basic competitive model	time constraints	sunk costs
price system	production possibilities	marginal costs
rationing systems	trade-offs	marginal benefits
opportunity set	diminishing returns	

REVIEW QUESTIONS

1. What are the essential elements of the basic competitive model?

2. Consider a lake in a state park where everyone is allowed to fish as much as he wants. What outcome do you predict? Might this problem be averted if the lake were privately owned and fishing licenses were sold?

3. Why might government policy to make the distribution of income more equitable lead to less efficiency?

4. List advantages and disadvantages of rationing by queue, by lottery, and by coupon. If the government permitted a black market to develop, might some of the disadvantages of these systems be reduced?

5. What are some of the opportunity costs of going to college? What are some of the opportunity costs a state should consider when deciding whether to widen a highway?

6. Give two examples of a sunk cost, and explain why they should be irrelevant to current decisions.

7. How is marginal analysis relevant in the decision about which car or which house to purchase: After deciding the kind of car to purchase, how is marginal analysis relevant?

Problems

1. Imagine that many businesses are located beside a river, into which they discharge industrial waste. There is a city downstream, which uses the river as a water supply and for recreation. If property rights to the river are ill-defined, what problems may occur?

2. Suppose an underground reservoir of oil may reside under properties owned by several different individuals. As each well is drilled, it reduces the amount of oil that others can take out. Compare how quickly the oil is likely to be extracted in this situation with how quickly it would be extracted if one person owned the property rights to drill for the entire pool of oil.

3. In some states, hunting licenses are allocated by lottery; if you want a license, you send in your name to enter the lottery. If the purpose of the system is to ensure that those who want to hunt the most get a chance to do so, what are the flaws of this system? How would the situation improve if people who won licenses were allowed to sell them to others?

4. Imagine that during time of war, the government imposes coupon rationing. What are the advantages of allowing people to buy and sell their coupons? What are the disadvantages?

5. Kathy, a college student, has $20 a week to spend; she spends it either on junk food at $2.50 a snack, or on gasoline at $1 per gallon. Draw Kathy's opportunity set. What is the trade-off between junk food and gasoline? Now draw each new budget constraint she would face if
    (a) a kind relative started sending her an additional $10 per week;
    (b) the price of a junk food snack fell to $2;
    (c) the price of gasoline rose to $1.20 per gallon.
In each case, how does the trade-off between junk food and gasoline change?

6. Why is the opportunity cost of going to medical school likely to be greater than the opportunity cost of going to college? Why is the opportunity cost of

a woman with a college education having a child greater than the opportunity cost of a woman with just a high school education having a child?

7. Bob likes to divide his recreational time between going to movies and listening to compact discs. He has 20 hours a week available for recreation; a movie takes two hours, and a CD takes one hour to listen to. Draw his "time budget constraint." Bob also has a limited amount of income to spend on recreation. He has $60 a week to spend on recreational activities; a movie costs $5, and a CD costs $12. (He never likes to listen to the same CD twice.) Draw his budget constraint. What is his opportunity set?

APPENDIX: READING GRAPHS

Whether the old saying that a picture is worth a thousand words under- or overestimates the value of a picture, economists find graphs extremely useful.

For instance, look at Figure 2.5; it is a redrawn version of Figure 2.1, showing the budget constraint—the various combinations of CDs and cassettes he can purchase—of an individual, Alfred. More generally, a graph shows the relationship between two variables, here, the number of CDs and the number of cassettes that can be purchased. The budget constraint gives the maximum number of cassettes that can be purchased, given the number of CDs that have been bought.

In a graph, one variable (here, CDs) is put on the horizontal axis and the other variable on the vertical axis. We read a point such as E by looking down

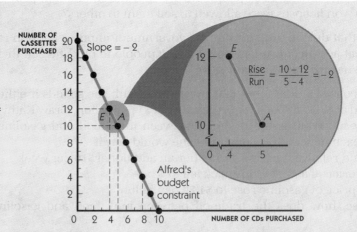

Figure 2.5 READING A GRAPH: THE BUDGET CONSTRAINT

Graphs can be used to show the relationship between two variables. This one shows the relationship between the variable on the vertical axis (the number of cassettes Alfred can buy) and the variable on the horizontal axis (the number of CDs).

The slope of a curve like the budget constraint gives the change in the number of cassettes that can be purchased as Alfred buys one more CD. The slope of the budget constraint is negative.

to the horizontal axis and seeing that it corresponds to 4 CDs, and by looking across to the vertical axis and seeing that it corresponds to 12 cassettes. Similarly, we read point *A* by looking down to the horizontal axis and seeing that it corresponds to 5 CDs, and by looking across to the vertical axis and seeing that it corresponds to 10 cassettes.

In the figure, each of the points from the table has been plotted, and then a curve has been drawn through those points. The "curve" turns out to be a straight line in this case, but we still use the more general term. The advantage of the curve over the individual points is that with it, we can read off from the graph points on the budget constraint that are not in the table.

Sometimes, of course, not every point on the graph is economically meaningful. You cannot buy half a cassette or half a CD. For the most part, we ignore these considerations when drawing our graphs; we simply pretend that any point on the budget constraint is actually possible.

Slope

In any diagram, the amount by which the value along the vertical axis increases from a change in a unit along the horizontal axis is called the **slope,** just like the slope of a mountain. Slope is sometimes described as "rise over run," meaning that the slope of a line can be calculated by dividing the change on the vertical axis (the "rise") by the change on the horizontal axis (the "run").

Look at Figure 2.5. As we move from *E* to *A*, increasing the number of CDs by 1, the number of cassettes purchased falls from 12 to 10. For each additional CD bought, the feasible number of cassettes that can be purchased falls by 2. So the slope of the line is

$$\frac{\text{rise}}{\text{run}} = \frac{10 - 12}{5 - 4} = \frac{-2}{1} = -2.$$

When, as in Figure 2.5, the variable on the vertical axis falls when the variable on the horizontal axis increases, the curve, or line, is said to be **negatively sloped.** A budget constraint is always negatively sloped. But when we describe the slope of a budget constraint, we frequently omit the term "negative." We say the slope is 2, knowing that since we are describing the slope of a budget constraint, we should more formally say that the slope is negative 2. Alternatively, we sometimes say that the slope has an absolute value of 2.

Figure 2.6 shows the case of a curve that is **positively sloped.** The variable along the vertical axis, income, increases as schooling increases, giving the line its upward tilt from left to right.

In later discussions, we will encounter two special cases. A line that is very steep has a very large slope; that is, the increase in the vertical axis for every unit increase in the horizontal axis is very large. The extreme case is a perfectly vertical line, and we say then that the slope is infinite (Figure 2.7, panel A). At the other extreme is a flat, horizontal line; since there is no increase in the vertical axis no matter how large the change along the horizontal, we say that the slope of such a curve is zero (panel B).

Figure 2.6 POSITIVELY SLOPED CURVE

Incomes increase with the number of years of schooling.

Figure 2.7 LIMITING CASES

In panel A, the slope of a vertical line is infinite. In panel B, the slope of a horizontal line is zero.

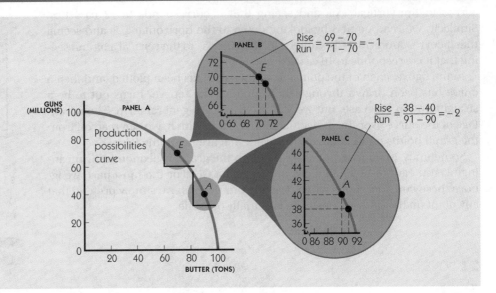

Figure 2.8 THE GUNS AND BUTTER TRADE-OFF

Panel A shows a trade-off between military spending ("guns") and civilian spending ("butter"), where society chooses point E. Panel B is an enlargement of the area around E, which focuses on the slope there, which also measures the marginal trade-offs society faces near that point. Similarly, panel C is an enlargement of the area around A and shows the marginal trade-offs society faces near that point

Figures 2.5 and 2.6 both show straight lines. Everywhere along the straight line, the slope is the same. This is not true in Figure 2.8, which repeats the production possibilities curve shown originally in Figure 2.3. Panel B of the figure blows up the area around point E. From the figure, you can see that if the output of butter increases by 1 ton, the output of guns decreases by 1 million guns. Thus, the slope is

$$\frac{\text{rise}}{\text{run}} = \frac{69 - 70}{71 - 70} = -1.$$

Now look at point A, where the economy is producing more butter. The area around A has been blown up in panel C. Here, we see that when we increase butter by 1 more unit, the reduction in guns is greater than before. The slope at A (again, millions of fewer guns produced per extra ton of butter) is

$$\frac{\text{rise}}{\text{run}} = \frac{38 - 40}{91 - 90} = -2.$$

With curves such as the production possibilities curve, the slope differs as we move along the curve.

INTERPRETING CURVES

Look at Figure 2.9. Which of the two curves has a larger slope? The one on the left appears to have a slope that has a larger absolute value. But look carefully at the axes. Notice that in panel A, the vertical axis is stretched relative to panel B. The same distance that represents 20 cassettes in panel B represents only 10

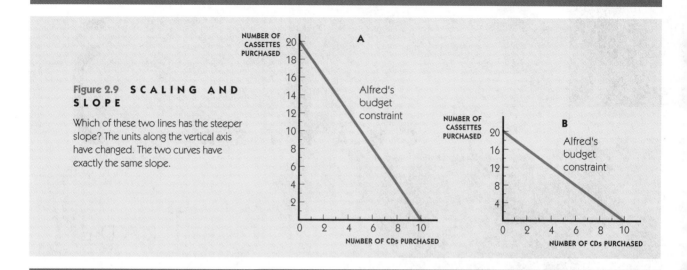

Figure 2.9 SCALING AND SLOPE

Which of these two lines has the steeper slope? The units along the vertical axis have changed. The two curves have exactly the same slope.

cassettes in panel A. In fact, both panels represent the same budget constraint. They have exactly the same slope.

This kind of cautionary tale is as important in looking at the graphs of data that were common in Chapter 1 as it is in looking at the relationships presented in this chapter that produce smooth curves. Compare, for instance, panels A and B of Figure 2.10. Which of the two curves exhibits more variability? Which looks more stable? Panel B appears to show that car production does not change much over time. But again, a closer look reveals that the axes have been stretched in panel A. The two curves are based on exactly the same data, and there is really no difference between them.

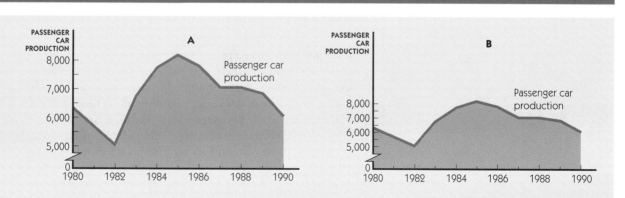

Figure 2.10 SCALING AND GRAPHS OF DATA

Which of these two curves shows greater variability in the output of cars over time? The two curves plot the same data. The vertical scale has again been changed. *Source: Ward's Automotive Reports* (1991).

CHAPTER 3

TRADE

A creature on another planet looking down at a developed modern economy on earth might compare human activity to an enormous ant colony. Each ant seemingly has an assigned task. Some stand guard. Some feed the young. Some harvest food and others distribute it. Some shuffle paper, scribble notes in books, and type on computer keyboards at computer consoles. Others work in factories, tightening screws, running machines, and so on. How is all of this activity coordinated? No dictator or superintelligent computer is giving instructions. Yet somehow an immense amount is accomplished in a reasonably coordinated way. Understanding how a complex economy operates—how it is that certain individuals do one task, others do another, how information is communicated and decisions made—is a central objective of economics.

This chapter discusses the problem of economic interdependence at two levels: individuals and firms within a country, and countries within the world economic community. Many of the same principles apply at both levels.

KEY QUESTIONS

1. Why is trade (exchange) mutually beneficial?

2. What are the similarities and differences between trade (exchange) between individuals within a country and trade between countries?

3. What determines what any particular country produces and sells on the international market? What is meant by

comparative advantage, and why does it play such an important role?

4. What are the gains from specialization?

5. How valid is the argument, so often heard in political circles, that trade should be restricted?

THE BENEFITS OF ECONOMIC INTERDEPENDENCE

We begin by considering the benefits of trade, specifically the exchange of those goods that are already available in the economy.

THE GAINS FROM TRADE

When individuals own different goods, have different desires, or both, there is an opportunity for trades that benefit all parties to the trade. Kids trading baseball cards learn the basic principles of exchange. One has two Ken Griffey, Jr. cards, the other has two Barry Bonds cards. A trade will benefit both of them. The same lesson applies to countries. Nigeria has more oil than it can use, but it does not produce enough food to feed its populace. The United States has more wheat than Americans can consume, but needs oil. Trade can benefit both countries.

Voluntary trade involves only winners. If the trade would make a loser of any party, that party would choose not to trade. Thus, a fundamental consequence of voluntary exchange is that it benefits everyone involved.

"FEELING JILTED" IN TRADE

In spite of the seemingly persuasive argument that individuals only voluntarily engage in trade if they think they will be better off as a result, people often walk away from a deal believing they have been hurt. It is important to understand that when economists say that a voluntary trade makes the two traders better off, they do not mean that it makes them both happy.

Imagine, for example, that Frank brings an antique rocking chair to a flea market to sell. He is willing to sell it for $100 but hopes to sell it for $200. Helen comes to the flea market planning to buy such a chair, hoping to spend only $100, but willing to pay as much as $200. They argue and negotiate, eventually settle on a price of $125, and make the deal. But when they go home, they both complain. Frank complains the price was too low, and Helen that it was too high.

From an economist's point of view, such complaints are self-contradictory. If Frank *really* thought $125 was too low, he would not have sold at that price. If Helen *really* thought $125 was too high, she would not have paid the price. Economists argue that people reveal their preferences not by what they say, but by what they do. If one voluntarily agrees to make a deal, one also agrees that the deal is, if not perfect, at least better than the alternative of not making it.

Two common objections are made to this line of reasoning. Both involve Frank or Helen "taking advantage" of the other. The implication is that if a buyer or a seller can take advantage, then the other party may be a loser rather than a winner.

The first objection is that either Frank or Helen may not really know what is being agreed to. Perhaps Helen recognizes the chair is an antique, but by neglecting to tell Frank, manages to buy it for only $125. Perhaps Frank knows the rockers fall off, but sells the chair without telling this to Helen, thus keeping the price high. In either case, lack of relevant information makes someone a loser after the trade.

The second objection concerns equitable division of the **gains from trade.** Since Helen would have been willing to pay as much as $200, anything she pays less than that is **surplus,** the term economists use for a gain from trade. Similarly, since Frank would have been willing to sell the chair for as little as $100, anything he receives more than that is also surplus. The total dollar value of the gain from trade is $100—the difference between the maximum price Helen was willing to pay and the minimum price at which Frank was willing to sell. At a price of $125, $25 of the gain went to Frank, $75 to Helen. The second objection is that such a split is not fair.

Economists do not have much patience with these objections. Like most people, they favor making as much information public as possible, and they think vendors and customers should be made to stand behind their promises. But economists also point out that second thoughts and "If only I had known" are not relevant. If Frank sells his antique at a flea market instead of having it valued by reputable antique dealers, he has made a voluntary decision to save his time and energy. If Helen buys an antique at a flea market instead of going to a reputable dealer, she knows she is taking a risk.

The logic of free exchange, however, does not say that everyone must express happiness with the result. It simply says that when people choose to make a deal, they prefer making it to not making it. And if they prefer the deal, they are by definition better off *in their own minds* at the time the transaction takes place.

The objections to trade nonetheless carry an important message: most exchanges that happen in the real world are considerably more complicated than the Frank-Helen chair trade. They involve problems of information, estimating risks, and expectations about the future. These complications will be discussed throughout the book. So without going into too much detail at the moment, let's just say that if you are worried that you do not have the proper information to make a trade, shop around, get a guarantee or expert opinion, or buy insurance. If you choose to plunge ahead without these precautions, don't pretend you didn't have other choices. Like those who buy a ticket in a lottery, you know you are taking a chance.

ECONOMIC RELATIONS AS EXCHANGES

Individuals in our economy are involved in masses of voluntary trades. They "trade" their labor services (time and skills) to their employer for dollars. They then trade dollars with a multitude of merchants for goods (like gasoline and groceries) and services (like plumbing and hair styling). The employer trades the goods it produces for dollars, and trades those dollars for labor services. Even your savings account can be viewed as a trade: you give the bank $100 today in exchange for the bank's promise to give you $105 at the end of the year (your original deposit plus 5 percent interest).

TRADE BETWEEN COUNTRIES

Why is it that people engage in this complex set of economic relations with others? The answer is that people are better off as a result of trading. Just as individuals *within* a country find it advantageous to trade with one another, so too do countries find trade advantageous. Just as it is impossible for any individual to be self-sufficient, it is impossible for a country to be self-reliant without sacrificing its standard of living. The United States has long been part of an international economic community. This participation has grown in recent decades increasing the interdependence between the United States and its trading partners. How has this affected the three main markets in the U.S. economy?

Interdependence in the Product Market   Foreign-produced goods are commonplace in U.S. markets. In the 1990s, for instance, more than a quarter of the cars sold in the United States were **imported** (imports are goods produced abroad but bought domestically), along with a third of apparel items, a third of the oil, and virtually all of the diamonds. Many of the minerals essential for the U.S. economy must also be imported from abroad. At the same time, U.S. farmers **export** almost two-fifths of the agricultural goods they produce (exports are goods produced domestically but sold abroad), including almost three-fourths of the wheat and one-third of the cotton.

Imports have grown in recent decades, not only in dollars, but also as a percentage of overall production. Exports have grown almost commensurately. Figure 3.1 shows how exports and imports have grown relative to the nation's total output: as a percentage of national output, both have more than doubled over the last twenty-five years. Smaller countries are typically even more

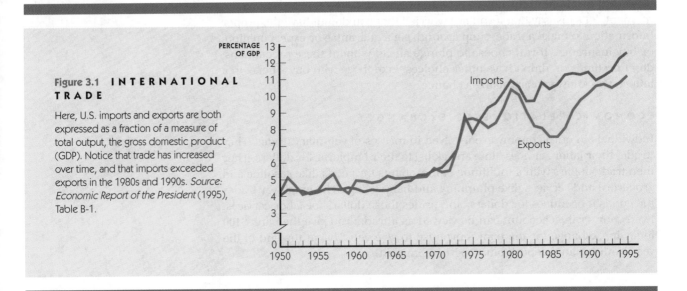

Figure 3.1 INTERNATIONAL TRADE

Here, U.S. imports and exports are both expressed as a fraction of a measure of total output, the gross domestic product (GDP). Notice that trade has increased over time, and that imports exceeded exports in the 1980s and 1990s. *Source: Economic Report of the President* (1995), Table B-1.

dependent on international trade than the United States. Britain and Canada import a quarter of their goods, France a fifth.

Earnings from abroad constitute a major source of income for some of our largest corporations; exports account for 45 percent of sales for Boeing, 20 percent for Hewlett-Packard, and 12 percent for Ford.

Interdependence in the Labor Market International interdependence extends beyond simply the shipping of goods between countries. More than 99 percent of U.S. citizens either immigrated here from abroad or are descended from people who did. Though the flow of immigrants, relative to the size of the population, has slowed since its peak at the turn of the century, it is still substantial, numbering in the millions every year. Today many rural American areas are dependent upon foreign-born doctors and nurses. Half of the engineers currently receiving doctorates at American universities are foreign-born. The harvests of many crops are highly dependent on migrant laborers from Mexico.

The nations of Europe have increasingly recognized the benefits that result from this international movement of workers. One of the important provisions of the treaty establishing the European Union, an agreement among most of the countries within Western Europe, allows for the free flow of workers within the member countries.

Interdependence in the Capital Market The United States has become a major borrower from abroad, but the country also invests heavily overseas. In 1995, for example, U.S. private investors owned approximately $2.5 trillion of assets (factories, businesses, buildings, loans, etc.) in foreign countries, while foreign investors owned $2.8 trillion of assets in the United States. American companies have sought out profitable opportunities abroad, where they can use their special skills and knowledge to earn high returns. They have established branches and built factories in Europe, Japan, Latin America, and elsewhere in the world.

Just as the nations of Western Europe have recognized the advantages that follow from the free flow of goods and labor among their countries, so too they have recognized the gains from the free flow of capital. Funds can be invested where they yield the highest returns. Knowledge and skills from one country can be combined with capital from another to produce goods that will be enjoyed by citizens of all countries. Though the process of liberalizing the flow of goods, labor, and capital among countries of the European Union has been going on for more than twenty years, 1992 marked the crucial date at which all remaining barriers were officially removed.

MULTILATERAL TRADE

Many of the examples to this point have emphasized two-way trade. Trade between two individuals or countries is called **bilateral trade.** But exchanges between two parties is often less advantageous than trade between several parties, called **multilateral trade.** Such trades are observed between sports teams. The New York Mets send a catcher to the St. Louis Cardinals, the Cardinals send a pitcher to the Los Angeles Dodgers, and the Dodgers send an outfielder to the Mets (see Figure 3.2A). No two of the teams was willing to make a two-way trade, but all can benefit from the three-way swap.

Countries function in a similar way. Japan has no domestic oil; it imports oil from Arabian countries. The Arabian countries want to sell their oil, but

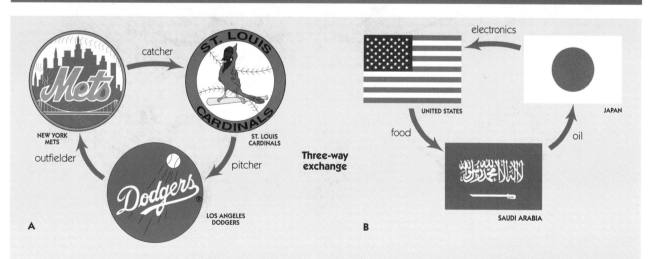

Figure 3.2 MULTILATERAL EXCHANGE

Panel A shows a multilateral, three-way trade between baseball teams. Notice that no two of the teams have the ingredients for a mutually beneficial exchange. Panel B illustrates a multilateral exchange in international trade.

they want wheat and food, not the cars and television sets that Japan can provide. The United States can provide the missing link by buying cars and televisions from Japan and selling food to the Arab nations. Again, this three-way trade, shown in Figure 3.2B, offers gains that two-way trade cannot. The scores of nations active in the world economy create patterns far more complex than these simplified examples.

Figure 3.3 illustrates the construction of a Ford Escort in Europe, and dramatizes the importance of multilateral and interconnected trade relations. The parts that go into an Escort come from all over the world. Similar diagrams could be constructed for many of the components in the diagram; the aluminum alloys may contain bauxite from Jamaica, the chrome plate may use chromium from South Africa, the copper for wiring may come from Chile.

Multilateral trade means that trade between any two participants may not balance. In Figure 3.2B, the Arab countries send oil to Japan but get no goods (only yen) in return. No one would say that the Arab countries have an unfair trade policy with Japan. Yet some congressional representatives, newspaper

Figure 3.3 THE MAKING OF A MODERN AUTOMOBILE

The ingredients for a Ford Escort are gathered from all over the world. *Source: World Development Report* (1990).

columnists, and business executives complain that since the United States imports more from a particular country (often Japan) than it exports to that country, the trade balance is "unfair." A misguided popular cliché says that "trade is a two-way street." But trade in the world market involves hundreds of possible streets between nations. While there are legitimate reasons to be concerned with the overall U.S. trade deficit, there is no reason why U.S. exports and imports with any particular country should be balanced.

COMPARATIVE ADVANTAGE

We have so far focused on exchanges of existing goods. But clearly, most of what is exchanged must first be produced. Trade allows individuals and countries to concentrate on what they produce best.

Some countries are more efficient at producing almost all goods than are other countries. The possession of superior production skills is called having an **absolute advantage,** and these advanced countries are said to have an absolute advantage over the others. How can the countries with disadvantages successfully engage in trade? The answer lies in the principle of **comparative advantage,** which states that individuals and countries specialize in producing those goods in which they are *relatively,* not absolutely, more efficient.

To see what comparative advantage means, let's say that both the United States and Japan produce two goods, computers and wheat. The amount of labor needed to produce these goods is shown in Table 3.1. (These numbers are all hypothetical.) The United States is more efficient (spends fewer worker hours) at making both products. America can rightfully claim to have the most efficient computer industry in the world, and yet it imports computers from Japan. Why? The *relative* cost of making a computer (in terms of labor used) in Japan, relative to the cost of producing a ton of wheat, is low, compared with the United States. That is, in Japan, it takes 15 times as many hours (120/8) to produce a computer as a ton of wheat; in the United States, it takes 20 times as many hours (100/5) to produce a computer as a ton of wheat. While Japan has an absolute *dis*advantage in producing computers, it has a *comparative* advantage.

Table 3.1 **LABOR COST OF PRODUCING COMPUTERS AND WHEAT (worker hours)**

	United States	Japan
Labor required to make a computer	100	120
Labor required to make a ton of wheat	5	8

The principle of comparative advantage applies to individuals as well as countries. The president of a company might type faster than her secretary, but it still pays to have the secretary type her letters, because the president may have a comparative advantage at bringing in new clients, while the secretary has a comparative (though not absolute) advantage at typing.

PRODUCTION POSSIBILITIES SCHEDULES AND COMPARATIVE ADVANTAGE

The easiest way to understand the comparative advantage of different countries is to use the production possibilities schedule first introduced in Chapter 2. Figure 3.4 depicts parts of hypothetical production possibilities schedules for two countries, China and the United States, producing two commodities, textiles (garments) and airplanes. In both schedules, point E represents the current level of production. Let us look at what happens if each country changes its production by 100 airplanes.

China has a **comparative** advantage in producing textiles. If it reduces its airplane production by 100, its textile production can be increased by 10,000 garments. This trade-off between airplanes and garments is called the **marginal rate of transformation.** By contrast, if the United States reduces its airplane production by 100 airplanes, its textile production can be increased by only 1,000 garments. Conversely, if it increases its airplane production by 100, it will have to reduce its garment production by only 1,000 garments. We can now see why the world is better off if each country exploits its comparative advantage. If China moves from E to E' (decreasing airplane production by 100), 10,000 more garments can be produced. If the United States at the same time increases its airplane production by 100 from E to E'', it will produce only 1,000 fewer garments. In the new situation, the world production of airplanes is unchanged, but world production of garments has increased by 9,000. So long as the production trade-offs differ—that is, so long as the mar-

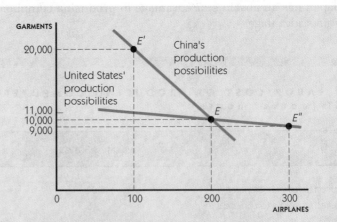

Figure 3.4 EXPLOITING COMPARATIVE ADVANTAGE

The production possibilities schedules for China and the United States, each manufacturing two commodities, textiles and airplanes, illustrate the trade-offs at different levels of production. Point E shows the current level of production for each country; E' and E'' illustrate production decisions that better exploit each country's comparative advantage.

Problem: Using the earlier example of Japan and the United States producing wheat and computers, calculate the trade-offs and the gains from specialization. Assume that both countries have 240,000 worker hours, initially divided equally between producing wheat and computers.

Solution: First, draw the production possibilities curves, as in the figure below. Since the costs (in worker hours) of producing each unit of each commodity are fixed, the production possibilities schedule is a straight line. If the United States used all its labor to produce computers, it would produce 2,400 computers; if it used all its labor to produce wheat, it would produce 48,000 tons of wheat. If Japan used all its labor to produce com-

puters, it would produce 2,000 computers; if it used all its labor to produce wheat, it would produce 30,000 tons of wheat.

In both curves, use point A to mark the current point of production, at which labor is equally divided between computers and wheat.

Next, calculate the slope of the production possibilities curve, giving the trade-offs: in the United States, increasing wheat output by 1,000 tons leads to a reduction of computers by 50, while reducing wheat output by 1,000 tons in Japan leads to an increase in computers of 66⅔. Thus, each shift of wheat production by 1,000 tons from Japan to the United States increases world computer production by 16⅔.

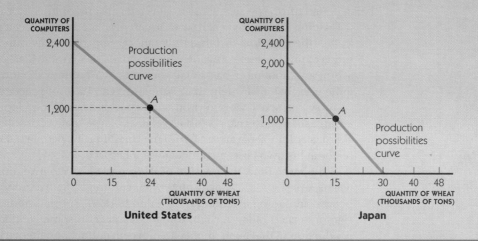

Though it pays countries to increase production and export of goods in which they have a comparative advantage and to import goods in which they have a comparative disadvantage, this may not lead to complete specialization. Thus the United States continues to be a major producer of textiles, in spite of heavy imports from the Far East. This does not violate the principle of comparative advantage: not all textiles require the same skill and expertise in manufacturing. Thus, while China may have a comparative advantage in inexpensive textiles, the United States may have a comparative advantage in higher quality textiles. At the same time, the comparative advantage of other countries is so extreme in producing some goods that it does not pay for the United States to produce them at all: TVs, VCRs, and a host of other electronic gadgets, for example.

COMPARATIVE ADVANTAGE AND SPECIALIZATION

To see the benefits of specialization, consider the pencil. A tree, containing the right kind of wood, must be felled; it must be transported to a sawmill, and there cut into pieces that can be further processed into pencil casings. Then the graphite that runs through the pencil's center, the eraser at its tip, the metal that holds the two together must each be produced by specially trained people. The pencil is a simple tool. But to produce it by oneself would cost a fortune in money and an eternity in time.

Why Specialization Increases Productivity   Specialization increases productivity, thus enhancing the benefits of trade, for three reasons. First, specializing avoids the time it takes a worker to switch from one production task to another. Second, by repeating the same task, the worker becomes more skilled at it. And third, specialization creates a fertile environment for invention.

Dividing jobs so that each worker can practice and perfect a particular skill (called the **division of labor**) may increase productivity hundreds or thousands of times. Almost anyone who practices simple activities—like sewing on a button, shooting a basketball, or adding a column of numbers—will be quite a lot better at them than someone who has not practiced. Similarly, a country that specializes in producing sports cars may develop a comparative advantage in sports cars. With its relatively large scale of production, it can divide tasks into separate assignments for different people; as each becomes better at his own tasks, productivity is increased.

At the same time, the division of labor often leads to invention. As someone learns a particular job extremely well, she might figure out ways of doing it better—including inventing a machine to do it. Specialization and invention reinforce each other. A slight initial advantage in some good leads to greater production of that good, thence to more invention, and thence to even greater production and further specialization.

Limits of Specialization   The extent of division of labor, or specialization, is limited by the size of the market. There is greater scope for specialization in mass-produced manufactured goods like picture frames than in custom-made items like the artwork that gets framed. That is one reason why the costs of production of mass-produced goods have declined so much. Similarly, there is greater scope for specialization in a big city than a small town. That is why small stores specializing in a particular food or type of clothing thrive in cities but are rare in smaller towns.

The very nature of specialization limits its benefits. Repetitive jobs can lead to bored and unproductive workers. And single-track specialization inhibits the new insights and ideas that can come from engaging in a variety of work activities.

WHAT DETERMINES COMPARATIVE ADVANTAGE?

Earlier we learned that comparative advantage determines the pattern of trade. But what determines comparative advantage? In the modern world, this turns out to be a complex matter.

Natural Endowments   In first laying down the principle of comparative advantage in the early 1800s, the great British economist David Ricardo used the example of Portugal's trade with Britain. In Ricardo's example, Portugal had an absolute advantage in producing both wool and wine. But it had a comparative advantage in producing wine, and Britain had a comparative advantage in producing wool. In this and other early examples, economists tended to assume that a nation's comparative advantage was determined largely by its **natural endowments.** Countries with soil and climate that are *relatively* better for grapes than for pasture will produce wine; countries with soil and climate that are relatively better for pasture than for grapes will produce sheep (and hence wool).

In the modern economy, natural endowments still count: countries that have an abundance of low-skilled labor relative to other resources, such as China, have a comparative advantage in producing goods like textiles, which require a lot of handwork. But in today's technological age nations can also act to *acquire* a comparative advantage.

Acquired Endowments   Japan has little in the way of natural resources, yet it is a major player in international trade, in part because it has **acquired endowments.** Japan's case underscores the principle that by saving and accumulating capital and building large factories, a nation can acquire a comparative advantage in goods, like steel, that require large amounts of capital in their production. And by devoting resources to education, a nation can develop a comparative advantage in those goods that require a skilled labor force. Thus, the resources—human and physical—that a country has managed to acquire for itself can also give rise to comparative advantage.

Superior Knowledge   In the modern economy, comparative advantage may come simply from expertise in using resources productively. Switzerland has a comparative advantage in watches because, over the years, the people of the country have accumulated superior knowledge and expertise in watch making. Belgium has a comparative advantage in fine lace; its workers have developed the requisite skills. A quirk of fate might have led Belgium to acquire a comparative advantage in watches and Switzerland in lace.

Although patterns of specialization sometimes occur as an accident of history, in modern economies they are more likely to be a consequence of deliberate decisions. The United States' semiconductor industry is a case in point.

CLOSE-UP: THE COMPARATIVE ADVANTAGE OF THE UNITED STATES

What is the U.S. comparative advantage? Looking at the strengths of the United States in comparison with the rest of the world, one thinks of high technology. With over three-fourths of the world living in poor countries, without access even to the capital required for manufacturing, it would seem that these countries would have a *comparative* advantage in agriculture. Thus agriculture would be an area in which the United States had a comparative disadvantage. This intuitive answer is half right. The United States does export high technology products, like computing equipment, aircraft and aircraft engines, industrial organic chemicals, plastics and resins, and pharmaceuticals (drugs). In addition, the United States receives two billion dollars in payments from other countries using its patents.

But the United States is also a major exporter of agricultural goods, dominating world exports of wheat, corn, and cereals. It also exports rice, dairy products, and a host of other agricultural commodities.* For some commodities, this is a consequence of governmental intervention overruling the workings of the market: the costs of production of dairy products exceeds what is received on the international market, with the taxpayer making up the difference through subsidies to exports. In most cases, however, the United States has a true comparative advantage: American farmers substitute sophisticated knowledge of farming, using skilled labor, advanced seeds, fertilizers, pesticides, and equipment instead of unskilled labor.

*The seemingly paradoxical observation that the United States was exporting less-capital-intensive goods, and importing more-capital-intensive goods, was first noted by Nobel Prize-winning economist Wassily Leontief, in a famous paper written in 1953. It is referred to as the Leontief paradox in his honor.

This industry manufactures the tiny silicon brains that control computers. Semiconductors were invented by an American, Robert Noyce, and in the 1970s, the United States had a powerful comparative advantage in manufacturing semiconductors; but Japan managed to become a close competitor in the 1980s. The rise of the U.S. semiconductor industry was built in part on decisions by the federal government to fund the necessary research (primarily so the semiconductors could be used in guided missiles and other weapons). The rise of the Japanese industry was similarly based on decisions by that government to support its semiconductor industry.

Stories like that of the semiconductor industry have led some economists to argue that government should encourage certain industries, in order for them to gain a technological advantage, for instance, through the support of research relevant to that industry.

Specialization   Earlier we saw how comparative advantage leads to specialization. Specialization may also lead to comparative advantage. The Swiss make fine watches, and have a comparative advantage in that market based on years of unique experience. Such superior knowledge, however, does not explain why Britain, Germany, and the United States, which are at roughly the same level of technological expertise in building cars, all trade cars with one another. How can each country have a comparative advantage in making cars? The answer lies in specialization.

Both Britain and Germany may be better off if Britain specializes in producing sports cars and Germany in producing luxury cars, or conversely, because specialization increases productivity. Countries enhance, or simply develop, a comparative advantage by specializing just as individuals do. As a result, similar countries enjoy the advantages of specialization even when they specialize in different variations of basically similar products.

THE FOUR BASES OF COMPARATIVE ADVANTAGE

Natural endowments, which consist of geographical determinants such as land, natural resources, and climate

Acquired endowments, which are the physical capital and human skills a nation has developed

Superior knowledge, including technological advantages, which may be acquired either as an accident of history or through deliberate policies

Specialization, which may create comparative advantages between countries that are similar in all other respects

THE PERCEIVED COSTS OF INTERNATIONAL INTERDEPENDENCE

If the argument that voluntary trade must be mutually beneficial is so compelling, why has there been, from time to time, such strong antitrade sentiment in the United States and many other countries? This antitrade feeling is often labeled **protectionism,** because it calls for "protecting" the economy from the effects of trade. Those who favor protectionism raise a number of concerns. Some of the objections to international trade parallel the objections to trade among individuals noted earlier. Was the trade a fair deal? Was the seller in a stronger bargaining position? Such concerns, for individuals and countries, revolve around how the *surplus* associated with the gains from trade is divided. Weak countries may feel that they are being taken advantage of by stronger countries. Their weaker bargaining position may mean that the stronger countries get *more* of the gains from trade. But this does not contradict the basic premise: both parties gain from voluntary exchange. All countries—weak as well as strong—are better off as a result of voluntary exchange.

But an important difference exists between trade among individuals and trade among countries. Some individuals within a country benefit from trade and some lose. Since the trade as a whole is beneficial to the country, the gains to the winners exceed the losses to the losers. Thus, in principle, those who benefit within the country could more than compensate those who lose. In practice, however, those who lose remain losers and obviously oppose trade, using the argument that trade results in lost jobs and reduced wages. These concerns have become particularly acute as unskilled workers face competition with low-wage unskilled workers in Asia and Latin America: how can they compete, without lowering their wages?

These concerns played a prominent role in the debate in 1993 over ratification of the North American Free Trade Agreement (NAFTA), which would allow Mexican goods into the United States with no duties at all. Advocates of NAFTA pointed out that (1) more jobs would be created by the new export opportunities than would be lost through competition from Mexican firms; and (2) the jobs created paid higher wages, reflecting the benefits from specialization in areas where the United States had a comparative advantage.

Opponents of NAFTA, in particular, and trade, in general, are not swayed by these arguments, but instead stress the costs to workers and communities as particular industries shrink in response to foreign imports. The textile worker in North Carolina who loses his job as a result of imports of inexpensive clothing from China cannot instantly convert himself into a computer programmer in California or an aircraft engineer working for Boeing. But the fact is that jobs are being destroyed and created all the time, irrespective of trade. And over the long run, the economic incentive of the new jobs at Boeing may induce someone in the Midwest to leave his semi-skilled job and get the training that makes him eligible for one of the skilled jobs at Boeing. The vacancy created may be filled by someone who moves in from Kentucky, leaving a vacancy there for the laid-off textile worker in North Carolina.

Because of the practical complications and the very real costs of retraining and relocation, there is increasing recognition that government may need to play a role in facilitating job movements. To the extent that such assistance increases the number of winners from trade, it should reduce opposition to trade.

The North American Free Trade Agreement (NAFTA)—which will eliminate all trade barriers between the United States, Canada, and Mexico within fifteen years—will result in the largest free trade zone in the world, embracing 380 million people and a gross national product of $8 trillion. NAFTA was so vehemently opposed, however, that it was in grave danger of being defeated in the U.S. Congress. Two opponents in particular —labor unions and environmental groups—commanded enough votes in Congress that the potential gains from free trade were in danger of being lost—until a set of side agreements allayed their concerns.

Both groups feared the effects of competition from Mexico, in spite of evidence—consistent with the law of comparative advantage—that freer trade would increase national income, perhaps substantially. Labor unions were against NAFTA because they feared competition from Mexico's low-wage economy. Environmentalists were against NAFTA because they feared that competition with

Mexico (and its low environmental standards) would force the United States to lower its environmental standards to remain competitive.

For the Clinton administration, it was clear that quoting the law of comparative advantage was not going to be effective in disarming these critics. The administration pushed to have the three countries sign side agreements ensuring that each country abided by its own labor and environmental laws, changing enough votes to secure passage. A particularly important safeguard was the establishment of a joint U.S.-Mexico air-quality board to help alleviate the severe environmental problems along the Mexican-American border. With this and other safeguards in place, NAFTA promises to improve labor and environmental standards south of the border.

While NAFTA is thought primarily as reducing barriers in the product market, it has important effects on labor and capital markets. Ross Perot, in his attacks on NAFTA, conjured up a strong image of jobs and investment flowing south of the border, in what he dramatically described as a "giant sucking sound." Fortunately, his premonitions have not been realized. In the long run, access to the American market will make investments in Mexico far more attractive; but the funds for investing will be attracted from throughout the global capital market. And increased access to Mexico will make investments in many industries in the United States more attractive. Higher wages in Mexico will reduce the immigration pressure on the United States. Finally, concerns about job loss are greatly exaggerated. It is not only that exports to Mexico will, in the long run, create more American jobs than will be lost through competition from Mexican imports; most of those jobs would have been lost anyway, to competition from Mexico or Asia or other Latin American countries. Though Mexico pays lower wages, its workers on average are less productive. It is precisely because American workers are more productive that American firms can pay higher wages.

Overall, America and Mexico both benefit from NAFTA, as each takes advantage of its comparative advantage, and living standards in both countries increase as a result.

While the perceived costs of economic interdependence cannot be ignored—especially when they become the subject of heated political debate—the fact that the country as a whole benefits from freer trade is one of the central tenets in which there is a consensus among the vast majority of economists. Trade is the subject of our third consensus point.

3 Trade

There are gains from voluntary exchanges. Whether between individuals or across national borders, all can gain from voluntary exchange. Trade allows parties to specialize in activities in which they have a comparative advantage.

REVIEW AND PRACTICE

SUMMARY

1. The benefits of economic interdependence apply to individuals and firms within a country as well as to countries within the world. No individual and no country is self-sufficient.

2. Both individuals and countries gain from voluntary trade. There may be cases when there are only limited possibilities for bilateral trade (exchange between two parties), but the gains from multilateral trade (exchange between several parties) may be great.

3. The principle of comparative advantage asserts that countries should export the goods in which their production costs are *relatively* low.

4. Specialization tends to increase productivity for three reasons: specializing avoids the time it takes a worker to switch from one production task

to another; workers who repeat a task become more skilled at it; specialization creates a fertile environment for invention.

5. A country's comparative advantage can arise from natural endowments, acquired endowments, superior knowledge, or specialization.

6. There is a basic difference between trade among individuals and trade among countries: with trade among countries, some individuals within the country may actually be worse off. Though in principle, those who gain could more than compensate those who lose, such compensations are seldom provided. Though free trade enhances national income, fears about job loss and wage reductions among low-skilled workers have led to demands for protection. Government assistance to facilitate the required adjustments may be desirable.

KEY TERMS

gains from trade
surplus
imports
exports
bilateral trade
multilateral trade

absolute advantage
comparative
    advantage
marginal rate of
    transformation
division of labor

natural endowments
acquired
    endowments
protectionism

REVIEW QUESTIONS

1. Why are all voluntary trades mutually beneficial?

2. Describe a situation (hypothetical, if need be) where bilateral trade does not work, but multilateral trade is possible.

3. What are some of the similarities of trade between individuals and trade between countries? What is a key way in which they differ?

4. Does a country with an absolute advantage in a product necessarily have a comparative advantage in that product? Can a country with an absolute disadvantage in a product have a comparative advantage in that product? Explain.

5. Why does specialization tend to increase productivity?

6. "A country's comparative advantage is dictated by its natural endowments." Discuss.

7. "If trade with a foreign country injures anyone in this country, the government should react by passing protectionist laws to limit or stop that particular trade." Comment.

PROBLEMS

1. Four players on a Little League baseball team discover that they have each been collecting baseball cards, and they agree to get together and trade. Is it possible for everyone to benefit from this agreement? Does the fact that one player starts off with many more cards than any of the others affect your answer?

2. Leaders in many less developed countries of Latin America and Africa have often argued that because they are so much poorer than the wealthy nations of the world, trade with the more developed economies of North America and Europe will injure them. They maintain that they must first become self-sufficient before than can benefit from trade. How might an economist respond to these claims?

3. If the United States changes its immigration quotas to allow many more unskilled workers into the country, who is likely to gain? Who is likely to lose? Consider the impact on consumers, on businesses that hire low-skilled labor, and on low-skilled labor in both the United States and the workers' countries of origin.

4. David Ricardo illustrated the principle of comparative advantage in terms of the trade between England and Portugal in wine (port) and wool. Suppose that in England it takes 120 laborers to produce a certain quantity of wine, while in Portugal it takes only 80 laborers to produce that same quantity. Similarly, in England it takes 100 laborers to produce a certain quantity of wool, while in Portugal it takes only 90. Draw the opportunity set for each country, assuming that each has 72,000 laborers. Assume that each country commits half its labor to each product in the absence of trade, and designate that point on your graph. Now describe a new production plan, with trade, that can benefit both countries.

5. Relate the comparative advantage of two countries to differences in the slope of their production possibilities schedules. In what sense might a small, poor country trading with a much larger, rich country be at a disadvantage? How might the differences affect how the gains from trade are divided?

6. In 1981, the U.S. government prodded Japanese automakers to limit the number of cars they would export to the United States. Who benefited from this protectionism in the United States and in Japan? Who was injured in the United States and in Japan? Consider companies that produce cars (and their workers) and consumers who buy cars.

7. For many years, an international agreement called the Multifiber Agreement has limited the amount of textiles that the developed economies of North America and Europe can buy from poor countries in Latin America and Asia. Textiles can be produced by relatively unskilled labor with a reasonably small amount of capital. Who benefits from the protectionism of the Multifiber Agreement, and who suffers?

4

DEMAND, SUPPLY, AND PRICE

C hoice in the face of scarcity, as we have seen, is the fundamental concern of economics. The **price** of a good or service is what must be given in exchange for the good. When the forces of supply and demand operate freely, price measures scarcity. As such, prices convey critical economic information. When the price of a resource used by a firm is high, the company has a greater incentive to economize on its use. When the price of a good that the firm produces is high, the company has a greater incentive to produce more of that good, and its customers have an incentive to economize on its use. In these ways and others, prices provide our economy with incentives to use scarce resources efficiently. This chapter describes how prices are determined in competitive market economies.

KEY QUESTIONS

1. What is meant by demand? Why do demand curves normally slope downward? On what variables, other than price, does the quantity demanded depend?

2. What is meant by supply? Why do supply curves normally slope upward? On what variables, other than price, does the quantity supplied depend?

3. Why do economists say that the equilibrium price occurs at the intersection of the demand and supply curves?

4. How do shifts in the demand and supply curves affect the equilibrium price?

THE ROLE OF PRICES

Prices are the way participants in the economy communicate with one another. Assume a drought hits the country, reducing drastically the supply of corn. Households will need to reduce their consumption of corn or there will not be enough to go around. But how will they know this? Suppose newspapers across the country ran an article informing people they would have to eat less corn because of a drought. What incentive would they have to pay attention to it? How would each family know how much it ought to reduce its consumption? As an alternative to the newspaper, consider the effect of an increase in the price of corn. The higher price conveys all the relevant information. It tells families corn is scarce at the same time as it provides incentives for them to consume less of it. Consumers do not need to know anything about why corn is scarce, nor do they need to be told by how much they should reduce their consumption of corn.

Price changes and differences present interesting problems and puzzles. In the early 1980s, while the price of an average house in Los Angeles went up by 41 percent, the price of a house in Milwaukee, Wisconsin, increased by only 4 percent. Why? During the same period, the price of computers fell dramatically, while the price of bread rose, but at a much slower rate than the price of housing in Los Angeles. Why? The "price" of labor is just the wage or salary that is paid. Why does a physician earn three times as much as a college professor, though the college professor may have performed better in the college courses they took together? Why did average wage rates fall in the United States between 1973 and 1983? Why is the price of water, without which we cannot live, very low in most cases, but the price of diamonds, which we can surely live without, very high? The simple answer to all these questions is that in market economies like the United States, price is determined by supply and demand. Changes in prices are determined by changes in supply and demand.

Understanding the causes of changes in prices and being able to predict their occurrence is not just a matter of academic interest. One of the events that precipitated the French Revolution was the rise in the price of bread, for which the people blamed the government. Large price changes have also given rise to recent political turmoil in several countries, including Morocco, the Dominican Republic, Russia, and Poland.

Noneconomists see much more in prices than the impersonal forces of supply and demand. It was the landlord who raised the rent on the apartment; it was the oil company or the owner of the gas station who raised the price of gasoline. These people and companies *chose* to raise their prices, says the noneconomist, in moral indignation. True, replies the economist, but there must be some factor that made these people and companies believe that a higher price was not a good idea yesterday, but is today. And economists point out that at a different time, these same impersonal forces can force the same landlords and oil companies to cut their prices. Economists see prices, then, as symptoms of underlying causes, and focus on the forces of demand and supply behind price changes.

DEMAND

Economists use the concept of **demand** to describe the quantity of a good or service that a household or firm chooses to buy at a given price. It is important to understand that economists are concerned not just with what people desire, but with what they choose to buy given the spending limits imposed by their budget constraint and given the prices of various goods. In analyzing demand, the first question they ask is how the quantity of a good purchased by an individual changes as the price changes, keeping everything else constant.

THE INDIVIDUAL DEMAND CURVE

Think about what happens as the price of candy bars changes. At a price of $5.00, you might never buy one. At $3.00, you might buy one as a special treat. At $1.25, you might buy a few, and if the price declined to $.50, you might buy a lot. The table in Figure 4.1 summarizes the weekly demand of one individual, Roger, for candy bars at these different prices. We can see that the lower the price, the larger the quantity demanded. We can also draw a graph that shows the quantity Roger demands at each price. The quantity demanded is measured along the horizontal axis, and the price is measured along the vertical axis. The graph in Figure 4.1 plots the points.

A smooth curve can be drawn to connect the points. This curve is called the **demand curve.** The demand curve gives the quantity demanded at each price. Thus, if we want to know how many candy bars a week Roger will demand at a price of $1.00, we simply look along the vertical axis at the price

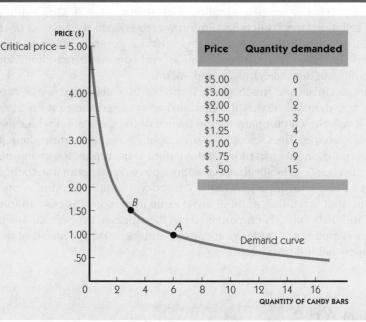

Price	Quantity demanded
$5.00	0
$3.00	1
$2.00	2
$1.50	3
$1.25	4
$1.00	6
$ .75	9
$ .50	15

Figure 4.1 AN INDIVID-UAL'S DEMAND CURVE

This demand curve shows the quantity of candy bars that Roger consumes at each price. Notice that quantity demanded falls as the price increases, and the demand curve slopes down.

$1.00, find the corresponding point *A* along the demand curve, and then read down to the horizontal axis. At a price of $1.00, Roger buys 6 candy bars each week. Alternatively, if we want to know at what price he will buy just 3 candy bars, we look along the horizontal axis at the quantity 3, find the corresponding point *B* along the demand curve, and then read across to the vertical axis. Roger will buy 3 candy bars at a price of $1.50.

As the price of candy bars increases the quantity demanded decreases. This can be seen from the numbers in the table in Figure 4.1, and in the shape of the demand curve, which slopes downward from left to right. This relationship is typical of demand curves and makes common sense: the cheaper a good is (the lower down we look on the vertical axis), the more of it a person will buy (the farther right on the horizontal axis); the more expensive, the less a person will buy.

DEMAND CURVE

The demand curve gives the quantity of the good demanded at each price.

Figure 4.2 DERIVING THE MARKET DEMAND CURVE

The market demand curve is constructed by adding up, at each price, the total of the quantities consumed by each individual. The curve here shows what market demand would be if there were only two consumers. Actual market demand, as depicted in Figure 4.3, is much larger because there are many consumers.

THE MARKET DEMAND CURVE

Suppose there was a simple economy made up of two people, Roger and Jane. Figure 4.2 illustrates how to add up the demand curves of these two individuals to obtain a demand curve for the market as a whole. We "add" the demand curves horizontally by taking, at each price, the quantities demanded by Roger and by Jane and adding the two together. Thus, in the figure, at the price of $.75, Roger demands 9 candy bars and Jane demands 11, so that the total market demand is 20 candy bars. The same principles apply no matter how many people there are in the economy. The **market demand curve** gives the total quantity of the good that will be demanded at each price. The table in Figure 4.3 summarizes the information for our example of candy bars; it gives the total quantity of candy bars demanded by everybody in the economy at various prices. If we had a table like the one in Figure 4.1 for each person in the economy, we would construct Figure 4.3 by adding up, at each price, the total quantity of candy bars purchased. Figure 4.3 tells us, for instance, that at a price of $3.00 per candy bar, the total market demand for candy bars is 1 million candy bars, and that lowering the price to $2.00 increases market demand to 3 million candy bars.

Figure 4.3 also depicts the same information in a graph. As with Figure 4.1, price lies along the vertical axis, but now the horizontal axis measures the quantity demanded by everyone in the economy. Joining the points in the figure together, we get the **market demand curve.** If we want to know what the total demand for candy bars will be when the price is $1.50 per candy bar, we

Figure 4.3 THE MARKET DEMAND CURVE

The market demand curve shows the quantity of the good demanded by all consumers in the market at each price. The market demand curve is downward sloping, for two reasons: at a higher price, each consumer buys less, and at high enough prices, some consumers decide not to buy at all—they exit the market.

Price	Quantity demanded (millions)
$5.00	0
$3.00	1
$2.00	3
$1.50	4
$1.25	8
$1.00	13
$ .75	20
$ .50	30

look on the vertical axis at the price $1.50, find the corresponding point *A* along the demand curve, and read down to the horizontal axis; at that price, total demand is 4 million candy bars. If we want to know what the price of candy bars will be when the demand equals 20 million, we find 20 million along the horizontal axis, look up to find the corresponding point *B* along the market demand curve, and read across to the vertical axis; the price at which 20 million candy bars are demanded is $.75.

Notice that just as when the price of candy bars increases, the individual's demand decreases, so too when the price of candy bars increases, market demand decreases. Thus, the market demand curve also slopes downward from left to right. This general rule holds both because each individual's demand curve is downward sloping and because as the price is increased, some individuals will decide to stop buying altogether. In Figure 4.1, for example, Roger **exits the market**—consumes a quantity of zero—at the price of $5.00, at which his demand curve hits the vertical axis. At successively higher prices more and more individuals exit the market.

SHIFTS IN DEMAND CURVES

When the price of a good increases, the quantity demand for that good decreases—when everything else is held constant. But in the real world, everything is not held constant. Any changes other than the price of the good in question shift

In the second half of 1993, oil prices fell dramatically, by nearly 25 percent. For consumers, this was good news, but for the Clinton administration, it presented a problem. In August 1992, the United States had signed the Framework Convention on Climate Change, known as the Rio convention, committing the country by the year 2000 to reduce its emissions of greenhouse gases to the level they had been in 1990. (Greenhouse gases, such as carbon dioxide, contribute to global warming.) Since the economy in 2000 would be substantially larger than in 1990, there would have to be corresponding increases in energy efficiency to meet this goal. In September 1993, the United States had outlined an ambitious "National Action Plan" for fulfilling the country's commitments. But the plan was predicated on oil prices remaining the same. Falling oil prices would increase demand. Demand curves of the kind discussed in this chapter enabled analysts to calculate the increased energy consumption—and greenhouse gas emissions—that could be expected. These calculations indicated that there would be a substantial shortfall in meeting U.S. commitments, unless further steps were taken.

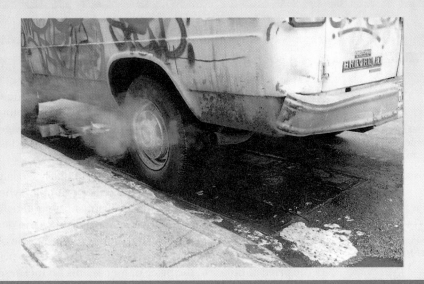

the (whole) demand curve—that is, change the amount that will be demanded at each price. How the demand curve for candy has shifted as Americans have become more weight conscious provides a good example. Figure 4.4 shows hypothetical demand curves for candy bars in 1960 and in 1995. We can see from the figure, for instance, that the demand for candy bars at a price of \$.75 has decreased from 20 million candy bars (point E_{1960}, the original equilibrium) to 10 million (point E_{1995}), as people have reduced their "taste" for candy.

Figure 4.4 SHIFTS IN THE DEMAND CURVE

A leftward shift in the demand curve means that a lesser amount will be demanded at every given market price.

SOURCES OF SHIFTS IN DEMAND CURVES

Two of the factors that shift the demand curve—changes in income and in the price of other goods—are specifically economic factors. As an individual's income increases, she normally purchases more of any good. Thus, rising incomes shift the demand curve to the right, as illustrated in Figure 4.5. At each price, she consumes more of the good.

Changes in the price of other goods, particularly closely related goods, will also shift the demand curve for a good. For example, when the price of margarine increases, some individuals will substitute butter. Two goods are **substitutes** if an increase in the price of one *increases* the demand for the other. Butter and margarine are thus substitutes. When people choose between butter and margarine, one important factor is the relative price, that is, the ratio of the price of butter to the price of margarine. An increase in the price of butter and a decrease in the price of margarine both increase the relative price of butter. Thus, both induce individuals to substitute margarine for butter.

Candy bars and granola bars can also be considered substitutes, as the two goods satisfy a similar need. Thus, an increase in the price of granola bars makes candy bars relatively more attractive, and hence leads to a rightward shift in the demand curve for candy bars. (At each price, the demand for candy is greater.)

Sometimes, however, an increase in a price of other goods has just the opposite effect. Consider an individual who takes sugar in her coffee. In deciding on how much coffee to demand, she is concerned with the price of a cup of coffee *with* sugar. If sugar becomes more expensive, she will demand less

Figure 4.5 A RIGHT-WARD SHIFT IN THE DEMAND CURVE

If, at each price, there is an increase in the quantity demanded, then the demand curve will have shifted to the right, as depicted. An increase in income, an increase in the price of a substitute, or a decrease in the price of a complement can cause a rightward shift in the demand curve.

CLOSE-UP: GASOLINE PRICES AND DEMAND FOR SMALL CARS

When demands for several products are intertwined, conditions affecting the price of one will affect the demand for the other. When gasoline prices in the United States increased in the 1970s, for example, the change affected the demand for small cars.

Actually, the price of gasoline soared twice in the 1970s: once when the Organization of Petroleum Exporting Countries (OPEC) shut off the flow of oil to the United States in 1973, and again when the Shah of Iran was driven from power in 1979, leading to a disruption in oil supplies. The price of gasoline at the pump rose from $.27 a gallon in 1973 to $1.40 a gallon by 1981. How could Americans conserve on gasoline? The distance from home to office was not going to shrink, and people had to commute to their jobs. One solution found by American drivers was that when the time came to replace their old cars, they purchased smaller cars that offered more miles to the gallon.

Analysts classify car sales according to car size. Just after the first rise in gas prices, about 2.5 million large cars, 2.8 million compacts, and 2.3 million subcompacts were bought per year. By 1985, the proportions had shifted drastically. About 1.5 million large cars were sold that year, a significant decline from the mid-1970s. The number of subcompacts sold was relatively unchanged at 2.2 million, but the number of compacts sold soared to 3.7 million.

The demand curve for any good (like cars) assumes that the price of complementary goods (like gasoline) is fixed. The rise in gasoline prices caused the demand curve for small cars to shift out to the right and the demand curve for large cars to shift back to the left.

The reason is easy to see. Imagine that you drive 15,000 miles per year. A large car gets 15 miles to the gallon, meaning that you would need to buy 1,000 gallons of gasoline per year, while a small car gets 30 miles to the gallon, meaning that you would only have to buy 500 gallons of gas per year. When the price of gasoline was at its 1981 peak of $1.40 per gallon, this higher mileage translated into a savings of $700 per year.

Sources: Gasoline prices taken from various issues of *Survey of Current Business;* auto sales figures from Linda Williams and Patricia Hu of Oak Ridge National Laboratory; *Light Duty Vehicle Summary: Model Year 1976 to the First Half of Model Year 1989.*

coffee. For this person, sugar and coffee are **complements;** an increase in the price of one *decreases* the demand for the other. A price increase of sugar shifts the demand curve of coffee to the left: at each price, the demand for coffee is less. Similarly a *decrease* in the price of sugar shifts the demand curve for coffee to the right.

Noneconomic factors can also shift market demand curves. The major ones are changes in tastes and in composition of the population. The candy example shown earlier was a change in taste. Other taste changes over the past decade in the United States include a shift from hard liquor to wine and from fatty meats to low-cholesterol foods. Each of these taste changes has shifted the whole demand curve of the goods in question.

Population changes that shift demand curves are often related to age. Young families with babies purchase disposable diapers. The demand for new houses and apartments is closely related to the number of new households, which in turn depends on the number of individuals of marriageable age. The U.S. population has been growing older, on average, both because life expectancies are increasing and because birthrates fell somewhat after the baby boom that followed World War II. So there has been a shift in demand away from diapers and new houses. Economists working for particular firms and industries spend considerable energy ascertaining population effects, called **demographic effects,** on the demand for the goods their firms sell.

Sometimes demand curves shift as the result of new information. The shifts in demand for alcohol and meat—and even more so for cigarettes—are related to improved consumer information about health risks.

Changes in the availability of credit also can shift demand curves—for goods like cars and houses that people typically buy with the help of loans. When banks, for example, reduce the money available for consumer loans, the demand curves for cars and houses shift.

SOURCES OF SHIFTS IN MARKET DEMAND CURVES

A change in income

A change in the price of a substitute

A change in the price of a complement

A change in the composition of the population

A change in tastes

A change in information

A change in the availability of credit

A change in expectations

Finally, what people think will happen in the future can shift demand curves. If people think they may become unemployed, they will reduce their spending. In this case, economists say that their demand curve depends on expectations.

SHIFTS IN A DEMAND CURVE VERSUS MOVEMENTS ALONG A DEMAND CURVE

The distinction between changes that result from a *shift* in the demand curve and changes that result from a *movement along* the demand curve is crucial to understanding economics. A movement along a demand curve is simply the change in the quantity demanded as the price changes. Figure 4.6A illustrates a movement along the demand curve from point *A* to point *B; given a demand curve,* at lower prices, more is consumed. Figure 4.6B illustrates a shift in the demand curve to the right; *at a given price,* more is consumed. Quantity again increases from Q_0 to Q_1, but now the price stays the same.

In practice, both effects are often present. Thus, in panel C of Figure 4.6, the movement from point *A* to point *C*—where the quantity demanded has been

Figure 4.6 MOVEMENT ALONG THE DEMAND CURVE VERSUS SHIFT IN THE DEMAND CURVE

Panel A shows an increase in quantity demanded caused by a lower price—a movement along a given demand curve. Panel B illustrates an increase in quantity demanded caused by a shift in the entire demand curve, so that a greater quantity is demanded at every market price. Panel C shows a combination of a shift in the demand curve (the movement from point *A* to *B*) and a movement along the demand curve (the movement from *B* to *C*).

increased from Q_0 to Q_2—consists of two parts: a change in quantity demanded resulting from a shift in the demand curve (the increase in quantity from Q_0 to Q_1), and a movement along the demand curve due to a change in the price (the increase in quantity from Q_1 to Q_2).

SUPPLY

Economists use the concept of **supply** to describe the quantity of a good or service that a household or firm would like to sell at a particular price. Supply in economics refers to such seemingly disparate choices as the number of candy bars a firm wants to sell and the number of hours a worker is willing to work. As with demand, the first question economists ask is how does the quantity supplied change when price changes, keeping everything else the same?

Figure 4.7 shows the number of candy bars that the Melt-in-the-Mouth Chocolate Company would like to sell, or supply to the market, at each price. As the price rises, so does the quantity supplied. Below $1.00, the firm finds it unprofitable to produce. At $2.00, it would like to sell 85,000 candy bars. At $5.00, it would like to sell 100,000.

Figure 4.7 also depicts these points in a graph. The curve drawn by connecting the points is called the **supply curve.** It shows the quantity that Melt-

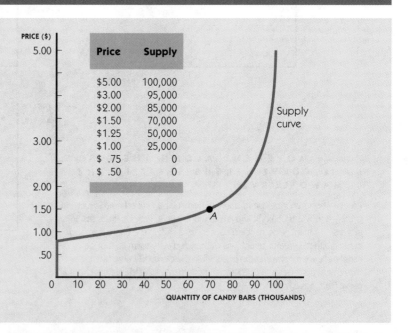

Figure 4.7 ONE FIRM'S SUPPLY CURVE

The supply curve shows the quantity of a good a firm is willing to produce at each price. Normally a firm is willing to produce more as the price increases, which is why the supply curve slopes upward.

Price	Supply
$5.00	100,000
$3.00	95,000
$2.00	85,000
$1.50	70,000
$1.25	50,000
$1.00	25,000
$ .75	0
$ .50	0

in-the-Mouth will supply at each price, holding all other factors constant. As with the demand curve, we put the price on the vertical axis and the quantity supplied on the horizontal axis. Thus, we can read point A on the curve as indicating that at a price of $1.50 the firm would like to supply 70,000 candy bars.

In direct contrast to the demand curve, the typical supply curve slopes upward from left to right; at higher prices, firms will supply more.[1] This is because higher prices yield suppliers higher profits—giving them an incentive to produce more.

SUPPLY CURVE

The supply curve gives the quantity of the good supplied at each price.

MARKET SUPPLY

The **market supply** of a good is simply the total quantity that all the firms in the economy are willing to supply at a given price. Similarly, the market supply of labor is simply the total quantity of labor that all the households in the economy are willing to supply at a given wage. Figure 4.8 tells us, for instance, that at a price of $2.00, firms will supply 70 million candy bars, while at a price of $.50, they will supply only 5 million.

Figure 4.8 also shows the same information graphically. The curve joining the points in the figure is the **market supply curve.** The market supply curve gives the total quantity of a good that firms are willing to produce at each price. Thus, we read point A on the market supply curve as showing that at a price of $.75, the firms in the economy would like to sell 20 million candy bars.

As the price of candy bars increases, the quantity supplied increases, other things equal. The market supply curve slopes upward from left to right for two reasons: at higher prices, each firm in the market is willing to produce more; and at higher prices, more firms are willing to enter the market to produce the good.

The market supply curve is calculated from the supply curves of the different firms in the same way that the market demand curve is calculated from the demand curves of the different households: at each price, we add horizontally the quantities that each of the firms is willing to produce.

[1]Chapter 9 will describe some unusual situations where supply curves may not be upward sloping.

Figure 4.8 THE MARKET SUPPLY CURVE

The market supply curve shows the quantity of a good all firms in the market are willing to supply at each price. The market supply curve is normally upward sloping, both because each firm is willing to supply more of the good at a higher price and because higher prices entice new firms to produce.

Price	Total market supply (millions)
$5.00	82
$3.00	80
$2.00	70
$1.50	59
$1.25	47
$1.00	34
$ .75	20
$ .50	5

Figure 4.9 shows how this is done in a market with only two producers. At a price of $1.25, Melt-in-the-Mouth Chocolate produces 50,000 candy bars, while the Chocolates of Choice Company produces 40,000. So the market supply is 90,000 bars. The same principle applies to markets with many firms.

Figure 4.9 DERIVING THE MARKET SUPPLY CURVE

The market supply curve is constructed by adding up the quantity that each of the firms in the economy is willing to supply at each price. The figure here shows what market supply would be if there were only two producers. Actual market supply, as depicted in Figure 4.8, is much larger because there are many producers.

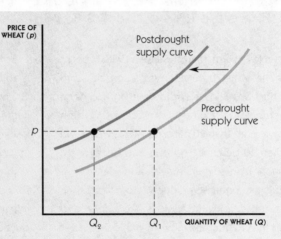

Figure 4.10 SHIFTING THE SUPPLY CURVE TO THE LEFT

A drought or other disaster (among other possible factors) will cause the supply curve to shift to the left, so that at each price, a smaller quantity is supplied.

SHIFTS IN SUPPLY CURVES

Just as demand curves can shift, supply curves too can shift, so that the quantity supplied at each price increases or decreases. Suppose a drought hits the breadbasket states of mid-America. Figure 4.10 illustrates the situation. The supply curve for wheat shifts to the left, which means that at each price of wheat, the quantity firms are willing to supply is smaller.

SOURCES OF SHIFTS IN SUPPLY CURVES

There are several sources of shifts in market supply curves, just as in the case of the market demand curves already discussed. One is changing prices of the inputs used to produce a good. Figure 4.11 shows that as corn becomes less expensive, the supply curve for cornflakes shifts to the right. Producing cornflakes costs less, at every price, firms are willing to supply a greater quantity. That is why the quantity supplied along the curve S_1 is greater than the quantity supplied, at the same price, along the curve S_0.

Another source of shifts is changes in technology. The technological improvements in the computer industry over the past two decades have led to a rightward shift in the market supply curve. Yet another source of shifts is nature. The supply curve for agricultural goods may shift to the right or left depending on weather conditions, insect infestations, or animal diseases.

Figure 4.11 SHIFTING THE SUPPLY CURVE TO THE RIGHT

An improvement in technology or a reduction in input prices (among other possible factors) will cause the supply curve to shift to the right, so that at each price, a larger quantity is supplied.

Reduction in the availability of credit may curtail firms' ability to borrow to obtain inputs needed for production, and this too will induce a leftward shift in the supply curve. Finally, changed expectations can also lead to a shift in the supply curve. If firms believe that a new technology for making cars will become available in two years' time, this belief will discourage investment today and will lead to a temporary leftward shift in the supply curve.

SOURCES OF SHIFTS IN MARKET SUPPLY CURVES

A change in the prices of inputs

A change in technology

A change in the natural environment

A change in the availability of credit

A change in expectations

Figure 4.12 MOVEMENT ALONG THE SUPPLY CURVE VERSUS SHIFT IN THE SUPPLY CURVE

Panel A shows an increase in quantity supplied caused by a higher price—a movement along a given supply curve. Panel B illustrates an increase in quantity supplied caused by a shift in the entire supply curve, so that a greater quantity is supplied at every market price.

SHIFTS IN A SUPPLY CURVE VERSUS MOVEMENTS ALONG A SUPPLY CURVE

Distinguishing between a movement *along* a curve and a *shift* in the curve itself is just as important for supply curves as it is for demand curves. In Figure 4.12A, the price of candy bars has gone up, with a corresponding increase in quantity supplied. Thus, there has been a movement along the supply curve.

By contrast, in Figure 4.12B, the supply curve has shifted to the right, perhaps because a new production technique has made it cheaper to produce candy bars. Now, even though the price does not change, the quantity supplied increases. The quantity supplied in the market can increase either because the price of the good has increased, so that for a *given supply curve*, the quantity produced is higher; or because the supply curve has shifted, so that at a *given price*, the quantity supplied has increased.

LAW OF SUPPLY AND DEMAND

This chapter began with the assertion that supply and demand work together to determine the market price in competitive markets. Figure 4.13 puts a market supply curve and a market demand curve on the same graph to show how this happens. The price actually paid and received in the market will be determined by the intersection of the two curves. This point is labeled E_0, for equilibrium, and the corresponding price ($.75) and quantity (20 million) are called, respectively, the **equilibrium price** and the **equilibrium quantity.**

Since the term **equilibrium** will recur throughout the book, it is important to understand the concept clearly. Equilibrium describes a situation where

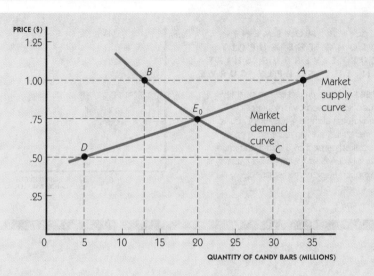

Figure 4.13 SUPPLY AND DEMAND EQUILIBRIUM

Equilibrium occurs at the intersection of the demand and supply curves, at point E_0. At any price above E_0, the quantity supplied will exceed the quantity demanded, the market will be out of equilibrium, and there will be excess supply. At any price below E_0, the quantity demanded will exceed the quantity supplied, the market will be out of equilibrium, and there will be excess demand.

there are no forces (reasons) for change. No one has an incentive to change the result—the price or quantity consumed or produced in the case of supply and demand.

Physicists also speak of equilibrium in describing a weight hanging from a spring. Two forces are working on the weight. Gravity is pulling it down; the spring is pulling it up. When the weight is at rest, it is in equilibrium, with the two forces just offsetting each other. If one pulls the weight down a little bit, the force of the spring will be greater than the force of gravity, and the weight will spring up. In the absence of any further intrusions, the weight will bob back and forth and eventually reach its equilibrium position.

An economic equilibrium is established in the same way. At the equilibrium price, consumers get precisely the quantity of the good they are willing to buy at that price, and producers sell precisely the quantity they are willing to sell at that price. Neither producers nor consumers have any incentive to change.

But consider the price of $1.00 in Figure 4.13. There is no equilibrium quantity here. First find $1.00 on the vertical axis. Now look across to find point A on the supply curve, and read down to the horizontal axis; point A tells you that at a price of $1.00, firms want to supply 34 million candy bars. Now look at point B on the demand curve. Point B shows that at a price of $1.00, consumers only want to buy 13 million candy bars. Like the weight bobbing on a spring however, this market will work its way back to equilibrium, in the following way. At a price of $1.00, there is **excess supply.** As producers discover that they cannot sell as much as they would like at this price, some of them will lower their prices slightly, hoping to take business from other producers. When one producer lowers prices, his competitors will have to respond, for fear that they will end up unable to sell their goods. As prices come

Every economic model, including the model of how supply and demand determine the equilibrium price and quantity in a market, is constructed of three kinds of relationships: identities, behavioral relationships, and equilibrium relationships. Recognizing these component parts will help in understanding not only how economists think but also the source of their disagreements.

The market demand is equal to the sum of individual demands. This is an identity. An identity is a statement that is true simply because of the definition of the terms. In other words, market demand is *defined* to be the sum of the demands of all individuals. Similarly, it is an identity that market supply is equal to the sum of the supplies of all firms; the terms are defined in that way.

The demand curve represents a relationship between the price and the quantity demanded. Normally, as prices rise, the quantity of a good demanded decreases. This is a description of how individuals behave, and is called a behavioral relationship. The supply curve for each firm is also a behavioral relationship.

Economists may disagree over behavioral relationships. They may agree about the direction of the relationship but disagree about the strength of the connection. For any given product, does a change in price lead to a large change in the quantity demanded or a small one? But they may even disagree over the direction of the effect. As later chapters will discuss, in some special cases a higher price may actually lead to a *lower* quantity supplied.

Finally, an equilibrium relationship exists when there are no forces for change. In the supply and demand model, the equilibrium occurs when the quantity demanded is equal to the quantity supplied. An equilibrium relationship is not the same as an identity. It is possible for the economy to be out of equilibrium, at least for a time. Of course, being out of equilibrium implies that there are forces for change pushing toward equilibrium. But an identity must always hold true at all times, as a matter of definition.

Economists usually agree about what an equilibrium would look like, but they often differ on whether the forces pushing the markets toward equilibrium are strong or weak, and thus on whether the economy is typically close to equilibrium or may stray rather far from it.

---

down, consumers will also buy more, and so on until the market reaches the equilibrium price and quantity.

Similarly, assume that the price is lower than $.75, say $.50. At the lower price, there is **excess demand:** individuals want to buy 30 million candy bars (point C), while firms only want to produce 5 million (point D). Consumers unable to purchase all they want will offer to pay a bit more; other consumers, afraid of having to do without, will match these higher bids or raise them. As prices start to increase, suppliers will also have a greater incentive to produce more. Again the market will tend toward the equilibrium point.

To repeat for emphasis: at equilibrium, no purchaser and no supplier has an incentive to change the price or quantity. In competitive market economies actual prices tend to be the equilibrium prices, at which demand equals supply.

This is called the **law of supply and demand.** Note: this law does not mean that at every moment of time the price is precisely at the intersection of the demand and supply curves. As with the example of the weight and the spring, the market may bounce around a little bit when it is in the process of adjusting. What the law of supply and demand does say is that when a market is out of equilibrium, there are predictable forces for change.

USING DEMAND AND SUPPLY CURVES

The concepts of demand and supply curves—and market equilibrium as the intersection of demand and supply curves—constitute the economist's basic model of demand and supply. This model has proven to be extremely useful. It helps explain why the price of some commodity is high, and that of some other commodity is low. It also helps *predict* the consequences of certain changes. Its predictions can then be tested against what actually happens. One of the reasons that the model is so useful is that it gives reasonably accurate predictions.

Figure 4.14 repeats the demand and supply curve for candy bars. Assume, now, however, that sugar becomes more expensive. As a result, at each price, the amount of candy firms are willing to supply is reduced. The supply curve shifts to the left, as in panel A. There will be a new equilibrium, at a higher price and a lower quantity of candy consumed.

Alternatively, assume that Americans become more health conscious, and as a result, at each price fewer candy bars are consumed: the demand curve shifts to the left, as shown in panel B. Again, there will be a new equilibrium, at a lower price and a lower quantity of candy consumed.

This illustrates how changes in observed prices can be related either to shifts in the demand curve or shifts in the supply curve. When the war in

Figure 4.14 USING SUPPLY AND DEMAND CURVES TO PREDICT PRICE CHANGES

Initially the market for candy bars is in equilibrium at E_0. An increase in the cost of sugar shifts the supply curve to the left, as shown in panel A. At the new equilibrium, E_1, the price is higher and the quantity consumed is lower. A shift in taste away from candy results in a leftward shift in the demand curve as shown in panel B. At the new equilibrium, E_1, the price and the quantity consumed is lower.

Kuwait interrupted the supply of oil from the Middle East in 1990, that was a shift in the supply curve. The model predicted the result: an increase in the price of oil. This increase was the natural process of the law of supply and demand.

Consensus on the Determination of Prices

The law of supply and demand plays such a prominent role in economics that there is a joke about teaching a parrot to be an economist simply by teaching it to say "supply and demand." That prices are determined by the law of supply and demand is one of the most long-standing and widely accepted ideas of economists. It forms our fourth point of consensus.

4 Prices

In competitive markets, prices are determined by the law of supply and demand. Shifts in the demand and supply curves lead to changes in the equilibrium price. Similar principles apply to the labor and capital markets. The price for labor is the wage, and the price for capital is the interest rate.

PRICE, VALUE, AND COST

Price, to an economist, is what is given in exchange for a good or service. Price, in this sense, is determined by the forces of supply and demand. Adam Smith, often thought of as the founder of modern economics, called our notion of price "value in exchange," and contrasted it to the notion of "value in use":

> The things which have the greatest value in use have frequently little or no value in exchange; and, on the contrary, those which have the greatest value in exchange have frequently little or no value in use. Nothing is more useful than water, but it will purchase scarce any thing; scarce any thing can be had in exchange for it. A diamond, on the contrary, has scarce any value in use; but a very great quantity of other goods may frequently be had in exchange for it.[2]

The law of supply and demand can help to explain the diamond-water paradox, and many similar examples where "value in use" is very different from "value in exchange." Figure 4.15 presents a demand and a supply curve for water. Individuals are willing to pay a high price for the water they need to live, as illustrated by point *A*, on the demand curve. But above some quantity, *B*, people will pay almost nothing more for additional water. In most of the

[2]*The Wealth of Nations* (1776), Book I, Chapter IV.

Figure 4.15 SUPPLY AND DEMAND FOR WATER

Point A shows that people are willing to pay a relatively high price for the first few units of water. But to the right of B, people have plenty of water already and are not willing to pay much for an additional amount. The price of water will be determined at the point where the supply curve crosses the demand curve. In most cases, the resulting price is extremely low.

inhabited parts of the world, water is readily available, so it gets supplied in plentiful quantities at low prices. Thus, the supply curve of water intersects the demand curve to the right of *B,* as in the figure; hence the low equilibrium price. Of course, in the desert, the water supply may be very limited and the price, as a result, very high.

To an economist, the statements that the price of diamonds is high and the price of water is low are statements about supply and demand conditions. They say nothing about whether diamonds are "more important" or "better" than water. In Adam Smith's terms, they are not statements about value in use.

Price is related to the *marginal* value of an object, that is, the value of an additional unit of the object. Water has a low price not because the *total* value of water is low—it is obviously high, since we could not live without it—but because the marginal value, what we would be willing to pay to be able to drink one more glass of water a year, is low.

Just as economists take care to distinguish the words "price" and "value," they also distinguish the *price* of an object (what it sells for) from its *cost* (the expense of making the object). This is another crucial distinction in economics. The costs of producing a good affect the price at which firms are willing to supply that good. An increase in the costs of production will normally cause prices to rise. And in the competitive model, *in equilibrium,* the price of an object will normally equal its (marginal) cost of production (including the amount needed to pay a firm's owner to stay in business rather than seek some other form of employment). But there are important cases—as we shall see in later chapters—where price does not equal cost.

In thinking about the relationship of price and cost, it is interesting to consider the case of a good in fixed supply, such as land. Normally, land is something that cannot be produced, so its cost of production can be considered infinite (though there are situations where land can be produced, as when Chicago filled in part of Lake Michigan to expand its lake shore). Yet there is still an equilibrium price of land—where the demand for land is equal to its (fixed) supply.

REVIEW AND PRACTICE

SUMMARY

1. An individual's demand curve gives the quantity demanded of a good at each possible price. It normally slopes down, which means that the person demands a greater quantity of the good at lower prices and a lesser quantity at higher prices.

2. The market demand curve gives the total quantity of a good demanded by all individuals in an economy at each price. As the price rises, demand falls, both because each person demands less of the good and because some people exit the market.

3. A firm's supply curve gives the amount of a good the firm is willing to supply at each price. It is normally upward sloping, which means that firms supply a greater quantity of the good at higher prices and a lesser quantity at lower prices.

4. The market supply curve gives the total quantity of a good that all firms in the economy are willing to produce at each price. As the price rises, supply rises, both because each firm supplies more of the good and because some additional firms enter the market.

5. The law of supply and demand says that in competitive markets, the equilibrium price is that price at which quantity demanded equals quantity supplied. It is represented on a graph by the intersection of the demand and supply curves.

6. A demand curve *only* shows the relationship between quantity demanded and price. Changes in tastes, in demographic factors, in income, in the prices of other goods, in information, in the availability of credit, or in expectations are reflected in a shift of the entire demand curve.

7. A supply curve *only* shows the relationship between quantity supplied and price. Changes in factors such as technology, the prices of inputs, the natural environment, expectations, or the availability of credit are reflected in a shift of the entire supply curve.

8. It is important to distinguish movements along a demand curve from shifts in the demand curve, and movements along a supply curve from shifts in the supply curve.

KEY TERMS

demand curve   **demographic effects**   **excess supply**
substitutes   **supply curve**   **excess demand**
complements   **equilibrium price**

REVIEW QUESTIONS

1. Why does an individual's demand curve normally slope down? Why does a market demand curve normally slope down?

2. Why does a firm's supply curve normally slope up? Why does a market supply curve normally slope up?

3. What is the significance of the point where supply and demand curves intersect?

4. Explain why, if the price of a good is above the equilibrium price, the forces of supply and demand will tend to push the price toward equilibrium. Explain why, if the price of the good is below the equilibrium price, the market will tend to adjust toward equilibrium.

5. Name some factors that could shift the demand curve out to the right.

6. Name some factors that could shift the supply curve in to the left.

PROBLEMS

1. Imagine a company lunchroom that sells pizza by the slice. Using the following data, plot the points and graph the demand and supply curves. What is the equilibrium price and quantity? Find a price at which excess demand would exist and a price at which excess supply would exist, and plot them on your diagram.

Price per slice	Demand (number of slices)	Supply (number of slices)
$1	420	0
$2	210	100
$3	140	140
$4	105	160
$5	84	170

2. Suppose a severe drought hit the sugarcane crop. Predict how this would affect the equilibrium price and quantity in the market for sugar and the market for honey. Draw supply and demand diagrams to illustrate your answers.

3. Imagine that a new invention allows each mine worker to mine twice as much coal. Predict how this will affect the equilibrium price and quantity in the market for coal and the market for heating oil. Draw supply and demand diagrams to illustrate your answer.

4. Americans' tastes have shifted away from beef and toward chicken. Predict how this change affects the equilibrium price and quantity in the market for beef, the market for chicken, and the market for roadside hamburger stands. Draw supply and demand diagrams to illustrate your answer.

5. During the 1970s, the postwar baby boomers reached working age, and it became more acceptable for married women with children to work. Predict how this increase in the number of workers is likely to affect the equilibrium wage and quantity of employment. Draw supply and demand curves to illustrate your answer.

Using Demand and Supply

The concepts of demand and supply are among the most useful in economics. The demand and supply framework explains why doctors are paid more than lawyers, or why the income of unskilled workers has increased less than that of skilled workers. It can also be used to predict what the demand for condominiums or disposable diapers will be fifteen years from now, or what will happen if the government increases the tax on cigarettes. Not only can we predict that prices will change, we can predict by how much they will change.

This chapter has two purposes. The first is to develop some of the concepts required to make these kinds of predictions, and to illustrate how the demand and supply framework can be used in a variety of contexts.

The second is to look at what happens when people interfere with the workings of competitive markets. Rents may seem too high for poor people to afford adequate housing. The price of corn may seem unfairly low, not adequate to compensate farmers for their work. Political pressure constantly develops for government to intervene on behalf of the group that has been disadvantaged by the market—whether it be poor people, farmers, or oil companies (which ask for government help when the price of oil falls). The second part of this chapter traces the consequences of political interventions into the workings of some markets.

1. What is meant by the concept of elasticity? Why does it play such an important role in predicting market outcomes?

2. What happens when market outcomes are interfered with, as when the government imposes price floors and ceilings? Why do such interferences give rise to shortages and surpluses?

SENSITIVITY TO PRICE CHANGES: THE PRICE ELASTICITY OF DEMAND

If tomorrow supermarkets across the country were to cut the price of bread or milk by 5 percent, the quantity demanded of these items would not change much. If stores offered the same reduction on premium ice cream, however, demand would increase substantially. Why do price changes sometimes have small effects and at other times large ones? The answer lies in the shape of the demand and supply curves.

The demand for ice cream is more sensitive to price changes than is the demand for milk, and this is reflected in the shape of the demand curves as illustrated in Figure 5.1. The demand curve for ice cream (panel A) is much flatter than the one for milk (panel B). When the demand curve is somewhat flat, a change in price, say from $2.00 a gallon to $2.10, has a large effect on the quantity consumed. In panel A, the demand for ice cream decreases from 100 million pints at a price of $2.00 a pint to 90 million pints at a price of $2.10 per pint.

By contrast, when the demand curve is steep, it means that a change in price has little effect on quantity. In panel B, the demand for milk decreases from 100 million gallons at $2.00 per gallon to 99 million gallons at $2.10 per gallon. But saying that the demand curve is steep or flat just pushes the question back a step: why are some demand curves steeper than others?

The answer is that though substitutes exist for almost every good or service, substitution will be more difficult for some goods and services than for others. When substitution is difficult, when the price of a good increases the quantity demanded will not decrease by much, and when the price falls the quantity demanded will not increase much. The typical consumer does not substitute milk for beer—or for anything else—even if milk becomes a good deal cheaper.

When substitution is easy, on the other hand, a fall in price may lead to a large increase in quantity demanded. For instance, there are many good substitutes for ice cream, including sherbets and frozen yogurts. The price decrease for ice cream means that these close substitutes have become relatively more expensive, and the demand for ice cream would thus increase significantly.

For many purposes, economists need to be precise about how steep or how flat the demand curve is. For precision they use the concept of the **price elasticity of demand** (for short, the price elasticity or the elasticity of demand). The price elasticity of demand is defined as the percentage change in the quantity demanded divided by the percentage change in price. In mathematical terms,

$$\text{elasticity of demand} = \frac{\text{percentage change in quantity demanded}}{\text{percentage change in price}}.$$

If the quantity demanded changes 8 percent in response to a 2 percent change in price, then the elasticity of demand is 4.

(Price elasticities of demand are really *negative* numbers; that is, when the price increases, quantities demanded are reduced. But the convention is to simply refer to the elasticity as a number with the understanding that it is negative.)

It is easiest to calculate the elasticity of demand when there is just a 1 percent change in price. Then the elasticity of demand is just the percent change in the quantity demanded. In the telescoped portion of Figure 5.1A, we see that increasing the price of ice cream from $2.00 a pint to $2.02—a 1 percent

Figure 5.1 ELASTIC VERSUS INELASTIC DEMAND CURVES

Panel A shows a hypothetical demand curve for ice cream. Note that quantity demanded changes rapidly with fairly small price changes, indicating that demand for ice cream is elastic. The telescoped portion of the demand curve shows that a 1 percent rise in price leads to a 2 percent fall in quantity demanded. Panel B shows a hypothetical demand curve for milk. Note that quantity demanded changes very little, regardless of changes in price, meaning that demand for milk is inelastic. The telescoped portion of the demand curve shows that a 1 percent rise in price leads to a .2 percent fall in quantity demanded.

increase in price—reduces the demand from 100 million pints to 98 million, a 2 percent decline. So the price elasticity of demand for ice cream is 2.

By contrast, assume that the price of milk increases from $2.00 a gallon to $2.02 (again a 1 percent increase in price), as shown in the telescoped portion of Figure 5.1B. This reduces demand from 100 million gallons per year to 99.8 million. Demand has gone down by .2 percent, so the price elasticity of demand is therefore .2. Larger values for price elasticity indicate that demand is more sensitive to changes in price. Smaller values indicate that demand is less sensitive to price changes.

PRICE ELASTICITY AND REVENUES

The revenue received by a firm in selling a good is price times quantity. We write this in a simple equation. Letting R denote revenues, p price, and Q quantity:

$$R = pQ$$

This means that when price goes up by 1 percent, whether revenues go up or down depends on the magnitude of the decrease in quantity. If quantity decreases by more than 1 percent, then total revenues decrease; by less than 1 percent, they increase.

We can express this result in terms of the concept of price elasticity. When the elasticity of demand is greater than unity, the change in quantity more than offsets the change in prices, we say that the demand for that good is **relatively elastic,** or *sensitive* to price changes, and revenues decrease as price increases and increase as price decreases.

In the case where the price elasticity is **unity,** or 1, the decrease in the quantity demanded just offsets the increase in the price, so price increases have no effect on revenues. If the price elasticity is less than unity, then when the price of a good increases by 1 percent, the quantity demanded is reduced by less than 1 percent. Since there is not much reduction in demand, elasticities in this range, between 0 and 1, mean that price increases will increase revenues. And price decreases will decrease revenues. We say the demand for that good is **relatively inelastic,** or *insensitive* to price changes.

Business firms must pay attention to the price elasticity of demand for their products. Suppose a cement producer, the only one in town, is considering a 1 percent increase in price. The firm hires an economist to estimate the elasticity of demand, so that the firm will know what will happen to sales when it raises its price. The economist tells the firm that its demand elasticity is 2. This means that if the price of cement rises by 1 percent, the quantity sold will decline by 2 percent.

The firm's executives will not be pleased by the findings. To see why, assume that initially the price of cement was $1,000 per ton, and 100,000 tons were sold. To calculate revenues, you multiply the price times the quantity sold. So initially revenues were $1,000 × 100,000 = $100 million. With a 1 percent increase, the price will be $1,010. If the elasticity of demand is 2, then a

Table 5.1 **SOME PRICE ELASTICITIES IN THE U.S. ECONOMY**

Industry	Elasticity
Elastic demands	
Purchased meals	2.27
Metals	1.52
Furniture, timber	1.25
Motor vehicles	1.14
Transportation	1.03
Inelastic demands	
Gas, electricity, water	.92
Oil	.91
Chemicals	.89
Beverages	.78
Tobacco	.61
Food	.58
Housing services	.55
Clothing	.49
Books, magazines, newspapers	.34
Meat	.2

Sources: Ahson Mansur and John Whalley, "Numerical Specification of Applied General Equilibrium Models: Estimation, Calibration, and Data," in Scarf and Shoven, eds., *Applied General Equilibrium Analysis* (New York: Cambridge University Press, 1984), p. 109; Hendrik S. Houthakker and Lester D. Taylor, *Consumer Demand in the United States: Analysis and Projections* (Cambridge: Harvard University Press, 1970).

1 percent price increase results in a 2 percent decrease in the quantity sold. With a 2 percent quantity decrease, sales are now 98,000 tons. Revenues are down to $98.98 million ($1,010 × 98,000), a fall of just slightly over 1 percent. Because of the high elasticity, this cement firm's price *increase* leads to a *decrease* in revenues.

The price elasticity of demand works the same way for price decreases. Suppose the cement producer decided to decrease the price of cement 1 percent, to $990. With an elasticity of demand of 2, sales would then increase 2 percent, to 102,000 tons. Thus, revenues would *increase* to $100,980,000 ($990 × 102,000), that is, by a bit less than 1 percent.

EXTREME CASES

There are two extreme cases that deserve attention. One is that of a flat demand curve, a curve that is perfectly horizontal. We say that such a demand curve is perfectly elastic, or has **infinite elasticity,** since even a slight increase in the price results in demand dropping to zero. The other case is that of a steep demand curve, a curve that is perfectly vertical. We say that such a demand curve is perfectly inelastic, or has **zero elasticity,** since no matter what the change in price, demand remains the same.

PRICE ELASTICITIES IN THE U.S. ECONOMY

The elasticity of demand for most foods is low (an increase in price will not affect demand much). The elasticity of demand for most luxuries, such as perfume, ski trips, and Mercedes cars, is high (an increase in price will lead to much less demand). Table 5.1 gives the elasticities of demand for some important goods. For example, the price elasticity of food and of tobacco is about .6, in contrast to the price elasticity for motor vehicles, which is 1.14. The table also shows the price elasticities for broad groups of goods. It may be easy to substitute purchased meals for home-cooked food, but it is difficult to do without food. Thus, the price elasticity of purchased meals is 2.27, while the price elasticity of all food is much lower, at .58. More generally, goods for which it is easy to find substitutes will have high price elasticities; goods for which substitutes cannot easily be found will have low price elasticities.

ELASTICITY AND SLOPE

The elasticity of a curve is not the same as its slope. The best way to see the distinction is to look at the **linear** demand curve. The linear demand curve is a straight line, depicted in Figure 5.2. With a linear demand curve, the quantity demanded is related to the price by the equation

$$Q = a - bp.$$

If $a = 120$, and $b = 2$, at a price of 10, $Q = 100$; at a price of 11, $Q = 98$; at a price of 12, $Q = 96$, and so forth.

The demand curve also gives the price at which a particular quantity of the good will be demanded. Thus, we can rewrite the equation to read

$$p = \frac{a}{b} - \frac{Q}{b},$$

so that (with $a = 120$, $b = 2$ as before), at $Q = 100$, $p = 10$; at $Q = 99$, $p = 10.5$; at $Q = 98$, $p = 11$.

Slope gives the change along the vertical axis per unit change along the horizontal axis. Recall that when we draw the demand curve, we put price on the vertical axis and output on the horizontal axis.

$$\text{slope} = \frac{\text{change in price}}{\text{change in quantity}} = \frac{\Delta p}{\Delta Q}.$$

where the symbol Δ—the Greek letter delta—signifies a change. Thus, ΔQ means the change in quantity and Δp means the change in price. Equivalently, slope is the change in price for a unit change in quantity. In our example, as we

Figure 5.2 LINEAR DEMAND CURVE

The linear demand curve is a straight line; it is represented algebraicly by the equation $Q = a - bp$. The slope of the demand curve is a constant. However, the elasticity varies with output. At low outputs (high prices) it is very high. At high outputs (low prices) it is very low.

PRICE ELASTICITY OF DEMAND

Elasticity	Description	Effect on Quantity Demanded of 1% Increase in Price	Effect on Revenues of 1% Increase in Price
Zero	Perfectly inelastic (vertical demand curve)	Zero	Increased by 1%
Between 0 and 1	Inelastic	Reduced by less than 1%	Increased by less than 1%
1	Unitary elasticity	Reduced by 1%	Unchanged
Greater than 1	Elastic	Reduced by more than 1%	Reduced; the greater the elasticity, the more revenue is reduced
Infinite	Perfectly elastic (horizontal demand curve)	Reduced to zero	Reduced to zero

change quantity by 1, price changes by ½. More generally, the slope of the linear demand equation above is ⅙.[1]

The elasticity, as we know, is given by

$$\text{elasticity} = \frac{\text{percentage change in quantity}}{\text{percentage change in price}}.$$

The percentage change in quantity is

$$\text{percentage change in quantity} = \frac{\text{change in quantity}}{\text{quantity}} = \frac{\Delta Q}{Q}.$$

Similarly,

$$\text{percentage change in price} = \frac{\text{change in price}}{\text{price}} = \frac{\Delta p}{p}.$$

We can now rewrite the expression for elasticity as

$$\text{elasticity} = \frac{\Delta Q/Q}{\Delta p/p} = \frac{\Delta Q}{\Delta p} \times \frac{p}{Q}$$

$$= b \times \frac{p}{Q}$$

$$= \frac{1}{\text{slope}} \times \frac{p}{Q}.$$

Everywhere along a linear demand curve, the slope is the same; but the elasticity is very high at low levels of output and very low at high levels of output.

The formula for elasticity has one other important implication, illustrated in Figure 5.3. Of two demand curves going through the same point, the flatter demand curve has the higher elasticity at the point of intersection. At the point where they intersect, p and Q (and therefore %) are the same. Only the slopes differ. The one with the smaller slope has the greater elasticity.

Figure 5.3 COMPARING ELASTICITIES

If two demand curves intersect, at the point of intersection, the flatter demand curve has the greater price elasticity.

[1]To see this, observe that at $Q + 1$, the price is

$$\frac{a}{b} - \frac{Q+1}{b}.$$

The change in price is

$$\frac{a}{b} - \frac{Q}{b} - \left(\frac{a}{b} - \frac{Q+1}{b} \right) = \frac{a}{b} - \frac{Q}{b} - \frac{a}{b} + \frac{Q+1}{b} = \frac{1}{b}.$$

SMALL VERSUS LARGE PRICE CHANGES

Often, economists are interested in what would happen if there is a large price change. For instance, if a 50 percent tax is imposed on cigarettes, what will happen to demand?

When price changes are small or moderate, we can *extrapolate*. That is, often we have information about the effect of a small price change. We then extrapolate, assuming that a slightly larger price change will have proportionately larger effects. For example, if a 1 percent change in price results in a 2 percent change in quantity, then a 3 percent change in price will probably result in an approximately 6 percent change in quantity.

With large price changes, however, such extrapolation becomes riskier. The reason is that *price elasticity is typically different at different points along the demand curve.*

THE DETERMINANTS OF THE ELASTICITY OF DEMAND

In our earlier discussion, we noted one of the important determinants of the elasticity of demand: the availability of substitutes. There are two important determinants of the degree of substitutability: the relative price of the good consumed and the length of time it takes to make an adjustment.

When the price of a commodity is low, and the consumption is high, a variety of substitutes exist. Figure 5.4 illustrates the case for aluminum. When the price of aluminum is low, it is used as a food wrap (aluminum foil), as con-

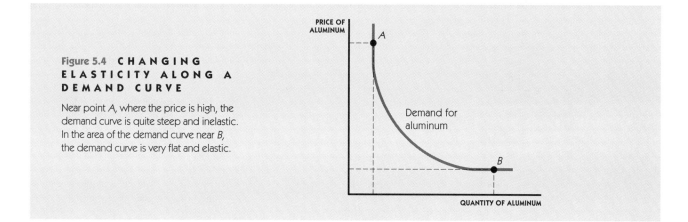

Figure 5.4 CHANGING ELASTICITY ALONG A DEMAND CURVE

Near point A, where the price is high, the demand curve is quite steep and inelastic. In the area of the demand curve near B, the demand curve is very flat and elastic.

tainers for canned goods, and in airplane frames because it is lightweight. As the price increases, customers seek out substitutes. At first, substitutes are easy to find, and the demand for the product is greatly reduced. For example, plastic wrap can be used instead of aluminum foil. As the price rises still further, tin is used instead of aluminum for cans. At very high prices, say near point *A*, aluminum is used only where its lightweight properties are essential, such as in airplane frames. At this point, it may take a *huge* price increase before some other material becomes an economical substitute.

A second important determinant of the elasticity of demand is time. Because it is always easier to find substitutes and to make other adjustments when you have a longer time to make them, the elasticity of demand is normally larger in the *long run*—in the period in which all adjustments can be made—than it is in the *short run*, when at least some adjustments cannot be made. Figure 5.5 illustrates the difference in shape between short-run and long-run demand curves for gasoline.

The sharp increase in oil prices in the 1970s provides an outstanding example. The short-run price elasticity of gasoline was .2 (a 1 percent increase in price led to only a .2 percent decrease in quantity demanded), while the long-run elasticity was .7 or more; the short-run elasticity of fuel oil was .2, and the long-run elasticity was 1.2. In the short run, consumers were stuck with their old gas-guzzling cars, their drafty houses, and their old fuel-wasting habits. In the long run, however, consumers bought smaller cars, became used to houses with slightly lower temperatures, installed better insulation in their homes, and turned to alternative energy sources. The long-run demand curve was therefore much more elastic (flat) than the short-run curve. Indeed, the long-run elasticity turned out to be much larger than anticipated.

How long is the long run? There is no simple answer. It will vary from product to product. In some cases, adjustments can occur rapidly; in other cases, they are very gradual. As old gas guzzlers wore out, they were replaced with

Figure 5.5 ELASTICITY OF DEMAND OVER TIME

Demand curves tend to be inelastic in the short run, when there is little time to adapt to price changes, but more elastic in the long run.

PRICE OF GASOLINE

Short-run demand for gasoline

Long-run demand for gasoline

QUANTITY OF GASOLINE

fuel-efficient compact cars. As furnaces wore out, they were replaced with more efficient ones. New homes are now constructed with more insulation, so that gradually, over time, the fraction of houses that are well insulated is increasing.

THE PRICE ELASTICITY OF SUPPLY

Supply curves normally slope upward. As with demand curves, they are steep in some cases and flat in others. The degree of steepness reflects sensitivity to price changes. A steep supply curve, like the one for oil in Figure 5.6A, means that a large change in price generates only a small change in the quantity firms want to supply. A flatter curve, like the one for chicken in Figure 5.6B, means that a small change in price generates a large change in supply. Economists have developed a precise way of representing the sensitivity of supply to prices in a way that parallels the one already introduced for demand. The **price elasticity of supply** is defined as the percentage change in quantity supplied divided by the percentage change in price (or the percentage change in quantity supplied corresponding to a price change of 1 percent).

$$\text{Elasticity of supply} = \frac{\text{percentage change in quantity supplied}}{\text{percentage change in price}}.$$

The elasticity of supply of oil is low—an increase in the price of oil will not have a significant effect on the total supply. The elasticity of supply of chicken is high, as President Nixon found out when he imposed price controls in August 1971. When the price of chicken was forced lower than the market equilibrium price, less than 10 percent lower, farmers found it was simply unprofitable to produce chickens and sell them at that price; there was a large decrease in the quantity supplied, and the result was huge shortages.

As is the case with demand, if a 1 percent increase in price results in more than a 1 percent increase in supply, we say the supply curve is elastic. If a 1 percent increase in price results in less than a 1 percent increase in supply, the supply curve is inelastic. In the extreme case of a vertical supply curve—where the amount supplied does not depend at all on price—the curve is said to be perfectly inelastic, or to have *zero* elasticity; and in the extreme case of a horizontal supply curve, the curve is said to be perfectly elastic, or to have *infinite* elasticity.

Just as the demand elasticity differs at different points of the demand curve, so too does the supply curve. Figure 5.7 shows a typical supply curve in manufacturing. An example might be ball bearings. At very low prices, plants are just covering their operating costs. Some plants shut down. In this situation, a small increase in price elicits a large increase in supply. The supply curve is relatively flat (elastic). But eventually, all machines are being worked, and factories are

Figure 5.6 DIFFERING ELASTICITIES OF SUPPLY

Panel A shows a supply curve for oil. It is inelastic: quantity supplied increases only a small amount with a rise in price. Panel B shows a supply curve for chicken. It is elastic: quantity supplied increases substantially with a rise in price.

Figure 5.7 CHANGING ELASTICITY ALONG A SUPPLY CURVE

When output is low and many machines are idle, a small change in price can lead to a large increase in quantity produced, so the supply curve is flat and elastic. When output is high and all machines are working close to their limit, it takes a very large price change to induce even a small change in output; the supply curve is steep and inelastic.

also working all three shifts. In this situation, it may be hard to increase supply further, so that the supply curve becomes close to vertical (inelastic). That is, however much the price increases, the supply will not change very much.

PRICE ELASTICITY OF SUPPLY

Elasticity	Description	Effect on Quantity Supplied of 1% Increase in Price
Zero	Perfectly inelastic (vertical suppply curve)	Zero
Between 0 and 1	Inelastic	Increased by less than 1%
1	Unitary elasticity	Increased by 1%
Greater than 1	Elastic	Increased by more than 1%
Infinite	Perfectly elastic (horizontal supply curve)	Infinite increase

SHORT RUN VERSUS LONG RUN

Economists distinguish between the responsiveness of supply to price in the short run and in the long run, just as they do with demand. The long-run supply elasticity is greater than the short-run. We define the short-run supply curve as the supply response *given the current stock of machines and build-ings.* The long-run supply curve assumes that firms can adjust the stock of machines and buildings.

Farm crops are a typical example of a good whose supply in the short run is not very sensitive to changes in price; that is, the supply curve is steep (inelastic). After farmers have done their spring planting, they are committed to a certain level of production. If the price of their crop goes up, they cannot go back and plant more. If the price falls, they are stuck with the crop they have. In this case, the supply curve is relatively close to vertical, as illustrated by the steeper curve in Figure 5.8.

The long-run supply curve for many crops, in contrast, is very flat (elastic). A relatively small change in price can lead to a large change in the quantity supplied. A small increase in the price of soybeans relative to the price of corn may induce many farmers to shift their planting from corn and other crops to soybeans, generating a large increase in the quantity of soybeans. This is illustrated in Figure 5.8 by the flatter curve.

Earlier, we noted the response of consumers to the marked increase in the price of oil in the 1970s. The long-run demand elasticity was much higher than the short-run. So too for supply. The higher prices drove firms, both in the United States and abroad in places like Canada, Mexico, and the North Sea off the coast of Great Britain, to explore for more oil. Though the alternative supplies could not be increased much in the short run (the short-run supply curve was inelastic, or steep), in the long run new supplies were found. Thus, the long-run supply elasticity was much higher (the supply curve was flatter) than the short-run supply elasticity.

Figure 5.8 ELASTICITY OF SUPPLY OVER TIME

Supply curves may be inelastic in the short run and very elastic in the long run, as in the case of agricultural crops like soybeans.

USING DEMAND AND SUPPLY ELASTICITIES

When the demand curve for a good such as wine shifts to the right—when, for instance, wine becomes more popular, so that at each price the demand is greater—there is an increase in both the equilibrium price of wine and the quantity demanded, or consumed. Similarly, when the supply curve for a good such as corn shifts to the left—because, for instance, of a drought that hurt the year's crop, so that at each price farmers supply less—there is an increase in the equilibrium price of corn and a decrease in quantity. Knowing that the shifts in the demand or supply curve will lead to an adjustment in both price *and* quantity is helpful, but it is even more useful to know whether most of the impact of a change will be on price or on quantity. For this, we have to consider the price elasticity of both the demand and supply curves.

Figure 5.9 illustrates the typical range of outcomes. If the supply curve is highly elastic (approaching the horizontal, as in panel A), shifts in the demand curve will be reflected more in changes in quantity than in price. If the supply curve is *relatively* inelastic (approaching the vertical, as in panel B), shifts in the demand curve will be reflected more in changes in price than in quantity.

Figure 5.9 ELASTICITY OF DEMAND AND SUPPLY CURVES: THE NORMAL CASES

Normally, shifts in the demand curve will be reflected in changes in both price and quantity, as seen in panels A and B. When the supply curve is highly elastic, shifts in the demand curve will result mainly in changes in quantities; if it is relatively inelastic, shifts in the demand curve will result mainly in price changes. Likewise, shifts in the supply curve will be reflected in changes in both price and quantity, as seen in panels C and D. If the demand curve is highly elastic, shifts in the supply curve will result mainly in changes in quantities; if it is relatively inelastic, shifts in the supply curve will result mainly in price changes.

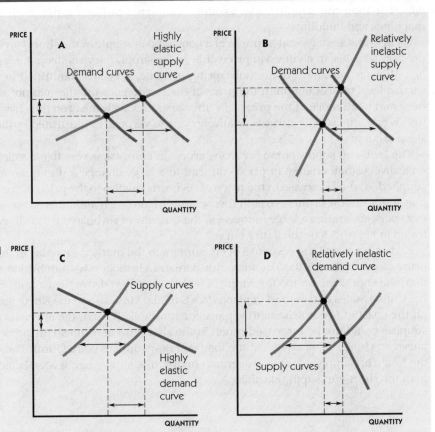

If the demand curve is highly elastic (approaching the horizontal as in panel C), shifts in the supply curve will be reflected more in changes in quantity than in price. Finally, if the demand curve is *relatively* inelastic (approaching the vertical as in panel D), shifts in the supply curve will be reflected more in changes in price than in quantity.

The extreme cases can be easily seen by extending the graphs in Figure 5.9. If one tilts the supply curve in panel A to be completely flat (perfectly elastic), a shift in the demand curve will have no effect on price. If one tilts the supply curve in panel B to be vertical (perfectly inelastic), a shift in the demand curve will have no effect on quantity.

LONG-RUN VERSUS SHORT-RUN ADJUSTMENTS

Because demand and supply curves are likely to be less elastic (more vertical) in the short run than in the long run, shifts in the demand and supply curves are more likely to be reflected in price changes in the short run, but in quantity changes in the long run. In fact, price increases in the short run provide the signals to firms to increase their production. Therefore, short-run price increases can be thought of as responsible for the output increases that occur in the long run.

TAX POLICY AND THE LAW OF SUPPLY AND DEMAND

For many questions of public policy, understanding the law of supply and demand is vital. One of the important ways economists use this law is in projecting the effect of taxes. Assume that the tax on a pack of cigarettes is increased by 10 cents, that the tax is imposed on cigarette manufacturers, and that all the companies try to pass on the cost increase to consumers, by raising the price of a pack by 10 cents. At the higher price, fewer cigarettes will be consumed, with the decrease in demand depending on the price elasticity of demand. With lower demand, firms must reduce their price if demand is to equal supply; by how much depends on the price elasticity of supply. The new equilibrium is depicted in Figure 5.10A.

For firms to produce the same amount as before, they must receive 10 cents more per pack (which they pass on to the government). Thus, the supply curve is shifted up by 10 cents. Since the demand for cigarettes is relatively inelastic, this shift will result in a large increase in price and a relatively small decrease in quantity demanded.

When a tax on producers results in consumers paying a higher price, economists say the tax is "passed on" or "shifted" to consumers. The fact that the consumer bears the tax (even though it is collected from the producers) does not mean that the producers are "powerful" or have conspired together. It simply reflects the system of supply and demand. Note, however, that the price did not rise the full 10 cents. Producers receive slightly lower after-tax prices and therefore bear a small fraction of the tax burden.

A tax imposed on a good for which the demand is very elastic leads to a different result. Assume, for instance, that the government decides to tax cheddar cheese (but no other cheeses). Since many cheeses are almost like cheddar, the demand curve for cheddar cheese is very elastic. In this case, as Figure 5.10B makes clear, most of the tax is absorbed by the producer, who receives (net of tax) a lower price. Production of cheddar cheese is reduced drastically as a consequence.

SHORTAGES AND SURPLUSES

The law of supply and demand works so well in a developed modern economy, most of the time, that everyone can take it for granted. If you are willing to pay the "market price"—the prevailing price of the good, determined by the

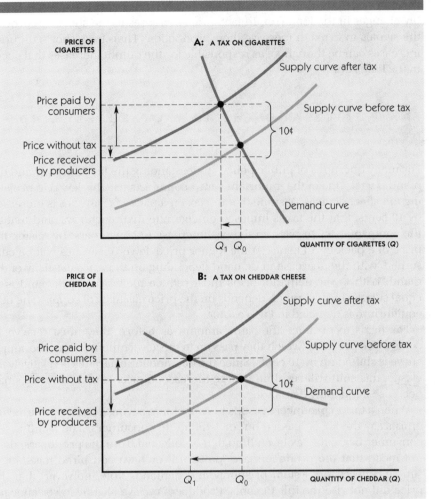

Figure 5.10 PASSING ALONG A TAX TO CONSUMERS

A tax on the output of an industry shifts the supply curve up by the amount of the tax. Panel A shows that if the demand curve is relatively inelastic, as it is for cigarettes, then most of the tax will be passed on to consumers in higher prices. Panel B shows that if the demand curve is relatively elastic, as it is for cheddar cheese, then most of the tax cannot be passed along to consumers in higher prices, and must instead be absorbed by producers.

intersection of demand and supply—you can obtain almost any good or service. Similarly, if a seller of a good or service is willing to charge no more than the market price, he can always sell what he wants to.

When the price is set so that demand equals supply—so that any individual can get as much as she wants at that price, and any supplier can sell the amount he wants at that price—economists say that the **market clears.** But when the market does not clear, there are shortages or surpluses. To an economist, a <u>**shortage**</u> means that people would like to buy something, but they simply cannot find it for sale at the going price. A <u>**surplus**</u> means that sellers would like to sell their product, but they cannot sell as much of it as they would like at the going price. These cases where the market does not seem to be working are often the most forceful reminders of the importance of the

Figure 5.11 SHORTAGES AND SURPLUSES

In panel A, the actual price p_1 is below the market-clearing price p^*. At a price of p_1, quantity demanded exceeds quantity supplied, and a shortage exists. In panel B, the actual price p_1 is above the equilibrium price p^*. In this case, quantity supplied exceeds quantity demanded, and there is a surplus, or glut, in the market.

law of supply and demand. The problem is that the "going price" is not the market equilibrium price.

Shortages and surpluses can be seen in the standard supply and demand diagram shown in Figure 5.11. In both panels A and B, the market equilibrium price is p^*. In panel A, the going price, p_1, is below p^*. At this price, demand exceeds supply; you can see this by reading down to the horizontal axis. Demand is Q_d; supply is Q_s. The gap between the two points is the "shortage." With the shortage, consumers scramble to get the limited supply available at the going price.

In panel B, the going price, p_1, is above p^*. At this price, demand is less than supply. Again we denote the demand by Q_d and the supply by Q_s. There is a surplus in the market of $Q_s - Q_d$. Now sellers are scrambling to find buyers.

At various times and for various goods, markets have not cleared. There have been shortages of apartments in New York; farm surpluses have plagued both Western Europe and the United States; in 1973, there was a shortage of gasoline, with cars lined up in long lines outside of gasoline stations. Unemployment is a type of surplus, when people who want to work find that they cannot sell their labor services at the going wage.

In some markets, like the stock market, the adjustment of prices to shifts in the demand and supply curves tends to be very rapid. In other cases, such as in the housing market, the adjustments tend to be sluggish. When price adjustments are sluggish, shortages or surpluses may appear as prices adjust. Houses tend not to sell quickly, for instance, during periods of decreased demand, which translate only slowly into lower housing prices.

When the market is not adjusting quickly toward equilibrium, economists say that prices are sticky. Even in these cases, the analysis of market equilibrium is useful. It indicates the direction of the changes—if the equilibrium price exceeds the current price, prices will tend to rise. Moreover, the rate at

POLICY PERSPECTIVE: ILLUSORY GAINS FROM TAXING LUXURIES?

No government likes to increase taxes. It doesn't sit well with voters. In 1990, as pressures to reduce the mounting federal deficit increased, and the scope for expenditure reduction seemed to be exhausted, there was an attempt to find the least painful way of increasing taxes. A 10 percent luxury tax was imposed on such big ticket items as pleasure boats, private airplanes, high-priced cars, jewelry, and furs. Such luxury taxes are often popular because no one *has* to pay them: rich people pay them only because they *choose* to buy these goods. All taxes are painful to someone, but a tax that weighs only on rich people who are buying frivolous luxuries is one of the more socially painless ways to raise money.

But the success of these taxes depends on the elasticity of demand. If the demand is highly elastic, slight increases in the price resulting from the tax will drive demand down, so little revenue would be raised.

As it turned out, the demand for these luxury goods was reasonably elastic. Sales of pleasure boats fell by nearly 90 percent in south Florida in early 1991, as prospective buyers bought boats in the Bahamas to avoid paying the tax. Sales of high-priced cars like Mercedes and Lexus also fell substantially. The situation of sellers of luxury goods was made even worse by the recession in 1991, which reduced the income of many prospective buyers, thus shifting the demand curve for luxuries back to the left as well.

This unexpected high elasticity of demand carried two bits of bad news for the economy. First, rather than falling on the wealthy as had been hoped, the burden of the new luxury tax actually ended up falling on the workers and retailers who manufacture and sell these luxury items. Second, the luxury tax raised far less money than had been expected. The Congressional Budget Office had forecast that the tax would raise about $1.5 billion over five years. But in 1991, it raised only about $30 million. Once the costs of setting up and enforcing the new tax were considered, it probably lost money for the government in its first year. Not surprisingly, the tax was repealed in 1993.

Sources: Bernard Baumohl, "Tempest in a Yacht Basin," *Time,* July 1, 1991, p. 52; Nick Ravo, "Big Boats Take It on the Chin," *New York Times,* April 14, 1991, sec. III, p. 9.

which prices fall or rise is often related to the gap, at the going price, between the quantity demanded and the quantity supplied.

INTERFERING WITH THE LAW OF SUPPLY AND DEMAND

The law of supply and demand, which governs how prices are set, can produce results that some individuals or groups do not like. For example, a reduced supply of oil may lead to a higher equilibrium price for oil. The higher price is not a malfunction of the law of supply and demand, but this is little comfort to those who use gasoline to power their cars and oil to heat their homes. Low demand for unskilled labor may lead to very low wages for unskilled workers. An increase in the demand for apartments in New York City leads, in the short run (with an inelastic supply), to an increase in rents—to the delight of landlords, but the dismay of renters.

In each of these cases, pressure from those who did not like the outcome of market processes has led government to act. The price of oil and natural gas was, at one time, regulated; minimum wage laws set a minimum limit on what employers can pay, even if the workers are willing to work for less; and rent control laws limit what landlords can charge. The concerns behind these interferences with the market are understandable, but the agitation for government action is based on two errors.

First, someone (or some group) was assigned blame for the change: the oil price rises were blamed on the oil companies, low wages on the employer, and rent increases on the landlord. As already explained, economists emphasize the role of anonymous market forces in determining these prices. After all, if landlords or oil companies are basically the same people today as they were last week, there must be some reason that they started charging different prices this week. Sometimes the price increase is the result of producers colluding to raise prices. This was the case in 1973, when the oil-exporting countries got together to raise the price of oil. The more common situation, however, is illustrated by the increase in the price of oil in August 1990, after Iraq's invasion of Kuwait. There was no collusion this time. The higher price simply reflected the anticipated reduction in the supply of oil. People rushed to buy, increasing short-term demand and pushing up the equilibrium price.

The second error was to forget that as powerful as governments may be, they can no more repeal the law of supply and demand than they can repeal the law of gravity. When they interfere with its working, the forces of supply and demand will not be balanced. There will either be excess supply or excess demand. Shortages and surpluses create problems of their own, often worse than the original problem the government was supposed to resolve.

Two straightforward examples of government overruling the law of supply and demand are **price ceilings,** which impose a maximum price that can be charged for a product, and **price floors,** which impose a minimum price. Rent control laws are price ceilings, and minimum wage laws and agricultural

CLOSE-UP: RENT CONTROL IN NEW YORK CITY

New York City adopted rent control on a "temporary" basis during World War II. Half a century later, it is still in effect. Journalist William Tucker has been collecting stories of well-to-do New Yorkers who benefit from this situation. The minority leader in the state senate, for example, pays $1,800 a month for a *ten-room* apartment overlooking Central Park. A newcomer pays $1,500 for a one-bedroom apartment in midtown Manhattan. A housing court judge who hears rent-control cases pays $93 a month for a two-bedroom apartment in a building where studio apartments (with no separate bedroom) rent for $1,200.

Of course, people who have been able to pay far below market value for decades tend to favor rent control. But since rent control is effectively a price ceiling, economists, looking to the law of supply and demand, would expect it to lead to problems and indeed it has.

For example, despite a serious shortage of housing in New York City, over 300,000 rental units have simply been abandoned. Almost no new rental housing is being built. Only about 2 percent of the apartments in New York are vacant at any time, as opposed to vacancy rates averaging 6 percent in East Coast cities, like Baltimore, that do not have rent control. When many people are struggling to obtain one of the few available apartments, poor people tend to lose out.

Even with rent control, the *average* rent in New York City is little different from some other large cities, like Chicago. But in Chicago, a newcomer can find an apartment at something close to the average rent. In New York, newcomers often have to make special payments to secure an apartment, and then pay extraordinarily high rents that help to subsidize those who have been living there for a long time.

Attempting to provide moderate and low-cost housing is a worthy public goal. But the example of New York and other rent-controlled cities shows that even when the goal is worthy, the law of supply and demand does not simply fade away.

Sources: William Tucker, "We All Pay for Others' Great Apartment Deals," *Newsday,* May 24, 1986; Tucker, "Moscow on the Hudson," *The American Spectator* (July 1986), pp. 19–21; Tucker, "Where Do the Homeless Come From?" *National Review,* September 25, 1987, pp. 32–43.

price supports are price floors. A closer look at each will help highlight the perils of interfering with the law of supply and demand.

PRICE CEILINGS: THE CASE OF RENT CONTROL

Price ceilings—setting a maximum charge—are always tempting to governments because they seem an easy way to assure that everyone will be able to afford a particular product. Thus, in the last couple of decades in the United States, price ceilings have been set for a wide range of goods, from chickens to oil to interest rates. In each case the result has been to create shortages at the controlled price. People want to buy more of a good than producers want to sell, because producers have no incentive to produce more of the good. Those who can buy at the cheaper price benefit; producers and those unable to buy suffer.

The effect of **rent control** laws—setting the maximum rent that a landlord can charge for a one-bedroom apartment, for example—is illustrated by Figure 5.12. In panel A, R^* is the market equilibrium rental rate, at which the demand for housing equals the supply. However, the local government is concerned that at R^*, many poor people cannot afford housing in the city, so it imposes a law that says that rents may be no higher than R_1. At R_1, there is an excess demand for apartments. While the motives behind the government

Figure 5.12 A PRICE CEILING: RENT CONTROL

Rent control laws limit the rents apartment owners may charge. If rents are held down to R_1, below the market-clearing level R^*, as in panel A, there will be excess demand for apartments. Panel B shows the long-run response. The supply of rental housing is more elastic in the long run, since landlords can refuse to build new apartment buildings, or they can sell existing apartments as condominiums. The price ceiling eventually leads to the quantity supplied being even farther below the quantity demanded.

action may well have been praiseworthy, the government has created an artificial scarcity.

The problems caused by rent control are likely to be worse in the long run than in the short run, because long-run supply curves are more elastic than short-run supply curves. In the short run, the quantity of apartments does not change much. But in the long run, the quantity of apartments can decline for several reasons, as landlords try to minimize the losses from rent control. Apartments may be abandoned as they deteriorate; they can be converted to condominiums and sold instead of rented; and apartment owners may not wish to construct new ones if they cannot charge enough in rent to cover their costs.

Figure 5.12B illustrates how the housing shortages under rent control will increase over time. Rent control results in all *existing* renters being better off, at least as long as the landlord stays in the business. But the quantity of available rental housing will decrease, so that many would-be residents will be unable to find rental housing in the market. Since renters tend to be poorer than those who can buy a home, a shortage of rental housing will tend to hurt the poor most.

PRICE FLOORS: THE CASE OF AGRICULTURAL SUPPORTS

Just as consumers try to get government to limit the prices they pay, sellers would like the government to put a floor on the prices they receive: a minimum wage for workers and a minimum price on wheat and other agricultural products for farmers. Both groups appeal to fairness. The price they are receiving is inadequate to cover the effort (and other resources) they are contributing.

Farmers, because of their political influence, have succeeded in persuading government to impose a floor on the prices of many agricultural products—a price which is above the market equilibrium, as illustrated in Figure 5.13. The consequences should be obvious: supply exceeds demand. To sustain the price, government has had to purchase and stockpile huge amounts of agricultural goods. The cost of supporting the price at these above market levels has been in the billions—at the peak, in 1986, the government spent over $25 billion, or an average of more than $11,000 for every farmer.

As government interferes with the law of supply and demand, it is led into a labyrinth of problems. To reduce supplies, it has imposed production limitations. Imposing limitations is not only administratively cumbersome, but impedes the adaptability of the market. This is because quotas are based on past production, but some areas should be expanding, and others contracting, in response to changed circumstances. The quota system does not allow this to happen easily. Worse still, wheat farmers have to keep producing wheat, lest they lose their quota. But this means that they cannot rotate their crops—and this is bad for the soil and the environment. To avoid the build up of surpluses, Congress has enacted a program to subsidize exports. But these subsidies have angered other countries, which view it as unfair competition. Our

Figure 5.13 PRICE FLOORS

If the government imposes a price floor on, say, wheat—at a price in excess of the market equilibrium—there will be excess supply. Either the government will have to purchase the excess, putting it into storage or discarding it in some way, or it will have to limit production.

subsidies of wheat exports to Mexico have hurt our economic relations with Argentina. Even Mexico has viewed them with alarm, as they have interfered with Mexico's attempts to reform its agricultural sector.

Government is aware of these problems, but the political pressures to maintain high prices kept the price support program in place for a long time. The agricultural bill passed in 1996 is intended to lead to a phase-out for most major crops.

ALTERNATIVE SOLUTIONS

Large changes in prices cause distress. It is natural to try to find scapegoats and to look to the government for a solution. Such situations call for compassion, and the economists' caution can seem coldhearted. But the fact remains

USING ECONOMICS: CALCULATING RESPONSES TO OIL PRICE CHANGES

As oil prices have fluctuated during the past decade, government analysts have repeatedly had to calculate the implications of those changes for oil consumption. If the United States consumes more oil, it will need to import more, and that in turn affects the balance of payments.

Assume prices of oil are expected to rise by 10 percent over the next two years. What will this do to the consumption of oil in the United States, if the elasticity of demand is .7? An elasticity of demand of .7 means that a 1 percent increase in price reduces demand by .7 percent. So a 10 percent increase in price will reduce demand by 7 percent. If the initial level of demand is 100 million barrels, demand will fall to 93 million.

What happens to total expenditures? If the initial price was $20 a barrel, total expenditures initially were $2 billion. Now, with a price of $22 a barrel (a 10 percent increase from $20), they have gone up to $22 × 93 million = $2.04 billion.

What happens to imports? The United States imports oil from abroad, and because the price of each barrel it imports has increased, it is worse off. But this is partly offset by the decreased use of oil. Assume the United States produces 50 million barrels, and that production remains unchanged. Initially, it imported 50 million, but now, it imports only 43 million. U.S. expenditures on imports actually fall: before the expenditures were 50 million × $20 = $1 billion; now they are 43 million barrels × $22 per barrel = $946 million.

In the long run, the elasticity of demand is greater, so the reduction in consumption is larger. If the long-run elasticity is 1, then consumption falls to 90 million barrels, and expenditures remain unchanged. Imports fall to 40 million barrels, with a value of $880 million.

that in competitive markets, price changes are simply the impersonal work-ings of the law of supply and demand; without price changes, there will be shortages and surpluses. The examples of government attempts to interfere with the workings of supply and demand provide an important cautionary tale: one ignores the workings of the law of supply and demand only at one's peril. This does not mean, however, that the government should simply ig-nore the distress caused by large price and wage changes. It only means that government must take care in addressing the problems; price controls, in-cluding price ceilings and floors, are unlikely to be effective instruments.

Later chapters will discuss ways in which the government can address dis-satisfaction with the consequences of the law of supply and demand—by making use of the power of the market rather than trying to fight against it. For example, if the government is concerned with low wages paid to unskilled workers, it can try to increase the demand for these workers. A shift to the right in the demand curve will increase the wages these workers receive. The government can do this either by subsidizing firms that hire unskilled work-ers or by providing more training to these workers and thus increasing their productivity.

If the government wants to increase the supply of housing to the poor, it can provide housing subsidies for the poor, which will elicit a greater supply. If government wants to conserve on the use of gasoline, it can impose a tax on gasoline. Noneconomists often object that these sorts of economic incentives have other distasteful consequences, and sometimes they do. But government policies that take account of the law of supply and demand will tend to be more effective, with fewer unfortunate side effects, than policies that ignore the predictable economic consequences that follow from disregarding the law of supply and demand.

REVIEW AND PRACTICE

SUMMARY

1. The price elasticity of demand describes how sensitive the quantity de-manded of a good is to changes in the price of the good. When demand is inelastic, an increase in the price has little effect on quantity demanded and the demand curve is steep; when demand is elastic, an increase in the price has a large effect on quantity demanded and the curve is flat. De-mand for necessities is usually quite inelastic; demand for luxuries is elas-tic.

2. The price elasticity of supply describes how sensitive the quantity sup-plied of a good is to changes in the price of the good. If price changes do not induce much change in supply, the supply curve is very steep and is said to be inelastic. If the supply curve is very flat, indicating that price changes cause large changes in supply, supply is said to be elastic.

3. The extent to which a shift in the supply curve is reflected in price or quantity depends on the shape of the demand curve. The more elastic the demand, the more a given shift in the supply curve will be reflected in changes in equilibrium quantities and the less it will be reflected in changes in equilibrium prices. The more inelastic the demand, the more a given shift in the supply curve will be reflected in changes in equilibrium prices and the less it will be reflected in changes in equilibrium quantities.

4. Likewise, the extent to which a shift in the demand curve is reflected in price or quantity depends on the shape of the supply curve.

5. Demand and supply curves are likely to be more elastic in the long run than in the short run. Therefore a shift in the demand or supply curve is likely to have a larger price effect in the short run and a larger quantity effect in the long run.

6. Elasticities can be used to predict to what extent consumer prices rise when a tax is imposed on a good. If the demand curve for a good is very inelastic, consumers in effect have to pay the tax. If the demand curve is very elastic, the quantities produced and the price received by producers are likely to decline considerably.

7. Government regulations may prevent a market from moving toward its equilibrium price, leading to shortages or surpluses. Price ceilings lead to excess demand. Price floors lead to excess supply.

KEY TERMS

price elasticity of demand	price elasticity of supply	price ceilings price floors
infinite elasticity	market clearing	
zero elasticity	sticky prices	

REVIEW QUESTIONS

1. What is meant by the elasticity of demand and the elasticity of supply? Why do economists find these concepts useful?

2. Is the slope of a perfectly elastic demand or supply curve horizontal or vertical? Is the slope of a perfectly inelastic demand or supply curve horizontal or vertical? Explain.

3. If the elasticity of demand is unity, what happens to total revenue as the price increases? What if the demand for a product is very inelastic? What if it is very elastic?

4. Under what condition will a shift in the demand curve result mainly in a change in quantity? in price?

5. Under what condition will a shift in the supply curve result mainly in a change in price? in quantity?

6. Why do the elasticities of demand and supply tend to change from the short run to the long run?

7. Under what circumstances will a tax on a product be passed along to consumers?

8. Why do price ceilings tend to lead to shortages? Why do price floors tend to lead to surpluses?

PROBLEMS

1. Suppose the price elasticity of demand for gasoline is .2 in the short run and .7 in the long run. If the price of gasoline rises 28 percent, what effect on quantity demanded will this have in the short run? in the long run?

2. Imagine that the short-run price elasticity of supply for a farmer's corn is .3, while the long-run price elasticity is 2. If prices for corn fall 30 percent, what are the short-run and long-run changes in quantity supplied? What are the short- and long-run changes in quantity supplied if prices rise by 15 percent? What happens to the farmer's revenues in each of these situations?

3. Assume that the demand curve for hard liquor is highly inelastic and the supply curve for hard liquor is highly elastic. If the tastes of the drinking public shift away from hard liquor, will the effect be larger on price or on quantity? If the federal government decides to impose a tax on manufacturers of hard liquor, will the effects be larger on price or on quantity? What is the effect of an advertising program that succeeds in discouraging people from drinking? Draw diagrams to illustrate each of your answers.

4. Imagine that wages (the price of labor) are sticky in the labor market, that is, wages do not change in the short run, and that a supply of new workers enters that market. Will the market be in equilibrium in the short run? Why or why not? If not, explain the relationship you would expect to see between the quantity demanded and supplied, and draw a diagram to illustrate. Explain how sticky wages in the labor market affect unemployment.

5. For each of the following markets, explain whether you would expect prices in that market to be relatively sticky or not:
    (a) the stock market;
    (b) the market for autoworkers;
    (c) the housing market;
    (d) the market for cut flowers;
    (e) the market for pizza-delivery people.

6. Suppose a government wishes to assure that its citizens can afford adequate housing. Consider three ways of pursuing that goal. One method is

to pass a law requiring that all rents be cut by one-quarter. A second method offers a subsidy to all builders of homes. A third provides a subsidy directly to renters equal to one-quarter of the rent they pay. Predict what effect each of these proposals would have on the price and quantity of rental housing in the short run and the long run.

CHAPTER 6

TIME AND RISK

When Bill Clinton ran for the presidency in 1992, a central part of his platform was that the country was not investing enough in its future. The *choices* we make today affect living standards in the future. Much of economics is thus *future oriented.* The basic principles of markets and making choices—the law of supply and demand—apply here as well. But there are some distinctive aspects of future-oriented choices that contrast with the static nature of the conventional supply and demand equilibrium analysis. The first part of this chapter focuses on those aspects. We show how prices in the present, for instance, are linked to expectations of prices in the future.

While the Republicans and Democrats differ on many issues, they are united on the importance of encouraging entrepreneurship. A large percentage of new jobs are created in new and small businesses. But starting new businesses is risky—one of the many risks that permeate the economy. How do individuals and firms respond to risks? And how does uncertainty affect markets? The function of insurance is to protect against risk. Homeowners typically buy fire insurance, for instance. But many risks cannot be protected against so easily. A firm planning to bring out a new product, for example, cannot buy insurance to protect against the risk that it will fail in the marketplace. How well market economies handle the problems created by risk has much to do with their successes. The second part of this chapter investigates insurance and other markets that protect against risk.

1. How do we compare a dollar received next year or in five years' time with a dollar received today?

2. What determines the demand for an asset like gold, which is purchased mainly with the intent of selling it at some later date? What determines shifts in the demand curve for assets?

3. How do individuals, firms, and markets respond to risk?

4. What are some of the central problems facing insurance firms? Why are there many risks for which insurance is not available?

5. Why is entrepreneurship so important?

INTEREST

When you put money into a bank account you are involved in a future-oriented transaction. You have loaned your money to the bank, and the bank has promised to pay you back. But banks offer more than security; they offer you a *return* on your savings. This return is called **interest.** If you put $1,000 in the bank at the beginning of the year, and the interest rate is 10 percent per year, you will receive $1,100 at the end of the year. The $100 is the payment of interest, while the $1,000 is the repayment of the **principal,** the original amount lent to the bank.

To an economist, the interest rate is a price. Normally, we express prices in terms of dollars. If the price of an orange is $1.00, that means we must give up $1.00 to get one orange. Economists talk about the relative price of two goods as the amount of one good you have to give up to get one more unit of the other. The relative price is the ratio of the two "dollar" prices.

For example, if the price of an apple is $.50 and the price of an orange is $1.00, then the relative price (that is, the ratio of the prices) is 2. If we wish to consume one more orange, we have to give up two apples. Thus, the relative price describes a trade-off. Similarly, if the interest rate is 10 percent, by giving up $1.00 worth of consumption today, a saver can have $1.10 worth of consumption next year. Thus, the rate of interest tells us how much future consumption we can get by giving up $1.00 worth of current consumption. It tells us the relative price between the present and the future.

THE TIME VALUE OF MONEY

Interest rates are normally positive. If you have $1.00 today, you can put it into the bank and, if the interest rate is 5 percent, receive $1.05 at the end of next year. In short, $1.00 becomes, in this example, $1.05 next year.

A dollar today is worth more than a dollar in the future. Economists call this the **time value of money.** The concept of **present discounted value** tells us precisely how to measure the time value of money. The present discounted value of $100 a year from now is what you would pay today for $100 a year from now. Suppose the interest rate is 10 percent. If you put $90.91 in the bank today, at the end of the year you will receive $9.09 interest, which together with the original amount will total $100. Thus, $90.91 is the present discounted value of $100 a year from now, if the interest rate is 10 percent.

There is a simple formula for calculating the present discounted value of any amount to be received a year from now: just divide the amount by 1 plus the annual rate of interest. The annual rate of interest is often denoted by r.

To check this formula, consider the present discounted value of $100. According to the formula, it is $100 / (1 + r)$. In other words, take the present discounted value, $100 / (1 + r)$, and put it in the bank. At the end of the year you will have

$$\frac{\$100}{1+r} \times (1+r) = \$100,$$

confirming our conclusion that $100 / (1 + r)$ today is the same as $100 one year from now.

PRESENT DISCOUNTED VALUE

Present discounted value of $1.00 next year $= \dfrac{\$1.00}{1 + \text{interest rate}}$.

Equivalently, denoting the interest rate by r, the right-hand side of the equation

becomes $\dfrac{\$1.00}{1 + r}$.

If the interest rate increases, the present discounted value of $100 a year from now will decrease. If the interest rate should rise to 20 percent, for example, the present discounted value of $100 a year from now becomes $83.33 $(100/1.2)$.

The concept of present discounted value is important because so many decisions in economics are oriented to the future. Whether the decision is made by a person buying a house or saving money for retirement, or by a company building a factory or making an investment, the decision maker must be able to value money that will be received one, two, five, or ten years in the future.

USING ECONOMICS: THE VALUE OF WINNING A LOTTERY

We have all heard about those $10 million jackpot lottery winners. What many people don't realize is that the winner doesn't get $10 million in cash on the spot. Rather, she typically gets a measly $500,000 a year for twenty years. While this is no reason to turn down the prize, the present discounted value of the prize is worth much less than $10 million in cash today.

In calculating the present discounted value of the whole jackpot, we add up the present discounted value of $500,000 next year, plus the present discounted value of $500,000 in two years, plus the present discounted value of $500,000 in three years, and so on. If we assume a 10 percent interest rate, the grand total comes to $4,256,781.86, far less than $10 million in cash today. (To learn how to do the calculation yourself, see the appendix to this chapter.)

THE MARKET FOR LOANABLE FUNDS

The previous section explained how the interest rate is a price, similar to the price of any other good, like apples and oranges. The price of borrowing a dollar (what you have to pay back in a year) is the dollar plus the annual rate of interest. In calculating the present discounted values, firms or individuals take the interest rate as given. But obviously the interest rate changes over time. How is the interest rate determined? Like other prices, the interest rate is determined by the law of supply and demand.

At any given time, there are some people and companies who would like to borrow, so they can spend more than they currently have. Rachel has her first job and knows she needs a car for transportation; George needs kitchen equipment, tables, and chairs to open his sandwich shop. Others would like to save, or spend less than they currently have. John is putting aside money for his children's college education and for his retirement; Bill is putting aside money to make a down payment on a house.

Exchanges that occur over time are called **intertemporal trades.** The gains from trade discussed in Chapter 3 apply equally well here. When one individual lends money to another, both gain. John and Bill can lend money to Rachel and George. John and Bill will get paid interest in the future, to compensate them for letting Rachel and George use their funds now. Rachel and George are willing to pay the interest because to them, having the funds today is worth more to them than waiting. The borrower may be a business firm like the one owned by George, who believes that with these funds he will be able to make an investment that will yield a return far higher than the interest rate he is charged today. Or the borrower may be an individual facing some emergency, such as a medical crisis, that requires funds today. The borrower may simply be a free spirit, wishing to consume as much as he can (as much as lenders are willing to give him), and letting the future take care of itself.

How is the supply of funds to be equated with the demand? As the interest rate rises, some borrowers will be discouraged from borrowing. Rachel may decide to ride her bicycle to work and postpone buying a new car until she can save up the money herself (or until interest rates come down). At the same time, as the interest rate rises, some savers may be induced to save more. Their incentives for savings have increased. John realizes that every extra dollar he saves today will produce more money in the future, so he may put more aside.[1] Figure 6.1 shows the supply and demand curves for loanable funds. Here the interest rate is the "price," and the amount of money loaned and borrowed is the quantity. At r^*, the demand for funds equals the supply of funds.

We can now explain why the equilibrium interest rate is positive. If it were zero or negative, prospective borrowers would demand more funds than prospective savers would be willing to supply. Indeed, negative interest rates would mean that people could borrow to consume today and pay back less in the future, and that savers would receive less in the future than the amount they saved. Only at a positive interest rate can the demand for loans be equated to the supply.

In our economy, borrowers and lenders do not usually meet face to face. Instead, banks and other financial institutions serve as intermediaries, collecting savings from those who want to save and disbursing money to those who want to borrow. These intermediaries help make the market for loans work smoothly. For their services, the intermediaries charge fees, which can be measured as the difference between the interest rate they pay savers and the interest rate they charge borrowers.

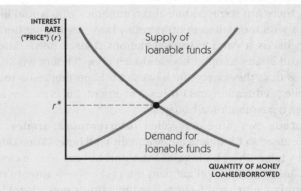

Figure 6.1 **SUPPLY AND DEMAND FOR LOAN-ABLE FUNDS**

The amount of money loaned and borrowed is the quantity, and the interest rate is the price. At the equilibrium interest rate r^*, the supply of loanable funds equals the demand.

[1]In Chapter 9, we will see that there is some controversy about whether higher interest rates always induce people to save more.

INFLATION AND THE REAL RATE OF INTEREST

The interest rate, we have seen, is a price. It tells how many dollars next period we can get if we give up one dollar today. But except for misers like Scrooge who store money for its own sake, dollars are of value only because of the goods that can be bought with them. Because of inflation—the increase in prices over time—dollars in the future buy fewer goods than dollars today. In deciding both whether to borrow and whether to lend, individuals want to know how much *consumption* they get tomorrow if they give up a dollar's worth of consumption today. The answer is given by the **real rate of interest.** This is distinguished from the **nominal rate of interest,** the rate one sees posted at one's bank and in the newspaper, which simply describes the number of dollars one gets next year in exchange for a dollar today. There is a simple relationship between the real interest rate and the nominal interest rate: the real interest rate equals the nominal interest rate minus the rate of inflation (the annual rate of change of prices on average). If the nominal interest rate is 10 percent and the rate of inflation is 6 percent, then the real interest rate is 4 percent. By lending out (or saving) a dollar today, you can increase the amount of goods that you get in one year's time by 4 percent.

Consider an individual who decides to deposit $1,000 in a savings account. At the end of the year, at a 10 percent interest rate, she will have $1,100. But prices meanwhile have risen by 6 percent. A good that cost $1,000 in the beginning of the year now costs $1,060. In terms of "purchasing power," she has only $40 extra to spend ($1,100 − $1,060)—4 percent more than she had at the beginning of the year. This is her real return. In an inflationary economy, a borrower is in a similar situation. He knows that if he borrows money, the dollars he gives back to repay the loan will be worth less than the dollars he receives today. Thus, what is relevant for individuals to know when deciding either how much to lend (save) or how much to borrow is the *real* interest rate, which takes account of inflation. It is the real interest rate that should appear on the vertical axis of Figure 6.1.

REAL INTEREST RATE

Real interest rate = nominal interest rate − rate of inflation

THE MARKET FOR ASSETS

Gardeners today would have been shocked at the price of tulip bulbs in early seventeenth-century Holland, where one bulb sold for the equivalent of $16,000 in today's dollars. The golden age of tulips did not last long, however, and in 1637, prices of bulbs fell by over 90 percent. Dramatic price swings are not only curiosities of history. Between 1973 and 1980, the price of gold rose from $98 to $613, or by 525 percent; then from 1980 to 1985, it fell to $318. Between 1977 and 1980, the price of farmland in Iowa increased by 40 percent, only to fall by over 60 percent from 1980 to 1987. On October 19, 1987, prices in the U.S. stock market fell by one-half *trillion* dollars, almost 25 percent. Even a major war would be unlikely to destroy a quarter of the U.S. capital stock in a single day. But there was no war or other external event to explain the 1987 drop.

How can the demand and supply model of Chapters 4 and 5 explain these huge price swings? Supply curves for these goods certainly could not have shifted so dramatically. Nor could changes in tastes, incomes, or other goods have caused such fantastic shifts in demand. The solution to this puzzle does lie in shifts of the demand curve, but not directly for the reasons we saw in Chapter 4.

The first step in the solution is to recognize that the goods in the examples above are unlike ice cream cones, newspapers, or any other goods that are valued by the consumer mainly for their present use. Gold, land, stock, and even tulips in seventeenth-century Holland are all examples of **assets.** Assets are long-lived and thus can be bought at one date and sold at another. For this reason, the price individuals are willing to pay for them today depends not only on today's conditions—the immediate return or benefits—but also on some expectation of what tomorrow's conditions will be; in particular, on what the assets can be sold for in the future.

The concept of present discounted value tells us how to measure and compare returns anticipated in the future. Changes in present discounted value shift demand curves, as shown in Figure 6.2, because the amount that someone is willing to pay today depends on the present discounted value of what she believes she can get for it in the future.

Present discounted values can change for two reasons. First, they can change because the interest rate changes. An increase in the interest rate reduces the present discounted value of the dollars you expect to receive in the future. This is one reason why increases in the interest rate are often accompanied by drops in the price of shares on the stock market, and vice versa. Smart investors thus try to forecast interest rates accurately. Second, present discounted values can change because of a change in the expected price of an asset at the time one expects to sell it. Again, this will lead to a shift in the demand curve. Such **expectations** can be quite volatile, which explains a great deal of the volatility in asset prices.

**Figure 6.2 HOW EXPECTA-
TIONS CAN SHIFT DE-
MAND**

Expectations that the price of an asset will
rise in the future can cause the demand
curve to shift out to the right, thus raising
the current price.

To see how expectations concerning future events affect *current* prices,
consider a hypothetical example. People suddenly realize that new smog-
control devices will, ten years from now, make certain parts of Los Angeles
much more attractive places to live than they are today. As a result, future-
oriented individuals will think that ten years from now the price of land in
those areas will be much higher, say $1 million an acre. But, they also think,
nine years from now it will already be recognized that in one short year an
acre will be worth $1 million. Hence, nine years from now investors will be
willing to pay almost $1 million for the land—even if, at that date (nine years
from now), the smog has not yet been eliminated. But then, these same individuals think, eight years from now investors will realize that in one short year
the price will rise to almost $1 million and will pay close to that amount.
Working backward like this makes it apparent that if people are confident
land is going to be much more valuable in ten years, its price rises today.

Thus, while changes in tastes or technology or incomes or the prices of
other goods *today* could not account for some of the sharp changes in asset
values described at the start of this section, changes in expectations concerning any of these variables in the future will have an effect *today* on the demand. Markets for assets are linked together over time. An event that is expected to happen in ten or fifteen or even fifty years can have a direct bearing
on today's market.

FORMING EXPECTATIONS

Changes in expectations about future returns or interest rates, then, can be
reflected in large changes in asset prices today. How do individuals and firms
form expectations? Partly by looking at past experience. If a company has

steadily grown more valuable, investors may come to expect that pattern to continue. If every time inflation rates increase the banking authorities act to slow the economy by raising interest rates, people come to expect inflation to be followed by higher interest rates.

Psychologists and economists have studied how individuals form expectations. Sometimes people are **myopic,** or short-sighted. They expect what is true today to be true tomorrow. The price of gold today is what it will be tomorrow. Sometimes they are **adaptive,** extrapolating events of the recent past into the future. If the price of gold today is 5 percent higher than it was last year, they expect its price next year to be 5 percent higher than it is today.

When people make full use of all relevant available data to form their expectations, economists say that their expectations are **rational.** While the price of gold rises during an inflationary period, the price of gold also goes down when inflation subsides. Thus, if a person knows that economic analysts are predicting lower inflation, he will not expect the gold price increases to continue. Even when individuals form their expectations rationally, they will not be right all the time. Sometimes they will be overly optimistic, sometimes overly pessimistic (although in making their decisions, they are aware of these possibilities). But the assumption of rational expectations is that on average they will be right.

The 1970s were a period when adaptive expectations reigned. Many investors came to expect prices of assets such as land and housing to continue to rise rapidly. The more you invested, the more money you made. The idea that the price of a house or of land might fall seemed beyond belief—even though history is full of episodes (most recently during the 1930s) when such prices fell dramatically. The weak real estate markets of the 1980s in many regions reminded investors of the importance of incorporating historical data in forming expectations.

But in this, as in all types of fortune-telling, history never repeats itself exactly. Since the situation today is never precisely like past experience, it is never completely clear which facts will be the relevant ones. Even the best-informed experts are likely to disagree. When it comes to predicting the future, everyone's crystal ball is cloudy.

THE MARKET FOR RISK

Most of us do not like the risk that accompanies most future-oriented economic activity. We might spend a few dollars on some lottery tickets or playing the slot machines at Las Vegas or Atlantic City, but for the most part, we try to avoid or minimize serious risks. Psychologists who have studied this "risk-avoidance behavior," focus on the anxiety to which uncertainty gives rise. Economists refer to risk-avoidance behavior by saying that individuals are **risk averse.**

RESPONDING TO RISK

Even though most individuals are risk averse, our economy needs to encourage risk taking. New ventures are risky, but they are the engine of economic growth. Our economy has developed a number of ways by which risks are transferred, transformed, and shared. The institutions and arrangements by which this is done are known collectively as the **market for risk.**

AVOIDING AND MITIGATING RISKS

The simplest way to respond to risk is to avoid it: don't gamble. But if everyone avoided all risks, economic activity would come to a standstill. No investments would be made. Firms wouldn't even hire workers: there is always the chance that an employee won't work out.

So risks cannot be avoided. But there is much individuals and firms can do to reduce the degree of risk and soften its impact. Firms invest in fire detection and suppression equipment to reduce the damage from a fire. Thorough research—obtaining as complete information as possible—before undertaking an investment project reduces the risk.

MAINTAINING OPTIONS

A second way to respond to risk is to keep one's options open. Many uncertainties get resolved over time. At the beginning of the week, Tim doesn't know whether it will rain on Saturday. By Friday, the weather forecasters will have provided him with much better information—a better estimate of the probability of rain. By Saturday morning, he will have a still better estimate. Tim would like to go to the football game Saturday afternoon, provided it does not rain. If it rains, he would rather go to the movies. But by Friday all the football tickets will be sold out. He has to make his decision earlier. He may decide to buy the ticket on Monday, knowing that there is a chance that he will not use it (if it rains). Buying the ticket on Monday maintains his options. Failing to buy the ticket forecloses the option of going to the football game. On Saturday morning it does rain. Tim recognizes that the expenditure on the football ticket is a sunk cost. Even though he spent the money, he prefers spending an extra $5 and going to the movies, than getting cold and drenched at the football game. It was worth spending the money to keep his options open.

Businesses often spend considerable amounts to maintain options. They may enter a market, for example, knowing they will lose money for the next year or two. But they hope to learn a lot from the experience, and they know that if they fail to enter the market, it will be much harder (costlier) to enter later. It is worth losing money for a while to keep their options open.

DIVERSIFYING

A third response to risk is: don't put all of your eggs in the same basket. Firms, for instance, may enter several lines of business to reduce risk. Farmers may grow several different crops. If things go badly in one area, there is a good chance they will go better in some other area.

TRANSFERRING AND SHARING RISKS

A fourth response to risk is to transfer or share it. If I have no homeowner's insurance and my house burns down, I would suffer a financial calamity. But if some rich person agrees to pay me $100 if my house burns down, his $100 loss would not have a major effect on his finances. He will be willing to accept the small risk, for a fee a bit above the average payment he expects to make in the event of my house burning down. Thus, if there is a 1 percent chance that my house will burn down, the "expected" payment of someone who agrees to pay me $100 if that happens is

$$\text{expected payment} = \text{probability of loss} \times \text{payment in event of loss}$$
$$= .01 \times \$100 = \$1.$$

The *risk premium* is the *extra* payment an individual or firm must receive to be willing to bear risks. If he were willing to accept the risk in return for a payment of $1.10, then the $.10 is the risk premium. I would be more than willing to pay him $1.10 to absorb the risk. Ideally, I would like to find 1,000 such people to insure my $100,000 house; for then, I would have completely transferred the risk of a fire to them.

Insurance Firms   Insurance firms are the institutions in our economy that specialize in absorbing risks. The earliest insurance firms—collectively known as Lloyd's of London—did nothing more than pull together a group of investors willing to absorb large risks, such as those associated with shipwrecks. Today, insurance firms absorb risk directly.

LIMITS ON INSURANCE AS PROTECTION AGAINST RISK

Even though insurance companies specialize in absorbing risks, individuals and firms cannot buy insurance to protect themselves against all types of risk. A business, for example, cannot buy insurance that protects it against the risk that the demand for its product will fall, or the risk that a competitor will develop a better product that will drive the company into bankruptcy. Economists have identified two inherent problems that limit the use of insurance as a mechanism for handling risk: adverse selection and moral hazard. Although the following discussion focuses on these problems in the context of insurance, they apply more generally to methods of sharing risk, including stocks and bonds.

Adverse Selection   The probability that an individual will have an accident depends on characteristics of that individual's life and behavior that an insurance firm cannot perfectly observe. If the accident probabilities of different individuals could be accurately estimated, then in a competitive insurance market, premiums would accurately reflect those accident probabilities. For example, "hot dog" skiers would pay higher medical insurance rates than people with safer pastimes, reflecting the higher average medical expenses.

What do you do as a policymaker to combat the practice of "cream skimming" in the health insurance industry? This is the practice of providing insurance to those who are in good health and have a low health-risk profile (inexpensive to insure) and refusing insurance to those who are already sick or who are at known high risk for future health problems (expensive to insure). This type of adverse selection in the health insurance industry adds to the problem of the medically uninsured in the United States today.

Among proposed reforms are (1) making it illegal for firms to refuse insurance to those with "pre-existing conditions," that is, medical conditions that existed prior to the purchase of insurance, and (2) requiring community rating, a risk-rating scheme that requires the insurance industry to charge the same premium, regardless of medical condition, age, or sex.

Such reforms may help, but they are unlikely to solve the problem because insurance companies can still select the favorable risks. They can, for example, locate their offices on the fifth floor of a building with no elevator and make prospective customers apply in person. They can also design their insurance packages to appeal to the young and healthy—by providing especially generous "sports medicine" benefits, for example, or giving free memberships to health clubs.

One way to prevent cream skimming would be to tax or subsidize insurance firms depending on the health risks of their particular client pool. These tax/subsidy arrangements are called "risk adjustments" and remove the cost advantage of selecting the best risks. Another way is to standardize benefits, thus preventing the use of special benefit packages to attract lower risk groups. These and similar proposals to regulate the insurance market have problems of their own, however. Most are imperfect, and some would require extensive and expensive bureaucracies to develop, administer, and enforce.

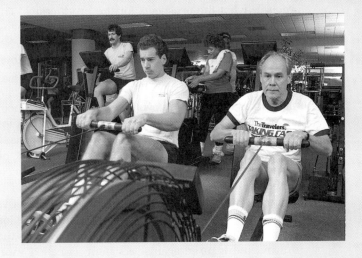

But insurance firms do not know everything about each individual's risks. Insurance rates can only be based on observable factors; auto insurance rates, for example, depend on the record of past accidents, age of driver, and type of vehicle. The same rate is charged to all people with identical observable traits. When an insurance company perceives that the premiums it is charging for a particular group of individuals is too low for the risks of the group, it raises the premiums. This is when the problem of adverse selection can appear.

The **adverse selection** problem arises when insurance companies try to raise their premiums and the best risks stop buying insurance. The best risks may either decide to self-insure (not buy insurance from any company) or switch to another company. The worst risks—those who know that they really need insurance because they are unhealthy, for example, and so will not self-insure, or those who cannot get insurance elsewhere—stick with the firm. As the best risks leave, the *average* riskiness of the insured risks worsens. It may deteriorate so much that average profits actually fall—the increased average riskiness more than offsets the increased premiums.

Though the term adverse selection was coined to capture this *adverse* effect on the mix of those buying insurance as premiums increase, it has come to refer to the whole array of actions which can affect the mix of those buying insurance.

For many kinds of insurance, such as fire insurance, adverse selection problems may not be too bad. The critical information (determining the likelihood of a fire) can easily enough be observed—for instance, by building inspectors. But for many of the kinds of risks against which individuals would like to buy insurance, adverse selection effects are important. With health or automobile insurance, for instance, an insurance firm is likely to find it difficult to determine any particular individual's risk. Even worse, consider the problem of measuring the risk that a firm's new product will fail to meet expectations. It would be nearly impossible for an insurance company to decide precisely what the prospects for the product are. The business firm itself is certainly more likely to be better informed than the insurance company about the markets in which it is trying to sell the product. Not surprisingly, then, because of their disadvantage in obtaining crucial information, insurance firms do not supply insurance against such business risks.

Moral Hazard   A second problem faced by insurance companies is an incentive problem: insurance affects people's incentives to avoid whatever contingencies they are insured against. A person who has no fire insurance on a house, for example, may choose to limit the risk of fire by buying smoke alarms and home fire extinguishers and being especially cautious. But if that same person had fire insurance, he might not be so careful. Indeed, if the insurance would pay more than the house's market value, he might even be tempted to burn his own house down to collect the insurance.

This general feature of insurance, that it reduces the individual's incentives to avoid the insured-against accident, is called **moral hazard.** Of course, from an economist's point of view, what is at issue is not a question of morality, but only a question of incentives. If a person bears only a portion, or none, of the consequences of his actions—as he does when he has purchased insurance—his incentives are altered.

In the late 1960s, after urban riots plagued many major cities in the United States, inner-city property values plunged. Insurance coverage adjusted, but slowly. In the meantime many buildings were insured at amounts that considerably exceeded their reduced market value. Was it purely coincidental that the value of fire losses nationwide increased 55 percent between 1966 and 1970?

Moral hazard concerns may not be important for many kinds of insurance; an individual who buys a large life insurance policy and thus knows that her children will be well cared for in the event of her demise is hardly likely to take much bigger risks with her life. (There was, however, a grisly case in California some years ago in which a person cut off one foot with an axe to try to collect on disability insurance.) But for many kinds of risks against which a firm's managers would *like* to buy insurance, moral hazard concerns are important. For example, if a company could buy insurance to guarantee a minimum level of profit, managers would have less incentive to exert effort. When moral hazard problems are strong, insurance firms will offer limited—or even no—insurance.

THE RISK-INCENTIVE TRADE-OFF

We have seen that insurance reduces incentives. The greater the insurance coverage, the more incentives are reduced. If my house is insured for only 50 percent of any loss, I have a strong incentive to make sure that there is no fire. If it is insured for 100 percent of any loss, I have little incentive to expend any resources to avoid a fire.

There is thus a risk-incentive trade-off. The more the individual divests himself of risk, the weaker his incentives to avoid "bad results" and to foster "good results." This principle applies in many contexts other than simple insurance markets. A store manager whose salary is guaranteed faces little risk, but also has little incentive. If his pay depends on the store's sales, he has stronger incentives, but faces greater risk. In spite of his best efforts, sales may be low—perhaps because of an economic downturn, perhaps because buyers have simply turned away from his products; in either case, his income will be low.

In many cases, the market reaches a compromise: partial insurance, providing the purchaser of insurance with some incentives, but making her also bear some risk. With medical insurance, for example, it is common for an insurance company to pay only some percentage (like 80 percent) of expenses (this is called coinsurance). In this case, an individual will have a financial motivation to be cautious in the use of medical care, but still be largely protected.

Similarly, a firm that borrows money for a project is generally required to invest some of its own funds in the project, or to supply the lender with collateral; that is, provide the lender with an asset that the firm forfeits if it fails to repay the loan. Lenders know that with more of their own money at stake, borrowers will have better incentives to use the funds wisely.

CLOSE-UP: AUTO INSURANCE AND ADVERSE SELECTION IN NEW JERSEY

The charge for private passenger automobile insurance in the United States skyrocketed during the mid- and late 1980s. The general price level rose by 3.5 percent per year during that time. Auto insurance prices rose by 9 percent per year. Perhaps no state had worse auto insurance problems than New Jersey.

New Jersey was a likely candidate for several reasons. It has the highest population per square mile of any state in the country crowding the highways. Nine of the nation's top twenty-five cities for car theft are in New Jersey. New Jersey was one of only two states with no upper limit on the medical costs that could be claimed from any accident. It cost $1,000 a year on average to insure a car in New Jersey at the start of the 1990s, more than double the national average.

But New Jersey contributed to its own woes. In 1983, the state set up a Joint Underwriting Authority (JUA), which was intended to offer auto insurance to those too risky for private companies to insure. JUA rates were supposed to be comparable to those in private companies, which is a bit difficult to figure, since the private insurance companies did not want to insure these risky drivers at all. In practice, anyone could be insured by the JUA at rates not much different from the average for low-risk drivers.

This law, though well-meant, set up what should have been anticipated patterns of adverse selection. Private insurance companies directed their worst risks to the JUA, insuring only the lower risks themselves. By the end of the 1980s, half of New Jersey's drivers were enrolled in the JUA, which had accumulated a deficit of $3 billion that was growing by $1 billion a year. Extra taxes were needed to cover the lost money, creating a political furor in the Garden State.

As is so often the case, the insurance industry got blamed for the mess. The government started regulating insurance premiums and compelling the insurance firms to insure high-risk cars. These constraints had the predictable effects. Insurance companies sued the state, and several, like Allstate, left the state altogether rather than sell insurance at a loss. Insurance spreads and shares risk, but it cannot provide something for nothing.

Sources: Insurance Information Institute, *1990 Property/Casualty Insurance Facts;* "Insurers Under Siege: Lawmakers, Consumers, and Corporate Customers Are Fighting Mad," *Business Week,* August 21, 1989, pp. 72–79; Joseph J. Sullivan, "Compromise on Insurance Isn't Working in New Jersey," *New York Times,* January 15, 1989, p. D6; Jay Romano, "Why Auto Insurance Costs So Much," *New York Times,* October 22, 1989, sec. XII, p. 1; Romano, "New Law on Auto Insurance Draws Fire," *New York Times,* March 18, 1990, sec. XII, p. 1.

ENTREPRENEURSHIP

Innovation gives life to a capitalist economy. It also demonstrates the vital roles played by time and risk. Consider for a moment the many new products and new processes of production that have so enriched (or at least altered) everyone's life in the last century: fast food, transistors, computers, airplanes, cars, televisions—the list is endless. Each of these innovations required more than just an idea. It needed people willing to follow the advice of David Lloyd George, once prime minister of Great Britain, who said: "Don't be afraid to take a big step if one is indicated. You can't cross a chasm in two small jumps."

Innovations require people and businesses to take risks. Innovators need capital too, since those who have innovative ideas, like Henry Ford, often do not have the capital to carry them out. They must turn to others to supply them with resources, generally in exchange for part of any eventual return. After all, someone who lends to an innovator bears a risk, and he must receive compensation to be willing to undertake these risks.

In forming judgments about whether to pursue a possible innovation, innovators and investors form expectations about the future. But because they are dealing with new ideas, products, and processes, the expectations of reasonable men and women may differ. When the returns are in and the project has proved to be a success or a failure, it is often difficult to ascertain the reasons why, even with the wisdom of hindsight. Thus, those whose jobs require them to make decisions—the lending officers of banks, the managers of pension funds and other financial institutions, the leaders of corporations—face a difficult task. But lack of any simple formula does not mean that there are not better and worse ways of making these decisions. Forming expectations and evaluating risks are like playing football in a fog; you cannot always tell what is going on, but skilled players with good foresight still have an advantage.

Thus, **entrepreneurs**—the individuals responsible for creating new businesses, bringing new products to market, developing new processes of production—face all the problems we have discussed. All business decision making involves risk taking. But entrepreneurs who take responsibility for managing a new business generally face more risk than established companies. Businesses often require additional financing for new projects, but new enterprises almost always require extensive outside financing. The problem of selection, of determining which of a set of potential investment projects and entrepreneurs ought to receive funds, is particularly acute, since because these projects are new, they have yet to establish a reputation. Lenders may be reluctant, for instance, to provide funds for fear of default.

Since entrepreneurs cannot buy insurance to cover most of the risks they face, they must also be willing to bear the risks themselves. Entrepreneurs need a return to compensate them for their efforts and the risks they undertake. Similarly, those who provide these new enterprises with capital must receive a return greater than they might receive elsewhere, to compensate them for the additional risks they have to bear. There has been ongoing concern about the effect of a variety of public policies, especially tax policy, on these returns. Does the current tax system discourage entrepreneurship? Can policies be designed to encourage it? These questions will be addressed later in the book.

AN OVERVIEW OF FINANCIAL MARKETS

Our economic system is often referred to as capitalism, reflecting the importance that capital markets—or more generally, financial markets—play in our economy. The central role of these markets constitutes another major area of consensus among economists. Here is our fifth consensus point:

5 Financial Markets

> *Financial markets are a central part of modern economies. They are essential for raising capital for new enterprises, expanding on-going businesses, and sharing risks.*

REVIEW AND PRACTICE

SUMMARY

1. Much of economics is future oriented, which means that households and firms must form expectations about the future and cope with problems of risk and uncertainty.

2. The interest rate is a price. It equates the supply of funds by savers and the demand by borrowers. Savers receive interest for deferring consumption, and borrowers pay interest so that they can consume or invest now and pay later.

3. The fact that the market interest rate is positive means that a dollar received today is worth more than a dollar received in the future. This is the time value of money. The present discounted value of a dollar in the future is the value in dollars today of receiving a dollar in the future, given the prevailing rate of interest.

4. The real interest rate, which measures a person's actual increase in buying power when she saves money, is equal to the nominal interest rate (the amount paid in dollars) minus the inflation rate.

5. What investors are willing to pay today for an asset depends largely on what they believe they can sell it for in the future. Changes in expectations can thus shift the demand curve for an asset and change current prices.

6. Most people are risk averse. They respond to risks by trying to avoid them and mitigate their impacts; by keeping options open; by diversifying; and by transferring risks to and sharing risks with others.

7. Among the most important institutions for absorbing risks are insurance firms. Insurance firms face two problems. One is that people who buy insurance tend to be those most at risk, and charging higher prices for insurance will discourage those less at risk from buying insurance at all. This effect is called adverse selection. The second problem is that insurance reduces the incentives individuals have to avoid whatever they are insured against. This is called moral hazard.

8. Entrepreneurial innovation plays a central role in modern economies.

KEY TERMS

interest	nominal rate of interest	rational expectations
principal		risk averse
present discounted value	assets	adverse selection
intertemporal trades	expectations	moral hazard
real rate of interest	myopic expectations	entrepreneurs
	adaptive expectations	

REVIEW QUESTIONS

1. Who is on the demand side and who is on the supply side in the market for loanable funds? What is the price in that market?

2. Would you prefer to receive $100 one year from now, or five years from now? Why? Does your answer change if the rate of inflation is zero?

3. What is the relationship between the nominal interest rate and the real interest rate?

4. True or false: "Demand curves depend on what people want now, not on their expectations about the future." Explain your answer.

5. What is meant by risk aversion? What are some consequences of the fact that most people are risk averse?

6. Why do people pay insurance premiums if they hope and expect that nothing bad is going to happen to them?

7. What is moral hazard? What is adverse selection? How do they affect insurance markets?

8. Why is there a trade-off between risk and incentives? Give an example of this trade-off.

PROBLEMS

1. Occasionally, firms issue bonds that promise to pay a fixed amount, say, in one year, but pay no interest in the interim. What is the market value today of a bond that promises to pay $1,000 next year, if the interest rate is 5 percent? 10 percent? 20 percent?

2. A machine costs $1 million and produces output of $1.1 million (net of other costs) next year, at which point it will be worn out and useless. At what rate of interest is the present discounted value of the return ($1.1 million) equal to the cost of the machine? If the current interest rate in the economy is higher than the rate for the present discounted value of the return, would you buy the machine? Why or why not?

3. Many states have passed laws that put a ceiling on the rate of interest that can be charged; these laws are called usury laws. Using a supply and demand diagram, show the effect of interest rate ceilings on the quantity (supply) of lending. Who is better off as a result of usury laws? Who is worse off?

4. Suppose the workers at a particular company have been complaining that their medical insurance does not cover enough items. To help build loyalty among the staff, the company agrees to cover more items. However, it finds that the number of sick days taken and its expenses for health care both rise sharply. Why might this happen? What is the name for it?

5. You hire someone to paint your house. Since it is a large job, you agree to pay him by the hour. What moral hazard problem must you consider? Explain the trade-off between risk and incentives in this situation.

6. (This problem depends on the chapter appendix below.) Imagine that $1,000 is deposited in an account for five years; the account pays 10 percent interest per year, compounded annually. At the end of the first year, the account is credited with $100 interest, and then starts earning interest on the interest, and similarly at the end of each successive year. How much money will be in the account after five years? What if the rate of interest is 12 percent? What if the annual rate of interest is 12 percent, but the interest is compounded monthly?

7. (This problem depends on the chapter appendix below.) Suppose you want to buy a car three years from now, and you know that the price of a car at that time will be $10,000. If the interest rate is 7 percent per year, how much would you have to set aside today to have the money ready when you need it? If the interest rate is 5 percent, how much would you have to set aside today?

APPENDIX: CALCULATING PRESENT DISCOUNTED VALUE

In the text, we described how to calculate the present discounted value (PDV) of a dollar received a year from now. The present discounted value of a dollar received two years from now can be calculated in a similar way. But how much *today* is equivalent to, say, $100 two years from now? If I were given $PDV today, and I put it in the bank, at the end of the year, I would have PDV(1 + r)$. If I left it in the bank for another year, in the second year I would earn interest on the total amount in the bank at the end of the first year, $r \times$ PDV$(1 + r)$. Therefore, at the end of the two-year period I would have:

$$\text{PDV}(1 + r) + [r \times \text{PDV}(1 + r)]$$
$$= \text{PDV}(1 + r)(1 + r)$$
$$= \text{PDV}(1 + r)^2.$$

Thus, the $PDV of $100 in two years is $100 / (1 + r)^2$. If I put $100 / (1 + r)^2$ in the bank today, I would have $100 / (1 + r)^2 \times (1 + r)^2 = \$100$ in two years. In performing these calculations, we have taken account of the interest on the interest. This is called **compound interest.**

(By contrast, **simple interest** does not take into account the interest you earn on interest you have previously earned.) If the rate of interest is 10 percent and is compounded annually, $100 today is worth $110 a year from now and $121 (*not* $120) in two years' time. Thus, the present discounted value today of $121 two years from now is $100. Table 6.1 shows how to calculate the present discounted value of $100 received next year, two years from now, and three years from now.

Table 6.1 **PRESENT DISCOUNTED VALUE OF $100**

Year received	Present discounted value
Next year	$\dfrac{1}{1 + r} \times 100 = \dfrac{100}{1 + r}$
Two years from now	$\dfrac{1}{1 + r} \times \dfrac{100}{1 + r} = \dfrac{100}{(1 + r)^2}$
Three years from now	$\dfrac{1}{1 + r} \times \dfrac{100}{(1 + r)^2} = \dfrac{100}{(1 + r)^3}$

We can now see how to calculate the value of an investment project that will yield a return over several years. We look at what the returns will be each year, adjust them to their present discounted values, and then add these values up. Table 6.2 shows how this is done for a project that yields $10,000 next year and $15,000 the year after, and that you plan to sell in the third year for $50,000. The second column of the table shows the return in each year. The third column shows the discount factor—what we multiply the return by to obtain the present discounted value of that year's return. The calculations assume an interest rate of 10 percent. The fourth column multiplies the return by the discount factor to obtain the present discounted value of that year's return. In the bottom row of the table, the present discounted values of each year's return have been added up to obtain the total present discounted value of the project. Notice that it is much smaller than the number we obtain simply by adding up the returns, which is the "undiscounted" yield of the project.

Table 6.2 CALCULATING PRESENT DISCOUNTED VALUE OF A THREE-YEAR PROJECT

Year	Return	Discount factor $(r = 0.10)$	Present discounted value $(r = 0.10)$
1	$10,000	$\dfrac{1}{1.10}$	$ 9,091
2	$15,000	$\dfrac{1}{(1.10)^2} = \dfrac{1}{1.21}$	$12,397
3	$50,000	$\dfrac{1}{(1.10)^3} = \dfrac{1}{1.331}$	$37,566
Total	$75,000	—	$59,054

7

THE PUBLIC SECTOR

Most Americans have a great deal of faith in our economic system, with its primary reliance on private markets. Yet despite this basic faith, the United States has a public, or governmental, sector that reaches out into all spheres of economic activity. How do economists explain the role of government in the economy?

In earlier chapters, we have seen how the profit system provides firms with the incentive to produce the goods consumers want. Prices give firms the incentive to economize on scarce resources. Prices also coordinate economic activity and signal changes in economic conditions. Private property provides incentives for individuals to invest in and to maintain buildings, machines, land, cars, and other possessions. Chapter 3 demonstrated the incentives individuals and countries have to engage in mutually advantageous trades and

KEY QUESTIONS

1. What distinguishes the private from the public sector?

2. What explains the economic roles the government has undertaken?

3. What are externalities and public goods, and why do they imply that markets may not work well?

4. What are the various ways the government can affect the economy and attempt to achieve its economic objectives?

5. How has the role of government changed in recent decades? And how does the role of government in the United States compare with its role in other industrial countries?

6. What are some of the current controversies concerning the roles of government? Why do failures of the market system not necessarily imply that government action is desirable?

to specialize in areas of comparative advantage. Chapters 4 and 5 showed how, in free markets, prices are determined by the interaction of demand and supply.

We have thus seen how the private market answers the four basic questions set out in Chapter 1: *What is produced and in what quantities* is determined by the interaction of demand and supply, reflecting both the goods consumers want and what it costs firms to produce those goods. *How it is produced* is determined by competition among firms, which must produce the goods in the least expensive way possible in order to stay in business. *For whom it is produced* is determined by the incomes of individuals in the economy. Those with high incomes get more of the economy's goods and services, and those with low incomes get less. These incomes, in turn, are established by the demand and supply for labor, which determines what workers are paid, and the demand and supply for capital, which determines the return people get on their savings. *Who makes the decisions?* Everyone. Which goods are produced depends on millions of decisions made in households and firms throughout the economy. Moreover, firms, competing against one another, have incentives to choose as managers those most able to make the hard decisions—whether to enter some new market or develop some new product—that every firm must face if it is to survive.

If this private-market system works so well, what role do economists see for the government? Economists recognize that the government must set and enforce the basic laws of society, and provide a framework within which firms can compete fairly against one another. Beyond this, however, economists' understanding of the market's ability to answer the basic economic questions leads them to look hard at any additional function the government serves: why are private markets not serving that function? This chapter will explore the roles the government has undertaken, and how and why it carries out those roles.

THE CHANGING ROLES OF GOVERNMENT

The appropriate balance between the public and private sectors is a subject of constant debate, with different countries giving different answers to this question. In Switzerland, the public sector is small and government economic activities are severely limited. In the Soviet Union before its collapse and China before its reforms, the government tried to control or **nationalize** virtually all aspects of economic activity, though the difficulty of doing this created increasing pressures for change. Between these extremes lies a wide spectrum: free market economies like Hong Kong, where businesses do not face many of the regulations facing businesses in the United States and Western Europe; welfare state economies like Sweden, where the government takes major responsibilities for health care, child care, and a host of other social services, but where there is also a large private sector; and a number of European economies, like Great Britain, where the government until recently dominated major industries like steel, coal, railroads, airlines, and public utilities. The United States is nearer the free market end of this spectrum than most countries with industrialized, developed economies.

Government has almost always been responsible for certain activities that the vast majority of citizens believe are fundamentally public functions—the justice system, police protection, and national defense, for example. But government's role in other areas has changed over time, usually in response to perceived failures of the market economy. In the late nineteenth century, the U.S. government began regulating railroads and breaking up huge monopolies such as Standard Oil, in response to concerns that they were ruthlessly using their market power to control the economy and exploit consumers. In the 1930s, the economic havoc inflicted by the Great Depression—one out of four Americans was out of work, banks failed and the stock market crashed, plummeting agricultural prices forced farmers to default on their loans and lose their farms—led government into a whole new set of responsibilities known collectively as the New Deal.

In 1946, with the Full Employment Act, the U.S. government extended its role to include responsibility for maintaining the economy at full employment. This commitment contributed in part to a period of unprecedented prosperity. But the fruits of that prosperity were distributed very unequally. Many Americans were born into squalor and poverty. Their educational prospects were dim, as were their chances of getting good jobs. In the 1960s, the government responded by again increasing its responsibility, this time in the form of President Johnson's Great Society programs, including the War on Poverty.

The 1970s saw a change in direction: government regulations were seen as excessively burdensome, interfering with rather than helping the economy. There was, in fact, a worldwide movement toward **deregulation**—eliminating, for instance, the regulations that controlled airline and trucking prices—

and **privatization**—relying on the private sector to provide services that were formerly provided by the government. In the late 1980s, a new set of concerns emerged having to do with the competitiveness of the American economy. Americans were saving less than were citizens of other industrialized powers. The rapid increases in productivity that had marked the 1950s and early 1960s slowed. There were new calls for government activity to spur the economy. Government increased its support for research and development (R & D) aimed at commercial rather than defense objectives, which had been the primary focus of public R & D funding in previous periods.

THE PICTURE IN STATISTICS

Changes in the size and role of government can be seen clearly in government statistics measuring the share of the total output of the economy (gross domestic product or GDP) devoted to government expenditures. In 1900, government spending accounted for 8 percent of GDP. By 1950, this share had grown to 21 percent, and by 1980—the year before Ronald Reagan took office—to 32 percent. Today it stands at 34 percent.

Figure 7.1 shows where federal dollars go. In 1950, just over half went to defense, and about an eighth each to Social Security/welfare and to interest pay-

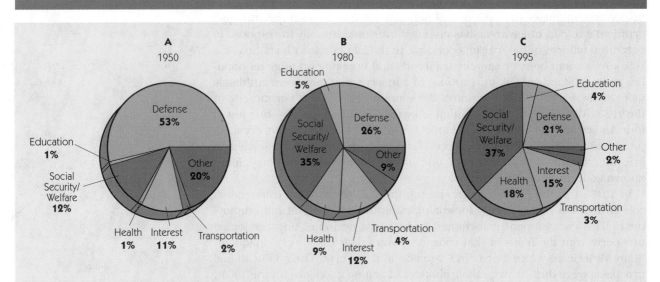

Figure 7.1 THE CHANGING PATTERN OF FEDERAL EXPENDITURES

Since 1950, there has been a steady increase in the share of federal funds allotted to health, Social Security, and welfare coupled with a marked decrease in the share allotted to defense. The share going for interest on the debt rose between 1980 and 1995 as a result of soaring deficits during the 1980s and early 1990s. *Sources: Statistical Abstract of the United States (1995), Table 520, Mid-Session Review of the 1997 Budget,* July 16, 1996.

POLICY PERSPECTIVE: THE "PEACE DIVIDEND"—NOW YOU SEE IT, NOW YOU DON'T

A dramatic event ushered in the decade of the 1990s—the end of the Cold War. With it came the promise of what came to be known as the "peace dividend." The arms race would be replaced with international cooperation, and the resources that had formerly been dedicated to the arms buildup could be spent on domestic needs for a change. But discussions of how to spend the peace dividend have turned into a consensus that there is no dividend to spend. Advocates of U.S. military strength argued that new weapons were required to face the new challenges of the post-Cold War world. The United States had to be able to fight in two regions simultaneously. While the need for nuclear deterrence was undoubtedly reduced, the need for conventional forces was possibly increased.

So far, in spite of the widespread consensus of the importance of unmet social needs, investments in education and research, and deficit reduction, the views of advocates of continued defense spending have prevailed. In real terms defense is projected to decline only slightly over the next ten years. Somehow, the peace dividend disappeared before anyone saw it.

The Berlin Wall, after it fell in November 1989.

ments on the national debt, leaving the remaining quarter to finance all other government programs. Since then, the share of federal spending going to defense has fallen dramatically: in 1995 only one in five federal dollars went to defense. The shares going for Social Security/welfare and health programs, on the other hand, have steadily increased, to the point where today they account for half of the total. In 1950, interest payments were relatively high as a result of the huge debt accumulated to fight World War II. But the deficit increases of the Reagan and Bush years caused interest payments on the national debt to rise to record levels, currently 15 percent of all federal expenditures. After defense, Social Security/welfare, health, and interest payments, only 9 percent of the budget is left to spend on everything else, including running the government itself!

STATE AND LOCAL GOVERNMENT

Most of the services that people look for from government—police protection, schools, fire, libraries, parks—are provided largely by states and localities, which account for 40 percent of public sector spending in the United States. In many areas state and local responsibility is growing. For a few services, such as education, federal funding has increased. For instance, today, while states and localities remain *responsible* for elementary and secondary education, the federal government provides about 6 percent of the funds.

WHAT DISTINGUISHES THE PRIVATE AND PUBLIC SECTORS?

In a democracy, two important features distinguish private from public institutions. First, the people responsible for running public institutions are elected or appointed by someone who is elected. The legitimacy of the person holding the position is derived directly or indirectly from the electoral process. Second, any government has certain rights of compulsion. For instance, the U.S. government has the right to force its citizens to pay taxes; if they fail to do so, it can confiscate their property and even imprison them. The government has the right to force its young people to serve in the armed forces at wages below those that would induce them to volunteer. The government also has the right of **eminent domain,** which is the right to seize private property for public use, provided it compensates the owner fairly.

Its ability to use compulsion means that the government can do things private institutions cannot do. Once a decision has been made to build a public road, for instance, a local government can make sure that everyone in town helps to pay for it. Sometimes governments create rules to bind their own hands, so that they cannot do *anything* they wish. For instance, the government has established elaborate hiring procedures for itself that private firms generally do not find worthwhile. The owner of a private firm can decide whom she wants to hire; if she hires someone incompetent, she and her firm suffer. If the manager of a public enterprise hires someone incompetent, however, the public pays. The government's strict hiring procedures help avoid bad hiring, but they may also result in rigidities that make it difficult for government enterprises to compete against private firms for the most talented individuals.

These and other constraints imposed on the public sector—as well as the absence of the profit motive which provides the private sector with strong in-

The increase in central (federal) government expenditures during the twentieth century has been dramatic, but expenditures in the United States are still among the smallest of any of the major industrial countries in proportion to the size of the economy. In the Netherlands and the United Kingdom, government expenditures are approximately half of GDP as compared to about one-quarter for the United States. Of the major developed countries, only Japan and Australia spend under one-third of GDP on the public sector. As a significant portion of U.S. federal expenditures goes to defense (about 4 percent of GDP), the relative size of nondefense expenditures is particularly low viewed from this international perspective.

In the United States federal spending on nondefense public sector programs amounts to about 19 percent of GDP. In the Netherlands and the United Kingdom this figure is 50 and 39 percent respectively. The key difference is that Social Security and welfare programs are much larger in those countries relative to the United States.

These foreign comparisons prove different things to different people. Advocates of more government spending argue that the United States is out of step. Opponents of more government spending argue that all of these countries would do better to reduce public expenditures.

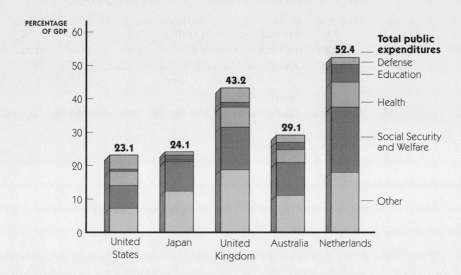

Source: Government Finance Statistics Yearbook (1995).

centives to be efficient, reduce costs, and produce what consumers want—put the public sector at a general disadvantage relative to the private sector in markets that work well. Economists, concerned with the most efficient solutions to economic problems ask: When do markets work well? When do they fail? And, when they fail, when might government improve matters?

ADAM SMITH'S "INVISIBLE HAND" AND THE CENTRAL ROLE OF MARKETS

The modern economic faith in private markets can be traced back to Adam Smith's 1776 masterpiece *The Wealth of Nations*. Smith argued that workers and producers, interested only in helping themselves and their families, were the basis of the success of the economy. The public interest would best be promoted by individuals pursuing their own self-interest. As Smith put it:

> Man has almost constant occasion for the help of his brethren, and it is in vain for him to expect it from their benevolence only. He will be more likely to prevail if he can interest their self-love in his favor, and show them that it is for their own advantage to do for him what he requires of them. . . . It is not from the benevolence of the butcher, the brewer, or the baker, that we expect our dinner, but from their regard to their own interest. We . . . never talk to them of our own necessities but of their advantages.[1]

Smith's insight was that individuals work hardest to help the overall economic production of society when their efforts help themselves. He argued that an "obvious and simple system of liberty" provided the greatest opportunities for people to help themselves and thus, by extension, to create the greatest wealth for a society.

Smith used the metaphor of the **"invisible hand"** to describe how self-interest led to social good: "He intends only his own gain, and he is in this as in many other cases led by an invisible hand to promote an end which was no part of his intention . . . By pursuing his own interest he frequently promotes that of the society more effectually than when he really intends to promote it."

Economics has progressed since Adam Smith, but his fundamental argument still has great appeal. Greater liberty for individuals in country after country has indeed led to huge increases in production that have benefited if not everyone, almost everyone. Nevertheless, it is not difficult to find discontent with the market. There is concern that markets produce too much of some things, like air and water pollution, and too little of other things, such as support for the arts or child care facilities. Generally, concern with market outcomes can be placed into three broad categories: those that are based on ignorance of the laws of economics, those having to do with redistribution of income, and those having to do with genuine failures of private markets.

[1]Book 1, Chapter 2.

CLOSE-UP: ADAM SMITH—FOUNDER OF MODERN ECONOMICS

Adam Smith, the founder of modern economics, was a professor of moral philosophy at the University of Glasgow, in the latter part of the eighteenth century. His great masterpiece, *The Wealth of Nations,* was published in 1776, the year the United States signed the Declaration of Independence. The American Revolution coincided with two other revolutions. The industrial revolution marked the transformation of the economy both from agriculture to industry and from rural to urban life. A revolution in ideas and ideology began to question the earlier view in which social institutions had been accepted as a matter of course, as part of a God-given order. Intellectuals began to inquire into the functions of social institutions (schools, churches, government) and to consider changes that could make society better off. This thinking is strongly reflected in the Federalist papers that form the background of the U.S. Constitution, and in the French Revolution at the turn of the nineteenth century.

No precise date or place marks the beginning of either the industrial or the ideological revolution. Glasgow was at the center of both, and this was perhaps no accident: both revolutions fed upon each other. The key idea in Adam Smith's economics was that individuals, in pursuing their self-interest, could more assuredly attain the common interest than if it were pursued by government (at that time, a monarch). This view contrasted with the earlier *mercantilist* view, which held that government should actively pursue the commercial interests of the country, particularly by promoting exports. Because of his emphasis on markets, Adam Smith is often held up as a champion of very limited government. A closer look at his *Wealth of Nations* shows a far more balanced view. Though he did not use the modern "market failures" vocabulary, he recognized many limitations of markets, and he saw government as performing an important role, such as supporting education. He also recognized the tendencies for firms to try to reduce or suppress competition, as well as the adverse consequences of lack of competition.

Adam Smith

GOVERNMENT AND IGNORANCE OF ECONOMICS

"Wouldn't the world be a better place if we still lived in the Garden of Eden?" epitomizes complaints about markets that ignore the laws of economics. Things have a price because they are scarce. If the price of oil is high, it is because oil is scarce and the high price reflects that scarcity. In Chapter 4, we saw that economists regard such situations not as market failures but as the hard facts of economic life. Much as everyone would like to live in a world where all individuals could have almost everything they wanted at a price they could afford, this is simply unrealistic. Those calling on government to "solve" the problem of scarcity by passing laws about prices simply shift the problem. They reduce prices for some and cause shortages for everyone else.

GOVERNMENT AND REDISTRIBUTION

A second category of complaints against the market represents a dissatisfaction with the distribution of income. Market economies may be productive and efficient at producing wealth, but they may also cause some people to get very rich and others to starve. Someone who has a rare and valuable skill will, by the laws of supply and demand, receive a high income. Someone else who has few skills, and common ones at that, will find his wage low—perhaps even too low for survival. The economy may have a very unequal distribution of income.

Most economists see an important role for the government in income redistribution, taking income from those who have more and giving it to those who have less. In their view, society need not accept whatever distribution of income results from the workings of private markets. Federal income and estate taxes on the rich and welfare programs for the poor are part of the government's role in redistribution.

Concern for greater economic equality is a generally accepted role for government, but there is still much disagreement about the benefits and costs of programs aimed at reducing inequality. And even if government reaches agreement on the degree to which income inequality should be reduced, economists will disagree as to what is the best method because income redistribution affects incentives.

Questions of redistribution are often posed as, How should the economy's pie be divided? What size slice should each person get? By looking at the pie in panel A of Figure 7.2, you can see that the poorest 20 percent of the population

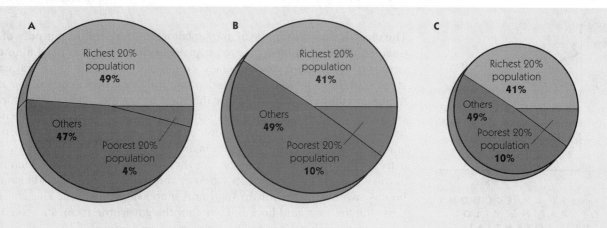

Figure 7.2 REDISTRIBUTION AND GROWTH

Panel A shows that the poor receive only a small share of the economy's output. Plans for redistribution often assume the situation in panel B, where the poor simply receive a larger share. But if the redistribution is poorly managed or too great, it may substantially reduce the size of the overall pie, as in panel C, making all groups worse off. *Source: 1994 Current Population Reports,* Bureau of the Census (June 1996).

get a relatively small slice—that is, 20 percent receive only 4 percent of the economy's income—while the richest 20 percent of the population get a relatively large slice, 49 percent of the economy's income. Often redistribution is viewed as simply cutting the pie differently, giving the poor somewhat larger slices and the rich somewhat smaller, as in panel B. But if the process of redistributing income weakens economic incentives and makes the economy less productive, the size of the whole pie will shrink, as illustrated in panel C. There the poor get a larger share of a smaller pie. The rich are much worse off now—they get a smaller share of a smaller pie. If the size of the pie has shrunk enough, even the poor may be worse off. By designing government redistribution programs appropriately, it may be possible to limit the size of these effects on productivity.

GOVERNMENT AND MARKET FAILURES

The final category of discontent with private markets represents cases where the market does indeed fail in its role of producing economic efficiency. Economists refer to these problems as **market failures,** and have studied them closely. When there is a market failure, government may be able to correct the market failure and enhance the economy's efficiency.

Figure 7.3 AN ECONOMY OPERATING BELOW FULL POTENTIAL

The economy is at point *E*, below the edge of its production possibilities curve. The government seeks to have it operate closer to the curve, at point *E'*, for instance.

STABILIZATION OF THE ECONOMY

The most dramatic example of market failures is the periodic episodes of high unemployment that have plagued capitalist economies. It is hard to tout the virtues of an efficient market when a quarter of the labor force and capital stock sits idle, as it did during the depth of the Great Depression of the 1930s. Although many economists believe there are forces that eventually restore the economy to full employment, the costs of waiting for the economy to correct itself—in terms of both forgone output and human misery—are enormous, and virtually all governments today take it as their responsibility to *try* to avoid extreme fluctuations in economic activity—both the downturns (when much of the economy's resources, its workers and machines, remain idle) and the booms (which may result in high and increasing inflation). The causes of these fluctuations, and how and whether the government can succeed in significantly reducing them, are topics in macroeconomics.

When the economy's scarce resources are idle, the economy is operating below its production possibilities curve, as shown in Figure 7.3. As usual, the curve has been simplified to two goods, guns and butter, which represent the general output levels in the public and private sectors. The government attempts to move the economy from point *E* to a point closer to the production possibilities curve, *E'*.

Even when the economy is at full employment, resources will not be efficiently allocated (1) if competition is limited, (2) if there are externalities, (3) if public goods are involved, (4) if markets are missing, and (5) if information is limited.

LACK OF COMPETITION

Competition is essential for a market to function efficiently. Competition is what forces firms to look for more efficient ways of producing goods and to meet the desires of consumers more effectively. Without competition, prices will be higher and production lower than with competition. But life for the firms themselves is easier without competition, and profits are higher. Thus, firms try to reduce the extent of competition. Governments have passed numerous laws, called antitrust and fair competition laws, attempting to enhance competition in the market economy.

EXTERNALITIES

But even when there is competition, the market may supply too much of some goods and too little of others. One of the reasons for this is the presence of **externalities.** Externalities are present whenever an individual or firm can take an action that directly affects others but for which it neither pays nor is paid compensation. It therefore does not bear all the consequences of its action. (The effect of the action is "external" to the individual or firm.) Externalities are pervasive. A hiker who litters, a driver whose car emits pollution, a child who leaves a mess behind after he finishes playing, a person who smokes a cigarette in a crowded room—all create externalities. In each case, the actor is not the only one who must suffer the consequences of his action; others suffer them too. Externalities can be thought of as instances when the price system works imperfectly. The hiker is not "charged" for the litter she creates, nor does the car owner pay for the pollution his car makes.

The examples so far are negative externalities. A common example of a negative externality is a factory that emits air pollution. The factory benefits from emitting the pollution, since by doing so, the company can make its product more cheaply than if it put in pollution-control devices. Society as a whole bears the negative external costs of pollution. If the factory had to pay for its pollution, it would find ways to produce less of it. And indeed, government environmental regulations are often aimed at just that goal.

Externalities can also be positive. A common example of a positive externality is a new invention. When someone makes a new discovery that leads to greater economic productivity, other people (or companies) benefit. The inventor receives, through the prices he charges, only a fraction of the total gains to society from the invention. Other firms will copy it and learn from it. Inventions like the laser and the transistor have benefited consumers, both by providing new products and allowing other products to be made less expensively. While the individual researcher bears the costs of making a discovery, society receives positive external benefits. If everyone who benefited from an invention had to pay money to the inventor, there would be far higher incentives for research and development. And indeed, patents and other government laws aimed at protecting intellectual property enable the investors to get a larger return than they otherwise would.

When externalities are present, the market's allocation of goods will be inefficient. When the production of a good such as steel entails a negative externality—like smoke and its effect on the air—the market level of production is too high. This is because the producer fails to take into account the "social costs" in deciding how much to produce. To put it another way, the price of steel determined in competitive markets by the law of supply and demand only reflects *private costs*, the costs actually faced by firms. If firms do not have to pay *all* of the costs (including the costs of pollution), equilibrium prices will be lower and output higher than they would be if firms took social costs into account.

The government can offset this effect in several ways. For instance, it might impose a tax. Panel A of Figure 7.4 shows the demand and supply curves for steel, and depicts the market equilibrium at the intersection of the two curves, Q_0. If the government imposes a tax on the production of steel, the supply curve will shift to the left—the quantity produced at each price will be lower—and the equilibrium level of production will be less, Q_1.

Figure 7.4 SUPPLY, DEMAND, AND EXTERNALITIES

The steel industry produces a negative externality of pollution. In panel A, a tax on steel production shifts the supply curve to the left, reducing both steel production and pollution. In panel B, a subsidy for rejuvenated buildings, which create the positive externality of neighborhood beautification, shifts the supply curve to the right, causing more buildings and neighborhoods to be renovated.

When the production of a good involves positive externalities, the market level of production is too low, and the government can try to enlarge the supply. The rejuvenation of an apartment building in a decaying part of a city provides an example of a positive externality; it will probably enhance the value of buildings around it. Panel B of Figure 7.4 shows the demand and supply curve for rejuvenated buildings. A government subsidy to rejuvenation shifts the supply curve to the right, increasing the number of rejuvenated buildings from Q_0 to Q_1.

PUBLIC GOODS

A particular category of goods, called **public goods,** is an extreme case of positive externalities. The consumption (or enjoyment) of a public good by one individual does not subtract from that of other individuals (consumption is accordingly said to be **nonrivalrous**). Public goods also have the property of **nonexcludability**—that is, it costs a great deal to exclude any individual from enjoying the benefits of a public good. The standard example of a public good is defense. Once the United States is protected from attack, it costs nothing extra to protect each new baby from foreign invasion. Furthermore, it would be virtually impossible to exclude a newborn from the benefits of this protection.

Public parks along the sides of a highway are another example. Anyone driving along the highway enjoys the view. The fact that one person is enjoying the view does not exclude others from enjoying it; and it would in fact be expensive to stop anyone who is driving along the highway from benefiting from the view. A lighthouse to guide ships around dangerous shoals or rocks is still another example of a public good. No additional costs are incurred as an additional ship navigates near the lighthouse, and it would be difficult to shut off the light in the lighthouse at just the right time to prevent a ship passing by from taking advantage of the lighthouse.

A **pure public good** is one where the marginal costs of providing it to an additional person are strictly zero and where it is impossible to exclude people from receiving the good. Many public goods that government provides are not *pure* public goods in this sense. The cost of an additional person using an uncrowded interstate highway is very, very small, but not zero, and it is possible, though relatively expensive, to exclude people from (or charge people for) using the highway.

Figure 7.5 compares examples of publicly provided goods against the strict definition of a pure public good. It shows the ease of exclusion along the horizontal axis and the (marginal) cost of an additional individual using the good along the vertical axis. The lower left-hand corner represents a pure public good. Of the major public expenditures, only national defense is close to a pure public good. Completely uncongested highways, to the extent they exist, are another example. The upper right-hand corner represents a pure private good (health services or education), where the cost of exclusion is low and the marginal cost of an additional individual using the good is high.

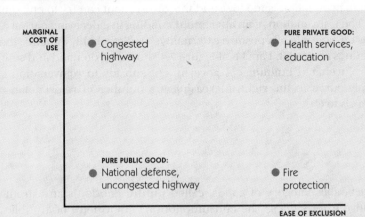

Figure 7.5 PUBLICLY PROVIDED GOODS

Pure public goods are characterized by nonrivalrous consumption (the marginal cost of an additional individual enjoying the good is zero) and nonexcludability (the cost of excluding an individual from enjoying the good is prohibitively high). Goods provided by the public sector differ in the extent to which they have these two properties.

Many goods are not pure public goods but have one or the other property to some degree. Fire protection is like a private good in that exclusion is relatively easy—individuals who refuse to contribute to the fire department could simply not be helped in the event of a fire. But fire protection is like a public good in that the marginal cost of covering an additional person is low. Most of the time, firefighters are not engaged in fighting fires but are waiting for calls. Protecting an additional individual has little extra cost. Only in that rare event when two fires break out simultaneously will there be a significant cost to extending fire protection to an additional person.

Sometimes the marginal cost of using a good to which access is easy (a good that possesses the property of nonexcludability) will be high. When an uncongested highway turns congested, the costs of using it rise dramatically, not in terms of wear and tear on the road but in terms of the time lost by drivers using the road. It is costly to exclude by charging for road use—as a practical matter, this can only be done on toll roads, and, ironically, the tollbooths often contribute to the congestion.

Many of the goods that are publicly provided, such as education and health services, have high costs associated with providing the service to additional individuals. For most of these goods, exclusion is also relatively easy. In fact, many of these goods and services are provided privately in some countries, or provided both publicly and privately. Though they are publicly provided in this country, they are not *pure* public goods, in the technical sense in which the term is defined.

Private markets undersupply public goods. If a single shipowner used the port near which a lighthouse is constructed, he could weigh the costs and benefits of the lighthouse. But if there were one large shipowner and many smaller owners, it would not pay any one of the small owners to build the lighthouse; and the large shipowner, in deciding whether to construct the lighthouse, would only take into account the benefits he would receive, not the benefits to the small shipowners. If the costs of construction exceeded the benefits that he alone would receive, he would not build the lighthouse. But if the benefits accruing to *all* the shipowners, large and small, were taken into account, those benefits might exceed the costs; it would then be desirable to build the lighthouse.

One can imagine a voluntary association of shipowners getting together to construct a lighthouse in this situation. But what happens if some small shipowner refuses to contribute, thinking that even if he does not contribute, the lighthouse will be built anyway? This is the **free-rider** aspect of public goods; because it is difficult to preclude anyone from using them, those who benefit from the goods have an incentive to avoid paying for them. Every shipowner has an incentive to "free ride" on the efforts of others. When too many decide to do this, the lighthouse will not be built.

Governments bring an important advantage to bear on the problem of public goods. They have the power to coerce citizens to pay for them. There might be *some* level of purchase of public goods—lighthouses, highway parks, even police or fire services—in the absence of government intervention. But society would be better off if the level of production were increased, and citizens were forced to pay for the increased level of public services through taxes.

MISSING MARKETS

Market economies only work well when there are, in fact, markets or good substitutes for markets. Before government provided unemployment insurance, disability insurance, and Social Security, individuals could not purchase these forms of insurance in the market.[2] In many areas, flood insurance, crop insurance, or even theft insurance is not available. Seventy-five years ago, before government became involved, many households could not obtain mortgages to buy a home. These are all examples of important **missing markets.** In later chapters, we will consider the reasons for these missing markets. For now, we simply note that the absence of these markets has served as an impetus for government programs to fill the gaps.

INFORMATION AND KNOWLEDGE

The efficiency with which it handles information is one of the great strengths of the market economy. Producers do not have to know what each consumer likes; and consumers do not have to know the details of production of any of the products which they consume. Prices convey information about scarcity. Working through the law of supply and demand, prices convey information from consumers to producers about how consumers value different goods, and from producers to consumers about the resources required (at the margin) to produce different goods.

---

[2]Even in those limited instances when insurance was available, the price was much higher than could be simply justified by the risks.

ECONOMIC ROLES FOR THE GOVERNMENT

Redistributing income
Correcting market failures

MAJOR MARKET FAILURES

Episodes of high unemployment
Lack of competition
Externalities
Public goods
Missing markets
Information and knowledge (including innovation)

But some kinds of information, like information about the weather, are public goods: the marginal cost of an additional individual benefiting from the information is negligible, and the cost of excluding individuals from this information may be considerable. This kind of information can also be important for efficient functioning of the economy, but markets do not produce efficient amounts of it. Thus, weather information is supplied by the U.S. Meteorological Service, an agency of the U.S. government.

Earlier, we saw how innovations typically give rise to externalities. Research can be thought of as the process of acquiring information, and innovation as the process of translating ideas, information, into new products. Later, we will discuss the array of government actions and programs that are trying to ensure not only that the level of resources allocated to knowledge acquisition is appropriate, but that it is directed in the right way.

BEYOND MARKET FAILURES

Markets, when they work well and do not suffer from one of the market failures described above, ensure that the economy is efficient—that resources are not wasted and that the economy operates on its production possibilities curve.

But efficiency is not everything. Even when a market is efficient, it may result in a distribution of income in which some individuals have hardly enough to live on, while others live in opulence.

Government actions are, of course, not limited to issues of economics. Governments try, for instance, to discourage robbery, rape, and murder. By and large, however, so long as an individual's action does not directly affect another, individuals are left to do what they please. I may think it strange that someone prefers vanilla to chocolate ice cream, or cherry to blueberry pie, but why should I impose my preferences? The principle that individuals are the best judges of what is in their own interests and that their preferences should be respected is called the **principle of consumer sovereignty.** There are, however, instances when government violates this principle: by smoking marijuana, an individual may cause no one else harm, yet governments in most states have made smoking marijuana illegal. Often, other rationales (such as externalities) for such actions are put forward; yet the underlying basis for government action remains inconsistent with the principle of consumer sovereignty. For instance, from 1920 to 1933, it was illegal to produce or sell alcoholic beverages in the United States. One of the reasons for this prohibition was the ill effects of drinking on others (such as alcohol-related accidents); but the view that drinking was *morally* wrong was what provided the fervor to the prohibition movement.

Government intervenes not only to discourage or prohibit certain actions, but to encourage or force others. It requires parents to send their children to school, for instance. Goods the government encourages because it believes there is some "public interest" in their consumption that is not an externality (although it goes beyond the private interests of those consuming the goods) are called **merit goods.**

GOVERNMENT'S OPTIONS

Once society has decided that government should do something, there is a second question: how can government accomplish society's ends most efficiently? The government has four choices. It can do something directly, it can provide incentives for the private sector to do something, it can mandate the private sector to do something, or it can take some combination of these.

TAKING DIRECT ACTION

One option is for government simply to take charge itself. If it believes there is a market failure in the provision of medical care, for instance, it can nationalize the medical sector, as Britain did after World War II. If the government believes there is a market failure in the airline or railroad industry, it can nationalize the industry, or the part of the industry with which it is discontent, and run the industry itself. If it believes there is a market failure in the provision of housing for the poor, it can build government housing projects.

Direct action does not require government to produce the good itself. It can also purchase the good from the private sector. Health care in the United States is an example. Although the government pays for much of the medical care of the poor and the elderly (through Medicaid and Medicare, respectively), it pays private doctors and hospitals to provide the actual care. Veteran's Hospitals, on the other hand, are run by the government.

PROVIDING INCENTIVES TO THE PRIVATE SECTOR

The government can also choose to operate at a distance, providing incentives to alter the workings of private markets in desirable ways. It can provide such incentives directly through subsidies, as it does for agriculture, or indirectly through the tax system, as is more commonly done in the United States. The government has used energy tax credits to encourage energy conservation. It has also used an investment tax credit, which gives firms a tax break for investing in new machines, to encourage investment. And special provisions of the tax code encourage employers to provide health insurance and pensions for their employees.

Subsidies and taxes put the government in the position of manipulating the price system to achieve its ends. If the government is worried about the supply of adequate housing for the poor, for example, it can provide builders with direct payments, or it can grant tax reductions for those who invest in slum areas. Both shift the supply curve of low cost housing to the right. If the government wants to encourage oil conservation, it can impose a tax on oil or gasoline, which will encourage conservation by raising the price of oil. It can also tax cars that are not energy efficient, raising their price.

MANDATING ACTION IN THE PRIVATE SECTOR

Concern about the effectiveness of incentives in achieving the desired result or about their cost (in tax forgiveness or outright payments) may lead government to mandate the desired action. A mandate is simply a requirement backed up by the threat of legal punishment. The government may mandate, for instance, that private firms provide health insurance to their employees.

GOVERNMENT'S OPTIONS

Taking direct action
    Production of a good or service
    Purchase of a good or service
Providing incentives to the private sector
    Direct subsidies
    Tax subsidies
Mandating private sector action

The government may mandate that automobile manufacturers produce fuel-efficient cars, specifying particular standards for miles per gallon of gas. Real estate developers who want to get a permit for a large housing project may be required to provide a certain number of units for low-income individuals, or to help improve a local road or build a loca l school. In all these cases, the government requirement does not show up as a cost on the government's budget. Mandates do have costs, however. These costs are borne indirectly by workers, firms, and consumers, and can be very high.

COMBINING OPTIONS

The government often combines two or more courses of action in its attempts to achieve some objective. Consider, for instance, the concern over medical care. The U.S. government pays for medical care for the aged and the poor; it provides actual medical care for veterans in hospitals it operates; it provides incentives for employers to offer health insurance by giving these expenditures favorable tax treatment; and there have been proposals to mandate firms to provide a minimum level of health insurance for employees. Different countries have chosen different mixes of these policies. In several countries, such as the United Kingdom, the government actually runs the entire health service; in other countries, government supplies health insurance to everyone and pays for that insurance with taxpayers' dollars.

GOVERNMENT FAILURES

Whenever there is a market failure, there is a *potential* role for government. Government needs to consider each of the alternatives discussed in the previous section, and assess the likelihood that one or the other alternative will succeed. Such an assessment may conclude that it is better not to intervene after all. Recent decades have provided numerous examples of government programs that have either not succeeded to the extent their sponsors had hoped, or have failed altogether. Urban renewal programs, meant to revive the inner cities and to provide housing for the poor, wound up destroying more low-income housing than they created. Welfare programs, intended to provide a safety net for the poor, are thought by some to have helped perpetuate the cycle of poverty. Out of the failures and limited successes of government programs has emerged a better understanding of the causes of government failure.

IMPERFECT INFORMATION

Imperfect information poses a problem in the public as well as the private sector. The government would like to make sure, for instance, that public welfare assistance goes only to those who really need it. But it is costly to sort out the truly deserving from those who are not. Spending more on screening applicants lets fewer of the undeserving through the application process. But spending more on administration leaves less to spend on benefits. As always, there are trade-offs.

INCENTIVES AND THE EFFICIENCY OF GOVERNMENT

Problems of incentives can be worse in the public than in the private sector. Homeowners, for example, have an incentive to maintain their property, not only because an attractive house is more enjoyable to live in, but also because when they sell, an attractive house will yield a higher price. Owners of a private apartment building, similarly, have incentives to maintain the building. And tenants in private apartments have an incentive not to abuse the property (they can be evicted or fail to have their lease renewed). Tenants in public housing have no such incentives. From their perspective, the quality of their apartment building is like a public good; each individual has too little incentive to maintain public amenities. Managers of public housing have no incentives comparable to private landlords, and they typically have limited discretion in evicting tenants or even in refusing to renew leases. The problem of incentives is made worse in the public sector because public officials work under a set of civil service rules about salary levels and job tenure that can make it difficult to hire first-rate workers or to reward workers for efficient performance. The rules make it difficult to pay good public officials a salary comparable to what similarly qualified and hardworking people receive in the private sector, or to offer them opportunities for rapid promotion. It is even more difficult to fire or demote incompetent and lazy workers.

Incentives in the public sector can actually lead to decisions that are not in the national interest in a broad sense. Legislators' concern about votes leads to "pork barrel" legislation, whose primary value is to create jobs or improve amenities in a legislator's home district. Presumably, most pork barrel projects would not be undertaken if those who lived in the district had to pay for it themselves, but the projects sound good if the rest of the country is footing the bill. It is widely believed, for instance, that a large number of unneeded military bases have been kept open because of congressional pressure.

Moreover, elected officials need funds to run their campaigns, and this makes them particularly attentive to those who can assist with campaign finances. The influence of the farm lobby in obtaining support, far out of proportion to the number of voters whose livelihood depends on agriculture, is frequently attributed to this sort of "special interest" lobbying. Unions and many other groups have formed Political Action Committees (PACs) to provide funds to congressional representatives who are sympathetic to their views. Naturally, lobbyists for these special interest groups claim they are not buying politicians but simply providing them with information needed to make an informed judgment—and then supporting those who have seen the truth. Some economists, including Nobel Prize winners James Buchanan and George Stigler, go so far as to see the problems of the public sector as perhaps the inevitable consequence of the political process.

WASTE IN GOVERNMENT

Whether for these or other reasons, many Americans view government as *necessarily* less efficient than private firms. These views have been supported by stories of government spending $1,000 for toilet seats and $200 for hammers, as well as some statistical studies which show systematic higher costs, associated with public housing (by as much as 20 percent) as opposed to private firms. While there are numerous instances of government inefficiency, the evidence casts doubt on the view that the public sector is inevitably less efficient than the private sector. When, for instance, government enterprises are subjected to competition—as in the case of the Canadian National Railroad (a government enterprise), which competes vigorously against the Canadian Pacific Railroad—the discipline of competition forces them to be equally efficient. The administrative costs of many private insurance companies—amounting to up to 30 percent or more of the premiums—are considerably higher than the administrative expenses of public social insurance, such as Social Security. France's state-run electricity company is reputedly as efficient as any private firm.

There are also theoretical reasons to question the conclusion that public enterprises are doomed to be less efficient. This is because *some* of the problems generating inefficiencies in the public sector plague the private sector also. Just as public sector employees typically do not receive any incentive pay (that is, pay is not linked to performance, so there are few *direct* returns to performing better), neither do most employees in the private sector. And large (with more than 500 employees) corporations—which still produce one-half of the economy's output—face bureaucratic problems no less than does government.

A consensus is thus emerging among economists that although the government is *often* less efficient than private firms performing similar tasks, it is not necessarily so. Major efforts are currently underway to increase government efficiency.

UNFORESEEN RESPONSES TO A PROGRAM

The success or failure of programs in the public sector depends not only on public officials, but also on how the private sector responds. Predicting those private responses is difficult, and many government programs have faced problems because of this difficulty. For example, providing almost free medical care to the aged, through Medicare, greatly increased the demand for medical services by the aged, leading to increases in costs well beyond those originally projected. In 1990, the government required that drug companies provide drugs to the government at the lowest price sold on the market. The government had observed that drug companies sold drugs to some customers at prices below those at which they were selling drugs to government under the Medicare program, and calculated that it could save billions of dollars by taking advantage of these discounts. But the drug companies cancelled

In 1993, President Clinton charged Vice President Al Gore with heading up a task force to identify systematically ways in which the government was doing its business inefficiently and recommend changes that would make it more efficient. This was the mandate to "reinvent government." The task force identified serious problems with procurement, how the government goes about buying goods from the private sector. For instance, when the government wants to buy a plain, ordinary T-shirt it takes more than thirty pages of fine print to describe the item in question. No wonder that a government-bought T-shirt costs more than its civilian counterpart, even if it is bought from the same dealer!

The government got itself into this mess with the best of motives. It puts up to competitive bidding most of what it purchases to ensure that it gets what it wants at the lowest price. But to get what it wants, the government must be precise in its specifications. Without such specifications for T-shirts, for example, a bidder might skimp on quality (cloth) or workmanship (stitching). Skimping might save only a dime a shirt. But if the government is in the market for a million shirts, the company that skimps stand to make an additional $100,000 in profits.

But drawing up specifications in such detail is almost certain to result in a T-shirt that is different from the standard T-shirts manufactured by the popular manufacturers—requiring a separate run, which raises the cost. Moreover, since most manufacturers simply do not find the inconvenience of filling a government contract worthwhile, the number of bidders is limited—raising the price still higher. Thus, rather than reducing prices, the competitive bidding process results in government actually paying higher prices.

The procurement reform proposed by the Gore task force to solve this general problem is simple.

It allows government to purchase off-the-shelf items through standard commercial channels, as long as the off-the-shelf prices are lower than the government can obtain through competitive bidding. Procurement reform may save the government several billion dollars a year. Other aspects of reinventing government entail efforts to get government to follow the best practices of America's most efficient companies—including a proposal to convert the nation's air traffic control system into a government-owned corporation.

Competition is enough to force the private sector constantly to "reinvent" itself, to look for better and more efficient ways of doing what it does. But it is political pressures—including the pressure of the huge government deficit—that provide the incentive to reinvent government.

all discounts, recognizing that it did not pay to discount at all if they had to give the government a discount every time they gave someone else a discount. As a result, instead of saving the government money, the legislation wound up costing other users of drugs more money!

Often a problem arises not from the overall design of a government program, but from a particular regulation. The Aid to Families with Dependent Children program (AFDC) used to have an eligibility requirement that there not be a man in the household (some states still have this requirement). The program may thus have contributed to the breakup of families. At other times, a problem occurs as an almost inevitable result of the program. Providing better Social Security benefits has enabled many elderly to live on their own, rather than being dependent on their children. These elderly, whose only or major source of income is Social Security, may (apart from the benefits of independence) be actually worse off than they were when they were living with their children. The true beneficiaries of increased Social Security may be not the elderly but their children, who have been relieved of a burden they otherwise would have assumed.

SOURCES OF PUBLIC FAILURES

Imperfect information

Problems of incentives, particularly for those charged with administering government programs, sometimes leading to waste

Failure to assess the full consequences of government programs, including responses of the private sector

AN APPRAISAL OF THE ROLE OF GOVERNMENT

The appropriate role of government is one of the most highly contested political issues. Consider the case of government's role in income redistribution. There are disagreements in assessing the trade-offs, such as the magnitude of the negative incentive effects arising from taxes upon the well-off to finance programs for the poor. And even if there were agreement about the magnitude of the incentive effects, there may be disagreements about whether the costs—in terms of reduced efficiency and reduced welfare of those who are hurt by higher taxes—are worth the gains—in terms of the benefits to the poor who are helped. Also, there are disagreements about basic values, such as whether the higher income of the well-off is their "just reward" for greater effort. Nonetheless, while there is disagreement about what role the government ought to play in the economy, there is general consensus among economists over the important role the government currently does play. This is our sixth consensus point:

6 The Role of Government

Government plays an important role in modern economies: it redresses market failures, redistributes income, and provides social insurance against risks such as unemployment, health care costs, disability, and retirement. Although the design and scope of government activity are often debated, there is broad agreement about the importance of the role of government in the economy.

REVIEW AND PRACTICE

SUMMARY

1. Government plays a pervasive role in the economy of almost every industrialized country. U.S. government expenditures are approximately one-third of national output—a much larger proportion than forty years ago, but a smaller proportion than in most countries of Western Europe. The major reason for the increase has been increased expenditures on Social Security/welfare, health programs, and interest payments.

2. In a democracy, the public sector differs from the private in two main ways. Its legitimacy and authority are derived from the electoral process; it also has certain powers of compulsion, such as requiring households and firms to pay taxes and obey laws.

3. By and large, private markets allocate resources efficiently. But in a number of areas they do not, as is the case with externalities and public

goods. Moreover, the economy sometimes fails to use the available resources fully; there may be idle industrial capacity and unemployed workers. Even when the economy is efficient, there may be dissatisfaction with the distribution of income.

4. Individuals and firms produce too much of a good with a negative externality, such as air or water pollution, since they do not bear all the costs. They produce too little of a good with a positive externality, such as a new invention, since they cannot receive all the benefits.

5. Public goods are goods that it costs little or nothing for an additional individual to enjoy, but that it costs a great deal to exclude any individual from enjoying. National defense and lighthouses are two examples. Free markets underproduce public goods.

6. Government has a variety of instruments it can use when markets are not functioning efficiently. It can take direct action, provide incentives to the private sector, or mandate action by the private sector.

7. While market failures provide a potential rationale for government action, government action may not provide an effective remedy. There are systematic reasons for "government failure" just as there are for "market failure."

8. The proper balance between the public and private sectors is a major concern of economics.

KEY TERMS

nationalization	market failures	missing markets
deregulation	externalities	principle of
privatization	public goods	consumer
"invisible hand"	free-rider problem	sovereignty

REVIEW QUESTIONS

1. Name some of the ways government touches the lives of all citizens, both in and out of the economic sphere.

2. "Since democratic governments are elected by the consent of a majority of the people, they have no need for compulsion." Comment.

3. How can individual selfishness end up promoting social welfare?

4. Name areas in which market failure can occur.

5. Why do goods with negative externalities tend to be overproduced? Why do goods with positive externalities tend to be underproduced? Give an example for each.

6. What two characteristics define a public good? Give an example.

7. What three broad types of instruments does government have to try to achieve its goals?

8. Does the presence of a market failure necessarily mean that government action is desirable? If not, why not?

PROBLEMS

1. In each of the following areas, specify how the government is involved, either as a direct producer, a regulator, a purchaser of final goods and services distributed directly to individuals or used within government, or in some other role:
   (a) education
   (b) mail delivery
   (c) housing
   (d) air travel
   (e) national defense.
In each of these cases, can you think of ways that part of the public role could be provided by the private sector?

2. Can you explain why even a benevolent and well-meaning government may sometimes have to use the power of eminent domain? (Hint: Consider the incentives of one person who knows that her property is the last obstacle to building a highway.)

3. Explain why government redistribution programs involve a trade-off between risk and incentives for *both* rich and poor.

4. Each of the situations below involves an externality. Tell whether it is a positive or negative externality, or both, and explain why free markets will overproduce or underproduce the good in question:
   (a) a business performing research and development projects
   (b) a business that discharges waste into a nearby river
   (c) a concert given in the middle of a large city park
   (d) an individual who smokes cigarettes in a meeting held in a small, unventilated room.

5. When some activity causes a negative externality like pollution, would it be a good idea to ban the activity altogether? Why or why not? (Hint: Consider marginal costs and benefits.)

6. Highways are often referred to as public goods. That designation is basically fair, but not perfect. What are the costs of "exclusion"? Can you describe a case where the marginal cost of an additional driver on a highway might be relatively high? How might society deal with this problem?

PART TWO

PERFECT MARKETS

art Two explores in depth the basic microeconomic assumptions of rational, well-informed consumers interacting with profit-maximizing firms in competitive markets. This set of assumptions, as we learned in Chapter 2, constitutes the economist's basic model. Here, we study the implications of this model and examine the powerful insights it affords. It turns out that while this basic model is a good starting point, consumers are often not as well-informed, and markets are often not as competitive, as the model assumes them to be. Part Three expands on and enriches the basic model in ways that make it more realistic.

The economy consists of three groups of participants—individuals or households, firms, and government—interacting in three markets, the labor, capital, and product markets. Part Two follows those divisions, with one important exception: the discussion of government is postponed to Part Three. The object in Part Two is to understand how a purely private market economy might operate. Chapters 8–10 discuss how individuals and households make their choices of what goods to consume, how much to save, how to invest their savings, and how much labor to supply. Chapters 11 and 12 analyze how firms make their decisions concerning how much to produce and how to produce it.

Finally, Chapter 13 brings households and firms together in the three markets. Households supply labor, and firms demand labor. The interaction of this supply and demand for labor determines wages. Similarly, households supply capital and firms demand capital to build factories and buy new machines. Their interaction in the capital market determines the interest rate and the equilibrium level of savings and investment in the economy. Households take their income, both what they earn as workers and the return on their savings, and use it to buy goods. They demand goods. With the workers they have hired, machines they have purchased, and factories they have built, firms produce goods. Firms' supply of goods and households' demand for goods interact in the product market, and this interaction determines the prices of the myriad of goods we consume.

CHAPTER 8

THE CONSUMPTION DECISION

More than 100 million U.S. households taken together make an astounding number of spending choices every day. These decisions contribute to the overall demand for cars and bicycles, clothes and housing, and masses of other products available on the market. The members of each household also make decisions that affect how much income they will have to spend, like whether to work overtime or whether both partners in a marriage should work. They decide how much of their income to save. And they decide where to put the nest eggs they do save.

These four sets of decisions—about spending, working, saving, and investing—represent the basic economic choices facing the household. This chapter focuses on spending decisions and how these decisions are affected by taxes and other government policies. Chapter 9 discusses working and saving decisions. Chapter 10 deals with household decisions concerning how to invest savings.

These microeconomic decisions have macroeconomic consequences as well. Household decisions about whether to buy a car that is imported from Japan or one that is American-made will affect the U.S. trade deficit. Choices about how much one should work will affect overall levels of unemployment and production. Household decisions about savings and investment will affect the future growth of the economy.

THE BASIC PROBLEM OF CONSUMER CHOICE

The first basic problem facing a consumer is easy to state, though hard to resolve: what should he do with whatever (after tax) income he has to spend. He must allocate (that is, divide) his available income among alternative goods. Should he buy CDs, go to the movies, eat candy bars, or purchase sweaters? In the absence of scarcity the answer would be easy: have it all!

Chapter 2 provided the basic framework for economic decision making. The consumer defines his opportunity set, what is *possible* given the constraints he faces, and then chooses the most preferred point within this set. This chapter begins by reviewing how we define the opportunity set, and then asks how it changes—and how what the individual chooses changes—when incomes and prices change.

THE BUDGET CONSTRAINT

The individual's opportunity set is defined by the budget constraint. If, after taxes, a person's weekly paycheck comes to $300 and he has no other income, this is his budget constraint. Total expenditures on food, clothing, rent, entertainment, travel, and all other categories cannot exceed $300 per week. (For now we ignore the possibilities that individuals may borrow money, or save money, or change their budget constraints by working longer or shorter hours.)

The line BC in Figure 8.1A shows a simplified individual budget constraint. A student, Fran, has a total of $300 each semester to spend on "fun" items. Figure 8.1 assumes that there are two goods, candy bars and compact discs. The simplified assumption of only two goods is an abstraction that highlights the main points of the analysis.

Let's say that a candy bar costs $1, while a compact disc costs $15. If Fran spent all her income on candy bars, she could purchase 300 candy bars (point B on the budget constraint). If she spent all her income on CDs, she could buy

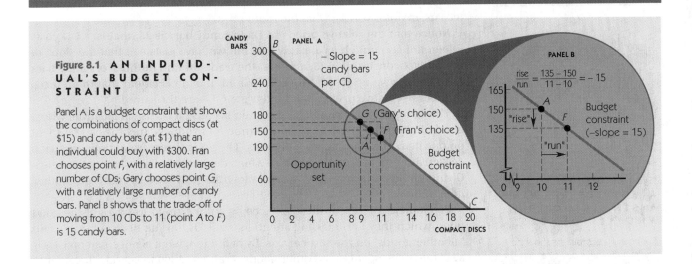

Figure 8.1 AN INDIVID-UAL'S BUDGET CON-STRAINT

Panel A is a budget constraint that shows the combinations of compact discs (at $15) and candy bars (at $1) that an individual could buy with $300. Fran chooses point F, with a relatively large number of CDs; Gary chooses point G, with a relatively large number of candy bars. Panel B shows that the trade-off of moving from 10 CDs to 11 (point A to F) is 15 candy bars.

20 CDs (point C on the budget constraint). Fran can also choose any of the intermediate choices on line BC. For example, she could buy 10 CDs (for $150) and 150 candy bars (for $150), or 15 CDs ($225) and 75 candy bars ($75). Each combination of purchases along the budget constraint totals $300.

As we learned in Chapter 2, a budget constraint diagram has two important features. First, although any point in the shaded area of Figure 8.1A is feasible, only the points on the line BC are really relevant. This is because Fran is not consuming her entire budget if she is inside her budget constraint. Second, by looking along the budget constraint, we can see the trade-offs she faces—how many candy bars she has to give up to get 1 more CD, and vice versa. Look at points F and A. This part of the budget constraint is blown up in panel B. At point A, Fran has 10 CDs; at F, she has 11. At F, she has 135 candy bars; at A, 150. To get 1 more CD, she has to give up 15 candy bars.

These are her trade-offs, and they are determined by the relative prices of the two goods. If one good costs twice as much as another, to get 1 more unit of the costly good, we have to give up 2 units of the cheaper good. If, as here, one good costs fifteen times as much as another, to get 1 more unit of the costly good, we have to give up 15 units of the less costly good.

The **slope** of the budget constraint also tells us what the trade-off is. The slope of a line measures how steep it is. As we move 1 unit along the horizontal axis (from 10 to 11 CDs), the slope measures the size of the change along the vertical axis. The slope is the rise (the movement up or down on the vertical axis) divided by the run (the corresponding horizontal movement). The slope of this budget constraint is thus 15.[1] It tells us how much of one good, at

[1]We ignore the negative sign. See the appendix to Chapter 2 for a more detailed explanation of the slope of a line.

Figure 8.2 ALLOCATING A BUDGET BETWEEN A SINGLE GOOD AND ALL OTHERS

Some budget constraints show the choice between a particular good, in this case CDs, and all other goods. The other goods that might be purchased are collectively measured in money terms, as shown on the vertical axis.

a given price, we need to give up if we want 1 more unit of the other good; it tells us, in other words, what the trade-off is.

Notice that the relative price of CDs to candy bars is 15; that is, a CD costs fifteen times as much as a candy bar. But we have just seen that the slope of the budget constraint is 15, and that the trade-off (the number of candy bars Fran has to give up to get 1 more CD) is 15. It is no accident that these three numbers—relative price, slope, and trade-off—are the same.

This two-product example was chosen because it is easy to illustrate with a graph. But this logic can cover any number of products. Income can be spent on one item or a combination of items. The budget constraint defines what a certain amount of income can buy, which depends on the prices of the items. Giving up some of one item would allow the purchase of more of another item or items.

Economists represent these choices by putting the purchases of the good upon which they are focusing attention, say CDs, on the horizontal axis and "all other goods" on the vertical axis. By definition, what is not spent on CDs is available to be spent on all other goods. Fran has $300 to spend altogether. A more realistic budget constraint for her is shown in Figure 8.2. The intersection of the budget constraint with the vertical axis, point *B*—where purchases of CDs are zero—is $300. If Fran spends nothing on CDs, she has $300 to spend on other goods. The budget constraint intersects the horizontal axis at 20 CDs (point *C*); if she spends all her income on CDs and CDs cost $15 each, she can buy 20. If Fran chooses a point such as *F*, she will buy 11 CDs, costing $165, and she will have $135 to spend on other goods ($300–$165). The distance 0*D* on the vertical axis measures what she spends on other goods; the distance *BD* measures what she spends on CDs.

CHOOSING A POINT ON THE BUDGET CONSTRAINT: INDIVIDUAL PREFERENCES

The budget constraint and a recognition of possible trade-offs is the starting point for the study of consumer behavior. The process of identifying the budget constraints and the trade-offs is the same for *any* two people. If a person walks into a store (that only accepts cash) with $300, any economist can tell you his budget constraint and the trade-offs he faces by looking at the money in his pocket and the prices on the shelves. What choice will he make? Economists narrow their predictions to points on his budget constraint; any individual will choose *some* point along the budget constraint. But the point actually chosen depends on the individual's preferences: Fran, who likes to listen to music, might choose point *F* in Figure 8.1, while Gary, who loves candy, might choose *G*.

Few people will choose either of the extreme points on the budget constraint, *B* or *C* in Figure 8.1, where only one of the goods is consumed. The reason for this is that the more you have of a good—say, the more CDs you have relative to another good such as candy—the less valuable is an additional unit of that good relative to additional units of another good. At points near *C*, it seems safe to assume that to most individuals, an extra CD does not look as attractive as some candy bars. Certainly, at B, most people would be so full of candy bars that an extra CD would look preferable.

Where the individual's choice lies depends on how she values the two goods. Chapter 2 emphasized the idea that in making decisions, people look at the *margin;* they look at the extra costs and benefits. In this case, the choice at each point along the budget constraint is between 1 more CD and 15 more candy bars. If Gary and Fran choose different points along the budget constraint, it is because they value the marginal benefits (how much better off they feel with an *extra* CD) and the marginal costs (how much it hurts to give up 15 candy bars) differently. Gary chooses point G in Figure 8.1 because that is the point where, for him, the marginal benefit of an extra CD is just offset by what he has to give up to get the extra CD, which is 15 candy bars. When Fran, who loves listening to music, considers point G, she realizes that for her, at that point, CDs are more important and candy bars less important than they are for Gary. So she trades along the line until she has enough CDs and few enough candy bars that, for her, the marginal benefits of an extra CD and the marginal costs of 15 fewer candy bars are equal. This point, as we have supposed, is F.

The same reasoning holds for a budget constraint like the one shown in Figure 8.2. Here, Gary and Fran are choosing between CDs and all other goods, measured in dollar terms. Now in deciding to buy an extra CD, each one compares the marginal benefit of an extra CD with the marginal cost, what has to be given in other goods. With CDs priced at $15, choosing to buy a CD means giving up $15 of other goods. For Gary, the marginal benefit of an extra CD equals the cost, $15, when he has only 9 CDs and can therefore spend $165 on other goods. For Fran, who has more of a taste for CDs, the marginal benefit of an extra CD does not equal this marginal cost until she reaches 11 CDs, with $135 to spend elsewhere. Thus, the price is a quantitative measure of the marginal benefit.

WHAT HAPPENS TO CONSUMPTION WHEN INCOME CHANGES?

When an individual's income increases, he has more to spend on consumption. Normally, he will buy a little more of many goods, although his consumption of some goods will increase more than that of others, and different individuals will spend their extra income in different ways. Jim may spend much of his extra income going out to eat in restaurants more often, while Bill may spend much of his extra income buying a more expensive car.

The **income elasticity of demand** (which parallels the *price* elasticity of demand presented in Chapter 5) measures how much the consumption of a particular good increases with income:

$$\text{income elasticity of demand} = \frac{\text{percentage change in consumption}}{\text{percentage change in income}}.$$

The income elasticity of demand, in other words, is the percentage change in consumption that would result from a one percent increase in income. If the income elasticity of demand of a certain good is greater than one, a 1 percent increase in an individual's income results in a more than 1 percent increase in expenditures on that good. That is, the amount he spends on that good increases more than proportionately with income. By definition, if the income elasticity of demand is less than one, then a 1 percent increase in income results in a less than 1 percent increase in expenditures. In this case, the share of income a consumer spends on that good decreases with a rise in income.

As people's incomes increase, the types of goods they choose to buy also change. In particular, they have more money to spend on goods other than those required just to survive. For instance, while they may spend some of the extra income to buy better-quality food and other necessities, more money goes toward movies, more expensive automobiles, vacations, and other luxuries. Accordingly, poor individuals spend a larger percentage of their income on food and housing and a smaller percentage of their income on perfume. In other words, the income elasticity of necessities is less than one, and the income elasticity of luxuries is greater than one.

The consumption of some goods actually decreases as income increases and increases as income decreases. These goods are called **inferior** goods. They are in sharp contrast to **normal** goods, the consumption of which increases with income. In other words, goods for which the income elasticity is *negative* are, by definition, inferior, while all other goods are called normal. For instance, if Fran, who has been riding the bus to work, gets a large raise, she may find that she can afford a car. After buying the car, she will spend less on bus tokens. Thus, in this particular sense, bus rides represent an inferior good.

Figure 8.3 shows how typical families at different income levels spend their income. In the figure, we see that *on average*, the poorest 20 percent of the population spend more than 100 percent of their before-tax income on housing—more than 100 percent is only possible because of government subsidies. This contrasts with the richest 20 percent, who spend only a fifth of their income on housing. Similarly, the poorest 20 percent spend nearly half their before-tax income on food, while the richest 20 percent spend less than a tenth.

Table 8.1 provides the income elasticities of some consumer goods. Chapters 4 and 5 pointed out that consumers and firms could make greater adjustments the longer the time they had to make changes. Thus, long-run price elasticities are normally larger—often much larger—than short-run price elasticities. The same is true for responses to changes in income. Long-run income elasticities are larger—often much larger—than short-run income elasticities. The data provided in the table are long-run elasticities. An example of the difference between long-run and short-run elasticity is provided by gasoline and oil; their long-run elasticity is 1.36; their short-run elasticity is only .55.

Note that the income elasticity of water is .59. It may seem surprising that water has any elasticity at all—don't poor people have to drink water just as much as rich people do to survive? The fact that there is a systematic relation-

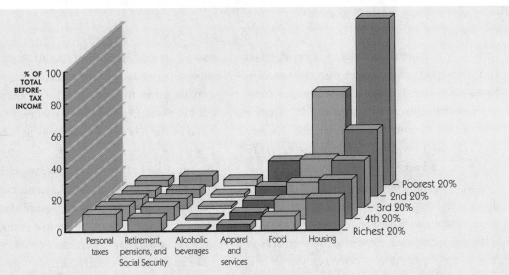

Figure 8.3 HOW HOUSEHOLDS OF DIFFERENT INCOMES SPEND THEIR MONEY

The poor spend far higher proportions of their income on basic necessities like food and housing than do the rich. *Note:* Before-tax income does not include borrowing or benefits received from government programs, which explains expenditures greater than 100 percent. *Source: Consumer Expenditure Survey Data,* 1984–87, Bulletin 2333.

Table 8.1 SOME INCOME ELASTICITIES OF DEMAND

Elastic (long-run)		Inelastic (long-run)	
Motion pictures	3.41	Car repairs	.90
Drugs and medicines	3.04	Tobacco products	.86
Owner-occupied housing	2.45	China, glassware, and utensils	.77
Nondurable toys	2.01	Shoe repairs	.72
Electricity	1.94	Alcoholic beverages	.62
Restaurant meals	1.61	Water	.59
Local buses and trains	1.38	Furniture	.53
Gasoline and oil	1.36	Clothing	.51
Car insurance	1.26		
Physicians' services	1.15		
Car purchases	1.07		

Source: H. S. Houthakker and Lester D. Taylor, *Consumer Demand in the United States* (Cambridge, Mass.: Harvard University Press, 1970).

POLICY PERSPECTIVE: THE FATE OF THE BTU TAX

Some of the differences in choices along a budget constraint reflect nothing more than differences in tastes—Fran likes CDs more than Gary. But some differences in choices are systematic, for instance representing differences in circumstances. Eleanor lives in New England and spends more on oil to heat her apartment than does Jim, who lives in Florida; Amy, who lives in Montana, 200 miles from the nearest town, buys more gas and spends more on cars than does someone from New York City.

Understanding such systematic determinants in how people spend their money helps us understand the markedly different responses in different regions of the country to government proposals to tax different goods. A case in point arose in 1993, after the Clinton administration took office with a pledge to reduce the huge federal deficit. Many policy analysts, both inside and outside government, favored a tax on energy. Most energy sources are relatively cheap in the United States compared to many other industrialized countries. Low energy prices lead Americans to consume high quantities of energy, thus increasing urban congestion, air pollution, and greenhouse gas emissions. A tax on energy would provide incentives to conserve energy—making such a tax an environmentally sound way of raising revenue and cutting the deficit.

The administration proposed a BTU tax—named after the British Thermal Unit, a standard measure of energy. The intent was to levy the tax on the basis of energy used, treating all energy sources alike. The tax proposal generated immediate opposition from heavy energy users. Americans living in the Northeast, who needed to heat their homes for much of the year, claimed that the tax would hit them unfairly. The aluminum industry, a heavy user of energy, strongly opposed it along with other energy-intensive industries.

In an effort to make the tax more politically palatable—and increase the chance of passage through the Congress—policymakers whittled it down to a single-form-of-energy tax—on gasoline. The proposal turned into an increase in the gasoline tax from 14.1 cents to 20.6 cents per gallon. Americans in the West, who drive much longer distances in a typical day than people in other parts of the country, were up in arms. Politics dictated a reduction in the proposed gas tax. Congress finally passed, and the President signed, a mere 4.3 cents per gallon increase in the tax on gasoline, which raises about $24 billion from 1993 to 1998, or less than $5 billion a year more in federal revenue than before the gas tax increase. This tax rate is too low to have a major effect on driving, let alone on energy use as a whole, and the extra revenues will have a similarly small effect on the federal deficit.

ship between income and water consumption simply emphasizes the point that, with effort, you can economize on almost any resource. At lower income levels, you may wash your car less often, water your lawn less often, and so on.

Information like that contained in Figure 8.3 is of great practical importance. For example, it helps determine how a tax will affect different groups. Anybody who consumes alcohol will be hurt by a tax on alcohol. But if the poor spend a larger fraction of their income on alcohol, as the figure suggests, they will bear a disproportionately large share of the tax.

A CLOSER LOOK AT THE DEMAND CURVE

In Chapter 4, we saw the principal characteristic of the demand curve: when prices rise, the quantity of a good demanded normally falls. Here, we take a closer look at why. This will help us understand why some goods respond more strongly to price changes, that is, have a greater price elasticity.

Let us return to our earlier example of Fran buying CDs in Figure 8.2. If the price of CDs rises from $15 to $20, Fran will face a new budget constraint. If she didn't buy any CDs, she would still have $300 to spend on other goods; but if she decided to spend all of her income on CDs, she could only buy 15 rather than 20. Her budget constraint is now the blue line in Figure 8.4.

The increase in the price of CDs has one obvious and important effect: Fran cannot continue to buy the same number of CDs and the same amount of other goods as she did before. Earlier, Fran bought 11 CDs. If she bought the same number of CDs, it would cost her $55 more, and she would have $55 less to spend on other goods. No matter what she does, Fran is worse off as a result of the price increase. It is *as if* she had less income to spend. When she has less income to spend, she reduces her expenditure on each good, including CDs. This part of the response to the higher price is called the **income effect.** An increase in income of about $55, or 18 percent ($55 out of $300), would offset the price increase.[2] Assume the income elasticity is approximately 1; that is, with income reduced by 18 percent, she would reduce purchases of CDs by 18 percent, which is about 2 CDs. This part of the reduction of the demand of CDs, from 11 to 9, is the income effect.

The magnitude of the income effect depends on two factors: how important the commodity is to the individual—that is, how large a fraction of the individual's income is spent on the good—and how large the income elasticity is. Since, in most cases, individuals spend a relatively small fraction of their income on any particular good, the income effect is relatively small. But in the case of housing, for example, on which individuals spend between a quarter

Figure 8.4 EFFECT OF PRICE INCREASE

An increase in the price of CDs moves the budget constraint down as shown. Fran must cut back on the consumption of some goods. Here, we show her cutting back both on the consumption of CDs and other goods.

---

[2]Actually, it would slightly overcompensate. With the $55 increase, Fran could buy exactly the same bundle of goods as before, but as we shall shortly see, she will *choose* to reallocate her spending. The reallocation will make her better off.

In recent years, the government has contemplated a variety of "sin" taxes—taxes on smoking and drinking—as well as environmental taxes—taxes on gasoline—as a way of raising revenue. To calculate the revenue raised from any tax, the government must estimate the elasticity of demand. If the elasticity of demand is high, then a tax which raises the price will reduce quantity consumed, and hence the revenue raised will be greatly reduced. Even if the elasticity is not high, if huge taxes are imposed—such as has been proposed for cigarettes—the reduction in consumption may be large.

For instance, the price elasticity of demand for cigarettes is estimated to be 0.3. In 1994, the tax stood at 24 cents, or 12 percent of the price. There have been proposals to raise the tax to 69 cents, 99 cents, or $2.00, raising the price (assuming that the tax is passed on to consumers) by 22.5, 37.5, or 88 percent. If the trend towards less smoking and other sources of price increases is ignored, the tax would thus reduce consumption by 6.8, 11.3, or 26.4 percent, and the estimated revenues would be far less than if there were no demand response. For instance, if the tax were quadrupled to 99 cents, rather than quadrupling tax revenue (as would be the case if demand remained unchanged), revenue would be increased only by a factor of 2.5.

and a third of their income on average, the income effect of an increase in the price of housing is significant.

Let us go back to Fran and the CDs. At the higher price, giving up one CD gets her more of other goods—more candy bars, more movies, more tapes, more sweaters. The relative price of CDs, or the trade-off between CDs and other goods has changed. At the higher price, she *substitutes* goods that are less expensive for the more expensive CDs. Not surprisingly, this effect is called the **substitution effect.** The magnitude of the substitution effect depends on how easily Fran can substitute other goods. If Fran still owns her tape player, and if the price of tapes remains unchanged, then the substitution effect might be large. She may drop the number of CDs she purchases to 2. But if Fran has no tape player, if the only entertainment she likes is listening to music, and if she dislikes all the music played by the local radio stations, then the substitution effect may be small. She may drop the number of CDs she purchases only to 8.

DERIVING DEMAND CURVES

We can now see both how to derive the demand curve and why it has the shape it does. At each price, we draw the budget constraint and identify the point along the budget constraint that is chosen. As the price of CDs increases, Fran will choose points along the successive budget constraints with fewer CDs purchased: higher prices mean she is less well off, and therefore, through the income effect, decrease her purchases of all goods. The higher price *relative to other goods* means she will substitute other goods for CDs.

THE IMPORTANCE OF DISTINGUISHING BETWEEN INCOME AND SUBSTITUTION EFFECTS

Distinguishing between the income and substitution effects of a change in price is important for two reasons.

Understanding Responses to Price Changes   First, the distinction improves our understanding of consumption responses to price changes. Thinking about the substitution effect helps us understand why some demand curves have a low price elasticity and others a high price elasticity. It also helps us understand why the price elasticity may well differ at different points along the demand curve. Recall from Chapter 5 that when an individual is consuming lots of some good, substitutes for the good are easy to find, and a small increase in price leads to a large reduction in the quantity demanded; but as consumption gets lower, it becomes increasingly difficult to find good substitutes.

Or consider the effect of an increase in the price of one good on the demand for *other* goods. There is always an income effect; the income effect, by itself, would lead to a reduced consumption of all commodities. But the substitution effect leads to *increased* consumption of substitute commodities. Thus, an increase in the price of Coke will lead to increased demand for Pepsi at each price; the demand curve for Pepsi shifts to the right, because the substitution effect outweighs the slight income effect.

Understanding Inefficiencies Associated with Taxes   A second reason to focus on income and substitution effects is to identify some of the inefficiencies associated with taxation. The purpose of a tax is to raise revenue so that the government can purchase goods; it represents a transfer of purchasing power from the household to the government. If the government is to obtain more resources, individuals have to consume less. Thus, any tax must have an income effect.

But beyond that, taxes often distort economic activity. The distortion caused by taxation is associated with the substitution effect. Take the window tax imposed in medieval England. It was intended to raise revenue. It led, instead, to the construction of windowless houses—a major distortion of the tax. Most of the distortions associated with modern taxes are somewhat more subtle. Take a tax on airline tickets or on telephone calls. Reducing consumption of things that are against society's interest can be a legitimate goal of taxation. But the government does not think flying or making telephone calls is a bad thing. The tax is levied to raise revenues. But it results in fewer air flights and telephone calls anyway—an unintentional consequence. Any tax leads to *some* reduction in consumption, through the income effect. But most taxes also

USING ECONOMICS: INCOME AND SUBSTITUTION EFFECTS

After the huge increase in oil prices in the late 1970s, President Carter wanted to conserve energy by discouraging the use of oil. One plan entailed the government raising the price of gasoline by imposing a tax, but then refunding the tax to consumers by reducing their income taxes. Some commentators ridiculed this idea. What's the point of collecting a tax and then refunding it? The answer is simple: the substitution effect.

Imagine that before this plan, Lucy has an income of $20,000. She spends $500 a year (2.5 percent of her income) on gasoline; at a price of $1.00 a gallon, she can buy 500 gallons of gasoline. Assume first that the tax on a gallon of gasoline is raised by $.20, increasing the price Lucy pays to $1.20 a gallon. If the price elasticity of demand for gasoline is .5, then this price increase will lead to a fall in quantity demanded of 10 percent

(20 percent × .5 = 10 percent). Now Lucy is buying 450 gallons (90 percent of 500) at a price of $1.20 a gallon—and spending a total of $540. Government revenue is $.20 × 450 = $90. Assume that the government refunds Lucy the $90. (The refund depends not on the actual amount of the gasoline tax paid by Lucy but on the average amount paid by all taxpayers. In this example, Lucy is an average person, so her refund is just equal to the gasoline tax she paid.) Is the government undoing the effect of the higher gasoline prices by giving consumers income? Not entirely. If Lucy continues to spend about 2.5 percent of her additional income on gasoline, her expenditure on gasoline goes up by just over $2 (2.5 percent × $90 refund). Her consumption of gasoline is still lower than it would have been without the tax combined with the rebate.

change relative prices; so they have a substitution effect. It is the substitution effect that gives rise to the distortion. If the substitution effect is small, the distortion is small; if the substitution effect is large, the distortion is large.

UTILITY AND THE DESCRIPTION OF PREFERENCES

We have seen that people choose a point along their budget constraint by weighing the benefits of consuming more of one good against the costs—what they have to forgo of other goods. Economists refer to the benefits of consumption as the **utility** that individuals get from the combination of goods they consume. Presumably a person can tell you whether or not he prefers a certain combination of goods to another. Economists say that the preferred bundle of goods gives that individual a higher level of utility than the other bundle of goods he could have chosen. Similarly, economists say that the individual will choose the bundle of goods—within the budget constraint—that maximizes his utility.

In the nineteenth century, social scientists, including the British philosopher Jeremy Bentham, hoped that science would someday develop a machine that could actually measure utility. A scientist could simply hook up some electrodes to an individual's head and read off how "happy" she was. Most modern economists believe that there is no *unique* way to measure utility, but that there are useful ways of measuring changes in how well-off a person is.

For our purposes, a simple way to measure utility will suffice: we ask how much an individual would be willing to pay to be in one situation rather than another. For example, if Joe likes chocolate ice cream more than vanilla, it stands to reason that he would be willing to pay more for a scoop of chocolate ice cream than for a scoop of vanilla. Or if Diane would rather live in California than in New Jersey, it stands to reason that she would be willing to pay more for the West Coast location.

Notice that how much a person is willing to pay is different from how much he *has* to pay. Just because Joe is willing to pay more for chocolate ice cream than for vanilla does not mean he will have to pay more. What he has to pay depends on market prices; what he is willing to pay reflects his preferences. Willingness to pay is a useful measure of utility, which is often helpful for purposes such as thinking about how an individual allocates his income along his budget constraint. But the hopes of nineteenth-century economists, that we could find some way of measuring utility that would allow us to compare how much utility Fran got from a bundle of goods with how much utility Gary obtained, are now viewed as pipe dreams.

Using willingness to pay as our measure of utility, we can construct a diagram like Figure 8.5A, which shows the level of utility Mary receives from sweatshirts as the number of sweatshirts she buys increases. This information is also given in Table 8.2. Here we assume that Mary is willing to pay $200 for 5 sweatshirts, $228 for 6 sweatshirts, $254 for 7 sweatshirts, and so on. Thus, 5 sweatshirts give her a utility of 200, 6 a utility of 228, and 7 sweatshirts a utility of 254. Mary's willingness to pay increases with the number of sweatshirts, reflecting the fact that additional sweatshirts give her additional utility. The extra utility of an additional sweatshirt, measured here by the additional amount she is willing to pay, is the **marginal utility.** The numbers in the third column of Table 8.2 give the marginal (or extra) utility she received from her last sweatshirt. When Mary owns 5 sweatshirts, an additional sweatshirt yields her an additional or marginal utility of 28 (228 − 200); when she owns 6 sweatshirts, an additional one gives her a marginal utility of only 26 (254 − 228). Panel B traces the marginal utilities of each of these increments.[3]

As an individual's bundle of goods includes more and more of a good, each successive increment increases her utility less. This is the law of **diminishing**

Figure 8.5 UTILITY AND MARGINAL UTILITY

Panel A shows that utility increases continually with consumption, but tends to level off as consumption climbs higher. Panel B explicitly shows marginal utility; notice that it declines as consumption increases.

---

[3]Since marginal utility is the extra utility from an extra unit of consumption, it is measured by the slope of the utility curve in panel A.

Table 8.2 **UTILITY AND MARGINAL UTILITY**

Number of sweatshirts	Mary's willingness to pay (utility)	Marginal utility	Number of pizzas	Mary's willingness to pay (utility)	Marginal utility
0	0		0	0	
		50			18
1	50		1	18	
		45			16
2	95		2	34	
		40			15
3	135		3	49	
		35			14
4	170		4	63	
		30			13
5	200		5	76	
		28			12
6	228		6	88	
		26			11
7	254		7	99	
		24			10
8	278		8	109	
		23			9
9	301		9	118	
		22			8
10	323		10	126	
		21			7
11	344		11	133	
		20			6
12	364		12	139	
		19			5
13	383		13	144	
		18			4
14	401		14	148	
		17			
15	418				
		16			
16	434				
		15			
17	449				
		14			
18	463				
		13			
19	476				
		12			
20	488				

marginal utility. The first sweatshirt is very desirable, and additional ones are attractive as well. But each sweatshirt does not increase utility by as much as the one before, and at some point, Mary may get almost no additional pleasure from adding to her sweatshirt wardrobe.

When Mary has a given budget and must choose between two goods that cost the same, say sweatshirts and pizza, each of which costs $15, she will make her choice so that the marginal utility of each good is the same. Table 8.2 shows Mary's willingness to pay (utility) for both sweatshirts and pizza. Look at what happens if Mary buys 20 sweatshirts with her $300 and no pizza. The marginal utility of the last sweatshirt is 12, and that of the first pizza is 18. If she switches $15 from sweatshirts to pizza, she loses a utility of 12 from the decreased sweatshirts, but gains 18 from her first pizza. It obviously pays for her to switch.

Now look at the situation when she has decreased her purchases of sweatshirts to 17 and increased purchases of pizza to 3. The marginal utility of the last sweatshirt is 15, and that of the last pizza is also 15. At this point, she will not want to switch anymore. If she buys another sweatshirt, she gains 14, but the *last* pizza, her 3rd, which she will have to give up, has a marginal utility of 15; she loses more than she gains. If she buys another pizza, she gains 14, but the last sweatshirt (her 17th) gave her 15; again, she loses in net. We can thus see that with her budget, she is best off when the marginal utility of the two goods is the same.

The same general principle applies when the prices of two goods differ. Assume that a sweatshirt costs twice as much as a pizza. So long as the marginal utility of sweatshirts is more than twice that of pizzas, it still pays for Mary to switch to sweatshirts. To get one more sweatshirt, she has to give up two pizzas, and we reason, as before, that she will adjust her consumption until she gets to the point where the marginal utilities of the two goods, *per dollar spent,* are equal. This is a general rule: in choosing between two goods, a consumer will adjust her choices to the point where the marginal utilities are proportional to the prices. Thus, the last unit purchased of a good that costs twice as much as another must generate twice the marginal utility as the last unit purchased of the other good; the last unit purchased of a good that costs three times as much must generate three times the marginal utility as the last unit purchased of the other good; and so on.

We can write this result simply as

$$\frac{MU_x}{p_x} = \frac{MU_y}{p_y}$$

where MU_x is the marginal utility of good x, MU_y is the marginal utility of good y, p_x is the price of good x, and p_y is the price of good y. The ratio of the marginal utility to price should be the same for all goods.

In the example we have just analyzed, we assumed Mary's willingness to pay for sweatshirts—her measure of utility—does not depend on how many pizzas, or other goods, she has. This is seldom the case. The utility, and hence marginal utility, of sweatshirts will depend on the number of pizzas, books, and other goods she has. Thus, even when the price of sweatshirts remains the same, if the price of other goods changes, she will change her consumption of those other goods *and* sweatshirts. The same thing will happen if Mary's income changes.

CONSUMER SURPLUS

Assume you go into a store to buy a can of soda. The store charges you 50 cents. You would have been willing to pay $1.00. The difference between what you paid and what you would have been willing to pay is called **consumer surplus.**

We can calculate the consumer surplus Mary gets from buying pizza from her demand curve. To see how we do this, use the marginal utility analysis of the previous section. We saw that at 11 pizzas, Mary is willing to pay $6 for one more; at 12, she is willing to pay $5.

Mary buys pizza up to the point where the price is equal to the marginal utility of the last pizza she chooses to buy. Of course, she pays the same price for each of the pizzas she purchases. Suppose pizzas cost $5 and Mary buys 13. The 13th pizza gives her a marginal utility of 5 and costs $5. Mary is getting a bargain: she would have been willing to pay more for the earlier pizzas. For her first pizza, she would have been willing to pay $18, for the second $16, and so forth. She would have been willing to pay a total of $144 ($18 + $16 + $15 + $14 + $13 + $12 + $11 + $10 + $9 + $8 + $7 + $6 + $5) for the 13 pizzas. The difference between what she *has* to pay for 13 pizzas—$5 × 13, or $65—and what she would have been willing to pay, $144, is her consumer surplus. In this case, her consumer surplus is $79.

There is always some consumer surplus, so long as a consumer has to pay only a fixed price for all the items she purchases. The fact that demand curves are downward sloping means that the previous units the consumer purchases are more valuable than the marginal units. She would have been willing to pay more for these earlier units than for the last unit, but she does not have to.

In Figure 8.6, the total amount Mary would have been willing to pay for 13 pizzas is the total area under the demand curve between the vertical axis and 13, the combination of the lightly and heavily shaded areas. This area is the sum of the willingness to pay for the 1st, 2nd, 3rd, and so on, up to 13 pizzas. The amount Mary actually has to pay is the heavily shaded area—the price, $5, times the quantity, 13 pizzas. Her consumer surplus is the *difference*, the lightly shaded area above the price line and below the demand curve, over the range of the quantity purchased.

Figure 8.6 CONSUMER SURPLUS

The demand curve plots the amount Mary would be willing to pay for her 1st, 2nd, 3rd, and so on, pizza. The total amount she is willing to pay for 13 pizzas is the area under the demand curve up to the 13th pizza. The amount she actually has to pay is the heavily shaded area. The consumer surplus is the difference between the two, the lightly shaded area above the line and below the demand curve, over the range of the quantity purchased.

LOOKING BEYOND THE BASIC MODEL: HOW WELL DO THE UNDERLYING ASSUMPTIONS MATCH REALITY?

In the market economy, "For whom are goods produced?" has a simple answer: goods are produced for consumers. A theory of consumer choice is, therefore, critical to understanding market economies. The model of budget constraints and individual preferences sketched in this chapter is the economist's basic model of consumer choice. It is a powerful one whose insights carry well beyond this course. Still, the model has been criticized. Four criticisms are summarized here. The first has no economic merit. The other three are somewhat relevant. The first criticism is that the model does not reflect the thought processes consumers really go through. This line of criticism is like criticizing the physicist's model of motion, which predicts with great precision how billiard balls will interact, simply because most pool players do not go through the equations before taking a shot. The appropriate question is whether the economic model of consumer choice can reliably be used to make predictions. By and large it can. Many businesses, for example, have found the model useful for predicting the demand for their products. And economists have used the model with remarkable success to predict consumer behavior in a variety of circumstances.

The second criticism questions the model's assumption that individuals know what they like, which is to say that they have well-defined preferences. This criticism has some merit. Having well-defined preferences means that if you gave someone a choice between two bundles of goods—one consisting of two apples, three oranges, and one pear and the other consisting of three apples, two oranges, and four pears—he could tell you quickly which he preferred. Furthermore, well-defined preferences imply that if you asked him tomorrow and the day after, he would give you the same answer. But in many cases, if you asked someone which of two things he preferred, he would say, "I don't know. Let me try them out." And what he likes may change from day to day. His preferences may, moreover, be affected by what others like. How else can we account for the frequent fads in foods and fashions as well as other aspects of our lives?

The third criticism has to do with the model's assumption that individuals know the prices of each good in the market. People often do not know prices. They know that there are bargains to be found, but they know it is costly to search for them. While we can talk meaningfully about the price of a bushel of wheat, what do we mean by the "price" of a couch, or a house? If we are lucky and stumble onto a deal, we might find a leather couch for $1,000. If unlucky, even after searching all day, we may not find one for under $1,500. When we

CLOSE-UP: INTERNATIONAL PRICE AND INCOME ELASTICITIES FOR FOOD

For many in the poorer nations, getting enough food to live on is a daily struggle. But for residents of wealthy nations, food is easy to come by. These differences in circumstances are reflected in differences in income and price elasticities. The left-hand column of the table below lists selected countries from the poorest to richest, with their per capita income given as a percentage of per capita income in the United States in the second column. The third column gives an income elasticity for food in that country, while the fourth column lists a price elasticity for food.

Notice that the income elasticity of demand for food declines as income rises. This makes intuitive sense: as poor people receive more income, they will tend to spend a larger proportion of their additional money on food than wealthier people will. In India, a 10 percent increase in income will lead to a 7.6 percent increase in the quantity of food demanded. Looking at the fourth column, we see that for the richer countries such as the United States and Canada, a 10 percent increase in the price of food leads only to a 1 percent reduction in the quantity of food purchased.

More of the expenditures on food in the richer countries are luxuries—restaurants, lobsters, steaks. One might have thought that this would imply that the price elasticity in richer countries would be larger than in poorer countries. But there is another effect that dominates. In poorer

Country	Per capita income (as % of U.S.)	Income elasticity of food	Price elasticity of food
India	5.2%	.76	−.32
Nigeria	6.7%	.74	−.33
Indonesia	7.2%	.72	−.34
Bolivia	14.4%	.68	−.35
Philippines	16.8%	.67	−.35
Korea	20.4%	.64	−.35
Poland	34.6%	.55	−.33
Brazil	36.8%	.54	−.33
Israel	45.6%	.49	−.31
Spain	55.9%	.43	−.36
Japan	61.6%	.39	−.35
Italy	69.7%	.34	−.30
United Kingdom	71.7%	.33	−.22
France	81.1%	.27	−.19
Germany	85.0%	.25	−.17
Canada	99.2%	.15	−.10
United States	100.0%	.14	−.10

Source: Ching-Fun Cling and James Peale, Jr., "Income and Price Elasticities," in Henri Thell, ed., *Advances in Econometrics Supplement* (Greenwich, CT: JAI Press, 1989). Data are from 1980.

countries, people spend a much larger fraction of their income on food. When the price of food goes up, they almost have to reduce food consumption. This is not the case in the wealthier countries. Because expenditures on food represent a larger fraction of total expenditures in poor countries, the income effect of a rise in the price of food there is larger.

get the bargain leather couch home, if we are lucky, we will find it is even better than we thought. If unlucky, the couch will fall apart.

The final criticism points out that sometimes prices and preferences interact in a more complicated way than this chapter has depicted. People's attitudes toward a good can depend on its price. More expensive goods may have snob appeal. And when the quality of certain goods cannot easily be checked, individuals may judge quality by price. Because, on average, better (more durable) things are more costly, a cheap item is assumed to be of poor quality and an expensive item of good quality. In either case, demand curves will look quite different from those described in this chapter. Lowering the price for a good may actually lower the demand.

The fact that the basic economic model needs to be extended or modified for some goods in some instances does not deny its usefulness in the vast majority of situations where it provides just the information that businesses and governments need for making important decisions. Even in those instances where the model does not work so well, it provides a basic framework that allows us to enhance our understanding of the behavior of households. By asking which of the assumptions underlying the model seems inappropriate in that particular situation, we are guided in our search for a better model of consumption.

REVIEW AND PRACTICE

SUMMARY

1. The amount of one good a person must give up to purchase another good is determined by the relative prices of the two goods, and is illustrated by the slope of the budget constraint.

2. As a good becomes more expensive relative to other goods, an individual will substitute other goods for the higher-priced good. This is the substitution effect.

3. As the price of a good rises, a person's buying power is reduced. The response to this lower "real" income is the income effect. Consumption of a normal good rises as income rises. Thus, normally, when price rises both the substitution and income effects lead to decreased consumption of that good.

4. When substitution is easy, demand curves tend to be elastic, or flat. If substitution is difficult, demand curves tend to be inelastic, or steep.

5. Economists sometimes describe the benefits of consumption by referring to the utility that people get from a combination of goods. The extra utility of consuming one more unit of a good is referred to as the marginal utility of that good.

KEY TERMS

slope	normal good	marginal utility
income elasticity of demand	income effect	diminishing marginal utility
inferior good	substitution effect	consumer surplus
	utility	

REVIEW QUESTIONS

1. How is the slope of the budget constraint related to the relative prices of the goods on the horizontal and vertical axes?

2. How can the budget constraint appear the same even for individuals whose tastes and preferences differ dramatically?

3. Is the income elasticity of demand positive or negative for a normal good?

4. If the price of a normal good increases, how will the income effect cause the quantity demanded of that good to change?

5. What is the substitution effect? Why do the substitution and income effects normally reinforce each other? Is this true for an inferior good?

6. Does a greater availability of substitutes make a demand curve more or less elastic? Explain.

7. Why does marginal utility tend to diminish?

8. What is meant by consumer surplus?

PROBLEMS

1. A student has an entertainment budget of $120 per term, and spends it on either concert tickets at $10 apiece or movie tickets at $6 apiece. Suppose movie tickets decrease in price, first falling to $4, then $3, then $2. Graph the four budget constraints, with movies on the horizontal axis. If the student's demand for movies, D, is represented by the function $D = 60 - 10p$, where p is the price, graph both the demand curve for movies and the point she will choose on the budget line corresponding to each price.

2. Choose two normal goods and draw a budget constraint illustrating the trade-off between them. Show how the budget line shifts if income increases. Arbitrarily choose a point on the first budget line as the point a particular consumer will select. Now find two points on the new budget line such that the new preferred choice of the consumer must fall between these points.

3. DINKs are households with "double income, no kids," and such households are invading your neighborhood. You decide to take advantage of this influx by starting a gourmet take-out food store. You know that the price elasticity of demand for your food from DINKs is .5 and the income elasticity of demand is 1.5. From the standpoint of the quantity that you sell, which of the following changes would concern you the most?

    (a) The number of DINKs in your neighborhood falls by 10 percent.

    (b) The average income of DINKs falls by 5 percent.

4. Compare one relatively poor person, with an income of $10,000 per year, with a relatively wealthy person who has an income of $60,000 per year. Imagine that the poor person drinks 15 bottles of wine per year at an average price of $10 per bottle, while the wealthy person drinks 50 bottles of wine per year at an average price of $20 per bottle. If a tax of $1 per bottle is imposed on wine, who pays the greater amount? Who pays the greater amount as a percentage of income? If a tax equal to 10 percent of the value of the wine is imposed, who pays the greater amount? Who pays the greater amount as a percentage of income?

    The data in Table 8.1 show an income elasticity of .62 for alcoholic beverages. Consider two people with incomes of $20,000 and $40,000. If all alcohol is taxed at the same rate, by what percentage more will the tax paid by the $40,000 earner be greater than that paid by the $20,000 earner? Why might some people think this unfair?

5. Consider two ways of encouraging local governments to build or expand public parks. One proposal is for the federal government to provide grants for public parks. A second proposal is for the government to agree to pay 25 percent of any expenditures for building or expansion. If the same amount of money would be spent on each program, which do you predict would be most effective in encouraging local parks? Explain your answer, using the ideas of income and substitution effects.

APPENDIX: INDIFFERENCE CURVES AND THE CONSUMPTION DECISION[4]

This chapter explained the consumption decision in terms of the budget constraint facing the individual and the individual's choice of her most preferred

---

[4]This appendix may be skipped without loss of understanding of later chapters.

Figure 8.7 BUDGET CON-STRAINT

The budget constraint defines the opportunity set. Fran can choose any point on or below the budget constraint. if she has strong preferences for CDs, she might choose B; if she has strong preferences for candy bars, she might choose point A.

point on the budget constraint. Effects of changes in prices on the quantity demanded were analyzed in terms of income and substitution effects.

To facilitate a more rigorous analysis of choices and the consequences of changes in prices, economists have developed an extremely useful tool called **indifference curves.** Indifference curves give the combinations of goods among which an individual is indifferent or which yield the same level of utility. This appendix shows how indifference curves can be used to derive the demand curve and to separate more precisely changes in consumption into income and substitution effects.

USING INDIFFERENCE CURVES TO ILLUSTRATE CONSUMER CHOICES

In this chapter solutions to consumer choice problems were characterized as having two stages: first, identify the opportunity set, and second, find the most preferred point in the opportunity set. For consumers with a given income to spend on goods, the budget constraint defines her opportunity set. Figure 8.7 repeats the budget constraint for Fran, who must divide her income between candy bars and CDs. In the chapter, we simply said that Fran chose the most preferred point along the budget constraint. If she likes CDs a lot, she might choose point B; if she has a stronger preference for candy, she might choose point A.

The concept of the indifference curve can help us see which of these points she chooses.

The indifference curve shows the various combinations of goods that make a person equally happy. For example, in Figure 8.8, the indifference curve I_0 gives all those combinations of candy bars and compact discs that Fran finds just as attractive as 150 candy bars and 10 CDs (point A on the curve). At B, for instance, she has 12 CDs but only 130 candy bars—not so much candy, but in

Figure 8.8 INDIFFER-ENCE CURVES

An indifference curve traces combinations of goods among which anindividual is indifferent. Each reflects Fran's taste for CDs and for candy bars. She is just as well off (has an identical amount of utility) at all points on the indifference curve I_0: A, B, C, D, or F.

her mind the extra CDs make up for the loss. The fact that *B* and *A* are on the same indifference curve means that Fran is indifferent. That is, if you asked her whether she preferred *A* to *B* or *B* to *A*, she would answer that she couldn't care less.

Indifference curves simply reflect preferences between pairs of goods. Unlike demand curves, they have nothing to do with budget constraints or prices. The different combinations of goods along the indifference curve cost different amounts of money. The indifference curves are drawn by asking an individual which he prefers: 10 candy bars and 2 CDs or 15 candy bars and 1 CD? or 11 candy bars and 2 CDs or 15 candy bars and 1 CD? or 12 candy bars and 2 CDs or 15 candy bars and 1 CD? When he answers, "I am indifferent between the two," the two points that represent those choices are on the same indifference curve.

Moving along the curve in one direction, Fran is willing to accept more CDs in exchange for fewer candy bars; moving in the other direction, she is willing to accept more candy bars in exchange for fewer CDs. Any point on the same indifference curve, by definition, makes her just as happy as any other— whether it is point *A* or *C* or an extreme point like *D*, where she has many candy bars and very few CDs, or *F*, where she has relatively few candy bars but more CDs.

However, if Fran were to receive the same number of candy bars but more CDs than at *A*—say 150 candy bars and 15 CDs (point *E*)—she would be better off on the principle that "more is better." The new indifference curve I_1 illustrates all those combinations of candy bars and CDs that make her just as well off as the combination of 150 candy bars and 15 CDs.

Figure 8.8 shows two indifference curves for Fran. Because more is better, Fran (or any individual) will prefer a choice on an indifference curve that is higher than another. On the higher indifference curve, she can have more of both items. By definition, we can draw an indifference curve for *any* point in the space of an indifference curve diagram. Also by definition, indifference curves cannot cross, as Figure 8.9 makes clear. Assume that the indifference curves I_0 and I_1 cross at point *A*. That would mean that Fran is indifferent between *A* and all points on I_0, and between *A* and all points on I_1. In particular, she would be indifferent between *A* and *B*, between *A* and *C*, and accordingly between *B* and *C*. But *B* is clearly preferred to *C*; therefore, indifference curves cannot cross.

INDIFFERENCE CURVES AND MARGINAL RATES OF SUBSTITUTION

The slope of the indifference curve measures the number of candy bars that the individual is willing to give up to get another compact disc. The technical term for the slope of an indifference curve is the **marginal rate of substitution.** The marginal rate of substitution tells us how much of one good an individual is *willing* to give up in return for one more unit of another. This concept is quite distinct from the amount a consumer *must* give up, which is determined by the budget constraint and relative prices.

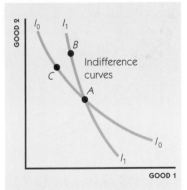

Figure 8.9 WHY INDIFFERENCE CURVES CANNOT CROSS

If two indifference curves crossed, a logical contradiction would occur. If curves crossed at point *A*, then Fran would be indifferent between *A* and *B*, between *A* and *C*, and therefore between *B* and *C*. But since *B* involves higher consumption of both goods than *C*, *B* is clearly preferred to *C*.

If Fran's marginal rate of substitution of candy bars for CDs is 15 to 1, this means that if she is given 1 more CD, she is willing to give up 15 candy bars. If she only had to give up 12 candy bars, she would be happier. If she had to give up 20, she would say, "That's too much—having one more CD isn't worth giving up twenty candy bars." Of course, Gary could have quite different attitudes toward CDs and candy bars. His marginal rate of substitution might be 25 to 1. He would be willing to give up 25 candy bars to get 1 more CD.

The marginal rate of substitution rises and falls according to how much of an item an individual already has. For example, consider point F back in Figure 8.8, where Fran has a lot of CDs and few candy bars. In this case, Fran already has bought all her favorite CDs; the marginal CD she buys now will be something she likes, but not something she is wild over. In other words, because she already has a large number of CDs, having an additional one is less important. She would rather have some candy bars instead. Her marginal rate of substitution of candy bars for CDs at F is very low; for the sake of illustration, let's say that she would be willing to give up the marginal CD for only 10 candy bars. Her marginal rate of substitution is 10 to 1 (candy bars per CD).

The opposite situation prevails when Fran has lots of candy bars and few CDs. Since she is eating several candy bars almost every day, the chance to have more is just not worth much to her. But since she has few CDs, she does not yet own all of her favorites. The marginal value of another candy bar is relatively low, while the marginal value of another CD is relatively high. Accordingly, in this situation, Fran might insist on getting 30 extra candy bars before she gives up 1 CD. Her marginal rate of substitution is 30 to 1 (candy bars per CD).

As we move along an indifference curve, we increase the amount of one good (like CDs) that an individual has. In Fran's case, she requires less and less of the other good (candy bars) to compensate her for each one-unit decrease in the quantity of the first good (CDs). This principle is known as the **diminishing marginal rate of substitution.** As a result of the principle of diminishing marginal rate of substitution, the slope of the indifference curve becomes flatter as we move from left to right along the curve.

USING INDIFFERENCE CURVES TO ILLUSTRATE CHOICES

By definition, an individual does not care where he sits on any *given* indifference curve. But he would prefer to be on the highest indifference curve possible. What pins him down is his budget constraint. As Figure 8.10 illustrates, the highest indifference curve that a person can attain is the one that just touches the budget constraint—that is, the indifference curve that is *tangent* to the budget constraint. The point of tangency (labeled E) is the point the individual will choose. Consider any other point on the budget constraint, say A. The indifference curve through A is below the curve through E; the individual is better off at E than at A. But consider an indifference curve above I_0, for instance I_1. Since every point on I_1 lies above the budget constraint, there is no point on I_1 that the individual can purchase given his income.

Figure 8.10 INDIFFERENCE CURVES AND THE BUDGET CONSTRAINT

The highest feasible indifference curve that can be reached is the one just tangent to the budget constraint, or indifference curve I_0 here. This individual's budget constraint does not permit her to reach I_1, nor would she want to choose point A, which would put her on I_2, since along I_2 she is worse off.

When a curve is tangent to a line, the curve and line have the same slope at the point of tangency. Thus, the slope of the indifference curve equals the slope of the budget constraint at the point of tangency. The slope of the indifference curve is the marginal rate of substitution; the slope of the budget constraint is the relative price. This two-dimensional diagram therefore illustrates a basic principle of consumer choice: *individuals choose the point where the marginal rate of substitution equals the relative price.*

This principle makes sense. If the relative price of CDs and candy bars is 15 (CDs cost $15 and candy bars cost $1) and Fran's marginal rate of substitution is 20, Fran is willing to give up 20 candy bars to get 1 more CD, but only *has* to give up 15; it clearly pays her to buy more CDs and fewer candy bars. If her marginal rate of substitution is 10, she is willing to give up 1 CD for just 10 candy bars; but if she gives up 1 CD, she can get 15 candy bars. She will be better off buying more candy bars and fewer CDs. Thus, if the marginal rate of substitution exceeds the relative price, Fran is better off if she buys more CDs; if it is less, she is better off if she buys fewer CDs. When the marginal rate of substitution *equals* the relative price, it does not pay for her to either increase or decrease her purchases.

$$U(x_1, x_2) = c$$

$$\frac{dU}{dx_1}dx_1 + \frac{dU}{dx_2}dx_2 = 0$$

$$\frac{dx_2}{dx_1} = \frac{-\left(\frac{dU}{dx_1}\right)}{\left(\frac{dU}{dx_2}\right)}$$

$$= \frac{-MU_1}{MU_2}$$

INCOME ELASTICITY

Budget constraints and indifference curves show why, while goods normally have a positive income elasticity, some goods may have a negative income elasticity. As incomes increase, the budget constraint shifts out to the right in a parallel line, say from BC in Figure 8.11 to B_1C_1 to B_2C_2. The choices—the points of tangency with the indifference curves—are represented by the points E_0, E_1, and E_2. In panel A, we see the normal case, where as the budget constraint shifts out, more of both candy bars and CDs are consumed. But panel B illustrates the case of inferior goods. Potatoes are on the horizontal

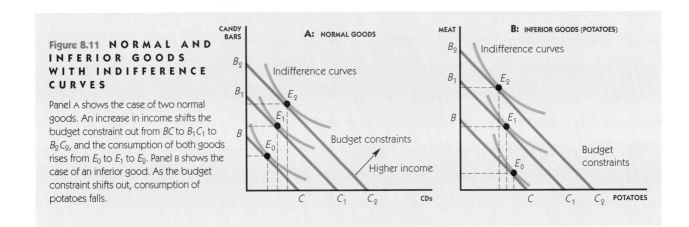

Figure 8.11 **NORMAL AND INFERIOR GOODS WITH INDIFFERENCE CURVES**

Panel A shows the case of two normal goods. An increase in income shifts the budget constraint out from BC to B_1C_1 to B_2C_2, and the consumption of both goods rises from E_0 to E_1 to E_2. Panel B shows the case of an inferior good. As the budget constraint shifts out, consumption of potatoes falls.

A: NORMAL GOODS

B: INFERIOR GOODS (POTATOES)

axis, and meat is on the vertical. As incomes rise, the points of tangency (E_1 and E_2) move to the left; potato consumption actually falls.

USING INDIFFERENCE CURVES TO DERIVE DEMAND CURVES

Indifference curves and budget constraints can be used to derive the demand curve, to show what happens when prices increase. The analysis consists of two steps.

First, we identify what happens to the budget constraint as, say, the price of CDs increases. In the budget constraint drawn in Figure 8.12A, we find CDs on the horizontal axis and all other goods on the vertical axis. If Fran buys no CDs, she has $300 to spend on all other goods. At a CD price of $15, she can

Figure 8.12 DERIVING DE- MAND CURVES FROM SHIFTING BUDGET CONSTRAINTS

In panel A, the budget constraint rotates down to the left as the price of CDs increases, leading Fran to change consumption from F to F_i. The budget constraint rotates to the right when the price of CDs decreases, and Fran moves from F to F_d. Panel B shows the corresponding demand curve for CDs, illustrating how the rising prices lead to a declining quantity consumed.

buy up to 20 CDs. As the price of CDs increases, the budget constraint rotates. If she buys no CDs, the amount of other goods she can purchase is unchanged, at $300. But if she buys only CDs, the number of CDs she can purchase decreases in proportion to the increase in price. If the price rises to $30, she can buy half the number of CDs.

For each budget constraint, we find the point of tangency between the indifference curve and the budget constraint, the points labeled F_i, F, and F_d. This shows the point chosen along each budget constraint. Looking at the horizontal axis, we see, at each price, the quantity of CDs purchased. Panel B then plots these quantities for each price. At the price of $15, Fran chooses 11 CDs, at a price of $30, only 6.

SUBSTITUTION AND INCOME EFFECTS

Indifference curves also permit a precise definition of the substitution and income effects. Figure 8.13 plots some of Jeremy's indifference curves between CDs and candy bars. Jeremy's original budget constraint is line BC and his indifference curve is I_0; the point of tangency, the point he chooses, is point E_0. Suppose the price of candy increases. Now he can buy fewer candy bars, but the number of CDs he can buy, were he to spend all of his income on CDs,

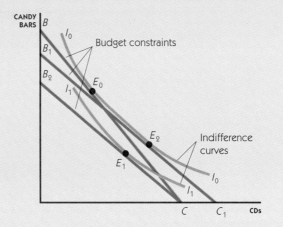

Figure 8.13 SUBSTITUTION AND INCOME EFFECTS WITH INDIFFERENCE CURVES

As the price of candy bars increases, the budget constraint rotates down. The change of Jeremy's choice from E_0 to E_1 can be broken down into an income and a substitution effect. The line $B_1 C_1$ shows the substitution effect, the change in the budget constraint that would occur if relative prices shifted but the level of utility remained the same. (Notice that Jeremy stays on the same indifference curve in this scenario.) The substitution effect alone causes a shift from E_0 to E_2. The shift in the budget constraint from $B_1 C_1$ to $B_2 C$ shows the income effect, the change that results from changing the amount of income but leaving relative prices unchanged. The income effect alone causes a shift from E_2 to E_1.

is unchanged. Thus, his budget constraint becomes flatter; it is now line B_2C. While Jeremy originally chose point E_0 on the indifference curve I_0, now he chooses E_1 on the *lower* indifference curve I_1.

The price change has moved Jeremy's choice from E_0 to E_1 for two reasons: the substitution effect and the income effect. To see how this has happened, let's isolate the two effects. First, we focus on the substitution effect by asking what would happen to Jeremy's consumption if we changed relative prices, but did not change how well off he was. To keep him just as well off as before the price change, we must keep him on the same indifference curve, I_0. Thus, the substitution effect is a movement along an indifference curve. As the price of candy rises, Jeremy, moving down the indifference curve, buys more CDs and fewer candy bars. The movement from E_0 to E_2 is the substitution effect. The budget constraint B_1C_1 represents the *new* prices, but it does not account for the income effect, by definition, since Jeremy is on the same indifference curve that he was on before.

To keep Jeremy on the same indifference curve when we increase the price of candy requires giving Jeremy more income. The line B_1C_1 is the budget constraint with the *new* prices that would leave Jeremy on the same indifference curve. Because prices are the same, the budget constraint B_1C_1 is parallel to B_2C. We now need to take away the income that left Jeremy on the same indifference curve. We keep prices the same (at the new levels), and we take away income until we arrive at the new budget constraint B_2C, and the corresponding new equilibrium E_1. The movement from E_2 to E_1 is called the income effect, since only income is changed. We have thus broken down the movement from the old equilibrium, E_0, to the new one, E_1, into the movement from E_0 to E_2, the substitution effect, and the movement from E_2 to E_1, the income effect.

CHAPTER

LABOR SUPPLY
AND SAVINGS

T he first of the four basic decisions of the household—how individuals choose to spend their money—was discussed in Chapter 8. How much money people have to spend depends, in turn, on two other basic decisions: how much they choose to work (and earn) and how much they save (or spend from savings). This chapter focuses on these two decisions. We will see that consumer theory can be applied directly to analyzing the work and saving decisions. We will also see how the supply curve for labor and the supply curve for savings can be derived, and why they have the shapes they do. Chapter 10 then focuses on the fourth basic decision: how individuals invest what they save.

KEY QUESTIONS

1. How can the basic tools introduced in Chapter 8 to analyze consumers' expenditure decisions be applied to such important aspects of life as work, education, and savings?

2. What determines the number of hours an individual works, or whether she chooses to work or not? How do income and substitution effects help us to understand why labor supply may not be very responsive to changes in wages, or savings to changes in interest rates?

3. Why do economists think of education as an investment, and refer to the result as human capital?

THE LABOR SUPPLY DECISION

Patterns of labor supply have changed greatly in the past three decades. The average work week for a production worker has declined by one-eighth since 1950. At the same time, the fraction of women in the labor force has increased enormously. As a result, the typical married household now devotes more hours to work outside the home than it did in 1900. The number of hours worked in different jobs and industries also varies. As Figure 9.1 shows, miners work 45 hours per week on average, for instance, while those in the retail sector work fewer than 30 hours.

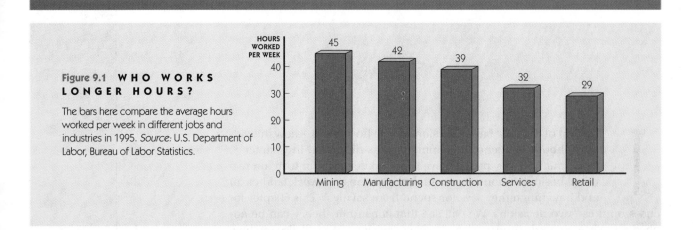

Figure 9.1 WHO WORKS LONGER HOURS?

The bars here compare the average hours worked per week in different jobs and industries in 1995. *Source:* U.S. Department of Labor, Bureau of Labor Statistics.

THE CHOICE BETWEEN LEISURE AND CONSUMPTION

Economists use the basic model of choice to help understand these patterns of labor supply. The decision about how much labor to supply is a choice between consumption, or income, and leisure. (Leisure to an economist means all the time an individual could potentially work for pay that he actually spends not working. The time parents spend caring for their children, for example, is leisure in this special sense.) By giving up leisure, a person receives additional income, and therefore increases his consumption. By working less and giving up some consumption, a person obtains more leisure. An increase in income does not necessarily translate *immediately* into consumption; the individual has to decide whether to spend his extra income now or in the future. We tackle this later in the chapter. Here we assume that the person spends all his income.

Even though the typical job seems to represent a fixed time requirement, there are a variety of ways in which people can influence how much labor they will supply. Many workers may not have discretion as to whether they will work full time, but they have some choice in whether or not they will work overtime. In addition, many individuals moonlight; they take up second jobs that provide them with additional income. Most of these jobs—like driving a taxi—provide considerable discretion in the number of hours worked. Hence, even when people have no choice about how much they work at their primary job, they still have choices. Further, the fact that jobs differ in their normal work week means that a worker has some flexibility in choosing a job that allows her to work the amount of hours she wishes. Finally, economists believe that the social conventions concerning the "standard" work week—the 40-hour week that has become the 35-hour week—respond over time to the attitudes (preferences) of workers.

We now apply the analysis of Chapter 8 to an individual's choice between work and leisure. Figure 9.2 shows the budget constraint of Steve, who earns an hourly wage of $5. Accordingly, for each hour less of leisure Steve enjoys—for each extra hour he works—he earns $5 more; that is, his consumption increases by $5. Underlying this budget constraint is his time constraint. He has only so many hours a day, say 16, to spend either working or at leisure. For each extra hour he works, he has 1 less hour of leisure. If he works 1 hour, his income is $5, if he works 2 hours, his income is $10, and so forth. If he works 16 hours—he has no leisure—his income is $5 \times 16 = 80. The budget constraint trade-off is $5 per hour.

Steve will choose a point on the budget constraint according to his own preferences, just as he chose between two goods in Chapter 8. He must choose the appropriate trade-off between consumption and leisure. Let's suppose that he chooses point E_0. At E_0, he has 10 hours of leisure, which means that he works 6 hours out of a total available time of 16 hours, and makes $30.

Figure 9.2 A BUDGET CONSTRAINT BE-TWEEN LEISURE AND INCOME

Individuals are willing to trade leisure for an increase in income, and thus in consumption. The budget constraint shows Steve choosing E_0, with 10 hours of daily leisure, 6 hours of work, and $30 in daily wages.

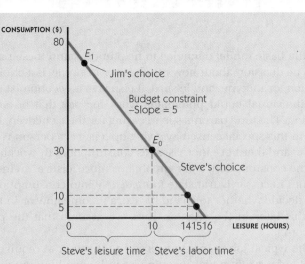

In deciding which of the points along the budget constraint to choose, Steve balances out the marginal benefits of what he can buy with an additional hour's wages with the marginal costs—the value of the hour's worth of leisure that he will have to forgo. Steve and his brother Jim assess the marginal benefits and marginal costs differently: Steve chooses point E_0, while his brother chooses point E_1. Jim values the material things in life more and leisure less.

For Steve, at E_0, the marginal benefit of the extra concert tickets or other goods he can buy with the money he earns from working an extra hour just offsets the marginal cost of that hour, the extra leisure he has to give up. At points to the left of E_0, Steve has less leisure (so the marginal value of leisure is greater) and he has more goods (so the marginal value of the extra goods he can get is lower). The marginal benefit of working more exceeds the marginal costs, and so he works more—he moves toward E_0. Converse arguments apply to Steve's thinking about points to the right of E_0.

We can use the same kind of reasoning to see why the workaholic Jim chooses a point to the left of E_0. At E_0, Jim values goods more and leisure less; the marginal benefit of working more exceeds the marginal cost. At E_1, the marginal benefit of working an extra hour (the extra consumption) just offsets the marginal cost.

This framework can be used to analyze the effect of changes in income and wages on the work–leisure decision in the same way that we discussed the effects of changes in income and prices on purchases of goods and services. For instance, an increase in nonwage income normally leads individuals to consume more of all "goods," including leisure: at fixed wages, as nonwage incomes rise, labor supply decreases.

Changes in wages have both an income effect and a substitution effect. An increase in wages makes individuals better off. When individuals are better off they work less. This is the income effect. But an increase in wages also changes the trade-offs. By giving up one more hour of leisure, the individual can get more goods. Because of this, individuals are willing to work more. This is the substitution effect.

In the case of the typical good, we saw that the income and substitution effects reinforced each other. A higher price meant individuals were worse off, and this lead to reduced consumption of the good; and a higher price meant that individuals substituted away from the good whose price had increased. *With labor supply, income and substitution effects work in opposite directions, so the net affect of an increase in wages is ambiguous.*

We derive the labor supply curve in the same way we derived the demand curve for a good in Chapter 8. Figure 9.3 shows two possible outcomes.

Figure 9.3A shows the normal case of an upward-sloping labor supply curve, where the substitution effect dominates. Panel B illustrates the case of a backward-bending labor supply curve. At high wages, the income effect of further increases in wages outweighs the substitution effect, so that labor supply decreases. Doctors, dentists, and other high-income professionals who work only a four-day week may be evidence of a labor supply curve that is backward bending at high-income levels.

If income and substitution effects just outweigh each other, then labor supply will be relatively unaffected by wage changes. The evidence is that, at least for men, the labor supply elasticity—the percentage increase in hours worked as a result of a 1 percent increase in real wages—is positive but small. That is

---

Figure 9.3 THE LABOR SUPPLY CURVE

Panel A shows the case where the substitution effect exceeds the income effect by just a bit, so increases in wages lead to only a small change in labor supply, and the labor supply curve is almost vertical. In panel B, the substitution effect dominates the income effect at low wages, so that the labor supply curve is upward sloping; and the income effect dominates the substitution effect at high wages, so that the labor supply is downward sloping over that range. Thus, the labor supply curve bends backward.

why in spite of the huge increase in wages over the past fifty years, average hours worked, for men, has not changed much.

WAGE CHANGES AND LABOR SUPPLY

As wages rise, individuals become better off. This income effect induces them to work less. Offsetting this is the substitution effect—the greater return to working provides an incentive to work longer hours. Either effect may dominate. Thus, the quantity of labor supplied may increase or decrease with wage increases.

LABOR FORCE PARTICIPATION

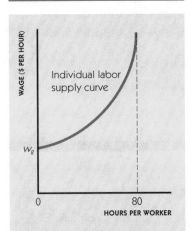

Figure 9.4 THE LABOR PARTICIPATION DECISION

The reservation wage W_R is the minimum wage at which an individual supplies labor.

The decision about how much labor to supply can be divided into two parts: whether to work and, if so, how much to work. The decision about *whether* to work is called the **labor force participation decision.** Figure 9.4 shows the labor supply curve for an individual, that is, how many hours he is willing to supply at each wage. The minimum wage at which the individual is willing to work, W_R, is called the **reservation wage.** Below the reservation wage, the individual does not participate in the labor force.

For men, the question of whether to work has traditionally had an obvious answer. Unless they were very wealthy, they have had to work to support themselves (and their families). The wage at which they would decide to work rather than not to was, accordingly, very low. For most men, a change in the wage still does not affect their decision of whether to work. It affects only their decision about how many hours to work, and even this effect is small.

Most women now work for pay too. Women, however, have faced different social expectations from those facing men. Only a few decades ago, not only was there some question as to whether women should work, the social presumption was that working women would drop out of the labor market when they had children. And many mothers did not reenter the market even after their children had grown. Whether by social convention or by choice, most women seemed almost indifferent about whether they worked for pay. Small changes in the wage rate thus had the potential of causing large changes in the fraction of women who worked. The labor supply curve for women appeared to be very elastic (flat). Some economists have estimated a female labor supply elasticity as large as .9; that is, a 1 percent increase in wages leads to a .9 percent increase in labor supply.

Today the traditional presumptions about the role of women have changed. Most women without small children participate in the labor market, and

Figure 9.5 **FEMALE LABOR FORCE PARTICIPATION**

While only one-third of all women were in the labor force in 1950, more than half are in the labor force today. *Source: ERP* (1996), Table B-35.

many with children leave only for relatively short periods of time. It is important to note here that the labor force, as economists define it, includes not only those who have jobs but also those who are looking for jobs. In 1890, only 17 percent of all women were in the labor force; the figure now stands at 57 percent. Figure 9.5 shows the dramatic increase in female labor force participation during the past 40 years.

This change can be viewed partly as a *shift* in the labor supply curve and partly as a *movement* along it. Figure 9.6 shows how the number of women participating in the labor force increases with the wage rate. Such a curve is called the labor force participation curve. If all women supplied a fixed number of hours (say, 35 hours per week), then the labor force participation curve and the female labor supply curve would look the same.

Job opportunities for women have increased enormously in the past thirty years, and relative wages have risen. Thus, the return to working has increased and the opportunity cost of being out of the labor force has gone up. Even in the absence of social change, these factors would be expected to lead to increased labor force participation by women. The increased participation of women as a result of higher wages is a *movement* along the labor force participation curve. This change is seen in Figure 9.6 as the increase in labor force participation from L_0 to L_1.

But two other changes have contributed to the trend as well. Beginning around 1973, (real) wages stopped growing at the rate they had been during the period following World War II. Individuals and families had come to expect regular increases in their income. When these increases stopped, they felt the loss. This development encouraged many married women to take part-time or full-time jobs as a way of keeping the family income increasing, and in some cases, to prevent it from decreasing.

There has also been a change in attitudes, both on the part of women and on the part of employers. Enrollments of women in professional schools increased dramatically, reflecting changed attitudes among the women themselves. And outright discrimination against women was barred by federal law

Figure 9.6 **EXPLAINING CHANGES IN LABOR FORCE PARTICIPATION**

The increased labor force participation of women results in part from a movement along the supply curve resulting from higher wages (the movement from L_0 to L_1), and in part from a shift of the supply curve itself (the movement from L_1 to L_2).

in 1963. Reduced discrimination made it more attractive for women to enter the labor force. These changes represent a *shift* in the labor force participation curve for women. Figure 9.6 shows the effect of the shift in the curve in the increased labor force participation from L_1 to L_2.

TAX POLICY AND LABOR SUPPLY

The effect of a change in wages on labor supply has important policy implications. For example, we often hear that an increase in taxes discourages people from working. An increase in tax rates is equivalent to a decrease in wages, since it decreases the after-tax wage received by the worker. But if the labor supply curve is backward bending, then a tax increase and its accompanying reduction in the after-tax wage can actually increase the labor supply.

Differences in views about the relative magnitudes of the income and substitution effects on labor supply have played an important role in recent debates over tax policy. When asked how they would respond to a tax increase, workers do not answer in terms of income and substitution effects. They say things like "I have to work longer hours to maintain my standard of living" or "I work less, because it doesn't pay to work so hard." But economists interpret these different responses in the analytical framework of income and substitution effects. In particular, economists are interested in what happens *on average*, and what happens to particular groups of people within the economy.

For men, the consensus is that the labor supply elasticity is relatively low, so that changing taxes has little effect on either labor force participation or hours worked. But some economists believe that men's labor supply elasticity is quite large, and that the 50 percent tax rate on high incomes that prevailed until 1986 had a strong adverse effect on labor supply. Indeed, some "Supply Siders" (named for their emphasis on incentives that affect supply) predicted that high-income groups would supply so much more labor in response to a tax reduction that government revenue would actually increase (even with lower tax *rates*). The evidence by and large indicates that the labor supply response elasticity for men is actually low. Hours worked increased little if at all as a result of the tax cuts of the 1980s, and overall tax revenues dropped. But tax revenues from *upper* income groups did increase. It is not clear that the rich worked more as a result of the reduced tax rates, however. Two other explanations are at least as plausible. First, the lower tax rates meant that the value of avoiding taxes through tax shelters fell, and investors moved their money back into taxable activities. Second, and more important, wage inequality continued to increase over the period. The rich became richer, not because they worked more hours but because they earned more per hour worked.

In contrast to the small labor supply response of men to tax rate changes, the labor supply response of women is large. Higher wages bring many more women into the labor force and higher taxes send many more women out of it. A look at the U.S. income tax makes it easy to see why taxes can have such a large effect on female labor force participation. For a family of four, no tax is

In 1993, Congress greatly expanded the earned income credit (EIC). With the EIC, low-income workers actually get a check from the government, rather than pay taxes. The intent of the EIC is to *make* work pay. Even a minimum wage worker with a family earns enough, with EIC, to bring him (almost) out of poverty. The government pays a subsidy of approximately 30 percent. Thus, a worker receiving $8,000 with two children would receive an additional $2,400. But above $11,000, the benefit is "phased out," that is, the size of the check received from the government becomes smaller. A family of four with a salary of $25,300 receives no benefit at all.

For low-wage workers, the EIC encourages labor force participation (the decision to look for a job rather than stay home). It succeeds in making work pay, at least pay more than before. But for workers in the phase-out range, the EIC discourages working long hours. The extra return for working an extra hour is greatly reduced. There is thus a strong substitution effect—the same effect that would have occurred if workers faced a 17.7 percent tax rate. After adjusting for the EIC phase-out, the *net* increase in income of a $5.00 per hour worker is only $4.12 for each hour worked. In addition, the worker may have to pay federal income tax of 15 percent, making the net income after adjustment for the EIC and income tax only $3.37 per hour—a marginal tax rate of 33 percent!

imposed on the first $16,000 of earned income. But if the household's primary breadwinner earns more than this, every dollar the spouse earns is taxed. In fact, if the primary breadwinner earns more than about $54,000, the household faces a federal income tax rate of 28 percent for every dollar the spouse earns (not to speak of the Social Security and state income taxes).

The situation is aggravated further because families in which both adults work have additional costs, like child care or the higher food bills from eating out or buying frozen dinners. Between the higher tax rate and the fact that much of the extra income may go to cover the extra expenses, the financial incentive for many secondary earners to work is low. Thus, changes in the after-tax wage rate can have large effects on the number of secondary earners who decide to work. A sobering fact of American life is that the spouse looking for the household's second job is usually the wife.

Before 1986, the tax laws recognized this problem, and did not tax the wages of the second worker in a family as heavily. But this tax provision created inequities as well. Consider a single-earner family where the father is working two jobs, one full-time and one part-time, for a total of 60 hours a week. Compare that with a two-earner family where the two wage earners' combined hours equal 60 hours a week. Why should the two-earner family deserve a lower tax rate than the man working overtime? Arguments like this one led to the 1986 repeal of the tax provision that benefited the second wage earner in a family.

THE RETIREMENT DECISION

Retirement is another important aspect of the labor force participation decision. In 1900, a 40-year-old American man could expect to live until age 68. At the same time, 68 percent of men over age 65 were in the labor force. Thus, the typical worker stayed on the job until he died, or until he was too sick to work. Today a 40-year-old man can expect to live to be 76, but only 16 percent of men over 65 are working or looking for work. In addition, only 67 percent of men between the ages of 55 and 64 are in the labor force. Retirement before 65 has become the expectation, and the number of middle-aged retirees is expected to continue to grow.

These retirement decisions too can be understood in terms of a basic economic model. Increased lifetime wealth has led individuals to choose more leisure over their lifetime. The fact that when people are better off they wish to enjoy more leisure is, as we saw earlier, the income effect. The decision to retire earlier can be thought of as a decision to enjoy more leisure. Indeed, it makes sense for people to choose more leisure in their later years, when their productivity has reached its peak and their wages are not going to increase much further.

At the same time, wages today are much higher than they were fifty years ago. This means that it is more costly for people to retire early—the amount of consumption (income) they have to give up is larger. This is the substitution effect. Evidently, for many people, the income effect dominates the substitution effect.

HUMAN CAPITAL AND EDUCATION

The nation's output depends not only on the number of hours people work but also on how productive those hours are. One of the important determinants of workers' productivity—and therefore wages—is education.

By staying in school longer, which usually means delaying entry into the labor force, people can increase their expected annual income. In addition, working *harder* in school and giving up leisure may result in better grades and skills, which in turn will result in higher wages in the future. Thus, students face a trade-off between leisure today and consumption, or income, in the future.

Spending a year in college has its obvious costs—tuition, room, and board. But there are also opportunity costs, such as the income that would have been received from a job. These opportunity costs are costs of going to school just as much as are any direct tuition payments. Economists say that the investment in education produces **human capital,** making an analogy to the **physical capital** investments that businesses make in plant and equipment. Human capital is developed by formal schooling, on-the-job learning, and many other investments of time and money that parents make in their children.

Table 9.1 YEARS OF SCHOOLING BY AGE

Age group (in 1993)	% with less than high school degree	% with a high school degree but no bachelor's degree	% with at least a bachelor's degree
25–44	12.3	62.5	25.2
45–64	19.8	57.8	22.4
65 and older	39.7	48.3	12.0

The United States invests an enormous amount in human capital. In fact, human capital is more significant than physical capital. As much as two-thirds to three-fourths of all capital is human capital. This investment is financed both publicly and privately. Local, state, and federal governments spend about one-quarter of a trillion dollars a year on education. Government expenditures on primary and secondary education are the largest category of expenditure at the local and state levels, accounting for more than 20 percent of total expenditures.

The enormous increase in education in the past fifty years is illustrated in Table 9.1. Among those 65 and older, nearly 40 percent do not have a high school degree; of those 25–44 only one in eight have not received a high school degree. Similarly the percentage with at least a bachelor's degree is twice as high for those 25–44 in relation to those 65 and older.

EDUCATION AND ECONOMIC TRADE-OFFS

The production possibilities curve introduced in Chapter 2 can illustrate how decisions concerning investments in human capital are made. To accomplish this, we divide an individual's life into two periods: "youth" and "later working years." Figure 9.7 depicts the relationship between consumption in youth and in later life. As the individual gives up consumption in his youth, staying in school longer increases his expected future consumption because he can expect his income to go up. The curve has been drawn to show diminishing returns: spending more on education today (reducing consumption) raises future income, but each additional investment in education provides a smaller and smaller return.

Point A represents the case where Everett is a full-time student through four years of college, with little income until graduation (his youth) but with a high income in later life. Point B represents the consequences of dropping out of school after high school. When he does this, Everett has a higher income in his youth but a lower income in later life. Other possible points between A and B represent cases where Everett drops out of college after one or two years.

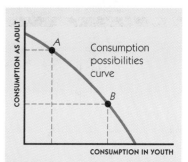

Figure 9.7 EDUCATION AND THE TRADE-OFF BETWEEN CURRENT AND FUTURE CONSUMPTION

Point A represents a choice of a reduced consumption and better education in the present, with a higher consumption in the future. Point B represents the choice of higher consumption and less education now, with a lower level of consumption in the future.

THE WIDENING WAGE GAP

Those who have a college education are paid more on average than those who fail to complete high school. The average wage of workers with at least four years of college is two-thirds greater than that of workers whose formal education ended with a high school diploma. Because unskilled workers generally cannot perform the same jobs as skilled workers, it is useful to think about the wages of the two groups as determined in separate labor markets, as illustrated in Figure 9.8. Panel A shows the demand and supply curves of unskilled workers, panel B those of skilled workers. The equilibrium wage for skilled workers is higher than that for unskilled workers.

What happens if a change in technology shifts the demand curve for skilled labor to the right, to DS_1, and the demand curve for unskilled labor to the left, to DU_1? The wages of unskilled workers will decrease from wu_0 to wu_1, and those of skilled workers will increase from ws_0 to ws_1. In the long run, this increased wage gap induces more people to acquire skills, so the supply of unskilled workers shifts to the left, and that of skilled workers shifts to the right. As a result, the wage of unskilled workers rises from wu_1 to wu_2, and that of skilled workers falls from ws_1 to ws_2. These long-run supply responses thus dampen the short-run movements in wages.

Over the past two decades, the ratio of wages of college graduates to high school graduates, and the ratio of wages of high school graduates to nongrad-

Figure 9.8 **THE MARKET FOR SKILLED AND UNSKILLED LABOR**

In panel A, new advanced technology shifts the demand curve for unskilled labor to the left, and reduces wages from wu_0 to wu_1. In panel B, the new technology shifts the demand curve for skilled labor out to the right, and thus raises wages from ws_0 to ws_1. Over time, this increased difference in wages may lead more individuals to obtain skills, shifting the supply curve for unskilled labor back to the left, raising wages for unskilled labor somewhat from wu_1 to wu_2, and shifting the supply curve for skilled labor to the right, reducing wages for skilled labor from ws_1 to ws_2.

Savings and labor supply are two of the key household decisions that can be analyzed using our basic model of consumer choice. But there are other important household decisions that can be analyzed using this model. Among the more important of these decisions is the number of children, a decision which affects the labor supply of the economy in the long run. Imagine the scene. A romantic, candlelit dinner, and two newlyweds discussing their future. They know about family planning and want to make a rational decision about the size of their future family. As their shared anticipation of the joys of parenthood increases, they push back their plates and bring out their calculators. Naturally, they have both taken economics.

As they consider all the costs of children—including the opportunity cost of wages lost from time the mother could otherwise spend working outside the home—they realize that the wife's expected earning power is an important part of their calculations. They structure their thinking about family size by weighing the marginal costs and marginal benefits of having children. From this per-spective they see the decision to have children as the demand for children, and higher earning power for the mother as increasing the "price" of a child, causing a downward movement along the demand curve.

In case you have any doubt, this is *not* how the typical family makes decisions about children, at least explicitly. But economists have noted that this model does explain the facts. Women with higher real wages have smaller families, on average. And birthrates in high-wage countries are lower than birthrates in countries with reduced earnings opportunities. This association has been confirmed repeatedly across time and across countries.

uates has increased enormously. Indeed, the real wages (that is, wages adjusted for changes in the cost of living) of unskilled workers has fallen dramatically (by as much as 30 percent). Though there have been shifts in both demand and supply curves, the primary explanation of these shifts is a change in the relative demand for skilled labor, probably attributable largely to changes in technology.

While we can be fairly confident of the predicted shifts in long-run labor supply, how fast they will occur is less clear. At the same time that these supply shifts occur, there may be further shifts in the demand curves, exacerbating wage differences. The question is how long will it take for the wage gap to be reduced to the levels that prevailed in the 1960s? In the meantime, many worry about the social consequences of steadily increasing wage (and income) inequality.

BUDGET CONSTRAINTS AND SAVINGS

The assumption that individuals spend their money in a rational manner, thinking through the alternatives clearly, holds for the savings as well as the spending and working decisions. In making their savings decisions, individuals are making a decision about *when* to spend, or consume. If they consume less today—if, that is, they save more today—they can consume more tomorrow.

We use the budget constraint to analyze this choice. Instead of showing the choice between two goods, the budget constraint now shows, as in Figure 9.9, the choice between spending in two time periods. This is similar to our discussion of human capital investment decisions. The only difference is that instead of "youth" and "later working years," the two time periods here are "working years" and "retirement years." Consider the case of Joan. She faces the lifetime budget constraint depicted in the figure. The first period is represented on the horizontal axis, the second on the vertical. Her wages during her working life (the first period) are w. Thus, at one extreme, she could consume all of w the first period (point C) and have nothing for her retirement. At the other extreme, she could consume nothing in the first period, save all of her income, and consume her savings with accumulated interest in the second (point B). If we use r to denote the rate of interest, her consumption in the second period is $w(1 + r)$. In between these extremes lies a straight line that defines the rest of her choices. She can choose any combination of first- and

Figure 9.9 THE TWO-PERIOD BUDGET CONSTRAINT

The two-period budget constraint *BC* describes the possible combinations of current and future consumption available. Wages not spent in period 1 become savings, which earn interest. As a result, forgoing a dollar of consumption today increases future consumption by more than a dollar.

SPENDING IN PERIOD 2 (JOAN'S RETIREMENT YEARS)

B $w(1 + r)$

High consumption in retirement years

D

Joan's two-period budget constraint

Trade-off: At every point on this budget constraint, Joan can trade $1 of consumption in period 1 for $(1 + r)$ in period 2.

"Smooth consumption" choice

E

High consumption in working years

F C

Wages (w)

SPENDING IN PERIOD 1 (JOAN'S WORKING YEARS)

Current consumption

Current savings

second-period consumption on this line. This is Joan's two-period budget constraint.

By postponing consumption—that is, by saving—Joan can increase the total amount of goods that she can obtain because she is paid interest on her savings. The cost, however, is that she must wait to enjoy the goods. But what is the relative price, the trade-off between future and current consumption? To put it another way, how much extra future consumption can she get if she gives up one unit of current consumption?

If Joan decides not to consume one more dollar today, she can take that dollar, put it in the bank, and get back at the end of the year that dollar plus interest. If the interest rate is 10 percent, for every dollar of consumption that Joan gives up today, she can get $1.10 of consumption next year. The relative price (of consumption today relative to consumption tomorrow) is thus 1 plus the interest rate. Because Joan must give up more than $1.00 of consumption in the second period to get an additional $1.00 worth of consumption today, current consumption is more expensive than future consumption. As was emphasized in Chapter 6, what Joan cares about in evaluating the trade-offs between consumption during her working years versus consumption in retirement is the *real* rate of interest, taking into account inflation.

In this example, where Joan's life is divided into a working period and a retirement period, what is relevant is the average length of time between the time that money is earned and saved, and the time that the savings are used in retirement. For an average person, this is perhaps 35 years. In making her calculations, Joan will take into account the fact that if she leaves her money in the bank, it will earn compound interest, meaning that interest will be paid on interest already earned, not just on the amount of principal saved.

In recent years, the real rate of interest has been around 4 percent a year. If interest were not compounded, earning 4 percent a year for 35 years would simply provide an overall return of 35×4 percent = 140 percent. If Joan puts $1.00 in the bank today, in 35 years, with no compounding of interest, she will get back $2.40 in real terms. However, if interest is compounded annually, for each dollar deposited the calculation is $(1 + .04)^{35}$.[1] So the total interest paid will be 294.6 percent. If she puts $1.00 in the bank today, in 35 years she will get back—in real terms—$3.94 (that is, her original dollar *plus* the interest). Compound interest makes a big difference.

Thus, the slope of Joan's budget constraint is 3.94—for every dollar of consumption she gives up during her working years, she gets $3.94 of additional consumption in retirement.

Joan chooses among the points on this budget constraint according to her personal preferences. Consider, for example, point *D*, where Joan is consuming very little during her working life. Since she is spending very little in the present, any additional consumption now will have a high marginal value. She will be relatively eager to substitute present consumption for future consumption. At the other extreme, if she is consuming a great deal in the pre-

---

[1]At the end of the first year, Joan has 1.04. In the second year, she earns 4 percent interest on this, so she has 1.04 *plus* $.04 \times \$1.04$, or $(1.04)^2$. In the third year, she earns 4 percent on this cumulated amount, or $.04 \times (1.04)^2$. Her total account is thus $(1.04)^2 + .04 \times (1.04)^2 = (1.04)^3$.

sent, say at point *F*, additional consumption today will have a relatively low marginal value, while future consumption will have a high marginal value. Hence, she will be relatively eager to save more for the future. She chooses a point in between, *E*, where consumption in the two periods is not too different. She has **smoothed** her consumption; that is, consumption in each of the two different periods is about the same. This kind of savings, motivated to smooth consumption over one's lifetime and to provide for retirement, is called **life-cycle** savings. In Figure 9.9, the difference between the first period income, *w*, and what she consumes is her savings.

SAVINGS AND THE INTEREST RATE

What happens to Joan's savings if the interest rate increases? Her new budget constraint is shown in Figure 9.10 as *B'C*. If she does no saving, the interest rate has no effect on her consumption. She simply consumes her income during her working years, with nothing left over for retirement. But for all other choices, she gets more consumption during her retirement years.

The increased interest rate has both an income and a substitution effect. Because Joan is a saver, higher interest rates make her better off. Because she is better off, she consumes more today, that is, she reduces savings. This is the income effect. But her return to savings—to postponing consumption—is increased. For each dollar of consumption she postpones, she gets more consumption when she retires. This induces her to consume less—to save more.

Figure 9.10 SAVINGS AND THE INTEREST RATE

An increase in interest rates rotates the budget constraint out from *BC* to *B'C* (panel A). The fact that the individual is better off means that there is an income effect, leading to greater consumption in the present (and the future). Higher current consumption implies lower savings. However, the higher interest rate makes future consumption cheaper; the substitution effect, associated with the changed slope, leads to greater savings now (panel B). The savings function in panel B gives the level of savings at each level of the real interest rate. The curve depicted has the typical shape: increases in the real interest rate lead to slight increases in savings; the substitution effect slightly outweighs the income effect.

SPENDING IN PERIOD 2 (FUTURE CONSUMPTION)

$w(1 + r)$

Joan's budget constraint with higher interest rates

E_0

E_1

Joan's budget constraint (original)

Wages (*w*)

SPENDING IN PERIOD 1 (CURRENT CONSUMPTION)

Current consumption

Current savings

A

REAL INTEREST RATE (*r*)

B

SAVINGS

This is the substitution effect. Thus, the substitution and income effects work in opposite directions, and the *net* effect is ambiguous. Either may dominate. A higher interest rate may lead to more or less savings. In the case shown, current consumption—and hence savings—is unchanged.

What happens on *average* is a difficult empirical question. Most estimates indicate that the substitution effect outweighs the income effect, so that an increase in real interest rates has a slightly positive effect on the rate of savings.

Panel B of Figure 9.10 shows the savings function, which gives the level of savings for each level of the real interest rate. It is derived by finding the choices between consumption today and in the future for different real interest rates, represented by rotating the budget constraint. The curve depicted has the typical shape. Increases in the real interest rate lead to slight increases in savings; the substitution effect slightly outweighs the income effect. But the savings curve could be vertical; the income effect just outweighs the substitution effect. Or it can even be backward bending; the income effect slightly outweighs the substitution effect.

The magnitude of the response of savings to interest rates is an important question. Government policies aimed at increasing the interest rate individuals receive, such as exempting certain forms of savings from taxation, are based on the belief that an increase in the interest rate on savings will significantly increase total (aggregate) savings in the economy. Since wealthy people save more, reducing taxes on interest—which increases the effective interest rate to the saver—obviously benefits them more, and increases the degree of income inequality.

THE SAVINGS DECISION

The savings decision is a decision of *when* to consume: today or tomorrow.

The slope of the budget constraint between consumption today and consumption tomorrow is determined by the rate of interest.

A principal motive of savings is to smooth consumption, so that consumption during working years and consumption during retirement years is about the same.

OTHER FACTORS AFFECTING SAVINGS

We have now seen how individuals' decisions about savings can be looked at using the techniques of consumer choice analysis presented in Chapter 8. For savings, the two basic determinants are income and interest rates. As incomes rise, individuals want to consume more in their retirement, and hence must save more. As interest rates change, the income and substitution effects work in different directions, so the net effect is ambiguous.

The savings decision in the United States also involves an even more important determinant: Social Security. How much individuals need to save for their retirement depends on how large a check they get from the Social Security Administration when they retire. A generous Social Security system reduces the need to save for retirement. If this is the case, why have private pension programs grown at the same time that Social Security payments have become more generous? Two explanations are commonly put forward. First, as individuals' life spans have increased well beyond the normal retirement age, the need for retirement income has increased faster than has the generosity of Social Security. Second, with higher incomes, as we saw earlier in the chapter, individuals decide to enjoy more leisure, one form of which is earlier retirement. With earlier retirement, the need for retirement income increases.

AGGREGATE SAVINGS

The sum of the savings of all individuals in society is **aggregate savings.** At any time, some individuals are saving and others are spending their savings (or, as economists say, **dissaving**). Aggregate savings is the two activities taken together. The **aggregate savings rate** is aggregate savings divided by aggregate income. **Demographic** factors, in particular the rate of growth of the population, are important determinants of the aggregate savings rate. Retirees typically dissave. That is, they withdraw from savings accounts and cash in stocks and bonds if they have any (to supplement their main income sources, Social Security and interest on investments). There is considerable concern about the low aggregate savings rate in the United States (discussed further below). Our aging population is one reason for this. A more slowly growing population, like that of the United States, has a larger proportion of elderly and, on

CLOSE-UP: WHY IS THE U.S. SAVINGS RATE SO LOW?

When Taiwan proposed becoming a major investor in McDonnell-Douglas in 1992, many observers got a jolt. Only a short while ago, Taiwan had been one of the poorer countries; now it was buying a major share of one of the world's premier aerospace firms. How come?

At one level the answer is easy. Households in Taiwan (and Japan, and many of the United States' major competitors) save a much larger proportion of their incomes than their U.S. counterparts. But the question still remains. Why? Several reasons are given by economists. First, U.S. Social Security benefits are relatively generous, reducing the need to save for retirement. Second, it has become much easier to borrow for all kinds of pur-

poses. In other words the capital market in this country has improved in its capacity to serve individual borrowers. Third, Americans have a greater taste than many for consumption now rather than later. If more people spend more, aggregate savings goes down. Fourth, the need to save for a rainy day has been reduced in this country with better medical insurance, unemployment insurance, and so on. Finally, the household wealth tied up in housing and corporate stocks in the United States rose dramatically through the 1980s—each by about $800 billion. As people saw their wealth embodied in real estate and stocks rise, they spent more of their income and saved less.

that account, a lower aggregate savings rate than faster-growing populations with higher birth rates.

The basic model provides great insight into the determinants of savings. But several motives for saving fall outside the basic model and have important implications for understanding the determinants of savings.

First, people typically want to leave something to their descendants. This is the **bequest savings motive.** Lawrence Summers, Deputy Secretary of the Treasury, and Laurence Kotlikoff, Boston University, argue that the sum of

One of the most popular policy programs designed to increase households' savings has been **individual retirement accounts** (IRAs). In its original form the tax law allowed people to deduct from their taxable income money invested in an IRA (up to an annual limit of say $2,000). **In** addition, the interest earned on this money is not taxed until it is withdrawn during retirement. Why are they popular? Because individuals rich enough to have savings can simply transfer money from a taxed account into their tax-free IRA account—they get a tax benefit without doing any additional saving. This may sound cynical but economic theory supports this reasoning. For anyone who is already saving more than the $2,000 per year allowed, there is no *marginal* incentive. The return from saving an additional dollar is unchanged. There is no substitution effect, and it is the substitution effect that drives additional savings. More generally, evidence indicates that interest elasticities of savings are low. In this case, even if there were no limit on the amount that could be deposited, savings would not be stimulated much. Moreover, poorer Americans are least likely to take advantage of IRAs, making the tax break for these accounts a benefit for the middle class and the wealthy.

Whether this is good or bad, of course, depends on the value one places on equity.

Despite the theoretical arguments suggesting that the IRAs would do little to stimulate savings, they are turning out to be more effective in increasing savings than expected. One reason is that banks advertise aggressively to recruit the IRA accounts. Advertisers "sell" savings, just as they sell cars and cigarettes.

More recently, a more tax-equitable IRA has been proposed. This would allow for tax deductibility for contributions to an IRA account that exceeded a target, say 10 percent of income. Richer individuals would thus have a higher target.

savings of the small group of very wealthy people exceeds that of the entire rest of the population, and the main reason for saving by the wealthy is the bequest motive. Another motive for savings is the **precautionary** motive. This "saving for a rainy day" protects against emergencies for which one has no insurance coverage. Precautionary savings is particularly important for owners of small businesses and farmers whose incomes can vary enormously from year to year. Still another (related) motive is to save for a particular purpose. **Target savings** is directed toward needs for which it may be hard to borrow sufficient funds, such as a down payment on a house or a college education for one's children.

REVIEW AND PRACTICE

SUMMARY

1. The decision about how to allocate time between work and leisure can be analyzed using the basic ideas of budget constraints and preferences. Individuals face a trade-off along a budget constraint between leisure and income. The amount of income a person can obtain by giving up leisure is determined by the wage rate.

2. In labor markets, the substitution and income effects of a change in wages work in opposite directions. An increase in wages makes people better off, and they wish to enjoy more leisure now as well as more consumption; this is the income effect. But an increase in wages raises the opportunity cost of leisure, and encourages more work; this is the substitution effect. The overall effect of a rise in wages will depend on whether the substitution or income effect is actually larger.

3. An upward-sloping labor supply curve represents a case where the substitution effect of higher wages outweighs the income effect. A relatively vertical labor supply curve represents a case where the substitution and income effects of higher wages are nearly equal. A backward-bending labor supply curve represents a case where the substitution effect dominates at low wages (labor supply increases as the wage increases), but the income effect dominates at high wages (labor supply decreases as the wage increases).

4. The basic model of choice between leisure and income also can be used to analyze decisions concerning labor force participation, including when to enter the labor force and when to retire.

5. Human capital adds to economic productivity just as physical capital does. It is developed by education, on-the-job learning, and investments of time and money that parents make in their children.

6. In making a decision to save, people face a trade-off between current and future consumption. The amount of extra consumption an individual can obtain in the future by reducing present consumption is determined by the real rate of interest.

7. An increase in the real rate of interest makes individuals who save better off. The resulting income effect leads to an increase in current consumption (*and* future consumption) and a decrease in savings. An increase in the real rate of interest also makes it more attractive to save; this is the substitution effect, and it leads to a decrease in current consumption. The net effect is thus ambiguous, though in practice it appears that an increase in the real interest rate has a slightly positive effect on savings.

KEY TERMS

labor force partici-
   pation decision
reservation wage
human capital

life-cycle savings
aggregate savings
bequest savings
   motive

precautionary
   savings motive
target savings
   motive

REVIEW QUESTIONS

1. How do people make choices about the amount of time to work, given their personal tastes and real wages in the market?

2. How will the income effect of a fall in wages affect hours worked? How will the substitution effect of a fall in wages affect hours worked? What does the labor supply curve look like if the income effect dominates the substitution effect? If the substitution effect dominates the income effect?

3. Describe how students invest time and money to acquire human capital.

4. How does a choice to consume in the present determine the amount of consumption in the future?

5. What is the price of future consumption in terms of present consumption?

6. For savers, how will the income effect of a higher interest rate affect current savings? How will the substitution effect of a higher interest rate affect current savings?

7. What are some of the other factors, besides incomes and interest rates, that affect savings?

PROBLEMS

1. Imagine that a wealthy relative dies and leaves you an inheritance in a trust fund that will provide you with $20,000 per year for the rest of your life. Draw a diagram to illustrate this shift in your budget constraint between leisure and consumption. After considering the ideas of income and substitution effects, decide whether this inheritance will cause you to work more or less.

2. Most individuals do not take a second job (moonlight), even if they could get one, for instance as a taxi driver. This is in spite of the fact that their "basic job" may require them to work only 37 hours a week. Most moonlighting jobs pay less per hour than the basic job. Draw a typical worker's budget constraint. Discuss the consequences of the kink in the budget constraint.

3. Under current economic conditions, let's say that an unskilled worker will be able to get a job at a wage of $5 per hour. Now assume the government decides to assure that all people with a weekly income of less than $150 will be given a check to bring them up to the $150 level. Draw one such worker's original budget constraint and the constraint with the welfare program. Will this welfare program be likely to cause a recipient who originally worked 30 hours to work less? How about a recipient who worked less than 30 hours? More than 30 hours? Explain how the government might reduce these negative effects by offering a wage subsidy that would increase the hourly wage to $6 per hour for each of the first 20 hours worked, and draw a revised budget constraint to illustrate.

4. This chapter analyzed the savings decision of an individual who worked for one period, and was retired the next, and received no social security payment in his retirement.
   (a) Show how the budget constraint changes if the individual receives a fixed social security payment in retirement. Discuss what this does to savings.
   (b) Show how the budget constraint changes if the individual is taxed the first period of his life and receives a fixed social security payment in retirement. Discuss what this does to savings.

5. This chapter focused on how interest rates affect savers. If an individual is a net debtor (that is, he owes money), what is the income effect of an increase in interest rates. Will an increase in the interest rates that he has to pay induce him to borrow more or less?

6. In the context of the life-cycle model of savings, explain whether you would expect each of the following situations to increase or decrease household savings.
   (a) More people retire before age 65.
   (b) There is an increase in life expectancy.
   (c) The government passes a law requiring private businesses to provide more lucrative pensions.

7. Explain how each of the following changes might affect people's saving.
   (a) Inheritance taxes are increased.
   (b) A government program allows college students to obtain student loans more easily.
   (c) The government promises to assist anyone injured by natural disasters like hurricanes, tornadoes, and earthquakes.
   (d) More couples decide against having children.
   (e) The economy does far worse than anyone was expecting in a given year.

8. Economists are fairly certain that a rise in the price of most goods will cause people to consume less of those goods, but they are not sure whether a rise in interest rates will cause people to save more. Use the ideas of substitution and income effects to explain why economists are confident of the conclusion in the first case, but not in the second.

9. There is a negative correlation between a woman's real wage and her family size. Two possible explanations have been put forward. One is that women with higher real wages *choose* to have smaller families. Explain why this might be so. The second is that larger family sizes might cause women to receive lower wages, for instance, because they have to accept jobs where they can be absent when their children are sick. What evidence might help you choose between these two explanations?

APPENDIX: INDIFFERENCE CURVES AND THE LABOR SUPPLY AND SAVINGS DECISIONS[2]

This appendix investigates the labor supply and savings decisions using the indifference curve approach applied in the appendix to Chapter 8 to the consumption decision. Let's first look at the choice between leisure and consumption.

Figure 9.11 shows Tom's budget constraint between leisure and consumption. The slope of the budget constraint is the wage. The figure also shows two indifference curves; each gives the combinations of leisure and consumption among which Tom is indifferent. As usual, since people prefer more of both consumption and leisure if that is possible, Tom will move to the highest indifference curve he can attain. This will be the one that is just tangent to the budget constraint.

The slope of the indifference curve is the marginal rate of substitution between leisure and consumption. It measures the amount of extra consumption Tom requires to compensate him for forgoing one additional hour of leisure. At the point of tangency between the indifference curve and the budget constraint, point E, both have the same slope. That is, the marginal rate of substitution equals the wage at this point.

As in the appendix to Chapter 8, we can easily see why Tom chooses this point. Assume his marginal rate of substitution is $15 (dollars per hour), while his wage is $20 (dollars per hour). If he works an hour more—gives up an hour's worth of leisure—his consumption goes up by $20. But to compensate him for the forgone leisure, he only requires $15. Since he gets more than he requires by working, he clearly prefers to work more.

Figure 9.11 INDIFFERENCE CURVES AND LEISURE-INCOME CHOICES

An individual will choose the combination of leisure and income at *E*. Point *A* would be more desirable, but it is not feasible. Other points on the budget line or inside it are feasible, but they lie on lower indifference curves and are therefore not as desirable.

DECIDING WHETHER TO WORK

Figure 9.12 shows how to use indifference curves to analyze how people decide whether to work or not. Consider a low-wage individual facing a welfare system in which there is a fixed level of benefits if one's income is below a

[2]You will need to have read the appendix to Chapter 8 in order to follow this appendix.

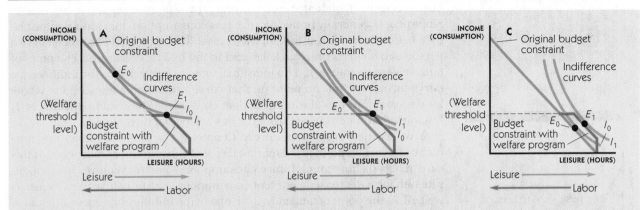

Figure 9.12 INDIFFERENCE CURVES AND WELFARE PROGRAMS

Panel A shows the case of an individual who chooses to work whether or not the welfare program exists. In panel B, before a welfare program is introduced, the individual is earning more than the welfare threshold. With the availability of welfare, she relies on welfare benefits to work less and move to a higher indifference curve. Panel C shows the case of someone who is earning less than the welfare threshold, but would choose to work still less if the welfare program existed.

threshold level. Benefits are cut off once income exceeds a certain level. The indifference curve I_0 is tangent to the budget constraint without welfare, and the point of tangency is E_0. The curve I_1 is the highest indifference curve consistent with the person receiving welfare.

The three possible cases are illustrated in panels A, B, and C. In panel A, the indifference curve through point E_0, I_0, is higher than the curve I_1. The individual chooses to work at E_0, and is unaffected by the welfare program. In panels B and C, the person works sufficiently little to be eligible for welfare; that is, I_1 is higher than I_0, and so he chooses point E_1. In panel B, the individual realizes that if he works more, he will lose his welfare benefits. He earns just (little) enough to be eligible for welfare. In panel C, the welfare system has only an income effect. If the welfare benefits are large enough, the individual may choose not to work at all (at E_1 there is zero labor).

DECIDING HOW MUCH TO SAVE

The decision of how much to save is a decision about how much of lifetime income to consume now and how much to consume in the future. This trade-off is summarized in the two-period budget constraint introduced in the chapter, with present consumption measured along the horizontal axis and future consumption along the vertical axis. The slope of the budget constraint is $1 + r$, where r is the rate of interest, the extra consumption we get in the future from forgoing a unit of consumption today.

Figure 9.13 shows three indifference curves. The indifference curve through point A gives all the combinations of consumption today and con-

Figure 9.13 INDIFFERENCE CURVES AND SAVINGS BEHAVIOR

An individual will choose the combination of present and future consumption at E. Point A would be more desirable, but it is not feasible. Point F is feasible, but it lies on a lower indifference curve and is therefore less desirable.

sumption in the future among which the individual is indifferent (she would be just as well off, no better and no worse, at any point along the curve as at *A*). Since people generally prefer more to less consumption, they would rather be on a higher than a lower indifference curve. The highest indifference curve a person can attain is one that is tangent to the budget constraint. The point of tangency we denote by *E*. The individual would clearly prefer the indifference curve through *A*, but no point on that curve is attainable because the whole indifference curve is above the budget constraint. She could consume at *F*, but the indifference curve through *F* lies below that through *E*.

As we learned in the appendix to Chapter 8, the slope of the indifference curve at a certain point is the marginal rate of substitution at that point. In this case, it tells us how much future consumption a person requires to compensate him for a decrease in current consumption by 1 unit, to leave him just as well off. At the point of tangency, the slope of the indifference curve is equal to the slope of the budget constraint. The marginal rate of substitution at that point, *E*, equals $1 + r$. If the individual forgoes a unit of consumption, he gets $1 + r$ more units of consumption in the future, and this is exactly the amount he requires to compensate him for giving up current consumption. On the other hand, if the marginal rate of substitution is less than $1 + r$, it pays the individual to save more. To see why, assume $1 + r = 1.5$, while the person's marginal rate of substitution is 1.2. By reducing his consumption by a unit, he gets 1.5 more units in the future, but he would have been content getting only 1.2 units. He is better off saving more.

CHANGING THE INTEREST RATE

With indifference curves and budget constraints, we can see the effect of an increase in the interest rate. Figure 9.14 shows the case of an individual, Maggie, who works while she is young and saves for her retirement. The vertical axis gives consumption during retirement years, the horizontal axis consumption during working years. An increase in the rate of interest rotates the budget constraint, moving it from BC to B_2C. It is useful to break the change down into two steps. In the first, we ask what would have happened if the interest rate had changed but Maggie remained on the same indifference curve. This is represented by the movement of the budget constraint from BC to B_1C_1. As a result of the increased interest rate, Maggie consumes less today—she saves more. This is the substitution effect, and it is seen in the movement from E_0 to E_2 in the figure.

In the second step we note that, since Maggie is a saver, the increased interest rate makes her better off. To leave Maggie on the same indifference curve after the increase in the interest rate, we needed to reduce her income. Her true budget constraint, after the interest rate increase, is B_2C, parallel to B_1C_1. The two budget constraints have the same slope because the after-tax interest rates are the same. The movement from B_1C_1 to B_2C is the second step. It induces Maggie to increase her consumption from E_2 to E_1. At higher incomes and the same relative prices (interest rates), people consume more every pe-

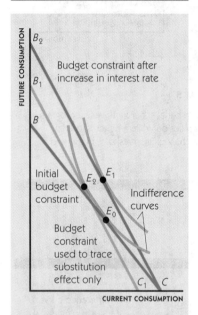

Figure 9.14 INCOME AND SUBSTITUTION EFFECTS OF A HIGHER INTEREST RATE

An increase in the interest rate rotates the budget constraint, moving it from BC to B_2C. The substitution effect describes what happens when relative prices are changed but Maggie remains on the same indifference curve; there is a shift in the budget line from BC to B_1C_1, and an increase in savings from E_0 to E_2. The income effect is the result of an outward shift of the budget line, keeping relative prices the same; the income effect is described by the shift from B_1C_1 to B_2C, and the increase in present consumption from E_2 to E_1.

riod, which implies that they save less. The movement from E_2 to E_1 is the income effect.

Thus, the substitution effect leads her to save more, the income effect to save less, and the net effect is ambiguous. In this case, there is a slight increase in savings.

CHAPTER 10

A STUDENT'S GUIDE TO INVESTING

E very decision to save is accompanied by a decision about what to do with the savings. They might go under a mattress, but usually savings are invested—in bank accounts, the stock or bond market, the real estate market, and other financial opportunities. Individually and collectively, these opportunities can be thought of as enticements to defer consumption—to save. Broadly speaking, an **investment** is the purchase of an asset in the expectation of receiving a return. For the economy as a whole, real investment must be distinguished from financial investment. Real investment includes the purchase of new factories and new machines. Financial investment includes bank accounts, stocks, bonds, and so on. The two markets are linked: the financial investments people make provide firms with the funds they need to undertake real investments.

This chapter is about financial investment. It first takes up the major alternatives available to savers and discusses the characteristics of the different alternatives that are important to investors. From these characteristics, we can establish a simple theory to explain how asset prices are determined. The chapter closes with strategies for intelligent investing.

KEY QUESTIONS

1. What are the principal alternatives available in which to invest savings?

2. What are the important characteristics of each?

3. Why do some assets yield a higher return than others?

4. What is meant by an efficient market? Is it possible to "beat the market"?

5. What are some of the basic ingredients in an intelligent investment strategy?

INVESTMENT ALTERNATIVES

Every saver faces a myriad of possibilities when it comes to investing her savings. The choices she makes depend on the amount of money she has to invest, her motivations to save, her willingness to bear risk, and her age and health. Of the seemingly endless array of places to put one's money, five are most important: bank deposits, including certificates of deposit (CDs); housing; bonds; stocks; and mutual funds. In making choices among them, investors focus on four characteristics: return, risk, liquidity, and tax liability.

BANK DEPOSITS

As a student, your major savings are likely to be earnings from a summer job that will be spent during the next school year. If so, the decision of where to invest is generally uncomplicated. A **bank savings account** (or a similar account) offers three advantages: it pays you interest, it allows easy access to your money, and it offers security, because even if the bank itself goes broke the federal government, through the Federal Deposit Insurance Corporation, insures bank deposits of up to $100,000.

After leaving school, investment decisions become more difficult. You may want to put away some savings to make a down payment on a house. (With the average house selling for $120,000, a 20 percent down payment would be $24,000.) As savings increase, the value of a few extra percentage points of interest also increases. A **certificate of deposit (CD)**, in which you deposit money in a bank for a preset length of time, is as safe as an ordinary bank account and yields a slightly higher return. The drawback of a CD is that if you withdraw the money before the preset time has expired, you pay a penalty. The ease with which an investment can be turned into cash is called its **liquidity.** Perfectly liquid investments can be converted into cash speedily and without any loss in value. CDs are less liquid than standard savings accounts.

HOUSING

Two-thirds of American households invest by owning their own homes. This investment is far riskier than putting money into a bank or a certificate of deposit. Home prices usually increase over time, but not always. In 1986, the price of housing in Houston declined by 11 percent, and in 1990, the price of housing in the Northeast and in the West declined by 6.8 percent and 3.5 percent, respectively. In addition, when prices do rise, the rate of increase is uncertain. Prices may be almost level for a number of years, and then shoot up by 20 percent in a single year. Note that while the bank may provide most of the funds for the purchase of a house, the owner bears the risk, since she is responsible for paying back the loan regardless of the market price of the house.

Housing as an investment has two other attributes—one attractive and one unattractive. On the positive side, real estate taxes, property taxes, and the interest on the mortgage are tax deductible, and the capital gains usually escape taxation altogether. On the negative side, housing is usually fairly illiquid. Houses differ one from another, and it often takes considerable time to find someone who really likes your house; if you try to sell your house quickly, on average you will receive less than you would if you had two or three months in which to sell it. Moreover, the costs of selling a house are substantial, often more than 5 percent of the value of the house—in any case more than the costs of selling stocks and bonds.

BONDS

Bonds are a way for corporations and government to borrow. The borrower—whether it is a company, a state, a school district, or the U.S. government—promises to pay the lender (the purchaser of the bond, or investor) a fixed amount in a specified number of years. In addition, the borrower agrees to pay the lender each year a fixed return on the amount borrowed. Thus, if the interest rate on a ten-year bond is 10 percent, a $10,000 bond will pay the lender $1,000 every year, and $10,000 at the end of ten years. The period remaining until a loan or bond is to be paid in full is called its **maturity.** Bonds that mature within a few years are called **short-term bonds;** those that mature in more than 10 years are called **long-term bonds.** A long-term government bond may have a maturity of 20 or even 30 years.

Bonds may seem relatively safe, because the investor knows what amounts will be paid. But consider a corporate bond that promises to pay $10,000 in 10 years and pays $1,000 every year until then. Imagine that an investor buys the bond, collects interest for a couple of years, and then realizes that he needs cash and wants to sell the bond. There is no guarantee that he will get $10,000 for it. He may get more and he may get less. If the market interest rate has fallen to 5 percent since the original bond was issued, a new $10,000 bond now would pay only $500 a year. Clearly, the original bond, which pays $1,000 a year, is worth considerably more. Thus, a decline in the interest rate leads to a rise in the value of bonds; and by the same logic, a rise in the interest rate leads to a decline in the value of bonds. This uncertainty about market value is what makes long-term bonds risky.[1]

Even if the investor holds the bond to maturity, that is, until the date at which it pays the promised $10,000, there is still a risk, since he cannot know for sure what $10,000 will purchase 10 years from now. If the general level of prices increases at a rate of 7 percent over these 10 years, the real value of the $10,000 will be just one-half what it would have been had prices remained stable during that decade.[2]

Because of the higher risk caused by these uncertainties, long-term bonds must compensate investors by paying higher returns, on average, than comparable short-term bonds. And because every corporation has at least a slight chance of going bankrupt, corporate bonds must compensate investors for the higher risk by paying higher returns than government bonds. The higher returns more than compensate for the additional bankruptcy risk, however, according to economic research. That is, if an investor purchases a very large number of good-quality corporate bonds, the likelihood that more than one or two will default is very small, and the overall return will be considerably higher than the return from purchasing government bonds of the same maturity (the same number of years until they come due).

Some corporate bonds are riskier than others—that is, there is a higher probability of default. These bonds must pay extremely high returns to induce investors to take a chance on them. When Chrysler looked on the verge of bankruptcy in 1980, Chrysler bonds were yielding returns of 23 percent. Obviously, the more a firm is in debt, the more likely it is to be unable to meet its commitments, and the riskier are its bonds. Especially risky bonds are called **junk bonds;** the yields on such bonds are much higher than those from a financially solid firm, but the investor must take into account the high probability of default.

SHARES OF STOCK

You might also choose to invest in shares of corporate stock. When a person buys shares in a firm, she literally owns a fraction (a share) of the total firm. Thus, if the firm issues 1 million shares, an individual who owns 100 shares

---

[1]The market price of the bond will equal the present discounted value of what it pays. For instance, a 3-year bond that pays $10 per year each of 2 years and $110 at the end of the 3rd year has a value of

$$\frac{10}{1+r} + \frac{10}{(1+r)^2} + \frac{110}{(1+r)^3},$$

where r is the market rate of interest. We can see that as r goes up, the value of the bond goes down, and vice versa.

[2]If prices rise at 7 percent a year, with compounding, the price level in 10 years is $(1.07)^{10}$ times the level it is today; $(1.07)^{10}$ is approximately equal to 2; prices have doubled.

owns .01 percent of the firm. Investors choose stocks as investments for two reasons.

First, firms pay some fraction of their earnings—its receipts after paying workers, suppliers of materials, and all interest due on bank and other loans—directly to shareholders. These payments are called **dividends.** On average, firms distribute one-third of earnings as dividends; the remainder, called **retained earnings,** is kept for investment in the company. The amount of a dividend, unlike the return on a bond, depends on a firm's earnings and on what proportion of those earnings it chooses to distribute to shareholders.

In addition to receiving dividends, those who invest in stocks hope to make money by choosing stocks that will appreciate in value, and then sell them at the higher price. The increase in the realized price of a share (or any other asset) is called a **capital gain.** (If the asset is sold at a price below that at which it was purchased, the investor realizes a **capital loss.**)

Shares of stock are risky for a number of reasons. First, the earnings of firms vary greatly. Even if firms do not vary their dividends, differences in profits will lead to differences in retained earnings, and these will be reflected in the value of the shares. In addition, the stock price of a company depends on the beliefs of investors as to, for instance, the prospects of the economy, the industry, and that particular firm. Loss of faith in any one could lead to a drop in the stock price. Thus, an individual who had to sell all his shares because of some medical emergency might find they had declined significantly in value. Even if the investor believes the shares will eventually return to a higher value, he may be unable to wait.

Shares of stock are riskier than bonds. This is because, when a firm goes bankrupt and must pay off its investors, the law requires bondholders to be paid off as fully as possible before shareholders receive any money at all. As a result, a bondholder in a bankrupt company is likely to be paid some share of her original investment, while a shareholder may receive nothing. Over the long run, shares of stock have yielded very high returns. While corporate bonds yielded on average an annual real rate of return of 2 percent in the period from 1926 to 1994, shares of stock yielded a real return of nearly 7 percent in the same period.

MUTUAL FUNDS

A **mutual fund** gathers funds from many different investors into a single large pool of funds, with which it can then purchase a large number of assets. A *money market* mutual fund invests its funds in CDs and comparably safe assets.

The advantage of a money market mutual fund is that you get higher rates of interest than on bank accounts and still enjoy liquidity. The fund managers know that most individuals will leave their money in the account, and some will be adding money to the account as others pull money out. They are thus able to put a large proportion of the fund in certificates of deposit and still not have to pay the penalties for early withdrawal. In this way, money market mutual funds give investors the easy access to their funds associated with banks, while providing them the higher returns associated with CDs.

Money market mutual funds may also invest their customers' money in short-term government bonds, called **Treasury bills, or T-bills.** Treasury bills are available only in large denominations ($10,000 or more). They promise to repay a certain amount (their face value, say, $10,000) in a relatively short period, less than 90 or 180 days, and investors buy them at less than their face value. The difference between the amount paid and the face value becomes the return to the purchaser.

With most money market mutual funds, you can even write a limited number of checks a month against your account. The major disadvantage of mutual funds is that they are not guaranteed by the federal government, as bank accounts are. However, some money market funds invest only in government securities or government-insured securities, making them virtually as safe as bank accounts.

Other mutual funds invest in stocks and bonds. Typically, they buy stock or bonds in dozens, sometimes hundreds, of different companies. Investors recognize the advantage of **diversification**—of not putting all their eggs in the same basket. If you put all your savings into a single stock and that firm has a bad year, you'll suffer a large loss. If you own stock in two companies, losses in one company may offset gains in the other. Mutual funds, in effect, allow much broader diversification. Of course, if the whole stock market does badly, a stock mutual fund will suffer too. When stocks go down, bonds often go up, so some mutual funds invest in both stocks and bonds. Others invest in risky ventures which, if successful, promise high returns; these are sometimes referred to as "growth" funds. There are many other specially designed mutual funds, and together they are enormously popular. For most investors, the first foray into the bond or stock market is through the purchase of a mutual fund.

DESIRABLE ATTRIBUTES OF INVESTMENTS

Table 10.1 sets forth the various investment opportunities we have described, with a list of their most important attributes. We now take a closer look at these attributes. As investors survey the broad range of opportunities available to them, they balance their personal needs against what the different investment options have to offer them. The ideal investment would have a high rate of return, be low risk, and be tax-exempt. But finding such an asset is as likely as finding the fountain of eternal youth. You can only expect to get more of one desirable property—say, higher returns—at the expense of another desirable property, such as safety. To understand what is entailed in these trade-offs, we need to take a closer look at each of the principal attributes.

Table 10.1 ALTERNATIVE INVESTMENTS AND HOW THEY FARE

Investment	Expected returns	Risk	Tax advantages	Liquidity
Bank savings accounts	Low	Low	None	High
CDs (certificates of deposit)	Slightly higher than savings	Low	None	Slightly less than savings accounts
Houses	High returns from mid-1970s to mid-1980s; in many areas, negative returns in late 1980s, early 1990s	Used to be thought safe; viewed to be somewhat riskier now	Many special tax advantages	Relatively illiquid; may take long time to find "good buyer"
Federal government long-term bonds	Normally slightly higher than T-bills	Uncertain market value next period; uncertain purchasing power in long run	Exempt from state income tax	Small charge for selling before maturity
Corporate bonds	Higher return than federal bonds	Risks of long-term federal bonds plus risk of default	None	Slightly less liquid than federal bonds (depends on corporation issuing bond)
Stocks	High	High	Capital gains receive slight tax preference	Those listed on major stock exchange are highly liquid; others may be highly illiquid
Mutual funds	Reflect assets in which funds are invested	Reflect assets in which funds are invested; reduced risk from diversification	Reflect assets in which funds are invested	Highly liquid
T-bills	About same as CDs	Low	Exempt from state income tax	Small charge for selling before maturity

EXPECTED RETURNS

First on the list of desirable properties are high returns. As we have noted, returns have two components: the interest (on a bond), dividend payments (on a stock), or rent (on real estate), and the capital gain. Thus, if you buy some stock for $1,000, receive $150 in dividends during the year, and at the end of the year sell the stock for $1,200, your total return is $150 + $200 = $350. If you sell the stock for $900, your total return is $150 − $100 = $50. If you sell it for $800, your total return is a *negative* $50.

In estimating the total return to an asset, the wise investor combines the asset's ongoing return (interest payments on a bank account or bond, dividends, rent, and so on) with its potential capital gain. But two problems still remain in comparing the returns to different assets. First, the returns may occur in different years. An asset that costs $1,000 and yields a $300 return next year is far preferable to one that costs the same amount and yields $300 in ten years. Dollars received at later dates are worth less than dollars today, as was demonstrated in Chapter 6. To make adjustments for the difference in timing, we need to compare the present discounted value of the returns.

The second problem is that, even if each of two assets will yield all of its returns next year, neither will have a guaranteed return. To make the right comparison in this case, we apply the concept of **expected returns.** The expected return to an asset is a statistical summing up—a single number that combines the various possible returns per dollar invested with the chances that each of these returns will actually be paid. Average returns *expected* in the future are the relevant focus here. Past returns should only be considered to the extent they give us a clue about expected future performance.

For simplicity, suppose that one of the two assets is a stock costing $100 that has a long tradition of paying $4 each year in dividends. The dividend thus supplies a 4 percent return; but some estimate is needed of its potential capital gain. Figure 10.1 plots the probabilities of different expected returns for this stock, and gives three possible outcomes for when the stock is sold a year from now. One possibility is that the stock will fetch only $97. The stock will nevertheless produce a 1 percent return ($97 + $4 = $101). Suppose, further, that experts give this outcome a 1 in 4 chance of occurring (a 25 percent probability). A second possibility is that the stock's price will be $104 and thus produce an 8 percent return ($104 + $4 = $108). This possibility is given a 2 in 4 chance of occurring (a 50 percent probability). The third possibility is that the stock will sell for $111, producing a return of 15 percent ($111 + $4 = $115). Like the first possibility, this is given a 1 in 4 chance of occurring (a 25 percent probability). (The sum of the probabilities, by definition, must add up to 1.)

The next step in calculating the expected return is to multiply each of the possible outcomes by the chance, or probability, that it will occur, as illustrated in Table 10.2. The sum of these products, 8 percent, is the expected

Figure 10.1 A PROBABILITY DISTRIBUTION OF POSSIBLE RATES OF RETURN

There are three possible levels of return for this asset: a 1 in 4 chance of a 1 percent return, a 2 in 4 chance of an 8 percent return, and a 1 in 4 chance of a 15 percent return. The expected return is calculated by multiplying the possible returns times their probability of happening, and adding the results.

Table 10.2 CALCULATING EXPECTED RETURNS

Outcome (return)	Probability	Outcome x probability
1 percent	25 percent	0.25 percent
8 percent	50 percent	4 percent
15 percent	25 percent	3.75 percent
		Sum = 8 percent

return. We would then go through the same series of calculations with the other investment opportunity. If all other important characteristics of the two opportunities were the same, we would presumably choose the one with the higher expected return.

Different individuals will differ in their judgments concerning the likelihood of various returns. To some extent, people's views are based on historical experience. When economists say that the average return to stocks is higher than the return to bonds, they mean that historically, on average, over the past century, the returns to stocks have been higher. This does not necessarily mean that the return to stocks next year will be higher than the return to bonds, or that the return to particular stocks will be higher than the return to particular bonds. An individual who believes that a major economic downturn is likely may believe that the expected return to stocks next year will be lower than the return to bonds, and will weight his expected return calculation accordingly.

An important first lesson in investment theory is: *If there were no differences between assets other than the ways in which they produce returns (interest, dividends, etc.), then the expected returns to all assets would be the same.* Why? Because investors seeing the return to an asset that yielded more than this average would bid more for the asset. If the 8 percent return given in the stock example above looked high relative to other options, investors desirous of that return would bid the stock price up above $100. As the price rose, the expected return would decline. The upward pressure would continue until the expected return declined to match the level of all other investments.

In fact, the expected returns per dollar invested for different assets differ markedly from one another. This is because a number of other important attributes affect an asset's return. These include the risk that it will not pay the expected return; its treatment under tax law; and its liquidity, or the ease with which it can be sold. An asset that is less risky or more liquid or receives favorable tax treatment will have higher demand. The higher demand will lead to higher prices and thus to lower returns. Therefore, the before-tax expected return will be lower on assets that are safer, more liquid, or tax-favored. Economists say that such desirable assets sell at a **premium,** while assets that are riskier or more illiquid sell at a **discount.** Still, market forces assure that assets of comparable risk, liquidity, and tax treatment must yield the same expected returns.

We can see the effect of changes in risk, taxes, or liquidity in Figure 10.2. A reduction in the riskiness of an asset, a reduction in the taxes that are imposed on it, or an increase in its liquidity shifts the demand curve for the asset to the right. In the short run, the supply of an asset is inelastic. Even in the longer run, supply is likely not to be perfectly elastic. Accordingly, as illustrated in the figure, the price of the assets goes up, from p_0 to p_1. Accompanying the increase in price is a reduction in the return per dollar invested.

The next three sections explore these three additional attributes of investments—risk, tax considerations, and liquidity—and how they create premiums and discounts.

Figure 10.2 EFFECTS OF DIFFERENCES IN RISK, LIQUIDITY, AND TAXES

Lowering risk, increasing liquidity, or granting more favorable tax treatment shifts the demand curve for the asset to the right, increasing the equilibrium price and lowering the average return.

RISK

It has been said that financial markets are the places where risk is bought and sold. A full appreciation of this insight is beyond our scope here; but it does underline the important risks associated with most assets. The investor may receive a high or a low return. She may even get back less than she put in—a loss. Often this uncertainty concerns what the asset will be worth next week, next month, or next year. The price of a stock may go up or down. Long-term bonds are risky; even though the interest they pay is known, their market value may fluctuate. Moreover, because there is uncertainty about future inflation, there is uncertainty about the *real* return paid by a bond, even though the nominal return is fixed.

A prime consideration for any investor, therefore, is the riskiness of any investment alternative. Bank accounts, in this regard, are safe. Since government deposit insurance came into play in the 1930s after the great stock market crash, no one in the United States has lost her money in an insured bank account. But investments in housing, stocks, bonds, and most other investments all involve risk. The return may be substantially lower than what you expected, or you may lose some or all of your money.

Some assets are riskier than others; that is, they may have a greater chance of very low returns and a greater chance of very high returns. Figure 10.3 provides a slightly more complex version of Figure 10.1. This time, instead of describing only three possible payoffs, the diagram depicts all possible payoffs for each of two stocks. The two stocks represented here have the same average return, but the stock whose return is described by curve *A* is riskier than the stock whose return is described by curve *B*. There is a greater chance of both very low and very high returns.

Figure 10.3 ILLUSTRATING RISK WITH PROBABILITY DISTRIBUTIONS

These two probability distributions are both symmetrical, around the same midpoint; thus, they both have the same expected return. However, the stock shown by curve A has a higher chance of very high or very low returns, and thus is riskier than the stock shown by curve B.

TAX CONSIDERATIONS

The government is a silent partner in almost all investments. It is not the kind of partner you would ordinarily choose—it takes a fraction of the profits, but leaves you with almost all the losses. Still, investors must take into account the fact that a substantial fraction of the returns to a successful investment will go to the government as taxes. Since different assets are treated differently in the tax code, tax considerations are obviously important in choosing a portfolio. After all, individuals care about after-tax returns, not before-tax returns. Investments that face relatively low tax rates are said to be **tax-favored.**

State and municipal bonds illustrate this point. These bonds yield a lower return than do corporate bonds of comparable risk and liquidity. So why do people buy them? The answer is that the interest on bonds issued by states and municipalities is generally exempt from federal tax. The higher your income, the more valuable this tax exemption is, because your tax savings are greater the higher your tax *rate*. The higher demand for these tax-exempt bonds from high-income investors drives up their price, which drives down the return received on the bonds. We can expect the return to decline to the point where the after-tax return for high-income individuals is at most only slightly higher than for an ordinary taxable bond of comparable risk.

Consider two bonds, identical in all respects except their tax treatment. Both promise to pay $110 next year, $10 of which is interest. The price of the taxable bond is $100. The equilibrium price for a municipal bond is greater than $100. This means that its average return, before tax, is less than 10 percent—less than the return on the taxable bond. If most investors have to pay 30 percent of any interest income in taxes, then the after-tax return is $7, not

CLOSE-UP: STOCK MARKET CRASHES

On the single day of October 19, 1987, stock prices fell by 22.6 percent on the New York Stock Exchange. It was the largest one-day crash in the history of the stock market.

Stock market crashes are difficult for economists to explain. Who can explain the exact path of a stampede or the precise direction of an avalanche? The Presidential Task Force on Market Mechanisms was appointed soon after the 1987 crash to give it a try. Headed by Nicholas Brady, later appointed secretary of the Treasury, the task force did offer some insight.

In an efficient stock market, one in which most information was widely distributed and new information was what caused prices to move, a stock market crash would make sense *if* it was preceded by some extremely bad news. However, while the weeks before October 19 held their share of bad news, there was no news bad enough—like an earthquake or a plague—to cause this sort of collapse. In fact, the economy continued to grow after the crash for almost another three years.

If the cause of the crash was not fundamental economic factors, the task force reasoned, it must have been related to the mechanisms through which stocks are traded. In theory, at least, it is conceivable that the existing mechanisms for trading stocks somehow pushed stock prices too high—higher than the underlying value of the company could justify—and then pushed them too low during the crash. Economists have been working for some time on how price movements might become exaggerated in this way.

One possible explanation is that a number of stock traders have a tendency to buy whatever stocks are going up and to sell whatever stocks are going down. In a rising stock market, these traders would bid stock prices still higher; in a falling market, they would push prices still lower.

This explanation may sound plausible, but a number of economists are not happy with it. It presumes, for example, that a high stock price leads to more purchasers for that stock, which violates the basic notion that demand curves slope down. And wouldn't these investors learn from the stock market crash that the market cannot be pushed higher forever? Perhaps most troubling, the worst days of the stock market since the Great Depression seem to be concentrated in the second half of the 1980s. Is there some factor in the modern stock market that is making crashes more likely?

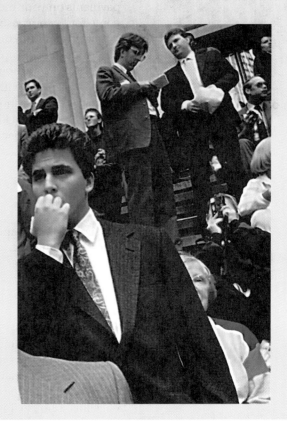

Some observers proposed to stop a future crash by shutting down the market whenever it declined substantially. Critics of this plan pointed out that stocks are traded worldwide, and the U.S. government has no power to shut down private trading. If shutting down the market leads to further panic, it could even prove counterproductive. Despite these doubters, in the aftermath of the 1987 crash, the New York Stock Exchange announced a rule that if stock prices move in a single day more than 50 points on the Dow Jones industrial average, trading will be interrupted.

Figure 10.4 EFFECT OF REMOVING TAX PREFERENCES FOR HOUSING

Removing tax preferences for housing will shift the demand curve for housing down, and this will, in the short run (with an inelastic housing supply), cause marked decreases in the price of housing.

$10. They will be willing to buy the tax-exempt bond so long as its yield is at least 7 percent. Below that level, they will buy the taxable bond instead. Thus, the equilibrium price of the tax-exempt bond is $110 ÷ 1.07 = $102.80. That is, the tax-exempt bond yields the same return at a price of approximately $103 as the taxable bond does at $100.

Investing in housing, particularly a house to live in, is another tax-favored form of investment enjoyed by most Americans. You can deduct the interest payments on your mortgage and real estate taxes when you calculate your income for tax purposes. In addition, the capital gain from owning the house is not taxed until the house is sold. Even then, if you use the money to buy another house or if you are above age fifty-five, the capital gain (up to $155,000) from selling your house is not taxed at all. If the tax advantages of home ownership were ever withdrawn, we could expect housing prices to decline precipitously in the short run (in which supply is inelastic), as illustrated in Figure 10.4. It is not likely that tax preferences for housing will be suddenly removed, however, because most voters own houses, and politicians are loathe to anger such a large number of their constituents.

LIQUIDITY

The fourth important attribute to consider is liquidity. An asset is liquid if the costs of selling it are very low. A bank account is completely liquid (except when the bank goes bankrupt), because you can turn it into cash at virtually no charge by writing a check. Corporate stock in a major company is fairly liquid, because the costs of selling at a well-defined market price are relatively small.

In the basic competitive model, all assets are assumed to be perfectly liquid. There is a well-defined price at which anything can be bought and sold; any household or firm can buy or sell as much as it wants at that price; and the transaction is virtually without cost. But these assumptions are not always met. There are often significant costs of selling or buying an asset. The costs of selling a house, for instance, can be 5 percent or more of the value of the house. At times, even municipal bonds have been fairly illiquid. The prices at which such bonds could be bought and sold have been known to differ by more than 20 percent.

Taxes not only reduce after-tax returns, but they also affect investment strategies in a variety of ways. This is particularly true of the capital gains tax.

The stock market was very successful in 1995. Though stockholders became much wealthier, they only had to pay taxes on these gains if they sold their stocks. As long as investors hold on to their investments, they can postpone the capital gains tax. This reduces the pain—or in more technical terms, the present discounted value—of the tax. Indeed, if a person holds the stock until death, the tax is completely avoided.[*] This can be looked at another way. If John acquired a stock for $100 that is now worth $1,100, if he sells it, he must pay a capital gains tax on the $1,000 gain; assuming he is in the 28 percent tax bracket, he will be left with $820 to reinvest. Suppose John puts the $820 in a new investment that yields a 10 percent before-tax return, but he needs the cash in one year to pay for his daughter's college education. He will end up with $879.[**] If he had left his money in the old stock—which he expected to grow by only 8 percent, far slower than the alternative investment—at the end of next year he would have $883.[†] The effect of the capital gains tax is to make holding the old stock more attractive for John, even though it returns less. This is called the *locked-in effect*.

Now suppose that instead of cashing in to pay for his daughter's education, John died, leaving his shares to his daughter. In this case, the locked-in effect would be even greater. If John switched to the higher return asset, his daughter could have sold the shares for a net proceed of $902—the capital gain on the new stock goes untaxed. But if he had left it in the old stock, she would have $1,188.

Temporarily lowering the capital gains tax induces people to sell shares in which they have unrealized capital gains. It is like a sale. And like a sale, so many people may sell their shares, and "realize" their gains that tax revenues may rise. Of course, though revenues are increased while the sale is on, they may be reduced later. A permanent lowering of the capital gains tax rate has a much smaller effect. There is considerable controversy over whether revenues will be increased in the short run, and even more controversy over whether they will be increased in the long run. When the Democrats controlled Congress, they calculated that a capital gains tax reduction would reduce revenues even in the short run; but when the Republicans took control of Congress in 1994, they calculated that it would increase revenues, at least in the short run.

As Congress focused on balancing the budget by the year 2002, attention was focused on the impact of tax policy in that year—and the fact that in the official calculations, a tax decrease raised revenue in that time horizon made a capital gains tax reduction seem particularly attractive. Although eliminating the loophole that allows capital gains accumulated over a lifetime to be completely avoided at death would be the most effective way of reducing the locked-in effect and, it is estimated, raise a considerable amount of revenue, proposals to do so received scant attention in the political debate.

---

[*] This loophole is called "step-up-in basis." The person inheriting the stock gets to treat it *as if* he had purchased it at the date of inheritance. His benefactor's capital gain is completely ignored.

[**] The $820 will generate a capital gain of $82, but he will have to pay $23 in taxes.

[†] The $1,100 will be worth $1,188. He will pay a capital gains tax of .28 × $1,088, or approximately $305.

EFFICIENT MARKET THEORY

The demand for any asset depends on all four of the attributes just discussed—average return, risk, tax treatment, and liquidity. In a well-functioning market, there are no bargains to be had; you get what you pay for. If some asset yields a higher average return than most other investments, it is because that asset has a higher risk, is less liquid, or receives less favorable tax treatment.

That there are no bargains does not mean the investor's life is easy. He still must decide what he wants, just as he does when he goes into a grocery store. Figure 10.5 shows the kind of choices he faces. For simplicity, we ignore liquidity and tax considerations and focus only on average returns and risk. Panel A shows the opportunity set in the way that is usual for this case. Because "risk" is bad, to get less risk we have to give up some average returns. That is why the trade-off has a positive slope. Panel B shows the more familiar version of an opportunity set, by putting a measure of "safety" on the horizontal axis. Greater safety can only be obtained at the expense of a lower average return. Reading from either panel, we can see that assets with greater risk (lower safety) have a higher average return. Point *A* represents a government T-bill—no risk but low return. Point *B* might represent a stock or mix of stocks of average riskiness, point *C* one of high risk. A very risk-averse person might choose *A*, a less risk-averse person *B*, a still less risk-averse person *C*.

The theory that prices perfectly reflect the characteristics of assets—there are no bargains—is called the **efficient market theory.** Since much of the work on efficient market theory has been done on publicly traded stocks, our discussion centers on them. The lessons, however, can be applied to all asset prices.

Figure 10.5 THE RISK-RETURN TRADE-OFF

To get a higher expected return, an investor must accept more risk, as is shown in panel A. Safety can be thought of as the inverse of risk. In panel B, the corresponding trade-off between safety and return is shown; to get more safety, an investor gives up some return.

The general presumption of the efficient markets theory is that high returns can only be obtained as a result of bearing high risks. Occasionally there are opportunities for making high returns at little or no risk—but competitive markets ensure that these opportunities quickly disappear. The most famous of these opportunities are called *arbitrage*. Arbitrage opportunities arise when the same item is being bought and sold at different prices. Thus, if gold can be bought or sold in New York at $350 an ounce, and in Zurich at $351 an ounce, it would pay someone to buy it in New York and sell it in Zurich, assuming that it is essentially costless to transfer gold from New York to Zurich. Arbitrage means that, at most, small price differences can survive long in the market. As investors buy gold in New York, the price there will be driven up; and as investors sell gold in Zurich, the price there will be driven down. The process stops when the prices are essentially the same.

Sometimes arbitrage takes on much more subtle forms. A closed-end mutual fund is a company that has bought stocks in a large number of other com-panies. Those are its only assets. The value of the company should be equal to the value of the shares it owns. Occasionally, closed-end funds have sold at a significant discount from the value of their shares. To see how arbitrage would work to eliminate this discount—at least shortly before the fund has announced that it will terminate, that is, sell its shares and send its owners a check for their value—notice that an investor could buy shares in the company and, at the same time agree to sell shares in the *underlying* stocks in a com-mensurate amount. For simplicity, assume the mu-tual fund owns only GM shares, and that there are a million shares in the mutual fund, and the fund owns 1 million GM shares. Buying a share in the mutual fund is *equivalent* to buying a share in GM. Assume a GM share sells for $30, and a share in the mutual fund sells for $25. An investor could buy a share in the mutual fund for $25 and agree to sell a share in GM, receiving $30, for a guaranteed profit of $5.

Good investors look for arbitrage opportunities, as elusive as they are.

EFFICIENCY AND THE STOCK MARKET

Most people do not think they can wander over to the racetrack and make a fortune. They are not so skeptical about the stock market. They believe that even if they themselves cannot sit down with the *Wall Street Journal* and pick out all the best stocks, someone who studies the stock market for a living could do so. But economists startled the investment community in the early 1960s by pointing out that choosing successful stocks is no easier—and no harder—than choosing the fastest horses.

The efficient market theory explains this discrepancy in views. When econ-omists refer to an efficient market, they are referring to one in which relevant information is widely known and quickly distributed to all participants. To oversimplify a bit, they envision a stock market where all investors have access to *Barron's* and *Fortune* magazines and many other sources of good information about business, and where government requires businesses to disclose certain information to the public. Thus, each stock's expected return, its risk, its tax treatment, and so on will be fully known by all investors. Because participants have all the information, asset prices will reflect it.

It turns out, however, that this broad dissemination of information is not only unrealistic but unnecessary. Economists have shown that efficient markets do not require that *all* participants have information. If enough participants have information, then prices will move as if the whole market had the information. All it takes is a few people knowledgeable enough to recognize a bargain, and prices will quickly be bid up or down to levels that reflect complete information. And if prices reflect complete information, even uninformed buyers, purchasing at current prices, will reap the benefit; while they cannot beat the market, neither do they have to worry about being "cheated" by an overpriced security.

You cannot "beat" an efficient market any more than you can beat the track. You can only get lucky in it. All the research done by the many big brokerage houses and individual investors adds up to a market that is in some respects like a casino. This is the irony of the view, held by most economists, that the stock market is an efficient one. If you are trying to make money in an efficient stock market, it is not enough to choose companies that you expect to be successful in the future. If you expect a company to be successful and everyone else also expects it to be successful, based on the available information, then the price of shares in that company will already be quite high. The only way to make abnormally high profits on stock purchases is to pick companies that will surprise the market by doing better than is generally expected.

The one exception is not really an exception because it involves trading with knowledge that other stock market participants do not have. **Inside traders** are individuals who buy and sell shares of companies for which they work. Studies show that their inside knowledge does in fact enable them to obtain above average returns. Federal law requires inside traders to disclose when they buy and sell shares in their own company. People who may not have the inside knowledge but imitate the stock market behavior of the insiders also do slightly above average. The law also restricts the ability of insiders to share their information with outsiders and profit from their extra knowledge, and exacts penalties for violations. Ivan Boesky made untold millions trading on insider information in the 1980s and paid large fines and even served time in jail.

Because prices in an efficient market already reflect all available information, any price changes are a response to *unanticipated* news. If it was already known that something good was going to occur, for instance some new computer model better than all previous computers was going to be unveiled, the price of the firm's stock would reflect this (it would be high) before the computer actually hit the market. You might not know precisely how much better than its competitors the new computer was, and hence you could not predict precisely by how much future earnings were likely to rise. You would make an estimate. The market will reflect the average of these estimates. When the new computer is introduced, there is some chance that it will be better than this average, in which case the price will rise further. But there is also a chance that it will not be quite as good as this average estimate, in which case the price will fall, even though the computer is in fact better than anything else on the market. In this case, the "surprise" is that the computer is not as good as the market anticipated.

Since tomorrow's news is, by definition, unanticipated, no one can predict whether it will cause the stock price to rise or fall. In an efficient stock market, prices will move unpredictably, depending on unexpected news. When a stock has an equal chance of rising or falling in value relative to the market as a whole, economists say that its price moves like a **random walk.** Figure 10.6 shows a computer-generated random walk, giving an idea of how unpredictable such a path is.

Random walk conjures up the image of a drunk who rambles down the street with generally unstable—and unpredictable—movements.

So too with the stock market. Although there is an upward drift in the level of all stock prices, whether any particular stock will do better or worse than that average is unpredictable. If the stock market is indeed a random walk, it is virtually impossible for investors to beat the market. You can do just as well by throwing darts at the newspaper financial page as you can by carefully studying the prospects of each firm. The only way to do better than the market, on average, is to take greater risks; but taking greater risks means that there is a larger chance of doing worse than the market too.

The randomness of the market has one important consequence: *some* individuals are going to be successful. This is bad news for people who want to believe that their insights, rather than luck, are what has enabled them to beat the market.

Figure 10.6 A COMPUTER-GENERATED RANDOM WALK

The series plotted here can be thought of as the closing price for a stock over 60 consecutive trading sessions. There is no predicting at the end of each day whether the stock will close higher or lower the next day.

EFFICIENT MARKETS OR RANDOM NOISE?

While most economists agree that there is little evidence individuals can, even by spending considerable money on information, consistently beat the market, there is controversy about how to interpret this finding. Some see it as evidence of the efficiency of the market, as we have seen. But some economists view it as evidence of nothing more than the market's randomness. Those who hold this view point out that there often seem to be large changes in stock market prices without any "news" of sufficient magnitude to account for these changes. For example, there are usually ten or fifteen days in the year when the stock market changes by more than 2 percent—a very large change for a single day—without any obvious news-related explanation.

The famous economist John Maynard Keynes compared predictions of the stock market to predictions of the winner of a beauty contest, where what one had to decide was not who was the greatest beauty, but who the other judges would think was the most beautiful. If investors suddenly "lose confidence" in a particular stock or in the whole stock market, or if they believe that others are losing confidence, share prices may fall dramatically.

STRATEGIES FOR INTELLIGENT INVESTING

So far, we have investigated major investment alternatives available to those who save, some of the important attributes of each, and the ways in which their prices reflect these attributes. If you are lucky enough (have enough money) to be considering some of these alternatives, keep in mind the following four simple rules. These rules will not tell you how to make a million by the time you are twenty-five, but they will enable you to avoid the worst pitfalls of investing.

1. *Know the attributes of each asset, and relate them to your personal situation.* Each asset has characteristic returns, risk, tax treatment, and liquidity. In making choices among different assets, your attitude toward each of these attributes should be *compared with the average attitudes reflected in the marketplace.* Most individuals prefer safer, tax-favored, more liquid assets. That is why those assets sell at a premium (and produce a correspondingly lower average return). Are you willing to pay the amount required by the market for the extra safety or extra liquidity? If you are less risk averse than average, you will find riskier assets attractive. You will not be willing to pay the higher price—and accept the lower return—for a safer asset. And if you are confident that you are not likely to need to sell an asset quickly, you will not be willing to pay the premium that more liquid assets require. If you are putting aside money for tuition next year, on the other hand, you probably will want to choose a relatively liquid asset.

2. *Give your financial portfolio a broad base.* In choosing among financial assets, you need to look not only at each asset separately, but at all of your assets together. A person's entire collection of assets is called her **portfolio.** (The portfolio also includes liabilities—what she owes—but they take us beyond the scope of this chapter.) This rule is seen most clearly in the case of risk. One of the ways you reduce risk is by diversifying your investment portfolio. With a well-diversified portfolio, it is extremely unlikely that something will go wrong with all the assets simultaneously. An investor with a diversified portfolio must still worry about events like recessions or changes in the interest rate, which will tend to make all stocks go up or down. But events that affect primarily one firm will have a small impact on the overall portfolio.

Many mutual funds claim more than just diversification: they claim that their research and insight into markets enable them to pick winners. Our discussion of efficient markets casts doubt on these claims. Many mutual funds do no research, claim no insights, and do nothing more than provide portfolio diversification. These are called **indexed funds.** There are several measures of the average price of stocks in the market. For instance, the Standard & Poor's (S&P) 500 index is the average price of 500 stocks chosen to be representative of the market as a whole. Other indices track prices of various categories of stocks, such as transportation, utilities, or high technology. Indexed funds link their portfolio to these stock market indexes. Thus, there are a number of index funds that buy exactly the same mix of stocks that constitute the S&P 500 index. Naturally, these indexed funds do about as well as—no better and no worse than—the S&P 500 index, after accounting for a small charge for managing the fund.

Because the index funds have low expenses, particularly in comparison with funds that are trying to outguess the market, they yield higher average returns to their investors than other funds with comparable risk.

3. *Look at* all *of the risks you face, not just those in your financial portfolio.* Many people may be far less diversified than they believe. For example, consider someone who works for the one big company in town. She owns a house, has a good job, has stock in the company, money in the bank, and a pension plan. But if that single company goes broke, she will lose her job, the value of her stock will fall, the price of her house is likely to decline as the local economy suffers, and even the pension plan may not pay as much as expected.

4. *Think twice before you think you can beat the market!* Efficient market theory delivers an important message to the personal investor. If an investment adviser tells you of an opportunity that beats the others on all counts, don't believe him. The bond that will produce a higher than average return carries with it more risk. The bank account that has a higher interest rate has less liquidity. The dream house at an unbelievable price probably has a leaky roof. The tax-favored bond will have a lower return—and so on. Efficient market theory, as we have seen, says that information about these characteristics is built into the price of assets, and hence built in to the returns. Basically, investors can adjust the return to their portfolio only by adjusting the risk they face. Burton Malkiel, author of the best-selling book

CLOSE-UP: JUST HOW SMART IS THE "SMART MONEY"?

The financial press pays attention to keeping track of the winners and losers in the investment world. Major newspapers, including the *Wall Street Journal,* regularly publish lists of the best- and worst-performing mutual funds for classes of investments. Now, everybody wants to put their investment money with the "smart money." But do the top experts really do that much better than average? One way to find out is to look at the return you would get if you followed the "dumb" strategy of buying and holding all the stocks on the S&P 500 list of the 500 largest U.S. companies. Since 1976, a mutual fund company has offered a fund that does exactly that—the Vanguard Index Trust 500 portfolio, which today has over $8 billion in assets. One advantage of such an "index fund" is that the amount the mutual fund spends on market research and buying and selling stocks is extremely low. The return to the investor of the Vanguard 500 over the last 10 years was 14.8 percent. This is a standard by which the "smart money" can be evaluated. One of the biggest success stories

has been the Fidelity Magellan fund managed by mutual fund guru Peter Lynch until his recent retirement. This fund beat the Vanguard 500 fund by about 3.8 percent per year. But is the Magellan fund the exception or the rule?

As we know, riskier investments require an added return, or risk premium. So, to compare apples to apples, we look at investment portfolios with riskiness similar to that of the S&P 500 list. The 10-year returns to investors from 52 actively managed mutual funds are shown in the figure. Their average return was only 13.9 percent per year, nearly one percentage point per year below that of the Vanguard 500 fund. The smart money was not so smart after all! In fact, less than 30 percent of the funds "beat the market." Economists see this as further support for the efficient market theory. Whether one fund does better than another is a matter of luck (and holding down costs).

Source: Morningstar (1994).

A Random Walk Down Wall Street, applies this theory to personal investing. "Every investor must decide the trade-off he or she is willing to make between eating well and sleeping well. The decision is up to you. High investment rewards can be achieved only at the cost of substantial risk-taking."[3]

REVIEW AND PRACTICE

SUMMARY

1. Investment options for individuals include putting savings in a bank account of some kind or using them to buy real estate, bonds, shares of stock, or mutual funds.

2. Returns on investment can be received in four ways: interest, dividends, rent, and capital gains.

3. Assets can differ in four important ways: in their average returns, their riskiness, their treatment under tax law, and their liquidity.

4. The expected return of an asset is calculated by multiplying each of the possible outcomes times the probability of its occurring, and adding the results.

5. By holding assets that are widely diversified, individuals can avoid many of the risks associated with specific assets, but not the risks associated with the market as a whole.

6. The efficient market theory holds that all available information is fully reflected in the price of an asset. Accordingly, changes in price reflect only unanticipated events and, therefore, are random and unpredictable.

7. There are four rules for intelligent investors: (1) evaluate the characteristics of each asset and relate them to your personal situation; (2) give your financial portfolio a broad base; (3) look at all the risks you face, not just those in your financial portfolio; (4) think twice before believing you can beat the market.

KEY TERMS

investment	capital gain	efficient market
certificate of deposit	mutual fund	theory
(CD)	Treasury bills	random walk
liquidity	(T-bills)	portfolio
dividends	expected returns	

[3]6th ed. (New York: Norton, 1995).

REVIEW QUESTIONS

1. Suppose an investor is considering two assets with identical expected rates of return. What three characteristics of the assets might help differentiate the choice between them?

2. List the principal alternative forms of investment that are available. What are the returns on each called? Rate them in terms of the characteristics described in question 1.

3. True or false: "Two assets must have equal expected returns." If we modify the statement to read "Two assets that are equally risky must have equal expected returns," is the statement true? Explain your answer.

4. If you found out that several company presidents were buying or selling stock in their own companies, would you want to copy their behavior? Why or why not?

5. What is the efficient market theory? What implications does it have for whether you can beat the market? Does it imply that all stocks must yield the same expected return?

6. Why do economists expect the market to be efficient?

7. What alternative interpretations are given to the observation that individuals cannot, even by spending considerable money on information, consistently beat the market?

8. List and explain the four rules for intelligent investing.

9. True or false: "A single mutual fund may be a more diversified investment than a portfolio of a dozen stocks." Explain.

PROBLEMS

1. Imagine a lottery where 1 million tickets are sold at $1 apiece, and the winning ticket receives a prize of $700,000. What is the expected return to buying a ticket in this lottery? Will a risk-averse person buy a ticket in this lottery?

2. Would you expect the rate of return on bonds to change with their length of maturity? Why or why not?

3. Why might a risk-averse investor put some money in junk bonds?

4. Would you predict that
   (a) the before-tax return on housing would be higher or lower than the before-tax return on other assets?
   (b) investors would be willing to pay more or less for a stock with a high return when the economy is booming and a low return when the economy is in a slump than they would pay for a stock with just the opposite pattern of returns?

(c) an investment with low liquidity would sell at a premium or a discount compared with a similar investment with higher liquidity?

5. Each of two investments has a 1 in 10 chance of paying a return of −10 percent; a 1 in 5 chance of paying 2 percent; a 1 in 3 chance of paying 6 percent; a 1 in 5 chance of paying 10 percent; and a 1 in 6 chance of paying 12 percent. Draw this probability distribution, and calculate the expected return for these two investments. If investment A is a house and investment B is a share of corporate stock, how might liquidity or tax considerations help you decide which of these investments you prefer?

6. Imagine a short-term corporate $1,000 bond that promises to pay 8 percent interest over three years. This bond will pay $80 at the end of the first year and the second year, and $1,080 at the end of the third year. After one year, however, the market interest rate has increased to 12 percent. What will the bond be worth to an investor who is not too concerned about risk at that time? If the firm appears likely to go bankrupt, how will the expected return on this bond change?

7. Golfer Lee Trevino once said: "After losing two fortunes, I've learned. Now, when someone comes to me with a deal that's going to make me a million dollars, I say, 'Tell it to your mother.' Why would a stranger want to make me a million?" Explain how Trevino's perspective fits the efficient market theory.

THE FIRM'S COSTS

The previous three chapters focused on the decisions of households and individuals. In this chapter, the focus shifts to the decisions of firms. Firms make decisions concerning what and how much to produce, and how to produce it, with the aim of maximizing their profits.

The basic competitive model is, once again, our starting point. Many firms, all making the same product, compete with one another to sell that product to well-informed customers, who instantaneously recognize and act upon any price differences. Because customers are well informed about prices, all firms in a competitive market must accept the price set for their product by the forces of supply and demand in the market as a whole. Any firm trying to sell above that price will lose all its customers. Firms in competitive markets are, therefore, **price takers.** The classic example of competitive markets are agricultural markets—thousands of farmers, say, producing milk. A dairy farmer does not waste time wondering what price to set for the milk he has to sell. He knows he will get the "going price."

A firm does, however, have some control over its costs. The firm's total costs are affected by, among other things, its level of production, and its choice of inputs (how to produce what it produces). Chapter 12 shows how a firm uses this relationship to choose the level of production that maximizes its profits. This chapter focuses on how firms minimize their costs, and how costs are affected by the level of production.

Even though we talk in terms of "production" and "goods," it is important to bear in mind that only one-third of the U.S. economy consists of industries

1. What do cost curves—curves relating costs to the level of production—look like in an economy where output depends on a single input to production?

2. What additional issues are raised when there are several inputs?

3. What is the relationship between long-run and short-run cost curves?

that produce goods in the conventional sense—manufacturing, mining, construction, and agriculture. The other two-thirds of the economy produces primarily services—industries like transportation, education, health care, wholesale and retail trade, and finance. The principles laid out here, however, apply equally to these other sectors.

PROFITS, COSTS, AND FACTORS OF PRODUCTION

A business that continually incurs losses over time will cease to exist because it will not have enough money to pay its bills. Businesses are under constant pressure to make money. The motivation of making as much money as possible—maximizing profits—provides a useful starting point for discussing the behavior of firms in competitive markets.

The definition of **profits** is simple:

profits = revenues − costs.

The **revenue** a business receives from selling its products are calculated as the quantity it sells of the product multiplied by the price of the product. A firm's **costs** are defined as the total expense of producing the good.

What the firm uses to produce the goods are called inputs or **factors of production**: labor, materials, and capital goods. The firm's total costs are simply the sum of the costs of these inputs. Labor costs are what the company pays for the workers it hires and the managers it employs to supervise the workers. The costs of materials include raw materials and intermediate goods. Intermediate goods are whatever supplies the company purchases from other firms—such as seeds, fertilizer, and gasoline for a farm; iron ore, coal, coke, limestone, and electric power for a steel company. The cost of capital goods include the cost of machinery and structures such as buildings and factories.

All firms work to keep their costs as low as possible. For given prices and levels of output, a firm maximizes its profits by finding the least costly way of producing its output. Thus, profit-maximizing firms are also cost-minimizing firms. Within limits, firms can vary the mix of labor, materials, and capital goods they use; and they will do so until they find the lowest cost method of producing a given quality and quantity of product. The simplest way of understanding how firms find the lowest cost point is to look at a firm with only two factors of production, one fixed, one variable. Not surprisingly, inputs which vary with the level of production are said to be variable.

PRODUCTION WITH ONE VARIABLE INPUT

A wheat farmer with a fixed amount of land who uses only labor to produce his crop is our example. The more labor he applies to the farm (his own time, plus the time of workers that he hires), the greater the output. Labor is the single variable factor (input).

The relationship between the quantity of inputs used in production and the level of output is called the **production function.** Figure 11.1 shows the farmer's production function; the data supporting the figure are set forth in Table 11.1. The increase in output corresponding to a unit increase in any factor of production, labor in this case, is the **marginal product** of that factor. For example, when the number of hours worked per year rises from 8,000 to 9,000, output increases by 10,000 bushels, from 155,000 to 165,000. The marginal product of an extra 1,000 hours of labor is, accordingly, 10,000 bushels. The marginal product is given in the last column of the table. Diagrammatically, it is given by the slope of the production function. The slope of a curve

Figure 11.1 PRODUCTION FUNCTION WITH DIMINISHING RETURNS TO AN INPUT

As the amount of the input (labor) increases, so does the output (wheat). But there are diminishing returns to labor; each increase in labor results in successively smaller increases in wheat output. Since the slope of the curve is the marginal product of labor, on the graph, this means the slope flattens out as the amount of labor increases.

OUTPUT OF WHEAT (IN THOUSANDS OF BUSHELS)

Production function

Slope in this region
= 15 bushels per hour of labor
= marginal product of an hour of labor (increasing labor input by 1,000 hours increases output by 15,000 bushels)

THOUSANDS OF HOURS WORKED

Table 11.1. **LEVEL OF OUTPUT WITH DIFFERENT AMOUNTS OF LABOR**

Number of hours worked	Amount of wheat produced (bushels)	Marginal product (additional bushels produced by 1,000 additional hours of labor)
5,000	95,000	25,000
6,000	120,000	20,000
7,000	140,000	15,000
8,000	155,000	10,000
9,000	165,000	5,000
10,000	170,000	0
11,000	170,000	

is the change along the vertical axis (the increase in output) from a unit increase along the horizontal axis (the increase in labor input).

DIMINISHING RETURNS

In the case of the wheat farmer, as more labor is added to a fixed amount of land, the marginal product of labor diminishes. This is another application of the concept of **diminishing returns,** which we originally encountered in Chapter 2. In the case of a firm's production function, diminishing returns implies that each additional unit of labor generates a smaller increase in output than the last. Increasing the number of hours worked from 7,000 to 8,000 raises output by 15,000 bushels, but increasing the hours worked from 8,000 to 9,000 raises output by only 10,000 bushels. Diminishing returns sets in with a vengeance at higher levels of input; moving from 10,000 to 11,000 hours worked adds nothing. Diagrammatically, diminishing returns are represented by the slope flattening out as the amount of labor increases. It is clear that, with diminishing returns, increases in output lead to less than proportionate increases in input; doubling the input results in output that is less than twice as large.

DIMINISHING RETURNS

As more and more of one input is added, *while other inputs remain unchanged,* the marginal product of the added input diminishes.

Figure 11.2 PRODUCTION FUNCTION WITH IN- CREASING RETURNS TO AN INPUT

As the amount of labor increases, so does output. But the returns to labor are increasing in this case; successive increases in labor result in successively larger increases in output. On the graph, this means the slope becomes steeper as the amount of labor increases.

Figure 11.3 PRODUCTION FUNCTION WITH CONSTANT RETURNS TO AN INPUT

The marginal product of labor is constant, neither increasing nor diminishing as the firm expands production. On the graph, this means that the slope does not change.

INCREASING RETURNS

Although a production function with diminishing returns is an important case, other cases do occur. Figure 11.2 shows a production function where increasing an input (here, labor) raises output more than proportionately. A firm with this kind of production function has **increasing returns.** In the single-input case depicted, it is clear that the marginal product of the input increases with the amount produced; that is, when the firm is producing a lot, adding one more worker increases output by more than it does when the firm is producing little.

Imagine a business that picks up garbage. If this business counts only one out of every five houses as customers, it will have a certain cost of production. But if the company can expand to picking up the garbage from two out of every five houses, while it will need more workers, the workers will be able to drive a shorter distance and pick up more garbage faster. Thus, a doubling of output can result from a less than doubling of labor. Many examples of increasing returns, like garbage collection, involve providing service to more people in a given area. Telephone companies and electric utilities are two other familiar instances.

CONSTANT RETURNS

In between the cases of diminishing and increasing returns lies the case of **constant returns,** shown in Figure 11.3. Each additional unit of input increases output by the same amount, and the relationship between input and output is a straight line.

FIXED VERSUS VARIABLE INPUTS

Firms typically require a certain level of input just to be in business. Before it can open its doors, for instance, a firm may need land (or space) and some machines. It will have to hire someone to run the personnel office and someone to supervise the workers. These are called **fixed inputs,** because they do not depend on the level of output. The quantities of **variable inputs,** in contrast, rise and fall with the level of production. For instance, the firm can work its space and machines for one shift a day, or it can run them for all twenty-four hours. It simply hires more workers and uses more materials. These workers and materials are variable inputs.

Figure 11.4 shows a production function with fixed and variable inputs. At L_0, the fixed inputs are in place. At first, when the firm increases inputs beyond L_0, output increases more than proportionately. Output at L_2 is more than twice output at L_1, even though L_2 is twice L_1. This is due to the effect of the fixed input. As the variable input is increased, the increase in output generated by each successive unit of input decreases due to diminishing returns. Beyond L_3, the effect of diminishing returns outweighs that of fixed inputs and output rises *less* than proportionately with inputs.

The ratio of output to input at any point on the production function is called the **average productivity.** At point *A*, for example, the average productivity is the distance up the vertical axis from the origin (Q_3) divided by the dis-

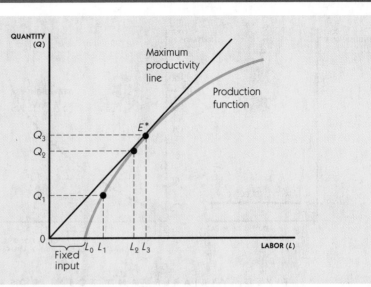

Figure 11.4 PRODUCTION FUNCTION WITH FIXED AND VARIABLE INPUTS

As the amount of labor increases, given the fixed inputs already in place, marginal returns to labor are decreasing, which is shown by the slope of the production function becoming flatter. Average productivity is given by the slope of a line from any point on the production function to the origin, and will be highest at E^*.

tance along the horizontal axis (L_3). This is the slope of the line from the origin to E^*. The steepest line from the origin to the production function touches the production function at E^*. This is the level of production at which output per unit of input is maximized. Notice that average productivity—the slope of the line from the origin to the production function—increases as output increases to point E^*, and falls thereafter. Marginal productivity—the slope of the production function itself—continuously decreases as employment increases beyond L_0.

COST CURVES

The production function is important to the firm because the inputs it depicts determine the costs of production. The case of the production function with fixed inputs described in Figure 11.4 is the most common production function in the economy, and a look at the kinds of costs it generates will give us an overview of the major categories of cost upon which economists concentrate.

FIXED AND VARIABLE COSTS

The costs associated with inputs that do not vary with the level of production are called **fixed costs.** Whether the firm produces nothing or produces at maximum capacity, it antes up the same fixed cost. Figure 11.5 shows how costs depend on output. Panel A depicts fixed costs as a horizontal line—by definition, they do not depend on the level of output. As an example, consider a would-be wheat farmer who has the opportunity to buy a farm and its equipment for $25,000. His fixed costs are $25,000.

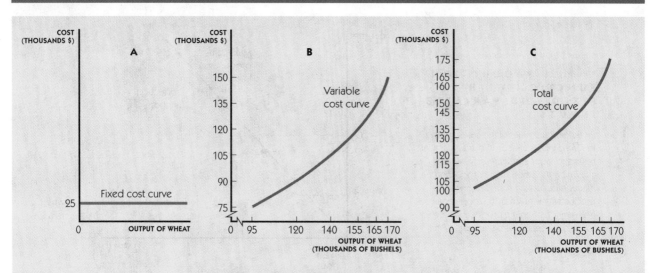

Figure 11.5 FIXED, VARIABLE, AND TOTAL COST CURVES

Panel A shows a firm's fixed cost; by definition, fixed costs do not depend on the level of output. Panel B shows a firm's variable costs, which rise with the level of production. The increasing slope of the curve indicates that it costs more and more to produce at the margin, which is a sign of diminishing returns. Panel C shows a total cost curve. It has the same slope as the variable cost curve, but is higher by the amount of the fixed costs.

Variable costs correspond to variable inputs. These costs rise or fall with the level of production. Any cost that the firm can change during the time period under study is a variable cost. To the extent that such items as labor costs or costs of materials can go up or down as output does, these are variable costs. If we give our farmer only one variable input, labor, then his variable costs would be, say, $15 per hour for each worker. The variable costs corresponding to levels of output listed in Table 11.1 are shown in Table 11.2 and plotted in Figure 11.5B. As output increases, so do variable costs, so the curve slopes upward.

TOTAL COSTS

Table 11.2 also includes a column labeled "Total cost." **Total costs** are defined as the sum of variable and fixed costs, so this column differs from the variable costs column by $25,000, the amount of the firm's fixed cost. The total cost curve, summarizing these points, is shown in Figure 11.5C.

MARGINAL COST AND MARGINAL PRODUCT

As with the economic decisions we have discussed earlier in this book, the most important cost for the firm's decision makers is the **marginal cost.** This is the extra cost corresponding to each additional unit produced. In the case

Table 11.2 **COST OF PRODUCING WHEAT**

Output (bushels)	Labor required (hours)	Total variable cost (at a wage of $15 per hour)	Total cost ($)	Marginal cost ($ per bushel)	Average cost ($ per bushel)	Average variable cost ($ per bushel)
95,000	5,000	75,000	100,000	—	1.05	.79
120,000	6,000	90,000	115,000	.60	.96	.75
140,000	7,000	105,000	130,000	.75	.93	.75
155,000	8,000	120,000	145,000	1.00	.94	.77
165,000	9,000	135,000	160,000	1.50	.97	.82
170,000	10,000	150,000	175,000	3.00	1.03	.88

of the wheat farmer's costs (Table 11.2), as he increases labor input from 7,000 hours to 8,000 hours, output increases by 15,000 bushels. Thus, to produce 1,000 extra bushels requires $1,000/15 = 66\frac{2}{3}$ extra hours. The cost of producing an extra 1,000 bushels is $66\frac{2}{3}$ hours $\times$ wage per hour. If the wage is $15 per hour, the marginal cost of 1,000 bushels is $1,000.

More generally, if *MPL* is the marginal product of labor (15 bushels per hour), and w is the (hourly) wage ($15 per hour), the marginal cost of producing an extra unit of output is just w/MPL ($1 per bushel).

The marginal cost curve depicted in Figure 11.6 is upward sloping, reflect-

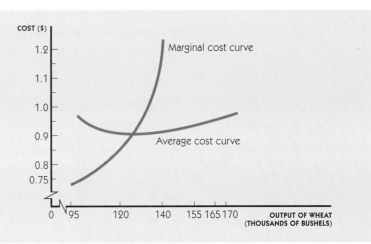

Figure 11.6 MARGINAL AND AVERAGE COST CURVES

The marginal cost is the extra cost of producing one more unit of output. With diminishing returns to an input, marginal costs increase with the level of output. Average costs, also shown here, are total costs divided by output.

ing the fact that as more is produced, it becomes harder and harder to increase output further—an example of the familiar principle of diminishing marginal returns.

RELATIONSHIP BETWEEN MARGINAL AND TOTAL COST CURVES

There is a simple relationship between the marginal cost curve and the total cost curve. The marginal cost is just the slope of the total cost—the change in total costs (movement along the vertical axis, in Figure 11.5C) resulting from a unit change in output (movement along the horizontal axis).

AVERAGE COST

The final set of costs that concern the business firm are its **average costs.** These are simply total costs divided by output. The average cost curve gives average costs corresponding to different levels of output. Figure 11.6 also shows the average cost curve corresponding to the total cost curve depicted in Figure 11.5C. To find the average cost for any level of output, we draw a line from the origin to the point on the total cost curve for that level of output. The slope of that line is

$$\frac{\text{total costs}}{\text{output}} = \text{average costs.}$$

AVERAGE VARIABLE COSTS

The concept of **average variable costs** will be useful in the next chapter when we discuss the production decision. These are total variable costs divided by output.

THE U-SHAPED AVERAGE COST CURVE

The typical average cost curve is U-shaped. To see why, we examine the typical production function in more detail. Shown in Figure 11.7A, it is a slight variant of the production function with a fixed input we saw earlier (Figure 11.4). Two properties of this production function stand out:

1. Just to start production requires a significant input of labor, marked by L_0 in the diagram.
2. Because of diminishing returns, beyond some level of output it requires more and more labor to produce each additional unit of output. It may be almost impossible to increase output beyond some point. That is why the production function flattens out.

Panel B shows what these properties imply for the total cost curve. First, there are fixed costs, c_0. Second, diminishing returns mean that not only do total costs rise as output increases, but the total cost curve becomes steeper

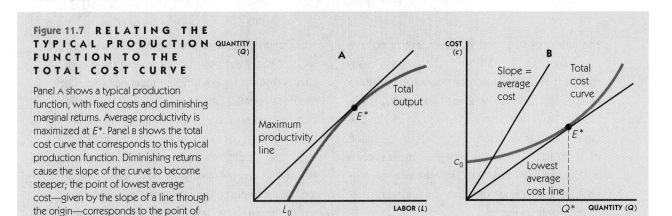

Figure 11.7 RELATING THE TYPICAL PRODUCTION FUNCTION TO THE TOTAL COST CURVE

Panel A shows a typical production function, with fixed costs and diminishing marginal returns. Average productivity is maximized at E^*. Panel B shows the total cost curve that corresponds to this typical production function. Diminishing returns cause the slope of the curve to become steeper; the point of lowest average cost—given by the slope of a line through the origin—corresponds to the point of highest average productivity.

and steeper. Third, average costs, total costs divided by output, are minimized at the output level Q^*. This is shown in Figure 11.8. Average cost is the sum of the average fixed cost—the fixed cost divided by output—and average variable cost. As output increases, average fixed cost declines. Average variable cost, on the other hand, increases with output as the law of diminishing returns sets in with strength. At low levels of output, the first effect dominates, so average costs declines. But once a high enough level of output is achieved, the second effect dominates, so average cost increases with output, as shown in Figure 11.8.

Even if the average cost curve is U-shaped, the output at which average costs are minimized may be very great, so high that there is not enough demand to justify producing that much. Thus, when economists refer to declining average costs, they mean that those costs are declining over the level of output that is likely to prevail in the market.

Relationship between Average and Marginal Cost Curves The relationship between average costs and marginal costs is reflected in Figure 11.8. The marginal cost curve intersects the average cost at the bottom of the U—the *minimum* average cost. To understand why the marginal cost curve will *always* intersect the average cost curve at its lowest point, consider the relationship between average and marginal costs. As long as the marginal cost is below the average cost, producing an additional unit will pull down the average. Thus, everywhere that the marginal cost is below average cost, the average cost curve is declining. If marginal cost is above average cost, then producing an additional unit will raise the average. So everywhere that the marginal cost is above average cost, the average cost curve must be rising. The point between where the U-shaped average cost curve is falling and where it is rising is the minimum point.

Figure 11.8 RELATING THE MARGINAL COST CURVE TO THE AVERAGE COST CURVE

The average cost curve is usually U-shaped. it initially declines as the fixed costs are spread over a larger amount of output, and then rises as diminishing returns to the variable input become increasingly important. With a U-shaped average cost curve, the marginal cost curve will cross the average cost curve at its minimum.

CLOSE-UP: HOW IMPORTANT IS THE FORTUNE 500?

The model of small and very competitive companies may seem like an abstraction. When many people think of the American economy, they think of huge companies like Exxon, IBM, and General Motors. Each year, *Fortune* magazine lists the 500 largest companies in the United States; it is a sort of honor roll of corporate America, where success is equated with size. But the existence of large companies does not disprove the importance of the competitive model.

Large firms are not immune from competition, either from other large firms or from upstarts. For the last few decades, the importance of the Fortune 500 has been declining relative to growth in the rest of the economy. Competitive pressure is eating away at even the largest companies, while the importance of small- and middle-sized companies has been increasing. In 1970, for example, the Fortune 500 employed a total of 14.6 million workers. About one worker in five was with a Fortune 500 company. By 1990, though, the Fortune 500 employed only 12.4 million, a decline of 15 percent from 1970. Since employment in the rest of the economy had been growing in that time, the share of total employment in the Fortune 500 fell. Only about one person in ten worked for one of the biggest 500 companies.

Sales figures tell a similar story. Between 1970 and 1990 sales reported by the Fortune 500 increased by 59 percent in real terms. However, the economy as a whole grew by 72 percent over that time, so the Fortune 500 was lagging well behind.

The reduced role of the biggest American corporations has given rise to considerable debate. Some argue that a globally connected economy increases the importance of bigness. Big compa-

nies can invest in larger projects, distribute and sell all over the globe, and compete with huge companies from other countries. Others respond that the rise of smaller, often new companies promotes competition and innovation and thus serves consumers better. For example, the David and Goliath story of Apple, whose first computer was launched from the garage of its founders, versus longtime computer giant IBM in the market for personal computers has fascinated industry observers. Confronted with a myriad of competitors in the personal computer market—including Compaq, Dell, Toshiba, and many others—IBM has not been able to dominate. Its share of the world market in personal computers has fallen to only 8 percent.

Sources: Fortune 500 numbers taken from April issues of *Fortune;* U.S. figures are from *Economic Report of the President* (1991).

Figure 11.9 COST CURVES WITH INCREASING OR CONSTANT RETURNS

Panels A and B show total, marginal, and average cost curves with increasing returns. Average costs decline as production increases. Panel C shows a total cost curve with constant returns; since returns to the variable factor are constant and fixed costs are zero, the total cost curve begins at the origin and its slope does not change. Panel D shows marginal and average costs with constant returns; marginal cost does not change, and so the average cost does not change either.

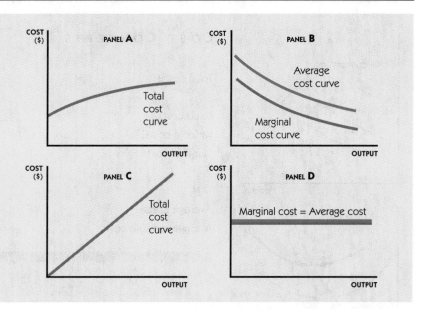

ALTERNATIVE SHAPES OF COST CURVES

Earlier, we saw that production functions may exhibit increasing or constant returns. If there are increasing returns, output increases more than proportionately with the input and total costs increase more slowly than output, as seen in panel A of Figure 11.9. In this case average costs decline, as illustrated in panel B. Marginal costs are also declining, corresponding to a situation where the marginal product of labor increases as output decreases.

If there are constant returns, doubling inputs doubles output, which will cost twice as much. In this case, total costs are simply proportional to output (panel C), and average and marginal costs are constant and equal (panel D).

CHANGING FACTOR PRICES AND COST CURVES

The cost curves shown thus far are based on the fixed prices of each of the inputs firms purchase. An increase in the price of a variable factor, such as the wage, or the price of some raw material, shifts the total, average, and marginal cost curves upward, as illustrated in Figure 11.10. An increase in the price of a fixed factor shifts only the total and average cost curves upward.

Figure 11.10 HOW CHANGING INPUT PRICES AFFECT COST CURVES

An increase in the price of a variable factor shifts the total, average, and marginal cost curves upward.

COST CONCEPTS

Total costs:	Total costs of producing output = fixed costs + variable costs
Fixed costs:	Costs that do not depend on output
Variable costs:	Costs that depend on output
Marginal costs:	Extra cost of producing an extra unit = total cost of ($Q + 1$) units minus total cost of Q units of output
Average costs:	Total costs divided by output
Average variable costs:	Total variable costs divided by output

PRODUCTION WITH MANY FACTORS

The basic principles of the case with only two factors—one fixed, one variable—apply also to firms producing many products with many different inputs. The only fundamental difference is that with many factors it becomes possible to produce the same output in several different ways. Cost minimization, therefore, involves weighing the costs of different mixes of inputs. (The analysis is somewhat more complicated, and is in the appendix to this chapter.)

COST MINIMIZATION

There are usually several ways a good can be produced, using different quantities of various inputs. Table 11.3 illustrates two alternative ways of making car frames, one a highly automated process requiring little labor and the other a less automated process that uses more assembly-line workers. The table shows the daily wage and capital costs for each process. Each method produces the same quantity of output (say, 10,000 car frames per day). In this simple example, we assume all workers are identical (of equal skill) and hence get paid the same wage, and that all machines cost the same. As we can see from the table, the less automated process clearly costs more at the given costs of labor ($20 per worker per hour) and machines (rental costs equal $1,000 per day).

Although this table provides only two stark alternatives, it should be clear that in some cases the alternative possibilities for production will form a con-

Table 11.3 **COSTS OF PRODUCTION**

Inputs	More automated process	Less automated process
Labor	50 man hours @ $20 = $1,000	500 man hours @ $20 = $10,000
Machines	5 machines @ $1,000 = $5,000	2 machines @ $1,000 = $ 2,000
Total	$6,000	$12,000

tinuum, where the input of one increases a bit, the input of another falls a bit, and output remains the same. In other words, the firm can smoothly substitute one input for another. For instance, in producing cars, different machines vary slightly in the degree of automation. Machines requiring less and less labor to run them cost more. When firms make their decisions about investment, they thus have a wide range of intermediate choices between the two described in the table.

THE PRINCIPLE OF SUBSTITUTION

One of the most important consequences of the principle of cost minimization in the case of multiple factors of production is that when the price of one input (say, oil) increases relative to that of other factors of production, the change in relative prices causes firms to substitute cheaper inputs for the more costly factor. This is an illustration of the general **principle of substitution** we encountered in Chapter 4.

THE PRINCIPLE OF SUBSTITUTION

An increase in the price of an input will lead the firm to substitute other inputs in its place.

In some cases, substitution is quick and easy; in other cases, it may take time and be difficult. When the price of oil increased fourfold in 1973 and doubled again in 1979, firms found many ways to economize on the use of oil. For instance, companies switched from oil to gas (and in the case of electric power companies, often to coal) as a source of energy. More energy-efficient cars and trucks were constructed, often using lighter materials like aluminum and plastics. These substitutions took time, but they did eventually occur.

The principle of substitution should serve as a warning to those who think they can raise prices without bearing any consequences. Argentina has almost a world monopoly on linseed oil. At one time, linseed oil was universally used for making high-quality paints. Since there was no competition, Argentina decided that it would raise the price of linseed oil and assumed everyone would have to pay it. But as the price increased, paint manufacturers learned to substitute other natural oils that could do almost as well.

Raising the price of labor (wages) provides another example. Unions in the auto and steel industries successfully demanded higher wages for their members during the boom periods of the 1960s and 1970s, and firms paid the higher wages. But at the same time, the firms redoubled their efforts to mechanize their production and to become less dependent on their labor force. Over time, these efforts were successful and led to a decline in employment in those industries.

DIAGRAMMATIC ANALYSIS

We can see the principle of substitution at work using our average cost diagrams. The car manufacturer described earlier has two alternative ways of producing cars, each with its own average cost curve. Both are shown in Figure 11.11. The general principle of cost minimization requires that the firm use the method of production with the lowest average costs at the planned level of production. In the figure, at high levels of production (above Q_1), the more mechanized process with average cost curve AC_2 dominates the less mechanized process with average cost curve AC_1. A smaller-scale producer, however, uses the less mechanized process. Assume now the cost of labor increases. This shifts up the cost curves for both ways of producing, but obviously, the less mechanized process—which is more dependent on labor—has its cost curve shifted up more. As a result, the critical output at

Figure 11.11 MINIMIZING COSTS AS INPUT PRICES CHANGE

With two production processes, as the price of an input increases—in this case, labor—both average cost curves shift up. However, AC_1 relies more heavily on labor, so it shifts up more. This means that firms will switch to the more mechanized technology of AC_2 at a lower level of output (Q_2 instead of Q_1), and there will tend to be a shift away from the more expensive input, labor, and toward the relatively cheaper capital.

COST ($)

Less mechanized process

AC'_1

AC_1

AC'_2

AC_2

More mechanized process

1. Higher labor costs shift AC of both processes up.

2. This shifts down the quantity at which it pays to use the more mechanized process.

Q_2 Q_1

QUANTITY (Q)

POLICY PERSPECTIVE: THE SUBSTITUTION PRINCIPLE AND GLOBAL WARMING

In the two hundred years since the beginning of the industrial revolution, there has been an enormous increase in the amount of carbon dioxide (CO_2) in the atmosphere; and concentrations are expected to increase rapidly over coming decades. There is an increasing consensus that the increased concentration of this and related gases (called greenhouse gases) will lead to global warming, with potentially significant impacts on the environment. Reflecting this consensus, the nation's of the world signed an agreement in Rio de Janeiro in 1992 to work towards limiting their growth. Slowing down the rate of increase of these greenhouse gases will entail using less energy, and substituting away from sources of energy that produce large amounts of greenhouse gases—like coal—towards sources of energy that produce less—like natural gas—or none at all, like hydroelectric power. A carbon tax, levied on various fuels in proportion to how much they contribute to greenhouse gases, has been suggested as one way of encouraging firms to substitute away from coal and toward fuels that are environmentally more sound.

which it pays to use the more mechanized production process is lowered, from Q_1 to Q_2. Thus, as the price of labor is increased, more firms switch to a more mechanized process—capital goods (machines) are substituted for labor.

An increase in the price of any input shifts the cost function up. The amount by which the cost function shifts up depends on several factors, including how much of the input was being used in the first place and how easy it is to substitute other inputs. If the production process uses a great deal of the input, then the cost will shift up a lot. If there is a large increase in the price of an input, and the firm cannot easily substitute other inputs, then the cost curve will shift up more than it would if substitution of other inputs were easy.

SHORT-RUN AND LONG-RUN COST CURVES

Up to this point, we have referred to the distinction between inputs that are fixed (their cost does not vary with quantity produced) and inputs that are variable (their cost does depend on quantity produced). We have sidestepped the fact that inputs, and costs, may be fixed for some period of time, but if the time period is long enough, they can vary with production. Take the inputs of labor and machines, for example. In the short run, the supply of machines may be fixed. Output is then increased only by increasing labor. In the longer run, both machines and workers can be adjusted. The short-run cost curve, then, is the cost of production with a *given* stock of machines. The long-run cost curve is the cost of production when all factors are adjusted.[1]

SHORT-RUN COST CURVES

If we think of the number of machines as being fixed in the short run, and labor as the principal input that can be varied, our earlier analysis of production with a single variable factor provides a good description of short-run cost curves. Thus, short-run *average* cost curves are normally U-shaped.

The short-run *marginal* cost curve in Figure 11.12 presents a pattern often seen in manufacturing. Marginal costs are approximately constant over a wide range. As long as their newest machines are not being fully used, firms find that increasing production by 10 percent requires increasing the number of production workers by 10 percent and the inputs of other materials (raw materials, intermediate goods) by 10 percent. Idle machines are simply put to work. Eventually, however, the cost of producing extra units goes up. Workers have to work more hours (and often they get paid more—time and a half or double time—for these extra hours). Overworked machines break down more frequently. Older, poorer machines have to be put to use. At some level of output, it may be impossible, without extraordinary costs, to push a factory to a higher level of production in the short run.

Figure 11.12 SHORT-RUN MARGINAL COSTS

When there is excess capacity, the marginal cost of producing an extra unit may not increase much, and so the marginal cost curve is flat. But when capacity is approached, marginal costs may rise rapidly.

[1]The distinction between short-run and long-run costs corresponds to the distinction between short-run and long-run supply curves introduced in Chapter 4. Chapter 12 will make clear the relationship. It is an exaggeration to think that only capital goods are fixed in the short run while all of labor is variable. In some cases, capital goods may easily be varied; a firm can, for instance, rent cars. And in some cases, as when a company has long-term contracts with its workers, it may be very difficult to vary labor in the short run.

We have thus identified two key properties of the short-run marginal cost curve. (1) When there is unused or excess capacity, the marginal cost of producing each extra unit does not increase much; the marginal cost curve is relatively flat. (2) But eventually the marginal cost curve becomes steeply upward sloping. (Remember, we are focusing here on the short run, so we assume the number of machines is fixed; there is a particular capacity for which the plant was designed.)

Before we turn to the long run, it is useful to rethink the meaning of fixed costs. So far, we have used the term to mean costs that do not depend on the level of output. This in fact blurs the distinction between two related concepts. Even if a firm could instantaneously adjust all factors of production, some overhead costs would still be required for the company to exist at all. From now on, **overhead costs** will be defined as costs that a firm must bear simply to operate, whether or not they can be varied in the short run. For a firm to be in business at all, for example, it probably needs telephone service. **Fixed costs** will be defined as costs that are fixed in the short run, whether or not they represent overhead costs. For example, if a firm signs a contract to rent a warehouse at $5,000 a month for ten years, its warehouse rental costs are fixed in the short run.

LONG-RUN COST CURVES

Even if the short-run average cost curves for a given manufacturing facility are U-shaped, the long-run average cost curve may not have the same shape. As production grows, it will pay at some point to build a second plant, and then a third, a fourth, and so on. Panel A of Figure 11.13 shows the total costs of producing different levels of output, assuming that the firm builds one plant. This curve is marked TC_1. It also shows the total costs of producing different levels of output assuming the firm builds two plants (TC_2) and three plants (TC_3). How many plants will the company build? Clearly, the firm wishes to minimize the (total) costs of producing at any level of output. Thus, the *relevant* total cost curve is the lower boundary of the three curves, which is heavily shaded. Between 0 and Q_1, the firm produces using one plant; between Q_1 and Q_2, it uses two plants; and for outputs larger than Q_2, it uses three plants.

We can see the same results in panel B, using average cost curves. Obviously, if the firm minimizes the total costs of producing any particular output, it minimizes the average cost of producing that output. The figure shows the average cost curves corresponding to the firm's producing with one, two, and three plants. The company chooses the number of plants that minimizes its average costs, given the level of output it plans to produce. Thus, if the firm plans to produce less than Q_1, it builds only one plant; AC_1 is less than AC_2 for all outputs less than Q_1. If the firm plans to produce between Q_1 and Q_2, it builds two plants, because AC_2 is, in this interval, less than either AC_1 or AC_3. Similarly, for outputs greater than Q_2, the firm builds three plants.

In this case, the long-run average cost curve is the shaded bumpy curve in

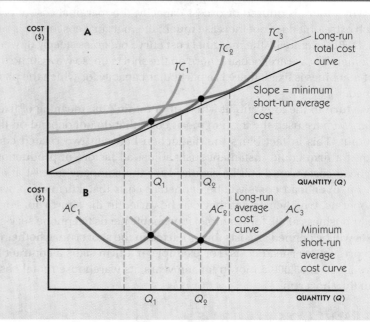

Figure 11.13 SHORT-RUN AND LONG-RUN COST CURVES

Panel A shows a series of short-run total cost curves, TC_1, TC_2, and TC_3, each representing a different level of fixed capital input. In the long run, a cost-minimizing firm can choose any of these, so the long-run total cost curve will be the lowest cost of producing any level of output, as shown by the heavily shaded lower boundary of the curves. Panel B shows a series of short-run average cost curves, AC_1, AC_2, and AC_3, each representing a different level of fixed capital input. In the long run, a cost-minimizing firm can choose any of these, so the long-run average cost curve will be the shaded lower boundary of the curves.

Figure 11.13B. For large outputs, the bumps look very small. In drawing long-run average cost curves, therefore, we typically ignore the bumps and draw smooth curves.

We now need to ask whether long-run average cost curves are normally flat or slope upward or downward. To answer this question, remember how we analyzed the shape of the short-run average cost curve, or the average cost curve with a single variable input. We first described the production function, relating the level of input to the level of output. If output increases less than proportionately with the input because there are diminishing returns, the average cost curve is rising. If output increases more than proportionately with the input, there are increasing returns, and the average cost curve is falling.

Exactly the same kind of analysis applies when there are many inputs. We ask, what happens when all of the inputs increase together? If, when all of the inputs increase together and in proportion, output increases just in proportion, there are **constant returns to scale;** if output increases less than proportionately, there are **diminishing returns to scale;** and if output increases more than proportionately, there are **increasing returns to scale,** or **economies of scale.**

Many economists argue that constant returns to scale are most prevalent in manufacturing; a firm can increase its production simply by replicating its plants. Then the long-run average and marginal costs equal minimum short-run average costs. The average and marginal cost curves for such a case are depicted in Figure 11.14, where there are many, many plants, and the long-run average cost curve is flat. (The small "bumps" are caused by the fact that output may not be a simple multiple of the output at which a plant attains its

Figure 11.14 THE SHAPE OF THE LONG-RUN AVERAGE COST CURVE

If there are many possibilities for varying the scale of the firm, such as by adding new machines and thus many short-run average cost curves, the long-run average cost curve defined by their joint boundary can be thought of as very flat, or smooth. In this case, the long-run average cost curve is drawn as horizontal. The firm can increase output simply by replicating identical plants, and there are constant returns to scale.

minimum average costs; but, as the figure shows, these bumps become relatively insignificant if output is very large.)

There are, however, also costs to running a firm—the overhead costs. The firm must bear these costs whether it operates 1, 2, or 100 plants. These overhead costs include not only the costs of the corporate headquarters, but also the basic costs of designing the original plant. Thus, we commonly think of the long-run average cost curve as slightly downward sloping, as in Figure 11.15A.

But sometimes small is beautiful, and big is bad. In these cases there are diminishing returns to scale. As the firm tries to grow, adding additional plants, it faces increasing managerial problems; it may have to add layer upon layer of management, and each of these layers increases its cost. When the firm is very small, the owner can watch all his workers. When the firm has grown to 10 employees, the owner can no longer supervise his workers effectively; a new supervisor may be needed every time his firm hires 10 more workers. By the time the firm has grown to 100 workers, he has 10 supervisors. Now the owner spends most of his time looking after the supervisors, not the workers directly.

Eventually, the owner finds it difficult to keep tabs on the supervisors, so it becomes necessary to hire a manager for them. Notice that in this pattern, the number of supervisors and managers is a growing proportion of the workers in the firm. An organization with 10 workers requires only 1 supervisor; with 100 workers, it requires 10 supervisors and a manager; with 1,000 workers, 100 supervisors, 10 managers, and 1 supermanager. Besides the raw numbers of administrative people, decisions now must pass through a number of layers of bureaucracy, and communication will often be slower.

Eventually, average costs may start to increase, as illustrated in Figure 11.15 B. Whether any particular industry is best described by Figure 11.14, 11.15A, or 11.15B depends on the importance of overhead costs and the extent to which managerial problems grow with size.

Increasing returns to scale are also possible in some industries, even for

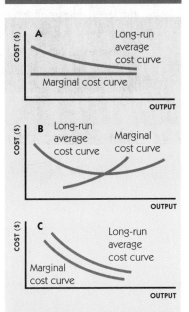

Figure 11.15 LONG-RUN AVERAGE COSTS

Panel A shows that with overhead costs, long-run average costs may be declining, but they flatten out as output increases. In panel B, with managerial costs increasing with the scale of the firm, eventually average and marginal costs may start to rise. Panel C shows that if there are increasing returns to scale, long-run costs may be continuously falling.

very large outputs. As the firm produces a higher output, it can take advantage of larger and more efficient machines, which it would not pay a small firm to purchase. If there are increasing returns to scale, then the long-run average cost curve and the marginal cost curve will be downward sloping, as in Figure 11.15c.

LOOKING BEYOND THE BASIC MODEL: COST CURVES AND THE COMPETITIVENESS OF MARKETS

The degree of competition in an industry depends to a considerable degree on the structure of costs in that industry. This leads us to several insights that take us beyond the basic model. Consider the case of one company that is producing all the market wants in an industry with declining average costs. If any new company wishes to enter this market and produce less than the incumbent firm, its average costs will be higher than that of the incumbent company. So long as the original firm produces more than the entrant, its costs will be lower, so it can undercut the newcomer—and in fact charge a price so low that the new firm suffers a loss while the incumbent firm still makes a profit. Indeed, if the original merchant charges a price just equal to his average costs (or threatens to do so if an entrant tries to crash into his market), there is no way that a rival can profitably enter.

If, in contrast, the incumbent firm is the only firm producing for the entire market but is on the upward-sloping portion of an average cost curve, a new company might aim at producing less with a lower average cost. Now, at least one new company will be able to undersell the original firm, and competitive forces will have some power.

The magnitude of the output at which average costs are minimized depends largely on the size of overhead costs, relative to total costs. In industries in which overhead costs are low, there will normally be many firms, since average costs will reach their minimum value at a relatively low level of output. Since the average cost curve may begin to rise quite rapidly beyond a relatively small output, small firms have the power to undersell larger firms, and there will be many firms in the market. Businesses with low overhead costs include real estate and travel agencies. In these industries, the typical firm is small, and there are thousands of them.

In industries in which overhead costs are high, however, the minimum average costs will be attained at a very high output, so there will be relatively few firms. Low-cost producers in these industries tend to be large firms, and relatively few fill the market demand. Makers of automobiles and household appliances are examples. In some industries, overhead average costs are declining throughout the output levels demanded in the market. In these cases, at least within any locality, there will be only one firm. Examples include electricity and other utility companies and cement plants. A main cost for most utilities is the cost of the wires (for electricity and telephone) or pipes (for water and sewage).

Expenditures to develop a new product are like high overhead costs in their effect on entry into a market. Firms can, of course, choose to spend more or less on research or on developing new products, but these costs do not increase with the firm's level of output. It is not surprising, then, that in many of the sectors of the economy in which research and development expenditures are important, there are relatively few firms. For example, the chemical industry is dominated by a small number of large firms.

ECONOMIES OF SCOPE

Most firms produce more than one good. Deciding which goods to produce and in what quantities, and how to produce them (the first and second basic economic questions), are central problems facing firm managers. The problems would be fairly straightforward, were it not for some important interrelations among the products. The production of one product may affect the costs of producing another.

In some cases, products are produced naturally together; we say they are **joint products.** Thus, a sheep farm naturally produces wool, lamb meat, and mutton. If more lambs are slaughtered for meat, there will be less wool and less mutton.

If it is less expensive to produce a set of goods together than separately, economists say that there are **economies of scope.** The concept of economies of scope helps us understand why certain sets of activities are often undertaken by the same firms. Issues of economies of scope have also played an important role in discussions of regulation over the past two decades. At the time of the breakup of AT&T, which previously had dominated both local and long-distance telephone service as well as research in telecommunications, some economists argued against the breakup on the grounds that there were important economies of scope among these activities.

REVIEW AND PRACTICE

SUMMARY

1. A firm's production function specifies the level of output resulting from any combination of inputs. The increase in output corresponding to a unit increase in any input is the marginal product of that input.

2. Short-run marginal cost curves are generally upward sloping, because diminishing returns to a factor of production imply that it will take ever increasing amounts of the input to produce a marginal unit of output.

3. The typical short-run average cost curve is U-shaped. With U-shaped average cost curves, the marginal and average cost curves will intersect at the minimum point of the average cost curve.

4. When a number of different inputs can be varied, and the price of one input increases, the change in relative prices of inputs will encourage a firm to substitute relatively less expensive inputs; this is an application of the principle of substitution.

5. Economists often distinguish between short-run and long-run cost curves. In the short run, a firm is generally assumed not to be able to change its capital stock. In the long run, it can. Even if short-run average cost curves are U-shaped, long-run average cost curves can take on a variety of shapes. They can, for instance, be flat, continuously declining, or declining and then increasing.

6. Economies of scope exist when it is less expensive to produce two products together than it would be to produce each one separately.

KEY TERMS

profits
revenues
production function
marginal product
fixed inputs
variable inputs
average productivity

fixed costs
overhead costs
variable costs
total costs
marginal cost
average costs
average variable
   costs

constant, diminish-
   ing, or increasing
   returns to scale
   (economies of
   scale)
economies of scope

REVIEW QUESTIONS

1. What is a production function? When there is a single (variable) input, why does output normally increase less than in proportion to input? What are the alternative shapes that the relationship between input and output takes? What is the relationship between these shapes and the shape of the cost function?

2. What is meant by these various concepts of cost: total, average, average variable, marginal, and fixed? What are the relationships between these costs? What are short-run and long-run costs? What is the relationship between them?

3. Why are short-run average cost curves frequently U-shaped? With U-shaped average cost curves, what is the relationship between average and marginal costs? If the average cost curve is U-shaped, what does the total cost curve look like?

4. What happens to average, marginal, and total costs when the price of an input rises?

5. If a firm has a number of variable inputs and the price of one of them rises, will the firm use more or less of this input? Why?

6. What are diminishing, constant, and increasing returns to scale? When might you expect each to occur? What is the relationship between these properties of the production function and the shape of the long-run average and total cost curves?

7. What are economies of scope, and how do they affect what a firm chooses to produce?

PROBLEMS

1. Tom and Dick, who own the Tom, Dick, and Hairy Barbershop, need to decide how many barbers to hire. The production function for their barbershop looks like this:

Number of barbers	Haircuts provided per day		Marginal product
		AP	
0	0	—	—
1	12	12	12
2	36	18	24
3	60	20	24
4	72	18	12
5	80	16	8
6	84	14	4

Calculate the marginal product of hiring additional barbers, and fill in the last column of the table. Over what range is the marginal product of labor increasing? constant? diminishing? Graph the production function. By looking at the graph, you should be able to tell at what point the average productivity of labor is highest. Calculate average productivity at each point to illustrate your answer.

2. The overhead costs of the Tom, Dick, and Hairy Barbershop are $160 per day, and the cost of paying a barber for a day is $80. With this information, and the information in problem #1, make up a table with column headings in this order: Output, Labor required, Total variable cost, Total cost, Marginal cost, Average variable cost, and Average cost. If the price of a haircut is $10 and the shop sells 80 per day, what is the daily profit? 240

Q	L	TVC	TC	MC	AVC	AC
0	0	0	160	—	—	∞
12	1	80	240	6.66	6.66	20
36	2	160	320	3.33	4.44	8.88
60	3	240	400	3.33	4	6.66
72	4	320	480	6.66	4.44	6.66
80	5	400	560	10	5	7
84	6	480	640	20	5.71	7.62

3. Using the information in problems #1 and #2, draw the total cost curve for the Tom, Dick, and Hairy Barbershop on one graph. On a second graph, draw the marginal cost curve, the average cost curve, and the average variable cost curve. Do these curves have the shape you would expect? Do the minimum and average cost curves intersect at the point you expect?

4. Suppose a firm has the choice of two methods of producing: one method entails a fixed cost of $10 and a marginal cost of $2; the other entails a fixed cost of $20 and a marginal cost of $1. Draw the total and average cost curves for both methods. At what levels of output will the firm use the low fixed-cost technology? At what levels of output will it use the high fixed-cost technology?

5. A firm produces cars using labor and capital. Assume that average labor productivity—total output divided by the number of workers—has increased in the last few months. Does that mean that workers are working harder? Or that the firm has become more efficient? Explain.

APPENDIX: COST MINIMIZATION WITH MANY INPUTS

This appendix shows how the basic principles of cost minimization can be applied to a firm's choice of the mix of inputs to use in production. To do this, we make use of a set of concepts and tools similar to those presented in the appendix to Chapter 8, in the analysis of how households make decisions about what mix of goods to purchase.

ISOQUANTS

The alternative ways of producing a particular quantity of output can be graphically represented by **isoquants.** The first part of the term comes from the Greek word *iso,* meaning "same," while "quant" is just shorthand for quantity. Thus, isoquants illustrate the different combinations of inputs that produce the same quantity.

Consider this simple extension of the example of Table 11.3 on page 263. A firm can buy three different kinds of machines, each of which produces car frames. One is a highly mechanized machine that requires very little labor. Another is much less automated and requires considerably more labor. In between is another technique. These represent three different ways of producing the same quantity.

Assume the firm wishes to produce 10,000 car frames a day. It could do this by using highly mechanized machines, moderately mechanized machines, or nonmechanized machines. The total capital and labor requirements for each of these possibilities are represented in Figure 11.16. The horizontal axis shows the capital requirements, while the vertical axis shows the labor requirements. The labor and capital associated with the highly mechanized production process is shown by point *A*, the moderately mechanized by point *B*, and the low mechanized by point *C*.

If the firm wishes, it can produce half of its output on the highly mechanized machines and half on the moderately mechanized machines. If it chooses this option, its capital requirements will be halfway between the capital that would be required if it used only *A* or only *B*, and its labor requirements will also be halfway between. This halfway-between choice is illustrated by point *X*. By similar logic, the firm can achieve any combination of capital and labor requirements on the straight line joining *A* and *B* by changing the proportion of highly mechanized and moderately mechanized machines. And by changing the proportion of moderately mechanized and low-mechanized machines, it can achieve any combination of capital and labor requirements on the straight line joining *B* and *C*. The curve *ABC* is the isoquant. It gives all those combinations of capital and labor that can produce 10,000 automobile frames per day. All of these input combinations give the same output.

Figure 11.16 THREE ALTERNATIVE METHODS OF PRODUCING A CERTAIN AMOUNT

Point *A* represents the inputs for a highly mechanized way of producing a certain number of car frames; point *C* represents a technique of production that uses a much less expensive machine, but more labor; point *B* represents a technique that is in between. By using different techniques in different proportions, the firm can use a combination of labor and capital on the line joining *A* and *B*, such as point *X*. The curve *ABC* is an isoquant.

Figure 11.17 ISOQUANTS AND THE MARGINAL RATE OF SUBSTITUTION

Panel A shows an isoquant defined with many alternative techniques of production. Panel B shows that as the number of production techniques increases, isoquants appear as a smooth curve. The slope of the isoquant tells how much of one input must be added to make up for the loss of a unit of the other input; this is the marginal rate of technical substitution.

Consider now what happens if many techniques are available instead of only three. The isoquant consists of points designating each of the techniques, and the short line segments connecting these points that represent combinations of two techniques, as shown in Figure 11.17A. When many, many production techniques are available, the isoquant looks much like a smooth curve, and economists often draw it that way, as in panel B.

Many different isoquants can be drawn, each representing one particular level of output, as in panel B. Higher isoquants represent higher levels of production; lower isoquants represent lower levels.[2] There is also a simple relationship between the production functions discussed above and isoquants. The production function gives the output corresponding to each level of inputs. The isoquant tells what are the levels of inputs that can yield a given level of output.

MARGINAL RATE OF TECHNICAL SUBSTITUTION

The idea of marginal rate of substitution was introduced in the appendix to Chapter 8 to describe how individuals are willing to trade off less of one good for more of another. The concept is also useful in analyzing what technology firms will choose. In the case of firms, the marginal rate of substitution is defined not by individual preferences but by actual physical facts. If a firm reduces one input by a unit and then raises another input enough so that the final output remains the same, the amount of extra input required is called the **marginal rate of technical substitution.**

An example should help to clarify this idea. If a firm can reduce the amount of capital it uses by 1 machine, hire 2 more workers, and produce the same quantity, then it is possible for 2 workers to replace 1 machine. In this case, the marginal rate of technical substitution between workers and machines is 2/1. The marginal rate of technical substitution is just the slope of the isoquant, as Figure 11.17B shows diagrammatically: the slope simply tells how much of an increase in labor is needed to offset a one-unit decrease in capital to produce the same amount of output.[3]

Notice that the marginal rate of technical substitution and the slope of the isoquant change with the quantities of labor and capital involved. With fewer and fewer machines, it becomes increasingly difficult to substitute workers for machines. The marginal rate of technical substitution rises, and the slope of the isoquant becomes steeper and steeper. At the other end of the isoquant, with more and more machines, it becomes easier and easier to replace one of

[2]Readers who have read the Chapter 8 appendix on indifference curves should recognize the similarities between isoquants and indifference curves: while indifference curves give those combinations of goods that yield the individual the same level of utility, the isoquant gives those combinations of goods (inputs) that yield the firm the same level of output.

[3]Again, readers who earlier studied indifference curves will recall that the slope of the indifference curve is also called the marginal rate of substitution; it tells us how much extra of one good is required when consumption of another good is reduced by one unit, if we wish to leave the individual at the same level of welfare—on his indifference curve.

them. The marginal rate of technical substitution diminishes as the number of machines increases, and the slope of the isoquant becomes flatter. There is a **diminishing marginal rate of technical substitution** in production, just as there was a diminishing marginal rate of substitution in consumption.

The marginal rate of technical substitution can be calculated from the marginal products of labor and capital. If adding 1 more worker increases the output of automobile frames by 1, the marginal product of an extra worker in this industrial process is 1 (car frame). Let us also imagine that adding 1 machine leads to an increase in car output of, say, 2 a day. So in this industrial process, the marginal product of a machine is 2. In this example, adding 2 workers and reducing machine input by 1 leaves output unchanged. Thus, the marginal rate of technical substitution is 2/1. In general, the marginal rate of technical substitution is equal to the ratio of the marginal products.

The principle of diminishing returns explains why the marginal rate of technical substitution diminishes as a firm adds more and more machines. As it adds more machines, the marginal product of an additional machine diminishes. As the number of workers is reduced, the marginal product of an additional worker is increased. As workers are becoming more productive at the margin and machines are becoming less productive at the margin, it becomes increasingly easier to replace machines with additional workers.

Notice that calculating the marginal rate of substitution does not tell the firm whether it *should* substitute workers for machines, or machines for workers. The number itself only provides factual information about what the trade-off would be, based on the technology available to the firm. To decide which combination of inputs should be chosen, the firm must also know the market prices of the various inputs.

$$Q(k, l) = c$$

$$\frac{dQ}{dk} \, dk + \frac{dQ}{dl} \, dl = 0$$

$$\frac{dl}{dk} = \frac{-\frac{dQ}{dk}}{\frac{dQ}{dl}}$$

$$\frac{dl}{dk} = \frac{-MP_k}{MP_l}$$

COST MINIMIZATION

Minimizing costs requires marginal decision making. Firms know the technology they are currently using and can consider changing it by trading off some inputs against others. To decide whether such a trade-off will reduce costs, they calculate the marginal rate of technical substitution and simply compare the market price of the input they are reducing with the price of the input they are increasing. If a firm can replace 1 machine with 2 workers and maintain the same output, and if a worker costs $12,000 a year and a machine costs $25,000 a year to rent, then by reducing machines by 1 and hiring 2 workers, the firm can reduce total costs. On the other hand, if a worker costs $13,000, it would pay to use 2 fewer workers (for a saving of $26,000) and rent 1 machine (for a cost of $25,000).

The only time that it would not pay the firm either to increase labor and reduce the number of machines or to decrease labor and increase the number of machines is when the marginal rate of technical substitution is equal to the relative price of the two factors. The reason for this is similar to the reason why individuals set their personal marginal rates of substitution equal to the ratio of market prices. The difference is that the individual's marginal rate of substitution is determined by individual preferences, while the firm's marginal rate of technical substitution is determined by technology.

Figure 11.18 COST MINI-MIZATION

Cost-minimizing firms will wish to produce as much output as they can given a particular level of expenditure, so they will choose the highest isoquant they can reach with a given isocost curve, which will be the isoquant tangent to the isocost curve.

ISOCOST CURVES

The **isocost** curve gives those combinations of inputs that cost the same amount. The isocost curve is analogous to an individual's budget constraint, which gives those combinations of goods that cost the same amount. If a firm faces fixed prices for its inputs, the isocost curve is a straight line, whose slope indicates the relative prices; that is, if each worker costs, say, $50 per day, then if the firm reduces the labor used by one, it could spend $50 per day on renting more machines. If renting a machine for a day costs $100, then the firm can rent one more machine with the amount it would save by reducing the input of labor by two. There are, of course, many isocost lines, one for each level of expenditure. Lower isocost lines represent lower expenditures on inputs. Costs along line C_1C_1 in Figure 11.18 are lower than costs along CC. The different isocost lines are parallel to one another, just as different household budget constraints representing different income levels are parallel.

Notice that all firms facing the same prices for inputs will have the same isocost lines. Similarly, different individuals with the same income face the same budget constraint, even when their preferences differ. However, the isoquant curves that describe each firm are based on the product the firm is making and the technology and knowledge available to the firm. Thus, isoquant curves will differ from firm to firm.

Isoquant curves and isocost lines can illuminate the behavior of a cost-minimizing firm. For example, any efficient profit-maximizing firm will wish to maximize the output it obtains from any given expenditure. Or to rephrase the same point, the firm must reach the highest possible isoquant, given a particular level of expenditure on inputs, represented by a particular isocost line. The highest possible isoquant will touch the isocost line at a single point; the two curves will be tangent.

The problem of cost minimization can be described in a different way. Consider a firm that has a desired level of output and wishes to minimize its cost. The firm chooses an isoquant, and then tries to find the point on the isoquant that is on the lowest possible isocost line. Again, the cost-minimizing firm will choose the point of tangency between the isocost line and the isoquant.

At the point of tangency, the slopes of the two curves are the same. The slope of the isoquant is the marginal rate of substitution. The slope of the isocost line is the relative price. Thus, *the marginal rate of technical substitution must equal the relative price.*

APPLYING THE DIAGRAMMATIC ANALYSIS

The isoquant/isocost diagram can be used to show how a change in relative prices affects the optimal mix of inputs. A change in relative prices changes the isocost line. In Figure 11.19, an increase in the wage makes the isocost curves flatter. CC is the original isocost curve that minimizes the costs of producing output Q_0 (that is, CC is tangent to the isoquant Q_0). C_1C_1 is the isocost line with the new higher wages that is tangent to the original isoquant. Obviously, to produce the same level of output will cost more if wages are in-

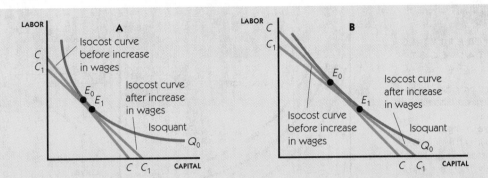

Figure 11.19 CHANGING FACTOR PRICES

This firm has chosen the level of production associated with the isoquant shown, and the cost-minimizing combination of labor and capital for producing that amount is originally at E_0. But as wages rise, relative prices shift, and the cost-minimizing method of producing the given amount becomes E_1. In panel A, an increase in wages leads to little substitution. But in panel B, an increase in wages leads to a much larger amount of substitution.

creased. The figure also shows what this change in relative prices in the form of higher wages does to the cost-minimizing combination of inputs: as one would expect, the firm substitutes away from labor toward capital (from point E_0 to E_1).

Of course, the magnitude of the substitution will differ from industry to industry, depending on an industry's isoquant. In addition, substitution is likely to be much greater in the long run than in the short run, as machines wear out, firms try to find out how to conserve on the more expensive inputs, and so on. The figure represents these different possibilities for substitution. In panel A, the possibilities for substitution are very limited. The isoquant is very "curved." This figure illustrates a case where it is very difficult to substitute (at least in the short run) machines for labor (illustrated, perhaps, by the use of blast furnaces in producing steel). In panel B, substitution is very easy; the isoquant is very flat. This illustrates an opposite case; it is relatively easy for a firm to substitute machines for labor, say, by using robots.

DERIVING COST CURVES

The cost curves in this chapter represent the minimum cost of producing each level of output, at a particular level of input prices. Figure 11.20A shows the cost-minimizing way of producing three different levels of output, Q_1, Q_2, and Q_3. Panel B then plots the actual level of costs associated with each of these levels of output. That is, the isocost curves tangent to the isoquants in panel A show the minimum level of costs associated with each output. Tracing out the costs associated with each level of output provides the total cost curve.

Figure 11.20 DERIVING THE TOTAL COST CURVE

The total cost curve describes how total cost changes at different levels of output. Panel A shows three isoquants representing different levels of output, and three isocost curves tangent to those isoquants, representing the least-cost way of producing each of these amounts. Panel B plots the actual level of costs for each of these levels of output, producing the familiar total cost curve.

And once we have the total cost curve, we know how to derive the marginal cost curve (the slope of the total cost curve) and the average cost curve (the slope of a line from the origin to the total cost curve).

PRODUCTION

C hapter 11 defined profits as the difference between revenues and costs. We learned the basic tools for assessing the costs of production. In this chapter, we learn how to calculate the benefits from production, and examine how firms weigh costs against these benefits. This balancing process dictates the profit-maximizing firm's production decision.

This chapter rounds out the discussion of markets because, in making their production decisions, firms provide the final ingredients for a complete model of the economy. With all the ingredients in hand—the basic economic decisions of individuals and households to maximize satisfaction, and the basic economic decisions of firms seeking to maximize profits—we will be able to construct a complete model of the economy in Chapter 13.

KEY QUESTIONS

1. What determines the level of output a firm will supply at any given price? How do we derive, in other words, the firm's supply curve?

2. What determines whether or when a firm will enter or exit a market?

3. How do the answers to these questions enable us to analyze the market supply curve, why it is upward sloping and why it may be more elastic than the supply curve of any single firm?

4. How do we reconcile economists' view that competition drives profits to zero with accountants' reports showing that most of the time most firms earn positive profits?

5. What determines a firm's demand for inputs, such as labor or capital? Why is a firm's demand curve for labor downward sloping?

REVENUE

Consider the hypothetical example of the High Strung Violin Company, manufacturers of world-class violins. The company hires labor; it buys wood, utilities, and other materials; and it rents a building and machines. Its violins sell for $40,000 each. Last year the company sold 7 of them, for a gross revenue of $280,000. Table 12.1 gives a snapshot of the firm's financial health, its profit-and-loss statement for last year.

We see that High Strung's revenues were $280,000, and its costs were

Table 12.1 PROFIT-AND-LOSS STATEMENT FOR THE HIGH STRUNG VIOLIN COMPANY

Gross revenue		$280,000
Costs		$180,000
Wages (including fringe benefits)	$150,000	
Purchases of wood and other materials	$ 20,000	
Utilities	$ 1,000	
Rent of building	$ 5,000	
Rent of machinery	$ 2,000	
Miscellaneous expenses	$ 2,000	
Profits		$100,000

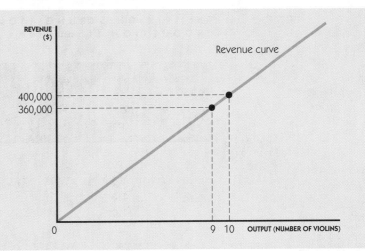

Figure 12.1 THE REVENUE CURVE

The revenue curve shows a firm's revenues at each level of output. For the firm in a competitive industry, price does not change as more is produced, so the revenue curve is a straight line with a constant slope. In this example, the revenue of each additional violin is always $40,000.

$180,000, so its profits were $100,000. If its costs had been $400,000 instead of $180,000, its profits would have been −$120,000. The firm would have made a negative profit, in other words, a loss.

The relationship between revenue and output is shown by the **revenue curve** in Figure 12.1. The horizontal axis measures the firm's output, while the vertical axis measures the revenues. When the price of a violin is $40,000 and the firm sells 9 violins, its revenue is $360,000; when it sells 10, revenue rises to $400,000.

The extra revenue that a firm receives from selling an extra unit is called its **marginal revenue.** Thus, $40,000 is the extra (or marginal) revenue from selling the tenth violin. It is no accident that the marginal revenue equals the price of the violin. A fundamental feature of competitive markets is that firms receive the same market price for each unit they sell, regardless of the number of units they sell. Thus, the extra revenue that firms in competitive markets receive from selling one more unit—the marginal revenue—is the same as the market price of the unit.

COSTS

High Strung's costs increase as it expands its level of output. Total costs are given in column 1 of Table 12.2 and depicted diagrammatically in Figure 12.2A. Panel B shows the corresponding average and marginal costs. High Strung's average cost curve exhibits the typical U-shape that we associate with manufacturing firms.

Even before it builds its first violin, the company must spend $90,000. Space must be rented. Some employees will have to be hired. Equipment must be

Table 12.2 **HIGH STRUNG VIOLIN COMPANY'S COSTS OF PRODUCTION (thousands of dollars)**

Output	(1) Total cost	(2) Average cost	(3) Marginal cost	(4) Total variable cost	(5) Average variable cost
0	90				
1	100	100	10	10	10
2	110	55	10	20	10
3	120	40	10	30	10
4	130	32.5	10	40	10
5	140	28	10	50	10
6	150	25	10	60	10
7	175	25	25	85	12.1
8	215	26.9	40	125	15.6
9	270	30	55	180	20
10	400	40	130	210	21

purchased. No matter how many or how few violins High Strung produces, its fixed costs will remain $90,000.

The *extra* cost of producing an additional violin, the marginal cost, is shown in column 3. Marginal cost is always associated with the additional cost of producing a *particular* unit of output. The marginal cost of increasing production from 1 to 2 violins, for example, is $10,000. Each additional violin costs $10,000 more until production reaches 6 violins. The extra (or marginal) cost of producing the seventh violin is $25,000. The marginal cost of producing the eighth violin is $40,000.

The High Strung Violin Company's average costs initially decline as its production increases, since the fixed costs can be divided among more units of production. But after 7 violins, average costs begin to increase, as the effect of the increasing average variable costs dominates the effect of the fixed costs.

BASIC CONDITIONS OF COMPETITIVE SUPPLY

In choosing how much to produce, a profit-maximizing firm will focus its decision at the margin. Having incurred the fixed cost of getting into this market, the decision is generally not the stark one of whether or not to produce, but

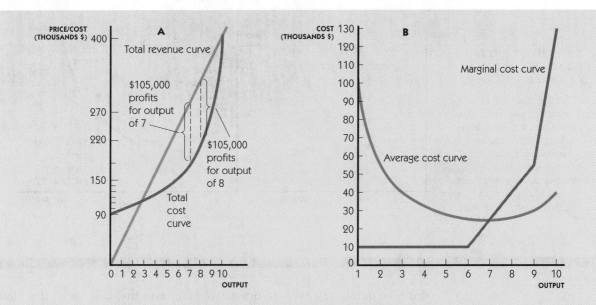

Figure 12.2 RELATING REVENUES AND COSTS

The firm's revenue and total cost curves can be diagrammed on the same graph, as in panel A. When total revenue exceeds total costs, the firm is making profits at that level of output. Profits, the difference between revenues and costs, are measured by the distance between the two curves; in this case, the highest level of profit is being made at a production level of 7 or 8. When total costs exceed total revenue, the firm is making losses at that level of output. When the two lines cross, the firm is making zero profits. The marginal and average cost curves for this company have their expected shape in panel B. Marginal costs are constant until a production level of 6, and then they begin to increase. The average cost curve is U-shaped.

whether to produce one more unit of a good or one less. For a firm in a competitive market, the answer to this problem is relatively simple: the company simply compares the marginal revenue it will receive by producing an extra unit—which is just the price of the good—with the extra cost of producing that unit, the marginal cost. As long as the marginal revenue exceeds the marginal cost, the firm will make additional profit by producing more. If marginal revenue is less than marginal cost, then producing an extra unit will cut profits, and the firm will reduce production. In short, the firm will produce to the point where the marginal cost equals marginal revenue, which in a competitive market is equal to price.

The profit-maximizing level of output, where price equals marginal cost, can be seen in panel A of Figure 12.3, which shows the marginal cost curve for a firm facing increasing marginal costs. The firm produces up to the point where price (which equals marginal revenue) equals marginal cost. If it produces more than that, the extra cost will be greater than the extra revenue received. The figure shows how much output the firm will produce at each price. At the price p_1, it will produce the output Q_1. At the price p_2, it will pro-

Figure 12.3 THE PROFIT-MAXIMIZING LEVEL OF OUTPUT

A competitive firm maximizes profits by setting output at the point where price equals marginal cost. In panel A, at the price of p_1, this quantity is Q_1. Panel B shows total revenue and total costs. Profits are maximized when the distance between the two curves is maximized, which is the point where the two lines are parallel (and thus have the same slope).

duce the output Q_2. With an upward-sloping marginal cost curve, it is clear that the firm will produce more as price increases.

The marginal cost curve is upward sloping, just as the supply curves in Chapter 4 were upward sloping. This too is no accident: a firm's marginal cost curve is actually the same as its supply curve. The marginal cost curve shows the additional cost of producing one more unit at different levels of output. A competitive firm chooses to produce at the level of output where the cost of producing an additional unit (that is, the marginal cost) is equal to the market price. We can thus read from the marginal cost curve what the firm's supply will be at any price: it will be the quantity of output at which marginal cost equals that price.

Figure 12.2A shows total revenues as well as total costs of the High Strung Violin Company. We can see that profits—the gap between revenues and costs—are maximized at an output of either 7 or 8. If the price were just slightly lower than $40,000, profits would be maximized at 7, and if the price were just slightly higher than $40,000, profits would be maximized at 8.

The profit-maximizing level of output can also be seen in panel B of Figure 12.3, which shows the total revenue and total cost curves. Profits are the dif-

EQUILIBRIUM OUTPUT FOR COMPETITIVE FIRMS

In competitive markets, firms produce at the level where price equals marginal cost.

ference between revenues and costs. In panel B, profits are the distance be-tween the total revenue curve and the total cost curves. The profit-maximizing firm will choose the output where that distance is greatest. This occurs at Q_1. Below Q_1, price (the slope of the revenue curve) exceeds marginal costs (the slope of the total cost curve) so profits increase as output increases; above Q_1, price is less than marginal cost, so profits decrease as output increases.

ENTRY, EXIT, AND MARKET SUPPLY

We are now in a position to tackle the market supply curve. To do so, we need to know a little more about each firm's decision to produce. First let's con-sider a firm that is currently not producing. Under what circumstances should it incur the fixed costs of entering the industry? This is a relatively easy problem: the company simply looks at the average cost curve and the price. *If price exceeds minimum average costs, it pays the firm to enter.* This is because if it enters, it can sell the goods for more than the cost of producing them, thus making a profit.

Figure 12.4A shows the U-shaped average cost curve. Minimum average cost is c_{min}. If the price is less than c_{min}, then there is no level of output at which the firm could produce and make a profit. If the price is above c_{min}, then the firm will produce at the level of output at which price (p) equals mar-ginal cost, Q^*. At Q^*, marginal cost exceeds average costs. (This is always true

Figure 12.4 COST CURVES, PROFITS, AND ENTRY

Panel A shows that if price is above the minimum of the average cost curve, profits will exist. Profits are measured by the area formed by the shaded rectangle, the profit per unit (price minus average cost, corresponding to the distance AB) times the output, Q^*. Panel B shows average cost curves for three different firms. At price p_1, only one firm will enter the market. As price rises to p_2 and then to p_3, first the firm whose cost curve is AC_2 and then the firm whose cost curve is AC_3 will enter the market.

at output levels greater than that at which average costs are minimum.) Profit per unit is the difference between price and average costs. Total profits are the product of profit per unit and the level of output (the shaded area in the figure).

Different companies may have different average cost curves. Some will have better management. Some will have a better location. Accordingly, firms will differ in their minimum average cost. As prices rise, additional firms will find it attractive to enter the market. Figure 12.4B shows the U-shaped average cost curves for three different firms. Firm 1's minimum average cost is AC_1, firm 2's minimum average cost is AC_2, and firm 3's minimum average cost is AC_3. Thus, firm 1 enters at the price p_1, firm 2 at the price p_2, and firm 3 at the price p_3.

SUNK COSTS AND EXIT

The converse of the decision of a firm to enter the market is the decision of a firm already producing to exit the market. **Sunk costs** are costs that are not recoverable, even if a firm goes out of business. The High Strung Violin Company, for example, may have had an extensive television advertising campaign. The cost of this campaign is a sunk cost. There is no way this expenditure can be recouped even if production ceases. If there were no sunk costs the decision to enter and the decision to exit would be mirror images of each other. Firms would exit the market when their average costs rose above the price. But if some costs remain even if a firm exits the market, the question facing that firm is whether it is better off continuing to produce or exiting.

Let us assume for simplicity that all fixed costs are sunk costs. A firm with no fixed costs has an average cost curve that is the same as its average variable cost curve. It will shut down as soon as the price falls below minimum average costs—the cost at the bottom of its U-shaped variable cost curve. But a firm with fixed costs has a different decision to make. Figure 12.5A depicts both the average variable cost curve and the average cost curve for such a case. As in the case with no sunk costs, the firm shuts down when price is below minimum average *variable* costs (costs that vary with the level of output), p_1. But if the price is *between* average variable costs and average costs, the firm will continue to produce, even though it will show a loss. It continues to produce because it would show an even bigger loss if it ceased operating. Since price exceeds average variable costs, the revenues it obtains exceed the additional costs it incurs from producing. (Later in the chapter we will discuss the case when fixed costs are not necessarily sunk costs.)

Different firms in an industry will have different average variable costs, and so will find it desirable to exit the market at different prices. Figure 12.5B shows the average variable cost curves for three different firms. Their cost curves differ; some may, for instance, have newer equipment than others. As the price falls, the firm with the highest minimum average variable costs finds it is no longer able to make money at the going price, and decides not to operate. Thus, firm 3 (represented by the curve AVC_3) shuts down as soon as the

Figure 12.5 **AVERAGE VARIABLE COSTS AND THE DECISION TO PRODUCE**

Panel A shows a firm's average variable cost curves. In the short run, firms will produce as long as price exceeds average variable costs. Thus, for prices between p_1 and p_2, the firm will continue to produce, even though it is recording a loss (price is less than average cost). Panel B shows that firms with different average variable cost curves will decide to shut down at different price levels. As price falls below c_3, the minimum average variable cost for firm 3, firm 3 shuts down; as price falls still lower, below c_2, firm 2 shuts down. Finally, when price falls below c_1, firm 1 shuts down.

price falls below c_3, firm 2 shuts down as soon as the price falls below c_2, and firm 1 shuts down as soon as the price falls below c_1.

THE FIRM'S SUPPLY CURVE

We can now draw the firm's supply curve. As Figure 12.6A shows, for a firm contemplating entering the market, supply is zero up to a critical price, equal to the minimum average cost. Thus, for prices below $c_{min} = p$, the firm produces zero output. For prices greater than $c_{min} = p$, the firm produces up to the point where price equals marginal cost, so the firm's supply curve coincides with the marginal cost curve. For a firm that has incurred sunk costs of entering the market (panel B), the supply curve coincides with the marginal cost curve so long as price exceeds the minimum value of average *variable* costs; when price is below the minimum value of average variable costs, the firm exits, so supply is again zero.

THE MARKET SUPPLY CURVE

With this information about the cost curves of individual firms, we can derive the overall market supply curve. Back in Chapter 4, the market supply curve was defined as the sum of the amounts that each firm was willing to supply at

USING ECONOMICS: ENTERING THE PAINTING BUSINESS

House painting is a summer business, for days that are hot and long, and with available low-skilled labor on vacation from high school and college. As a way of picking up some cash, Michael decided to start Presto Painters during the summer after taking introductory economics.

Just getting started involves some substantial fixed costs. Michael ran the business out of his parents' home so he had no costs for office space. His fixed costs ended up looking like this:

Fixed costs	
Used van	$5,000
Paint and supplies	$2,000
Flyers and signs	$1,200
Business cards and estimate sheets	$ 500
Phone line and answering machine	$ 300
Total	$9,000

Michael went to work drumming up business. He took calls from potential customers and knocked on doors, made estimates of what he thought it would cost to paint someone's home, and then offered them a price. Of course, he was in direct competition with many other painters and had to meet the competition's price to get a job.

Michael found that the going rate for labor was $10 per hour. In the real world, labor is not the only variable input required for house painting. There are also costs from buying additional paint and brushes, but for the sake of simplicity, let's assume that he started off the summer with all the paint he needed. Thus, his variable costs were re-

lated to the labor he needed to hire.

Variable costs are also related to the amount of time it takes to paint a house, which varies depending on the quality of the labor you can find. The variable costs for Presto Painters were as follows:

Houses painted	Hours of labor hired	Payroll cost
5	100	$ 1,000
10	300	$ 3,000
15	600	$ 6,000
20	1,000	$10,000
25	1,500	$15,000
30	2,100	$21,000

Given this information, Michael could calculate cost curves for Presto Painters (see next page).

Based on his marginal and average cost curves, Michael figured that if market conditions allowed him to charge $1,000 or more for a typical house, then he could make a profit by painting at least 25 houses. Roughly speaking, that is how his summer worked out; painting 25 houses for $1,000 apiece. Thus, he earned $1,000 in profits.

Or so he thought. Nowhere in this list of costs did Michael consider the opportunity cost of his time. He was not getting paid $10 an hour for painting houses; he was out there stirring up business, hiring and organizing workers, taking calls from customers, dealing with complaints.

Imagine that Michael had an alternate job possibility waiting on tables. He could earn $6 per hour (including tips) and work 40-hour weeks during a

12-week summer vacation. Thus, he could have earned $2,880 during the summer with little stress or risk. If this opportunity cost is added to the fixed costs of running the business, then his apparent profit turns into a loss. Since Presto Painters did not cover Michael's opportunity cost *and* compensate him for the risk and aggravation of running his own business, he would have been financially better off sticking to the business of filling people's stomachs rather than painting their houses.

Number of homes	Total cost	Average cost	Marginal cost (per house)
0	$ 9,000		
			$ 200
5	$10,000	$2,000	
			$ 400
10	$12,000	$1,200	
			$ 600
15	$15,000	$1,000	
			$ 800
20	$19,000	$ 950	
			$1,000
25	$24,000	$ 960	
			$1,200
30	$30,000	$1,000	

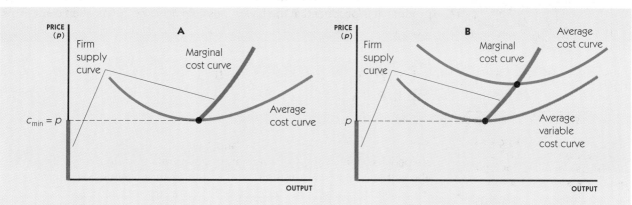

Figure 12.6 **THE SUPPLY CURVE FOR A FIRM**

Panel A shows that for a firm contemplating entering the market, supply is zero up to a critical price, equal to the firm's minimum average cost, after which the firm's supply curve coincides with the marginal cost curve. Panel B shows a firm that has already entered the market, incurring positive sunk costs; this firm will produce as long as price exceeds the minimum of the average variable cost curve.

Figure 12.7 THE MARKET SUPPLY CURVE

The market supply curve is derived by horizontally adding up the supply curves for each of the firms. More generally, as price rises, each firm produces more and new firms enter the market.

any given price. Figure 12.7 provides a graphical description of the supply curve for a market with two firms. More generally, if the price rises, the firms already in the market (firms 1 and 2) will find it profitable to increase their output and new firms (with higher average variable cost curves) will find it profitable to enter the market. Because higher prices induce more firms to enter a competitive market, the market supply response to an increase in price is greater than if the number of firms were fixed. In the same way, as price falls, there are two market responses. The firms that still find it profitable to produce at the lower price will produce less, and the higher cost firms will exit the market. In this way, the competitive market ensures that whatever the product, it is produced at the lowest possible price by the most efficient firms.

LONG-RUN VERSUS SHORT-RUN SUPPLY

Figure 12.8 ELASTICITY OF SHORT-RUN AND LONG-RUN SUPPLY CURVES FOR A FIRM

Because there is a greater chance for a firm to adjust to changes in price in the long run, the price elasticity of the supply curve is greater in the long run than in the short run.

As we saw in Chapter 11, in the short run the typical firm will have a U-shaped average cost curve, and a rising marginal cost curve at output levels above the lowest point of the U. But its long-run marginal cost curve is flatter. This is because adjustments to changes in market conditions take time, and some adjustments take longer than others. In the short run, you can add workers, work more shifts, run the machines harder (or reduce the rate at which these things are done), but you are probably stuck with your existing plant and equipment. In the long run, you can acquire more buildings and more machines (or sell them). Thus, the long-run supply curve for a firm is more elastic (flatter) than the short-run supply curve, as shown in Figure 12.8.

The same thing is true, only more so, for the industry—again because the number of firms is not fixed. Even if each firm can operate only one plant, the industry's output can be increased by 5 percent by increasing the number of firms by 5 percent. The extra costs of increasing output by 5 percent are approximately the same as the average costs. Accordingly, the long-run market supply curve is approximately horizontal. Under these conditions, even if the demand curve for the product shifts drastically, the market will supply much more of the product at pretty much the same price, as additional plants are constructed and additional firms enter the market.

Thus, the market supply curve is much more elastic in the long run than in the short run. Indeed, in the *very* short run, a firm may find it impossible to hire more skilled labor or to increase its capacity. Its supply curve, and the market supply curve, would be nearly vertical. In the short run machines and the number of firms are fixed, but labor and other inputs can be varied. Figure 12.9A shows the short-run supply curve. Contrast the short-run market supply curve with the long-run market supply curve. The short-run curve slopes up much more sharply. A shift in the demand curve has a larger effect on price and a smaller effect on quantity than it does in the long run. In the long run, the market supply curve may be horizontal. In this case, shifts in the demand curve have an effect *only* on quantity, as in panel B. Price remains at the level of minimum average costs; competition leads to entry to the point where there are zero profits.

Again, it is worth asking, "How long is the long run?" That depends on the industry. It takes an electric power company years to change its capacity. For most other firms, buildings and equipment can be added, if not within months, certainly within a year or two. Recent improvements in technology, like computer-aided design and manufacturing, have made it possible for many companies to change what they are producing more rapidly, and thus have reduced the length of the long run and made supply curves more elastic than in the past.

Figure 12.9 MARKET EQUILIBRIUM IN THE SHORT RUN AND LONG RUN

In panel A, the market equilibrium is originally at a price p_0 and an output Q_0. In the short run, a shift in the demand curve from D_0 to D_1 raises the price to p_1 and quantity to Q_1. In the long run, the supply elasticity is greater, so the increase in price is smaller—price is only p_2—and quantity is greater, Q_2. If supply is perfectly elastic in the long run, as shown in panel B, shifts in demand will only change the quantity produced in the long run, not the market price.

ADJUSTMENTS IN THE SHORT RUN AND THE LONG RUN

In the very short run, firms may be unable to adjust production at all; only the price changes.

In the short run, firms may be able to hire more labor and adjust other variable inputs.

In the long run, firms may be able to buy more machines, and firms may decide to enter or to exit.

The times required for these adjustments may vary from industry to industry.

Between January and April of 1996, gasoline prices soared, increasing by nearly 20 percent. One reason was the unusually cold winter, which had diverted more crude oil into the production of heating oil. But a more important factor was uncertainty concerning oil from Iraq. After the 1991 Gulf War, Iraq had been barred from selling oil on the international market. In early 1996, in the face of increasing evidence of food shortages in Iraq, there seemed to be significant progress in negotiations which would allow Iraq to sell $2 billion of oil in exchange for food. This additional oil would have depressed world oil prices, and American importers were clearly nervous about holding large inventories of oil under these circumstances. But by April, no agreement had been reached.

One proposed response to ease the burden on consumers was to reduce the gasoline tax temporarily by 4.3 cents a gallon,. Most economists believed that in the short run, the reduction would have little effect. They believed that the short-run supply curve for gasoline was very inelastic; American refineries were working to capacity. In this view, the price was high because of the limited supply. Any lowering of the prices consumers paid would result in demand exceeding supply in the short run. In this view, all the benefits of the reduced tax would accrue to the oil companies, in the form of higher profits.

Eventually, of course, more gasoline could and would be imported from abroad. In this case, the long-run supply curve—taking into account the response of imports—would come into play within a month or two.

LOOKING BEYOND THE BASIC MODEL: SUNK COSTS, ENTRY, AND COMPETITION

The degree of competition envisioned in the basic competitive model requires a large number of firms, vying with one another to sell a product. Competition among these firms drives the market price down to a level where there are no profits (as economists define them) in the market. (Recall that opportunity costs of the owners of the business and the cost of capital are included in the costs.)

Even without a large number of firms in the market, the predictions of the basic competitive model may still hold. Here is where the distinction between overhead (or *fixed*) and *sunk* costs becomes important. Overhead costs are costs that are incurred regardless of the scale of production of the firm. A company's headquarters is an overhead cost in this sense. But if a company ceases to operate, it can resell the building and might well recover its cost. The cost of the building in this case, though fixed, is not sunk. Now take the case of a company that not only bought a building but spent a lot of money commissioning a logo, which it then mounted conspicuously on its building. If this firm went out of business it could recover the cost of its building but *not* its logo. Who wants the secondhand logo of a bankrupt company? Advertising expenditures are typically sunk costs. Expenditures on assets that can readily be put to other uses—buildings and cars—are, for the most part, not sunk.

The theory of **contestable markets** predicts that even in a market with only one firm, that firm will make zero profits, just as in a market with many firms, *if* sunk costs are low. The threat that other firms will enter is sufficient to deter the single firm from raising its price beyond average cost. This result holds even in the presence of high fixed or overhead costs, so long as those costs consist of buildings, cars, airplanes, and other assets that can be easily sold. A firm entering the industry has little to lose, since it can always reverse its decision and recover its investment.

But when the assets include major ones with no alternative use—such as a nuclear power plant—then these costs become sunk costs, and the threat of competition diminishes. The firm that would otherwise have entered the market might now worry that if it enters, competition will get fierce. And the firm would be right to worry, as high sunk costs will make all firms reluctant to exit. If competition is fierce enough, the price might even drop below average costs, and still the firm's rivals may not leave. With prices below average costs, the new firm will not be able to get a return on its investment. Until it enters the market, the firm has an advantage: it has not taken on the sunk costs. Given the scenario just described, it may very well avert its gaze from the lure of high profits, knowing they are like a mirage. The profits will disappear if the new firm tries to grab them by entering the market, but will remain for the limited number of firms already in the market if they can keep the would-be newcomer out. Thus, markets with high sunk costs may be able to sustain high profits without much fear of entry—a clear departure from the basic competitive model.

CLOSE-UP: PAN AM'S EXIT

Pan American World Airways passed away on December 4, 1991. The company had been flying since 1927, and for many decades had been the dominant global airline. In fact, some said that the Pan Am logo may have been the most widely recognized corporate logo in the world at one time.

The death came as no surprise. Pan Am had lost money in every year except one between 1980 and 1991—losses that totaled nearly $2 billion. It had officially declared bankruptcy in January 1991. But what life support system delayed the exit of Pan Am from commercial aviation? How can our economic model account for a company that makes losses for a decade and even continues to operate after it has officially declared bankruptcy?

The model of entry and exit based on cost curves gives a useful explanation of why Pan Am would not exit after a single year of losses. As long as a firm can charge a price above average variable costs, it makes economic sense to stay in business, even if the price is below average total costs and the firm is making losses.

In fact, Pan Am seems to have continued to operate even when price was less than average variable cost. It hoped that market conditions would improve, and it wanted to keep alive its option. But it paid a high price for doing so.

To stay in business while making losses, though, a company must have assets to sell. In its many profitable years, Pan Am had built up many such assets, and in the 1980s it proceeded to sell them off. The company sold the Pan Am Building to Metropolitan Life Insurance for $400 million; its Intercontinental Hotels subsidiary for $500 million; its Pacific operations and later its London routes to United Airlines; and a considerable amount of Tokyo real estate. By the end of 1991, Pan Am was proposing to sell off most of its other routes to Delta and become a small airline based in Miami, serving mainly Latin American destinations. In other words, although Pan Am continued to fly during the 1980s while losing money, it was slowly exiting during most of that time.

In fact, economists sometimes disagree over whether a market economy forces exit to happen quickly enough. As the case of Pan Am demonstrates, exit can be a drawn-out process. This surely benefits some workers who could avoid switching jobs for a longer time. But shareholders in Pan Am would have been better off if the company had been sold off in the early 1980s before it had a chance to lose more money.

Sources: Brett Pulley, "Pan Am Ceases Operations, Race Opens to Get Its Valuable Latin American Routes," *Wall Street Journal,* December 5, 1991, p. A7; Agis Salpukas, "Its Cash Depleted, Pan Am Shuts," *New York Times,* December 5, 1991, p. D1; Severin Borenstein, "The Evolution of U.S. Airline Competition," *Journal of Economic Perspectives* (Spring 1992).

ACCOUNTING PROFITS AND ECONOMIC PROFITS

We have learned in previous chapters that firms maximize profits, but now it appears that with competition, profits are driven to zero. To most individuals, this seems like a contradiction: if profits were truly zero, why would firms ever produce? How do we reconcile the conclusion that competition drives profits to zero with the fact that, throughout the economy, firms regularly report making profits?

The answer is that accountants and economists think about profits differently in two important respects. The first is that economists take opportunity costs into account. The second has to do with the economic concept of rent. Both deserve a closer look.

OPPORTUNITY COSTS

To begin to see how opportunity costs affect the economist's view of profits, consider a small firm in which the owner has invested $100,000. Assume the owner receives a small salary, and devotes sixty hours a week to running the enterprise. An economist would argue that the owner ought to calculate his opportunity costs related to his investment of time and money into the business. The opportunity cost of his time is the best wage available to him if he worked sixty hours a week at an alternate job. The opportunity cost of his capital is the return that the $100,000 invested in this enterprise would produce in another investment. These are the true costs of the owner's time and capital investment. To calculate profits of the firm as the economist sees them, these opportunity costs have to be subtracted out.

One can easily imagine a business whose accountant reports a profit equal to 3 percent of the capital investment. An economist would note that if the investment capital had been put in a bank account, it would have earned at least 5 percent. Thus, the economist would say the business is making a loss. Failure to take into account opportunity costs means that reported profits often overstate true economic profits.

Taking opportunity costs into account is not always a simple matter; it is not always easy to determine the alternative uses of a firm's resources. Managerial time spent in expanding the firm in one direction, for example, might have been spent in controlling costs or expanding the firm in another direction. Land that is used for a golf course for the firm's employees might have been used for some other purpose, which could have saved more than enough money to buy golf club memberships for all who want them. In making decisions about resources like these, firms must constantly ask what price the resources might fetch in other uses.

Sometimes market data can provide appropriate prices for calculating opportunity costs. For example, the opportunity cost of giving huge offices to top executives can be gauged by the money those offices would bring if they were rented to some other company. But often the calculation is more difficult: how can, for example, a company measure the opportunity cost of the vice-president who cannot be fired and will not retire for five years?

What about the costs associated with an expenditure already made, say on a building that is no longer really needed by the firm? The relevant opportunity cost of this building is not the original purchase or lease price, but instead the value of the building in alternate uses, such as the rent that could be earned if the building were rented to other firms.

The fundamental point is that you cannot use past expenditures to calculate opportunity costs. Consider an automaker that has purchased a parcel of land for $1 million an acre. It turns out, however, that the company made a mistake and the land is worth only $100,000 an acre. The firm now must choose between two different plants for producing new cars, one of which uses much more land than the other. In figuring opportunity costs, should the land be valued at the purchase price of $1 million an acre, or what the land could be sold for—$100,000 an acre? The answer can make a difference between whether or not the firm chooses to conserve on land. From an economics viewpoint, the answer to this valuation problem should be obvious: the firm should evaluate costs according to the *current* opportunity costs. The fact that the company made a mistake in purchasing the land should be irrelevant for the current decision.

Individuals and firms frequently do compound their economic errors, however, by continuing to focus on past expenditures. Business executives who were originally responsible for making a bad decision may be particularly reluctant to let bygones be bygones. Publicly announcing that the correct market price of land is $100,000 an acre, for example, would be equivalent to announcing that a major mistake had been made. Acknowledging such a mistake could jeopardize a business executive's future with the firm.

ECONOMIC RENT

A second difference between an economist's and an accountant's definition of profit concerns **economic rent.** Economic rent is the difference between the price that is actually paid and the price that would have to be paid in order for the good or service to be produced.

Although economic rent has far broader applications than its historic use to refer to payments made by farmers to their landlords for the use of their land, the example of rent for land use is still instructive. The critical characteristic of land in this regard is that its supply is inelastic. Higher payments for land (higher rents) will not elicit a greater supply. Even if landlords received virtually nothing for their land, the same land would be available. Many other factors of production have the same inelastic character. Even if you doubled his salary, Greg Maddux would not "produce" more pitches for the Atlanta Braves. The extra payments for this kind of rare talent fall into the economist's definition of rent. Anyone who is in the position to receive economic rents is fortunate indeed, because these "rents" are unrelated to effort. They are payments determined entirely by demand.

Firms earn economic rent to the extent that they are more efficient than other firms. We saw earlier that a firm is willing to produce at a price equal to its minimum average cost. Some firms might be more efficient than others, so their average cost curves are lower. Consider a market in which all firms except one have the same average cost curve, and the market price corresponds to the minimum average cost of these firms. The remaining firm is super-efficient, so its average costs are far below those of the other firms. The company would have been willing to produce at a lower price, at its minimum average cost. What it receives in excess of what is required to induce it to enter the market are rents—returns on the firm's superior capabilities.

Thus, when economists say that competition drives profits to zero, they are focusing on the facts that in competitive equilibrium, price equals marginal cost for every firm producing. A company will not increase profits by expanding production, and it will not pay for firms outside the industry to enter. We say that competition drives profits to zero at the margin.

In some cases, supplies of inputs are inelastic in the short run but elastic in the long run. An example is payment for the use of a building. In the short run, the supply of buildings does not depend on the return, and hence payments for the use of a building are rents, in the economist's sense. But in the long run, the supply of buildings does depend on the return—investors will not construct new buildings unless they receive a return equal to what they could obtain elsewhere. So the "rent" received by the building's owner is not really a rent, in the sense in which economists use the term.[1]

ACCOUNTANTS' VERSUS ECONOMISTS' PROFITS

Accounting profits: revenues minus expenditures

Economic profits: revenues minus rents minus economic costs (including opportunity costs of labor and capital)

FACTOR DEMAND

In the process of deciding how much of each good to supply and what is the lowest-cost method of producing those goods, firms also decide how much of various inputs they will use. This is called **factor demand.** It is sometimes

---

[1] Economists sometimes use the term "quasi-rents" to describe payments for the use of buildings or other factors that are inelastically supplied in the short run, but elastically supplied in the long run.

Figure 12.10 THE DE-MAND FOR LABOR

The demand for labor can be calculated from the firm's supply curve and the production function. Panel A shows how the firm, given a market price p_1, chooses a level of output Q_1 from its supply curve. Panel B shows that to produce the output Q_1 requires L_1 units of labor. L_1 is the demand for labor.

called a derived demand, because it flows from other decisions the profit-maximizing firm makes. In Chapter 11, the analysis of cost was broken up into two cases, one in which there was a single variable input, or factor of production, and one in which there were several factors. We proceed along similar lines here. Labor is used as our main example of an input. The same principles apply to any factor of production.

When there is only a single factor of production, say labor, then the decision about how much to produce is the same as the decision about how much labor to hire. As soon as we know the price of the good, we can calculate the supply (output) from the marginal cost curve; and as soon as we know the output the firm plans to produce, we know the labor required, simply by looking at the production function, which gives the output for any level of input of labor, or, equivalently, the labor required for any level of output. Thus, in Figure 12.10 at the price p_1, the output is Q_1 (panel A), and the labor required to produce that output (factor demand) is L_1 (panel B).

There is another way of deriving the demand for a factor. If a firm hires one more worker, for example, the extra cost is the wage, w. The extra benefit of the worker is the price of the good times the extra output. The extra output corresponding to the extra worker is the marginal product of labor. (Marginal products can be calculated for any other factor of production as well.) The price of the good thus produced times the marginal product of labor is re-ferred to as the **value of the marginal product of labor.** The firm hires labor up to the point where the value of its marginal product (the marginal benefit) equals its price, in this case, the wage.

Using p for the price of the good, MPL for the marginal product of labor, and w for the wage of the worker, we can write this equilibrium condition as

value of marginal product of labor $= p \times MPL = w =$ wage.

From this equilibrium condition we can derive the demand curve for labor. Figure 12.11 plots the value of the marginal product of labor for each level of

Figure 12.11 THE DEMAND CURVE FOR LABOR

The value of the marginal product of labor declines with the level of employment. Since labor is hired up to the point where the wage equals the value of the marginal product, at wage w_1, employment is L_1, and at wage w_2, employment is L_2. The demand curve for labor thus traces out the values of the marginal product of labor at different levels of employment.

Figure 12.12 EFFECT OF PRICE CHANGE ON THE DEMAND CURVE FOR LABOR

An increase in the price received by a firm shifts the value of the marginal product of labor curve up, so that at each wage, the demand for labor is increased. At wage w_1, employment rises from L_1 to L_4; at wage w_2, employment rises from L_2 to L_3.

labor. Since the marginal product of labor decreases as labor increases, the value of the marginal product of labor decreases. When the wage is w_1, the value of the marginal product of labor equals the wage with a level of labor at L_1. This is the demand for labor at a wage w_1. When the wage is w_2, the value of the marginal product of labor equals the wage with a level of labor at L_2. This is the demand for labor at a wage w_2. Thus, the curve giving the value of the marginal product of labor at each level of employment *is* the demand curve for labor.

It is easy to use this diagram to see the effect of an increase in the price of the good the firm produces. In Figure 12.12, the higher price increases the value of the marginal product of labor at each level of employment, and it immediately follows that at each wage, the demand for labor increases; the demand curve for labor shifts to the right.

Thus, the demand for labor depends on both the wage and the price the firm receives for the goods it sells. In fact, the demand for labor depends only on the ratio of the two, as we will now see.

If we divide both sides of the equation giving the equilibrium condition by the price, we obtain the condition

$MPL = w/p.$

The wage divided by the price of the good being produced is defined as the **real product wage.** It measures what firms pay workers in terms of the goods the worker produces rather than in dollar terms. Thus, the firm hires workers up to the point where the real product wage equals the marginal product of labor.

This principle is illustrated in Figure 12.13, which shows the marginal product of labor. Because of diminishing returns, the marginal product diminishes as labor (and output) increases. As the real product wage increases, the demand for labor decreases.

Figure 12.13 THE FIRM'S DEMAND CURVE FOR LABOR AND THE REAL PRODUCT WAGE

Firms hire labor up to the point where the real product wage equals the marginal product of labor. As the real product wage increases, the demand for labor decreases.

FACTOR DEMAND

A factor of production will be demanded up to the point where the value of the marginal product of that factor equals the price. In the case of labor, this is the same as saying that the marginal product of labor equals the real product wage.

FROM THE FIRM'S FACTOR DEMAND TO THE MARKET'S FACTOR DEMAND

Once we have derived the firm's demand curve for labor, we can derive the total market demand for labor. At a given set of prices, we simply add up the demand for labor by each firm at any particular wage rate. The total is the market demand at that wage rate. Since each firm reduces the amount of labor that it demands as the wage increases, the market demand curve is downward sloping. Figure 12.14 shows how we add up diagrammatically the demand curves for labor for two firms, the High Strung Violin Company and Max's Fine Tunes Violin Company. At a wage of w_1, High Strung demands 30

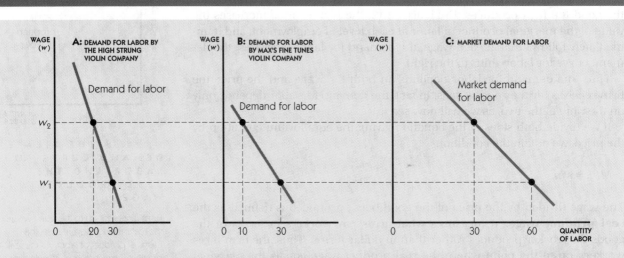

Figure 12.14 **THE MARKET DEMAND CURVE FOR LABOR**

The market demand curve for labor at each wage is obtained by horizontally adding up the demand curves for labor of each individual firm. As the wage rises, at a fixed price of output, less labor is demanded.

CLOSE-UP: FACTOR ELASTICITIES ON THE FARM

On the farm, basic inputs like durable equipment, real estate, and energy can be used to produce a variety of different outputs. However, as the price of an input rises, it may be harder to conserve on its use for some products than for others.

The elasticity relationships between three farm inputs and three outputs are shown in the table here. The first three rows of the table show how much the output of livestock, milk, and grains will change as the price of the three inputs changes. These figures allow an analyst to predict which products' supply would be affected most severely by changes in the price of various inputs. A 10 percent change in the price of durable equipment would have by far the smallest impact on the supply of grain, while a 10 percent change in the price of real estate would have the smallest effect on the supply of livestock.

Another result of a change in input prices will be that less of the input itself is demanded, because less of it will be used for every unit of output, and output will be lower; this is where the second three rows come in. The first column in the row for durable equipment shows that demand for durable equipment will fall 12.71 percent if the price of that equipment rises by 10 percent.

The third effect of a change in input prices will be on how much other inputs are demanded. In this example, raising the price of any input will lead to less of other inputs being used as well. This may seem surprising. As the price of one input increases, shouldn't a sensible farmer substitute other inputs? Such substitution is surely likely to occur. But the overall decrease in the amount produced will mean that fewer of all inputs are needed, even if the proportion of the inputs that are used shifts. If the price of energy increases by 10 percent, for example, the quantity of energy demanded will fall by 9.41 percent, the quantity of durable equipment demanded will fall by 3.21 percent, and the quantity of real estate by 2.06 percent. Since the amount of energy demanded will decline by the greatest amount, the production process will now be using relatively less energy than before. But since overall supply of all products will fall, fewer of all inputs will be needed.

Source: U. F. Ball, *American Journal of Agricultural Economics* (November 1988), p. 823. Data are from 1978 and 1979, and all elasticities are short-run.

| | Elasticity with respect to the price of | | |
	Durable equipment	Real estate	Energy
Livestock	−.534	−.275	−.286
Fluid milk	−.556	−.319	−.409
Grains	−.192	−.425	−.166
Durable equipment	−1.271	−.192	−.321
Real estate	−.237	−.584	−.206
Energy	−.647	−.336	−.941

workers and Max's Fine Tunes demands 30 workers, for a total demand of 60 workers. At a wage of w_2, High Strung demands 20 workers and Max's demands 10 workers, for a total demand of 30 workers.

FACTOR DEMANDS WITH TWO OR MORE FACTORS

It is now time to relax our assumption that firms require only one factor of production. With more than one factor, when the price of any input falls, the demand for that input will increase for two reasons. First, the firm (and the industry as a whole) substitutes the cheaper input for other inputs, so that for each unit of output produced, more of the cheaper input is employed. Second, the lower price of the input lowers the marginal cost of production at each level of output, and this leads to an increase in the level of production. Since

total demand for an input = demand for input per unit output × output,

and since both factor demand per unit of output and output have been increased, total demand for the input has increased.

When we draw the demand curve for labor, which shows the quantity of labor demanded at each wage, in the background we are keeping the price of output and the price of other inputs fixed. When any of these prices changes, the demand curve for labor shifts. For instance, as we have seen, if the price of output increases, the value of the marginal product of labor increases and the demand curve shifts to the right.

THE THEORY OF THE COMPETITIVE FIRM

We have now completed our description of the theory of the competitive firm. The firm takes the prices it receives for the goods it sells as given, and it takes the prices it pays for the inputs it uses, including the wages it pays workers and the costs of capital goods, as given. The firm chooses its outputs and inputs in order to maximize its profits.

We have seen where the supply curves for output and the demand curves for labor and capital that were used in Part One came from, and why they have the shape they do. As prices increase, output increases; firms produce more, and more firms produce. Thus, supply curves are upward sloping.

As wages increase, with the price of other inputs fixed, firms' marginal cost curve shifts up. This causes them to produce less at each price of their output. The higher *relative* price of labor induces firms to substitute other inputs for labor; they use less labor to produce each unit of output. Therefore, the demand curve for labor (and other inputs) is downward sloping.

In the next chapter, we will use these results, together with the analysis of the household's behavior in Chapters 8–10, to form a model of the entire economy.

REVIEW AND PRACTICE

Summary

1. A revenue curve shows the relationship between a firm's total output and its revenue. For a competitive firm, the marginal revenue it receives from selling an additional unit of output is the price of that unit.

2. A firm in a competitive market will choose the level of output where the market price—the marginal revenue it receives from producing an extra unit—equals the marginal cost.

3. A firm will enter a market if the market price for a good exceeds its minimum average costs, since it can make a profit by selling the good for more than it costs to produce the good.

4. If the market price is below minimum average costs and a firm has no sunk costs, the firm will exit the market immediately. If the market price is below minimum average costs and a firm has sunk costs, it will continue to produce in the short run as long as the market price exceeds its minimum average variable costs.

5. For a firm contemplating entering a market, its supply is zero up to the point where price equals minimum average costs. Above that price, the supply curve is the same as the marginal cost curve.

6. The market supply curve is constructed by adding up the supply curves of all firms in an industry. As prices rise, more firms are willing to produce, and each firm is willing to produce more, so that the market supply curve is normally upward sloping.

7. The economist's and the accountant's concepts of profits differ in how they treat opportunity costs and economic rents.

8. A firm's demand for factors of production is derived from its decision about how much to produce. Inputs will be demanded up to the point where the value of the marginal product of the input equals its price.

9. The demand curve for factors of production is downward sloping for two reasons. Output is reduced as the price of the factor increases, and at each level of output, the firm substitutes away from the factor whose price has increased.

Key Terms

sunk costs
revenue curve
marginal revenue

contestable markets
economic rents
factor demand

real product wage

REVIEW QUESTIONS

1. In a competitive market, what rule determines the profit-maximizing level of output? What is the relationship between a firm's supply curve and its marginal cost curve?

2. What determines firms' decisions to enter a market? to exit a market? Explain the role of the average variable cost curve in determining whether firms will exit the market.

3. What is the relationship between the way accountants use the concept of profits and the way economists use that term?

4. How do firms decide how much of an input to demand? Why is the demand curve for inputs (like labor) downward sloping?

PROBLEMS

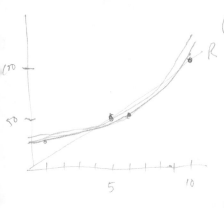

1. The market price for painting a house in Centerville is $10,000. The Total Cover-up House-Painting Company has fixed costs of $4,000 for ladders, brushes, and so on, and the company's variable costs for house painting follow this pattern:

Output (houses painted)	2	3	4	5	6	7	8	9	10
Variable cost (in thousands of dollars)	26	32	36	42	50	60	72	86	102

Calculate the company's total costs, and graph the revenue curve and the total cost curve. Do the curves have the shape you expect? Over what range of production is the company making profits?

2. Calculate and graph the marginal cost, the average costs, and the average variable costs for the Total Cover-up House-Painting Company. Given the market price, at what level of output will this firm maximize profits? What profit (or loss) is it making at that level? At what price will the firm no longer make a profit? Assume its fixed costs are sunk; there is no market for used ladders, brushes, etc. At what price will the company shut down?

3. Draw a U-shaped average cost curve. On your diagram, designate at what price levels you would expect entry and at what price levels you would expect exit if all the fixed costs are sunk. What if only half the fixed costs are sunk? Explain your reasoning.

4. José is a skilled electrician at a local company, a job that pays $50,000 per year, but he is considering quitting to start his own business. He talks it over with an accountant, who helps him to draw up the following chart with their best predictions about costs and revenues.

Predicted annual costs		Predicted annual revenues
Basic wage	$20,000	$75,000
Rent of space	$12,000	
Rent of equipment	$18,000	
Utilities	$ 2,000	
Miscellaneous	$ 5,000	

The basic wage does seem a bit low, the accountant admits, but she tells José to remember that as owner of the business, José will get to keep any profits as well. From an economist's point of view, is the accountant's list of costs complete? From an economist's point of view, what are José's expected profits?

APPENDIX: ALTERNATIVE WAYS OF CALCULATING THE DEMAND FOR LABOR

We have now seen three different ways for determining the demand for labor. One uses the condition for equilibrium output, that price equals marginal cost—to determine the equilibrium level of output and then determine the required labor. The second is derived directly from the profit-maximizing condition for the demand for labor: the value of the marginal product of labor is set equal to the wage. The third is to set the real product wage equal to the marginal product of labor. This appendix shows how these conditions are, in fact, alternative ways of writing the same condition.

With a single factor of production, labor, the extra cost of producing an extra unit of output is just the extra labor required times the wage. The extra labor required is $1/MPL$, 1 divided by the marginal product of labor. If 1 extra worker produces 2 violins a year, it takes ½ of a worker to produce an extra violin. Hence, the competitive equilibrium condition, price equals marginal cost, can be rewritten as

$$p = w/MPL.$$

If we multiply both sides of this equation by MPL, we obtain

$$p \times MPL = w,$$

the familiar condition that the value of the marginal product ($p \times MPL$)

equals the wage. And if we now divide both sides of the equation by p, we obtain

$$MPL = w/p,$$

the condition that the marginal product of labor equals the real product wage. All of these conditions are in fact three ways of writing the same equation.

Two important consequences follow from these conditions. First, note that the demand for labor depends only on the real product wage, that is, the wage divided by the price of the good produced. If wages and prices both double, then the demand for labor and the supply of output are unaffected. Second, an increase in the wage, keeping prices fixed, reduces the demand for labor. This effect can be seen in several different ways. The real product wage has increased. Therefore, for the condition "the marginal product of labor equals the real product wage" to be satisfied, the marginal product of labor must increase. But the principle of diminishing returns says that to increase the marginal product of labor, the input of labor must be reduced.

Alternatively, an increase in the wage can be seen as increasing the marginal cost of hiring an additional unit of labor, while with a fixed output price, the marginal benefit remains the same. Thus, at the old level of employment, the marginal benefit of the last worker hired is less than the marginal cost, and it pays firms to lower their level of production. At a high enough wage, the average variable costs of production may exceed the price, and the firm will shut down.

COMPETITIVE EQUILIBRIUM

Now that we have considered each aspect of the basic competitive model separately—the consumption decision, the work and savings decision, the investment decision, and the production decision—it is time to put the pieces together. In doing so, we will come to understand how markets answer the basic economic questions posed in Chapter 1: what is to be produced and in what quantities, how these goods are to be produced, for whom they are to be produced, and, most fundamental, how these resource allocation decisions are to be made.

This chapter also provides a first glance at the interconnectedness of a modern economy. In the giant web of transactions that is the U.S. economy, pressure on any one part will affect all the rest. In 1982, for example, the sharp fall in the price of oil reduced oil-drilling activity in the United States. This led to lower economic activity in oil-drilling states, most notably Texas, which resulted in lower real estate prices. Many real estate developers were unable to pay off the money they had borrowed to build new homes, and defaulted. Since most of these loans had been made through savings and loan associations (S & Ls), many S & Ls went bankrupt. The cost of rescuing the Texas S & Ls was so great that it threatened the nation's entire S & L system, requiring a federal bailout. Thus, a shiver in one part of the economy sent a chill through many other sectors.

Finally, this chapter explains why economists believe that, by and large, the market answers the fundamental economic questions efficiently.

GENERAL EQUILIBRIUM ANALYSIS

In Chapter 4 where we introduced the idea of a market equilibrium, we focused on one market at a time. The price of a good was determined when the demand for that good equaled its supply. The wage rate was determined when the demand for labor equaled its supply. The interest rate was determined when the demand for savings equaled its supply. This kind of analysis is called **partial equilibrium analysis.** In analyzing what is going on in one market, we ignore what is going on in other markets.

Interdependencies in the economy make partial equilibrium analysis overly simple because demand and supply in one market depend on prices determined in other markets. For instance, the demand for skis depends on the price of ski tickets, ski boots, and possibly even airline tickets. Thus, the equilibrium price of skis will depend on the price of ski tickets, ski boots, and airline tickets. But by the same token, the demand for ski tickets and ski boots will depend on the price of skis. Accordingly, the equilibrium price of ski tickets and ski boots will depend on the price of skis. **General equilibrium analysis** broadens the perspective, taking into account the interactions and interdependencies within the various parts of the economy.

EXAMPLE: THE CORPORATE INCOME TAX

Ascertaining the effect of the corporate income tax—the tax the federal government imposes on the net income of corporations—provides an example of why general equilibrium analysis is often essential. A partial equilibrium

Figure 13.1 PARTIAL EQUILIBRIUM ANALYSIS OF THE CORPORATE INCOME TAX

In panel A, the tax, viewed as a tax on the return to capital in the corporate sector, leads to a lower return to investors and a higher cost of capital to firms. In panel B, the tax simply results in a higher cost of capital to firms.

analysis of this tax is provided in Figure 13.1, where we have drawn the demand and supply curves for capital in the corporate sector. The corporate income tax is shown as a tax on capital because much of a corporation's income is, in fact, a return on the capital invested in it. As can be seen, this tax drives a wedge between the price of capital paid by the firm and the return received by investors.

Who bears the burden of the tax? The partial equilibrium analysis shown in panel A of Figure 13.1 makes it clear that investors bear only a part of the burden. Their after-tax return is lowered, but not by the full amount of the tax. Panel B of the figure, indeed, shows a case in which investors bear none of the burden, when the supply of capital is horizontal (infinitely elastic).

If investors do not bear the burden of the tax, who does? Because the interest rate which firms pay increases, firms' costs have gone up, and this will be reflected in higher equilibrium prices. Thus, consumers bear some of the costs. If sales decrease as a result, the demand for labor may decrease, and thus wages may fall, in which case workers will bear some of the burden. But other factors need to be taken into account as well. The higher cost of capital may induce firms to substitute labor for machines, in which case the demand for labor may actually increase. At higher prices to consumers, however, the return to working is reduced. In this case, workers might supply less labor.

Account must also be taken of the interactions between capital in the corporate and unincorporated sectors of the economy. Because over 80 percent of nonfarm business takes place in the corporate sector, activities in that sector have major ramifications on the rest of the economy. If investors find it less attractive to invest in the corporate sector, they will shift their savings from the corporate to the unincorporated sector. As capital flows into the unincorporated sector, the return to capital in that sector will be reduced to the point that it equals the rate of return in the corporate sector. A full general equilibrium analysis needs to take all these factors into account.

General equilibrium analysis focuses on the fact that, in equilibrium, the re-

turns to all investments throughout the economy must provide the same rate of return per dollar invested (adjusting for risk). An analysis of the corporate income tax that failed to take into account the responses in the unincorporated sector would be incomplete at best, and could be seriously misleading. (Most economists agree that, in the long run, most of the burden of the corporate income tax rests on workers and consumers, and relatively little on corporations, their shareholders, or others who have lent money—contrary to popular belief.)

WHEN PARTIAL EQUILIBRIUM ANALYSIS WILL DO

In the example of the corporate income tax just given, general equilibrium analysis is clearly important. But can we ever focus on what goes on in a single market, without worrying about the reverberations in the rest of the economy? Are there circumstances in which partial equilibrium analysis will provide a fairly accurate answer to the effect of, say, a change in a tax? Fortunately, the answer is yes.

Partial equilibrium analysis is adequate, for example, when the reverberations from the initial imposition of a tax are so dispersed that they can be ignored without distorting the analysis. Such is the case when individuals shift their demand away from the taxed good toward many, many other goods. Each of the prices of those goods changes only a very little. And the total demand for factors of production (like capital and labor) changes only negligibly, so that the prices of different factors are virtually unchanged. Moreover, the slight changes in the prices of different goods and inputs have only a slight effect on the demand and supply curve of the industry upon which the analysis is focusing. In these circumstances, partial equilibrium analysis will provide a good approximation to what will actually happen.

EXAMPLE: A TAX ON CIGARETTES

The effect of a tax on cigarettes is an example where partial equilibrium analysis works well. Back in 1951, the federal tax on a pack of cigarettes was worth 42 percent of the total price paid by a consumer. Since the tax has not been adjusted for inflation, while the price of cigarettes (and everything else) has increased, by the late 1980s, the tax had dropped to only about 15 percent of the market price of a pack. A case could be made for increasing the tax, particularly since even doubling the tax—still well within the 42 percent figure—on each pack of cigarettes would raise nearly $3 billion a year. What predictions can be made about the consequences of increasing the tax?

A tax paid by firms can be thought of as increasing the costs of production. Figure 13.2 shows the tax as shifting the supply curve of cigarettes up by the amount of the tax. Demand is reduced from Q_0 to Q_1. Since expenditures on cigarettes are a small proportion of anyone's income, a 15 percent increase in their price will have a small effect on overall consumption patterns. While the

Figure 13.2 PARTIAL EQUILIBRIUM ANALYSIS OF THE EFFECT OF A TAX ON CIGARETTES

A tax on cigarettes raises the price of cigarettes and reduces consumption slightly. The second-round reverberations of this tax are sufficiently slight that they can be ignored.

reduced quantity demanded of cigarettes (and the indirect changed demand for other goods) will have a slight effect on the total demand for labor, this effect is so small that it will have no noticeable effect on the wage rate. Similarly, the tax will have virtually no effect on the return to capital.

Under these circumstances, where more distant general equilibrium effects are likely to be so faint as to be indiscernible, a partial equilibrium analysis of a tax on cigarettes is appropriate.

THE BASIC COMPETITIVE EQUILIBRIUM MODEL

General equilibrium analysis requires a model of the entire economy. To analyze the effects of imposing a tax or the immigration of labor or any other change, one "solves" for the full equilibrium before and after the change, and looks at how each of the variables—wages, prices, interest rates, outputs, employment, and so forth—has changed.

To see how this is done, we focus on a simplified version of the full competitive equilibrium model.

In this simplified model, we assume all workers have identical skills. Ignoring differences in skill level enables us to talk about the labor market as if all workers received the same wage. Similarly, we ignore all aspects of risk in our analysis of the capital market. This allows us to use a single interest rate. Finally, we assume that all firms produce the same good; in other words, the product market consists of only one good. We now have an economy made up of three markets—the labor market, the capital market, and the product market—and can use general equilibrium analysis to trace through how they depend on one another.

In Chapter 9, we saw how households determine the amount of labor they wish to supply. Households supply labor because they want to buy goods. Hence, their labor supply depends on both wages and prices. It also depends on other sources of income. If we assume, for simplicity, that households' only other source of income is the return to their investments (their return to capital, or the interest on their investments), then we can see that the labor supply is connected to all three markets. It depends on the wage, the price of the single good, and the return to capital. Similarly, in Chapter 11, we saw that the demand for labor depends on the wage, on the interest rate, and on the price at which the firm sells its product.

Equilibrium in the labor market requires that the demand for labor equal the supply. Normally, when we draw the demand curve for labor, we simply assume that p, the price of the good(s) being produced, and the interest rate (here, r) are kept fixed. We focus our attention solely on the wage rate, the price of labor. *Given p and r,* we look for the wage at which the demand and supply for labor are equal. This is a partial equilibrium analysis of the labor market.

The labor market is only one of the three markets, even in our highly simplified economy. There is also the market for capital to consider. In Chapter 9, we saw how households determine their savings, which in turn determine the available supply of capital. The supply of capital is affected, in general, by the return it yields (the interest rate, r) plus the income individuals have from other sources, in particular from wages. Since the amount individuals are willing to save may depend on how well off they feel, and how well off they feel depends on the wage rate relative to prices, we can think of the supply of capital too as depending on wages, interest rates, and prices. In Chapter 11, we learned how to derive firms' demand for capital. This too will depend on the interest rate they must pay, the price at which goods can be sold, and the cost of other inputs.

Equilibrium in the capital market occurs at the point where the demand and supply for capital are equal. Again, partial equilibrium analysis of the capital market focuses on the return to capital, r, at which the demand and supply of capital are equal, but both the demand and the supply depend on the wage and the price of goods as well.

Finally, there is the market for goods. Chapters 8 and 9 showed how to derive households' demand for goods. We can think of the household as first deciding on how much to spend (Chapter 9), and then deciding how to allocate what it spends over different goods (Chapter 8). Of course, with a single consumption good, the latter problem no longer exists. In our simplified model, then, we can think of the demand for goods at any price as being determined by household income, which in turn depends on the wage and the interest rate.

Similarly, in Chapter 12, we analyzed how firms determine how much to produce: they set price equal to marginal cost, where marginal cost depends on wages and the interest rate. Equilibrium in the goods market requires that the demand for goods equal the supply of goods. Again, while in the simple partial equilibrium analysis we focus on how the demand and supply of goods depend on price, p, we know that the demand and supply of goods also depend on both the wage rate and the return to capital.

EQUILIBRIUM IN THE BASIC COMPETITIVE MODEL

The labor market clearing condition: The demand for labor must equal the supply.
The capital market clearing condition: The demand for capital must equal the supply.
The goods market clearing condition: The demand for goods must equal the supply.

The labor market is said to be in equilibrium when the demand for labor equals the supply. The product market is in equilibrium when the demand for goods equals the supply. The capital market is in equilibrium when the demand for capital equals the supply. The economy as a whole is in equilibrium only when all markets clear simultaneously (demand equals supply in all markets). The general equilibrium for our simple economy occurs at a common wage rate, w, price, p, and interest rate, r, at which all three markets are all in equilibrium.

In the basic equilibrium model, there is only a single good, but it is easy to extend the analysis to the more realistic case where there are many goods. The same web of interconnections exists between different goods and between different goods and different inputs. Recall from Chapter 4 that the demand curve depicts the quantity of a good—for instance, beer—demanded at each price; the supply curve shows the quantity of a good that firms supply at each price. But the demand curve for beer depends on the prices of other goods and the income levels of different consumers; similarly, the supply curve for beer depends on the prices of inputs, including the wage rate, the interest rate, and the price of hops and other ingredients. Those prices, in turn, depend on supply and demand in their respective markets. The general equilibrium of the economy requires finding the prices for each good and for each input such that the demand for each good equals the supply, and the demand for each input equals the supply.

THE CIRCULAR FLOW OF FUNDS

General equilibrium analysis is not the only way to think about the interrelations of the various parts of the economy. Another way is to consider the flow of funds through the economy. Households buy goods and services from firms. Households supply labor and capital to firms. The income individuals receive, whether in the form of wages or the return on their savings, is spent to buy the goods that firms produce. All these transactions constitute what is called the **circular flow.**

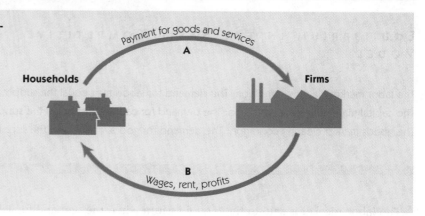

Figure 13.3 A SIMPLE CIR-CULAR FLOW DIA-GRAM

In this simple circular flow diagram, only labor and product markets and only the household and firm sectors are represented. It can be analyzed from any starting point. For example, funds flow from households to firms in the form of purchases of goods and services. Funds flow from firms to households in the form of payments for the labor of workers and profits paid to owners.

The circular flow for a simplified economy—in which there are only households and firms, households do not save, and firms do not invest—is shown in Figure 13.3. This circular flow diagram serves two purposes. First, it keeps track of how funds flow through the economy. We can see this by starting at point A and following the circular flow around to the right. The top arrow shows that households pay money to firms to buy goods for their consumption. The lower arrow (point B) shows that firms use the money to pay household members in the form of wages (for labor), rent (to the owners of land), and profit (to the owners of firms). The second purpose of the circular flow diagram is to focus on certain balance conditions in the economy that must always be satisfied. In the case of the simple flow in Figure 13.3, there is one balance condition. The income of households (the flow of funds from firms, lower arrow) must equal the expenditures of households (the flow of funds to firms, upper arrow).

Figure 13.4 expands the circular flow in three ways. First, savings and capital are included. Thus, the funds that flow from the firm to the household now include a return on capital (interest on loans and bonds, dividends on stocks). The funds that flow from the household to the firm now include savings, which go to purchase machines and buildings. And firms now retain some of their earnings to finance investment.

Second, the circular flow now includes funds flowing into and out of the government. Thus, some households receive transfer payments from the government (benefits like Social Security and welfare payments). Some sell their labor services to the government rather than private firms. Some receive interest on loans to the government (U.S. government bonds). And there is now an important additional outflow from households: income that goes to the government in the form of taxes. Similarly, firms have additional sources of inflow in the sales of goods and services they make to the government and in government subsidies to firms, and an additional outflow in the taxes they must pay to the government.

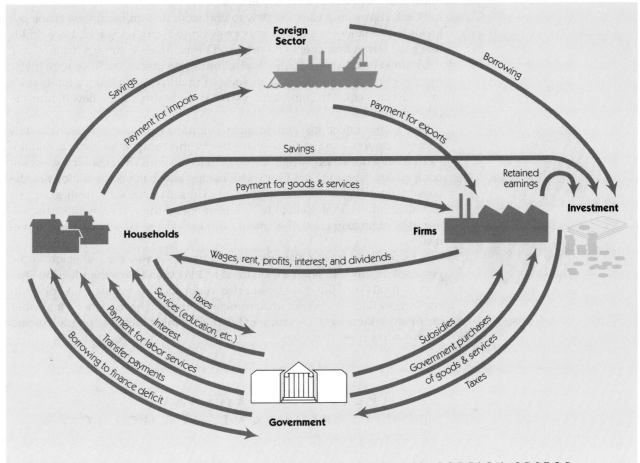

Figure 13.4 CIRCULAR FLOW WITH GOVERNMENT AND FOREIGN SECTOR ADDED

This expanded circular flow diagram shows the labor, capital, and product markets along with households, firms, government, and foreign countries; it too can be analyzed from any starting point. The flow of funds into each sector must balance the flow of funds out of each sector.

Just as the flow of funds into and out of households and firms must balance, the flow of funds into the government must balance the flow of funds out.[1] When there is a deficit—that is, when the government spends more than it collects in taxes, as has been the case in recent years—funds go into the gov-

---

[1]We ignore here the possibility that the government can simply pay for what it obtains by printing money. In the United States, the government always finances any shortfall in revenue by borrowing.

ernment as borrowings. The government finances the difference by borrowing (in our diagram, from households).

Third, Figure 13.4 adds the flow to and from foreign countries. Firms sell goods to foreigners (exports) and borrow funds from foreigners. Households buy goods from foreigners (imports) and invest funds in foreign firms. Again, there must be a balance in the flow of funds into and out of the country. U.S. exports plus what the country borrows from abroad (the flow of funds from abroad) must equal its imports plus what it lends abroad (the flow of funds to other countries).[2]

The interconnections and balance conditions making up circular flow analysis are the same as those that arise in the competitive general equilibrium model discussed earlier in the chapter. Even if the economy were not competitive, however, the interrelationships and balance conditions of the circular flow diagram would still be true. Thus, the circular flow diagram is a useful reminder that change in one element of the economy *must* be balanced by change in another element, whether or not the economy is competitive.

Let's put the circular flow diagram to work. Consider a reduction in the personal income tax, such as occurred in 1981 under President Reagan. The flow of funds into the government was reduced. The circular flow diagram reminds us flows in and out must remain balanced. That is, either some other tax must be increased, government borrowing must increase, or government expenditures must decrease.

COMPETITIVE GENERAL EQUILIBRIUM AND ECONOMIC EFFICIENCY

The first part of this chapter introduced the basic model of competitive general equilibrium. Competitive general equilibrium entails prices, wages, and returns to capital such that all markets—for goods, labor, capital (and other factors of production)—clear. A change in economic conditions, such as the imposition of a tax, a migration of labor, or a sudden decline in the quantity supplied of a good at each price, results in a new equilibrium to the economy. We have seen how the effects of such changes can be traced out.

Economists are interested, however, not only in describing the market equilibrium, but in evaluating it. Do competitive markets do a "good" job in allocating resources? Chapter 7 introduced the idea of Adam Smith's "invisible hand," which said that market economies are efficient. One of the most important achievements of modern economic theory has been to establish in what sense and under what conditions the market is efficient.

---

[2]This condition can be put another way. The difference between U.S. imports and exports must equal the net flow of funds from abroad (the difference between what the country borrows from abroad and what it lends).

CLOSE-UP: THE MINIMUM WAGE AND GENERAL EQUILIBRIUM

When the first minimum wage law was adopted by passage of the Fair Labor Standards Act of 1938, it had general equilibrium effects that altered the character of the country.

When enacted, the minimum wage law required that wages be no lower than 32.5 cents per hour. Because wages were much lower in the South than in the North, many more workers were affected there. For example, 44 percent of Southern textile workers were paid below the minimum wage, but only 6 percent of Northern textile workers were. African-Americans in the South were particularly affected. Many lost their jobs and migrated North. The economy of the South, no longer able to pay low wages, adapted by seeking out investment, which over the years has helped make states like Texas and Florida among the fastest-growing in the country.

Gavin Wright, professor of economics at Stanford University described the situation this way: "The overall effect of this history on black Americans is complex, mixed, and ironic. Displacement and suffering were severe. Yet in abolishing the low-wage South, the federal government also destroyed the nation's most powerful bastion of racism and white supremacy. The civil rights movement of the 1960s was able to use the South's hunger for capital inflows as an effective weapon in forcing desegregation. Similarly, migration to the North allowed dramatic increases in incomes and educational opportunities for many blacks; yet the same migration channeled other blacks into the high-unemployment ghettos which if anything have worsened with the passage of time."

A partial equilibrium analysis of the effects of enacting a minimum wage would only look at how the law affected labor markets. But for society as a whole, the effects of enacting such a law were far more momentous, touching on issues like racial desegregation and the growth of urban ghettos.

Source: Gavin Wright, "The Economic Revolution in the American South," *Journal of Economic Perspectives* (Summer 1987) 1:161–78.

PARETO EFFICIENCY

To economists, the concept of efficiency is related to concern with the well-being of those in the economy. When no one can be made better off without making someone else worse off the allocation of resources is called **Pareto efficient,** after the great Italian economist and sociologist Vilfredo Pareto (1848–1923). Typically when economists refer to efficiency, Pareto efficiency is what they mean. Saying that a market is efficient is a compliment. In the same way that an efficient machine uses its inputs as productively as possible, an efficient market leaves no way of increasing output with the same level of inputs. The only way one person can be made better off is by taking resources away from another, thereby making the second person worse off.

It is easy to see how an allocation of resources might not be Pareto efficient. Assume the government is given the job of distributing chocolate and vanilla ice cream and pays no attention to people's preferences. Assume, moreover, that some individuals love chocolate and hate vanilla, while others love vanilla and hate chocolate. Some chocolate lovers will get vanilla ice cream, and some vanilla lovers will get chocolate ice cream. Clearly, this is Pareto inefficient. Allowing people to trade resources, in this case, ice cream, makes both groups better off.

There is a popular and misguided view that *all* economic changes represent nothing more than redistributions. Gains to one only subtract from another. Rent control is one example. In this view, the only effect of rent control is redistribution—landlords receive less, and are worse off, by the same amount that their tenants' rents are reduced (and the tenants are better off). In some countries, unions have expressed similar views, and see wage increases as having no further consequences than redistributing income to workers from those who own or who manage firms. This view is mistaken, because in each of these instances, there are consequences beyond the redistribution. Rent control that keeps rents below the level that clears the rental housing market results in inefficiencies. For those concerned about renters who cannot afford the going rate, there are better approaches that make the renters as well as the landlords better off than under rent control. Thus, with rent control, the economy is not Pareto efficient.

CONDITIONS FOR THE PARETO EFFICIENCY OF THE MARKET ECONOMY

For the economy to be Pareto efficient, it must meet the conditions of exchange efficiency, production efficiency, and product-mix efficiency. Considering each of these conditions separately shows us why the basic competitive model attains Pareto efficiency. (Recall the basic ingredients of that model: rational, perfectly informed households interacting with rational, profit-maximizing firms in competitive markets, and in an environment in which the market failures discussed in Chapter 7 do not occur.)

EXCHANGE EFFICIENCY

Exchange efficiency requires that whatever the economy produces must be distributed among individuals in an efficient way. If I like chocolate ice cream and you like vanilla ice cream, exchange efficiency requires that I get the chocolate and you get the vanilla.

When there is exchange efficiency, there is no scope for further trade among individuals. Chapter 3 discussed the advantages of free exchange among individuals and nations. Any prohibition or restriction on trade results in exchange inefficiency. For instance, in war times, governments often ration scarce goods, like sugar. People are given coupons that allow them to buy, say, a pound of sugar a month. If sugar carries a price of $1 a pound, having $1 is not enough; you must also have the coupon. There is often considerable controversy about whether people should be allowed to sell their coupons, or trade their sugar coupons for, say, a butter coupon. If the government prohibits the sale or trading of coupons, then the economy will not be exchange efficient—it will not be Pareto efficient.

The price system ensures that exchange efficiency is attained. In deciding how much of a good to buy, people balance the marginal benefit they receive by buying an extra unit with the cost of that extra unit, its price. Hence, price can be thought of as a rough measure of the *marginal* benefit an individual receives from a good—that is, the benefit a person receives from one more unit of the good. For those who like chocolate ice cream a great deal and vanilla ice cream very little, this will entail consuming many more chocolate ice cream cones than vanilla. And conversely for the vanilla lover. Notice that no single individual or agency needs to know who is a chocolate and who is a vanilla lover for the goods to get to the right person. Not even the ice cream stores have to know individual preferences. Each consumer, by his own action, ensures that exchange efficiency is attained.

Notice too that if different individuals face *different* prices, then the economy will not, in general, be exchange efficient. This is because the difference in price opens up an opportunity for exchange. For example, Jim would love to fly to Hawaii but feels it is not worth it at the full fare offered. At the same time, Madeleine, whose mother is an airline executive and only has to pay half fares, is not keen on going to Hawaii but cannot pass up the good deal. Both can be made better off if they are allowed to make an exchange.

PRODUCTION EFFICIENCY

For an economy to be Pareto efficient, it must also be **production efficient.** That is, it must not be possible to produce more of some goods without producing less of other goods. In other words, Pareto efficiency requires that the economy operate along the production possibilities curve first introduced in Chapter 2.

Figure 13.5 shows the production possibilities curve for a simple economy that produces only two goods, apples and oranges. If the economy is at point *I*, inside the production possibilities curve, it cannot be Pareto efficient. Society could produce more of both apples and oranges, and by distributing them to

Figure 13.5 THE PRODUCTION POSSIBILITIES CURVE

The production possibilities curve shows the maximum level of output of one good given the level of output of other goods. Production efficiency requires that the economy be on its production possibilities curve. Along the curve, the only way to increase production of one good (here, apples) is to decrease the production of other goods (oranges).

CLOSE-UP: PARETO IMPROVEMENT IN THE SKIES

Airlines want their planes to fly as full as possible. They also know that a certain percentage of people who purchased a ticket for any given flight are not going to show up. This gives the airlines an incentive to "overbook" flights. They sell more tickets than there are seats in the reasonable expectation that there will be room to take everyone who actually shows up. But sometimes everyone does show up, and a decision must be made about who will be bumped from the flight. Several methods of making this choice are possible.

In the 1960s, the airlines simply bumped whoever showed up last, and gave those people tickets for a later flight. Bumped passengers had no recourse. This sort of policy causes high blood pressure.

To avoid imposing these costs on frustrated passengers, a second policy might be for the government to forbid airlines to overbook flights. But in this case, some planes will be forced to fly with empty seats that some people would have been willing to buy. Airlines would lose revenues, prices would have to rise to offset the lost revenue, and travelers who could have flown in the empty seat but could not get reservations under the no-overbooking rule would all be losers.

There is an alternative solution which is a Pareto improvement both over the practice of bumping and over rules forbidding overbooking. Today airlines offer a free ticket on a future flight or other bonus as compensation to anyone willing to wait. People willing to accept such a deal are clearly better off in their own estimation. The airlines benefit because they are allowed to continue their practice of overbooking and thus keeping their flights as full as possible. In fact, since the person who receives a free ticket will often occupy a seat that would have been vacant anyway, the marginal cost of offering the free ticket for the airline is very close to zero. This is a real-world Pareto improvement. Everyone involved is at least no worse off and many are better off.

Source: Julian L. Simon, "An Almost Practical Solution to Airline Overbooking," *Journal of Transport Economics and Policy* (May 1968), pp. 201–2.

different individuals, it could make people better off. Prices signal to firms the scarcity of each of the inputs they use. When all firms face the same prices of labor, capital goods, and other inputs, they will take the appropriate actions to economize on each of these inputs, ensuring that the economy operates along its production possibilities curve.

PRODUCT-MIX EFFICIENCY

The third condition for Pareto efficiency is **product-mix efficiency.** That is, the mix of goods produced by the economy must reflect the preferences of those in the economy. The economy must produce along the production possibilities curve at a point that reflects the preferences of consumers. The price system again ensures that this condition will be satisfied. Both firms and households look at the trade-offs. Firms look at how many extra oranges they can produce if they reduce their production of apples. The result is given by the slope of the production possibilities curve, and is called **the marginal rate of transformation.** Firms compare this trade-off with the relative benefits of producing the two goods—given by the relative prices. Similarly, households look at the relative costs of apples and oranges—again given by the relative prices—and ask, given those trade-offs, whether they would like to consume more apples and fewer oranges or vice versa.

Changes in preferences are reflected quickly—through the operation of demand and supply curves—in changes in prices. These changes are then translated into changes in production by firms. Assume that the economy is initially producing at a point along the production possibilities curve, E in Figure 13.5. Consumers decide that they like apples more and oranges less. The increased demand for apples will result in the price of apples increasing, and this will lead to an increased output of apples; at the same time, the decreased demand for oranges will result in the price of oranges falling, and this in turn will lead to a decreased output of oranges. The economy will move from E to a point such as E_1, where there are more apples and fewer oranges produced; the mix of goods produced in the economy will have changed to reflect the changed preferences of consumers.

THREE CONDITIONS FOR PARETO EFFICIENCY

1. Exchange efficiency: Goods must be distributed among individuals in a way that means there are no gains from further trade.

2. Production efficiency: The economy must be on its production possibilities curve.

3. Product-mix efficiency: The economy must produce a mix of goods reflecting the preferences of consumers.

POLICY PERSPECTIVE: THE COST OF AIR SAFETY FOR CHILDREN

Many states require small children in cars to ride in specially designed safety seats. So why shouldn't small children traveling by plane be required to ride in safety seats as well? Congressional hearings were held on this subject in the summer of 1990. Everyone agreed that in at least a few cases, such seats would save a child's life in an airplane crash. Nevertheless, after considering the potential consequences and side effects of such a rule, the Federal Aviation Administration (FAA) argued against it.

On the benefit side, the FAA estimated that mandatory safety seats would save the life of one child in one airline crash every 10 years. But parents would have to pay as much as $185 to buy the safety seats themselves, in addition to paying for a regular airplane seat for the child. Now, children under two years old are allowed to sit in their parents' laps, avoiding the expense of an airline ticket. With those extra costs, the FAA estimated that 20 percent of the families who now fly with small children would either stay home or drive. The additional driving would lead to 9 additional highway deaths, 52 serious injuries, and 2,300 minor injuries over the same ten-year period, according to FAA estimates.

Even those who feel that saving an additional child's life has a value that cannot be reduced to a price tag, however high, must look beyond the market being regulated. Looking beyond airlines makes it clear that reducing airline deaths by requiring child safety seats for infants and toddlers is almost certain to cause even greater loss of life.

COMPETITIVE MARKETS AND PARETO EFFICIENCY

We now know that when economists say that market economies are efficient, or that the price system results in economic efficiency, they mean that the economy is Pareto efficient: no one can be made better off without making someone else worse off. We have also learned why competitive markets ensure that all three of the basic conditions for Pareto efficiency are attained: exchange efficiency, production efficiency, and product-mix efficiency.

The argument that competitive markets ensure Pareto efficiency can be put somewhat loosely in another way: a rearrangement of resources can only benefit people who voluntarily agree to it. But in competitive equilibrium, people have already agreed to all the exchanges they are willing to make; no one wishes to produce more or less or to demand more or less, given the prices he faces.

Pareto efficiency does *not* say that there are no ways to make one or many individuals better off. Obviously, resources could be taken from some and given to others, and the recipients would be better off. We have seen how, for instance, government interventions with the market, such as rent control, do benefit some individuals—those who are lucky enough to get the rent-controlled apartments. But in the process, someone is made worse off.

COMPETITIVE MARKETS AND INCOME DISTRIBUTION

Efficiency is better than inefficiency, but it is not everything. In the competitive equilibrium, some individuals might be very rich, while others live in dire poverty. One person might have skills that are highly valued, while another does not. Competition may result in an efficient economy with a very unequal distribution of resources.

The law of supply and demand in a competitive economy determines how the available income will be divided up. It determines how much workers get paid for their labor and the return to owners of capital on their investments. By determining wages and the return to capital, the market thus determines the distribution of income.

Knowing how the distribution of income is determined is important, because it tells us how the nation's economic pie is divided: it provides the answer to the question: "For whom are goods produced?" While competitive markets produce economic *efficiency*—no one can be made better off without making someone else worse off—competitive markets may also produce distributions of income that seem, at least to some, morally repugnant. An economy where some individuals live in mansions while others barely eke out a living may be efficient, but that still hardly makes the situation desirable. Left to themselves, competitive markets may provide an answer to the question "For whom are goods produced?" that seems unacceptable.

This unacceptable response does not mean that the competitive market mechanism should be abandoned, at least not under the conditions assumed in our basic model, with perfectly informed, rational consumers and firms interacting in perfectly competitive markets. Even if society as a whole wishes to redistribute income, it should not dispense with competitive markets. Instead, all that is needed is to redistribute the wealth that people possess, and then leave the rest to the workings of a competitive market. With appropriate redistributions of wealth, the economy can achieve any desired distribution of income.

As a practical matter, perhaps the most important impact of government on the distribution of "wealth" is through education—in providing everyone a certain amount of human capital. By providing all individuals, regardless of the wealth of their parents, with a free basic education, government reduces the degree of inequality that otherwise would exist. Still, as we shall see in Chapter 23, the magnitude of inequality in the United States remains high—larger than in most other developed countries.

Frequently government interferences with the market are justified on the grounds that they increase equality. These government policies are often based on the widely held but mistaken (as we have already seen) view that all redistributions are just that, some individuals get more, others get less, but there are no further repercussions. We now know that changing relative prices to achieve redistribution—such as rent control—will have effects in addition to redistributing income. Such changes interfere with the economy's efficiency. One consequence of lower rents for apartments, for example, is that the return on capital invested in rental housing will fall, and the economy will as a result invest too little in rental housing. Because of this underinvestment, the economy is not efficient.

Thus, interventions in the economy justified on the grounds that they increase equality need to be treated with caution. To attain an efficient allocation of resources with the desired distribution of income, *if* the assumptions of the competitive model are satisfied by the economy, the *sole* role of the government is to redistribute initial wealth. Not only can one rely on the market mechanism thereafter, but interfering with the market may actually result in the economy not being Pareto efficient.

Both of the results just presented—that competitive markets are Pareto efficient, and that every Pareto-efficient allocation, regardless of the desired distribution of income, can be obtained through the market mechanism—are **theorems.** That is, they are logical propositions that follow from basic definitions and assumptions, such as what is meant by a competitive economy and what is meant by Pareto efficiency. These theorems are based on other assumptions as well, such as the absence of externalities. When their assumptions are not satisfied, market economies may not be Pareto efficient, and more extensive government interventions may be required to obtain Pareto-efficient allocations. Later chapters will explore these circumstance in greater detail.

LOOKING BEYOND THE BASIC MODEL: MARKET FAILURES AND THE ROLE OF GOVERNMENT

This chapter has brought together the pieces of the basic competitive model. It has shown how the competitive equilibrium in an ideal economy is achieved. To the extent that conditions in the real world match the assumptions of the basic competitive model, there will be economic efficiency.

Government will have little role in the economy beyond establishing a legal framework within which to enforce market transactions.

One group of economists, referred to as **free-market economists** for their strong faith in unfettered markets as the path to economic efficiency, believe that the competitive model provides a good description of most markets most of the time. These economists, who include Nobel laureates Milton Friedman of Stanford University's Hoover Institution and the late George Stigler of the University of Chicago, believe that there is a very limited role for government in economic affairs. In their view, government intervention should be restricted mainly to changing unacceptable distributions of income, and even in this area government should operate with restraint.

Another group of economists, called **imperfect-market economists,** see significant discrepancies between the basic competitive model and the conditions they observe when they study actual consumers, firms, and markets. Such discrepancies lead them to question whether private markets, left to operate on their own, will produce economically efficient outcomes.

Imperfect-market economists would not, however, discard the model. For them, it is an important baseline for investigation. For example, many economists who specialize in the study of the economy's industrial structure, such as Joseph Bain of the University of California at Berkeley or F. M. Scherer of Harvard, argue that competition is limited, and explain why this is so. If the cigarette market is not competitive, the competitive model will yield incorrect predictions concerning, for instance, the consequences of an increase in the tax on cigarettes.

Other economists, such as Nobel laureate Kenneth J. Arrow of Stanford University, contend that firms do not have perfect information about the quality of their workers and investors do not have perfect information about the returns to different investment opportunities. This imperfect information, they argue, results in capital and labor markets functioning in ways quite different from that described by the basic competitive model.

Still other economists, such as MIT's Nobel laureate Robert Solow, argue that the model is generally appropriate, but there are important instances where markets cannot be relied upon without government intervention. They are concerned about pollution of the environment and about unemployment. Further, economists such as Paul Romer of the University of California at Berkeley and Paul David of Stanford University worry that firms on their own will invest too little in research, and as a result, economic growth will be hampered. These economists believe that these are instances where one or more of the assumptions of the basic competitive model are violated and that there is, therefore, scope for government intervention to increase economic efficiency.

What are the consequences when the underlying assumptions are not valid? Which of the assumptions are most suspect? What evidence do we have with which we can assess either the validity of the model's underlying assumptions or its implications? The next part of this book is devoted to these questions, and to the role of government that emerges from the answers.

A warning is in order before we embark on our study of market imperfections. That markets do not work perfectly—suggesting a possible role for government—does not necessarily mean that government intervention will improve matters.

TWO VIEWS OF THE BASIC COMPETITIVE MODEL

Free-market view: The competitive model provides a good description of the economy, and government intervention is not required.

Imperfect-market view: In many markets, the competitive model does not provide a good description—for instance, because competition is limited and information is imperfect. There are important market failures, evidenced by unemployment and environmental pollution, requiring at least selective government intervention.

Free-market and imperfect-market economists continue to debate the extent to which the basic competitive model provides a good description of the economy. However, these disagreements should not mask the large, and growing areas of consensus about the efficiency of competitive markets, which we highlight with our seventh consensus point:

7   The Efficiency of Competitive Markets

> *At the center of the modern economy are competitive markets. Through the profit motive and the price system, competitive markets lead to economic efficiency. However, there are important exceptions, where markets fail to produce efficient outcomes. For instance, markets may not be competitive, and markets produce too much of goods with negative externalities (like pollution), and too little of goods with positive externalities (like basic research).*

REVIEW AND PRACTICE

SUMMARY

1. When an economic change affects many markets at once, general equilibrium analysis is used to study the interactions among various parts of the economy. But when the secondary repercussions of a change are small, partial equilibrium analysis, focusing on only one or a few markets, is sufficient.

2. General equilibrium in the basic competitive model occurs when wages, interest rates, and prices are such that demand is equal to supply in all labor, capital, and product markets. All markets clear.

3. Circular flow of funds diagrams show capital, labor, and product market interrelationships between households, firms, government, and the foreign sector. The flow of funds in and out of each sector must balance.

4. Under the conditions of the basic competitive model, the economy's resource allocation is Pareto efficient; that is, no one can be made better off without making someone else worse off.

5. The distribution of income that emerges from competitive markets may possibly be very unequal. However, under the conditions of the basic competitive model, a redistribution of wealth can move the economy to a more equal allocation that is also Pareto efficient. No further government intervention is required.

6. Some economists hold that the basic competitive model provides an essentially accurate view of most of the economy; markets ensure economic efficiency, and there is only a limited role for government. Others maintain that many markets are quite imperfect, the basic competitive model provides no more than a starting point for analysis, and government intervention is required to deal with some of society's problems.

KEY TERMS

partial equilibrium analysis	circular flow	production efficiency
general equilibrium analysis	Pareto-efficient allocations	product-mix efficiency
	exchange efficiency	

REVIEW QUESTIONS

1. What is the difference between partial and general equilibrium analysis? When is each one especially appropriate?

2. List the principal flows into and out of firms, households, government, and the foreign sector.

3. How does the economy in general equilibrium answer the four basic economic questions: What is produced, and in what quantities? How are these goods produced? For whom are they produced? Who decides how resources are allocated?

4. What is meant by Pareto efficiency? What is required for the economy to be Pareto efficient? If the conditions of the basic competitive model are satisfied, is the economy Pareto efficient?

5. If the distribution of income in the economy is quite unequal, is it necessary to impose price controls or otherwise change prices in the competitive marketplace to make it more equal?

PROBLEMS

1. Decide whether partial equilibrium analysis would suffice in each of these cases, or whether it would be wise to undertake a general equilibrium analysis:
   (a) a tax on alcohol;
   (b) an increase in the Social Security tax;
   (c) a drought that affects farm production in the Midwestern states;
   (d) a rise in the price of crude oil;
   (e) a major airline going out of business.
Explain your answers.

2. Use the extended circular flow diagram, with the foreign sector included, to trace out the possible consequences of the following:
   (a) a law requiring that businesses raise the wages of their employees;
   (b) a decision by consumers to import more and save less;
   (c) an increase in government expenditure financed by a corporate income tax;
   (d) an increase in government expenditure without an accompanying increase in taxes.

3. Explain how each of the following might interfere with exchange efficiency:
   (a) airlines that limit the number of seats they sell at a discount price;
   (b) doctors who charge poor patients less than rich patients;
   (c) firms that give volume discounts.
In each case, what additional trades might be possible?

4. Assume that in the steel industry, given current production levels and technology, 1 machine costing $10,000 can replace 1 worker. Given current production levels and technology in the automobile industry, 1 machine costing $10,000 can replace 2 workers. Is this economy Pareto efficient; that is, is it on its production possibilities curve? If not, explain how total output of both goods can be increased by shifting machines and labor between industries.

5. Consider three ways of helping poor people to buy food, clothing, and shelter. The first way is to pass laws setting price ceilings to keep these basic goods affordable. The second is to have the government distribute coupons that give poor people a discount when they buy these necessities. The third is for the government to distribute income to poor people. Which program is more likely to have a Pareto-efficient outcome? Describe why the other programs are not likely to be Pareto efficient.

APPENDIX: PARETO EFFICIENCY AND COMPETITIVE MARKETS

The concept of the marginal rate of substitution, introduced in the appendices to Chapters 8 and 9, can be used to see more clearly why competitive markets are Pareto efficient.

EXCHANGE EFFICIENCY

Exchange efficiency can be achieved only when all individuals have the same marginal rate of substitution, the amount of one good a person is willing to give up to get one unit of another. In competitive markets, individuals choose a mix of goods for which the marginal rate of substitution is equal to relative prices. Since all individuals face the same relative prices, they all have identical marginal rates of substitution, ensuring the exchange efficiency of the economy.

To see why exchange efficiency requires that all people have the same marginal rate of substitution, let's look at a simple example of Crusoe and Friday and their island economy. Assume that Crusoe's marginal rate of substitution between apples and oranges is 2; that is, he is willing to give up 2 apples for 1 extra orange. Friday's marginal rate of substitution between apples and oranges is 1; he is willing to give up 1 apple for 1 orange. Since their marginal rates of substitution are not equal, we can make one of them better off without making the other worse off (or we can make both of them better off). The allocation is not Pareto efficient.

To see how this is done, suppose we take 1 orange away from Friday and give it to Crusoe. Crusoe would then be willing to give up 2 apples, and be just as well off as before. If he gave up only 1½ apples to Friday, Friday would also be better off. Friday would have given up 1 orange in return for 1½ apples; he would have been willing to make the trade if he had received just 1 apple in return.

It is easy to see that Crusoe and Friday will continue to trade until their marginal rates of substitution are equal. As Friday gives up oranges for apples, his marginal rate of substitution increases; he insists on getting more and more apples for each orange he gives up. Similarly, as Crusoe gives up apples and gets more oranges, his marginal rate of substitution decreases; he is willing to give up fewer apples for each extra orange he gets. Eventually, the two will have identical marginal rates of substitution, at which point further trade will stop. Thus, the basic condition for exchange efficiency is that the marginal rates of substitution of all individuals must be the same.

PRODUCTION EFFICIENCY

The condition of production efficiency—when the economy is on its production possibilities curve—is very similar to the condition of exchange efficiency. An economy can only be productively efficient if the marginal rate of technical substitution between any two inputs in any two firms is the same. The marginal rate of technical substitution is the amount that one input can be reduced if another input is increased by one unit, while output remains constant (see appendix to Chapter 11).

Profit-maximizing firms in a competitive economy choose a mix of inputs such that the marginal rate of technical substitution of different inputs is equal to the relative prices of those inputs. If all firms face the same relative prices of inputs, their marginal rates of technical substitution will all be the same, and production efficiency will result.

For example, consider a case involving the steel and auto industries. Assume that in steel, the marginal rate of technical substitution between capital expenditures and labor is $2,000; that is, if a company uses one more worker, it can save $2,000 on equipment (or equivalently, two $1,000 machines substitute for one worker). In the auto industry, the marginal rate of technical substitution is $1,000; one $1,000 machine substitutes for one worker. The marginal rates of technical substitution between inputs are not equal, which means that the economy is not productively efficient.

Consider a worker moving from the auto to the steel industry. If the steel industry keeps its output at the same level, the additional worker in that industry frees up two machines. One of those machines can be transferred to the auto industry, and production in that industry would stay at the same level. (We are assuming that in the auto industry one $1,000 machine substitutes for one worker.) But one machine is left over. It can be used in the steel industry, the auto industry, or both to increase production.

As we increase the number of workers in the steel industry, the marginal productivity of labor in that industry will diminish, while as we reduce workers in the automobile industry, the marginal productivity of labor in that industry will increase; conversely for machines. As a result, the marginal rates of technical substitution will shift in the two industries, so that they are closer. Spurred on by the profit motive of the individual companies in competitive markets, labor and capital will tend to move between companies until marginal rates of technical substitution are equated, and production efficiency is reached. Thus, production efficiency, which means that the economy is on its production possibilities curve, requires that the marginal rate of technical substitution between any two inputs be the same in all uses.

PRODUCT-MIX EFFICIENCY

This third condition of Pareto efficiency requires that the economy operate at the point along the production possibilities curve that reflects consumers' preferences. Look at a particular point on the production possibilities curve in Figure 13.5, say point E. The **marginal rate of transformation** tells us how many extra units of one good the economy can get if it gives up one unit of another good—how many extra cases of beer the economy can produce if it reduces production of potato chips by a ton, or how many extra cars the economy can get if it gives up one tank. The slope of the production possibilities curve is equal to the marginal rate of transformation. The slope tells us how much of one good, measured along the vertical axis, can be increased if the economy gives up one unit of the good along the horizontal axis.

Product-mix efficiency requires that consumers' marginal rate of substitution equal the marginal rate of transformation. To see why this is so, and how competitive economies ensure product-mix efficiency, consider an economy producing two fruits, apples and oranges. Assume that the marginal rate of substitution between apples and oranges is 2—that is, individuals are willing to give up 2 apples for an additional orange; while the marginal rate of transformation is 1—they only have to give up 1 apple to get an additional orange. Clearly, it pays firms to increase orange production and reduce apple production.

The competitive price system ensures that the economy satisfies the condition for product-mix efficiency. We know that consumers set the marginal rate of substitution equal to the relative price. In a similar way, profit-maximizing firms have an incentive to produce more of some goods and less of others according to the prices they can sell them for, until their marginal rate of transformation is equal to the relative price. If consumers and producers both face the same relative prices, the marginal rate of substitution will equal the marginal rate of transformation. Thus, product-mix efficiency comes about when both consumers and firms face the same prices.

To see more clearly why competitive firms will set the marginal rate of transformation equal to relative prices, consider a firm that produces both apples and oranges. If the company reallocates labor from apples to oranges, apple production is reduced and orange production is increased. Assume apple production goes down by 2 cases and orange production goes up by 1 case. The marginal rate of transformation is 2. If a case of apples sells for $4 and a case of oranges sells for $10, the firm loses $8 on apple sales but gains $10 on orange sales. It is clearly profitable for the firm to make the switch. The firm will continue to switch resources from apples to oranges until the marginal rate of transformation equals the relative price. The same result will occur even if oranges and apples are produced by different firms.[3]

Thus, the basic condition for product-mix efficiency, that the marginal rate of substitution must equal the marginal rate of transformation, will be satisfied in competitive economies because firms set the marginal rate of transformation equal to relative prices, and consumers set their marginal rate of substitution equal to relative prices.

[3]The concept of product-mix efficiency can be illustrated by superimposing a family of indifference curves (Chapter 8, appendix) in the same diagram with the production possibilities curve. Assume, for simplicity, that all individuals are the same. The highest level of welfare that one representative individual can attain is represented by the tangency of her indifference curve with the production possibilities curve. The slopes of two curves that are tangent to each other are equal at the point of tangency. The slope of the indifference curve is the consumer's marginal rate of substitution; the slope of the production possibilities curve is the marginal rate of transformation. Thus, the tangency—and Pareto efficiency—requires that the marginal rate of substitution equal the marginal rate of transformation.

PART THREE

IMPERFECT MARKETS

n Part Two, the basic model of perfectly competitive markets was developed. If the real world matched up to its assumptions, then markets could be given free rein. They would supply efficient outcomes. If an outcome seemed inequitable, society would simply redistribute initial wealth and let markets take care of the rest.

In the two centuries since Adam Smith enunciated the view that markets ensure economic efficiency, economists have investigated the model with great care. Nothing they have discovered has shaken their belief that markets are, by and large, the most efficient way to coordinate an economy. However, they have found significant departures between modern economies and the competitive model. Still, its insights are powerful, and most economists use the basic competitive model as the starting point for building a richer, more complete model. In Part Three, and later in Part Four, we will explore many of the ways in which the real world deviates from the competitive model. We can enumerate the basic differences here.

1. Most markets are not as competitive as those envisioned by the basic model. For evidence, one need look only as far as the nearest brand name. When we think of beer, we think of Budweiser, Miller, and Coors (among domestic beers). Automobiles bring to mind Chevrolets, Fords, Chryslers, and Toyotas. The examples go on forever; in fact, it is hard to think of a consumer product without attaching a brand name to it. The basic competitive model focuses on products like wheat or pig iron, for which the products produced by different firms are essentially identical, and are perfect substitutes for one another. In that model, there is no room for brand names. In the basic competitive model, if a firm raises its price slightly above that of its rivals, it loses all of its customers, as they switch; in the real world, a firm that raises its price slightly above that of its rivals loses some, but far from all, of its customers. A Budweiser enthusiast would probably pay 10 cents more for a six-pack of Bud than for one of Coors. In the basic competitive model, when firms contemplate how much to produce, they take the market price as given, and do not need to consider how their rivals will react. In the real world, many firms spend enormous energies trying to anticipate the actions and reactions of rivals. In Chapters 14–16, we will take up failures of competition in product markets and government responses to them. In Chapter 19, we will also encounter restricted competition in the labor market.

2. The basic model simply ignores technological change. It tells us about the striving for efficiency that occurs as consumers and firms meet in competitive markets, but it assumes that all firms operate with a given technology. Competition in the basic model is over price, yet in the real world, a primary focus of competition is the development of new and better products and the improvements in production, transportation, and marketing that allow products to be brought to customers at lower costs and thus at a lower price. This competition takes place not between the multitude of small producers envisaged in the basic competitive model, but often between the industrial giants like Du Pont and Dow Chemical, and between the industrial giants and upstarts, like IBM and the slew of small computer firms that eventually

took away a major share of the computer market. Chapter 17 will enrich the model to help us understand better this more general view of competition, and to enable us to see how technological change can be encouraged.

3. The individuals and firms envisioned in the basic model have easy and inexpensive access to the information they need in order to operate in any market they enter. Buyers know that they are buying, whether it is stocks or bonds, a house, a car, or a refrigerator. Firms know perfectly the productivity of each worker they hire, and when a worker goes to work for a firm, he knows precisely what is expected of him in return for his promised pay.

Imperfections of information and competition arise in all markets—in product, labor, and capital markets—and in each they take on different forms. Consider, for instance, the product market (Chapter 18). Consumers cannot ascertain all the characteristics of a product before they buy it; they rely in part on the seller's reputation. They may worry that if the price is too low, the product is likely to be shoddy; they use price in part to *judge* quality—a quite different role from that upon which Part Two focused, with important consequences.

Or consider the labor market, discussed in Chapter 19: in the basic model, the employer knows precisely what he wants the worker to do, and he knows whether the worker has done what he is supposed to do. The employer pays the worker if and only if he does what he was contracted for. Issues of incentives, of motivating workers, simply never arise. In practice, designing compensation schemes—often based on performance—to motivate workers is a central concern of management.

Or consider the capital market: a central issue facing firms is how best to meet their capital requirements, whether by borrowing or issuing new equity. A somewhat surprising implication of the basic competitive model is that how the firm raises its capital makes no difference. Chapter 20 explains how factors not taken into account in that basic model help us understand why it does make a difference, and how firms actually make these crucial decisions.

There are other important questions which the basic model does not address—because in that model the answer is either trivial or unimportant. For instance, *who* makes economic decisions makes no difference, when the outcome of that decision-making process would be the same whoever sat in the managers' chair. It would make no difference whether one firm took over another because the profit-maximizing decisions—what and how much should be produced and how it should be produced—would be the same in either case. But the decision about who manages a firm *is* an important decision; the takeover of one firm by another *can* have important consequences. Chapter 20 discusses some of the key issues concerning controlling and managing firms.

While beyond the scope of Part Three, the following points are noted here to complete our comparison of the competitive model and the real world.

4. The competitive model assumes that the costs of bringing a good to market accrue fully and completely to the seller, and that the benefits of consuming a good go fully and completely to the buyer.

In Chapter 7, however, we encountered the possibility of externalities, which are extra costs or benefits that do not figure in the market calculation. There may be positive externalities (such as national defense) and negative externalities (such as pollution). We will return to negative externalities in Part Four.

5. The basic model answers the question "What goods will be produced, and in what quantities?" by assuming that all desired goods that *can* be brought to market *will* be brought to market. Trees that bloom in gold coins and tablets that guarantee an eternal youth are out of the question. But if customers want to buy green hair coloring, cancer-causing tobacco products, or life insurance policies overladen with extras, then producers can be expected to supply such goods. However, there are many cases where markets have not provided goods or services that could be provided at a cost consumers would be willing to pay. Some of the most obvious examples are in insurance markets, where government has intervened with such programs as unemployment insurance, Social Security, and medical insurance for the aged. We first considered this problem of missing markets in Chapter 7, and will return to it in Part Four.

6. In the basic model, all markets clear—supply meets demand at the market price. Decades of evidence, however, suggest that labor markets often do not clear. The result is involuntary unemployment, sometimes on a massive scale. During the Great Depression, for instance, one out of four workers was out of a job. While beyond our scope in Part Three, the recurrence of involuntary unemployment in the economy is an important deviation from the competitive model of Part Two.

7. Even if markets are efficient, the way they allocate resources may appear to be socially unacceptable. We addressed this issue in Chapter 7, in the discussion of how government may redistribute income when the distribution produced by the market is deemed socially unacceptable. We will return to this subject in Part Four.

In the competitive model, there is little role for government, because markets ensure economic efficiency. The foregoing discussion highlights several reasons why there may be dissatisfaction with markets—why they may not in fact ensure efficiency or why, even if markets were efficient, the outcomes may not be acceptable. In each of these instances, government may be called upon. In each of the ensuing chapters, we will not only explore the limitations of the markets, but also describe and assess the roles government has undertaken to address those limitations.

THE BASIC MODEL VERSUS THE REAL WORLD

The Basic Model	The Real World
1. All markets are competitive.	1. Most markets are *not* characterized by the degree of competition envisioned in the basic model.
2. Technological know-how is fixed and cannot change.	2. Technological change is a central part of competition in modern industrial economies.
3. Firms, consumers, and any other market participants have easy access to information that is relevant to the markets in which they participate.	3. Good information may be impossible to come by, and in most cases is costly to obtain. In many markets, buyers of products know less than the sellers.
4. Sellers bear the full and complete costs of bringing goods to market, and buyers reap the full benefit.	4. Externalities mean that market transactions may not accurately account for costs and benefits and the private market provides an inadequate supply of public goods.
5. All desired markets exist.	5. Some markets may not exist, even though goods or services in that market might be provided at a cost consumers would be willing to pay.
6. There is no involuntary unemployment.	6. There is involuntary unemployment.
7. Competitive markets provide an efficient allocation of resources.	7. Efficiency is not enough. The income distribution generated by the market may be socially unacceptable.
8. There is little role for government.	8. Government plays an important role in the economy. Among its roles are correcting market failure, providing social insurance, and redistributing income.

CHAPTER 14

MONOPOLIES AND IMPERFECT COMPETITION

In the competitive model discussed in Part Two, markets have so many buyers and sellers that no individual household or firm believes its actions will affect the market equilibrium price. The buyer or seller takes the price as given, and then decides how much to buy or sell. At the "market" price, the seller can sell as much as she wants. But any effort to outfox the market has dramatic consequences. If, for instance, she raises her price above that of her competitors, her sales will be zero.

Not all markets are very competitive, however. For years, AT&T was the only long distance telephone carrier. Kodak controlled the market for film, and Alcoa the market for aluminum. Some firms so dominated a product that their brand name became synonymous with the product, as with Kleenex and Jell-O.

In some industries, such as soft drinks (Coca-Cola, Pepsi, Canada Dry), a handful of firms dominate a market, producing similar but not identical products. When one such firm raises its price a little—say, by 2 or 3 percent—it loses some customers but far from all. If it lowers its price by 2 or 3 percent, it gains additional customers, but not the entire market. As a result, these companies do not simply "take" the price as dictated to them by the market. They "make" the price. They are the **price makers.** Markets in which competition is limited are the subject of this chapter and the next.

KEY QUESTIONS

1. If there is only one firm in a market—a monopoly—how does it set its price and output? In what sense is the monopoly price too high?

2. Why do firms with no competition or imperfect competition face downward-sloping demand curves?

3. What are the barriers to entry that limit the number of firms in a market?

4. What does equilibrium look like in a market with imperfect competition, where barriers to entry are small enough that profits are driven to zero, yet in which there are few enough firms that each faces a downward-sloping curve?

MARKET STRUCTURES

One way to simplify an economy is to break it up into its constituent markets. One market in the United States is the passenger car market, with Ford, General Motors, Chrysler, and various foreign firms the suppliers.

When economists look at markets, they look first at the **market structure,** that is, at how that market is organized. The market structure that forms the basis of the competitive model of Part Two is called perfect competition. For example, there are so many wheat farmers (producers) that no individual wheat farmer can realistically hope to move the price of wheat from that produced by the law of supply and demand.

Frequently, however, competition is not "perfect." Rather, it is limited. Economists group markets in which competition is limited into three broad structures. In the most extreme, there is no competition. A single firm supplies the entire market. This is called **monopoly.** Your local electric company probably has a monopoly in supplying electricity in your area. Since one would expect the profits of a monopolist to attract entry into that market, for a firm to maintain its monopoly position, there must be some barrier to entry. Below, we learn what these barriers are.

In the second structure, several firms supply the market, so there is *some* competition. This is called **oligopoly.** The automobile industry is an example, with three main producers in the United States. The defining characteristic of oligopolies is that the small number of firms forces each to be concerned with how its rivals will react to any action it undertakes. If General Motors offers low-interest-rate financing, for instance, the other companies may feel compelled to match the offer; and before making any such offer, GM will have to take this into account. By contrast, a monopolist has no rivals and thus considers only whether special offers help or hurt itself. And a firm facing perfect competition can sell as much as it wants at the market price without having to resort to any special offers.

In the third market structure, there are more firms than in an oligopoly, but not enough for perfect competition. This is called **monopolistic competition.** An example is the market for moderately priced clothing as represented by J. C. Penney, Sears, Kmart, and other such chains of stores. Each chain has its own make of clothing, which no other chain sells. But the clothing in each chain is similar enough to that supplied by other chains that there is considerable competition. Even so, the clothing supplied by the different chains is different enough to make competition limited, so that the chain is not a price taker. The degree of competition under monopolistic competition is greater than that of oligopoly. This is because monopolistic competition involves a sufficiently large number of firms that each firm can ignore the reactions of any rival. If one company lowers its price, it may garner for itself a large number of customers. But the number of customers it takes away from any single rival is so small that none of the rivals is motivated to retaliate.

With both oligopolies and monopolistic competition, there is some competition, but it is more limited than under perfect competition. These in-between market structures are referred to as **imperfect competition.**

ALTERNATIVE MARKET STRUCTURES

Perfect competition: Many, many firms; each believes that nothing it does will have any effect on the market price.

Monopoly: One firm.

Imperfect competition: Several firms, each aware that its sales depend on the price it charges and possibly other actions it takes, such as advertising. There are two special cases:

  Oligopoly: Sufficiently few firms that each worries about how rivals will respond to any action it undertakes.

  Monopolistic competition: Sufficiently many firms that each believes that its rivals will not change the price they charge should it lower its own price.

This chapter focuses on monopoly and monopolistic competition. Oligopolies are left for Chapter 15. We begin with an analysis of how a monopolist sets its price and quantity, and how monopoly outcomes compare with competitive outcomes. We then switch to imperfect competition, a more common structure, and analyze the principal determinants of competition within any market. We follow this with an analysis of the barriers to entry that enable imperfectly competitive firms to sustain higher than normal profits for long periods of time. The final section looks at the case where barriers to entry are weak enough that profits are driven to zero, but competition is still sufficiently limited that each firm can change its prices without losing all its customers.

MONOPOLY OUTPUT

Figure 14.1 THE DEMAND CURVE FACING A PERFECTLY COMPET-ITIVE FIRM AND A MONOPOLIST

A price-taking, perfectly competitive firm can sell any quantity it wishes at the market price, but cannot raise the price at all without losing all its business. It faces the horizontal demand curve shown in panel A. A monopolist provides all the output in a market, so an increased amount can only be sold at a reduced price. Panel B shows the downward-sloping demand curve—the market demand curve—faced by a monopolist.

Economists' concerns about monopolies and other forms of restricted competition stem mainly from the observation that the output, or supply, of firms within these market structures is less than that of firms faced with perfect competition. To address these concerns, we consider a monopolist that charges the same price to all its customers and show how it determines its level of output.

A monopolist and a competitive firm are similar in some ways. Both try to maximize profits. In determining output, they compare the extra (or marginal) revenue they would receive from producing an extra unit of output with the extra (or marginal) cost of producing that extra unit. If marginal revenue exceeds marginal cost, it pays to expand output. Conversely if marginal revenue is less than marginal cost, it pays to reduce output. Thus, the basic principle for output determination for both a competitive firm and a monopolist is the same. Each produces at the output level at which marginal revenue equals marginal cost.

The essential difference between a monopolist and a competitive firm is that a competitive firm takes the price set by market forces. When such a firm increases production by one unit, its marginal revenue is just the price. For instance, the marginal revenue a wheat farmer receives from producing one more bushel of wheat is the price of a bushel of wheat. But the only way a monopolist can sell more is to lower the price it charges, so marginal revenue is *not* equal to the present market price.

The difference can be put another way. The demand curve facing a competitive firm is perfectly horizontal, as illustrated in Figure 14.1A. The price, p^*, is the "market price." The firm can sell as much as it wants at that price, and nothing at any higher price. In an industry such as wheat farming, if there are one million wheat farmers, each farmer on average accounts for one-millionth of the market. If a single average farmer even doubled his production, the total production would increase by one-millionth—a truly negligible amount that could be absorbed by the market with no perceptible change in price.

The demand curve facing a monopolist, in contrast, is downward sloping, as illustrated in Figure 14.1B. By definition, the monopolist controls the entire industry, so that a doubling of *its* output is a doubling of industry output, which will have a significant effect on price. If Alcoa, in the days when it had a monopoly on aluminum, had increased its production by 1 percent, the total supply of aluminum would have increased by 1 percent. Market prices would have fallen observably in response to a change in supply of even that magnitude.

The marginal revenue a monopolist receives from producing one more unit can be broken into two separate components. First, the firm receives revenue from selling the additional output. This additional revenue is just the market price. But to sell more, the firm must reduce its price. Unless it does so, it cannot sell the extra output. Marginal revenue is the price it receives from the sale of the one additional unit *minus* the loss in revenues from the price reduction on all other units. Thus, for a monopolist, the marginal revenue for producing one extra unit is always less than the price received for that extra unit. (Only at the "first" unit produced are marginal revenue and price the same.)

This can be represented by a simple equation:

marginal revenue = net increase in revenue from selling one more unit

$$= \text{price} + \Delta p \times Q$$

where Δp represents the change in price and Q represents the initial quantity sold. For a competitive firm, $\Delta p = 0$, so marginal revenue equals price. For a monopolist, Δp is negative, so marginal revenue is less than the price.

Figure 14.2A shows the output decision of a competitive firm. Marginal revenue is just equal to the market price, $p*$. Panel B shows the output decision of a monopolist. Marginal revenue is always less than price. Note that with a monopoly, since marginal revenue is less than price and marginal revenue equals marginal cost, marginal cost is less than price. The price is what individuals are willing to pay for an extra unit of the product; it measures the marginal benefit to the consumer of an extra unit. Thus, the marginal benefit of

$$R = p(Q) \cdot Q$$

$$\frac{dR}{dQ} = \frac{dp}{dQ} Q + p$$

$$(-)$$

Figure 14.2 MARGINAL REVENUE EQUALS MARGINAL COST

A perfectly competitive firm gains or loses exactly the market price ($p*$) when it changes the quantity produced by one unit. To maximize profits, the firm produces the quantity where marginal cost equals marginal revenue, which in the competitive case also equals price. Panel B shows the downward-sloping marginal revenue curve for a monopolist. A monopolist also chooses the level of quantity where marginal cost equals marginal revenue. In the monopolistic case, however, marginal revenue is lower than price.

Figure 14.3 MONOPOLY AND THE ELASTICITY OF DEMAND

In panel A, a monopoly faces a very elastic market demand, so prices do not fall much as output increases, and monopoly price is not much more than the competitive price. In panel B, a monopoly faces a less elastic market demand, so price falls quite a lot as output increases, and price is substantially above the competitive price.

an extra unit exceeds the marginal cost. This is the fundamental reason that monopolies reduce economic efficiency.[1]

The extent to which output is curtailed depends on the magnitude of the difference between marginal revenue and price. This in turn depends on the shape of the demand curve. When demand curves are very elastic (relatively flat), prices do not fall much when output increases. As shown in Figure 14.3A, marginal revenue is not much less than price. The firm produces at Q_m, where marginal revenue equals marginal cost. Q_m is slightly less than the competitive output, Q_c, where price equals marginal cost. When demand curves are less elastic, as in panel B, prices may fall a considerable amount when output increases, and then the extra revenue the firm receives from producing an extra unit of output will be much less than the price received from selling that unit.

The larger the elasticity of demand, the smaller the discrepancy between marginal revenue and price. This can be seen simply by using the definitions of the elasticity of demand and marginal revenue:

$$\text{elasticity of demand} = -\frac{\text{change in market quantity}}{\text{market quantity}} \bigg/ \frac{\text{change in price}}{\text{price}}$$

$$= -\frac{\Delta Q}{Q} \bigg/ \frac{\Delta p}{p}.$$

If we consider a change in quantity by 1 (as we do when we calculate marginal revenue), so that $\Delta Q = 1$,

$$\text{elasticity of demand} = -\frac{1}{Q} \bigg/ \frac{\Delta p}{p} = -\frac{p}{\Delta p \times Q}, \text{ and}$$

[1]Chapter 16 will describe more precisely how the magnitudes of the losses associated with monopoly can be quantified.

marginal revenue = price + change in price × quantity sold

$$= p + (\Delta p \times Q)$$

$$= p \left(1 + \frac{\Delta p \times Q}{p} \right)$$

$$= p \, (1 - 1/\text{elasticity of demand}).$$

Hence, if the elasticity of demand is 2, marginal revenue is ½ of price. If the elasticity of demand is 10, marginal revenue is 9/10 of price.

$$MR = p + Q \frac{dp}{dQ}$$
$$= p \left(1 + \frac{Q}{p} \frac{dp}{dQ} \right)$$
$$= p \left(1 - \frac{1}{e_D} \right)$$

THE FIRM'S SUPPLY DECISION

All firms maximize profits at the point where marginal revenue (the revenue from selling an extra unit of the product) equals marginal cost.

For a competitive firm, marginal revenue equals price.

For a monopoly, marginal revenue is less than price.

AN EXAMPLE: THE ABC-MENT COMPANY

Table 14.1 gives the demand curve facing the ABC-ment Company, which has a monopoly on the production of cement in its area. There is a particular price at which it can sell each level of output. As it lowers its price, it can sell

Table 14.1 DEMAND CURVE FACING ABC-MENT COMPANY

Cubic yards (thousands)	Price	Total revenues	Marginal revenues	Total costs	Marginal costs
1	$10,000	$10,000		$15,000	
			$8,000		$2,000
2	$ 9,000	$18,000		$17,000	
			$6,000		$3,000
3	$ 8,000	$24,000		$20,000	
			$4,000		$4,000
4	$ 7,000	$28,000		$24,000	
			$2,000		$5,000
5	$ 6,000	$30,000		$29,000	
			0		$6,000
6	$ 5,000	$30,000		$35,000	

more cement. Local builders will, for instance, use more cement and less wood and other materials in constructing a house.

For simplicity, we assume cement is sold in units of 1,000 cubic yards. At a price of $10,000 per unit (of 1,000 cubic yards), the firm sells 1 unit, at a price of $9,000, it sells 2 units, and at a price of $8,000, 3 units. The third column of the table shows the total revenues at each of these levels of production. The total revenues are just price times quantity. The marginal revenue from producing an extra unit (of 1,000 cubic yards) is just the difference between, say, the revenues received at 3 units and 2 units or 2 units and 1 unit. Notice that in each case, the marginal revenue is less than the price.

Figure 14.4 shows the demand and marginal revenues curves, using data from Table 14.1. At each level of output, the marginal revenue curve lies below the demand curve. As can be seen from the table, not only does price decrease as output increases, but so does marginal revenue.

The output at which marginal revenues equal marginal costs—the output chosen by the profit-maximizing monopolist—is denoted by Q_m. In our example, $Q_m = 4,000$ cubic yards. When the number of cubic yards increases from 3,000 to 4,000, the marginal revenue is $4,000, and so is the marginal cost. At this level of output, the price, p_m, is $7,000 (per 1,000 cubic yards), which is considerably in excess of marginal costs, $4,000. Total revenues, $28,000, are also in excess of total costs, $24,000.[2]

Figure 14.4 DEMAND AND MARGINAL REVENUE

At each level of output, the marginal revenue curve lies below the demand curve.

[2]In this example, the firm is indifferent between producing 3,000 or 4,000 cubic yards. If the marginal cost of producing the extra output exceeds $4,000 by a little, then it will produce 3,000 cubic yards; if the marginal cost is a little less than $4,000, then it will produce 4,000 cubic yards.

MONOPOLY PROFITS

Monopolists maximize their profits by setting marginal revenue equal to marginal cost. The total level of monopoly profits can be seen in two ways, as shown in Figure 14.5. Panel A shows total revenues and total costs (from Table 14.1) for each level of output of the ABC-ment Company. The difference between revenues and costs is profits—the distance between the two curves. This distance is maximized at the output $Q_m = 4,000$ cubic yards. We can see that at this level of output, profits are $4,000 ($28,000 − $24,000). Panel B calculates profits using the average cost diagram. Total profits are equal to the profit per unit multiplied by the number of units produced. The profit per unit is the difference between the unit price and the average cost, and total monopoly profits is the shaded area $ABCD$. Again, the sum is $4,000: ($7,000 − $6,000) × 4.

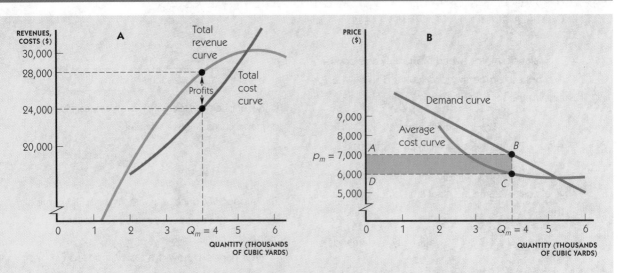

Figure 14.5 **PRICE EXCEEDING AVERAGE COST MEANS PROFIT**

Panel A shows profits to be the distance between the total revenue and total cost curves, maximized at the output $Q_m = 4,000$ cubic yards. Profits occur when the market price is above average cost, as in panel B, so that the company is (on average) making a profit on each unit it sells. Monopoly profits are the area *ABCD*, which is average profit per unit times the number of units sold.

A monopolist enjoys an extra return because it has been able to reduce its output and increase its price from the level that would have prevailed under competition. This return is called a **pure profit.** Because these payments are not required to elicit greater effort or production on the part of the monopolist (in fact, they derive from the monopolist's *reducing* the output from what it would be under competition), they are also called **monopoly rents.**

PRICE DISCRIMINATION

The basic objective of monopolists is to maximize profits, and they accomplish this by setting marginal revenue equal to marginal cost, so price exceeds marginal cost. Monopolists can also engage in a variety of other practices to increase their profits. Among the most important is **price discrimination,** which means charging different prices to different customers or in different markets.

Figure 14.6 shows a monopolist setting marginal revenue equal to marginal cost in the United States and in Japan. The demand curves the firm faces in the two countries are different. Therefore, though marginal costs are the same, the firm will charge different prices for the same good in the two countries. (By contrast, in competitive markets, price equals marginal cost, so that regardless of the shape of the demand curves, price will be the same in the

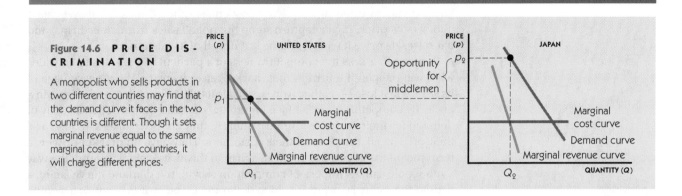

Figure 14.6 PRICE DIS-CRIMINATION

A monopolist who sells products in two different countries may find that the demand curve it faces in the two countries is different. Though it sets marginal revenue equal to the same marginal cost in both countries, it will charge different prices.

two markets, except for the different costs of delivering the good to each market.) With prices in the two countries differing, middlemen firms will enter the market, buying the product in the country with the low price and selling it in the other country. A company may attempt to thwart the middlemen—as many Japanese companies do—by, for instance, having distinct labels on the two products and refusing to provide service or honor any guarantees outside the country in which the good is originally delivered.

Within a country, a monopolist can also price discriminate *if* resale is difficult and *if* it can distinguish between buyers with high and low elasticities of demand. An electricity company can make its charge for each kilowatt hour depend on how much electricity the customer uses, because of restrictions on the retransmission of electricity. If the company worries that large customers faced with the same high prices that it charges small customers might install their own electric generators, or switch to some other energy source, it may charge them a lower price. An airline with a monopoly on a particular route might charge business customers a higher fare than vacationers. They do so knowing that business customers have no choice but to make the trip, while vacationers have many alternatives. They can travel elsewhere, on another day, or by car or train. Such business practices enable the monopolist to increase its profits relative to what they would be if it charged a single price in the market. Firms facing imperfect competition also engage in these practices as we will see. Airlines again provide a telling example. Though the Robinson-Patman Act, which Congress passed in 1936, was designed to restrict price discrimination, it is only partially successful.

IMPERFECT COMPETITION

In most markets, there is more than a single firm. In the perfectly competitive model of Part Two, firms compete against one another while believing they cannot affect the price—that if they raise their price, they will lose all their business. But outside agriculture, imperfect competition is more typical. Firms compete, often vigorously, against one another. But each believes that if it lowers its price, it can capture some but not all sales from other firms; and if it raises its price it will lose some but not all of its customers.

One way to assess the competitiveness of a particular market is to consider what will happen if a firm in that market raises its price. What percentage of its sales will it lose—in other words, what is its elasticity of demand? Firms in a perfectly competitive market face horizontal demand curves. The elasticity of demand for their output is infinite. Similarly, they are price takers. If they raise their price at all, they lose all their customers. They have no **market power,** a term meant to suggest the ability of a firm to throw its weight around, the way a monopoly can. As imperfect competition sets in, the demand curve facing a firm in the industry begins to slope downward. The more downward sloping the demand curve, the more market power the firm has.

Two factors affect the elasticity of the demand curve facing a firm, and, therefore, its market power. The first is the number of firms in the industry—more generally, how concentrated is production within a few firms. The second is how different are the goods produced by the various firms in the industry.

Table 14.2 DEGREE OF COMPETITION IN VARIOUS INDUSTRIES

	Market share of top 4 firms (percent)
Breakfast cereals	81
Burial caskets	53
Motor vehicles and car bodies	92
Primary copper	92
Semiconductors and related devices	36
Women's suits and coats	14
Wood household furniture	15

Source: Census of Manufacturing (1982), vol. 7, Table 6.

NUMBER OF FIRMS IN THE INDUSTRY

Competition is likely to be greater when there are many firms in an industry (textiles, shoes) than when a few companies dominate (home refrigerators and freezers, greeting cards, soft drinks). Table 14.2 gives the percentage of output that is produced by the top four firms in a variety of industries ranging from breakfast cereals to wood household furniture. The fraction of output produced by the top four firms in an industry is called the **four-firm concentration ratio,** one of several measures used to study industry concentration. When the four-firm percentage is high, as in the automobile or copper industry, companies have considerable market power. This is true even when they produce similar or identical products, as in the case of copper. When it is low, as in the case of furniture or women's clothes, market power is low; each firm faces a practically horizontal demand curve.[3]

PRODUCT DIFFERENTIATION

In addition to the number of firms in a market—and how concentrated production is—the amount of competition depends on how similar are the goods produced by different firms. In some industries, the goods produced are essentially identical—copper produced by Kennecott Copper is essentially identical to that produced by Anaconda Copper. More typically, the firms in an in-

---

[3]In both theory and practice, a critical issue in evaluating the extent of competition is defining the relevant market, an issue taken up in Chapter 16.

dustry with imperfect competition produce goods that are **imperfect substitutes**—goods sufficiently similar that they can be used for many of the same purposes, but different enough that one may be somewhat better than another, at least for some purposes or in some people's minds. Kellogg's Corn Flakes and the store brand may look alike. But more people purchase the Kellogg's version, even though it is more expensive.

The fact that similar products nonetheless differ from one another is referred to as **product differentiation.** Firms in imperfect markets spend considerable effort to produce goods that are slightly different from those of their competitors.

SOURCES OF PRODUCT DIFFERENTIATION

Many of the differences between products can be seen, heard, or tasted by consumers. But geography can also provide the basis for product differentiation. People are willing to pay more for service at a neighborhood garage, rather than drive fifty miles to a discount garage. They are willing to pay more for milk at the neighborhood grocery store than at the supermarket out on the main road.

In cases where consumers find it difficult to assess the quality of a product before they purchase it, they rely heavily on firm reputations. They may buy Bayer aspirin even though it is more expensive than the store brand, because they believe it is of a higher quality. (In fact, aspirin itself is just acetylsalicylic acid, nothing more or less. Still, the binding agents that hold the pill together may differ, so the effects may differ.) Consumers are often willing to pay more for goods with a trademark than for generic brands.

Ignorance and the costs of obtaining information often make the products of one firm an imperfect substitute for another. A consumer sees a dress for $45. She might know or suspect that some other store is selling the same dress for $35, but she does not know where, she is not sure it is in stock there, it will cost her money to drive around looking for it, and so she buys the dress at $45 anyway. If the store had raised its price to $55, she probably would have made the effort to search. If a store raises its prices, more customers decide to search out the bargains, and sales go down.

HOW PRODUCT DIFFERENTIATION IMPLIES IMPERFECT COMPETITION

When goods are perfect substitutes, individuals will choose whichever is cheapest. In an imaginary world where all brands of cornflakes really are perfect substitutes for all consumers, they would all sell at the same price. If one brand lowered its price slightly, all consumers (assuming they knew this) would switch to it. If it raised its price slightly, all consumers would switch to the rival brand. That is why the demand curve facing the manufacturer of a perfectly substitutable good is horizontal, as illustrated in Figure 14.7A.

By contrast, if most consumers view the different brands as imperfect substitutes, the demand curve facing each firm will be downward sloping as in panel B. This, we have already learned, implies a departure from perfect competition. Some individuals may prefer sogginess and be willing to pay more for cornflakes that rapidly become soggy. Others may prefer crispness and be

Figure 14.7 DEMAND CURVES WITH PERFECT AND IMPERFECT COMPETITION

Panel A shows the demand curve for a perfectly competitive firm: if it raises its price, all its customers will find substitutes. The marginal revenue curve for the firm is the same as its demand curve. Panel B shows the demand curve and marginal revenue curve facing a firm with only imperfect substitutes for its products.

willing to pay more for cereal that does not become soggy. Assume that Kellogg's Corn Flakes become soggy more slowly than the store brand. As the price for Kellogg's increases above that of the store brand, individuals who care less about crispness will switch to the store brand. They are not willing to pay the price differential. But some are willing to pay a lot more for crisp flakes. Hence, Kellogg's does not lose all its customers, even if it charges considerably more than the store brand. By the same token, when Kellogg's lowers its price below that of the store brand, it does not steal all the customers. Those who love sogginess will pay more for the store brand.

It matters little whether the differences between the brands are true or simply perceived differences. The store brand and Kellogg's Corn Flakes could be identical, but if Kellogg's advertisements have convinced some consumers that there is a difference, they will not switch even if the price of Kellogg's is higher. Numerous studies attest to the fact that consumers often see differences where none exist. One study put the same soap into two kinds of packages, one marked Brand A, the other marked Brand B. Homemakers were asked to judge which brand cleaned their clothes more effectively. Half saw no difference, but the other half claimed to see significant differences. Another study put the same beer into three kinds of bottles, one labeled premium, the second labeled standard, the third labeled discount. After drinking the differently bottled beers over an extended period of time, consumers were asked which they preferred. The "premium" beer was chosen consistently.

BASES OF PRODUCT DIFFERENTIATION

1. Differences in characteristics of products

2. Differences in location of different firms

3. Perceived differences, often induced by advertising

BARRIERS TO ENTRY: WHY IS COMPETITION LIMITED?

Normally, profits attract other firms to enter the market. For a monopoly to persist, some factors must prevent competition from springing up. Similarly, when there are profits with imperfect competition, some factors must prevent other firms' entering and eroding those profits. Such factors are called **barriers to entry.** They take a variety of forms, ranging from government rules that prohibit or limit competition (for reasons that may be good or bad), to technological reasons that naturally limit the number of firms in a market, to market strategies that keep potential competitors at bay.

When there are few barriers to entry, a monopoly can only be temporary—the profits of the monopolist will attract entry, and the firm's monopoly position will be lost. When there are many barriers, even if they only serve to delay entry, there *is* cause for concern, particularly when firms themselves take actions to create the barriers.

GOVERNMENT POLICIES

Many early monopolies were established by governments. In the seventeenth century, the British government gave the East India Company a monopoly on trade with India. The salt monopoly in eighteenth-century France had the exclusive right to sell salt. Even today, governments grant certain monopoly franchises; for example, government grants monopolies for electric and telephone service within a locality.

The most important monopolies granted by government today, however, are patents. As we learned in Chapter 1, a patent gives inventors the exclusive right to produce or to license others to produce their discoveries for a limited period of time, currently seventeen years. The argument for patents is that without them, copycat firms would spring up with every new invention, inventors would make little money from their discoveries, and there would be no economic incentive to invent. The framers of the U.S. Constitution thought invention so important that they included a provision enabling the newly created federal government to grant patents.

Occasionally governments set policies that restrict entry, allowing some, but only limited, competition. Licensing requirements in many of the professions (law, accounting, medicine), whose ostensible purpose is to protect consumers against incompetent practitioners, may at the same time limit the number of qualified practitioners, and thus limit competition.

SINGLE OWNERSHIP OF AN ESSENTIAL INPUT

Another barrier to entry and source of monopoly power is a firm's exclusive ownership of something that is not producible. For example, an aluminum company might attempt to become a monopolist in aluminum by buying all the sources of bauxite, the essential ingredient. A single South African company, De Beers, has come close to monopolizing the world's supply of diamonds. There are in fact relatively few instances of such monopolies.

INFORMATION

Information does not pass through the economy in the full and complete way envisioned in the basic competitive model of Part Two. In considering barriers to entry, we encounter two of many ways that information—and the lack

Market strategies and patents can be—and have been—used in combination by companies to maintain a dominant position long after the initial patent has expired. While patents encourage innovation, abuses can lead not only to higher prices, but in some cases even a slower pace of innovation. But identifying abuses is not always easy.

You may have heard someone say, "I'm going to Xerox that document." What that person usually means is, "I'm going to photocopy that document on a machine that may or may not have been made by Xerox." Until the early 1970s, the Xerox company was almost synonymous with photocopying. The company had invented the photocopier; it held a group of more than 1,700 closely interrelated patents on the photocopying process; and it received about 95 percent of all copying machine sales in the United States.

In 1972, the Federal Trade Commission charged that Xerox was using its many patents as a way of monopolizing the photocopy market. Instead of using the patents to protect a new invention for a limited amount of time, the FTC argued, Xerox was making them part of a strategy to monopolize the market indefinitely.

After several years of investigation and argument, a "consent order" was announced. Essentially, Xerox did not admit it had done anything wrong, but it agreed to change anyway. In July 1975, Xerox agreed to allow other competitors to use its patents and even to give its competitors access to some future patents. In addition, Xerox was required to drop all outstanding lawsuits against other companies for infringing on its patents. A spokesman for the FTC maintained that these steps (and some others) would "eliminate the principal sources of Xerox's dominance of the office copier industry."

No longer fearing a lawsuit for infringing on a Xerox patent, entrants started pouring into the photocopy market, led by the Japanese firm

Ricoh. Prices for photocopiers fell sharply. By 1980, Xerox was receiving only 46 percent of U.S. copier sales. Among the cheaper machines, the company held only 31 percent of the market. And the downward trend was continuing.

The ensuing years saw a rush of innovations, with not only copiers becoming less expensive, but new products, like color copiers and copiers linked to fax machines, coming on line.

Sources: Business Week, December 16, 1972, p. 24, October 12, 1981, p. 126, February 13, 1989, p. 90; *Wall Street Journal,* April 17, 1975, p. 8, July 31, 1975, p. 7; *Fortune,* June 17, 1991, p. 38.

thereof—affects market outcomes. First, firms engage in research to give them a technological advantage over competitors. Even if they do not get a patent, it will take time before what they learn disseminates to rivals. The fact that firms outside the industry do not know the trade secrets of the industry provides an important barrier to entry. Coca-Cola helps maintain its position in the soft drink market by guarding its formula with the greatest care.

Second, consumers have imperfect information concerning the products being sold by different firms. As a new firm, you must not only let potential buyers know about your product, you must convince them that the product is a better value than that of your rivals. When goods differ markedly in qualities that cannot easily be detected, it may not suffice simply to sell at a lower price. Customers may interpret the lower price as signaling lower quality. Thus, to get customers to try your product, you may have to advertise heavily and give away free samples. Entry costs like these constitute another significant barrier to entry.

ECONOMIES OF SCALE AND NATURAL MONOPOLIES

The technology needed to produce a good can sometimes result in a market with only one or very few firms. For example, it would be inefficient to have two firms construct power lines on each street in a city, with one company delivering electricity to one house and another company to the house next door. Likewise, in most locales, there is only one gravel pit or concrete plant. These situations are called **natural monopolies.**

A natural monopoly occurs whenever the average costs of production for a single firm are declining up to levels of output beyond those likely to emerge in the market. When the average costs of production fall as the scale of production increases, we say there are economies of scale, a concept first introduced in Chapter 11. In Figure 14.8, the demand curve facing a monopoly intersects the average cost curve at an output level at which average costs are still declining. At large enough outputs, average costs might start to increase, but that level of output is irrelevant to the actual market equilibrium. For instance, firms in the cement industry have U-shaped average cost curves, and

Figure 14.8 NATURAL MONOPOLY

In a natural monopoly, market demand intersects average cost in the downward-sloping portion of the average cost curve, at quantity Q_r and price p_r. Any firm that attempts to enter the market and produce less than Q_r will have higher average costs than the natural monopoly. Any firm that tries to enter the market and produce more than Q_r will find that it cannot sell all its output at a price that will cover its average costs.

the level of output at which costs are minimized is quite high. Accordingly, in smaller, isolated communities, there is a natural monopoly in cement.

A natural monopolist is protected by the knowledge that it can undercut its rivals should they enter. Since entrants typically are smaller and average costs decline with size, their average costs are higher. Therefore the monopolist feels relatively immune from the threat of entry. So long as it does not have to worry about entry, it acts like any other monopolist, setting marginal revenue equal to marginal cost, as in Figure 14.8, where it produces at the output Q_m and charges p_m.

Whether a particular industry is a natural monopoly depends on the size of the output at which average costs are minimized relative to the size of the market. With high enough demand, the monopolist will be operating along the rising part of the average cost curve. At this point, the monopolist can be undercut by an entrant, since a new firm that enters at the output at which average costs are minimized has costs that are lower. Thus, with high enough demand, the industry is no longer a natural monopoly. In medium-sized cities, there may be several producers of cement, so that instead of a monopoly, there is an oligopoly.

Among the most important determinants of market size are transportation costs. Among the most important determinants of the quantity of output at which average costs are minimized is the size of the fixed costs. The larger the expenditures of the firm just to begin production, the larger the scale of production at which average costs are minimized.

ECONOMIES OF SCALE AND IMPERFECT COMPETITION

Fixed costs also help explain why only a limited number of firms produce each variety of a good, and why the variety of goods is limited. Setting up dies to make a slight variant of an existing car, for example, may be very expensive. Similarly, automobile companies tend to produce cars in only a limited range of colors. Some individuals might prefer a car that is bright orange but most car manufacturers do not offer this option. Presumably this is because they realize that additional costs to paint some cars bright orange would exceed the marginal revenue they would receive from providing this option.

Because both technology and transportation costs may change over time, the number of firms in a market may change. Long-distance telephone service used to be a natural monopoly. Telephone messages were transmitted over wires, and it would have been inefficient to duplicate wires. As the demand for telephone services increased, and as alternative technologies like satellites developed, long-distance service ceased to be a natural monopoly. Today, a large number of firms compete to provide long-distance services.

Market Strategies

Some monopolies and oligopolies cannot be explained by any of the factors discussed so far. They are not the result of government policies and are not natural monopolies; nor can information problems explain the lack of entry. Many firms, whose original monopoly position may have been based on some technological innovation or patent, manage to maintain their dominant positions even after their patents expire, at least for a time. IBM, Kodak, and Polaroid are three examples. These firms maintained their dominant positions by the pursuit of market strategies that deterred other firms from entering the market.

When a company thinks about entering an industry dominated by a single firm, it must assess not only the current level of profits being earned by that firm but also what profits will be like after it has entered. If a potential entrant believes that the incumbent firm is likely to respond to entry by lowering its price and fighting a fierce competitive battle, then the potential newcomer may come to believe that while prices and profits look high now, they are likely to drop precipitously if it actually does enter the market.

Established firms would thus like to pursue a strategy to convince potential entrants that even though they are currently making high levels of profit, these profits will disappear should the new firm enter the market. There are three major ways to create this belief, collectively called **entry-deterring practices:** predatory pricing, excess capacity, and limit pricing.

Predatory Pricing If prices have fallen drastically in a certain market every time there has been entry in the past, then new firms may be reluctant to enter. An incumbent firm may deliberately lower its price below the new entrant's cost of production, in order to drive the new arrival out and discourage future entry. The incumbent also may lose money in the process, but it hopes to recoup the losses when the entrant leaves and it is free to raise prices to the monopoly level. This practice is called **predatory pricing** and is an illegal trade practice. However, shifting technologies and shifting demand often make it difficult to ascertain whether a firm has actually engaged in predatory pricing or simply lowered its price to meet the competition. Firms that lower their prices always claim that they were "forced" to do so by their competitors.

While allegations of predation are not uncommon, the courts have set high standards of proof. Thus, in one of the more recent cases, Liggett, a tobacco company that sells low-priced generic cigarettes that cut into name-brand sales, claimed that Brown & Williamson had engaged in predation. The charge was that B&W wanted Liggett to raise its prices and thus shift demand back to B&W's name brands. B&W lowered prices on its brands as a warning to Liggett to do B&W's bidding. In the lower court a jury found in favor of Liggett. The Supreme Court reversed the lower court's judgment, however, in a 1993 decision.

Excess Capacity   Another action firms can take to convince potential rivals that prices are likely to fall if they enter the market is to build up production facilities in excess of those currently needed. By building extra plants and equipment, even if they are rarely used, a firm poses an extra threat to potential entrants. A newcomer will look at this **excess capacity** and realize that the incumbent firm can increase production a great deal with minimal effort. The excess capacity serves as a signal that the incumbent is willing and able to engage in fierce price competition.

Limit Pricing   Other strategies for deterring entry involve clever patterns of pricing. A potential entrant may know what price is charged on the market and may have a good idea of its own costs of production. But it is not likely to know precisely the cost curve of the incumbent firm. The established firm can try to persuade potential entrants that its marginal costs are low, and that it could easily reduce its price if threatened with a new entrant to the market.

Suppose a potential entrant knows that a monopolist firm's marginal revenue is 70 percent of price. If the monopolist charges a price of $10, then the marginal revenue (the extra revenue from selling one more unit) is $7. Reasoning that the monopolist is setting marginal revenue equal to marginal cost, the potential entrant might use a $7 marginal cost figure in deciding whether it pays to enter.

The monopolist is aware that such a calculation is probably going on. Thus, it has an incentive to make its costs look lower than they are—and hence to make entry look less attractive than it really is. It can do this by lowering the price it charges. If it can persuade the potential entrant that marginal costs have to be below $6 (rather than $7) for entry to be profitable, it has protected its monopoly position that much better. This is an example of a broader practice known as **limit pricing,** in which firms charge less than the ordinary monopoly price and produce at a level beyond that at which marginal revenue equals marginal cost because they are afraid that at higher prices, entry will be encouraged. This may happen simply because a firm realizes that high profits attract attention. The more attention is focused on a market, the more likely it is that some entrepreneur will believe that entry is profitable.

Some entry-deterring devices, such as maintaining excess capacity, may be socially wasteful. Others, such as limit pricing, will benefit consumers, and partially temper deleterious effects of monopoly or limited competition.

BARRIERS TO ENTRY

Government policies: These include grants of monopoly (patents) and restrictions on entry (licensing).

Single ownership of an essential input: When a single firm owns the entire supply of a nonproducible input, entry is by definition precluded.

Information: Lack of technical information by potential competitors inhibits their entry; lack of information by consumers concerning the quality of a new entrant's product discourages consumers from switching to the new product, and thus inhibits entry.

Economies of scale: With a natural monopoly, economies of scale are so strong that it is efficient to have only one firm in an industry.

Market strategies: These include actions (such as predatory pricing, excess capacity, and limit pricing) aimed at convincing potential entrants that entry would be met with resistance, and thus would be unprofitable.

EQUILIBRIUM WITH MONOPOLISTIC COMPETITION

Barriers to entry are sufficiently weak in some markets that firms enter to the point where profits are driven to zero. But even then competition is imperfect, if products are differentiated. With each firm producing a slightly different product, each faces a downward-sloping demand curve. In this section, we analyze the case where fixed costs are sufficiently large to ensure that each firm faces a downward-sloping demand curve, but where there are *enough* firms so that each firm can ignore the consequences of its actions on others. This is the case of monopolistic competition, first analyzed by Edward Chamberlin of Harvard University in 1933.

Figure 14.9 illustrates a market in which there is monopolistic competition. Assume initially that all firms are charging the same price, say p_1. If one firm were to charge a slightly lower price, it would steal some customers away from other stores. If there were twenty firms in the market, this price-cutting firm would attract more than one-twentieth of the total market demand. And if it should raise its price above that of its rivals, it would lose customers to them. Each firm assumes that the prices charged by other firms will remain unchanged as it changes its price or the quantity it produces. The demand curve facing each firm is thus the one shown in the figure.

Figure 14.9 PROFIT-MAXIMIZING FOR A MONOPOLISTIC COMPETITOR

A monopolistic competitor chooses the quantity it will produce by setting marginal revenue equal to marginal cost (Q_1), and then selling that quantity for the price given on its demand curve (p_1). In panel A, the price charged is above average cost, and the monopolistic competitor is making a profit, enticing other firms to enter the market. As firms enter, the share of the market demand of each firm is reduced, and the demand curve facing each firm shifts to the left. Entry continues until the demand curve just touches the average cost curve (panel B). When the firm produces Q_e, it just breaks even; there is no incentive either for entry or exit.

In deciding how much to produce, the firm sets marginal revenue equal to marginal cost. The market equilibrium is (p_1, Q_1), with marginal revenue equaling marginal cost. In the equilibrium depicted in the figure, price exceeds average costs. One can think of this situation as a sort of minimonopoly, where each firm has a monopoly on its own brand name or its own store location.

But if existing firms are earning monopoly profits, there is an incentive for new competitors to enter the market until profits are driven to zero, as in the perfectly competitive model. *This is the vital distinction between monopolies and monopolistic competition.* In both cases, firms face downward-sloping demand curves. In both cases, they set marginal revenue equal to marginal cost. But in monopolistic competition, there are no barriers to entry. Entry continues so long as profits are positive. As firms enter, the share of the industry demand of each firm is reduced. The demand curve facing each firm thus shifts to the left, as depicted in panel B. This process continues until the demand curve just touches the average cost curve, at point (p_e, Q_e). At that point, profits are zero.

The figure also shows the firm's marginal revenue and marginal cost curves. As we have said, the firm sets its marginal revenue equal to its marginal cost. This occurs at exactly the level of output at which the demand curve is tangent to the average cost curve. This is because at any other point, average costs exceed price, so profits are negative. Only at this point are profits zero. Accordingly, this is the profit-maximizing output.

The monopolistic competition equilibrium has some interesting character-

CLOSE-UP: IBM—FROM THE EDGE OF MONOPOLY TO THE EDGE OF COMPETITION

IBM committed itself to computers in the 1950s, and rapidly asserted its dominance in the business of large "mainframe" computers. IBM machines were often the most technologically advanced, and in the few cases where they might not have been the best, they still had an extraordinary reputation for great service and support. Back in the days when computers were more than a little mysterious to most of their users, that reputation mattered a lot.

IBM was never a literal monopoly. Throughout the 1960s and 1970s, competition came from firms like Control Data, Honeywell, Sperry Univac, Burroughs, and NCR. But by 1980, IBM still had over 80 percent of the world market for mainframe computers. It was common for the company's sales to grow every year by double-digit percentages.

But by the early 1990s, its market share had slipped dramatically. In 1990, it had only 15 percent of the fastest-growing segment of the market, personal computers. Upstarts—Apple, Compaq, Dell, AST—as well as foreign producers—NEC and Toshiba—dominated the market. IBM was forced to make dramatic cutbacks. For the first time in its

history, there were massive layoffs. It engaged in large-scale restructuring, trying to make itself "nimble" enough to compete in the fast-moving market. Less than two decades after the Justice Department had tried to break up IBM, charging that it was too close to a monopoly, it was scrambling for market share. It is a real world example of Joseph Schumpeter's vision of markets with dominant firms only able to maintain their position temporarily in the face of intense technological competition from new entrants (see page 358).

istics. Notice that in equilibrium, price and average costs exceed the minimum average costs at which the goods could be produced. *Less is produced at a higher price.* But there is a trade-off here. Whereas in the perfectly competitive market every product was a perfect substitute for every other one, in the world of monopolistic competition there is variety in the products available. People value variety, and are willing to pay a higher price to obtain it. Thus, the fact that goods are sold at a price above the minimum average cost does not necessarily mean that the economy is inefficient.

Whether the market results in too little or too much product variety remains a contested subject. Either can occur. The important point to realize here is that there is a trade-off. Greater variety can only be obtained at greater cost.

SCHUMPETERIAN COMPETITION

The famous Harvard economist Joseph Schumpeter envisaged a rather different form of monopolistic competition. He saw different markets dominated at different times by one or two firms, those that had technological superiority. The dominant firms were constantly subjected to competition for supremacy as new innovations supplanted old. Even when the lead firm is not supplanted by another, the threat of entry keeps it on its toes. While each company dominates the market, it acts like a monopolist: it sets marginal revenue equal to marginal cost, producing less than would be produced under perfect competition. But if it wishes to maintain its position, the firm must reinvest profits in further expenditures to make new products and to develop new, cheaper ways of producing. In Schumpeter's view, the disadvantage of the monopoly aspects of imperfect markets—the reduction in output—was more than offset by the advantages of the greater research the extra profits funded. Chapter 17 will take a closer look at these questions.

REVIEW AND PRACTICE

SUMMARY

1. Economists identify four broad categories of market structure: perfect competition, monopoly, oligopoly, and monopolistic competition (the last two are collectively referred to as imperfect competition).

2. A perfectly competitive firm faces a horizontal demand curve; it is a price taker. In markets in which there is imperfect or no competition, each firm faces a downward-sloping demand curve, and is a price maker.

3. Both monopolists and firms facing perfect competition maximize profit by producing at the quantity where marginal revenue is equal to marginal cost. However, marginal revenue for a perfect competitor is the same as the market price of an extra unit, while marginal revenue for a monopolist is less than the market price.

4. Since with a monopoly price exceeds marginal revenue, buyers pay more for the product than the marginal cost to produce it; there is less production in a monopoly than there would be if price were set equal to marginal cost.

5. Imperfect competition occurs when a relatively small number of firms dominate the market and/or when firms produce goods that are differentiated by their characteristics, by the location of the firms, or in the perception of consumers.

6. Monopolies and imperfect competition may be sustained by either natural or manmade barriers to entry.

7. With monopolistic competition, barriers to entry are sufficiently weak that entry occurs until profits are driven to zero; there are few enough firms that each faces a downward-sloping demand curve, but a sufficiently large number of firms that each ignores rivals' reactions to what it does.

KEY TERMS

monopoly
oligopoly
monopolistic
   competition
imperfect
   competition

pure profit or
   monopoly rents
price discrimination
product
   differentiation
barriers to entry

natural monopoly
predatory pricing
limit pricing

REVIEW QUESTIONS

1. What is the difference between perfect and imperfect competition? between oligopoly and monopolistic competition?

2. Why is price equal to marginal revenue for a perfectly competitive firm, but not for a monopolist?

3. How should a monopoly choose its quantity of production to maximize profits? Explain why producing either less or more than the level of output at which marginal revenue equals marginal cost will reduce profits. Since a monopolist need not fear competition, what prevents it from raising its price as high as it wishes to make higher profits?

4. What are the primary sources of product differentiation?

5. What are barriers to entry? Describe the principal ones.

6. What is a natural monopoly?

7. Describe market equilibrium under monopolistic competition. Why does the price charged by the typical firm exceed the minimum average cost, even though there is entry?

PROBLEMS

1. Explain how it is possible that at a high enough level of output, if a monopoly produced and sold more, its revenue would actually decline.

2. Assume there is a single firm producing cigarettes, and the marginal cost of producing cigarettes is a constant. Suppose the government imposes a

10-cent tax on each pack of cigarettes. If the demand curve for cigarettes is linear (that is, $Q = a - bp$, where Q = output, p = price, and a and b are constants), will the price rise by more or less than the tax?

3. With what strategies might a furniture firm differentiate its products?

4. Suppose a gas station at a busy intersection is surrounded by many competitors, all of whom sell identical gas. Draw the demand curve the gas station faces, and draw its marginal and average cost curves. Explain the rule for maximizing profit in this situation. Now imagine that the gas station offers a new gasoline additive called zoomine, and begins an advertising campaign that says: "Get zoomine in your gasoline." No other station offers zoomine. Draw the demand curve faced by the station after this advertising campaign. Explain the rule for maximizing profit in this situation, and illustrate it with an appropriate diagram.

5. Explain how consumers may benefit from predatory pricing in the short run, but not in the long run.

6. Why might it make sense for a monopolist to choose a point on the demand curve where the price is somewhat lower than the price at which marginal revenue equals marginal costs?

7. Assume the demand curve for some commodity is linear
$$Q = a - bp.$$
  (a) Express how the price depends on the quantity produced.
  (b) What is the relationship between revenue and the quantity produced?
  (c) Assume that output increases slightly from Q to $(Q + \Delta Q)$. What happens to revenue? If ΔQ is a small number (much less than 1), then $(\Delta Q)^2$ is a *very* small number. Ignoring terms in $(\Delta Q)^2$, what is the relationship between marginal revenue and output?
  (d) Show that the expression for marginal revenue can be reexpressed as
$$MR = 2p - a/b$$
  (e) Assume that $b = 1$ and $a = 100$. Draw the demand and marginal revenue curves.
  (f) If marginal cost is \$1, what is the equilibrium competitive price and the monopoly price?
  (g) If the producer is required to pay a tax of \$.10 per unit of output produced, what happens to the price under monopoly? under perfect competition?

APPENDIX A: MONOPSONY

In any market, imperfections of competition can arise on either the buyer or seller side. In this chapter, we have focused on imperfect competition among the sellers of goods. When there is a single buyer in a market, the buyer is called a **monopsonist.** Though monopsonies are relatively rare, they do exist. The government is a monopsonist in the market for a variety of high-technology defense systems.

In some labor markets, a single firm may be close to a monopsonist. In many markets, an employer may face an upward-sloping supply curve for labor, or at least labor with particular skills. Firms in one-company towns—like Gary, Indiana, which was founded and is dominated by U.S. Steel—particularly when they are geographically isolated, are most likely to face such upward-sloping supply curves for labor.

The consequences of monopsony are similar to those for monopoly. The basic rule remains: produce at the point where marginal revenue equals marginal cost. The buyer firm is aware, however, that if it buys more units, it will have to pay a higher price. Then if the firm cannot price discriminate, the marginal cost of buying one more unit is not only what the company has to pay for the last unit, but also the higher price it must pay for all previously purchased units.

In the case of a labor market, Figure 14.10 illustrates the consequence. Chapter 12 showed that in competitive markets, firms hire labor up to the point where the value of the marginal product of labor *(MPL)* equals the wage, the marginal cost of hiring an additional worker. The figure shows the curve that represents the value of the marginal product of labor; it declines as the number of workers hired increases. The figure also shows the labor supply curve, which is upward sloping. From this, the firm can calculate the marginal cost of hiring an additional worker, the wage *plus* the increase in wage payments to all previously hired workers. Clearly, the marginal cost curve lies above the labor supply curve. The firm hires workers up to the point L^*, where the value of the marginal product of labor is equal to the marginal cost. Employment is lower than it would have been had the firm ignored the fact that as it hires more labor, the wage it pays increases.

Figure 14.10 MONOP-SONY

As a monopsonist buys more of an input, it must pay not only a higher price for the marginal unit but a higher price for all the units it buys; thus, the marginal cost of buying an input exceeds the price. The monopsonist sets the marginal cost of the input equal to the value of its marginal product at employment level L^*, and sets the wage at w_m. In a competitive labor market, a firm hires labor up to L_c, at wage w_c. Thus, a monopsonist hires less labor at a lower wage than competitive firms would.

APPENDIX B: DEMAND FOR INPUTS UNDER MONOPOLY AND IMPERFECT COMPETITION

In Chapter 12, we saw that competitive firms hire labor up to the point where the value of the marginal product (the value of what an extra hour of labor would produce) is equal to the wage. Similarly, any other factor of production is demanded up to the point where the value of its marginal product is equal to its price. From this, we could derive the demand curve for labor (or any other input).

A quite similar analysis applies with imperfect competition. A monopolist hires labor up to the point where the extra revenue it produces—what economists call the marginal revenue product—is equal to the wage. In competitive markets, the value of the marginal product is just equal to the

Figure 14.11 MARGINAL REVENUE PRODUCT CURVE

Firms hire labor up to the point where the marginal revenue product of an extra worker equals the marginal cost. In a competitive labor market, the marginal cost of labor is just the wage.

price of the output times the marginal physical product, the extra quantity that is produced. In a monopoly, the marginal revenue product (MRP) is equal to the marginal revenue yielded by producing one more unit (MR) times the marginal physical product (MPP): $MRP = MR \times MPP$.

The quantity of labor that will be hired is illustrated in Figure 14.11, which shows the marginal revenue product curve. It is downward sloping, for two reasons: the more that is produced, the smaller the marginal physical product (this is just the law of diminishing returns), and the more that is produced, the smaller the marginal revenue. The firm hires labor up to the point where the marginal revenue product equals the wage, point L_0. If the wage increases from w_0 to w_1, the amount of labor hired will fall, from L_0 to L_1. Thus, the demand curve for labor is downward sloping with imperfect competition, just as it is with perfect competition.

CHAPTER 15

OLIGOPOLIES

In industries characterized by monopolistic competition, there are enough firms that each assumes its actions have no effect on the actions of its competitors. But in many industries, called oligopolies, there are so few firms that each worries about how its rivals will react to anything it does. This is true of the airline, cigarette, aluminum, automobile, and a host of other industries. Airlines that offer frequent flier bonuses, for instance, can expect their competitors to respond with similar offers.

If an oligopolist lowers its price, it worries that rivals will do the same and it will gain no competitive advantage. Worse still, a competitor may react to a price cut by engaging in a price war and cutting the price still further. Different oligopolies behave in quite different ways. The oligopolist is always torn between its desire to outwit competitors and the knowledge that by cooperating with other oligopolists to reduce output, it will earn a portion of the higher industry profits.

This chapter examines the key question facing an oligopolistic firm—whether it will earn higher profits colluding with rivals to restrict output or competing with rivals by charging lower prices. The analysis of oligopoly behavior is divided into three sections. The first discusses collusion, or cooperation, and the problems firms confront in colluding. The second shows how firms may restrict competition, even when they do not formally collude. The third describes what happens if firms in an oligopoly compete.

KEY QUESTIONS

1. In what ways do oligopolies differ from the other market structures—monopoly, perfect competition, and monopolistic competition?

2. What are the incentives for the firms in an oligopoly to collude? Why is it hard to maintain the cooperative behavior required for cartels to be effective?

3. What practices do firms in an oligopoly engage in that facilitate collusion and, in the absence of collusion, that restrict the force of competition?

4. What are some of the different forms that competition among oligopolists takes?

COLLUSION

In some cases, oligopolists try to **collude** to maximize their profits. In effect, they act jointly as if they were a monopoly, and split up the resulting profits. The prevalence of collusion was long ago noted by Adam Smith, the founder of modern economics: "People of the same trade seldom meet together, even for merriment and diversion, but the conversation ends in a conspiracy against the public, or in some contrivance to raise prices."[1] A group of companies that formally operate in collusion is called a **cartel.** The Organization of Petroleum Exporting Countries (OPEC), for instance, acts collusively to restrict the output of oil, to raise oil prices and hence the profits of member countries.

In the late nineteenth century, two or more railroads ran between many major cities. When they competed vigorously, profits were low. So it did not take them long to discover that if they acted collusively, they could raise profits by raising prices.

In the steel industry at the turn of the century, Judge Elbert H. Gary, who headed the U.S. Steel Company, the largest of the steel firms, regularly presided over Sunday dinners for prominent members of his industry at which steel prices were set. But while cartels increase industry profits, it is hard to maintain the cooperative behavior required. We now look at three problems facing cartels.

THE PROBLEM OF SELF-ENFORCEMENT

Cartels seek to restrict output and thus to raise prices above marginal costs. The central difficulty facing cartels is that it pays any single member of the cartel to cheat. That is, if all other members of the cartel restrict output, so

[1]*Wealth of Nations* (1776), Book 1, Chapter 10, Part II.

that price exceeds marginal cost, it pays the last member of the cartel to increase its output and take advantage of the higher price. This firm is said to be free riding on the cartel—the other firms pay the price of collusion by restricting their output, while the free rider gets the higher price without giving up any sales. But if too many members of a cartel cheat by increasing their output beyond the agreed-upon levels, the cartel breaks down. This happened to the OPEC oil cartel during the 1980s. Producers (other than Saudi Arabia) systematically increased production beyond their allotted quotas.

The incentives for any member of a cartel to cheat are illustrated in Figure 15.1, in which all members of a cartel face the same constant marginal costs. The figure shows the market demand curve and the output, Q_c, and price, p_c, at which the cartel's joint profits are maximized—that is, where marginal revenue for the cartel as a whole equals marginal costs. But the marginal revenue for the cartel as a whole is not the marginal revenue for any one firm. Any firm thinks it can cheat on the cartel and get away with it. If it shaves its price just lower than p_c and increases its production, it makes a profit of approximately p_c minus the marginal cost on that additional unit. With a large gap between price and marginal costs, the incentives to cheat are strong.

A factor that further encourages some members of a cartel to cheat on the collusive agreement is that members frequently believe they are not getting their fair share. This problem has plagued the OPEC oil cartel. Each country within the cartel faces different economic circumstances. Oil-rich sheikdoms have per capita incomes among the highest in the world. But for poor countries like Indonesia, oil revenues are a potential resource for development. No simple principles exist to help these countries decide how much each should produce, or who should bear the burden of cutting back production in order to sustain a high market price. Those who feel they are being unfairly treated are most likely to try to cheat on the collusive agreement.

Thus, the first major problem facing cartels is how to enforce their collu-

Figure 15.1 INCENTIVES TO CHEAT ON A CARTEL

The existence of a large gap between price and marginal costs provides a strong incentive for each member of a cartel to cheat; p_c is the cartel price.

Maintaining collusive behavior is difficult, particularly given the laws aimed at restricting it. Ironically, government is sometimes an accomplice in restricting competition. Such is commonly the case in alcoholic beverages, where state laws make it difficult for distributors in one state to sell in another. The dramatic effect of restrictions on selling across state lines was recently demonstrated by New York in the case of milk.

In the 1930s, the state passed a law prohibiting dairies outside New York from selling milk in the state. The law benefited New York milk producers at the expense of its consumers and milk producers in other states. In 1979, New Jersey–based Farmland Dairies challenged the New York law. After an eight-year legal battle, it won the right to sell milk in New York City. Before the decision, five milk producers controlled over 90 percent of the milk market in the city. After the decision, when

Farmland and others entered the market, milk prices in the city tumbled by as much as 70 cents a gallon. The new competition saves New York consumers as much as $100 million every year in lower milk prices.

sive arrangement on their members. This self-enforcement is a particular problem in the United States because both state and federal governments have passed **antitrust laws** prohibiting collusive behavior. This makes it impossible for firms to get together and sign legally binding contracts that would require each firm to keep output low and prices high.

But the profits from collusion can be so great that firms have taken the risks involved in violating the law. One of the most famous cases involved manufacturers of electrical machinery, including Westinghouse and General Electric, who were caught conspiring in their bids for major projects, like the electric turbines for a dam. The companies arranged to take turns winning, using an elaborate scheme that involved the phases of the moon and the lunar calendar. Their scheme was so clever that the conspiracy went on for years before they were caught.

THE PROBLEM OF COORDINATION

In countries where explicit collusion is illegal, members of an oligopoly who wish to take advantage of their market power must rely on **tacit collusion.** Tacit collusion is an implicit understanding that the oligopoly's interests are best served if its members do not compete too vigorously and particularly if they avoid price cutting. However, the interests of particular firms may not coincide exactly. And an implicit agreement by its very nature makes it difficult to specify what each firm should do in every situation. When cost or demand curves shift, perhaps because of changes in technology or changes in tastes, the members of a cartel need to get together to agree upon the appropriate changes in output and prices. A new technology or development may benefit one firm more than another, and that firm will wish to increase output more than the others. If the oligopolists could bargain together openly, they might be able to cut a deal. But since the law prohibits them from such a straightforward solution, inventive oligopolists have developed a number of ways to circumvent this coordination problem.

One approach is for a particular firm to become the **price leader.** That firm, often the second- or third-largest member of the industry, sets the price, and others follow. According to some economists, American Airlines used to be the price leader in its industry. As costs (say, of fuel) or demand conditions changed in the airline industry, American would announce new fare structures, and the other airlines would simply match them. It is hard to prove that collusion has occurred in this type of sequence—the firms simply claim that they are responding to similar market forces.

Sometimes communication among firms of an industry can be so subtle as to be almost undetectable. The Justice Department caught firms in the airline industry communicating through the airline reservation system. Farecodes are normally used to identify when a particular fare will be in effect, and other restrictions on availability. But the airlines devised a way (using farecodes for fares that were not actually being offered) in which they would communicate how they would respond to a proposed change in the fare in a particular market.[2]

Yet another approach is to develop **facilitating practices** that serve to make collusion easier. One example is the "meeting-the-competition clause," in which at least some members of the oligopoly commit themselves, often in advertisements, to charging no more than any competitor. Electronics shops often make such claims. To the consumer, this looks like a great deal. To see why this practice may actually lead to higher prices, think about it from the perspective of rival firms. Assume that the electronics store is selling for $100 an item that costs the store $90; its selling costs are $5, so it is making a $5 profit on the sale. Consider another store that would like to steal some customers away. It would be willing to sell the item for $95, undercutting the first store. But then it reasons that if it cuts its price, it will not gain any customers, since the first store has already guaranteed to match the lower price. Further, the second store knows that it will make less money on each sale to its current customers. Price cutting simply does not pay. It thus appears that a practice that seemingly is highly competitive in fact may facilitate collusion.

In many cases, oligopolists create a variety of cooperative arrangements that involve sharing inventories, research findings, or other information. In electronics and other high-technology industries, exchanging research

---

[2]Not surprisingly, the airlines denied the charge. But in 1993 they signed an agreement to no longer engage in the practice.

information is particularly important. In retail and wholesale markets, helping one another out in the case of inventory shortages is important. For example, one distributor of beer may provide beer to another when the latter's inventory is insufficient to meet his retailers' demand. Any firm that cheated on the collusive price arrangement would find itself cut out from these cooperative arrangements.

THE PROBLEM OF ENTRY

The third major problem cartels face is similar to the problem faced by a monopolist. High profits enjoyed by the members of the cartel attract entry from other firms or cause nonmembers of the cartel to expand production. This was one of the fates that befell OPEC. When its members raised the price of oil, noncartel countries like Britain, Canada, and Mexico increased their production of oil.

Some economists, such as William Baumol of New York and Princeton Universities, have argued that in some markets just the threat of entry is strong enough to keep prices low, even if a firm controls over 90 percent of the market. If prices were ever so slightly above costs of production, there would be rapid entry, forcing prices down. In these cases, **potential competition,** the possibility of entry, is sufficient to keep prices low. The costs of entry and exit have to be relatively small, however, for potential competition to be effective. Otherwise, firms will not enter, even when they see high prices, unless they have reason to believe that prices will remain high after entry.

Markets such as these, in which potential competition suffices to ensure competitive prices, are called **contestable.** At one time, advocates of the theory of contestable markets used airlines as the basic example of a contestable market. An airline could easily enter a market in which price exceeded costs (for example, the San Francisco–Los Angeles market), and thus potential competition would ensure low prices, even when there were only one or two airlines flying a particular route. But by the end of the 1980s, as airline prices skyrocketed on many routes on which competition was limited, potential competition did not seem strong enough to keep prices down. Potential entrants recognized that there were significant costs to entering a market—customers had to be informed, they had to be persuaded to switch from the usual carrier, airline offices had to be opened, and so forth—and experience had taught them that once they entered, prices would fall, making it impossible for them to recover these costs.

It is remarkable how many oligopolies persist with limited entry. There has been some entry into the film industry (Fuji), but it remains dominated by a few firms. Other oligopolies, such as the automobile, cigarette, and aluminum industries, have remained relatively intact over long periods of time. Even the number of attempts at entry has been limited; Tucker and Kaiser represent the two most famous cases of failure in automobiles. This suggests that if the barriers to entry discussed in Chapter 14 are strong enough, as appears to be the case in many situations, potential entry may not provide an adequate threat to prevent firms from charging prices in excess of marginal costs.

CLOSE-UP: PRICE FIXING IN ACTION

Price-fixing cases are often hard to prosecute, since the parties go to great lengths to hide their activities. Occasionally, however, a private conversation becomes public, as happened in a 1983 antitrust suit against American and Braniff Airlines. The following is part of a recorded telephone call between Robert Crandall, president of American Airlines, and Howard Putnam, president of Braniff Airlines, that was introduced at the trial. (The two companies had been acting as oligopolistic competitors and cutting prices as they competed in the Dallas market.)

CRANDALL: I think it's dumb as hell . . . to sit here and pound the (deleted) out of each other and neither one of us making a (deleted) dime. . . . We can both live here and there ain't no room for Delta. But there's, ah, no reason that I can see, all right, to put both companies out of business.

PUTNAM: Do you have a suggestion for me?

CRANDALL: Yes, I have a suggestion for you. Raise your goddamn fares twenty percent. I'll raise mine the next morning. . . . You'll make more money, and I will too.

PUTNAM: We can't talk about pricing.

CRANDALL: Oh (deleted), Howard. We can talk about any goddamn thing we want to talk about.

The Justice Department released a transcript of the conversation as it charged American Airlines and Crandall with an attempt to monopolize airline routes and fix prices with Braniff. However, after some months of litigation, a federal judge dismissed the charge. The decision held that while the conversation was clearly an offer to raise prices, it was not an attempt to monopolize according to the meaning of the law. The judge also wrote that "Crandall's conduct was at best unprofessional and his choice of words distasteful," but concluded that since Putnam turned down the offer, no conspiracy to monopolize existed.

Crandall was lucky. If his phrasing had been a bit different, or if Putnam had taken him up on his offer, he could easily have been found guilty. But how many other, similar conversations are occurring among other executives today, without any government recording devices on the line?

Sources: Robert E. Taylor and Dean Rotbart, "American Air Accused of Bid to Fix Prices," *Wall Street Journal,* February 24, 1983, p. 2; Dean Rotbart, "American Air, Its President Gets Trust Suit Voided," *Wall Street Journal,* September 14, 1983, p. 2.

LIMITS TO COLLUSION

Self-enforcement; incentives for each firm to cheat
Coordination problems in responding to changed economic circumstances
Entry

GAME THEORY: THE PRISONER'S DILEMMA

In recent years, economists have used a branch of mathematics called game theory to study collusion among oligopolists. The participants in a game are allowed to make certain moves, defined by the rules of the game. The outcomes of the game—what each participant receives—are referred to as its payoffs, and depend on what each player does. Each participant in the game chooses a strategy; he decides what moves to make. In games in which each player has the chance to make more than one move (there is more than one round, or period), moves can depend on what has happened in previous periods. Game theory begins with the assumption that each player in the game is rational and knows that his rival is rational. Each is trying to maximize his own payoff. The theory then tries to predict what each player will do. The answer depends on the rules of the game and the payoffs.

One example of such a game is called the **Prisoner's Dilemma.** Two prisoners, A and B, alleged to be conspirators in a crime, are put into separate rooms. A police officer goes into each room and makes a little speech: "Now here's the situation. If your partner confesses and you remain silent, you'll get five years in prison. But if your partner confesses and you confess also, you'll only get three years. On the other hand, perhaps your partner remains silent. If you're quiet also, we can only send you to prison for one year. But if your partner remains silent and you confess, we'll let you out in three months. So if your partner confesses, you are better off confessing, and if your partner doesn't confess, you are better off confessing. Why not confess?" This deal is offered to both prisoners.

The diagram below shows the results of this deal. The upper left-hand box, for example, shows the result if both A and B confess. The upper right-hand box shows the result if prisoner A confesses but prisoner B remains silent. And so on.

	Prisoner B	
	Confesses	Remains silent
Confesses	A gets 3 years B gets 3 years	A gets 3 months B gets 5 years
Prisoner A **Remains silent**	A gets 5 years B gets 3 months	A gets 1 year B gets 1 year

From the combined standpoint of the two prisoners, the best option is clearly that they both remain silent and each serve their one year. But the self-interest of each individual prisoner says that confession is best, whether his partner confesses or not. However, if they both follow their self-interest and confess, they both end up worse off, each serving three years. The Prisoner's Dilemma is a simple game in which both parties are made worse off by independently following their own self-interest. Both would be better off if they could get together to agree on a story, and to threaten the other if he deviated from the story.

The Prisoner's Dilemma comes up in a variety of contexts. For example, during the years of the Cold War, the arms race between the United States and the former USSR was described in these terms. Each party reasoned that if the other side built weapons, it needed to match the buildup. And if the other side did not build, it could acquire an advantage by building. Even though both sides might have been better off by agreeing not to build, their incentives pushed them toward a situation where both continued to do so.

The game can also be directly applied to collusion between two oligopolists. (A market with two firms is called a duopoly.) Assume that both firms agree to cut back their production, so they obtain higher prices and higher profits. But each oligopolist reasons the following way. Whether my rival cheats or not, it pays for me to expand production. If my rival cheats, then he gets all the advantages of my restricting output but pays none of the price. And if he does not cheat and keeps production low, it pays for me to cheat. As both firms reason that way, production expands and prices fall to a level below that at which their joint profits are maximized.

In the examples of the Prisoner's Dilemma presented so far, each party makes only one decision. But if firms (or countries) interact over time, then they have additional ways to try to enforce their agreement. For example, suppose each oligopolist announces that it will refrain from cutting prices as long as its rival does. But if the rival cheats on the collusive agreement, then the first oligopolist will respond by increasing production and lowering prices. Won't this threat ensure that the two firms cooperate?

Consider what happens if the two firms expect to compete in the same market over the next ten years, after which time a new product is expected to come along and shift the entire configuration of the industry. It will pay each firm to cheat in the tenth year, when there is no possibility of retaliation, because the industry will be completely altered in the next year. Now consider what happens in the ninth year. Both firms can figure out that it will not pay either one of them to cooperate in the tenth year. But if they are not going to

USING ECONOMICS: GAME THEORY AND COLLUSION

Game theory helps explain why, in spite of the obvious advantages of collusion, cartels have a hard time maintaining themselves. The box below shows the problem of a duopoly, where each of the duopolists can either collude, restricting output, or compete. Numbers in the upper left triangle are the first duopolist's profits and in the bottom right triangle the second duopolist's profits.

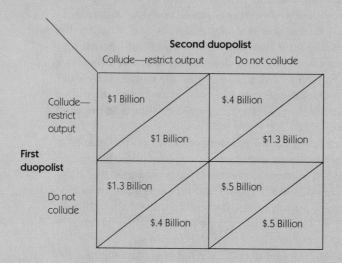

When they both collude, profits are high—in this example, each receives a profit of $1 billion. If the first duopolist restricts his output, and the second duopolist takes advantage of that, the first duopolists' profit falls to $400 million, while the second duopolists' profit increases to $1.3 billion. Industry profits are down ($1.7 billion versus $2 billion before); because only one firm is restricting its output, output is higher and price lower. The outcomes are symmetric, if the second duopolist restricts his output and the first does not. Finally, if both compete vigorously, price falls precipitously, and profits of each fall to $500 million. The gains from collusion in this example are enormous: profits are doubled. But in spite of that, in equilibrium, they will compete.

The first firm reasons: if my rival restricts his output, and I do too, my profits are $1 billion; but if I do not restrict my output, I can increase my profits to $1.3 billion. Clearly, in this case, I am better off not restricting my output. If my rival does not restrict his output, but I do, my profits are $400 million; but if I do not restrict my output, my profits increase to $500 million. In either case—no matter what my rival does—I am better off not restricting my output. The second firm reasons exactly the same way, and the outcome is clear: neither restricts his output, and each earns a profit of $500 million, half of what they would have earned had they colluded.

cooperate in the tenth year anyway, then the *threat* of not cooperating in the future is completely ineffective. Hence in the ninth year, each firm will reason that it pays to cheat on the collusive agreement by producing more than the agreed-upon amount. Collusion breaks down in the ninth year. Reasoning backward through time, this logic will lead collusion to break down almost immediately.

Economists have set up laboratory experiments, much like those used by other sciences, to test how individuals actually behave in these different games. The advantage of this sort of **experimental economics** is that the researcher can change one aspect of what is going on at a time, to try to determine what are the crucial determinants of behavior. One set of experiments has looked at how individuals cooperate with one another in situations like the Prisoner's Dilemma. These experiments have a tendency to show that participants often evolve simple strategies that, although they may appear irrational in the short run, can be effective in inducing cooperation (collusion) as the game is repeated a number of times. One common strategy is "tit for tat." If you increase your output, I will do the same, even if doing so does not maximize my profits. If the rival firm believes this threat, especially after it has been carried out a few times, the rival may decide that it is more profitable to cooperate and keep production low rather than to cheat. In the real world, such simple strategies may play an important role in ensuring that firms do not compete too vigorously in those markets where there are only three or four dominant firms.

RESTRICTIVE PRACTICES

If members of an oligopoly could easily get together and collude, they would. Their joint profits would thereby be increased. They would have a problem of how to divide the profits, but each of the members of the oligopoly could be better off than it would be if they competed. We have seen, however, that there are significant impediments to collusion. If the members of an industry cannot collude to stop competition and cannot prevent entry, at least they can act to reduce competition and deter entry.

Chapter 14 described some of the ways firms act to deter entry. Here, we look at practices firms engage in that may serve to *restrict* competition, called **restrictive practices.** Some of these practices were made illegal by the Federal Trade Commission Act of 1914. While these practices may not be quite as successful in increasing profits for the firms as the collusive arrangements discussed above, they do succeed in raising prices. In some cases, consumers may be even worse off than with outright collusion. Many restrictive practices are aimed at the wholesalers and retailers who sell a producer's goods. When one firm buys or sells another firm's products, the two companies are said to have a "vertical" relationship. Such restrictive practices are called **vertical restrictions,** as opposed to the price-fixing arrangements among producers or

Microsoft is the dominant producer of personal computer software in the world. Microsoft products account for almost two-thirds of installed PC operating systems and more than half of all spreadsheet applications. Its profits soared close to a billion dollars in 1993, and its market value is larger than that of GM. On July 16, 1994, Microsoft signed an out-of-court settlement of a case brought by the European Union and the U.S. Department of Justice alleging Microsoft engaged in practices designed to reduce competition. This marked the first time that two major law enforcement agencies from different parts of the world had collaborated in bringing and settling a suit.

Largeness in itself is not a crime. So why the suit? Competitors claimed, and the Department of Justice agreed, that Microsoft was engaging in unfair trade practices to establish and maintain its dominant market position. The contract it signed with PC manufacturers that installed programs like Microsoft Windows and DOS on their computers was cited as an example. Microsoft was basing its charges simply on the scale of the PC manufacturer's sales volume—such as the number of PCs delivered—not on the number on which Microsoft's programs were actually installed. Thus, if a competitor were to come up with a program that was in fact just as good, a manufacturer would have no incentive to install it, because it would have already paid for Microsoft's Windows and DOS programs. Microsoft denied any wrongdoing, but signing the consent decree involved an agreement to stop engaging in such practices.

Were the European Union and the U.S. Department of Justice right to accept the consent decree, or should they have gone farther? Critics say that the consent decree would not lessen Microsoft's hold on the market by much, because it was still allowed to use volume discounts, which kept the *marginal* charge for installing Windows and DOS very low. Since designing the operating system gave it a distinct advantage in developing applications programs for use with the system, some critics wanted Microsoft divided into two companies. One would develop operating systems and the other applications, and what is called a Chinese wall would separate them. This would put competitors on a level playing field in developing applications.

Microsoft supporters say the outcome represented an appropriate balance between concerns about innovation and competition. Their position is that the dominant position of Microsoft results from (1) its price competitiveness—it had been able to bring down the price of the operating systems to under $100—and (2) its innovativeness—new features were continually being added.

Source: *New York Times*, July 18, 1994, pp. D1–4.

among wholesalers selling in the same market, which are referred to as **horizontal restrictions.**

One example of a vertical restriction is that of **exclusive territories,** in which a producer gives a wholesaler or retailer the exclusive right to sell a good within a certain region. Beer and soft drink producers, for instance, typically give their distributors exclusive territories. Coca-Cola manufactures its own syrup, which it then sells to bottlers who add the soda water. Coca-Cola gives these bottlers exclusive territories, so the supermarkets in a particular area can buy Coke from only one place. A store in Michigan cannot buy the soft drink from Coca-Cola bottlers in New Jersey, even if the price in New Jersey is lower. Indiana passed a law prohibiting exclusive territories for beer within the state. As a result, beer prices there are substantially lower (adjusting for other differences) than in other states.

Another example of a restrictive practice is **exclusive dealing,** in which a producer insists that any firm selling its products not sell those of its rivals. When you go into an Exxon gas station, for instance, you can be sure you are buying gas refined by the Exxon Corporation, not Texaco or Mobil. Like most refiners, Exxon insists that stations that want to sell Exxon sell only its brand of gasoline.

A third example of a restrictive practice is **tie-ins,** in which a customer who buys one product must buy another. Mortgage companies, for example, used to insist that those who obtained mortgages from them purchase fire insurance as well. Nintendo designs its console so that it can only be used with Nintendo games. In effect, it forces a tie-in sale between the console and the computer games. In the early days of computers, IBM designed its computers so that they could only be used with IBM "peripherals," such as printers.

A final example of a restrictive practice is **resale price maintenance.** Under resale price maintenance, a producer insists that any retailer selling his product must sell it at the "list" price. Like exclusive territories, this practice is designed to reduce competitive pressures at the retail level.

CONSEQUENCES OF RESTRICTIVE PRACTICES

Firms engaging in restrictive practices *claim* they are doing so not because they wish to restrict competition, but because they want to enhance economic efficiency. Exclusive territories, they argue, provide companies with a better incentive to "cultivate" their territory. Exclusive dealing contracts, they say, provide incentives for firms to focus their attention on one producer's goods.

Regardless of these claims, restrictive practices often reduce economic efficiency. Exclusive territories for beer, for example, have limited the ability of very large firms, with stores in many different territories, to set up a central warehouse and distribute beer to their stores in a more efficient manner.

Regardless of whether they enhance or hurt efficiency, restrictive practices may lead to higher prices by limiting competitive pressures.

Some restrictive practices work by increasing the costs of, or otherwise impeding, one's rivals. In the 1980s, several major airlines developed computer reservation systems that they sold at very attractive prices to travel agents. If the primary goal of these systems had been to serve consumers, they would

FORMS OF RESTRICTIVE PRACTICES

Exclusive territories

Exclusive dealing

Tie-ins

Resale price maintenance

have been designed to display all the departures near the time the passenger desired. Instead, each airline's system provided a quick display for only its own flights—United's, for instance, focused on United flights—although with additional work, the travel agent could find out the flights of other airlines. Airlines benefited from these computer systems, not because they best met the needs of the consumer, but because they put competitors at a disadvantage and thereby reduced the effectiveness of competition.

An exclusive dealing contract between a producer and a distributor is another example of how one firm may benefit from hurting its rivals. The contract may force a rival producer to set up its own distribution system, at great cost. The already-existing distributor might have been able to undertake the distribution of the second product at relatively low incremental cost. The exclusive dealing contract increases total resources spent on distribution.

Courts have taken varying attitudes toward the legality of these and similar practices—in some circumstances ruling that they are illegal because they reduce competition, while in others allowing them, having been persuaded that they represent reasonable business practices.

THE MANY DIMENSIONS OF COMPETITION AMONG OLIGOPOLISTS

In the perfectly competitive markets of Part Two, competitive behavior is clear and simple. Firms work to lower their costs of production. They can sell as much as they want at the going market price. They don't have to worry about clever marketing strategies, new products, advertising: but these, and a host of other decisions, are the battlefields on which competition among oligopolists occurs. This competition is fierce with firms constantly trying to outwit rivals and anticipate their responses. It is like a game, but one in which not all the rules are clear, let alone written down. American Airlines might have thought it was getting a leg up on its rivals when it introduced its frequent flier program, and Delta Air Lines might have thought it was doing likewise when it offered triple mileage. But some of the rival airlines had more empty seats than either American or Delta. Since giving away free tickets may have been less costly for them, they could respond by offering even more attractive programs. Were American and Delta, then, really better off?

PRICE AND OUTPUT COMPETITION

Even in the limited domain on which we have focused so far, determining prices and output, the life of an oligopolist is complicated. At one level of analysis, the oligopolist firm is just like a firm facing monopolistic competition. The oligopolist faces a demand curve specifying how much output it believes it can sell at each price it charges, or what the firm believes it will receive if it tries to sell a particular quantity. The oligopolist chooses the point along that demand curve at which its profits are maximized. It sets, in other words, marginal revenue equal to marginal cost. But while true, this statement hides all the real difficulties in an analysis of oligopoly. What an oligopolist will sell at any particular price, or what the market price will be if it produces a particular level of output, depends on what its rivals do.

Economists have investigated the behavior of oligopolies under different assumptions concerning what each firm believes about what his rival will do.

COURNOT COMPETITION

An oligopolist firm may believe that its rivals are committed to producing a given quantity and selling it on the market, and that they will keep this quantity fixed no matter what level of output the firm chooses to produce. If the firm considers producing more, it expects that its rivals will cut their prices until they sell the production level to which they are committed. Competition where an oligopolist firm assumes its rivals' output levels are fixed is called **Cournot competition,** after Augustin Cournot, a French economist and engineer, who first studied it in 1838. Industries such as aluminum or steel, where the major part of the cost of production is the cost of machinery, and once capital goods are in place, variable costs are relatively unimportant, are often thought of as industries where Cournot competition prevails. Adding new machinery would be expensive, and not using machinery to its capacity would save the firm relatively little money. Output is then determined, at least in the short run, by the production capacity of the firm's capital goods.

BERTRAND COMPETITION

In Cournot competition, each firm maximizes profits by choosing what it will produce. In making its calculations, it assumes the level of output of its rivals is fixed. This assumption, we saw, is plausible for industries in which it takes time to change production capacity, and in which capital goods represent the bulk of all production costs. But in many industries it is easy to expand capacity. A taxicab company in a large city can easily buy a new car and hire new drivers. While increasing the total number of planes in service may take some time, an airline that wishes to increase the number of planes flying the Chicago–New York route can do so quickly. Firms in these industries can be thought of as choosing a price to charge, and adjusting their output to meet whatever demand arises at that price. They choose the price so as to maximize their profits, given their beliefs about the behavior of their rivals. One commonly made assumption is that rivals' prices are fixed. Oligopolies in which each firm chooses its price to maximize its profits on the assumption that rivals' prices are fixed are said to be characterized by **Bertrand competition,** after the French economist Joseph Bertrand, who first studied this form of competition in 1883.

If rivals keep their prices unchanged, then the oligopolist may steal many of its rivals' customers when it lowers its price. But as long as the goods produced by two rivals are imperfect substitutes (for any of the reasons discussed in Chapter 14), when one firm lowers its price below that of its rivals, it does not capture *all* the customers.

KINKED DEMAND CURVES

A third hypothesis about how oligopolistic rivals may respond says that rivals match price cuts but do not respond to price increases. In this situation, an oligopolist believes that it will not gain much in sales if it lowers its price, because rivals will match the price cut, but it will lose considerably if it raises its price, since it will be undersold by rivals who do not change their prices. The demand curve facing such an oligopolist appears kinked, as in Figure 15.2. The curve is very steep below the current price, p_1, reflecting the fact that few sales are gained as price is lowered. But it is relatively flat above p_1, indicating that the firm loses many customers to its rivals, who refuse to match the price increases.

The figure also presents the marginal revenue curve, which has a sharp drop at the output level corresponding to the kink. Why does the marginal revenue curve have this shape, and what are the consequences? Consider what happens if the firm wants to increase output by one unit. It must lower its price by a considerable amount since, as it does so, its rivals will match that price. Accordingly, the marginal revenue it garners is small. If the firm contemplates cutting back on production by one unit, it needs to raise its price only a little since rivals will not change their prices. Thus, the loss in revenue from cutting back output by a unit is much greater than the gain in revenue from increasing output by a unit. With a flat demand curve, price and marginal revenue are close together.

The drop in the marginal revenue curve means that at the output at which the drop occurs, Q_1, the extra revenue lost from cutting back production is much greater than the extra revenue gained from increasing production. This has one important implication. Small changes in marginal cost, from

Figure 15.2 A KINKED DE-MAND CURVE

The demand curve facing a firm is relatively flat at price levels above the current level (p_1), showing that an oligopolist will lose a large amount of sales if it increases its price and rivals do not. However, the demand curve is relatively steep at prices below the current level, showing that the oligopolist will not gain much in sales if it lowers its price, since rivals will follow. The sharp drop in marginal revenue means that a firm may not change its level of price or output, even if marginal costs shift.

MC_1 to MC_2, have no effect on output or price. Thus, firms that believe they face a kinked demand curve have good reason to hesitate before changing their prices.

COMPETITION AMONG OLIGOPOLISTS

Cournot competition: Each firm believes its rivals will leave their output unchanged in response to changes in the firm's output.

Bertrand competition: Each firm sets its price believing its rivals will leave their own price unchanged in response to changes in the firm's price.

Kinked demand curves: Each firm believes its rivals will match price cuts but not price increases.

THE IMPORTANCE OF IMPERFECTIONS IN COMPETITION

Many of the features of the modern economy—from frequent-flyer mileage awards to offers to match prices of competitors, from brand names to the billions spent every year on advertising—not only cannot be explained by the basic competitive model, but are inconsistent with it. They reflect the imperfections of competition which affect so many parts of the economy. Most economists agree that the extreme cases of monopoly (no competition) and perfect competition (where each firm has *no* effect on market prices) are rare, and that most markets are characterized by some, but imperfect, competition. However, there is disagreement about the accuracy of the predictions of the perfectly competitive model, with advocates of that model claiming that in many, if not most situations, it provides a good approximation. Even so, there is broad consensus among economists that various phenomena and markets can only be understood in terms of limitations of competition. Imperfect competition is the subject of our eighth consensus point.

8 Imperfect Competition

There is limited competition in many markets. In imperfectly competitive markets, firms are aware that how much they sell, or other actions they take, may affect the price they receive. In many cases, firms must think strategically, considering how their rivals may react to their actions.

REVIEW AND PRACTICE

SUMMARY

1. Oligopolists must choose whether to seek higher profits by colluding with rival firms or by competing. They must decide what their rivals will do in response to any action they take.

2. A group of firms that have an explicit and open agreement to collude is known as a cartel. While the gains from collusion can be significant, there are important limits posed by the incentives to cheat and the necessity to rely on self-enforcement, by the coordination problems arising out of the necessity to respond to changing economic circumstances, and by new entry attracted by the cartel profits. Although cartels are illegal under U.S. law, firms have tried to find tacit ways of facilitating collusion—for example, by using price leaders and "meeting the competition" pricing policies.

3. If the threat of potential entry is sufficient to cause firms to set price and output at competitive levels, the industry is said to be contestable.

4. Even when they do not collude, firms attempt to restrict competition with practices like exclusive territories, exclusive dealing, tie-ins, and resale price maintenance. In some cases, a firm's profits may be increased by raising its rival's costs and making the rival a less effective competitor.

5. In Cournot competition, an oligopolist chooses its output under the assumption that its rivals' output levels are fixed.

6. In Bertrand competition, each firm chooses the price of its product on the assumption that its rivals' prices are fixed.

7. If the rivals to an oligopolist match all price cuts but do not match any price increases, then the oligopolist faces a kinked demand curve. A kinked demand curve will lead to a marginal revenue curve with a vertical segment, which implies that the firm will often not change its level of output or its price in response to small changes in costs.

KEY TERMS

cartel
antitrust laws
Prisoner's Dilemma
Cournot competition

Bertrand
  competition
kinked demand
  curve

contestable markets
potential
  competition

REVIEW QUESTIONS

1. Why is the analysis of oligopoly more complicated than that of monopoly, perfect competition, or monopolistic competition?

2. What are the gains from collusion? Why is there an incentive for each member of a cartel to cheat, to produce more than the agreed upon amount? What is the "Prisoner's Dilemma" and how is it related to the problem of cheating? What are the other problems facing cartels?

3. Name some ways that firms might use tacit collusion, if explicit collusion is ruled out by law.

4. What is a contestable market?

5. Name and define three restrictive practices.

6. What are the different forms of competition among oligopolies? How do they relate to *expectations* concerning how rivals will respond? Under what circumstances might each be more likely to be observed?

7. What expectations must an oligopolist have about the behavior of its rivals if it believes that it faces a kinked demand curve? Why might a firm that faces a kinked demand curve not change its price even when its costs change?

PROBLEMS

1. Explain why every member of a cartel has an incentive to cheat on its agreement. How does this fact strengthen the ability of antitrust laws that outlaw explicit collusion to do their job?

2. How might cooperative agreements between firms—to share research information, share the costs of cleaning up pollution, or help avoid shortfalls of supplies—end up helping firms to collude in reducing quantity and raising price?

3. Explain why each of the following might serve to deter entry of a competitor:
   (a) Maintaining excess production capacity.
   (b) Promising customers that you will undercut any rival.
   (c) Selling your output at a price below that at which marginal revenue equals marginal cost. (Hint: Assume entrants are unsure about what your marginal costs are. Why would they be deterred from entering if they believed you have low marginal costs? Why might a lower price lead them to think that you had low marginal costs?)
   (d) Offering a discount to customers who sign up for long-term contracts.

4. Explain why frequent-flyer programs (in which airlines give credits for each mile traveled, with the credits being convertible into travel awards) might reduce competition among airlines. Put yourself in the role of consultant to one of the airlines in the days before any airline had such programs. Would you have recommended that the airline adopt the program? What would you have *assumed* about the responses of other airlines? Would this have been important to your assessment?

5. At various times, Nintendo has been accused of trying to stifle its competitors. Among the alleged practices have been (a) not allowing those who produce games for Nintendo to produce games for others; and (b) discouraging stores that sell Nintendo from selling competing games, for instance, by not fulfilling their orders as quickly, especially in periods of shortages. Explain why these practices might increase Nintendo's profits.

6. Some industries are characterized by one large, highly efficient firm, and many smaller, less-efficient firms. Describe the equilibrium in this market. How does it depend on the level of demand? If the large firm becomes more efficient, what happens to price? profits?

7. Consider two oligopolists, with each choosing between a "high" and a "low" level of production. Given their choices of how much to produce, their profits will be:

		Firm A	
		High production	Low production
Firm B	High production	A gets $2 million profit B gets $2 million profit	A gets $1 million profit B gets $5 million profit
	Low production	A gets $5 million profit B gets $1 million profit	A gets $4 million profit B gets $4 million profit

Explain how firm B will reason that it makes sense to produce the high amount, regardless of what firm A chooses. Then explain how firm A will reason that it makes sense to produce the high amount, regardless of what firm B chooses. How might collusion assist the two firms in this case?

8. Use the Prisoner's dilemma analysis to describe what happens in the following two situations:

(a) Consider two rivals, say producers of cigarettes. If Benson and Hedges alone advertises, it diverts customers from Marlboro. If Marlboro alone advertises, it diverts customers from Benson and Hedges. If they both advertise, they retain their customer base.

Are they genuinely unhappy with government regulations prohibiting advertising? In practice, they have complained quite bitterly about such government restrictions, including those aimed at children. Why?

(b) Consider two rivals, say producers of camera film, Fuji and Kodak. Consumers want a film that accurately reproduces colors and is not grainy. Assume that initially, they had products that were comparable. If one does R & D and improves its product, it will steal customers from its rival. If they both do R & D, and develop comparable products, then they will continue to share the market as before. Thus, the hypothetical pay-off matrix (in millions of dollars) appears as below (the profits in the case of research take into account the expenditures on research):

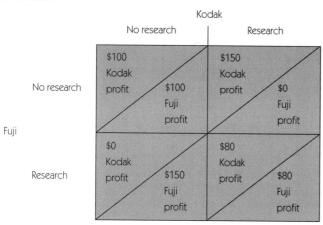

Explain why both will engage in research, even though their profits are lower. Could society be better off, even though profits are lower?

9. In 1990, Iraq invaded Kuwait, destroyed much of its oil fields, and, after losing a war, was essentially barred from selling oil. Assume Kuwait and Iraq were low-cost producers of oil. If OPEC, the oil cartel, operated to maximize joint profits, what would have been the effect of this on international oil prices? In 1996, there were plans to allow Iraq to sell a limited quantity of oil. What kind of response would one expect from OPEC?

10. Explain how exclusive territories, exclusive dealing, tie-ins, and resale price maintenance might help an oligopolist to make higher profits. How might a firm make the case that these practices add to efficiency?

APPENDIX: DESCRIBING THE MARKET EQUILIBRIUM FOR OLIGOPOLY

In this appendix, we take a closer look at how firms in an oligopoly behave and interact to determine the market equilibrium.

COURNOT COMPETITION

Under Cournot competition, each firm assumes its rival's output is constant. For simplicity, we focus on the case of a duopoly, a market in which there are only two firms, as illustrated in Figure 15.3.

The duopolist's demand curve in this case is simply the market demand curve shifted over to the left by the amount of output the rival is committed to producing.[3] Given this demand curve, we can draw the marginal revenue curve, and the firm produces at the point where marginal revenue equals marginal cost.

Figure 15.3 COURNOT COMPETITION IN A DUOPOLY

For a duopolist in a situation of Cournot competition, the firm's demand curve and the market demand curve are parallel, separated by the amount that the rival firm is committed to producing. Given the demand curve, the duopolist maximizes profit in the usual way, by setting its marginal revenue equal to marginal cost.

[3]This demand curve is sometimes referred to as the residual demand curve.

Figure 15.4 THE RE-ACTION FUNC-TION

The reaction function in panel A shows how much Alcoa will choose to produce for every level of output by Reynolds. Note that Alcoa's output declines as Reynolds' increases. Panel B shows why this is so. An increase in the rival's output shifts the demand curve facing the firm to the left. Similarly, the marginal revenue curve shifts to the left, and as a result, output is reduced.

Normally, the equilibrium output with Cournot competition is less than with perfect competition but greater than with monopoly. Recall a firm sets marginal revenue equal to marginal cost. With perfect competition, marginal revenue is just price. With a monopoly, marginal revenue is lower than price. It is price minus what the firm loses on its earlier sales; that is, the reduction in price from producing one more unit. This is also the case with Cournot competition. Thus, output is lower than it is with perfect competition. But if there are two identical firms, each is producing only half the total output. Hence, what it loses in profits on earlier sales is smaller than under monopoly. Part of the lost revenue from lower prices is borne by the rival firm, which, under the Cournot assumption is expected to maintain its output. Marginal revenue is closer to price. So, because at any level of output the marginal revenue is higher with Cournot competition than with monopoly, equilibrium output is also higher.

To describe the market equilibrium, we need to see how the firms interact. The central tool in this analysis is the **reaction function,** which specifies the level of output of each firm given the level of output of the other firm. It shows, in other words, the reaction of one firm to the actions of the other. Consider the aluminum industry in the period after World War II; the two largest firms were Alcoa and Reynolds. The reaction function for Alcoa is plotted in Figure 15.4A. It is downward sloping.

To see why this is so, we need to recall how each Cournot oligopolist decides how much to produce. It sets marginal revenue equal to marginal cost, as in panel B. If Reynolds increases production, the demand facing Alcoa at any given price is reduced. Equivalently, if Alcoa wants to sell the same amount as before, it must lower its price. The figure shows the new demand and marginal revenue curves; they are to the left of the corresponding curves when Reynolds produced less. Accordingly, the optimal

Figure 15.5 MARKET EQUILIBRIUM WITH COURNOT COMPETITION

Equilibrium will be at the intersection of the two reaction functions, where each firm is maximizing its profits given its belief that the output of the other firm is fixed. At that point, there is no pressure for either firm to change output.

level of output is lower: as Reynolds increases production, Alcoa decreases production.

We can apply the same analysis to Reynolds, in Figure 15.5. The reaction curve shows Reynolds' level of output along the horizontal axis, given Alcoa's output along the vertical axis. The market equilibrium is the intersection of the reaction functions, point E. This point depicts the equilibrium output of Alcoa given the output of Reynolds, and it depicts the output of Reynolds given the output of Alcoa. The intersection of the reaction functions is an equilibrium because, given each firm's beliefs about the behavior of its rival, neither firm wishes to change what it does. There are, in short, no pressures to change. Each firm is maximizing its profits, given its belief that the rival is committed to producing its current level of output. The equilibrium price is given by the market demand curve for aluminum at a quantity equal to the sum of Alcoa's and Reynolds' output.

BERTRAND COMPETITION

Figure 15.6 uses reaction functions to describe the market equilibrium of a Bertrand duopoly. A Bertrand duopolist assumes that its rival's price is fixed. This duopoly consists of two mattress companies, Supersleeper and Heavenlyrest, which produce imperfect substitutes. The reaction function in this case gives the price charged by one firm, given the price charged by its rival. As Supersleeper increases its price, Heavenlyrest finds it optimal to increase its own price. That is why the reaction function is positively sloped. The equilibrium is at E.

With price-setting (Bertrand) competition, firms believe that they face more elastic demand curves than they do with quantity-setting (Cournot) competition. This can easily be seen when we consider the extreme case where the two goods produced by two different firms are perfect substi-

Figure 15.6 MARKET EQUILIBRIUM WITH BERTRAND COMPETITION

Equilibrium will be at the intersection of the two reaction functions, where each firm is maximizing its profits given its belief that the price of the other firm is fixed. As one firm increases its price, the profit-maximizing price of its rival increases, so the reaction functions are positively sloped.

tutes. Then if one firm charges slightly less than its rival, it garners for itself the entire market; if it charges slightly more, it loses all of its sales. Each firm faces a horizontal demand curve. Thus, even when there are only two firms, if each believes the other has fixed its price and will not change the price in response to changes in prices it charges, and if the two firms produce *perfect* substitutes, the market outcome is competitive.

We can see this process of competition as follows. Assume both firms have constant marginal and average costs of production. Since each company believes its rival will not budge its price so long as price exceeds marginal costs, each one will find that it pays it to shave its price by a small amount. By doing so, it steals the whole market. But the rival firm, thinking the same way, then undercuts still further. The process continues until the price is bid down to the point where there are zero profits. It does not pay to cut prices any further.

In general, the products produced by two duopolists are not perfect substitutes but differ somewhat, so that each firm faces a downward-sloping demand curve. In equilibrium, price exceeds marginal costs. Output is less than it would be with perfect competition, but more than it would be with Cournot competition.

16

GOVERNMENT POLICIES TOWARD COMPETITION

n the minds of most Americans, monopolies are not a good thing. They smell of income inequities and undemocratic concentrations of political power. To economists, however, the concern is economic efficiency. Motivated by both political and economic concerns, government has taken an active role in promoting competition and in limiting the abuses of market power. In this chapter, we review the economic effects of limited competition and look at government policies to reduce its negative effects.

1. Why is government concerned with monopolies and imperfect competition? In what sense do markets with monopolies and imperfect competition result in inefficiency?

2. How have different governments attempted to address the problem posed by a natural monopoly?

3. How have governments used antitrust policies to break up monopolies, to impede the ability of any single firm to attain a dominant position in a market, and to outlaw practices designed to restrict competition?

THE DRAWBACKS OF MONOPOLIES AND LIMITED COMPETITION

Four major sources of economic inefficiency result from monopolies and other imperfectly competitive industries: restricted output, managerial slack, insufficient attention to research and development, and rent-seeking behavior. The problems can be seen most simply in the context of monopolies (the focus here), but they also arise in imperfectly competitive markets.

RESTRICTED OUTPUT

Monopolists, like competitive firms, are in business to make profits by producing the kinds of goods and services customers want. But monopolists can make profits in ways not available to competitive firms. One way is to drive up the price of a good by restricting output, as discussed in Chapter 14. They can, to use the popular term, gouge their customers. Consumers, by *choosing* to buy the monopolist's good, are revealing that they are better off than they would be without the product. But they are paying more than they would if the industry were competitive.

A monopolist who sets marginal revenue equal to marginal cost produces at a lower level of output than a corresponding competitive industry—an industry with the same demand curve and costs but in which there are many producers rather than one—where price equals marginal cost. Figure 16.1 shows that the monopoly output, Q_m, is much smaller than the competitive output, Q_c, where the price under competition, p_c, equals marginal cost. The price under monopoly, p_m, is much higher than p_c.

The price of a good, by definition, measures how much an individual is willing to pay for an extra unit of a good. It measures, in other words, the marginal benefit of the good to the purchaser. With perfect competition, price

Figure 16.1 WHY MONOPOLY OUTPUT IS INEFFICIENT

With perfect competition price is set equal to marginal cost, with output at quantity Q_c and price p_c. A monopolist will set marginal revenue equal to marginal cost, and produce at quantity Q_m and price p_m, where the market price exceeds marginal cost.

equals marginal cost, so that in equilibrium the marginal benefit of an extra unit of a good to the individual (the price) is just equal to the marginal cost to the firm of producing it. At the monopolist's lower level of output, the marginal benefit of producing an extra unit—the price individuals are willing to pay for an extra unit—exceeds marginal cost.

By comparing the monopolist's production decision to the collective output decisions of firms in a competitive market, we can estimate the value of the loss to society when there is a monopoly. To simplify the analysis, in Figure 16.2 marginal cost is assumed to be constant, the horizontal line at the competitive price p_c. The monopolist produces an output of Q_m, at the point where marginal revenue equals marginal cost, and finds that it can charge p_m, the price on the demand curve corresponding to the output Q_m.

Two kinds of loss result, both related to the concept of consumer surplus introduced in Chapter 8. There we learned that the downward-sloping demand curve implies a bounty to most consumers. At points left of the intersection of the price line and demand curve, people are willing to pay more for the good than they have to. With competition, the consumer surplus in Figure 16.2 is the entire shaded area between the demand curve and the line at p_c.

The monopolist cuts into this surplus. First, it charges a higher price, p_m, than would be obtained in the competitive situation. This loss is measured by the rectangle *ABCD*, the extra price times the quantity actually produced and consumed. This loss to consumers is not a loss to society as a whole. It is a transfer of income as the higher price winds up as revenues for the monopoly. But second, it reduces the quantity produced. While production in a competitive market would be Q_c, with a monopoly it is the lower amount, Q_m. This second kind of loss is a complete loss to society, and is called the **dead-**

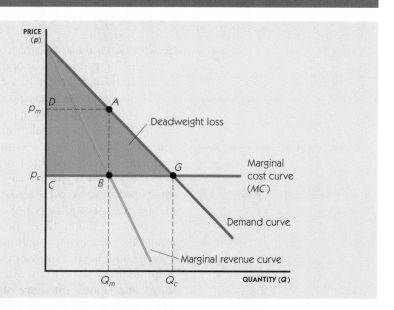

Figure 16.2 MEASURING THE SOCIAL COST OF MONOPOLY

The higher, monopoly price removes some of the consumer surplus. Part of this loss (the rectangle *ABCD*) is simply a transfer of income from consumers to the monopolist; the remainder (the triangle *ABG*) is known as the deadweight loss of monopoly.

weight loss of a monopoly. Consumers lose the surplus to the right of Q_m, denoted by *ABG*, with no resulting gain to the monopolist.

Some economists, such as Arnold Harberger of UCLA, have argued that these costs of monopoly are relatively small, amounting to perhaps 3 percent of the monopolist's output value. Others believe the losses from restricting output are higher. Whichever argument is right, output restriction is only one source of the inefficiencies monopolies introduce into the economy.

MANAGERIAL SLACK

Chapter 11 argued that any company wants to minimize the cost of producing whatever level of output it chooses to produce. But in practice, companies already making a lot of money without much competition often lack the incentive to hold costs as low as possible. The lack of efficiency when firms are insulated from the pressures of competition is referred to as **managerial slack.**

In the absence of competition, it can be difficult to tell whether managers are being efficient. How much, for instance, should it cost for AT&T to put a call through from New York to Chicago? In the days when AT&T had a monopoly on long-distance telephone service, it might have claimed that its costs were as low as possible. However, not even trained engineers could really tell whether this was true. When competition developed for intercity telephone calls, shareholders in AT&T could compare its costs with those of Sprint, MCI, and other competitors, and competition provided each company with an incentive to be as efficient as possible.

REDUCED RESEARCH AND DEVELOPMENT

Competition motivates firms to develop new products and less expensive ways of producing goods. A monopoly, by contrast, may be willing to let the profits roll in, without aggressively encouraging technological progress.

Not all monopolists stand pat, of course. Bell Labs, the research division of AT&T, was a fountain of important innovations throughout the period during which AT&T was a virtual monopolist in telephone service. The laser and the transistor are but two of its innovations. But AT&T was also in a unique position. The prices it charged were set by government regulators, and those prices were set to encourage the expenditure of money on research. From this perspective, AT&T's research contribution was as much a consequence of government regulatory policy as of anything else.

In contrast to Bell Labs, the American automobile and steel industries are often blamed for falling behind foreign competition because of their technological complacence. By the end of World War II, these industries had attained a dominant position in the world. After enjoying high profits for many years, they lost a significant share of the market to foreign firms in the 1970s and 1980s. Foreign automobile and steel firms, for example, were able to undersell their U.S. counterparts during the 1980s, not only because they paid lower wages but also because their technological advances had made production processes more efficient.

RENT SEEKING

The final source of economic inefficiency under monopoly is the temptation for monopolists to expend resources in economically unproductive ways. A major example is devoting resources to obtaining or maintaining their monopoly position by deterring entry. Since the profits a monopolist receives are called monopoly rents, the attempt to acquire or maintain already existing rents by acquiring or maintaining a monopoly position in some industry is referred to as **rent seeking.**

Sometimes a firm's monopoly position is at least partly the result of government protection. Many less-developed countries grant a company within their country a monopoly to produce a good, and they bar imports of that good from abroad. In these circumstances, firms will give money to lobbyists and politicians to maintain regulations that restrict competition so that they can keep their profits high. Such activities are socially wasteful. Real resources (including labor time) are used to win favorable rules, not to produce goods and services. There is thus legitimate concern that the willingness of governments to restrict competition will encourage firms to spend money on rent-seeking activities rather than on making a better product.

How much would a firm be willing to spend to gain and hold a monopoly position? The firm would be willing to spend up to the amount it would receive as monopoly profits. The waste from this rent-seeking activity can be much larger than the loss from the reduced output.

FURTHER DRAWBACKS OF LIMITED COMPETITION

We saw in Chapters 14 and 15 that markets in which a few firms dominated were more prevalent than monopolies. Relative to monopolies, some of the inefficiencies discussed above are smaller under limited competition. Output is lower than under perfect competition, but higher than under monopoly, for example. And competition to produce new products (research and development) is often intense, as we shall see in the next chapter. But other inefficiencies are worse in markets with limited competition than in monopoly markets. Firms under imperfect competition, for example, expend major resources on practices designed to deter entry, to reduce the force of competition, and to raise prices. Such expenditures may increase profits but they waste resources and make consumers worse off. Under imperfect competition firms may, for instance, maintain excess capacity to deter entry. A firm may gain a competitive advantage over its rival, not by lowering its own costs but by raising the rival's—for instance, by depriving it the use of existing distribution facilities. A firm may also spend money on uninformative (but persuasive) advertising.

POLICIES TOWARD NATURAL MONOPOLIES

If imperfect competition is as disadvantageous as the previous analysis has suggested, why not simply require that competition be perfect? To answer this question, we need to recall the reasons, discussed in Chapter 14, why competition is imperfect.

One reason is government-granted patents. Monopoly profits provide the return to inventors and innovators that is necessary to stimulate activities vital to a capitalist economy. We will discuss these issues more extensively in Chapter 17.

A second reason is that the cost of production may be lower if there is a single firm in the industry. This is the case with natural monopoly. In the case depicted in Figure 16.3, average costs are declining throughout the relevant levels of output, though marginal costs are constant. This is a case where there are very large fixed (overhead) costs. Natural monopolies present a difficult policy problem. Like any other firm, a natural monopolist will produce at the level where marginal revenue equals marginal cost, at Q_m in Figure 16.3. At this level, it will charge a price of p_m, which is higher than the marginal cost at that point. Thus, it will produce less and charge more than it would if price were equal to marginal cost, as would be the case with perfect competition (the output level Q_c and the price p_c in the figure).

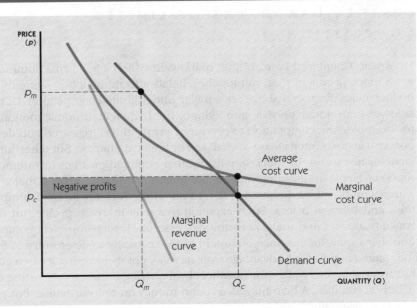

Figure 16.3 A PROBLEM WITH REGULATING NATURAL MONOPOLY

A natural monopoly will set marginal revenue equal to marginal cost, and produce at quantity Q_m and price p_m. In perfect competition, price would be equal to marginal cost, at Q_c and p_c. However, the perfectly competitive outcome is not possible in this case, since it would force the natural monopoly to produce at below its average cost, and thus to be making losses.

But in the case of natural monopoly, the very nature of the decreasing cost technology precludes perfect competition. Indeed, consider what would happen if price were set equal to marginal cost. With a natural monopoly, average costs are declining, and marginal costs are below average costs. Hence, if price were equal to marginal cost, it would be less than average costs, and the firm would be losing money. Profits would be negative, as shown by the shaded area in the figure. If the government wanted a natural monopoly to produce at the point where marginal cost equaled price, it would have to subsidize the company to offset these losses. Taxes would have to be raised to generate the money for the subsidies, which imposes other economic costs. Moreover, the government would likely have a difficult time ascertaining the magnitude of the subsidy actually required. Managers and workers in such a firm have a way of exaggerating their estimates of the high wages and other costs they "need" to produce the required output.

Following are three different solutions government has found to the problem of natural monopolies.

PUBLIC OWNERSHIP

In many foreign countries, government simply owns natural monopolies, such as electric power, gas, and water. There are problems with public ownership, however. Governments often are not particularly efficient as producers. Managers often lack adequate incentives to cut costs and modernize vigorously, particularly given the fact that government is frequently willing to sub-sidize the industry when it loses money. In addition, public ownership brings with it a number of political pressures. Political pressure may affect where public utilities, for example, locate their plants—politicians like to see jobs created in their home districts—and whether they prune their labor force to increase efficiency. Publicly run firms may also be under pressure to provide some services at prices below marginal cost, and make up the deficit from revenues from other services, a practice referred to as **cross subsidization.** Thus, business customers of utilities are sometimes charged more, relative to the costs of serving them, than are households. There is in effect a hidden tax and a hidden subsidy; businesses are taxed to subsidize households. The same phenomenon can be seen in our most important public monopoly, the U.S. postal service. It charges the same price for delivering mail to small rural communities as it does to major cities, in spite of the large differences in costs. Small communities have their mail services subsidized by larger ones.

How much less efficient the government is as a producer than the private sector is difficult to determine. Efficiency comparisons between government-run telephone companies in Europe and America's private firms provided much of the motivation for the **privatization** movement—the movement to convert government enterprises into private firms. Britain sold its telephone services and some other utilities, Japan its telephones and railroads, France its banks and many other enterprises. Not all publicly run enterprises are less efficient than their private counterparts, however. For example, Canada has two major rail lines, one operated by the government and one private, which differ little in the efficiency with which they are run. This may be because competition between the two forces the government railroad to be as efficient as the private. Many of the publicly owned enterprises in France seem to run as efficiently as private firms. This may be because of the high prestige af-forded to those who work in the French civil service, which allows them to re-cruit from among the most talented people in their country. There may also be less difference between government enterprises and large corporations—particularly when both are subjected to some market pressure and competi-tion—than popular conceptions of inefficient government would suggest.

REGULATION

Some countries leave the natural monopolies in the private sector but regu-late them. This is generally the U.S. practice. Local utilities, for instance, re-main private, but their rates are regulated by the states. Federal agencies reg-ulate interstate telephone services and the prices that can be charged for interstate transport of natural gas.

The aim of regulation is to keep the price as low as possible, commensurate with the monopolist's need to obtain an adequate return on its investment. In other words, they try to keep price equal to average costs—where average costs include a "normal return" on what the firm's owners have invested in the firm. If the regulators are successful, the natural monopoly will earn no

Everyday 66 thousand planes fly across the country. With planes crisscrossing each other constantly in the sky, why are there not more collisions? The reason is the air traffic control system, currently run by the Federal Aviation Administration.

The system has not been kept up to date, however, because of budget pressure. Though it was one of the first government agencies to use computers on a large scale, many of its original outdated computers are still in use. The failure to make long-run investments, combined with government restrictions on procurement and personnel, have increased the cost of running the air traffic control system, and throw into question its capacity to meet the needs of the future.

In April 1994 the Clinton administration sent to Congress a proposal to **corporatize** the air traffic control system. Corporatization represents a halfway house towards privatization. Under the corporatization plan, the air traffic control system would be run much like a private corporation. Its revenues would come from "user fees" charged to the airlines and airplanes that use the system, and a ticket tax. Like regular corporations it could borrow funds. It would have a board of directors, composed, among others, of representatives from the airlines and government. Just as the government exercises safety supervision of private airlines, the government would continue to exercise safety supervision over the air traffic control system. The main difference between it and a private corporation would be that this "public" corporation could not sell shares. And its mandate would not be to maximize profits, but to provide the most efficient air traffic control services—for instance, minimizing unnecessary delay—at the lowest costs.

The privatized air traffic control system would, of course, be a monopolist, but since its major customers—the airlines—would serve on its board of directors, the scope for abusing its monopoly power would be limited. Still, there is concern that it could choose pricing or other policies that favor one group of users over another. Concern about such potential abuses provided the motivation for corporatization, as opposed to privatization, keeping the system within the public sector, with a strong public role in policy determination.

The major airlines were enthusiastic about the proposal. But supporters of general aviation—individually owned airplanes and corporate jets—were monopoly profits. Such a regulated output and price are shown in Figure 16.4 as Q_r and p_r.

Two criticisms have been leveled against regulation as a solution to the natural monopoly problem. The first is that regulations often take an inefficient form. The sources of inefficiency are several. The intent is to set prices so that firms obtain a "fair" return on their capital. But to make the highest level of profit, firms respond by increasing their amount of capital as much as possible, which can lead to too much investment. In addition, the structure of prices may be set so that some groups, often businesses, may be charged extra-high prices to make it possible to subsidize other groups. This problem of cross subsidies is no less a problem for natural monopolies if they are privately owned and regulated than it is if they are owned and operated by the government. Further, firms' incentives to innovate are weakened if every time they lower costs, regulated prices are reduced commensurately. Recently regulators have recognized that unless they reward innovation, it will not happen. They have agreed to allow the utilities to retain much of the increased profits they obtain from improved efficiency, at least for a few years.

The second criticism is that the regulators lose track of the public interest. The theory of **regulatory capture** argues that regulators are pulled frequently

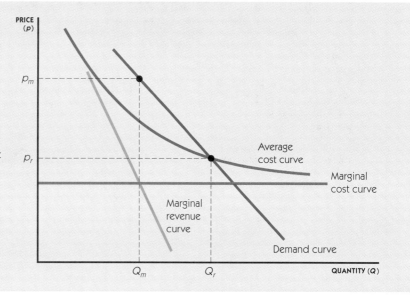

Figure 16.4 REGULATING NATURAL MONOPOLY

Government regulators will often seek to choose the point on the market demand curve where the firm provides the greatest quantity at the lowest price consistent with the firm's covering its costs. The point is the quantity Q_r and price p_r, where the demand curve intersects the average cost curve.

into the camps of those they regulate. This could happen through bribery and corruption, but the much likelier way is just that over time, employees of a regulated industry develop personal friendships with the regulators, who in turn come to rely on their expertise and judgment. Worse, regulatory agencies (of necessity) tend to hire from among those in the regulated industry. By the same token, regulators who demonstrate an "understanding" of the industry may be rewarded with good jobs in that industry after they leave government service.

ENCOURAGING COMPETITION

The final way government deals with the hard choices posed by natural monopolies is to encourage competition, even if imperfect. To understand this strategy, let us first review why competition may not be viable when average costs are declining over the relevant range of output.

If two firms divide the market between them, each faces higher average costs than if any one firm grabbed the whole market. As illustrated in Figure 16.5, Q_d denotes the output of each firm in the initial duopoly and AC_d its average costs. By undercutting its rival, a firm would be able to capture the entire market *and* have its average costs reduced. By the same token, a natural monopolist knows that it can charge a price above its average cost, AC_m, without worrying about entry. Rivals that might enter, trying to capture some of the profits, know that the natural monopolist has lower costs because of its larger scale of production, and so can always undercut them.

Even under these conditions, some economists have argued (as noted in

Figure 16.5 WHY COMPETITION MAY NOT BE VIABLE WITH DECREASING AVERAGE COSTS

If two firms share a market, each producing Q_d, one firm could double its output to Q_m, lower its cost, and undercut its rival. The larger firm has a cost advantage over the smaller competitor.

Chapter 15) that a monopolist would not in fact charge higher than average costs, because a rival could enter any time and grab the whole market. (The zero profit equilibrium is shown in the figure at output Q_r and price $AC_r = p_r$.) On this argument, all that is required to keep prices low is potential competition. Potential competition forces prices down to p_r, where the demand curve intersects the average cost curve.

Most economists are not so sanguine about the effectiveness of potential, as opposed to actual, competition. As we saw in Chapter 15, potential competition has not been able to keep airline prices down in those markets in which actual competition is limited to one or two carriers.

In the late 1970s and 1980s, as many governments became convinced that competition, however imperfect, might be better than regulation, and there began a process of deregulation. Deregulation focused on industries such as airlines, railroads, and trucking, where competition had a chance—there were, at most, limited increasing returns to scale. Government also sought to distinguish parts of an industry where competition might work from parts where competition was unlikely to be effective. In the telephone industry, for example, competition among several carriers was strong for long-distance telephone service, and there were few economies of scale in the production of telephone equipment. Accordingly, regulation of these parts of the industry was reduced or eliminated.

The virtues of competition have been borne out for the most part. Trucking—where the arguments for government regulation seemed most suspect—was perhaps the most unambiguous success story, with prices falling significantly. Railroads appear more financially sound than they did under regulation. But coal producers, who rely on railroads to ship their coal, complain that railroads have used their monopoly power to charge them much higher tariffs.

Airline deregulation has become more controversial in recent years. After its initial success—with new firms, lower fares, and more extensive routings—a rash of bankruptcies has reduced the number of airlines. Many airports, including those at St. Louis, Atlanta, and Denver, are dominated by one or two carriers, and these communities often face extremely high fares. A pattern of discriminatory pricing has developed, with businessmen who cannot make reservations weeks in advance paying four or more times the fare for the same seat as a vacationer.

APPROACHES TO NATURAL MONOPOLY

Public ownership
Regulation
Encouraging competition

CLOSE-UP: THE BREAKUP OF AT&T

When AT&T was broken up and the telephone industry partially deregulated in 1984, the general tone of discussion was resigned cynicism. The federal government had sought out one of the few things in life that worked—phone service—and decided to muck it up. AT&T had provided local and long-distance service to essentially everyone. After deregulation, a regional phone company (sometimes called a "Baby Bell") provided local phone service as a regulated monopoly, while the long-distance market was opened up to competition between AT&T, MCI, Sprint, and others. From the public reaction, you would have thought it was the end of modern communication. People complained about how confusing it was to receive two phone bills, one for local service and one for long-distance, and how phone service declined.

Well, fair is fair. The results are now coming in on how phone deregulation has worked, and they are reasonably positive. It is time to give the deregulation decision a little credit.

The technological story is clear. In the five years following deregulation, the cost of leasing a phone fell by half. New phone services like call waiting, phone mail, three-way calling, automatic redialing, and call forwarding have become popular. Of course, many of these technological changes would have happened over time, with or without phone deregulation. But the increased competitive pressure helped speed them up.

The price story, however, is a little more ambiguous. The price of long-distance service fell as much as 40 percent in these five years. However, local phone bills increased substantially; not enough to absorb all of that 40 percent, but enough to absorb much of it. Much of this change had been predicted by economists. Before deregulation, AT&T charged long-distance callers more heavily in order to subsidize local phone service. With deregulation, both local and long-distance service are now closer to paying their own way. Overall phone service (combining local and long-distance) was slowly getting cheaper before deregulation; it has continued to gradually fall in price.

Clearly, phone deregulation has had its benefits. Just as clearly, the main benefits have gone to those who make the most use of the new phone services and who use long-distance heavily. In 1996 Congress passed a new regulatory program for the telecommunications industry.

Deregulation has not yet extended to natural monopolies like water. But in the case of electricity a process for introducing some deregulation has begun. Some competition may be viable in electric power generation, which in general is not a natural monopoly, necessitating less government regulation. On the other hand, the transmission of electricity will continue to be a natural monopoly subject to regulation.

ANTITRUST POLICIES

Only some of the failures of competition arise from natural monopolies. Other imperfections, as we have seen, are the result of sharp business practices to develop market power by deterring entry or promoting collusion. When encouraging competition doesn't work, government sometimes resorts to enforcing competition through **antitrust policy.**

As we will see, these policies have often been controversial. Consumer groups and injured businesses tend to support them, arguing that, without them, firms would focus more on competition-reducing strategies than on efficiently producing products that customers like. Many businesses, however, claim that such policies interfere with economic efficiency. For instance, even if the most efficient way to distribute its products is through exclusive territories for distributors, the firm might worry that such a contract might be illegal under **antitrust law,** the body of law designed to restrict anticompetitive practices. Government antitrust efforts have followed the ebb and flow of concern about competition versus concern about the efficiency costs of antitrust restrictions.

The U.S. government has been officially concerned about the negative consequences of imperfect competition since the late nineteenth century. Table 16.1 lists the major landmarks of antitrust policy. These take the form of legislation and relevant judicial decisions. They fall into two categories: (1) limiting market domination, and (2) curbing restrictive practices.

LIMITING MARKET DOMINATION

In this section, we look at how government tries to limit economic power. In the decades following the Civil War, entrepreneurs in several industries attempted to form **trusts.** These were organizations that controlled a market. One individual has a controlling interest in a firm, which in turn had a controlling interest in all the other firms in the industry. By adding more layers—firms that controlled firms that controlled firms, and so on—a relatively small ownership stake could be leveraged into enormous economic power.

A controlling interest need not be a majority interest when the shares of a company are widely held. An individual or group of individuals owning only 10 or 20 percent of the shares can frequently exercise control, since the rest of the shareholders will either split their votes or be apathetic about the outcome. Among the most famous of the nineteenth-century trusts was the oil industry trust, with Rockefeller and his partners eventually controlling 90 percent of oil sold in America between 1870 and 1899. In the early 1900s, Andrew Carnegie and J. P. Morgan merged many smaller steel companies to form U.S. Steel, which in its heyday sold 65 percent of all American steel.

Concern about these robber barons led to passage of the Sherman Antitrust Act of 1890, which outlaws "every contract, combination in the form

Table 16.1 MAJOR ANTITRUST LEGISLATION AND LANDMARK CASES

Sherman Antitrust Act, 1890	Made acts in restraint of trade illegal.
Standard Oil and American Tobacco Cases, 1911	Broke up both firms (each of which accounted for more than 90% of their industry) into smaller companies.
Clayton Act, 1914	Outlawed unfair trade practices. Restricted mergers that would substantially reduce competition.
Establishment of the Federal Trade Commission, 1914	The Federal Trade Commission was established to investigate unfair practices and issue orders to "cease and desist."
Robinson-Patman Act, 1936	Strengthened provisions of the Clayton Act, outlawing price discrimination.
Alcoa Case, 1945	Alcoa, controlling 90% of the aluminum market, was found to be in violation of the Sherman Act.
Tobacco Case, 1946	The tobacco industry, a concentrated oligopoly, was found guilty of violation of the Sherman Act on the basis of tacit collusion.
Celler-Kefauver Act, 1950	Placed further restrictions on mergers that would reduce competition.
Du Pont Cellophane Case, 1956	Broadened the definition of market. Ruled that a 20% market share was insufficient to establish market power.

of a trust or otherwise, or conspiracy in restraint of trade or commerce." Further, "every person who shall monopolize, or attempt to monopolize, or combine or conspire with any other person or persons, to monopolize any part of the trade or commerce among the several States, or with foreign nations, shall be deemed guilty of a misdemeanor." (A 1974 amendment made violations felonies.) Two important decisions based on the Sherman Act were the breakups of Standard Oil and American Tobacco in 1911, each of which had dominated their respective industries.

The Sherman Act was supplemented by the Clayton Act in 1914, which forbade any firm to acquire shares of a competing firm when that purchase would substantially reduce competition. The act also outlawed interlocking directorates (in which the same individuals serve as directors of several firms) among firms that were supposedly in competition. These antimerger provisions were further strengthened in 1950 by the Celler-Kefauver Antimerger Act.

The government does not care about absolute size itself. In the 1960s, huge firms called conglomerates were formed, which brought together such disparate enterprises as a steel company, an oil company, and a company making films. For example, United Airlines bought Hertz rental cars and Westin

Hotels. But while large, these conglomerates generally did not have a dominant position in any one market, and thus the antitrust laws were not concerned with them. The early antitrust laws were particularly concerned with **horizontal mergers,** with competition within a market. These are distinguished from **vertical mergers,** in which a firm buys a supplier or a distributor, amalgamating the various stages in the production process within a firm. Thus, Ford made its own steel, and General Motors bought out Fisher Body (the maker of GM's car bodies), as well as many of the specialized firms that produced batteries, spark plugs, and other components.

Under current court interpretations, market power *per se* (by itself) is also not the primary concern. To be convicted of an antitrust violation, one must show that the firm acquired its market position by anticompetitive practices or that it used its market power to engage in anticompetitive practices.

DEFINING MARKETS

The question of whether a firm dominates a market is usually phrased, "What is its size relative to the market?" The debate thus centers on what is the relevant market. We have learned that the extent to which a firm's demand curve is downward sloping, so it can raise prices without losing all its customers— its market power—is related to both the number of firms in the industry and the extent of product differentiation. The problem of defining markets for the purposes of antitrust enforcement is related to both factors.

Market Bounds During the last quarter century, international trade has become ever more important to the United States and the world economy. This change has affected all aspects of economic analysis, including the extent of competition in many markets. Today, imports exceed 9 percent of national output—three times the level in the 1950s and 1960s.

Thus while the degree of concentration among domestic producers of automobiles has increased—three firms are responsible for more than 90 percent of all U.S. auto production—the industry has become more competitive in the 1980s and 1990s, as foreign competition has increased and as foreign companies such as Toyota and Honda have established plants in the United States. It used to be that American firms could increase their price without worrying about their consumers switching to Japanese or European imports, but no longer. Today, the degree of competition in a market must be assessed from a global viewpoint, rather than looking simply at how many firms produce a good in the United States.

Product Differentiation While all firms that produce the same good and sell in the same location are clearly in the same market, when the goods produced by different firms are imperfect substitutes, the definitional problem is more ambiguous.

What is the market for beer? Those in the industry might claim that premium beers and discount beers are really two different markets, with relatively few customers crossing over from one to the other. In the early 1950s,

Du Pont's cellophane had a virtual monopoly on the market for clear wrapping paper. In 1956, the company managed to fight off charges of monopoly by claiming that this market was part of a larger one for "wrapping materials." It claimed that brown paper was a good, though not perfect, substitute for cellophane, and in this broader market, Du Pont did not have a particularly large share (roughly 18 percent).

Legal Criteria   Today the courts look at two criteria for defining a market and market power. First, they consider the extent to which the change in prices for one product affects the demand for another. If an increase in the price of aluminum has a large positive effect on the demand for steel, then steel and aluminum may be considered to be in the same market—the market for metals. Second, if a firm can raise its price, say by 10 percent, and lose only a relatively small fraction of its sales, then it is "large"—that is, it has market power. (In a perfectly competitive market, a firm that raised its price by 10 percent would lose all its customers, so this is a workable approach to measuring the degree of competitiveness in the market.)

Before one large company can acquire a competitor or merge with another, it must convince the government that the acquisition would not seriously interfere with competition. Thus, although Dr. Pepper made up only a small part of the soft drink market, the government was concerned that the proposed acquisition of Dr. Pepper by Coca-Cola would have a significantly adverse affect on competition in a market that was already highly concentrated.

CURBING RESTRICTIVE PRACTICES

In addition to promoting competition by limiting the extent of concentration within an industry, the government works to limit restrictive practices. The history here begins with the 1914 Federal Trade Commission Act. The first ten words of the act read: "Unfair methods of competition in commerce are hereby declared unlawful." President Wilson defined the purpose of the new commission to "plead the voiceless consumer's case." Since then, a number of laws have been passed by Congress to make these general statements more specific.

Many of the restrictive practices targeted by the government involve the relations between a firm and its distributors and suppliers. Such practices include tying, exclusive dealing, and price discrimination. We have already encountered all three. Tying requires a buyer to purchase additional items when she buys a product. Exclusive dealing is when a producer says to a firm that wants to sell its product, "If you want to sell my product, you cannot sell that of my rival." Price discrimination entails charging different customers different prices, when those price differences are not related to the costs of serving those customers. The Robinson-Patman Act of 1936 strengthened the provisions outlawing price discrimination, making it easier to convict firms engaged in the practice. Other practices discussed in Chapters 14 and 15 designed to deter entry or promote collusion are illegal as well.

The precise definition of an illegal restrictive practice has changed over time with varying court interpretations of the antitrust laws. Some practices are illegal *per se*—firms conspiring together to fix prices, for example. In 1961, General Electric, Westinghouse, and other producers of electrical equipment were found guilty of this practice. They paid millions of dollars in fines, and some of their officials went to prison. Today, however, for most practices a "rule of reason" prevails. Under a rule of reason, the practice is acceptable if it can be shown to be reasonable business practice, designed to promote economic efficiency. The efficiency gains are balanced against the higher prices resulting from the reduced competition.

Thus, Budweiser beer delivers its product through distributors. In any area, there is only one distributor, and the distributors are not allowed to compete against one another. The New York attorney general has argued that this system, by restricting competition, raises prices. Anheuser-Busch has replied that the system of exclusive territories enhances the efficiency with which beer is delivered and is necessary to ensure that customers receive fresh beer. They have maintained that their distribution system satisfies the rule of reason, and thus far their view has been upheld by the courts.

ENFORCING THE ANTITRUST LAWS

Today antitrust laws are on the books at both state and federal levels, and are enforced by both criminal and civil courts. The government takes action not only to break up existing monopolies but also to prevent firms from obtaining excessive market power.

The Federal Trade Commission and the Antitrust Division of the Department of Justice are at the center of the government's efforts to promote competition. The FTC works like a law enforcement agency, investigating complaints it receives. It can provide advisory opinions on how an individual business should interpret the law, provide guidelines for entire industries, or even issue specific rules and regulations that businesses must follow. When necessary, the FTC enforces these decisions in court.

One interesting and controversial aspect of the antitrust laws is the use they make of *private* law enforcement. Any firm that believes it has been injured by the anticompetitive practices of another firm can sue, and if successful, can receive three times the dollar value of the damages and attorney fees incurred. The treble damage provision helps encourage private firms to call violations to the attention of the government. For example, MCI sued AT&T, claiming that the latter had used unfair trade practices to hurt MCI in its attempt to enter the long-distance telephone business. The jury estimated that MCI had, as a result of AT&T's activities, lost $600 million in profits, and ordered AT&T to pay triple that amount—$1.8 billion—in damages to MCI. The award was subsequently reduced on appeal to higher courts.

Two arguments favor private enforcement of antitrust laws. First, those who are injured by anticompetitive practices are in the best position to detect a violation of the law. Second, government may be lax in the enforcement of

Using Economics: Coke and Pepsi Play Merger Mania

Coca-Cola Company and PepsiCo, Inc., dominate the market for carbonated soft drinks. Early in 1986, each proposed to grow larger through acquisition. In January, PepsiCo proposed buying 7-Up, the fourth largest soft drink manufacturer, for $380 million. In February, Coca-Cola proposed buying Dr. Pepper, the third largest, for $470 million.

The mergers would have made the big even bigger. Coca-Cola and PepsiCo already held 39 percent and 28 percent of the market, respectively, while Dr. Pepper had 7 percent and 7-Up had 6 percent. The next largest firm in the market after 7-Up was R. J. Reynolds (known for Canada Dry and Sunkist), which held 5 percent of the soft drink market.

The Federal Trade Commission announced that it would oppose the mergers. To assess the impact on competition, the government often uses in such cases what is called the Herfindahl-Hirschman Index (HHI). The HHI is calculated by summing the squares of the market shares. If the industry consists of a single firm, then the HHI is $(100)^2 = 10,000$. If the industry consists of 1,000 firms, each with .1 percent of the market, then the HHI is $(.1)^2 \times 1,000 = 10$. Thus, higher values of the HHI indicates less competitive industries.

Merger guidelines adopted by the federal government in 1982 divided markets into three categories, with different policy recommendations.

Before the mergers, a somewhat simplified HHI for the soft drink industry was (assuming that the 15 percent of the market not accounted for by the big four was divided equally among 15 small producers)

Level of HHI	Policy recommendation
Less than 1,000, unconcentrated	Mergers allowed without government challenge
Between 1,000 and 1,800, moderately concentrated	Mergers challenged if they raise the industry HHI by more than 100 points
Above 1,800, concentrated	Mergers challenged if they raise the industry HHI by more than 50 points

$$\text{HHI} = 39^2 + 28^2 + 7^2 + 6^2 + 5^2 + 15\,(1)^2$$
$$= 2,430.$$

If we plug in the 34 percent share that PepsiCo would have after acquiring 7-Up, the PepsiCo–7-Up merger would raise the HHI to 2,766. The two proposed mergers together would raise the HHI to 3,312.

With the announced FTC opposition to the merger, PepsiCo immediately gave up on purchasing 7-Up. Coca-Cola pushed ahead with its plan to buy Dr. Pepper until a federal judge ruled in August 1986 that it was a "stark, unvarnished" attempt to eliminate competition that "totally [lacked] any apparent redeeming feature."

The court case did bring a secret to the surface, however. The trial disclosed certain Coca-Cola company memos written after PepsiCo's offer for 7-Up had been made. In the memos, Coca-Cola executives expressed fear that the FTC might allow the PepsiCo merger, despite the merger guidelines. By announcing plans to buy Dr. Pepper, Coca-Cola hoped that the FTC would step in and these laws because of the potential political influence of cartels and dominant firms.

On the other side of the argument are concerns about the rising costs of antitrust litigation—the number of private suits doubled between the 1960s and the 1970s. And many worry that businesses use the threat of an antitrust suit as a way of raising a rival's costs. Thus, Chrysler charged General Motors with an antitrust violation when GM proposed a joint venture with a Japanese firm, only to drop the action when it found a Japanese partner for its own joint venture. Also, whenever a firm is successful in winning customers from a rival, the rival may accuse the firm of unfair practices and bring suit. Thus, firms may be reluctant to lower their prices when their efficiency has increased for fear they will be accused of predatory pricing.

CURRENT ANTITRUST CONTROVERSIES

Exactly how and when antitrust laws should be enforced remains one of the most controversial subjects of economic policy. In recent years, controversy has focused on two major issues.

First, how stringent should the standards be for allowing mergers of competing firms? In 1982, the government adopted new guidelines for such mergers, which many critics thought to be too lax. Those who favored the more lax rules argued that in today's international markets, competition is almost always sufficiently keen to ensure low prices and economic efficiency. Any firm that tried to exercise monopoly power by charging too high a price or that was slack in keeping costs down would be faced with an onslaught of competition. At most, the firm could enjoy a monopoly position for only a short time. For example, Ricoh, Canon, and a host of other firms unseated Xerox's monopoly position in copiers, and Fuji is now challenging Kodak's dominant position in film. Moreover, these advocates argue, attempts to restrict size penalize the more successful firms and inhibit their ability to take advantage of economies of scale and scope. Since foreign governments do not put similar restrictions on their own firms, American companies find themselves at a disadvantage. Size is particularly important for financing large-scale research endeavors, necessary if America is to keep its competitive edge.

Critics of this view contend that international competition cannot be relied upon—though admittedly, markets are more competitive with than without international competition. Furthermore, they question the importance of the economies of scale and scope. Many of America's leading exporters are relatively small companies, such as Compaq Computer. And the enhanced competition among firms in the United States not only makes consumers better off, through lower prices, but also sharpens the edge of businesses, making the more successful firms better able to compete not only at home but also abroad.

The second major controversial issue concerns what governmental policies should be toward restrictive practices—in particular, the contractual arrangements between firms and their suppliers and customers, such as exclusive dealing, tying, and exclusive territories—the so-called vertical restrictions discussed in Chapter 15. Those who, like Richard Posner (formerly of the University of Chicago, now a federal judge), believe that by and large competition is effective think there should be a presumption that such practices are legal. Others, like Steven Salop of Georgetown Law School, believe that frequently, while there is competition, it is limited. A review of the alleged "efficiency" gains of such practices suggests to these observers that the typical motive is to restrict competition further. If a change is needed from the current rule of reason, they argue, the presumption should be that these practices are restrictive. The burden would then be on any firm engaging in restrictive practices to show that the efficiency gains outweigh the losses from reduced competition.

ANTITRUST POLICIES

OBJECTIVE: ENSURE COMPETITIVE MARKETPLACE

Limit market domination

Curb restrictive practices

PROBLEMS

Defining markets

Practices may *both* reduce competition *and* enhance efficiency

Per se: practice is illegal (price fixing)

Rule of reason: balance anticompetitive and efficiency effects

ENFORCEMENT

Criminal

Civil–private law enforcement, treble damages

CURRENT CONTROVERSIES

Stringency of standards for allowing mergers

Policies toward vertical restraints

REVIEW AND PRACTICE

SUMMARY

1. Economists have identified four major problems resulting from monopolies and imperfect competition: restricted output; managerial slack; lack of incentives for technological progress; and wasteful rent-seeking expenditures.

2. Since for a natural monopoly average costs are declining over the range of market demand, a large firm can undercut its rivals. And since marginal cost for a natural monopoly lies below average cost, an attempt by regulators to require it to set price equal to marginal cost (as in the case of perfect competition) will force the firm to make losses.

3. Taking ownership of a natural monopoly allows the government to set price and quantity directly. But it also subjects an industry to political pressures and the potential inefficiencies of government operation.

4. In the United States, natural monopolies are regulated. Government regulators seek to keep prices as low and quantity as high as is consistent with the natural monopolist covering its costs. However, regulators are under political pressure to provide cross subsidies and are prone to being "captured" by the industry they are regulating.

5. In some cases, competition may be as effective as public ownership or government regulation at keeping prices low.

6. Antitrust policy is concerned with promoting competition, both by making it more difficult for any firm to dominate a market and by restricting practices that interfere with competition.

7. Under the "rule of reason," companies may seek to defend themselves from accusations of anticompetitive behavior by claiming that the behavior also leads to greater efficiency. In such cases, courts must often decide whether the potential efficiency benefits of restrictive practices outweighs their potential anticompetitive effects.

KEY TERMS

managerial slack	cross subsidization	vertical mergers
rent seeking	horizontal mergers	

REVIEW QUESTIONS

1. What does it mean when an economist says that monopoly output is "too little" or a monopoly price is "too high"? By what standard? Compared with what?

2. Why might a monopoly lack incentives to hold costs as low as possible?

3. Why might a monopoly lack incentives to pursue research and development opportunities aggressively?

4. What might an economist regard as a socially wasteful way of spending monopoly profits?

5. Explain why the marginal cost curve of a natural monopoly lies below its average cost curve. What are the consequences of this?

6. If government regulators of a natural monopoly set price equal to marginal cost, what problem will inevitably arise? How might government ownership or regulation address this problem? What are the problems of each?

7. What is the regulatory capture hypothesis?

8. Explain the difference between a horizontal and a vertical merger.

9. Explain how the government uses antitrust policies to encourage competition, by making it more difficult for a firm to dominate a market and by curbing restrictive practices. What are some of the problems in implementing antitrust policy and some of the current controversies surrounding it?

PROBLEMS

1. Before deregulation of the telephone industry in 1984, AT&T provided both local and long-distance telephone service. A number of firms argued that they could provide long-distance service between major cities more cheaply than AT&T, but AT&T argued against allowing firms to enter only the long-distance market. If those other firms (which had no technological advantage) could actually have offered long-distance service more cheaply, what does that imply about cross subsidies in AT&T's pricing of local and long-distance service? What would have happened if AT&T had been required to continue offering local service at the same price, but competition had been allowed in the long-distance market?

2. "The stories of $400 hammers and $1,000 toilet seats purchased by the Department of Defense prove that the private sector is more efficient than the public sector." Comment.

3. Explain the incentive problem involved if regulators assure that a natural monopoly will be able to cover its average costs.

4. Explain how some competition, even if not perfect, may be an improvement for consumers over an unregulated natural monopoly. Explain why such competition will not be as good for consumers as an extremely sophisticated regulator, and why it may be better than many real-world regulators.

5. Should greater efficiency be a defense against an accusation of an antitrust violation?

TECHNOLOGICAL
CHANGE

F or much of the twentieth century, the United States has led in discovering and applying new technologies. Alexander Graham Bell and the telephone, the Wright brothers and the airplane, Thomas Edison and a host of electric devices—all are familiar early success stories. This tradition of innovation and invention continued as American inventors came up with products like the transistor and the laser. U.S. companies such as IBM, Eastman Kodak, and Xerox grew to become household names mostly because of the new products they brought to the market. More recently, Intel, Microsoft, and Genentech have experienced rapid growth and financial success based on their innovations.

The great strength of the market economy has been its ability to increase productivity, raise living standards, and innovate. Yet, the basic competitive model upon which we focused in Part Two simply *assumed* the state of technology as given.

If we are to understand what determines the pace of innovation, we must go beyond the standard competitive model.

1. In what ways is the production of knowledge—including the knowledge of how to make new products and how to produce things more cheaply—different from the production of ordinary goods, like shoes and wheat?

2. Why is the patent system important in providing incentives to engage in research and development?

3. How may patents, as essential as they are for encouraging competition in research, at the same time reduce some aspects of competition?

4. How can government encourage technological progress?

First, industries in which technological change is important are almost necessarily imperfectly competitive. Second, the basic competitive model of Part Two assumes that individuals and firms receive all the benefits and pay all the costs of their actions. This assumption takes no account of the externalities produced by technological change. There is little doubt that we have all benefited from the multitude of inventions that have occurred in the last century. Just imagine what life would be like without the radio, television, cars, airplanes, washing machines, dishwashers—the list is endless. Alexander Graham Bell, Henry Ford, the Wright brothers were all rewarded for their inventions, some richly so. But the creation of these new products confers benefits beyond what consumers have to pay for them. Inventions possess certain characteristics of public goods and generate externalities.

This chapter shows why technological change is inevitably linked to imperfect competition. It then discusses the public good aspects of technological change and alternative ways to promote it.

LINKS BETWEEN TECHNOLOGICAL CHANGE AND IMPERFECT COMPETITION

In modern industrialized economies, much competition takes the form of trying to develop both new products and new ways of making existing products. Firms devote considerable resources to R & D—research (discovering new ideas, products, and processes) and development (perfecting, for instance, a new product to the point where it is brought to the market). In industries in which technological change and R & D is important, such as computers and drugs, firms strive to earn profits by introducing new and better (at least in the eyes of consumers) goods, or less costly methods of production. Only through such profits can the investment in R & D payoff.

Technological change and imperfect competition are inevitably linked for four major reasons. First, to make R & D expenditure pay, and therefore stimulate innovation, inventions are protected from competition by patents. Patents are specifically designed to limit competition. Second, industries where technological change is important typically have high fixed costs—costs that do not change as output increases. This implies decreasing average costs over a wide range of output, another characteristic that limits competition. Third, industries characterized by rapid technological change are also industries where the benefits of increasing experience in a new production technique can lead to rapidly decreasing costs. Finally, because banks are generally unwilling to lend funds to finance R & D, raising capital for new and small firms is difficult. All these make entry difficult, and reduce competition in the sense defined by the basic competitive model.

PATENTS

The U.S. Constitution, as noted in Part One, enables Congress to grant "for limited time to authors and inventors the exclusive right to their respective writing and discoveries." Economists refer to the output of this creative action as **intellectual property.** The "limited time" for inventors is currently seventeen years. During this period, other producers are precluded from producing the same good, or even making use of the invention in a product of their own, without the permission of the patent holder. A patent holder may allow others to use its patent or sell its product; in return the patent holder receives a payment called a royalty.

THE TRADE-OFF BETWEEN SHORT-RUN EFFICIENCY AND INNOVATION

The patent system grants the inventor a temporary monopoly, allowing her to appropriate some part of the returns on her inventive activity. In Chapter 16, we learned that, relative to a competitive market a monopoly produces a lower level of output that sells at a higher price. In spite of this, and in spite of the antitrust policies discussed there, why does government sanction these monopolies?

In Chapter 13, where we explained why competitive markets, with price equal to marginal cost, ensure economic efficiency, we assumed that the technology was given. We refer to the kind of economic efficiency that ignores concerns about innovation and invention as **static efficiency.**

But the overall efficiency of the economy requires balancing these short-run concerns with the long-run objectives of stimulating research and innovation. Innovation requires firms to reap a return on their investment, and that in turn requires some degree of monopoly power. An economy in which the balancing of short- and long-run concerns is appropriately done is said to be **dynamically efficient.**

A key provision of the patent law affecting the static efficiency versus the incentives for innovation necessary for dynamic efficiency is the **life of the patent.** If the life of a patent is short, then firms can appropriate the returns from their innovation for only a short time. There is less incentive to innovate than if the patent protection (and monopoly) lasted longer, but the economy has greater static efficiency. If the life of a patent is long, then there are large incentives to innovate, but the benefits of the innovation are limited. Consumers, in particular, must wait a long time before prices fall. The seventeen-year patent period is intended to strike a balance between the benefits to consumers and the return to investments in R & D.

AN EXAMPLE: THE SWEET MELON COMPANY

Figure 17.1 illustrates the effect of a patent owned by the Sweet Melon Company on a new, cheaper process for producing frozen watermelon juice. To make it simple, the marginal cost of production is constant in this example. Before the innovation, all producers face the same marginal cost of c_0. Sweet Melon's innovation reduces the marginal costs of production to c_1. Imagine that this industry is perfectly competitive before the innovation, so that price equals marginal cost, c_0. But now Sweet Melon is able to undercut its rivals. With patent protection, the firm sells the good for slightly less than p_0. Its rivals drop out of the market because at the new, lower price, they cannot break even. Sweet Melon now has the whole market. The company sells the quantity Q_1 at the price p_1, making a profit of AB on each sale. Total profits are shaded area $ABCD$ in the figure. The innovation pays off if the profits received exceed the cost of the research. (These profits may be thought of as "rents" associated with its superior technology.)

Figure 17.1 ECONOMIC EFFECT OF PATENTS

Here, an innovation has reduced the marginal cost of production from c_0 to c_1. Before the innovation, the equilibrium price is p_0, which equals c_0. However, an innovator with a patent will drop the price to p_1, just below p_0, and sell the quantity Q_1. Total profits are the shaded area $ABCD$. When the patent expires, competitors reenter the market, price falls to p_2, which equals c_1, and profits drop to zero.

What happens when the patent expires? Other firms enter the industry, using the less expensive technology. Competition forces the price down to the now lower marginal costs, c_1, and output expands to Q_2. The new equilibrium is at E. Consumers are clearly better off. Static economic efficiency is enhanced, because price is now equal to marginal cost. But Sweet Melon reaps no further return from its expenditures on research and development.

If no patent were available, competitors would immediately copy the new juice-making process, and the price would drop to c_1 as soon as the innovation became available. Sweet Melon would receive absolutely no returns. (In practice, of course, imitation takes time, during which the company would be able to obtain *some* returns from the innovation.) If the patent were made permanent, consumers would benefit only a small amount from the innovation, since other companies could not compete. Output would remain at Q_1, slightly greater than the original output, and the price would remain high.

BREADTH OF PATENT PROTECTION

How broad a patent's coverage should be is as important as its duration. If an inventor comes up with a product quite similar to, but still slightly different from, one that has already been patented, can this inventor also get a patent for his variant? Or does the original patent cover "minor" variants? Chapter 1 discussed the patent claim of George Baldwin Selden, who argued that his patent covered all self-propelled, gasoline-powered vehicles. He tried to force Henry Ford and the other pioneers of the automobile industry to pay royalties to him, but Ford successfully challenged the patent claim. Recently controversies over patents have hit genetic engineering and superconductivity. Does a firm that decodes a fraction of a gene and establishes a use for that information, for example, get a patent? If so, does the patent cover the fraction in question or the whole gene?

The original innovators have every incentive to claim broad patent coverage, affecting their own product and those that are in any way related. Later entrants argue for narrow coverage, so that they will be allowed to produce variants and applications without paying royalties. As usual in economics, there is a trade-off. Broad coverage ensures that the first inventor reaps more of the returns of her innovation. But excessively broad coverage inhibits follow-on innovation, as others see their returns to further developing the idea squeezed by the royalties they must pay to the original inventor.

TRADE SECRETS

If patents protect the profits of innovation, why do many firms not bother to seek patent protection for their new products and processes? A major reason is that a firm cannot get a patent without disclosing the details of the new product or process—information that may be extremely helpful to its rivals in furthering their own R & D programs.

To prevent such disclosure, companies sometimes prefer to keep their own innovations a **trade secret.** A trade secret is simply an innovation or knowledge of a production process that a firm does not disclose to others. The formula for Coca-Cola, for example, is not protected by a patent. It is a trade secret. Trade secrets play an important role in metallurgy, where new alloys are usually not patented. Trade secrets have one major disadvantage over patents. If a rival firm *independently* discovers the same new process, say for making an alloy, it can use the process without paying royalties, even though it was second on the scene.

Some of the returns to an invention come simply from being first in the market. Typically, the firm that first introduces a new product has a decided advantage over rivals, as it builds up customer loyalty and a reputation. Latecomers often have a hard time breaking in, even if there is no patent or trade secret protection.

R & D AS A FIXED COST

Patents and trade secrets are not the only reason that industries in which technological change is important are generally not perfectly competitive. A second explanation is that R & D expenditures are fixed costs. That is, the cost of inventing something does not change according to how many times the idea is used in production.[1] The size of fixed costs helps determine how competitive an industry is. The larger the fixed costs relative to the size of the market the more likely that there will be few firms and limited competition.

Because expenditures on research and development are fixed costs, industries with large R & D expenditures face declining average cost curves up to relatively high levels of output. We saw in Chapter 11 that firms typically have U-shaped average cost curves. The presence of fixed costs means that average costs initially decline as firms produce more, but for all the reasons discussed in Chapter 11, beyond some level of output average costs increase. When there are large fixed costs, large firms will have lower average costs than small firms and enjoy a competitive advantage. (See Figure 17.2.) Industries with large fixed costs thus tend to have relatively few firms and limited competition. It is not surprising, therefore, that the chemical industry—where R & D is tremendously important—is highly concentrated.

Increased size also provides firms with greater incentives to undertake research. Suppose a small firm produces 1 million pens a year. If it discovers a better production technology that reduces its costs by $1 per pen, it saves $1 million a year. A large firm that makes the same discovery and produces 10 million pens a year will save $10 million a year. Thus, large firms have more incentive to engage in research and development, and as they do, they grow more than their smaller rivals do.

But while a large firm's research and development department may help the firm win a competitive advantage, it may also create managerial problems. Bright innovators can feel stifled in the bureaucratic environment of a large corporation, and they may also feel that they are inadequately compensated for their research efforts. In the computer industry, for example, many capable people have left the larger firms to start up new companies of their own.

---

[1] R & D expenditures can themselves be varied. Differences in the expenditure level will affect when new products will be brought to market and whether a firm will beat its rivals in the competition for new products.

Figure 17.2 COSTS OF RE-SEARCH AND DEVEL-OPMENT

R & D costs are fixed costs—they do not vary with the scale of production. In industries that are R & D intensive, average costs will be declining over a wide range of outputs. Firms with low levels of output (Q_1) have higher average costs than those with higher output (Q_2).

Thus, size has both its advantages and disadvantages when it comes to innovation. Important inventions and innovations, such as nylon, transistors, and the laser have been produced by major corporations; on the other hand, small enterprises and individual inventors have produced Apple computers, Polaroid cameras, and Kodak film, all of which became major corporations as a result of their success. One objective of antitrust policies is to maintain an economic environment in which small, innovative firms can compete effectively against established giants.

LEARNING BY DOING

Some increases in productivity occur not as a result of explicit expenditures on R & D, but as a by-product of actual production. As firms gain experience from production, their costs fall. This kind of technological change is called **learning by doing.** This systematic relationship between cumulative production experience and costs—often called the **learning curve**—was first discovered in the aircraft industry, where as more planes of a given type were produced, the costs of production fell dramatically.

This is the third reason why technological change and imperfect competition go together—because the marginal cost falls as the scale of production (and the experience accumulated) increases. The first firm to enter an industry has a particular advantage over other firms. Even if some of what the first company has learned spills over into other firms, not all of it does. Because of the knowledge the first firm has gained, its costs will be below those of potential rivals, and thus it can always undercut them. Since potential entrants know this, they are reluctant to enter industries where learning by doing has a significant impact on costs. By the same token, companies realize that if they can find a product that provides significant benefits from learning by doing,

Obtaining a patent does not necessarily guarantee that the inventor will receive a return on her discovery. Others may "infringe" on her patent— that is, use the idea without paying for it—in which case the inventor will have to sue. Suits for patent infringement are common. In recent years, Apple Computer sued Microsoft and Polaroid sued Kodak, to name but two such cases. One of the most famous examples of an inventor who found it difficult to enforce his patents is Eli Whitney and the cotton gin.

Late in the eighteenth century, the textile mills of England and the northern American states were up and humming, but there seemed to be a perpetual shortage of cotton. The kind of cotton grown in the southern United States could have filled the need, but someone had to find an inexpensive way to separate the seeds from the cotton. Eli Whitney invented the cotton gin to perform that task. Whitney did what an inventor is supposed to do. He applied for a patent and received one in 1794. He found a partner to put up the money, and then started a business to make machines that would clean the seeds out of cotton. The cotton gin turned out to be a wonder, bringing prosperity to the American South. But Whitney received little of the benefit.

The problem was that Whitney's machine was both very effective and very simple. Cotton planters found it easy to copy the cotton gin and make a few minor changes. When Whitney sued in court for patent infringement, courts in cotton-growing states tended to find that his patent had not actually been infringed. Eventually, the states of South Carolina, North Carolina, Tennessee, and Georgia agreed to pay a lump sum to Whitney to purchase the rights to his invention. The amount paid, though, was barely enough to allow Whitney and his partner to recoup their expenses.

Whitney continued his lifelong career as an inventor, but he never bothered to patent an invention again. As he once wrote: "An invention can be so valuable as to be worthless to the inventor." Whitney's experience was extreme. Today patent

Whitney's cotton gin

laws provide essential protection for scientific firms engaged in producing new and better products. They may choose to share their new technology by selling their patent rights in return for royalties. Royalties represent a substantial fraction of the revenues of some firms, such as Texas Instruments.

the profits they earn will be relatively secure. Hence, just as firms race to be the first to obtain a patent, so too they race to be the first to enter a product market in which there is a steep learning curve. This behavior is commonly displayed in the computer chip industry.

When learning by doing is important, firms will produce beyond the point where marginal revenue equals *current* marginal costs, because producing more today has an extra benefit. It reduces future costs of production. How much extra a firm produces depends on the steepness of the learning curve.

ACCESS TO CAPITAL MARKETS

Banks are generally unwilling to lend funds to finance R & D expenditures, because they are often very risky and these risks cannot be insured. When a bank makes a loan for a building, if the borrower defaults, the bank winds up with the building. If the bank lends for R & D and the research project fails, or a rival beats the firm to the patent office, the bank may wind up with nothing. Banks also often have a hard time judging the prospects of an R & D endeavor—inventors are always optimistic about their ideas. This difficulty is compounded because an inventor may be reluctant to disclose all the information about his idea, either to banks or potential investors, lest some among them steal his idea and beat him either to the market or the patent office.

For established firms in industries with limited competition and growing demand, financing their research expenditures presents no serious problem. They can pay for R & D out of their profits. That is why, for the economy as a whole, most research and development occurs in such firms. But raising capital is a problem for new and small firms, and also for firms in industries where intense competition limits the profits that any one company can earn. Thus, a firm's dominant position in an industry may be self-perpetuating. Its greater output means that it has more to gain from innovations that reduce the cost of production. And its greater profits give it more resources to expend on R & D.

Today much of the research and development in new and small companies is financed by venture capital firms. These firms raise capital, mainly from pension funds, insurance companies, and wealthy individuals, which they then invest in the most promising R & D ventures. Venture capital firms often demand, as compensation for their risk taking, a significant share of the new enterprise, and they usually keep close tabs on how their money is spent. They often specialize in particular areas, such as computer technology or biotechnology. In less glamorous industries, it is often difficult to find financing for research and development, because venture capital firms may be hesitant to invest in a higher-risk venture.

CLOSE-UP: JOSEPH SCHUMPETER AND SCHUMPETERIAN COMPETITION

The economist most known for emphasizing the role of innovation in market economies is Joseph Schumpeter. Schumpeter began his career in Austria (serving from spring to October 1919 as Minister of Finance to the Emperor of the Austro-Hungarian Empire), and ended his career as a distinguished professor of economics at Harvard. His vision of the economy was markedly different from that of the competitive equilibrium model. That model focuses on equilibrium, a state of the world in which there is no change. He questioned the very concept of equilibrium. To him the economy was always in flux and the economist's role was to understand the forces driving those changes.

Schumpeter argued that the economy was characterized by a process of creative destruction. An innovator could, through his new product or lower costs of production, establish a dominant position in a market. But eventually, that dominant position would be destroyed, as a new innovator took his place.*

He worried that the giant corporations he saw being formed during his life would stifle innovation and end this process of creative destruction. His fears, so far, have been unfounded; indeed, many of the largest firms, like IBM, have not been able to manage the innovative process in a way that keeps up with upstart rivals.

Modern day Schumpeterians often turn to biology to help them understand the process of change. They describe changes as *evolutionary*. They see a slow process of change, with many random elements, with firms that are the fittest—who, by luck or skill manage to discover new products or new ways of doing business that are better, in the particular environment, than their rivals—managing to survive and their practices spreading to other firms.

As respect for and understanding of the importance of innovation has grown, so too have the number of economists who think of themselves as Schumpeterians. And the Schumpeter Society of Austria provides an award every year to honor someone in the "Schumpeterian tradition." In 1994, the award went to an American, Ted Turner, founder of CNN.

Joseph Schumpeter

*We discussed this kind of competition—a succession of monopolies—in Chapter 14, under the topic of **Schumpeterian competition.**

COMPETITION AND TECHNOLOGICAL CHANGE

HOW COMPETITION AFFECTS TECHNOLOGICAL CHANGE

Competition spurs R & D:
   A new innovation enables firms to enjoy profits (profits are driven to zero in standard markets).
   Unless firms innovate, they will not survive.

Competition impedes R & D:
   Competitors may imitate, thus eroding returns from innovation.
   Competition erodes the profits required to finance R & D.

HOW TECHNOLOGICAL CHANGE AFFECTS COMPETITION

R & D spurs competition:
   R & D provides an alternative to prices as a way for firms to compete; it is one of the most important arenas for competition in modern economies.

R & D impedes competition:
   Patents give a single firm a protected position for a number of years.
   The fixed costs of R & D give large firms an advantage, and mean that industries in which R & D is important may have few firms.
   Learning by doing gives a decided advantage to the first entrant into a market.
   Limited access to capital markets for financing R & D is a disadvantage to new and small firms.

BASIC RESEARCH AS A PUBLIC GOOD

R & D expenditures on inventions or innovations almost always give rise to externalities. Externalities arise, as we learned in Chapter 7, whenever one individual's or firm's action produces costs or benefits to others. The total benefits produced by an R & D expenditure are referred to as its **social benefit.** Even with patents, inventors appropriate only a fraction of the social benefit of an invention. A firm that discovers a cheaper way of producing is likely to lower its price during the life of the patent to steal customers away from its rivals. This benefits consumers. After the patent expires, consumers benefit even more as rivals beat the price down further. And the benefits of an invention in one area spill over to other areas. The transistor, which revolutionized electronics, was invented at AT&T's Bell Laboratories. AT&T reaped the benefits from its direct application to telephone equipment. But the benefits in better radios, television sets, and other products accrued to others.

From society's viewpoint, a particularly valuable kind of R & D is **basic research.** Basic research is the kind of fundamental inquiry that produces a wide range of applications. Basic research in physics, for example, led to the ideas behind so many of the things we take for granted today—the laser, the transistor, atomic energy. The private returns to firms from any basic research they might undertake—which would dictate the amount of R & D spent on basic research in the absence of government intervention—are negligible in comparison to its social benefits. Indeed, the externalities flowing from basic research are so extreme that it can be considered a public good.

Public goods are defined by two properties. First, it is difficult to exclude anyone from the benefits of a public good. Basic research involves the discovery of underlying scientific principles or facts of nature. Such facts—like superconductivity, or even the fact that there exist certain materials that exhibit superconductivity at temperatures considerably above absolute zero—cannot be patented.

Second, the marginal cost of an additional individual enjoying a public good is zero. We say that consumption is nonrivalrous. An additional person being informed of a basic discovery does not detract from the knowledge that the original discoverer has, though it may, of course, reduce the profits the original discoverer can make out of the discovery. Indeed, sharing the fruits of basic research as soon as they are available can yield enormous benefits—as other researchers use this knowledge in their quest for innovations.

As with all public goods, private markets yield an undersupply of basic research. Accordingly, the government supports basic research through the National Science Foundation, the National Institutes of Health, and other organizations. Some of the expenditures of the Department of Defense on R & D also go into basic research. Still, there is increasing concern among economists that expenditures on basic research are inadequate.

Figure 17.3 shows that support by the federal government for R & D, outside of defense, has not increased, as a percentage of the nation's output, over

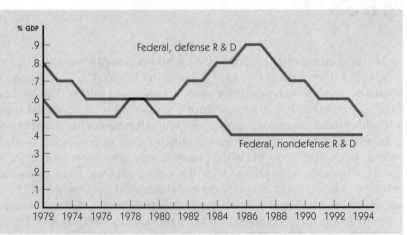

Figure 17.3 FEDERAL EXPENDITURES ON RESEARCH AND DEVELOPMENT

The figure shows federal expenditures as a percentage of the nation's output. Expenditures on R & D for nondefense purposes have been flat since 1972, while expenditures on defense research increased during the 1980s. *Source: Statistical Abstract of the United States, 1995,* Table 979.

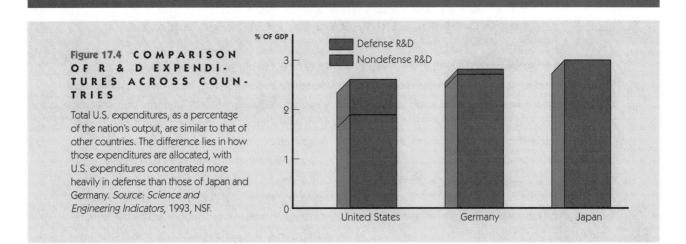

Figure 17.4 COMPARISON OF R & D EXPENDITURES ACROSS COUNTRIES

Total U.S. expenditures, as a percentage of the nation's output, are similar to that of other countries. The difference lies in how those expenditures are allocated, with U.S. expenditures concentrated more heavily in defense than those of Japan and Germany. *Source: Science and Engineering Indicators*, 1993, NSF.

the last two decades. With the end of the Cold War, there has been an attempt to shift more of the federal government's support of R & D away from defense towards civilian or **dual use** technologies (technologies which have both civilian and military use). Still, 55 percent of government R & D expenditures remain defense related. This explains why, while the United States devotes about the same proportion of its economy to R & D as do Japan and Germany, as shown in Figure 17.4, less of the total is spent in developing new products and processes to make American industry more competitive. And more is spent in developing better and more effective weapons. This may also partly explain why today foreigners are getting almost one out of every two patents granted by the U.S. Patent Office. (Inventors have the right to obtain a patent from a foreign country as well as their own.)

GOVERNMENT PROMOTION OF TECHNOLOGICAL PROGRESS

While there is widespread agreement that government should encourage innovative activity through the protection of intellectual property rights and through support of basic R & D, other ways by which the government promotes R & D have been more controversial.

SUBSIDIES

One way in which government has sought to encourage new technologies is through subsidies. This approach has been criticized with the argument that the government has a bad record in picking what to subsidize. As evidence,

Government programs are often criticized as wasteful and unproductive. But government-sponsored research programs have had a remarkable and long history of successes, and should be given their due.

In the nineteenth century, agriculture was at the center of the economy. Government research efforts were accordingly focused there—and are given a large share of the credit for the impressive increase in productivity in agriculture over the last century.

Today telecommunications is one of the sectors at the forefront, and government has played an effective role in promoting this sector, sometimes referred to as the information superhighway. In 1842, the federal government supported Samuel Morse's first telegraph line, between Baltimore and Washington. More recently the federal government developed the Internet, which has linked people and computers throughout the world.

One indicator of the importance of federal support—and its success—is that virtually all of the American winners of the Nobel Prize in science and medicine have been supported by the federal government. The basic research of these scientists has spawned new industries, such as biotechnology, and has solidified America's technological leadership.

they note that the Concorde, the supersonic airplane developed with the support of the French and British governments, has never been able to pay for itself. Closer to home, the government spent billions of dollars in an unsuccessful attempt to develop synthetic fuels. Broad-based subsidies, such as R & D tax credits, do not depend on government selection of particular projects, but are controversial due to their relatively high cost to the government. Critics claim that little additional research is generated per dollar of tax revenue lost.

But there are still supporters of more active involvement of government in R & D, who claim there are large positive externalities associated with applied research, implying that the private sector underinvests in applied research. Policies aimed to support particular sectors of the economy are called **industrial policies,** even if those sectors are not industries as we conventionally think of them, such as agriculture.

Advocates of public support of applied R & D admit that government has not always picked winners. But they claim R & D is by its very nature risky, and a record of complete success cannot be expected. They also claim that, in fact, government's success record has been impressive. They point, for example, to the over 1,000 percent increase in the productivity of agriculture over the past century. This has resulted not only from research undertaken at the state agricultural colleges (which the federal government has helped for more than a century) but also from government-supported diffusion of knowledge, through the agricultural extension service.

Advocates of a more active government role in promoting technology argue that the objective is not so much to pick winners as to identify areas where, in the absence of government support, there would be significant underinvestment, for instance because there are large externalities or spillovers. There is not a sharp demarcation between basic and applied research, but rather a continuum, with many applied projects generating large knowledge spillovers. Substantial underinvestment is likely in sectors, such as agriculture, where there are a large number of small producers (in contrast to the chemical industry, for instance, where there are a few dominant firms.) Well-designed government research programs serve as a complement to private sector efforts, rather than as a substitute for them. On average, increases in government expenditures are associated with increases, not decreases, in private research expenditures.

Advocates of government technology programs argue, further, that government should work in partnership with industry to increase the effectiveness of its R & D investment. They advocate requiring industry to put up money of its own, and making the competition for funds very broad. New technology programs, established since the Clinton administration has taken office, take this approach. And hundreds of partnership agreements between private firms and government-run laboratories have been recently signed. It is too soon to assess the performance of these new efforts, but experience with earlier, similar programs has been encouraging. Sematech—a cooperative research venture of the electronics industry centered in Austin, Texas, and supported with $90 million annually in government subsidies—while it played an important role in the recovery of that industry in the 1980s, announced in October 1994 that it would no longer need government assistance as of fiscal 1997.

INTERNATIONAL COMPLICATIONS

Subsidies have, however, raised the specter of unfair competition in the international arena. Countries facing competition from foreign firms with government subsidies often impose countervailing duties, that is, taxes on imports that are intended to offset the benefits of these subsidies. The concern is if, for instance, Europe and the United States become engaged in a contest to support some industry, the industry will benefit, but at the expense of the taxpayers in both countries. Thus, international agreements have tried to reduce the extent of subsidization. Broad-based R & D subsidies (such as through the tax system) are still permitted, but more narrowly focused subsidies are either prohibited or put into the category of questionable practices.

PROTECTION

Firms in less developed countries often argue that they need to be insulated from competition from abroad in order to develop the knowledge base required to compete effectively in world markets. This is the **infant industry argument for protection.** Most economists are skeptical. They see this argument mainly as an attempt by rent-seeking firms who will use any excuse to insulate themselves from competition so they can raise prices and increase profits. The best way to learn to compete is to compete, not to be isolated from competition. If some help is needed to enable firms to catch up, it should be provided in the form of subsidies, the costs of which are explicit and obvious, unlike the hidden costs of higher prices that result from protection.

RELAXING ANTITRUST POLICIES

The antitrust policies explored in Chapter 16 were founded on the belief that government should push markets toward the model of perfect competition. But an increasing awareness of the importance of R & D in modern industrial economies has led some to argue for change.

A major argument for change is that cooperation aimed at sharing knowl-edge and coordinating research among firms in an industry has the effect of internalizing the externalities of R & D. But antitrust authorities long worried that cooperation in R & D could easily grow into cooperation in other areas, such as price setting, which would not serve the public interest. Public policy has tried to find an effective balance. In 1984, the National Cooperative Research Act was passed to allow some cooperative ventures. Ventures regis-tered under the act are shielded from the risk of paying triple damages in a private antitrust suit, but not shielded from all antitrust risk. By the end of the 1980s, over a hundred such ventures had been registered. Among the best known are the Electric Power Research Institute, formed by electric power companies; Bell Communications Research, formed by local telephone com-panies; and Sematech.

TECHNOLOGICAL CHANGE AND THE BASIC COMPETITIVE MODEL

Basic competitive model	Industries in which technological change is important
Assumes fixed technology.	The central question is what determines the pace of technological change. Related issues include what determines expenditure on R & D and how learning by doing affects the level of production.
Assumes perfect competition, with many firms in industry.	Competition is not perfect; industries where technological change is important tend to have relatively few firms.
Perfect capital markets.	Firms find it difficult to borrow to finance R & D expenditures.
No externalities.	R & D confers benefits to those besides the inventor; even with patents, the inventor appropriates only a fraction of the social benefits of an invention.
No public goods.	Basic research is a public good: the marginal cost of an additional person making use of a new idea is zero (nonrivalrous consumption), and it is often difficult to exclude others from enjoying the benefits of basic research.

TECHNOLOGICAL CHANGE AND ECONOMIC GROWTH

Living standards in the United States are far higher today than they were 100 years ago. The reason is that productivity—output per hour—has increased enormously. Underlying these increases is technological change. While there are many stories of discoveries that occurred almost by accident (such as Fleming's discovery of penicillin), in the modern economy, most advances are a result of the deliberate allocation of resources to research and development. The importance—and consequences—of technological change constitutes our ninth point of consensus among economists.

9   Innovation

Modern economies are based on innovation. Imperfect competition is widespread in the sectors of the economy in which innovation is most important. Government plays a crucial role in innovation, not only protecting intellectual property (through patents and copyrights) but also in supporting basic research.

REVIEW AND PRACTICE

SUMMARY

1. Industries in which technological change is important are almost necessarily imperfectly competitive. Patents are one way the government makes it difficult and costly for firms to copy the technological innovations of others. A firm with a patent will have a government-enforced monopoly. The expenditures on R & D are fixed costs; when they are large, there are likely to be few firms in the industry, and price competition is more likely to be limited.

2. Long-lived and broad patents reduce competition (at least in the short run), but provide greater incentives to innovate. Excessively broad patent coverage may discourage follow-on innovation.

3. Learning by doing, in which companies (or countries) that begin making a product first enjoy an advantage over all later entrants, may be a source of technological advantage.

4. Research and development generally provides positive externalities to consumers and other firms. But since the innovating firm cannot capture all the social benefits from its invention, it will tend to invest less than a socially optimal amount.

5. Basic research has both the central properties of a public good: it is difficult to exclude others from the benefits of the research, and the marginal cost of an additional person making use of the new idea is zero.

6. A number of governmental policies encourage technological advance: patents; direct spending on research; tax incentives to encourage corporate R & D; temporary protection from technologically advanced foreign competitors; and relaxing antitrust laws to allow potential competitors to work together on research projects.

KEY TERMS

patent	learning curve	infant industry
trade secret	industrial policy	argument for
learning by doing		protection

REVIEW QUESTIONS

1. In what ways do industries in which technological change is important not satisfy the assumptions of the standard competitive model?

2. Why do governments grant patents, thereby conferring temporary mo-

nopoly rights? Explain the trade-off society faces in choosing whether to offer long-lived or short-lived patents, and whether to offer broad or narrow patents.

3. How does the existence of learning by doing provide an advantage to incumbent firms over prospective entrants?

4. Why might it be harder to raise capital for R & D than for other projects? How can established firms deal with this problem? What about start-up firms?

5. How do positive externalities arise from research and development? Why do externalities imply that there may be too little expenditure on research by private firms?

6. Explain how basic research can be thought of as a public good. Why is society likely to underinvest in basic research?

7. What are the arguments for and against industrial policies?

8. What possible trade-off does society face when it considers loosening its antitrust laws to encourage joint research and development ventures?

Problems

1. Imagine that Congress is considering a bill to reduce the current seventeen-year life of patents to eight years. What negative effects might this change have on the rate of innovation? What positive effect might it have for the economy?

2. Suppose that many years ago, one inventor received a patent for orange juice, and then another inventor came forward and requested a patent for lemonade. The first inventor maintained that the orange juice patent should be interpreted to cover all fruit juices, while the second inventor argued that the original patent included only one particular method of making one kind of juice. What trade-offs does society face in setting rules for deciding cases like these?

3. Although a patent assures a monopoly on that particular invention for some time, it also requires that the inventor disclose the details of the invention. Under what conditions might a company (like Coca-Cola) prefer to use trade secrets rather than patents to protect its formulas?

4. Why might a company invest in research and development even if it does not believe it will be able to patent its discovery?

5. Learning by doing seems to be important in the semiconductor industry, where the United States and Japan are the main producers. Explain why U.S. and Japanese firms may race to try to bring out new generations of semiconductors. If learning by doing is important in the semiconductor industry, why might other nations try to use an infant industry strategy to develop their own semiconductor industry?

CHAPTER 18

IMPERFECT INFORMATION IN THE PRODUCT MARKET

t was never any secret to economists that the real world did not match the model of perfect competition. Theories of monopoly and imperfect competition such as those covered in Chapters 14–17 have been propounded from Adam Smith's time to the present.

Another limitation of the model of perfect competition has recently come to the fore: its assumption of **perfect information**—that market participants have full information about the goods being bought and sold. By incorporating **imperfect information** into their models, economists have come a long way in closing the gap between the real world and the world depicted by the perfect competition, perfect information model of Part Two.

This chapter provides a broad overview of the major information problems of the product market, the ways in which market economies deal with them, and how the basic model of Part Two has to be modified as a result. In the following chapters, we will see how information problems affect labor markets (Chapter 19), and capital markets and the management of firms (Chapter 20). In Parts Four and Five, we will see how many of the most important macroeconomic problems may be traced, at least in part, to information problems.

KEY QUESTIONS

1. Why is information different from other goods, such as hats and cameras? Why, in particular, do markets for information often not work well?

2. When does the market price affect the quality of what is being sold? How does the fact that consumers believe price affects quality influence how firms behave?

3. When customers have trouble differentiating good from shoddy merchandise, what are the incentives firms have to produce good merchandise? What role does reputation play?

4. Why is it that, in the same market, identical or very similar goods will sell at different prices? How does the fact that search is costly affect the nature of competition?

5. How does advertising affect firms' demand curves and profits? Why may the firms in an industry be better off if they collectively agree not to advertise?

6. What has government done to address some of the problems resulting from imperfect information? Why do these efforts have only limited success?

THE INFORMATION PROBLEM

The basic competitive model assumes that households and firms are well informed. This means that they know their opportunity set, or what is available and at what price. More striking, they know every characteristic of every good, including how long it will last. Were these assumptions true, shopping would be easy!

The model also assumes that consumers know their preferences, that is, they know what they like. They know not only how many oranges they can trade for an apple, but also how many oranges they are willing to trade. In the case of apples and oranges this may make sense. But how do students know how much they are going to enjoy, or even benefit from, a college education before they have experienced it? How does an individual know whether she would like to be a doctor or a lawyer? She gets some idea about what different professions are like by observing those who practice them, but her information is at best incomplete.

According to the basic model, firms too are perfectly well-informed. They all know the best available technology. They know the productivity of each applicant for a job. They know the prices at which inputs can be purchased from every possible supplier (and all of the inputs' characteristics). And they know the prices at which they can sell the goods, not only today, but in every possible circumstance in the future.

How Big a Problem?

That individuals and firms are not perfectly well informed is, by itself, not necessarily a telling criticism of the competitive model, just as the criticism that markets are not perfectly competitive does not cause us to discard the model. The relevant issue is, are there situations where the competitive model will mislead us? Are there important economic phenomena that can be explained only by taking into account imperfect information? Are there important predictions of the model that are incorrect as a result of the assumptions concerning well-informed consumers and firms?

Increasingly, over the past two decades, economists have come to believe that the answer to these questions is yes. For example, college graduates may receive a higher income than high school graduates not only because they have learned things in college that make them more productive, but because their college degree helps them through a sorting process. Employers cannot glean from an interview which applicants for a job will be productive workers. They therefore use a college degree to help them identify those who are better at learning. College graduates *are*, on average, more productive workers. But it is wrong to conclude from this that college has necessarily *increased* their productivity. It may simply have enabled firms to sort out more easily the more productive from the less productive.

How Prices Convey Information

The price system provides brilliant solutions for some information problems. We have seen how prices play an important role in coordinating production and communicating information about economic scarcity. Firms do not have to know what John or Julia likes, what their trade-offs are. The price tells the producer the marginal benefit of producing an extra unit of the good, and that is all he needs to know. Similarly, a firm does not need to know how much iron ore is left in Minnesota, the cost of refining iron ore, or a thousand other details. All it needs to know is the price of iron ore. This tells the company how scarce the resource is, how much effort it should expend in conserving. Prices and markets provide the basis of the economy's incentive system. But there are some information problems that markets do not handle, or do not handle well. And imperfect information sometimes inhibits the ability of markets to perform the tasks it performs so well when information is complete.

Markets for Information

Information has value; people are willing to pay for it. In this sense, we can consider information as a good similar to any other good. There is a market for information, with a price—just as there is a market for labor and a market for capital. Indeed, our economy is sometimes referred to as an information economy. Every year, investors spend millions of dollars on newsletters that give them information about stocks, bonds, and other investment opportunities. Magazines sell specialized information about hundreds of goods.

However, the markets for information are far from perfect, and for good reasons. The most conspicuous one is that information is *not* just like any other good. When you buy a chair, the furniture dealer is happy to let you look at it, feel it, sit on it, and decide whether you like it. When you buy information, you cannot do the same. The seller can either say, "Trust me. I'll tell you what you need to know," or show you the information and say, "Here's what I know. If this is what you wanted to know, please pay me." You would rightfully be skeptical in the first scenario, and might be unwilling to pay in the second. After you were given the information, what incentive would you have to pay?

In some cases, there is a basic credibility problem. You might think, if a stock tipster *really* knows that a stock is going to go up in price, why should he tell me, even if I pay him for the information? Why doesn't he go out and make his fortune with the information? Or is it that he really is not sure, and would just as soon have me risk my money rather than risk his?

Most important, even after the firm or consumer buys all the information he thinks is worth paying for, his information is still far from perfect. Some information is simply too costly to obtain relative to the benefit of having it. Let's look now at some of the consequences of imperfect information.

THE MARKET FOR LEMONS AND ADVERSE SELECTION

Have you ever wondered why a three-month-old used car sells for so much less—often 20 percent less—than a new car? Surely cars do not deteriorate that fast. The pleasure of owning a new car may be worth something, but in three months, even the car you buy new will be "used." But a couple of thousand dollars or more is a steep price to pay for this short-lived pleasure.

George Akerlof of the University of California at Berkeley has provided a simple explanation, based on imperfect information. Some cars are worse than others. They have hidden defects which become apparent to the owner only after she has owned the car for a while. Such defective cars are called lemons. One thing after another goes wrong with them. While warranties may reduce the financial cost of having a lemon, they do not eliminate the bother—the time it takes to bring the car into the shop, the anxiety of knowing there is a good chance of a breakdown. The owners, of course, know they have a lemon and would like to pass it along to someone else. Those with the worst lemons are going to be the most willing to sell their car. At a high used car price, they will be joined by owners of better quality cars who want to sell their cars, say, to buy the latest model. As the price drops, more of the good cars will be withdrawn from the market as the owners decide to keep them. And the average quality of the used cars for sale will *drop*. We say there is an

Figure 18.1 A MARKET WITH LEMONS

Panel A shows the average quality of a used car increasing as the price increases. Panel B shows a typical upward-sloping supply curve, but a backward-bending demand curve. Demand bends back because buyers know that quality is lower at lower prices, and they thus choose to buy less as the price falls. Panel B shows the market equilibrium is at point E.

adverse selection effect. The mix of those who elect to sell changes adversely as price falls. We encountered adverse selection in the insurance market in Chapter 6. We will encounter adverse selection again in our discussion of labor market (Chapter 19) and capital market (Chapter 20) imperfections.

Figure 18.1 shows the consequences of imperfect information for market equilibrium in the used car market. Panel A depicts, for each price (measured along the horizontal axis), the average quality of used cars being sold in the market. As price increases, average quality increases. Panel B shows the supply curve of used cars. As price increases, the number of cars being sold in the market increases, for all the usual reasons. The demand curve is also shown. This curve has a peculiar shape: upward as well as downward sloping. The reason is that as price increases, the average quality increases. But demand depends not just on price but on quality—on the "value" being offered on the market. If, as price falls, quality deteriorates rapidly, then quantity demanded will actually *fall* as price falls—consumers are getting less for their dollars. The equilibrium is depicted in panel B.

The situation just described is characterized by **asymmetric information** between sellers and buyers. That is, the seller of the used car has more information about the product than the buyer. Many markets are characterized by asymmetric information. One of the consequences of asymmetric information is that there may be relatively few buyers and sellers, far fewer than there would be with perfect information. Economists use the term **thin** to describe markets in which there are relatively few buyers and sellers. In some situations, a market may be so thin as to be essentially nonexistent. When there are important markets missing from an economy, it is said to have an **incomplete** set of markets. The used car market, for example, is a thin one. Buyers may know that there are some legitimate sellers, those who for one reason or another always want to drive a new car. But mixed in with these are people who are trying to dump their lemons. The buyers cannot tell the lemons apart from the good cars. Rather than risk it, they simply do not buy. (Of course, the fact that demand is low drives down the price, increasing the proportion of lemons. It is a vicious cycle.)

SIGNALING

If you have a good car and you want to sell it, you would like to persuade potential buyers that it is good. You could tell them that it is not a lemon, but why should they believe you? There is a simple principle: *actions speak louder than words.* What actions can you take that will convince buyers of the quality of your car?

The fact that Chrysler is willing to provide a five-year, fifty-thousand-mile warranty on its cars says something about the confidence Chrysler has in its product. The warranty is valuable, not only because it reduces the risks of having to spend a mint to repair the car, but also because the buyer believes that Chrysler would not have provided the warranty unless the chances of defects were low. Actions such as this are said to **signal** higher quality. A signal is effective if it differentiates goods—here between high-quality cars and low-quality cars. The cost to the producer of a five-year guarantee is much higher for a car that is likely to fall apart within five years than for a car that is unlikely to break down. Customers know this, and thus can infer that a firm willing to provide this warranty is selling high-quality cars.

When you go to a car dealer, you want to know that it will still be around if you have trouble. Some firms signal that they are not fly-by-nights by spending a great deal of money on their showroom. This indicates that it would be costly for them to just pack up and leave. (There are, of course, other reasons why they may spend money on a fancy showroom.)

Actions such as providing a better guarantee or a larger showroom are taken not just for the direct benefit that the consumer receives from them, but because those actions make consumers believe that the product is a better product or the firm is a better firm to deal with. In a sense, the desire to convey information "distorts" the decisions made relative to what they would have been in a perfect-information world. For example, if customers receive no direct benefit from the quality of the showroom, the cost of building and maintaining a luxurious showroom is a waste of resources.

JUDGING QUALITY BY PRICE

There is still another clue that buyers use to judge the quality of what they are about to purchase. This is price. Consumers make inferences about the quality of goods based on the price charged. For example, they know that on average, if the price of a used car is low , the chance of getting a lemon is higher. Many if not most sellers know that buyers know this.

In markets with imperfect information, firms *set* their prices. And in setting

CLOSE-UP: AUTOMOBILE BROKERS AND IMPERFECT INFORMATION

A broker is someone who arranges contracts between two parties. In older times, marriage brokers brought together prospective couples. Stockbrokers bring together buyers and sellers of stocks. Car brokers bring together buyers and sellers of cars.

In every case, though, a broker is someone whose job exists only because of imperfect information. After all, why can't a person just go out and choose a spouse or a stock or a car? The obvious problem is that many different varieties are available, and it costs time and energy and money to collect the information to make an informed decision. A good broker is out there in the market all the time, keeping track of what is going on. Having a relatively small number of people keeping track of buyers and sellers is certainly more efficient than having all buyers and sellers duplicating one another's efforts.

Consider how car brokers work, for example. You call up a broker (usually they are listed in the Yellow Pages of the phone book) and describe what sort of car you want—make, model, year, accessories. The broker then finds you the best deal.

Working as a broker may seem like a funny way to make a living. How can someone get paid for shopping for cars? The answer is that shopping for a car involves time and the energy of confronting dealers and haggling over price. Even if the buyer spends several days or weeks shopping, it is not clear she will find the best deal. Paying a knowledgeable broker will certainly save time and energy, and might result in a cheaper price too. A good broker will know the sales representative's typical commission or the "preparation fee" that dealers receive for getting a car ready to sell. By taking factors like this into account, the broker can often negotiate a better price.

Not everyone will need or want an automobile broker. But for those who feel their information about the car market is extremely imperfect, a broker may be a wise choice.

Source: "A Better Way to Buy a Car?" *Consumer Reports,* September 1989, pp. 593–95.

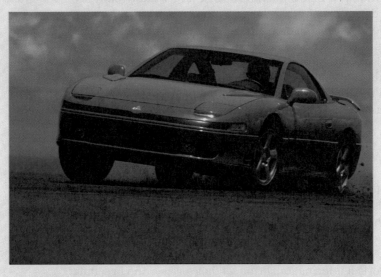

their prices, they take into account what customers will think about the quality of the good being sold. Concerns about consumers (correctly or incorrectly) making inferences about quality impede the effectiveness of price competition. In the used car example, we saw that, as price rose, the average quality of cars on the market increased. But if firms think customers believe that cars being sold at a lower price are lemons—that the quality deteriorates more than the price declines—they will not lower the price because to do so would scare away customers who perceive that such "bargains" must be lemons. Under such circumstances, even if firms cannot sell all they would like at the going price, they will still not cut prices.

A situation can be sustained in which there is a seeming excess supply of goods. Imperfect information means that equilibrium will be achieved away from the intersection of supply and demand curves. This is a profound result, one we will trace through many of the chapters that follow.

Information problems fascinate economists because they turn the basic competitive model upside down. Economists have long recognized that prices convey critical information about scarcity in a market economy. But only recently have the other informational roles of prices—and their consequences—become clear. Sellers will manipulate prices when they can to control the information conveyed. Buyers, for their part, see through these manipulations. And their concern that the seller is trying to pass off a lemon discourages trade. When information problems like these are severe, markets are thin or even nonexistent. Alternatively, price competition may be limited. Even when there is an excess supply of goods, firms may not cut their prices and the market may not clear.

SOLUTIONS TO ADVERSE SELECTION PROBLEMS IN MARKET ECONOMIES

Signaling

Judging quality by price

THE INCENTIVE PROBLEM

We have seen throughout this book that providing incentives that motivate individuals to make the best choices is one of the central economic problems. The central problem of incentives, in turn, is that individuals do not bear the full consequences of their actions. The multi-billion-dollar collapse of the savings and loan associations—though fraud may have played a part—is attributable largely to incorrect incentives. Because S & L deposits were guaranteed by the government, depositors had no incentives to check on what the S & Ls were doing. For the same reason, the owners of many S & Ls had an incentive to take high risks. If they were successful, they kept the gains. If they failed, the government picked up the loss.

When there is a misalignment of incentives such as occurred in the S & Ls, we say there is a problem of moral hazard, as noted in Chapter 6. The term originated in the insurance industry. Individuals who purchased insurance had an inadequate incentive to avoid the insured-against event—indeed, if they were insured for more than 100 percent of the loss, they would have an incentive to bring about the event. Doing so was considered immoral, hence the term. Today, economists think of these simply as incentive problems, with no moral overtones. Thus, an individual who has fire insurance has less of an incentive to avoid a fire. The benefit to him, for instance, of putting in a sprinkler system may not be worth the cost—though it would if he took into account the expected cost to the fire insurance company. That is why the fire insurance company is likely to require a sprinkler system, or to give a discount on the premium if an individual has one. It would thus pay to have a sprinkler system installed.

In the basic competitive model of Part Two, private property and prices provide incentives. Individuals are rewarded for performing particular tasks. The problem arises when an individual is not rewarded for what he does, or when he does not have to pay the full costs for what he does. In our economy, incentive problems are pervasive.

In product markets, firms must be given the incentive to produce quality products. Again, the incentive problem is an information problem. If customers could always tell the quality of the product they were getting, firms that produced higher-quality products would always be able to charge a higher price, and no company could get away with producing shoddy goods. Most of us have had the experience of going to a newly established restaurant, having a good meal, and then returning to find that the quality had deteriorated. Evidently something went wrong with incentives.

MARKET SOLUTIONS

In simple transactions, incentive problems can be solved by stipulating penalties and rewards. You would like a document typed. You sign a contract with someone to pay him $25 to deliver the typed document by tomorrow at 5:00 P.M. The contract stipulates that $.50 will be deducted for each typographical error, and $1.00 for every hour the paper is late. The contract has built-in incentives for the paper to be delivered on time and without errors.

But most transactions, even relatively simple ones, are more complicated than this one. The more complicated the transaction, the more difficult it is to solve the incentive problem. You want your grass mowed, and your neigh-

The soaring costs of Medicare (the government program providing health insurance for the aged) have prompted a number of proposals from policy makers, among these a proposal to establish *medical savings accounts* (MSAs). MSAs would encourage individuals to buy health insurance with large deductibles and co-payments. For instance, the insurance company would only pay 80 percent of the amount in excess of $1,000; in that case, there is a $1,000 deductible and a 20 percent co-payment. With such insurance, individuals have an incentive to economize on their use of health care, and the premium would, presumably, be considerably lower than the costs under the current system. Each individual would receive a check, representing the difference between what it costs the government under the old system and the premium under the new privately provided policies. Individuals could deposit this money in a tax-exempt medical savings account, and use it to pay for the uninsured costs, deductible, and co-payments.

Sounds like a good system: improved incentives reduce costs for both government and individuals. But the problems of adverse selection and incentives are often intertwined, and critics say that adverse selection effects will dominate the incentive effects. The rich and healthy will take the MSA option, transferring to the standard option when their health deteriorates. Thus, the *apparent* cost under the new option will be lower, but mostly because of the adverse selection effect, not improved incentives. Meanwhile, the same adverse selection effect will drive up the average costs of those remaining under the standard option. Thus, the net costs to the government could actually increase. This problem could be rectified if there were some way of adjusting payments to reflect the health condition of the individual. Such "risk adjusters" have been discussed for several years, but so far, no one has devised a satisfactory method of making the appropriate risk adjustments.

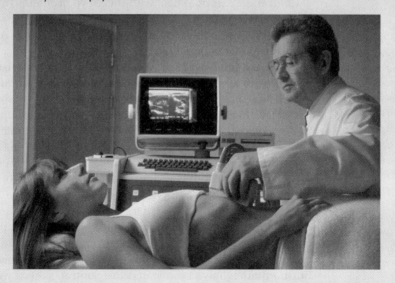

bor's twelve-year-old son wants to mow it. You want him to take care of your power mower. When he sees a rock in the mower's path, he should pick it up. But what incentive does he have to take care of the mower? If you plan to charge him for repairs if the mower does hit a rock, how can you tell whether the rock was hidden by the grass? If he owned his own mower, he would have the appropriate incentives. That is why private property combined with the price system provides such an effective solution to the incentive problem. But your neighbor's son probably does not have the money to buy his own power mower. Then an incentive problem is inevitable. Either you let him use your lawn mower and bear the risk of his mistreating it. Or you lend him money to buy his own, in which case you bear the risk of his not paying you back.

Many private companies must hire people to run machinery worth hundreds or thousands of times more than a lawn mower. Every company would like its workers to exert effort and care, to communicate clearly with one another and take responsibility. Beyond private property and prices, the market economy has other partial solutions to these incentive problems, loosely categorized as contract solutions and reputation solutions.

CONTRACT SOLUTIONS

When one party (firm) agrees to do something for another, it typically signs a contract, which specifies the conditions of the transaction. For example, a firm will agree to deliver a product of a particular quality at a certain time and place. There will normally be "escape" clauses. If there is a strike, if the weather is bad, and so on, the delivery can be postponed. These **contingency clauses** may also make the payment depend on the circumstances and manner in which the service is performed.

Contracts attempt to deal with incentive problems by specifying what each of the parties is to do in each situation. But no one can think of every contingency. And even if they could, it would take them a prohibitively long time to write down all the possibilities.

There are times when it would be extremely expensive for the supplier to comply with all the terms of the contract. He could make the promised delivery on time, but only at a very great cost; if the buyer would only accept a one-day delay, there would be great savings. To provide suppliers with the incentive to violate the terms only when it is really economically worthwhile, most contracts allow delivery delays, but with a penalty. The penalty gives the supplier the incentive to deliver in a timely, but not overly costly, way.

Sometimes the supplier may think it simply is not worth complying with the contract. If he violates the agreement, he is said to be in **breach** of the contract. When a contract has been breached, the parties usually wind up in court, and the legal system stipulates what damages the party breaking the contract must pay to the other side. Contracts, by stipulating what parties are supposed to do in a variety of circumstances, help resolve incentive problems. But no matter how complicated the contract, there will still be ambiguities and disputes. Contracts are incomplete and enforcement is costly, and thus they provide only a partial resolution of the incentive problem.

REPUTATION SOLUTIONS

Reputations play an extremely important role in providing incentives in market economies. A reputation is a form of guarantee. Even though you may know that you cannot collect from this guarantee yourself—it is not a "money-back" guarantee—you know that the reputation of the person or company will suffer if it does not perform well. The incentive to maintain a reputation is what provides firms with an incentive to produce high-quality goods. It provides the contractor with an incentive to complete a house on or near the promised date.

For reputation to be an effective incentive mechanism, firms must lose something if their reputation suffers. The "something" is, of course, profits. For reputations to provide incentives, there must be profits to lose.

Thus, we see another way that markets with imperfect information differ from markets with perfect information. In competitive markets with perfect information, competition drives price down to marginal cost. In markets in which quality is maintained as the result of a reputation mechanism, whether competitive or not, price must remain above marginal cost.

Why, in markets where reputation is important, doesn't competition lead to price cutting? If price is "too low," firms do not have an incentive to maintain their reputation. Consumers, knowing this, come to expect low-quality goods. This is another reason that cutting prices will not necessarily bring firms more customers. Most consumers, at one time or another, have encountered companies that tried to live off their reputation. For example, Head skis were the high-quality skis in the early 1970s. At high prices, of course, demand was limited. When the company lowered its price, sales increased. Consumers, knowing about the high quality, bought the skis thinking they were getting a bargain. But bargains are not so easy to come by. At the lower prices, profits were lower and Head had little incentive to maintain its reputation.

Reputation as a Barrier to Entry   Competition is frequently very imperfect in markets where reputation is important. The necessity of establishing a reputation acts as an important barrier to entry, and limits the degree of competition in these industries. Given a choice between purchasing the product of an

SOLUTIONS TO INCENTIVE PROBLEMS IN MARKET ECONOMIES

Private property and prices

Contracts

Reputations

One of the key issues in the 1992 U.S. presidential campaign was reform of the medical care industry. The United States spends a larger fraction of its national income on health care, but has a lower life expectancy and greater infant mortality rate than many other developed countries. Information problems and associated market failures are a large part of the reason. Moral hazard—the reduced incentive to economize on health care expenditures when a large fraction of the tab is picked up by insurance firms—is one source of market failure. Adverse selection—the attempt of each insurance firm to take the lowest-risk patients, leaving those with high medical costs to others—is another.

In the standard model, consumers are assumed to be well informed. But, consumers go to the doctor for information to find out what is wrong with them. Moreover, they typically must rely on the doctor's advice. Economists worry that under the fee-for-service system, where doctors are paid for each of the services they perform, there is an incentive to provide excessive care. Excessive means the marginal cost exceeds the marginal benefit to the patient.

Today, more and more doctors work in "managed care" organizations, where they are paid a flat fee up front. They then provide whatever care is needed and receive no extra income from doing extra procedures. On average, doctors working in managed care cost less and perform fewer surgeries, with no noticeable effect on patient health. Critics worry that with managed care, doctors have an incentive to underprovide, since they receive no compensation at all for providing care at the margin. But advocates argue that any managed care organization that did so would quickly lose its patients. Reputations provide effective discipline. When employers provide a level playing field between fee-for-service and managed care plans—contributing an equal amount for each, and making the employee pay for the extra cost if they choose the more expensive fee-for-service plans—more than half their employees, on average, choose the managed care plan. Evidently, the employees do not feel the benefits of the extra services provided under fee-for-service are worth the extra costs.

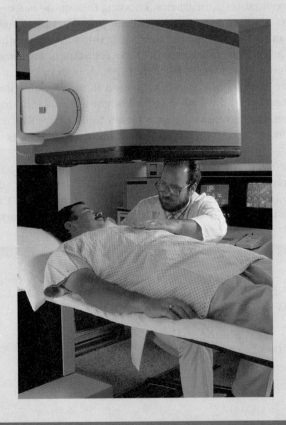

established firm with a good reputation and the product of a newcomer with no reputation at the same price, consumers will normally choose the established firm's good. In choosing a new TV you may choose a Sony over an equally priced new brand with no track record for quality and reliability. The newcomer must offer a sufficiently low price, often accompanied with strong guarantees. In some cases, newcomers have almost to give away their product in order to establish themselves. Entering a market thus becomes extremely expensive.

THE SEARCH PROBLEM

A basic information problem is that consumers must find out what goods are available on the market, at what price, and where. Households must learn about job opportunities as well as opportunities for investing their savings. Firms, by the same token, have to figure out the demand curve they face, and where and at what price they can obtain inputs. Both sides of the market need, in other words, to find out about their opportunity sets.

In the basic competitive model of Part Two, a particular good sells for the same price everywhere. If we see what look like identical shoes selling for two different prices at two neighboring stores—$25 at one and $35 at the other—it must mean (in that model) that the stores are really selling different products. If the shoes are in fact identical, then what the customer must be getting is a combination package, the shoes plus the service of having the shoes fitted. And the more expensive store is providing a higher quality of service.

In fact, however, essentially the same good may be sold at different stores for different prices. And you may not be able to account for the observed differences in prices by differences in other attributes, like the location of the store or the quality of the service provided. In these cases, we say there is **price dispersion.** If the act of finding out all prices were costless (or information perfect, as in the standard competitive model), consumers would search until they found the cheapest price. And no store charging more than the lowest price on the market would ever have any customers. But with costly information, a high-price store may still be able to keep some customers—and its higher profit per sale offsets its lower level of sales. Thus, price dispersion can persist.

do Bttere model.

Price dispersion, combined with variations in quality, means that households and firms must spend considerable energies in searching. Workers search for a good job. Firms look for good workers. Consumers search for the lowest prices and best values. The process by which this kind of information is gathered is called **search.**

Search is an important, and costly, economic activity. Because it is costly, a search stops before you have *all* the relevant information. You know there are bargains out there to be found, but it is just too expensive to find them. You might worry that you will be disappointed the day or week after buying a new computer, if you find it for sale at 10 percent less. But in truth, there should be no regrets. There was a chance that you would not find a better buy, or that

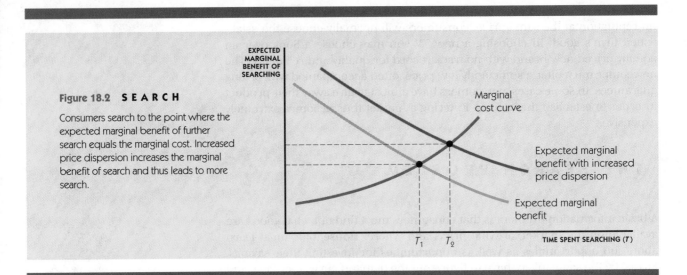

Figure 18.2 SEARCH

Consumers search to the point where the expected marginal benefit of further search equals the marginal cost. Increased price dispersion increases the marginal benefit of search and thus leads to more search.

next week you would not even be able to buy it at the price offered today. You looked at these risks, the costs of further search, the benefits of being able to get the computer today and use it now (compared with the benefits of waiting and the chance of finding it at a still lower price). After a careful balancing of the benefits and costs of further waiting, you decided to purchase now.

In Figure 18.2 the horizontal axis plots the time spent in searching, while the vertical axis measures the expected marginal benefit of searching. On the one hand, the expected marginal benefit of searching declines with the amount of search. In general, people search the best prospects first. As they search more and more, they look at less and less likely prospects. Say you are looking to buy a used car. You might first look in the newspaper, then go to local car dealers. Finally, you might drive the streets looking for cars with "for sale" signs. On the other hand, the marginal cost of additional search rises with increased search. This reflects the fact that the more time people spend in search, the less time they have to do other things. The opportunity cost of spending an extra hour searching thus increases. The amount of search chosen will be at the point where the expected marginal benefit just equals the marginal cost.

An increase in price (or quality) dispersion will normally increase the return to searching—there is a chance of picking up a really good bargain, and the difference between a good buy and a bad buy is larger. Thus, the expected marginal benefit curve shifts up, and the amount of search will increase from T_1 to T_2.

SEARCH AND IMPERFECT COMPETITION

Firms know search is costly, and take advantage of that fact. They know they will not lose all their customers if they raise their prices. And if a store lowers its price slightly, it will not immediately attract *all* the customers from the other stores. Customers have to learn about the competitive price advantage, and this takes time. Moreover, even when people do hear of the lower price, they may worry about the quality of the goods being sold, the nature of the service, whether the goods will be in stock, and so on.

The fact that search is costly means that the demand curve facing a firm will be downward sloping. Competition is necessarily imperfect.

Consider, for instance, the demand for a Walkman. When you walk into a store, you have some idea what it should sell for. The store asks $70 for it. You may know that somewhere you might be able to purchase it for $5 less. But is it worth the additional time, trouble, and gasoline to drive to the other stores that might have it, looking for a bargain? Some individuals are willing to pay the extra $5 simply to stop having to search. As the store raises its price to, say, $75, $80, or $85, some people who would have bought the Walkman at $70 decide that it is worth continuing to shop around. The store, as it raises its price, loses some but not all of its customers. Thus, it faces a downward-sloping demand curve. If search were costless, everyone would go to the store selling the Walkman at the lowest price, and any store charging more than that would have no sales. Markets in which search is costly are, accordingly, better described by the models of imperfect competition introduced in Chapters 14 and 15.

SEARCH AND INFORMATION INTERMEDIARIES

Some firms play an important role by gathering information and serving as intermediaries between producers and customers. These firms are part of the market for information discussed in the beginning of the chapter. One of the functions of good department stores, for example, is to economize on customers' search costs. The stores' buyers seek out literally hundreds of producers, looking for the best buys and the kinds of goods that their customers will like. Good department stores earn a reputation for the quality of their buyers. Customers still have a search problem—they may have to visit several department stores—but doing so is far less costly than if they had to search directly among producers. In addition magazines like *Consumer Reports* provide readers with detailed information on product quality and price, saving consumers considerable search cost.

ADVERTISING

Customers have an incentive to find out where the best buys are. Firms have a corresponding incentive to tell customers about the great deals they are providing. Companies may spend great sums on advertising to bring information about their products, prices, and locations to potential customers.

In the classic joke about advertising, an executive says, "We know half the money we spend on advertising is wasted, but we don't know which half."

The economics of search—a comparison of the costs and benefits of search—has important applications in the labor market. New entrants into the labor market typically have much higher job turnover than older workers. While older workers typically stay with an employer for years, younger workers often leave after a period of a few weeks or months. How can we explain these differences?

To begin, contrast a job search for a sixty-year-old and a thirty-year-old. Even should the sixty-year-old find a better job, he is likely to enjoy the job for at most a few years. For the thirty-year-old, the marginal benefit of additional search is much greater: there is at least the *possibility* that he will stay with the new employer for two decades or more. Each worker evaluates the marginal benefit and the marginal cost of additional search, but their evaluations yield different answers.

Two other factors reinforce these outcomes. First, the younger worker is likely to be less informed both about her own preferences (what she likes and does not like) and about the job market. Moving from job to job provides additional information about both. Secondly, employers recognize this, so there is little stigma associated with a younger worker moving about. By contrast, employers worry that an older worker who is looking for a new job may know that he is about to be dismissed or demoted, because of inadequate job performance. Excessive job mobility for an older worker is often interpreted as a "bad" signal.

That joke says a lot about the economics of advertising. In the United States, many firms spend 2 percent, 3 percent, or more of their total revenues on advertising. Today, total expenditures on advertising are over $130 billion, with slightly more than half spent on national advertising. To add some perspective, these expenditures are only slightly less than spending on all federal, state, and local public assistance.

Advertising can serve the important economic function of providing information about what choices are available. When a new airline enters a market, it must convey that information to potential customers. When a new product is developed, that fact has to be made known. When a business is having a sale, it must let people know. A firm cannot just lower its price, sit on its haunches, and wait, if it wants to be successful. Companies need to recruit new customers and convey information in an active way.

But not all advertising is designed to convey factual information about product prices or characteristics. Take the typical beer or car advertisement. It conveys almost no information about the product, but seeks to convey an image, one with which potential buyers will identify. That these advertisements succeed in persuading individuals either to try a product or to stick with that product and not try another—is a reminder that consumer behavior is much more complicated than the simple theories of competitive markets suggest. Few people decide to go out and buy a car or a new suit solely because they saw a TV ad. But decisions about what kinds of clothes to wear, what beer to drink, what car to drive, are affected by a variety of considerations, including, how peers view them or how they see themselves. These views, in turn, can be affected by advertising.

To emphasize the different roles played by advertising, economists distinguish between **informative advertising** and **persuasive advertising.** The intent of the former is to provide consumers with information about the price of a good, where it may be acquired, or what its characteristics are. The intent of persuasive advertising is to make consumers feel good about the product. This can even take the form of providing "disinformation"—to confuse consumers into thinking there is a difference among goods when there really is not.

ADVERTISING AND COMPETITION

Advertising is both a cause and a consequence of imperfect competition. In a perfectly competitive industry, where many producers make identical goods, it would not pay any single producer to advertise the merits of a good. You do not see advertisements for wheat or corn. If such advertising were successful, it would simply shift the demand curve for the product out. The total demand for wheat might increase, but this would have a negligible effect on the wheat grower who paid for the advertisement. If all wheat farmers could get together, it might pay them to advertise as a group. In recent years, associations representing producers of milk, oranges, almonds, raisins, and beef have done just that.

If, however, advertising can create in consumers' minds the perception that products are different, then firms will face downward-sloping demand curves. There will be imperfect competition. If imperfect competition exists, advertising can be used to increase the demand for a firm's products.

ADVERTISING AND PROFITS

The objective of advertising is not only to change the slope of the demand curve—by creating the perception of product differences—but also to shift the demand curve out, as in Figure 18.3. The increase in advertising by one firm may divert customers away from rivals, or it may divert customers away from other products. Advertising a particular brand of cigarettes may be successful in inducing some smokers to switch brands and in inducing some nonsmokers to smoke.

The increase in profits from shifting the demand curve consists of two parts. First, the firm can sell the same quantity it sold before but at a higher price— p_3, rather than p_1. Profits then increase by the original quantity (Q_1) times the change in price ($p_3 - p_1$), the rectangle $ABCD$ in the figure. Second, by adjusting the quantity it sells, it can increase profits still further. This is because the advertising has shifted the firm's marginal revenue curve up. As usual, the imperfectly competitive firm sets marginal revenue equal to marginal cost, so it

CLOSE-UP: ADVERTISING ORANGE JUICE

In the simple model of perfect competition, a new orange juice company would announce that its product was ready, match or beat the price prevailing in the market, and sell its product. When Procter and Gamble entered the orange juice business in 1983, it competed by setting the price for its Citrus Hill juice a little lower than the price for established competitors like Tropicana and Minute Maid, and by blanketing the country with Citrus Hill coupons. But Procter and Gamble evidently felt that something more was needed to get its product started. According to *Business Week,* it set an advertising and promotion budget of $75 to $100 million. (By comparison, only $2.5 billion worth of orange juice was being sold in a year by all existing companies.)

There are two lessons to be drawn from this and many similar episodes. First, by spending significant amounts of money on advertising, manufacturers demonstrate their belief that offering a lower price is not a sufficient way of competing. Second, manufacturers must believe that advertising helps to make people perceive their product as unique, even when, as in the case of orange juice, most consumers probably can barely distinguish the different brands. Companies are able to take advantage of such perceptions to earn higher profits.

Source: Business Week, October 31, 1983.

Figure 18.3 HOW ADVERTISING CAN SHIFT THE DEMAND CURVE

Successful advertising shifts the demand curve facing a firm. When the imperfect competitor equates its new marginal revenue with its old marginal cost, it will be able to raise both its price and its output.

increases output from Q_1 to Q_2. The additional profits thus generated are measured by the area between the marginal revenue and marginal cost curves between Q_1 and Q_2. Marginal cost remains the same, so the second source of extra profits is the shaded area *EFG*. The net increase in profits is the area *ABCD* plus the area *EFG* minus the cost of advertising.

So far, in studying the effect of an increase in advertising on one firm's profits, we have assumed that other firms keep their level of advertising constant. The effect of advertising on both industry and firm profits is more problematical once the reactions of other firms in the industry are taken into account. To the extent that advertising diverts sales from one firm in an industry to another, advertising may, in equilibrium, have little effect on demand. For example, assume that Nike shoe ads divert customers from Reeboks to Nike and vice versa for Reebok ads. Figure 18.4 shows the demand curve facing Reebok (1) before advertising, (2) when only Reebok advertises, and (3) when both companies advertise. The final demand curve is the same as the initial demand curve. Price and output are the same; profits are lower by the amount spent on advertising. We have here another example of a Prisoner's Dilemma. If the firms could cooperate and agree not to advertise, they would both be better off. But without such cooperation, it pays each to advertise, regardless of what the rival does. The government-mandated ban on cigarette advertising on radio and TV may have partially solved this Prisoner's Dilemma for the tobacco industry—in the name of health policy.

In practice, when all cigarette firms advertise, the ads do more than just

Figure 18.4 HOW ADVERTISING CAN CANCEL OTHER ADVERTISING

If only one company advertises, the demand curve for its product may shift out. But if both companies advertise, the resulting demand curve may be the same as it would if neither advertised.

CONSEQUENCES OF IMPERFECT INFORMATION

Adverse selection problems—quality may be affected by price

    Thin or nonexistent markets

    Signaling

    Markets may not clear

Incentive problems—weak or misdirected incentives

    Importance of contingency contracts, with contingency clauses

    Reputations, with price exceeding marginal cost

Search problems

    Price dispersion

    Imperfect competition

Advertising

    To change slope of demand curve—create perception of product differences

    To shift demand curve

cancel each other out. Some people who might not otherwise have smoked are persuaded to do so, and some smokers are induced to smoke more than they otherwise would have. But the shift in the demand curve facing a particular firm when all companies advertise is still much smaller than it is when only that firm advertises.

THE IMPORTANCE OF IMPERFECT INFORMATION

The modern economy has sometimes been called "the information economy." This is partly because the major advances in computer technology have greatly enhanced the capacity to process information, and partly because such a large fraction of economic activity revolves around collecting, processing, and disseminating information. Personnel officers focus on finding out about potential employees; lending officers attempt to assess the likelihood of default of potential borrowers; market researchers try to determine the potential market for some new product; large retail stores have buyers scouring the world for new suppliers of the clothes they sell. But no matter how much information we have, we seldom have as much as we would like.

Not only is information imperfect, but different people have different information. Information is asymmetric. The seller of a car knows more about his car's problems than the buyer. The worker may know more about his strengths and weaknesses than does the firm where he is interviewing for a job. The borrower may know more about some of the contingencies that may affect his ability to repay the loan than the lender. Because the parties to a transaction do not always have an incentive to be perfectly truthful, it may be difficult for the more informed party to convey convincingly what he knows to others.

In recent years, economists have come to agree that such imperfections of information fundamentally alter how individuals and markets behave. This agreement forms the basis of our tenth consensus point in economics.

10 Imperfect Information

The fact that individuals and firms typically make decisions based on imperfect information affects the behavior of markets in various ways. Firms and individuals compensate for the scarcity of information. In many markets where problems of adverse selection and moral hazard arise, firms adjust prices to convey information about quality. Individuals and firms may attempt to signal information about their characteristics and work to establish a reputation.

GOVERNMENT AND INFORMATION

The market inefficiencies resulting from information problems can take a number of forms. Governmental concern for the consequences of ill-informed consumers has motivated a number of pieces of **consumer protection legislation.** For example, the Wheeler-Lea Act of 1938 made "deceptive" trade practices illegal and gave the Federal Trade Commission power to stop false and deceptive advertising. Truth-in-lending legislation requires lenders to disclose the true interest rate being charged. Truth-in-packaging legislation makes it less likely that consumers will be misled by what is printed on the package. And the Securities and Exchange Commission, which regulates the sale of stocks and bonds, requires firms selling these securities to disclose a considerable amount of information.

Yet much of this legislation is of only limited effectiveness. One problem occurs when consumers try to absorb and process the information. A cereal manufacturer may disclose not only what is required, but a host of other information, which may or may not be of importance. How is the consumer to know what to pay attention to? He cannot absorb everything. Occasionally, as in the case of warnings about the dangers from smoking, government regulators, aware of these problems of information absorption, have required the disclosures to be of a specific form and size lettering to make them stand out. But that kind of intervention on a more massive scale would probably be, at the very least, extremely costly.

Another problem with outlawing deceptive advertising is the difficulty of drawing a clear line between persuasion and deception. Advertisers are good at walking along the edge of any line—a suggestive hint may do where an explicit claim might be called deceptive. Having congressmen or the courts draw a line between informative and noninformative advertising seems an impossible task.

REVIEW AND PRACTICE

SUMMARY

1. The basic competitive model assumes that participants in the market have perfect information about the goods being bought and sold and their prices. In the real world, information is often imperfect. Economists have modified the basic model to include a number of limitations on information.

2. A problem of adverse selection may arise when consumers cannot judge the true quality of a product. As the price of the good falls, the quality

mix changes adversely, and the quantity demanded at a lower price may actually be lower than at a higher price.

3. Producers of high-quality products may attempt to signal that their product is better than those of competitors, for instance by providing better warranties.

4. When consumers judge quality by price, there may be some price that offers the best value. Firms will have no incentive to cut price below this "best value" price, even when, at this price, the amount they would be willing to supply exceeds demand. As a result, the market can settle in an equilibrium with an excess supply of goods.

5. When there is perfect information, private property and prices provide correct incentives to all market participants. When information is imperfect, two methods of helping to provide correct incentives are contracts with contingency clauses, and reputations. For firms to have an incentive to maintain a reputation, there must be profits. The equilibrium price can exceed marginal cost. Reputation may serve as a barrier to entry.

6. With costly search, there may be price dispersion and imperfections of competition as each firm faces a downward-sloping demand curve.

7. Advertising attempts to change consumers' buying behavior, either by providing relevant information about prices or characteristics, by persuasion, or both.

KEY TERMS

imperfect information	thin or incomplete markets	contingency clauses
asymmetric information	adverse selection	price dispersion
	signal	consumer protection legislation

REVIEW QUESTIONS

1. Why are markets for information not likely to work as well as markets for goods like wheat?

2. Why would "lemons" not be a problem for consumers in a world of perfect information? Why do they lead to a backward-bending demand curve in a world of imperfect information?

3. Why is signaling unnecessary in a world of perfect information? What does it accomplish in a world of imperfect information?

4. Explain why, if consumers think that quality increases with price, there will be cases where firms will have no incentive to cut prices in an attempt to attract more business.

5. How do contingency clauses in contracts help provide appropriate incentives? What are some of the problems in writing contracts that provide for all the relevant contingencies?

6. What role does reputation have in maintaining incentives? What is required if firms are to have an incentive to maintain their reputations? How might the good reputation of existing firms serve as a barrier to the entry of new firms?

7. What are the benefits of searching for market information? What are the costs? How does the existence of price dispersion affect the benefits? Could price dispersion exist in a world of perfect information? How does the fact that search is costly affect the nature of competition in a market?

8. Describe how advertising might affect the demand curve facing a firm. How do these changes affect prices? profits?

9. "For most practical purposes, information problems can be solved by government requirements that information be disclosed to potential buyers and investors." Discuss.

PROBLEMS

1. The We Pick 'Em Company collects information about horse races, and sells a newsletter predicting the winners. Why might you possibly be predisposed to distrust the accuracy of the We Pick 'Em newsletter?

2. How might a house cleaning service try to signal that it will promptly and carefully clean your house every time?

3. Explain how the incentives of someone to look after a car she is renting may not suit the company that is renting the car. How might a contingent contract help to solve this problem? Is it likely to solve the problem completely?

4. L. L. Bean, a mail order company, has a long-standing policy that it will take back anything it has sold, at any time, for any reason. Why might it be worthwhile for a profit-maximizing firm to enact such a policy?

5. Would you expect to see greater price dispersion within a metropolitan area, or between several small towns that are fifty miles apart? Why?

6. How do costs of search help to explain the success of department stores?

CHAPTER 19

IMPERFECTIONS IN THE
LABOR MARKET

Part Two emphasized the similarity between the labor market and markets for goods. Households demand goods and firms supply them, with the price system as intermediary. Likewise, firms demand labor and workers supply it, with the wage as intermediary. Firms hire labor up to the point where the value of the marginal product of labor is equal to the wage, just as they would buy coal up to the point where the value of the marginal product of coal is equal to the price of coal.

This chapter takes another look at the labor market. Just as we saw in the preceding five chapters some of the ways in which product markets differ from the way they are depicted in the basic competitive model, here we will see important ways in which labor markets differ from the way they are depicted in the basic competitive model. We will see that labor markets, like

KEY QUESTIONS

KEY QUESTIONS

1. How do unions affect the wages of their workers? of workers in general? What limits the power of unions? Why have unions been declining in strength?

2. How do we explain the large differences in wages paid to different workers, even to workers that appear to have similar abilities? What role does discrimination play?

3. How do firms seek to motivate their workers, to ensure that they put out effort commensurate with their pay? In what sense can the problem of providing workers incentives be viewed as a consequence of imperfect or limited information?

product markets, are characterized by imperfect competition. Unions are the most obvious manifestation, and we will take a look at their history as well as their impact on wages and employment—the prices and quantities of the labor market.

Information problems have an even more significant impact on the labor market than on product markets. This is partly because workers are not like lumps of coal. They have to be motivated to work hard. And they are concerned with work conditions and how their pay compares with that of other firms. Firms are aware of the importance of these considerations in attracting and keeping employees and design employment and compensation policies that take them into account.

LABOR UNIONS

Labor unions are organizations of workers, formed to obtain better working conditions and higher wages for their members. The main weapon they have is the threat of a collective withdrawal of labor, known as a **strike.**

A BRIEF HISTORY

Labor unions are less important institutions in our economy than they used to be, and have always played a smaller role in the United States than they do in many European countries. Unionization in the United States began in the late nineteenth and early twentieth centuries. A variety of craft unions were established, consisting of skilled workers such as carpenters, plumbers, and printers. In 1886, the American Federation of Labor (AFL) was formed. Led by Samuel Gompers, the AFL gathered together a number of these craft unions to enhance their bargaining power.

The Rise of Unions In the 1930s, two events strengthened union power: the confederation of major industrial unions into the Congress of Industrial Organizations (CIO) and the passage of the Wagner Act, which provided legal status to unions. The CIO represented a major change in two respects. First, it embraced all workers, unskilled as well as skilled; and second, it represented all the workers in a company. These industrial unions, by uniting all workers together, enhanced workers' bargaining strength. The leaders of these unions, such as Walter Reuther of the United Automobile Workers (UAW), attained national prominence, and the unions were able to obtain for their workers substantial wage increases and improvements in working conditions. The 1935 Wagner Act set up the National Labor Relations Board, which established procedures for certification of labor unions and prevention of certain practices on the part of firms trying to prevent workers from unionizing.

The Decline of Unions Prompted by concern that the balance had swung too far in favor of unions, Congress passed the Taft-Hartley Act in 1947. This law addressed two issues. First, unions had claimed that when they negotiated a better contract or better working conditions, they were providing benefits to all workers at an establishment. Thus, they required all laborers at unionized companies to join the union, a requirement that established **union shops.** Critics of union shops thought that the right to work should not be limited to members of unions. The Taft-Hartley law left it to the individual states to decide whether to outlaw union shops, and many states subsequently passed **right-to-work laws.** The laws gave workers the right to hold a job without belonging to a union—or, to put it the way unions do, the right to receive union pay without paying union dues.

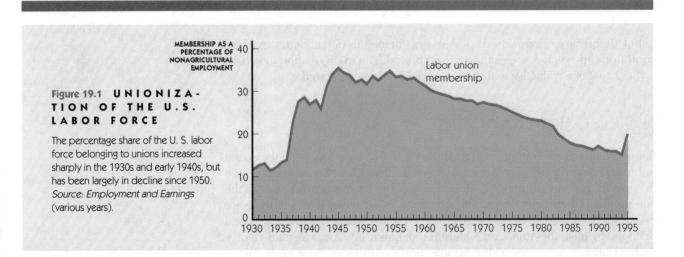

Figure 19.1 UNIONIZATION OF THE U.S. LABOR FORCE

The percentage share of the U. S. labor force belonging to unions increased sharply in the 1930s and early 1940s, but has been largely in decline since 1950. *Source: Employment and Earnings* (various years).

MEMBERSHIP AS A PERCENTAGE OF NONAGRICULTURAL EMPLOYMENT

Labor union membership

The second concern addressed by the Taft-Hartley Act was the devastating effect on the country of strikes by national unions. A shutdown of the railroads or the steel or coal industry could have ramifications far beyond the firms directly involved. The Taft-Hartley law gave the president the power to declare, when national welfare was at stake, an eighty-day cooling-off period, during which workers had to return to work.

Since the mid-1950s, union power has declined steadily in the United States. Figure 19.1 traces out the sharp increases of union membership in the 1930s, and again during World War II, when the government encouraged unionization in all military plants. But since then, unions have had only limited success in recruiting new members, so the union share of nonagricultural employment has been falling. It fell below 20 percent in 1984, where it remains today. In fact, not only has the union share been declining, the actual number of unionized workers has been falling. Today there are about seventeen million union members, 1 million less than there were in 1960.

These figures hide the even greater decline of unions in the private sector. In 1960 the percentage of union members working in the public sector was only 6 percent. Today it is more than 35 percent. Today only one out of ten nongovernment workers belongs to a union. Why the recent and continuing decline?

One explanation is that, whether as a result of union pressure or technological progress, working conditions for workers have improved enormously. Workers see less need for unions.

A second reason is related to the changing nature of the American economy. Unions have declined as the traditionally unionized sectors (like automobiles and steel) have weakened, and the service sector, in which unions have been and continue to be weak, has grown.

Third, unions may be less effective in competitive markets. When competition is limited, there are monopoly (or imperfect competition) profits or rents. Unions may be successful in obtaining for their workers a share in those rents. But when markets are competitive, firms cannot charge more than the market price for their goods, and if they are to survive, they simply cannot pay their workers more than the competitive wage.

In the late nineteenth and early twentieth centuries, for example, high wages in shoe and textile mills in New England drove plants to the nonunionized South. High wages also drive American firms to manufacture abroad. Unless unions manage to ensure that their workers are more productive than average, it is only when these sources of competition are restricted that unions can succeed in keeping their wages above average for long. In this view, the increased competition to which American industry was subjected in the 1970s and 1980s, both from abroad and from the deregulation of trucking, oil, airlines, banking, telephone service, and so on, led to a decline in the ability of unions in the private sector to garner higher wages for their workers.

A final explanation of the growth and decline of unions is the changing legal atmosphere. When laws support or encourage unions, unions prosper. When they do not, unions wither. Thus, the Wagner Act set the stage for the growth of unions in the 1930s. The Taft–Hartley Act paved the way for their decline in the post-World War II era.

Figure 19.2 THE UNION AS A MONOPOLY SELLER OF LABOR

Unions can be viewed as sellers of labor, with market power. When they increase their wage demands, they reduce the demand for their members' labor services.

ECONOMIC EFFECTS

The source of union power is collective action. When workers join together in a union, they no longer negotiate as isolated individuals. The threat of a strike (or a work slowdown) poses many more difficulties for an employer than does the threat of any single employee quitting.

In the perfectly competitive model of labor markets, workers are price takers, facing a given market wage. But in situations where there is a downward-sloping demand curve for labor, as in Figure 19.2,[1] unions have some power to be price setters. As a result of this power, a worker at a given level of skill who works in a unionized establishment will be paid more than a comparable worker in a competitive industry. The firm would like to hire that lower-priced, nonunion worker, and the nonunionized worker could easily be induced to move, but the firm has a union contract that prevents it from doing so. But as the union raises the price of labor (the wage), firms will employ fewer workers. Higher wages are obtained at the expense of lower employment. In the figure, when wages rise from the competitive level w_c to w_m, employment is reduced from L_c to L_m.

SHORT-RUN GAINS AT THE EXPENSE OF LONG-RUN LOSSES

Sometimes unions can increase both employment and wages, at least for a time. They present the employer with, in effect, two alternatives: either pay a high wage *and* maintain an employment level above the labor demand curve for that wage, or go out of business. If the employer already has sunk costs in machines and buildings, he may concede to the union demands. In effect, the union takes away some of the employer's monopoly profits and/or return to capital. In competitive markets, where there are no monopoly profits, the higher wages can only come out of employers' return to capital. But these employers will lose interest in investing in more capital. As capital wears out, the employer has less and less to lose from the union threat. As he refuses to invest more, jobs decrease. Even if the union makes short-run gains, they come at the expense of a long-run loss in jobs.

EFFECTS ON NONUNION WORKERS

The gains of today's union members may not only cost future jobs, they may also be at the expense of those in other sectors of the economy, for two reasons. First, the higher wages may well be passed on to consumers in the form

[1]Chapter 12 showed how the demand curve for labor is derived in competitive markets. Firms hire labor up to the point where the wage equals the value of the marginal product of labor. The derivation of the demand curve for labor in monopolies and imperfectly competitive markets follows along similar lines. Firms hire labor up to the point where the marginal revenue, the extra revenue they obtain from selling the extra output they produce from hiring an extra unit of labor, is equal to the wage.

of higher prices, particularly if product markets are not perfectly competitive. Second, the increased wages (and reduced employment) in the union sector drives down wages in the nonunionized sector, as the supply of nonunion labor increases. Some argue the opposite—that high union wages "pull up" wages in nonunion firms. The nonunion firms may, for instance, pay higher wages to reduce the likelihood of unionization. In particular sectors this effect is important, but most economists believe that the overall effect on nonunion workers is negative.

JOB SECURITY AND INNOVATION

As explained in Chapter 17, the economy as a whole benefits from innovation, but particular groups are likely to suffer. In an innovative economy, those workers who are dislocated by new inventions are expected to learn new skills and seek out new jobs. Without labor shifting in response to changes in demand (resulting either from new technologies or changes in tastes), the economy will be inefficient.

Technological changes may threaten the job security unions seek for their members. As a result, unions have attempted to retard innovations that might decrease the demand for their members' labor services. Job transitions are necessary for economic efficiency, but they are costly and the costs are borne largely by the workers. Before the advent of unions and laws providing unemployment compensation, the human toll was considerable. Individuals could not buy insurance against these employment risks, but they could form unions, and union attempts to enhance job security were a response to this important problem. Today many countries are looking for ways of insulating workers against the risks of job transition without impeding the labor mobility that is so important for economic efficiency. For instance, the Swedish government has set up major programs to facilitate job transitions and job retraining.

UNIONS AND POLITICS

We have seen that the fortunes of unions depend, to a large extent, on the legal environment in which they operate. Unions have also learned that what they cannot get at the bargaining table they may be able to obtain through the political process. For example, they have actively campaigned for higher minimum wages.

At the same time, unions have shown in their political stances that they recognize the economic forces that determine both the strength of their bargaining positions and, more generally, the level of wages. Thus, they have been active supporters of policies of high employment. They have sought to restrict imports from abroad (believing that this will increase the demand for American products and therefore the demand for labor). And they have been proponents of restrictions on immigration (recognizing that increases in the supply of labor lead to reductions in wages).

Finally, unions have been strong advocates, through the political process, of safer working conditions. Today, the Occupational Safety and Health Administration (OSHA) attempts to ensure that workers are not exposed to unnecessary hazards. OSHA seeks to make the kinds of episodes such as occurred in the asbestos industry, where workers were exposed to life-threatening risks, much less likely today.

LIMITS ON UNION POWER

In the United States, no union has a monopoly on *all* workers. At most, a union has a monopoly on the workers currently working for a particular firm. Thus, the power of unions is partly attributable to the fact that a firm cannot easily replace its employees. When a union goes on strike, the firm may be able to hire some workers, but it is costly to bring in and train a whole new labor force. Indeed, most of the knowledge needed to train the new workers is in the hands of the union members. While one bushel of wheat may be very much like another, one worker is not very much like another. Workers outside the firm are not perfect substitutes for workers, particularly skilled ones, inside.

THE THREAT OF REPLACEMENT

In those industries in which skills are easily transferable across firms, or where a union has not been successful in enlisting the support of most of the skilled workers, a firm can replace striking workers, and union power will be limited. Caterpillar, a manufacturer of tractors and road-making equipment, weathered a prolonged strike by the United Auto Workers beginning June 21, 1993. Eventually management announced that if workers did not return to their jobs, they would be replaced. The union caved in shortly after the firm made good on its threat.

In many cases, however, workers' skills are firm-specific. Just as, from the employers' perspective, workers outside the firm are not perfect substitutes for workers within, from the workers' perspective, one job is not a perfect substitute for another. Thus, there is often value both to workers and firms in preserving ongoing employment relationships. The two parties are tied to each other in what is referred to as a bargaining relationship. The bargaining strengths of the two sides are affected by the fact that a firm, at a cost, can obtain other employees, and employees, at a cost, can get other jobs. The total amount by which the two sides together are better off continuing their relationship than ending it is referred to as the "bargaining surplus." A large part of the negotiations between unions and management are about how to split this surplus.

THE THREAT OF UNEMPLOYMENT

Unions have come to understand that in the long run, higher wages—other things being equal—mean lower levels of employment. When job opportunities in general are weak, concern about the employment consequences of union contracts increases. This was evident in the early 1980s, as a deep recession threatened a number of union jobs, especially in the automobile industry, which also faced the threat of Japanese imports.

CLOSE-UP: LESSONS FROM UNIONS IN OTHER COUNTRIES

Unions have been blamed for declining productivity growth in the United States, even though only one in six workers belongs to a union. This share is less than the share of the work force that in unionized in most developed countries. In Japan, for example, one in four workers belong to unions. The share in Germany is more than one third; Canada and the United Kingdom, 42 percent; and in Denmark and Sweden, it is over 70 percent.

Those who blame American unions for the decline of U.S. economic power must explain how nations like Japan and Germany have increased their rates of productivity with higher rates of unionization. And those who blame the decline in unionization on the growth of the service sector or greater global competition must explain why those factors have led to lower union membership in the United States but much higher levels in other countries.

Part of the explanation is the different nature of unions in different countries. In Finland and Portu-

gal, for example, unions negotiate with employers and the government on overall national policy. And in Germany, union negotiations tend to happen one industry at a time. By contrast, U.S. and Japanese unions tend to negotiate one *company* at a time.

In addition, a nation's legal environment can either encourage workers to form unions or make it easier for management to fight unions off. Margaret Thatcher, as prime minister of Britain in the 1970s, took as one of her main goals the redressing of what she saw as an imbalance of power in favor of unions.

This international perspective suggests that asking whether unions are generically "good" or "bad" is too simplistic. Instead, the question should be whether unions, in some form, have a potentially useful role to play in the U.S. economy. Richard Freeman, of Harvard University, thinks so. He argues: "Although Scandinavian levels of unionization seem to me to be infeasible and undesirable in a large, diverse country like the United States . . . research supports the view that greater unionization is needed to give workers alternatives to the market or to governmental intervention in workplace arrangements." Freeman suggests that in the future, American unions will have to focus less attention on demanding higher wages and benefits and more on improving working conditions.

Just as American firms have been looking abroad to find alternative models for what makes success, unions in other countries may provide some alternative models for how American unions might help increase the country's productivity.

Sources: International Labour Office, *World Labour Report* (1992). Richard Freeman, "Is Declining Unionization of the U.S. Good, Bad, or Irrelevant?" in Lawrence Mishel and Paula Voos, eds., *Unions and Economic Competitiveness* (Armonk, N.Y.: Sharpe, 1992), pp. 143–72.

In the round of union negotiations that began in 1981, Ford Motor Company was the first auto company to settle with the United Automobile Workers. In the new thirty-month contract, the UAW agreed to give up annual wage increases for two years, to defer what had been automatic increases in wages in response to increases in the cost of living, and to eliminate a number of paid personal holidays. The contract also provided for new employees to be paid at only 85 percent of the normal rate, thus creating a two-tier wage system. For its part, Ford offered a moratorium on closing any plants, a guarantee that extra profits arising during the term of the contract would be shared with workers, increased worker participation in decision making, and greater job security for workers. General Motors made a similar deal a few months later, and Chrysler was able to negotiate a better deal because of its even

UNIONS AND IMPERFECT COMPETITION IN THE LABOR MARKET

Economic effects:

Higher wages for union members, with fewer union jobs and lower wages for nonunion members

Improved job security, sometimes at the expense of innovation and economic efficiency

Minimum wages, restrictions on imports, improved working conditions, other gains achieved through the political process

Determinants of union power:

Political and legal environment

Economic environment: threat of replacement and unemployment worse financial condition. The dollar value of the total concessions from the union was estimated at about $3 billion for the contract period. Similar wage cuts occurred in the airline and steel industries, among others.

The deal between Ford and the UAW set the pattern for auto labor contracts in the 1980s. Unions made wage concessions in return for job security. For example, in 1984, in return for wage concessions, GM agreed not to lay off for the next six years any worker with at least one year's seniority who was displaced by new technology. Instead, such workers would stay on at their full salary while they were retrained and relocated.

WAGE DIFFERENTIALS

The basic competitive model suggests that if the goods being sold are the same, prices will also be the same. Wages are the price in the labor market; but even in the absence of unions, similar types of workers performing similar types of jobs are sometimes paid quite different wages. For example, some secretaries are paid twice as much as others. How can economists explain differences like these?

They begin by pointing to **compensating wage differentials.** Understanding compensating wage differentials begins with the observation that although different jobs may have the same title, they can be quite different. Some jobs are less pleasant, require more overtime, and are in a less convenient location. These are **nonpecuniary** attributes of a job. Other nonpecuniary attributes include the degree of autonomy provided the worker (that is, the closeness with which her actions are supervised) and the risk she must bear, whether in a physical sense or from the variability in income. Economists expect wages to adjust to reflect the attractiveness or unattractiveness of these nonpecuniary characteristics. Compensating wage differentials arise because firms have to compensate their workers for the negative aspects of a job.

Other differences are accounted for by differences in the productivity of workers. These are **productivity wage differentials.** Some workers are much more productive than others, even with the same experience and education.

Compensating and productivity wage differentials fall within the realm of the basic competitive model analysis. But other wage differentials are due to imperfect information. It takes time to search out different job opportunities. Just as one store may sell the same object for a higher price than another store, one firm may hire labor for a lower wage than another firm. The worker who accepts a lower-paying job simply because he did not know about the higher-paying one down the street faces an **information-based differential.**

Limited information has important implications for firms. First, in the standard competitive model, firms face a horizontal supply curve for labor. If they raise wages slightly above the "market" wage, they can obtain as much labor as they want. In practice, mobility is more limited. Even if workers at other firms knew about the higher wage offer, they might be reluctant to switch. They may worry that they are not well matched for the job, or that the employer is offering high wages because the work is unattractive.

Second, firms worry about the quality of their work force. If an employer offers a higher wage to someone working for another firm, and the worker accepts, the employer might worry about the signal his action sends about the quality of the worker. Did the worker's current employer—who presumably knows a lot about the worker's productivity—fail to match the job offer because the worker's productivity does not warrant the higher wage? Does the worker's willingness to leave demonstrate a "lack of loyalty," or an "unsettled nature"—in which case, he may not stick with the new firm long enough to make his training worthwhile? These concerns again impede labor mobility—as employers prefer to keep their existing labor force even when there are lower-paid workers with similar credentials whom they might recruit at a lower wage.

There are a variety of other impediments to labor mobility, including the costs of moving from one city to another.

Different groups of individuals may differ in their mobility. For instance, older workers may be much more reluctant to move than younger workers. Sometimes, firms take advantage of these differences, to pay lower wages. Knowing that older workers will not leave even if wages fail to keep pace with inflation, employers may hold back raises from them. This provides a rationale for employers to engage in age discrimination in wage setting.

DISCRIMINATION

Discrimination is said to occur if two workers of seemingly similar *work-related* characteristics are treated differently. Paying higher wages to more educated workers is not discrimination, as long as the higher level of education is related to higher productivity. If older workers are less productive, then paying them lower wages is not discrimination. But if older workers are just as productive as younger workers, then taking advantage of their lower mobility *is* discrimination.

Forty years ago, there was open and outright discrimination in the labor market. Some employers simply refused to hire African-Americans. Today much of the discrimination that occurs is more subtle. Firms seek to hire the best workers they can for each job at the lowest cost possible, operating with imperfect information. In making predictions about future performance, employers use whatever information they have available. On average, employers may have found that those receiving a degree from a well-established school are more productive than those receiving a degree from a less-established college. Of those African-Americans and Hispanics who have managed to get a college education, more may have gone to the less-established schools. Screening the applicant pool to pick those with degrees from well-established colleges effectively screens out many African-Americans and Hispanics. This more subtle form of discrimination is called **statistical discrimination.**

Some discrimination is neither old-fashioned prejudice nor statistical discrimination. Employers may just feel more comfortable dealing with people with whom they have dealt in the past. In a world in which there is so much uncertainty about who is a good worker, and in which a bad worker can do enormous damage, top management may rely on certain trusted employees for recommendations. And such judgments are inevitably affected by friendships and other ties. Many claim that if discrimination is to be eliminated, this form of discrimination, based on "old boy networks," has to be broken.

When firms pay lower wages to, say, women or minorities, it is called **wage discrimination.** Today, wage discrimination is perhaps less common than **job discrimination,** where disadvantaged groups have less access to better-paying jobs. Women are often said to face a "glass ceiling": they can climb up to middle management jobs, but can't get beyond that to top management.

Some market forces tend to limit the extent of discrimination. If a woman is paid less than a man of comparable productivity, it pays a firm to hire the woman. Not to hire her costs the firm profits. To put it another way, the firm pays a price for discriminating. If there are enough firms that put profits above prejudice, then the wages of women will be bid up toward the level of men of comparable productivity.

Beginning in the 1960s, the government has taken an increasingly active stance in combatting discrimination. In 1964, Congress passed the Civil Rights Act, which prohibited employment discrimination and set up the Equal Employment Opportunity Commission to prosecute cases of discrimination. The reach of these laws was extended in 1975 when the government banned age discrimination.

EXPLANATIONS OF WAGE DIFFERENTIALS

Unions: Unions may succeed in obtaining higher wages for their workers.

Compensating differentials: Wage differences may correspond to differences in the nature of the job.

Productivity differentials: Wage differences may correspond to differences in the productivity between workers.

Information-based differentials: Wage differences may reflect the fact that workers do not have perfect information about the opportunities available in the market, and employers do not view all workers as perfect substitutes.

Imperfect labor mobility: Differentials will not be eliminated by individuals moving between jobs.

Discrimination: Wage differentials and hiring and promotion decisions can sometimes be traced to nothing more than racial or gender differences.

Beyond this, the government has required its contractors to undertake **affirmative action.** They must actively seek out minorities and women for jobs, and actively seek to promote them to better-paying positions. In order to be effective, affirmative action has occasionally taken the form of quotas that specify that a certain number or fraction of positions be reserved for minorities or women. Critics claim that quotas are discriminatory—they imply that a minority individual would be chosen over a more qualified white male. One of the objectives of antidiscrimination laws was to discourage thinking in racial or gender terms. Courts have reaffirmed this, allowing quotas only in special circumstances such as redressing the effects of specific instances of past discrimination.

MOTIVATING WORKERS

The discussion to this point has treated workers as if they were machines. Workers have a price—the wage—analogous to the price of machines. But even to the most profit-hungry and coldhearted employer, people are different from machines. They bring adaptability and a multitude of skills and experiences to a job. Most machines can only do one task, and even robots can only do what they are programmed to do. However, machines have one advantage over humans. Except when they break down, they do what they are told. But workers have to be motivated if they are to work hard and to exercise good judgment.

This can be viewed as an information problem. In the basic competitive model of Part Two, workers were paid to perform particular tasks. The employer knew perfectly whether the worker performed the agreed-upon task in the agreed-upon manner. If the worker failed to do so, he did not get paid. The pay was the only form of motivation required. But in reality, workers frequently have considerable discretion. Employers have limited information about what a worker is doing at each moment. So they have to motivate their work force to exercise their abilities to the fullest.

To motivate workers, employers use both the carrot and the stick. They may reward workers for performing well by making pay and promotion depend on performance, and they may punish workers for shirking by firing them. Sometimes a worker is given considerable discretion and autonomy; sometimes he is monitored closely. The mix of carrots and sticks, autonomy and direct supervision, varies from job to job and industry to industry. It depends partly on how easy it is to supervise workers directly and how easy it is to compensate workers on the basis of performance.

PIECE RATES AND INCENTIVES

When workers can be paid for exactly what they produce, with their pay increasing for higher productivity and falling for lower productivity, they will have appropriate incentives to work hard. The system of payment in which a worker is paid for each item produced or each task performed is called a **piece-rate system.** But relatively few Americans are paid largely, let alone exclusively, on a piece-rate system. Typically, even workers within a piece-rate system get a base pay *plus* additional pay, which increases the more they produce.

Why don't more employers enact a piece-rate system, if it would improve incentives? One major reason is that piece rates leave workers bearing considerable risk. A worker may have a bad week because of bad luck. For example, salesmen, who are often paid commissions on the basis of sales—a form of piece rate—may simply find the demand for their products lacking.

A firm, by providing a certain amount of guaranteed pay, gives the worker a steady income and reduces the risk she must bear. But with lower piece-rate compensation, the worker has less incentive to work hard. There is thus a trade-off between risk and incentives. Compensation schemes must find some balance between offering security and offering incentives linked to worker performance. In many jobs, employers or managers achieve this balance by offering both a guaranteed minimum compensation (including fringe benefits) and bonuses that depend on performance.

A second reason more employers do not use piece-rate systems is a concern for quality. For workers on an assembly line, for example, the quantity produced may be easily measured, but quality cannot. If the workers' pay just depends on the number of items produced, the worker has an incentive to emphasize quantity over quality. The result may be less profitable for the firm than a lower level of higher-quality output.

In any case, most workers are engaged in a variety of tasks, only some of which can easily be defined and rewarded by means of a piece-rate system. For example, although employers would like experienced workers to train new workers, employees who are paid on a piece-rate system have little incentive to do this, or to help their co-workers in other ways. Similarly, when salesmen are paid on the basis of commissions, they have little incentive to provide information and service to potential customers whom they perceive as not likely to be immediate buyers. Even if providing information enhances the likelihood that a customer will return to the store to buy the good, there is a fair chance that some other salesperson will get the commission. To see this effect at work, visit a car dealer's showroom, make it clear that you are not going to buy a car that day, and see what service you get.

EFFICIENCY WAGES

When output is easily measured, then the carrot of basing pay at least partially on performance makes sense. And when effort is easily monitored, then using the stick of being fired for failure to exert adequate effort makes sense. But monitoring effort continuously is often expensive. An alternative is to monitor less frequently, and impose a big penalty if the worker is caught shirking. One way of imposing a big penalty is to pay above-market wages. Then, if a worker is fired, he suffers a big income loss. The higher the wage, the greater the penalty from being fired. Similarly, rewarding workers with higher pay who are observed to be working hard whenever they are monitored, provides incentives for workers to continue to work hard.

These are examples where higher wages help motivate workers and lead to increased productivity. There are additional reasons why it may pay a firm to pay high wages. High wages reduce labor turnover, lead to more loyalty and higher quality work by employees, and enable the firm to attract more productive workers. For all of these reasons it may pay firms to pay high wages—higher than are absolutely necessary to recruit the desired number of workers. The theory that higher wages increases workers' net productivity, either by reducing labor turnover, by providing better incentives, or by enabling the firm to recruit a higher quality labor force, is called the **efficiency wage theory.** While conventional theory emphasizes that increased productivity leads to higher wages, efficiency wage theory emphasizes that higher wages lead to increased productivity.

Efficiency wage theory provides an explanation for some wage differentials. In jobs where it is very costly to monitor workers on a day-to-day basis, or where the damage a worker can do is very great (where, for instance, by punching one wrong button the worker can destroy a machine), employers are more likely to rely on high wages to ensure workers perform well.

These "wages of trust" may explain why wages in more capital-intensive industries (that require massive investments) are higher for workers with otherwise comparable skills than wages in industries using less capital. They may also explain why workers entrusted with the care of much cash (which they could abscond with) are paid higher wages than are other workers of comparable skills. It is not so much that they receive high wages because they are trustworthy, but that they become more trustworthy because they receive high wages—and the threat of losing those high wages encourages honest behavior.

OTHER INCENTIVES

Other important incentives to increase job performance are enhanced promotion possibilities for those who perform well, with pay rising with promotions. But it is often hard to determine the difficulty of the task a worker is performing. One way to figure out who is performing well is to set up a contest among workers, with the winner receiving some valuable prize, like a cash bonus. Consider a firm trying to figure out how much to pay its sales force when it is promoting a new product. If a salesperson is successful, does that represent good salesmanship, or is the new product able to "sell itself"? All sales representatives are in roughly the same position. The representative who sells the most gets a bonus—and wins the contest.

At the top end of the corporate hierarchy, the top executives of America's largest firms are paid much higher average salaries than their counterparts in many other industrial economies, often running into the millions of dollars. Why is this? Economists continue to debate the issue. Some interpret these salaries as the payoffs of contests, others as reflecting the large contributions of these managers or wages of trust. But some suspect that top managers have

Legislating a minimum wage below which it is illegal to hire workers has been sharply criticized by economists as hurting exactly the people it is designed to help—those at the bottom of the wage scale.

Critics base their reasoning on the traditional demand and supply model of Part Two. There, an increase in wages above the market equilibrium results in lower employment. Those who manage to get jobs are better off; those who are forced into unemployment are worse off. If the objective is to reduce poverty, the minimum wage, in this perspective, seems counterproductive.

But as this chapter has pointed out, markets for labor are different from markets for many other commodities. Workers have to be motivated to work hard. High wages lead to increased productivity, less absenteeism, and lower labor turnover. Presumably, rational firms would take this into account in their wage setting. Even so, if the government forces firms to pay higher wages through minimum wage legislation, the increased productivity may largely offset the increased wages, so that the employment effect may be very small.

In labor markets in which there is imperfect competition, minimum wages could actually lead to increased employment. Because of imperfect mobility, firms face an upward-sloping supply schedule. Since all workers in a similar job have to be treated the same, the cost of hiring an additional worker may be high, above the wage it pays to its new employee. Not only must the firm raise the wage offered to the *new* worker, it must raise the wage paid to all existing workers. This discourages the firm from hiring additional employees. With a minimum wage, the cost of hiring an additional worker is just the minimum wage. Accord-

ingly, the marginal cost of hiring an additional worker when there is a minimum wage may actually be lower than when there is not, in which case firms will actually hire more workers.

These perspectives are consistent with several recent empirical studies which have shown there to be negligible, or even positive, employment effects from a minimum wage.

Some economists have also pointed to broader, positive consequences of minimum wages: they induce firms to invest more in their workers, to increase their workers' productivity. Gavin Wright, a distinguished economic historian at Stanford University, has argued that minimum wages played a vital role in the transformation of the South. It was

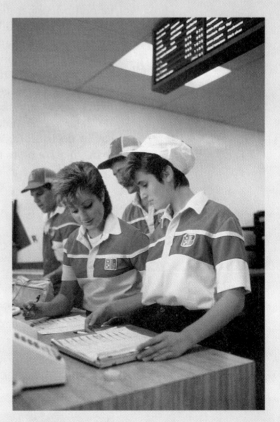

a region that had been vastly poorer than the North from the end of the Civil War to the Great Depression, with an economy largely based on very low wages. The minimum wage catalyzed changes which had dramatic effects on the South's economy, shifting them away from those low wage industries to dynamic industries paying higher wages.

A further alleged advantage of raising the minimum wage is that it increases the incentives to work, by increasing the difference between what someone on welfare receives and what a worker gets.

enough control over the firm to divert a considerable amount (though but a small fraction) of a firm's resources to their own betterment in the form of higher compensation.

In recent years, firms have explored the consequences of alternative ways of encouraging worker motivation and hence worker productivity. Some use teams. When pay depends on team performance, members of a team have an incentive to monitor and help one another. The Swedish automaker Volvo believes that such team arrangements have increased the productivity of its own work force. Some firms have encouraged worker participation in decision making. Such participation may help both sides see that there is more to be gained by cooperation than by conflict. For instance, new ways of producing goods can make both the firm and the workers better off; if the company sells more goods, all share in the benefits.

At least in the long run, wages and labor costs respond to reflect the attitudes of workers. If workers find that a certain firm provides an attractive workplace, the wages it must pay to recruit people may be lower than other firms' wages, and the people that it recruits will work harder and stay longer. If workers as a whole become concerned about having more autonomy, more say in decision making, or any other attribute of the workplace, it will pay firms to respond to their concerns.

WAYS OF MOTIVATING WORKERS

Piece rates, or pay based on measured output.

The threat of firing workers whose efforts or performance are deemed inadequate.

Efficiency wages introduce an extra cost to those dismissed for unsatisfactory performance.

Relative performance: promotions, contests.

Team rewards, pay based on team performance.

CLOSE-UP: FRINGE BENEFITS

The monetary pay a worker receives is often only a portion of his total compensation received. In 1993, for example, the average wage (or salary) received by a private industry worker in the United States was $11.90 per hour. However, the total compensation received was $16.70 per hour, a full 40 percent higher.

The difference is "fringe benefits." U.S. employers paid an average of $1.11 per hour to each employee for paid leave, including vacation time, paid holidays, and absence for illness, $.42 per hour for special bonuses and incentives, $1.19 per hour for insurance, mainly health insurance, and $.48 an hour for company pensions. Employers also paid $1.52 per hour per employee for government-required programs like Social Security and unemployment insurance. These payments clearly have value to workers, but they do not show up in take-home pay.

Fringe benefits complicate the straightforward model of the labor market presented earlier in this book. In that model, workers try to seek out the firm that will give them the highest pay, while employers try to seek out those who will work for the lowest pay. The existence of fringe benefits means that workers must look beyond take-home pay and take all forms of compensation into account.

Why do employers offer fringe benefits, rather than simply paying a straight salary to workers? One main reason involves the tax code; if employees are paid income and then purchase health insurance on their own, they must pay income tax on the money. But if the company buys the insurance for them, the fringe benefit is not counted as income. In addition, many employers use fringe benefits to offer an incentive for employees to stay with the company. For example, companies often require that the employee remain with the company for a period of several years before becoming eligible for the company pension plan. Such

"We have something with terrific fringe benefits. No salary—just fringe benefits."

benefits show that employers are not eager to lose their long-term employees, and would rather offer some added benefits than go through the cost and trouble of hiring and training new workers. But why—other than for tax reasons—they should rely so heavily on rewarding these workers through better fringe benefits rather than through cash bonuses remains unclear.

Source: Statistical Abstract of the United States (1994).

REVIEW AND PRACTICE

SUMMARY

1. The proportion of U.S. workers in unions has declined since the 1950s. Possible reasons include laws that have improved working conditions in general; the decline of manufacturing industries, where unions have traditionally been strong, relative to service industries; increased competition in the product market, providing firms with less latitude to pay above market wages; and a more anti-union atmosphere in the U.S. legal structure.

2. Union gains in wages are typically at the expense of lower employment, at least in the long run, and lower wages in the nonunion sector. Unions also have played an important role in enhancing job security, though sometimes at the expense of innovation. Some of the gains they have accomplished for workers have been through the political process, for instance, in pushing legislation that promotes occupational safety and health and the minimum wage.

3. Union power is limited by the ability of companies to bring in new, nonunion workers and by the threat of unemployment to union workers.

4. Explanations for wage differentials include compensating differentials (differences in the nature of jobs), productivity differentials (differences in productivity between workers), imperfect information (workers do not know all the job opportunities that are available), and discrimination.

5. Employers try to motivate workers and induce high levels of effort through a combination of direct supervision, incentives for doing well, and penalties for doing badly. They pay wages higher than workers could get elsewhere (efficiency wages), give promotions and bonuses, base pay on relative performance (contests), and grant team rewards.

KEY TERMS

union shops	**compensating wage**	**piece-rate system**
right-to-work laws	**differentials**	**efficiency wage theory**

REVIEW QUESTIONS

1. Has the power of unions in the U.S. economy been shrinking or growing in the last few decades? Why? In what sector has union growth been largest? Why might this be so?

2. What effect will successful unions have on the level of wages paid by unionized companies? on the capital investment for those companies? What effect will they have on wages paid by nonunionized companies?

3. How might greater job security for union workers possibly lead them to become less efficient?

4. Does it make sense for a union to resist the introduction of an innovation in the short run? in the long run?

5. What are alternative explanations for wage differentials?

6. How do piece rates provide incentives to work hard? Why is there not a greater reliance on piece-rate systems?

7. What is efficiency wage theory?

PROBLEMS

1. In what ways are labor markets similar to product markets? In what ways are they different?

2. Explain how both these points can be true simultaneously:
    (a) unions manage to raise the wage paid to their members;
    (b) unions do not affect the average level of wages paid in the economy.

3. How might each of the following factors affect the power of unions?
    (a) A state passes a right-to-work law.
    (b) Foreign imports increase.
    (c) The national unemployment rate falls.
    (d) Corporate profits increase.

4. Suppose a worker holding a job that pays $15 per hour applies for a job with another company that pays $18 per hour. Why might the second company be suspicious about whether the worker is really worth $18 per hour? How might the worker attempt to overcome those fears?

5. Imagine that a company knows that if it cuts wages 10 percent, then 10 percent of its employees will leave. How might adverse selection cause the amount of work done by the company to fall by more than 10 percent?

6. Advances in computer technology have allowed some firms to monitor their typists by a system that counts the number of keystrokes they make in a given workday. Telephone operators are sometimes monitored according to how many calls they take, and how long they spend on an aver-

age call. Would you expect these changes to increase productivity? Why or why not?

7. When someone is promoted from middle-management to top executive, his salary often doubles or more. Why does this seem puzzling, from the perspective of the theory of competitive markets? Why might a profit-maximizing firm do this?

CHAPTER 20

FINANCING, CONTROLLING, AND MANAGING THE FIRM

Who controls a company? The simple answer is the executives do. Presidents, vice presidents, chief executive officers—these are the people who make decisions, and they deserve a major share of the responsibility for a company's actions. But executives of most corporations are not entirely autonomous. There is an old saying: "He who pays the piper calls the tune." In the context of corporate behavior, investors who provide money to a firm certainly have some control over the executives who manage it.

In Chapter 9 we looked at equity and debt from the perspective of the household investing its funds. Here we use the perspective of the corporation that issues securities and receives the money. The branch of economics concerned with how firms raise capital—and the consequences of alternative methods—is called **corporate finance.** The importance of this topic to modern economics was recognized by the Nobel Foundation in 1990, when it awarded the Nobel Memorial Prize in economics to William Sharpe of Stanford University, Merton Miller of the University of Chicago, and Harry Markowitz of the City College of New York for their pioneering work in the field.

KEY QUESTIONS

1. What difference does it make whether a firm raises capital through debt or through equity? How do concerns about taxes, bankruptcy, and managerial incentives affect firms' choices of financial structure?

2. Why is credit frequently rationed? And why, in spite of the advantages in risk sharing, is so little new capital raised in the form of equity?

3. What is the relationship between financial structure and control of the firm?

4. What role do takeovers play in enhancing the efficiency of the economy? Why is there such criticism of takeovers?

5. What are the central problems facing organizations in which the manager is not the sole owner?

6. What difference does it make whether decision making is centralized or decentralized? What are the pros and cons to each?

7. What determines what a firm produces itself as opposed to what it purchases from other companies? What determines, in other words, the boundaries of the firm?

Curiously enough, none of the issues we will be concerned with here arises in the basic competitive model of Part Two. There, firms all have a single objective, to maximize their profits or market value. That is also what all investors want. And because there is unanimity about what firms should do, the issue of "control" never arises. Indeed, even the issue of how the firm should raise its capital—through debt or equity financing—turns out to make no difference in the basic competitive model. In the real world, issues of finance and control not only grab headlines but also absorb the attention of Wall Street and firm managers. And for a good reason, as we will see.

THE FIRM'S LEGAL FORM

Business firms in the United States take one of three legal forms: proprietorship, partnership, or corporation. A **proprietorship** is the simplest form. The firm has a single owner. If you went into business selling class notes to other students, your business would be listed as a proprietorship by the IRS. Because of the advantages of incorporation (which we will see below), only the smallest firms remain proprietorships.

When two or more individuals decide to go into business together, they typically form a **partnership.** As with proprietorships, most partnerships are small—Sally and Sue's Delicatessen, or Bob and Andy's Laundromat. However, some partnerships are much larger. Many of the major national accounting firms are organized as partnerships, with hundreds of partners. Likewise, many law firms with one hundred or more lawyers are organized as partnerships.

The final form of organization is the **corporation.** Corporations divide ownership into shares, also known as the stock of a company. The purchase of a corporation's stock entitles the purchaser to a corresponding share of ownership in the firm with proportional voting rights and entitlements to the firm's profits. The key feature of the corporation, and the one that has made possible the huge firms we know today—like IBM, General Motors, and Exxon—is **limited liability.**

With proprietorships and partnerships, there is no limit to the liability of the owner(s). Consider Joe Smith, who decides to open up a restaurant and has not yet hired a lawyer to advise him of the advantages of the corporate form of business. He invests $50,000 of his savings and borrows $200,000 to buy furniture for the restaurant, to decorate it, and to pay for a five-year lease. Unfortunately, he has limited talents both as a chef and as a businessman, and fails to attract customers. After trying it for a year, he closes his business. But he is still responsible for the debts of the firm. Not only has he lost the $50,000 he took out of his savings, but he may be forced to sell his home to repay the $200,000 in loans because he is fully liable for them.

In partnerships, each partner is fully liable for all the debts of the firm. Now, when Joe Smith and his partner, Alfred Jones, go into business together, they each put up $25,000 and together borrow $200,000. If Alfred has no house or other form of wealth and thus cannot help to pay off the debt when the restaurant goes bankrupt, Joe will again find himself fully liable for the $200,000 debt.

By choosing the corporate form, owners avoid full liability. If Joe Smith sets his restaurant up as a corporation (and he can invite Alfred Jones and any others to purchase shares and join him as owners of the company), he can put his $50,000 into the corporation and have the corporation borrow the $200,000. The corporation is liable for all the debts it incurs, and in the case of bankruptcy, its assets will be sold. The money recouped in this way will go first to those who have lent the firm money (banks, bondholders), and then, if any is left over, to Joe and his fellow shareholders. In the event of bankruptcy, the shareholders are likely to lose all the money they invested in the corporation, but *they will not lose any more.* When Eastern Airlines declared bankruptcy in March 1989, the airline's shareholders did not have to worry about selling their houses to help pay off the billions of dollars of Eastern's debts.

Limited liability provides larger corporations with another important advantage over other forms of organization: it facilitates public trading of the company's shares. Buying such a share always involves the risk that the investor will lose all the money invested, as we have seen. Yet this risk may be tiny compared with the risk faced by the investor in a partnership. In the latter, each partner is liable for all the partnership's bills, if his fellow partners cannot pay their share. Therefore, an investor purchasing a partnership share needs to know something about the wealth of each of the other partners in order to know how much risk he faces. Such information is unnecessary to the investor in a corporation, which means the potential pool of investors in corporations is much, much larger. The limited liability feature of corporations is attractive enough that today most businesses, small and large, are set up as corporations. Even the single proprietor, if he has a good lawyer, is likely to set his business up as a corporation to protect his family's assets.

There is another important distinction among the three legal forms. When there is a single proprietor, there is no question about who makes the final decisions. When there are many owners, whether they are partners or shareholders, there are potential disagreements. There must be a set of rules concerning how these disagreements are to be resolved. For instance, shareholders elect directors, who choose managers. If a majority of shareholders do not like what their board of directors is doing, they can elect new directors—though this seldom happens.

CORPORATE FINANCE

Corporations can finance their investments in many ways. We focus on three alternatives. A corporation can borrow funds, either from a bank or directly from investors by issuing bonds. It can issue new shares of stock, the buyers of which become entitled to a share of whatever profits the firm distributes to its owners in dividends. Or, if its profits are high enough, the corporation can finance its investment with its own earnings, rather than paying them out in dividends.

Figure 20.1 provides a schematic representation of a corporation's cash flow. The corporation receives cash in three forms: income from the sale of

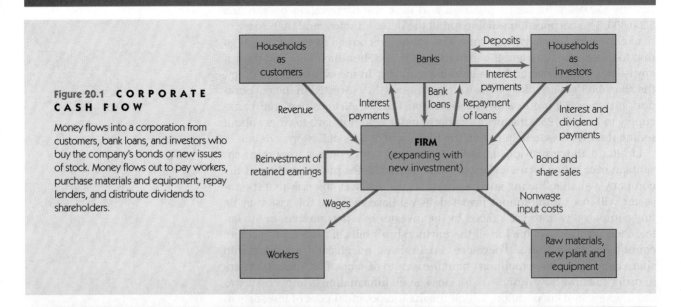

Figure 20.1 CORPORATE CASH FLOW

Money flows into a corporation from customers, bank loans, and investors who buy the company's bonds or new issues of stock. Money flows out to pay workers, purchase materials and equipment, repay lenders, and distribute dividends to shareholders.

its products, borrowed funds from banks and bond sales, and funds from sales of new shares. The corporation uses its cash to pay its expenses—wages, raw materials, and other costs of production. It also pays back outstanding loans. Any cash left over after expenses and debt payments may be distributed to the shareholders as dividends. Or some cash—called **retained earnings**— may be kept by the firm for the corporation to use for further investments or as a cash reserve.

In Chapters 6 and 9, we learned the attributes of investments: average return, risk, tax treatment, and liquidity. There we took the perspective of the investor. Bonds yielded a lower average return and had lower risks than stocks. Stocks yielded returns in the form of both dividends and capital gains. And capital gains had major tax advantages.

Here, we take the corporation's perspective. A corporation's management wants to raise capital in a way that best serves the interests of its shareholders. In particular, managers want to maximize the value of the firm's shares. Traditional theory reasons that in deciding between debt and equity financing, a firm's treasurer focuses on two issues. First is the cost of capital, what the firm must pay to *new* investors in return for using their funds—the "average return" to investors. The average return paid to those who supply debt capital is lower than the average return paid to those who supply equity capital. Thus, debt is less attractive from the viewpoint of new investors but more attractive from the viewpoint of the firm.

The second issue is risk, particularly the risk of bankruptcy. While firms do not have to pay their shareholders on any fixed schedule, they do have fixed obligations to pay certain amounts at certain times to bondholders and other lenders. Debt therefore imposes greater risks on the firm. If it does not have the cash to meet those obligations, and cannot get the cash by borrowing from someone else, then the company goes into bankruptcy. The more the firm borrows, the greater these fixed obligations, and the greater the chance that it will not be able to meet them. Thus, while to the investor debt appears safer, to the firm debt is riskier. On this account equity is preferable to the firm.

The traditional analysis of corporate finance sees the firm as facing a risk-return trade-off. In general, the greater the debt, the lower the costs (lower payments, on average, to those who provided the capital), but the higher the risk, in terms of the likelihood of bankruptcy. The problem of the corporate treasurer in this scenario is to choose the appropriate balance between risk and return.

The nature of the trade-off between risk and return is complicated. Assume the firm only cares about its *average* cost of capital. Since what it pays to bondholders is less than what it pays to equity holders, it might be tempted to issue more and more debt. But as it borrows more—that is, as it becomes more **highly leveraged**—the equity becomes riskier. The return on equity is simply what is left over after paying debtholders. The more it borrows, the more likely it is that there will be nothing left over for equity holders. As a result, the return it has to pay in order to raise equity must be increased.

In 1958, Franco Modigliani of MIT and Merton Miller of the University of Chicago proved a remarkable theorem. They showed that under what seemed like quite general conditions, how firms raised funds still made no difference, because the increasing cost of equity, as more debt is issued, just offsets the savings from the reduced cost of capital raised from debt.

We can liken the firm in the Modigliani-Miller perspective to a pie. Bondholders and shareholders get different pieces of the pie. But the size of the pie—the real value of the firm—is not affected at all by how it is sliced. The corporation's financial structure affects *who* gets the dollars earned by the corporation—how the profits pie is divided and who bears the risk of the firm—but that is all.

WHY CORPORATIONS CARE ABOUT FINANCIAL STRUCTURE

The Modigliani-Miller theorem is like the simple model of profit-maximizing firms in perfectly competitive markets. It provides a useful starting point and organizing framework for thinking about the central issues. Describing when the corporate finance decision does not matter helps focus attention on what is truly important about corporate financial structure. The sections that follow examine the confounding factors of bankruptcy, taxation, management incentives, the market perception of a firm's value, and corporate control. Each provides an explanation of why, in particular cases, a firm may care a great deal about its financial structure, its blend of debt and equity.

CONSEQUENCES FOR BANKRUPTCY

As we have already seen, increased debt imposes a greater risk of bankruptcy on a corporation. Modigliani and Miller's analysis ignored any direct costs associated with bankruptcy. And there are hundreds of thousands of bankruptcies a year. Bankruptcy has high *direct* costs—to shareholders, creditors, and managers. While 700,000 new businesses were incorporated in 1993, there were 86,000 filings of bankruptcy in that year. These statistics are typical. And they include major firms like International Harvester, once one of the world's largest manufacturers of agricultural machinery, Western Union, Railroad Express, Pennsylvania Central Railroad, and Eastern Airlines. Were it not for the fact that lenders limit the amounts they are willing to lend and monitor closely the firms to which they have lent money, bankruptcy rates might be substantially higher.

Concerns about bankruptcy thus provide an important limit on the use of debt. Banks are likely to limit the amount they are willing to lend. And even if they were willing to lend more, at high enough interest rates to compensate them for the risk of default, borrowers would limit the amount they borrow, recognizing that borrowing more exposes them to an excessively high risk of bankruptcy.

TAX CONSEQUENCES

Taxes affect a firm's choice of financial structure because, while interest payments are tax deductible, payments to shareholders (dividends) are not. Thus, the firm would rather pay interest than dividends, if these are its options. Of

Consider a firm with a perfectly safe investment prospect costing a billion dollars, and yielding a 10 percent return (equal to the rate of interest). It can finance the investment by issuing either bonds (debt) or stocks (equity). What are the tax considerations for each alternative?

If the firm issues bonds, paying out the $100 million return as interest, it pays no corporate income tax (since interest payments are tax deductible), but investors pay individual income taxes on their interests receipts. Assume the total marginal income tax rate is 50 percent. Tax payments would amount to $50 million.

If the firm issues equity, paying out the $100 million return as a dividend, it first pays a corporate income tax of 35 percent, leaving $65 million to be distributed as profits. Individuals then pay 50 percent of that as individual income taxes, so the total tax bill (individual plus corporate) is $67.5 million ($35 million plus $32.5 million), $17.5 million more than if it had issued debt.

But there is one more alternative: it can issue equity, and rather than paying dividends, keep the extra value inside the firm (say in the form of another investment). The investor can realize his return by selling his shares, paying only a capital gains tax. The capital gains tax rate for upper income individuals is lower than for ordinary income (interest or dividends). And by postponing selling his shares, he can postpone paying the tax. In fact, if he holds onto his shares until he dies, he can completely escape taxation—which won't do him much good, but will leave more money for his heirs. As a result, the *effective* capital gains tax rate on average is quite low. For simplicity, assume it is 10 percent. Then the total tax is $41.5 million ($35 million corporate plus $6.5 million capital gains), lower than it would have been had the firm financed the investment by issuing bonds.

Thus, the nature of the tax advantages associated with issuing debt or equity depend on the investors' circumstances as well as what the firm does with its returns—whether it distributes the returns as dividends or retains them within the corporation.

course, the firm also should take into account the taxes that its investors have to pay on their individual incomes. The tax law treats differently capital gains, dividends, and interest. Under the current tax law, capital gains receive slightly favored treatment. Since much of the return to stocks takes the form of capital gains, this aspect of the tax code gives shares a slight advantage over debt to individuals. Still, the net effect of the tax code appears to be in favor of corporate borrowing.

MANAGERIAL INCENTIVES

Another reason a firm cares about how it is financed is that debt and equity provide managers with different incentives. A backs-to-the-wall theory of corporate finance holds that firms should be encouraged to borrow, so that managers are forced to work hard to avoid bankruptcy. If a firm is financed by equity and is making at least some money, according to this theory, managers have little incentive to push for greater efficiency.

In the 1970s, for example, the sharp increase in the price of oil yielded enormous profits to oil companies. Flush with profits, the firms invested unwisely, resulting in a rash of takeovers, financed largely with debt. There is evidence that under the pressure of the increased debt, the management of these firms did become more effective.

But the higher chance of bankruptcy that accompanies high debt loads can also cause a problem. All the managers' efforts may be directed at keeping the firm alive, not at making the sound investments necessary for long-run prosperity. Firms near the threshold of bankruptcy may also undertake excessive risks. Management may gamble—knowing that if they fail they won't lose much since they probably would have gone broke anyway, but if the gamble pays off they may be able to get the firm back on its feet. Thus, finding the right financial structure represents a real challenge. Too little debt, and the firm's resources may be inefficiently used; too much debt, and the bankruptcy threat will distort the incentives to invest wisely for the longer term.

CONSEQUENCES FOR MARKET PERCEPTION OF VALUE

A firm's financial structure may also affect the market's beliefs about the firm's prospects. Most investors believe that a firm's managers are in a better position to judge the company's prospects than outsiders are. If the managers believe there is little risk, they will be willing to issue more debt, because they can do so without incurring a risk of bankruptcy. Their willingness to issue debt thus conveys in a forceful and concrete way management's confidence in the firm—a far more convincing display of confidence than a glossy and glowing report on the firm's future. Because debt both leads managers to work hard and convinces prospective shareholders about the value of the firm's prospects, issuing debt reduces the overall cost of capital to the firm and increases the company's market value.

We have seen that three of the factors discussed so far—tax considerations, managerial incentives, and market perceptions of value—tend to steer firms in the direction of debt financing, when they can obtain it. In practice, established firms finance most of their investments, in excess of retained earnings, by borrowing from banks or issuing bonds.

FINANCE AND CONTROL

There is a final, important respect in which debt and equity financing differ, and it relates to who controls the firm.

Previous chapters treated the "firm" as a monolithic entity. The firm decided what to produce, how to produce it, and how much to produce in order to maximize profits or the market value of the firm. In practice, however, individuals within the firm make these decisions. The interests and beliefs of different individuals differ. The interests of individuals within the firm may not be perfectly aligned with the objectives of profit maximization. And even if they are aligned, it may not be obvious what actions the firm should take to accomplish those goals. In the world of perfect information of Part Two, it was easy to answer the basic questions of what to produce, how to produce it, and how much to produce. But in practice, even the simplest question is fraught with uncertainties. Should GM invest more in robotics? (In this particular case, GM took a gamble of heavy investment in robotics in the 1980s, which, at least so far, does not appear to have paid off.) Can machines really replace men? Should we wait until the technology improves? Or should we invest now to get ahead of our competitors?

Because different individuals might answer the basic questions of what the firm should do differently, it matters who makes these decisions. Who controls the firm and how it is controlled are key issues to understanding how firms behave.

How firms raise capital has implications for control. An entrepreneur needing additional cash often is reluctant to issue equity, since shareholders have the right to elect the board of directors—which nominally controls the firm by appointing the officers who run it. Every entrepreneur is familiar with the story of Steven Jobs, who co-founded Apple Computer, but was pushed out of the company a few years later when Apple faced financial problems. By contrast, bondholders and banks have no formal role in the management of the corporation, except when there is a bankruptcy.

In reality, however, shareholders may have less control over a firm's decisions than banks and other lenders. This is because information and incentive problems weaken shareholders' control. They have to rely on managers for information, who will, to the extent possible, tell them what they want them to hear. And they have little incentive to invest the effort and resources required to become really well informed about management quality, because they typically own such a small proportion of the shares. In most large American firms, no shareholder has more than a few percent of the outstanding shares. This is a classic public goods problem. All shareholders would benefit from better management, but none has the full incentive to get the information necessary to make informed judgments about management.

WHY FINANCIAL POLICY MATTERS

The amount of debt affects the likelihood of bankruptcy.

Debt and equity receive different tax treatment.

The amount of debt affects managerial incentives.

The firm's choice of financial structure may affect the market's perception of the firm's value and risk.

Bonds, bank finance, and new equities have different implications for who controls the firm.

Banks and other lenders are in a more powerful position, because most firms are critically dependent on them for funds—at least from time to time—and lenders at any time can withdraw the credit they have extended. Corporation managers, accordingly, pay close attention to their bankers' views. Because banks often lend considerable amounts to a large firm, they have both the incentive and capacity to keep abreast of the firm's financial state and the quality of management decisions.

The safest course for an entrepreneur who worries about the loss of control is to finance her investments with retained earnings. But if her retained earnings are small, as is typically the case with new firms, and if she believes that the return to additional investment is high enough, she will be tempted to turn to outside sources for funds. In this case, she believes the expected return is worth risking loss of control.

LIMITED FINANCIAL OPTIONS

We have seen that the advantages and disadvantages of raising funds by alternative means help explain the choices that individual firms make in financing new investments. But in many circumstances, firms may not be able to borrow or issue new equities, except at very disadvantageous terms. A company may then be forced to limit its investment to retained earnings.

CREDIT RATIONING

When individuals or firms are willing to pay the current interest rate but simply cannot obtain funds at that rate, they are said to be **credit rationed.** To understand credit rationing, picture a medium-sized corporation, Checkout Systems, that produces software. This software, when used with retailers' checkout registers, handles inventory and all other accounting functions as well. The software has been popular, but Checkout Systems realizes that it would be much more successful if it also sold the hardware—computer systems, terminals, and cash register drawers—that stores must have in order to use the software. Checkout can get the hardware from a computer manufacturer, but it needs $2 million for warehouse and inventory. The company is fully confident that the $2 million expansion will produce a steady return of at least 30 percent. However, it has no retained earnings with which to pay for the expansion.

This is only the beginning of Checkout's problems. Let the going interest rate for loans to small firms be 14 percent. The company has a line of credit at the going rate of $400,000. But its banker refuses to make a loan to finance expansion. Checkout executives offer to pay a higher price—16 percent interest for the $2 million. The bank turns the company down. Is there any interest rate at which the bank would be willing to lend, the Checkout executives ask? The bank replies no.

The bank knows that some borrowers are more likely to default than others, but it has no way of knowing which ones are most likely to do so. Thus, it faces an adverse selection problem. As it raises interest rates to accommodate firms like Checkout, its average returns may actually decrease. The reason for this is that at higher interest rates, the "best" borrowers—those with the lowest likelihood of default—decide not to borrow.

Figure 20.2 shows the return to a lender being maximized at the interest rate r_0. The bank will not raise its interest rates beyond this level, even though at this rate the demand for funds may exceed the supply.

Let's look now at the market for funds for a particular category of loans, say small mortgages (under $100,000) for owner-occupied houses. The supply curve for funds for loans differs from the supply curve depicted in the basic model. Figure 20.3, which is based on the information in Figure 20.2, shows the supply curve for funds as backward bending. This shape reflects the reasonable assumption that as the average return to loans (which should not be confused with the interest rate charged for these loans) increases, the supply of funds increases. The supply curve thus bends backward beyond r_0. As the interest rate charged rises to this point, average returns increase and so does the supply of funds; but at interest rates beyond this point, average returns decline and so does the supply of funds.

Credit rationing takes three forms. Some borrowers get funds, but less than they would like. Some loan applicants are denied credit, even though similar applicants receive credit. And some whole categories of applicants are simply denied credit. A bank may, for instance, refuse to give loans for vacations or to finance a college education or to buy a house in a particular part of the town. In each of these cases, those who have their credit denied or limited will not be any more successful in obtaining credit if they offer to pay a higher interest rate.

If lenders had perfect information, there would be no rationing. They would charge higher interest rates to reflect differences in the likelihood of default, but all applicants willing to pay the appropriate rate would get loans. Thus, underlying credit rationing is lack of information. No matter how many

Figure 20.2 HIGHER INTEREST RATES, LOWER RETURN

As the interest rate increases, safe borrowers tend to drop out of the market, and only risky borrowers remain. Beyond some point, rises in the interest rate increase defaults on loans by enough to reduce the expected return to a lender. At higher interest rates, borrowers may also undertake greater risks, again lowering lenders' expected returns.

Figure 20.3 SUPPLY AND DEMAND FOR CAPITAL WITH CREDIT RATIONING

The supply of funds depends on the expected return. If that return begins to fall when the interest rate charged gets high, the supply of funds will be backward bending. Even if demand for funds exceeds supply at interest rate r_0, the lender will not raise his interest rate, since that would reduce expected returns. As a result, an excess demand for funds can exist in equilibrium.

forms are filled out, references requested, or interviews held, lenders know there is a residual amount of missing information. They therefore develop rules of thumb for loans. Yes to well-run, small businesses. No to vacation loans for college students or to new high-tech computer software firms, both of whom typically have high rates of default.

The lower the interest rate charged, of course, the greater the demand for funds. As the demand curve is drawn in Figure 20.3, average returns are maximized at interest rate r_0, but the supply of funds is less than the demand at this point. There is credit rationing; L_0 loans are actually made, while total demand is L_1. Many qualified borrowers would like to take out loans at the going interest rate but cannot. The magnitude of the credit rationing is measured by the gap between the demand, L_1, and the supply, L_0.

In addition to imperfect information, there is a second reason for credit rationing. Let's return to the example of Checkout Systems. The bank knows that Checkout's executives can engage in excessively risky behavior, some of which the bank will find impossible to monitor. It may worry that the higher the interest rate charged, the more likely that such risk-taking behavior occurs. The greater the risk taking, the higher the probability of bankruptcy, the lower the possibility that the lender will be able to recoup his funds, and thus the lower the expected return to the loan. As in Figure 20.2, expected returns to the bank may actually decrease as the interest rate charged increases, because of this adverse incentive effect.

EQUITY RATIONING

We might suppose that firms that are unable to borrow would raise money by issuing more stock. However, established firms seldom raise capital in this way. In recent years, less than a tenth of new financing has occurred through the sale of equity. The reason is not hard to see—when firms issue new equity, the price of existing shares tends to decline, often by a significant amount. For example, say that a firm worth $1 million issues $100,000 worth of new shares, and the price of the stock falls by 5 percent. The firm's existing shareholders have to give up $50,000 to raise $100,000 in funds from new investors. This is clearly an unattractive deal.

There are several reasons why issuing more equity frequently has such an adverse effect on the price of shares. First, issuing equity reduces the market's perception of a firm's value. Investors reason that the firm's original owners and its managers will be most anxious to sell shares when these well-informed individuals think the market is overvaluing the shares currently outstanding. These concerns are compounded by the fact that the market is well aware that firms normally turn first to banks to raise funds. Investors wonder, "Is the reason the firm is trying to issue new shares that banks will not lend to it, or at least not on very favorable terms, or at least not as much as the firm wants? If banks are reluctant to lend, why should I turn over my money?" Reasoning this way, they will only invest in the firm if they believe they are getting a good enough deal, that is, if the price of the shares is low enough.

Also, as we saw earlier, debt has a positive incentive effect on managers. By the same token, giving the firm more money to play with, without any fixed commitment to repay—which is exactly what new issues of equity do—may have an adverse effect on incentives.

For these and other reasons, the issue of new shares on average depresses the share value. Accordingly, only infrequently do established firms raise new capital by issuing shares.

OVERVIEW: THE LIFE CYCLE OF A FIRM

We have now identified various considerations affecting the relative attractiveness of different ways of raising capital. In the life cycle of a firm these considerations play out in different ways. In its early days, a firm typically finds it impossible to issue shares and has difficulty borrowing. Owners must rely on their own savings and investments of friends and relatives. In some high technology areas, they may turn to providers of venture capital (see Chapter 6). Such businesses provide not only capital but also managerial help, in return for a substantial share in the firm. As the young firm gets more established, it will find access to borrowing easier, and eventually, it may issue an IPO (initial public offering) on the stock market. Throughout the remainder of its life, it will finance much of its investment through retained earnings. In its later years, it may even turn to buying back its shares.

TAKEOVERS, CONTROL OF FIRMS, AND THE MARKET FOR MANAGERS

If you are a small shareholder, and you think management is not using the company's assets in ways that maximize profits, there is little you can do other than sell your shares. But if you are rich—or if you have access to others' capital—you can attempt to buy enough of the shares to gain control of the firm. This need not be a majority of the shares. You may be able to persuade other shareholders to vote their shares in support of you. You may even be able to persuade the existing management to leave quietly (by providing them with generous pensions) and to support the change in control. When one management team (one firm) takes over the control of another, it is called a **takeover.** When the second firm resists, it is called a **hostile takeover.** Sometimes takeovers occur through mergers. That is, the two firms combine, with shareholders in the new firm getting shares in the new combined firm in exchange for their shares in the original firm. Sometimes takeovers occur through acquisitions, when one firm buys another outright.

Takeovers increased sharply in the 1980s, as seen in Figures 20.4 and 20.5. So did the size of the companies taken over. It used to be thought that a company the size of TWA, Marathon Oil, or Nabisco would be immune from a takeover attempt. Who, after all, had the capital required to buy the shares? But size has not turned out to be a barrier—in 1988, RJR Nabisco was bought for over $20 billion.

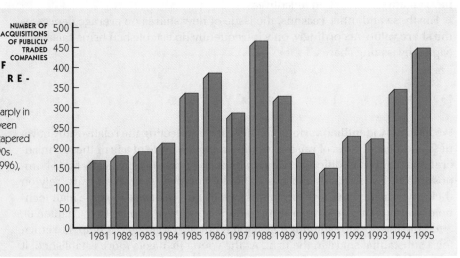

Figure 20.4 NUMBER OF ACQUISITIONS IN RECENT YEARS

The number of acquisitions rose sharply in the mid-1980s, nearly tripling between 1981 and 1988. Acquisitions then tapered off before resurging in the mid-1990s. *Source: Mergerstat Review 1995* (1996), p. 35.

Figure 20.5 VALUE OF ACQUISITIONS IN RECENT YEARS

The value of publicly traded companies acquired also rose sharply in the mid-1980s, nearly tripling from 1981 to 1988. The dollar value of acquisitions dropped after 1988, but returned to a high level in 1995. (The dollar values given are adjusted for inflation, reflecting 1995 dollars.) *Source: Mergerstat Review 1995* (1996), p. 35.

Mergers and acquisitions began to decline after 1988, for a variety of reasons. Many of the mergers and acquisitions had been financed by **junk bonds** carrying interest rates of 15 percent or higher. Even these seemingly high interest rates underestimated the true risk of default. Company after company found itself unable to meet its debt obligations, particularly as the economy began to go into recession in 1990. After the recession, takeovers returned to high levels in 1994 and 1995. Changes in economic structure and industrial regulations may explain the resurgence. For instance, rapid changes in the telecommunications industry, including anticipated changes in government regulations, spawned a series of mergers and acquisitions by telecommunications firms.

The takeover movement of the mid-1980s got a bad reputation because of the unsavory practices of some of its leading practitioners. Several, such as Michael Milken, wound up in jail. The government—in order to ensure that the markets are viewed as a "level playing field"—does not allow managers of firms who have access to inside information about their firms to trade on their information (as noted in Chapter 9). Thus, if you are president of an oil company, and you know that your firm has just made a major oil discovery, you cannot go out and buy more shares of the firm's stock. Nor can you tell your wife and family to do the same. The courts have extended this basic "insider" principle to those involved in buying and selling companies. If you know that your firm is about to make an offer to acquire another firm, which will send that firm's share prices soaring, you cannot use that information for private gain. In one year alone, Milken made more than a billion dollars, at least some of which was attributed to exactly this kind of insider trading.

Another unsavory practice was **greenmail,** so called because of its similarity to blackmail. Takeover artists would buy shares in a firm and then threaten a takeover. Their intent was not to actually buy the company but to get a "bribe" to go away—to get the company to buy back their shares at a premium to ward off a takeover.

Opposition to takeovers came not only from the management that was displaced, but also from workers in the affected firms. Often, following a takeover, faced with heavy debt, firms tightened their belts, laying off workers and even shutting down whole plants. Of course, some of these changes were exactly the reason for the takeover: previous management had not been effective in minimizing costs.

TAKEOVERS: PROS AND CONS

The debate about takeovers is often a debate about how well markets work— in this case the markets for managers and for financial assets.

The central argument in favor of takeovers is that they represent a successful way to replace ineffective managers. Under existing management, a firm may be worth $1 million, with 100,000 shares that trade at $10. An alternative management team may be able to use the firm's resources better, raising its value to $2 million ($20 per share). Even if the acquiring firm (the firm making the takeover) pays a 10 percent premium for the shares—that is, pays $1.1 million for the firm—it makes a profit of $900,000 on the deal. From this perspective, takeover battles are like auctions. The firm is sold to the bidder willing to pay the highest price, the one that thinks it can most effectively utilize the firm's resources.

Having won the auction, the highest bidder must get the company to earn enough money to justify its bid. If the post-takeover managers can indeed do a better job, the takeover firm realizes a profit. From this perspective, then, takeovers reflect the competition to be managers. They are evidence that the market for managers works. Much of the takeover activity of the 1980s in the oil industry was an attempt by various investors to redirect America's oil companies toward more profitable activities.

Thus, takeovers provide an important discipline device even for managers not threatened with one. Managers know that if they do not work hard, they may be threatened with a hostile takeover. They also know that a well-managed firm is unlikely to be taken over, because outsiders will recognize the quality of the management and know they are unlikely to raise the firm's profits. Even if the typical small shareholder does not look over the shoulder of the existing management team, an army of corporate raiders is always on the lookout for a mismanaged firm that could be turned around under new management.

Takeovers are particularly important, because the other methods of controlling managers of large corporations are relatively ineffective. We saw earlier, for instance, that most shareholders have neither the information, the incentives, nor the tools to exercise much control over management. The one way they have of exercising control is voting to elect members of the board of directors. Most investors, if they become dissatisfied with how the firm is being run, just sell their shares. In addition, supporters of takeovers (and of free markets) tend to believe that since shareholders are the real owners of a company, they should have a chance to sell what they own to the highest bidder when they desire to do so.

PUBLIC POLICY TOWARD TAKEOVERS

During their heyday in the late 1980s, takeovers became a source of public policy concern. As the memory of the collapse of the junk bond market and the unsavory practices fades, the takeover movement may well recover, and with it the public policy debate.

Many economists believe that the virtues of takeovers have been overstated. They argue that takeovers do not necessarily replace one management with a more efficient management, but rather often represent the unbridled quest of one firm's management to aggrandize more power for itself. There is some evidence for this view. On average, the shares of the firms taking over do not increase as a result of the takeover activity. This is particularly true in companies where management owns a relatively small share of the stock—in which case management may have little incentive to pay close attention to how their activities affect the market price. Professor Andrei Shleifer of Harvard University has shown that managers with large egos—who, for instance, place their picture prominently within the company's annual report—are more likely to engage in takeovers.

Critics claim that even the threat of a takeover has bad consequences, because it forces companies to make themselves look like unattractive candidates for a takeover. To accomplish this, a corporation may do several things. On the positive side, it can try to make itself more efficient. But it may choose efficiency-reducing alternatives instead. It may be tempted, for example, to sacrifice long-term projects for short-term profits, in the hope that short-term profits will trick investors into thinking the company is better managed than it actually is. Additionally, since corporations with a lot of free cash are particularly attractive takeover targets, the corporation might be induced to

POLICY PERSPECTIVE: WHY PENNSYLVANIA COMPANIES DO NOT WANT PROTECTION AGAINST TAKEOVERS

In early 1990, Pennsylvania passed a law aimed at allowing companies to block takeovers. The new law had three main provisions. One made it very difficult for anyone who bought a large block of stock within twelve months of a takeover bid to vote either for or against the takeover. A second provision allowed corporate directors to put the interests of a firm's employees and customers above the interests of the company's shareholders. A third provision required that if a raider made any profits while attempting a takeover that turned out to be unsuccessful, those profits would have to be given to the target of the takeover.

One might think that companies would welcome this sort of protection. However, the law also allowed companies to choose to be exempt from any or all of the antitakeover provisions if they wished. About two dozen of Pennsylvania's largest companies (including Westinghouse, H. J. Heinz, Mellon Bank, Allegheny Ludlum, and Quaker Chemical) chose not to be protected against takeovers in at least one of these ways.

Why would any company choose to remain vulnerable? Many shareholders, especially big institutional investors like state pension funds, shy away from owning the stock of companies that are sheltered against takeovers, since eliminating the threat of a takeover may mean less pressure for efficiency. When a number of large buyers no longer demand a company's stock, the share price falls. Indeed, the stocks of Pennsylvania-based companies did 7 percent worse than the average performance of stocks from the time the antitakeover law was first proposed until it was passed.

With passage of the antitakeover law, Pennsylvania companies faced a trade-off. They could be protected against takeovers but know that some investors would be reluctant to invest in their company and their stock price would suffer. Or they could remain vulnerable to a takeover but manage their business in such a way that their stock price stayed high, making them an unattractive target.

Source: Leslie Wayne, "Many Companies in Pennsylvania Reject State's Takeover Protection," *New York Times,* July 20, 1990, p. A1.

Slab casting at U.S. Steel

spend its free cash so quickly that it makes bad investment decisions. Or it may take on huge debts so that the return on the stock becomes riskier. Such actions rarely accord with the long-run interests of the corporation.

Finally, critics point out that a company that spends its scarce management time thwarting takeovers is less able to spend its time increasing efficiency and making better products.

Curiously, both those who believe strongly in the competitive model and those who have great reservations about that model often side together in opposing legislation curbing takeovers. Economists who believe strongly in the market system argue that hostile takeovers, like any change, produce gainers and losers, and that overall, the discipline that the market imposes makes the economy more efficient and most individuals better off.

Economists with less faith in the perfectly competitive markets envisioned in Part Two, including Andrei Shleifer of Harvard University and Rob Vishny of the University of Chicago Business School, argue that without the threat—and reality—of hostile takeovers, management would be even more entrenched, more pursuant of its own interests, than it is today. While they recognize potential abuses of a system that permits takeovers, such as greenmail, they argue, in the imperfect world we live in, the gains from the discipline provided by takeovers exceed the costs of any of the abuses.

Despite these concerns, legislation has been enacted that would alter market outcomes. Some states have allowed corporations to create "poison pills," devices that provide for the partial destruction of the firm in the event of a successful takeover, making the takeover less attractive. And Congress—motivated partly by interest-group politics and partly by concern that the large debts accumulated to finance the takeovers might increase the chance of a wave of bankruptcies—has debated whether to remove some of the tax advantages of debt when used as part of a hostile takeover. But the fact is that laws restricting takeovers work to the detriment of shareholders for several reasons. Shareholders do not benefit from the competition for shares that results from takeover battles. The likelihood of incompetent management being replaced through takeover is reduced. And current management, freed from the admittedly limited discipline provided by the takeover mechanism, is more likely to take actions that benefit the managers at the expense of shareholders.

MAKING DECISIONS

In Chapter 1, we listed four basic questions: What and how much is to be produced, how it is to be produced, for whom it is produced, and *who makes these decisions*. Most of this book focuses on the first three questions. The question of who controls the firm goes to the heart of the final question: Who makes these decisions? The rest of this chapter addresses how the organization of the firm, and of the economy, determines who makes the decisions and how they make them.

DELEGATION AND THE PRINCIPAL-AGENT PROBLEM

Even if the firm were owned by a single individual, there would be a problem of control, because the owner cannot make all the decisions himself. He must *delegate* some to subordinates, who, in turn, must engage in further delegation. The central problem is how to ensure that these managers act in the same way that the owner would have acted. This is an example of a broad class of incentive problems.

Chapter 6 noted that incentive problems arise whenever an individual does not bear, or receive, the full consequences of her action. If the manager makes a good decision, the firm prospers and the shareholders benefit. If she makes a bad decision, they suffer. Thus, shareholders would like to motivate the manager to act in a way that maximizes the value of their shares. In this form, the incentive problem is referred to as the **principal-agent problem.** The principal (here, the owner) would like to motivate the agent (here, the manager) to act in the principal's interests. But both parties know the owner cannot judge whether the manager has taken the appropriate action simply by the observable results.

The interests of managers and owners frequently differ. The manager going on a business trip may choose to buy a ticket on a more expensive airline because he is trying to accumulate frequent flier points for himself on that airline, rather than a cheaper alternative. The sales representative for a computer firm may give some account especially close attention, not because of the prospects of increased sales but because he is trying to land a new job.

There are two important aspects of the principal-agent problem: how hard the agent works, and what risks the agent takes. If a manager works especially hard, for example, the owners of the firm (often the shareholders) will receive some of the reward. But because the manager does not receive all the reward, she may have insufficient incentives for exerting maximum effort.

The manager's taste for risk will rarely match the owner's interests. On the one hand, managers may act in a more risk-averse (cautious) manner than the owners of the firm might like. After all, the managers know that should projects under their supervision fail, they may be denied promotions or even lose their jobs. On the other hand, managers may be willing to take risks when the owners would not be willing to do so. They are gambling with someone else's money. If the project is a flop, the firm loses money; if it is successful, the manager will be called a "genius." The consensus among economists is that under most circumstances, managers act in a way that is *more* risk averse than the owners would like.

Ownership as a Solution   The most obvious solution to the principal-agent problem would be for the owner of the firm to sell each manager the portion of the firm under his responsibility. As the owner, the manager would have all the right incentives. If he worked harder, he would reap the rewards. If he took more risks, he would receive the gains and bear the losses. In general,

CLOSE-UP: THE BEST EXECUTIVES FOR THE MONEY?

As the table here shows, some top executives earn mind-bending sums of money, sometimes millions of dollars a year. Defenders of these high salaries point out that top executives make life-or-death decisions for their companies and that they deserve to be compensated for making those decisions wisely. Much of top executive pay comes in the form of stock options. Their high pay is therefore due in part to the fact that the company's stock did well, which offers an incentive for top management to look out for the interests of shareholders.

However, in the past few years, critics of high executive salaries have become considerably more vocal. Here are some of their main arguments:

1. Pay for top executives has grown disproportionately. In 1974, for example, the typical chief executive officer (CEO) received pay that was 35 times that of the average manufacturing worker. In the early 1990s, the typical CEO earned about 120 times the pay of an average manufacturing worker.

2. Pay for U.S. top executives is out of line with what foreign companies pay. In Japan, the average CEO earns 20 times the pay of the average worker;

in the United Kingdom, he earns 35 times the pay of the average worker. These large differences from U.S. practice are not reflected in productivity differences.

3. Pay for top executives does not offer a true incentive, because it often rises even when the company does badly. During the recession in 1990, for example, average corporate profits fell by 7 percent, but compensation for top executives rose by 7 percent.

Critics of high executive pay point out that compensation levels are often set by a board of directors chosen by the top executive, with the help of an outside consultant who is also chosen by the top executive. They argue that, although a well-designed plan of linking the top executives' pay to the long-term price of the company's stock can provide useful incentives, too many stock plans have become a way to funnel money to the top executive, without limit or control.

Sources: "How High can CEO Pay Go?," *Business Week,* April 22, 1996; Graef Crystal, *In Search of Excess* (New York: Norton, 1991).

THE 10 HIGHEST-PAID CHIEF EXECUTIVES FOR 1995

Name	Company	Total pay in 1995
1. Lawrence Coss	Green Tree Financial	$65.6 million
2. Sanford Weill	Travelers Group	$49.8 million
3. John Welch Jr.	General Electric	$22.1 million
4. Gordon Binder	Amgen	$21.5 million
5. James Donald	DSC Communications	$19.2 million
6. Casey Cowell	U. S. Robotics	$18.6 million
7. Floyd English	Andrew Corp.	$17.7 million
8. Howard Solomon	Forest Laboratories	$17.0 million
9. Stanley Gualt	Goodyear Tire and Rubber	$16.6 million
10. Edward Brennan	Sears, Roebuck	$16.4 million

however, the manager does not have the requisite capital to buy the firm, and even if he did, he might not be willing to buy it. An owner's income is a lot more variable than a paycheck, depending not only on his own efforts but also on the vagaries of the market. A manager may not be willing to take that risk.

In any case, most modern corporations cannot be split into the right parts to make each manager an owner and still operate efficiently. We can sometimes divide a large corporation into several parts, each run separately. But within each of these parts, there remain large principal-agent problems.

Incentive Pay as a Solution A second-best solution to the principal-agent problem is to include in the agent's compensation package incentives that reflect the principal's interest. Thus, sales representatives earn commissions, and many workers can qualify for performance bonuses if they or their department exceeds production quotas. One form of incentive program for top managers is the **stock option** bonus, the value of which depends on how well their firms perform. Suppose stock in a particular company is currently selling for $30. The stock option allows the manager to purchase a specified number of shares at $30 for a specified period of time. For instance, the manager may be given the option to buy 100,000 shares at $30 any time during the next three years. If the firm's shares rise in value to $40, the manager can purchase the shares for $3 million and then immediately resell them for $4 million, receiving a bonus—presumably as a reward for her contribution in increasing the value of the firm—of $1 million. It is common for firms to provide their top managers with stock option bonuses valued in the millions of dollars.

Monitoring as a Solution Appropriately designed compensation schemes help align the interests of the agent with that of the principal. But they do not fully resolve the problem. Principals further reduce the scope for agents to take actions which are not in their interests by monitoring and obtaining information not only about what the agent *is* doing, but also about what she *should* be doing.

It is not easy for owners or top management to know what is going on in a large corporation. They can, of course, easily tell whether the factories are producing, but are they really doing what it takes to maximize profits? An

DELEGATION

The principal-agent problem

    Work effort of agent

    Risk taking of agent

Solutions

    Ownership

    Incentive pay

    Monitoring

CLOSE-UP: WHAT IS GOOD MANAGEMENT?

Despite conflicts of interests between managers and shareholders, American managers do see themselves as trying quite hard to do the best job that they can for their firm. The bestseller list for books almost invariably includes one or two that promise a better way to manage a firm. The popularity of these books is testimony to the widespread concern about how to be a good manager; the fact that one book is followed by another with contradictory advice is testimony to the everlasting hope of American managers that the promised success formulas are just around the corner.

Back in the 1950s and 1960s, books often taught management skills as if following a few basic steps would always lead to a correct decision. Managers were urged to clarify their objectives, outline how best to attain those objectives, and constantly monitor the extent to which their objectives were being attained; good advice, but of only limited help. The simple prescriptions of forty years ago offered no assistance in dealing with the uncertainty and limited information that pervade decision making within firms; neither did they offer solutions for the difficulties of motivating individuals—the principal-agent problem.

More recent examples of this genre of books do not have a much better record of success. In 1983, Tom Peters and Robert Waterman wrote a bestseller, *In Search of Excellence.* The book's main theme was that managers of businesses should learn from the example of the excellent companies identified in the book. The distinguishing feature of these companies was their commitment to excellence and the concern they showed for their employees.

However, the next couple of years were not kind to many of the "excellent" companies identified by Peters and Waterman. For example, an airline called People Express, which had been growing like a weed for several years by offering no-frill flights, was cited as an excellent company with innovative personnel policies. It went bankrupt and was bought by Continental Airlines two years after the book came out. In fact, the firms selected as role models for excellence fared not much better over the five years following the book's publication than any randomly chosen group of firms.

But only five years later, both authors were back with new books that contained new guesses for success. In 1988, Tom Peters's, *Thriving on Chaos* argued that "there are no excellent companies."

Instead, it listed forty-five guidelines for dealing with a frenzied and chaotic business environment. Robert Waterman's 1988 book, *The Renewal Factor,* offered examples of companies that had achieved excellence by seeking out new products and strategies and renewing themselves. Of course, the list of companies were not the same as the list of five years earlier.

There are many other management books available, with a variety of themes. Some want U.S. firms to model themselves after Japanese firms. Others stress the need to build worker loyalty or customer loyalty.

These books illustrate the difference between useful anecdotes and serious economic research. Systematic study of a subject requires looking at all the cases together, failures as well as successes.

essential aid in gathering requisite information are the accounting systems that all modern corporations employ. They are intended to provide top management with essential information concerning, for instance, the relative profitability of each of its parts.

Still, monitoring is imperfect. Long-term relationships between most principals and agents improve the effectiveness of even imperfect monitoring because both sides see the gains from continuing the relationship. An employee will not take advantage of every opportunity to gain at the expense of the firm. She knows that even if the firm does not detect self-serving behavior every time, it is likely to observe it some of the time, and that even if the firm does not fire her, her behavior might affect prospects for promotion.

CENTRALIZATION AND DECENTRALIZATION

The most basic issue in a firm's decision-making structure is the extent to which decision making is **centralized** or **decentralized.** A firm in which the president or chief executive officer (CEO) makes all decisions is highly centralized, just as an economy where all decisions are made by a central Ministry of Economics is highly centralized. However, all large organizations involve some degree of decentralization. The president of a corporation simply does not have the time, much less the information, with which to make all the day-to-day decisions.

The consequence of decentralization is that the firm's subunits have considerable autonomy—freedom to make their own decisions. Should the Chevrolet division of General Motors be allowed to make its own decisions concerning what kind of new car to develop, or should the corporation's CEO be consulted? Which decisions are of sufficient importance that the CEO needs to be involved? Which decisions should the CEO actually make? These fundamental decisions are faced by every economic organization.

There are trade-offs to differing degrees of centralization and decentralization. Centralized decision making usually involves a hierarchical structure. A project must pass through a set of well-defined approval layers, like a fine sieve. This reduces the likelihood that bad projects are approved. But the process of sifting also leads to good projects being rejected. Decentralized decision making provides fewer checks on any project. Some bad projects are more likely to get adopted. By the same token, fewer good projects are rejected.

ADVANTAGES OF CENTRALIZATION

Hierarchical decision making may allow for better coordination across the divisions of a large corporation; this may be important in instances where there are externalities—where, for instance, the fruits of research in one part of the firm may be of benefit to another. Thus, in developing a new motor—an expensive endeavor—it might pay the different divisions of General Motors to coordinate their research and development efforts. Even if, in the end, the different units decide to produce different motors, they will still find it profitable to coordinate their research programs and develop, for instance, new, lighter materials from which to make a motor.

Another argument in favor of centralized decision making is that it avoids the duplication that results from operating autonomous corporate divisions, where personnel from several units are often engaged in quite similar activities. Thus, advocates of centralization claim that it is inefficient for each division of a firm to have its own legal staff or its own marketing department.

ADVANTAGES OF DECENTRALIZATION

Some of the arguments used by advocates of greater centralization can be turned on their head and used as arguments for decentralization. For example, supporters of decentralization point out that having different units within an organization doing similar things may have decided advantages: the resulting competition not only provides a strong motivation for members of the different production units, but also provides a basis for judging whether one unit is doing better than another, and hence for making decisions about who is performing well and who should receive more funds.

Decentralized decision making also enables a production unit to adapt decisions to its own particular circumstances, so that they reflect the diversity of attitudes and skills among workers. As hard as they may try, centralized authorities have difficulty in obtaining the requisite information from those who are actually engaged in the production process. Decentralization also allows a range of experimentation greater than that found under more centralized regimes, and enables projects to be approved more quickly.

Its advantages are sufficiently great that many firms have considerable decentralization. Large corporations, like General Motors, are separated into divisions, each of which may have considerable autonomy, at least over some functions (such as marketing). While there may be centralization in certain issues—like the design of a new motor or body frame—there is great decentralization in others. Pontiac and Buick see their markets as slightly different, and even if they have the same basic engineering, each division believes it can adapt the car—with its own interior design, for example—and adopt a marketing strategy aimed at its part of the market far better than central headquarters could do. The computer company Hewlett-Packard divides itself into a large number of units, each of which has the authority to undertake research projects.

CENTRALIZATION AND DECENTRALIZATION WITHIN THE ECONOMY AS A WHOLE

The advantages and disadvantages of centralization within firms parallel those of the economy as a whole. The U.S. economy is characterized by a high degree of decentralization. Each firm in the economy decides for itself which projects to undertake. Projects and ideas that are rejected by one firm are taken up by others. There is a widespread consensus that decentralization is desirable. The gains in increasing the likelihood that good projects get developed outweigh the disadvantages of having the same idea reexamined in what appears to be a duplicative manner. There are many stories of inventors and entrepreneurs who needed the chances provided by a decentralized system in order to find one backer for their brilliant idea.

Despite the decentralization of the U.S. economy as a whole, many of its autonomous firms have only limited decentralization and retain a fairly strong hierarchy. Even multibillion-dollar companies like Exxon maintain a fairly high degree of centralization. Thus, our economy can be viewed as involving a mixture of decentralization and centralization. The question is one of balance. And the balance between centralization and decentralization is one that will continually be debated, both within firms and, more broadly, within society as a whole.

CENTRALIZED VERSUS DECENTRALIZED DECISION MAKING

CENTRALIZED	DECENTRALIZED
Fewer bad projects are accepted.	More good projects are accepted.
There is greater coordination; externalities are taken into account.	Comparison between competing units provides (a) incentives and (b) bases of selection.
Duplication is avoided.	There is greater diversity and experimentation

THE BOUNDARIES OF THE FIRM

Many firms sell personal computers. Most of them are "assemblers." They buy circuit boards, cases, monitors, and keyboards in bulk, assemble the parts into personal computers, and sell them. Why don't they expand, and make their own circuit boards, cases, monitors, and keyboards? To turn the question around, why don't those who make these parts assemble them? After all, firms always want more profits, and these expansions seem to be prime areas for growth.

Economists are interested in the conditions that cause a firm to limit itself in size or in the number of products it manufactures. What determines the boundaries of firms? Or to put the same question in a different way, when does a company find it easier to deal with another company through the market, rather than produce what it needs itself? What are the advantages and disadvantages of markets? In modern economies, the degree of centralization and decentralization is closely related to the issue of what is produced within the firm, and what each firm purchases from other firms.

In the case of the personal computer market, there is a great deal of decentralization. Companies make extensive use of the market. The circuit board manufacturers have a much larger market than just personal computers, so they can achieve economies of scale they would not enjoy if they restricted their output to supplying circuit boards for personal computers. They also fear the risk entailed in putting all their eggs in the personal computer market "basket." The same is true for those who make the other parts. This pattern of specialization, however, leaves a profit opportunity for the assemblers, who can buy the parts from outside and still wind up with a computer they can sell at a good profit.

But the degree of decentralization within the personal computer market is unusual. Much economic activity occurs within firms, rather than between firms. That is, companies produce intermediate products that are used as inputs for the goods the company eventually sells, and firms may even produce the inputs that are used in these intermediate products. Such activity is known as **vertical integration.** (By contrast, **horizontal integration** involves bringing together firms producing the same goods.) At one time, U.S. Steel owned its own iron ore mines and its own fleet of vessels to transport the iron ore. It not only produced the pig iron, it also used the pig iron to make more finished steel products, such as the beams used in construction. Ford Motor Company at one time owned its own steel mill, for producing the steel used in making its cars.

Table 20.1 shows that the output of several large, vertically integrated firms is as large as the entire output of several medium-sized countries.[1] Within these firms, relationships are controlled by commands—direct decisions by the managers—though those commands themselves may be affected by accounting profits and prices (which can differ significantly from market prices and profits).

There are a number of factors that go into the decisions about whether to vertically integrate—that is, whether to produce the inputs used to produce the goods—or whether to use the market. One important factor is **transactions costs**—the extra costs (beyond the price of the purchase) of conducting

Table 20.1 COMPARING LARGE CORPORATIONS AND SMALL COUNTRIES

1993 sales of large U.S. corporations	
General Motors	$134 billion
Ford	$109 billion
Exxon	$ 98 billion
IBM	$ 63 billion
1992 national output of medium-sized economies	
Norway	$113 billion
Thailand	$110 billion
Greece	$ 67 billion
Egypt	$ 34 billion

Source: Fortune, April 18, 1994; World Development Report (1994).

[1] The comparison is not perfect. The appropriate comparison would be between the value added of U.S. corporations—the difference between their sales and the goods and services they purchase from other firms. Even in these terms, General Motors and Ford are larger than Egypt and Greece.

a transaction, whether those costs are money, time, or inconvenience. Ronald Coase of the University of California at Los Angeles was awarded the Nobel Prize in 1991 partly for his work in identifying the role of transactions costs in determining the "boundaries" of the firm—what activities occur within a firm and what activities occur between firms.

Consider, for instance, the problem of a large manufacturing company that offers health insurance to its employees. The company could continue to pay premiums to an outside insurance company that would then be liable for any claims. Because of its large work force, however, the option of paying its employees' medical bills directly has become economically viable. The company could set up a division to run its health insurance, but then it will face all the managerial problems discussed in this chapter. Although this company is good at manufacturing, it has no comparative advantage at running a health insurance company, and its managerial talent is scarce. Accordingly, the firm may find it cheaper, once these transactions costs are taken into account, to continue with the outside health insurance company. It is more efficient to make use of the market in obtaining health insurance services.

In other cases, transactions costs may be lower if the firm vertically integrates. Consider a chemical firm eager for new products to sell. It could hire an outside laboratory to try to develop a new drug, and use outside sales representatives to sell existing ones. But how can the company make sure that the outside laboratory really tries to make a breakthrough discovery? How can the company make sure that the outside sales firm makes a sincere effort to sell its products?

Transactions costs are every bit as real as the costs of production. Indeed, as innovations in manufacturing (such as the invention of the assembly line) have reduced production costs, transactions costs have taken on increasing importance. Many of the innovations of the past two decades, in turn, have reduced transactions costs. Computers, for example, have enhanced our ability to keep track of records and process other information required for engaging in transactions.

Finding a balance between centralization and decentralization and between what the firm produces and what it purchases from other firms are thus two of the central problems facing managers of all large enterprises.

REVIEW AND PRACTICE

SUMMARY

1. The three main forms of business ownership are proprietorships, partnerships, and corporations. Only corporate ownership has the advantage of limited liability, which means that investors are not liable for debts incurred by the company.

2. The Modigliani-Miller theorem argues that under a simplified set of conditions, the manner in which a firm finances itself is a matter of

indifference. However, issues of bankruptcy, taxation, management incentives, and corporate control mean that firms care about their financial structure.

3. Shareholders have nominal control of corporations, but when share ownership is widely distributed, shareholders may not exercise effective control. While lenders (like banks) have nominal control over a corporation only if it declares bankruptcy, their ability to control the immediate flow of capital to the firm may give them a fair amount of say in what the firm does.

4. Credit rationing occurs when a borrower cannot find a source of funds even when he is willing to pay a higher-than-market interest rate. Lenders fear their average return may *decrease* (the chance of default is greater) as the nominal interest rate increases.

5. Firms will not be willing to issue new equity if doing so results in large decreases in the market value of outstanding shares.

6. The argument for takeovers is that they provide a means by which less efficient management teams can be replaced by more efficient teams. The argument against is that takeovers often are more matters of power or ego rather than efficiency, and that the threat of takeovers diverts companies from focusing on their actual business.

7. The problem owners of firms have in motivating the managers to work hard and make decisions about risk in the general interests of the firm, rather than in their own personal interest, is known as the principal-agent problem.

8. A major problem facing all economic organizations (firms or whole economies) is the extent of centralization or decentralization. In principle, greater centralization can improve coordination, provide a more effective way of dealing with externalities, reduce duplication, and reduce the chances of "bad" projects being adopted. Decentralization provides a basis for experimentation and comparison, allows for greater adaptability and faster decision making, and increases the chances that "good" projects will be adopted.

9. Every firm must decide whether to make a product or provide a service inside the firm or buy it in the marketplace. The choice depends, in part at least, on transactions costs.

KEY TERMS

proprietorship	Modigliani-Miller theorem	centralization
partnership	credit rationing	decentralization
corporation	principal-agent problem	transactions costs

REVIEW QUESTIONS

1. Explain the difference between a proprietorship, a partnership, and a corporation.

2. Explain how the risk of bankruptcy and the tax treatment of dividends and interest payments affect the attractiveness of equity to a business. How does debt provide incentives for management to work harder?

3. Why might the market interpret the issue of new equity as a negative signal concerning the value of a company?

4. Do banks or small shareholders have greater effective control over a corporation? Is your answer the same for large shareholders?

5. What is credit rationing? Why does it occur?

6. What are the arguments for and against takeovers?

7. What is a principal-agent problem? How might ownership and incentive pay address this problem?

8. What are the advantages and disadvantages of centralized and decentralized decision making within a firm?

9. When will a firm try to do a job itself, and when will it try to hire someone to do it in the market?

PROBLEMS

1. Consider a firm that needs $350,000 in capital to get started. First, think about this firm organized as a proprietorship, where you put up $50,000 and borrow the rest from a bank. Second, think about this firm organized as a partnership, where you and nine friends each put up $5,000 and borrow the rest from a bank. Third, think about the firm organized as a corporation, where you and nine friends each buy $5,000 worth of stock and then borrow the rest from a bank. If the firm goes broke without earning any money, how large are your potential losses in each case?

2. The bankruptcy laws of the United States were changed in the mid-1980s to make it easier and less costly for a firm to declare bankruptcy. Would you expect these laws to lead to more partnerships or to more corporations? Why?

3. Speak Software, a small firm attempting to design new computer software, applies for a bank loan to purchase some new computer hardware. The bank turns the company down for the loan. When Speak Software offers to pay a higher interest rate, the bank still turns it down. Explain why the bank might practice this form of credit rationing, using a diagram that compares the interest rate charged with the bank's expected return.

4. The Kitbits Company, which makes cat treats, has a stock price of $40 per share. A raider is trying to take over the company and is offering $50 per share. Shareholders must decide whether to sell their stock to the raider and take a $10 per share gain, or to hold on to the stock. Consider the effect of future management of the company. When might it make sense to hold on to the stock?

5. How might a firm harm itself in attempting to avoid a takeover? How might it strengthen itself in attempting to avoid a takeover?

6. Think up an incentive scheme that would encourage managers to take more risks.

7. A company is considering setting up two new divisions. One division would own a corporate fleet of cars, as an alternative to renting cars from existing firms. The other division would be an R & D laboratory, as an alternative to contracting out projects to labs. Consider issues of transactions costs and comparative advantage, and analyze why these functions might be set up inside the company or bought from outside.

8. In several European countries, there have been strong movements for worker participation in management, entailing, for instance, unions sending representatives to sit on the board of directors. Discuss the problem of getting worker representatives to act in the interests of the workers in terms of the principal-agent problem.

PART FOUR

Policy Issues

T he basic competitive model presented in Part Two focused on the private sector—on firms and households. Yet government plays a central role in our modern economy. About a third of the economy's output passes through the hands of the government (at the local, state, or federal level). Government programs touch our lives—and our economy—in myriad ways. Chapter 7 presented a brief overview of the economic role of government, and in Part Three we saw how government sought to encourage competition and promote technological change. But we have yet to discuss some of the most important activities of the government—both what the government does, and why.

In Chapter 21 we return to the subject of externalities—introduced in Chapter 7—considering the impact of negative externalities upon the environment. In the last twenty-five years, government efforts to limit environmental degradation have enjoyed great success. We will explore the market failures which give rise to pollution, and review the alternative ways in which governments have attempted to remedy those failures. We will also examine the depletion of natural resources, a growing concern in recent years. Do markets provide adequate incentives to conserve natural resources such as oil and mineral resources? Chapter 21 answers this question. Finally, Chapter 21 discusses an important category of circumstances in which the consumption of certain products is mandated (as in compulsory education) or prohibited (as in illegal narcotics) by government. Here, government intervention is not only based on economic efficiency, but stands on other grounds.

Even when markets are efficient, how they allocate resources among individuals may appear to be socially unacceptable. Such concerns are raised by poverty, homelessness, and limited access to health care, to name but a few examples. The distribution of income is a major concern of modern societies and their governments, one that has grown in the United States due to the increasing disparity of income and wealth between the most well off and the least well off. Of course, what individuals have to spend depends not only on how much they earn, but how much they have to pay in taxes. Chapter 22 discusses recent changes in U.S. income distribution. It also provides a description of the U.S. tax system, and evaluates that system in terms of certain basic criteria.

Government social insurance programs are also discussed in Chapter 22. Markets often fail to provide insurance against some of the most important risks which individuals face, including the loss of a job, being disabled so that one cannot work, and the coverage of medical needs of the elderly. Chapter 22 looks at these social insurance programs, and the problems they face today, as well as the broader role of government in redistribution.

Government differs from households and firms in many ways, not the least of which is the form of decision making. In a democratic society, different individuals have different preferences. Some would like the government to spend more money on education, others on parks, others on building bombers. How *collective* decisions are made, and the influences upon those decisions, have significant effects on the allocation of resources. Chapter 23 discusses these issues and some of the problems facing collective decision making. While we have seen that markets often fail to provide efficient resource allocations, or socially acceptable resource allocations, government interventions are also subject to failure. Chapter 23 analyzes some of the systematic reasons for these public failures.

In Part Four we will complete our discussion of the many ways in which the real world is different from the basic model—except for one. The basic model assumes that all markets clear, including the labor market. But at times involuntary unemployment becomes a fact of life. At times, such as during the Great Depression when one out of four workers was without a job, there is massive unemployment. Later parts of the book will address the causes of this unemployment, and what government can do about it.

CHAPTER 21

EXTERNALITIES AND THE ENVIRONMENT

I n this and the next two chapters, we probe the economic role of government, a topic first treated in broad terms in Chapter 7. Beyond providing a legal framework within which economic relations take place, government may have an economic role to play when markets fail to produce efficient outcomes. This justification is known as the **market failures approach** to the role of government.

We already know several ways in which markets can fail to produce efficient outcomes. For example, competition may be less than envisaged by the basic model, and less-than-perfect competition produces inefficient economic outcomes. Competitive markets may, for all the reasons set forth in Chapter 17, fail to produce the technological innovation needed by a thriving economy. Government has responded with patent laws and other legislative efforts to spur innovation.

Markets may also fail in the face of information problems described in Chapters 18 and 19. For instance, producers tend to know more about their products than they reveal to customers. Government has responded with truth-in-advertising laws.

One market failure has not yet been adequately discussed. This failure arises when there are externalities—costs and benefits of a transaction that are not fully reflected in the market price. When we first encountered externalities in Chapter 7, our focus was on positive externalities, such as those associated with goods that are publicly provided. Here we shift the focus to negative externalities and the issues of environmental protection.

1. Why do externalities such as pollution result in a market failure? What alternatives can government employ to remedy this market failure?

2. What are the market forces that lead to an efficient use of society's natural resources? What may impede markets from using scarce natural resources efficiently?

NEGATIVE EXTERNALITIES AND OVERSUPPLY

The basic competitive model assumes that the costs of producing a good and the benefits of selling it all accrue to the seller, and that the benefits of receiving the good and the costs of buying it all accrue to the buyer. This is often not the case. As was explained in Chapter 7, the extra costs and benefits not captured by the market transaction are called externalities.

Externalities can be either positive or negative, depending on whether individuals enjoy extra benefits they did not pay for or suffer extra costs they did not incur themselves. Goods for which there are positive externalities—such as research and development—will be undersupplied in the market. In deciding how much of the good to purchase, each individual or firm thinks only about the benefits it receives, not the benefits conferred upon others. By the same token, goods for which there are negative externalities, such as air and water pollution, will be oversupplied in the market. The fact that the market might not fully capture the costs and benefits of a trade provides a classic example of a market failure and a possible role for the public sector.

Figure 21.1A shows the demand and supply curves for a good, say steel. Market equilibrium is the intersection of the curves, the point labeled E, with output Q_p and price p_p. Chapter 13 explained why, in the absence of externalities, the equilibrium E is efficient. The price reflects the marginal benefit individuals receive from an extra unit of steel (it measures their marginal willingness to pay for an extra unit). The price also reflects the marginal cost to the firm of producing an extra unit. At E, marginal benefits equal marginal costs.

Consider what happens if, in the production of steel, there is an externality—producers are polluting the air and water without penalty. The **social marginal cost**—the marginal cost borne by all individuals in the economy—will now exceed the **private marginal cost**—the marginal cost borne by the producer alone. Note that in a competitive industry, the supply curve corresponds to the horizontal sum of all producers' *private* marginal cost curves. Panel B contrasts the two situations. It shows the social marginal cost curve for producing steel lying above the private marginal cost curve. Thus, with so-

Figure 21.1 HOW NEGATIVE EXTERNALITIES CAUSE OVERSUPPLY

In a perfectly competitive market, the market supply curve is the (horizontal) sum of the marginal cost curves of all firms, while market demand reflects how much the marginal consumer is willing to pay or how much the marginal unit is worth to any consumer. In panel A, the intersection or equilibrium, at quantity Q_p and price p_p, will be where private marginal cost is equal to the marginal benefit.

The private marginal cost includes just the costs actually paid by the producing firm. If there are broader costs to society as a whole, like pollution, then the social marginal costs will exceed the private costs. If the supplier is not required to take these additional costs into account (as in panel B), production will be at Q_p, greater than Q_s, where price equals social marginal cost, and the quantity produced will exceed the amount where marginal cost is equal to marginal benefit for society as a whole.

cial marginal costs equated to social marginal benefits, the economically efficient level of production of steel will be lower, *at Q_s,* than it would be, at Q_p, if private costs were the only ones.

Thus, the level of production of steel, which generates negative externalities, will be too high in a free market. We can also ask, what about the level of expenditure on pollution abatement? Such expenditures confer a positive externality on others—the benefits of the equipment, the cleaner air, accrue mainly to others. Figure 21.2 shows a firm's demand curve for pollution-abatement equipment in the absence of government regulation. It is quite low, reflecting the fact that the firm itself derives little benefit. That is, the firm's marginal private benefit from expenditures on pollution-abatement equipment are small. The firm sets its marginal private benefit equal to the marginal cost of pollution abatement, which results in a level of expenditure on pollution abatement at *E*. The figure also depicts the marginal social benefit of pollution abatement, which is far greater than the marginal private benefit. Efficiency requires that the marginal social benefit equal the marginal cost, point *E'*. Thus, economic efficiency requires greater expenditures on pollution abatement than there would be in the free market.

One of government's major economic roles is to correct the inefficiencies resulting from externalities. Among the many types of negative externalities, perhaps the most conspicuous are those that harm the environment.

Figure 21.2 HOW POSITIVE EXTERNALITIES CAUSE UNDERSUPPLY

The private marginal benefit includes just the benefits received by the firm, but since pollution-abatement equipment provides a positive externality, it will have a social marginal benefit that is higher. If the firm takes only its private benefit into account, it will operate at point E, using less equipment than at the point where marginal benefits are equal to marginal costs for society as a whole (E').

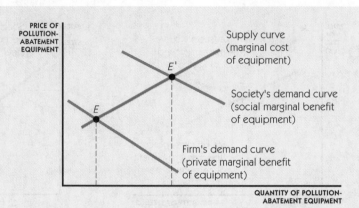

PRICE OF POLLUTION-ABATEMENT EQUIPMENT

Supply curve (marginal cost of equipment)

Society's demand curve (social marginal benefit of equipment)

Firm's demand curve (private marginal benefit of equipment)

QUANTITY OF POLLUTION-ABATEMENT EQUIPMENT

ENVIRONMENTAL PROTECTION AND CONSERVATION: EXAMPLES

Freon gas, used as the propellant in aerosol cans and as a coolant in air conditioners, appears to have destroyed some of the ozone layer of the atmosphere—risking major climatic changes and possibly exposing individuals to radiation that may cause cancer. This is a worldwide externality. A major treaty among the nations of the world was signed in early 1990 that would eventually ban the use of this and related gases. The nature of the externality in this case was clear: the use of the gas anywhere could have disastrous effects on everyone.

Another major international treaty was signed in Rio de Janeiro in 1992. Since the beginning of the industrial revolution, enormous quantities of fossil fuels—coal, oil, and gas—have been burned. When they burn, they produce carbon dioxide (CO_2). Carbon dioxide is absorbed into the oceans and used by plants in photosynthesis. But the rate of emissions in recent decades has been far greater than the rate of absorption—so much so that the concentration of CO_2 in the atmosphere is 25 percent higher than it was at the beginning of the industrial revolution. Worse, in the next few decades, it is projected to double, or more, unless strong actions are taken. The United Nations convened an international panel of scientists to assess both the extent of these dramatic changes in the earth's atmosphere and their consequences. Their findings were alarming. These and other gases create a "greenhouse gas" effect, trapping radiation arriving at the earth, and leading to global warming. While the magnitude of the warming effect is likely to be small—only a few degrees—the potential harm is great: a partial melting of the earth's ice caps, a rise in sea levels, a flooding of low-lying countries such as Bangladesh, an increase in the spread of deserts.

At Rio, the developed countries agreed to restrain their level of emissions, returning them to their 1990 level by the year 2000. Since emissions increase with energy use, and energy use normally increases with economic growth, achieving this goal will require both substantial increases in energy efficiency and switching from energy sources (such as coal) that produce high levels of emissions to those that produce little or none (such as hydroelectric power).

These are examples of global externalities. Most externalities are more local. Many of the world's cities are choking with smog, for example, caused largely by automobile exhausts. Many rivers, streams, and lakes are so polluted that they are unsafe to drink from or to swim in.

POLICY RESPONSES TO PROBLEMS IN THE ENVIRONMENT

As the negative externalities associated with pollution and other environmental issues are increasingly recognized, the alternative ways government can curtail their bad effects have received considerable attention from economists and others. This section evaluates several of the major options.

PROPERTY RIGHTS RESPONSES

Large-scale environmental degradation is a conspicuous form of negative externalities. Having identified them as market failures, what can the government do to improve matters? Some economists, led by Nobel laureate Ronald Coase of the University of Chicago Law School, argue that government should simply rearrange property rights. **Coase's theorem** says that, with appropriately designed property rights, markets could take care of externalities without direct government intervention. Consider, for example, the case of a small lake in which anyone can fish without charge. Each fisherman ignores the fact that the more fish he takes out of the lake, the fewer fish there are for others to take out. If the government were to rearrange property rights and grant to a single individual the right to fish, then he would have every incentive to fish efficiently. There would be no externalities. He would take into account the long-run interests as well as the short-run. He would realize that if he fished too much this year, he would have fewer fish next year. If it were a large lake, he might let others do the fishing and charge them for each fish caught or regulate the amount of fish they could catch. But the prices he charged and the regulations he imposed would be designed to ensure that the lake was not overfished.

The point of this example is that the problem of overfishing is solved with only limited government intervention. All the government has to do is assign the property rights correctly.

This kind of problem arises repeatedly. The U.S. government leases public land to cattle ranchers. Since the ranchers only lease the land, they often impose a negative externality on future potential users by overgrazing the land, which leads to environmental damage like soil erosion. If the property rights were altered so that the land was sold to the ranchers, they would have reason to look after the land. In deciding on how many cattle to graze this year, they would take into account the effect on the pasture, and thus on the number of cattle they could graze next year.

Coase envisioned that once property rights were assigned, market solutions or bargaining among potential users would ensure efficient outcomes. Consider the conflict between smokers and nonsmokers over whether to allow smoking in a room. Smokers confer a negative externality on nonsmokers. Coase suggests a simple solution. Give the rights to the air to one individual, say a smoker. He has the right to decide whether to allow smoking or not. For simplicity, assume that there are only two individuals in the room, one a smoker and the other a nonsmoker. If the value of fresh air to the nonsmoker exceeds the value of smoking to the smoker, the nonsmoker would offer the smoker enough money to compensate him not to smoke. Conversely, if the property rights were given to the nonsmoker, and if the value of smoking to the smoker exceeded the value of fresh air to the nonsmoker, then the smoker could compensate the nonsmoker.

Coase argued not only that assigning property rights ensures an efficient outcome, but that how the property rights are assigned affects only the distribution of income, not economic efficiency. Whether smoking would be allowed would depend simply on whether the value of smoking to smokers exceeded or was less than the value of fresh air to nonsmokers.

The appeal of Coase's theorem is that it assigns a minimal role to government. Government simply makes the property rights clear, and leaves the efficient outcome to private markets. Opportunities to apply the theorem are limited, however, because the costs of reaching an agreement may be high, particularly when large numbers of individuals are involved. Imagine the difficulties of assigning property rights to the atmosphere, and having all the individuals adversely affected by air pollution negotiating with all those contributing to it!

Today there is general agreement that while assigning property rights clearly may take care of some externality problems, most externalities, particularly those concerning the environment, require more active government intervention. Some forms this intervention might take include regulatory measures, financial penalties, subsidization of corrective measures, and creating a market for the externality.

REGULATION

Government's first response to the need for intervention to address environmental externalities was to regulate. Electric utilities that burned high-sulfur coal would not be allowed to emit sulfur dioxide into the atmosphere. They would be required to install scrubbers, devices that removed the sulfur from

CLOSE-UP: THE MARKET FOR WHALES

The average American eats sixty-three pounds of beef, fifty pounds of pork, and forty-six pounds of chicken in a year, and one never hears concerns that this consumption will drive cows or pigs or chickens into extinction. Relatively few Americans eat whale meat, yet in certain countries like Japan, whale meat is considered a delicacy. In 1986, fearing that whales were being hunted into extinction, an international convention passed a moratorium on all commercial whaling. Why does the market system work to assure plenty of cows and pigs and chickens, but threaten to exterminate certain breeds of whales?

Economists approach this question by analyzing the property rights in each case. The farmers who raise cows and pigs and chickens own them, and thus have an incentive to build up the supply of animals. But no country or individual owns the ocean or the whales in it. Thus, although there is an economic incentive to hunt whales and sell their meat, there is no individual or company with a direct economic incentive to help nurture and increase the overall number of whales.

This pattern has been called "the tragedy of the commons." When an area is owned in common, like the ocean, everyone has an economic incentive to exploit it, but no one has an economic incentive to care for it. The result can be the disappearance of the whales in the ocean.

Of course, the problem of the commons is not limited to whales. The decimation of the bison on the commonly owned American prairie is another example, as is the pollution in the commonly owned air and water.

Soon after the moratorium on whaling for commercial purposes was passed in 1986, several countries felt a sudden need to hunt whales for scientific purposes. Japan, for example, announced in 1987 an urgent need to kill for research purposes nearly half the number of whales they had been catching for commercial purposes. Iceland announced that it would be shipping much of the whale meat from its "research whales" to Japan, where the meat would sell at premium prices. More recently, international agreements have placed tight limits on the number of whales that can be caught. As a result, the number of Minke whales quickly made a recovery, to the point where limited commercial whaling has begun once again.

Sources: Figures on meat consumption from *Statistical Abstract of the United States* (1994) information about whaling in 1986 and 1987 comes from Timothy Appel, "Japan Finds Loophole in Whaling Ban," *Christian Science Monitor,* April 15, 1987, p. 1.

the fumes. And cars would be required to have catalytic converters. This approach is sometimes called the **command and control approach.**

It quickly ran into problems. The same environmental benefits often could be achieved at much lower costs than the specificity of the regulations demanded. This was partly because the regulations did not (and could not) allow for the myriad of variations in circumstances facing different firms, and partly because the regulatory process is always slow (at best) in incorporating newly developing technologies. Worse still, the command and control approach failed to provide incentives for the development of new technologies to reduce environmental damage, since it often would not allow the technologies, even if they did a better job.[1]

Moreover, politics inevitably intrudes into the setting of regulations, resulting in higher than necessary costs. High-sulfur coal producers worried that the cost of scrubbers would put them at a competitive disadvantage relative to low-sulfur coal producers. (This is the correct market outcome from the viewpoint of economic efficiency, of course, because the social cost of high-sulfur coal—including the negative environmental impacts—was greater than that of the low-sulfur coal.) So they succeeded in getting Congress to mandate that low-sulfur coal also had to have unnecessary scrubbers. In another example, ethanol producers (dominated by a single firm, ADM) succeeded in getting regulators to require a corn-based gasoline additive to reduce pollution rather than an oil-based one—even though the latter was cheaper, and may be better environmentally.[2]

TAXES AND SUBSIDIES

Most economists believe that taxes and subsidies provide a better way than regulation to encourage the behavior society wants. Taxes are the stick, while subsidies are the carrot. Both share the aim of adjusting private costs to account for social costs.

Taxes on pollution are similar to fines for violating regulations in one respect—they both increase the cost of and thereby discourage pollution. But taxes differ from regulation in a fundamental way. Regulations are a clumsy weapon. They penalize firms for polluting over a specified level, but polluters who stay just below that level get off scot-free. Pollution taxes can be set so that they reduce aggregate pollution by the same amount as a regulator would under a command and control system. But the economic effects are very different. Taxes add the cost of pollution to the costs a company has to cover to remain in business. As a result, companies have the incentive to reduce their pollution as far as possible and to find new, low-cost ways of reducing pollution, rather than keeping it just below the legal standard. This is "efficient pollution abatement," with the producers who pollute less having their reward in lower costs.

[1]On the other side, advocates argue that in some cases the tight regulations have "forced" development of new technologies to meet environmental standards that could not be met with existing technologies.

[2]As this book goes to press, the courts have issued a stay on this regulation.

Subsidies such as tax credits for pollution-abatement devices are an alternative way of providing incentives to reduce pollution. Subsidies are economically inefficient. Take the case of a steel firm. With subsidies, firms are not paying the full costs. Part of the costs are being picked up by the government. This allows producers to sell (and users to buy) steel at lower than its full cost of production, and it keeps steel and pollution production above the socially efficient level. Clearly, firms prefer subsidies to taxes.

THE MARKETABLE PERMIT RESPONSE

Still another approach to curbing pollution is **marketable permits.** Companies purchase (or are granted) a permit from the government that allows them to emit a certain amount of pollution. Again, the government can issue the amount of permits so that the company produces the same level of pollution that there would be under the command and control approach. However, companies are allowed to sell their permits. Thus, if a company cuts its pollution in half, it could sell some of its permits to another company that wants to expand production (and hence its emission of pollutants).

The incentive effects of marketable permits are very much like those of taxes. A market for pollution permits encourages development of the best possible antipollution devices, rather than keeping the pollution just under some government-set limit. If the government wishes to reduce pollution over time, the permits can be designed to reduce the amount of pollution they allow by a set amount each year. In the United States, this sort of shrinking marketable permit was used to reduce the amount of lead in gasoline during the early 1980s. Variants of this idea have recently been adopted to help control other forms of air pollution, such as sulfur dioxide.

WEIGHING THE ALTERNATIVE APPROACHES

Incentive programs, such as taxes or marketable permits, have an important advantage over direct controls, like regulations. The issue of pollution is not whether it should be allowed—after all, it is virtually impossible to eliminate all pollution in an industrial economy. Nor would it be efficient; the costs of doing so would far exceed the benefits. The real issue is how sharply pollution should be limited. The *marginal* benefits have to be weighed against the marginal costs. This is not done under regulation. If government ascertains the marginal social cost of pollution and sets charges or marketable permits accordingly, private firms will engage in pollution control up to the point at which the marginal cost of pollution control equals the marginal social return of pollution abatement (which is, of course, just the marginal cost of pollution). Each firm will have the correct marginal incentives.

Governments often prefer direct regulations because they believe that they can control the outcomes better. But such control can be illusory. If an unreachable standard is set, it is likely to be repealed. For example, as automobile companies have found the costs of various regulations to be prohibitive, they have repeatedly appealed for a delay in the enforcement of the regulations, often with considerable success.

It must also be kept in mind that choosing the socially efficient method of pollution abatement is the easy part of the policy problem. Figuring out the

SOLVING THE PROBLEM OF EXTERNALITIES

Externalities, which occur when the extra costs and benefits of a transaction are not fully reflected in the market price, give rise to market failure. Four main solutions have been proposed and used:

1. The reassignment of property rights
2. Regulations that outlaw the negative externality
3. Tax and subsidy measures to encourage the behavior society wants
4. Marketable permits

In the new, Republican-controlled Congress that convened in January 1995, three issues dominated the environmental debate: unfunded mandates (federal requirements laid on states and localities without accompanying funding); takings (a legal term meaning reduction in property value because of government regulations); and cost-benefit analysis (verifying the costs and benefits in assessing whether—and how—to regulate).

Unfunded Mandates The federal government imposes certain environmental regulations on states and localities that entail costs for which the federal government does not provide funds. Critics of environmental regulation said that if the government imposed mandates, it should provide the money. Environmentalists worried that, since federal funding is hard to come by, such a requirement would end environmental regulation. Economists tried to point out that, when well designed, environmental regulations align social and private costs. This is true whether the action is one undertaken by a private firm or a municipal sewage authority. If the sewage authority is imposing externalities on others, through its effect of discharges on water quality, it should bear some extra costs, such as those required to stop the externality. (To be sure, not all of the federally imposed mandates were correcting an externality.)

Takings The takings, for the private sector, are what the unfunded mandate is for the public sector. Take the case of a farmer being ordered not to drain a wetlands area and plant on it. Critics said

that if the government took actions that had adverse effects on property values, the government should provide compensation. Environmentalists again worried that, without funds, such a requirement would end environmental regulation. They agreed that the Constitution prohibited the taking of private property without compensation, but said that the courts should adjudicate whether and when a taking occurred. Courts in fact have taken a fairly narrow view: only in extreme cases would they declare that a taking had occurred. The problem is that virtually every government action affects property values. A change in the interest rates engineered by the Federal Reserve Board can have huge effects on market values. These are not actionable as takings. Where do you draw the line?

Cost-Benefit Analysis The rising costs of environmental regulation, now estimated to exceed $100 billion a year, have made the demand for better analysis when designing regulation almost irresistible. Such analysis should look at the cost and benefit of regulations, encouraging government to only undertake regulations where benefits exceed costs, and to focus on areas where environmental risks are greatest. These principles, supported by most economists, would seem to be unexceptional, and are in fact reflected in Executive Orders issued by both President Bush and President Clinton to guide the implementation of regulations. But some environmentalists take a "purist" stand. They argue that a child's health is not an issue for the cold calculus of costs and benefits. And they worry about "paralysis by analysis"—that the process of doing the cost-benefit analysis studies will effectively bring environmental regulation to a halt.

"right" level of pollution to aim for is much harder. Uncertainty about the consequences of pollution abounds and how to value certain options is an issue of hot debate. To what extent can environmental degradation be reversed? How much value should be placed on the extinction of a species like the spotted owl, or the preservation of the Arctic wilderness? No matter what approach is chosen to externalities and the environment, such questions will remain controversial.

NATURAL RESOURCES

A recurrent theme among environmentalists is that our society is squandering its natural resources too rapidly. We are using up oil and energy resources at an alarming rate, hardwood timber forests that took hundreds of years to grow are being cut down, and supplies of vital resources like phosphorus are dwindling. There are repeated calls for government intervention to enhance the conservation of our scarce natural resources. Those who believe in the infallibility of markets reply, nonsense! Prices give the same guidance to the use of natural resources that they give to any other resource, these people say. Prices measure scarcity, and send consumers and firms the right signals about how much effort to expend to conserve resources, so long as consumers and firms are well informed, and so long as there is not some other source of market failure.

There is, in fact, some truth in both positions. Prices, in general, do provide signals concerning the scarcity of resources, and *in the absence of market failures*, those signals lead to economic efficiency. We have seen some cases where a private market economy without government intervention will not be efficient—when there are negative externalities (pollution) or when a resource (like fish in the ocean) is not priced.

But what about a privately owned resource, like bauxite (from which aluminum is made) or copper? The owner of a bauxite mine has a clearly defined property right. Let's assume that he pays a tax appropriate to any pollution his mining operation causes. Thus, the price he charges will reflect both social and private costs. The question of resource depletion now boils down to the question of whether his bauxite is worth more to him in the market today or left in the ground for future extraction. The answer depends on what bauxite will be worth in the future, say thirty years from now. If it is worth enough more thirty years from now (to compensate for waiting), he will keep the bauxite in the ground even though he may not be alive. That way he maximizes the value of his property, and he can enjoy his wise decision by selling the mine when he retires. The price at which he sells it should reflect the present discounted value of the bauxite.

If this miner and all other bauxite producers choose to bring the bauxite to market today, depleting the world's supply of bauxite, there are two possible reasons. Either, this is the socially efficient outcome—society values bauxite more highly today than it will tomorrow. Or, the miners have miscalculated the value of bauxite thirty years from now and underestimated future prices, though they have every incentive to get as accurate a forecast as they can. If they have indeed miscalculated, we might view the result as a market failure; but there would be no reason to expect a government bureaucracy to do any better than the firms at guessing future prices.

However, from society's viewpoint there are two plausible reasons why private owners may undervalue future benefits of a natural resource. First, in countries where property rights are not secure, owners of a resource may feel that if they do not sell it soon, there is a reasonable chance that the resources will be taken away from them. There may be a revolution, for example, in which the government will take over the resource with no or only partial compensation to the owners. Even in countries like the United States, where owners are not worried about government confiscating their property, increased regulations might make it more expensive to extract the resource in the future, or higher taxes might make it less attractive to sell the resource in the future. Second, individuals and firms often face limited borrowing opportunities and very high interest rates. In these circumstances, capital markets discount future returns at a high rate, far higher than society or the government would discount them.

Higher interest rates induce a more rapid depletion of resources. Suppose an oil company is deciding whether to extract some oil today or to wait until next year. For simplicity, assume there are no extraction costs, so the net return to selling the oil is just its price. If the price of a barrel of oil is the same today as a year from now, the firm's decision is simple. The firm will sell the oil today. But what if the price of oil is expected to go up 10 percent? Now the firm must compare the present discounted value of the oil sold a year from now with what it could receive today. To calculate the present discounted value, we simply divide next year's price by 1 plus the interest rate. If the interest rate is 10 percent, then a dollar a year from now is worth 10 percent less than a dollar today. So if the interest rate is less than 10 percent, it pays the firm to wait; if the interest rate is more than 10 percent, it pays the firm to extract the oil today. At higher interest rates, firms have a greater incentive to extract oil earlier.

Sometimes government has aggravated the waste of natural resources. In the United States, for example, much of the timber lies on government lands. The government, in making the land available, has paid less attention to concerns about economic efficiency than it has to the pleading of timber interest groups. Government policies aimed at restricting the import of foreign oil have also encouraged the use of domestic resources, a seemingly perverse policy of "drain America first." Government policies in keeping the price of water for farmers low has led to many negative outcomes: excessive use of water, draining water from underground basins built up over centuries, lowering the water table, and in some cases, leaching out the soil. In each of these cases, private property rights and market outcomes would have supplied solutions that almost everyone in society would regard as better than what happened.

MERIT GOODS AND BADS

In this chapter, we have explained why market failures—such as externalities—provide a rationale for government intervention. To some people, how we treat the environment and the earth's natural resources is not just a matter of economic efficiency; it is a moral issue. They argue that the issue of allowing whaling should not be approached narrowly from the perspective of economic costs and benefits. This is but one of many examples in which government becomes involved not just because markets have failed to produce efficient outcomes, but because government believes there are values that supersede those reflected in individual preferences, and it has the right and duty to impose those values on its citizens. It rejects the basic premise of *consumer sovereignty*, which holds that individuals are the best judges of their own welfare, and argues that in certain selected areas, there is a role for *paternalism*—government can make better choices in some matters than individuals. Goods that the government mandates to be consumed—like compulsory education—are called **merit goods,** and goods that it prohibits on these grounds—such as drugs, pornography, and, from 1919 to 1933, alcohol—are called **merit bads.** These goods are proscribed not just because of their adverse effects on others (externalities).

REVIEW AND PRACTICE

SUMMARY

1. Government may have a role in the economy when markets fail to produce an efficient outcome. When positive or negative externalities exist, markets will not provide an efficient outcome.

2. One way to deal with externalities is to assign clear-cut property rights.

3. Governments may deal with environmental externalities by imposing regulatory measures (the command and control approach), levying taxes and granting subsidies, or issuing marketable permits.

4. In a perfect market, natural resources are used up at an efficient rate. However, privately owned resources may be sold too soon, for two reasons. First, owners may fear that if they do not sell the resources soon, new government rules may prevent them from selling at all or, in any case, lower the return from selling it in the future. Second, interest rates facing owners may be high, so they may value future income less than society in general. High interest rates lead to a faster exploitation of natural resources.

KEY TERMS

market failure approach	**private marginal cost**	**command and control approach**
social marginal cost	**Coase's theorem**	

REVIEW QUESTIONS

1. Name several market failures. Why do economists see the existence of these market failures as a justification for government action?

2. Why will a free market produce too much of goods that have negative externalities, like pollution? Why will a free market produce too little of goods that have positive externalities, like pollution control?

3. What are the advantages and limitations of dealing with externalities by assigning property rights?

4. What are the advantages of marketable permits over command and control regulation? What are the advantages of using taxes for polluting rather than subsidies for pollution-abatement equipment?

5. How do markets work to allocate natural resources efficiently? In what cases will markets fail to give the correct signals for how quickly a resource like oil should be depleted?

PROBLEMS

1. Marple and Wolfe are two neighboring dormitories. Wolfe is considering giving a party with a very loud band, which will have a negative externality, a sort of sound pollution, for Marple. Imagine that the school

administration decides that any dormitory has the right to prevent another dorm from hiring a band. If the band provides a negative externality, how might the residents of Wolfe apply the lessons of Coase's theorem to hire the band they want?

Now imagine that the school administration decides that no dormitory can prevent another dorm from hiring a band, no matter how loud. If the band provides a negative externality, how might the residents of Marple apply the lessons of Coase's theorem to reduce the amount of time they have to listen to the band? How would your answer change if the band provided a positive externality?

2. The manufacture of trucks produces pollution of various kinds; for the purposes of this example, let's call it all "glop." Producing a truck creates one unit of glop, and glop has a cost to society of $3,000. Imagine that the supply of trucks is competitive, and market supply and demand are given by the following data:

Price (thousand $)	19	20	21	22	23	24	25
Quantity supplied	480	540	600	660	720	780	840
Quantity demanded	660	630	600	570	540	510	480

Graph the supply curve for the industry and the demand curve. What are equilibrium price and output? Now graph the social marginal cost curve. If the social cost of glop were taken into account, what would be the new equilibrium price and output?

If the government is concerned about the pollution emitted by truck plants, explain how it might deal with the externality through fines or taxes and through subsidies. Illustrate the effects of taxes and subsidies by drawing the appropriate supply and demand graphs. (Don't bother worrying about the exact units.) Why are economists likely to prefer fines to subsidies?

3. Consider a small lake with a certain number of fish. The more fish that one fisherman takes out, the fewer fish are available for others to take out. Use graphs depicting private and social costs and benefits to fishing to describe the equilibrium and the socially efficient level of fishing. Explain how a tax on fishing could achieve the efficient outcome. Explain how giving a single individual the property right to the fish in the lake might also be used to obtain an efficient outcome.

The more fish taken out this year, the less fish will be available next year. Explain why if there is a single owner for the lake, the fish will be efficiently extracted from it. Assume that anyone who wants to fish can do so. Would you expect that too many fish would be taken out this year?

4. Consider a crowded room with an equal number of smokers and nonsmokers. Each smoker would be willing to pay $1.00 to have the right to smoke. Each nonsmoker would be willing to pay $.50 to have the room free from smoke. Assume there is a rule that says than no smoking is allowed. Could everyone be made better off if smoking is allowed? How? If property rights to clean air are assigned to the nonsmokers, how might

the efficient outcome be obtained? What difference does it make to the outcome whether there is initially a rule that smoking is allowed or smoking is not allowed? What problems might you envision occurring if no smoking is allowed unless all the nonsmokers agree to allow smoking?

22

TAXES, TRANSFERS, AND REDISTRIBUTION

D uring this century, governments have become increasingly involved in reducing inequality in the distribution of income provided by the market. Without help, some families have too little income to do more than barely survive. Children who have the bad fortune to be born into impoverished families face bleak life prospects. Most developed countries have therefore sought to provide a safety net for the poor. Some have taken the more active stance of promoting equality of opportunity. Many have also developed benefit programs that help people, regardless of income, in times of need (such as illness, unemployment, or old age).

Income redistribution is inextricably linked to taxation. After a look at the case for income redistribution, this chapter takes up the two major ways government alters the distribution of income: taxes and public benefit programs (transfers).

KEY QUESTIONS

1. What are the characteristics of a good tax system, and how does America's current tax system fare under these criteria? What are the various ways government raises revenues?

2. What do economists mean when they talk about a fair or equitable tax system? What arguments are used to decide how the burden of taxation should be shared among various groups in the population?

3. What are the basic programs designed to provide assistance for the poor? What are the trade-offs between equity and efficiency in the design of these programs?

4. What is the rationale for social insurance programs? What are some of the current public policy controversies surrounding them?

THE CASE FOR INCOME REDISTRIBUTION

Income redistribution policies are justified in ways different from other governmental economic policies. The roles of government developed in earlier chapters are based on the premise that public sector intervention may be appropriate to ensure efficient outcomes when there are market failures—whether from lack of competition, imperfect information, or the presence of externalities. In such situations, markets fail to provide completely satisfactory answers to some of the basic economic questions: "What goods are produced, and in what quantities?" and "How are the goods produced?"

When it comes to the question "For whom are the goods produced?," to which this chapter is devoted, the rationale for public sector intervention is different. Individuals' incomes determine who consumes the goods produced in a market economy. People with higher skills or more capital, for instance, earn higher incomes and therefore get to consume more of the goods produced. Labor and capital markets may be efficient, in the sense that wages and returns to capital get the incentive structure right for the economy. But the market-determined distribution of income may result in some individuals having billions of dollars and others being homeless, with inadequate food and medical care. Thus, the case for income redistribution is not based on the pursuit of economic efficiency. It is based on overriding social values. There is a general consensus that when the market results in incomes so low that people cannot sustain a minimally decent standard of living, government should help out. *How* it helps out is crucial, however, because redistribution programs often interfere with economic efficiency.

THE CHANGING U.S. INCOME DISTRIBUTION

Concern about income distribution has risen as the wage differential between skilled and unskilled workers has become more pronounced over the past two decades. Real wages of unskilled workers have fallen dramatically over this time span. At the same time, real wages of skilled workers have held steady or fallen modestly, increasing the wage differential between skilled and unskilled workers. (See Figure 22.1.) Though lower-income families have made up for some of the difference by working longer hours (often with both parents working), the poorest families have still seen a decline in their real incomes. Moreover, changing family structures have increased the proportion of single-parent households. These patterns, in turn, have increased the number of poor children to the point where almost one in four children in this country now lives below the poverty threshold.

What to do about the increased inequality depends on the time frame. The long-run strategy focuses on improved education and training. In the short run, attention focuses on tax and benefit programs.

TAXES

The U.S. government raises tax revenues from a variety of sources. There are taxes on the earnings of individuals and corporations, known as **individual income taxes** and **corporation income taxes.** Real estate—buildings and

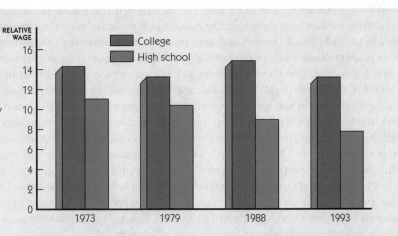

Figure 22.1 INCREASING INCOME INEQUALITY

During the past two decades the wage differential between skilled and unskilled workers has become more pronounced. This trend is evident in a comparison of the average real wages of high school and college graduates who recently entered the labor force. The real wages of high school graduates have decreased consistently since 1973, falling a total of 30 percent between 1973 and 1993. During the same period, the average real wages of college graduates changed little. *Source:* John Bound and George Johnson, "What Are the Causes of Rising Wage Inequality in the United States?", *FRBNY Economic Policy Review* (January 1995), p. 11.

Figure 22.2 THE IMPORTANCE OF VARIOUS TAXES

At the federal level, the largest share of taxes come from the individual income tax, followed by the payroll tax and the corporate income tax, as shown in panel A. Sources of revenue at the state and local level are more fragmented, as seen in panel B, but include sales and property taxes, as well as revenue received from other levels of government. *Source: Economic Report of the President* (1996), Tables B-78, B-82.

land—is subject to taxation by most states; these taxes are known as **property taxes.** Large bequests and gifts are taxed, through **gift** and **estate taxes.** There are special provisions relating to the taxation of capital gains (the increase in value of an asset between the time an individual purchases it and the time she sells it). Furthermore, wage income is subject not only to the income tax, but also to the **payroll tax** (the tax levied on a company's payroll, half of which is deducted from employees' paychecks). Revenues from the payroll tax are intended to finance the Social Security (retirement income) and Medicare (medical care for the aged) programs.

There are also taxes on the purchase of specific goods and services, known as **excise taxes.** The two heaviest excise taxes are on alcohol and tobacco, also known as **sin taxes.** The excise taxes on air travel and gasoline are sometimes called **benefit taxes** because the proceeds go for benefits, like airports and roads, to those who purchase the good. Excise taxes on perfume, large cars, yachts, and expensive fur coats, targeted to the rich, are referred to as **luxury taxes.** Other excise taxes, such as the one on telephone services, have no particular justification other than raising revenue. Most states impose a general tax on purchases of goods and services, known as a **sales tax,** though typically a wide variety of items (such as food) are exempted.

As this list indicates, few transactions in our economy escape taxation. Figure 22.2 shows the relative importance of various taxes at the federal and the state/local levels. At the federal level (panel A), the single most important source of revenue is the tax on individuals' income (contributing almost half of total revenue), followed by the payroll tax. At the state/local levels (panel B), the sales tax is the most important revenue source.

CHARACTERISTICS OF A GOOD TAX SYSTEM

One out of every three dollars of total output of the U.S. economy goes to the government. Not surprisingly, there is great concern about how the government raises its revenue. At one time, the art of taxation was likened to the problem of how to pluck a goose without making it squawk. The basic fact of life is that everyone enjoys government services but few enjoy paying taxes. Even so, there is substantial agreement about what constitutes a "good" tax system. It has five characteristics.

Fairness   In most people's minds, the first criterion is fairness. But fairness, like beauty, is often in the eyes of the beholder. In trying to define fairness, economists focus on two principles: **horizontal equity,** which says that individuals who are in identical or similar situations should pay identical or similar taxes, and **vertical equity,** which says that people who are better off should pay more taxes.

Tax systems in which the rich pay a larger fraction of their income than the poor are said to be **progressive,** while those in which the poor pay a larger fraction of their income than the rich are called **regressive.** If rich people pay more taxes than the poor but not proportionately more, the tax system is still considered regressive.

The U.S. income tax is progressive, since the rates that apply to higher incomes are larger than for lower incomes. Taxes on tobacco and alcohol are examples of regressive taxes, since poor individuals spend a larger fraction of their income on these goods. States sales taxes, on the whole, are regressive, since in general not all goods—such as vacations in Europe—are taxed, and the fraction of income of the rich that thus escapes taxation is larger than that of the poor.

Efficiency   The second criterion for a good tax system is efficiency. The tax system should interfere as little as possible with the way the economy allocates resources, and it should raise revenue with the least cost to taxpayers. Very high taxes may discourage work and savings, and therefore interfere with the efficiency of the economy. Taxes that select out particular goods to be taxed—such as excise taxes on perfume, boats, and airline tickets—discourage individuals from purchasing those goods, and therefore also interfere with efficiency.

The U.S. income tax system has many provisions that have the effect of encouraging some types of economic activity and discouraging others. For instance, the U.S. income tax allows certain child care payments to be taken as a credit against tax payments owed. The government thus subsidizes child care. Similarly, when firms spend money on R & D, their expenditures may reduce the amount they have to pay in taxes. Such arrangements are called **tax subsidies.** These subsidies cost the government money just as if the government paid out money directly for child care or research. Accordingly, the revenue lost from a tax subsidy is called a **tax expenditure.**

Today, capital gains received favorable treatment in a number of ways. The maximum tax rate is 28 percent, rather than the 39.6 percent tax rate on other income. In addition, taxes are paid only when assets are sold, not when the gain is accrued. This postponement of payment is equivalent to a reduction in the tax rate of a quarter or more (7 percentage points). In addition, when an individual dies, the assets are passed on to his or her heirs and the accrued capital gain completely escapes taxation—at an estimated cost to the Treasury of $30 billion a year. And there are major tax breaks if you hold investments in new companies for at least five years.

But prior to 1986, capital gains received even more favorable treatment—they were taxed at 40 percent of the rate of ordinary income. Many investors would like a return to the good old days. Reinforcing that perspective is a bit of budget gimmickry. When capital gains taxes are lowered (particularly if the reduction is viewed to be temporary), some households are induced to sell their assets earlier than they otherwise would. This yields a temporary *increase* in tax revenues. Of course, though households pay their taxes earlier, the total taxes they pay is reduced. Thus, in the long run, government revenues are lowered (and the deficit increased). There is another possibility: some individuals who would have held assets until death—and thus managed to escape taxation— might be enticed by the lower capital gains tax rates to sell their assets early. Even so, the statistical evidence that tax revenues would increase is, at best, weak.

Advocates for cutting the capital gains tax believe that lower taxes will provide a greater stimulus to the economy, and the higher rate of growth will itself generate more revenues. This is the same argument as was used in 1981 when taxes were lowered. At the time, the economy was operating far below full employment, so there was room for expansion; even under these conditions, the tax cut did not generate increased tax revenues.

Critics of a capital gains tax cut argue that with the economy at full employment, there is little room for extra expansion. And in any case, capital gains taxation distorts the pattern of investment. If greater investment is desired, the best way to elicit efficient investment is through lowering interest rates. The focus should be on policies, such as deficit reduction, which allow lower interest rates. The benefits of capital gains tax reductions go disproportionately to the rich, since wealth is even more concentrated than income; and, extending the preferential tax treatment to investments already made has no incentive effect.

In spite of these criticisms, as this book goes to press, the prospects of a capital gains tax cut remain good. In an era of budget stringency, the official accounting of the cost of capital gains tax reductions focuses only on the impact over seven years, and employs high estimates of induced realizations of capital gains. This accounting method makes the capital gains tax cut appear to be one of the most affordable forms of tax reduction. In some versions, cutting the tax actually provides more revenue within the seven-year period.

Administrative Simplicity   The third criterion is administrative simplicity. It is costly—to the government and to those who must pay taxes—to collect taxes and administer a tax system. In addition to the costs of running the IRS, billions of hours are spent each year in filling out tax forms, hours that might be spent producing goods and services. Billions of dollars are spent on accountants and lawyers by taxpayers and by the IRS in the annual ritual of preparing and processing tax forms. Finally, with a good tax system, it should be difficult to evade the taxes imposed.

Flexibility   The fourth criterion is flexibility. As economic circumstances change, it may be desirable to change tax rates. With a good tax system, it should be relatively easy to do this.

Transparency   The fifth criterion is transparency. A good tax system is one in which it can be ascertained what each person is paying in taxes. The principle of transparency is analogous to the principle of "truth in advertising." Taxpayers are consumers of public services. They should know what they (and others) are paying for the services they are getting.

GRADING THE U.S. TAX SYSTEM

How well does the U.S. tax system fare, based on these five criteria? Equally important, have the major changes in the tax laws over the past decade improved the tax system?

Fairness   As noted, the U.S. federal income tax system is, over all, progressive. Low-income individuals are exempted from paying any income tax whatsoever. Beyond a certain level of income (depending on the size of the family—for a family of four, the critical level in 1995 was $16,550), the tax rate is 15 percent. This means that for each extra $100 an individual earns, he must pay an extra $15 of taxes; this is his **marginal tax rate.** At a still higher level of income, the marginal tax rate increases to 28 percent, then to 39.6 percent.

The **average tax rate** gives the ratio of taxes to taxable income. While there are big jumps in the marginal tax rate, the average tax rate increases smoothly. Figure 22.3 shows the 1995 marginal and average income tax rates for a typical family of four that did not itemize its deductions.

The income tax is only one of several income-related taxes that U.S. citizens pay. The payroll (Social Security) tax is another one that increases with income up to some level. An **earned-income tax credit** is designed to supplement the income of low-income workers with families; as a person's income increases beyond some level, the payments he *receives* under this program decrease. Figure 22.4 collects together all income-related federal taxes: the income tax, the earned-income credit, and the payroll tax. The figure is remarkable because of its irregular shape—a consequence of the interaction of the various parts of the tax system—but also because for so much of the income distribution, there is so little variability in the marginal tax rate.

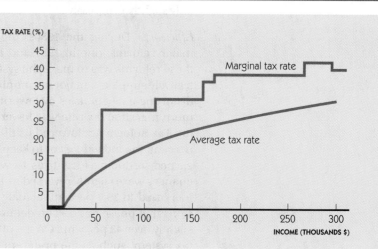

Figure 22.3 MARGINAL AND AVERAGE TAX RATES

Marginal tax rates change by jumps, as shown in the table, but average tax rates increase gradually. *Source:* Internal Revenue Service, Form 1040 (1995).

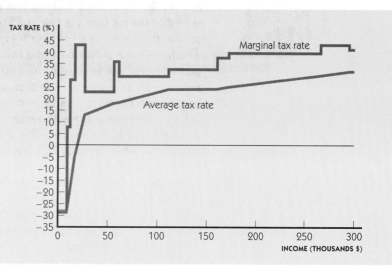

Figure 22.4 AVERAGE AND MARGINAL TAX RATES, TAKING INTO ACCOUNT VARIOUS FEDERAL TAXES

The individual income tax is only one of the taxes people pay. As incomes rise, there are changes in payroll taxes, income taxes, and earned-income tax credits, resulting in a complicated pattern of marginal tax rates. *Source:* Internal Revenue Service, Form 1040 (1995).

To assess the overall progressiveness of the U.S. tax system, we have to look not only at the federal income tax but at all taxes—including the corporation income tax and state and local taxes.

Many state and local taxes are regressive. This is because lower- and middle-income individuals spend a larger fraction of their income on items that are subject to state sales taxes than do the rich. Our current *total* tax system—combining the slightly progressive federal tax system with the slightly regressive state and local tax system—is, in the judgment of most economists, only slightly progressive.

Efficiency During the 1980s, the U.S. income tax system underwent two major reforms, one in 1981 and another in 1986. The announced intent of these reforms was to make the system more efficient, more fair, and administratively simpler. A major accomplishment of these reforms was to reduce the distorting effect of taxes by lowering the marginal tax rate. In 1981, the maximum marginal tax rate was lowered from 70 percent to 50 percent. In 1986, the Tax Reform Act lowered it still further to 33 percent. With a tax rate of 70 percent, the individual got to keep less than one out of every three dollars she earned, reducing incentives to work harder and increase earnings. These changes were slightly reversed in 1993, when the top marginal tax bracket was increased to 39.6 percent (actually, when the medicare insurance and provisions that phase out certain deductions are included, the top marginal rate is slightly over 42 percent). On the other hand, several distorting elements of the tax system, such as the preferential treatment of gas and oil, were retained. Thus, in the area of efficiency, the U.S. tax system today, while considerably better than it was fifteen years ago, still has much room for improvement.

Administrative Simplicity Americans live in a complex society, and their tax laws reflect and contribute to this complexity. As they have sought to make sure that the tax laws are fair and apply uniformly to all people in similar situations, the laws have become increasingly complex. High tax rates make it worthwhile for individuals and businesses to think hard about how to avoid taxes (legally, without going to jail). With high tax rates, it may pay a businessperson to devote almost as much energy to how he can avoid taxes as to how he can produce a better product. The tax law has evolved out of this constant battle between the government and taxpayers; as each new way of reducing taxes is discovered, the law is modified to close the loophole. Inevitably another hole is discovered, and another repair job is attempted. Today the federal tax law amounts to a multitude of volumes.

The objective of administrative simplicity seems to have been an elusive one. Many economists are convinced that the United States could have a tax system that is truly administratively simple, but to do so, other objectives would have to be given up. Some of the complexity derives from the attempt to have a progressive income tax and to tax the income from capital. But preferential treatment of capital income is also a major source of complexity, as rules have to be made to stop the conversion of other income into forms receiving preferential treatment.

Flexibility One of the weakest aspects of the U.S. tax system is its lack of flexibility. Any time a tax change is proposed, all of the issues discussed here are raised. There are debates about how different groups would be affected and about how efficiency is affected. Basic issues of values—how progressive should the tax system be?—are aired once again. Special-interest groups try to take the opportunity of any change in the tax law to get favorable treatment. It has turned out to be extremely difficult—and time-consuming—to change the tax law.

Transparency   Of all the parts of the tax system, the ultimate burden of corporation income tax is perhaps the least transparent. Although corporations write the check to the IRS, most economists agree that much of the burden is shifted to individuals and households, through reduced wages and/or higher product prices. The 1986 Tax Reform Act increased the relative importance of the corporation income tax, and thus on average made the tax system less transparent. The sales tax ranks second lowest on the transparency scale. Politicians love the sales tax, because they know that many, perhaps most, individuals never figure out the total amount they are actually spending on government services.

TRANSFERS

In addition to tax policy, government affects the income distributions through **transfer programs.** Transfers are payments that households receive without having to engage in any current productive activity in return. Transfer payments can be private, such as company pensions or scholarships from private universities. Government engages in a wide range of transfer programs. Two major groups of government transfer programs concern us here: **income-tested transfers,** the direct purpose of which is to redistribute income from upper-income to lower-income Americans, and **social insurance,** which protects individuals, irrespective of income, in times of need.

NEED-BASED TRANSFER PROGRAMS

Politicians frequently appeal to voters by expressing their concern for the poor. Compassion for others not as fortunate is a fundamental human value. Government programs to aid the poor reflect the belief that all citizens have a collective responsibility to take care of those among them who are in need. Though the extent to which responsibility should be borne by government or by voluntary charities is a matter of debate, governments in all the developed countries have assumed a major role in providing at least a safety net to protect the most disadvantaged.

There are currently five major public benefit programs for low-income Americans. AFDC (Aid to Families with Dependent Children), what most people refer to as "welfare," provides cash assistance to poor families (mostly households with only one parent present). Medicaid provides health care for those on AFDC and to other poor children as well. The food stamp program provides vouchers for the purchase of food. SSI (supplemental security income) provides cash assistance to the low-income elderly and disabled, to supplement their social security benefits. Housing assistance programs include public housing and rental vouchers. In addition to these five program areas, states and localities provide general assistance to those who fall between the cracks. Food stamps and SSI are federal programs (states can supplement SSI benefits). The other programs vary from state to state, with the federal government typically providing only broad program guidelines, but footing much of the bill.

Our discussion here focuses on the two most controversial program areas: welfare and housing.

WELFARE

AFDC is the most controversial of the programs providing benefits that depend on income. In his 1992 campaign, President Clinton promised to "end welfare as we know it," a sentiment shared by many Republicans. In 1996 Congress passed, and the president signed, major welfare reform legislation, which ended the federal entitlement to welfare, left most of the details of welfare programs up to the states, and provided the states with a fixed amount of money (bloc grants) with which to run the programs. Underlying the reforms were three principles:

1. Encouraging work. There is now a strong consensus that welfare should be, for all who are capable, a transition to work. Recipients need incentives to work—carrots and sticks. The earned income tax credit (EITC) provides a big carrot by subsidizing the wages of low-income workers. The stick embodied in the new welfare legislation is the threat to cut off welfare payment after two years of receipt ("time-limited welfare").
2. Increasing opportunity. To obtain work, individuals must have the skills required by the marketplace. Hence, most welfare reform proposals include provision for training and job search.
3. Fostering responsibility. Most proposals also include measures designed to make parents provide financial support for their children, and to encourage a sense of responsibility—in particular, the responsibility that comes with parenthood.

A goal of the 1996 reform was the reduction of welfare costs, but the success of the initiative may require new expenditures, such as spending on child care and training.

HOUSING

Public housing projects have been described as "warehouses of the poor," and the description has merit. By failing to integrate the poor more thoroughly into the communities in which they live, public housing projects help perpetuate the cycle of poverty. Moreover, many housing programs are inequitable. They provide generous benefits to those lucky enough to receive them, but many with the same income and family size get nothing. Worse still, providing a subsidy that is tied to a particular dwelling impedes labor mobility. Finally, the costs of public housing are high, and its quality is often much lower than housing of similar cost in the private sector.

All these drawbacks to public housing have led the government to reduce its role in directly supplying low-income housing and to turn increasingly to more market-based solutions. This is done by subsidizing the cost of housing for the poor through rental vouchers. As recipients use the vouchers, increasing demand for low-income housing, more builders are induced to provide

The official poverty line determines how many people the government counts as "poor." But what determines the poverty line itself?

In the late 1960s, an official at the Social Security Administration, Molly Orshansky, developed a method of measuring poverty from a survey of household expenditures. She found that a typical family spent one-third of its income on food. She then gathered information on minimum food budgets for families of various sizes, and multiplied that number by three to get an estimate of the poverty line for the different family sizes. With minor changes, Orshansky's poverty line was officially adopted in 1969 and has been increased by the overall rate of inflation since then.

There are a number of questions one can ask about how poverty is measured: here are three.

First, the survey Orshansky relied on to find that households spent one-third of their income on food was taken in 1955. Since then, household expenditures have shifted. Households now spend a much lower percentage of income on food, perhaps one-fourth or one-fifth. If the minimum food budget were accordingly multiplied by four or five, the poverty line would be much higher.

Second, the poverty line does not take in-kind benefits into account. In-kind benefits include any benefits that are not received in cash form, like Medicaid, food stamps, and subsidized school lunches. If those benefits are measured as additional income, the number of people below the poverty line falls by about 20 percent.

Finally, some critics have proposed that poverty should be thought of as a relative rather than an absolute concept. They argue that those at the bottom of society, say the bottom 5 or 10 or 20 percent, are poor relative to everyone else. Poverty is more appropriately viewed as an extreme case of inequality.

For many, this last criticism goes too far. They fear that a relative concept of poverty might reduce the moral urgency of fighting poverty. There is broad social support for efforts to assure that people have basic levels of food, housing, clothing, and medical care, even if defining those amounts is controversial.

In 1995, a National Academy of Sciences study proposed major revisions in how we measure poverty. While there was agreement about including noncash income, the difficult problems of how best to include health care expenditures were not

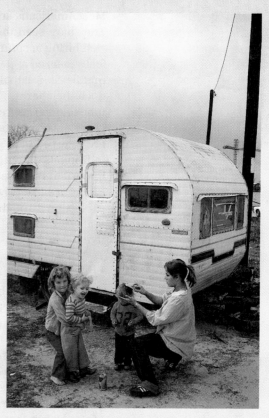

fully resolved. Should a sick, poor person who receives $150,000 for a kidney transplant have that added to his income, in which case he now appears to be in an upper income bracket? The study proposed an adjustment in the poverty level that went beyond just taking into account inflation, but it did not propose increasing the poverty level in proportion to increases in average income, which would have made poverty a purely relative phenomenon. But even this compromise generated a strong dissent from one of the members of the Academy's panel.

Sources: Joyce E. Allen and Margaret C. Simms, "Is a New Yardstick Needed to Measure Poverty?" *Focus,* February 1990, pp. 6–8; *Measuring Poverty: A New Approach,* National Academy of Sciences, 1996.

housing for them. Vouchers have several other advantages. They allow for individuals to shop for their housing over broader areas, not just the inner cities, and they can be made "portable," so that individuals can relocate due to job opportunities without losing their housing subsidy.

SOCIAL INSURANCE

Most Americans are neither rich nor poor. They belong to the "middle class." They have seen the poor get free medical care. They have heard about the rich hiring accountants to duck taxes by taking advantage of loopholes. They feel squeezed and unfairly treated. Some of this is a matter of perception. The middle class actually receives the benefits of many "hidden" loopholes that reduce their taxes. For instance, fringe benefits (health insurance, retirement funds), often representing between a quarter to a third of a person's salary, generally escape taxation. In addition, the United States has a variety of what are referred to as **middle-class entitlement programs,** so named because individuals do not have to demonstrate poverty to receive benefits. The most important of these are the social insurance programs. Social insurance programs are like private insurance, in that people nominally pay for their own protection through a tax on wage income, the payroll tax. But in other, important ways, they are *not* like private insurance, as we will see in the paragraphs that follow.

THE BURDEN OF SOCIAL INSURANCE PROGRAMS

The first myth about social insurance concerns who pays for it. Social Security is supported by a tax on wages, 50 percent paid by the employer, 50 percent by the employee. This division of the tax is entirely superficial; the consequences of the tax are essentially the same as they would be if the worker paid the entire tax.

Figure 22.5 uses demand and supply curves for labor to show this. Consider a payroll tax imposed on the employer based on what she pays her workers. The vertical axis measures the wage *received* by the employee. Since the cost of a worker is the wage received by the employee *plus* the tax, the tax shifts the demand curve down. In the new equilibrium, workers' wages have fallen.

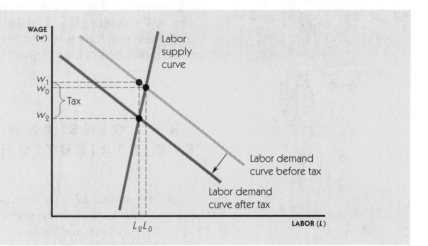

Figure 22.5 THE INCIDENCE OF PAYROLL TAXES

The payroll tax introduces a wedge between the cost to an employer of an individual working an hour more (wage plus tax) and what the worker receives. The magnitude of the wedge does not depend on whether the tax is levied on the employer or employee. The tax leads to fewer workers being hired at the equilibrium wage, reduced from w_0 to w_2.

The wage received by a worker is precisely the same as it would have been had the same tax been imposed on the worker directly. While normally the wage falls by less than the amount of the tax, the extent to which it falls depends on the elasticity of the demand and supply curves. The figure shows the "normal" case where the supply of labor is relatively inelastic, in which case wages fall almost by the full amount of the tax.

HOW SOCIAL INSURANCE IS MORE THAN AN INSURANCE PROGRAM

The second myth about social insurance programs is that they have no redistribution effect. In any insurance program, some individuals receive back more than they contribute, some less. That, in a sense, is the whole purpose of insurance. No one knows whether she will be sick enough next year to need hospitalization. So people buy hospital insurance. Those who are lucky enough not to need hospitalization in effect help pay for the hospitalization of those who need it. But with private insurance, on average, the premiums (what you pay for the insurance) cover the costs of what you receive (including the costs of administration, which are often substantial). With the social insurance programs, however, there is often no close connection between the amount contributed and the amount received back. For instance, on average, single high-wage earners receive less back per dollar contributed than do low-wage families with a single earner. Thus, Social Security performs a redistributive as well as an insurance function.

To the extent that social insurance provides insurance that individuals want and the market has failed to provide, it performs an important economic function. To the extent that social insurance is popular because everyone believes someone else is picking up the tab, its role and function need to be reexamined. Social insurance is popular partly because it seems to benefit the majority of the population, the middle class. The problem facing the middle class, however, is that there are not enough "rich" people to pay for these programs, so the middle class must pay for them itself. And the taxes required to finance them may have serious disincentive effects. These have to be balanced against the benefits of their redistributive role.

THE COSTS AND BENEFITS OF REDISTRIBUTION

Tax, welfare, and social insurance programs in the United States all play an important role in answering one of the fundamental questions posed in Chapter 1: For whom are goods produced (who gets to enjoy the goods that are available)? Each group in society would like to pay as little in taxes as possible and receive as many benefits as possible, and complaints about fairness abound. But issues of what is fair may never be resolved. And economists worry that at least some attempts to make sure everyone has a fair slice may so reduce the size of the economic pie to be divided that almost everyone is worse off.

EQUITY-EFFICIENCY TRADE-OFFS

Economists enter the discussion of redistribution to clarify the costs and consequences of various programs, including different tax systems. Systems that tax the rich more heavily or provide support for poor people even if they could work (but only if they remain unemployed) are likely to have adverse effects on incentives. Economists try to calculate precisely how important these effects are.

All economists agree that as government redistributes more income to the poor, it has to raise taxes on the rich and middle-income individuals, which weakens their incentives to work. But economists disagree about the magnitudes of the trade-offs. Most economists agree that at high enough tax rates, incentives are greatly reduced. The high marginal tax rates of 60 percent or more that used to prevail in Europe probably had large negative effects on efficiency. But whether at current marginal tax rates in the United States, an increase in taxation would have a *large* effect on incentives is much more debatable.

Economists focus on the trade-offs—between equity (how the pie is divided) and efficiency (the size of the pie); and between reductions in the risks of life (through the provision of social insurance) and economic incentives. Beyond these trade-offs lie basic issues of social values, of what kind of society we want to have *recognizing the economic constraints on the choices that we can make.* These values touch not only on issues of efficiency, equality, and risk protection (economic security), but also on individual rights and social responsibilities.

HOW WELL DOES THE UNITED STATES DO?

Taking all of the government programs into account—the tax system, welfare, social insurance—does the government succeed in changing the answer to the question "Who gets the goods produced in the economy?" To answer this question, we need some way of measuring the distribution of income.

Economists often represent the degree of inequality in an economy by a diagram called the **Lorenz curve.** The Lorenz curve shows the cumulative fraction of the country's total income going to the poorest 5 percent, the poorest 10 percent, the poorest 15 percent, and so on. Figure 22.6A shows Lorenz curves for the United States, both before and after government tax and transfer programs have had their effect. If there were complete equality, then 20 percent of the income would accrue to the lowest 20 percent of the population, 40 percent to the lowest 40 percent, and so on. The Lorenz curve would be a straight 45-degree line. If incomes were very concentrated, then the lowest 80 percent might receive almost nothing, and the top 5 percent might receive 80 percent of total income; in this case, the Lorenz curve would be very bowed. Twice the

Figure 22.6 INEQUALITY MEASURES

Taxes and subsidies affect the distribution of income. Panel A shows two Lorenz curves for the United States in 1989, one for income before taxes have been levied and government transfers have been received, and the other after. Clearly, some redistribution does take place through these mechanisms, as they move the Lorenz curve toward greater equality. Panel B shows how other developed countries rank relative to the United States on one standard measure of inequality, the Gini coefficient. The United States ranks number one: it has the most unequal distribution of income among the ten. *Sources: Current Population Reports* (1990), p. 5, Table B; *Luxembourg Income Study Database* (1989).

area between the 45-degree line and the Lorenz curve is a commonly employed measure of inequality, called the **Gini coefficient.**

As can be seen, the after-tax curve for the United States is decidedly inside the pre-tax, indicating that the combined effect of government redistribution programs is to make incomes more equal than the market would have made them. Thus, while the efficiency costs are a matter of debate, the redistributive gains are undeniable.

Still, income inequality in the United States remains much larger than in other developed economies. Panel B of Figure 22.6 gives the measure of inequality for ten developed countries. The United States ranks number one: it has the most *unequal* distribution of income among the ten.

THE ROLES OF GOVERNMENT: A REVIEW

Part Two, which set forth the basic competitive model, closed with a chapter that explained how the market system envisioned by that model will produce efficient economic outcomes. Beyond establishing a legal framework within which markets could operate, the only role seen for government in Part Two was possibly to correct the unacceptable distributions of income that have also been the subject of this chapter.

In Parts Three and Four, we have learned of many instances in which markets in the real world can be expected to depart from the basic competitive model. Failures of competition were discussed in Chapters 14 and 15, and government responses to them formed the subject of Chapter 16. Chapter 17 pointed out the absence of any analysis of technological advance in the basic model, and discussed the patent system and government support of research and development as responses to this shortcoming.

The basic model assumes that parties to transactions are armed with all the information they need about the goods being traded. Chapter 18 pointed out why this might not be the case in the product market, and Chapters 19 and 20 discussed problems of imperfect information in the labor and capital markets. Consumers may be ill-informed, for instance, because information is costly to obtain, so that it is seldom optimal to become perfectly informed; moreover, sellers tend to have better information than buyers and may try to take advantage of this. Government has responded with truth-in-advertising laws designed to protect consumers from this information imbalance. Similarly, the regulations surrounding securities trading were promulgated largely out of concern that buyers needed more information than they were given. In certain insurance and loan markets, where systematic information problems create a thin market—or no market at all—government has stepped in to supply the insurance or loans itself.

Chapter 21 discussed another market failure, externalities, which have so adversely affected our environment in recent decades, and the steps government has taken to remedy the situation.

When the market is efficient—or when government interventions successfully correct market failures—no one can be made better off without someone being made worse off. But even under these circumstances, there may be dissatisfaction with the market which leads to government action. For instance, sometimes there is a profound distrust of consumer sovereignty—as in the case of merit goods. But the most important reasons for government action is its role in income distribution and social insurance. Even when markets produce economically efficient outcomes, there is no guarantee that the income shares they produce will be socially acceptable. As we have seen in this chapter, both taxes and expenditures—including the important social insurance programs—are sensitive to concerns about income distribution. Progressive taxes are designed to ensure that upper income individuals pay a larger fraction of their income and taxes, and the social insurance and welfare programs are designed to provide a safety net for poorer households, and especially for poor children and the elderly.

GOVERNMENT RESPONSES TO MARKET FAILURES

Market failures	Government responses
Failure to ensure efficiency	
Market not competitive Product markets (Chapters 14–17) Labor markets (Chapter 19)	Antitrust policies
Public goods and externalities (Chapters 7, 21)	Regulation of pollution; provision of national defense
Basic research as a public good; externalities associated with R & D (Chapter 17)	Public support of basic research; patents
Imperfect information and thin or nonexistent markets (Chapters 18, 20)	Consumer protection legislation (including securities regulations); government loan and insurance programs
Imperfect annuity markets (Chapter 22)	Social Security
Absence of unemployment and disability insurance (Chapter 22)	Unemployment and disability insurance programs
Problems in health insurance market for the aged (Chapter 22)	Medicare
Failure to produce socially desirable outcomes	
Merit goods and bads; distrust of consumer sovereignty (Chapter 21)	Compulsory education; prohibition against drugs
Socially unacceptable income distribution (high levels of poverty) (Chapter 22)	Welfare and other safety net programs; social insurance programs; tax structure reflecting redistributive objectives

Finally, we should note one more category of market failures. Even though resources are scarce, periodically, the economy fails to utilize them fully. The result is unemployment—occasionally massive unemployment. The reason for this market failure, and what governments can do about it, are among the central questions of macroeconomics, and lie beyond our concerns here.

REVIEW AND PRACTICE

SUMMARY

1. Even if markets are efficient, there may be dissatisfaction with the resulting distribution of income.

2. Inequality—both in terms of wages and income—in the United States has been increasing.

3. At the federal level, the largest share of taxes comes from the individual income tax. At the state level, the main source of revenue is the sales tax.

4. A tax system can be judged by five criteria: horizontal and vertical equity, efficiency, administrative simplicity, flexibility, and transparency.

5. All public assistance programs force society to balance the concerns of equity, which involve helping those in need, with the concerns of efficiency, which involve making sure that both poor people and taxpayers have good incentives to work and invest.

6. Social insurance programs, like Social Security and Medicare, are entitlement programs for everyone, regardless of income. But although everyone is entitled to benefits, some redistribution takes place, with some people getting back more than they contribute.

KEY TERMS

individual income tax	payroll tax	regressive tax
corporate income tax	excise tax	transfer programs
property tax	horizontal equity	Lorenz curve
	vertical equity	Gini coefficient
	progressive tax	

REVIEW QUESTIONS

1. Will an efficient market necessarily produce a fairly equal distribution of income? Discuss.

2. What is the main source of federal revenue? of state revenue?

3. What are the five characteristics of a good tax system? How well does the U.S. tax system fare in terms of these criteria? What is the difference between horizontal equity and vertical equity? What is the difference between a progressive and a regressive tax?

4. How can redistribution take place through an entitlement program like Social Security, where all workers contribute and all retirees receive benefits?

5. How do tax and redistribution programs affect incentives? How do social insurance programs affect incentives? Describe some of the trade-offs involved?

6. What is a Lorenz curve? What does it reveal?

PROBLEMS

1. Explain how a tax subsidy for a good with positive externalities (like research and development) can help economic efficiency. Then explain how a tax subsidy for other goods without such externalities could injure efficiency.

2. Assume that a country has a simple tax structure, in which all income over $10,000 was taxed at 20 percent. Evaluate a proposal to increase the progressivity of the tax structure by requiring all those with incomes over $100,000 to pay a tax of 80 percent on income in excess of $100,000. Draw a high-wage earner's budget constraint. How does the surtax affect his budget constraint? What happens to his incentives to work? Is it possible that imposing the tax actually will reduce the tax revenues the government receives from the rich?

3. Imagine that Congress decided to fund an increase in Social Security benefits by increasing the payroll tax on employers. Would this prevent employees from being affected by the higher tax? Draw a diagram to illustrate your answer.

4. Draw Lorenz curves for the following countries. Which country has the greatest and least inequality?

	Percentage of total income received by				
	Lowest fifth	Second fifth	Third fifth	Fourth fifth	Top fifth
United States	4.7	11.0	17.4	25.0	41.9
Japan	8.7	13.2	17.5	23.1	37.5
Germany	6.8	12.7	17.8	24.1	38.7

5. Consider an individual contemplating whether to quit her job and go on welfare. How might the fact that welfare is time limited affect her decision? Is it possible that time-limited welfare may not only lead people to leave welfare, but reduce the number who go on welfare?

23

PUBLIC DECISION MAKING

xcept in a dictatorship, government actions do not reflect the preference of any single individual. Rather, they are the result of public choices. The importance of public choice theory was recognized when James Buchanan of George Mason University was awarded the Nobel Prize for his pioneering work on this topic.

In this chapter we look at how public choices are made. We look at some of the problems, at both the theoretical and practical levels, facing public decision making in a democracy. What are the problems associated with majority voting? What role do interest groups play and why? In recent years, there has been considerable dissatisfaction with government. The analysis of this chapter may provide insights into why government often fails to live up to our expectations. Also, in recent years, there has been a strong movement to give government "back to the people," by giving more responsibility to the state and local governments, and taking responsibility away from the federal government. In this chapter, we see what economic analysis has to say about the appropriate assignment of responsibilities for different functions of government.

1. How does majority voting provide answers to questions about the public allocation of resources? Why may voting fail to give clear answers?

2. What is the role of bureaucrats and interest groups in decision making in a democracy?

3. Why does government frequently fail to achieve its stated objectives? What are the sources of government failure?

4. What should be the relationship between federal and state governments? What activities should be undertaken at each level?

DECISION MAKING IN A DEMOCRACY

In a democracy, the wishes of the majority are supposedly reflected in the actions government takes. But the United States is not a direct democracy, where citizens vote for or against each law. Rather Americans vote for the president and members of Congress, along with state and local elected officials, who, in turn, make our laws. Federal laws have to be introduced and passed by both houses, and signed by the president. The president can veto the legislation, and that veto can be overridden by a two-thirds vote in each house. Political scientists focus on the whole range of issues and actors that define the political process, including coalition formation, interest groups, and the media. Economists have a narrower focus, analyzing how rational individuals express their preferences through the political process of voting, and how, in models of the political process, their votes are reflected in the public choices that mark collective decision making.

COLLECTIVE DECISION MAKING

Chapter 8 provided a simple description of how an individual allocates his income: he chooses the most preferred point along his budget constraint. Communities, states, and the federal government also face budget constraints in allocating public resources. For example, they can buy more bombers and spend less on schools, or provide better Social Security benefits and spend less on medical care for the aged. The big difference between individual and collective decision making is that individuals may have different views about public decisions. The aged may want more spending on Social Security; the family with children may want more on education; and the businessperson may see more profits from increased defense spending. Somehow, from these disparate views, a decision must be formed.

There are many theories describing how public decision making occurs—including those that focus on the role of interest groups—but the simplest theory focuses directly on the voting process. In a democracy, the majority is supposed to rule. What does this imply for resource allocation?

MAJORITY VOTING AND THE MEDIAN VOTER

Consider a simple issue like how much to spend on public schools. Some individuals want more to be spent, some less. Whose preferences dominate? The **median voter theory** provides a remarkably simple prediction of the outcome in the case of majority voting. It is the median voter—half of the population want more to be spent than this voter, and half want less—whose preferences dominate. For instance, assume the median voter wants $5,000 to be spent per pupil and there are 40,001 voters. In any vote between $5,000 per pupil and a lesser amount, say $3,000, $5,000 will win. Likewise, in any vote between $5,000 and a greater amount, $5,000 will win again. The median voter will always join those wanting the amount closest to $5,000, ensuring that $5,000 wins. This is the choice the median voter would have made if the decision had been left to her.

Voters, of course, do not decide most issues directly, but elect politicians who vote on issues. Politicians, however, want to get elected. To increase the likelihood that they get elected, they take positions that will increase the amount of votes they receive. If politicians of both parties take positions to maximize their votes, both will take positions reflecting the views of the median voter.

To understand this point, imagine that the amounts different individuals would like the government to spend are arranged from the smallest to the largest. Suppose there are two parties, and one party takes the position reflecting the individual at the 40th percentile. That is, 40 percent would like the government to spend less, 60 percent would like it to spend more. The other party will win simply by taking a position close to that of the voter representing the 41st percentile. That party would get 59 percent of the vote—a landslide. Of course, the first party knows this and tries to find a position such that the opposition cannot undercut it and win a majority. There are thus strong incentives for both parties to take positions closely reflecting the views of the median voter.

This theory explains why voters often feel that they do not have a choice: the two parties are both trying to find the middle position, so that they will not be defeated. It also gives us a way of forecasting government behavior: government will approximate the interests of the median voter.[1]

---

[1] The principle that both parties will gravitate toward the center (reflecting the views of the median voter) was first analyzed by the economist-statistician Harold Hotelling, who taught at Columbia University and North Carolina State.

THE VOTING PARADOX

Governments are not always consistent in their actions. This may not be surprising, given that government choices do not reflect the preferences of a single individual. More fundamentally, majority voting may not yield a determinate outcome even when only three people choose among only three alternatives, as was noted more than two hundred years ago by the Frenchman Marquis de Condorcet. This is referred to as the **voting paradox.** Consider the simple example of three people who want to go to a movie together. They have narrowed their choices down to three movies, which they rank in this way.

	Jessica's preferences	Ralph's preferences	Brutus's preferences
First choice:	Young and Romantic	Third and Goal to Go	Automatic Avengers
Second choice:	Third and Goal to Go	Automatic Avengers	Young and Romantic
Third choice:	Automatic Avengers	Young and Romantic	Third and Goal to Go

When they compare each of the movies, they find that *Young and Romantic* is preferred over *Third and Goal to Go* by a 2–1 margin and *Third and Goal to Go* is preferred to *Automatic Avengers,* also by a 2–1 margin. Taking this information alone, they might reason that—since *Young and Romantic* is preferred over *Third and Goal to Go* and *Third and Goal to Go* is preferred over *Automatic Avengers*—*Young and Romantic* is also preferred to *Automatic Avengers.* But when they put it to a vote, they find that *Automatic Avengers* is preferred to *Young and Romantic* by a 2–1 margin. There is no majority winner. Majority voting can compare any two of these choices, but is incapable of ranking all three of them.

Nobel laureate Kenneth Arrow proved an even more remarkable result. All voting systems (two-thirds majority, weighted majority, or any other), under some circumstances, yield the same kind of indecision. Inconsistencies are simply inherent in the decision-making process of any democratic government. The only way around this problem, to ensure that consistent choices are made, is to entrust a single individual with all decisions. Such a system yields consistent choices, but is hardly democratic!

Inconsistencies in democratic decision making, such as illustrated by the above example, are fortunately not inevitable. For instance, with majority voting, if there is a single variable being voted upon—say, the level of expenditure on education—and different individuals have a "most preferred" level and vote for outcomes closer to that level, then the median voter will always determine the outcome. But some preferences are more complicated—for instance, some individuals prefer a high level of expenditures on public education, in which case they send their children to public schools. But if expenditures are viewed to be inadequate, they send their children to private schools, and so would vote for a very low level of expenditures over a "moderate" level. When alternatives cannot be simply ranked in terms of "more" or "less" (as in the three-movie example given earlier) the voting paradox will arise and there is no clear theoretical prediction of the outcome of the electoral process.

INTEREST GROUPS AND RENT SEEKING

The median voter theory provides a clear answer to how decisions are made in a democracy, but frequently government action does not even remotely reflect the interests of the median voter. Rather, it more nearly represents interests of particular groups.

One economic explanation for this has to do with the increasing needs of candidates for funds to run successfully for election, and the willingness of special-interest groups to provide those funds as long as their interests are served. In American politics, these groups argue that it is in the general interest for their special interests to be served. Thus, the gas and oil industries argue for huge subsidies through the tax system, stressing the importance of energy for the American economy.

Economists refer to these activities as rent seeking. Rents, as we learned in Chapter 12, are returns enjoyed by a factor of production that go beyond those required to elicit its supply. As we saw in Chapter 16, the term rent seeking is used when individuals or firms devote their energies to the procurement of rents or other special favors from the government. Government, through its power to tax, set tariffs, provide subsidies, and intervene in other ways in private markets, can affect the profitability of various enterprises enormously. For example, the attempt by U.S. car producers in the 1980s to restrict foreign competition is a case of rent seeking. As a result of protection from foreign competition, they can get higher prices for their products and make bigger profits.

In the budget debates of 1995 and 1996, attention was drawn to special interest provisions under the title of "corporate welfare." In a period in which sacrifices were being asked from a wide range of groups—such as welfare, Medicaid, and Medicare recipients—it was argued that it was only fair for corporations to pay their fair share. While much of the cost of tariffs and other restrictions is borne directly by consumers in the form of higher prices, the Treasury loses billions of dollars each year from preferential tax provisions and other subsidies, often hidden (such as the sale of timber at below market price). The Clinton administration, as part of its plan to reduce the deficit, proposed eliminating more than $40 billion of such subsidies over a seven-year period.

As long as the government has the discretion to grant rents and other special favors, firms and individuals will find it pays to engage in rent-seeking behavior—that is, to persuade government to grant them tariffs or other benefits—and the decisions of government accordingly get distorted. It makes little difference whether this behavior comes in the form of direct bribes, as is frequently the case in less developed countries, or campaign contributions that serve to influence how congressional representatives vote. Either way,

POLICY PERSPECTIVE: MOTOR VOTERS

The most important determinant of political outcomes often comes down to the simple question of who turns out to vote. In some sense, it is not *rational* for an individual to vote. It is costly to become informed. It is costly, in terms of time, to vote. And the likelihood that any individual will have an effect on the outcome is negligible. Ensuring that government is well run is a public good—all benefit when governments function well—and like any public good, there is a tendency for undersupply.

The fact that individuals have so little incentive to vote—and that who votes makes a big difference to outcomes—has not gone unnoticed by politicians. Although all parties pay lip service to the principle that everyone should be encouraged to vote, the party that expects to gain from partic-

ipation of the nonvoter is more likely to go after those votes. Thus, soon after he took office in 1993, President Clinton proposed a law that would make it easier for individuals to register to vote. The bill, called the Motor Voter bill—because it would enable people to register at the same time they got their driver's license—was opposed by some Republicans. The reason given was that more noncitizens, not eligible to vote, might slip through onto the electoral rolls. The Republican governor of California, Pete Wilson, also claimed the law was a case of an unfunded mandate: a requirement placed on states without funds to carry it out. But Democratic skeptics suspected that the real concern was its effect on the electoral process.

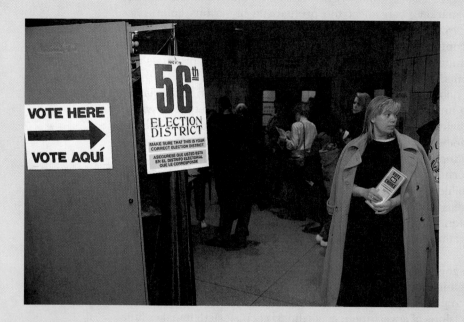

the consequences are likely to be similar: governments respond to the rent-seeking behavior of special-interest groups.

BUREAUCRACIES

The final aspect of government behavior that we will take up is the theory of bureaucracy, which involves a principal-agent problem. The government consists not only of elected officials, but also of those appointed by elected officials and the civil service, whose job it is to administer government programs. Just as in the private sector managers' interests may not perfectly coincide with those of shareholders, in the government sector public managers may not do what the electorate, or their elected representatives would ideally like—or what is, in some broader sense, in the public interest.

Even if they are partly concerned with doing a good job, bureaucrats are also concerned with their own careers. For instance, concern about making mistakes may lead them to act in a risk-averse manner. Because it is so difficult to assess the "output" of administrators, performance may be judged more on the extent to which an individual has conformed to certain "bureaucratic" procedures, which partially accounts for the proliferation of red tape. Bureaucrats may have an interest in expanding their spheres of influence, just as any businessperson has an interest in the growth of her business. But while a businessperson expands her business by providing a good at a cheaper price, bureaucrats expand their influence by persuading the legislature either that they need more funds or personnel to do what has to be done, or that there should be more of whatever it is they do. This leads to a form of competition among bureaucrats that may have deleterious effects.

AGRICULTURE: A CASE STUDY IN MIXED MOTIVES

Government agricultural programs provide an opportunity for studying the mixed motives of government as well as the public and market failures that so frequently characterize government activities. The United States has a major program of subsidies for agriculture—amounting, at their peak in 1986, to more than $25 billion per year. The total cost to the American consumer, however, is far higher, because a major objective of the program is to raise the prices farmers receive—and therefore the prices consumers pay.

Government gives two justifications for its agriculture programs. One is the enormous variability of prices and output in agriculture, risks against which a farmer cannot obtain adequate insurance. Thus, the programs are sometimes rationalized on the basis of "stabilizing" prices. But prices are not just stabilized around an average market price, as they would be if the objective were truly risk reduction. Rather, prices are stabilized around a higher level, necessitating huge government purchases of some goods in order to sustain the prices and restrictions on production. Moreover, the risk that farmers really

CLOSE-UP: ECONOMICS, LIABILITY, AND LEGAL REFORM

When the Republican members and prospective members of Congress signed their "Contract with America," prior to the November 1994 election, among their pledges was reform in the U.S. liability laws that compensate someone for damages as a result of another's actions.

Through the nineteenth century, one could only be held liable in a court case for behavior that deviated greatly from the norm—for example, if you kept explosives in your back garden and they blew up the neighbor's house. By definition, actions that are very different from normal do not happen all that often, so liability law was quite restricted. By the early twentieth century, this sort of liability law was felt to be inadequate. After all, many people are injured in the normal course of events—in the workplace, while driving, while using various products, and so on. If liability only applied to the ab-

normal, most people injured through no fault of their own would receive no compensation.

In the 1930s and 1940s economists pointed out that if employers, drivers, or manufacturers could impose negative externalities on others without having to pay a price, they would have insufficient incentives to avoid negligence. Moreover, the liability system could be viewed as a sort of insurance system. To "insure" against liabilities for injuries caused by products, for example, manufacturers would charge a little more to everyone (like an insurance premium) and use the money to pay off the lawsuits of those who were injured.

By the 1960s, the legal rule had evolved into "strict" liability, under which all parties were held responsible for *all* harm they did, whether they had behaved abnormally or not. This was viewed as a useful way to encourage safer behavior and assure that victims of accidents received compensation. But strict liability ran into problems. While it reduced the occurrence of negative externalities, it led to an explosion of lawsuits, some of them frivolous, with a corresponding increase in liability insurance premiums. Moreover, since manufacturers were held liable for any harm resulting from a product, no matter how carefully they had tested it beforehand, they became more hesitant to innovate.

These were among the motivations for inclusion of liability reform in the list of ten major initiatives in the Contract with America. Courts have even allowed "punitive damages"—damages in excess of the losses incurred—as a way of providing further incentives for firms to ensure that the products they produce are safe. But critics worry that juries have gone too far. The Contract with America attempts to restore balance, by restricting punitive damages. Whether the proposal will restore a balance, or tilt the balance the other way, is the central question at issue.

care about is the risk to their income. Price stabilization programs do not eliminate *income* risk. Income depends on the price of outputs, the level of output, and costs. Price stabilization programs only affect one of the three variables. If risk reduction were really the objective, it would be possible to design a better program to meet that objective. Indeed, today there are markets where farmers can effectively ensure that they get a certain price when they harvest their crop, making the role of government even more questionable.

The second justification given is to help the rural poor (small farms). This justification has little merit because, by their very nature, programs that provide support by raising the prices result in large farmers receiving more than small farmers. This is because the more farmers sell, the greater their subsidy. In assessing whether poverty alleviation is really the objective, one needs to ask two questions. Is there any reason why the United States should be more concerned about the poor in the rural sector than poor elsewhere in the economy? And even if a reason could be found for a program directed at poor farmers, couldn't a program be designed that got at this problem more directly, rather than also providing large subsidies to large farmers? In fact, average farm income today is higher than average nonfarm income, and, while in recent years, total farm payments have declined, the average *payment* per farm household now exceeds $30,000, close to the U.S. average family *income*.

Worse still, the farm programs have in many instances contributed to environmental degradation. Because of peculiar provisions in the farm law, farmers' benefits are often reduced when they engage in crop rotation, even though crop rotation increases soil fertility. The high payment rates also often encourage excessive use of fertilizer and pesticides. The new farm legislation passed in 1996 went some way in reducing these distortions.

The explanation for the farm programs is simple: special-interest groups try to increase the income of their members, at the expense of taxpayers and consumers at large. Consider the rice and tobacco programs. Many of the rice farms are in California, on irrigated land. Even with large government subsidies, rice farming is profitable largely because the price of water is heavily subsidized. Why, in a state that is facing major water shortages, is the government subsidizing rice production? And why did the government spend large amounts of money on the message that smoking is bad for your health at the same time it spent money subsidizing tobacco farmers?

More generally, how can we explain the seeming disproportionate influence of certain small interest groups, like farmers, who constitute less than 2 percent of Americans and have succeeded in getting huge subsidies from the federal government? The answer suggested by Nobel laureate Gary Becker is that the free-rider problem is smaller the smaller the group. "Bribing" representatives to support one's special interest is a public good. All wheat farmers benefit from a wheat subsidy. All steel or car producers benefit from trade barriers that keep out less expensive foreign steel or cars. But these are small groups, making it easier to persuade all to contribute to the cost of lobbying. Each of these programs also has losers. And the losers are not only far more numerous, but together, they lose more than the special-interest groups gain. But each of the losers loses a little, while each of the gainers gains a lot. Opposing the special-interest groups is also a public good, and each opponent has an incentive to be a free rider. As a result, it is harder for groups representing broad groups, such as consumers, to be organized than it is for special-interest groups representing industries or other concentrated beneficiaries.

PUBLIC FAILURES

That markets are, by and large, the most efficient way of providing goods and services is well accepted today, as is the idea that there are particular circumstances—such as the externalities associated with environmental pollution—in which markets fail. The role of government in correcting such market failures is more hotly debated, with many Americans believing that—no matter how bad the market failure—government is likely to make matters worse, not better.

The evidence is more mixed than much of the antigovernment rhetoric suggests. Government has long played an important role in the economy, and the list of commonly accepted successes is correspondingly long. The amazing increase in agricultural productivity over the past seventy-five years is generally attributed to the government's support of research, and its dissemination of knowledge of new technologies to farmers. Major scientific breakthroughs, from atomic energy to the discovery of the AIDS virus, occurred in government laboratories. Key advances in computer technology and jet engines were the result of government support. The development of the important telecommunications sector has been based on government support—from Samuel Morse's first telegraph line between Baltimore and Washington in 1842 to the development of the Internet in the 1970s and 1980s. America was brought together as a nation in part through the intercontinental railroads, made possible through huge land grants. We are better able to breathe the air in our cities and to drink and swim in the water from our lakes and rivers, largely because of actions undertaken by government.

Even the evidence on the comparative inefficiency of government is mixed. The government-run Canadian National Railroad appears to be as efficient as the privately run Canadian Pacific Railroad. And even the much maligned post office has managed to score productivity improvements in the past fifteen years that exceed the average for the U.S. economy.

Still, failures of government are impressive, from public housing projects that rival the worst provided by any slumlord, to cost overruns on defense projects. And some of the government successes have had questionable side effects: the interstate highway system, while greatly reducing transportation time, contributed to the urban sprawl that plagues many of our cities. Many of the worst problems have been the result of complex interactions between the private and public sectors. The failure of savings and loan associations, costing U.S. taxpayers upwards of $200 billion, was the result of excessively speculative investments made by *private* S & Ls. But government-provided deposit insurance allowed depositors to give their money to S & Ls without worrying how the money would be used. Thus, S & Ls undertook increasingly speculative investments without considering their depositors. And government regulators failed to take strong actions in the face of worsening balance sheets, increasing the final costs of the debacle to the taxpayers.

What should be the role of government? And how can it perform better? To answer these questions, we have to understand the *systemic* reasons for government failure. Three major factors underlie systemic government failure: incentive problems, budgeting problems, and unintended consequences of government action.

INCENTIVES AND CONSTRAINTS

Unlike private organizations, government has the power of coercion. It can force people to pay taxes. It can prohibit people from paying less than the minimum wage if they engage in interstate commerce. And so on. But since this power carries with it enormous potential for abuse, certain procedures have been developed to protect the public against arbitrary use of government power. These procedures are called **due process.**

A good example to illustrate the potential incentive problems of due process procedures is the set of rules governing civil service employment. These rules are designed to ensure that there is no discrimination or other arbitrary treatment of government workers. But the rules are often inflexible and make it difficult to pay comparable salaries to public officials who do their jobs as well as similarly qualified and dedicated persons in the private sector—or to offer them the same opportunities for rapid promotion. It is even more difficult for government to demote or fire incompetent and lazy workers. Thus, the public sector's ability to recruit and manage staff for maximum efficiency is typically limited.

In addition to the constraints of due process, the government has trouble making long-term commitments that are perceived to be binding. The

Republicans who signed the 1994 Contract with America—with its guarantees about taxes, the deficit, and the like—may or may not live up to their contract. But if they do not, the American voters will have no *legal* recourse. Any Congress can reverse decisions made by previous Congresses, though it may try to design both legislation and legislative rules in ways that make it more difficult to do so. Such limitations on the government's ability to make binding commitments can have major economic consequences. Take, for example, a government promise that it will pursue a policy of interest rate stability. The current government may convince investors of its commitment to keeping interest rates low. But it has no control at all over what happens in the next election. Investors know that and make their own assessments of interest rate risk, which may interfere with the effectiveness of what the government is trying to do today. The government today can make it more costly for future governments to increase the rate of inflation; for instance, it can issue short-term bonds, so that the interest cost to the government would rise quickly if inflation started to pick up.

Another factor that can undermine government efficiency, and lead to perverse decisions against the broad interests of society, is the political pressures inherent in the democratic process. A prime example here is legislators' concerns about the next election. These can lead to so-called "pork barrel" projects that create jobs in a pivotal legislator's home district but make no economic sense from a national perspective. In addition to the incentives to invest in projects that will aid the reelection chances of politicians, the enormous cost of running for office provides incentives for elected officials to pay particular attention to the views and needs of those who contribute to their campaign funds. Through this route, lobbyists, for example, can wield influence way out of proportion to the importance of the interests they represent.

BUDGETING AND SPENDING PROCEDURES

The budgeting and spending constraints facing government decision makers differ from those of the private sector in three major ways. The first is the severity of the budget constraint facing public decision makers. Unlike a private firm, which faces the prospect of bankruptcy if enough of its ventures yield losses, a public enterprise can more easily turn to the government for budgetary help. This is the problem of **soft budget constraints.** Amtrak, for example, continues to make losses in its overall railroad operations, in spite of government promises to the contrary. A major reason for the continuing loss is a set of labor rules *imposed by the government*—which require that workers be compensated if they are laid off or forced to relocate even a short distance. Soft budget constraints such as these weaken the incentives for public management to be efficient. There is nothing quite like the threat of bankruptcy to focus managerial attention.

The second budgetary difference between the private and public sectors—a factor that works in the opposite way from the soft budget constraints—is the annual appropriations process. This can force short-term spending constraints on the public sector that are not cost-effective in the long run. Limited investment flexibility is a particularly unfortunate fallout from the annual appropriations system. One of the major reasons the Clinton administration proposed corporatizing the air traffic control system, for example, was to remove this rigidity. Although the air traffic control system had done a truly impressive job in preventing accidents, many saw a disaster waiting to happen. The computers used by the system were so outmoded that many still used vacuum tubes—indeed they were probably the largest purchaser of these outmoded products, which are no longer manufactured in the United States, and must be imported from Poland. The government simply did not have the estimated $30 billion on hand in a given year to update the system.

The third budgetary constraint on government is the antiefficiency effects of some of the procedures implemented to ensure strict cost control. No one likes to see public money wasted, least of all taxpayers or the congressional representatives who risk the taxpayers' wrath. Government has instituted detailed accounting, competitive bidding, and other procurement procedures to avoid waste and corruption. Yet these procedures can cost more than they save and not only because of the extra bureaucracy involved. Competitive bidding is an example highlighted by Vice President Gore's National Performance Review. When purchasing T-shirts, for example, the government in its efforts to ensure that the specifications were accurate and precise—so that bidders were competing to supply *exactly* the same product—created 30 pages of fine print documentation which prospective bidders have to follow carefully. These types of bureaucratic red tape reduce the supply of bidders willing to sell to the government and increase the cost to the government of goods and services. Gore's project recommended, among many other things, that the government purchase such ordinary items "off the shelf." Procurement reforms such as this were enacted into law in the 1994 Federal Acquisitions Streamlining Act, and are expected to save billions of dollars a year.

UNINTENDED CONSEQUENCES

Information problems plague government just as they plague the private sector. But one aspect of uncertainty is much more problematic for government—the problem of unforeseen consequences, particularly the unanticipated effects of government actions on incentives, both public and private. For example, subsidizing medical care for the elderly through Medicare greatly increased the elderly's demand for medical services, leading to increases in costs far beyond those originally projected. (Since the Medicare program was passed in the 1960s, the ability to project behavioral consequences and their cost implications has vastly improved. But the problem of unanticipated consequences has by no means been solved.)

Two frequently cited examples are the interstate highway program and the urban renewal programs. The interstate highway program was designed to provide a suitable highway system for the rapid expansion of automobiles after World War II. But the expansion of the highways made it easier for people

POLICY PERSPECTIVE: REINVENTING GOVERNMENT

Recognizing a problem is only the first step in addressing it. There has been wide recognition that government often fails to deliver on its promise, and the government is often inefficient. But addressing the problem is a greater challenge—one which Vice President Gore set out to meet in his National Performance Review (NPR) in 1993, often referred to as his initiative to "reinvent government."

The basic thrust of his recommendations was that government should organize itself more like successful firms. Government should think of those they serve as their "customers" or "clientele." They should be customer oriented, taking into account the costs they impose on those with whom they deal (such as waiting time) and the kinds of services that their customers want. As a result of the emphasis on customer orientation, one survey noted that the Social Security Administration's telephone service rivaled that of the best private companies.

The NPR also emphasized that, where possible, performance criteria should be developed, and agencies and managers should be evaluated in terms of how well they do on these performance criteria.

The NPR also recommended that, where possible, government activities should be corporatized or privatized. In corporatization, a government agency functions like a corporation, though ownership remains with the government. Government corporations include the TVA (the Tennessee Valley Authority), the postal service, and the Uranium Enrichment Corporation (the USEC, which produces nuclear fuel for electric power plants). NPR recommended that the air traffic control system be corporatized. Privatization entails going one step further—turning over ownership to the private sector. The most recent privatization has been the sale of the U.S. government's helium production. Some have recommended that USEC be privatized, though others have worried that doing so might have adverse security consequences; and others have recommended that the air traffic control system be privatized, though this proposal also has its strong critics.

to commute from the suburbs and thereby facilitated the widespread movement of people from cities to suburbs. This suburban flight—with the associated decay of the inner city—was thus an unintended consequence of a program designed to improve our highway system.

Urban renewal programs were designed to stop urban decay, by tearing down old buildings and putting in their place new housing and facilities for new businesses. But the housing that was destroyed was low-income housing, and the housing with which it was replaced was largely housing for middle and upper-income households. Thus, the urban renewal programs unintentionally contributed to the plight of the poor—the shortage of housing which they could afford—and, over time, to homelessness.

SOURCES OF PUBLIC FAILURES

Incentives and constraints
> Due process
> Constrained ability to make long-term commitments
> Political pressures
>> Pork barrel projects
>> Power of lobbyists who make campaign contributions

Budgeting and spending constraints
> Soft budget constraints
> Annual appropriations process
> Rigid procurement rules

Unintended consequences
> Unforeseen changes in behavior resulting from government action

DECENTRALIZATION AND THE FEDERAL ROLE

Ever since the United States was first formed, debate has raged not only about government's role generally, but also about the role of the federal government in contrast to the role of states and localities. The U.S. Constitution provided that those activities not explicitly delegated to the federal government were reserved to the states and the people. This provision has been interpreted in different ways over the years, changing the role of government as economic circumstances have changed. The "interstate commerce clause," which gives the federal government the right to regulate interstate commerce, has been used very flexibly to cover a host of activities.

The fundamental debate is over the virtues of centralization versus decentralization in government decision making and action. **Decentralization** in this context refers to provision of government goods and services at the state or local levels. Since markets are a decentralized way of producing private goods and services, market failure analysis provides insight into why decentralization will *not* work.

First, when there are externalities, leaving matters to the states or localities will *not* result in efficient outcomes. Pollution in Chicago leads to acid rain in New York. Children who receive an inadequate education in one state may become a welfare burden in another state when they grow up and move. This is a negative externality. There are also positive externalities. Again, education is an example. Some states, such as Wisconsin, provide strong support to their state university systems. These systems yield benefits that extend far beyond the state residents whose taxes make them possible.

Second, although some public goods benefit only residents of a particular area—called **local public goods** (such as local libraries and local roads)—others benefit the whole nation. Protection against foreign aggression, for example, is a national public good. Efficiency requires that national public goods be provided at the federal level.

Third, just as we cannot count on markets to yield a socially acceptable distribution of income, we cannot rely on particular states and localities to ensure an acceptable distribution of income. By lowering benefits to the poor, for example, each state or locality can reduce its poor population as they move elsewhere to survive. This has been called "a race to the bottom."

The instances just listed—of circumstances when decentralization does not yield the outcomes society wants—are matched by circumstances in which decentralization has marked advantages. The first important point here is that federal responses may be clumsy solutions to problems that require adaptation to different community preferences and different state or local needs. States and localities have good incentives to be aware of and respond to needs that are specific to their communities' political, social, and economic conditions. The second major point is that decentralization allows different states to try out different solutions to common problems. In this sense, the states are like a set of laboratories, with the successful experiments providing examples for imitation elsewhere. To take one example, the Medicaid program is partly funded and regulated by the states. This has allowed individual states to experiment with cost controls. Minnesota, for example, is one of the states pushing Health Maintenance Organizations (HMOs) as part of Medicaid. These HMOs reduce the incentive to overtreat by charging a fixed fee per enrollee, regardless of medical condition or services received. Oregon has reduced the range of services provided in exchange for expanding the number of individuals covered.

Many public programs entail shared responsibilities among different levels of government. A typical form of sharing is for the federal government to pick up much of the tab and set broad guidelines, but for the states/localities to implement the programs within these guidelines. This type of sharing does not always work well. If the federal government pays most of the bill, the incentives for state and local bureaucrats to spend the money cost-effectively are correspondingly weakened. The federal government currently picks up as much as 90 percent of highway maintenance costs. This gives the states a strong incentive to use their allotment fully, even when they know the money is not being used cost-effectively (the states would not spend the money in this manner if they had the alternative of using it elsewhere).

Twice in recent times, debate over the federal role has taken center stage. Early in his presidency, Ronald Reagan proposed a New Federalism—a redefinition that proposed transferring responsibility for a number of then-federal social programs to the states. Overshadowing the debate over principles at that time were the potential fiscal consequences for states. The governors did not mind taking over the responsibilities for running programs but they were very concerned that the federal government was also transferring to the states the responsibility for paying a greater share of the costs.

The election of November 1994, which ended with Republican majorities in both the House and Senate, brought principles of decentralization to the forefront of policy debate: (1) states should be given more flexibility to use funds as they want; (2) many of what are now separate programs should be consolidated into grants to the states; and (3) performance measures should be used to measure program performance, both to provide efficiency incentives for states and localities and to evaluate their success in meeting federal objectives. There are large elements of a consensus on these principles, but many disputed issues remain. For instance, Congress passed, and the president signed, a measure limiting legislation which imposes costs on states and localities without providing funds (the so-called unfunded mandates). Information about the magnitude of the costs must be made available before the legislation may be passed. Critics said this did not go far enough; others argued that in some cases, unfunded mandates were just like federal requirements on private producers not to pollute—that the federal government should have the right to impose restrictions against one state dumping garbage in the water of a neighboring state.

Perhaps the most contentious issues in the 1995 to 1996 debate concerned Medicaid: should there be a *national* entitlement, for instance, for children to receive a minimal level of health care, or should the federal government simply provide funds for states to spend on health care however they wished? Providing funds without restrictions is called **bloc granting.** Clearly, there is a wide range between the extremes—no restrictions or no state discretion. Much of the real debate concerns where in that range to place various programs in which there is a shared federal and state responsibility.

DECENTRALIZATION

Limitations
  Externalities
  National public goods
  Income redistribution
    Race to the bottom
Advantages
  Local public goods
  Adaptation to local preferences and needs
  Experimentation
    Different solutions to common problems

The debate over the appropriate federal–state division of responsibilities—in particular the activities for which lower levels of government should take fiscal responsibility—has been going on since the colonies split from the British crown. It is unlikely to stop any time soon.

REVIEW AND PRACTICE

SUMMARY

1. Different voters have different views about what the government should do. In some cases majority voting may not yield a determinate outcome. In other cases the choices made in majority voting reflect the preferences of the median voter.

2. Government actions sometimes reflect the interests of particular groups, who seek special favors. The activities they engage in to get these special favors are called rent-seeking activities.

3. Sources of systemic public failure include weak or distorted incentives, budgeting and spending rigidities, and inability to foresee fully the consequences of government programs, particularly changes in behavior.

4. Centralized (federal) provision of public goods and services is preferred in the case of externalities extending beyond a state's jurisdiction and national public goods or when income distribution issues are involved. Decentralized (state and local) provision is preferred for local public goods, may be more responsive to community preferences and needs, and facilitates experimentation in different ways to solve common problems.

KEY TERMS

voting paradox	public choice theory	due process
median voter theory	public failure	soft budget
rent seeking		constraints

REVIEW QUESTIONS

1. What is the voting paradox?

2. What is the median voter? Why does the median voter matter so much in a system of majority rule?

3. What role do special-interest groups and bureaucrats play in determining what government does?

4. In what ways do government enterprises face different constraints from those facing firms in the private sector? What effects do the differences have on incentives?

5. Describe the advantages and disadvantages of providing public goods and services at the local or state level versus the national level?

PROBLEMS

1. The president is trying to decide which of three goals he should put at the top of his agenda—deficit reduction (d), a middle-class tax cut (m), and preserving the safety net for the poor (p). He puts the matter before his advisers in three separate meetings. Assume he has three advisers, and he takes a vote in each meeting. His political adviser's ranking is {m–d–p}, his economic adviser's ranking is {d–p–m}, and his health care adviser's ranking is {p–m–d}. What is the outcome?

2. Suppose you are considering building a food stand along a mile-long strip of beach, but you know that one other vendor is planning to build a stand too. If visitors are evenly distributed along the beach, and people will buy from whichever food stand is closest to them, where should you decide to build your stand? If the goal is to have the shortest possible average distance for people to get to food, where should the two stands be located? (Hint: Think about the situation of two political parties competing for the median voter.)

3. While the median voter theory predicts that the two political parties will converge toward the center, in practice the two parties often seem far apart. Use median voter theory to predict the outcome of a two-stage election. In the first stage, voters within each party choose their candidate. If, in the first stage, voters do not vote strategically—that is they vote for their preferred candidate, not for the candidate that they think will win—describe the outcome of the political process. How might the fact that voters at the extremes of the political spectrum are more likely to vote affect the outcome?

4. In some programs, the federal government pays half of all expenditures but leaves it to the states to decide how much will be spent. How might this cost-sharing arrangement affect the level of expenditure? How might the wealth of a state affect the extent to which it takes advantage of such programs?

5. Evaluate the advantages and disadvantages of transferring responsibility to states and localities for the following programs: (a) interstate highways; (b) local streets; (c) welfare programs; (d) cash assistance to the poor; (e) assistance to the poor for medical expenses; (f) job training programs.

6. In 1996, the welfare system was reformed. Each state was given a bloc grant (a fixed sum of money), where previously it had been given a match-

ing grant, with the fraction paid by the federal government somewhat higher for poor states than for rich states. Focusing on incentives and marginal costs, explain why a state that received exactly as much as before might *choose* to spend less on welfare. Some critics worried that matters would be worse: there would be a race to the bottom, with each state lowering welfare payments to encourage welfare recipients to move to a neighboring state. Explain why this is consistent with median voter theory.

7. In virtually every election, there are complaints about the undue influence of special interest groups, resulting from their large campaign contributions. Prohibiting an individual from spending money on his own behalf is viewed as interfering with First Amendment rights of free speech; prohibiting campaign contributions is viewed as putting those who are not rich at an unfair disadvantage in the political arena, relative to those who can pay for their campaigns. Discuss the consequences and desirability of (a) public financing of campaigns; or (b) prohibiting campaign contributors from lobbying the person to whom they have contributed for a period of, say, one year after the contribution.

8. Special interest groups often are thought of as representing particular industries, like steel or automobiles. More recently, however, attention has turned to the American Association of Retired Individuals (AARP), which tries to represent the interests of the retired. There has been increasing concern among economists about the long-term fiscal situation of the United States. As the baby boomers reach retirement age, enormous demands will be placed on Social Security, Medicare, and Medicaid. Why might median voter theory give a different prediction about how the political system responds to this problem than do theories focusing on special interests?

PART FIVE

Full-Employment Macro-economics

P eace and prosperity" is the slogan on which many political candidates have run for office, and the failure to maintain prosperity has led to many a government's defeat. There is widespread belief among the citizenry that government is responsible for maintaining the economy at full employment, with stable prices, and for creating an economic environment in which growth can occur. This belief is reflected in the Full Employment Act of 1946, which stated that "it is the continuing policy and responsibility of the Federal Government to use all practicable means . . . to promote maximum employment, production, and purchasing power."

Although most economists still agree with these sentiments, there are dissenting views. Some claim that the government has relatively little power to control most of the fluctuations in output and employment; some argue that, apart from isolated instances such as the Great Depression of the 1930s, neither inflation nor unemployment is a major *economic* problem (though they obviously remain political problems); and some believe that government has been as much a cause of the problems of unemployment, inflation, and slow growth as part of their solution. We will explore these various interpretations in greater depth in the chapters that follow.

The problems of unemployment, inflation, and growth relate to the performance of the entire economy. Earlier in the book, we learned how the law of supply and demand operates in the market for oranges, apples, or other goods. At any one time, one industry may be doing well, another poorly. Yet to understand the forces that determine how well the economy as a whole is doing, we want to see beyond the vagaries that affect any particular industry. This is the domain of macroeconomics. Macroeconomics focuses not on the output of single products like orange juice or peanut butter, nor on the demand for masons or bricklayers or computer programmers. Rather, it is concerned with the characteristics of an entire economy, such as the overall level of output, the total level of employment, and the stability of the overall level of prices. What accounts for the "diseases" that sometimes affect the economy—the episodes of massive unemployment, rising prices, or economic stagnation—and what can the government do, both to prevent the onset of these diseases and to cure them once they have occurred?

Macroeconomic *theory* is concerned with what determines the level of employment and output as well as the rate of inflation and the overall growth rate of the economy; while macroeconomic *policy* focuses on what government can do to stimulate employment, prevent inflation, and increase the economy's growth rate.

We begin our study of macroeconomics in Chapter 24 by learning the major statistics used to assess the state of the economy—the rates of unemployment, inflation, and growth. Chapter 25 then builds on the microeconomic analysis of Part Two to construct an *aggregate* model of the economy. Paralleling our earlier discussions, we focus on labor, product, and capital markets. We see how the demand and supply for labor determines the real wage, and how the real wage changes in response to shifts in either of these curves. We then see how the price level and the interest rate are determined in the product and capital markets. In this basic aggregate model, we assume there is full employment. The rate of growth is determined, in part, by the level of investment that emerges from the market equilibrium. And changes in the price level (and the rate of inflation) are determined by changes in the money supply.

International trade plays an increasingly important role in the U.S. economy. Exports have been expanding far faster than the economy as a whole has been growing. And the United States has been borrowing annually billions of dollars from abroad. Thus, international economic relations affect both the product and capital markets, as Chapter 25 also discusses.

One of the most frequently discussed issues of the U.S. economy in the last few years has been the soaring trade deficit and the soaring fiscal deficit—the huge excess of federal expenditures over taxes, reaching almost 5 percent of the economy's output in 1992. Chapter 26 uses the full-employment model of Chapter 25 to address these and several important questions. It shows, for instance, that to a large extent, the trade deficit is a *consequence* of the fiscal deficit, and that another consequence of the fiscal deficit is lower economic growth.

CHAPTER 24

MACROECONOMIC GOALS AND MEASURES

J ust as doctors take a patient's temperature to help them determine just how sick the patient is, economists use statistics to get a quantitative measure of the economy's performance. This chapter introduces the major statistics that summarize the overall condition of the economy. In studying these measures, economists look for patterns. Are good years regularly followed by lean years? Does inflation usually accompany high employment levels? If they find patterns, they ask why.

This chapter also discusses problems of measurement that affect almost every economic variable. When the rate of unemployment or inflation changes by a few tenths of a percent it often means little, just as there is rarely cause for alarm when a person's temperature changes by a tenth of a degree. But over time, the statistics describing the economy may change more dramatically. When unemployment statistics show an increase from 5 percent to 10 percent (that is, a change from one out of twenty workers without jobs to one out of ten), few would doubt that there has been a sizable increase in unemployment.

The sections below discuss unemployment, inflation, and growth, and explain how each is measured.

1. What are the main objectives of macroeconomic policy?

2. How are unemployment, output, growth, and inflation measured?

3. What are some of the central problems in measuring these variables?

THE THREE MACROECONOMIC ILLS

Chapter 1 characterized the economy in terms of a set of interconnected labor, product, and capital markets. The diagram often referred to as the circular flow diagram in Figure 1.5 shows firms obtaining labor and capital from households and using it to produce goods, which are then sold to households, who buy the goods with the income they earn providing labor and capital to firms. Given these interconnections, it is not surprising that problems in one part of the economy may be manifested in other parts. The symptoms in one part may indicate disease elsewhere in the system.

Later chapters will enable us to understand the entire system. Here we focus on the symptoms, each of which is most closely associated with a particular part of the system.

In the 1992 presidential election campaign, two slogans struck a responsive chord: "It's the economy, stupid!" and "Jobs, Jobs, Jobs." America was entering the third year of an economic slowdown. Even though by historical standards, the **unemployment rate** was not very high—one out of thirteen workers was without a job—many faced the threat of unemployment, and anxiety levels were high. And even this level of unemployment represented a significant departure from the basic competitive model, which assumes that all resources—including labor—are fully employed, with demand equaling supply.

Two years later, policymakers began to worry about another problem: **inflation,** or rising prices. These price increases were, again by historical standards, moderate, about 2 to 4 percent a year. But policymakers feared the rate of inflation would grow. Only fifteen years earlier, inflation had hit double digit levels (13.3 percent in 1979). Still, the U.S. experience has been tame compared to that in other countries. In Ukraine, the inflation rate recently hit 10,000 percent a year! Inflation—the continual increase in prices month to month—means the demand and supply of goods in the product market are not in equilibrium at a stable price level.

Although we may focus on unemployment or inflation at any given moment, the real long-run concern is living standards. In the early 1970s, average Americans expected not only their children to enjoy better living standards, but also expected their own incomes to rise continually over time—a pattern that had held true for more than a century. But things started unraveling around 1973. Average family incomes stagnated, and those at the lower part of the income distribution fell, sometimes dramatically. The problem was inadequate **economic growth.** It was partly due to insufficient amounts of money going from the capital market to fund new investments and new innovations.

These three ills, unemployment, inflation, and lack of growth, are the diseases that macroeconomists are constantly trying to fight, with varying degrees of success.

THREE GOALS OF MACROECONOMIC POLICY

Full employment
Low inflation
Rapid growth

GROWTH

For generations, Americans had simply taken for granted that each generation would be better off than the previous one, and for decades Americans had presumed that their firms would be the most competitive and productive in the world. The continued increases in productivity (output per hour) provided the basis for continued increases in standards of living. Beginning around 1973, doubts arose concerning these expectations. The rate of increase in productivity slowed down: from around 3 percent per year from 1950 to 1973, to about 1 percent per year from 1973 to 1995. These changes were reflected in slow growth of standards of living for ordinary Americans.

In comparing countries, as well as comparing output within the same country over time, we have to adjust for differences in population. **Output per capita** simply divides total output by the population. As Figure 24.1 shows, Japan and several other countries of East Asia in the past two decades experienced far more rapid growth in output per capita than the United States. For years, Americans could take comfort in the idea that they were simply catching up. But by the 1980s, in some industries productivity in Japan exceeded that in the United States.

Figure 24.1 INTERNATIONAL COMPARISONS OF RATES OF GROWTH IN OUTPUT PER CAPITA

Other countries have been growing more rapidly in recent decades than the United States.

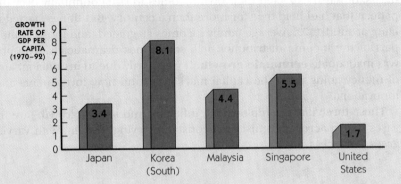

MEASURING OUTPUT

The output of the economy consists of millions of different goods. We could report how much of each good the economy produced: 1,362,478 hammers, 473,562,382 potatoes, 7,875,342 wristwatches, and so forth. Such data may be useful for some purposes, but they do not provide us with the information we want. If next year the output of hammers goes up by 5 percent, the output of potatoes goes down by 2 percent, and the output of wristwatches rises by 7 percent, has total output gone up or down? And by how much?

We need a single number that summarizes the output of the economy. But how do we add up the hammers, potatoes, wristwatches, and billions of other products produced in the economy? We do this by adding the money value of all the final goods (goods that are not used to make other goods) produced and arriving at a single number that encapsulates the production of the economy. This number is called the **gross domestic product,** or **GDP.** It is the standard measure of the output of an economy, and sums up the total money value of the goods and services produced by the residents of a nation during a specified period. GDP includes everything from buttons to air travel, and from haircuts to barrels of oil. It makes no difference whether the production takes place in the public or private sector, or whether the goods and services are purchased by households or by government.[1]

There is one problem with using money as a measure of output. The value of a dollar changes over time. Candy bars, books, movie tickets, hammers, all cost more today than they did ten years ago. Another way of saying this is that a dollar does not buy as much as it did ten years ago. We do not want to be misled into believing that the output is higher when in fact only prices have risen.

[1]We use prices not only because they are a convenient way of making comparisons, but also because prices reflect how consumers value different goods. If the price of an orange is twice that of an apple, it means an orange is worth twice as much (at the margin) as an apple.

To keep the comparisons of different years straight, economists adjust GDP for changes in the average level of prices. Unadjusted GDP is known as **nominal GDP.** The term **real GDP** is used for inflation-adjusted GDP figures, which are truer year-to-year measures of what the economy actually produces. To calculate real GDP, economists simply take the nominal value of GDP—the money value of all the goods and services produced in the economy—and divide it by a measure of the price level. Thus, real GDP is defined by the equation

$$\text{real GDP} = \frac{\text{nominal GDP}}{\text{price level}}.$$

If nominal GDP has risen 3 percent in the past year but inflation has also increased prices by 3 percent, then real GDP is unchanged.

Another way of thinking about real GDP is to ask, what would GDP be if prices had remained unchanged; that is, simply add up the number of apples produced today times the price of apples (in the "base" year, a year which is used as a point of reference) plus the number of oranges produced today times the price of oranges (in the base year). This calculation gives the *real value* of GDP today using base year prices.

This approach encounters a problem when *relative* prices change dramatically. If the price of computers should fall rapidly as the output of computers increases—as has happened over the past two decades—then real output, using an earlier base year, such as 1987, will look like it is increasing very rapidly. When the base year is changed—as is done periodically—the growth of the economy will appear to diminish suddenly; in the *new* base year, computer prices are lower so each computer "counts" for less in GDP. Of course, the growth of the economy did not really diminish; it was only that our yardstick distorted the picture.

To avoid this problem, the Bureau of Economic Analysis, the government agency responsible for the GDP numbers, changed its methodology in January 1996. It now provides a measure which is called the **chain-weighted real GDP.** It uses 1995 prices to calculate real income in 1996; 1996 prices to calculate real income in 1997; and so forth. This measure allows us to say how much GDP would have grown this year, if prices had remained unchanged at last year's levels. If output in 1997 is 3 percent higher than output in 1996, and output in 1996 is 2 percent higher than that in 1995, then 1997 output is 5 percent higher than 1995 output.

POTENTIAL GDP

GDP measures how much the economy actually produces. But sometimes the economy is capable of producing more than it actually does. Another measure, **potential GDP,** indicates what the economy *could* produce if labor and machines were used fully to their capacity.

Figure 24.2 POTENTIAL AND ACTUAL GDP

Potential GDP measures how much the economy would produce if it used all its resources. Actual GDP shows what the economy actually produces. Notice that both have been growing over time.
Source: ERP (1996), Tables B-2, B-50.

Figure 24.2 shows how potential (real) GDP and actual (real) GDP have increased over the past quarter century.[2] Output does not grow smoothly, and there have been periods in which actual output has been far below potential output. The jagged progression in the figure shows the effect of short-term fluctuations around an upward trend. Sometimes these fluctuations represent only a slowdown in the rate of growth; sometimes output actually falls. The dips in real GDP from 1971 to 1973, from 1980 to 1981, and from 1990 to 1991 represent periods when U.S. economic output actually declined. Strong upward fluctuations are called **booms,** and downward ones are called **recessions.** Severe downturns are referred to as **depressions.** The last depression, called the Great Depression because of its length and depth, began in 1929. The economy did not fully recover from it until World War II. While there is no technical definition of a boom, a recession is said to have occurred when GDP falls for at least two consecutive quarters. (For statistical purposes, the year is divided into quarters.)

The economy's fluctuations are sometimes referred to as **business cycles.** But the term cycle suggests a degree of regularity that is not really present. Though it is true that every so often the economy has a downturn, the time between one **trough** (the bottom of a recession) and another, or one **peak** (the top of a boom) and another, is highly variable, from just a few years, to as many as eight. Indeed, the likelihood of a downturn in the economy after, say, five years from the previous trough is no greater than three years from the

[2]Figure 24.2 shows actual GDP exceeding potential GDP in a few years. How is this possible, if potential GDP really measures what the economy *could* produce? The answer is that the estimates of potential GDP are based on assumptions about normal levels of unemployment and on the fact that even when the economy is quite strong, some capacity is not fully utilized. In fact, for short spurts of time, such as when a country goes to war, actual GDP can exceed estimates of potential GDP by a considerable amount.

Figure 24.3 CAPACITY UTILIZATION

Capacity utilization measures the fraction of machines and buildings that are actually in use. Notice that the figure fluctuates between about 70 and 90 percent as the economy moves between booms and recessions. *Source: ERP (1996), Table B-50.*

previous trough, and even sophisticated statistical models cannot predict accurately the next turning point in the economy.

In recessions the economy operates well below its potential. Unemployment is high and a large fraction of machines remain idle. Figure 24.3 shows the percentage of America's industrial capacity that was utilized for the past several decades. The figures vary from slightly more than 70 percent of industrial capacity in a recession to over 90 percent of industrial capacity in a boom. (Because some machines are being repaired and maintained, while other are idle because they are not suited for the economy's current structure, the economy never shows a 100 percent capacity utilization rate.) Low-capacity utilization, like unemployment of workers, represents a waste of scarce economic resources.

MEASURING GDP: THE VALUE OF OUTPUT

There are three approaches to measuring GDP (whether real or nominal), each of which yields the same result. Two concentrate on output data. The third—relying on the fact that the value of output all becomes income to someone—uses income figures to obtain a measure of output.

THE FINAL GOODS APPROACH

On the face of it, measuring GDP is a straightforward task, albeit massive. One gathers together the dollar values of all goods and services sold in a country, and then adds them up. Unfortunately, matters are not this simple, because it is first necessary to distinguish between final goods and intermediate goods. Final goods—like automobiles, books, bread, and shoes—are sold to consumers. Intermediate goods are used to produce outputs—such as coal when used to make steel, or apples when used to make applesauce. A good such as an apple can be either a final or an intermediate good, depending on how it is used. The **final goods approach** to GDP adds up the total dollar value of goods and services produced, categorized by their ultimate users.

The reason it is so important to distinguish between final and intermediate goods is that the value of final goods *includes* the value of the intermediate goods that went into making them. When Ford sells a car for $12,000, that figure may include $100 worth of Uniroyal tires. It would be double counting to list in GDP the revenues of both the car maker and the tire producer. Likewise for the steel, plastic, and other components that go into the car. In fact, cases where some intermediate goods are used to produce other intermediate goods could even lead to triple or quadruple counting.

One way of calculating the value of the final goods of the economy is to consider where those goods go. There are four possibilities. Some final goods are consumed by individuals—we call this aggregate **consumption** (and we include all consumption goods, regardless of where they are produced). Some are used by firms to build buildings and make machines—this is called aggregate **investment** (again, we include all investment goods, regardless of where they are produced). Some are purchased by government, and are called **government spending.** And, some of the goods, called **exports,** go abroad. If we didn't import (that is, buy from abroad) any goods, then GDP would simply consist of goods that went for private consumption, private investment, to the government, or for export. But not all consumption, investment, or government purchases is produced at home. We, therefore, need a final step to get GDP by this method. We have to subtract the amount imported. Thus,

$$GDP = C + I + G + X - M$$

where C = consumption, I = investment, G = government purchases, X = exports, and M = imports. The difference between exports and imports is referred to as **net exports.** This equation is an **identity,** that is, it is always true (by definition) that GDP equals consumption plus investment plus government expenditures plus net exports.

GDP equals consumption plus investment plus government expenditures plus exports minus imports.

THE VALUE-ADDED APPROACH

A second way to calculate the value of GDP is to study the intermediate goods directly. The production of most items occurs in several stages. Consider the automobile. At one stage in its production, iron ore, coal, and limestone are mined. At a second stage, these raw materials are shipped to a steel mill. A third stage finds a steel company combining these ingredients to make steel.

POLICY PERSPECTIVE: A SLOWDOWN IN ECONOMIC GROWTH?

In early 1996, a controversy broke out over whether the U.S. economy could grow faster than it had been growing over the last twenty years. Growth since 1973 had been markedly slower than in the 1950s and 1960s. While the policy discussion focused on how to make the economy grow faster, economists pointed out that some of the apparent slowdown might only be a statistical artifact, arising from well-known measurement problems.

MEASURING QUALITY CHANGES

With many products, such as computers, quality changes almost every year. GDP statisticians try to make adjustments for changes in quality. For example, when antipollution devices were first required in automobiles in the early 1970s, the price of cars rose. The national income accountants decided that the increased cost was a quality improvement and effectively added to real output: consumers were buying a better car. But in some sectors, such as the financial and health sectors and the computer industry, the adjustments may be inadequate. The real growth of GDP is accordingly understated, and because these sectors are expanding rapidly, the magnitude of the understatement may be larger today than it was thirty years ago.

MEASURING GOVERNMENT SERVICES

The standard GDP calculation measures price and quantity at the point of sale. But what about goods that are not sold, at least not directly?

One important category of such goods is government-produced services. Imagine that state government bureaucrats become more efficient and are able to process automobile registrations faster. This might mean that the state can hire fewer workers to do the same job. But GDP statistics simply reflect the number of hours worked by government officials, not the actual value of what they produce. If the government becomes more efficient, measured GDP might go down, even though actual output—the number of registrations—increases. In this case, the conventional GDP measure would again understate the real growth of the economy.

MEASURING NONMARKETED GOODS

Nonmarketed goods and services, like housework done by family members, present similar problems. The statistics underestimate the true level of production in the economy, because they ignore such economic activity. For example, if one spouse stays at home and cleans and cooks, that would not be measured in GDP. However, if that spouse leaves home to take a job and hires someone else to do the cleaning and cooking, then both the spouse and the housekeeper would be measured in GDP.

If, in this way, more and more previously nonmarketed goods and services become part of the economy's measured output, then measured growth will overstate the actual growth of the economy.

Finally, the steel and other inputs, such as rubber and plastics, are combined by the automobile firm to make a car. The difference in value between what the automaker pays for intermediate goods and what it receives for the finished cars is called the firm's **value added.**

Value added = firm's revenues − cost of intermediate goods. GDP can be measured by calculating the value added at each stage of production.

GDP = sum of value added of all firms.

THE INCOME APPROACH

The third method used to calculate GDP involves measuring the income generated by selling products, rather than the value of the products themselves. This is known as the **income approach.** Firms do five things with their revenues. They pay for labor, they pay interest, they buy intermediate goods, they pay indirect taxes such as excise taxes, and they enjoy what is left over as profits.

Revenues = wages + interest payments + cost of intermediate inputs + indirect taxes + profits.

But we already know that the firm's value added is its revenue minus the cost of intermediate goods. Therefore, value added = wages + interest payments + indirect taxes + profits. And since the value of GDP is equal to the sum of the value added of all firms, GDP must also equal the sum of the value of all wage payments, interest payments, taxes, and profits for all firms:

GDP = wages + interest payments + indirect taxes + profits.

People receive income from wages, from capital, and from profits of the firms they own (or own shares in). Thus, the right-hand side of this identity is just the total income of all individuals plus government revenue from indirect taxes. This is an extremely important result, one economists use frequently, so it is worth highlighting: *aggregate output equals aggregate income.*

Differences between Individual Incomes and National Income   The notion of income used above to calculate GDP differs slightly from the way individuals commonly perceive income, and it is important to be aware of the distinction.

First, people are likely to include in their view of income any capital gains they earn. **Capital gains** are increases in the value of assets, and accordingly do not represent production (output) in any way. The national income accounts used to calculate GDP, which are designed to focus on the production of goods and services, do not include capital gains.

Second, profits that are retained by a firm are included in national income, but individuals may not perceive these retained profits as part of their own income. Again, this is because the GDP accounts measure the value of production, and profits are part of the value of production, whether those profits are actually distributed to shareholders or retained by firms.

COMPARISON OF THE FINAL GOODS AND INCOME APPROACHES

Earlier we learned how to break down the output of the economy into four categories—consumption, investment, government expenditures, and net exports. We break down the income of the economy into three categories—

Table 24.1 TWO APPROACHES TO U.S. GDP, 1995

Final goods	Billions $	Income	Billions $
Consumption	4,923.4	Employee compensation	4,209.4
Investment	1,067.5	Profits, rents, interest, etc.	2,442.5
Government expenditures	1,358.5	Indirect taxes	595.9
Net exports	−101.7	Total	7,247.8
Total	7,247.8		

payments to workers, consisting mainly of wages; payments to owners of capital, including profits, interest, and rents; and taxes. As Table 24.1 shows, the value of GDP is the same whether calculated in output or income terms: in 1995, U.S. GDP was approximately $7,248 billion.

That the value of output is equal to the value of income—that GDP measured either way is identical—is no accident. It is a consequence of the circular flow of the economy. What each firm receives from selling its goods must go back somewhere else into the economy—as wages, profits, interest, or taxes. The income to households flows back in turn either to firms—in consumption goods households purchase or in savings, which eventually are used to purchase plant and equipment by firms—or to government, in the form of taxes or newly issued government bonds. Similarly, the money spent by the government must have come from somewhere else in the economy—either from households or corporations in the form of taxes, or through borrowing.

ALTERNATIVE APPROACHES TO MEASURING NATIONAL OUTPUT

Measuring output of final goods
> Value of final output:
>> Consumption + Investment + Government Expenditures + Net Exports
> Sum of value added in each stage of production

Measuring income
> Employee compensation + Profits, Rents, Interest + Indirect taxes

Output = Income

ALTERNATIVE MEASURES OF OUTPUT

The U.S. government has used GDP as its main statistical measure of output since 1991. Before then, **gross national product (GNP)** was used. Gross national product is a measure of the incomes of residents of a country, including income they receive from abroad (wages, returns on investment, interest payments), but subtracting similar payments made to those abroad. By contrast, GDP ignores income received from or paid overseas. It is thus a measure of the goods and services actually produced *within* the country. GDP was the standard measure of output used by most European countries, in which trade had traditionally been far more important than in the United States. As international trade became more important for the United States, it was natural for the country to switch. Besides, the switch made comparisons with the performance of other countries easier.

The treatment of machines and other capital goods (buildings) is another problem in measuring national output. As machines are used to produce output, they wear out. Worn-out machines are a cost of production that should be balanced against total output.

As an example, consider a firm that has a machine worth $1,000 and uses that machine, with $600 of labor, to produce $2,000 worth of output. Furthermore, assume that at the end of the year the machine is completely worn out. The firm then has a *net* output of $400: $2,000 minus the labor costs *and* minus the value of the machine that has worn out.

The reduction in the value of the machine is called the machine's **depreciation.** Since machines wear out at all sorts of different rates, accounting for how much the machines in the economy have depreciated is an extremely difficult problem. The GDP figures take the easy road and make no allowance for depreciation. The term "gross" in "gross domestic product" should serve as a reminder that the statistic covers all production. Economists sometimes use a separate measure that includes the effects of depreciation, called **net domestic product (NDP),** which subtracts an estimate of the value of depreciation from GDP:

$$NDP = GDP - depreciation.$$

The problem is that economists have little confidence in the estimates of depreciation. For this reason they usually use the GDP figure as the measure of the economy's output. Since GDP, GNP, and NDP go up and down together, for most purposes, it does not much matter which one you use as long as you are consistent.

MEASURING THE STANDARD OF LIVING

GDP tells something about the overall level of a nation's economic activity, the goods and services produced in market transactions. But it is only part of the measure of a society's overall well-being. Other social indicators are often employed for this, such as literacy rates (the percentage of the population that can read or write), infant mortality rates (the fraction of infants that die), and life expectancy.

GDP does not reflect environmental degradation which may accompany economic growth. And GDP statistics may be misleading: consider a poor country that decides to harvest its hardwood forests to increase its income. These forests take centuries to grow. Harvesting the forest increases the measured output of the economy, but decreases the country's assets. The output is not sustainable. The United Nations is creating a new set of national accounts, called **Green GDP,** which attempts to incorporate some of the effects on the environment and natural resources. In the above example, Green GDP would subtract from conventional GDP the decrease in the natural resource base. Policymakers would then know that the conventionally measured increase in GDP from cutting down the hardwood forest is short-lived. It is based not on an addition to society's wealth, but rather a subtraction from it.

UNEMPLOYMENT

While increasing living standards is the central economic goal over the long run, when the economy goes into a downturn, unemployment becomes a source of immediate concern. To an economist, unemployment represents an underutilization of resources. People who are willing and able to work are not being productively employed. To the unemployed individuals and their families, unemployment represents economic hardship and changes in their way of life. If a person is unemployed for a long time, he will be unable to meet his current expenses—like utilities and rent—and will have to move to cheaper housing and reduce other aspects of his standard of living.

Unemployment not only costs individuals their paychecks, it can deal a powerful blow to their self-respect. Unemployed workers in today's urban America cannot fall back on farming or living off the land as they might have done in colonial times. Instead, they and their families may be forced to choose between poverty and the bitter taste of government or private charity. Many of these families break up under the strain.

Unemployment presents different problems for each age group of workers. For the young, having a job is necessary for developing job skills, whether they are technical skills or such basic work prerequisites as punctuality and responsibility. Persistent unemployment for them not only wastes valuable human resources today but also reduces the future productivity of the labor force. Individuals fail to obtain critical on-the-job training that improves their skills, and to develop work habits that improve their on-the-job productivity. Furthermore, young people who remain unemployed for an extended period are especially prone to becoming alienated from society and turning to anti-social activities such as crime and drug abuse.

For the middle-aged or elderly worker, losing a job poses different problems. Despite federal and state prohibitions against age discrimination, employers are often hesitant to hire an older worker. They may fear she is more likely than a younger person to become sick or disabled. They may worry about being able to "teach old dogs new tricks." If older workers are unemployed for long periods of time, they may have lost some of their skills. Even if the unemployed older worker succeeds in getting a job, it often entails reduced wages and lower status than in her previous job and may make less than full use of her skills. The toll of such changes is a heavy burden of stress on the dislocated worker and her family.

In addition to these personal losses, unemployment poses heavy costs for communities. If people in a town are thrown out of work—say, because a big employer closes down or decides to move—everyone else in town is likely to suffer as well, since there will be fewer dollars circulating to buy everything from cars and houses to gasoline and groceries. As more unemployment results in fewer people paying local taxes, the quality of schools, libraries, parks, and police can be threatened.

Unemployment may also reinforce racial divisions in society as a whole. The rate of unemployment for blacks is generally more than twice that for whites. During the 1980s and early 1990s, among blacks between the ages of sixteen and nineteen who were just beginning to look for work, unemployment averaged 37 percent, nearly reaching 50 percent in the recession years of 1982 to 1983.

Unemployment represents a tragedy for the individual and the family, a source of dislocation and stress for a community, and a waste of productive resources for society as a whole.

THE MAGNITUDE OF THE PROBLEM

Living in the midst of the approximately 125 million people who get up and go to work every morning is a fluctuating group of several million healthy people who do not. During the recession year of 1991, 8.5 million people were out of work, and one-fourth of those people were jobless for fifteen weeks or more. From the standpoint of the economy as a whole, the potential production of workers who cannot find jobs is a major loss. One calculation puts the loss in output from the high unemployment of the early 1980s at between $122 billion and $320 billion a year, for a per capita loss of between $500 and somewhat more than $1,300.[3] In other words, using the latter number, every man, woman, and child in the United States would have had (on average) an additional $1,300 to spend if the unemployed workers had been gainfully employed.

UNEMPLOYMENT STATISTICS

In the United States, unemployment data are collected by the Department of Labor, which surveys a representative mix of households and asks each whether a member of the household is currently seeking employment. The

[3]A. Blinder, *Hard Heads, Soft Hearts* (Reading, Mass.: Addison-Wesley, 1987).

unemployment rate is the ratio of the number seeking employment to the total labor force. If there are 120 million Americans employed and 10 million say they are looking for a job but cannot find one, then the total labor force is 130 million, and the

$$\text{unemployment rate} = \frac{\text{number unemployed}}{\text{labor force}}$$

$$= \frac{\text{number unemployed}}{\text{number employed} + \text{number unemployed}}$$

$$= \frac{10 \text{ million}}{120 \text{ million} + 10 \text{ million}} = 7.7 \text{ percent.}$$

Figure 24.4 plots the unemployment rate for the United States since 1960. The figure illustrates two facts. First, unemployment is persistent. Second, the level of unemployment can fluctuate dramatically. In the worst days of the Great Depression, over one quarter of the U.S. labor force was unemployed. The unemployment rate among those who worked in manufacturing was even worse—at one point, one out of three workers in manufacturing had lost their jobs. As recently as 1983, the unemployment rate in the United States was nearly 10 percent. The level of unemployment in the early 1990s, at 5.4 to 7.4 percent, while much lower than that of the early 1980s, is still higher than the rate that prevailed in the mid-1960s, around 4 percent.

Unemployment in other countries has often been worse than in the United States (Figure 24.5). In European countries, it reached over 10 percent during much of the 1980s, and in many developing countries over 20 percent.

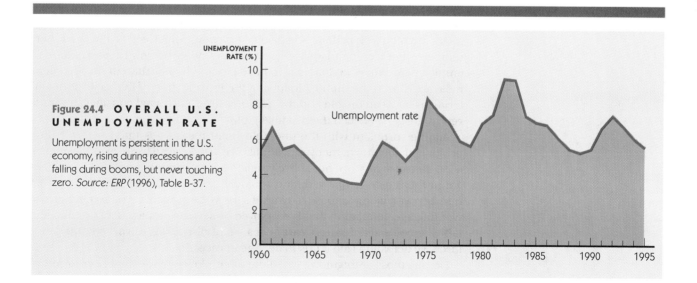

Figure 24.4 OVERALL U.S. UNEMPLOYMENT RATE

Unemployment is persistent in the U.S. economy, rising during recessions and falling during booms, but never touching zero. *Source: ERP* (1996), Table B-37.

**Figure 24.5 INTERNA-
TIONAL UNEMPLOY-
MENT COMPARISONS**

In other developed countries, the unemployment rate is often much higher than has been observed in the United States in recent years. *Source: ERP* (1996), Table B-105.

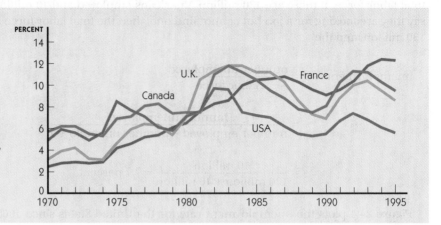

PROBLEMS WITH THE UNEMPLOYMENT STATISTICS

Unemployment statistics are supposed to measure the number of workers who are actively seeking employment but cannot find a job. Information is obtained from a survey of households, and the results of such survey often depend on how the survey is conducted. For instance, in January 1994, the Bureau of Labor Statistics changed the manner in which it conducted its monthly survey. The timing could not have been worse: the economy was pulling out of a recession and a major policy initiative, the 1993 deficit reduction, was just going into effect. Policymakers wanted to know how the economy was doing. It was as if at the very moment a physician tried a new medicine on a sick patient, she also used a new, imperfectly calibrated thermometer. Early comparisons suggested that under the new measure, the unemployment rate would appear to be .6 percent higher than under the older measure. But in the months following the introduction of the survey, the differences between the old and the new measures narrowed considerably; currently, the gap between them is negligible.

Another problem with the unemployment measure is that, especially in a prolonged downturn, many individuals are *discouraged* from even looking for a job. Because they are not actively seeking employment, the statistics will not count them as unemployed, and thus will provide an underestimate of the number who would choose to work if a job were available. The fraction of the working age population that is employed or seeking employment is called the **labor force participation rate.** Because of discouraged workers, the labor force participation rate tends to decline in recessions.

Despite these ambiguities, when the unemployment rate increases by more than a trivial amount, it is safe to conclude that the economy has slowed down. Some individuals have been laid off and have not found new jobs, and firms may have slowed down the pace at which they hire new workers.

FORMS OF UNEMPLOYMENT

Economists distinguish between different kinds of unemployment. Right before Christmas, there is a huge demand for retail salespeople to work in department stores and shopping malls across the country. In many parts of the country, construction slows down in the winter because of the climate. For the same reason, tourism often increases in the summer, and so does the number of jobs that cater to tourists. The supply of labor also increases in the summer, as high school and college students enter the labor force on a temporary basis. Unemployment that varies with the seasons is called **seasonal unemployment.** Since these movements in employment and unemployment reflect normal seasonal patterns, the unemployment rate you see reported on the news is adjusted according to the average amount of seasonal unemployment. These adjustments are called seasonal adjustments. Thus, if, on average, the unadjusted unemployment rate is normally .4 percent higher in the summer than at other times, the seasonally adjusted unemployment rate for July will be the measured unemployment rate minus .4 percent.

While workers in construction, agriculture, and tourism regularly face seasonal unemployment, other workers become unemployed only as part of a normal transition from one job to another. This kind of unemployment is referred to as **frictional unemployment.** If people could move from job to job instantaneously, there would be no frictional unemployment. In a dynamic economy such as America's, with some industries growing and other declining, there will always be movements from one job to another, and hence there will always be frictional unemployment.

Most bouts of unemployment are short-lived; the average person who loses a job is out of work for only three months. However, about 10 percent of the jobless have been unemployed for more than six months. This kind of long-term unemployment often results from structural factors in the economy, and is called **structural unemployment.** Substantial structural unemployment is found quite often side by side with job vacancies, because the unemployed lack the skills required for the newly created jobs. For example, there may be vacancies for computer programmers, while construction workers are unemployed. By the same token, there may be job shortages in those parts of the economy that are expanding (as in the Sunbelt) and unemployment in areas that are suffering decline (as in Michigan during the period of decline in demand for U.S. cars).

Unemployment that increases when the economy goes into a slowdown and decreases when the economy goes into a boom is called **cyclical unemployment** and is the fundamental concern of this part of the book. Government policy is particularly interested in reducing both the frequency and magnitude of this kind of unemployment, by reducing the frequency and magnitude of the recessions that give rise to it. Government also seeks to reduce its impact, by providing unemployment compensation for those temporarily thrown out of work.

As the economy goes into a recession, the demand for labor—the number of hours to be worked—decreases; if the decreased demand were spread uniformly among all workers, the social disruption would be limited; but in

FORMS OF UNEMPLOYMENT

Seasonal

Frictional

Structural

Cyclical

fact, most workers have a slight reduction in work, while a few workers simply lose their jobs. And unskilled workers and minorities are especially likely to become unemployed. Unemployment rates among these groups often soar in a downturn.

INFLATION

In the 1920s, the years of silent pictures, a movie ticket cost a nickel. By the late 1940s, in the heyday of Hollywood, the price was up to $.50. By the 1960s, the price of a movie was $2.00, and now it is over $7.00. This steady price rise is no anomaly. Most other goods have undergone similar increases over time. This increase in the general level of prices is called inflation. While unemployment tends to be concentrated in certain groups within the population, everyone is affected by inflation. Thus, it is not surprising that when inflation becomes high, it almost always rises to the top of the political agenda.

It is not inflation if the price of only one good goes up. It *is* inflation if the prices of *most* goods go up. The **inflation rate** is the rate at which the *general level* of prices increases.

MEASURING INFLATION

If the prices of all goods rose by the same proportion, say by 5 percent, over a period of a year, measuring inflation would be easy: the rate of inflation for that year would be 5 percent. The difficulties arise from the fact that the prices of different goods rise at different rates, and some goods even decline in price. Over the past twenty years, while the price of fruits and vegetables has increased by 220 percent, the price of gasoline by 138 percent, and the price of medical care by 383 percent, the price of computers has declined by over 90 percent. To determine the change in the overall price level, economists calculate the *average* percentage increase in prices. But since some goods loom much larger in the typical consumer's budget than others, this calculation must reflect the relative purchases of different goods. A change in the price of housing, for example, is much more important than a change in the price of pencils. If the price of pencils goes down by 5 percent but the price of housing goes up by 5 percent, the overall measure of the price level should go up.

Economists have a straightforward way of reflecting the differing importance of different goods. They ask, what would it cost consumers to purchase the same bundle of goods this year that they bought last year? If, for example, it cost $22,000 in 1996 to buy what it cost consumers only $20,000 to purchase in 1995, we say that prices, *on average,* have risen by 10 percent. Such results are frequently expressed in the form of a **price index,** which, for ease of comparison, measures the price level in any given year relative to a common base year.

The price index for the base year is, by definition, 100. The price index for any other year is calculated by taking the ratio of the price level in that year to the price level in the base year and multiplying it by 100. For example, if 1995 is our base year and we want to know the price index for 1996, we first calculate the ratio of the cost of a certain bundle of goods in 1996 ($22,000) to the cost of the same bundle of goods in 1995 ($20,000), which is 1.1. The price index in 1996 is therefore $1.1 \times 100 = 110$. The index of 110, using 1995 as a base, means that prices are 10 percent higher, on average, in 1996 than in 1995.

There are several different price indices, each using a different bundle of goods. To track the movement of prices that are important to American households, the government collects price data on the bundle of goods that represents how the average household spends its income. This index is called the **consumer price index,** or CPI. To determine this bundle, the government, through the Bureau of Labor Statistics of the Department of Labor, conducts a Consumer Expenditure Survey, which is updated once a decade or so.

THE AMERICAN EXPERIENCE WITH INFLATION

As we have learned, the inflation rate is the percentage increase in the price level from one year to the next. Figure 24.6 shows the inflation rate for the United States during this century. Three interesting features stand out.

First, prices were relatively stable for much of the century, with the inflation rate under 5 percent except in three periods: around World War I, around World War II, and during the period 1973–1981. Indeed, from the start of the twentieth century until the early 1960s, average inflation ran at only about 1 percent per year.

Second, prices can actually come down. During the recession that followed World War I, prices fell by more than 15 percent, and in the Great Depression of the 1930s by more than 30 percent. It may seem hard to believe in an era when inflation seems the ever-present threat, but at the end of the nineteenth century, the concern was **deflation,** which is a steady decline of the price

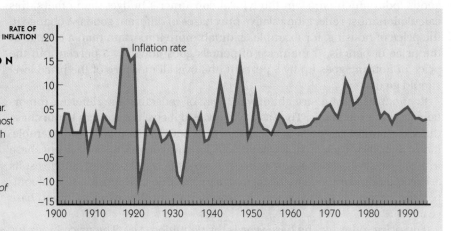

Figure 24.6 THE INFLATION RATE

The inflation rate is the percentage increase in the price level in a given year. Notice that inflation was low through most of the early part of this century (although high during World Wars I and II), rose sharply in the 1970s, and then fell somewhat in the 1980s. *Sources: ERP* (1996), Table B-60; *Historical Statistics of the United States.*

level. Borrowers at that time who were in debt and had not anticipated the fall in prices found that the dollars they had to pay back were worth far more than the dollars that they had borrowed. They were as upset about this as investors (lenders) are today when inflation makes the value of the dollars they get back from an investment or loan worth less than the value of the dollars they originally put in.

Finally, while prices on average have been stable and there have even been periods of price decline, there have also been a few periods of high inflation, when prices increased rapidly. The most notable recent episode was in the late 1970s and early 1980s. In 1980 alone, prices rose by more than 13 percent.

THE IMPORTANCE OF INFLATION

In modern economies, much has been done to ease the pain of inflation. For workers, rising levels of prices are usually accompanied by higher wages, and if a worker faces higher prices but has commensurately more money in her pocket, she is just as well off. The U.S. government has taken steps to adjust the income of retirees to changes in the price level. Most significant, Social Security payments are now "indexed," that is, adjusted, to keep up with changes in the cost of living.

Why, then, does fighting inflation rank so high as a priority in economic policy? There seem to be three answers.

The first is that some groups still suffer. Anyone whose income does not adjust fully is made worse off by increases in the price level. Second, when the rate of inflation suddenly increases, those who have lent money find that the dollars they are being paid back with are worth less. Thus, creditors (those

Using Economics: Calculating the Consumer Price Index

Encapsulating the movements of masses of prices into an index provides an easy way to look at price trends over time. Suppose that in 1990 the average American family spent $1,000 per month to buy a basket of goods. Assume that in 1996 it cost $1,200 to buy the same basket. Then the price index for 1996 is just the ratio of the cost in 1996 to the cost in 1990, times 100. That is,

$$\text{CPI for 1996} = {}^{1,200}\!/_{1,000} \times 100 = 120.$$

The advantage of an index is that once there is an index number for any given year, we can compare it with any other year. The CPI for 1973 was 44, and for 1994 it was 148. Between those years, the index rose by 104, so the increase was

$$100 \times {}^{104}\!/_{44} = 236 \text{ percent.}$$

On average, prices rose by 236 percent from 1973 to 1994.

The figure below shows the level of the consumer price index from 1900 to the present, using 1983 as the base year. For example, prices in 1920 were 20 percent of what they were in 1983.

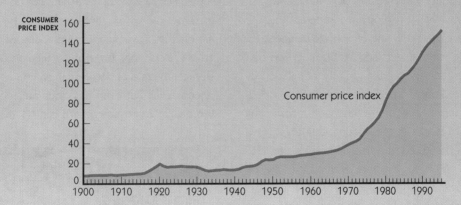

Source: ERP (1996), Table B-56.

who lend money) are worse off, while debtors are better off. When the inflation rate varies, both borrowing and lending become riskier.

Third, many feel that something is fundamentally wrong with the economy when what cost $1 five years ago costs $2 today. Sometimes these observers are right. Inflation can reflect gross errors in government economic policy, such as spending that is far in excess of revenues, or excessive provision of credit. But frequently inflation gets the blame when something else is the underlying problem. The steep increase in oil prices in 1973 set off a worldwide inflationary spiral. With Americans paying more to the oil-exporting countries, the United States was, in a sense, poorer. Someone had to take a cut. Furthermore, the worldwide economic downturn set off by the 1973 oil price rise made the cut that had to be taken that much larger. Thus, workers' real

POLICY PERSPECTIVE: THE PRICE INDEX MAKES A DIFFERENCE!

Price indices have increasingly come to play an important role in economic life, in spite of the dry, technical flavor that seems to pervade most discussion of them. The Social Security benefits of the elderly increase with the cost of living index, and tax brackets and tax exemptions also change with the index. If the index overstates the cost of living (rate of inflation) increases, the real benefits (purchasing power) of the elderly increase, and real inflation-adjusted tax revenues decrease. Both distortions increase the budget deficit of the government—the first by increasing the outlays, the second by reducing the receipts of government.

By early 1994, it had become apparent that the price index used by the federal government for adjusting both benefits and tax brackets was seriously flawed—overstating the rate of inflation by between .5 and 1.5 percent a year. Several scheduled changes will go part of the way in correcting those errors. But in the interim, until those revisions are instituted, the Treasury will lose an estimated $100 billion or more as a result of the biased index.

The upward bias stems from three problems. The first is the "fixed basket problem." Price indices are generally calculated by comparing how much it costs to purchase a particular market basket of goods that represents an average consumer's expenditure pattern. But expenditure patterns change steadily over time, while the market basket is revised only infrequently (for instance, 1997 will be the first revision since 1982 through 1984). As people buy more of the goods which have become relatively less expensive, and less of the goods which have become relatively more ex-

pensive, the index increasingly overweights goods whose prices are rising.

The second major problem is "quality adjustments." New products, which can do new and better things than older products, constantly enter the market. To compare the prices of the new products with the old, some quality adjustment must be made. If the price goes up by 10 percent, but the product lives longer and does better than the old one, in a real sense the price increase is less than 10 percent and may even be a price reduction. The quality adjustments may sometimes be easy: one machine can do what two machines did before. But usually the comparisons are difficult. If we measure the quality of computers by calculations per minute, memory, and disk storage, the rate of decrease in computer prices is phenomenal. But even this does not fully reflect the quality improvement. We can do things with

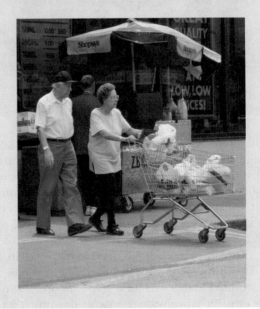

the computer now that were unimaginable twenty-five years ago at any price. And how do we treat a new drug that cures a previously incurable disease? The Bureau of Labor Statistics tries to make adjustments for quality. But the consensus is that these adjustments are imperfect and result in an overestimate in the inflation rate of between a few tenths of a percent to more than 1 percent.

A third set of problems is technical, having to do with the way the data are collected and the details of the calculation.

But many economists believe that the scheduled revisions will not fully eliminate the CPI bias. They argue that, as a result, Social Security and taxes should be indexed to the CPI rate of inflation minus 1 or .5.

wages fell. They blamed inflation for their declining standard of living. But inflation was not really the culprit—higher oil prices were.

As the economy has adapted to inflation, economists have increasingly debated about how concerned we should be about moderate rates of inflation—the 3 to 6 percent inflation that has occurred regularly during the past few decades. They worry that the cures for moderate inflation may be worse than the disease. Still, most economists think that double-digit inflation levels, at the very least, are symptomatic of some kind of malfunction in the economy. Certainly there is a consensus that the kinds of rapid inflation experienced in Israel and some Latin American countries are extremely disruptive to the economy.

ALTERNATIVE MEASURES OF INFLATION

The consumer price index is one measure of inflation, based on what the average consumer pays. Other price indices can be calculated using different market baskets. A different measure of prices is the **producer price index,** which measures the average level of prices of goods sold by producers. This index is useful because it gives us an idea of what will happen to consumer prices in the near future. Usually, if producers are receiving higher prices from their sales to wholesalers, eventually retailers will have to charge higher prices. This will be reflected in a higher consumer price index.

Earlier in the chapter we observed that real GDP is nominal GDP adjusted for the price level. The price index we use for calculating real GDP is called the **GDP deflator.** It represents a comparison between what it would cost to buy the total mix of goods and services within the economy today and in a base year. In other words, the GDP deflator is a weighted average of the prices of different goods and services, where the weights represent the importance of each of the goods and services in GDP.

CONNECTING THE THREE MAJOR VARIABLES

Often the major macroeconomic variables move together in systematic ways. For example, when the economy is in a recession, as it was in 1982, unemployment tends to be higher, inflation tends to be lower, and growth comes to a standstill. These connections make sense. After all, when the economy is suffering tough times, businesses reduce their output, lay off workers, and do not hire new workers. In addition, businesses that are having a hard time selling products in a competitive market are less likely to raise prices.

FLOWS AND STOCKS

GDP, GNP, and NDP are all measures of output *per year*. Rate measurements such as these are called **flows.** When a news report says, "The quarterly GDP statistic, just released, shows that GDP was $4 trillion per year," it does not mean that $4 trillion of goods and services was produced during the quarter. Rather, it means that $1 trillion was produced during the quarter, so that if that rate of production were maintained for a whole year, the total value of goods and services would be $4 trillion.

Flow statistics need to be contrasted with **stock** statistics, which measure an item at a single point in time. Among the most important stocks is the capital stock—the total value of all the buildings and machines that underlie the productive potential of the economy.

The relationships between stocks and flows are simple. The stock of capital at the end of 1996, for example, consists of the stock of capital at the end of 1995 plus or minus the flows into or out of this stock during 1996. Investment is the flow into the capital stock. Depreciation is the flow out of the capital stock.

Similarly, we can look at the *number* of unemployed individuals as a stock. This number at the end of 1996 consists of the number at the end of 1995 plus or minus the flows into or out of the unemployment pool during 1996. Layoffs, firings, resignations, and new entry into the labor force can be thought of as flows into the unemployment pool; new hires represent flows out of the unemployment pool.

REVIEW AND PRACTICE

SUMMARY

1. The three central macroeconomic policy objectives of the government are low unemployment, low inflation, and high growth. Macroeco-

nomics studies how these aggregate variables change as a result of household and business behavior, and how government policy may affect them.

2. Productivity has not been increasing as rapidly in the United States in the last two decades as it had earlier.

3. Gross domestic product (GDP) is the typical way of measuring national output. Real GDP adjusts GDP for changes in the price level.

4. GDP can be calculated in three ways: the final goods approach, which adds the value of all final goods produced in the economy; the value-added approach, which adds the difference between firms' revenues and costs of intermediate goods; and the income approach, which adds together all income received by those in the economy. All three methods give the same answer.

5. Unemployment imposes costs both on individuals and on society as a whole, which loses what the unemployed workers could have contributed and ends up supporting them in other ways.

6. Seasonal unemployment, such as construction in areas with harsh winters, occurs regularly depending on the season. Frictional unemployment results from people being in transition between one job and another. Structural unemployment refers to the unemployment generated as the structure of the economy changes, with the new jobs being created having requirements different from the old jobs being lost. Cyclical unemployment increases or decreases with the level of economic activity.

7. The inflation rate is the percentage increase of the price level from one year to the next. U.S. inflation was low through most of the early part of this century, rose sharply in the 1970s and early 1980s, and then fell somewhat in the later 1980s and early 1990s. In different countries at different times, inflation has sometimes been very high, with prices increasing by factors of tens or hundreds in a given year.

8. The amount of inflation between two years is measured by the percentage change in the amount it would cost to buy a given basket of goods in those years. Different baskets define different price indexes, such as the consumer price index and the producer price index.

9. Many macroeconomic variables seem to move together in systematic ways. For example, in a boom, unemployment tends to fall, inflation tends to rise, and productivity tends to rise. In a recession, the reverse happens.

10. Economists distinguish between flows—such as output per year—and stocks—such as the stock of capital.

KEY TERMS

unemployment rate	gross domestic	nominal GDP
inflation	product (GDP)	real GDP

chain-weighted real
  GDP
potential GDP
business cycles
boom
recession
trough
peak
value added
capital gains
gross national
  product (GNP)

depreciation
net domestic
  product (NDP)
Green GDP
labor force
  participation rate
seasonal
  unemployment
frictional
  unemployment
structural
  unemployment

cyclical
  unemployment
consumer price
  index
deflation
producer price
  index
GDP deflator
flows
stocks

REVIEW QUESTIONS

1. What are the three main goals of macroeconomic policy?

2. What is the difference between nominal GDP, real GDP, and potential GDP?

3. What is the difference between the final outputs approach to measuring GDP, the value-added approach, and the income approach?

4. What is the difference between GDP, GNP, and NDP?

5. What has happened in the last two decades to the rate of change of productivity?

6. What is the difference between frictional unemployment, seasonal unemployment, structural unemployment, and cyclical unemployment?

7. When there is a reduction in the number of hours worked in the economy, is this normally shared equally by all workers? Are workers in some groups more impacted by increased unemployment than those in other groups?

8. When the prices of different goods change at different rates, how do we measure the rate of inflation?

9. Are all groups of people affected equally by inflation? Why or why not?

PROBLEMS

1. Which would you expect to fall fastest in a recession, real GDP or potential GDP? Could potential GDP rise while real GDP fell?

2. Geoffrey spends his allowance on three items: candy, magazines, and renting VCR movies. He is currently receiving an allowance of $30 per month, which he is using to rent 4 movies at $2 apiece, buy 10 candy bars

at $1 apiece, and purchase 4 magazines at $3 apiece. Calculate a Geoffrey price index (GPI) for this basket of goods, with the current price level equal to 100, in the following cases.

(a) The price of movies rises to $3.

(b) The price of movies rises to $3, and the price of candy bars falls by $.20.

(c) The price of movies rises to $3, the price of candy bars falls by $.20, and the price of magazines rises to $4.

3. An increase in the consumer price index will often affect different groups in different ways. Think about how different groups will purchase items like housing, travel, or education in the CPI basket, and explain why they will be affected differently by increases in components of the CPI. How would you calculate an "urban CPI" or a "rural CPI"?

4. Given the information below about the U.S. economy, how much did real U.S. GDP grow between 1965 and 1975? between 1975 and 1985?

	1965	1970	1975	1980	1985	1990	1995
Nominal GDP (billions)	$700	$1,000	$1,600	$2,700	$4,000	$5,500	$7,000
Consumer price index	100	115	160	250	320	415	480

5. Much of this chapter has discussed how economists adjust the data to find what they want to know—for example, by adjusting for inflation or dividing by the population level. What adjustments might you suggest for analyzing education expenditures? Social Security expenditures?

6. Firms typically do not fire workers quickly as the economy goes into a recession—at least not in proportion to the reduction in their output. How might you expect output per worker and output per hour to move over the business cycle?

CHAPTER 25

THE FULL-
EMPLOYMENT
MODEL

I f we look at history in decades, the market economy creates jobs for almost all who seek them. In the 1980s, for example, the American labor force increased by 19 million people, and the number of people employed increased by the same amount. But sometimes the markets fail, as is evident when one out of ten, one out of five, or even (during the Great Depression) one out of four job seekers cannot find jobs. Yet every period in which the market has failed to create enough jobs for those who seek them has been followed by a period in which the economy catches up. Thus, while the economy stalled from 1991 to 1992, creating only 1 million jobs, in the two and a half years from January 1993 until July 1995, more than 7 million new jobs were created.

The economic theories in the next part of the book explain why there are important episodes in which markets fail to create enough jobs and what the government can do about them. In this part of the book, we will see how the economy works in the long run—when it creates jobs at the rate of new entry into the labor force. We focus on the aggregate behavior of the economy—on movements of such macroeconomic variables as output and wages—when resources are fully employed. We show how competitive markets, when they work well, help explain the vitality of the American economy. No government official can calculate where to place the 7 million new workers who are expected to enter the labor force between 1996 and the year 2000. Indeed, if anyone from the president on down, had been asked where all the new entrants

KEY QUESTIONS

1. In an economy operating at full employment, what determines real wage, level of output, and investment?

2. How is the economy affected by government expenditures and international trade? When government increases its expenditures, but raises taxes to pay for the increased expenditures, what happens to investment? How might the answer differ between a small country like Switzerland and a large country like the United States?

3. How are markets in the economy interlinked?

would find jobs in the 1993 to 1994 growth spurt, no one would have known the precise answer, though they could have pointed to particular parts of the economy that would be the most likely sources of job growth. But they would have said, on the basis of past experience, that somehow, somewhere, the economy would create the jobs. The economic theories that we explore in this and the following chapters help explain this job growth.

MACROECONOMIC EQUILIBRIUM

The model we employ here is the basic competitive model described in earlier chapters. In it, large numbers of households and firms interact in the labor, product, and capital markets. Households supply labor to firms that use the labor to produce goods and compensate workers by paying them wages. Households also save, and those savings finance firms' investments such as the plant and equipment that firms need to produce. For the use of their funds, households receive interest and dividends from firms. With the income they earn from working and the return they earn from their savings, households buy the products that firms produce.

Two key lessons emerge from the basic competitive model. First, all markets are interrelated. What goes on in one market has an impact on others. The demand for labor, for instance, depends on the level of output (the product market). Second, wages, interest rates, and prices adjust to equate demand and supply. In this part of the book, we continue to focus on product, labor, and capital markets, and to assume that the adjustments in wages, interest rates, and prices are sufficiently rapid that, for practical purposes, all markets are always in equilibrium. That is, they all clear, with demand equal to supply. This assumption is not only a convenient starting point, but it gives us powerful insights into some of the basic macroeconomic questions. We began the chapter with the observation that *somehow* the economy creates jobs for the millions of new entrants into the labor force each year. It has done

Close-up: The Birth of the Micro–Macro Division

Today even noneconomists have heard the terms "microeconomics" and "macroeconomics." But economists did not actually begin thinking in those terms until the 1930s, when the global economy suffered the collapse that became known as the Great Depression. In the United States, the economy shrank 30 percent from 1929 to 1933; the unemployment rate hit 25 percent in 1933. Attention shifted to what determined aggregate variables like the unemployment rate and GDP.

John Maynard Keynes expressed the general idea when he wrote in 1936: "The division of Economics . . . is, I suggest, between the Theory of the Individual Industry or Firm and of the rewards and the distribution of a given quantity of resources on the one hand, and the Theory of Output and Employment *as a whole* on the other hand."

The first known written use of the words "micro-economic" and "macroeconomic" was by P. de Wolff, a little-known economist at the Netherlands Statistical Institute. In a 1941 article, de Wolff wrote: "The micro-economic interpretation refers to the relation . . . for a single person or family. The macro-economic interpretation is derived from the corresponding relation . . . *for a large group of persons or families (social strata, nations, etc.).*"

In the 1960s and 1970s, many economists became concerned that macroeconomic thinking had strayed too far from its microeconomic roots. Interestingly, some of the most important economic work of the last twenty years—which will be described in the following chapters—has sought to break down that wall and explain how rational, well-informed consumers and profit-maximizing firms can work together in a way that sometimes creates unemployment, inflation, or fluctuations in growth.

Source: Hal R. Varian, "Microeconomics," in Eatwell, Milgate, and Newman, eds., *The New Palgrave: A Dictionary of Economics* (1987), 3:461–63.

this without any government official or private individual managing the whole process. The magic of the market—the adjustment of wages and prices equilibrating the labor market—guides this process, and the model we present here explains how this happens.

The analysis here differs in one important way from the kind of microeconomic analysis we have seen previously. In macroeconomics, we focus on aggregates, on total output, rather than the output of individual products. We focus on total employment, and on average prices, which we refer to as the price level. We also proceed as if there is a single good being produced or a single kind of labor. That is, we can picture the economy as if all firms produced the same commodity and all workers are identical. In looking at these aggregates, we ignore the richness of the microeconomic detail we dealt with earlier. Hidden behind an increase in the price level are a myriad of changes in relative prices. Some prices have gone up faster than this average, some have gone up more slowly, some may have even decreased. The basic premise of macroeconomics is that we can say a great deal about the aggregates without inquiring into the smaller details.

THE LABOR MARKET

By assumption, in the basic competitive model, all markets clear. In the labor market, the fact that the demand for labor equals the supply implies that there is full employment. No worker who wishes to get a job (for which she is qualified) at the going market wage will fail to get one. Adjustments in wages ensure that this will occur. Of course, when economists say that there is full employment of the labor force—that the demand for labor is equal to the supply—there is still a small amount of unemployment. As we learned in Chapter 24, there is always some frictional unemployment in modern economies, as workers in transition between jobs, or just entering the labor force search for new positions. Thus, full employment should not be equated with an unemployment rate of zero.

The assumption of zero unemployment, while it is clearly unrealistic, is a useful simplification, particularly for studying changes in the economy in periods in which unemployment is relatively low, or for comparing the economy at different periods in which unemployment was low, such as 1989 and 1995.

In the aggregate labor market, the relationship between wages (w) and the price level (P) is very important. Economists distinguish between real and nominal wages. The real wage is the nominal wage adjusted for increases in the price level. Dividing the nominal wage by the price level gives us the real wage, or w/P. This means that if wages and the price level change together, the real wage will remain the same. For example, suppose that nominal wages and the price level both increase by 2 percent during the course of a year. The real wage would be exactly the same as it was at the beginning of the year, because the increase in the nominal wage would be offset by a proportional increase in prices. Alternatively, if the price level is held constant, changes in the nominal wage represent changes in the real wage, and if the nominal wage is held constant while the price level increases (or decreases), the real wage will fall (or rise).

Figure 25.1 shows the aggregate labor market, with the real wage (w/P) on the vertical axis, the quantity of labor (L) on the horizontal axis, and the aggregate demand and supply curves for labor. With a given set of machines and technology, the aggregate demand for labor depends on the wages firms must pay, the prices firms receive for the goods they produce, and the prices they have to pay for other inputs, including raw materials and machines. Holding the prices of goods and inputs constant, the aggregate demand curve traces out the quantity of labor demanded by firms at different wages. At lower wages, the quantity of labor demanded is greater. There are two reasons for this. First, as wages fall relative to the cost of machines, it pays firms to substitute workers for machines. Second, as the wage falls, labor becomes relatively less expensive compared with the price of the goods it produces (so at the old level of employment, the value of the marginal product of the last unit of labor hired would exceed the wage), and again employers will hire more workers.

Figure 25.1 EQUILIBRIUM IN THE LABOR MARKET

Equilibrium in the labor market is at the intersection of the aggregate demand and supply curves for labor. If the real wage is above w_1/P where demand equals supply, there will be unemployment, putting pressure on wages to fall as workers compete to offer their services. Below w_1/P there will be excess demand for labor, which will put pressure on wages to rise.

Thus, the demand curve for labor slopes down, as shown in the diagram.

The figure also shows an aggregate labor supply curve. To simplify matters, we assume that labor supply is inelastic.[1] That is, individuals are either in the labor force, working a full (forty-hour) work week, or they are not. They do not enter and exit the market as wages go up and down, nor do they reduce or increase the hours they work in response to such changes. One advantage of making the assumption that the hours worked per week is fixed is that we can put *either* the number of hours worked (per week) or the number of workers hired on the horizontal axis of the figure. The demand and supply of labor hours (per week) is simply forty times the demand and supply of workers.

Basic supply and demand analysis implies that market equilibrium should occur at the intersection of the demand and supply curves, point E. The reason for this is simple: if the wage happens to be above the equilibrium wage w_1/P, say at w_2/P, the demand for labor will be L_2, much less than the supply, L_1. There will be an excess supply of workers. Those without jobs, who want jobs, will offer to work for less than the going wage, bidding down the wages of those already working. The process of competition will lead to lower wages, until eventually demand again equals supply. Likewise, if the wage is lower than w_1/P, say at w_3/P, firms in the economy will demand more labor than is supplied. Competing with one another for scarce labor services, they will bid the wage up to w_1/P.

[1] Recall the definition of elasticity from Chapter 5: the percentage change in quantity divided by the percentage change in price. Thus, an inelastic labor supply means that a 1 percent increase in wages results in a small percentage increase in supply. A perfectly inelastic labor supply curve is vertical: that means the labor supply does not change at all when wages increase.

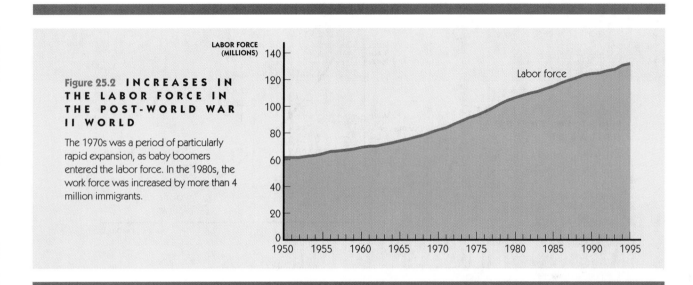

Figure 25.2 INCREASES IN THE LABOR FORCE IN THE POST-WORLD WAR II WORLD

The 1970s was a period of particularly rapid expansion, as baby boomers entered the labor force. In the 1980s, the work force was increased by more than 4 million immigrants.

SHIFTS IN THE DEMAND AND SUPPLY OF LABOR

The basic competitive model makes clear predictions of the consequences of shifts in the demand and supply of labor. Consider first shifts in the supply curve of labor. This can occur because there are more young people reaching working age than there are old people retiring, or because of new immigrants, or because of social changes which lead more women to join the labor force. Figure 25.2 shows the increase in the labor force over the last forty-five years. It shows, in particular, a rapid expansion in the 1970s. The consequences of such a large shift in the labor supply curve are depicted in Figure 25.3. The supply curve (here depicted as vertical) shifts to the right. The equilibrium real wage falls. The economy responds to the lower wages by creating more jobs. The wages (the price of labor) indicate to firms that labor is less scarce, in a sense, than it was before, and so firms should economize less in the use of labor.

Consider now the effects of a shift in the demand curve for labor. First consider the case of a decrease in investment leading to a reduction in the quantity of machines available for use by workers. This reduces the productivity of workers, thereby shifting the demand curve for labor to the left, as depicted in panel A of Figure 25.4. For a given real wage, firms want to hire fewer workers than before.

Panel B depicts the effects of technological progress on the demand for labor. Workers are more productive and the labor demand curve shifts to the right.

These examples suggest that increases in investment and improvements in technology imply an increase in the demand for labor represented by a

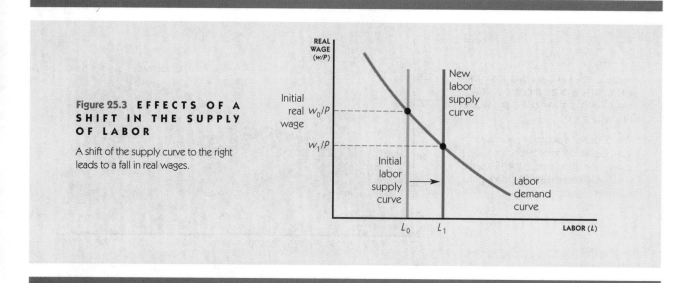

Figure 25.3 EFFECTS OF A SHIFT IN THE SUPPLY OF LABOR

A shift of the supply curve to the right leads to a fall in real wages.

rightward shift in the labor demand curve. Although this is generally true, it may be the case that the demand for some types of labor, especially unskilled labor, actually declines with investment in new machines and technology, while the demand for skilled workers may increase. In this case, the labor market is really made up of two markets: that of skilled and that of unskilled workers. An increase in investment or technology may increase the demand

Figure 25.4 EFFECTS OF CHANGES IN INVESTMENT AND TECHNOLOGY

New investment or technological change shifts the demand curve for labor. Panel A shows a reduction in investment. Workers have fewer machines to work with, and the demand curve for labor shifts to the left, lowering real wages. Panel B shows an improvement in technology. The demand curve shifts to the right, as workers' marginal productivity increases, leading to higher real wages.

for skilled workers as in panel B, but decrease the demand for unskilled workers as in panel A. This represents one of the cases where merely studying the market for all labor is not sufficient to understand an interesting macroeconomic phenomenon—the increase in wage inequality based on skill levels.

LABOR MARKET EQUILIBRIUM

Real wages adjust to equate labor demand with labor supply.

A rightward shift in labor supply lowers the real wage, inducing firms to create additional jobs equal to the increased labor supply.

Technological change or new investment induces changes in the real wage, so that all workers remain fully employed. The real wage adjusts to equate supply and demand.

THE PRODUCT MARKET

Just as the real wage adjusts to ensure that the demand for labor equals the supply, so too—in our basic competitive model—prices adjust to ensure that the demand for goods equals the supply.

AGGREGATE SUPPLY

At any point in time, the economy has a certain capital stock, a set of machines and buildings that, together with labor and materials, produces output. If more workers are hired, output increases. The relationship between employment and output is called the **short-run production function,** depicted in Figure 25.5. There are diminishing returns. As more workers are hired, output goes up, but at a diminishing rate. The most productive machines are used first; if more labor is put to work, it is assigned to older and less productive machines.

We have been assuming that there is a fixed supply of labor. With this fixed supply of labor, the economy has a certain productive capacity, also referred to as the potential GDP or the **full-employment level of output.** This level of output is also referred to as the **aggregate supply.** It represents the amount of goods that firms would be willing to supply, given their plant and equipment, assuming wages and prices are flexible, and adjust so that everyone is fully employed.

Figure 25.5 SHORT-RUN PRODUCTION FUNCTION

In the short run, with given technology and a given set of plant and equipment, as more labor is employed, output increases, but with diminishing returns. (Each successive increase in input results in smaller increases in output.) L_f is the full-employment level of employment, so Y_f is the full-employment level of output. An increase in the labor supply generates a movement along the short-run production function; the full-employment level of output will increase to y_f'.

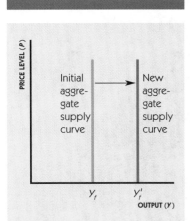

Figure 25.6 AGGREGATE SUPPLY CURVE

If real wages adjust to clear the market, the aggregate supply curve is vertical. If the labor force grows, the aggregate supply curve shifts to the right.

Figure 25.7 AGGREGATE DEMAND CURVE

The aggregate demand curve is downward sloping. Equilibrium in the product market occurs at the intersection of the aggregate demand and supply curves.

Output can occasionally exceed capacity: for short spurts, such as during wars, output can be increased further, by deferring maintenance, running machines three shifts, and so forth.

If the labor supply increases, even with a fixed stock of machines, the capacity of the economy increases. This is a movement along the short-run production function. Figure 25.5 shows that if employment increases from L_f to L_f', then output increases from Y_f to Y_f'.

The **aggregate supply curve** gives the level of aggregate supply at each price level. Note that if real wages adjust to clear the labor market, then the level of aggregate supply does not depend at all on price. Thus, Figure 25.6 depicts the aggregate supply curve (sometimes referred to as the **long-run aggregate supply curve,** since it is based on the long-run assumption that labor markets clear) as vertical. We have seen that an increase in the labor force leads to a shift in the aggregate supply curve to the right, as depicted.[2]

AGGREGATE DEMAND AND EQUILIBRIUM OUTPUT

Aggregate demand is the sum total of the goods and services demanded by all the households and firms in the economy and by government—plus foreigners wishing to buy the country's goods and services. In Chapter 24, we divided aggregate output into four components: consumption, investment, government expenditures, and (net) exports. Analyses of aggregate demand thus focus on identifying the demand for each of these components.

The **aggregate demand curve** gives the quantity of goods and services demanded at each price level, and has the shape of the demand curves encountered earlier in the book. In particular, it is downward sloping, as depicted in Figure 25.7. The reason for this can be seen by focusing on consumption, which accounts for 70 percent of aggregate demand. Households' demand for real consumption (that is, consumption, taking into account changes in the price level) depends on their real wealth. When individuals are wealthier, they purchase more goods. An important part of individuals' wealth is their money and other financial assets denominated in dollars, for instance, government savings bonds promising to pay $100 in ten years. When the price level increases, the real value of these assets decreases. Households' real wealth thus decreases and hence their consumption decreases. Higher price levels will be associated with lower levels of consumption and lower levels of aggregate demand, as depicted in the figure.[3]

The equilibrium, the intersection of the aggregate demand and supply curves, determines the price level and output. Since we know that, in equilibrium, demand equals supply, and supply is fixed at Y_f, equilibrium output equals Y_f.

---

[2]Later, we will see how technological change and investment shift the short-run production function out, and even with a fixed labor supply, also shift the aggregate supply curve to the right.

[3]Later, we will see that there are other reasons why the aggregate demand curve may have the shape depicted.

PRODUCT MARKET EQUILIBRIUM

In equilibrium, output is equal to the full-employment level of output, that is, the output which can be generated by the available labor force working with the given set of plant and equipment.

Increases in the labor supply (rightward shifts in the labor supply curve), increases in the stock of plant and equipment as a result of net investment, and technological change all increase the full-employment level of output.

THE CAPITAL MARKET

We turn now to the capital market. Equilibrium in the capital market requires that savings (the supply of funds) equal investment (the demand for funds).

SAVINGS

The most important determinants of savings are income and interest rates. Each year, families have to decide how much of their income they spend on current consumption, and how much they save for future consumption, for retirement, for emergencies, to pay for their children's college education, or to buy a new car or a new home. On average, families with higher incomes spend more and save more. Of course, what is relevant is how much income households have to spend; this is called their **disposable income**—their income after taxes. Thus, when the government increases taxes, it reduces disposable income, and when disposable income is reduced, household savings will be reduced.

In this chapter, we assume that the stock of plant and equipment as well as the labor supply are given. With wages and prices adjusting to ensure that the labor market clears, aggregate output is fixed. We now make use of an important result from Chapter 24: we saw there that national income equals aggregate output. The money that is used to purchase goods has to go into somebody's pockets, and thus becomes income. If aggregate output is given, so is aggregate income. Here, we also assume that taxes are fixed, so that with aggregate income given, so is aggregate disposable income.

With taxes fixed, our focus is on the interest rate, which is the return on savings. Figure 25.8 shows two different possibilities. In panel A, savings increase

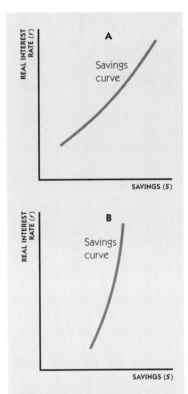

Figure 25.8 SAVINGS AND THE REAL INTEREST RATE

Different savings curves are shown in panels A and B. In panel A, savings increase with the interest rate. In panel B, savings are only slightly sensitive to the interest rate, a relationship which is supported by empirical evidence.

significantly with the interest rate, while in panel B, savings respond only slightly to changes in the interest rate. Empirical studies suggest that savings are only slightly sensitive to interest rates, that is, the savings curve is almost vertical—it looks more like panel B than panel A. For simplicity, in the rest of the chapter we depict the savings curve as completely inelastic—that is, as a vertical straight line.

But doesn't a higher interest rate provide greater incentives to save? Yes, but at higher interest rates, individuals who save are better off, and as a result, consume more, and save less. This is the income effect, in contrast to the incentive or substitution effect. The two effects pull in opposite directions, and essentially offset each other. That is why savings are not very sensitive to the interest rate.

Of course, when individuals look at the return to savings, they take into account inflation—the fact that a dollar in the future may buy less than a dollar today. Thus the relevant interest rate for savings is the *real* interest rate, which is just the nominal interest rate minus the rate of inflation. If the nominal interest rate is 10 percent, and the rate of inflation is 4 percent, then the real interest rate is 6 percent. As in the macroeconomic analysis of the labor and product markets, where we ignore differences between the variety of wages and prices, here we ignore the differences between the various interest rates at play in the economy. We simply refer to the interest rate in general.

INVESTMENT

Economists use the word investment in two different ways. Households think of the stocks and bonds they buy as investments—**financial investments.** These financial investments provide the funds for firms to buy capital goods—machines and buildings. The purchases of new machines and buildings represent firms' investments, referred to as **capital goods investments.** In macroeconomics, when we refer to investments, it is to capital, not financial, investments.

Firms invest in order to increase their capacity to produce, enabling them to produce more goods. They expect returns from the sale of these extra goods to cover the cost of additional workers and raw materials required to increase production, as well as the cost of the funds to finance the investment, leaving them with a profit.

There are thus two key determinants of investment: firms' expectations concerning the future, which we will assume for now to be fixed, and the interest rate. Many firms borrow to finance their investment. The cost of these funds—what they have to pay the bank for using its funds—is the interest rate. Since a firm pays back a debt with dollars that have less purchasing power due to inflation, the relevant cost of funds is the real interest rate.

The higher the interest rate, the fewer investment projects are profitable—that is, the fewer the projects which, after paying the bank its interest, will yield a return to the investor sufficient to compensate him for the risks he undertakes. Even if the firm is flush with cash, the interest rate matters. The interest rate then becomes the opportunity cost of the firm's money, what it could have obtained if, instead of making the investment, it had simply decided to lend the money to the government or some other firm.

The **investment function** gives the level of (real) investment at each value of the real interest rate. The investment function slopes downward to the right: investment increases as the real interest rate decreases. This is depicted in Figure 25.9, which shows the real interest rate on the vertical axis and the real investment level on the horizontal axis.

There is another way of seeing why the interest rate matters: while the firm puts out money today to buy machines, the returns it receives, in increased profits, do not occur until the future. A dollar received in the future is not worth as much as a dollar today, because of the time value of money: a dollar today could have been put in the bank and earned interest; if the interest rate is 7 percent, in ten years, the dollar will have doubled to $2. We thus say that the **present discounted value** of $2 ten years from now is a dollar. (The present discounted value of a dollar in the future is what someone would be willing to pay today for that dollar.) An increase in the interest rate reduces the present discounted value of future dollars. At a 14 percent interest rate, a dollar put in the bank today has doubled to $2 in five years and quadrupled to $4 in ten years. Thus, a dollar in ten years is worth only a quarter, while at 7 percent it is worth fifty cents. An investment is undertaken if the present discounted value of (expected) profits is more than the cost; with an increase in the interest rate, fewer investments meet this criterion. The aggregate level of investment thus decreases.

Figure 25.9 THE INVESTMENT FUNCTION

The investment function slopes downward to the right, tracing out the levels of real investment at different real interest rates. As the interest rate falls, investment increases.

EQUILIBRIUM IN THE CAPITAL MARKET

The equilibrium real interest rate is the rate at which savings equal investment, depicted in Figure 25.10. Panels A and B show the effect of an increased demand for investment at each real interest rate. In panel A, both the equilibrium real interest rate and the equilibrium level of savings and investment are increased, while in panel B, only the equilibrium real interest rate is changed.

CAPITAL MARKET EQUILIBRIUM

In equilibrium, savings equal investment.

Increases in savings (shifts to the right in the savings curve) lead to lower real interest rates and higher levels of investment.

Shifts to the right in the investment schedule lead to higher real interest rates, but unchanged or higher levels of investment.

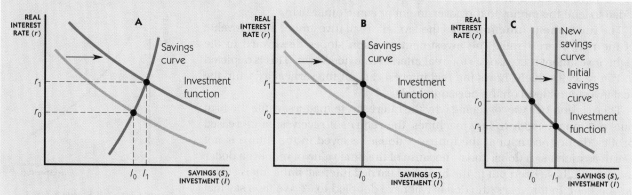

Figure 25.10 EQUILIBRIUM IN THE CAPITAL MARKET

Equilibrium requires the demand for funds (investment) equal the supply (savings). The level of desired investment decreases as the real interest rate increases.

We assume the economy is at full employment. In panel A, savings increase slightly with increases in the real interest rate. In panels B and C, savings are not interest sensitive, so the savings curve is a vertical straight line. The equilibrium level of investment is simply equal to the full employment level of savings.

A shift in the investment function—so that at every real interest rate the demand for investment is increased—is depicted in panels A and B. In panel A, investment is increased from I_0 to I_1, while in panel B, with inelastic savings, the only effect is to increase the real interest rate from r_0 to r_1, leaving investment (and savings) unchanged. Panel C shows a rightward shift in the savings curve. The level of savings increases at each real interest rate, resulting in a decrease of the real interest rate from r_0 to r_1, and an increase in investment from I_0 to I_1.

Because savings are not sensitive to the real interest rate, and savings must equal investment, investment remains unchanged. By contrast, a rightward shift in the savings curve, so that at every real interest rate savings increase, results in a reduction in the real interest rate and an increase in investment (panel C). Because the savings curve is almost vertical, the shift in the savings curve translates to a corresponding change in investment.

THE GENERAL EQUILIBRIUM

We can now describe the general equilibrium of the economy, the real wages, price level, and interest rate at which the labor, product, and capital markets all clear:

The real wage adjusts to ensure the demand for labor equals the supply. This determines the equilibrium real wage. The price level adjusts to ensure that aggregate demand equals aggregate supply, which in turn is equal to the full-employment level of output. Thus, equilibrium output is equal to potential GDP, the output which the labor supply, working with the available capital

Figure 25.11 EFFECTS OF INTRODUCING PERSONAL COMPUTERS INTO THE ECONOMY

Panel A depicts the labor market. Personal computers increase the marginal product of workers, resulting in a rightward shift of the labor demand curve and an increase in the equilibrium real wage from w_0 to w_1. Panel B depicts the product market. With the increased productivity of workers, the aggregate supply curve shifts to the right. Output increases from Y_0 to Y_1. If aggregate demand increases (due to an increase in investment and an increase in consumption from higher incomes) the aggregate demand curve will shift to the right. If at P_0 the increase in aggregate demand is the same as the increase in aggregate supply, the price level will remain at P_0. Panel C depicts the capital market. Investment increases as firms purchase computers, and savings increase as a result of increased income. Both the investment and savings curves shift to the right. There may be no net effect on the interest rate (r_0), as shown here.

stock, can produce. Finally, the real interest rate adjusts to ensure that, at this full-employment level of output, savings are equal to investment.[4]

USING THE GENERAL EQUILIBRIUM MODEL

The general equilibrium model is useful because it allows us to understand the effects of various changes in the economy—from the market in which these changes originate to all the other markets in the economy.

Consider the effect of the introduction of personal computers to the economy. The marginal product of workers increases, causing a shift in the demand curve for labor to the right. The equilibrium real wage increases as shown in Figure 25.11, panel A.

[4]We can, in fact, show that if savings are equal to investment at the full-employment level of output, then aggregate demand equals aggregate supply at that level of output.

In our simplified model with no government and no foreign trade, there are two sources of aggregate demand, investment and consumption:

$Y^d = C + I.$

Since national output *always* equals national income, full-employment output, Y_f, equals full-employment income, and full-employment incomes are either saved or consumed:

$Y_f = C + S$ or $S = Y_f - C.$

Given the greater productivity of workers and the fixed labor supply, full-employment output increases as shown by a rightward shift in the aggregate supply curve (panel B). Aggregate demand may rise due to an increase in investment (at every value of the real interest rate) as firms take advantage of the available profit opportunities opened up by the new computer technology. At the same time, the increase in income leads to increases in consumption and in savings at each interest rate. If aggregate demand rises by the same amount as aggregate supply, the price level is unchanged. Of course, the shift in the aggregate demand curve at P_0 may be greater or less than the increase in aggregate supply, so the price level might either increase or decrease.

The increased investment and savings at each interest rate are represented by a rightward shift in both the investment and savings functions (panel C). In equilibrium the real interest rate may rise, fall, or stay the same (though panel C depicts a stable interest rate).

We have focused here on the current effects of these changes, but there are important future effects. In the future, there will be more plant and equipment. The economy's future capacity will increase. Thus, not only are all markets linked today, but markets today are linked with markets in the future.

EXTENDING THE BASIC FULL-EMPLOYMENT MODEL

Macroeconomics is concerned with policy: what are the impacts, for instance, of increasing government expenditure or increasing the money supply. The basic full-employment aggregate model can incorporate government expenditures, money, and international trade, and thus be used to address these policy questions.

GOVERNMENT

Introducing government into the analysis affects both the product market and the capital market. In the product market, government expenditures add to aggregate demand, but taxes reduce disposable income and thus subtract from aggregate demand. In the capital market, an increase in taxes to fund

---

Thus, when desired investment (as reflected in the investment schedule) equals full-employment savings,

$I = S^d,$

where we use the superscript to remind us that this is the desired level of savings, then from the second equation,

$I = Y_f - C.$

Substituting the fourth equation back into the first equation gives

$Y^d = C + I = C + Y_f - C = Y_f;$

thus, aggregate demand equals full-employment output, the aggregate supply. There is equilibrium in the product market.

increased government expenditures affects savings, investment, and the interest rate. In Figure 25.12, the reduction in disposable income from taxes shifts the savings curve to the left, reducing equilibrium savings, from S_0 to S_1. With an unchanged investment schedule, the equilibrium interest rate rises and the equilibrium investment level falls.

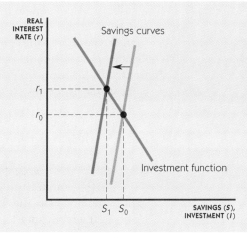

Figure 25.12 GOVERNMENT EFFECTS ON THE CAPITAL MARKET

Government taxes reduce disposable income and savings, resulting in a leftward shift of the savings curve from S_0 to S_1. The equilibrium interest rate rises from r_0 to r_1, and the investment level falls.

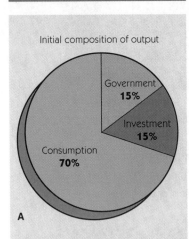

Initial composition of output

Government
15%

Investment
15%

Consumption
70%

A

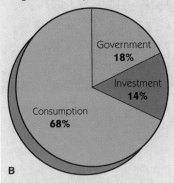

Composition of output after increase
in government expenditure and taxes

Government
18%

Investment
14%

Consumption
68%

B

Figure 25.13 EFFECT OF AN EQUAL INCREASE IN GOVERNMENT EXPENDITURES AND TAXES ON THE COMPOSITION OF OUTPUT

An increase in government expenditure financed by an increase in taxes leads to a decrease in consumption and investment. Government expenditure is said to crowd out private expenditure.

Government also affects the composition of output. Figure 25.13 shows how an increase in government expenditure matched with an increase in taxes changes the composition of output. The total size of the pie is unchanged; we assume that the economy remains at full employment. Thus, the effect of government is simply to change how the pie is divided. Investment and consumption are both lowered—or **crowded out**—to make room for increased government expenditures. Even if government increases taxes by an amount to pay fully for the increased expenditure—in our example, by 3 percent of GDP—consumption is reduced by less, as individuals adjust in part by reducing savings.

THE MONEY SUPPLY

Government may also play a role in the economy by changing the amount of money in circulation. This is done through monetary policy, a subject we will consider later in the book. For now, it is important to understand the consequences of changes in the money supply for the full-employment model.

By and large, economists agree that in a full-employment economy, money affects the price level, but little else. In particular, it does not affect the quantity of goods produced or the number of workers employed. We can use an imaginative example to understand the point. Suppose that instantaneously, the entire supply of money in the economy was increased by a multiple of ten. In effect, we have tacked a zero onto the money supply. Dollar bills are now worth $10; five-dollar bills are now worth $50; ten-dollar bills are now worth $100; your checking account of $250 is now worth $2,500, and so on. Stores, acting perfectly efficiently, and knowing that the money supply has multiplied by ten, would increase their prices tenfold. Thus, the actual amount of goods and services produced and consumed would be the same; there would be no real effect. The only difference would be the numbers on the bills, bank statements, and price tags.

The lesson is more general: an increase in the supply of money accompanied by a proportionate increase in the price level has no real effects on the economy. When changing the money supply has no real effects we say that money is *neutral*. If the economy is at full employment and prices are perfectly flexible, prices will increase proportionally with the money supply. Thus, the **neutrality of money** is a basic property of the full-employment model. We can see this by tracing through the effects of an increase in the money supply in the product, labor, and capital markets, as shown in Figure 25.14.

Panel A of Figure 25.14 shows the aggregate supply and aggregate demand curves. An increase in the money supply represents an increase in money balances held by the public, so private wealth increases. This results in a rightward shift of the aggregate demand curve. The price level increases from P_0 to P_1, but the equilibrium level of output remains at Y_0.

In panel B we see the aggregate supply and aggregate demand curves for labor. In the labor market, the increase in the price level will be matched by an increase in the nominal wage, from w_0 to w_1, so that the real wage remains at its original level, $w_0/P_0 = w_1/P_1$. At this real wage, the demand for labor continues to equal its supply. Thus the effect on the labor market of an increase in

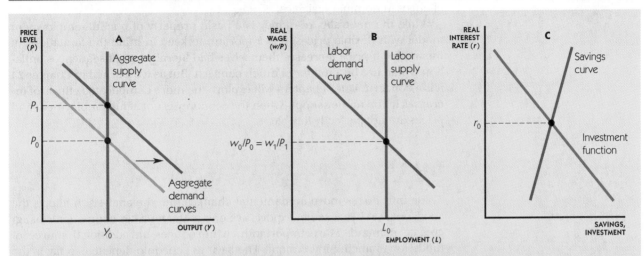

Figure 25.14 EFFECTS OF AN INCREASE IN THE MONEY SUPPLY

Panel A shows the product market. The increase in the money supply results in a rightward shift of the aggregate demand curve. The price level rises from P_0 to P_1, and the equilibrium level of output remains at Y_0. Panel B shows the labor market. The nominal wage (w) increases in proportion to the increase in the price level, so that the real wage is unaffected. Panel C shows the capital market. The savings and investment curves giving the *real* levels of those variables remain unchanged. The real interest rate, r_0, is unaffected.

the price level is simply a proportionate increase in the nominal wage. There are no real effects—the equilibrium real wage and the equilibrium level of employment L_0 are not affected.

In the capital market, real savings and investment both depend on the real interest rate, which is not affected by the increase in the price level. Accordingly, in panel C, neither the savings curve nor the investment function shifts. At each real interest rate, *nominal* savings and investment would increase by an amount exactly proportional to the increase in the money supply. Why? Because households and firms must increase the dollar amount of savings and investment in order to maintain the value of savings and investment relative to the higher price level. But panel C shows the levels of *real* savings and investment at each real interest rate. The equilibrium real interest rate, r_0, remains the same. The overall result once again displays the neutrality of money because there are no real effects in the capital market. Only the *nominal* levels of savings and investment change in proportion to the change in the price level.

The neutrality of money highlights the important distinction economists make between real and nominal phenomena. As we have seen here and in earlier chapters, in referring to nominal variables, such as nominal GDP and nominal wages, we mean the current money value of those variables, that is, the value *without* adjustments for changes in the price level. As this example shows, our full-employment model with flexible prices makes a perfect distinction between real and nominal phenomena. Relationships between real variables—which are the focus of the model—are completely independent of changes in nominal variables.

While the neutrality of money is a basic property of our full-employment model with flexible prices, it is important to keep in mind the limitations of the model. If price increases themselves had literally no consequences, inflation would not be a matter of much concern. But as we learned in Chapter 24 it is a concern. Later chapters will explore the more complicated effects of increases in the money supply when the economy is not at full employment and prices are not perfectly flexible.

TRADE

Trade introduces more fundamental changes into the analysis. It affects the goods market because net exports are one of the four key components of aggregate demand. More importantly, it introduces an additional source of funds for financing investment. The savings schedule depicted so far is the domestic source of funds. If investment, the demand for funds, exceeds domestic savings, firms can borrow abroad.

We say that an economy which trades with other countries and borrows from and lends to other countries is an **open economy.** A small open economy like Switzerland faces an essentially horizontal supply curve of funds at a given real interest rate. If Switzerland pays a slightly higher interest rate than that paid in other countries, those with capital divert their funds to Switzerland. If Switzerland pays slightly less than the interest rate available in other countries (adjusted, of course, for risk) it can obtain no capital. Those who have capital in Switzerland can take their funds and invest them abroad. For a small country, the interest rate is determined by the international capital market. Effectively, such a country takes the interest rate as fixed. This is shown in Figure 25.15, where the interest rate is fixed at r^*. A fixed interest rate, in turn, means that the level of investment is fixed, at I^* in Figure 25.15. A short-

Figure 25.15 SUPPLY OF SAVINGS IN A SMALL OPEN ECONOMY

In a small open economy, the real interest rate, r^*, is determined by the international capital market. That in turn determines the level of investment, I^*. In the figure, savings are assumed to be fixed, unaffected by the interest rate. If domestic savings equal S_0, the shortfall, B_0, is made up by borrowing from abroad. A reduction in savings to S_1 leads to increased borrowing, B_1, but leaves investment unchanged.

POLICY PERSPECTIVE: A GLOBAL CAPITAL SHORTAGE?

No sooner had the world economy begun showing signs of recovery from the recession of the early 1990s than the newspapers sounded a new alarm: a global capital shortage.

Of course, economists are reluctant to refer to shortages, because they recognize that prices (here interest rates) adjust to demand and supply. What was really worrying people was the possibility that the world's savings curve was shifting left and the world's investment curve was shifting right —and the combination was driving up real interest rates. The reason for the anxiety was not hard to see. In the space of a year, real interest rates rose from 1 percent to 4 percent, far higher than the average real interest rates that had prevailed over the first nine decades of the century (between .5 percent and 1.5 percent).

And several factors suggested that the situation might not be simply a temporary aberration. First, national savings rates in Europe, the United States, and Japan were all down significantly from what they had been a decade or so earlier—on average by perhaps 4 percent of GDP. Second, Eastern Europe and Russia represented a vast area of potential investment that was at last opening up to the world's capital market. And the reforms required to make these economies more hospitable to foreign investment were occurring, albeit at a slower pace than had been anticipated. Third, many less developed countries that had previously discouraged foreign investment were now actively seeking it. While these emerging markets remained small on the scale of the world capital market, they represented an enormous potential increase in demand. Some of the fastest-growing countries, like Singapore and China, have managed to sustain savings rates roughly commensurate with their high investment rates (exceeding 25 percent of GDP). But in South Asia and Latin America, investment demand could easily exceed savings by a substantial amount.

It is too soon to tell whether the higher real

interest rates are to remain a feature of the world's capital market in coming decades. If so, American firms will have to pay higher real interest rates. Higher real interest rates in turn will lead to lower levels of investment, unless a rightward shift of the investment curve offsets the higher real interest rates. (Such a shift of the investment curve could arise if technological change and new business practices sufficiently increased the returns to new investment.)

fall (B_0) between the level of savings and that level of investment is funded by borrowing from abroad. A reduction in the amount of savings increases the amount of foreign borrowing (B_1), but leaves investment unaffected.

This result contrasts markedly with our earlier result for a **closed economy,** one in which there was no foreign borrowing or lending. There, we noted that lower savings (a shift to the left in the savings curve) result in less investment. There is a similar contrast in the effect of an increase in government expenditure matched by an increase in taxes. In a closed economy, increased taxes reduce household and thus national savings, and hence, reduce investment. In an open economy, investment is unchanged.

Though investment is unaffected, the increased foreign borrowing has consequences for the future. In the future, interest will have to be paid to foreigners on this debt, and this will lower future standards of living, much as the lower level of investment would have. These effects will be discussed at greater length in the next chapter.

THE U.S. ECONOMY

The United States is an open economy. But it is such a large part of the world scene, that—unlike in the case of a small country like Switzerland—changes in the U.S. savings function affect the international interest rate, with global ramifications. The U.S. economy represents about one-quarter of world output and one-fifth of world savings. Thus, a shift to the left in the U.S. savings function (so less is saved at each interest rate) raises world real interest rates and leads to less investment in the United States. Because the full impact is spread throughout the world, the effect on U.S. investment is far less than it would be if the United States were a closed economy.

The discussion so far has assumed that the world's capital markets are fully integrated. However, the world capital market is far from fully integrated. Individuals know more about what is going on in their own country than what is going on abroad. American investors require slightly higher return on foreign investments to compensate them for this increased risk. In recent years, with the greater flow of information, the magnitude of this risk premium—the extra return they must earn—has decreased. But it is still the case that capital does not flow perfectly freely, so that interest rates are not equalized and a decrease in U.S. savings is not made up fully by an increased flow of capital from abroad.

NAFTA, the North American Free Trade Agreement, eliminated all trade barriers in North America. During the national discussion leading up to the ratification of NAFTA, Vice President Al Gore debated Ross Perot, who opposed the agreement. One of Perot's most notable lines referred to "a giant sucking sound," as Mexico attracted investment and jobs out of the United States. He conveyed an image of Mexico attracting thousands of factories with its cheap labor, leaving hundreds of thousands of Americans without jobs. His predictions proved wrong, partly because the slight reduction in tariffs has negligible effects. Moreover, labor-intensive firms (that is, firms that required a lot of unskilled labor) were already in the process of shifting operations to abroad, for instance to Malaysia, China, and Korea; NAFTA might induce some of these firms to move to Mexico, but was unlikely to have much effect on the overall flow.

But Perot was correct in emphasizing an important aspect of NAFTA: it was not only a trade agreement, but also an investment agreement. Increasingly, countries have recognized the importance not only of free trade, but also of open capital markets, where capital can flow to wherever returns are highest. By allowing the free flow of capital, world GDP is increased. If the return to investment in one country is 8 percent and in another it is 24 percent, a billion dollars invested in the second country yields an extra $160 million a year. Moreover, trade and investment flows are often interlinked. American firms investing, say, in Asia often turn to other firms in the United States to supply parts and components.

International investment agreements focus on two issues. The first is called national treatment. American firms investing abroad should not be dis-criminated against; they should be given exactly the same treatment that the country's own firms receive. The second is called reciprocity. Foreign governments should extend to our firms the same treatment that we extend to theirs. While there is general agreement about the first principle, the second is more contentious. For instance, formerly, Japan did not allow American banks to open up branches in certain rural areas; and Japan requires rigorous testing of automobile parts from sources other than the original car manufacturer before they can be used by repair shops. National treatment says that these practices are permissible, so long as Japanese firms are subjected to the same requirements. Similarly, the United States used to have a law forbidding banks from opening up branches in more than one state. Again, under national treatment, such restrictions would be permissible, if applied uniformly. Often, however, national treatment can still result in effective discrimination. Almost all cars sold in Japan are Japanese, so that the Japanese manufacturers can supply parts for repair shops; but the testing process is so long that American parts firms are effectively precluded from the market. The greater openness of the U.S. economy, including the relative absence of regulations, means that foreign firms find it easier to enter the United States than American firms find it to open shop abroad. Reciprocity is required to restore a level playing field.

However, less developed countries often argue persuasively that the kinds of regulations that are appropriate for more developed countries would not be appropriate for them. International agreements working towards harmonization of regulations is the way that principles of national treatment and reciprocity can be reconciled.

How much does U.S. investment decrease as a result of a shift to the left of the U.S. savings curve by, say, $1 billion? Early estimates, for the decades immediately following World War II, suggested that U.S. investment would decrease by $800 million to $1 billion—by almost the full amount of the change in savings. Current estimates indicate that the effect would be much smaller, somewhere between $350 and $500 million.

OPEN ECONOMY INVESTMENT

The United States is a large open economy. Reductions in the U.S. savings rate are reflected in increases in the real interest rate internationally (and therefore in the United States), and reduced levels of investment. But the effects on investment in the United States are smaller than would be the case if the economy were closed.

CONSENSUS IN MACROECONOMICS

Macroeconomic issues are often front and center in newspapers and nightly newscasts on television. There is good reason for this. As we learned in Chapter 24, the macroeconomic problems of unemployment, slow growth, and inflation have substantial, widespread consequences. With modest productivity gains, the concern is with slow economic growth; when the unemployment rate increases, the focus is on impending recession; when the consumer price index goes up faster, attention shifts to inflation. These problems, and the ways to address them, are often hotly debated, giving rise to controversy. In this context, the views of economists often appear to be contradictory, and the old saw about how any two economists will give you three opinions may seem true. But in fact, there is remarkable consensus among economists about basic macroeconomic principles. In this chapter we have encountered our eleventh and twelfth points of consensus:

11 Effects of Government Expenditures at Full Employment

When the economy is at full employment, and the economy is closed, increases in government expenditures must come at the expense of private consumption and/or investment. Even when matched with increases in taxes, such increases crowd out private investment, since the increased taxes will normally lead to a reduction in savings. If the economy is open, government expenditures lead to increased foreign borrowing, but in the United States, the increased borrowing does not fully offset the reduced savings, so investment is decreased.

12 Neutrality of Money

> *At full employment, an increase in the money supply only leads to a proportionate increase in prices and wages, with no real consequences.*

LOOKING FORWARD

This chapter has used the basic competitive model to analyze the full-employment macroeconomic equilibrium of the economy. We have seen how real wages adjust to ensure that the demand for labor always equals the supply, even in the face of changes in technology and new investments which might replace workers. We have seen how prices and interest rates adjust in the face of shifts in the demand for investment so that the economy continues to produce at its productive capacity and so that savings continue to equal investment at the full-employment level of output.

In the long run, wages, prices, and interest rates do adjust in much the manner described here. In the short run, however, they may not. If they did adjust to shifts instantaneously, then the full-employment model would not only be a good description of how the economy in the long run is able to create enough new jobs to match the increase in labor supply, but it would also be a good description of the economy in the short run. But wages and prices in particular may be sticky, that is, fail to adjust to the market-clearing levels. This has profound implications for how the economy behaves in the short run, as we shall see in the following two parts. First, however, we take a closer look at some of the important implications of our full-employment model.

REVIEW AND PRACTICE

SUMMARY

1. Macroeconomic equilibrium focuses on equilibrium levels of aggregates: employment, output, and investment. In a full-employment competitive equilibrium, each is determined by equating demand and supply. Full employment is attained as a result of flexible wages and prices.

2. The real wage equates the demand for labor with the supply of labor. Increases in the labor supply are reflected in lower real wages, which induce firms to create additional jobs to match the increased supply.

3. The full-employment level of output is that level of output which the economy can produce with its given stock of plant and equipment, when labor is fully employed. It will increase with increases in the labor supply.

4. The price level adjusts to equate aggregate demand to aggregate supply.

5. The real interest rate (which takes account of inflation) equates investment and savings. The desired level of investment decreases with increases in the real interest rate. Savings depend on disposable income and the real interest rate. With flexible wages and prices, labor is fully employed, so output is always at the full-employment level. Since aggregate output equals national income, if taxes are fixed, disposable income will be fixed. Hence, in a full-employment economy the interest rate is the main variable of concern in determining savings. Savings increase slightly with increases in the real interest rate.

6. In a closed economy, government expenditures, when paid for by increases in taxes, crowd out consumption and investment. In a small open economy, investment is unchanged and foreign borrowing increases. The United States is a large open economy—with effects somewhere between a closed economy and a small open economy.

7. Shifts to the left in the savings curve lead to reduced investment in a closed economy, and to increased foreign borrowing in a small open economy.

8. All the markets in the economy are interlinked. Changes in one market have effects on all other markets.

9. In a full-employment economy with perfectly flexible wages and prices, money is neutral: increases in the money supply are simply reflected in increases in prices.

KEY TERMS

short-run production function	aggregate demand curve	investment function
full-employment level of output	disposable income	present discounted value
aggregate supply curve	financial investments	crowding out
	capital goods investments	neutrality of money
		open economy
		closed economy

REVIEW QUESTIONS

1. How do competitive markets with flexible wages and prices ensure that labor is always fully employed? What induces firms to create just the right number of additional jobs to match an increase in the number of workers?

2. Describe the effects of shifts in the labor supply curve on equilibrium real wages and potential GDP (full-employment level of output).

3. What determines the economy's productive capacity or aggregate supply or potential GDP? How does aggregate supply increase when labor supply increases?

4. What is the aggregate demand curve? Why is it downward sloping? Why is the aggregate supply curve vertical? What determines the price level?

5. What is the investment schedule? Why does investment decrease when the real interest rate increases? What role do expectations play in investment?

6. What determines the level of savings? Explain why, if taxes are fixed, disposable income in a full-employment economy is fixed. Explain why savings may not be very sensitive to the real rate of interest.

7. How is the equilibrium rate of interest determined?

8. How do government expenditures matched by taxes affect the market equilibrium?

9. What difference does it make whether the economy is closed or open? Illustrate by examining the effects of an increase in government expenditure.

10. How does the U.S. economy differ from a closed economy? from a small open economy such as Switzerland?

PROBLEMS

1. In the text, we assumed that the labor supply did not depend on the real wage. Assume that at higher real wages, more individuals wish to work. Trace through how each of the steps in the analysis has to be changed. (Show the equilibrium in the labor market. What happens to real wages, employment, GDP, and savings if the labor supply curve shifts to the right?)

2. An increase in capital resulting from an increase in investment allows a given number of workers to produce more. Show the effect on the short-run production function and the full-employment level of output.

3. Firms hire workers up to the point where the real wage equals the marginal product of labor, the extra output that an extra worker produces. Explain why the slope of the short-run production function is the marginal product of labor. Explain why, with diminishing returns, an increase in the real wage leads to a lower level of demand for labor. Draw an example of a shift outward in the short-run production function, caused by technological change, which causes (at any real wage) the demand for labor to decrease; to increase.

4. Explain how income and substitution effects offset each other in the

supply curve of labor; in the supply curve for savings. Is it possible for an improvement in technology to lead to a lower real wage?

5. Trace through how the effects of a change in one market—such as an increase in the supply of labor—has effects on other markets. How was it possible for there to be a large increase in the labor supply, such as occurred during the 1970s and 1980s, and yet real wages changed relatively little.

6. Trace through the effects of an increase in taxes without a corresponding increase in government expenditures, or an increase in government expenditures without a corresponding increase in taxes.

7. What are some of the reasons that, even in an open economy, investment and savings might be highly correlated.

8. "Even if, in an open economy, a decrease in savings does not decrease investment, future generations are worse off." Discuss.

9. Consider a closed economy initially in equilibrium with $400 billion in savings (investment) and a real interest rate of 4 percent. Households save 10 percent of their $4 trillion income. The government imposes a $100 billion additional tax on households, used to finance $100 billion additional government expenditures. If the interest elasticity of savings is zero, and if a 10 percent increase in the real interest rate (from 4 to 4.4 percent) decreases investment by 2.6 percent, what are the new equilibrium level of investment, savings, and the real interest rate? Show that if the interest elasticity of savings is .1 (so an increase of the interest rate to 4.4 percent generates $4 billion in increased savings), the new equilibrium entails the real interest rate rising by 7 percent, to 4.28 percent. What happens to investment in this case?

26

USING THE FULL-
EMPLOYMENT
MODEL

T he federal budget deficit ballooned during the 1980s and emerged
from being a problem that mainly interested economists and political pundits into the national spotlight. By the 1992 presidential
election, public opinion polls were persistently ranking the huge
deficits among the central problems facing the country. In this
chapter we use the model developed in Chapter 25 to elucidate the consequences of the deficit. Another big problem in the 1980s was the huge trade
deficit; every year we imported billions of dollars more than we exported. The
full-employment model can also be used to help us understand the trade
deficit, and how it might be affected by various policies.

In Chapter 24, we described the three fundamental economic problems of
growth, unemployment, and inflation. By assumption, the full-employment
model of Chapter 25 cannot directly shed light on the problem of unemployment, though in the next chapter we will explain how simply by changing one
of the critical assumptions of that model, there can be unemployment. In the
last chapter we saw how the full-employment model provides us with useful
insights into inflation—with the price level increasing in proportion to the
money supply. In this chapter, we also show how the full-employment model
provides us with useful insights into the problem of growth.

KEY QUESTIONS

1. What are the consequences of the huge fiscal deficits of the 1980s?

2. What gave rise to the huge trade deficits of the 1980s

and 1990s? What are their consequences?

3. How do deficits affect economic growth? What are some other policies that can help promote growth?

THE DEFICIT

When the government spends more than it receives in taxes and other revenues in any given year, it has a deficit, often referred to as the **fiscal deficit,** to distinguish it from the gap between imports and exports, which is called the trade deficit. It must borrow to finance the deficit. In 1981, taxes were cut, but expenditures were not cut commensurately. Figure 26.1 shows the result-

Figure 26.1 **THE FEDERAL DEFICIT**

No matter how it is measured, federal borrowing increased dramatically during the 1980s. Panel A shows the nominal deficit; panel B the real deficit, adjusting for inflation. *Source: ERP* (1996), Tables B-3, B-74.

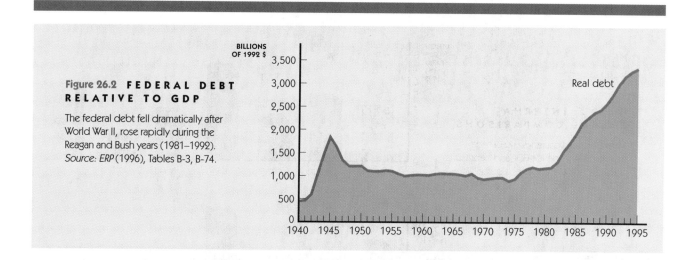

Figure 26.2 FEDERAL DEBT RELATIVE TO GDP

The federal debt fell dramatically after World War II, rose rapidly during the Reagan and Bush years (1981–1992). *Source: ERP* (1996), Tables B-3, B-74.

ing increase in the deficit. In twelve years, from 1981 to 1992, the federal deficit more than quadrupled, from $60 billion to $280 billion. Even adjusting for inflation, the increase in the deficit was dramatic. These represented the first major peacetime deficits in the country's history.

The **federal debt** is the cumulative amount that the government owes. Figure 26.2 shows that the federal debt, after falling dramatically after World War II, rose rapidly during the Reagan and Bush years.

The Clinton administration managed to bring the deficit as a percentage of GDP down from 4.9 percent in 1992 to 1.6 percent in 1996. As a result of these efforts, even by 1995, neither the deficits nor the debt are as large as those of many European countries or Canada—as Figure 26.3 illustrates.

In Chapter 37 we will discuss at greater length some of the political and economic events that gave rise to the deficit, as well as the debates about precisely how deleterious the deficit is for the economy's well-being. Here, we use the model of Chapter 25 to give us a qualitative picture of the consequences. In Chapter 25 we discussed the effects of an increase in government expenditures matched with an increase in taxes. Here, we look at the effect of an increase in government expenditures not matched with an increase in taxes. (The same results hold for a decrease in taxes—as in 1981—unmatched with a decrease in expenditures.) Our earlier analysis identified the openness of the economy as a critical determinant. We examine the two extreme cases—a closed economy and a small open economy—remembering that the U.S. economy lies between these extremes.

A CLOSED ECONOMY

If the government increases its expenditures without increasing taxes, it must borrow the difference.[1] Now private savings, S_p, has two purposes—to

[1]It used to be that some governments simply printed money to pay for the difference. Today, within developed countries, printing money to finance deficits is more the exception than the rule.

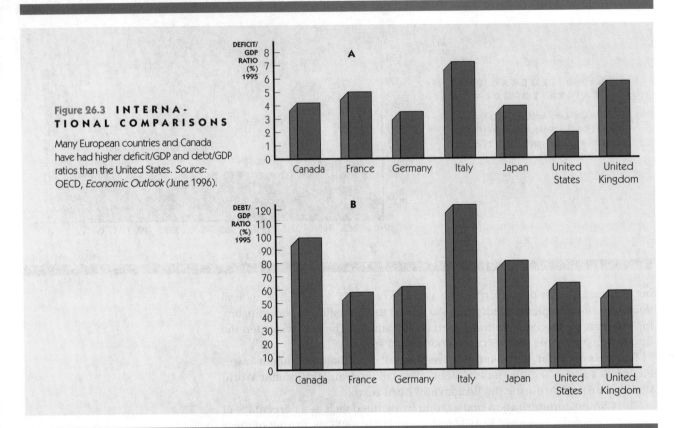

Figure 26.3 INTERNATIONAL COMPARISONS

Many European countries and Canada have had higher deficit/GDP and debt/GDP ratios than the United States. *Source:* OECD, *Economic Outlook* (June 1996).

finance the deficit, *D,* and to finance investment, *I:*

$$S_p = D + I.$$

Alternatively, we can think of the deficit as **negative public savings**

$$D = -S_g.$$

From this perspective, we can rewrite the first equation as

$$S_p - D = I$$

or

$$S = S_p + S_g = I.$$

National savings, *S,* consisting of private (household and business) savings, S_p, plus government savings, S_g, equal investment.

In Figure 26.4, the increased deficit is reflected as a shift to the left of the savings curve, decreasing the equilibrium level of investment and increasing

Figure 26.4 EFFECTS OF INCREASED DEFICITS IN A CLOSED ECONOMY

Increased deficits reduce national savings. With a leftward shift in the savings curve, the equilibrium level of interest rates is higher and the equilibrium level of investment is lower.

the equilibrium real interest rate. Because investment is lower, output and living standards in the future will be lower.

A SMALL OPEN ECONOMY

The difference between an open economy and a closed economy is that when national savings are reduced in an open economy, it can turn to other countries to finance its investment. Figure 26.5 shows the increased deficit reducing national savings, and shifting the savings curve to the left. The leftward shift leaves investment unchanged—this is determined simply by the international

Figure 26.5 EFFECTS OF INCREASED DEFICITS IN AN OPEN ECONOMY

Increased deficits shift the national savings curve to the left. Investment is unaffected, but foreign borrowing increases.

real interest rate. But it increases borrowing from abroad—in future years the country will be poorer as it has to pay interest on this indebtedness. Once again, living standards in the future are lower than they would have been in the absence of the deficit.

A LARGE OPEN ECONOMY

We saw in Chapter 25 that the United States is a large open economy—with features that represent a cross between a closed economy and a small open economy. When the United States has a deficit, it borrows more from abroad, but interest rates rise, and some investment is crowded out. A rough rule of thumb is that between one-third and one-half of the deficit is offset by increased foreign borrowing.

If we look at who has bought the additional bonds the government has been issuing in recent years, we note that some but not all of the higher deficit has been financed by foreigners. But the consequences are equally or even more disturbing if foreigners do not *directly* finance the deficit. A high deficit can lead to increased foreign indebtedness directly as the government borrows directly from abroad, or it can increase foreign debt indirectly by sopping up available domestic savings so that Americans no longer have the money to invest in U.S. businesses and foreigners come in to fill the gap. Some economists have described the latter situation by saying that government borrowing can *crowd in* foreign investment.

In a closed economy, an increase in government expenditure not accompanied by an increase in taxes (or a decrease in taxes, not accompanied by a corresponding decrease in government expenditures) results in higher interest rates and decreased investment, while in a small, open economy, interest rates and investment remain unchanged but foreign borrowing increases.

THE TRADE DEFICIT

The **trade deficit** is the difference between imports and exports in any given year. At the same time that the budget deficit was exploding, so was the trade deficit. From about $20 billion a year from 1977 to 1982, it soared (in nominal terms) to $102 billion in 1984, $142 billion in 1987, and back down to $96 billion in 1995—though as a percentage of GDP, it declined from 3 percent in 1987 to 1.4 percent in 1995.

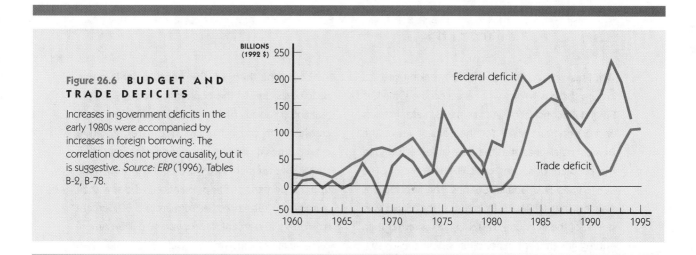

Figure 26.6 BUDGET AND TRADE DEFICITS

Increases in government deficits in the early 1980s were accompanied by increases in foreign borrowing. The correlation does not prove causality, but it is suggestive. *Source: ERP* (1996), Tables B-2, B-78.

Figure 26.6 shows the trade and federal deficits. The two have moved together. This is no accident: the two are in fact closely related. The reason for this we already noted: for an open economy, an increase in government expenditure not matched by an increase in taxes (or a decrease in taxes, not matched by a reduction in government expenditures) results in an increased deficit and increased foreign borrowing. We will now see why increased foreign borrowing implies an increase in the trade deficit.

CAPITAL FLOWS

To see the relationship between foreign borrowing and the trade deficit, we first need to see the links between trade flows and capital flows. Let's trace what happens when an American buys a German car. It seems like a simple matter: he pays good American dollars to his dealer. His dealer buys the car—in dollars—from an importer. The importer buys the car from the German manufacturer, who wants to be paid in German marks. For the importer, this is no problem: he goes to a bank, say in Germany, and exchanges his dollars for marks. But the bank won't just hold those dollars. It will sell them, either to someone wanting to purchase U.S. goods or to someone wanting to invest in a dollar-denominated asset.

We call the money coming into the United States to buy investments, to be deposited in U.S. banks, to buy U.S. government bonds, or to lend to Americans for any reason—including buying a German car—**capital inflows.** U.S. dollars going to other countries for similar purposes are called **capital outflows.** For most purposes, we are interested in **net capital inflows,** the inflows minus the outflows.

As we have seen, every dollar an American spends to buy a foreign import eventually comes back, either to buy American exports or to buy an investment in the United States. We can express this relation by a simple equation:

Vice President Al Gore cast a tie-breaking vote to ensure the passage of what is called the Omnibus Budget Reconciliation Act of 1993, setting taxes and expenditure levels for the coming years. The Democrats claimed that they had at last addressed the problem of soaring deficits, the legacy of the Reagan and Bush administrations. The Republicans claimed that OBRA 93 threatened the underlying health of the economy, by raising taxes rather than cutting government expenditures. Some even suggested that the deficit would become worse: that the reduced economic activity resulting from the increased taxes would actually lead to reduced tax revenues.

As it turned out, the deficit reduction was genuine. While the deficit had been projected to increase without OBRA 93 to as much as $350 billion by 1996, the actual deficit, after OBRA 93 was implemented, was about $140 billion. The economy had a healthy recovery, and this by itself contributed significantly to the deficit reduction. The Clinton administration, of course, said that the deficit reduction, by restoring confidence in the economy and leading to reduced interest rates, spurred investment and the recovery; critics claimed that the recovery was based on the underlying strength of the American economy, and had occurred in spite of the tax increase.

About one-third of the improvement in the deficit was due to the economic recovery. Of the remainder, about half of that was due to tax increases, with the other half due to expenditure cuts. Besides a relatively moderate gasoline tax increase, the tax increases were concentrated in the upper 2 percent of the population, who saw their marginal tax rate increase from around 30 percent to around 40 percent. Moreover, 40 million Americans—families with incomes below $28,000—had an effective tax decrease. Still, a large percentage of Americans believed that they had a tax increase. This belief contributed strongly to demands for a middle-class tax cut.

imports into the United States = exports + capital inflows.

Subtracting exports from both sides of this equation, we obtain the basic trade identity:

trade deficit = imports − exports = capital inflows.

Thus, a trade deficit and an inflow of foreign capital are two ways of saying the same thing. This can be put another way: the only way that American consumers and businesses can import more from abroad than they export abroad is if foreigners are willing to make up the difference by lending to or investing in the United States.

In a world of multilateral trade, the accounts between any particular country and the United States do not have to balance. Assume Japan and Europe are in trade balance and the United States and Europe are in trade balance, but Japanese investors like to put their money into Europe and Europeans like to invest in the United States. Europe has zero net capital inflows with a positive capital inflow from Japan offset by a capital outflow to the United States. In this situation, the U.S. trade deficit with Japan is offset by a capital inflow from Europe. But what must be true for any country is that total imports minus total exports (the trade deficit) equal total capital inflows.

The basic trade identity can describe a capital outflow as well as a capital inflow. In the 1950s, the United States had a substantial trade surplus, as the country exported more than it imported. Europe and Japan did not receive enough dollars from selling exports to the United States to buy the imports that they desired, and they borrowed the difference from the United States. There was a net capital outflow from America, which gradually accumulated. Japan now exports more than it imports, with the difference equal to its capital outflows.

EXCHANGE RATES

If a country borrows more (or less) from abroad, the **exchange rate** ensures that net imports adjust. The exchange rate tells how much of one currency exchanges for a given amount of another. For instance, in October 1995, one dollar could be exchanged for approximately 100 yen. Exchange rates may change rapidly. In 1992 a dollar was worth 126 yen. At the beginning of 1995, a dollar was worth only 100 yen. It then fell to only about 85 yen in March: a fall in value of 15 percent in three months. When the dollar has become less valuable relative to the yen, we say it has **depreciated;** the yen has become more valuable—it has **appreciated.**

The exchange rate is thus a price—the relative price of two currencies. Like any price, the exchange rate is determined by the laws of supply and demand. For simplicity, let us continue to focus on the exchange rate between the dollar and the yen (ignoring the fact that, in the world trading system, all exchange markets are interlinked). Figure 26.7 depicts the market for dollars in terms of the exchange rate with the yen. The exchange rate in yen per dollar is on the vertical axis, and the quantity of U.S. dollars is on the horizontal axis. The supply curve for dollars represents the quantity of dollars supplied by Americans to purchase Japanese goods and to make investments in Japan. At higher exchange rates—when the dollar buys more yen—Americans will supply higher quantities of dollars. The supply curve for dollars thus slopes upward to the right. The demand curve for dollars represents the dollars

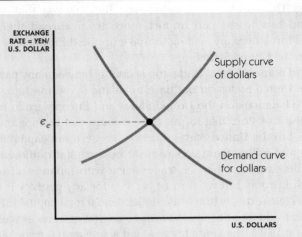

Figure 26.7 EQUILIBRIUM IN THE MARKET FOR DOLLARS

The exchange rate is the relative price of two currencies. The equilibrium exchange rate, e_e, occurs at the intersection of the supply and demand curves for dollars.

demanded by the Japanese to purchase American products and to make investments in the United States. At higher exchange rates—when it takes more yen to buy one dollar—the Japanese demand lower quantities of dollars, resulting in a demand curve which slopes downward to the right. The equilibrium exchange rate, e_e, lies at the intersection of the supply and demand curves for dollars.

Now we can see how the exchange rate connects the flow of capital and goods between countries. We continue with the case of the United States and Japan. Suppose the United States wants to borrow more from Japan. Higher U.S. interest rates will attract more Japanese investment to the United States. Japanese demand for dollars increases at each exchange rate, shifting the demand curve for dollars to the right, as depicted in Figure 26.8. The higher interest rates will also make Japanese investments relatively less attractive to American investors, who will therefore increase their investments at home. Americans will be willing to supply fewer dollars at each exchange rate, shifting the supply curve for dollars to the left. These shifts in the supply and demand curves for dollars cause the exchange rate to rise from e_0 to e_1—the dollar appreciates and the yen depreciates.[2] Since the dollar can now buy more Japanese products, U.S. imports increase (Japanese exports increase). Changes in the exchange rate thus ensure that the trade deficit moves in tandem with foreign borrowing.

THE SAVINGS-INVESTMENT IDENTITY

We can now return to the issue discussed at the beginning of this section, where we saw that in the 1980s, both the trade and fiscal deficit increased.

[2]Later, in Chapter 33, we shall see that matters are somewhat more complicated. Investors have to take into account expectations concerning changes in the exchange rates as well.

Figure 26.8 EXCHANGE RATE EFFECTS OF INCREASED FOREIGN BORROWING

The equilibrium exchange rate is e_0 before the increase in U.S. borrowing from Japan. Higher interest rates in the United States attract Japanese investment to the U.S., shifting the demand curve for U.S. dollars to the right. At the same time, more Americans decide to invest in the U.S. rather than abroad, represented by a shift to the left of the supply curve for dollars. The exchange rate rises from e_0 to e_1. At the higher exchange rate, the dollar buys more yen, so U.S. imports of Japanese products increase. Conversely, U.S. exports decrease.

The fact that they moved together was no accident: as the United States needed to borrow more to finance the increased deficit, interest rates increased. The higher interest rates attracted foreign investors; the foreign borrowing helped finance the deficit. But at the same time, the dollar appreciated (from increased demand for dollars to invest in the United States), which reduced exports and increased imports, and hence increased the U.S. trade deficit.

The relationship between the fiscal deficit and the trade deficit (or foreign borrowing) can be seen another way using the savings and investment identity:

private (household and business) savings + capital flows (borrowing) from abroad = investment in machines and equipment + federal budget deficit.

Private savings and capital flows from abroad can be thought of as the "sources" of funds; and investment and budget deficits can be thought of as the uses of funds. A slightly different approach is to think of the fiscal deficit as dissaving, or negative savings. Just as when a household spends less than its income it is saving, and when it spends more than its income it is dissaving, so too with government. The savings-investment identity can thus be rewritten:

private savings + government savings + capital flows from abroad = investment.

The savings-investment identity says that if there is an increase in the deficit and if private savings and investment are unchanged, capital flows from abroad must increase and foreigners must end up holding more American assets. But the identity does not specify which assets they will hold. They may buy some of the newly issued government bonds or they may buy U.S. companies, letting Americans use their savings to buy the newly issued bonds.

BASIC TRADE IDENTITIES

Capital inflow = Trade deficit

Investment = Private saving + Government savings + Capital inflows

WHY TRADE DEFICITS ARE A PROBLEM

Borrowing from abroad is not necessarily bad, any more than borrowing in general is necessarily bad. In its first century, America borrowed heavily from abroad. For most of this century, the United States has loaned more money to foreign countries and investors than it has borrowed. This pattern is typical. In the early stages of development, countries borrow to build up their economies, and repay the loans with a portion of their economic gains. More mature economies typically lend capital.

The enormous U.S. trade deficits in the 1980s reversed this pattern. Just as when the government borrows year after year the cumulative budget deficits lead to a high level of government debt, when the country borrows from abroad year after year, the cumulative trade deficits (cumulative capital inflows) also lead to a high level of debt to foreigners.

The effect of the trade deficits of the 1980s was to convert the United States from the world's largest creditor nation at the beginning of the 1980s to the world's largest debtor nation by the end of the 1980s. The sum of U.S. indebtedness equals the combined amount owed by the three huge Latin American debtor countries, Mexico, Brazil, and Argentina. Figures on how much private parties in one country owe or have borrowed from another country are not fully reliable, yet it is clear that the U.S. debt is huge and growing.

Figure 26.9 shows that in the mid-1980s the United States slipped from being a creditor nation to being a debtor nation. At the beginning of the decade, the net international investment position of the United States—the value of all of America's assets abroad plus what others owe it minus the value of all assets within the United States owned by foreigners minus what it owes others—was positive.[3] But the cumulative effect of the trade deficits was to make this posi-

[3]One has to be careful about interpreting the figures. Critics of such figures point out that many of the assets that the United States owns abroad have greatly increased in value since it obtained those assets, but the data do not adequately reflect these increases. Still, there is little doubt about the general picture—there is a definite deterioration in America's net investment position.

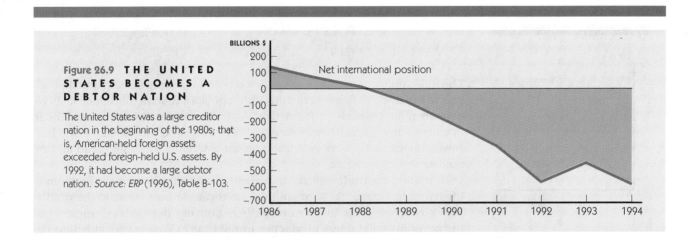

Figure 26.9 THE UNITED STATES BECOMES A DEBTOR NATION

The United States was a large creditor nation in the beginning of the 1980s; that is, American-held foreign assets exceeded foreign-held U.S. assets. By 1992, it had become a large debtor nation. *Source: ERP* (1996), Table B-103.

tion negative by the end of the decade. As a result, the U.S. economy will have to pay interest, dividends, and profits to foreign investors each year. The effects are readily apparent: for the first time since World War I, America is sending more dollars abroad in payment of interest and dividends than it is receiving.

The consequences for the nation are little different from those you would experience if you borrowed a large amount from the bank. In the future, unless you used the borrowed funds to make an investment that yielded a return at least equal to the interest you had to pay, you would be unable to consume as much as you would otherwise, because you must pay the bank interest as well as the principal. Consider this rough calculation: if the nation's debt to foreign investors reaches $1 trillion by the year 2000 and the average rate of interest is 6 percent, the interest payments alone work out to over $200 for every man, woman, and child in the United States *every year.*

LONG-RUN CONSEQUENCES OF PERSISTENT TRADE DEFICITS

Increased foreign indebtedness, leading eventually to

Increased interest and dividend payments abroad, and if foreign borrowing is not used to finance additional investments that yield returns sufficient to pay the increased interest and dividend payments,

Lower living standards

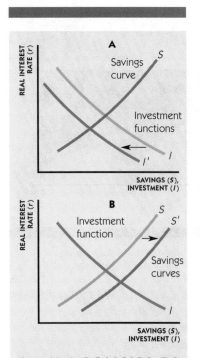

Figure 26.10 POLICIES TO REDUCE THE TRADE DEFICIT

The trade deficit can be reduced either by shifting the investment function to the left (panel A) or the savings function to the right (panel B).

USING THE BASIC MODEL TO ANALYZE THE TRADE DEFICIT

The full-employment model can be used both to provide insights into the origins of the trade deficit and to think about policies that might reduce it. As we have seen, an increase in the deficit—a decrease in national savings—in an open economy leads to more foreign borrowing; and increased foreign borrowing leads to an increased trade deficit. Exchange rates adjust to accommodate the trade deficit.

To reduce the trade deficit, we can either shift the investment function to the left as in Figure 26.10A or shift the aggregate savings curve to the right as in Figure 26.10B. The former obviously is not very desirable—it means that the economy will be less productive in the future. That is why attention has focused on shifting the aggregate savings curve. There are two ways to do this: either increase government savings (reduce the deficit) or increase private savings.

REDUCING THE TRADE DEFICIT

Increase private savings
Reduce the fiscal deficit
Reduce investment

GROWTH

The full-employment model can also be used to analyze policies that might promote economic growth. There are three keys to increased growth: (1) a more productive labor force—the result of improved education and training; (2) more and better capital—the result of increased investment in plant and equipment and investment in **infrastructure,** such as roads and airports; and (3) technological progress—partially the result of public and private expenditures on research and development. Expenditures in all three categories are referred to as **investments,** which are expenditures made today that reap benefits in the future. Investments in people are often called **human capital.** All three of these investments shift future short-run production func-

Figure 26.11 INCREASING THE ECONOMY'S PRODUCTIVE POTENTIAL

Improved education and training, the result of investments in people, more and better capital, the result of investments in plant and equipment, and improved technology, the result of investments in research and development and technology, all shift the short-run production function out, so that the level of output produced by any level of employment is increased.

tions out, as depicted in Figure 26.11, so that the level of output that can be obtained at any level of employment is increased.

In a closed economy, there are basically two ways to increase investment: shift the investment function or the savings function to the right.

STIMULATING INVESTMENT

Governments have used tax policy as a way of shifting the investment function, as illustrated in Figure 26.12. With an **investment tax credit,** firms can subtract a fraction of the cost of the investment from their taxes, so that, in effect, the government is paying part of the cost of the investment. For example, with a 10 percent investment tax credit, a machine costing $100 results in a reduction in tax payments of $10, so the net cost of the machine is only $90. Naturally, the firm will invest more.

Another way that the government encourages investment through the tax system is through **accelerated depreciation.** When a firm buys a machine that lasts, say, ten years, in calculating its taxable income it is allowed to deduct 10 percent of the cost of the machine each year, to reflect the fact that over time, the machine is becoming worth less and less. The deduction is called a **depreciation allowance.** In 1981, the government passed a law allowing firms to accelerate their depreciation. Thus, they might be able to pretend that a machine that lasted ten years only lasted five, deducting 20 percent of the value in each of the first five years of its life. This meant that taxes they paid in the first five years were lower. Obviously, a dollar today is worth far more than a dollar five years from now: with accelerated depreciation, the present discounted value of the tax reductions associated with depreciation allowances is greatly increased. This makes investments more attractive, shifting the investment function to the right.

Figure 26.12 EFFECT OF INVESTMENT TAX CREDIT IN A CLOSED ECONOMY

An investment tax credit shifts the investment schedule to the right, resulting in a higher equilibrium interest rate and more investment. The higher level of investment increases the rate of growth, at least in the short run.

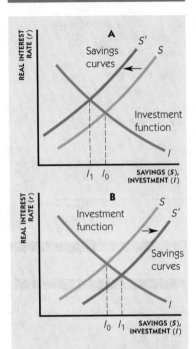

Figure 26.13 EFFECT OF SAVINGS INCENTIVES IN A CLOSED ECONOMY

IRAs increase the incentive for households to save, but the tax preferences mean a loss of government revenues, and hence an increased deficit. In panel A, private savings increase by an insufficient amount to offset the increased deficit, so that the aggregate savings curve shifts to the left. Investment is actually lowered. In panel B, the increased private savings more than offset the increased deficit; the aggregate savings curve shifts to the right, leading to lower interest rates, increased investment, and higher growth.

STIMULATING SAVINGS

The government has also tried a variety of ways of shifting the savings function, again largely by providing tax preferences, including individual retirement accounts (IRAs) and 401K and 403B plans. IRAs may have been successful in encouraging savings, not so much because of the extra incentives they provide, but because of the advertising that banks did to recruit new IRA accounts. Critics of IRAs argue, however, that even if IRAs have succeeded in increasing private savings, the net effect on national savings is negative. With any tax preference—IRAs included—government loses tax revenues, and the lost tax revenue contributes to the deficit. And the deficit, we have seen, is equivalent to *negative* government savings. If the lost tax revenue exceeds the increased private savings, national savings actually decrease. How much private savings increase with low taxes depends on the **interest elasticity of savings,** that is, if the after-tax interest rate (what savers care about) is increased by 1 percent, by what percentage do savings increase? Most estimates suggest that savings are relatively inelastic, that is, lowering the tax rate to zero—and thus increasing the after-tax return substantially—will not induce even an individual facing a 40 percent marginal tax rate to save much more. The reason is simple: if he is saving for his retirement, the amount he has to save, to provide any level of retirement income, will be reduced as the after-tax interest rate increases.[4] If savings are relatively inelastic, then the increase in private savings is insufficient to offset the increased deficit, and national savings are reduced. Figure 26.13 illustrates the two possible cases.

REDUCING THE DEFICIT

We saw earlier that reducing the deficit is equivalent to shifting the aggregate savings curve to the right. But we need to emphasize that the net effect on growth depends on how the deficit is cut. In Figure 26.14 we illustrate a case where deficit reduction actually leads to lower growth. As we saw earlier, the shift in the aggregate savings curve to the right leads to lower interest rates and increased private investment. This shifts the economy's future short-run production function out to $0P'$. But if the government reduces the deficit by cutting back on productive public investments, such as research, investments in education, or infrastructure, the future short-run production function shifts in, to $0P''$—below where it was before the deficit reduction. If private savings is responsive to after-tax interest rates, as in Figure 7.13, a dollar of deficit reduction does not, in general, result in an increase of private invest-

---

[4]Higher interest rates mean that savers are better off, so they consume more today. This is the income effect. At the same time, a higher after-tax interest rate increases the incentive to save; this is the substitution effect—for every dollar of consumption forgone today, the individual can consume more dollars of consumption in the future. The income and substitution effects largely offset each other.

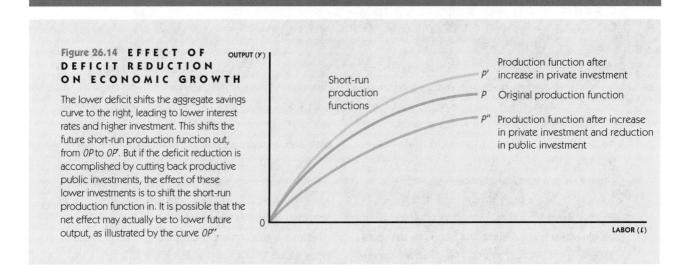

Figure 26.14 EFFECT OF DEFICIT REDUCTION ON ECONOMIC GROWTH

The lower deficit shifts the aggregate savings curve to the right, leading to lower interest rates and higher investment. This shifts the future short-run production function out, from OP to OP'. But if the deficit reduction is accomplished by cutting back productive public investments, the effect of these lower investments is to shift the short-run production function in. It is possible that the net effect may actually be to lower future output, as illustrated by the curve OP".

ment by a dollar (because the investment function is downward sloping[5]). Thus, even if public investment is *less* productive than private investment, deficit reduction attained through investment reduction can lower economic growth. And there is evidence that public investments in education, research, and infrastructure may actually yield higher marginal returns than private investment.

OPEN ECONOMY

In an open economy, investment may differ from domestic savings, since the country can always borrow to finance its investment. By the same token, changes in domestic savings need not equal changes in investment. For a small open economy, with a perfectly elastic supply of funds at the international interest rate, r^*, the level of investment is determined by that interest rate.

In a large open economy like the United States, however, savings and investment tend to move together, with increases in savings leading to increases in investment, but not on a dollar-for-dollar basis. As we have noted, today most estimates suggest that an increase in domestic savings by a dollar increases investment by between 35 and 50 cents.

If a small open economy wishes to increase its growth rate, it focuses its attention on shifting its investment function; changes in the savings curve only affect the amount it borrows from abroad (though, as we have seen, this will have important consequences for the economy's future well-being).

---

[5]Only if the investment function were a horizontal straight line would a shift in an upward-sloping savings curve to the right by a dollar result in an increase in investment by a dollar.

Using Economics: Estimating the Effect of Deficit Reduction on Growth

In 1995 there seemed to be a bipartisan consensus that the deficit should be reduced to zero. Still, there were sharp disagreements about the best way to reduce it. The Republicans wanted deep cuts in expenditure that would finance large tax cuts. What can one say about the effects of the alternative programs on economic growth?

Consider first a program that entailed $200 billion in expenditure cuts—a quarter of which were cuts in investment. Assume the economy manages to remain at full employment, and there are no tax cuts, so consumption remains unchanged. Based on historical experience, the $200 billion increased national savings will result in $100 billion increased private investment. (For the economy to remain at full employment when government expenditures decrease by $200 billion, and consumption is unchanged, if investment increases by $100 billion, net exports must increase by $100 billion. Exchange rates must change to accommodate the increase in net exports and interest rates must change to generate the increased investment.*) Thus, aggregate investment increases by $50 billion per year (private investment increases by $100 billion, offset by a reduction of $50 billion in public investment). The $50 billion per year, cumulated over ten years, assuming no depreciation, yields at the end of a decade $500 billion more capital, which, with a return of approximately 7 percent, will mean that national income will be $35 billion higher than it otherwise would have been. GDP in ten years is estimated to be approximately $10 billion (in 1995 dollars), so that GDP will be .35 percent higher than it otherwise would have been, representing an increase in the expected growth rate of less than .1 percent.

Consider an alternative plan that had an extra $50 billion annually of tax cuts, financed half by cuts in public investments and half by cuts in non-investment government expenditures, and assume labor supply is unchanged. The extra $50 billion in tax cuts—because they are fully financed by expenditure cuts—leaves public savings unchanged. But since a household's disposable income has increased by the amount of the tax cut, its savings increase. Typically, an increase in household income of $50 billion yields an increase in savings of somewhat less than $5 billion. An increase in national savings of $5 billion generates an extra $2.5 billion in private investment. Thus aggregate investment (public plus private) is reduced by $22.5 billion. Thus, almost half of the gain in growth from the original deficit reduction package is lost with the tax cuts that are partially financed by reductions in public investment.

*This analysis assumes that the savings rate is not sensitive to the interest rate. If lowering the interest rate leads to reduced savings—and increased consumption—then the requisite adjustments in investment and net exports will be accordingly reduced.

CONSENSUS IN MACROECONOMICS

From this chapter emerges a thirteenth point of consensus in macroeconomics:

13 Growth

> *Increases in standards of living require increases in productivity; increases in productivity require expenditures on research and development, investments in new technology, plant, equipment, and infrastructure, and increases in the skills of the labor force.*

In a closed economy, investment can be increased either by shifting the investment curve to the right (such as by an investment tax credit) or the savings curve to the right (such as by preferential tax treatment). Some preferential tax treatments may actually lower national savings, since the induced private savings are less than the increased deficit. Similarly, deficit reduction, in a closed economy, will result in increased private investment, but if the deficit reduction is attained through reducing public investment, future output and living standards may actually be reduced.

REVIEW AND PRACTICE

SUMMARY

1. The early 1980s were marked by a surge in the size of federal budget deficits in the United States, leading to marked increases in the national debt. Beginning in 1993, the deficit began to be substantially reduced.

2. In a closed economy, increases in the deficit lead to lower private investment and increased interest rates. The net effect of reductions in the deficit depend on how it is reduced. If generated by reductions in public investment, growth is likely to be reduced, as the increased private investment is unlikely to be sufficient to offset the reduced public investment.

3. In a small open economy, increases in the deficit have no effect on investment, but lead to increased foreign indebtedness and larger trade deficits. Cumulative increases in foreign indebtedness will make future citizens worse off, as they have to pay interest on the foreign indebtedness.

4. The large increases in the trade deficit that began in the 1980s were largely explained by the large increases in the fiscal deficit which began at that time. The trade deficit must equal capital inflows. Policy options for reducing the U.S. trade deficit and foreign borrowing include decreasing investment (a bad idea for long-term growth), increasing household and business savings (a good idea if the government could do it), or reducing the federal deficit.

5. The savings-investment identity for an open economy says that the sum of private savings, capital flows from abroad, and government savings is equal to investment. This identity implies that a change in any one factor must also involve offsetting changes in other factors.

6. Increases in investments in human capital, plant and equipment, infrastructure, and improved technology all shift out the short-run production curve, increasing the full-employment output of the economy and the economy's rate of growth. Investment can be stimulated either through investment tax credits or accelerated depreciation, or, in a closed economy, by increasing the rate of savings through tax preferences. Because of a low interest elasticity of savings, tax preferences may not be very effective.

KEY TERMS

fiscal deficit	appreciate	interest elasticity of
trade deficit	investment tax	savings
capital flows (capital	credit	infrastructure
outflow, inflow)	accelerated	human capital
exchange rates	depreciation	
depreciate	depreciation	
	allowance	

REVIEW QUESTIONS

1. What happened to the size of the budget deficits in the 1980s? What is the relationship between the deficit and the level of the debt?

2. What are the consequences of an increased deficit for private investment in an open economy and in a closed economy?

3. Why do the consequences for growth of deficit reduction depend on whether the deficit reduction is accomplished by cutting government investment, by cutting government consumption expenditures, or by raising taxes?

4. What happened to the trade deficit during the 1980s? How did the foreign indebtedness of the U.S. economy change during the 1980s? What is the relationship between these two changes?

5. What is the relationship between the trade deficit and an inflow of foreign capital?

6. What is the relationship between the trade deficit and the fiscal deficit?

7. What is the exchange rate? How is it determined? What role do adjustments in the exchange rate play in ensuring that capital inflows equal the trade deficit?

8. What are the consequences of persistent trade deficits?

9. What is the savings-investment identity for an open economy?

10. How may government stimulate investment and savings?

11. How do efforts to increase economic growth differ in a small open economy compared to a large open economy?

PROBLEMS

1. Suppose a certain country has private savings of 6 percent of GDP, foreign borrowing of 1 percent of GDP, and a balanced budget. What is its level of investment? If the budget deficit is 1.5 percent of GDP, how does your answer change?

2. Why does it make a difference if a country borrows abroad to finance the expansion of its railroads, or to finance increased Social Security benefits for the elderly?

3. Assume investments in human capital yield a return of 15 percent, private investments yield a total return of 10 percent, and public investments in research yield a return of 25 percent. Assume the deficit is $100 billion per year, and the government wishes to eliminate it. What will be the impact on economic growth of a deficit reduction package which consists of reducing Medicare expenditures by $50 billion, education expenditures by $40 billion, and research expenditures by $10 billion?

4. The primary deficit is defined as the difference between government expenditures *excluding interest payments* and tax revenues; it represents what the deficit would have been, has the government not inherited any debt. The table below shows the primary deficit over time. (A negative deficit means the government is running a surplus.) Discuss why the concept of a primary deficit may or may not be useful or relevant.

Year	Primary deficit	Actual deficit
1980	21.3	73.8
1985	82.8	212.3
1990	37.2	221.4
1995	−68.4	163.8

5. If the economy is growing at 5 percent per year, and the debt/GDP ratio is 50 percent, what is the critical value of the deficit/GDP ratio, such that if the deficit/GDP ratio exceeds that number, the debt/GDP ratio will increase, and if the deficit/GDP ratio falls short of that number, the debt/GDP ratio decreases.

6. U.S. foreign indebtedness is greater than that of Mexico, Brazil, and Argentina combined. But does this necessarily mean that the United States has a larger debt problem than those countries? Why or why not? Can you think of a situation in which an individual with debts of larger value may actually have less of a debt problem?

7. If Congress were to pass a law prohibiting foreigners from buying U.S. Treasury bills, would this prevent government borrowing from leading to capital inflows? Discuss.

8. Japan had large trade surpluses during the 1980s. Would this cause Japan to be a borrower or a lender in international capital markets?

9. If a nation borrowed $50 billion from abroad one year and its imports were worth $800 billion, what would be the value of its exports? How does the answer change if, instead of borrowing, the nation loaned $100 billion abroad?

10. Since other countries benefit from exporting their products to the United States, why shouldn't the U.S. government charge them for the privilege of selling in the United States?

PART SIX

Unemployment MACROECONOMICS

art Five explored full-employment macroeconomics. The basic assumption there was that the economy operates as envisioned in the basic competitive model: prices, wages, and interest rates adjust quickly and fully to ensure that all markets clear. Most importantly, the demand for labor equals the supply of labor. The assumption may be unrealistic, but the model is instructive. We saw how deficits crowd out investment and increase foreign borrowing, and we got to look more closely at economic growth.

The full-employment model needs to be modified to take up two further, fundamental macroeconomic questions: unemployment and inflation. In this part, we take up unemployment, reserving inflation for Part Seven. Over the long run, as we have seen, the economy has managed to create jobs to keep pace with the increasing number of workers. But in the short run, mismatches between demand and supply not only give rise to public outcries, but are among the most important determinants of the fates of elected officials. Today, government is viewed as having the responsibility for keeping the economy on an even keel, which means avoiding the pitfalls of excessive unemployment.

Here, in Part Six, we examine the problem of maintaining the economy at full employment. The most fundamental difference in our analysis in this part of the book is that we drop the assumption that wages and prices instantaneously adjust to clear all markets. For simplicity, we will assume that they do not adjust at all, that they are fixed. In Part Seven, we will take up the in-between case, exploring how wages and prices adjust, and why they often change so slowly.

Chapter 27 provides an overview of the macroeconomics of unemployment, and introduces some of the basic concepts. The next two chapters focus on the product market. Chapter 28 looks at aggregate demand—which, as we will see, in situations of unemployment, determines the level of aggregate output. Chapter 29 looks more closely at two of the most important components of aggregate demand, consumption and investment.

Chapters 30–32 then focus on the capital market, and the links between that market and the product market. We begin with a discussion, in Chapter 30, of money. Chapter 31 then discusses monetary theory—how changes in the supply of money and the availability of credit affect the level of economic activity, and how government changes the supply of money and credit availability. Chapter 32 puts the entire unemployment model with fixed prices and wages together, focusing on how fiscal and monetary policy can be used to restore the economy to full employment. To reach a better understanding of the roles these two alternative policy instruments play, it contrasts both their consequences and the difficulties that are faced in using them effectively.

CHAPTER 27

OVERVIEW

OF UNEMPLOYMENT

MACROECONOMICS

P eople worry about jobs. They worry about layoffs. If they are laid off, they worry about how long it will take to get another job. In all market economies, there is some unemployment. In a dynamic economy, some firms and industries are shrinking—jobs are being lost—at the same time that new jobs are being created. It takes time for individuals to switch from one job to another. But at times, as we saw in Chapter 24, the unemployment rate becomes very high. Labor markets do not clear: the demand for labor is much less than the supply. In such situations, governments take on the responsibility of reducing the unemployment rate—not necessarily to zero, but at least to a low level.

We have seen how all markets of the economy are interlinked. The labor market is linked to the product market and the product market to the capital market. The labor market is particularly sensitive to changes in the product market: if output goes down, so too will the demand for labor. If real wages adjust too slowly, there will be unemployment. In this chapter, we do not ask why they adjust slowly—that is a question postponed until Part Seven. We focus instead on the consequences. After a few words about the nature of macroeconomic models, we discuss the labor market, then the product market, and finally the capital market. The chapter closes by applying the framework to discuss some recent macroeconomic events.

1. How do economists analyze what determines levels of aggregate output and employment in the short run, when wages and prices are fixed?

2. What causes shifts in the aggregate demand and supply curves for labor? Why may unemployment result if wages fail to adjust in response to these shifts?

3. What is the aggregate demand curve? What happens when the price level is fixed at a level at which aggregate demand is less than aggregate supply? What are the consequences of a shift in the aggregate demand curve in these circumstances?

4. How can we use aggregate demand curves to interpret some of the major macroeconomic episodes of the past fifty years?

MORE ABOUT MACROECONOMIC MODELS

Part Five developed the full-employment macroeconomic model. The critical assumption of Part Five was that wages and prices adjust so that all markets—including the labor market—clear: there is no unemployment. The basic way in which this part differs from Part Five is that here, we are concerned about the problem of unemployment. The basic explanation for unemployment is that wages do not adjust quickly enough to shifts in either the demand or supply curve for labor, so that *at least for a while, and sometimes for extended periods of time,* the demand for labor at market wages and prices may be less than the supply. In this part of the book, to simplify matters, we assume wages and prices are fixed; that is, they do not adjust at all. Economists say that such wages and prices are **rigid.** The results are much the same as they would be if they adjusted slowly—that is, adjusted in the direction required by market clearing, but too slowly to ensure that the demand and supply for, say, labor were equated. While some prices—such as those on the stock market—adjust quickly, others—wages in particular—adjust slowly. Unions, for instance, often sign three-year contracts, and even nonunionized firms let workers know their wages at the beginning of the year, and are reluctant to lower wages quickly in response to either the availability of cheaper labor elsewhere or a decrease in the demand for their products. At the bottom, minimum wage laws prevent employers from lowering wages, even if they wanted to. Over the last fifteen years, much of Europe has had much higher rates of unemployment, and this is widely attributed, in part at least, to their greater wage rigidity.

The fact that slow adjustments can lead to persistent unemployment is one of the reasons that macroeconomists focus so much on dynamics—how, and in particular, *how fast* things change. In Part Seven of the book, we will describe the dynamics of the economy, focusing in particular on price and wage adjustments. We will analyze how and how fast the economy adjusts.

This part of the book focuses on the short run, a time span that might range from a week or a month up to a few years. Although investment is occurring in the economy, we assume the net change in the capital stock is so small in the short term that it can be ignored. Except when we focus explicitly upon *changes* in government actions, we will also assume that tax rates, levels of expenditures, and the money supply are all fixed.

THE LABOR MARKET

Since unemployment is our key concern in this part of the book, our discussion naturally begins with the labor market. In Chapter 25, we described equilibrium in the labor market as the intersection of the aggregate demand and supply curves for labor. Both depended on real wages. We are assuming now that prices are fixed, so we do not have to distinguish between nominal and real wages.

In the earlier discussion of the labor market, we simplified the analysis in two ways. We assumed that each worker supplied exactly 40 hours of labor—no more and no less—per week, and that real wages did not affect aggregate supply.[1] Thus, the aggregate labor supply curve was vertical. Wages were flexible, so that they adjusted to equate demand and supply, to w_1/P in Figure 27.1.

But what happens if wages do not adjust quickly? Assume, for some reason, that the demand curve for labor suddenly shifts to the left, so that at each

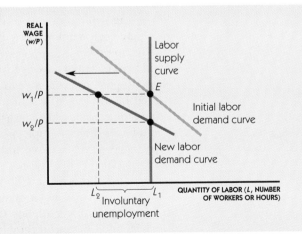

Figure 27.1 **EFFECTS OF A SHIFT IN THE DEMAND FOR LABOR WITH FIXED WAGES**

Equilibrium in the labor market is at the intersection of the aggregate demand and supply curves for labor. If the demand for labor decreases and the wage is fixed, employed labor decreases from L_1 to L_2.

[1] The fact that each worker works 40 hours means that we can put on the horizontal axis either the number of workers or the number of hours worked.

wage, fewer workers are demanded. At the old equilibrium wage, w_1/P, the supply for labor exceeds the demand. However, if the wage is stuck at the original level, w_1/P—above the wage at which the demand for labor equals the supply—firms will still only hire the amount demanded. More workers will be willing to work than can get jobs at that wage. Those without jobs will be involuntarily unemployed. In Figure 27.1 the demand for labor will only be L_2, while the supply is L_1. The distance between these two points measures the amount of involuntary unemployment. At this high wage, the supply of labor exceeds the demand.

Involuntary unemployment arising from reductions in the demand for labor (combined with wage rigidity) would be much less of a social problem if the impact could be spread over the entire population. Even if the demand for labor were reduced by 10 percent and wages did not fall, the consequences would be limited if each worker worked 10 percent fewer hours. The problem in that case would be *underemployment*. Each person in the economy might work only 36 hours per week, when she wished to work 40 hours.

In the modern industrial economy, the problem is different. Most workers continue to work the same, or only a slightly reduced, number of hours when the labor market goes out of equilibrium, but an unfortunate few will find no full-time job at all at the going wage. This is the problem of unemployment. Whenever the supply of labor exceeds the demand at the going wage, there will be "rationing"—some individuals will not be able to sell all the labor they would like. But the impact of this rationing is not evenly spread in the economy; some workers will manage to sell little if any of their labor services, while others will be fully employed. Many of the social problems associated with a reduced demand for labor result from the fact that the economic burden is so concentrated.

The analysis is little different if we assume an upward-sloping, rather than vertical, labor supply curve. This would mean that workers change the number of hours they work in response to wage changes, supplying less labor at lower wages and more labor at higher wages. And at low wages, some individuals may decide not to work at all. Consider Figure 27.2, which shows an upward-sloping labor supply curve and a labor demand curve, LD_1. The initial equilibrium, entails a wage of w_1/P and employment of L_1 (hours worked). Now suppose there is a reduction in labor demanded at each wage, represented by the leftward shift of the labor demand curve from LD_1 to LD_2. If wages adjusted quickly, there would be a new equilibrium with wages at w_2/P and a lower level of employment at L_2. In this case, the reduction in employment is referred to as **voluntary unemployment.** At the lower wage w_2/P fewer people wish to work—those who wish to work have jobs, and those who are unemployed have chosen not to work.

By contrast, if wages remain at w_1/P after the shift of the labor demand curve, then employed labor falls to L_3. At this wage, the number willing to work is much higher: it remains at L_1. The workers who cannot get jobs represent **involuntary unemployment.** They are willing and able to work at the going wage, w_1/P, but simply cannot find jobs.

Most economists believe that the individual's labor supply curve, while not perfectly inelastic (or vertical), is relatively inelastic, and that much of the re-

Figure 27.2 THE EFFECTS OF A SHIFT IN THE DEMAND FOR LABOR WITH FIXED WAGES AND ELASTIC LABOR SUPPLY

If wages do not fall when the demand for labor shifts to the left, involuntary unemployment results. If wages adjust, employment decreases, but this is a voluntary change.

sponsiveness of the aggregate labor supply to wages comes from decisions to participate in the labor force (rather than in the desired number of hours worked per week). Moreover, as we have noted, when demand for labor is less than the supply, the shortfall usually takes the form mostly of reduction in employed workers, rather than hours worked per worker. For simplicity, in the following analysis, we shall assume that the hours worked per worker are fixed, and reductions in the demand for labor hours are translated directly into reductions in employment.

UNEMPLOYMENT AND WAGE RIGIDITIES

If we look at data on real wages—the wage adjusted for changes in the price level—we see that wages vary little with economic conditions. Figure 27.3 plots the real wage and unemployment rate during 1982 through 1994. During that period the unemployment rate fluctuated between 5.3 and 9.7 percent, yet the real wage was almost constant. Even in the Great Depression, with massive unemployment, real wages did not fall, or fell very little.

Given the relatively small changes in real wages, the magnitude of the changes in employment cannot be explained by movements along a fixed, steep labor supply curve. Then how can we account for such large changes in employment?

There are but two possibilities. One is that the labor market always remains in equilibrium. Thus, the labor supply curve is not only not fixed, but shifts dramatically—in a way just offsetting shifts in the labor demand curve—so that in spite of large variations in employment, real wages remained unchanged. Few economists accept this account. Even if there are sudden, dramatic shifts in the labor supply curve, it is hard to believe they would occur in just the right amount to offset shifts in the labor demand curve.

Figure 27.3 REAL WAGES AND UNEMPLOYMENT

During 1982–1995 the unemployment rate fluctuated between 5.3 and 9.7 percent. The real wage was almost constant.

Economists have focused their attention on the other possible explanation: at least at times, demand for labor is less than supply—the labor market is not in equilibrium. How does such a situation arise? First, there is a shift in the demand curve for labor, as we illustrated in Figures 27.1 and 27.2. Such shifts can occur fairly rapidly, mainly because of changes in output. Second, wages fail to fall enough to restore equilibrium (where demand for labor equals supply), resulting in involuntary unemployment. Because there is widespread agreement over this explanation, we may present it as our fourteenth point of consensus:

14 Unemployment

Unemployment is typically generated by shifts in the aggregate demand curve for labor when wages fail to adjust. The shifts in the aggregate demand curve for labor typically arise from changes in aggregate output.

UNEMPLOYMENT AND THE AGGREGATE SUPPLY OF LABOR

While most unemployment arises from sudden leftward shifts in the demand curve for labor, occasionally large rightward shifts in the supply curve for labor can also give rise to unemployment, as illustrated in Figure 27.4. Normally, aggregate labor supply changes only slowly, such as through demographic changes or changes in labor force participation rates. But there are circumstances in which aggregate supply can shift dramatically in a short span of time. For instance, in the early 1990s, Israel was faced with a flood of Jewish immigrants from Russia, increasing its labor force by more than 10 percent. In the short run, real wages did not adjust quickly enough, and unemployment rose. Remarkably, within five years, the unemployment rate was

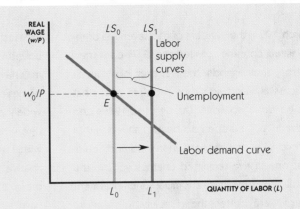

Figure 27.4 UNEMPLOYMENT AND THE AGGREGATE SUPPLY OF LABOR

Unemployment may arise from rightward shifts of the aggregate supply curve for labor, when wages fail to adjust. The initial equilibrium wage is w_0/P, at the intersection of the aggregate demand curve for labor and the initial aggregate supply curve for labor (LS_0). The aggregate supply curve for labor then shifts from LS_0 to LS_1. The real wage remains at w_0/P, where the quantity of labor demanded, L_0, is less than the quantity of labor supplied, resulting in unemployment.

back down—though the adjustment seems to have been more through a compensating shift in the aggregate demand curve for labor than a lowering of the real wage. Another instance of *potentially* rapid shifts in the labor supply curve are associated with changes in tax laws, which might induce a smaller or larger fraction of the population to join the labor force—though in practice such changes appear to take place more gradually.

BASIC ISSUES IN THE ANALYSIS OF UNEMPLOYMENT

1. What causes shifts in the demand curve for labor?
2. Why do wages fail to adjust?

THE PRODUCT MARKET IN THE SHORT RUN

To understand unemployment we must understand what causes changes in output. Thus, we now turn to the product market. Later, in Part Four, we will return to another basic issue of unemployment—what causes real wages to adjust slowly.

In March 1994, the leaders of the seven major industrialized countries (called the G-7) convened in Detroit. Their agenda: the first ever jobs summit to discuss a worldwide jobs problem and what might be done about it. Through the 1980s and into the 1990s, Europe had been plagued with a high level of unemployment. In Ireland and Spain, almost one in five remained unemployed. In the Netherlands, though the official unemployment statistics were better, the disability rolls—again, one in five—disguised what was really going on; more generous disability benefits and an absence of tight screening led many who were thrown out of jobs to apply for disability rather than unemployment benefits. The United States was beginning to control unemployment, but in many other countries unemployment remained a problem, as the figure on the next page indicates.

All countries agreed that the major source of the problem was with low-skilled and unskilled workers. The demand curve for these workers had not shifted to the right enough to offset the increased supply of such workers—and in some countries, the demand curve for these workers may have even shifted to the left. Though a variety of explanations have been put forward, the most widely accepted focus is on changes in technology, which have increased the demand for those with skills (such as the ability to use computers) relative to those without skills. The responses to these shifts in labor supply and demand curves have varied from country to country. In the United States, real wages of unskilled labor fell. In Europe, higher minimum wages helped prevent such a drop in real wages at the bottom of the skill distribution. Real wages of those employed in Europe increased over the 1970s through the 1990s by about 2 percent per year, in contrast to the virtual stagnation in the United States.

While the focus of attention was on unskilled workers, in Europe the problem seemed to be more widespread. Total job creation in the private sector in the first half of the 1990s was virtually nil—in contrast to the United States where more

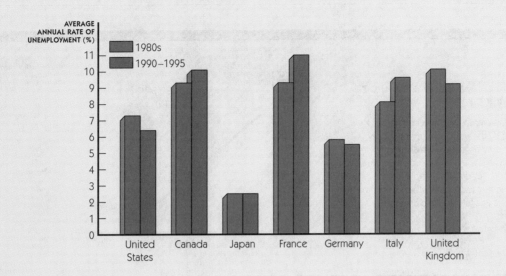

AVERAGE ANNUAL RATE OF UNEMPLOYMENT (%)

than seven million jobs were created in the private sector from 1993 through 1995. While there is no universally accepted explanation of Europe's poor job performance, one widely held view focuses on their more rigid labor markets, in which it is harder for firms to fire workers. But the flip side of greater job security is that firms become more nervous about taking on more workers.

Thus, in Europe fewer people had jobs, but those that did did better. The European solution involved greater inequality among the unskilled workers (higher wages versus no wages) and a loss of economic efficiency, as human resources were vastly underutilized.

Just as the demand and supply curves for labor were the basic tools for analyzing the labor market, the aggregate supply and demand curves for goods provide the framework for analyzing the product market. Recall the graph of the product market from Chapter 25. Redrawn here as Figure 27.5, it shows the vertical aggregate supply curve and the downward-sloping aggregate demand curve intersecting at point E. As we know from Chapter 25, the aggregate supply curve defines the economy's full-employment level of output, denoted as Y_s. At point E the economy is at full employment at the price level, P_0.

Like the assumption of fixed wages in our short-run analysis of the labor market, we assume that prices are fixed in the short-run analysis of the product market. In the short run, prices change little in response to movements of the aggregate demand and supply curves. Automobile manufacturers, for instance, typically change their prices only when new models come out. There are costs to changing prices—such as those of printing new catalogues and price lists—and risks—if a firm raises its price and its rival does not, it might price itself out of the market and lose customers. While there are a few markets, such as the stock market or the market for gold, in which prices adjust to shifts in the demand and supply curves on a daily or faster basis, for most

Figure 27.5 THE PRODUCT MARKET

The full-employment level of output, Y_s, is given by the vertical aggregate supply curve. The aggregate demand curve intersects the aggregate supply curve, at the price level P_0. Full-employment equilibrium is at point E, the intersection of the aggregate demand and supply curves.

goods and services, whether sold by producers, wholesalers, or retailers, there is considerable price rigidity.

Consider what happens in the short run if aggregate demand shifts to the left, as depicted in Figure 27.6. At price level P_0, firms will produce only the quantity that they can sell, the quantity Y_1, below the full-employment level of output. One result of the reduced output will be a decrease in the demand for labor. Because of fixed wages in the labor market, this results in involuntary unemployment. Eventually, prices and wages may adjust, and if the aggregate demand curve remains in its new position (AD_1), the economy may move down the aggregate demand curve toward the future full-employment equi-

Figure 27.6 OUTPUT BELOW CAPACITY

With the price level fixed at P_0, if the aggregate demand curve shifts to the left, the economy will fall below the full-employment level of output, Y_s. Output will be given by the aggregate demand curve at P_0, the level of output, Y_1. Eventually, if the aggregate demand curve remained at AD_1, the economy will move down the aggregate demand curve toward the future full-employment equilibrium, E_f.

Figure 27.7 EXCESS DEMAND

If the aggregate demand curve shifts to the right (from AD_0 to AD_1), aggregate demand will exceed the economy's capacity to produce at P_0. There will be excess demand and upward pressure on prices. Eventually, the economy will move up the aggregate supply curve toward the future full-employment equilibrium at E_f.

librium, E_f. But this process of adjustment is beyond the scope of our concern here. In the short run, which may span a year or more, the economy will be stuck at P_0, with output below capacity and involuntary unemployment.

Another scenario is also possible, and is illustrated in Figure 27.7. What happens if the aggregate demand curve shifts to the right, when the economy is initially in equilibrium at full employment? At price level P_0, demand exceeds supply, output is limited by aggregate supply (Y_s), and there is upward pressure on prices, anticipating the economy's eventual movement up the aggregate supply curve toward the future full-employment equilibrium, E_f. Under such circumstances the problem is not unemployment, but inflation, a subject we will consider in detail in later chapters. For now, the point to remember is that inflation becomes a concern when demand exceeds supply at a given price level; unemployment is the opposite problem, when demand at a given price level is less than the full-employment supply, Y_s.

THE ECONOMY BELOW CAPACITY

The economy may fall below the full-employment level of output for any number of reasons. Anything that decreases the demand (at a given price level) for consumption, investment, government expenditures, or net exports can give rise to a leftward shift in the aggregate demand curve, bringing the economy to a level of output below the full-employment level. For instance, an economic downturn in Mexico, Japan, or Europe will decrease their demand for American goods, decreasing our exports to them at any price level. Or, if businesses lose confidence in the future, they will be less willing to invest. Such unexpected shifts in the aggregate demand curve are referred to as **demand shocks.**

Occasionally, shifts in the supply schedule can also give rise to excess capacity—a wave of immigration faster than the economy can absorb or improvements in technology that increase the economy's productive capacity, even with an unchanged labor supply. When such shifts are sudden and unanticipated, they are referred to as **supply shocks.**

However it gets there, when the economy falls below the full-employment level of output, the options for policymakers are clear: either wait for the economy to adjust to a new full-employment equilibrium, or take action to shift the aggregate demand curve to the right, reestablishing the full-employment level of output at the existing price level. Policymakers have tended to take action. As the economist John Maynard Keynes once said: "In the long run, we are all dead." That the economy will resume full employment in the long run offers little solace to the unemployed. Figure 27.8 depicts the economy beginning at a level of output below capacity at Y_0. By shifting the aggregate demand curve to the right, the economy can be brought to the full-employment level of output, or at least closer to it—and faster than if markets were allowed to adjust on their own.

Anything that increases the demand (at a given price level) for consumption, investment, government expenditures, and net exports may lead to a rightward shift in the aggregate demand curve. One option for government is to increase its expenditures. For instance, by increasing defense expenditures, aggregate demand at each price level would increase, shifting the aggregate demand curve to the right. With excess capacity in the economy, this would result in increased output.

Raising government expenditures in response to involuntary unemployment is an act of **fiscal policy.** By fiscal policy, economists refer to changes in government expenditures and taxes directed at improving macroeconomic performance, including increasing output when there is excess capacity. Economists sometimes refer to a government effort to stimulate the economy through fiscal policy as a **fiscal stimulus.**

Figure 27.8 ATTAINING FULL EMPLOYMENT

At price level P_0, if the government can shift the aggregate demand curve enough to the right, the economy can be moved to operate at full capacity. When the aggregate demand curve shifts from AD_0 to AD_1, output increases from Y_0 to Y_1. With the aggregate demand curve, AD_2, the economy attains the full-employment equilibrium at P_0.

Figure 27.9 INCREASING AGGREGATE SUPPLY

At the current price level P_0, aggregate demand is less than Y_s, so that an increase in the economy's productive capacity has no effect on output in the short run.

THE SUPPLY SIDE OF THE MARKET

So far we have focused on the demand side of the market, and shifts in aggregate demand. What effect do increases in aggregate supply have on involuntary unemployment when the economy is below capacity?

Increased capacity of the economy may result from new investment or new technology. This shifts Y_s to the right. Figure 27.9 shows a rightward shift of the aggregate supply curve when the economy is initially below capacity at the price level, P_0. The result is only an increase in the amount by which aggregate supply exceeds aggregate demand at P_0. There is no effect on output.

On the other hand, when there is excess demand for goods (see Figure 27.7), an increase in aggregate supply will reduce the magnitude of the excess demand for goods, and thus the magnitude of the inflationary pressures. This was part of the rationale for the "supply-side" policies of the early 1980s, in which lower taxes were supposed to lead to increased labor supply and increased investment. As it turned out, the supply-side effects were small, and were overwhelmed by demand effects arising out of monetary policy.

THREE MORE POINTS OF CONSENSUS

The important results of this analysis of aggregate demand and supply can be summarized in our fifteenth, sixteenth, and seventeenth points of consensus.

15 Stimulating the Economy when It Is Below Capacity

When the economy has excess capacity, an increase in aggregate demand at each price level results in an increase in aggregate output, with relatively little effect on prices.

The increase in aggregate demand can, of course, come from any source: an increase in consumption by households, expenditure by government, investment by firms, or net exports.

16 The Effect of Overstimulating the Economy

When the economy is close to capacity, with most machines and workers fully employed, then a further increase in the demand for goods and services at each price level results in upward pressure on prices and has little effect on output.

17 Supply-Side Effects when There Is Excess Capacity

When the economy has excess capacity, increases in capacity have little effect on output.

LINKS WITH THE CAPITAL MARKET

We have now discussed the labor and product markets, two of the three central markets of the economy. These are both linked to the capital market in important ways.

In the capital market, interest rates are influenced by **monetary policy**—the actions of the **Federal Reserve Board,** which is the government agency responsible for controlling the money supply and interest rates. The Federal Reserve can lower and raise interest rates, with important consequences for the product and labor markets. Consider first the product market. Low interest rates may encourage home construction and investment, leading to a higher demand for goods and a higher level of output. If the Federal Reserve detects a lull in economic activity, it may choose to lower the interest rate. Figure 27.10 shows the effect of lower interest rates on the product market. There is a rightward shift of the aggregate demand curve. If the economy is initially operating with excess capacity, the shift in the aggregate demand curve leads to an increase in aggregate output. We could then trace through the effects on the labor market: higher aggregate output leads to a higher level of employment.

On the other hand, if the Federal Reserve is worried that the inflation rate is about to increase, it typically raises the interest rate. A situation with inflationary pressure is typically one where, at the current price level, aggregate demand exceeds the economy's full-employment level of output, as we depicted earlier in Figure 27.7. A higher interest rate dampens the level of aggregate demand—at each price, the quantity of investment that firms wish to make is reduced, so that the aggregate demand curve shifts to the left. If the Federal Reserve Board's assessment of the economic situation is correct, then the leftward movement of the aggregate demand curve simply decreases the upward pressure on prices, without having much effect on output. But if it increases

Figure 27.10 THE LINK BETWEEN THE CAPITAL MARKET AND THE PRODUCT MARKET

Lower interest rates lead to increased investment. This in turn leads to a rightward shift in the aggregate demand curve. If the economy is initially operating with excess capacity, aggregate output increases.

interest rates too far, it will shift the aggregate demand curve too much to the left, so that aggregate demand at the current price level P_0 will be less than Y_s: output will fall and unemployment will increase.

We have thus come full circle: all the markets of the economy are interconnected. So too are all the major policy concerns. The Federal Reserve may stimulate the economy by cutting the interest rate. On the other hand, aggressive action to contain inflation by restraining the economy—by raising the interest rate—discourages investment, and may lead to lower growth. If the Federal Reserve acts excessively aggressively, it may overshoot, lowering output and inducing unemployment. Rather than just curtailing inflation, it may actually push the economy into a recession. Later chapters will pursue these links, as well as the trade-offs for policymakers.

INTERDEPENDENCIES AMONG MARKETS

Changes in the capital market—such as lower interest rates—have immediate and direct impacts on the product market, shifting the aggregate demand curve.

Changes in the product market—such as increased aggregate demand—have impacts on the labor market, shifting the demand curve for labor.

Economic policymakers need to know more than just that an increase in output will translate into an increase in employment. They need to know something about the quantitative relationship: If they succeed in reducing unemployment by 1 percentage point, say from 7 percent to 6 percent, how much will output increase? If they succeed in reducing interest rates by 1 percentage point, say from 4 percent to 3 percent, how much will output increase? In making their calculations, they often use simple rules of thumb, based on historical experience. The most famous of these is called Okun's law, after Arthur Okun, who served as chairman of the Council of Economic Advisers under President Johnson. He calculated that the percentage increase in output was approximately twice the percentage decrease in the unemployment rate. Thus, lowering the unemployment rate from 7 percent to 6 percent will increase output by 2 percent.

Thus, in early 1996, there was widespread support for the view that the Federal Reserve Board should lower interest rates, given the absence of any inflationary pressures. This would stimulate economic growth. In February 1996, the unemployment rate stood at 5.5 percent. If lower interest rates succeeded in lowering unemployment to 5.2 percent, then, according to Okun's law, output would increase by approximately .6 percent (over what it otherwise would have been). Given that the economy had been forecast to grow at about 2 percent for the year, this represented a substantial increase in the growth rate *for that year.*

Okun's law can also be used in reverse. In early 1993, the unemployment rate stood at slightly more than 7 percent. Policymakers wanted to know how much would output have to increase in order to get the unemployment rate down to 6 percent. Okun's law gave them an answer: it would have to grow by about 2 percent *more* than the amount by which output would increase simply from the increase in productivity and the increase in employment that would result from the increased labor force with a *fixed* unemployment rate. With GDP at the time of approximately $6.5 trillion, this meant that aggregate demand would have to be increased by an additional amount of approximately $130 billion.

MACROECONOMIC LESSONS FROM THE POSTWAR PERIOD

The wide areas of macroeconomic consensus have been developed in part through a series of hardlearned lessons in the decades following World War II. The brief historical sketches that follow highlight some of the major policy discussions of the period.

THE KENNEDY TAX CUT

In 1963, the unemployment rate seemed to be stuck at an unacceptably high level, 5.5 percent. Ten years before it had been 2.8 percent. By 1959, it was 5.3 percent. President Kennedy's economic advisers believed that a cut in the individual income tax would cause households to consume more. This in turn would lead to a rightward shift in the aggregate demand curve. A shift in the aggregate demand curve, Kennedy's advisers believed, would result in increased output—not higher prices. This is because they believed that the economy had excess capacity, that productive workers and machines were lying idle. As a result, the shift in the aggregate demand curve would be translated into increases in output, as shown in Figure 27.11.

Increases in output, as we have learned, imply increases in employment. The predictions of Kennedy's advisers turned out to be correct. Unemployment fell to 4.4 percent in 1965 and stayed under 4 percent for the rest of the 1960s. In addition, real GDP grew at the remarkable average rate of 5.5 percent from 1964 to 1966.

THE REAGAN PROGRAM

When President Reagan took office in 1981, there was a widespread view that something should be done to stop inflation, which was high and appeared to be moving higher. Paul Volcker, chairman of the Federal Reserve Board, is generally given credit for doing so—though in the process he caused the worst recession in the postwar period. The Fed took strong actions to tighten the availability of credit and to raise interest rates—interest rates reached

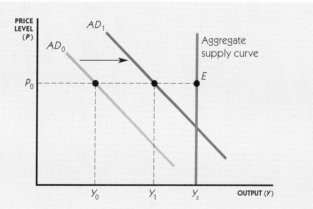

Figure 27.11 THE KENNEDY TAX CUT

The 1963 tax cut shifted the aggregate demand curve to the right and increased output from Y_0 to Y_1.

Figure 27.12 MONETARY POLICY CONTROLS INFLATION BUT CAUSES A RECESSION

Beginning in the late 1970s and early 1980s, the Federal Reserve Board, worried about runaway inflation, acted to restrict credit and thus consumption and investment. The resulting leftward shift in the aggregate demand curve caused a major recession. The effects were so strong that they more than offset the increased expansionary effects from the 1981 tax cut. The downward price pressures did, however, serve to reduce the pace of inflation.

record levels in excess of 20 percent before Volcker deemed inflation defeated. (How the Fed does this and the broader impact of such measures will be the subject of Chapters 30 and 31.) As a result of the Fed's actions, firms cut back their investments, and households cut back their purchases of items like cars and houses. Interestingly, at the same time that the Fed was taking these actions to restrict aggregate demand, fiscal policy was stimulating the economy. Reagan cut taxes, without cutting expenditures an offsetting amount. But the contractionary effect of higher interest rates more than offset the expansionary effect of lower taxes, and the aggregate demand curve shifted to the left, as shown in Figure 27.12. There, the initial upward pressure on prices is reflected by aggregate demand exceeding aggregate supply at the initial price level P_0 in the original situation. But the leftward shift in the aggregate demand curve was so large that at P_0, aggregate demand was much less than aggregate supply: the economy was thrown into a major recession. The national unemployment rate exceeded 11 percent, and climbed as high as 20 percent in certain parts of the country. However, the recession did have the effect of curbing inflation, which fell from around 13 percent in 1980 to just 3.2 percent in 1983.

THE 1991 RECESSION

The origins of the 1991 recession remain somewhat controversial. In perhaps the standard interpretation, inflation increased gradually from 1989 to 1991. As the Fed again became increasingly worried about inflation, it stepped on the brakes—raising interest rates. The large leftward shift in the aggregate demand curve had the predictable effect of lowering equilibrium output. But when the Fed subsequently loosened interest rates—lowering them to 3 percent—to restart the economy, the impacts were smaller, and took longer to take effect, than it had anticipated. The slow recovery is often thought to have contributed to President Bush's defeat in 1992.

Two factors complicate this story. The Persian Gulf War, beginning in August 1990 with Iraq's invasion of Kuwait, almost coincided with the recession; the sudden increase in oil prices is sometimes given credit for stalling out the economy. Most observers, however, note that the slowdown of the economy had actually set in slightly before. Still, the economic disruption of the war may have contributed to the downturn.

Secondly, when President Bush came into office, he found a fragile banking system. Part of it—the savings and loan associations—was on the verge of bankruptcy, and required a bailout costing taxpayers upward of $150 billion. Lax enforcement of regulations during the preceding years had contributed to the debacle. Regulators, worried about repeating the mistake, became overzealous, and banks were forced to cut back on lending to marginal borrowers. And the weakened financial shape of banks in many parts of the country made them less willing to make loans that they considered in any way risky. The result was a cutback in lending, which shifted the aggregate demand curve to the left. Whether this shift by itself would have thrown the economy into a recession is debatable, but what is clear is the weakened financial condition of the banks made them less willing and able to respond to the easing of the Fed, and this accounts in part for why it was unable to engineer a recovery with the speed that it would have liked.

DEFICIT REDUCTION TO STIMULATE THE ECONOMY

The final episode which we will discuss was a drama played out in 1993 and 1994. Clinton took office on a promise to restart the economy. Clinton's 1993 budget, which narrowly passed Congress, included about $250 billion of expenditure cuts and $250 billion of tax increases over the following five years, for a total deficit reduction of $500 billion. Many economists were worried: both expenditure cuts and tax increases reduce aggregate demand. Potentially, they could have made the economic downturn even worse. But there was another effect: the lower demand for borrowing (and the anticipated decreases in future years) led to lower interest rates, and the lower interest rates stimulated investment. The *net* effect was a shift in the aggregate demand curve to the right. The economy took off. Indeed, in a span of two years, more than five million new jobs were created.

Notice that both in this episode and that at the beginning of the Reagan administration, interest rate effects overwhelmed fiscal policy effects. In the former case, high interest rates led to a recession, even though fiscal policy was expansionary; in the more recent case, low interest rates led to recovery, even though fiscal policy was contractionary.

As is so often the case, the evidence is consistent with more than one interpretation: some believe that what really happened was a normal recovery from an economic downturn. If anything, the deficit reduction dampened the recovery, rather than causing it. In this interpretation, the dampening effects of expenditure cuts and tax increases more than offset the stimulating effect of increased investment due to lower interest rates, but the economy's momentum of recovery overcame the government's policy.

REVIEW AND PRACTICE

SUMMARY

1. Unemployment macroeconomics assumes that wages and prices are fixed in the short run.

2. To explain unemployment, we need to explain why the aggregate labor market does not clear. If real wages do not adjust to shifts in the aggregate supply and demand curves for labor, and either the demand curve for labor shifts to the left or the supply curve for labor shifts to the right, then the quantity of labor supplied will exceed the quantity demanded at the prevailing wage, and there will be involuntary unemployment.

3. The demand curve for labor shifts because of a fall in the production of goods by firms, as a result of a decrease in the demand for their products at each price level.

4. In the product market, if aggregate demand at a given price level is less than the economy's full-employment output (capacity), output will be limited by aggregate demand. Shifting the aggregate demand curve to the right will increase output and employment, and may restore the economy to full employment.

5. If, at a given price level, aggregate demand exceeds aggregate supply, output will be limited by aggregate supply, and there will be upward pressure on prices.

6. All markets in the economy are interrelated. Thus disturbances in the product market have consequences for the labor market, and disturbances in the capital market have consequences for the product market. For instance, when there is involuntary unemployment, lower interest rates may result in increased investment, increasing output and employment.

KEY TERMS

voluntary
   unemployment
involuntary
   unemployment

demand shocks
supply shocks
fiscal policy
fiscal stimulus

monetary policy
Federal Reserve
   Board

REVIEW QUESTIONS

1. If the labor market always cleared, would there be any unemployment? What does it mean for the labor market not to clear? What gives rise to unemployment?

2. If the labor market always cleared, can there be variations in the level of employment?

3. What inferences do you draw from the following two facts?
   (a) The labor supply curve is relatively inelastic.
   (b) Large variations in employment coexist with relatively small variations in real wages.

4. What might shift the aggregate demand curve for labor?

5. If prices are rigid, and at a level *above* that at which aggregate demand equals supply, what will be the level of output? What will happen if the aggregate demand curve shifts to the left? To the right? If the aggregate supply curve shifts to the left? To the right?

6. If prices are rigid, and at a level *below* that at which aggregate demand equals supply, what will be the level of output? What will happen if the aggregate demand curve shifts to the left? To the right? If the aggregate supply curve shifts to the left? To the right?

7. What are some of the ways in which the various markets of the economy are interlinked?

8. Use the aggregate demand and supply curve framework to describe some of the major macroeconomic episodes of the postwar period.

PROBLEMS

1. In the 1970s, a large number of new workers entered the U.S. economy from two main sources. The baby boom generation grew to adulthood and the proportion of women working increased substantially. If wages adjust, what effect will these factors have on the equilibrium level of wages and quantity of labor? If wages do not adjust, how does your answer change? In which case will unemployment exist? Draw a diagram to explain your answer. What is the effect of the increased labor supply on the product market? Illustrate your answer diagrammatically.

2. Soon after Iraq invaded Kuwait in August 1990, many firms feared that a recession would occur. Anticipating a lack of demand for their goods, they began cutting back on production. If wages adjust, what will happen to the equilibrium level of wages and employment? If wages do not adjust, how does your answer change? In which case will unemployment exist?

3. In early 1995, Mexico faced a financial crisis, which led to a major economic downturn in that country. Exports to Mexico exceed those to any other country except Canada. If nothing else had happened, what effect would you expect this to have on the aggregate demand curve and on the level of national output in the short run, at a given price level?

4. In the early 1990s, there was a massive wave of Russian immigrants into Israel. Yet, within a few years, unemployment returned to normal levels and real wages had not fallen. Using aggregate demand and supply curves for goods and labor, explain how this could have occurred. (Hint: new immigrants generate additional demand for goods as well as additional supplies of labor.)

5. When Bill Clinton became president in early 1993, the unemployment rate was in excess of 7 percent. There was worry about the speed of economic recovery. He proposed—but Congress rejected—a small "stimulus" package, consisting mainly of increased investment. Show diagrammatically what this might have done to the aggregate demand curve and the level of output at a given price level. Critics worried that the government would have had to borrow more money to pay for the additional expenditures, and that this would drive up interest rates, discouraging private investment. If this happened, show what would have happened to the aggregate demand curve and the level of output at a given price level.

6. While for the most part, macroeconomics focuses on aggregate employment, ignoring distinctions among different categories of workers, it sometimes focuses on broad categories, such as skilled and unskilled

workers. Assume, for simplicity, that there are just these two categories, and that for the most part, they cannot be substituted for each other.

(a) Draw demand and supply curves for skilled and unskilled workers, marking the initial equilibrium in each market.

(b) Assume now that there is a technological change which increases the demand for skilled labor at each wage, while it shifts the demand curve for unskilled labor to the left. If wages do not adjust, can there be vacancies of one type of labor at the same time there is unemployment of another type?

28

AGGREGATE
DEMAND

I n Chapter 27 we learned that the major cause of unemployment
was a shift in the demand curve for labor, without a commensurate fall in the real wage. We also learned that the major cause of a
shift in the demand curve for labor was a reduction in aggregate
output. Thus, to understand events in the labor market, we must
understand the product market—what determines the level of output and its
changes.

The objective of this and the following chapters is to answer that question,
focusing on those circumstances where supply imposes no constraints—that
is, where there is excess capacity of machines and unemployment of labor. In
this simple scenario, output is determined entirely by aggregate demand.

The task of this chapter is to explain what determines the level of aggregate
demand at any particular set of wages and prices, what causes changes in aggregate demand, and why output can be so volatile.

tures schedule is flatter than the 45-degree line since aggregate expenditures increase less than dollar for dollar with increased income.

Third, even if national income were zero, aggregate expenditures would remain positive. This is reflected in the fact that the aggregate expenditures schedule intercepts the vertical axis at a positive level, point A. (We will discuss the reasons for this later in the chapter.)

The facts that (a) the aggregate expenditures schedule is flatter than the 45-degree line through the origin and (b) aggregate expenditures are positive, even when income is zero, imply that the aggregate expenditures schedule intersects the 45-degree line, as seen in the figure.

What is the relationship between the aggregate expenditures schedule and the aggregate demand schedule discussed in the last chapter? The aggregate expenditures schedule shows expenditures, at each level of price and income; the aggregate demand curve shows aggregate demand (or expenditures) at each level of price—when the level of income has been adjusted to its (short-run) equilibrium level. This brings us to our central question: What determines the (short-run) equilibrium level of output, when there is excess capacity? Besides the aggregate expenditure schedule, we need two more concepts for our analysis.

THE NATIONAL INCOME-OUTPUT IDENTITY

National income is equal to national output (as shown in Chapter 24). This reflects the fact that when a good is purchased, the money that is paid must eventually wind up as someone's income—as wages, in the pockets of workers in the firm that produced the good (or of workers who produced the intermediate goods that were used in the production of the final good); as interest payments, in the pockets of those who have lent the firm money; or as profits, in the pockets of the owners of the firm. For simplicity, we will assume that the residents of the country neither receive money (net) from abroad nor pay money (net) to abroad, so GNP and GDP coincide. If Y is used to represent national income, this identity can be written

GDP = national income = Y.

This identity is our second necessary concept. It allows us to interpret the horizontal axis in Figure 28.2 in two different ways. We can say the aggregate expenditures schedule gives the level of expenditures at each level of national *income*. We can also say it gives the level of expenditures at each level of national *output*.

EQUILIBRIUM OUTPUT

Normally, firms will only produce what they believe they can sell. This means that the total output produced by all firms will equal the total demand for output. This is our third necessary concept, and it can be put another way. In equilibrium, aggregate expenditures, which we denote by AE, must equal aggregate output (GDP). Since aggregate output equals national income (Y), we have the simple equation

$$AE = \text{GDP} = Y.$$

In Figure 28.2, the 45-degree line through the origin is labeled "Aggregate expenditures = output." The line traces all points where the vertical axis (aggregate expenditures) equals the horizontal axis (national income, which equals aggregate output).

Equilibrium lies at the point on the aggregate expenditures schedule that also satisfies the aggregate-expenditures-equal-output condition. That is, equilibrium occurs at the intersection of the aggregate expenditures schedule and the 45-degree line. The corresponding equilibrium value of aggregate output is denoted by Y^*.

The analysis that determines equilibrium output by relating income (output) to aggregate expenditures is called **income-expenditure analysis.** We can see that Y^* is the equilibrium in two different ways. The first way is to note that it is the only point that satisfies the two conditions for equilibrium. In equilibrium, everything produced must be purchased. Thus, aggregate expenditures must be equal to national output (income), as represented by the 45-degree line. In equilibrium, the level of aggregate expenditures must also be what households, firms, and government want to spend in total at that level of national income, given by the aggregate expenditures schedule.

The second way is to consider what happens at a level of income Y_1, in excess of Y^*. At that point, the aggregate expenditures schedule lies below the 45-degree line. What households, firms, and government would like to spend at that level of national income, as reflected in the aggregate expenditures schedule, is less than national income (output). More goods are being produced than individuals want to buy. Some of the goods, like strawberries, cannot be stored. They simply spoil. The goods that can be stored go into inventories.

Economists distinguish between **planned inventories** and **unplanned inventories.** Firms choose to have some inventory on hand because it makes business more efficient. Planned inventories are considered an investment, and their buildup is therefore counted as part of investment spending in the aggregate expenditures schedule. Unplanned inventories are simply the goods firms are producing but cannot sell. In Figure 28.2, at Y_1, above the 45-degree line, firms find that unplanned inventories are piling up—they are producing goods that cannot be sold, which are either spoiling or increasing inventories beyond the desired level. They respond by cutting back production until they reach Y^*. At Y_2, the aggregate expenditures schedule lies above the 45-degree line. Households, firms, and government are spending more than national income (output). They are, in other words, purchasing more than the economy is producing. This is possible because firms can sell out of inventories. With planned inventories being depleted, firms increase production until equilibrium is restored, with output (income) again equal to Y^*.

Figure 28.3 EFFECT OF A SHIFT IN THE AGGRE-GATE EXPENDITURES SCHEDULE

An upward shift in the aggregate expenditures schedule results in an increase in the equilibrium level of output. The magnitude of the increase in equilibrium output from a given upward shift in the aggregate expenditures schedule is greater than the magnitude of the upward shift; that is, $Y_1 - Y_0$ exceeds S, the magnitude of the shift.

SHIFTS IN THE AGGREGATE EXPENDITURES SCHEDULE

The aggregate expenditures schedule can shift through a variety of changes in the economy that lead households, firms, and government to decide, *at each level of income,* to spend more or less. Figure 28.3 shows what happens if the level of aggregate expenditures increases at each level of national income by the amount S. The new aggregate expenditures schedule is denoted by AE_1.

INCOME-EXPENDITURE ANALYSIS

1. Equilibrium output is at the point where the aggregate expenditures schedule equals output (income).
2. Upward shifts in the aggregate expenditures schedule result in increases in equilibrium output. The increases in equilibrium output are larger than the initial shift in the aggregate expenditures schedule. How much larger depends on the slope of the aggregate expenditures schedule. The steeper the slope, the greater the increase.

Figure 28.4 THE IMPOR-TANCE OF THE SLOPE OF THE AGGREGATE EXPENDITURES SCHEDULE

The flatter the aggregate expenditures schedule, the smaller the magnitude of the increase in output resulting from a given upward shift in the schedule.

The equilibrium output increases from Y_0 to Y_1, *which is greater than the amount S.* How much greater depends on the slope of the aggregate expenditures schedule. In Figure 28.4, the aggregate expenditures schedule shifts up by the same amount it did in Figure 28.3, but the aggregate expenditures schedule is flatter. Consequently, the increase in equilibrium output is much smaller.

MATHEMATICAL FORMULATION

We can describe the equilibrium using simple algebra. The aggregate expenditures equation can be written:

$$AE = b + cY,$$

where b is the vertical intercept of the aggregate expenditures schedule (the value of AE when $Y = 0$); and c is the slope of the aggregate expenditures schedule (an increase in Y of \$1 increases AE by \$$c$). The fact that the slope is less than 45 degrees implies that c is between 0 and 1. Equilibrium requires aggregate expenditures to equal income—which, under our simplifying assumptions, equals Y:

$$AE = Y.$$

Substituting the second equation into the first equation yields

$$Y = b + cY,$$

which can be solved for Y:

$Y = b/(1 - c).$

An upward shift in the aggregate expenditures schedule corresponds to an increase in b, say to $b + 1$. Then Y increases by an amount $1/(1 - c)$. Since c is less than 1, $1/(1 - c)$ is greater than 1. If $c = .9$, then $1 - c = .1$ and $1/(1 - c) = 10$, so that an upward shift in the aggregate expenditures schedule by \$1 increases GDP by \$10. This basic property is called the multiplier. Later in the chapter we will take a closer look at it.

A LOOK FORWARD

We have just learned two of the central principles of macroeconomics: (1) shifts in the aggregate expenditures schedule determine changes in the equilibrium output of the economy, and (2) the magnitude of those changes is greater than the magnitude of the shift up or down in the aggregate expenditures schedule and increases with the slope of the aggregate expenditures schedule. The remainder of this chapter explores the implications of these principles. Two questions are addressed.

The first question is: What determines the slope of the aggregate expenditures schedule—that is, the extent to which aggregate expenditures increase as income increases? As we have seen, the greater that slope, the larger the increase in output from any upward shift in the schedule. The second question is: What causes shifts in the aggregate expenditures schedule? And what, if anything, can the government do to shift the schedule? The possibilities for government are an important issue. In the last chapter, we saw that unemployment is created when there is a shift in the demand curve for labor without a corresponding downward adjustment of wages. The primary reason for a shift in the demand curve for labor is a change in the equilibrium level of output. When output is low, the demand for labor is low. If government can increase the equilibrium level of output by somehow shifting the aggregate expenditures schedule, then it can increase the level of employment.

To answer these questions, we need to take a closer look at each of the four components of aggregate expenditures: (1) consumption goods, such as food, television sets, or clothes, all of which are purchased by consumers; (2) investment in capital goods, machines or buildings that are bought by firms to help them produce goods; (3) government purchases, both goods and services bought for current use (public consumption) and goods and services like buildings and roads, bought for the future benefits they generate (public investment); and (4) net exports. We say net exports, because we have to subtract from the value of goods sold abroad the value of those goods and services bought by U.S. households, businesses, and government that are produced abroad, that is, imports.

Using *AE* for aggregate expenditures, *C* for consumption spending, *I* for investment spending, *G* for government spending, and *E* for net exports, we can set out the components of aggregate expenditures in equation form:

$$AE = C + I + G + E.$$

This equation is nothing more than a definition. It says that consumption spending, investment spending, government spending, and net exports add up to aggregate expenditures. Net exports is sometimes written as $X - M$, where X stands for exports and M for imports. These symbols represent near-astronomical numbers for the U.S. economy. In 1995, *AE* was $7,248 billion, of which *C* was $4,923 billion (67.9% of *AE*), *I* was $1,067 billion (14.7% of *AE*), *G* was $1,359 billion (18.8% of *AE*), *X* was $805 billion, and *M* was $906 billion (so *E* was −1.4% of *AE*). We now take a brief look at each of these categories.

Table 28.1 RELATIONSHIP BETWEEN INCOME AND CONSUMPTION

Income	Consumption
$ 5,000	$ 6,000
10,000	10,500
20,000	19,500
30,000	28,500

Table 28.2 AGGREGATE CONSUMPTION AND NATIONAL INCOME (billions of dollars)

National income	Consumption (*C*)
$ 1,000	$ 1,050
2,000	1,950
3,000	2,850
4,000	3,750
6,500	6,000
10,000	9,150
20,000	18,150

CONSUMPTION

The most important determinant of consumption is income. On average, families with higher incomes spend more. Table 28.1 shows the relationship between consumption and income for a hypothetical family. The same information is depicted graphically in Figure 28.5A, with the amount of consumption given along the vertical axis and income along the horizontal axis. The upward slope of the line indicates that consumption for this family increases as income does. The relationship between a household's consumption and its income is called its **consumption function.** Every family has different consumption patterns because the tastes and circumstances of families differ, but the pattern shown in Table 28.1 is typical.

Aggregate consumption is the sum of the consumption of all the households in the economy. Just as when a typical family's income rises its consumption increases, when the total income of the economy rises, aggregate consumption increases. For purposes of macroeconomics, it is the **aggregate consumption function,** the relationship between aggregate consumption and aggregate income, that is of importance. And the measure of income that is important is disposable income, or what people have after paying taxes. But because we are assuming no government for the moment, disposable income equals national income. The relationship between aggregate consumption and national income is given in Table 28.2, and the aggregate consumption function is depicted graphically in Figure 28.5B.

THE MARGINAL PROPENSITY TO CONSUME

The amount by which consumption increases when disposable income increases by a dollar is called the **marginal propensity to consume** (*MPC*). For the United States as a whole, the marginal propensity to consume in recent

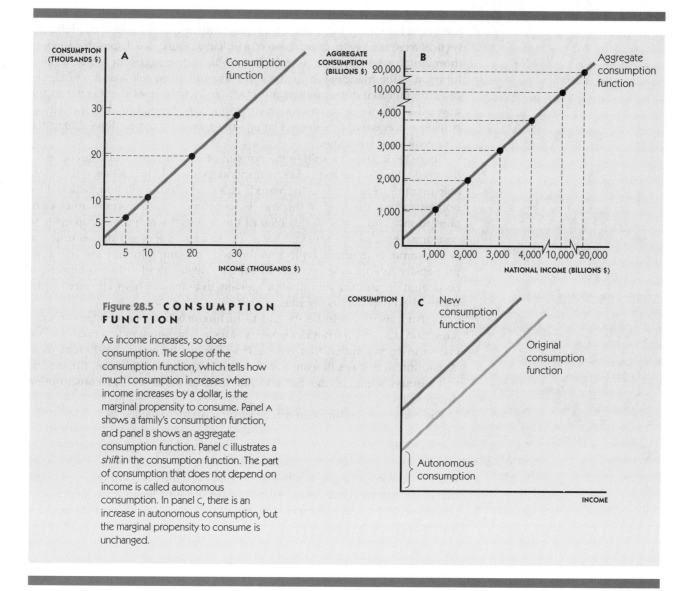

Figure 28.5 CONSUMPTION FUNCTION

As income increases, so does consumption. The slope of the consumption function, which tells how much consumption increases when income increases by a dollar, is the marginal propensity to consume. Panel A shows a family's consumption function, and panel B shows an aggregate consumption function. Panel C illustrates a *shift* in the consumption function. The part of consumption that does not depend on income is called autonomous consumption. In panel C, there is an increase in autonomous consumption, but the marginal propensity to consume is unchanged.

years has been somewhere between .9 and .97. That is, of each extra dollar of income households receive, they spend on average between 90 and 97 percent.[1] If aggregate income increases by $100 billion, then aggregate consumption will increase by between $90 and $97 billion. In the hypothetical consumption function illustrated in Figure 28.5B, the marginal propensity to consume is .9: when disposable income goes up by $1 trillion, aggregate consumption goes up by $900 billion.

[1] In the late 1980s, consumption was sometimes as high as 97 percent of household income. More recently, consumption has been somewhat lower. These statistics give the *average* ratio of consumption to disposable income. The *marginal* propensity to consume is somewhat smaller.

The slope of the aggregate consumption function conveys important information. It tells us by how much aggregate consumption (measured along the vertical axis) rises with an increase of a dollar of aggregate disposable income (horizontal axis). In other words, the slope of the aggregate consumption function is the marginal propensity to consume. In panels A and B of Figure 28.5, the fact that consumption increases as income rises is reflected in the upward slope of the consumption function, and the marginal propensity to consume is equal to this slope. Flatter slopes would illustrate lower marginal propensities to consume.

Figure 28.5C shows a shift in the consumption function. The intercept with the vertical axis—the level of consumption that would prevail even if disposable income were zero—is increased. This part of consumption, which does not depend on the level of income, is sometimes called **autonomous consumption**.[2] With the shift depicted in the figure, the marginal propensity to consume remains unchanged; that is, the slope of the consumption function is the same. Sometimes both autonomous consumption and the marginal propensity to consume change. In the late 1980s, the level of autonomous consumption and the marginal propensity to consume both appeared to be higher than in previous decades.

As usual, we have to be careful to distinguish between changes in consumption that result from *movements along a consumption function*—the increase in consumption that results from higher incomes—and changes in consumption that result from a *shift in the consumption function*. Chapter 29 will discuss some of the factors that lead to shifts in the consumption function.

The consumption function can be written mathematically as

$$C = a + mY_d,$$

where C is consumption, a is the level of autonomous consumption, m is the marginal propensity to consume (the extra amount spent on consumption when disposable income increases by a dollar), and Y_d is disposable income, income after paying taxes.

THE MARGINAL PROPENSITY TO SAVE

Individuals have to either spend or save each extra dollar of disposable income, so savings and consumption are mirror images of each other. The definition "income = consumption plus savings" tells us that when disposable income rises by a dollar, if aggregate consumption increases by 90 cents, aggregate savings increase by 10 cents. The higher level of savings stemming from an extra dollar of income is called the **marginal propensity to save** (*MPS*). This is the counterpart to the marginal propensity to consume, and the

---

[2]People can consume even when their income is zero by using up savings.

two must always sum to one:

marginal propensity to save + marginal propensity to consume = 1.

The high marginal propensity to consume today means that there is a low marginal propensity to save. Fifty years ago, the marginal propensity to consume was smaller than it is today, somewhere between .8 and .9; of each extra dollar of disposable income, between 80 and 90 cents was spent on consumption. By the same token, the marginal propensity to save was larger; between 10 and 20 cents of each extra dollar of disposable income went into savings.

INVESTMENT

We now turn to the second major component of GDP—investment. Investment varies greatly from year to year, and, as we learned in Chapter 25, depends on the level of interest rates. Now, however, our focus is on the relationship between aggregate expenditures and national income as described by the aggregate expenditures schedule. We assume the level of investment is unrelated to the level of income this year. This assumption is made largely to simplify the analysis, but it also reflects the view that investment is primarily determined by firms' estimates of the economic prospects over the future. Accordingly, investment levels are not greatly affected by what happens this year and, in particular, not greatly affected by the level of national income. (See Table 28.3.) We can now analyze equilibrium output in a simplified economy

Table 28.3 **SOME COMPONENTS OF AGGREGATE EXPENDITURES** (billions of dollars)

Disposable income (Y_d)	Consumption expenditures (C)	Investment spending (I)	Total aggregate expenditures
$ 1,000	$ 1,050	$500	$ 1,550
2,000	1,950	500	2,450
3,000	2,850	500	3,350
4,000	3,750	500	4,250
6,500	6,000	500	6,500
10,000	9,150	500	9,650
20,000	18,150	500	18,650

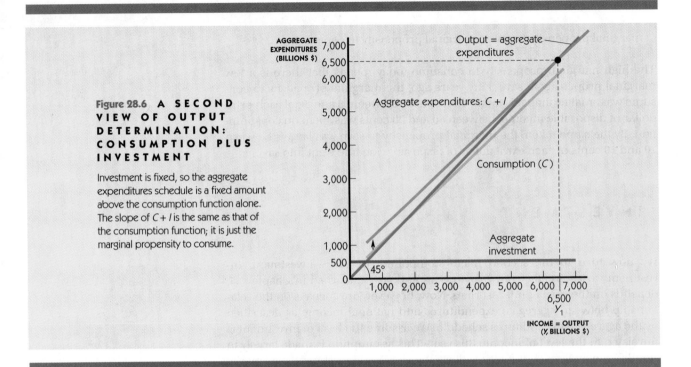

Figure 28.6 A SECOND VIEW OF OUTPUT DETERMINATION: CONSUMPTION PLUS INVESTMENT

Investment is fixed, so the aggregate expenditures schedule is a fixed amount above the consumption function alone. The slope of $C + I$ is the same as that of the consumption function; it is just the marginal propensity to consume.

with no government and no foreign trade. Aggregate expenditures thus consist only of consumption and investment.

Table 28.3 combines the information from Table 28.2 with a fixed level of investment, $500 billion. Because we have assumed away government—both taxes and expenditures—disposable income is the same as national income. The table shows the level of aggregate expenditures for various levels of national income. Aggregate expenditures consist of the sum of consumption and investment, shown in the fourth column of the table and plotted in Figure 28.6. Because we assume investment does not depend on current income, the slope of the upper line in the figure is exactly the same as the slope of the consumption function: as income increases, aggregate expenditures increase by the same amount that consumption does, that is, by the marginal propensity to consume. The slope of the aggregate expenditures schedule is still the marginal propensity to consume. The equilibrium—the intersection of the aggregate expenditures schedule and the 45-degree line—is at Y_1 ($6,500 billion).

THE MULTIPLIER

One of the fundamental insights of income-expenditure analysis is that factors shifting the aggregate expenditures schedule will have a compound effect on output. Consider, for instance, an upward shift in the aggregate expenditures schedule induced by an increase in investment of $1 billion. We continue to assume that the marginal propensity to consume (MPC) is .9. The first-round effect of the extra investment spending, shown in Table 28.4, is straightforward: output increases by $1 billion as firms purchase capital goods. This is only the beginning, however. The value of this increased output is distributed to the members of the economy as income, in the form of either higher wages, higher interest payments, of higher profits that become income to the firms' owners. Given that the marginal propensity to consume is .9, this will lead consumption demand to increase by .9 × $1 billion = $900 million. This second-round effect creates a $900 million increase in output and thus income, which in turn brings on a third-round increase of consumption of .9 × $900 million = $810 million. In the next round, output is increased by .9 × $810,000, then by .9 times that amount, then by .9 times that amount, and so on. In this example, when all the increases are totaled, a $1 billion increase in investment will lead to a $10 billion rise in equilibrium output.

Unfortunately, the multiplier process also works in reverse. Just as an increase in investment leads to a multiple increase in national output, a decrease in investment leads to a multiple decrease in national output. In our example, with an MPC of .9, if investment decreases by $1 billion, national output will decrease by $10 billion. The relationship between any change in investment expenditures and the resulting eventual change in national output is called the investment multiplier, or just **multiplier** for short. An increase in government expenditures or net exports has a similar multiplier effect.

In our simple model, with no trade and no government, the multiplier has a simple mathematical form: $\frac{1}{1 - MPC}$. As we learned earlier, any income an individual does not consume is saved, and an increase of income by a dollar must be spent either on consumption or on savings. Therefore,

$1 - MPC = MPS$, the marginal propensity to save.

Table 28.4 EFFECTS OF AN INCREASE IN INVESTMENT OF $1 BILLION (millions of dollars)

First round	$ 1,000
Second round	900
Third round	810
Fourth round	729
Fifth round	656
Sixth round	590
Seventh round	531
Eighth round	478
Ninth round	430
Tenth round	387
Eleventh round	349
Sum of twelfth and successive rounds	$ 3,140
Total increase	$10,000

The basic lesson of the multiplier is that a little stimulus can go a long way—at least a longer way than it would without the multiplier. In 1993, with the economy still in an economic downturn, and unemployment in excess of 7 percent, newly elected President Clinton argued for a small stimulus package, consisting largely of investments, of approximately $16 billion. Sixteen billion dollars in a six trillion dollar economy seems like a small number—about a quarter of one percent. But with a multiplier of 2, that could add $32 billion to national output. A $32 billion increase in output in turn would lop off two- to three-tenths of a percentage point from the unemployment rate—not enough by itself to bring the economy's unemployment rate down to the target of 6 percent or below, but enough to speed the recovery and show that the administration was doing something about the slowdown which by then had lasted close to two years. Indeed, the small size was viewed as a virtue: it posed little threat of overheating the economy, should the economy's recovery take hold on its own faster than had been forecast.

This result allows us to rewrite the basic formula for the multiplier:

$$\text{multiplier} = \frac{1}{1 - MPC} = \frac{1}{MPS}.$$

In other words the multiplier is the reciprocal of the marginal propensity to save. If the marginal propensity to consume is .9, the marginal propensity to save is $1 - .9 = .1$, and the multiplier is 10.

USING ECONOMICS: CALCULATING THE MULTIPLIER

Earlier, we showed that

$$y = \frac{a + I}{1 - m}.$$

To see the multiplier, assume that I increases by a dollar. Now

$$Y_1 = \frac{a + I + 1}{1 - m}.$$

The change in Y, $Y_1 - Y$ is found by subtraction:

$$Y_1 - Y = \frac{1}{1 - m}.$$

The smaller m, the marginal propensity to consume, is the flatter the aggregate expenditures schedule is, and the smaller the multiplier is. If $m = .9$, the multiplier is 10. If $m = .8$, the multiplier is 5.

THE MULTIPLIER

An increase in investment leads to an increase in output that is a multiple of the original increase.

The multiplier equals $1/(1 - MPC)$, or $1/MPS$.

GOVERNMENT AND TRADE

The basic operation of the multiplier is unchanged when government and foreign trade are included in the analysis. Changes in government expenditure and net exports lead, through a multiplier, to larger changes in equilibrium output. But, as we will see, the effects of government and trade change the size of the multiplier.

THE EFFECTS OF GOVERNMENT

Government serves as a double-edged sword in the macroeconomy: its spending increases aggregate expenditures at the same time that its taxes reduce the amount of people's income. Let us take taxes first. Since consumption depends on individuals' disposable income—the amount of income they have available to spend after paying taxes—government taxes also reduce consumption.

Total income equals total output, denoted by Y. Disposable income is simply total income minus taxes, T:

disposable income $= Y - T$.

Taxes do two things. First, since at each level of national income disposable income is lower with taxes, consumption is lower. Taxes shift the aggregate expenditures schedule down. Second, when taxes increase with income, the multiplier is lower (the slope of the aggregate expenditures schedule is smaller). This is because taxes typically go up with income. When total income increases by a dollar, therefore, consumption increases by less than it otherwise would, since a fraction of the increased income goes to government.

Without taxes, when investment goes up by a dollar, income rises by a dollar, which leads to an increase in consumption determined by the marginal propensity to consume. This increase in consumption then sets off the next round of increases in national income. If, when income goes up by a dollar,

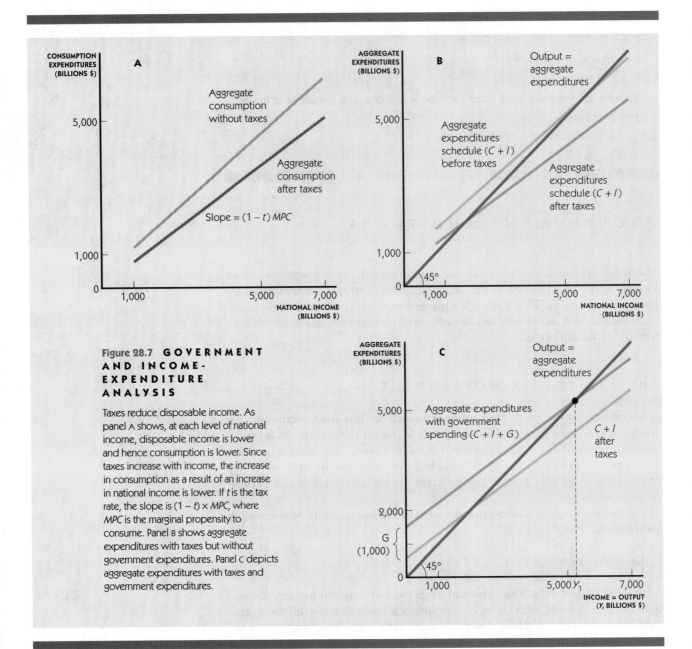

Figure 28.7 GOVERNMENT AND INCOME-EXPENDITURE ANALYSIS

Taxes reduce disposable income. As panel A shows, at each level of national income, disposable income is lower and hence consumption is lower. Since taxes increase with income, the increase in consumption as a result of an increase in national income is lower. If *t* is the tax rate, the slope is $(1 - t) \times MPC$, where *MPC* is the marginal propensity to consume. Panel B shows aggregate expenditures with taxes but without government expenditures. Panel C depicts aggregate expenditures with taxes and government expenditures.

government tax collections increase by 25 cents, then disposable income increases by only 75 cents. So the increase in consumption with taxes is one quarter smaller than it is without. In other words, the consumption function is flatter, as shown in panel A of Figure 28.7. Because the slope of the aggregate consumption function is flatter, the slope of the aggregate expenditures schedule is flatter, as illustrated in panel B. And because the slope of the aggregate expenditures schedule is flatter, the multiplier is smaller.

How about government spending? The answer to this question would be simpler if the government's expenditures moved in lockstep with its revenues. However, the government can spend more than it raises in taxes, by borrowing. When annual government expenditures exceed tax revenues, there is a **deficit.** There is some debate about the effects of deficits. Here we make the simplifying assumption that the deficit itself (as opposed to the spending imbalance that created the deficit) has no *direct* effect on either consumption or investment.

We also assume that government expenditures do not increase automatically with the level of income; they are assumed to be fixed, say at $1,000 billion. Thus, while taxes shift the aggregate expenditures schedule down and flatten it, government expenditures shift the aggregate expenditures schedule up by the amount of those expenditures, as shown in panel c of Figure 28.7. In this panel, the upward shifts in the aggregate expenditures schedule from government expenditures have been superimposed on the downward shifts in the aggregate expenditures schedule from taxes depicted in panel B. Note that the contributions of investment, I (which, in the example of Figure 28.7, are still assumed to be $500 billion), and government expenditures, G, raise the schedule but do not change its slope. The slope in panel c is the same as in panel B. Equilibrium again occurs at the intersection of the aggregate expenditures schedule and the 45-degree line. Increased government expenditures can have a powerful effect in stimulating the economy. But if the economy is in a serious recession, the government may have to increase expenditures a great deal to raise output to the full-employment level.

THE EFFECTS OF INTERNATIONAL TRADE

The analysis so far has ignored the important role of international trade. This is appropriate for a closed economy, an economy that neither exports nor imports, but not for an open economy, one actively engaged in international trade. Today the United States and other industrialized economies are very much open economies.

International trade can have powerful effects on national output. To begin with, exports expand the market for domestic goods. In recent years, the American economy has exported goods and services amounting to approximately 10 percent of national output. For smaller countries, exports amount to a much larger percentage of output: 26 percent for the United Kingdom and 12 percent for Japan, for instance.

But just as exports expand the market for domestic goods, imports decrease it. Therefore, imports and exports affect the aggregate expenditures schedule in different ways. In recent years, net exports—the appropriate concept when looking at the overall effect on aggregate expenditures—have turned sharply negative in the United States. That is to say, imports have exceeded exports. In the late 1980s, net exports amounted to *minus* 2 to 3 percent of U.S. GDP. Trade not only has increased in size relative to the economy, but net exports have changed dramatically, as illustrated in Figure 28.8.

Figure 28.8 U.S. NET EXPORTS SINCE 1950

U.S. net exports were generally positive through the 1950s and 1960s, before turning sharply negative in the 1980s. *Source: ERP* (1996), Table B-1.

IMPORTS

When households' incomes rise, they not only buy more American-made consumer goods, they also buy more goods from abroad. We can illustrate an **import function** in much the same way that we illustrated a consumption function. (We have assumed investment and government expenditures to be fixed here, so for now there is no schedule relating either of these to income.) The import function shows the levels of imports corresponding to different levels of income. Table 28.5 shows hypothetical levels of imports for different

---

USING ECONOMICS: PUTTING GOVERNMENT INTO THE EQUATION

When we add government, the equation for aggregate expenditures becomes

$$AE = C + I + G = a + mY_d + I + G,$$

where Y_d is disposable income. For simplicity, we assume a given fraction, t, of income is paid in taxes, so

$$Y_d = Y(1 - t).$$

Hence, in equilibrium, with aggregate expenditures equaling income

$$AE = Y = a + mY(1 - t) + I + G$$

or

$$Y = \frac{a + I + G}{1 - m(1 - t)}.$$

Hence,

$$\text{multiplier} = \frac{1}{1 - m(1 - t)}.$$

If $m = .8$ and $t = .25$, the multiplier $= 2.5$. By contrast, the multiplier without taxes is 5, twice as large. The reason that the multiplier is larger without taxes than with is simple. Without taxes every dollar of extra income translates into 80 cents of extra expenditure. With taxes, when income goes up by a dollar, consumption increases by only $.8 \times (1 - .25) = 60$ cents.

Figure 28.9 THE IMPORT FUNCTION

Imports *(M)* increase steadily as disposable income *(Y)* rises. The slope of the import function is equal to the marginal propensity to import.

levels of income. For simplicity, we assume that imports are bought by consumers and that, accordingly, it is disposable income that determines their level. The import function is depicted in Figure 28.9.

Imports increase with income. The **marginal propensity to import** gives the amount of each extra dollar of income spent on imports. If the marginal propensity to import is .1, then if income goes up by $1,000, imports go up by .1 × $1,000 = $100. In Figure 28.9, the marginal propensity to import is given by the slope of the import function.

EXPORTS

What foreigners buy from the United States depends on the income of foreigners and not directly on income in the United States. Exports may also depend on other factors, such as the marketing effort of American firms and the prices of American goods relative to those of foreign goods. Our focus here is to determine output in the United States. For simplicity, we assume that these other factors are fixed and do not depend on what happens in the United States. In particular, we assume that foreigners' incomes do not depend significantly on incomes in the United States. Hence, the level of exports is taken as fixed at $400 billion.

Exports minus imports (net exports) is sometimes referred to as the **balance of trade.** Net exports at each level of national income are given in Table 28.6. At very low levels of income, net exports are positive. That is to say, exports exceed imports. As income increases, imports increase, with exports remaining unchanged. Eventually imports exceed exports; the balance of trade becomes negative.

Trade, like taxes, has the effect of flattening the aggregate expenditures schedule. This is because as income increases, some of it goes to buy foreign goods rather than domestically produced goods. Hence, aggregate expenditures—spending for goods produced within the country—increase by a smaller amount. In a closed economy, when income increases by a dollar aggregate expenditures increase by the marginal propensity to consume. In an open economy, when income increases by a dollar, aggregate expenditures increase by the marginal propensity to consume *minus* the marginal propensity to import. The difference between the two can be thought of as the marginal propensity to consume domestically produced goods.

This can be seen in Table 28.7, which calculates, for different levels of national

Table 28.5 IMPORTS AND DISPOSABLE INCOME (billions of dollars)

Disposable income	Imports
$ 1,000	$ 100
2,000	200
3,000	300
4,000	400
5,000	500
10,000	1,000
20,000	2,000

Table 28.6 NET EXPORTS (billions of dollars)

Disposable income	Exports	Imports	E (exports – imports)
$ 1,000	$400	$ 100	$ 300
2,000	400	200	200
3,000	400	300	100
4,000	400	400	0
5,000	400	500	–100
10,000	400	1,000	–600
20,000	400	1,800	–1,400

income, the level of disposable income, consumption, investment, government expenditures, and net exports. Every time aggregate income increases by $1,333 billion, disposable income increases by only $1,000 billion; and while consumption increases by $900 billion, net exports *fall* (because imports increase) by $100 billion, so the net increase in aggregate expenditures is only $800 billion. In a closed economy with government, aggregate expenditures would have increased by $900 billion.

At an income of $5,333 billion (a disposable income of $4,000 billion), net exports are zero. At higher levels of income, net exports are negative. At lower levels, they are positive. Thus, trade increases aggregate expenditures at lower levels of national income, and decreases aggregate expenditures at higher lev-

Table 28.7 AGGREGATE EXPENDITURES SCHEDULE
(billions of dollars)

Income	Disposable income	Consumption	Investment	Government	Net exports	Aggregate expenditures
$ 1,333	$ 1,000	$ 1,050	$500	$1,000	$ 300	$ 2,850
2,666	2,000	1,950	500	1,000	200	3,650
4,000	3,000	2,850	500	1,000	100	4,450
5,125	3,844	3,609	500	1,000	16	5,125
5,333	4,000	3,750	500	1,000	0	5,250
13,333	10,000	9,150	500	1,000	–600	10,050
26,666	20,000	18,150	500	1,000	–1,400	18,250

Note: The numbers in the table are constructed under the following assumptions: a tax rate of .25, a marginal propensity to consume of .9, and a marginal propensity to import of .1.

Figure 28.10 INCOME-EXPENDITURE ANALYSIS WITH A FOREIGN TRADE SECTOR

Adding a fixed level of exports raises the aggregate demand function. But adding imports makes the slope of the function flatter, since some of national income is now going to buy products produced outside the country. The multiplier is reduced.

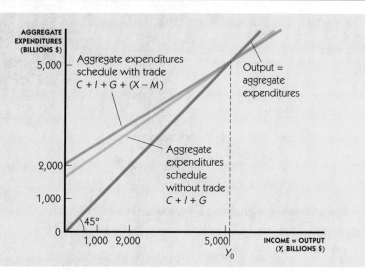

els of national income. At low levels of income, the stimulation provided by exports more than offsets the losses from imports; at higher levels of income just the opposite happens.

In Figure 28.10, the income-expenditure analysis diagram is again used to show how the level of output is determined. As before, the equilibrium condition that output equals aggregate expenditures, $Y = AE$, is represented by the 45-degree line. The aggregate expenditures schedule now adds all of its components: $C + I + G + (X - M)$. The slope of this line is even flatter than in Figure 28.7C. This is because, as income increases, net exports—one of the components of aggregate expenditures—actually decrease. Equilibrium again occurs at the intersection of the aggregate expenditures schedule and the 45-degree line, the output level Y_0 (equal to $5,125) in the figure.

We know that whenever the aggregate expenditures schedule is flattened, the multiplier is lowered. To see precisely how this works in the case of trade, think again about how the multiplier works through various rounds in the economy. The first-round effect of the increase in investment is augmented by the second-round effect of the rise in consumption induced by the higher income of those producing the investment goods. This is augmented by the third-round effect of the increase in consumption induced by the higher income of those involved in producing the second round. And so on. But now, when investment rises by $1 billion, the second-round effect is only the increase in consumption of domestically produced goods. If the marginal propensity to consume is .9, the tax rate is .25, and the marginal propensity to import is .1, the increase in *domestically produced* consumption goods is $600 million (not $675 million, as it would be without trade, or $900 million, as it would be without taxes or trade).[3] Not only is the second-round effect

---

[3]Of the $1 billion, the government takes 25 percent, leaving households with $750 million. Households consume 90 percent of this amount, but 10 percent of their income is spent on imports, so 80 percent of

When we add trade, aggregate expenditures are given by

$$AE = C + I + G + X - M.$$

Imports are now related to disposable income by the import function

$$M = MPI \times Y_d,$$

where MPI is the marginal propensity to import; exports are assumed to be fixed. Hence, aggregate expenditures are

$$AE = a + mY(1 - t) + I + G + X - MPI(1 - t) Y.$$

Since aggregate expenditures equal income, in equilibrium

$$y = \frac{a + I + G + X}{1 - (1 - t)(m - MPI)},$$

so the multiplier is

$$\frac{1}{1 - (1 - t)(m - MPI)}.$$

If $t = .25$, $m = .8$, $MPI = .1$, then the multiplier is

$$\frac{1}{1 - .75(.8 - .1)} = 2.1,$$

much smaller than in the absence of trade (2.5).

smaller, the third-round effect is also smaller. The increase of $600 million in the second round leads to increased consumption of domestically produced goods of $360 million in the third round.

If more of the income generated on each successive round is not spent on goods produced within the country, the multiplier will be smaller. When income generated in one round of production is not used to buy more goods produced within the country, economists say there are **leakages.** In a closed economy there are two leakages: savings and taxes. In an open economy there are three leakages: savings, taxes, and imports.

BACK TO THE AGGREGATE DEMAND CURVES

We began the chapter with an aggregate demand and supply schedule. The objective of this chapter was to show how at any price level aggregate demand—and equilibrium output—is determined. We can use the analysis to *derive* the aggregate demand curve simply by asking, what happens to aggregate demand—and equilibrium output—when the price level changes? To answer that question, all we have to ascertain is, how does the aggregate expenditures schedule shift when the price level increases or decreases? When

---

their income is spent on domestically produced consumer goods. The increase in demand for domestically produced consumer goods is .8 × $750 million = $600 million.

Figure 28.11 DERIVING THE AGGREGATE DEMAND CURVE

Panel A shows the effect of an increase in the price level from P_0 to P_1 on the aggregate expenditures schedule. It decreases equilibrium output from Y_0 to Y_1. Panel B traces out the equilibrium values of aggregate demand (and output) corresponding to different price levels.

the price level rises, at each level of income, consumers will consume less, since the real value of their bank balances will have decreased. Also, if *current* price levels are higher relative to (fixed beliefs about) *future* price levels, then households may *substitute* against current consumption (which has become relatively expensive) for future consumption. In either case, the aggregate expenditures schedule shifts down, as depicted in Figure 28.11, and equilibrium output falls. Thus, while Y_0 is the point on the aggregate demand schedule corresponding to P_0, Y_1 is the point on the aggregate demand schedule corresponding to P_1. Later chapters will explore more fully how changes in the price level shift the aggregate expenditures schedule.

LIMITATIONS OF THE INCOME-EXPENDITURE APPROACH

This chapter has analyzed the determination of national output by focusing exclusively on the aggregate expenditures schedule, which underlies the aggregate demand curve. But what happened to aggregate supply? Isn't that important too?

Recall that aggregate demand rules the roost when there is excess capacity. That is, changes in aggregate demand alone determine what happens to national output when there are idle machines and workers that could be put to work if only there were sufficient demand to purchase the goods they produce.

There are many times when there is excess capacity in the economy, and when the approach taken here, ignoring capacity constraints, makes perfect sense. There are other times, however, when the economy is working close to capacity. Then aggregate supply has to be brought into the picture.

REVIEW AND PRACTICE

SUMMARY

1. Income-expenditure analysis shows how the equilibrium level of output in the economy is determined when there is excess capacity, so that aggregate demand determines the level of output. Throughout the analysis, the price level is taken as fixed.

2. Equilibrium output is determined by the intersection of the 45-degree line and the aggregate expenditures schedule. The aggregate expenditures schedule shows the level of aggregate expenditures at each level of national income, while the 45-degree line represents the points where aggregate expenditures equal output (income).

3. Shifts in the aggregate expenditures schedule give rise to changes in the equilibrium level of output. The magnitude of the increase in output resulting from an upward shift in the aggregate expenditures schedule depends on the slope of the schedule. Much of macroeconomic analysis focuses on what determines the slope of the aggregate expenditures schedule, what causes shifts in the schedule, and how government can shift the schedule.

4. Aggregate expenditures are the sum of consumption, investment, government expenditures, and net exports. Net exports are the difference between exports and imports.

5. Consumption increases as disposable income increases, and the relationship between income and consumption is called the consumption function. The amount by which consumption increases when disposable income increases by a dollar is called the marginal propensity to consume (MPC). The amount by which savings increase when disposable income increases by a dollar is called the marginal propensity to save (MPS). Since all income must be saved or consumed, the sum of the MPC and MPS must be 1.

6. The multiplier is the factor by which a change in investment or government expenditures must be multiplied to get the resulting change in

national output. In a simple model without government spending, taxes, or net exports, the multiplier for changes in investment is $1/(1 - MPC)$, or $1/MPS$.

7. Government spending increases aggregate expenditures, and taxes reduce disposable income and therefore consumption. When taxes increase with income, consumption increases by less than it otherwise would, since a fraction of the increased income goes to government. The aggregate expenditures schedule is flatter, and the multiplier is smaller.

8. Exports increase aggregate demand, and imports reduce aggregate demand. Imports increase with income, but exports are determined by factors in other countries. Trade flattens the aggregate expenditures schedule, because as income increases some of it goes to buy foreign rather than domestic goods. As a result, the multiplier is smaller.

9. The aggregate expenditures schedule is used to derive the equilibrium level of output at each price level (assuming that there is excess capacity in the economy). As the price level increases, the aggregate expenditures schedule shifts down and equilibrium output decreases. The aggregate demand curve then traces out the equilibrium level of output at each price level.

KEY TERMS

aggregate expenditures schedule	consumption function	multiplier import function
income-expenditure analysis	marginal propensity to consume	marginal propensity to import
planned and unplanned inventories	autonomous consumption	balance of trade
	marginal propensity to save	

REVIEW QUESTIONS

1. What is the aggregate expenditures schedule? What are the components of aggregate expenditures?

2. How is the equilibrium level of output determined? Why are points on the aggregate expenditures schedule above the 45-degree line not sustainable? Why are points on the aggregate expenditures schedule below the 45-degree line not sustainable?

3. What is a consumption function? What determines its slope? What is an import function? What determines its slope?

4. What is the consequence of a shift in the aggregate expenditures schedule? Give examples of what might give rise to such a shift.

5. Illustrate the difference between a change in consumption resulting

from an increase in income with a given consumption function and a change in consumption resulting from a shift in the consumption function.

6. Why is the sum of the marginal propensity to save and the marginal propensity to consume always 1?

7. Show that the magnitude of the effect of a given shift in the aggregate expenditures schedule on equilibrium output depends on the slope of the aggregate expenditures schedule. What determines the slope of the aggregate expenditures schedule? How is it affected by taxes? by imports?

8. How can changes of a certain amount in the level of investment or government spending have a larger effect on national output? What is the multiplier?

9. What is the relationship between the aggregate expenditures schedule and the aggregate demand curve? How does the aggregate expenditures schedule shift when the price level increases? How can the aggregate demand curve be derived?

PROBLEMS

1. In the economy of Consumerland, national income and consumption are related in this way:

National income	$1,500	$1,600	$1,700	$1,800	$1,900
Consumption	$1,325	$1,420	$1,515	$1,610	$1,705

Calculate national savings at each level of national income. What is the marginal propensity to consume in Consumerland? What is the marginal propensity to save? If national income rose to $2,000, what do you predict consumption and savings would be?

2. To the economy of Consumerland add the fact that investment will be $180 at every level of output. Graph the consumption function and the aggregate expenditures schedule for this simple economy. What determines the slope of the aggregate expenditures schedule? What is the equilibrium output?

3. Calculate the first four rounds of the multiplier effect for an increase of $10 billion in investment spending in each of the following cases:
    (a) a simple consumption and investment economy where the MPC is .9;
    (b) an economy with government but no foreign trade, where the MPC is .9 and the tax rate is .3;
    (c) an economy with an MPC of .9, a tax rate of .3, and a marginal propensity to import of .1.

4. If, at each level of disposable income, savings increase, what does this imply about what has happened to the consumption function? What will be the consequences for the equilibrium level of output?

5. Use the income-expenditure analysis diagram to explain why a lower level of investment, government spending, and net exports all have similar effects on the equilibrium level of output.

6. In a more stable economy (where national output is less vulnerable to small changes in, say, exports), government policy is less effective (changes in government expenditures do not do much to stimulate the economy); in a less stable economy, government policy is more effective. Explain why there is a trade-off between the stability of the economy and the power of government policy.

CHAPTER 29

CONSUMPTION
AND INVESTMENT

Now that we have developed the overall framework of income-expenditure analysis, we take a closer look at two of the components of aggregate expenditures, consumption and investment. Examining them will help us understand both why the level of economic activity fluctuates and what policies the government might pursue to reduce those fluctuations or to stimulate the economy.

*This chapter may be skipped or taken up after subsequent chapters without loss of continuity.

1. Why may current consumption not be very dependent on current income, and what implications does this have for the use of tax policy to stimulate the economy?

2. What other factors determine the level of aggregate consumption?

3. What are "consumer durables," and why are expenditures on them so volatile?

4. What are the major determinants of the level of investment? What role do variations in real interest rates and the availability of credit play? What role is played by changing perceptions of risk and the ability and willingness to bear risk?

5. Why is the variability in investment and expenditures on consumer durables so important?

CONSUMPTION

The consumption function presented in Chapter 28 said that the demand for goods and services by households is determined by the level of disposable income. As disposable income goes up, so does consumption. Knowing this year's disposable income, then, an economist can use the consumption function to predict this year's consumption spending.

This simple consumption function, often referred to as the Keynesian consumption function, is a good starting point, as Figure 29.1 illustrates. Income varies from year to year, and so does consumption. If they moved in lockstep as the simple consumption function predicts, a straight line could be drawn through all the points in the figure. The relationship is remarkably close to the linear relationship predicted by the theories. Still, economists have sought to develop even better predictors of consumption.

FUTURE-ORIENTED CONSUMPTION FUNCTIONS

In the decades after Keynes's time, many economists questioned his notion that current consumption depends primarily on current income. They argued that individuals, in making consumption decisions, look at total income over their lifetime, averaging good years with bad, and recognizing that income typically increases with experience.

Nobel laureate Franco Modigliani, for instance, emphasized that people save for retirement. He called this motive **life-cycle savings,** to convey the notion that individuals will save during their working years so they will not have to curtail their consumption after they retire. Milton Friedman, also a

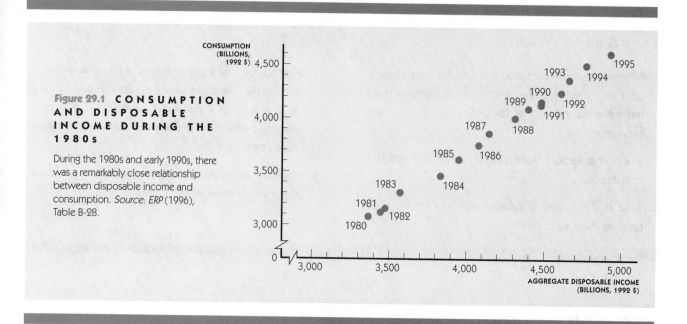

Figure 29.1 CONSUMPTION AND DISPOSABLE INCOME DURING THE 1980s

During the 1980s and early 1990s, there was a remarkably close relationship between disposable income and consumption. *Source: ERP (1996),* Table B-28.

Nobel laureate, emphasized how the future affects consumption today by pointing out that people save in good years to carry them through bad years. His view is called the **permanent income hypothesis.** Permanent income is a person's average income over her lifetime. Friedman stressed that consumption depends not so much on current income as on total lifetime income, averaging good years with bad. While Modigliani emphasized the role of savings in smoothing consumption between working and retirement years, Friedman emphasized its role in smoothing consumption between good and bad years. Underlying both views is the notion that people like their consumption patterns to be stable.

These future-oriented theories of savings and consumption yield different consequences from the basic Keynesian or traditional theory that consumption simply depends on this year's income. Consider an individual who happens to get a windfall gain in income one year—perhaps he wins $1 million in the state lottery. If the marginal propensity to consume is .9, the Keynesian consumption function predicts that he will consume $900,000 of his winnings that year. The future-oriented consumption theories suggest that the lucky winner will spread the extra income over a lifetime of consumption. Similarly, if the government temporarily lowers taxes for one year, the future-oriented consumption theories predict that a taxpayer will not dramatically increase consumption in that year but will spread over his lifetime the extra consumption that the one-year tax reduction allows. Thus, they suggest that *temporary* tax changes will be much less effective in stimulating consumption than the Keynesian model predicts.

Figure 29.2 compares the future-oriented consumption function and the Keynesian consumption function for the household. Suppose a household were to have a onetime increase in its disposable income. If consumption responds according to the Keynesian consumption function, it will increase from C_0 to C_1 as shown in panel A.

The future-oriented theories predict that consumption will not change very much. We can see this in two different ways. Panel B shows consumption depending on average disposable income over a person's lifetime. Now the change in this year's income from Y_0 to Y_1 has little effect on average disposable income, and hence little effect on consumption. Panel C put this year's disposable income on the horizontal axis, as does panel A. The difference in slope between the consumption functions in panels A and C reflects the difference between Keynes's views and those of the future-oriented theorists. Consumption, in the latter view, is not very sensitive to current disposable income, which is why the line is so flat.

The principle that consumption depends not just on income this year but also on longer-run considerations holds at the aggregate level as well. Figure 29.3 shows the implications of future-oriented theories for aggregate expenditures and the determination of equilibrium output. Since the relationship between changes in today's income and changes in consumption is weaker than in the Keynesian model, the aggregate expenditures schedule is now much flatter, that is, increases in current income lead to relatively small changes in consumption and aggregate expenditures. This in turn has strong implications for the multiplier. An increase in, say, investment, which shifts the aggregate expenditures schedule up, increases equilibrium output by an amount only slightly greater than the original increase in investment. The multiplier is very small.

WEALTH AND CAPITAL GAINS

The future-oriented consumption theories suggest not only that current income is relatively unimportant in determining consumption but also that variables Keynes ignored may be important. For instance, wealthier people consume more (at each level of current income). Since consumption is related to wealth, changes in consumption will be affected by changes in wealth.

The distinction between income and wealth as a determinant of consumption is important. It corresponds to the distinction between flows and stocks. Flows are measured as "rates." Both income and consumption are flow variables. They are measured as dollars *per year.* Wealth is a stock variable.[1] It is measured simply by the total value ("dollars") of one's assets. Future-oriented theories emphasize that there is no reason that an individual's current consumption should be related to his current income. What he consumes should be related to how well off he is, and that is better measured by his wealth.[2]

[1] Other stock variables in macroeconomics include capital stock; other flow variables include the interest rate.
[2] Future-oriented theories take an expansive view of what should be included in wealth: they include *human capital*, the present discounted value of future wage income. (See Chapter 25 for a definition of present discounted value.)

Figure 29.2 EFFECT OF A TEMPORARY INCOME CHANGE IN THE LIFE-CYCLE MODEL

With the Keynesian consumption function, panel A, a temporary change in income results in a large change in consumption. In the life-cycle model, panel B, a temporary change in income has only a small effect on average annual income over a lifetime, and thus leads to only a small change in consumption. Panel C shows how the life-cycle model predicts that consumption will react in response to *this year's income*. Since consumption does not change by much, the life-cycle consumption function is very flat.

Figure 29.3 THE LIFE-CYCLE MODEL AND DETERMINING NATIONAL OUTPUT

Since changes in today's income have much weaker effects on current consumption in the life-cycle model, the aggregate expenditures schedule is much flatter, which implies that the multiplier is lower.

Capital gains, or changes in the value of assets, change an individual's wealth. Thus, these theories predict that when stock or real estate prices rise in value and people expect this change to last for a long time, individuals who own these assets will increase their level of consumption. They will do so because their overall wealth has grown, even if they do not immediately receive any income from the increase in value.

There is some evidence to support this view. Many economists believe that the stock market crash of 1929, which preceded the Great Depression, contributed to that Depression by generating a downward shift in the consumption function. On the other hand, when the stock market fell by over 22 percent on a single day in October 1987, consumption did not decline sharply in the way one might have expected. People responded only slightly to this capital loss. One reason for this is that individuals respond to changes in wealth only slowly, and in 1987 their consumption had not yet fully responded to the increases in stock market prices that had occurred during the preceding few years. A prolonged and persistent decline in the stock market might, however, have an extremely depressing effect on consumption.

RECONCILING CONSUMPTION THEORY WITH FACTS

The permanent income and life-cycle hypotheses contain large elements of truth. Families do save for their retirement, so life-cycle considerations are important. And households do smooth their consumption between good years and bad, so permanent income considerations are relevant. Even so, household consumption appears to be more dependent on current income than either theory would suggest. There are two reasons for this, durable goods and credit rationing. Each plays an important role in consumption.

DURABLE GOODS

Goods such as cars, refrigerators, and furniture are called **durable goods.** Purchasing a durable good is like an investment decision, because such goods are bought for the services they render over a number of years. Decisions to postpone purchasing a durable good have quite different consequences from decisions not to buy food or some other nondurable. If you do not buy strawberries today, you will have to do without them. But not buying a durable does not mean you will do without. It simply means you may have to make do with the services provided by an older durable. The costs of postponing the purchase of a new car are often relatively low; you can make do with an old car a little bit longer.

When a household's income is temporarily low, rather than borrowing to purchase durables, the household simply postpones the purchase. Similarly, if a worker worries about losing his job, he may cut back durable purchases. Figure 29.4 traces the purchases of durables as a percentage of disposable income during the postwar period. These fluctuations in purchases of durables, together with the variations in investment, seem to account for much of the variation in economic activity over the business cycle. Variations in the

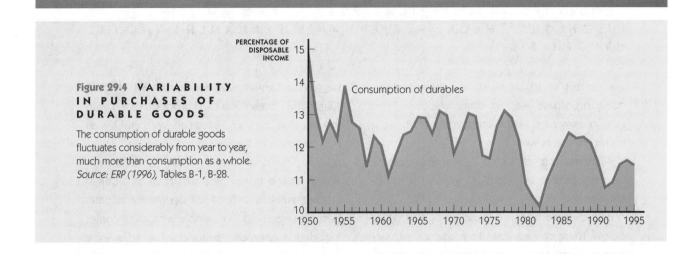

Figure 29.4 **VARIABILITY IN PURCHASES OF DURABLE GOODS**

The consumption of durable goods fluctuates considerably from year to year, much more than consumption as a whole. *Source: ERP (1996),* Tables B-1, B-28.

services provided by durable goods—and hence in true consumption—are much smaller.

CREDIT RATIONING

Empirical studies show that even nondurable consumption expenditures seem more dependent on current income than the future-oriented theories suggest. These theories, in particular the permanent income hypothesis, assume that when an individual has a bad year, he can maintain his consumption at a steady level. They assume, in other words, either that the household has a large stock of savings to draw on while its income is temporarily low, or that the household can easily borrow.

For many people, neither of these conditions is true. Most individuals, even in the United States, have few liquid assets upon which to draw. They may have considerable savings tied up in a pension scheme, but they cannot draw upon these until they retire. They may have some equity in their house, but the last thing they want to do is sell their home. Moreover, it is precisely in times of need, when a person is unemployed or a business is doing badly, that banks are least forthcoming with funds. (As the saying goes, banks only lend to those who don't need the money!)

Credit rationing occurs when people are unable to obtain funds at the market rate of interest, because of the risks associated with lending to them. Many people are credit rationed. For those who have no assets and are credit rationed, cutting back on consumption when income declines is not a matter of choice. For these individuals, consumption depends heavily on current income.

If people were not credit rationed, short-term unemployment would not be as important a problem as it appears to be. The suffering caused by temporary layoffs would be much less. To see why, we need to look again at the concept of total wealth. Assume, for instance, that Evan will work for forty years,

Close-up: An Empirical Puzzle and an Ingenious Theory—Friedman's Permanent Income Hypothesis

The genesis of Milton Friedman's permanent income hypothesis was an empirical puzzle. The story of how he solved it illustrates insightful economic analysis at work.

When economists plotted aggregate disposable personal income in various years with the corresponding level of aggregate consumption, they obtained something like panel A of the figure below. These data suggested a consumption function in which consumption increases proportionately with income. But, when economists plotted the consumption of different income groups against their current income for any particular year, they obtained something more like panel B. This

suggests a consumption function in which consumption increases less than proportionately with income. The problem Friedman set himself was how to reconcile the data.

His ingenious solution was to say that consumption is related to people's long-term or "normal" income, what he called their permanent income. Friedman observed that people with low incomes included a disproportionate number who were having unusually bad years. And correspondingly, those with very high incomes included a disproportionate number having unusually good years. Those having a bad year did not reduce their consumption proportionately; those having a particu-

Panel A shows that as income has increased over time, consumption has increased almost in proportion. Panel B illustrates the fact that individuals with higher income increase their consumption somewhat less than proportionately, especially at the highest income levels. *Sources: ERP* (1995), Table B-28; *Consumer Expenditure Survey* (1988).

larly good year did not increase their consumption proportionately. Friedman was thus able to explain how, over time, aggregate consumption could rise in proportion to income for the population as a whole, even though the consumption of any particular household increased less than proportionately with current income.

Stanford University economist Robert Hall has pointed out an unsettling consequence of the permanent income hypothesis. If the level of consumption a person chooses depends on permanent income, which incorporates all information about what future *expected* income will be, changes in consumption are related only to *unexpected* changes. By definition, unexpected changes are random and unpredictable. Thus, the permanent income theory predicts that changes in consumption are largely random and unpredictable—not good news for economists trying to understand and forecast such patterns.

that his initial salary is $25,000 per year, that his salary increases in real terms at 5 percent per year, and that 5 percent is the real rate of interest. Then the present discounted value of his lifetime earnings is $1 million. This is his wealth, assuming that he has no unexpected windfall, no inheritance from his great-aunt, and no other assets. Imagine that Evan loses his job and is unemployed for half a year. At first glance, that looks like a personal calamity. But upon closer inspection, we see that it represents a loss of only a bit more than 1 percent of his lifetime wealth.

If Evan could borrow six months' pay, he would have no trouble paying it back, and the period without work would be no tragedy—his life-style would be constrained, but insignificantly. Since he would have to cut expenditures by only a bit more than 1 percent, cutting out a few movies, a fancy restaurant meal or two, and a few other activities would do the trick. However, for most people, losing a job for half a year would in fact be a major disaster—not because of the reduction in total lifetime wealth, but because most individuals face important constraints on the amount they can borrow. Without a job, they cannot obtain loans, except possibly at very high interest rates. Because of these credit constraints, for most lower- and many middle-income individuals, the traditional Keynesian consumption function is all too relevant. When their current income is reduced, their consumption is necessarily reduced.

MACROECONOMIC IMPLICATIONS OF CONSUMPTION THEORIES

The alternative theories of consumption we have explored so far have two sets of macroeconomic implications. First, the future-oriented theories of consumption, in arguing that consumption does not depend heavily on current income, maintain that the aggregate expenditures schedule is flat and therefore the multiplier is low. This is both good news and bad news for the economy. It is good news because a small multiplier means that decreases in the level of investment lead to much smaller decreases in the level of national income than they would if the multiplier were large. It is bad news because it

POLICY PERSPECTIVE: A QUICK STIMULUS IN THE FACE OF AN IMPENDING ELECTION TESTS THE FUTURE-ORIENTED THEORIES

In late 1991 and early 1992, as the presidential election neared and the economy remained stubbornly stuck in an economic downturn, President Bush decided the economy needed a quick stimulus. He did two things.

First, he reduced IRS tax-withholding rates (which postponed payment of taxes without altering the amount of ultimate tax liability). With more money in their pockets, he hoped people would spend more, even though the day of reckoning was only postponed. This provided a clear test of the future-oriented theories. Disposable income was increased in 1992, but permanent income was not changed in any way. If the future-oriented theories were correct, there should have been no effect. In fact, there was a significant positive effect on consumption.

Second, government departments were required to increase the pace of their spending. Again, total spending (over the course of the year) would not be changed, but outlays would be made at a faster pace. This could give a temporary boost to the economy.

Many derided these actions as gimmicks, but they seemed to work—though not fast enough for the president. The economy had a strong fourth quarter in 1992, too late to have much effect on voters.

means that government efforts to stimulate the economy through temporary reductions in taxes—or to dampen an overheated economy through temporary increases in taxes—will be less effective than if the multiplier were larger.

Second, by identifying other determinants of consumption, future-oriented theories help explain why the ratio of consumption to disposable income may shift from year to year. Expectations concerning future economic conditions, changes in the availability of credit, or variations in the price of houses or shares of stock are among the factors that can give rise to such shifts in the consumption function. These shifts in turn give rise to larger variations in the equilibrium level of national output. Indeed, they help explain how a slight downturn in economic activity can become magnified. With a downturn, consumers may lose confidence in the future. They worry about layoffs, and cut back on purchases of durables. At the same time, banks, nervous about the ability of borrowers to repay loans should the downturn worsen, become more restrictive. Even those adventurous souls willing to buy a new car in the face of the uncertain future may find it difficult to find a bank willing to lend to them. The net effect is a downward shift in the consumption function, exacerbating the initial decline in national income.

DETERMINANTS OF CONSUMPTION

1. Keynesian consumption function: stresses the dependence of consumption on current disposable income
2. Future-oriented consumption theories: stress the dependence of consumption on total lifetime wealth and the role of savings in smoothing consumption
   a. Life-cycle theory: stresses the importance of savings for retirement
   b. Permanent income theory: stresses the role of savings in smoothing consumption between good and bad years
   c. Implications
      i. Consumption not very dependent on current income: small multipliers
      ii. Consumption sensitive to capital gains and losses
3. Explanations of why consumption seems to be more dependent on current income than future-oriented theories predict
   a. Durable goods
   b. Credit constraints

INVESTMENT

Variations in the level of investment are probably the principal cause of variations in aggregate expenditures, and hence in national output. Just how volatile investment is can be seen in Figure 29.5. In recent years, investment has varied from 13 to 18 percent of GDP.

The investment spending relevant for aggregate expenditures includes three broad categories. The first is firms' purchases of new capital goods, which includes, besides buildings and machines, the automobiles, cash registers, and desks that firms use. These make up the **plant and equipment** portion of overall investment. Firms also invest in **inventories** as they store their output in anticipation of sales or store the raw materials they will need to produce more goods. The third investment category consists of households' purchases of new homes. The purchases of previously owned capital goods or houses do not count, because they do not increase output. Households' financial investments such as stocks and bonds are a related but different concept. Usually when an individual buys, say, a share of stock, she buys it from someone else. She makes an investment, but someone else makes a "disinvestment." There is simply a change in who owns the economy's assets. There is, however, a close relationship between investment in new capital goods and the capital market in general: when firms issue new shares or borrow funds

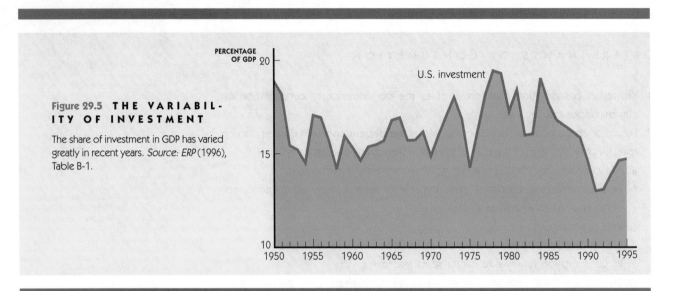

Figure 29.5 THE VARIABIL-ITY OF INVESTMENT

The share of investment in GDP has varied greatly in recent years. *Source: ERP* (1996), Table B-1.

by issuing bonds, they procure the resources with which to purchase new capital goods. (In this way, financial investments and capital investments—with which we are concerned here—are closely linked.)

We restrict our focus in this discussion to business investment, which includes two of our three major investment categories: plant and equipment, and inventories. The third major investment category—consumers' demand for new housing—is best analyzed as a very long-lived durable good, using the principles governing the demand for durable goods developed earlier in this chapter.

Three questions concern us here. What determines the level of business investment? Why is it so variable? And how does government influence it? We direct these questions first to plant and equipment investment and then to inventory investment.

INVESTMENT IN PLANT AND EQUIPMENT

To undertake an investment, firms must believe that the expected future returns will be large enough to compensate them for the risks of the investment. Moreover, firms are aware that a dollar in the future is worth less than a dollar today; if they have a dollar this year, they can put it in the bank and get back the dollar *with interest* next year. As the interest rate rises, future dollars are worth less relative to today's dollars. That means there will be fewer projects with future returns large enough to offset forgone interest. To put it another way, think of the firm as having to borrow the money for the investment project. Higher interest rates increase the cost of undertaking the project. Fewer projects will have a sufficiently high return to pay these higher interest costs. Thus, higher interest rates lead to lower levels of investment. The rela-

CLOSE-UP: THE CORPORATE VEIL

When firms have money left over after paying all their bills, they can either use the funds to pay dividends to stockholders or retain the earnings and invest them. Retained earnings, which can be thought of as a firm's savings, are more than triple the savings of households.

When a firm saves through retained earnings, the future profits of the firm should be higher as it begins to receive a return from this investment. Anticipation of these higher profits should raise the price of shares of stock in the firm, and shareholders should accordingly feel wealthier.

Strictly rational shareholders would treat the increased stock value due to retained earnings just as if they had saved the money themselves. Thus, they will incorporate this wealth gain into their *overall* savings decisions. But will they? Only if they are fully informed about and fully understand what happens inside the corporation—they see through the "corporate veil," as economists would say. Recent economic theories emphasize the consequences for the economy if shareholders have only blurry vision through the veil.

Much more than idle curiosity motivates this discussion. The extent to which people see through the veil affects the size of the multiplier—the factor by which an initial change in spending is transformed into a larger change in aggregate demand. Assume that firms increase their investment, but finance the additional investment with retained earnings, forgoing an increase in dividends. If people perceive only that their dividends have not increased—without fully realizing that the corporation is putting their money into productive investments—they may reduce their consumption and the total increase in aggregate demand resulting from the increase in investment will be much smaller than predicted by traditional Keynesian theory.

The Tax Reform Act of 1986 provided a test of the corporate veil theory. This act reduced taxes levied on individuals and increased taxes on corporations by a corresponding amount (roughly $120 billion over a five-year period). Those who believed people can see through the corporate veil argued that the increase in disposable income would have little effect, since people would realize that total tax burdens were unchanged. However, consumption did increase somewhat, implying that a corporate veil does exist.

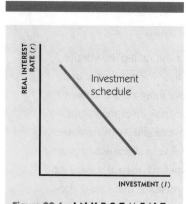

Figure 29.6 INVESTMENT SCHEDULE

At higher real interest rates, firms are willing to invest less.

tionship between interest rates and investment is the investment schedule introduced in Chapter 25, and is depicted as the downward-sloping curve in Figure 29.6. Of course, what matters for investment is the real interest rate, the cost of funds taking into account the effect of inflation. If the *nominal* interest rate increases but future prices increase in an offsetting way, firms' investment will be unaffected. (The real interest rate is the nominal interest rate minus the rate of inflation.) And, of course, what matters for long-term investments is the long-term real interest rate—over the period of the investment.

EXPECTATIONS AND RISK

Perhaps the hardest part of the firm's investment decision is predicting future returns. In some cases, there are **technological risks**—the firm may be using a new technology which could prove unreliable. In most cases, there are **market risks.** Will there be a market for the product? At what price will it sell? What wage will workers demand in the future? What will be the price of electricity and other inputs? The firm has no crystal ball: it has to make an educated guess, recognizing that there is uncertainty.

Typically, firms insist on being compensated for bearing risks. There are three major determinants of the amount that firms require to compensate them for bearing risks: the magnitude of the risks, their ability to share the risks, and their willingness to bear the risks. When the economy goes into a recession, typically firms perceive that the risks of investing are greater. The primary way that firms share risks is through the stock market. In companies whose share are widely held, large numbers of individuals share risks. When the stock market is booming, firms find it easy to issue new shares and thus to spread risks more widely. Finally, the ability and willingness of firms to bear risks depends on their own financial strength. If their net worth has been eroded by a series of losses, and if they have had to borrow to remain afloat, their ability and willingness to bear risks will be reduced.

THE ACCELERATOR

One of the most important determinants of expectations of returns to investment is future sales. When sales are up today, firms may expect future sales to be high, and perhaps even increasing. With high and increasing sales, firms will want to have more capital—that is, they want to invest more. Thus, an increase in government expenditures today not only gives rise to an even larger increase in output through the multiplier, but to a still larger increase, as the higher output generates more investment, which further stimulates the economy. The fact that increases in output beget further increases in output as a result of increased investment is referred to as the **accelerator.**

AVAILABILITY OF FUNDS

There is one more important determinant of investment. The analysis so far has assumed that firms can borrow funds, if they wish to, at the market rate of interest. Particularly in economic downturns, many firms *claim* they cannot borrow as much as they would like. When they cannot borrow, they must resort to **retained earnings**—their profits, less what they pay out to shareholders in dividends—to finance their investment.

For instance, in the 1992 economic downturn, many builders claimed that they could not obtain funds to continue their construction activities. Banks simply would not lend to them. At that time, many banks had been badly hurt by high defaults. With their capital eroded, they were less willing to bear the risks of lending. Even if they had wanted to, bankers said that bank regulators prohibited them from making many loans that had previously been made. However, some banks—and many economists—argued that the issue was not banks' unwillingness to make loans. The problem was a shortage of good borrowers, and an unwillingness of many borrowers to pay an interest rate commensurate with banks' perceptions of the riskiness of the loans.

In fact, most firms—even those that can easily borrow—finance most of their investments out of retained earnings. But even if they cannot borrow from banks, large firms have two other sources of funds—they can issue new shares on the stock market, or they can issue new bonds on the bond market. But typically, in an economic downturn, the stock market does not fare well, so that firms would have a hard time issuing new shares; current owners would have to give up a large share of their firm—more than they think it is worth—to raise a limited amount of funds. And the bond market is likely to be no more friendly, requiring what the borrower may feel is an exorbitant interest rate to compensate them for what they perceive as the high risk of lending in the midst of a recession. Thus, as a practical matter, particularly in an economic downturn, many firms view the availability of funds as a major constraint on their investment.

RECESSIONS

As the economy goes into a recession, typically the investment schedule shifts to the left, as depicted in Figure 29.7. Expectations of profits decrease, risks appear larger, the ability to share risks is decreased, and the ability and willingness to bear risks is reduced. Moreover, firms that are not able to borrow and have to use retained earnings to finance investment, have fewer funds available for investment. And banks—with their capital base eroded from higher defaults and with a perception of a greater risk of default for new loans—may be less willing to make loans. Under these circumstances, even large changes in (real) interest rates may be unable to generate much additional investment.

Figure 29.7 THE EFFECT OF A RECESSION ON INVESTMENT

As the economy enters a recession, expectations of profits decrease, the ability to share risks decreases, and the availability of financing decreases. This leads to a shift in the investment schedule to the left.

WHY INVESTMENT MAY BE LOW IN RECESSIONS

Low expectations of future profits

Banks unwilling to lend and low firm profits make it impossible for firms to finance investment projects

Perceptions of greater risk and lower ability to bear risk make banks less willing to lend and firms less willing to invest

Upon assuming office in 1993, the Clinton administration faced two economic problems: reducing the deficit and stimulating the economy to lower the unemployment rate. It proposed a five-year $500 billion deficit reduction package, roughly divided evenly between tax increases and expenditure reductions. Assume it proposed lowering expenditures in 1993 by $50 billion and raising taxes by $50 billion. How much would interest rates have had to fall just to offset the contractionary effects of fiscal policy?

The tax increase was concentrated on the upper 2 percent of the population, whose marginal propensity to consume may be slightly lower than the average for the economy. If the marginal propensity to consume is .9, then fiscal policy would have reduced aggregate demand a total of $95 billion ($45 billion reduced consumption plus $50 billion reduced government expenditures).

It was estimated that a .1 percentage point reduction in interest rates would increase investment by $10 billion. Thus, long-term interest rates would have to fall by .95 percentage points just to offset fiscal policy.

Clinton tried to "backload" the deficit reduction: more of the expenditure cuts were imposed in later years, so that the fiscal drag on the economy in 1993 would be smaller. It was hoped that long-term interest rates would respond to the long-term commitment of credible deficit reduction. In fact, long-term interest rates fell by one percentage point from 7.3 to 6.3, and investment increased substantially.

Combined with increasing exports, aggregate demand increased sufficiently to reduce the unemployment rate from 7.3 percent at the end of 1992 to 6.4 percent at the end of 1993.

A LOOK AT THE DATA

There is considerable evidence that lowering interest rates does stimulate investment. Some kinds of investment—such as investment in housing—are viewed to be more interest sensitive than others (such as inventories, which we will discuss shortly). When, for instance, interest rates increased in late 1994, there was a quick reduction in the number of new housing starts. By the same token, when interest rates fell in early 1995, housing construction quickly picked up.

While interest rates are an important determinant of investment, they are not the only determinant: as we have seen, changes in expectations, perceptions of risk, and willingness to bear risk may all shift the investment schedule. Indeed, in certain periods of time, most of the variations in investment appear related to these other variables. Figure 29.8 illustrates this. Panel A shows investment and long-term real interest rates for 1954 through 1969; panel B shows the same for 1930 through 1995. Two observations emerge: there have been long periods of time (such as the 1950s and 1960s) when real interest rates varied little—from slightly below 2 percent to slightly below 3

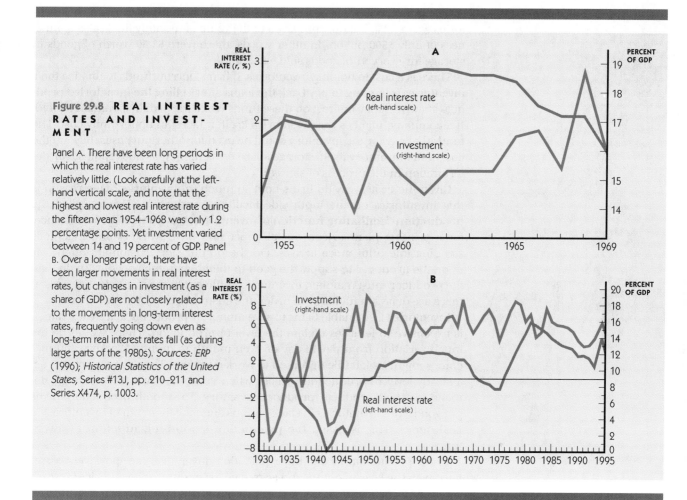

Figure 29.8 REAL INTEREST RATES AND INVEST-MENT

Panel A. There have been long periods in which the real interest rate has varied relatively little. (Look carefully at the left-hand vertical scale, and note that the highest and lowest real interest rate during the fifteen years 1954–1968 was only 1.2 percentage points. Yet investment varied between 14 and 19 percent of GDP. Panel B. Over a longer period, there have been larger movements in real interest rates, but changes in investment (as a share of GDP) are not closely related to the movements in long-term interest rates, frequently going down even as long-term real interest rates fall (as during large parts of the 1980s). *Sources: ERP* (1996); *Historical Statistics of the United States,* Series #13J, pp. 210–211 and Series X474, p. 1003.

percent. Almost none of the volatility in investment in this period can be attributed to interest rate changes. In the early 1980s, real interest rates were substantially higher than in the 1960s, yet investment (relative to GDP) was not substantially lower.

We now know why investment in plant and equipment can be volatile: changes in expectations, availability of funds, a firm's net worth, as well as interest rates can affect investment. Indeed, Keynes thought firms' investment decisions were so unpredictable as to be based on "animal spirits."

INVENTORY INVESTMENT

One of the most volatile components of investment are inventories—the materials that are held in storage either awaiting use in production or for sale to customers.

Inventories are typically very large. In 1995, for example, the value of inventories was $1,250 billion, compared to the value of monthly final sales of business of only $500 billion. In other words, there were $2.50 worth of goods in storage for every $1 of goods sold each month.

There is a cost to holding inventories. If firms borrow funds to finance their inventories, planning to pay back the loans after selling the inventoried products, they must pay interest on these funds while the products remain unsold. If a company finances the inventories itself, it faces an opportunity cost. The funds that pay for the inventory could be used for other purposes. Beyond the cost of the inventory itself, storage space costs money, as does spoilage or deterioration in the process of storage.

Given the costs, why do firms hold so much in inventories? One reason is that inventories on the input side facilitate production. This is called the **production-facilitating function** of inventories. It is very costly, for instance, for a printing plant to run out of paper and have workers and machines standing idle until more arrives. On the output side, customers often rely upon the producer to supply the good to them when they need it. To do that, the producer must maintain inventories sufficient to meet anticipated sales. If there are delays in fulfilling an order, the customer may turn elsewhere.

Inventories also enable firms to save money by producing at a steady rate. It is expensive to let sales dictate the level of production. There would be too much variation from day to day or even month to month. Workers and machines might be left idle or forced to work overtime. Thus, firms prefer to set a steady level of production, which, when combined with the unsteady demand for their products, produces inventory. To smooth production, firms put goods into inventories in slack periods and take them out of inventories in peak times. This is called the **production-smoothing function** of inventories.

In the production-facilitating explanation, inventories are positively correlated with the level of output and aggregate expenditures: inventories increase when the level of output is high. In the production-smoothing explanation, inventories are negatively correlated with aggregate expenditures: they go up when expenditures go down. This pattern would seem to suggest that inventories reduce fluctuations in national output, by allowing firms to keep an even level of production.

In fact, however, rather than serving to dampen business fluctuations, inventories seem to exacerbate them. Inventories vary far more than output, and as was mentioned earlier, they seem to be a major contributing factor to fluctuations in aggregate expenditures. This is true even for inventories of consumer goods, which should serve a particularly smoothing role.

One reason for the variability of investment in inventories may again be the risk-averse behavior of firms and the availability of credit. When the economy enters a recession, firms often find that their net worth is decreased. They are less willing to make any kind of investment, including inventory investment. Where possible, they would like to "disinvest," or convert their assets back into cash. By far, the easiest kind of disinvestment is to sell off inventories. When a business faces credit rationing, it may be forced to sell its inventories to raise the requisite capital. And even if it is not yet forced to sell off its inventories, it

CLOSE-UP: JUST-IN-TIME INVENTORY MANAGEMENT

Simmons is the firm that makes the well-known "Beautyrest" mattress. But in the mid-1980s, the company was anything but relaxed. Its costs were high enough to threaten its financial stability. It was operating a network of 19 manufacturing facilities and 67 warehouses, linked together by 128 truck tractors and 250 trailers. The company's freight bill alone was 6 percent of total sales, and inventory costs were high. The solution? A "just-in-time" manufacturing system. Simmons would only produce *after* receiving an order.

Simmons reorganized the company to eliminate all its warehouses, five of its plants, and 43 of its trucks.

The Simmons plan was based on the just-in-time inventory system pioneered by Toyota in 1972. The idea was to hold inventories to a bare minimum by providing inputs only when they were immediately needed. The system spread throughout Japanese industry during the rest of the 1970s. During the 1980s, it was adopted in the United States, with big companies like General Motors, IBM, Hewlett-Packard, General Electric, and Black and Decker among those who tried it first.

Besides saving on the costs of carrying inventory, just-in-time systems help companies modernize in other ways. *The Economist* magazine described it this way: "A favorite analogy is with water in a river. When the level of water falls, rocks start to appear. The rocks can be removed rather than hit." In other words, carrying big inventories can allow a company to cover up a variety of other organizational problems. Thinking about how to cut inventories can be a powerful tool for overall efficiency.

The widespread adoption of just-in-time systems may have significant effects on macroeconomic stability. For instance, within two weeks of the be-

ginning of a strike at two GM brake plants in March 1995, GM's entire production was brought to a halt: there were no inventories of brakes, and without brakes, no cars could be constructed. More than 200,000 workers were laid off.

At the same time, the overall stability of the economy may be enhanced. Under standard systems with large inventories, when sales dip, a business may cut down purchases and production drastically while inventories are depleted. A business with just-in-time inventories will reduce purchases only a little, and will cut production just by the amount of the reduction in sales.

Sources: The Economist, April 25, 1987, p. 68; Richard J. Schonberger, "The Transfer of Japanese Manufacturing Management Approaches to U.S. Industry," *Academy of Management Review* (1982) 7:479–87; "Bringing JIT's Benefits to the Bottom Line," *Traffic Management* (November 1991), p. 57.

may fear future credit rationing and, in anticipation, seek to reduce its inventories.

UNINTENDED INVENTORY ACCUMULATIONS

Often, as the economy goes into a recession, inventories build up "involuntarily." Retail stores, for instance, make orders based on expected sales; if the sales fail to materialize, the store holds the unsold merchandise as "inventories." This unintended inventory accumulation can feed back quickly into production, as stores reduce their factory orders in response to their larger than desired inventories. Lower orders lead quickly to a cutback in production. The cutbacks in production as firms try to restore inventories to normal size relative to sales are referred to as "inventory corrections." Cyclical variability induced by inventories are called inventory cycles.

POLICIES TO STIMULATE INVESTMENT

While the government cannot control all of the determinants of investment, it has a variety of instruments that may affect it. If the business community is convinced of the government's commitment to economic stability, businesses may perceive less risk and be more willing to invest. But predicting, let alone controlling, the psychology of business executives is at best a tricky business.

The government can change the tax code to make investment more attractive. It can, for instance, provide an **investment tax credit.** With an investment tax credit, a fraction (say 6 percent) of the amount spent on investment is deductible from the tax bill. It is *as if* the government were paying 6 percent of the cost of the machine (for corporations and individuals who have sufficiently large tax liabilities). Temporary tax changes can be particularly effective; a temporary tax credit has the same effect as a sale: a firm that buys a machine during the period of the temporary tax credit saves money, just as it would if the firm temporarily lowered its price. The effects of such temporary tax changes are more predictable than the effects of policies aimed at changing the psychological climate. But temporary tax changes are a cumbersome tool, requiring action by Congress and the president. Temporary tax changes may also distort how resources are allocated, though the macroeconomic gains—in higher levels of output—may well be worth the microeconomic losses from these distortions.

For the most part, however, the government relies on monetary policy, which affects both the availability of credit and the terms on which firms can borrow. Firms raise funds through the capital market. How and when the government, through monetary authorities, affects the capital market (interest rates and availability of credit) are important, complex questions that we will explore in the next three chapters. For now, it is worth noting once again the interrelationships among all the pieces of the macroeconomic puzzle. What goes on in the product market (the determination of the equilibrium level of output) affects the labor market (the level of unemployment in the economy), and what goes on in the capital market (interest rates and the availability of credit) affects investment and thus the product market.

WAYS OF STIMULATING INVESTMENT

1. Increasing business confidence: government demonstrating a commitment to maintaining high levels of employment and output
2. Lowering the cost of investment: subsidies to investment through the tax system
3. Increasing the availability of credit or making it available on more attractive terms (monetary policy)

REVIEW AND PRACTICE

SUMMARY

1. The Keynesian consumption function stresses the importance of current disposable income in determining consumption. In contrast, future-oriented consumption theories focus on an individual's total wealth, including what he will receive as income over his entire life; savings serves to smooth consumption. Thus, the life-cycle hypothesis says that people save during their life so that they can spend after retirement. The permanent income hypothesis argues that people save in good years to offset the bad years.

2. In the traditional (Keynesian) consumption function, the government could manipulate this year's consumption by changing this year's tax rate. In the future-oriented theories, temporary tax reductions would have a limited effect in stimulating consumption, since people are considering a longer horizon than this year for their consumption decisions.

3. Both the life-cycle and permanent income models predict that consumption will depend on lifetime wealth, and that changes in wealth (including capital gains) will therefore affect consumption.

4. Household consumption appears to be more dependent on current income than either the life-cycle or permanent income theory suggests. Consumers can easily postpone the purchase of durables when current income falls. Also, limitations on their ability to borrow (credit rationing) may keep the consumption of many people with little savings close to their current income.

5. Future-oriented theories of consumption suggest that the aggregate expenditures schedule is flat and the multiplier is low.

6. Variations in the level of investment are probably the principal reason for variations in total aggregate expenditures. The three main categories of investment are firms' purchases of plant and equipment, firms' increase or decrease of inventories, and households' purchases of new homes.

7. While investment depends on the real rate of interest, historically, much if not most of the variation in investment is attributed to other factors, such as changes in expectations, perceptions of risk, and willingness and ability to bear risk, all of which shift the investment schedule.

8. As income increases, investment tends to increase, partly because expectations of future sales increases, partly because as GDP increases, profits increase, increasing the availability of funds for investment. The relationship between income and investment is called the accelerator.

9. Most firms finance most of their investment out of retained earnings. When firms cannot borrow, or raise money in the stock market—or can do so only at very unattractive terms—firms may perceive lack of availability of funds as limiting their investment.

10. Investment is low in a recession because of low expectations of future profits, an unwillingness of banks to lend, a lack of profits, which makes it impossible for firms to finance investment projects on their own, and perceptions of greater risk and a lower ability to bear risk, which make banks less willing to lend and firms less willing to invest.

11. Inventories both serve to facilitate production and smooth production. Variations in inventory accumulation contribute to the economy's fluctuations; a slight unanticipated downturn in the economy leads to unintended inventory accumulation, and as firms cut back orders to reverse this unintended inventory accumulation, output falls.

12. Government can stimulate investment by increasing business confidence, especially through a demonstrated commitment to maintain the economy at high levels of employment and output, by subsidizing investment through the tax system, and by lowering interest rates and increasing the availability of credit.

KEY TERMS

life-cycle savings

permanent income hypothesis

durable goods

accelerator

retained earnings

production-facilitating function

production-smoothing function

investment tax credit (ITC)

REVIEW QUESTIONS

1. What is the difference between the Keynesian model of consumption, the life-cycle model, and the permanent income model?

2. Why do the life-cycle and permanent income hypotheses predict that temporary tax changes will have little effect on current consumption?

3. What factors affect consumer expenditures on durables? Why are these expenditures so volatile?

4. How will the existence of credit rationing make consumption more dependent on current income than the future-oriented consumption theories would suggest?

5. What are the principle forms of investment? Why does the level of investment depend on the real interest rate? What are other important determinants of the level of investment in plant and equipment? Historically, what role have these various determinants played in variations in the level of investment?

6. What is the accelerator, what gives rise to it, and what are its consequences?

7. What are the possible sources of funds for firms that wish to invest? Why might availability of funds play an important role in investment?

8. Why does investment tend to fall in a recession?

9. Why do firms hold inventories? What are the costs and benefits of holding inventories? What are unintended inventory accumulations, and what role do they play? Why might inventory investment be as volatile as it is?

10. How can government stimulate investment?

PROBLEMS

1. Under which theory of consumption would a temporary tax cut have the largest effect on consumption? Under which theory would a permanent rise in Social Security benefits have the largest effect on consumption? Under which theory would permanently higher unemployment insurance benefits have the largest effect on consumption? Explain.

2. Which theory of consumption predicts that aggregate savings will depend on the proportion of retired and young people in the population? What is the relationship? Which theories predict that consumption will not vary a great deal according to whether the economy is in a boom or recession? Why?

3. If the government made it easier for people to borrow money, perhaps by enacting programs to help them get loans, would you expect consumption behavior to become more or less sensitive to current income? Why?

4. How would you predict that a crash in the stock market would affect the relationship between consumption and income? How would you predict that rapidly rising prices for homes would affect the relationship between consumption and income? Draw shifts in the consumption function to illustrate. How do your predictions differ depending on whether the consumer is a Keynesian, life-cycle, or permanent income consumer?

5. A company that expects the long-term real interest rate to be 3 percent is considering a list of projects. Each project costs $10,000, but they vary in the amount of time they will take to pay off, and in how much they will pay off. The first will pay $12,000 in two years; the second, $12,500 in three years; the third, $13,000 in four years. Which projects are worth doing? If the expected interest rate was 5 percent, does your answer change? You may assume that prices are stable.

6. Take the projects in problem 5 and reevaluate them, this time assuming that inflation is at 4 percent per year and the payoffs are in nominal dollars at the time they occur. Are the projects still worth doing?

7. Draw a diagram to show how investment is affected in each of the following situations.
   (a) The government passes an investment tax credit.
   (b) Businesses believe the economic future looks healthier than they had previously thought.
   (c) The government reduces the real interest rate.

8. Imagine that the government raises personal income taxes, but also enacts an investment tax credit for a corresponding amount. Describe under what circumstances this combination of policies would be most effective in stimulating aggregate demand. Consider differing theories of consumption, and the choice between permanent and temporary changes in the tax code.

9. Explain how purchasing a durable good is like an investment. How might an increase in the interest rate or a change in credit availability affect the demand for durables?

10. Explain why if most inventories were held for reasons of production smoothing, inventory accumulation would actually serve to stabilize the economy. Why do economists focus on movements in inventories of consumption goods to argue that there are important factors other than production smoothing that determine patterns of inventory holding? What is one possible explanation of the observed pattern?
   Why would you expect the desired level of inventory holdings to increase with the level of output? Explain why this accelerator relationship might contribute to economic instability. How would you expect changes in the rate of interest, changes in the costs of storage, and innovations in

inventory management techniques to affect the desired inventory-sales ratio?

APPENDIX: THE INVESTMENT-SAVINGS IDENTITY

We typically think of savings and investment together. Both are virtues: "A penny saved is a penny earned." Increased investment enhances the future productivity of the economy. It has frequently been suggested that Americans should encourage savings, the presumption being that savings are automatically converted into investment.

When a *closed* economy is operating along its production possibilities curve, with all resources fully utilized, increased savings—reduced consumption—mean that more capital goods can be produced. Then savings and investment will move together. But when the economy is operating below its production possibilities curve, increased savings—reduced consumption—may simply push the economy further below that curve.

In *open* economies, savings and investment do not have to change together even when the economy is on its production possibilities curve. This is because the economy can undertake investment, even when there is little domestic saving, by borrowing from abroad.

The income-expenditure analysis of Chapter 28 focused on the relationship between aggregate expenditures and income. Equilibrium occurs when aggregate expenditures equal national income. An alternative way of describing how national output is determined focuses on savings and investment. We look at a simple model first, in which disposable income equals national income. For this to be the case, we assume that taxes are zero and all of a firm's profits are paid out as dividends. To simplify further, we assume there are no government savings or dissavings, or any flow of funds from abroad. Later we will loosen up these assumptions to get a fuller picture.

By definition individuals can either spend their income today or save:

$$\text{income} = \text{consumption} + \text{savings}. \tag{29.1}$$

With no government purchases or net exports, we know from the components of aggregate expenditures that firms can produce only two kinds of goods: consumer goods and investment goods. Thus, output, Y, can be broken into its two components:

$$Y = \text{consumption} + \text{investment}. \tag{29.2}$$

These two identities can be combined to form a new one. Since the value of national output equals national income,

$$Y = \text{income}, \tag{29.3}$$

we can use the right-hand side of (29.1) and (29.2) to get

consumption + savings = consumption + investment. (29.4)

Subtracting consumption from both sides of the equation yields

savings = investment. (29.5)

One way to understand this identity is to think of firms as producing a certain amount of goods, the value of which is just equal to the income of the individuals in the economy (because everything firms take in they pay out as income to someone). The income that is not consumed is, by definition, saved. On the output side, firms either sell the goods they produce or put them into inventory for sale in future years. Some of the inventory buildup is planned, because businesses need inventories to survive. Some of it is unplanned—businesses may be surprised by an economic downturn that spoils their sales projections. Both intended and unintended inventory buildups are considered investment. Thus, the goods that are not consumed are, by definition, invested.

This identity (29.5) can be transformed into an equation determining national output, once it is recognized that in equilibrium firms will cut back production if there is unintended inventory accumulation. Because firms will cut back, in equilibrium the amount companies invest is the amount they wish to invest (including inventories), given current market conditions. The equilibrium condition, then, is that

investment = desired investment. (29.6)

Now switch over to the savings side of the identity (29.5). The consumption function presented earlier tells how much people wish to consume at each level of income. But since what is not consumed is saved, the consumption function can be transformed into a savings function, giving the level of savings at each level of income. Savings is income minus consumption:

savings = income (Y) − consumption. (29.7)

Figure 29.9 shows the savings function. The slope of this curve, the amount by which savings increase with income, is the marginal propensity to save, which is 1 minus the marginal propensity to consume.

Since savings must equal investment, and in equilibrium investment must equal desired investment, then in equilibrium

savings = desired investment. (29.8)

The figure shows a fixed level of desired investment, I_1. Desired investment is horizontal because investment is assumed to be unaffected by the level of income. Equilibrium occurs at the intersection of the desired investment curve and the savings curve, point E.

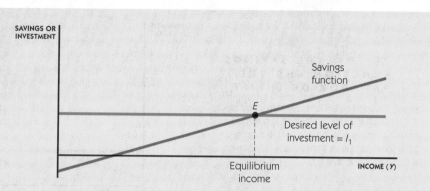

Figure 29.9 THE SAVINGS FUNCTION AND NATIONAL INCOME

As income increases, the amount individuals desire to save increases. The amount by which savings increase as the result of a $1 increase in income—the slope of the savings function—is called the marginal propensity to save. In equilibrium, savings equal desired investment. Thus, equilibrium occurs at the intersection of the savings function and the level of investment.

As with income-expenditure analysis, savings-investment analysis shows how an increase in investment leads to an increase in output that is a multiple of itself. Figure 29.10 shows that as investment shifts up from I_1 to I_2, the equilibrium shifts from E_1 to E_2, and output increases from Y_1 to Y_2. The change in output is again larger than the change in investment, ΔI. This should not surprise us, since income-expenditure analysis and savings-investment analysis are two ways of looking at the same thing.

The Paradox of Thrift   We can use a similar diagram to illustrate what may seem a paradoxical result. When the economy's resources are not fully employed, an increase in thrift—the level of savings at each level of income—may have no effect at all on the equilibrium level of savings or investment. The

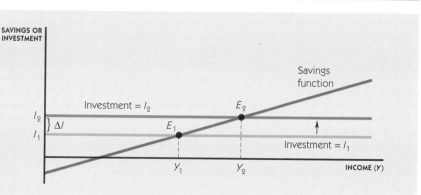

Figure 29.10 USING THE SAVINGS-INVESTMENT DIAGRAM

A shift in investment from I_1 to I_2 leads to an increase in output from Y_1 to Y_2; the increase in output is a multiple of the original increase in investment.

Figure 29.11 **THE SAVINGS FUNCTION AND THE PARADOX OF THRIFT**

Given a level of investment fixed by other factors, increased thriftiness, reflected in an upward shift in the savings function, lowers output from Y_1 to Y_2, but leaves savings unchanged.

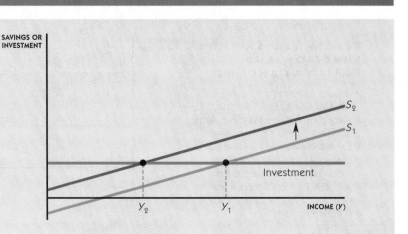

only effect of greater thrift is to lower national income and output. Figure 29.11 shows the effect of an upward shift in the savings function—at each level of income, savings are higher. But in equilibrium, savings equal investment. With investment fixed, savings, in equilibrium, must also be fixed. To attain that level of savings (equal to the level of investment), income must be lowered from Y_1 to Y_2.

CHAPTER

MONEY, BANKING, AND CREDIT

S ome say money is the root of all evil. Some say money makes the world go 'round. Actually, money does not *do* anything, in and of itself. Part of the economy is made up of real people working with real machines to make goods that satisfy needs directly. Money for the most part is just paper and a ledger mark in a bank account. It satisfies needs only indirectly, when it is spent.

In Chapter 25 we encountered the principle of money neutrality. At full employment, an increase in the money supply only leads to a proportionate increase in prices and wages, with no real consequences. Yet controlling the supply of money is considered such an important function of government that failure to exercise that control properly has been blamed not only for inflations, but also for depressions. In the short run, the economy may deviate significantly from full employment, and under such conditions monetary policy may affect output and employment substantially.

We have emphasized that all markets are interlinked. Fluctuations in aggregate output cause fluctuations in employment. Changes in aggregate output can be traced to changes in the level of aggregate demand, which in turn can be related to changes in the level of investment. Investment depends on interest rates and other aspects of the capital market.

So it is to the capital market that we now turn. We will see in this and the next two chapters how government can—through monetary policy—affect interest rates and the availability of credit, and thus the level of investment in

KEY QUESTIONS

1. What *is* money? What economic functions does it serve?

2. What is meant by the money supply, and how is it measured?

3. What institutions in our economy are responsible for controlling the money supply and determining monetary policy?

4. How do modern economies create money through the banking system? How do monetary authorities affect the creation of money and the availability of credit? How do they, in other words, affect the supply of money and credit?

the short term. This chapter will explain what money is, what it does, and why it is so important. The following two chapters will show how, why, and when monetary policy affects the level of economic activity.

MONEY IS WHAT MONEY DOES

We use the term "money" to mean much more than just currency and coins. When someone asks how much money you make, he means what is your income. When someone says, "He has a lot of money," she means he is wealthy, not that he has stashed away lots of currency. When someone accuses corporations of being "interested only in making money," she means they are interested only in making profits.

Economists define money by the functions it serves, and we must look at these functions before we can develop a formal definition of money.

MONEY AS A MEDIUM OF EXCHANGE

Money's first function is to facilitate trade—the exchange of goods or services for mutual benefit. This is called the **medium of exchange** function of money. Trade that occurs without money is called **barter.** Barter involves a direct exchange of one good or service for another. Two families agree to take turns baby-sitting for each other, or a doctor and a lawyer agree to trade consultations. Nations sometimes sign treaties phrased in barter terms. A certain amount of oil, for example, might be traded for a certain amount of machinery or weapons.

Barter works best in simple economies. One can imagine an old-style farmer bartering with the blacksmith, the tailor, the grocer, and the doctor in his small town. For simple barter to work, however, there must be a **double-coincidence of wants.** That is, one individual must have what the other wants, and vice versa. Henry has potatoes and wants shoes, Joshua has an extra pair of shoes and wants potatoes. Bartering can make them both happier. But if Henry has firewood and Joshua does not need any of that, then bartering for Joshua's shoes requires one or both of them to go searching for more people in the hope of making a multilateral exchange. Money provides a way to make multilateral exchange much simpler. Henry sells his firewood to someone else for money and uses the money to buy Joshua's shoes. The convenience of money becomes even clearer when one considers the billions of exchanges that take place in a modern economy.

Any easily transportable and storable good can, in principle, be used as a medium of exchange. And a wide variety of items have served that function. Indeed, the item chosen as "money" can be thought of as a social convention. The reason you accept money in payment for what you sell is that others will accept it for things you want to buy. Different cultures in different times have used all sorts of items as money. American Indians used wampum, South Sea Islanders used cowrie shells. In World War II prisoner-of-war camps and in many prisons of today, cigarettes serve as a medium of exchange.

For a long time, gold was the major medium of exchange. However, the value of a gold coin depends on its weight and purity, as well as on the supply and demand for gold in the gold market. It would be expensive to weigh and verify the quality of gold every time you engaged in a transaction. So one of the functions of governments, right up until the twentieth century, was to mint gold coins, certifying their weight and quality. But because gold is soft, it wears thin with use. Criminals have also profited by shaving the edges off gold coins. The ridges on U.S. dimes and quarters are a carryover from coins developed to deter this practice.

Today all the developed countries of the world use paper (printed by the government specially for this purpose) as well as metal coins for currency. However, most business transactions use not currency but checks drawn on banks, credit cards whose balances are paid with checks, or funds wired from one bank to another. Economists consider checking account balances to be money, just as currency is, because they are accepted as payment at most places and thus serve the medium of exchange function. Since most people have much more money in their checking accounts than they do in their wallets, it should be evident that the economists' measure of the money supply is much larger than the amount of coins and other currency in circulation.

MONEY AS A STORE OF VALUE

People will only be willing to exchange what they have for money if they believe they can later exchange the money for the goods or services they want. Thus, for money to serve its role as a medium of exchange, it must hold its value, at least for a short while. This function is known as the **store of value** function of money. There was a time when governments feared that paper money by itself would not be accepted in the future and so paper money was not as good a store of value as gold. People had confidence in paper dollars only because they were backed by gold (if you wished, you used to be able to exchange your paper dollars for gold).

Today, however, all major economies have **fiat money**—money that has value only because the government says it has value and because people are willing to accept it in exchange for goods. The dollar bill in your pocket recognizes this need for security with its message: "This note is legal tender for all debts, public and private." The fact that it is legal tender means that if you owe someone $100, you have fully discharged that debt if you give her a hundred-dollar bill.

There are many other stores of value. Gold, which is no longer "money" because it no longer serves as a medium of exchange, nevertheless continues to serve as a store of value. In India, for instance, people hold much of their savings in the form of gold. Land, corporate stocks and bonds, oil and minerals—all are stores of value. None of them is perfectly safe, in the sense that you cannot be precisely sure what they can be exchanged for in the future. But currency, checking account balances, and other forms of money are not a perfectly safe store of value either. If prices change, then what you can buy with the dollars in your pocket or bank account will change.

MONEY AS A UNIT OF ACCOUNT

In performing its roles as a medium of exchange and a store of value, money serves a third purpose. It is a way of measuring the relative values of different goods. This is the **unit of account** function of money. If a banana costs 25 cents and a peach 50 cents, then a peach is worth twice as much as a banana. A person who wishes to trade bananas for peaches can do so at the rate of two bananas for one peach. Money thus provides a simple and convenient yardstick for measuring relative market values.

Imagine how difficult it would be for firms to keep track of how well they were doing without such a yardstick. The ledgers might describe how many of each item the firm bought or sold. But the fact that the firm sold more items than it purchased would tell you nothing about how well that firm was doing. You need to know the value of what the firm sells relative to the value of what it purchases. Money provides the unit of account, the means by which the firm and others take these measurements.

We are now ready for the economic definition of **money.** Money is anything that is generally accepted as a medium of exchange, a store of value, and a unit of account. Money is, in other words, what money does.

MEASURING THE MONEY SUPPLY

The quantity of money is called the **money supply,** a stock variable like the capital stock. Most of the other variables discussed in this chapter are stock variables as well, but they have important effects on the flow variables (like the level of economic activity, measured as dollars *per year*).

Close-up: When Atlanta Printed Money

In the nineteenth and early twentieth centuries, in the rural South and West, there was often a shortage of cash for everyday transactions. Workers could not shop for food or clothing, bills were not paid, and the local economy lurched sideways or backward.

It was common in such cases for towns, private companies, and sometimes states to print their own currency, known politely as "scrip" and less politely as "soap wrappers," "shinplasters," "doololly," and many less printable names. The idea was that issuing scrip could keep the local economy going until official currency became available again, at which point people could cash in their scrip.

The last major issue of scrip in the United States came during the Great Depression of the early 1930s. Banks were crashing right and left, and bank runs were a daily occurrence. Remember, these were the days before deposits were insured. When President Franklin Roosevelt took office early in 1933, one of his first major actions was to declare a "bank holiday" for the week of March 6–12. He closed all the banks for a week to give everyone time to relax and get their bearings.

But these were also the days before checking accounts had become widespread, when workers were paid weekly, in cash. If firms could not get to the bank, they could not pay their workers. How could the local economy react to these sorts of financial disturbances?

Each area adapted in its own way. Let's consider Atlanta. The city issued about $2.5 million in scrip, in eight different issues made during the first half of the 1930s. One of the first payments was to schoolteachers, and the city made sure that Rich's, a prominent local department store, would take the scrip at full face value. Many other stores, however, would count the scrip only at 75 percent or less of face value. Notice that by taking scrip, which it would later turn in to the city for cash, stores were effectively loaning money to the city that issued the scrip.

Such stories of scrip may sound antiquated today (though in its 1992 financial crisis, California paid its workers with something akin to scrip). But they emphasize the fact that without something to serve as a medium of exchange, a yardstick for measurement, and a (short-term) store of value, an economy simply cannot function. Today the Federal Reserve acts to ensure that currency is available. But in the 1930s, issuing scrip was one thing a city could do on its own to cushion the ravages of the Great Depression.

Source: William Roberds, "Lenders of the Next-to-Last Resort: Scrip Issue in Georgia During the Great Depression," *Economic Review of the Federal Reserve Bank of Atlanta* (September–October 1990), pp. 16–30.

What exactly should be included in the money supply? A variety of items serve some of the functions of money, but not all of them. For example, the chips issued in casinos for gambling serve as a medium of exchange inside the casino and perhaps even in some nearby stores and restaurants. But no place outside the casino is obligated to take them; they are neither a generally accepted medium of exchange nor a unit of account.

The economists' measure of money begins with the currency and coins that we carry around. Economists then expand the measure of money to include other items that serve the three functions of money. Checking accounts, or **demand deposits** (so called because you can get your money back upon demand), are included in the money supply, as are some other forms of bank accounts. But what are the limits? There is a continuum here, running from items that everyone would agree should be called money to items that can work as money in many circumstances, to items that can occasionally work as money, to items that would never be considered money.

Economists have developed several measures of the money supply to take account of this variety. The narrowest, called **M1,** is the total of currency, traveler's checks, and checking accounts. In other words, M1 is currency plus items that through the banking system can be treated like currency. In late 1995, MI totaled $1,123 billion.

A broader measure, **M2,** includes everything that is in M1 plus some items that are *almost* perfect substitutes for M1. Savings deposits of $100,000 or less are included. So are certificates of deposit (deposits put in the bank for fixed periods of time, between six months and five years); money market funds held by individuals; and Eurodollars, U.S. dollars deposited in European banks. In late 1995 M2 totaled $3,781 billion.

The common characteristic of assets in M2 is that they are very *liquid,* or easily convertible into M1. You cannot just tell a store that the money it requires in exchange for a shirt or a dress is in your savings account. But if you have funds in your savings account it is not hard to turn those into something the store will accept. You can transfer funds from your savings account into your checking account, or withdraw them as currency.

A third measure of the money supply, **M3,** includes everything that is in M2 (and thus everything that is in M1) plus large-denomination savings accounts (over $100,000) and institutional money market mutual funds. M3 is just about as liquid as M2. In late 1995, M3 totaled $4,564 billion.

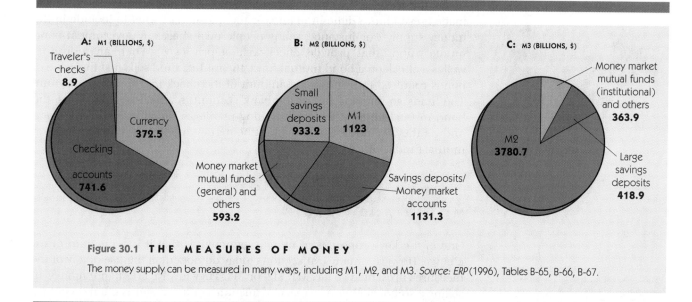

Figure 30.1 THE MEASURES OF MONEY

The money supply can be measured in many ways, including M1, M2, and M3. *Source: ERP* (1996), Tables B-65, B-66, B-67.

Figure 30.1 shows the relative magnitude of these three different measures of the money supply. Figure 30.2 shows that the different measures grow at different rates.

Recent changes in financial institutions—such as the growth of mutual

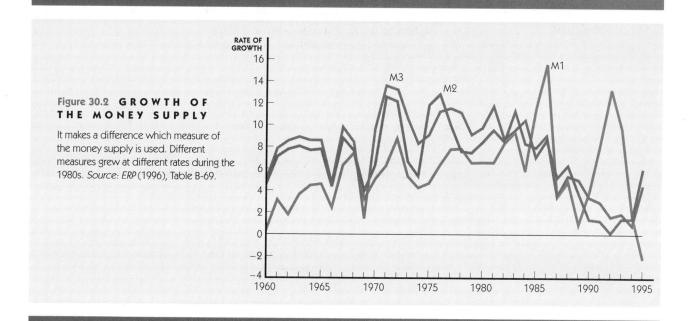

Figure 30.2 GROWTH OF THE MONEY SUPPLY

It makes a difference which measure of the money supply is used. Different measures grew at different rates during the 1980s. *Source: ERP* (1996), Table B-69.

funds, the more extensive use of credit cards, and home equity loans—have made it even more difficult to answer the question of what to include in the money supply. For instance, many people own shares in government-bond mutual funds that provide check-writing privileges. When an individual writes a check on a bond mutual fund, the mutual fund sells just the value of bonds required to transfer the amount of the check into the bank account. The funds go into and out of the bank account in a split second. Thus, the bond mutual funds with check-writing privileges function just like money. And yet they are not included within the money supply, while money market mutual funds are.

MONEY AND CREDIT

One of the key properties of money, as noted, is that it is a medium of exchange. However, many transactions today do not entail the use of any of the measures presented so far: M1, M2, or M3. They involve credit, not money. In selling a suit of clothes or a piece of furniture or a car, stores often do not receive money. They receive rather, a promise from you to pay money in the future. Credit is clearly tied to money: what you owe the store is measured in dollars. You want something today, and you will have the money for it tomorrow. The store wants you to buy today and is willing to wait until tomorrow or next week for the money. There is a mutually advantageous trade. But because the exchange is not *simultaneous,* the store must rely on your promise.

Promises, the saying goes, are made to be broken. But if they are broken too often, stores will not be able to trust buyers, and credit exchanges will not occur. There is therefore an incentive for the development of institutions, such as banks, to ascertain who is most likely to keep economic promises and to help ensure that once such a promise has been made it is kept.

When banks are involved, the store does not need to believe the word of the shopper. Rather, the shopper must convince the bank that he will in fact pay. Consider a car purchase. Suppose a bank agrees to give Luke a loan, and he then buys the car. If he later breaks his promise and does not pay back the loan, the car dealer is protected. It is the bank that tries to force Luke to keep his commitment.

Modern economies have relied increasingly on credit as a basis of transactions. Banks have a long tradition of extending **lines of credit** to firms. This means that a bank agrees to lend a business money automatically (up to some limit), as it is needed. With Visa and MasterCard and the variety of other national credit cards that came into widespread use in the 1970s and 1980s, lines of credit have also been extended to millions of consumers, who now can purchase goods even when they have no currency or checking account balances on hand. Today individuals can also easily get credit based on the equity in their houses (the difference between the value of the house and what they owe on their mortgage, which is the loan taken out to buy the house). This type of credit is called home equity loans. When house prices increased

CLOSE-UP: GLOSSARY OF FINANCIAL TERMS

One of the problems in defining money is the wide variety of assets that are not directly used as a medium of exchange but can be readily converted into something that *could* be so used. Should they be included in the money supply? There is no right or wrong answer. Below are definitions of nine terms, some of which were defined in earlier chapters. Each of these assets serves, in progressively less satisfactory ways, the function of money.

Currency and coins	One-, five-, ten-, twenty-, and hundred dollar bills; pennies, nickels, dimes, quarters, and half dollars.
Traveler's checks	Checks issued by a bank or a firm such as American Express that you can convert into currency upon demand and are widely accepted.
Demand deposits, or checking accounts	Deposits that you can withdraw upon demand (that is, convert into currency upon demand), by writing a check.
Savings deposits	Deposits that technically you can withdraw only upon notice; in practice, banks allow withdrawal upon demand (without notice).
Certificates of deposit	Money deposited in the bank for a fixed period of time (usually six months to five years), with a penalty for early withdrawal.
NOW (negotiable order of withdrawal) accounts	A kind of account that breaks through legislative loopholes to allow customers to write checks on interest-bearing deposits.
Money market accounts	Another category of interest-bearing bank checking accounts, often paying higher interest rates but with restrictions on the number of checks that can be written.
Money market mutual funds	Mutual funds that invest in Treasury bills, certificates of deposit, and similar safe securities. You can usually write checks against such accounts; they are thus similar to NOW and other interest-bearing bank checking accounts.
Eurodollars	U.S. dollar bank accounts in banks outside the United States (mainly in Europe).

rapidly in the 1980s, they provided a ready source of credit for millions of home owners.

These innovations make it easier for people to obtain credit. But they have also altered the way economists think about the role of money in the economy—blurring definitions that once seemed quite clear.

THE FINANCIAL SYSTEM IN MODERN ECONOMIES

Broadly speaking, a country's **financial system** includes all institutions involved in moving savings from households and firms whose income exceeds their expenditures and transferring it to other households and firms who would like to spend more than their income allows. Here we take a closer look at the most important of these institutions.

The financial system in the United States not only allows consumers to buy cars, televisions, and VCRs even when they do not have the cash to do so. It also enables firms to invest in factories and new machines. Sometimes money goes directly from, say, a household doing some saving to a firm that needs some additional cash. For example, when Ben buys a new bond from General Motors that promises to pay a fixed amount in 90 or 180 days (or in 5 or 15 years), he is lending money directly to GM.

But most of the funds flow through **financial intermediaries.** These are firms that stand in between the savers, who have the extra funds, and the borrowers, who need them. The most important group of financial intermediaries is the banks, but there are many other groups of financial intermediaries as well, including life insurance companies, credit unions, and savings and loan associations. All are engaged in looking over potential borrowers, ascertaining who are good risks, and monitoring their investments and loans. The intermediaries take "deposits" from consumers and invest them. By putting the funds into many different investments, they diversify and thus reduce the risk. One investment might turn sour, but it is unlikely that many will. This provides the intermediary with a kind of safety it could not obtain if it put all its eggs in one basket. Financial institutions differ in who the depositors are, where the funds are invested, and who owns the institutions.

FEDERAL RESERVE SYSTEM

Just as there is a continuum—from currency and demand deposits to money market accounts—that serves in varying degrees the functions of money, so too is there a continuum of financial intermediaries that perform in varying ways the functions that banks perform. For instance, savings and loan associations (S & L's) accept deposits and make loans today in a way that is almost identical to that of banks. Financial intermediaries play an important role in our financial system. Their actions affect the supply of money (particularly money in the broader definitions, such as M2 and M3). For simplicity, the discussion here focuses on commercial banks and the narrower definition of money, M1. Traditionally, banks have been the most important way in which businesses raise capital and by which the government attempts to control the level of investment and hence the level of national economic activity.

Governments today have two objectives in their involvement with the bank portion of the financial system. The first is to protect consumers: when banks go bankrupt, depositors stand to lose their life's savings. The typical saver is not in a position to audit a bank's books to see whether it is really sound. During the Depression of the 1930s, hundreds of banks closed, leaving thousands destitute. Today banks are more tightly regulated. In addition, depositors are insured by government agencies, to limit their losses should a bankruptcy occur.

The second objective of government involvement in the banking system is to stabilize the level of economic activity. We have seen the important role that the banking system plays in taking funds from savers and providing them to investors. When the banking system collapses, firms cannot obtain funds to make their investments, and the entire economy suffers. More broadly, the banking system, by its actions, affects the level of investment, and this affects the level of economic activity. Sharp declines in investment can throw the economy into a recession; sharp increases can set off an inflationary spiral.

CENTRAL BANK

Different economies have developed a variety of institutions and laws for accomplishing these twin objectives. The most important institution in each country is its **central bank.** The central bank is a bank from which other banks can borrow. But it is more than a banker's bank. It is also responsible for stabilizing the level of economic activity by controlling the money supply and the availability of credit, and for regulating the banking system to ensure its financial health. In the United States, the central bank is called the **Federal Reserve,** which was established in 1913. The Federal Reserve consists of a Board of Governors, also known as the **Federal Reserve Board,** which, with their staff, supervises a system of twelve regional **Federal Reserve banks,** and with them, monitors the operations of six thousand member banks. The collection of governors and Federal Reserve banks, often simply referred to as the "Fed," is at the heart of the **Federal Reserve System,** which includes all of the member banks.[1]

The structure of the system is depicted in Figure 30.3. The Board of Governors consists of seven members who are appointed for fourteen-year terms (although the average length of service is about seven years). While in theory each member of the Board of Governors has one vote, the chairman of the board has traditionally wielded enormous power. The chairman is appointed by the president to serve a four-year term, with that term of office intentionally set so as not to coincide with the term of the president. Once appointed, the chairman is theoretically fully independent of the president or Congress. Indeed, because the funding of the Fed comes from the profits it earns on its operations, Congress and the president cannot even threaten to reduce the Fed's funding. Still, the chairman must report regularly to Congress on the Fed's actions and budget.

CONTROLLING THE MONEY SUPPLY

The country is divided into twelve Federal Reserve districts, as shown in Figure 30.4, each with its own bank. But responsibility for stabilizing the economy through controlling the money supply is vested in a committee of the Federal Reserve called the **Federal Open Market Committee.** This commit-

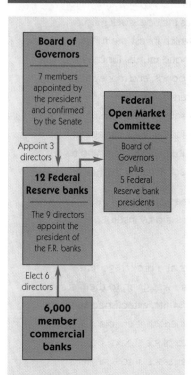

Figure 30.3 STRUCTURE OF THE FEDERAL RESERVE SYSTEM

The Federal Reserve operates at both a national level and a district level. The Board of Governors are appointed by the president; the district level includes some directors appointed nationally and some from within the district; the Open Market Committee includes the presidentially appointed governors and representatives from the district banks.

---

[1]While the Federal Reserve banks are officially "owned" by the member banks and therefore in a technical sense are not really part of the government, most of the profits of the Fed—which generally amount to about $25 billion a year—are turned over to the U.S. Treasury.

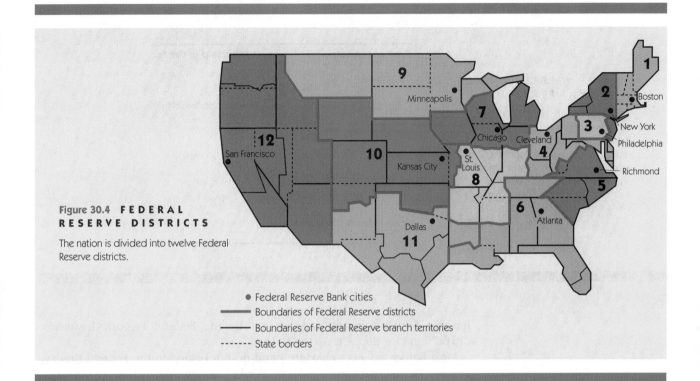

Figure 30.4 FEDERAL RESERVE DISTRICTS

The nation is divided into twelve Federal Reserve districts.

• Federal Reserve Bank cities
— Boundaries of Federal Reserve districts
— Boundaries of Federal Reserve branch territories
------ State borders

tee consists of the Board of Governors plus five of the twelve Federal Reserve bank presidents (on rotating duty). The name comes from the way the committee operates. The Fed engages in **open market operations**—so called because they involve the Fed entering the capital market directly, much as a private individual or firm would, buying or selling government bonds. (Later in the chapter, we will see how these actions translate into changes in the money supply, and look at other ways that the Fed controls the money supply.) Once the Open Market Committee has set its goals, its operations are carried out by the Federal Reserve Bank of New York, because of that bank's proximity to the huge capital markets in New York.

REGULATING BANKS

The other primary objective of central banks is ensuring the financial soundness of the other banks in the country. To open its doors, a U.S. bank must receive a charter, from either the federal government or one of the states. Figure 30.5 shows that two-thirds of all banks are state-chartered. All the federally chartered banks, and some of the state-chartered banks, belong to the Federal Reserve System; they are called **member banks,** in contrast to **nonmember banks,** which do not belong to the Federal Reserve System. Depositors in virtually all U.S. banks, whether they belong to the Federal

Figure 30.5 WHERE BANKS ARE CHARTERED

Two-thirds of banks are state-chartered. All federally chartered banks and some state-chartered banks are members of the Federal Reserve System. Depositors in almost all banks, whether state or federal, are insured by the Federal Deposit Insurance Corporation. *Source: Statistics on Banking* (1995), Table 104.

Type of charter	Membership in the Fed
National banks •3,075 ••(56%)	Member banks 4,050 (77%)
State banks 7,375 (44%)	Nonmember banks 6,400 (23%)

• Total number
•• Percentage of total commercial banking assets held

Reserve System or not, are insured by the Federal Deposit Insurance Corporation for deposits up to $100,000.

Most banks are state-chartered and do not belong to the Federal Reserve System. These are for the most part small banks with the important exception of large state-chartered banks in New York. A few large banks control most of the assets within the banking system; 3 percent control more than 70 percent of the assets. The smallest 60 percent control less than 8 percent of the assets. The sixteen largest banks, each with assets of over $20 billion, control one-third of the assets in the entire banking system.

The banks that are members of the Federal Reserve System are subject to three layers of regulation. The U.S. Treasury, through the comptroller of the currency, the Federal Deposit Insurance Corporation, and the Federal Reserve itself all share the job of supervision. Even so, in the late 1980s and early 1990s, a rash of bankruptcies and near bankruptcies, some in fairly large banks, raised questions about the adequacy of the banking regulations.

CREATING MONEY IN MODERN ECONOMIES

In order to understand how the Fed goes about its task of controlling the money supply, we need to know more about how a bank runs its business, particularly how banks create money. The money supply of today is created not by a mint or printing press but largely by the banking system. When you put money into the bank, the bank does not simply take the currency down to its vault, put it into a little slot marked with your name, and keep it there until

Savings and loan associations (S & L's) have traditionally been one of America's most staid and trusted institutions—using people's savings to finance mortgages, with savings deposit accounts insured against default by the federal government. Tradition came to an abrupt halt in the mid- and late 1980s, as a major part of the S & L industry went belly up. Bank failures soared, reaching 221 in 1988, more than 20 times the number in 1980. Greed and corruption were widely cited as the cause of the problem. The solution was expensive. The government bailout which began in 1989 ultimately cost taxpayers more than $100 billion.

What really happened? Almost everyone now agrees that, though unscrupulous S & L's certainly exploited the system, the crisis had roots in Washington. In fact, the problem had been brewing since the 1970s, when the Fed suddenly began raising interest rates. S & L's were left paying far more in interest on deposit accounts than they were earning on the fixed-rate mortgages issued in years past. The government responded by relaxing the regulations governing how S & L's could use depositors' funds, and allowing S & L's to invest in higher-risk, potentially higher-return investments. Higher returns did stave off the crisis for a few years. But the downside of high-risk investments is the greater likelihood that they will go sour. And sour they went in the late 1980s—both the real estate markets and the market for high-risk bonds (sometimes called junk bonds) in which S & L's had invested heavily.

The fundamental, if unpalatable truth is that S & L managers and depositors were responding rationally to the misguided incentives built into deposit insurance. Facing bankruptcy, S & L's had little choice but to pursue the risky course—at least the high returns would enable them to continue operating—and they had little trouble obtaining the funds. After all, depositors didn't have to worry about how the S & L's handled their money (at least up to the guarantee limit of $100,000). Those S & L's paying the highest interest rates—and taking the highest risks—attracted the most deposits.

Government regulators multiplied the problem. When the problem first arose, they should have recognized that the S & L's worsening financial situation required increased scrutiny. The S & L's were paying higher interest rates on deposits while the returns on old mortgages were fixed at low levels. Regulators should have feared the S & L's might take undue risk to bail themselves out. Instead, the government loosened the regulations. Then, as the crisis mounted in the mid-1980s, with an ever-rising number of bankruptcies they overreacted. Lest regulators be accused of regulatory laxity, they became ruthless in tightening and enforcing the regulations. Banks and S & L's responded by becoming even more conservative in their lending than the new standards required. The reduced lending contributed greatly to the economic downturn of the early 1990s.

you are ready to take it out. Instead, banks realize that not all their thousands of depositors will withdraw their money on any given day. Some will come by next week, some in two weeks, some not for a year or more. In the meantime, the bank can lend out the money deposited in its vault and charge interest. The more money the bank can persuade people to deposit, the more can be loaned out and thus the more money the bank will earn. To attract depositors, the bank pays interest on its deposits, effectively passing on (after taking its cut) the interest earned on its loans.

How much can safely be lent out? Money retained by a bank in case those who have deposited money want it back is called its **reserves.** How much needs to be kept as reserves? Should the bank keep reserves of 5 percent of deposits? 20 percent of deposits? The less it keeps as reserves, the more money it can earn, but the greater the possibility that it will not have enough funds on hand if a large number of depositors want their deposits back at the same time. To understand how these reserves work and how they affect the supply of money and credit available in the economy, we need to take a close look at the typical bank's balance sheet.

THE BANK'S BALANCE SHEET

Bankers see the world backward. Where else would loans be called "assets" and deposits be called "liabilities"? This is the perspective shown on a bank's **balance sheet.** Like any firm's balance sheet, it describes the bank's **assets** and **liabilities.** Assets are what the firm owns, including what is owed to it by others. That is why the bank's loans appear as assets on its balance sheet. Liabilities are what it owes to others. We can think of the bank's depositors as having loaned money to the bank. They can get their money back when they wish. That is why deposits are treated by the bank as liabilities.

Table 30.1 shows the balance sheet of AmericaBank. Its assets are divided into three categories: loans outstanding, government bonds, and reserves, in-

Table 30.1 **AMERICABANK BALANCE SHEET**

Assets		Liabilities	
Loans outstanding	$28 million	Deposits	$30 million
Government bonds	$ 2 million		
Reserves	$ 3 million	Net worth	$ 3 million
Total	$33 million	Total	$33 million

cluding cash in the vault. Least secure are the loans outstanding. These consist of loans to business firms, real estate loans (mortgages), car loans, house-remodeling loans, and so on. Government bonds are more secure than loans to households or firms. Most banks' holdings of government bonds are typically concentrated in Treasury bills (or T-bills), short-term bonds maturing in thirty, sixty, or ninety days after the date of issue.[2] Most secure are the reserves that are held on deposit at the "banker's bank," the local Federal Reserve bank, and the cash in the vault.

The amount of money people need to set aside for a rainy day depends (in part) on how easily they can borrow. The same is true for banks. If they can borrow easily from other banks to meet any shortfall of reserves, they need to keep very little in reserves. In the United States, the Federal Reserve banks act as the banker's bank, lending money to other banks. (Banks do not, however, have an automatic right to borrow; the Fed must concur with the request. Many central banks use this discretionary power to elicit desired behavior.) But banks need to hold reserves for an additional reason other than caution. The Fed imposes reserve requirements on banks. Today, the amount of reserves banks hold is dictated more by regulations than by the banks' own perceptions of what is prudent. After all, holding T-bills is just as safe as holding reserves with the Fed—and yields higher returns. And the level of reserves required by the Fed is designed primarily from the perspective of controlling the money supply and thereby the level of economic activity. Table 30.2 shows the current reserve requirements. This system of banking, in which banks hold a fraction of the amount on deposit in reserves, is called the **fractional reserve system.**

The liability side of AmericaBank's balance sheet consists of two items: deposits and net worth. Deposits include checking accounts, which are technically known as demand deposits, and the variety of forms of savings accounts,

[2]Long-term bonds are volatile in price, because their price changes with changes in interest rates. Banks typically hold short-term government bonds because the risk of such changes over a relatively short period of time is low, and banks wish to avoid risk.

Table 30.2 REQUIRED RESERVES

Type of deposit	Minimum reserve required (percentage of deposits)
Very large checking accounts (over $54 million)	3
Other checking accounts (under $54 million)	10
All other deposits	0

Source: *Federal Reserve Bulletin* (1995).

which are technically known as time deposits. The bank's net worth is simply the difference between the value of its assets and the value of its liabilities. In other words, if the bank's assets were sold and its depositors paid off, what remained would equal the net worth of the bank.

Since net worth is *defined* as the difference between the value of the liabilities and the value of the assets, the numbers on both sides of the balance sheet always balance.

HOW BANKS CREATE MONEY

As we have seen, the coins and currency manufactured by the Treasury are a relatively small part of the money supply. Who creates the rest of the money? Banks.

To see how banks create money, let's consider all 10,450 U.S. banks as one huge superbank. Assume the Fed is requiring that reserves be 10 percent of deposits. Now suppose that a multi-multi-millionaire deposits $1 billion in currency in her account.

The bank reasons as follows. It knows it must keep a reserve-to-deposit ratio of 1 to 10, and it has a long line of loan applicants. When the bank makes a loan, it does not actually give the borrower currency. It credits him with funds in his checking account. It does this by placing an entry into its books on both the left- and right-hand side of the ledger: there is a loan on the asset side and a deposit on the liability side. If it makes $9 billion worth of loans, it liabilities will have gone up to $10 billion (the $1 billion in currency originally deposited by the millionaire plus the $9 billion worth of loans). On the asset side, the bank takes the $1 billion in currency to the Fed and is credited with the amount, so that it now has $1 billion in reserves. Thus, its reserves have increased by $1 billion, its deposits by $10 billion; it has satisfied the reserve requirement.

We can reach the same result by a slower route, as shown in Table 30.3. The

Table 30.3 SUPERBANK BALANCE SHEET

Before-deposit equilibrium			
Assets		**Liabilities**	
Loans outstanding	$ 91 billion	Deposits	$100 billion
Government bonds	2 billion		
Reserves	10 billion	Net worth	3 billion
Total	103 billion	Total	103 billion

First round (Add $1 billion deposits, $.9 billion loans)			
Assets		**Liabilities**	
Loans outstanding	$ 91.9 billion	Deposits	$101 billion
Government bonds	2 billion		
Reserves	10.1 billion	Net worth	3 billion
Total	104 billion	Total	104 billion

Second round (Add $.9 billion deposits, $.81 billion loans to previous round[a])			
Assets		**Liabilities**	
Loans outstanding	$ 92.71 billion	Deposits	$101.9 billion
Government bonds	2 billion		
Reserves	10.19 billion	Net worth	3 billion
Total	104.9 billion	Total	104.9 billion

Third round (Add $.81 billion deposits, $.73 billion loans to previous round[a])			
Assets		**Liabilities**	
Loans outstanding	$ 93.44 billion	Deposits	$102.71 billion
Government bonds	2 billion		
Reserves	10.27 billion	Net worth	3 billion
Total	105.71 billion	Total	105.71 billion

After-deposit equilibrium (Add $10 billion new deposits, $9 billion new loans to original equilibrium)			
Assets		**Liabilities**	
Loans outstanding	$100 billion	Deposits	$110 billion
Government bonds	2 billion		
Reserves	11 billion	Net worth	3 billion
Total	113 billion	Total	113 billion

[a]In each subsequent round, new deposits equal new loans of the previous round; new loans equal .9 × new deposits.

bank might reason, now that its deposits have gone up by $1 billion, that it must send $100 million to the Federal Reserve as part of its reserve requirements. But it can lend out the remaining $900 million (.9 × $1 billion). This is the first-round balance sheet that appears in the table. Deposits have increased $1 billion (compared with the initial situation), loans have increased $.9 billion, and reserves have increased $.1 billion.

For simplicity, let's assume that the lending is all made to one customer. Desktop Publishing borrows $900 million so that it can purchase new computers from ComputerAmerica. When Desktop pays $900 million for the computers, ComputerAmerica deposits the money in its account. Thus, the loan of $900 million is reflected in the addition of $900 million in deposits. This is shown on the right-hand side of the second-round balance sheet in the table, where deposits have now risen from $101 billion to $101.9 billion.

But with the $900 million additional deposits, the bank is allowed to increase its lending by .9 × $900 million, or $810 million, putting $90 million into reserves. These changes are shown in the left-hand side of the second-round balance sheet. Assume that all $810 million is lent out to various companies, each of which uses the money to purchase new goods. In each case, some other firm will sell its good and will put these new funds into the superbank. As a result, new deposits at the superbank will again grow by $810 million. As the third round begins, deposits are once again increased.

But the bank is still not in equilibrium. Because of the increase in deposits of $810 million, it can lend out .9 × $810 million = $729 million. And so the process continues. Notice that on each round, the increase in deposits is smaller than in the previous round. In the second round, the increase in deposits was $900 million, in the third round $810 million, and so on. The after-deposit equilibrium balance sheet in the last part of the table shows that the bank has increased its deposits by ten times the original deposit ($100 billion to $110 billion) and increased its lending by nine times the original deposit ($91 billion to $100 billion). The $1 billion injection into the banking system has turned into a $10 billion increase in the money supply.

In the new situation, the banking system is in equilibrium. Its reserves of $11 billion are precisely equal to 10 percent of its $110 billion deposits. It cannot lend out any more without violating the reserve requirements.

In this way, any new deposit into the banking system results in a multiple expansion of the number of deposits. This is the "miracle" of the fractional reserve system. Deposits increase by a factor of 1/reserve requirement. In the superbank example, the reserve requirement was 10 percent; 1/reserve requirement is 10. If the reserve requirement had been 20 percent, deposits would have increased by 1/.2, or 5. Note that as the deposits increased, so did the supply of outstanding loans.

In this example, there were no "leakages" outside the system. That is, no one decided to hold currency rather than put his money back into the bank, and whenever sellers were paid, they put what they received into the bank. With leakages, the increase in deposits and thus the increase in money will be smaller. In the real world these leakages are large. The ratio of M1 to reserves is only around 3, and even for M2 the ratio is only between 11 and 12. Nevertheless, the increase in bank reserves will lead to some multiple increase in the money supply. This relationship between the change in reserves and the final change in deposits is called the **money multiplier.**[3]

MONEY MULTIPLIERS WITH MANY BANKS

The money multiplier works just as well when there is more than one bank involved. Assume that Desktop Publishing and ComputerAmerica have their bank accounts in two separate banks, BankNational and BankUSA, respectively. When Desktop Publishing writes a check for $900 million to ComputerAmerica, $900 million is transferred from BankNational to BankUSA. Once that $900 million has been transferred, BankUSA will find that it can lend more than it could previously. As a result of the $900 million increase in deposits, it can lend .9 × $900 = $810 million. Suppose it lends the $810 million to the NewTelephone Company, which uses the money to buy a machine for making telephones from Equipment Manufacturing. If Equipment Manufacturing has its bank account at BankIllinois, after Equipment Manufacturing has been paid, BankIllinois will find that because its deposits have increased by $810 million, it can lend .9 × $810 = $729 million. The process continues, until the new equilibrium is identical to the one described earlier in the superbank example, where there is a $10 billion increase in the money supply. The banking system as a whole will have expanded the money supply by a multiple of the initial deposit, equal to 1/reserve requirement.

It should be clear that when there are many banks, no individual bank can create multiple deposits. Individual banks may not even be aware of the role they play in the process of multiple-deposit creation. All they see is that their deposits have increased and therefore they are able to make more loans.

The process of multiple-deposit creation may seem somewhat like a magician pulling rabbits out of a hat: it seems to make something out of nothing. But it is, in fact, a real physical process. Deposits are created by making entries in records; today electronic impulses create records on computer tapes. The rules of deposit creation are rules specifying when you may make certain entries in the books. It is these rules—in particular, the fractional reserve requirements—that give rise to the system's ability to expand deposits by a multiple of the original deposit increase.

MONEY MULTIPLIER

An increase in reserves by a dollar leads to an increase in total deposits by a multiple of the original increase.

---

[3]This multiplier should not be confused with the (investment) multiplier introduced in Chapter 9. That multiplier showed that an increase in investment or government expenditures leads to a multiple increase in the equilibrium level of aggregate expenditures. There are clearly similarities in the way we go about calculating the two multipliers, however.

THE INSTRUMENTS OF MONETARY POLICY

Most changes in the money supply are not the result of someone depositing a billion dollars of currency in a bank. Nor any longer do they involve someone selling gold to or depositing gold in a bank. Instead, they are the result of actions by the Federal Reserve Board. The Fed creates reserves. It does so deliberately, in order to increase the supply of money and credit. By such action, the Fed affects the level of economic activity. The connections between the actions the Fed takes and their effect on the level of economic activity are the subject of the next two chapters. Here, our concern is simply with the supply of money and credit. Money and credit, as we have seen, represent the two sides of a bank's balance sheet. When deposits (money) increase, either bank loans (credit) or bank holdings of T-bills must increase. Frequently both will. Though ultimately our concern will be with bank lending, bank lending is not directly under the control of the Fed, so it must affect bank lending through the money supply. The Fed has three tools with which it can change the money supply: reserve requirements, discount rate, and open market operations.

RESERVE REQUIREMENTS

The simplest tool available to the Fed is to alter **reserve requirements.** The Fed sets the minimum amount of money each bank is required to hold in reserves. While in principle the government could require banks to hold reserves in a variety of forms (cash, government bonds, gold), the Fed actually requires that the reserves be held as deposits with the Federal Reserve—partly because this stipulation facilitates monitoring of the reserve requirement.

Assume that banks are initially required to maintain reserves equal to 10 percent of deposits, and consider what happens if reserve requirements are lowered to 5 percent. Each bank will find that it now has **excess reserves** or **free reserves**—reserves in excess of the amount required. This means that each bank will be in a position to lend more. Where a lack of funds may have caused the bank to reject loans to projects it considered worthy, now it will make these loans. The new loans get spent, creating new deposits and allowing still further loans, and the multiplier process is once again set in motion.

DISCOUNT RATE

The second tool of monetary policy is the **discount rate.** This is the interest rate banks must pay when they borrow from the Federal Reserve banks. As explained earlier in this chapter, the Federal Reserve banks are called the banker's banks because they lend money to banks and hold their deposits.

When the discount rate is high, interest rates charged by banks tend to be high, and banks make loans less available.

Consider an aggressive bank that always keeps just the minimum amount of reserves, lending out all the rest of its funds. If a major depositor suddenly wishes to withdraw funds, the bank is forced to borrow funds to cover this withdrawal, either from other banks or from the Federal Reserve banks. When the discount rate increases, the interest rate the bank must pay for borrowing from other banks increases in tandem. The discount rate affects this bank as a direct cost of doing business. If it has to pay the Fed more to borrow itself, it must charge its own customers more.

If the bank pursues a less aggressive policy and holds more funds in the form of Treasury bills or other liquid assets, a large withdrawal causes only a minor adjustment: the bank simply sells some of its liquid assets. Raising the discount rate makes it more expensive to call upon the Fed in the event of a shortfall of funds, and this induces banks to hold more liquid assets and more T-bills, which in turn means that the bank will be lending less.

The Fed not only uses a higher discount rate to discourage banks from lending, it also rations access to the discount "window." That is, it may refuse to lend to a bank, even at the announced discount rate. This action forces the bank to take more costly remedial actions to satisfy the reserve requirements set by the Fed. Banks in good financial condition can usually borrow from each other, so today this instrument has only limited effectiveness.

The discount rate is the only interest rate the Fed directly sets. All other interest rates are set in the market, by the forces of demand and supply. But as the Fed affects banks' willingness to lend, it may at the same time indirectly affect the interest rates they charge and the rates they pay depositors. The interest rates the government pays on both short-term borrowing (T-bills) and longer-term borrowing are also determined in the market. The Fed's actions also affect these interest rates only indirectly.

The Fed often uses the discount rate, not so much for its direct effects, but as a signal of its intentions. When the Fed lowers the discount rate, the market knows the Fed is serious about making credit more available in the economy. When it raises the discount rate, the market knows the Fed means to restrict credit. But the Fed also changes the discount rate to reflect changes in interest rates that have already occurred. If market interest rates have risen but the Fed has failed to increase the discount rate in tandem, the difference between the discount rate—the rate banks have to pay to obtain funds from the Fed—and the rate they can receive on loans may be large. This will tempt banks to try to borrow excessively from the Fed. Thus, while changes in the discount rate sometimes signal a change in policy, at other times the changes just reflect the Fed's catching up with the market.

OPEN MARKET OPERATIONS

Open market operations are the most important instrument the Fed uses to control the money supply. In open market operations, the Federal Reserve enters the market directly to buy or sell government bonds. Imagine that it buys $1 million of government bonds from wealthy Joe Brown (or a thousand different Joe Brown families), paying him with a $1 million check. Joe Brown takes the check down to his bank, AmericaBank, which credits his account with $1 million. AmericaBank presents the check to the Fed, which credits the bank's account with $1 million. AmericaBank now has $1 million of new deposits (which is matched by $1 million in new reserves) and it can accordingly lend out an additional $900,000. A money multiplier goes to work, and the total expansion of the money supply will be equal to a multiple of the initial $1 million increase in deposits. And credit—the amount of outstanding loans—will also have increased by a multiple of the initial increase in deposits.

The purchase of bonds from Joe Brown by the Federal Reserve has a quite different effect from a purchase of the same bonds by a private citizen, Jill White. In the latter case, Jill White's deposit account goes down by $1 million, and Joe Brown's deposit account goes up by $1 million. The funds available in the system as a whole remain unchanged. The money multiplier goes to work only when funds enter from "outside," in particular from the Federal Reserve banks.

Thus, the Fed has three indirect ways in which it controls the money supply and credit-creating activities of banks. Through reserve requirements, it affects the amount of reserves that banks must have, relative to their deposits. Through the discount rate, it affects the cost of having too few reserves. Through open market operations, it affects the supply of reserves. By changing the required amount of reserves, the cost of not having sufficient reserves, or the supply of reserves, the Fed affects the amount that banks can lend, and the attractiveness to banks of making loans as compared with holding their assets in a liquid form, such as T-bills.

INSTRUMENTS OF MONETARY POLICY

1. Reserve requirements—the required ratio of reserves to deposits. The Fed can change the reserve requirement, the amount that banks must hold as reserves.
2. Discount rates—the rate the Fed charges for loans made to member banks. The Fed can change the discount rate and thus change the amount that banks wish to hold as reserves and the interest rate charged on loans.
3. Open market operations—by buying and selling Treasury bills, the Fed changes the supply of reserves and thus the money supply.

Assume, for one reason or another, the government wished to increase the money supply by $1 billion. How large of an increase in reserves will be required to generate the desired increase in money supply?

If the money multiplier is 20, then an increase in reserves of $50 million will generate an increase in money supply of $1 billion.

But what determines the money multiplier? If there is a 5 percent reserve requirement, banks hold no excess reserves, and individuals always redeposit in banks any money they receive, then the money multiplier is 20.

In practice, there is some variability in the money multiplier. As the economy goes into a recession, banks might want to *hold* excess reserves—though there are usually safe investments yielding a positive return (such as U.S. Treasury bills) so that it does not pay to leave reserves at the Fed yielding zero return. Moreover, individuals may decide to hold currency, rather than redeposit funds in the banking system. A central concern of central bankers is increasing their ability to predict changes in the money supply.

SELECTING THE APPROPRIATE INSTRUMENT

Of the three instruments, the Federal Reserve uses open market operations most frequently. Changes in discount rates and in reserve requirements are blunt tools compared with the fine-tuning that open market operations make possible. Thus, changes in reserve requirements and in discount rates are used to announce major shifts in monetary policy, but not on a regular basis. Such changes can be quite effective in signaling tighter credit (that is, changes in monetary policy that entail higher interest rates and reduced credit availability) or looser credit (that is, changes in monetary policy that have the reverse effect). Banks, foreseeing a tightening of credit, may cut back their lending, and firms may postpone investment plans.

THE STABILITY OF THE U.S. BANKING SYSTEM

The fractional reserve system explains how banks create money, and it also explains how, without the Fed, banks can get into trouble. Well-managed banks, even before the advent of the Fed and its reserve requirements, kept reserves equal to some average expectation of day-to-day needs. A bank could get into trouble in a hurry if one day's needs exceeded its reserves.

If (for good reasons or bad) many depositors lose confidence in a bank at the same time, they will attempt to withdraw their funds all at once. The bank simply will not have the money available, since most of the money will have been lent out in loans that cannot be called in instantaneously. This situation is called a **bank run.** Bank runs were as common in nineteenth-century America as they were in the old Western movies, where customers in a small town would line up at the bank while it paid out what reserves it had on a first-come, first-served basis until there was no more left. Such a run could quickly drive even a healthy bank out of business. If a rumor spread that a bank was in trouble and a few savers ran to the bank to clean out their accounts, then other investors would feel they were foolish not to run down to the bank themselves and withdraw their deposits. One vicious rumor could result in a healthy bank shutting down, and the panic setting off a run on other banks, thus destabilizing the banking system and the whole local economy.

REDUCING THE THREAT OF BANK RUNS

Bank runs and panics have periodically afflicted the American banking system. In fact, one reason the Fed was set up in 1913 was to make them less likely. The last major panic occurred in the midst of the Great Depression in 1933. Since then, the modern banking system has evolved a variety of safeguards that have ended the threat of bank runs for most banks. There are four levels of protection.

First, the Fed acts as a "lender of last resort." If a bank faces a run, it can turn to the Fed to borrow funds, to tide it over. Knowing that the bank could meet its obligations means, of course, that there is no need to run to the bank. The Fed lends money when a bank faces a liquidity problem; that is, it has a temporary shortage of funds, but its assets still exceed its liabilities. It is, in other words, solvent. The objective of the next two measures is to reduce the likelihood that banks face problems of illiquidity or insolvency.

Second, the Fed sets reserve requirements. Even those bank executives who might like to live recklessly, getting along on minuscule reserves, are unable to do so.

The third level of protection is provided by the owners of the bank. Most banks are started by investors who put up a certain amount of money in exchange for a share of ownership. The net worth of the firm—the difference between the bank's assets and its liabilities—is this initial investment, augmented or decreased over time by the bank's profits or losses. If the bank makes bad investment decisions, then these shareholders can be forced to bear the cost. This cushion provided by shareholders not only protects depositors, it also encourages the bank to be more prudent in its loans. If the bank makes bad loans, the owners risk their entire investment. But if the owners' net worth in the bank is too small, the owners may see themselves in a "Heads I win, tails you lose" situation. If risky investments turn out well, the extra profits accrue to the bank; if they turn out badly, the bank goes bankrupt, but since the owners have little at stake, they have little to lose. To protect against this danger, the government requires banks to maintain certain ratios of net worth to deposits. These are called **capital requirements.** Capital requirements protect against insolvency; they mean that if the bank invests badly and many of its loans default, the bank will still be able to pay back depositors. (By contrast, reserves and the ability to borrow from the Fed protect against illiquidity; they ensure that if depositors want cash, they can get it.) On occasion —more frequently in recent years—a bank will make so many bad loans that its net worth shrinks to the point where it can no longer satisfy the capital requirements.

As a fourth and final backstop, the government introduced the Federal Deposit Insurance Corporation (FDIC) in 1933. Since then, federal banks and savings and loans have had to purchase insurance, which ensures that depositors can get all their money back, up to $100,000 per account. Since deposits are guaranteed by the federal government, depositors fearing the collapse of a bank have no need to rush to the bank. The deposit insurance thus not only protects depositors, it has an enormous impact in increasing the stability of the banking system. Simply because it exists, the threat against which it insures is much less likely to occur. It is as if life insurance somehow prolonged life.

Deposit insurance has an offsetting disadvantage, however. Depositors no longer have any incentive to monitor banks, to make sure that banks are investing their funds safely. Regardless of what the bank does with their funds, the funds are protected. Thus—to the extent that capital requirements fail to provide banks with appropriate incentives to make good loans—bank regulators must assume the full responsibility of ensuring the safety and soundness of banks.

Chapter 31 takes a closer look at the relations between monetary policy, the financial position of banks, money and credit, and the level of economic activity.

REVIEW AND PRACTICE

SUMMARY

1. Money is anything that is generally accepted in a given society as a medium of exchange, store of value, and unit of account.

2. There are many ways of measuring the money supply, with names like M1, M2, and M3. All include both currency and checking accounts. They differ in what they include as assets that are close substitutes to currency and checking accounts.

3. A buyer does not need money to purchase a good, at least not right away, if the seller or a financial institution is willing to extend credit.

4. Financial intermediaries, which include banks, savings and loans, mutual funds, insurance companies, and others, all have in common that they form the link between savers who have extra funds and borrowers who desire extra funds.

5. Government is involved with the banking industry for two reasons. First, by regulating the activities banks can undertake and providing deposit insurance, government seeks to protect depositors and ensure the stability of the financial system. Second, by influencing the willingness of banks to make loans, government attempts to influence the level of investment and overall economic activity.

6. By making loans, banks can create an increase in the supply of money that is a multiple of an initial increase in the banks' deposits. If every bank loans all the money it can and every dollar lent is spent to buy goods, purchased from other firms who deposit the check in their account, the money multiplier is 1/the reserve requirement imposed by the Fed. In practice, the money multiplier is considerably smaller.

7. The Federal Reserve Board can affect the money supply by changing the reserve requirement, by changing the discount rate, or by open market operations.

8. Reserve requirements, capital requirements, the Fed's acting as a lender of last resort, and deposit insurance have made bank runs rare.

KEY TERMS

medium of exchange	financial	fractional reserve
store of value	intermediaries	system
unit of account	central bank	money multiplier
money	open market	reserve
demand deposits	operations	requirements
M1, M2, M3	reserves	discount rate

REVIEW QUESTIONS

1. What are the three characteristics that define money?

2. What are the differences between M1, M2, and M3?

3. When consumers or businesses desire to make a large purchase, are they limited to spending only as much as the M1 money that they have on hand? Explain.

4. What is the Federal Reserve System?

5. What are the two main reasons for government involvement in the banking system?

6. What are three ways for the Federal Reserve to reduce the money supply?

7. What has the government done to make bank runs less likely?

PROBLEMS

1. Identify which of money's three traits each of the following assets shares, and which traits it does not share:
    (a) a house;
    (b) a day pass for an amusement park;
    (c) German marks held by a resident of Dallas, Texas;
    (d) a painting;
    (e) gold.

2. How might bank depositors be protected by legal prohibitions on banks' entering businesses like insurance, or selling and investing in stocks or venture capital? What are the possible costs and benefits of such prohibitions for depositors and for the government?

3. Down Home Savings has the following assets and liabilities: $6 million in government bonds and reserves; $40 million in deposits; $36 million in outstanding loans. Draw up a balance sheet for the bank. What is its net worth?

4. What factors might affect the value of a bank's loan portfolio? If these factors are changing, explain how this would complicate the job of a bank examiner trying to ascertain the magnitude of the bank's net worth. Why would the bank examiner be concerned about the value of the net worth?

5. While gardening in his backyard, lucky Bob finds a mason jar containing $100,000 in currency. After he deposits the money in his lucky bank, where the reserve requirement is .05, how much will the money supply eventually increase?

6. Why is it that if the Fed sells Treasury bonds the money supply changes, but if a big company sells Treasury bonds (to anyone other than the Fed) the money supply does not change?

7. "So long as the central bank stands ready to lend to any bank with a positive net worth, reserve requirements are unnecessary. What underlies the stability of the banking system is the central bank's role as a lender of last resort, combined with policies aimed at ensuring the financial viability of the banks—for instance, the net worth requirements." Comment.

MONETARY THEORY

In Chapter 30 we saw the close link between the creation of money and credit (loans). This chapter explains why the money supply and the availability of credit are important to the economy. Knowing this, we can understand how monetary policy—the collection of policies aimed at affecting the money supply and the availability of credit—works.

Changes in the money supply and in the availability of credit are really two sides of the same coin. We begin by looking at the Fed's direct effects on the money supply, then turn to its effects on credit availability.

KEY QUESTIONS

1. What determines the demand for money? How and why does it depend on the interest rate and the level of income?

2. How is the demand for money equilibrated to the supply of money?

3. What are the consequences of changes in the supply of money when prices are fixed? When will it lead to a change in real output? When will it largely lead to a change in the amount of money that individuals are willing to hold?

4. What are the channels through which monetary policy affects the economy? What role is played by changes in the real interest rate? the availability of credit?

5. How does monetary policy work differently in an open economy than in a closed one?

MONEY SUPPLY AND ECONOMIC ACTIVITY

In this chapter, we continue with our assumption that the price level is fixed. (Recall that if prices are completely flexible, changes in the money supply elicit proportionate changes in the price level, leaving the real stock of money unchanged.) In the case of fixed prices, if the Fed increases the money supply, there are only two possible results. First, people who get the additional money could just hold on to it. Their bank balances would grow, but nothing would happen to the rest of the economy. In this case, monetary policy will be relatively ineffective—an outcome that is most likely when the economy is in a deep recession. Second, those who get the additional money could spend it. If the economy has excess capacity and prices are fixed, this increased spending (aggregate expenditures) will increase incomes and output.

What actually happens when the money supply is increased (assuming prices are fixed) is a combination of changed holdings of money and changed output. One of the purposes of this chapter is to understand the circumstances under which each of these effects predominates.

In Chapter 30, we learned several different ways of measuring the money supply—M1, M2, and M3. For much of our discussion, we do not have to be precise about which definition we have in mind. But it is natural to focus our attention on M1, for two reasons. First, M1 is the supply of money most directly under the control of the Fed. It is through the banking system that monetary policy has its most direct impact. M2 and M3 include such items as money market mutual fund balances which are not directly related to the banking system. Second, our primary focus here is on money's role as a medium of exchange. Money facilitates transactions. M1, which includes checking accounts and currency, is the definition of money most directly related to its use as a medium of exchange.

Within M1, we will focus on the portion most directly under the Fed's control: demand deposits and other checking-account deposits. This is also appropriate because they are the most important component of M1, accounting for more than 70 percent of the M1 total.

THE VELOCITY OF MONEY

The speed with which money circulates in the economy, its **velocity,** is as important to monetary policy as the money supply itself. If people keep money under the mattress for weeks after being paid, money circulates very slowly. In a bustling city, where money changes hands quickly, a given money supply supports many more transactions. The velocity of money is formally defined as the ratio of GDP to the money supply. If Y represents the real output of the economy, the quantity of goods produced in the economy, and P is a weighted average of their prices (the price level), PY is equal to nominal GDP (which, as we know, equals nominal aggregate income). Using the symbol V to denote velocity and M as the money supply, we get[1]

$$V \equiv PY/M.$$

This equation is sometimes referred to as the **equation of exchange.**

Let's use this equation of exchange to look at what happens when the money supply increases. If M increases, with the price level fixed, either V must decrease or Y must increase. This matches the possible consequences of an increase in the money supply with which we began the chapter. Individuals could simply hold the extra money, which would decrease velocity, or the amount bought, Y, may increase.

The essential problem of monetary theory is to understand when each of these outcomes will result. When the *only* effect is on money holdings, monetary policy is completely ineffective in stimulating aggregate output and employment. But if there is *some* effect on output as well, then monetary policy can be a useful instrument in stimulating the economy. It may take a large dose of the medicine—a large increase in the money supply—to achieve any desired goal, but it can be done. To answer the question of when individuals will simply be willing to hold any additional supply of money, we have to understand the determinants of the demand for money.

THE DEMAND FOR MONEY

The velocity of money depends on how willing people are to hold, or keep, money. Because currency is an asset that bears no interest, it is like a hot potato—there are strong incentives to pass it along. Preferring to earn inter-

---

[1]The symbol "≡" means "is defined as" or "is identical to."

est, people have an incentive to exchange currency for either goods or an interest-bearing asset like a Treasury bill (T-bill). The only reason to hold currency is its convenience. You can buy groceries with currency, but not with a T-bill, unless you convert your T-bill back to currency, for which there are costs (transaction costs).

THE EFFECT OF INTEREST RATES

People's willingness to hold money is a result of their balancing the benefits of holding money—the convenience—against the opportunity cost or the forgone interest—the interest that could have been earned if the money in their checking accounts (or the currency in their pockets) had been invested in some other asset. If checking deposits pay interest of 0 percent and very short-term government bonds (Treasury bills) pay 4 percent per year, then the cost of holding money is 4 percent per year. Today checking accounts pay interest, so the opportunity cost of holding funds in them is lower than it used to be. Nevertheless, the difference between the interest paid on checking accounts and the return to other assets of similar risk deters people from holding money. We focus on the interest rate paid on T-bills for a simple reason: they are just as safe as money. The only difference is that T-bills yield a higher interest rate, but money is better as a medium of exchange.

The demand for money is much like the demand for any other good; it depends on the price. The nominal interest rate (i) the individual could have earned on a government bond can be thought of as the price of money, since it measures the opportunity cost of holding money. As the nominal interest rate rises, the amount of money demanded declines, as shown in Figure 31.1.

THE EFFECT OF INCOME

The benefits of holding money are related to money's use as a medium of exchange. The more transactions people engage in, the more money they will want to hold. The demand for money arising from its use in facilitating

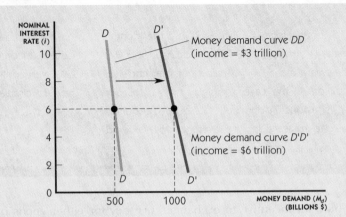

Figure 31.1 DEMAND CURVE FOR MONEY

The quantity demanded of money slopes down as the opportunity cost of holding funds—that is, the interest rate—increases. An increase in income causes a shift in the money demand function from *DD* to *D'D'*.

transactions is called the **transactions demand for money.** This demand for money rises with *nominal* income: higher incomes mean that the value of goods bought will be greater, which implies that the value of transactions will be greater. In fact, the demand for money increases proportionately with the nominal value of income, which equals the value of output, *PY*: if prices double, then other things being equal, people will need to have twice the amount of money to engage in the same transactions. This is illustrated in Table 31.1, which shows a hypothetical example. Figure 31.1 shows that an increase in income shifts the demand curve to the right. With an income level of $3 trillion, the demand for money is given by the curve on the left. Doubling the income level to $6 trillion shifts the demand curve for money out to the right. The table and figure illustrate the two basic properties of the demand for money. It decreases as the interest rate rises. And it increases, at a fixed interest rate, in proportion to income.

Table 31.1 DEMAND FOR MONEY

	Money demand	
Nominal interest rate	Income: $3 trillion	$6 trillion
2%	550	1,100
4%	525	1,050
6%	500	1,000
8%	475	950
10%	450	900

Figure 31.2 EQUILIBRIUM INTEREST RATES

The interest rate adjusts to make the demand for money equal the supply. In this diagram, a government-induced shift in the supply of money from MS_0 to MS_1 has a large effect on the interest rate, since the demand for money is relatively inelastic with respect to the interest rate.

EQUILIBRIUM

In equilibrium, the interest rate adjusts to make the demand for money equal the supply. Figure 31.2 shows supply curves for money as well as a demand curve. The supply of money is controlled by the government (the Fed), through the instruments described in Chapter 30. The amount of money the government makes available does not depend at all on the interest rate. That is why the supply curves are vertical. The equilibrium interest rate with money supply MS_0 is i_0.

The principles described in this section—that the nominal interest rate is the opportunity cost of holding money, that the demand for money decreases as the interest rate rises, and that the interest rate is determined to equate the demand and supply of money—are together sometimes called **Keynesian monetary theory,** or **traditional monetary theory.** Keynes used this theory to explain how monetary policy works when it works, and why it sometimes does not work. To do this, he traced out the effects of a change in the supply of money on the interest rate, the effects of a change in the interest rate on investment, and the effects of a change in investment on the level of national income. We now take a closer look at each of the steps in this analysis.

MONETARY POLICY AND INTEREST RATES

Figure 31.2 can also be used to show how changes in the money supply can lead to changes in the interest rates. Initially, the money supply is at MS_0 and the equilibrium interest rate is i_0. When the government increases the money supply to MS_1, the interest rate falls to i_1. In the figure, the demand for money is relatively inelastic, so that an increase in the supply of money at a given level of income causes a large decrease in the interest rate. As the interest rate falls,

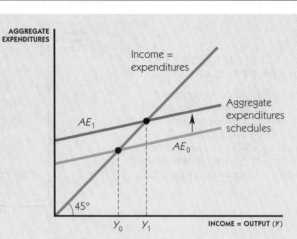

Figure 31.3 A MONETARY POLICY STIMULUS

An increase in the money supply shifts the aggregate expenditures schedule up, because of increased investment by firms, leading to an increased equilibrium output.

investment rises. As investment spending increases, income (which is the same as output) rises via the multiplier. (Actually, as discussed earlier, investment depends on the *real* interest rate, denoted by r, not the nominal interest rate. But in this part of the book, the price level is fixed, so the nominal and real interest rates are identical.)

The increase in investment shifts the aggregate expenditures schedule up, as depicted in Figure 31.3, and results in a higher equilibrium level of output. Output increases from Y_0 to Y_1.

When income increases, the money demand curve shifts to the right, as shown in Figure 31.4. Thus, the eventual equilibrium attained will involve a

Figure 31.4 SECOND-ROUND EFFECTS OF INCREASED MONEY SUPPLY

In the first round, the increased money supply led to lower interest rates (Figure 31.2), which led in turn to higher levels of national income (Figure 31.3). This higher level of income now shifts the money demand curve up (since the demand for money at each interest rate is higher). The equilibrium interest rate is i_2.

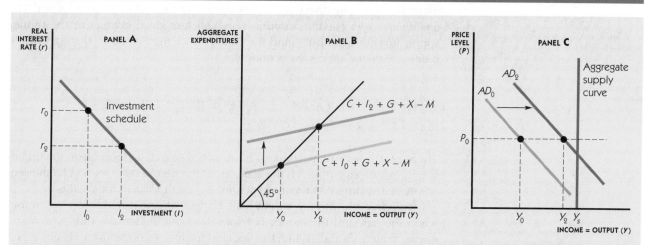

Figure 31.5 TRACING OUT THE FULL EFFECTS OF AN INCREASE IN MONEY SUPPLY

An increase in the money supply leads to a lower interest rate. Panel A shows that the lower interest rate leads to increased investment. Panel B shows that the increased investment shifts the aggregate expenditures schedule up, leading to a higher equilibrium output *at each price level*. Panel C shows that as a result, the aggregate demand curve shifts to the right.

smaller decrease in the rate of interest than i_1. The new equilibrium interest rate will lie somewhere between i_0 and i_1. In the figure, it is i_2.

We can trace out the equilibrium in the capital market at the new equilibrium interest rate: panel A of Figure 31.5 shows the level of investment, I_2, when the real interest rate is r_2 (which corresponds to the new equilibrium nominal interest rate, i_2), while panel B shows the aggregate expenditures schedule when investment is equal to I_2, and the equilibrium level of output Y_2.

The aggregate expenditures schedule assumes a particular price level. A similar effect of an increase in the money supply occurs at each price. In Chapter 28 we showed how to derive the aggregate demand curve by tracing out the intersection of the aggregate expenditures schedule with the 45-degree line at each price level. Since at each price level, the equilibrium level of output is higher, the aggregate demand curve has shifted to the right, as depicted in panel C. In this chapter, we are focusing on situations where price is fixed and there is excess capacity. We see clearly in panel C how the shift in the aggregate demand curve translates into an increase in aggregate output from Y_0 to Y_2.

The results of this section lead us to our eighteenth point of consensus in economics:

18 Using Monetary Policy to Stimulate the Economy

When there is excess capacity and prices are rigid, increasing the money supply normally stimulates the economy, leading to higher levels of output.

While there is consensus on the conclusion that monetary policy can stimulate the economy, there is far less agreement about two other issues: The *quantitative effects*—the amount by which any given change in the money supply increases output—and the *channels,* or mechanisms, through which monetary policy affects the economy.

WHAT DETERMINES THE EFFECTIVENESS OF MONETARY POLICY?

There are three principal determinants of how much an increase in the money supply increases output: (1) the elasticity of the demand for money, (2) the sensitivity of investment to the interest rate, and (3) the size of the multiplier.

Increasing the money supply will be less effective in increasing output when the demand for money is relatively elastic (when the money demand curve is relatively flat). When the demand for money is relatively elastic, an increase in the money supply has little effect on interest rates—interest rates decrease only slightly (see Figure 31.6, panel A). *Other things being equal,* when the interest rate decreases little, there is only a small increase in investment, resulting in a small increase in GDP.

Increasing the money supply will be less effective in increasing output when investment is not very sensitive to the interest rate (investment is inelas-

Figure 31.6 EFFECTS OF MONETARY POLICY IN A SEVERE RECESSION

Panel A shows that if the demand curve for money is flat, an increase in the money supply has little effect on interest rates. Panel B shows that if the investment schedule is steep, a decrease in interest rates has little effect on investment. Panel C shows that if the aggregate expenditures schedule is very flat, the multiplier is small, so that aggregate output increases very little.

tic). In this case a decrease in the interest rate resulting from an increase in the money supply will have little effect on investment, and therefore GDP (see Figure 31.6, panel B).

An increase in investment has less of an effect on output when the multiplier is small. For any given increase in investment, the smaller the multiplier, the smaller the increase in GDP. Thus, an increase in the money supply will result in a smaller increase in output when the multiplier is smaller. And, as we saw in Chapter 28, the multiplier is smaller if (1) the marginal propensity to save is large, (2) tax rates are large, or (3) the marginal propensity to import is large.

Many economists argue—as did Keynes—that when the economy is in a deep recession, monetary policy is relatively ineffective. They believe that the demand curve for money appears as in Figure 31.6A: at least at low interest rates it is relatively flat. As a result, monetary authorities have a hard time driving the interest rate down further. Exacerbating the problem facing monetary authorities is a fact that takes us beyond the model of this chapter—but is nonetheless real: in deep recessions, prices actually fall. In the Great Depression, prices fell by 25 percent. In the economic downturn in Japan in 1994 and 1995, prices fell slightly. What investors care about is *real interest rates*—the difference between the nominal interest rates and the rate of inflation. If the nominal interest rate falls, but the rate of inflation falls more, real interest rates rise. With falling prices, real interest rates exceed the nominal interest rates. If prices are falling at 10 percent a year, then even a zero nominal interest rate corresponds to a 10 percent real interest rate—by historical standards, an extremely high real interest rate.

Moreover, given investors' pessimism about economic prospects, it takes a large fall in interest rates to induce firms to invest much more. Since by definition, in a recession, there is considerable excess capacity, the marginal return from extra investment is close to zero. New machines simply add to excess capacity, not to profits. Only if the new machines are much better than the old (using so much less labor that the savings in labor more than offsets the additional capital costs) or if they are designed to make a new product, will it pay firms to make additional investments. Moreover, a lengthy period of losses will deplete a firm's cash reserves, and increase its indebtedness. Facing the threat of bankruptcy, the firm will be reluctant to undertake additional new investments, even if it could persuade banks to lend it money. As a result of these negative factors, as the economy goes into a recession, not only will the investment schedule shift down, but it also becomes relatively inelastic, that is, lower interest rates have only a small effect in inducing additional investment (Panel B, Figure 31.6).

Since increasing the money supply has a small effect on interest rates, and the decrease in interest rates has only a small effect on investment, increasing the money supply has a small effect on output, as illustrated in Figure 31.6C.

Some economists have described the ineffectiveness of monetary policy in deep recessions by saying that it is like pushing on a string. While economists differ in their judgments about how deep a recession it takes before monetary policy becomes relatively ineffective, they agree on the basic principle. This brings us to our nineteenth point of consensus in economics:

19 Monetary Policy in a Deep Recession

> *When the economy is in a deep recession, monetary policy is relatively ineffective in stimulating the economy to recover.*

Some advocates of monetary policy claim, however, that all that matters is that there be some effect of monetary policy. A weak effect—for a given percentage change in the money supply—simply means that monetary authorities have to take more aggressive actions, by increasing the money supply by a larger percentage.

TRADITIONAL MONETARY THEORY

The nominal interest rate is the opportunity cost of holding money.

The demand for money decreases as the interest rate rises.

The interest rate equates the demand and supply for money.

TRADITIONAL THEORY OF MONETARY POLICY

When monetary policy is effective in generating increased output, it is because the policy induces a lower interest rate.

Monetary policy is ineffective in deep recessions, because

1. The money demand curve is elastic, so changes in the money supply induce only small changes in interest rates; and

2. Even large changes in the interest rate induce little change in investment and hence in aggregate demand.

MONETARISM

While there is broad agreement on the two consensus points stated above—that monetary policy can be used effectively to stimulate the economy, except when there is a deep recession—some economists, called **monetarists,** argue that the *only* effect of monetary policy is on the price level. They believe that the basic assumption underlying this chapter—that prices are fixed—is simply wrong. They argue that prices are flexible, even in the short run. Thus, *all* that happens when the money supply increases is that the price level changes with no changes in output or employment. In fact they believe that prices move approximately in proportion to the change in the money supply. They believe that the full-employment model discussed in Chapter 25 applies at all times. Some monetarists believe that even if there is unemployment, and output is below the economy's capacity, increases in the money supply are still mostly reflected in changes in the price level.

To see how monetarists arrive at this conclusion, we need to return to the equation of exchange. The equation of exchange, as presented, was a *definition* of velocity. But they make one additional assumption—velocity is constant. Thus

$$M\bar{V} = PY$$

where the bar over the V reminds us that it is fixed. If Y is assumed fixed (say at its full-employment level), then increases in M get translated into proportionate increases in P.

This equation also gives us a simple rule for the expansion of the money supply. If we want prices to be stable, and real income is increasing at say 2 percent a year, then the money supply should increase at 2 percent a year. Monetarists believe that monetary policy should focus on the monetary aggregates (the measures of the money supply), and that money supply should increase in proportion to increases in real output. Doing this will lead to stable prices.

These are the *conclusions* of the monetarists. They can, however, be simply related to the traditional monetary theory. Monetarists believe that the demand for money is just proportional to nominal output (income). It does not depend on the interest rate. Note the contrast with traditional Keynesian theory. While Keynes assumed that in deep recessions the demand curve for money was almost horizontal (the elasticity was very large), monetarists assume that the demand curve is vertical (demand does not depend on the interest rate).

$$M_d = \text{(a constant)}Y_m,$$

that is, the demand for money, M_d, equals a constant times nominal income (output), Y_m. Since money demand equals money supply,

$$M_d = M_s,$$

increasing money supply increases nominal aggregate output (income) proportionately. Furthermore, since nominal income is the price level P times the real output, Y,

$$Y_m = PY,$$

if Y is *fixed*, then increasing nominal output (income) Y_m leads to an equiproportionate increase in the price level. In other words, if money supply doubles, in equilibrium, money demand must double. Money demand can

[handwritten marginalia: $M\bar{V} = P\bar{Y}$ implies P proportional to M.]

CLOSE-UP: EXPERIMENTING WITH A THEORY—THE FED CAUSES A RECESSION

Before the late 1970s, the focus of the Federal Reserve was mainly interest rates. When the Fed thought the economy needed a boost, it decided how low it wanted interest rates to go, and expanded the money supply (for instance, by engaging in open market operations) until the interest rate reached that target. Paul Volcker, when named chairman of the Federal Reserve Board in 1979, announced that henceforth the Fed would increase the money supply at a predetermined rate, regardless of what happened to the interest rate. He shifted the "target" from controlling the interest rate to controlling the money supply. The chosen rate of expansion of the money supply was set sufficiently low to bring down the rate of inflation, which had climbed from 6.7 percent in 1977 to 9.0 percent in 1978 and 13.3 percent in 1979.

Volcker's policy was based on the theory that velocity was constant (or at least predictable). If the money supply increased at a steady pace, enough to accommodate the increased production of goods (and any anticipated change in velocity), then the price level would be steady. Recall the definition of velocity (V): $V = PY/M$.

The Fed pursued this policy vigorously. When the money supply started to increase faster than the amount targeted, the Fed engaged in open market operations, selling government bonds. Growth in the money supply was reduced, but interest rates soared to 10, then 15, then 20 percent, pushing the economy into the recessions of 1980 and 1981–82.

The Fed abandoned this policy of targeting the money supply, for two reasons. First, the rate of inflation tumbled sharply, falling to 3.8 percent in 1982. With inflation much lower and the economy in a recession, it became important to try to stimulate the economy rather than harness inflation. Second, it became increasingly evident that the velocity of circulation was not constant, and the rapidly changing financial institutions also made the appropriate definition of money less and less clear. Saying that the money supply should expand at a constant rate was one thing, but in practice did that mean M1, M2, or M3? Today the monetary authorities keep an eye on interest rates and all of the indicators of the money supply, and search for an overall feel for what these sometimes conflicting indicators are telling them.

Paul Volcker, former chairman, Federal Reserve Board

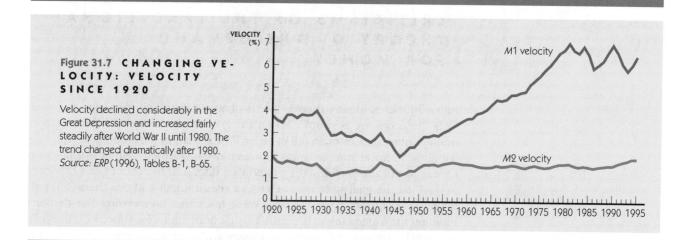

Figure 31.7 CHANGING VE-LOCITY: VELOCITY SINCE 1920

Velocity declined considerably in the Great Depression and increased fairly steadily after World War II until 1980. The trend changed dramatically after 1980. *Source: ERP* (1996), Tables B-1, B-65.

only double if nominal aggregate output (income) doubles, and nominal aggregate output (income) can double only if the price level doubles.

Thus, the assumption that the demand for money does not depend on the interest rate is equivalent to the assumption that velocity (PY/M) is constant. The theory that holds that because velocity is constant, increases in the money supply are reflected simply in proportionate increases in nominal income is called the **quantity theory of money.** While there have been long periods for which velocity has been nearly constant, in recent years it has changed, and often in ways that are hard to predict, as Figures 31.7 and 31.8 illustrate.

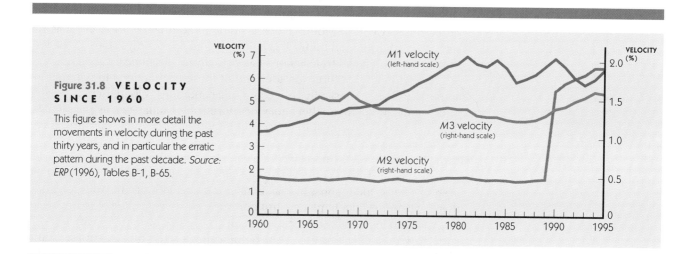

Figure 31.8 VELOCITY SINCE 1960

This figure shows in more detail the movements in velocity during the past thirty years, and in particular the erratic pattern during the past decade. *Source: ERP* (1996), Tables B-1, B-65.

CRITICISMS OF THE TRADITIONAL THEORY OF THE DEMAND FOR MONEY

In traditional monetary theory, the mechanism by which monetary policy affects the economy is simple. When the government increases the supply of money, interest rates must fall in order for the demand for money to equal the supply; and lower interest rates induce more investment and consumer purchases of durables, stimulating aggregate demand. In recent years, changes in the U.S. financial system have led to a reexamination of this theory. In particular, economists have raised several questions concerning the demand function for money underlying the theory. Some questions focus on the relationship between the demand for money and income, others on the effect of interest rates on the demand for money.

Relationship between Money and Income

Earlier we saw that what particularly distinguishes money from other assets such as government Treasury bills is its role as a medium of exchange in facilitating transactions. The traditional monetary theory implies that the higher their income, the more money people will want to hold. In other words, there is a simple relationship between the volume of transactions and the level of income. This would be the case if most transactions were directly related to output—employers paying wages and buying goods from suppliers, customers buying goods from firms, and so on.

But in fact, in terms of their dollar value, most transactions are for exchanges of financial assets, not the purchase of goods and services. One individual thinks General Motors stock is going to go down, and so he sells his shares. Another person thinks it is going up, and so she buys shares. The volume of these financial transactions has virtually no direct bearing on national output and income. Moreover, the *ratio* of these transactions to national income may change markedly with economic conditions. When there is greater uncertainty and change, there may be more such exchanges, as people take differing views of what the future holds and as individual circumstances change rapidly.

In the longer run, a number of other factors affect the relationship between money and income. For instance, not all transactions require payment by cash or check; today most transactions are made with credit. You need neither have money in a bank account nor currency in your pocket to buy a car or a vacation in Hawaii, so long as you can get credit. You can pay with a credit card or write a check against your home equity credit line. Of course, some kinds of transactions are still not easily done with credit. In most cities in the

United States, for example, you still have to pay for taxis with cash. But in Australia, taxis accept Visa, MasterCard, and American Express. The transactions that require money at the point of sale represent a relatively small and shrinking proportion of all transactions in the modern economy.

Indeed, technology has altered the whole idea of the role and velocity of money. Money market mutual funds invest in Treasury bills, but often allow individuals to write checks just like a banking account. What technically happens is that the mutual fund has an arrangement with a bank upon which the check is actually written. Assume Joe writes a check to Jim. Jim takes the check to his bank. When the check arrives at Joe's mutual fund's bank to be honored, the mutual fund instantaneously transfers the required amount of money into Joe's account, from which it is instantaneously transferred out to Jim's bank, so that Jim's bank can credit Jim's account. Recall we said before that the reason that people hold money rather than T-bills is because it is a better medium of exchange. The new technologies effectively allow people to use T-bills as a medium of exchange.

RELATIONSHIP BETWEEN INTEREST RATES AND THE DEMAND FOR MONEY

This brings us to the second set of criticisms: most money, as we have seen, is in the form of demand deposits, and today—unlike fifty years ago when traditional monetary theory was first formulated—demand deposits generally bear interest. Thus, the opportunity cost of holding "money" is not the interest rate, but the *difference* between the return to holding a government bond, for example, and the interest paid on demand deposits. That difference is generally small and relates primarily to the bank's cost of running the checking account. The existence of interest-bearing checking accounts calls into question the extent to which the demand for money will rise or fall in response to changes in interest rates.

OTHER CRITICISMS OF TRADITIONAL MONETARY THEORY

Traditional monetary theory assumed that changing the money supply affected the economy through changes in *real* interest rates. Yet there have been long periods in which real interest rates have varied very little (see Figure 29.8 on p. 705). Nominal interest rates tend to move up or down with inflation, so variations in real interest rates are far smaller than variations in nominal interest rates. Monetary policy seems to have effects that are far larger than would be indicated by the relatively small variations in real interest rates.

CRITICISMS OF TRADITIONAL MONETARY THEORY

There is no simple relationship between the demand for money and income.

Most transactions involve not goods and services (output) but the exchange of assets. The connection between transactions related to output and those related to exchange may not be stable.

Transactions do not necessarily need money; credit will do.

Today, more extensive use is made of credit (credit cards) and money market funds, which effectively allow people to use T-bills as a medium of exchange.

There is no simple relationship between real interest rates and money demand and supply.

Today, most money takes the form of demand deposits and is interest-bearing. Thus, the opportunity cost of holding money is low and is not directly related to the interest rate.

Changes in the rate of inflation may offset changes in the nominal interest rate.

ALTERNATIVE MECHANISMS

Traditional monetary theory has thus been questioned on several fronts—both the theory of demand for money, which underlies it, and the role of interest rates. But monetary policy does seem to matter. There are several alternative mechanisms through which monetary policy exercises its influence.

CREDIT AVAILABILITY

One channel is through credit availability. In Chapter 30, we looked at the two sides of the bank's balance sheet—its deposits (the money supply) and its assets, which include loans. Various actions of the Federal Reserve reduce both deposits (the money supply) and the supply of available loans. Figure 31.9 shows the demand and supply of "credit," both a function of the interest rate. Restrictive monetary policy has the effect of reducing banks' supply of loans—shifting the loan supply curve to the left, and increasing the equilibrium interest rate at which credit is made available, while decreasing the equilibrium level of lending.

At times, banks may ration the amount of credit they make available. They typically do not simply lend to anyone willing to borrow at the interest rates

Figure 31.9 EFFECT OF MONETARY POLICY VIEWED THROUGH IMPACT ON CREDIT AVAILABILITY

Restrictive monetary policy reduces the supply of loans available at any interest rate. Thus, the equilibrium interest rate increases (from r_0 to r_1) and the quantity of loans made is reduced from L_0 to L_1. In some circumstances, interest rates appear to be rigid, and do not adjust. There will then be credit rationing, with the demand for loans exceeding the supply. In that case, the decrease in loans may even be greater, to L_2.

they charge. At times, they may not even extend loans to all those deemed "credit-worthy" who would like loans. They could, of course, raise the interest rate charged; but they may worry that by doing so, the best risks—those most likely to repay the loan—will go elsewhere, or decide it is not worth borrowing at such interest rates. If interest rates—like other prices—remain fixed, then a shift in the loan supply curve has an even larger effect than when interest rates adjust, as Figure 31.9 illustrates.

Adverse selection

Even when credit is not being rationed, banks respond to a situation of tighter credit by adjusting terms of the loan contract other than the interest rate: they may, for instance, require more collateral.

In any case, the shift in the availability of credit (the shift of the loan supply curve to the left) results in lower investment, either because interest rates are higher (making it less attractive to undertake investments), because other terms of the loan contract are adjusted to make borrowing less attractive, or because funds required to undertake investments simply are not available.

PORTFOLIO THEORIES

An alternative channel by which monetary policy may affect the economy is through the price of shares and long-term bonds. At lower *nominal* interest rates, the value of long-term bonds typically increases. People feel wealthier, and because they feel wealthier, they consume more. Moreover, because bonds yield lower returns, investors turn to stocks. As the demand for stocks increases, their prices rise. Higher stock prices not only lead to increased consumption, but also to increased investment: at the higher stock prices, more firms believe that it is a good time to issue new shares, to raise additional capital, to finance new investments.

Portfolio theories argue that monetary policy affects the level of economic activity not only, or so much, through its *direct* impact on interest rates (as a

During 1992 and 1993, the banking system made a remarkable recovery. The Fed lowered short-term interest rates to 3 percent, and the rates banks paid depositors fell as well. But the rates banks charged borrowers remained high. Credit card rates, for instance, remained in the region of 16 to 20 percent. At these huge interest rate spreads, bank coffers were quickly replenished.

There was also a bit of good luck: with a large spread between long-term rates and short-term rates, many banks gambled, buying long-term government bonds. Long-term bonds yielded much higher returns than short-term bonds. Though there was no risk of default, there was a risk that the price of long-term bonds might fall, with disas-trous consequences for these banks. (At the time, bank regulations only focused on default risk, not price risk.) As it turned out, the price of these long-term bonds increased substantially in late 1992 and 1993. The banks thus enjoyed a large capital gain, in addition to the higher yields of the bonds. As the economy recovered, banks increased their loan portfolios and decreased their holding of long-term government bonds. Thus, the plummeting of long-term bond prices in 1994 had relatively little impact on the banking sector.

With higher net worths, banks were willing to make more credit available. Interest rates charged on loans fell, investment increased, and the economy expanded.

result of the interaction of the demand and supply of money), but through a variety of indirect mechanisms, as individuals adjust their **portfolios,** the bundle of assets—including stocks and bonds— that they hold. These adjust-ments in the demands for other assets result in changes in their prices, and it is through these changes that monetary policy ultimately has its most important effects.

MONETARY POLICY IN AN OPEN ECONOMY

In today's open, international economy, one of the most important ways by which monetary policy affects the level of economic activity is by affecting the exchange rate: lowering interest rates leads to a lower exchange rate—the number of yen that can be traded for a dollar. A lower exchange rate makes American goods more attractive abroad—and foreign goods less attractive here—and thus increases exports and decreases imports. For instance, between January and April 1995 the exchange rate between the dollar and the yen fell approximately 20 percent. Thus, to a Japanese consumer, a $100 American shirt fell in price by 20 percent, from 10,000 yen to 8,000 yen. And to an American consumer, the price of Japanese goods increased by 25 percent. A computer that sold in Japan for 100,000 yen—and thus cost $1,000 in the United States—would now cost Americans $1,250. (In practice, the changes were somewhat less dramatic, since in the short run, exporters and importers "absorb" some of the variation in exchange rates.)

As exports increase and imports decrease, *net* exports increase. As Figure 31.10 illustrates, an increase in net exports leads to an increase in aggregate output. In this section, we explain in more detail how monetary policy affects the exchange rate. We begin with a review of what determines the exchange rate.

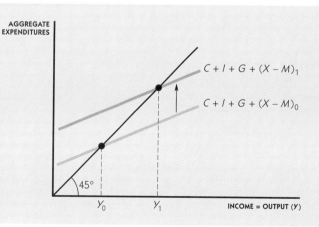

Figure 31.10 IMPACT OF AN INCREASE IN NET EXPORTS ON AGGREGATE OUTPUT

A depreciation of the exchange rate reduces the price of American goods relative to foreign-produced goods, increasing exports and reducing imports. An increase in net exports shifts the aggregate expenditures schedule up and results in an increased equilibrium level of output.

HOW MONETARY POLICY AFFECTS EXCHANGE RATES

In Chapter 26, we saw that the yen–dollar exchange rate (for example) is determined by the intersection of the demand and supply curves for dollars. The demand for dollars is determined in turn by Japan's demand for U.S. goods, and Japan's desire to invest in the United States. Similarly, the supply of dollars is determined by U.S. demand for Japanese goods and Americans' desire to invest in Japan. When the Fed lowers the interest rate, foreigners find it less attractive to invest in the United States, and Americans find it more attractive to invest abroad. This shifts the demand for dollars to the left and the supply of dollars to the right, as in Figure 31.11. The net result is a decrease in the exchange rate, an increase in exports, and a decrease in imports.

WHY TRADITIONAL CHANNELS OF MONETARY POLICY MAY BE LESS EFFECTIVE IN AN OPEN ECONOMY

While there is thus a new channel through which monetary policy exercises its influence, some of the other channels may in fact be much weaker in an open economy. One of the ways that we saw that monetary policy exercises its influence is in reducing the availability of credit. But if American firms can borrow abroad, then restricting credit from American banks simply induces borrowers to seek funds elsewhere. To be sure, not everyone has access to foreign banks. But the thousands of multinational firms do. And if enough of these firms switch their borrowing abroad, it frees up funds so American

Figure 31.11 IMPACT OF MONETARY POLICY ON EXCHANGE RATES

A lowering of interest rates in the United States induces more Americans to invest abroad, increasing the supply of dollars (at any exchange rate); and reduces the demand by foreigners to invest in the United States, reducing the demand for dollars (at any exchange rate). As a result, the new equilibrium exchange rate is lowered, falling from e_0 to e_1.

banks can continue their lending to those who do not have access to foreign banks.

REVIEW AND PRACTICE

SUMMARY

1. Theories concerning the effect of monetary policy on the economy focus on the two sides of the banks' balance sheet, on money and on credit.

2. When prices are fixed, changes in the supply of money can cause changes in holdings of money or changes in output. When the economy has considerable excess capacity, normally output will increase; in deep recessions, the effect on output may be minimal.

3. Traditional theories of the demand for money focus on its dependence on the (nominal) rate of interest and on the level of income. Equilibrium requires the demand for money to be equal to the supply. Changes in the supply of money result in changes in the interest rate and, through changes in the interest rate, in the level of aggregate expenditures and equilibrium output.

4. In severe recessions, the interest elasticity of the demand for money may be high and the interest elasticity of investment is low, so monetary policy may be relatively ineffective.

5. The quantity theory of money holds that the demand for money does not depend on the interest rate, and accordingly that the velocity of money is constant. Increases in money supply then result in proportionate increases in national income. In recent years, however, velocity has not only not been constant; it has changed in relatively unpredictable ways.

6. There are many difficulties with the traditional monetary theory. Money is not used for many transactions, and many transactions involve exchanges of assets, which have little to do with income generation. Changes in technology and the structure of the economy may alter the money-income relationship. Most money bears interest, and the opportunity cost is only the difference between the interest rate it pays and the interest rate on government Treasury bills.

7. Portfolio theories stress the effect of changes in monetary policy on the demand and supply of various assets (including money) and the resulting effect on prices of assets.

8. Credit availability theories stress the effects of monetary policy on the availability of credit (the supply of loans) by banks.

9. In an open economy, monetary policy is likely to have a smaller effect on interest rates and credit availability than it otherwise would. If the Fed

attempts to restrict credit or raise interest rates, American firms can borrow from abroad.

10. In an open economy, monetary policy has effects on exchange rates: a reduction in the money supply leading to higher interest rates leads to an appreciation of the dollar, a decrease in exports, and an increase in imports.

KEY TERMS

velocity	transactions demand	quantity theory of
equation of	for money	money
exchange	monetarists	portfolio theories

REVIEW QUESTIONS

1. What might happen in response to a change in the money supply?

2. Why does demand for money fall as the interest rate rises? What is the opportunity cost of holding money that pays interest (such as demand deposits)?

3. What might cause changes in the relationship between the demand for money and income besides changes in the interest rate?

4. Why might changes in the money supply not lead to increases in the level of investment in a severe recession?

5. What assumptions are involved in the quantity theory of money? What conclusion can be drawn on the basis of those assumptions? What is the evidence concerning the constancy of the velocity of circulation?

6. What are alternative mechanisms by which portfolio theories suggest that monetary policy affects the economy?

7. Describe how monetary policy might affect investment or consumption, *even if monetary policy has little effect at all on interest rates.*

8. How does the fact that an economy is open affect monetary policy? How do exchange rate changes affect equilibrium levels of output? How does monetary policy affect equilibrium exchange rates?

PROBLEMS

1. If GDP is $4 trillion and the money supply is $200 billion, what is velocity? How does your answer change if GDP rises to $5 trillion while the money supply remains the same? If GDP remains at $4 trillion while the money supply increases to $250 billion, how does velocity change?

2. Graph the money demand curve from the following data, with quantity of money demanded given in billions of dollars.

Interest rate	7%	8%	9%	10%	11%	12%
Money demand	900	880	860	840	820	810

How do changes in national income affect the demand curve?

3. Using money supply and demand diagrams, explain how the elasticity of the money demand curve determines whether monetary policy can have a substantial effect on the interest rate.

4. Explain how the elasticity of investment with respect to interest rates determines whether monetary policy can have a substantial effect on aggregate demand.

5. Explain how each of the following might affect the demand for money:
   (a) interest is paid on checking accounts;
   (b) credit cards become more readily available;
   (c) electronic fund transfers become common.
Would the changes in the demand for money necessarily reduce the ability of the Fed to use monetary policy to affect the economy?

6. How might an increase in national income affect the exchange rate? Before 1973 exchange rates were *fixed* by the government (with the government buying and selling dollars in order to maintain the set exchange rate). Contrast the effects of an increase in investment on equilibrium output assuming the exchange rate is fixed with the effects if exchange rates are *flexible*, that is, are allowed to vary freely to equilibrate demand and supply.

7. Describe the impact of the appreciation of the yen relative to the dollar on the Japanese economy, using the aggregate expenditures schedule.

8. In the text, we saw that if output was growing at 2 percent per year, and velocity is constant, if the government wanted stable prices, it should expand the money supply at 2 percent. In fact, velocity has been falling gradually over time. Assume that velocity in any year does not depend on the interest rate, but year after year, it falls at the rate of 1 percent per year. What does this imply about the rate at which the monetary authorities should expand the money supply if they wished to maintain stable prices?

9. Assume that banks are worried that if they raise the interest rate, they will attract borrowers who are riskier, that is, less likely to repay their loan. Borrowers who realize that there is a good chance that they will not repay their loan may be less sensitive to increases in interest rates, while borrowers who invest in conservative, safe projects will decide that at high interest rates, it simply does not pay to borrow and invest. Why might this mean that as the bank raises its interest rates, its expected return (taking into account the probability of default) might actually decrease? Assume there was an interest rate at which the expected return

was maximized, that is, further increases actually lead to a lowering of expected return. What would happen if at that interest rate, the demand for funds exceeds the supply? Would banks raise the interest rate they charged anyway?

10. Use the equation of exchange to explain the alternative possible effects of changing the money supply. (a) What happens if velocity and output are constant? (b) What happens if price and velocity are constant? (c) What does traditional monetary policy say about the normal effect of monetary policy on velocity? What does this do to the magnitude of the effect on output compared to what it would have been had velocity been constant (assuming price is constant)? (d) What does traditional monetary policy say about what happens when the economy is in a deep recession?

What do you think is the most plausible response of prices to an increase in the money supply when there is a large excess capacity and high unemployment in the economy?

11. Assume that for one reason or another, the interest rate on loans is fixed, and there is credit rationing. Show on a diagram what this implies. Assume that there are firms that rely on borrowing to finance their investment projects. They invest all of their cash flow, plus what they can borrow. What happens to investment if they have a bad year—say their sales drop because of a temporary recession in the countries to which they export goods? Show what happens to investment and GDP if as a result of monetary policy, the supply of funds at each interest rate increases? Use the diagram to explain why monetary policy may be even more effective in such situations than if the interest rate adjusts?

If the multiplier is 2, and the government increases credit availability by $100 billion, what happens to GDP if the interest rate does not adjust. Assume that the interest rate always adjusts to equate the demand and supply of funds (a closed economy), and that the interest rate elasticity of savings is 1, so that a lowering of the interest rate from 10 percent to 9 percent lowers savings by 10 percent. Assume that initially investment (equals savings) is $900 billion, and that as a result of monetary policy, at each interest rate, $100 billion more funds are available for lending, but that the interest rate falls from 10 percent to 9 percent. Calculate what happens to GDP now.

APPENDIX: AN ALGEBRAIC DERIVATION OF EQUILIBRIUM IN THE MONEY MARKET

The money demand equation can be written

$$M_d = M_d(r, PY),$$

where M_d is the demand for money. If M_s is the money supply, then the equilibrium condition that the demand for money equals the supply can be written

$$M_s = M_d(r, PY). \tag{31.1}$$

From Chapter 28, we know that

$$Y = C + I + G,$$

where I (investment) depends on the interest rate, r, and G (government expenditures) is assumed to be fixed. If consumption is just $(1 - s)$ times income Y, then

$$Y = (1 - s)Y + I(r) + G,$$

or

$$Y = [I(r) + G]/s. \tag{31.2}$$

Equations (31.1) and (31.2) provide us with two equations in two unknowns (assuming that the price level P is fixed). The solution gives us the equilibrium income and interest rate. An increase in the money supply results in a new solution, with a lower interest rate and a higher level of national income.

CHAPTER 32

FISCAL AND MONETARY POLICY

There are three principal objectives of monetary and fiscal policy: maintaining full employment, promoting economic growth, and maintaining price stability. In Chapters 25 and 26, we saw that when the economy is at full employment, government policy can have significant effects on the growth rate, by affecting the level of investment. At full employment, there is a fixed size pie, and government actions affect how that pie is divided. But when there is unemployment and resources are not fully utilized, government actions can affect both the size of the pie and how it is divided. Even if a smaller share of national output goes to investment, if national output is increased enough, the level of investment will actually increase, and long-run growth will be promoted.

This chapter pulls together the insights of earlier chapters of this part to see how fiscal and monetary policy may be used to stimulate the economy and promote economic growth. We will compare the effects of monetary and fiscal policy, and analyze several issues that arise in the application of policy today. Later chapters will explore how fiscal and monetary policy relate to the problem of maintaining price stability.

FISCAL POLICY

In Chapter 27 we defined fiscal policy as efforts to improve macroeconomic performance through changes in government expenditures and taxes. Faced with output below the full-employment level, policymakers may help restore the economy to full employment through an increase in government expenditures or a reduction in taxes. Recall our aggregate expenditures diagram from Chapter 28. An increase in government expenditures shifts the aggregate expenditures schedule up, as shown in Figure 32.1A. Equilibrium output at each price level increases, and the aggregate demand schedule shifts to the right, as illustrated in Figure 32.1B. A tax cut puts more money in the pockets of consumers, leading to an increase in consumption. This also shifts the aggregate expenditures schedule up and results in a rightward shift of the aggregate demand curve. Either way, the economy is brought closer to the full-employment level of output.

IS IT WORTH INCURRING A DEFICIT TO GET OUT OF A RECESSION?

The problem with an increase in government expenditures, or a tax cut, is that it increases the deficit. There are two concerns. First, even if the fiscal stimulus makes us better off now, future generations are saddled with debt, making them worse off. However, if government expands its investment—in infrastructure, human capital, or research—future generations may actually be better off, provided the return on those investments exceeds the interest rate. Estimated returns in many of these areas are very high. Most estimates put the return on investment in research in excess of 20 percent, and estimates of the return on investment in education greatly exceed the interest rate.

But even if increased expenditures are spent on consumption, the outcome appears favorable. Assume the government spends $1 billion in public consumption goods. As a result of the multiplier, the net increase in current income (consumption) is much higher. If the multiplier is 2, national income

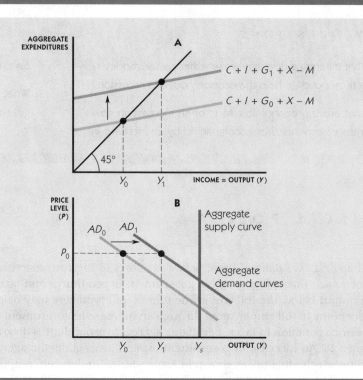

Figure 32.1 EFFECT OF INCREASED GOVERN- MENT EXPENDITURES

Increased government expenditures shift the aggregate expenditures schedule up, and hence increase the equilibrium level of output at each price level. Hence the aggregate demand schedule shifts to the right—by an amount equal to the multiplier times the increase in government expenditures. At the initial fixed price level, P_0, equilibrium output increases by the amount of the shift—the multiplier times the increase in government expenditures.

increases by $2 billion. At some future date—say in the next boom—the increased indebtedness has to be paid off, with interest. But there is only $1 billion in increased indebtedness. The trade-off between an increase in national income today of $2 billion, with a reduction in consumption in the future to repay $1 billion (plus interest) in indebtedness, seems a favorable one. Indeed, the trade-off may be more favorable still, if the government has borrowed money from its own citizens. In this case, the government will simply impose a tax on some individuals, in order to repay those who purchased bonds to finance the original expenditure. Then there would be a transfer of resources from taxpayers to bondholders, but no reduction in aggregate consumption.

The trade-off from a debt-financed fiscal stimulus is slightly less favorable than this calculation since the government's dissaving (deficit) soaks up some savings that would have been available for investment. The capital stock of the economy is thus smaller, and as a result, so is future national income, making future generations worse off.

FISCAL POLICY UNDER FISCAL CONSTRAINTS

In recent years, with governments in many countries running huge deficits, increasing government expenditures in a recession to stimulate the economy has often seemed politically impossible. Thus, in the United States, Congress now abides by a self-imposed constraint that it will not increase expenditures (over agreed-upon levels) unless there is an agreement to increase taxes by a corresponding amount. Such action is unlikely, given that raising new taxes is so politically unpopular, especially in an economic downturn. Similarly, the Maastricht Treaty, under which the countries of the European Union are supposed to form a common currency, calls for them to reduce their deficits to 3 percent of GDP by 1997. Achieving this goal requires cutting back on expenditures or raising taxes, but will leave little room for increasing expenditures or lowering taxes to stimulate the economy. In such situations, the government has no choice but to rely on monetary policy.

BALANCED BUDGET MULTIPLIERS

What happens if government matches increased expenditures with increased taxes? The **balanced budget multiplier** is the increase in GDP from a dollar increase in government expenditures matched by a dollar increase in taxes. The increased taxes reduce disposable income, and thus private consumption. This largely, but not completely, offsets the expansionary effect of the increased government expenditures. To see why it only partially offsets the expansionary effect, recall that a one dollar reduction in disposable income only reduces consumption by the marginal propensity to consume times one dollar. The net effect of the increased expenditure accompanied by matching increased taxes—after the multiplier has had a chance to run itself out—is that national income rises by the amount of the increased government expenditure (rather than a multiple of that amount, as would be the case if taxes were not raised). The balanced budget multiplier is unity.

Suppose that an increase in government expenditures of $1 billion is matched by an equal increase in taxes (ignoring, for simplicity, the dependence of taxes on income, and ignoring exports and imports). The first-round net effect is just:

$$\$1 \text{ billion} - MPC \times \$1 \text{ billion} = (1 - MPC) \times \$1 \text{ billion},$$

where MPC is the marginal propensity to consume. The multiplier, as we know from Chapter 28, is:

$$\frac{1}{1 - MPC}$$

so the net effect is:

$$\frac{1}{1 - MPC} \times 1 - MPC \times \$1 \text{ billion} = \$1 \text{ billion}.$$

The net effect is $1 billion. Figure 32.2 illustrates the effect of a balanced budget increase in government expenditures. The aggregate demand curve shifts to the right by the amount of the increased government expenditures, increasing output.

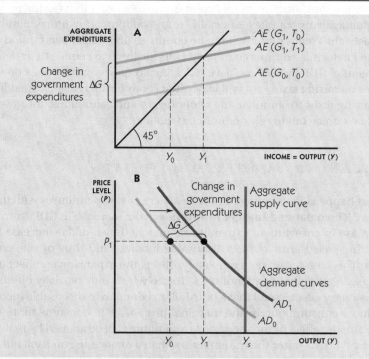

Figure 32.2 EFFECT OF INCREASED GOVERNMENT EXPENDITURES MATCHED BY TAX INCREASES

Three aggregate expenditures schedules appear in panel A. $AE(G_0, T_0)$ corresponds to aggregate expenditures before the increase in government spending and the matching tax increase. $AE(G_1, T_0)$ represents the effect of the increased government expenditures had there been no tax increase. $AE(G_1, T_1)$ shows the effect of the balanced budget increase in government spending; the balanced budget multiplier is unity, so the increase in output is equal to the increase in government spending. Panel B shows the aggregate demand curve shifting to the right by the amount of the increase in government spending.

MONETARY POLICY

In earlier chapters we have seen how monetary policy can stimulate the economy. An increase in the money supply leads to lower interest rates and increased credit availability, stimulating investment. This shifts the aggregate expenditures schedule up, and the aggregate demand schedule out, so that at any price level, aggregate output increases (see Figure 32.3). As we saw in Chapter 31, an additional mechanism is at play in an open economy: as interest rates fall, exchange rates decrease, and exports increase while imports decrease. Thus, net exports increase, and again, the aggregate expenditures schedule shifts up.

INTERACTIONS BETWEEN MONETARY AND FISCAL POLICY

So far, we have treated monetary and fiscal policy as if they were two distinct policies. In fact, there are important interactions between them. Consider the earlier discussion of a fiscal stimulus. If the monetary authorities simultaneously raise interest rates, monetary policy may partially or totally offset the expansionary effects of fiscal policy. The two are pulling in opposite directions. This happened in the early 1980s, where the restrictive monetary policy more than offset the expansive fiscal policy and the economy went into a major recession.

Sometimes the two policies work hand in hand. For instance, in 1993, the *direct* contractionary effects of deficit reduction were avoided in part by offsetting monetary policies. Unemployment actually fell. Economists sometimes refer to such monetary policies as **accommodative,** because the policies accommodate the changes in fiscal policy (or other changes in the economic environment) in ways which maintain the economy's macroeconomic performance.

Note that if the monetary authorities did nothing—that is, kept the money supply constant—in the presence of a fiscal expansion (an increase in government expenditures), interest rates would rise. The increase in national income would lead to an increase in the demand for money, and for the demand for money to equal the fixed supply, interest rates would have to rise. The rise in the interest rate would discourage investment. The increased government expenditure would have partially crowded out private investment. The net expansion in the economy is smaller—possibly far smaller—than if the monetary authorities had been more accommodative.

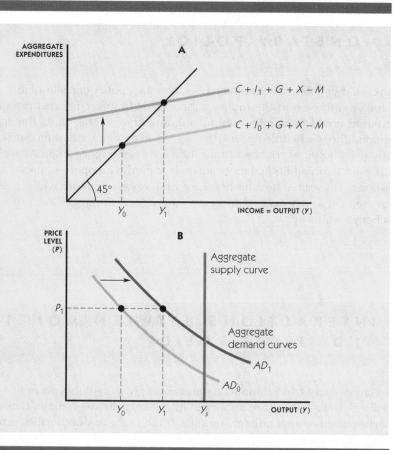

Figure 32.3 EFFECT OF MONETARY POLICY

An increase in the money supply leads to lower interest rates and increased credit availability, stimulating investment. This shifts the aggregate expenditures schedule up (panel A). The aggregate demand schedule shifts out, so that at any price level, aggregate output increases (panel B).

DIFFERENCES BETWEEN MONETARY AND FISCAL POLICY

There are major differences between monetary and fiscal policy, in their effects on the composition of output, their efficacy, and the lags with which their effects are felt.

EFFECTS ON THE COMPOSITION OF OUTPUT

Assume, first, that we could use either monetary or fiscal policy to stimulate the economy to the same extent. If we use monetary policy, we lower interest rates, stimulating investment. Thus, future levels of income will be higher. Using monetary policy, governments can pursue both a high-growth and a full-employment strategy. If we use fiscal policy, with a fixed money supply, as

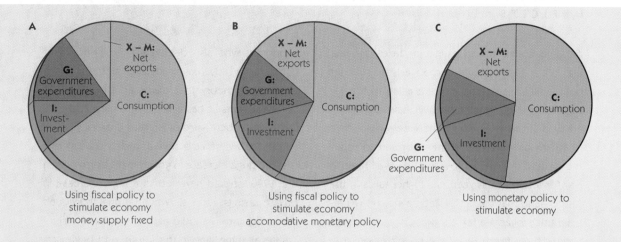

Figure 32.4 COMPARISON OF THE EFFECTS OF MONETARY AND FISCAL POLICIES

The share of investment is highest when monetary policy alone is used to restore full employment, and lowest when monetary authorities keep money supply constant, and increased government expenditures alone are used.

incomes increase, interest rates rise so that the demand for money remains equal to the supply. Figure 32.4 contrasts the composition of GDP under alternative policies, assuming part of the fiscal stimulus comes from tax cuts and part from expenditure increases. While either fiscal or monetary policy may be able to restore the economy to full employment, they have different effects on future economic growth.

But these differences become less clear if government expenditures are for investments. A substantial portion—in recent years, approximately 16 percent—of government expenditures go for physical investments, such as the construction of roads and buildings. Additionally, large amounts are devoted to investment in people (investment in human capital) and in technology, both of which serve to increase economic growth. If the government stimulates the economy by increasing public investment rather than lowering interest rates and stimulating private investment, the impact on growth will depend on the relative rates of return of these two forms of investment.

DIFFERENCES IN THE EFFICACY OF MONETARY AND FISCAL POLICY

Recall Consensus Point 19 from Chapter 31: when the economy is in a deep recession, monetary policy may be ineffective. Increases in the money supply may have little effect on interest rates, and decreases in the interest rate may have little effect on investment.

CLOSE-UP: THE PUBLIC VEIL AND THE IMPACT OF DEFICITS

If the government reduces income taxes this year but keeps expenditures unchanged, the budget deficit will increase. This deficit is a liability for taxpayers. In the future, taxes will have to be increased (from what they otherwise would have been) to pay interest on the debt and to repay the debt. If taxpayers know that they will have to pay for a tax cut this year with higher taxes in the future—and that their total lifetime income will remain unchanged—a tax cut (keeping government expenditures fixed) may have no effect on consumption. Clearly, this view goes beyond the permanent income and life-cycle models introduced earlier, which said a temporary tax cut would have an effect (if small) on total lifetime wealth, and therefore have a small effect on today's aggregate consumption.

The view that whether the government finances a given level of expenditures by taxes or by borrowing makes *no* difference to current consumption—that the two are perfectly equivalent—is called the Ricardian equivalence view, in honor of David Ricardo, the nineteenth-century English economist who also discovered the principle of comparative advantage. Ricardo described the equivalence theory, then dismissed it as irrelevant. In recent years, it has been resurrected and promoted by Robert Barro of Harvard University.

The theory of Ricardian equivalence suggests that the huge increase in government borrowing in the 1980s should have led to a huge increase in private savings. After all, when rational individuals see deficits, they should expect that taxes will increase at some time in the future, and begin setting aside funds to pay the bills. But instead of increasing, private savings rates in the United States continued at their low levels in the 1980s.

There are numerous reasons why Ricardian equivalence does not hold. Many individuals do not think and act in the way envisaged in the model. Many taxpayers have little idea about the true size of the deficit and do not take into account the consequences of higher future taxes. When individuals do not fully see and respond to these consequences in ways which fully offset them, we say there is a "public veil"—just as when they do not fully take into account what is going on inside corporations, we say there is a "corporate veil."

If the burden of repaying the public debt can be passed on to future generations—and if parents do not fully adjust bequests to their heirs to reflect this—then the tax reduction does represent an increase in the current generation's lifetime wealth, and accordingly aggregate consumption should rise for this generation.

Questions have also been raised about the efficacy of some fiscal policies. In some circumstances, a tax reduction may not stimulate much consumption. Consumers—worried about the future and thinking that the tax reduction may not be permanent—save the additional funds.[1] But if the economy has been in an extended downturn, leaving many individuals credit constrained, even temporary tax cuts are likely to be effective at increasing consumption.

Many economists worry that increased deficits—tax cuts not matched by expenditure cuts, or expenditure increases not matched by tax increases—themselves dampen the economy. Since the government will have to turn to capital markets to finance the deficit, some private investment will be crowded out. The net impact of fiscal policy must take this into account: if increased deficit-financed government expenditures crowd out an equivalent amount of private investment, there will be no stimulative effect. In the open economy of the United States, this crowding out effect is not likely to be so dramatic. Still, there may be some offsetting effects through changes in the exchange rate, but because imports and exports adjust so slowly—sometimes taking up to two years to adjust fully—the offsetting effects may not reduce by much the efficacy of fiscal policy in the very short run.

DIFFERENCES IN THE LAGS OF MONETARY AND FISCAL POLICY

Monetary and fiscal policy also differ in the speed with which they can take effect. Monetary policy stimulates the economy by lowering interest rates and increasing investment in equipment and housing. Even after firms see a decrease in interest rates, it may take some time before they place new orders for investment, and before the capital goods industry starts producing the newly ordered items. Similarly, though in the long run lower interest rates lead to increased demand for housing, it takes a while before plans are drawn up, permits are obtained, and construction starts. Typically, it takes six months or longer before the effects of monetary policy are realized. By contrast increased government expenditures have a direct and immediate effect in increasing incomes.

There is another important source of delay: governments must decide to take action. They must see that the economy is in a downturn, and that some

[1]Chapter 29 analyzed in more detail these future-oriented consumption decisions. Individuals base consumption not on their current income, but on their lifetime or permanent incomes, and a one-time, once-and-for-all, tax reduction has little effect on individual's lifetime or permanent income.

kind of stimulus is needed. These lags in taking action are often significant. The lags of government decision making are avoided through the use of **automatic stabilizers,** expenditures that automatically increase or taxes that automatically decrease when economic conditions worsen.

The economy has a number of these automatic stabilizers. Expenditures on unemployment compensation automatically go up in an economic downturn. So do other social insurance payments, as more individuals claim disability and more people retire early. Similarly, the federal income tax functions as an automatic stabilizer because of its progressive structure. A progressive tax system is one in which individuals with higher incomes pay a larger fraction of their income in taxes. As an individual's income increases, he moves into a higher tax bracket, and his average tax rate increases. Thus, when the total income (output) of the economy increases, average tax rates increase, and taxes as a fraction of GDP increase. Conversely, when the economy goes into a downturn, tax revenues would decline even if the tax rate were constant. But with a progressive tax system, they decline even more since the average tax rate declines. The fact that the tax system is progressive thus enhances its role as an automatic stabilizer.[2]

The government could, if it wanted, increase the degree of automatic stabilization. For instance, while the standard unemployment benefits last 26 weeks, during extended downturns these have been expanded to 39 or more weeks. Such extensions could be made automatic.

CONSEQUENCES OF A BALANCED BUDGET AMENDMENT

Many people have thought that it is irresponsible for government to have a deficit, reasoning that, like a business, government cannot permanently run at a loss.[3] The huge deficits of the 1980s brought the issue to a head: there was a strong political movement to adopt a constitutional amendment requiring a balanced budget, known as the **balanced budget amendment.** The proposal for such an amendment passed the House of Representatives in 1995, and failed by one vote to achieve the required two-thirds majority in the Senate.

Most economists opposed the balanced budget amendment, largely because they believed that it would eliminate the ability of automatic stabilizers to work. As we have seen, automatic stabilizers typically result in expenditures increasing and revenues falling in economic downturns, leading to deficits in recessions. But under a balanced budget amendment, the government would

[2]Before 1986, the tax system was largely unindexed, that is, it did not adjust for changes in the price level. In the 1970s, the economy experienced high unemployment together with high inflation, a condition known as stagflation. Thus, nominal GDP continued to rise even as real GDP declined. The progressivity of the unindexed tax system meant that the average tax rate increased, exacerbating the economic downturn. With indexing, average tax rates increase only when real GDP increases.

[3]A more in-depth discussion of the economic consequences of fiscal budget deficits is provided in Chapter 37.

When President Clinton came to office in January 1993, he faced two economic challenges: the huge deficits that had begun in 1981 and persisted since then had soared to 4.9 percent of GDP, and the economy remained in a prolonged slowdown, with unemployment still in excess of 7 percent. The two problems seemed to call for contradictory policies: increased deficits might stimulate the economy, but exacerbate the deficit problem. The Clinton administration chose to embark on a long-run deficit reduction program; it cut expenditures and increased taxes—policies which should have exacerbated the economic downturn. Yet the Clinton administration claimed its economic policies had helped turn the economy around. Did the economic policies fuel the recovery, or hinder it?

This episode demonstrates the complex relationships between monetary policy, expectations, and fiscal policy, as well as the potential importance of timing. The administration tried to structure the deficit reduction package so that more of the expenditure cuts occurred in 1995 and 1996—not so much because it wanted to postpone the political heat of expenditure cuts, but because it believed that by then, if its policies were in place, there would be an economic recovery that could withstand these expenditure cuts.

Clinton believed that the overall deficit reduction package would restore confidence in the economy—confidence that matters were being taken under control. The argument went like this. With smaller future deficits, there would be less federal debt competing for funds with private investment. Investors would anticipate this, and hence long-term interest rates would fall, even if

the Fed did nothing. The lower long-term interest rates, in turn, would help stimulate the economy. (Long-term interest rates did fall.) The Fed, in turn, recognizing that the economy was less likely to become overheated as a result of excessive fiscal deficits, would maintain an easier monetary policy than it otherwise would. Indeed, it kept interest rates at 3 percent throughout 1993, not raising them until February 1994, after signs that recovery was under way.

The hope of the administration was that lower short-term interest rates induced by the Fed and lower long-term interest rates induced by increased investor confidence would more than offset the direct depressing effects of fiscal policy. The economy did indeed recover. While most economists believe that eventually the economy would, in any case, have recovered, most also think that the reduction in the deficit probably ensured that the recovery occurred faster and more strongly than otherwise would have been the case.

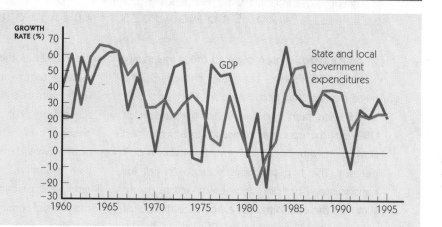

Figure 32.5 EXPENDITURES BY STATE AND LOCAL GOVERNMENTS

The figure compares the growth rate of GDP and expenditures of state and local governments. These expenditures tend to increase in booms and decrease in recessions, thus contributing to the volatility of the economy. *Source: ERP* (1995), Table B-2.

be forced to *destabilize* the economy—either raising taxes or cutting expenditures as the economy went into a recession, when just the opposite medicine is required. A look at the experience of the states, many of which have balanced budget requirements, supports this view. Figure 32.5 shows that typically, in economic booms, state expenditures increase, reinforcing the boom, and in economic downturns, they decrease, reinforcing the downturn.

With fiscal policy no longer being used to stabilize the economy—or worse, contributing to its instability—the burden of stabilization is put squarely on the shoulders of the monetary authorities. This means that interest rates will have to fluctuate more than they otherwise would, causing greater expansions and contractions in the interest-sensitive sectors (housing, durable goods, and plant and equipment). Since the lags in monetary policy—the time between when an action is undertaken and its effects are fully felt—are long and variable (typically six months or more), the economy itself will exhibit greater variability. And there are times when monetary policy is relatively ineffective in stimulating the economy (when the response of the economy to lowering interest rates is small, or smaller than anticipated), such as during the Great Depression and in the economic downturn of 1991. In such situations, the economic downturn will last longer and may be deeper than it would be if stronger automatic stabilizers were in place.

One proposal for reducing these destabilizing effects is to balance not the actual budget, but to set to zero the **full-employment deficit**—what the deficit would have been had the economy been operating at full employment. The full-employment deficit takes into account the changes in expenditures and revenues due to the current economic conditions. In a recession the full-employment deficit is smaller than the actual deficit. Most economists believe that the government is fiscally responsible so long as there is no full-employment deficit. Many argue that if there is to be a constitutional amendment regarding a balanced budget, it should be written in terms of the full-employment deficit.

The text described the importance of the concept of the full-employment deficit (sometimes called the structural deficit). Consider an economy which has 7 percent unemployment, when it is generally believed that the economy could operate at 5.5 percent unemployment without encountering inflationary pressures. From Chapter 24 we know that there are always some people without jobs in the economy, because of such factors as frictional and seasonal unemployment. Thus, we can assume that 5.5 percent unemployment corresponds to the full-employment level of output. Assume also that the deficit is $300 billion, output is $6 trillion, and that a 1 percentage point reduction in the unemployment rate will yield a 2 percent increase in output. What is the full-employment deficit?

Step 1. Calculate the full-employment level of out-

put. Reducing unemployment from 7 to 5.5 percent will yield an increase in output of $180 billion.

Step 2. Calculate the extent to which tax revenues increase and expenditures decrease as output expands. Federal tax revenues increase approximately $20 for every $100 increase in GDP, while expenditures are reduced (as demands for unemployment insurance decrease, as fewer people go on disability, etc.). For simplicity, we assume those expenditures decrease by $5 for every $100 increase in GDP. Thus, the increase in GDP of $180 billion increases revenues by $36 billion and reduces expenditures by $9 billion.

Step 3. Add those amounts to the original deficit. Full-employment deficit = $300 billion − $36 billion − $9 billion = $255 billion.

BALANCED BUDGETS AND STABILIZATION POLICY

1. An increase in government expenditure matched by an increase in tax revenues is expansionary.
2. Automatic stabilizers increase expenditures and reduce taxes automatically as the economy goes into a recession. Standard versions of the balanced budget amendment would preclude the use of automatic stabilizers as well as eliminate the possibility of using fiscal policy to stabilize the economy.
3. In practice, a balanced budget amendment would likely destabilize the economy, and force the entire burden of stabilization onto monetary policy.

REVIEW AND PRACTICE

SUMMARY

1. Increasing government expenditure (without increasing taxes) stimulates the economy, but generates a deficit. If the government spends the additional funds on investments which yield returns in excess of the interest rate, then increased government expenditure can make the economy stronger both today and in the future.

2. Increases in government expenditure matched by increases in taxes can still stimulate the economy, but there will be no multiplier effects.

3. Monetary policy stimulates the economy by increasing investment and net exports. Thus, stimulating the economy through monetary policy has a more positive effect on economic growth than doing so through fiscal policy unless the increased government expenditures are spent on investments. In deep recessions, however, monetary policy may not be very effective.

4. The lags associated with monetary policy may be longer than those associated with fiscal policy.

5. Automatic stabilizers help to stabilize the economy, without any policymaker making an active decision.

6. Most versions of a balanced budget amendment would circumscribe the operation of automatic stabilizers and thus serve to destabilize the economy. All the burden of stabilization would be placed on monetary policy.

KEY TERMS

balanced budget multiplier
accommodative monetary policy

automatic stabilizers
balanced budget amendment

full-employment deficit

REVIEW QUESTIONS

1. How does an increase in government expenditure shift the aggregate expenditures schedule and the aggregate demand curve? How does monetary policy shift the aggregate expenditures schedule and the aggregate demand curve?

2. If the economy is in a recession, describe the trade-off between today and the future associated with an increase in government expenditures. How does what the government spends its increased expenditures on affect the trade-off? If the government spends the funds on investments that yield high returns, is there still a trade-off? Even if the government spends the funds on public consumption, why might the trade-off still appear attractive?

3. What is the effect of an increase in government expenditure matched by an increase in taxes?

4. Compare the effects of monetary and fiscal policy on the level of investment and the composition of output.

5. What other factors are important in the choice between monetary and fiscal policy?

6. What effect might a balanced budget amendment have on the stability of the economy?

7. What are automatic stabilizers, and why are they important?

PROBLEMS

1. Show how a decrease in the price level leads to an increase in aggregate demand and equilibrium output if money supply remains unchanged and there is excess capacity in the economy.
   (a) Use the demand and supply curves for money to show the effect on interest rates.
   (b) Use the investment function to show the effect on investments.
   (c) Use the aggregate expenditures schedule to show the effect on equilibrium output.

2. Show the differences in the effect of an increase in government expenditure when monetary authorities (a) keep the money supply constant, and (b) expand the money supply to keep the interest rate constant. Trace out the effects on (a) the demand and supply curves for money and the equilibrium interest rate; (b) the level of investment; (c) the aggregate expenditures schedule and the equilibrium level of output at any fixed price; and (d) the aggregate demand curve.

3. Assume you are in charge of monetary policy. The economy is $60 billion below capacity, or 1 percent of its $6 trillion capacity. (a) You are told the government does not plan to increase government expenditures or change tax rates at all. How much must you increase the money supply? Assume: money demand has an interest elasticity of .8, an income elasticity of 1; investment elasticity is .8 and investment amounts to 10 percent of GDP ($540 billion); and the multiplier is 2. (b) In some countries, such as the United Kingdom, the monetary authorities are more directly under control of the government than in the United States. Assume the government says

that it plans to increase government expenditures to restore full employment, but it wants the monetary authorities to keep interest rates constant. By how much must they increase the money supply? (Use the same assumptions as in part a). Assuming the multiplier is 2, by how much must government expenditure be increased. (c) Now assume the monetary authorities are independent, and have announced that they will not change the money supply. By how much will interest rates rise if the government is successful in restoring the economy to full employment? How will that affect investment? What does this imply for the required magnitude of increase in government expenditure?

4. When individuals become wealthier they consume more. If prices fall, the *real value* of wealth which is denominated in monetary terms—like money and government bonds—increases. Would you expect this effect to be large or small? Assume government bonds and money represent 10 percent of national wealth, and that an increase in real wealth of 10 percent leads to a .6 percent increase in consumption. Assume consumption represents 90 percent of GDP and the multiplier is 2. Assume prices fall by 5 percent. By approximately what percent will GDP increase? Assume the economy is 10 percent below capacity. How long would it take the economy to be restored to full employment if prices continued to fall at the rate of 5 percent per year?

5. The economy is $60 billion below capacity, or 1 percent of its $6 trillion capacity. The government contemplates stimulating the economy by alternative policies. Assume the multiplier is 2, and that investment is completely interest inelastic. Calculate the required increase in government expenditures. Calculate the required increase in government expenditures if the government increases taxes in tandem. Can monetary policy be used to stimulate the economy?

6. Consider the extreme case where the individuals and firms within a country can borrow (or lend) abroad as much as desired at a fixed real interest rate. Can monetary authorities affect the level of real investment? Assume that as the monetary authorities try to raise interest rates, funds flow in from abroad; as they flow in, they bid up the exchange rate. Trace through the effects: (a) of the increased demand for U.S. dollars by foreign investors wishing to invest in the U.S. on the exchange rate; (b) the effect of the exchange rate on the aggregate expenditures schedule and on GDP.

7. Several European countries are scheduled to form a European Monetary Union (EMU), in which they would have a single currency. Effectively, this means that exchange rates between the countries would be fixed, and there would be a single interest rate for all the countries. The governments have agreed that certain criteria must be met to join the EMU. These include reducing the fiscal deficit as a share of GDP to below 3 percent. What might be the macroeconomic effects of this deficit reduction (a) if each country's monetary authorities do not adjust interest rates? (b) if interest rates are reduced? Why might the simultaneous reduction of

deficits by all the countries lead to a larger reduction in output than if only one country reduced its deficit, if interest rates do not fall? Use diagrams to illustrate your answer.

8. Assume that after the European Monetary Union is established, interest rates will be the same in all countries within the Union. Assume that unemployment in one country within the Union, say France, increases. What can the government do to restore full employment?

Contrast what might be done about unemployment in France within the European Monetary Union with what might be done about unemployment in California. In what ways will the situation be similar? How will they differ?

9. Compare the effects on longer term economic growth of using monetary rather than fiscal policy to stimulate an economy when capital flows freely internationally with the effects within a closed economy.

PART SEVEN

Dynamics and Macro Policy

So far, we have discussed two of the three key macroeconomic problems: growth and unemployment. We now turn to the third, *inflation*. What causes it? Why is it a problem? What can government do about it?

This part of the book does more, however, than just round out our discussion of the three key macroeconomic problems. It also describes and explains the *dynamics of wage and price adjustments*. Part Five focused on full-employment economies; Part Six on economies with unemployment. We emphasized that the key distinction between the two were assumptions about adjustments. In Part Five, wages and prices adjusted quickly so that the labor market was always in equilibrium. In Part Six, wages and prices were fixed. We were taking a snapshot of the economy, before the dynamic process unfolded. We recognized that when the demand for labor was less than the supply at the current wages, or when the demand for goods was less than the supply at the current price level, there were pressures for wages and prices to fall. But the adjustments do not occur instantaneously. Similarly, if initially the economy's resources were fully employed, and there was a rightward shift in the aggregate demand curve, there would be excess demand for goods at the going price level. This creates upward price pressure, but again, prices do not adjust instantaneously.

The fact that wages and prices do not adjust instantaneously—that they are sticky—means that after any disturbance, there will be at least a period in which demand does not equal supply. If at current prices and wages demand is less than supply, output is limited by aggregate demand, so that an increase in aggregate demand—say as a result of increased government expenditure—increases output and employment.

Understanding why unemployment persists and why prices may rise, not just once, but year after year entails understanding the dynamics of adjustment. In this part, we will *describe* observed regularities in wage and price adjustments and *explain* both the consequences of these observed patterns and the sources of wage and price stickiness.

Part Seven consists of three chapters. Chapter 33 provides the basic description of wage and price dynamics. It explains the major determinants of the rate of inflation. Chapter 34 takes a closer look at the labor market, to see why wages in particular often exhibit rigidities. Finally Chapter 35 brings together the insights of Parts One, Five, and Six to discuss some of the central policy issues in macroeconomics and the controversies surrounding them. Should the government intervene? And if so, what is the most effective form of intervention?

INFLATION: WAGE AND PRICE DYNAMICS

I t is an axiom of political rhetoric that inflation is bad. Popular sentiment runs so strongly against inflation that it is usually taken for granted that the government should do something about it. But if the government needs to do something about inflation, we need to know what causes it. How do we explain why some countries have higher inflation rates than others? Why does the United States have a lower inflation rate today than it did fifteen years ago?

If inflation is so disliked, why don't governments simply get rid of it? The answer is that, normally, inflation can only be reduced at a cost—only if the unemployment rate is allowed to increase. This chapter looks at the trade-off between inflation and unemployment, and how this trade-off can be changed. Many economists believe that in the long run, there is no trade-off: attempting to reduce unemployment to too low a level is a chimera. Not only does inflation increase, but it increases at a faster and faster rate, until inflation, not unemployment, becomes viewed as the central economic problem. This chapter explains these critical debates which underlie so much of current policy discussions.

KEY QUESTIONS

1. What are the costs of inflation? Why does it make a difference whether inflation is anticipated? How can the costs be ameliorated?

2. What is the trade-off between inflation and unemployment? How do expectations about inflation affect the level of inflation associated with any level of unemployment?

3. Why might inflation accelerate if the unemployment rate is kept at too low a level? How do these considerations affect government policies?

4. What are the factors that affect the critical unemployment rate below which inflation starts to increase? How has this critical unemployment rate changed over time?

5. Why is it that once inflation starts, it tends to persist?

6. What role does monetary policy play in initiating or perpetuating inflation?

7. What are some of the reasons for wage and price rigidities?

THE COSTS OF INFLATION

We identified growth, unemployment, and inflation as the three key macroeconomic problems. Part Five discussed issues of growth, and Part Six of unemployment. Here we focus on inflation and the relationship between inflation and unemployment. While the costs of unemployment are apparent—not only is there a loss in output, but the misery of those who cannot secure gainful employment is palpable—the costs of inflation are more subtle, and over the years have been greatly ameliorated.

People sense there is something wrong with the economy when there is high inflation. Workers worry that their paycheck will not keep pace with increases in the price level, and thus their living standards will be eroded. Investors worry that the dollars they receive in the future will be worth less than the dollars they invested, leaving them with less than enough to live comfortably in their old age.

When inflation is anticipated, many of its economic costs disappear. Workers who know that prices will be rising by 10 percent this year, for example, may negotiate wages that rise fast enough to offset the inflation. Lenders know that the dollars they will be repaid will be worth less than the dollars they lent, and they take this into account when setting the interest rate they charge or when deciding whether to make the loan.

But even when inflation is not perfectly anticipated, workers and investors can immunize themselves against the effects of inflation by having wages and returns **indexed** to inflation. For instance, when wages are perfectly indexed, a 1 percent increase in the price level results in a 1 percent increase in wages.

In recent years, Social Security payments and tax rates have both been indexed. Many countries, including the United Kingdom, Canada, and New Zealand, sell indexed government bonds so that savers can put aside money knowing that the returns will not be affected by inflation. In May 1996, the U.S. government announced its intention to begin selling indexed bonds.

WHO SUFFERS FROM INFLATION?

While indexing softens the effects of inflation, it is far from complete. So who suffers today from inflation? Many people may suffer a little, since indexing does not fully protect them, but some are more likely to suffer than others. Among the groups most imperfectly protected are lenders, taxpayers, and holders of currency.

Lenders Since most loans are not fully indexed, increases in inflation mean that the dollars that lenders receive back from borrowers are worth less than those they lent out. Many people put a large part of their savings for their retirement into bonds or other fixed-income securities. These people will suffer if an inflationary bout comes between them and their nest eggs. The extent to which they will suffer depends in large measure on whether the price changes were anticipated. After World War II, many people bought bonds yielding a 3 or 4 percent annual return. They did not anticipate much inflation. When inflation reached double-digit levels in the late 1970s, the rate of interest they received did not even come close to compensating them for the reduced value of the dollars they had invested. In real terms, they received a negative return on their savings.

Taxpayers Our tax system is only partially indexed, and inflation frequently hurts investors badly through the tax system. All returns to investment are taxed, including those that do nothing more than offset inflation. Consequently, real after-tax returns are often negative. Consider a rate of inflation of 10 percent and an asset that yields a return of 12 percent before tax. If the individual has to pay a 33 percent tax on the return, his after-tax yield is 9 percent—not enough to compensate him for inflation. His after-tax real return is minus 1 percent.

Holders of Currency Inflation also makes it expensive for people to hold currency because as they hold it, the currency loses its value. Since currency facilitates a variety of transactions, inflation interferes with the efficiency of the economy by discouraging the holding of currency. The fact that inflation takes away the value of money means that inflation acts as a tax on holding money. Economists refer to this distortionary effect as an **inflation tax.**

This distortion is not as important in modern economies, where checking accounts are frequently used instead of cash, and checking accounts typically pay interest. As the rate of inflation increases, the interest rate paid on checking accounts normally increases as well. Even in Argentina in the 1970s, when prices were rising at 800 percent a month, bank accounts yielded more than

CLOSE-UP: HYPERINFLATION IN GERMANY IN THE 1920s

Following World War I, Germany was required by the victorious Allied nations to make substantial "reparation" payments. But the sheer size of the reparations, combined with the wartime devastation of German industry, made payment nearly impossible. John Maynard Keynes, then an economic adviser to the British government, was among those who warned that the reparations were too large. To finance some of Germany's financial obligations, the German government started simply printing money.

The resulting increases in both the amount of circulating currency and the price level can be seen in the figure. From January 1922 to November 1923, the average price level increased by a factor of almost 20 billion.* People made desperate attempts to spend their currency as soon as they received it, since the value of currency was declining so rapidly. One story often told by Keynes was how Germans would buy two beers at once, even though one was likely to get warm, for fear that otherwise, when it came time to buy the second beer, the price would have risen.

At an annual inflation rate of 100 percent, money loses half its value every year. If you save $100 today, in five years it will have buying power equal to only 3 current dollars. It is possible for nominal interest rates to adjust even to very high inflation rates. But when those high inflation rates fluctuate in unanticipated ways, the effects can be disastrous.

Periods of hyperinflation create a massive redistribution of wealth. If an individual is smart or lucky

Inflation in Germany during the 1920s reached levels that may seem unbelievably high. At the end of 1923, prices were 10 billion times higher than they were two years earlier.

800 percent a month. Still, poorer individuals who do not have checking accounts—and therefore must hold much of what little wealth they have in the form of currency—are adversely affected.

The Economy   There are two costs of inflation to the economy as a whole. The first has to do with relative prices. Because price increases are never perfectly coordinated, increases in the rate of inflation lead to a greater variability of relative prices. If the shoe industry makes price adjustments only every three months, then in the third month, right before its price increase, shoes may be relatively cheap, while right after the price increase, shoes may be relatively expensive. On the other hand, the prices of groceries might change continually throughout the three-month period. Therefore, the ratio of the price of groceries to the price of shoes will continually be changing. When the average rate of inflation is only 2 or 3 percent per year, this does not cause much of a problem. But when the average rate of inflation is 10 percent per month, inflation causes real distortions in how society allocates its resources. When inflation gets very high, economies tend to allocate considerable resources to avoid the costs of inflation and to take advantage of the discrepancies in prices charged by different sellers. Rather than carrying money, which quickly erodes in value, people rush to deposit their money in interest-bearing bank accounts.

The second economy-wide cost of inflation arises from the risk and uncertainty that inflation generates. If there were perfect indexing, the uncertainty about the rate of inflation would be unimportant. But as indexing is not perfect, the resulting uncertainty makes it difficult to plan. People saving for their retirements cannot know what to put aside. Business firms borrowing money are uncertain about the price they will receive for the goods they produce. Firms are also hurt when they build wage increases into multiyear contracts to reflect *anticipated* inflation. If for any reason a firm finds that the prices it can charge increase less rapidly than anticipated in the contract, the employer suffers.

MISPERCEIVED COSTS OF INFLATION

We have discussed the significant costs of inflation, but much of the aversion to inflation comes from a variety of forms of misperceptions. If a poll were conducted asking people whether they were hurt or helped by inflation, most would say they were hurt. Much of this is simply *perception*. People "feel" price increases much more vividly than they do the corresponding income increases. They "feel" the higher interest rates they have to pay on loans more than they do the decrease in the value of the dollars with which they repay lenders. A closer look at who benefits and who loses from unanticipated inflation suggests that there are probably more gainers than there are losers. This is simply because there are probably more debtors than lenders, and debtors benefit from unanticipated inflation.

In many inflationary episodes, many individuals not only *feel* worse off, they *are* worse off—but inflation itself is not the culprit. The oil price increases of 1973 set off a widespread inflation in the United States. The higher price of oil also made the United States poorer than it had previously been, because it was an oil importer. Someone's standard of living had to be cut, and inflation did the cutting. Frequently those whose incomes were cut—unskilled workers, whose wages did not keep pace with prices—cited as the *cause* of their lower incomes the inflation that accompanied the oil price increases. However, generalized price inflation was only a symptom. The underlying cause of that particular inflation, and of the reduced real incomes, was a sharp rise in the price of oil.

It is clear that the costs of inflation are different, and undoubtedly lower, than they were before indexing was so extensive. Today economists do not agree on the *magnitude* of the adverse effects of inflation. There is considerable evidence that high rates of inflation have strongly adverse effects on economic performance. But there is little evidence that at the moderate rates of inflation that the United States has experienced in recent years there are any significant adverse effects.

COSTS OF INFLATION, ACTUAL AND PERCEIVED

Real costs

    Variability in relative prices

    Resources devoted to mitigating the costs of inflation and taking advantage of
        price discrepancies

    Increased uncertainty

Misperceptions

    Failing to recognize offsetting increases in income

    Blaming inflation for losses in real income that occur during inflationary episodes
        but are caused by other factors

INFLATION AND UNEMPLOYMENT

While there is some debate about the *magnitude* of the costs of inflation, if it were costless to reduce inflation, clearly governments would do so. But lower inflation can typically be obtained only through higher unemployment. In this section, we analyze the relationship between inflation and unemployment.

In the previous two parts of the book, we examined two different models of the economy: the full-employment and unemployment models. These models are based on opposite assumptions about prices and wages. In the full-employment model, we assumed that prices and wages are perfectly flexible. In the unemployment model, we assumed that prices and wages are fixed. The full-employment model gives us a useful picture of the economy in the long run. Eventually, prices and wages do adjust so that the economy returns to the full-employment level of output. The unemployment model is a closer picture of the economy in the very short run, in which prices and wages adjust very little, if at all. Our objective now is to understand the middle ground between the very short run of the unemployment model (with fixed wages and prices), and the long run of the full-employment model.

In Part Six we focused on the case when at the current price level, P_0, aggregate demand fell short of aggregate supply, as illustrated in Figure 33.1 by the aggregate demand curve AD_1. As we know, in this situation, output (Y_1) is limited by aggregate demand. When the economy is below the full-employment level of output, policymakers may attempt to shift the aggregate demand curve to the right, increasing output and reducing unemployment. But if the aggregate demand curve is shifted too far to the right, say to AD_2, at the current price level P_0, aggregate demand exceeds aggregate supply; upward price pressure is injected into the economy, and inflation rears its ugly head. On the other hand, if the initial situation is represented by AD_2, upward price pressure may be diminished by leftward shifts of the aggregate demand curve. If this is taken to extremes, the level of output may fall below the full-employment level.

The problems of inflation and unemployment lie on opposite sides of the aggregate supply curve. When aggregate demand exceeds aggregate supply at the current price level, the economy will experience inflation (rising prices) as it moves to the future equilibrium level. On the other hand, when aggregate demand is less than aggregate supply at the current price level, unemployment becomes the problem. In both cases, the size of the effects on the rates of inflation and unemployment will depend on the size of the gap between aggregate supply and aggregate demand; the larger the gap, the larger is the effect. This interconnection between inflation and unemployment is the key to understanding the dynamics of adjustment—the middle ground between the full-employment and unemployment models we have studied thus far.

The challenge for economists and policymakers is threefold: (1) to determine the state of the economy at any given time; (2) to determine how policy

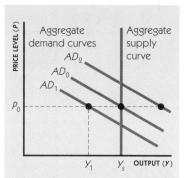

Figure 33.1 SHORT-RUN EQUILIBRIUM

When aggregate demand is less than aggregate supply at the current price level, output will be limited by aggregate demand (Y_1), and there will be involuntary unemployment. When aggregate supply is less than demand at the current price level, output will be limited by aggregate supply and there will be upward price pressure.

Figure 33.2 **THE PHILLIPS CURVE**

The Phillips curve shows that as the level of unemployment falls, the rate of inflation rises. Panel A shows the curve A. W. Phillips actually plotted in 1958 for the British economy. Panel B depicts the Phillips curve relationship for U.S. data in the 1960s, early 1980s, late 1980s, and early 1990s. Panel C gives the Phillips curve for Japan for 1970–1995. *Source: ERP* (1995), Tables B-40, B-63, B-110, B-111.

can change the state of the economy favorably; and (3) to determine how inflation and unemployment are likely to change in the future. Two of the key factors they look at in assessing the state of the economy are the unemployment rate—a measure of the "tightness" of the labor market—and the rate of change of wages. Economists and policymakers also examine conditions in the product and capital markets, but for various reasons, unemployment and wages are an especially good gauge of where the economy is and where inflation is heading.

THE PHILLIPS CURVE

The framework for thinking about the rate of change of wages is the same as that used for thinking about the rate of change of prices. Just as the greater the gap between demand and supply at the current price level, the more pressure there is for prices to increase, and so the *faster* will be the rate of price increases, so too in the labor market: the "tighter" the labor market, the faster we expect the price of labor—wages—to rise. This kind of relationship has been verified in a number of instances, as illustrated in Figure 33.2. The relationship is called the **Phillips curve** after A. W. Phillips, a New Zealander who taught economics in England in the 1950s.

The different panels of Figure 33.2 show Phillips curves for different countries and periods. In every case, the unemployment rate at which inflation is zero is positive. There are several reasons for this. In the economy, not every worker is qualified to do every job. There may be unemployment of autoworkers and excess demand for computer programmers. If wages respond upward to excess demand more strongly than they respond downward to excess supply, average wages will be rising even when the excess demand for one type of labor equals the excess supply of the other. Similarly, there may be unemployment in Detroit and vacancies in Seattle. But unemployed autoworkers in Detroit cannot simply walk into jobs making airplanes in Seattle. By the same token, there will always be some workers moving between jobs; in Chapter 24 we referred to this as frictional unemployment.

THE EXPECTATIONS-AUGMENTED PHILLIPS CURVE

In the 1970s, the stable relationship between unemployment and inflation seemed to disappear. The economy experienced high unemployment with high inflation. There was a simple explanation for this: the rate at which wages increase at any level of unemployment depends on expectations concerning inflation. If workers expect prices to be rising, they will demand offsetting wage increases; and employers will be willing to grant those higher wage increases, because they believe that they will be able to sell what they produce at higher prices.

Inflationary expectations ran high in the 1970s, resulting in higher rates of inflation coexisting with higher unemployment. This is represented diagrammatically in Figure 33.3. The Phillips curve shifts up, incorporating the inflationary

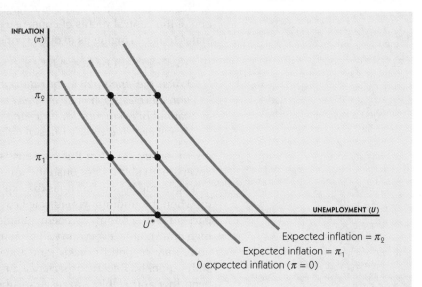

Figure 33.3 **THE EXPECTATIONS-AUGMENTED PHILLIPS CURVE**

The position of the Phillips curve depends on inflationary expectations. Increased expectations concerning inflation shifts the Phillips curve up. U^* is the natural or non-accelerating inflation rate of unemployment (NAIRU). At U^*, if expected inflation is π_1, actual inflation is π_1; when expected inflation is π_2, actual inflation is π_2. At lower umemployment rates, inflation exceeds inflationary expectations, and eventually the Phillips curve shifts up still more. At higher unemployment rates, inflation is less than the expectations concerning inflation, and the Phillips curve shifts down.

expectations. Because it includes inflationary expectations, the newly positioned Phillips curve is called the **expectations-augmented Phillips curve.** The Phillips curve shifted up successively during the 1970s, until it stabilized in the early 1980s. The Phillips curve stabilizes when actual inflation equals expected inflation. This occurs at a special level of unemployment sometimes called the **natural rate of unemployment,** indicated by U^* in Figure 33.3.

To better understand the role of the natural rate of unemployment, consider how expectations about inflation are affected both by recent experience and anticipated changes in policy and economic conditions. Take the simple case where expectations are simply adaptive, that is, they respond or adapt to recent experience. Assume the economy was initially in a situation where prices had been stable for an extended period of time. Given this historical experience, workers expect zero inflation, represented in Figure 33.3 by the Phillips curve labeled $\pi = 0$. Suppose the government reduces unemployment below the rate U^* (where inflation equals expected inflation), and keeps it at the lower rate. This induces an increase in the inflation rate. As the inflation rate increases, the expectations-augmented Phillips curve shifts up, so that there will be higher rates of inflation at each level of unemployment. If the government continues to maintain the unemployment rate below U^*, this will fuel higher expected inflation, resulting in another upward shift of the expectations-augmented Phillips curve. Thus, if the government attempts to maintain the unemployment rate below the natural rate, the inflation rate will continue to increase. As expectations adapt to each successive increase in the inflation rate, inflation increases still more. Accordingly, today, the natural rate is generally known as the **non-accelerating inflation rate of unemployment,** or NAIRU for short.

An economy cannot *permanently* lower its unemployment rate below the NAIRU without facing higher and higher rates of inflation. This has emerged as one of the central points of consensus among macroeconomists in the United States today, bringing us to our twentieth consensus point.

20 The Trade-off between Inflation and Unemployment

When the unemployment rate remains below the NAIRU the rate of inflation increases; when it remains above the NAIRU it decreases. An economy cannot permanently lower its unemployment rate below the NAIRU without facing ever-increasing rates of inflation.

An important result of this consensus is an emerging belief about policy: the government should not push the unemployment rate below the NAIRU.

A key issue is how fast does the expectations-augmented Phillips curve shift up when the unemployment rate is below the NAIRU? The answer depends in part on the economy's recent inflationary experience: if inflation has been high and volatile, everyone will be sensitized to inflation, inflationary expectations may respond quickly, and the expectations-augmented Phillips curve shifts quickly. Recent experience in the United States, where inflation has been low and stable, suggests a rather sluggish response: if the unemployment rate is kept below the NAIRU by 2 percentage points for one year, then the inflation rate will increase by 1 percentage point. Conversely, to bring the inflation rate down by 1 percentage point requires keeping the unemployment rate *above* the NAIRU by 2 percentage points for one year (or by 4 percentage points for six months). The amount by which the unemployment rate must be kept above the NAIRU for one year to bring down inflation by 1 percentage point is called the **sacrifice ratio.** In 1996, the sacrifice ratio for the United States was believed to be about 2.

SHIFTS IN THE NAIRU

Though the *concept* of the NAIRU is now well accepted, economists do differ in their estimate of what the critical level of unemployment is below which inflation begins. This is because the NAIRU itself may vary over time. In the late 1980s, most economists thought that the NAIRU was around 6 percent, or slightly higher. As the unemployment got pushed down to 5.8 percent, and then to 5.6 percent, and hovered in that range throughout 1994 and 1995, more and more economists believed the NAIRU had decreased. In its annual report issued in February 1995, President Clinton's Council of Economic Advisers concluded that the NAIRU had deceased to somewhere in the range of 5.5–5.8 percent. By February of 1996, they suggested that the range was probably even lower. Other economists worried that inflation would appear, but only with a long lag. Today, few economists believe that the evidence is strong enough to suggest a precise number for the NAIRU; the best that can be done is to identify a range of plausible values.[1]

---

[1] In Europe, the large structural changes that have occurred in the last fifteen years have increased the uncertainty surrounding the value of the NAIRU. Many economists in Europe believe that the uncertainty is so large as to make the concept of little use in policymaking.

Some of the changes in the NAIRU are predictable. There is always some frictional unemployment, people moving from job to job. Such movement is more common among new entrants into the labor force; in the 1970s, there were many new entrants, as the baby boomers reached working age and as more women entered the labor force. As a result the NAIRU increased. In the 1990s, these trends reversed themselves, partially accounting for the decline in the NAIRU. Government policies to help workers move quickly from one job to another may lower the NAIRU. Similarly, competitive pressures have increased, and unionization has decreased, so that wages more frequently fall, and are slower to rise. This too has helped lower the NAIRU.

THE LONG-RUN PHILLIPS CURVE

The relationship between unemployment and the inflation rate *in the long run* is called the long-run Phillips curve, shown in Figure 33.4. The long-run Phillips curve is vertical at the level of unemployment that we have identified as the NAIRU. An economy cannot *permanently* lower its unemployment rate below the NAIRU without facing faster and faster inflation. It cannot "buy" a

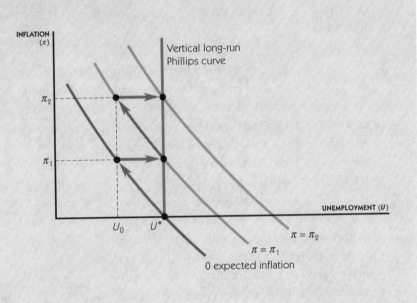

Figure 33.4 A VERTICAL LONG-RUN PHILLIPS CURVE

Assume initially there is no inflation, and that the government decides to "buy" less unemployment by allowing increased inflation. For a short time, unemployment is reduced to U_0, but then the inflationary expectations shift the expectations-augmented Phillips curve up, so that at π_1, unemployment increases back to U^*. If the government again attempts to lower the unemployment rate below U^*, it can only do so by allowing inflation to increase further, to π_2. But this raises the Phillips curve yet again. If it kept inflation fixed at π_2, unemployment would rise again to U^*. Only by allowing the inflation rate to continue to increase can an unemployment rate below U^* be sustained. The only unemployment rate that can be sustained with a fixed rate of inflation is U^*: the long-run Phillips curve is vertical.

lower unemployment rate by accepting just a slightly higher inflation rate. But there is still a short-term trade-off. In the short term, the economy may be able to obtain lower unemployment at the price of higher inflation.

RATIONAL EXPECTATIONS

In the example given above, the expectations-augmented Phillips curve shifts up gradually over time, as market participants experience higher inflation rates, and build those expectations into their wage bargains. Their expectations are assumed to *adapt* to what they actually experience; when expectations are formed in that way, they are said to be **adaptive.**

In path-breaking work done in the 1970s that earned him the Nobel Prize in 1995, Robert Lucas suggested that the upward shift in the expectations-augmented Phillips curve could occur much more rapidly. Market participants did not have to wait until inflation actually occurred to build it into their expectations. They could *rationally anticipate* it. If, for instance, the government tried to stimulate the economy by expanding the money supply, firms and workers would rationally expect that prices would increase, and they would build that expectation into their behavior. These expectations, based on an understanding of the structure of the economy, are referred to as **rational expectations.**

There is one very strong implication of rational expectations. Assume the government announced it was going to keep the unemployment rate below the NAIRU by expanding the money supply. Workers and firms would antici-

BASICS OF INFLATION AND UNEMPLOYMENT

PHILLIPS CURVE: Shows the relationship between inflation and unemployment; the lower the unemployment rate, the higher the inflation rate.

INFLATION EXPECTATIONS-AUGMENTED PHILLIPS CURVE: The level of inflation associated with any level of unemployment depends on expectations concerning inflation; the higher inflationary expectations, the higher the level of inflation associated with any level of unemployment. As inflationary expectations increase, the inflation expectations-augmented Phillips curve shifts up.

NAIRU: The NAIRU (non-accelerating inflation rate of unemployment) is the unemployment rate at which actual inflation equals expected inflation and both remain constant. It is positive. If the unemployment rate remains below the NAIRU level, the rate of inflation will continue to accelerate. To reduce the rate of inflation requires keeping the unemployment rate below the NAIRU.

LONG-RUN PHILLIPS CURVE: The relationship between the inflation rate and unemployment in the long run, with full adjustment of inflationary expectations. It is generally believed to be vertical.

pate the increased inflation, and this would instantaneously shift up the expectations-augmented Phillips curve. Indeed, if the impact of the faster expansion of the money supply was fully anticipated, prices would rise proportionately; there would be no increase in the real money supply, and hence no effect on the level of economic activity. In this case the vertical long-run Phillips curve applies even in a relatively short time span, possibly even less than a year.

How quickly expectations adjust depends on economic circumstances. When inflation has been stable for an extended period of time, households and firms are likely to take the inflation rate as given. They will change expectations only gradually. But in economies which have experienced high and variable inflation, households and firms realize the importance of forming accurate predictions of inflation, and in that case, expectations are more likely to be highly responsive to changes in government policy.

There is one curious aspect of highly responsive expectations. While the government cannot reduce unemployment below the NAIRU level without inflation increasing very rapidly, there may also be little cost to the government reducing the inflation rate. If firms and households believe that the government

In May 1996, Secretary of the Treasury Robert Rubin announced the United States' intention to join the small band of countries that issue indexed bonds. Such bonds guarantee a *real return,* independent of the rate of inflation. If an indexed bond promised to pay one percent real, and the inflation rate is 4 percent, it pays 5 percent total; if the inflation rate is 2 percent, it pays a total return of 3 percent.

Indexed bonds have a number of other important virtues. One is saving for retirement. Currently, people have no way of investing completely safely for their retirement. A bondholder faces significant risk from increases in the inflation rate. If a bond pays 7 percent, and inflation turns out to be 10 percent, the retiring individual may find himself much less well off than he had thought. Many pension funds provide pensions that rise with inflation. But individuals have no way of putting aside money to insure themselves against a high rate of inflation.

Yet another advantage would be a likely reduction in the government's cost of borrowing. Since individuals and pension funds dislike bearing the inflation risk, they would be willing to pay extra for inflation insurance, and the government is in a better position to bear this risk than anyone else.

There is a final advantage to policymakers and economic researchers. Looking at the difference in returns between indexed and nonindexed bonds can yield important information concerning inflationary expectations. For instance, if the interest rate on unindexed bonds increases by 1 percent, and the price of indexed bonds remains unchanged, we may infer that investors' expectations concerning inflation have increased by 1 percent.

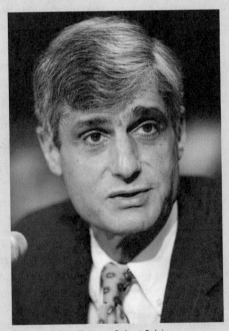

Secretary of the Treasury Robert Rubin

will reduce the inflation rate, inflationary expectations can be brought down almost overnight, with the consequent downward shift in the expectations-augmented Phillips curve. The trick, of course, is for the government to convince others that it will succeed in getting the inflation rate down. It may be difficult to establish such credibility, and the "price" may be high—running the economy at a high unemployment rate over an extended period of time.

INFLATION, AGGREGATE DEMAND, AND AGGREGATE SUPPLY

The previous section focused on the labor market—on unemployment—and described how the level of unemployment combines with inflationary expectations to determine the rate of inflation. Because wages and prices move in tandem, by studying the determinants of wage inflation, we are in fact studying the determinants of overall inflation. In this and the next section, we take a closer look at the linkage between labor and product markets. This will enable us to see more closely the relationship between the dynamic analysis that we have just described, focusing on the rate of change of wages and prices, and the static analysis of Parts Five and Six, which used the tools of the aggregate supply and demand curves.

AGGREGATE SUPPLY

We begin by focusing in on the product market, on aggregate demand and supply. In earlier chapters, we described the economy's potential GDP, Y_s, the amount of output it could produce using the available labor supply and stock of plant and equipment. For simplicity, we assumed that labor supply was inelastic. As a result, changes in the price level did not draw more people into the labor force, and thus the economy's potential output was not sensitive to the price level.

Another way of thinking of the economy's aggregate supply is that it is the level of output that would be produced if wages and prices were perfectly flexible, so that labor was always fully employed. Because of this assumption that wages and prices can adjust fully to ensure full employment, economists sometimes call the vertical aggregate supply curve the **long-run aggregate supply curve.**

Firms may not be willing to hire all the available workers if the price they receive for the goods is low *relative* to the wages they pay workers. The **short-run aggregate supply curve** assumes that wages are fixed—they do not fall to ensure that there is full employment. It asks: How much are firms willing to supply at each price level? Typically, it has the shape depicted in Figure 33.5. The curve has three parts. If there is excess capacity, then there can be large increases in output with little or no increase in the price level—the horizontal portion. If the economy is using all of its resources fully, then no increase in the price level can elicit an increase in output—the vertical portion. And in between, there is an upward-sloping portion, where higher prices can coax producers to work their machines harder.

The relationship between the vertical portion of the short-run aggregate supply curve, the long-run (vertical) aggregate supply curve, and the NAIRU requires some discussion. In the short run, as we saw in Chapter 24, the economy can operate at more than 100 percent of normal capacity, as maintenance

Figure 33.5 SHORT-RUN AGGREGATE SUPPLY CURVE

The short-run aggregate supply curve gives the level of output that will be produced at each price level, given a particular level of wages. By contrast, the long-run aggregate supply curve gives the level of output that will be produced when wages are flexible, and so labor and capital are working at what might be viewed a "normal" level of full capacity. Because for short periods of time, capital and labor can work more beyond this level, at high prices, short-run aggregate supply can exceed long-run aggregate supply.

The short-run aggregate supply curve has three portions: a flat portion where there is a large amount of excess capacity, a vertical portion when there is no spare capacity, and an upward-sloping portion in between.

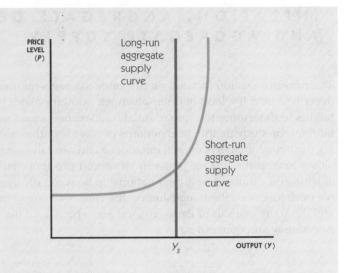

on machines is deferred. Moreover, for short periods of time workers may be induced to work overtime, and additional workers may be brought into the labor force temporarily. But it is not possible in the long run to defer maintenance or to induce workers to work, say, additional shifts. To the extent that one can work workers and machines "overtime" the vertical portion of the short-run aggregate supply curve lies to the right of the long-run aggregate supply curve, as depicted in Figure 33.5. The position of the long-run aggregate supply curve represents the *normal* capacity of the economy. When the economy is operating beyond normal full capacity, there will be upward pressure on prices, and when it is operating below normal full capacity, there will be downward pressure on prices. Thus, the output of the long-run aggregate supply curve is that corresponding to the NAIRU; at that unemployment rate, the inflation rate is neither increasing nor decreasing.

SHORT-RUN EQUILIBRIUM

We can now see how equilibrium output *(in the short run)* depends on the price level. When the price level is very high, as in Figure 33.6A, aggregate demand is less than aggregate supply—the familiar case of Part Six. Firms only produce what they can sell. Output is equal to aggregate demand.

Panel B illustrates a case where at the current price, P_1, the short-run aggregate supply exceeds the long-run aggregate supply, but aggregate demand is larger still. Output is determined by the short-run aggregate supply curve.

The general principle here is: the short side of the market always dominates.

Figure 33.6 SHORT-RUN OUTPUT DETERMINATION

The graphs in panels A and B show aggregate demand *(AD)*, long-run aggregate supply *(LRAS)*, and short-run aggregate supply *(SRAS)* curves. In panel A, at P_0, aggregate demand is less than aggregate supply. Output equals Y_0. In panel B, at the current price, P_1, the short-run aggregate supply exceeds the long-run aggregate supply, but aggregate demand is larger still. Output is determined by the short-run aggregate supply curve.

SHIFTS IN AGGREGATE DEMAND CURVES

We can use this framework to show the consequences of shifts in the aggregate demand curves on inflationary pressures. There are three situations. Panel A of Figure 33.7 shows the aggregate demand curve initially intersecting

SHORT-RUN OUTPUT DETERMINATION

When the price level fails to adjust to equate aggregate demand and aggregate supply, the short side of the market dominates:

(a) If at the given price level, aggregate demand is less than aggregate supply, the actual output will be given by aggregate demand.

(b) If at the given price level, the short-run aggregate supply is less than aggregate demand, the actual output will be given by the short-run aggregate supply.

Figure 33.7 SHIFTS IN THE AGGREGATE DEMAND CURVE

The graphs in panels A, B, and C show aggregate demand (AD), long-run aggregate supply (LRAS), and short-run aggregate supply (SRAS) curves. Panel A. The initial equilibrium is along the horizontal portion of the short-run aggregate supply curve, so that rightward shifts in the aggregate demand curve lead to increased output but no upward price pressure. Panel B. The initial equilibrium is along the vertical portion of the aggregate supply curve, so that rightward shifts in the aggregate demand curve lead to no increased output, but considerable upward price pressure. Panel C. The initial equilibrium is along the upward-sloping portion of the aggregate supply curve. Rightward shifts in the aggregate demand curve lead to upward pressures on prices. If nothing else changed, eventually equilibrium would be restored with aggregate demand equaling aggregate supply at P_1, and with output higher than before.

the short-run aggregate supply curve along the horizontal portion of the aggregate supply curve. The initial price level is P_0 and the initial output is Y_0. There is large excess capacity. A rightward shift in the aggregate demand curve leads to a new equilibrium output, Y_1. At Y_1, there is no excess demand for goods. There is no upward price pressure. Because there is so much excess capacity, the increase in aggregate demand has not resulted in any inflationary pressure.

Panel B shows the aggregate demand curve initially intersecting the short-run aggregate supply curve along the vertical portion of the aggregate supply curve. We assume initially that the price is P_0, so again, in the initial situation, aggregate demand just equals aggregate supply. Now, however, a rightward shift in the aggregate demand curve leads to no change in aggregate output—after all, the economy is already operating at full capacity. But there is large upward pressure on prices. Inflation that starts with a rightward shift in the aggregate demand curve is referred to as **demand-pull inflation.**

The situation depicted in Figure 33.7B occurred in 1965. At the time, the economy was operating at close to capacity. President Johnson wanted to fight a war in Vietnam, but did not want Americans to know how costly such a war might be. As a result, he decided not to raise taxes, at least not enough to pay for the war. In addition, he did not want to cut other government expenditures, including his War on Poverty. With the initial equilibrium along the vertical portion of the aggregate supply curve, the increased government expen-

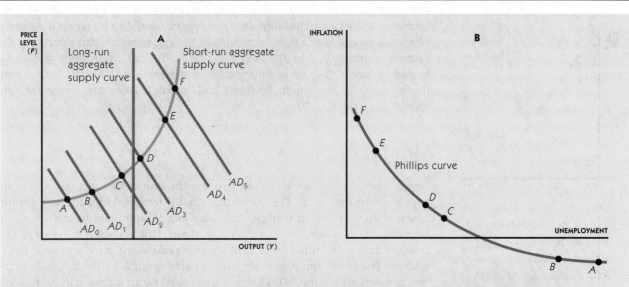

Figure 33.8 THE SHAPE OF THE PHILLIPS CURVE: TRANSLATING STATIC SHIFTS IN THE AGGREGATE DEMAND CURVE INTO MOVEMENTS ALONG THE PHILLIPS CURVE

When there is large excess capacity—when the unemployment rate is high—shifts in the aggregate demand curve result in large reductions in the unemployment rate and small increases in the inflation rate—the movement from *A* to *B*. When unemployment is very low, shifts in the aggregate demand curve result in small reductions in the unemployment rate and large increases in the inflation rate— the movement from *E* to *F*. In between, shifts in the aggregate demand curve result in moderate reductions in the unemployment rate and increases in the inflation rate—the movement from *C* to *D*.

ditures shifted the aggregate demand curve to the right, giving rise to inflationary pressures. The inflation rate, which had been running at an annual rate of between 1 and 2 percent in the early 1960s, climbed to the then staggering rate of almost 6 percent by 1970.

Panel c shows the aggregate demand curve initially intersecting the short-run aggregate supply curve along the upward-sloping portion of the aggregate supply curve. Again, we assume initially the price is P_0, where aggregate demand equals aggregate supply. Again, a rightward shift in the aggregate demand curve gives rise to upward price pressure; but now, as the price level increases, output actually increases, since the aggregate supply curve (in this region) is upward sloping.

Thus, the extent to which the shift in the aggregate demand curve gets reflected in increased prices or increased output depends on the slope of the short-run aggregate supply curve: when it is horizontal, output increases and there is no price pressure; when it is vertical, output cannot increase but there are large upward pressures on price; and when it is upward sloping, output increases *and* there is upward price pressure. This static picture translates into the shape of the typical Phillips curve shown in Figure 33.8. When the unemployment rate is high, a given rightward shift in the aggregate

Figure 33.9 SHIFTS IN THE SHORT-RUN AGGREGATE SUPPLY CURVE

The short-run aggregate supply curve may shift downward and to the right, due to increases in capacity or decreases in costs, or upward and to the left, due to decreases in capacity or increases in cost. Panel A shows the shift downward and to the right from AS_0 to AS_1, resulting in downward pressure at the original price level. As prices fall, output will increase. Panel B shows the shift upward and to the left from AS_0 to AS_1, resulting in upward price pressure at the original price level.

demand curve (say, increasing aggregate demand at a given price level by 1 percent) results in a large reduction in the unemployment rate and very little increase in the rate of inflation (the movement from A to B); when the unemployment rate is low, a rightward shift in the aggregate demand curve by the same amount results in a small reduction in the unemployment rate and a large increase in the rate of inflation (the movement from E to F); in between, the changes in the unemployment and inflation rates are moderate (the movement from C to D).

SHIFTS IN THE AGGREGATE SUPPLY CURVE

Panels A and B of Figure 33.9 show two ways in which the short-run aggregate supply curve may shift. The curve may shift downward and to the right because of an increase in capacity (say, because of additional investment) or a decrease in costs (say, a fall in the price of oil). This is shown in panel A. The result is that at the initial price level, there is downward price pressure. Panel B shows the short-run aggregate supply curve shifting in the opposite manner, upward and to the left. This may be caused by an increase in costs, such as occurred in the 1970s when oil prices rose dramatically. The result is upward price pressure at the initial price level, leading to inflation. Inflation that arises from this type of shift in the aggregate supply curve is called **cost-push inflation.**

In 1973, the Organization of Petroleum Exporting Countries (OPEC), consisting mainly of nations in the Middle East, decided to impose an embargo on the shipment of oil to certain Western nations, including the United States. Even after the embargo was lifted, OPEC restricted oil production, so that the price of oil rose dramatically. For the U.S. economy as a whole, the higher oil prices raised costs of production. The short-run aggregate supply curve shifted upward and to the left, resulting in inflationary pressures.

SHORT-RUN AGGREGATE SUPPLY

The short-run aggregate supply curve has three portions: a vertical segment, where the economy is operating at full capacity; a horizontal segment, along which output can be increased with little or no increase in the price level; and an upward-sloping portion joining the two.

Shifts in the aggregate supply curve result either from increased capacity (new investment), shifting the curve to the right; or changes in costs of production, for instance, as a result of increases in the price of imported oil, shifting the curve up, or technological change, shifting the curve down.

Figure 33.10 THE OIL PRICE SHOCK AND THE END OF THE VIETNAM WAR

The end of the Vietnam War shifted the aggregate demand curve to the left, from AD_0 to AD_1. If nothing else had happened, this would have put downward pressure on prices. But at the same time, the oil price shock shifted the short-run aggregate supply curve up, from $SRAS_0$ to $SRAS_1$. At the old price p_0, output was reduced, while upward price pressure persisted.

The timing could not have been worse. As we saw earlier, the increased government expenditure to finance the Vietnam War had ignited inflation. As the Vietnam War wound down, reduced government expenditures would have led to a leftward shift in the aggregate demand curve, resulting in downward price pressure. But the upward shift in the short-run aggregate supply curve more than offset this effect, and the economy had **stagflation**—inflation went up as unemployment went up. This is illustrated in Figure 33.10. The inflationary episode that had begun with a rightward shift in the aggregate demand curve as a result of the Vietnam War was carried forward with an upward shift in the aggregate supply curve as a result of the oil embargo. Moreover, as we saw earlier, inflationary expectations were raised during the period, exacerbating the inflationary episode.

INFLATION INERTIA

Earlier in the chapter, we described how if the unemployment rate remains at the NAIRU level, inflation will simply continue at a given rate. This tendency of inflation to persist is referred to as **inflation inertia.** Inflation inertia occurs because higher wages lead to higher prices (and expectations of higher prices), which in turn lead to higher wages. At the higher prices, firms are willing to pay, and workers demand, higher wages. And at higher wages firms demand higher prices, which consumers are willing to pay.

It makes little difference how inflation is started—whether through a shift in the aggregate demand curve that gives rise to demand-pull inflation or through a shift in the aggregate supply curve that gives rise to cost-push inflation. Once started, wage increases give rise to price increases which give rise to further wage increases, in a continuous cycle.

Expectations help to maintain inflation inertia. Workers base their demand for wage increases on their *expectations* of price increases; and firms may set their prices based on *expectations* of increases in wages and other costs.

When inflation inertia is strong, it can take long periods of unemployment to bring inflation down. With high unemployment, workers' moderate wage demands; lower wage demands translate into slower rates of increase in prices; as workers gradually realize that inflation is slowing down, this reinforces the moderation of their wage demands.

Sometimes, however, inflation can be stopped quickly, by reversing expectations. If the government puts into place policies that are thought to be effective in reducing inflation, then, for instance, workers may moderate their wage demands and firms will not be willing to grant increased wages since they do not anticipate that they will be able to get higher prices for the products they sell.

MONETARY POLICY

Inflation is often viewed as essentially a monetary phenomenon. In Part Five, where prices were perfectly flexible, we saw that this was the case. Increases in the money supply translated into increases in the price level, with no real effect on the economy. On the other hand, in Part Six, where prices were perfectly rigid, by assumption monetary policy did not have an *immediate* effect on inflation, but it did have an effect on output. In this part, which bridges the discussion between perfectly flexible and perfectly rigid prices, we will see that in general monetary policy has an effect both on output and inflation.

Figure 33.11A shows that an increase in the money supply shifts the aggregate demand curve to the right. Assume that initially aggregate demand equaled (both short-run and long-run) aggregate supply, and that initially there was no inflation. The shift in the aggregate demand curve leads at the current price level to upward price pressure, and, as we have seen, this upward price pressure gradually translates into higher prices. With higher prices, output increases along the short-run aggregate supply curve. As output increases, so does employment. Panel B shows that the unemployment rate falls below the NAIRU level, and as a result inflation sets in. Thus, an increase in the money supply can begin an inflationary episode.

Monetary policy may also play a role in sustaining inflation inertia. If the money supply is allowed to increase in tandem with prices, inflation can persist. However, with restrictive policies, inflation can be reduced.

Whether monetary policy is being restrictive depends to a large extent on the rate of increase in the money supply. In Chapter 12, we saw that normally the demand for money (at any interest rate) increases with *nominal* income. If the economy's real growth is, say, 2 percent, and prices are increasing at 3 percent, then if the money supply is increased at the rate of 5 percent per year, the increased supply of money will just equal the increased demand at an unchanged interest rate. If the money supply increases less rapidly, inter-

Figure 33.11 EXCESSIVELY EXPANSIONARY MONETARY POLICY SETS OFF INFLATION

Increasing the money supply shifts the aggregate demand curve to the right (panel A). There is upward price pressure. As prices rise, output increases along the short-run aggregate supply curve. As output increases, so does employment. In panel B the unemployment rate falls below the NAIRU level, and as a result inflation accelerates.

INFLATION INERTIA AND MONETARY POLICY

Inflation once started perpetuates itself:

> Increases in prices lead to increases in wages, which in turn lead to further increases in prices
>
> Expectations of inflation get built into wage formation

Monetary policy can dampen or accelerate inflation

est rates must rise for demand to equal supply, reducing investment. The aggregate demand curve shifts to the left and inflationary pressures are reduced.

EXPECTATIONS AND FOREIGN EXCHANGE RATES

In Chapter 31, we saw that there were two channels through which monetary policy affects the economy: it affects interest rates, and thus investment, and, in an open economy, it affects exchange rates, and thus net exports. In our earlier analysis, we noted that a decrease in the interest rate makes financial investment in the country less attractive, decreasing the demand for its currency and thereby decreasing the exchange rate. The lower exchange rate makes the country's goods more attractive abroad—increasing exports—and makes other countries' goods more expensive—decreasing imports. The result is an increase in net exports, shifting the aggregate demand curve to the right. The same logic applies to a restrictive monetary policy. Higher interest rates lead to a higher exchange rate and a decrease in net exports, shifting the aggregate demand curve to the left.

This analysis ignores one critical ingredient in the determination of exchange rates, a wild card which makes predicting the effect of monetary policy on exchange rates difficult: expectations. If American investors hold yen, and the dollar *appreciates*, they make a capital loss. Consider Jack who spent $1,000 to buy yen in April 1995, when the exchange rate was 80 yen to the dollar. He received 80,000 yen. Four months later, the exchange rate was 100 yen to the dollar. If he cashed in his yen, he would have received $800, for a 20 percent loss in only four months. If investors expect the dollar to appreciate, they sell yen and buy dollars, so the demand for dollars increases. Hence, the exchange rate rises—confirming their expectations. It is easy to see how a spiral of increasing exchange rates can emerge, as—at least up to a point—each rise of the dollar reinforces beliefs that the dollar will rise further.

How investors and speculators form their expectations—and how monetary policy affects those expectations—is a complicated matter that is not completely understood. But inflationary expectations are an important determinant. If the price level in the United States is expected to rise faster than the price level of Japan, investors will believe that *in the long run* the dollar must decline in value relative to the yen.

Expectations reinforce the dampening effect of tighter monetary policy when tighter monetary policy leads to an appreciation of the dollar because of its effects on inflationary expectations: if investors believe that the monetary authorities are taking actions to dampen the economy—and hence reduce inflation—they will expect the dollar to increase in value relative to the yen (compared to what it otherwise would have been), and this expectation of an increased value leads to higher demand for dollars today—and a higher exchange rate. The higher exchange rate makes imports more attractive to Americans, while Japanese consumers find American goods more expensive, and so the United States will export less.

CAUSES OF WAGE AND PRICE RIGIDITIES

We have *described* in this chapter how wages and prices adjust—how, for instance, wages increase faster the lower the unemployment rate. These empirical regularities make sense; after all, the tighter the labor market, the more likely employers will be scrambling to hire workers, and the more wages will rise. But to economic theorists, these explanations are not fully satisfactory. Why don't wages and prices adjust faster than they do? If they did, unemployment might not be able to persist as long. Economists have identified three key reasons why wages and prices adjust slowly—adjustment costs, risk and imperfect information, and imperfect competition that gives rise to kinked demand and labor supply curves.[2]

ADJUSTMENT COSTS

The first explanation for price rigidities emphasizes the costs of changing prices. When firms change their prices, they must print new menus and price lists or otherwise convey the change in prices to their customers. Changing prices costs money, and these costs are referred to as **menu costs.** Menu costs may be large, but advocates of the menu-cost explanation of price rigidities, who include Gregory Mankiw, George Akerlof, and Janet Yellen, point out

---

[2]In some cases, these explanations seem to explain too much—they suggest that under some circumstances, prices and wages will not adjust at all to, say, small changes in demand or costs. But the economy consists of many firms in different circumstances. Some may be in a situation where they do not respond at all, while others may respond fully. The *average* for the economy will reflect a slow response. In the next chapter, we consider a set of explanations that pertain particularly to the labor market.

that even small costs can have big effects. If each firm in the economy is slow to adjust its prices because of menu costs, even if these costs are small, the cumulative effects could still be significant. There could be powerful aggregate price rigidities.

Still, when firms face a shift in the demand curves for their products, as in Figure 33.12, they must choose whether to adjust quantity or price. While there are costs of adjusting either prices or quantity, the costs of adjusting quantity are almost always much greater. Facing such choices, firms will adjust prices rather than quantities. Accordingly, *in most instances* the direct costs of making adjustments do not provide a convincing explanation of price rigidities.

RISK AND IMPERFECT INFORMATION

Risk and imperfect information provide important reasons for price and wage rigidities. Firms experience a great deal of uncertainty about the consequences of price and wage changes. When a firm lowers its price, whether sales increase or not depends on how other firms in the industry respond and how its customers respond. If rivals respond by lowering their prices, the firm may fail to gain market share, and its profits simply plummet with the decline in prices. If rivals fail to respond, the firm may gain a competitive advantage. Customers may think that this is just the first of several price decreases, and decide to postpone purchases until prices get still lower; thus a decrease in price might even result in reduced sales. Similarly, the consequences of a firm lowering its wages depend on how its workers and rival firms respond. Other firms might leave wages unchanged, and use the opportunity to try to recruit the firm's best employees. Alternatively, they might respond by lowering wages in a corresponding manner. In one case profits would fall, in the other, they would rise.

The uncertainty associated with wage and price changes is often much greater than that associated with changing output and employment. When a firm cuts back on its production, provided it does not cut back too drastically, its only risk is that its inventories will be depleted below normal levels, in which case it simply increases production next period to replace the lost inventories. If production costs do not change much over time, there is accordingly little extra risk to cutting back production. Similarly, there is little risk to a firm decreasing its employment simply by not hiring new workers as older workers leave or retire—much less risk than associated with lowering wages.

Since firms like to avoid risks, they try to avoid making large changes to prices and wages; they would rather accept somewhat larger changes in quantities—in the amount produced or in the hours worked. As a result wages and prices are sticky.

KINKED DEMAND CURVES

A third group of explanations attribute price rigidities to the shape of demand curves facing firms under imperfect competition. Recall that with perfect competition, a firm faces a horizontal demand curve. With imperfect competition,

Figure 33.12 ADJUSTMENT COSTS

Shifts in the demand curve facing a firm necessitate adjustments in either the price charged or the quantity produced. How the firm adjusts depends in part on the costs of adjusting each and the risks associated. If the costs or risks of adjusting prices are high, and of adjusting quantities are low, then the firm will leave price unchanged, and lower quantity: there will be price rigidity.

Figure 33.13 KINKED DEMAND CURVES AND PRICE INFLEXIBILITY

If firms lose many more sales from price increases than they gain from price decreases, their demand curve will be kinked. When the demand curve is kinked, the marginal revenue curve has a vertical section, since the extra revenue from price decreases is less than the lost revenue from price increases, and small changes in marginal cost will not lead to any change in price or output.

a firm faces a downward-sloping demand curve; in particular, the demand curve may have a kink, as illustrated in Figure 33.13. The kink means that firms lose many more sales when they raise prices above the current price, p_0, than they gain when they lower prices below p_0.

There are two reasons why the demand curve may be kinked—that is, why there are very different responses to price increases and price decreases. First, companies believe that if they raise their prices, their own customers will immediately know it and will start searching for stores selling the good at a lower price. But if they lower their prices without heavy expenditures on advertising, customers at other stores may not find out about their lower prices, so they gain few new customers.

Second, firms worry that if they raise their prices their rivals will not match the increase, and hence they will lose customers from their relatively uncompetitive prices. But if they lower their prices, rivals will view this as a threat and will match the decrease and the firm will gain little from the attempt to beat the market.

Kinked demand curves have one dramatic implication: small changes in marginal costs may have no effect on the price firms charge. Even if the com-

SOURCES OF WAGE AND PRICE RIGIDITY

Adjustment costs

Risks associated with wage and price adjustments

Imperfect competition with kinked demand or labor supply curves pany's costs go down, it will continue to charge the price at the kink, p_0 in Figure 33.13. Firms worry, for instance, that if they cut their price in response to the lower marginal cost, other firms will simply match them and they will be no better off. Thus, kinked demand curves give rise to price rigidities: small changes, such as those resulting from a fall in wages, have no effect on either the output or pricing decisions of the firm.

A similar analysis applies to labor, in markets where firms have to pay higher wages to obtain more workers with required skills. There may be *different* responses to a firm's lowering or increasing its wages. If a firm raises wages, rival firms may match the increase out of fear of losing their best workers; but if a firm lowers wages, the rival firms may not respond, taking advantage of their higher wages to attract the best workers. Thus, the consequences of lowering wages may be costly.

REVIEW AND PRACTICE

SUMMARY

1. The costs of inflation increase with its level, the variability in its rate, whether it is anticipated, and the extent of indexation. Among the costs are the resources devoted to mitigating its effects and those associated with increased uncertainty. Increased indexation has lowered many of the costs.

2. Some of the antipathy to inflation is based on misperceptions, such as blaming inflation for losses in real incomes that occur during inflationary episodes but are caused by other factors.

3. *Other things equal,* lower levels of inflation are associated with higher levels of unemployment. This relationship is called the Phillips curve.

4. The level of inflation associated with any particular level of unemployment will increase as expectations of inflation increase. As a result, if the government tries to maintain unemployment at a very low rate, the inflation rate will continually increase, as each increase in inflation is built into individuals' expectations. The Phillips curve that reflects the effects of inflationary expectations is called the expectations-augmented Phillips curve.

5. The unemployment rate at which the inflation rate is stable—at which actual inflation is equal to expected inflation—is called the NAIRU, the non-accelerating inflation rate of unemployment.

6. The NAIRU can change because of changes in the structure of the labor force, and increasing competition in labor and product markets, which puts downward pressures on wages and prices.

7. With rational expectations, changes in policy can be reflected directly into inflationary expectations; the expectations-augmented Phillips curve can shift up immediately upon the announcement of a policy change.

8. The short-run aggregate supply curve gives the amount that firms are willing to supply at each price level (given current wages). It has three portions: a horizontal portion (with excess capacity, there can be large increases in output with little or no changes in price), a vertical portion (representing the full capacity of the economy), and an upward-sloping portion.

9. When at the current price level aggregate demand is greater than aggregate supply, there is upward pressure on prices. But wages and prices do not adjust instantaneously to clear labor and product markets. The rate of change in prices or wages is related to the magnitude of the gap between supply and demand.

10. There is considerable inflation inertia. Once started, inflation can persist, as increases in wages lead to increased prices, and increases in prices lead to increased wages.

11. Monetary policy may allow the money supply to increase in tandem with prices—and thus help perpetuate inflation; or, by restricting the rate of increase of the money supply, it may dampen inflation.

12. Prices and wages may be slow to adjust for three reasons. Firms may face large costs of adjustments. Firms may adjust output and employment rather than prices and wages because the uncertainties associated with changing prices and wages may be greater. And firms may face kinked demand and labor supply curves.

KEY TERMS

indexing	non-accelerating	short-run aggregate
inflation tax	inflation rate of	supply curve
Phillips curve	unemployment	demand-pull
expectations-	adaptive	inflation
augmented	expectations	cost-push inflation
Phillips curve	rational expectations	menu costs
natural rate of	long-run aggregate	
unemployment	supply curve	

REVIEW QUESTIONS

1. What are the costs, actual and perceived, of higher inflation? How has indexing affected the costs of inflation? What difference does it make whether inflation is anticipated or unanticipated, and why?

2. Why is there a trade-off between inflation and unemployment in the short run?

3. What role do changes in expectations play in shifting the Phillips curve? What difference does it make whether expectations are adaptive or rational?

4. What is the NAIRU? Why, if unemployment is kept below the NAIRU, will the rate of inflation accelerate? Why might the long-run Phillips curve be vertical?

5. What factors affect the NAIRU?

6. What is the shape of the typical short-run aggregate supply curve?

7. What is the relationship between the dynamic analysis of the Phillips curve and the static analysis of aggregate demand and supply curves?

8. What is inflation inertia? What factors contribute to its existence?

9. How does monetary policy affect inflation? What difference does it make whether there are rational expectations? whether the economy is open?

10. What are some explanations for wage and price rigidities?

PROBLEMS

1. Priscilla earns $40,000 per year, but her wages are not indexed to inflation. If over a period of three years inflation is at 5 percent and Priscilla receives raises of 2 percent, how much has the actual buying power of her income changed over that time?

2. Patrick receives a gift of two $100 bills for his birthday. Because he likes having the bills around to admire, he does not spend them for a year. With an inflation rate of 6 percent, what inflation tax does he pay? If he put them into a bank account paying 4 percent, what is the real value of his $200 at the end of the year? If he puts them into a money market fund paying 8 percent, what is the real value at the end of the year?

3. "It is unfair to tax capital gains—the increases in the value of stocks and bonds—at the same rate as ordinary income in inflationary situations." Discuss this statement, paying particular attention to a comparison of capital gains and interest income.

4. There have been proposals to increase Social Security benefits with the wages received by current workers, so that retired individuals do not fall behind those who are employed. What would be the consequences of increasing Social Security benefits *both* to compensate for increases in the price level and to match salary increases of the currently employed?

5. Social Security payments are currently indexed to the consumer price index (CPI). There is a widespread belief that the CPI overstates the true rate of inflation, because, for instance, it does not correctly account for improvements in quality. Assume that the overstatement is approximately

.5 percent per year. Discuss whether Social Security payments should be indexed to the CPI—.5 percent.

6. Why might the inflation effect of a onetime increase in a tax rate on final goods be different from other events that might start an inflationary spiral?

7. The sacrifice ratio measures the number of "unemployment years" required to bring down inflation by 1 percent. Thus, if the sacrifice ratio is 2, then one can bring down the inflation rate by .5 percent either by increasing the unemployment rate by .5 percent for two years, or by increasing the unemployment rate by 1 percent for one year, or by 2 percent for a half year. If the sacrifice ratio is 1, then how long will it take to bring down the inflation rate by 2 percent?

8. Assume the government maintained the unemployment rate above the NAIRU by 1 percent for 2 years, and the inflation rate increased by 1 percentage point, from 3 to 4 percent. Assume the costs to bringing down inflation are identical to the benefits (lower unemployment) associated with the increase in inflation. What must the government do to decrease the inflation rate to its original level? What is the sacrifice ratio?

9. If you were in the position of the Fed in 1994, with unemployment approaching 6 percent, and other indicators suggesting the economy had relatively little excess capacity, but had shown no strong signs of incipient inflation, would you have raised interest rates? Why or why not?

10. "If expectations adjust quickly to changes in economic circumstances, including changes in economic policy, then it is easy to start an inflationary episode. But under the same conditions, it is also easy to stop inflation." Discuss. If true, what implications might this finding have for economic policy?

11. Use aggregate supply and demand curves to explain whether (and when) the following events might trigger inflation:
   (a) an increase in business confidence;
   (b) an increase in the discount rate;
   (c) the development of important new technologies;
   (d) an increase in the price of imports;
   (e) an increase in government spending.

12. What would be the effect on the Phillips curve of an announcement that OPEC—the cartel of oil-producing countries—had fallen apart, and thus the price of oil was expected to fall dramatically?

13. While playing around with old economic data in your spare time, you find that in 1963, unemployment was 5.5 percent and inflation was 1.3 percent; in 1972, unemployment was 5.5 percent and inflation 3.2 percent; in 1979, unemployment was 5.8 percent and inflation 11.3 percent; in 1988, unemployment was 5.5 percent and inflation 3.6 percent. Does this evidence necessarily imply anything about the shape of the short-run or long-run Phillips curve? How might you interpret this data?

CHAPTER 34

UNEMPLOYMENT: UNDERSTANDING WAGE RIGIDITIES

L arge numbers of people collecting unemployment insurance, huge lines at firms that are hiring workers, plants closing down and laying off workers—all are symptoms of an economy in a recession. Even more than lost output and reduced profits, the human misery that results from unemployment is a poignant reminder of the political commitment to limit both the extent and the costs of unemployment in the economy. But if we are to understand how to reduce unemployment, we must first understand its causes.

Although unemployment represents a situation where the supply of labor exceeds its demand, the macroeconomics of unemployment in Part Six looked at the product rather than the labor market. The reason is simple. Variations in output underlie most variations in employment. And variations in aggregate demand underlie most variations in output. Still, one important fact remains, which we emphasized in Chapter 25. No matter what the source of variation in the aggregate demand for labor, if real wages adjusted, full employment could be sustained. Unemployment is fundamentally a labor market phenomenon. It reflects a failure of real wages to adjust to changes in economic circumstances. The last chapter gave several reasons why wages and prices may be sticky. This chapter focuses on special features of the labor market that may contribute to rigidities in wages, particularly in *real wages*.

KEY QUESTIONS

1. What are the reasons that wages may not fall even when there is excess supply of labor?

2. What policies might reduce either the extent of unemployment or the costs borne by those who are thrown out of work?

3. What are some of the problems facing the unemployment insurance system?

THE WAGE-EMPLOYMENT PUZZLE

It is difficult to reconcile observed changes in employment (or unemployment) and wages with the basic competitive model. If we applied the basic model to the labor market, we would predict that when the demand for labor goes down, as in a recession, the real wage also falls, as illustrated in Figure 34.1. A leftward shift in the demand for labor results in lower wages. If the supply of labor is unresponsive to wage changes (that is, the labor supply curve is inelastic), as depicted by the steepness of the line in the figure, the reduction in the real wage is large.

In the real world it doesn't seem to happen this way. In the Great Depression, for example, when the demand for labor fell, real wages in manufacturing actually rose. One estimate shows that while unemployment increased from 5.5 percent in 1929 to 22 percent in 1934, real wages *rose* by more than

Figure 34.1 CHANGES IN THE DEMAND FOR LABOR AND REAL WAGES

Traditional theory predicts that when the demand curve for labor shifts to the left, real wages fall.

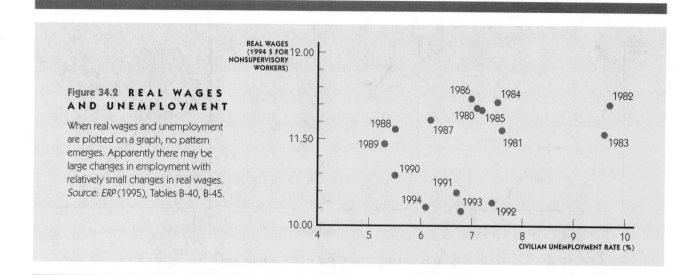

Figure 34.2 **REAL WAGES AND UNEMPLOYMENT**

When real wages and unemployment are plotted on a graph, no pattern emerges. Apparently there may be large changes in employment with relatively small changes in real wages. *Source: ERP* (1995), Tables B-40, B-45.

20 percent. In the 1980s, a much more recent example, real wages again rose as the unemployment rate increased, from 5.2 percent to 9.5 percent.

Figure 34.2 shows the real wage and unemployment rates during the 1980s and early 1990s. Real wages have not been much affected by changes in unemployment. There are three possible explanations. The first is that the supply curve for labor is horizontal and the demand curve for labor has shifted, as shown in Figure 34.3A. In this case, the labor market has moved along the labor supply curve to a new point of equilibrium. Almost all economists reject this interpretation, because of the huge amount of evidence suggesting that the labor supply curve is relatively inelastic (steep), not flat.

The second possible interpretation is that there are shifts in the labor supply curve that just offset the shifts in the labor demand curve, as depicted in panel B. The shifting demand and supply curves trace out a pattern of changing employment with little change in the real wage. Again, the labor market winds up at an equilibrium point. The reduced employment in the Great Depression was, in this view, due to a decreased willingness to supply labor—in other words, an increased desire for leisure. As we learned in Chapter 27, there have been marked changes in the supply of labor, as women and baby boomers have joined the labor force. But most economists do not see any persuasive evidence that the supply curve for labor shifts much as the economy goes into or comes out of a recession, let alone to the extent required in Figure 34.3B. And they see no reason why shifts in the demand curve for labor would normally be offset by shifts in the supply curve.

The third interpretation is that there has been a shift in the demand curve for labor, with no matching shift in the supply curve *and no corresponding change in the real wage,* depicted in Figure 34.3C. The labor market is stuck in disequilibrium. At the wage w_0/P, the amount of labor that workers would like to supply remains at L_0. But as the demand for labor shifts, the number of

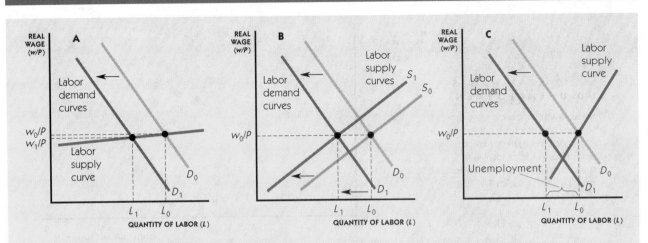

Figure 34.3 WHY WAGES DO NOT FALL WHEN DEMAND SHIFTS

Panel A shows a very elastic labor supply curve. A leftward shift in demand for labor from D_0 to D_1 will decrease employment without affecting wages. Panel B shows a shift in both supply and demand curves. Although the shift in demand for labor from D_0 to D_1 would reduce wages by itself, it is offset by a shift in the supply of labor from S_0 to S_1, leaving the wage level unchanged. In panel C, the demand for labor shifts from D_0 to D_1, but wages do not fall for some reason. Involuntary unemployment results.

workers hired at w_0/P falls from L_0 to L_1. The difference, $L_0 - L_1$, is the level of unemployment. If the wage does not fall, most economists—and virtually all of the general public—would say the unemployment is involuntary. People are willing to work *at the going wage,* but the work is not there. The same argument holds even if there is a slight shift in the labor supply curve and a slight change in the wage. The adjustment in the wage is too small to align demand with supply.

The question posed by panel C is fundamental to macroeconomics. How do we explain the apparent fact that wages do not fall in the face of a shift in the demand curve for labor? Reasons abound, as we will see in the following sections.

EXPLANATIONS OF WAGE RIGIDITIES

Why don't wages fall enough to eliminate unemployment quickly? We looked at several explanations in the previous chapter. Two possibilities are important for the current discussion. First, firms may not be allowed to lower wages, because of union pressure or government legislation. Second, the efficient wage for the firm (i.e., the wage at which profits are maximized) may be at the current wage level. It may not pay the firm to reduce wage levels, even if the supply curve for labor changes. The reasons for wage stickiness may vary from industry to industry and may overlap.

UNIONS, CONTRACTS, AND GOVERNMENT REGULATIONS

One reason real wages may not decline as employment declines is that contracts and regulations are in place that keep them from doing so. In effect, there are wage floors, like the price floors we encountered in Chapter 5. The most conspicuous example is union contracts.

Union Contracts   Labor union power explains wage rigidities in some industries. High wages in the U.S. steel industry, for example, undoubtedly contributed to the high costs of production in that industry, especially in the 1970s and 1980s—and to the decline of American companies in the world steel market in that period. Average wages in the steel industry in 1982 were $13.96 per hour, 64 percent more than the going wage in all manufacturing industries. (They fell sharply relative to average manufacturing wages after that.)

Unions and management share the blame when the high wages called for in their contracts make an industry uncompetitive. In many instances, unions have insisted on high wages even in the face of declining employment. Management has sometimes found it easier to pay the unions what they ask— even if doing so may not be good for the long-term health of the firm—rather than suffer the aggravation of a protracted negotiation or a strike.

It may even be in the interests of those currently employed in unionized industries to demand wages so high that they significantly reduce the demand for workers. If a union demands ever-higher wages, the employer will have an incentive to reduce the work force. But if the decline in the work force is slow enough, it can be accomplished by natural attrition (that is, by workers who choose to retire or quit). In that case, the job security of those still employed is not threatened. Nonunion workers who would be willing to work for less money are shut out by the union contract and have no way of offering to work for a lower wage.

Unions occasionally accept wage cuts in severe recessions. During the recession of the early 1980s, for example, unions in the airline, automobile, and steel industries accepted wage cuts rather than drive their firms into bankruptcy.

Economists do not agree about whether or not unions can obtain higher wages for their members over the long run than would be the case in a competitive labor market. But there is little doubt that unions slow the pace of wage adjustments. The first reason is that union contracts are for a fixed period—three years is typical. If the contract is signed just before an economic downturn, it may be more than two years before any wage adjustment, even if workers agree to one at that time. And if the economy is back on the road to recovery by the time the contract comes up for renewal, the workers' wages will have been largely insulated from the economic downturn.

The second reason union contracts may slow the adjustment process is through cost-of-living adjustment (COLA) clauses. In periods when there is high and variable inflation, union contracts frequently build in clauses that tie wage increases to the rate of inflation. Real wages are, in consequence, relatively unaffected by the rate of inflation or unemployment.

The final reason is that, to the extent that unions are sensitive in their collective bargaining to the unemployment rate, average union wages adjust slowly to changes in unemployment, since different contracts expire at different months and different years.

Union contracts, however, cannot provide the full explanation of rigid wages in the United States. There was high unemployment before unions became important, and there has been high unemployment recently, despite the steady decline of unions over the past thirty years. As the economy went into the Great Depression in 1929, only 7 percent of the labor force was unionized. In the recession of 1982, only 18.8 percent of the work force belonged to unions and the unemployment rate hit 10 percent.

UNION CONTRACTS

May reduce employment in unionized sectors.

May slow down real wage adjustment, thus contributing to cyclical unemployment.

Do not cover enough of the labor force to fully explain unemployment trends.

Implicit Contract Theory Union-contract-style wage rigidities may come about even in the absence of a union or an explicit labor contract. This is because the relations between an employer and her employees are governed by a host of implicit understandings developed over time between the firm and its workers. These implicit understandings are referred to as an **implicit contract.**

Workers are generally risk averse. Many have fixed financial commitments like monthly rent or car payments. They do not want their wages to fluctuate with every change in the demand and supply of labor. Firms can bear these market fluctuations more easily. First, the owners of firms tend to be wealthier, with a larger cushion for adjusting to variations in income. Second, in the event of a temporary shortfall of funds, companies can borrow more easily than can most workers.

Given that firms are less vulnerable to economic fluctuations than individual workers, it pays companies to provide at least some indirect "insurance" to their workers. Workers will be willing to work for a dependable firm that pays a steady wage, even if that wage is lower on average than the highly varying wages they could get elsewhere. Such a firm provides a form of insurance to its workers through an implicit contract—an understanding that the wages will not vary with the month-to-month, or even year-to-year, variations in the labor market. That is, the firm behaves *as if* it had a contract with its workers guaranteeing the wage. It is called an implicit contract because it is an understanding, not a formal or explicit contract. In these circumstances, the wage workers receive can be thought of as consisting of two parts: the "market" wage (the wage the worker could receive elsewhere) plus an adjustment for the implicit insurance component. When the market wage is relatively low, the wage received by the worker may be higher than the market wage. The worker is receiving a benefit on the implicit insurance policy. When the market wage is high, the wage received by the worker may be lower than the market wage. The difference is the premium the worker pays for wage stability.

For many industries in which long-term employment relations are common, implicit contract theory provides a convincing explanation of why wages do not vary much. But it does not explain layoffs. The risk of most concern to workers is the complete cessation of their income. Thus, implicit contract theory seems to predict that rather than laying people off, firms will engage in **work sharing;** they will reduce the hours each person works. Some firms have in fact experimented with work sharing, but it is not common. Layoffs are.

Proponents of the implicit contract theory try to explain layoffs in two ways. Both explanations are ultimately unsatisfactory. The first focuses on the fixed costs of employment and the idea that productivity shrinks more than proportionately with changes in the length of the workday. If a worker needs the first half-hour to settle into work, the last half-hour to get ready to leave, and a one-hour lunch break, then a six-hour day will lose the same two hours as an eight-hour day. So a firm seeking to cut its labor bill by 25 percent, by cutting its workday from 8 to 6 hours, would find its productivity reduced by 33 percent. This does not, in fact, explain layoffs, however, because the work sharing could simply take the form of fewer days a week rather than fewer hours a day.

The second explanation for layoffs given by implicit contract theorists is that unemployment insurance encourages layoffs. In most places, individuals are not eligible for unemployment compensation in the event of a layoff unless they work full time. (Some European countries now allow unemployment compensation for those who face reductions in their work week.) If a company trims the work week, it and its workers share the cost. If the company lays off workers instead, the government shares the cost. This is an unsatisfactory explanation because it once again only suggests a different form of work sharing—one in which there are short-term layoffs that take the form of job rotations. One group might be laid off for two months, the next group for the next two months, and so on. Job rotations such as these, in fact, are vary rare in the real world.

But the most telling criticism of implicit contract theory is that it does not really explain why wages of job seekers should fail to decline when there is unemployment. Even in the deepest recession, the labor market is like a revolving door, with people quitting jobs and some firms hiring new workers. Even if implicit contract theory could explain why some workers are laid off, it does not explain why employers do not pay new employees lower wages than they pay to their existing work force. If the wages paid to new employees fell sufficiently, presumably there would be no unemployment.

Insider-Outsider Theory   Seeking an explanation for why firms faced with recessionary conditions do not pay lower wages to new employees, economists have devised what is known as **insider-outsider theory.** Insiders in this case are those with jobs at a particular firm. Outsiders are people who want jobs at that firm.

Insider-outsider theory focuses on the importance of training costs. Each firm needs a labor force trained in the special ways that it operates. Most of the training is done by current employees, the insiders. The insiders recognize that by training new employees, outsiders, they are reducing their bargaining position with the firm. The company can promise to continue to pay them higher wages than the newcomers, but the insiders know this promise could be broken. In future bargaining situations, the employer can use the availability of the lower-wage workers to exert downward pressure on the wages of the other employees. Knowing this, the insiders refuse to cooperate with training the outsiders, unless the new employees' interests are made coincidental with their own. The firm can accomplish this only by offering similar pay. This results in wage stickiness and unemployment persists.

Insider-outsider theory holds, further, that even if the current employees were to train new, lower-paid workers, the firm should not take the new workers' willingness to work at a low wage seriously. For once an outsider has been trained, she becomes a trained insider able to extract from the firm higher wages.

Wage systems in which new workers are paid less than established workers doing the same job are called **two-tier wage systems.** Firms do not seem to like two-tier wage systems. Most such experiments—such as the contract between Ford and its workers signed in 1982, which provided that new workers be paid 85 percent of what previously hired workers received—are relatively short-lived. The Ford experiment was abandoned in 1984.

Minimum Wages   A minimum wage set by the government may result in unemployment. The minimum wage is a government-enacted price floor. To the extent that workers would accept and firms would offer wages below the minimum if they were allowed to, the minimum wage keeps the demand for labor from equaling supply. Most workers in the United States earn considerably more than the minimum wage, so minimum wage legislation has little effect on unemployment for these workers. However, many economists believe that minimum wage legislation probably does contribute *some* to the unemployment of unskilled workers, including teenagers just entering the labor force. This effect may not be strong, however. When, in 1990, the government set a special, lower minimum wage for teenagers, for example, relatively few firms availed themselves of this opportunity. They paid their teenaged employees wages that were in excess of the new minimum wage. Still, it is worth noting that in recessions, unemployment rates among unskilled workers and teenagers often increase much more than for the population as a whole.

EFFICIENCY WAGE THEORY

Even in a world without contracts, explicit or implicit, wages may not fall enough to eliminate unemployment because firms may find they make more profits by paying a wage higher than the one at which the labor market would clear. If paying higher wages leads to higher productivity, then higher wages may improve a firm's profits.

In Chapter 1, we learned that when Henry Ford opened his automobile plant in 1914, he paid his workers more than double the going wage. He wanted his workers to work hard. He knew that his new technique of production—the assembly line—when combined with motivated workers, would increase his profits. Many modern companies apply the same philosophy.

WHY DOES PRODUCTIVITY DEPEND ON WAGES?

Economists have identified three main reasons why firms may benefit if they pay high wages: wages affect the quality of the work force, the level of effort, and the rate of labor turnover. Each of these reasons has been extensively studied. In each, productivity may depend not just on the wage paid, but also on the wage paid relative to that paid by other firms and on the unemployment rate.

Quality of the Labor Force   It is all too common for companies to discover after a wage cut that they have lost the best of their workers. Indeed, this is the reason frequently given by firms for not cutting wages. This is an example of adverse selection: the average quality of those offering to work for a firm is affected adversely by a lowering of the wage.[1] If a firm lowers wages, its best workers will most likely find a new job at the old (higher) wage and therefore will most likely leave.

Level of Effort   We can easily see that it would not pay any worker to make any effort on the job if all firms paid the market-clearing wage. A worker could reason as follows: "If I shirk—put out a minimal level of effort—I will either be caught or not. If I don't get caught, I get my paycheck and have saved the trouble of making an effort. True, if I am unlucky enough to be caught shirking, I risk being fired. But by the terms of the basic competitive model, I can immediately obtain a new job at the same wage. There is, in effect, no penalty for having been caught shirking."

Firms that raise their wages above the market-clearing level will find that they have introduced a penalty for shirking, for two reasons. First, if their workers are caught shirking and are fired, they will have to take the lower wage being offered by other firms. Second, if many firms offer higher-than-market-clearing wages, unemployment will result, since at the higher wages firms as a whole will hire fewer workers. Now a worker who is fired may have to remain unemployed for a time.

[1]It should be clear that we have now moved away from the assumption that all workers are identical.

CLOSE-UP: EFFICIENCY WAGES IN TANZANIA

One of the implications of efficiency wage theory—that employers may be able to get work done more cheaply by *increasing* wages—can lead to some topsy-turvy implications. Or as Alfred Marshall, a famous economist of the late nineteenth and early twentieth centuries put it: "Highly paid labour is generally efficient and therefore not dear labour; a fact which though it is more full of hope for the future of the human race than any other that is known us, will be found to exercise a very complicating influence." The first chapter of this book gave the example of Henry Ford taking advantage of efficiency wage theory by paying higher wages in the automobile industry. But the theory can have striking implications in less developed countries too.

Consider the experience of the east African nation of Tanzania, formed by the union of Tanganyika and Zanzibar in 1964. When the area now known as Tanzania achieved independence in 1961, most wage earners worked on large plantations. Most of the workers were migrants, as is commonly the case in Africa, returning from the plantations to their home villages several times each year. The workers had low productivity and were not paid much. After independence, the government decreed that wage rates for the plantation workers would triple. Plantation owners predicted disaster; such a massive increase in the price they paid for labor, they thought, could only drive them out of business. But the government responded with predictions based on efficiency wage theory, that higher wages would lead to a more productive and stable work force.

The government predictions turned out to be correct. Sisal, for example, is a plant cultivated because it produces a strong white fiber that can be used for cord or fiber. Overall production of sisal quadrupled under the efficiency wage policy. This occurred not because of a change in the overall physical capital available, but because more motivated and highly skilled workers were better employed by the plantation owners. Over several years following the wage increase, however, employment in Tanzania's sisal industry fell from 129,000 to 42,000, thus illustrating how efficiency wages can increase unemployment.

Sources: Mrinal Datta-Chaudhuri, *Journal of Economic Perspectives* (Summer 1990), pp. 25–39; Richard Sabot, "Labor Standards in a Small Low-Income Country: Tanzania," Overseas Development Council (1988).

Consider a wage just high enough that workers are induced not to shirk. We know this wage must exceed the wage at which the demand for labor equals the supply. If one of the unemployed workers offers to work for a lower wage at a particular firm, he will not be hired. His promise to work is not credible. The firm knows that at the lower wage, it simply does not pay the worker to exert effort.

The no-shirking view of wages also provides a gloomy forecast for the consequences of well-intentioned unemployment benefits offered by government. Assume the government, concerned about the welfare of the unemployed, increases unemployment benefits. Now the cost of being unemployed is lower; hence the wage a firm must pay to induce workers to work—that is, not to shirk—is higher. As a result, wages are increased, leading to a lower level of employment. The higher unemployment benefits have increased the unemployment rate.

Higher wages may lead to higher levels of effort for another reason. They may lead to improved worker morale. If workers think the firm is taking advantage of them, they may reciprocate by taking advantage of the firm. If workers think their boss is treating them well—including paying them good wages—they will reciprocate by going the extra mile.

gift exchange

Rate of Labor Turnover   Lowering wages increases the rate at which workers quit. Economists refer to this rate as the **labor turnover rate.** It is costly to hire new workers, to find the jobs that best match their talents and interests, and to train them. So firms seek to reduce their labor turnover rate by paying high wages. The lower the wages, the more likely it is that workers will find another job more to their liking, either because it pays a higher wage or for some other reason. Thus, while firms may save a little on their direct labor costs in the short run by cutting wages in a recession, these savings will be more than offset by the increased training and hiring costs incurred as demand rises again and they have to replace lost workers. We can think of what workers produce net of the costs of hiring and training them as their *net* productivity. Higher wages, by lowering these turnover costs, lead to higher net productivity.

DETERMINING THE EFFICIENCY WAGE

If, as we have just seen, net productivity increases when a firm pays higher wages, then it may be profitable for an employer not to cut wages even if there is an excess supply of workers. This is because the productivity of the employer's work force may decline enough in response to a wage cut that the overall labor costs per unit of production will actually increase.

The employer wants to pay the wage at which total labor costs are minimized, called the **efficiency wage.** The wage at which the labor market clears —the wage at which the supply of labor equals the demand for labor—is called the market-clearing wage. There is no reason to expect the efficiency wage and the market-clearing wage to be the same. **Efficiency wage theory** suggests that labor costs may be minimized by paying a wage higher than the market-clearing wage.

If the efficiency wage is greater than the market-clearing wage, it will still pay any profit-maximizing firm to pay the efficiency wage. There will be unemployed workers who are willing to work at a lower wage, but it will not pay firms to hire them. At the lower wage, productivity will decline enough to more than offset the lower wage.

If productivity depends on wages because effort increases with the wage—the shirking view of wages—the efficiency wage *must* exceed the market-clearing level. But if productivity depends on wages for some other reason, the efficiency wage can be less than the market-clearing wage. In that case, competition for workers will bid up the wage to the competitive, market-clearing level. Firms would like to pay the lower, efficiency wage, but at that wage they simply cannot hire workers. In efficiency wage theory, the market-clearing wage thus forms a floor for wages.

In general, the efficiency wage for any firm will depend on two factors: the wage paid by other firms and the unemployment rate. The wage paid by other firms matters because if other companies pay a lower wage, a firm will find that it does not have to pay quite as high a wage to elicit a high level of effort. Workers know that if they are fired, the jobs they are likely to find will pay less. Thus, the cost of being fired is increased, and this spurs employees on to working harder. The wage paid by other firms matters for other reasons as well. If wages paid by other firms are low, then the firm will lose fewer workers to other firms if it lowers its wages, and thus the "cost" of lowering wages —increased turnover rate—will be lower. Also, firms will find it easier to hire high-quality workers at any wage if the wages paid by competitors are lower.

The unemployment rate comes into play because as it increases, firms will again find that they do not have to pay quite as high a wage to elicit a high level of effort. The workers know that if they are fired, they will have a harder time getting a new job.

Efficiency wage theory also suggests a slow adjustment process for wages. Each firm is reluctant to lower its wages until others do, for several reasons. The company worries that its best workers will be attracted by other firms. It worries that the morale of its workers, and thus their productivity, will be impaired if they see their wage is below that of similar firms. No company wants to be the leader in wage reductions. Each therefore contents itself with reducing its wage slowly, and never much below that of other firms. Gradually, as wages in all firms are lowered, employment is increased and unemployment reduced.

These patterns are in contrast to the basic competitive model, which predicts that with a relatively inelastic supply curve for labor, there will be large and quick changes in wages in response to changes in the demand for labor. It is these wage changes that prevent unemployment.

WHY ARE THERE LAYOFFS?

Efficiency wage theory also helps explain why, if the economy needs a 25 percent reduction in labor supplied, workers don't simply work thirty hours rather than forty, and save jobs for the 25 percent of their colleagues who otherwise would be laid off.

According to efficiency wage theory, the reason workers do not just work

To many Americans, it has long seemed that if you work full time fifty-two weeks a year at some job, you ought to earn enough to support yourself and your family. During the Great Depression of the 1930s, Congress gave force to that feeling by enacting the Fair Labor Standards Act of 1938. Among the provisions of the act was a requirement that most businesses pay at least a *minimum wage* to all workers. Since then, Congress has raised the minimum wage as the cost of living in the economy has increased. Because of these increases, the minimum wage has generally been about half the average wage for all workers. But during the 1980s, the minimum wage was not increased, and as it slipped to a near all-time low, it was increased with bipartisan support in 1991. But by the mid-1990s, it had again fallen to a near forty-year low. Whether it should be raised again became a heated political subject in 1996.

Economists had long opposed minimum wages, on the grounds that raising any price—including the price of labor—above the market-determined level introduced distortions; they worried that raising the minimum wage would increase unemployment among low-skilled workers. But studies conducted in the early 1990s, especially by Professors David Card and Alan Krueger of Princeton University, called into question these views. They looked for a natural experiment, two neighboring states in similar economic circumstances, but with different levels of the minimum wage. In 1992 New Jersey raised its minimum wage (but neighboring Pennsylvania did not). Focusing their attention on low-paid restaurant workers, they found no significant adverse effects. These and other studies have led to considerable agnosticism: it appears that a modest minimum wage is unlikely to have significant employment effects.

One reason suggested that employment effects might be small is the efficiency wage theory: higher wages lead to higher productivity, largely offsetting the additional costs of the higher wages. Indeed, during discussions over raising the minimum wage from \$4.25 to \$5.15 (over two years), it was estimated that at least 3 million workers earning between \$5.15 and \$5.75 an hour would also receive a pay raise. The fact that employers who do not have to raise wages *choose* to do so suggests that labor markets are not like the markets for ordinary commodities like steel; employers do worry about the impact of wages on productivity. Raising the minimum wage raises "norms" of how workers should be treated, and generates a ripple effect.

Many economists had also opposed minimum wage increases, believing that it was not a very effective way of targeting help to the poor. It used to be that many minimum wage workers were teenagers or secondary workers in families which were not poor. But increasingly, minimum wage workers have become the primary source of incomes for their families. Today, the average share of household income earned by a minimum wage worker is one-half.

A further advantage of raising the minimum wage is that it increases the incentives to work, by increasing the difference between what someone on welfare receives and what a worker gets.

Source: David Card and Alan Krueger, *Myth and Measurement,* (Princeton: Princeton University Press, 1995).

thirty hours rather than forty is that by reducing work proportionately among its workers, a firm will in effect be reducing overall pay proportionately. The company will fall back into the traps outlined above. If it lowers overall pay, it may lose a disproportionate fraction of its better workers. These workers can obtain offers of full-time work and full-time pay, and they will find this more attractive than a job with 80 percent of full-time work and 80 percent of the pay. (They may enjoy the extra leisure, but it will not help meet the mortgage payments.) Furthermore, workers now working part time will find that their incentives to exert high levels of effort decline. If they get fired, losing a part-time job is not as serious as losing a full-time job. This ability to explain concentrated layoffs is one feature that sets efficiency wage theory apart from some of the alternative views of wage rigidity.

THE IMPACT OF UNEMPLOYMENT ON DIFFERENT GROUPS

One striking aspect of unemployment in the United States is that it affects different groups in the population very differently. In competitive markets, wages will adjust to reflect productivity. Groups with higher productivity will have commensurately higher wage rates, while groups with lower productivity will have lower wage rates. But people in both groups will have jobs. There would be no reason for different groups to have different unemployment rates. Thus, we must go beyond the basic model of competitive markets to understand why unemployment affects different groups differently.

The efficiency wage theory argues that there may be some kinds of laborers—such as part-time workers or those with limited skills—who, at any wage, have sufficiently low productivity that it barely pays a firm to hire them. To put it another way, while they may receive a low wage, the wage is only just low enough to offset their low productivity. Paying higher wages would not increase productivity enough to offset the wage increase. And paying lower wages would reduce productivity, making that option unworkable as well.

It is these groups, who lie right at the margin of the firm's hiring decision, who will bear the brunt of the fluctuations in the demand for labor. Teenagers and young workers not only have higher average unemployment rates, they bear more than their proportionate share of the burden of variations in employment.

LIMITS OF EFFICIENCY WAGE THEORY

Efficiency wage theory may provide a significant part of the explanation for wage rigidities in a number of different situations: where training and turnover costs are high; where monitoring productivity is difficult; and where differences in individuals' productivity are large and important, but it is difficult to ascertain them before hiring and training them. But efficiency wage considerations are likely to be less important in situations where workers are paid piece rates on the basis of how much they produce, or in situations where training costs are low and monitoring is easy. These situations may indeed exhibit greater wage flexibility, at least if there are no union pressures, implicit contracts, or insider-outsider considerations.

OKUN'S LAW AND DISGUISED UNEMPLOYMENT

As high as the unemployment statistics sometimes climb, they still may not fully reflect the underutilization of labor. Firms find it costly to hire and train workers. When they have a temporary lull in demand, they may not even lay workers off, for fear that once laid off, the workers will seek employment elsewhere. Thus, firms keep the workers on the job, but may not fully utilize them. This is **labor hoarding,** and can be thought of as a form of disguised unemployment. Employees are not really working, though they are showing up for work. Like open unemployment, it represents a waste of human resources.

The importance of disguised unemployment was brought home by Arthur Okun, chairman of the Council of Economic Advisers under President Johnson. He showed that as the economy pulls out of a recession, output increases more than proportionately with employment; and as the economy goes into a recession, output decreases more than proportionately with the reduction in employment. This result is **Okun's law.** In Okun's study, for every 1 percentage point decrease in the unemployment rate, output increased by 3 percent. Today, most economists still think output increases more than proportionately with employment, though not as much as Okun suggested. Current estimates predict that a 1 percentage point increase in the unemployment rate will correspond to a 2 to 2.5 percent decrease in output (a 2 percent decrease in output is the rule of thumb used elsewhere in this text). This was a remarkable finding, for it seemed to run contrary to one of the basic principles of economics—the law of diminishing returns—which would have predicted that a 1 percentage point decrease in the unemployment rate would have less than a proportionate effect on output. The explanation for Okun's law, however, was simple. Many of those who were working in a recession were partially idle. As the economy heated up, they worked more fully, and this yielded the unexpected increase in output.

ALTERNATIVE EXPLANATIONS OF WAGE RIGIDITIES

1. Unions with explicit and implicit contracts prevent wages from falling. Insider-outsider theory explains why firms do not pay newly hired workers a lower wage. Minimum wages explain why wages for very low skilled workers do not fall.

2. Efficiency wage theory suggests that it is profitable for firms to pay above-market wages. This is because wages affect the quality of the labor force, labor turnover rates, and the level of effort exerted by workers.

POLICY ISSUES

This chapter has explored possible reasons why wages do not fall to the level where the demand for labor equals the supply. The truth involves a combination of all the explanations. Minimum wages may play a role among very low skilled workers. Unions play a role in some sectors of the economy. And in some jobs, firms do not cut wages because of efficiency wage considerations.

But wages do sometimes fall, as in the Great Depression. But what are important for firm decisions are wages *relative to* prices. Wages do not fall *fast enough* to equilibrate demand and supply. And all the reasons given in this chapter play a role, not only in explaining why wages do not fall, but also in helping us to understand why, when they fall, they fall slowly.

When the labor market does not clear and involuntary unemployment results, there may be an economic role for government. It is worth reviewing government policies designed to overcome failures in the labor market. Such policies have included increasing wage flexibility; reducing the costs of unemployment by providing replacement income to the unemployed; and increasing the efficiency of the labor market through reemployment programs.

INCREASING WAGE FLEXIBILITY

Those who see wage rigidities as a major cause of unemployment and believe that they are created by unions or implicit contracts have sought ways of increasing wage flexibility. In Japan, for example, large companies have long-term (lifetime) implicit contracts with their workers, but workers receive a substantial fraction of their pay in the form of annual bonuses. In effect, this means that the wage a worker receives varies from year to year depending on the fortunes of the firm. Unemployment in Japan is considerably less variable than in the United States, and many economists believe that flexible wages are an important part of the reason. In his book *The Share Economy*, Martin Weitzman of Harvard University has advocated that U.S. firms adopt a similar system.

Two features make wage flexibility unattractive to workers. First, workers would have to bear more risk in income fluctuations. Under the current U.S. system, workers who have considerable seniority, and who often dominate union negotiations, face little risk of being laid off during hard times. Their incomes are relatively secure, both from year-to-year variation and from the threat of complete cessation. With the bonus system, however, all employees, including the more senior ones, would face considerable risk. And as the discussion of implicit contracts pointed out, the firm is generally in a better position than the worker to bear the risk of economic fluctuations.

Second, workers worry that the firms most likely to be willing to give large profit shares to their employees in exchange for wage concessions may be those firms that expect the smallest profits. By giving up a share of the profit, they are giving the least away. In effect, when the workers' pay depends on the profits of the firm, workers become much like shareholders—what they receive depends on how well the company does. It does no good to own a large share in the profits of a firm that makes no profits.

This second reason makes it clear why unions do not trust wage flexibility systems. Their concern that firms without profits will be the most willing to offer to share them with their workers proved justified in 1985, when employees of Eastern Airlines actually accepted a pay reduction in return for a share of the profits. The airline went into bankruptcy soon after.

Still, the fact is that large segments of Japanese industry employ a system with greater wage flexibility, and that system seems to give rise to less variability in employment. Japan appears to have overcome the obstacles to making wages vary with profits. How this happened, whether it is possible for the United States to move to a system with more flexible wages, and what role government should play in encouraging such a move, remain questions of debate among economists.

REDUCING THE COSTS OF UNEMPLOYMENT

During the past half century, governments have made it their responsibility not only to reduce the level of unemployment but also to reduce the costs borne by those unfortunate enough to be unemployed. The difficulty is, how do we do this without giving rise to further economic problems?

UNEMPLOYMENT INSURANCE

The unemployment insurance program is the most important one for reducing the cost to the worker of being unemployed. It was started in the midst of the Great Depression with passage of the Social Security Act in 1935. Unemployment insurance programs are run by the states, within federal guidelines, and vary by state. The typical program pays up to 50 percent of a person's former salary for twenty-six weeks. In a number of instances, when the unemployment rate has increased, coverage has been extended to thirty-nine weeks or longer. To be eligible for the maximum, workers must have worked for a minimum number of weeks—forty out of the previous fifty-two, for example. Thus, new workers are not covered by unemployment insurance.

Critics of the program worry that it reduces the incentive of unemployed workers to search for jobs. There is some evidence for this. The number of people who get jobs just as their unemployment benefits expire is far greater than can be accounted for by chance. Others worry that when generous unemployment insurance is available, workers have less incentive to exert effort at any given level of wages and unemployment because the threat of being fired is not as fearsome as it would otherwise be. To restore the incentives of efficiency wages, firms must pay higher wages, but when they do, the higher cost of labor induces them to hire fewer workers. By this logic, high unemployment insurance actually contributes to increasing the unemployment rate.

What we have here is another illustration of a familiar basic trade-off. Economic arrangements that diminish risk also diminish incentives. A person who is guaranteed a job will have little incentive to work. If unemployment insurance were sufficiently generous that it fully replaced whatever income he lost if he were fired, a worker would not find any economic incentives for working. And a worker who is laid off would have no incentive to look for a new job. Thus, some critics of the current unemployment insurance system argue that we have gone too far in reducing risk—and reducing incentives.

Other critics argue that the current U.S. unemployment system is targeted to the wrong groups—that it does not provide enough support for either the long-term unemployed or new entrants into the labor force, but provides too much for the short-term unemployed. Insurance for unemployment periods of six or eight weeks may be unnecessary in the eyes of many economists. They argue that people should be able to finance these short-term spells out of savings or by borrowing. One recent study calculated that requiring an unemployed worker to wait two weeks before receiving any unemployment payments would save $1.1 billion a year in lower unemployment benefits, while still assuring a steady stream of income to the longer-term unemployed. These economists believe that in general, insurance should be designed to cover *large* losses, against which individuals cannot self-insure.

THE U.S. REEMPLOYMENT SYSTEM

In 1994 Secretary of Labor Robert Reich (who formerly taught at Harvard's Kennedy School) proposed redirecting America's unemployment system to create a "reemployment system," focusing on providing both incentives and resources to encourage more rapid transitions from one job to another. The objective of this system is to increase the efficiency of the labor market. A nationwide system of "one-stop job centers" would provide both job search and training information. Training would be directed toward available job opportunities. And to be eligible for extended unemployment insurance benefits (beyond the basic twenty-six weeks), workers would have to enroll in active training and job search programs.

REVIEW AND PRACTICE

SUMMARY

1. Involuntary unemployment exists when the supply of labor exceeds the demand for labor at the prevailing market wage. This happens when demand for labor at each wage level falls but real wages do not decline.

2. Explanations for why firms may be unable to reduce wages and thus unemployment include union contracts or implicit contracts, insider-outsider theory (which explains why firms do not pay lower wages to new hires), and minimum wage laws.

3. Reducing wages may actually lead to an increase in labor costs, because (a) it may result in a lower average quality of workers as the best workers leave; (b) it may result in lower effort; and (c) it may result in higher turnover costs.

4. Firms often do not fully utilize their labor force in economic downturns. This labor hoarding means that as the economy expands, output increases more than in proportion to increases in employment.

5. Making wages depend more on firm profits might result in less variability in employment. But workers would risk income reductions in hard times, and would worry that the firms most likely to give large profit shares to employees are those with the smallest profits to share.

6. Unemployment insurance reduces the costs to workers of being laid off, but it also reduces workers' incentives to work hard or to search for a new job. Firms' responses may lead to higher rather than lower unemployment.

KEY TERMS

implicit contract	labor turnover rate	Okun's law
work sharing	efficiency wage	
insider-outsider theory		

REVIEW QUESTIONS

1. What gives rise to involuntary unemployment?

2. List reasons why firms may be unable or unwilling to reduce wages.

3. True or false: "The prevalence of unions and minimum wage laws is the primary reason for wage stickiness, and therefore for unemployment, in the U.S. economy." Discuss your answer.

4. If an implicit contract is not written down, why would a firm abide by it? Why would a worker?

5. Why does implicit contract theory predict that work sharing is more likely than layoffs?

6. Give three reasons why productivity may depend on the level of wages paid.

7. How does an efficiency wage differ from a market-clearing wage?

8. How does efficiency wage theory help explain why different groups may have very different levels of unemployment?

9. What trade-off does society face when it attempts to expand economic security for workers with higher unemployment benefits or greater job security?

PROBLEMS

1. In 1996, Congress passed legislation increasing the minimum wage in two steps from $4.25 per hour to $5.15 per hour. Explain why efficiency wage theory suggests that the effect on employment may be relatively small.

2. Would you be more or less likely to observe implicit contracts in industries where most workers hold their jobs for only a short time? What about industries where most workers hold jobs a long time? Explain.

3. A number of businesses have proposed a two-tier wage scale, in which the wage scale for new employees is lower than the wage scale for current employees. Using the insights of insider-outsider theory, would you be more or less likely to observe two-tier wage scales in industries where a lot of on-the-job training is needed than in those where not much is needed?

4. The following figures represent the relationship between productivity and wages for the Doorware Corporation, which makes hinges.

Wage per hour	$ 8	$10	$12	$14	$16	$18	$20
Hinges produced per hour	20	24	33	42	52	58	60

Graph the productivity-wage relationship. From the graph, how do you determine the efficiency wage? Calculate output per dollar spent on labor for the Doorware Corporation. What is the efficiency wage?

5. Would you be more or less likely to see efficiency wages in the following types of industries?
   (a) industries where training and turnover costs are relatively low;
   (b) industries where it is difficult to monitor individual productivity;
   (c) industries that have many jobs where individual differences in productivity are relatively large.

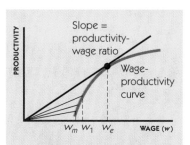

Figure 34.4 THE RELATIONSHIP BETWEEN PRODUCTIVITY AND WAGES

As wages rise, productivity increases, at first quickly and then more slowly. The efficiency wage is the wage at which the ratio of productivity to wage is highest. It is found by drawing a line through the origin tangent to the wage-productivity curve.

APPENDIX: DERIVATION OF THE EFFICIENCY WAGE

Figure 34.4 depicts a curve that represents one possible relationship between productivity and wages. We refer to this curve as the **wage-productivity curve.** Productivity here can be thought of as "the number of pins produced in an hour," or any similar measure of output. There is a minimum wage, w_m, below which the firm will find it difficult, if not impossible, to obtain labor. At a very low wage, w_1, the company can only hire the dregs of the labor market —those who cannot get jobs elsewhere. Worker morale is low, and effort is low. Workers quit as soon as they can get another job, so labor turnover is high.

As the firm raises its wage, productivity increases. The company earns a reputation as a high-wage firm, attracting the best workers. Morale is high, turnover is low, and employees work hard. But eventually, as in so many areas, diminishing returns set in. Successive increases in wages have incrementally smaller effects on productivity. The firm is concerned with wage costs per unit of output, not wage costs per employee. Thus, it wishes to minimize not the wage but the wage divided by productivity.

This can be put another way. The company wishes to maximize the output per dollar spent on labor (we are assuming that all other costs are fixed). Since productivity is defined as output per unit of time (pins per hour), and the wage is labor cost per unit of time (dollars per hour), dividing productivity by the wage produces the equation

$$\frac{\text{productivity}}{\text{wage}} = \frac{\text{output/unit of time}}{\text{dollars/unit of time}} = \frac{\text{output}}{\text{dollars spent on labor}}.$$

Thus, a decision to make the ratio of output to dollars spent on labor as high as possible is mathematically equivalent to a decision to make the ratio of productivity to wages as high as possible. To tell what level of wages will accomplish this goal, Figure 34.4 shows the productivity-wage ratio as the slope of a line from the origin to a point on the wage-productivity curve. The slope of this line is the ratio of productivity (the vertical axis) to the wage (the horizontal axis).

As we draw successive lines from the origin to points on the wage-productivity curve with higher wages, the slope first increases and then decreases. The slope is largest for the line through the origin that is just tangent to the wage-productivity curve. The wage at this point of tangency is the wage at which labor costs are minimized: the efficiency wage, w_e.

Figure 34.5 shows that changes in unemployment rates may shift the wage-

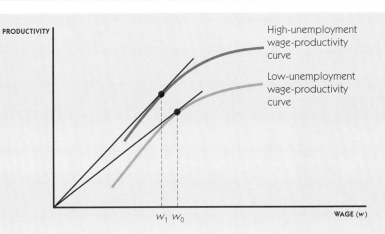

Figure 34.5 SHIFTING THE PRODUCTIVITY-WAGE RELATIONSHIP

If unemployment is low, workers have many alternative job possibilities. With the threat of being fired reduced, at each wage workers work less hard, so productivity is lower. In the case shown here, the efficiency wage will be lower when there is high unemployment than when there is low unemployment.

PRODUCTIVITY

High-unemployment wage-productivity curve

Low-unemployment wage-productivity curve

w_1 w_0

WAGE (w)

productivity curve. At each wage, the productivity of the labor force is higher at the higher unemployment rate. Also, the efficiency wage—the wage at which the ratio of productivity to the wage is maximized—is lowered slightly. It falls from w_0 to w_1. The change in the efficiency wage may be relatively small, even if the shift in the curve relating productivity to wages is relatively large.

CHAPTER 35

INFLATION VS. UNEMPLOYMENT: APPROACHES TO POLICY

Making economic policy can be like walking a tightrope. Lean too far one way, and unemployment increases. Lean too far the other way, and prices rise. It is even possible to have the worst of all worlds: simultaneous inflation, unemployment, and slow growth.

Many of the basic macroeconomic problems stem from variability in the level of economic activity. When the economy is dragging along, a jump start may be required to reignite it. But when the economy is racing, inflation may loom. Both unemployment and inflation cause economic hardship. Unemployment particularly affects the young, who have no cushion of accumulated savings to fall back upon, as well as blacks, Hispanics, and unskilled workers. Inflation takes its toll among those retired people whose incomes do not rise commensurately with inflation.

After briefly reviewing these costs, this chapter focuses on the major policy issues: Should the government intervene to stabilize the economy? If so, how? With monetary or fiscal policy? It then illustrates some of the basic issues by a historical review of the major policy debates over the past three decades.

KEY QUESTIONS

1. What are the key issues facing policymakers as they decide whether to stimulate (or dampen) the economy? What are the costs, actual and perceived, of inflation? Of unemployment?

2. What are the alternative explanations of the pronounced fluctuations in the level of economic activity in the economy? Why does the economy periodically experience a downturn in which unemployment is high, growth slows down, and output actually falls?

3. Why do some economists believe the government should not intervene to stabilize the economy? Why do they believe that such intervention is unnecessary, ineffective, or more likely to do harm than good? And why do other economists believe that intervention can be helpful?

4. How can government attempt to dampen economic fluctuations and reduce the NAIRU, below which inflation starts to accelerate?

5. What have been some of the major policy debates over the past three decades? How do they illustrate general principles?

THE IMPACT OF INFLATION AND UNEMPLOYMENT

When should policymakers act to stimulate or dampen the economy? Each decision involves a trade-off. Consider the problem facing U.S. policymakers in 1994 and 1995, as the unemployment rate decreased from 7 percent to 6 percent to 5.4 percent. Everyone agreed that at some point, inflationary pressures would set in. The question was, when? If, for instance, the Fed acted too early and raised interest rates too much, the recovery could stall, throwing the economy back into recession. If it waited too long, inflation would increase. How much would it cost to bring inflation down? What would be the costs of a higher level of inflation?

THE BASIC TRADE-OFFS

The discussions of earlier chapters have set the scene for how policymakers approach these decisions: the costs of high unemployment—including the loss in output—are apparent. Typically, lowering the unemployment rate by 1 percentage point (say from 7 to 6 percent) increases output by 2 percent. In a $10 trillion economy, this translates into $200 billion per year.

Inflation too has its costs, though the discussion of Chapter 33 suggested that at the low levels of inflation that have prevailed in the United States during the past fifteen years, some of those costs are more perceived than real.

Chapter 33 also clarified the trade-offs. Today, the focus is not so much on trading a little more inflation for a temporary lowering of the unemployment rate. Governments recognize that they cannot permanently run the economy at a rate lower than the NAIRU without inflation accelerating, and most do not seem even willing to take advantage of the short-run gains from reduced unemployment, which typically occur earlier than the inflation costs, which are felt only with a lag. Today, the debate focuses more on risk: if there is uncertainty about the NAIRU, how aggressive or conservative should government be? How willing should it be to risk an increase in inflation, at the cost of failing to use the economy's resources as fully as they might be used? But in assessing these risks, economists continue to evaluate the costs of inflation and of unemployment. Not surprisingly, those who worry more about unemployment argue for more aggressive policies, while those who worry about inflation argue for conservative policies.

DIFFERENT VIEWS OF TRADE-OFFS

Key in understanding these different positions is the recognition that unemployment and inflation impact different groups. Low-wage workers and other disadvantaged groups are the most likely to benefit from low unemployment policies. Since they have little savings, they bear little of the costs of inflation. The costs of *unanticipated* increases in inflation are typically borne most by those who hold long-term bonds—who see the value of those bonds decrease as nominal interest rates increase, as typically happens when inflation increases.

It is thus not surprising that unions typically push for more aggressive macroeconomic policies, and that Wall Street bondholders push for more conservative policies. Since more aggressive policies typically entail the Fed's lowering interest rates—a major cost for firms who typically borrow to finance inventories and purchases of plant and equipment—and lead to higher levels of output, both of which are good for business, it is also not surprising that businesses, such as the National Association of Manufacturers, also typically support more aggressive policies. The split in views is often characterized as a difference in views between Main Street and Wall Street.

PERSPECTIVES ON FLUCTUATIONS AND MACROECONOMIC POLICY

There is widespread agreement on the desirability of high growth, low unemployment, and low and stable inflation. But economists disagree about the role and means of government in pursuing these objectives. Some economists believe that government attempts at intervention have little effect, or worse, only destabilize the economy. Others argue that government interventions are generally successful.

For simplicity, we can split economists into two broad groups on these issues—interventionists and non-interventionists. Non-interventionists tend to have great faith in markets and little faith in government. Believing the economy adjusts quickly and efficiently to disturbances, non-interventionists see little role for government action. Interventionists argue that because markets adjust slowly, there may be extended periods of unemployment, and government policies can restore the economy to full employment faster than the market would do on its own.

Figure 35.1 shows the rate of change of output over the past 125 years. The figure illustrates the central challenge in "managing" the economy: its variability. It is not as if there is an isolated episode in which the aggregate demand curve shifts to the left, resulting in unemployment. The prescription then would be simple: use monetary or fiscal policy to shift the aggregate demand curve back to the right. The problem is that the economy is always changing, always fluctuating. Some non-interventionists accept that markets may adjust slowly, but argue that government efforts do more harm than good. There is a real fear that because of the length of time it takes for policies to be put into effect, the government will be stimulating the economy just when it should be dampening it, and vice versa. There are some economists

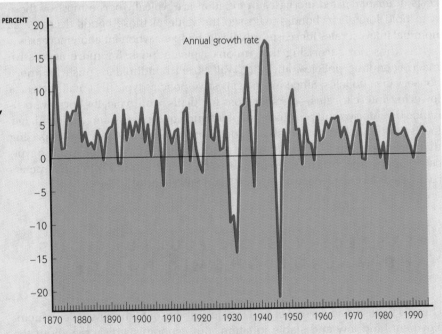

Figure 35.1 RATE OF CHANGE OF OUTPUT, 1870–1995

Output growth has varied markedly over the past 125 years, but appears to have been more volatile before World War II than after, when the government actively tried to stabilize the economy. *Sources:* Angus Maddison, *Dynamic Forces in Capitalist Development,* Oxford University Press, 1991; *ERP* (1996).

who think that government policies have actually contributed to the economy's fluctuations. Views concerning whether government should or should not intervene depend strongly on views concerning the origins and nature of the economy's fluctuations.

ECONOMIC FLUCTUATIONS

Figure 35.2A shows the movement of U.S. economic output over the past forty-five years. A smooth line has been drawn through the data, tracing out the path the economy would have taken had it grown at a steady rate. This line represents the economy's **long-term trend.** The economy is sometimes above the trend line and sometimes below. Panel B shows the percentage by which the economy has been below or above trend for the past sixty-five years. It also shows the unemployment rate, to illustrate the negative correlation between these deviations of output from trend and unemployment. The term "recession" is reserved for periods in which output actually declines, but even growth at a substantially lower rate represents an economic slowdown, with significant consequences.

Figure 35.2 ECONOMIC FLUCTUATIONS: OUTPUT

Panel A shows how real output has moved above and below a long-term trend line over the past forty-five years. Panel B compares the deviation of GDP from its long-term trend with the unemployment rate. Notice that when GDP is above its long-term rate, unemployment tends to be low; and when GDP is below its long-term rate, unemployment tends to be higher. *Source: ERP* (1995), Tables B-1, B-40, B-116.

Figure 35.3 THE DURATION OF ECONOMIC EXPANSIONS

Over the past fifty years, there has been a high variability in the length of time that economic expansions have lasted. The average is 50 months, the shortest 12 months, and the longest 106 months. As this book goes to press, the expansion that began in 1991 has lasted more than 68 months. *Source: ERP* (1996), Chart 2-11.

At one time, economists thought there was a certain inevitability to these economic fluctuations—they were so regular that they were called business cycles. But at least since World War II, the length of time between recessions has been extremely variable, as Figure 35.3 shows. Average duration of an expansion is 50 months, the shortest 12 months, and the longest 106 months. The expansion that began in 1991 has exceeded the postwar average.

It used to be thought that there *had* to be a downturn every four years. As an expansion entered its fourth year, everyone looked toward a recession around the corner. It was as if expansions *had* to die of old age. But there is little evidence that economic expansions die of old age—an economic downturn is almost as likely to occur after three years of an expansion as after five years, as Figure 35.4 shows. But Figure 35.4 also illustrates that economic downturns tend not only to be much shorter than expansions, but the longer they last, the more likely they are to end. The reason for this is partly that the longer the recession, the stronger the pressure for action to stimulate the economy.

While the length of downturns and upturns has been highly variable, there are still distinct patterns associated with the economy's fluctuations. In downturns, not only does output growth slow down (and sometimes even become negative), but unemployment increases. Hours worked per worker tend to decline, inflation tends to slow, and in some cases, prices even start to fall.

While economists agree that the economy has been marked by fluctuations exhibiting these distinctive patterns, they disagree about the *causes* and what government should do. Some believe that the underlying sources of the fluctuations are **exogenous** shocks—that is, disturbances originating outside the economy, such as wars that start a boom. Others focus on **endogenous** factors, that is, properties of the economy itself, such as a tendency of the economy to become overconfident in expansions, leading to overinvestment (including overinvestment in inventories), leading in turn to a downturn as

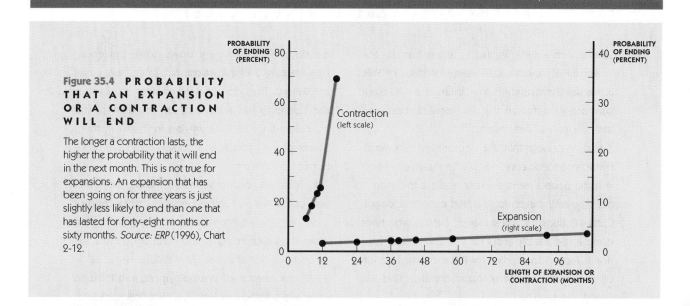

Figure 35.4 PROBABILITY THAT AN EXPANSION OR A CONTRACTION WILL END

The longer a contraction lasts, the higher the probability that it will end in the next month. This is not true for expansions. An expansion that has been going on for three years is just slightly less likely to end than one that has lasted for forty-eight months or sixty months. *Source: ERP* (1996), Chart 2-12.

investment slows down once the overinvestment is recognized. Today, most economists think economic fluctuations involve a mixture of exogenous and endogenous factors: an external shock (such as an increase in the price of oil) may hit an economy, but endogenous factors may sometimes amplify the initial effects and make them more persistent.

Some of the variation in economic activity is an inevitable consequence of people's inability to predict the future perfectly. There will be times in which firms overestimate demand and produce too much. When production exceeds sales, inventories build up. As inventories build up, firms are induced to cut back on their production. And by the same token, government interventions designed to stabilize the economy may not do so, and may even exacerbate the fluctuations, because government cannot predict perfectly where the economy is going. Indeed, in many cases, it may not even know with much precision where the economy is today. Data gauging the health of the economy become available only with a lag.

Most economic downturns in the postwar period in the United States have been associated with large increases in interest rates by the Fed; but these increases in turn have been motivated by evidence of actual or incipient inflation. In some cases, such as the oil price shock of 1973, exogenous shocks played a role in accelerating inflation. In other cases, the natural buoyancy of the economy has led aggregate demand to outpace aggregate supply. Economists disagree whether monetary policy could have more finely tuned the economy: By a timely raising of interest rates, could it have kept aggregate demand moving precisely in step with aggregate supply, so that inflation did not pick up, and so that the Fed could have avoided "slamming on the brakes"? Or, having failed to stop the inflation, could it have slowed down the economy

CLOSE-UP: THE POLITICAL BUSINESS CYCLE

Several economists, including Bruno Frey of the University of Zurich and William Nordhaus of Yale University, have argued that there is an intimate connection between the electoral process and the economy's fluctuations.

First, they note that the electorate is very sensitive to economic conditions. When unemployment is high, people tend to vote against the incumbents, blaming them for the bad economic conditions. Political scientists and economists have done a remarkably accurate job using these economic factors to predict, for instance, the fraction of seats in the House of Representatives that will change party.

Second, these economists note that politicians are aware of this. Since politicians like to get re-elected, they plan for economic policies to be favorable at the time of election.

The third part of the theory maintains that the electorate is shortsighted. These economists argue that it pays politicians to overstimulate the economy as elections approach, even though this may (and systematically does) have adverse effects after the election. The overheated economy generates inflation; to quell the inflation, after the election, the government slows down the economy, causing unemployment. But voters' memories are limited. They do not hold grudges. So long as the economy has recovered by the time of the *next* election, they are forgiving. In this view, then, the electoral process is a primary source of economic fluctuations.

Interestingly, economic models forecasting election outcomes performed badly in the election of 1992, in which Clinton defeated Bush, and 1994, when the Republicans took control of both houses of Congress for the first time in four decades. In 1992, the combined unemployment and inflation rates were sufficiently low by historical standards that Bush should have been re-elected, according to most of the models. In 1994, the economic conditions, as measured by those two variables, were at a three-decade high, so incumbents should have done extremely well. But in both 1992 and 1994 incumbents were defeated. One explanation sometimes made was that in both cases, voters were expressing dissatisfaction. Though macroeconomic statistics were favorable, real incomes of many Americans had stagnated—or even declined—from the early 1970s to the early 1990s.

President George Bush on the campaign trail in July 1992

more gradually, and thus avoided as deep a recession at the same time that it lowered inflation?

Interventionists believe that appropriate policies can both reduce the endogenous forces that either give rise to or help sustain fluctuations—for instance by strengthening the automatic stabilizers discussed in Chapter 32—and increase the likelihood that interventions actually stabilize the economy.

THE NON-INTERVENTIONIST PERSPECTIVE

Those who share the view that government should not intervene to stabilize the economy differ in their reasons. Some believe that the economy is efficient, so that there is little that government can add; others believe that government action is ineffective; while still others believe that governments do have significant effects—but more often make matters worse. We now take a closer look at each of these perspectives.

REAL BUSINESS CYCLE THEORY: INTERVENTION IS UNNECESSARY

Intervention is clearly unnecessary if the economy always operates efficiently, at full employment. **Real business cycle** theorists attribute the economy's fluctuations to exogenous shocks, such as the 1973 and 1979 oil price increases, but believe that markets adjust quickly—prices and wages are sufficiently flexible that full employment will be restored quickly—and certainly more quickly than it would take government to recognize a problem, take actions, and have an effect. Since the economy typically operates at full employment, government need only worry about inflation. But recall from our discussion of Part Five that when the economy is at full employment, prices tend to increase with the money supply. Price stability—and full employment—can be attained if the monetary authorities let the money supply expand at the rate of increase in real GDP.

NEW CLASSICAL MACROECONOMICS: INTERVENTION IS INEFFECTIVE

Some non-interventionists claim that the government cannot even have an effect on output in the short run, because the private sector largely undoes any government action. Thus, if the government increases the money supply, with rational expectations, all market participants recognize that this will simply have an effect on the price level. Price levels adjust instantaneously, so that the *real* money supply is unchanged. The expansionary effects of the increase in money supply are thus completely counteracted, and monetary policy has no *real* effects. Similarly, an increase in the government deficit is perfectly offset by an increase in private savings as households foresee the need for higher taxes in the future.

The view that policies are largely ineffective, and to the extent that they are effective, it is only in the very short run—with no permanent gains—was strongly advanced by the **new classical economists,** led by Robert Lucas of the University of Chicago.

INTERVENTION IS COUNTERPRODUCTIVE

Faith in markets is one thing; faith in the ability of government to improve on markets is another. Some non-interventionists see more shortcomings in markets than do real business cycle theorists and new classical economists, but nonetheless have little confidence in the ability of government to improve macroeconomic performance. Indeed, some hold the view that intervention is counterproductive, for two reasons.

First, they recognize that there are important **lags**—between the time the government recognizes a problem and takes action, and between the time the action occurs and its macroeconomic effects are fully realized. By the time the effects are fully realized, the action may no longer be appropriate. Lags by themselves would not be a problem if the government could accurately forecast where the economy is going and the exact effects of policy on the economy. But everyone—including the government—sees the future with a cloudy crystal ball, and as a result, governments risk taking the wrong action. In recent years, governments have become much more sensitized to the problem of timing. One of the reasons given for President Bush's reluctance to take strong actions to stimulate the economy in the midst of the economic downturn in 1991, was a worry that, given the shallowness of the recession, the economy might quickly recover on its own, making any extra government expenditures or reductions in taxes unnecessary and potentially harmful.

Second, critics of strong interventionist policies argue that there are systematic political reasons that interventions are often misguided. Politicians want the economy to be strong before an election. They thus tend to overheat the economy, with gains in employment showing up before the election, but costs, in terms of inflation, showing up (hopefully) only after the election.

RULES VS. DISCRETION: THE NON-INTERVENTIONIST PERSPECTIVE

Critics of intervention claim that historically, whether because of political motivations, or simply because of the lags described earlier, the government has actually exacerbated the economy's fluctuations. When the government attempts to dampen a boom, its policies reducing demand take effect just as the economy is weakening, reinforcing the downward movement. Conversely, when the government attempts to stimulate the economy, the increase in demand kicks in as the economy is strengthening on its own, thereby igniting inflation. Thus, critics of government action, such as Nobel Prize–winning economist Milton Friedman, now at Stanford's Hoover Institution, and formerly of the University of Chicago, conclude that economic policy should be based on simple *rules* rather than the *discretion* of government policymakers. For example, **monetarists** like Friedman believe the government should expand the money supply at a constant rate, rather than adjusting the money supply in response to specific economic events or conditions. According to Friedman and others, by sticking to such rules, the government would eliminate a major source of uncertainty and instability in the economy: uncertainty about future government policy.

Furthermore, they believe not only that government should pursue certain rules, but that it should have its hands tied, so that it has no choice. The reason for this is that even if the government today promised to follow certain rules—such as not trying to stimulate the economy should there be a downturn—it will not (or politically, cannot) follow those rules. The problem of whether the government will actually carry out a promised course of action is called the problem of **dynamic consistency.** The government may announce that a particular tax change is permanent—and it might even deceive itself into believing that the tax change is permanent. But when circumstances change, policies will change. And the fact that policies will change—and that individuals and firms expect them to change—has enormous consequences for the behavior of individuals and firms. In 1981, for instance, new legislation gave special tax breaks to the real estate industry. These breaks were intended (by the legislation) to be permanent. A real estate boom resulted. The boom is partly attributed to builders rushing to take advantage of the tax break which they believed would eventually be repealed. They were right: the tax advantages were repealed in 1986.

THE INTERVENTIONIST PERSPECTIVE

The most compelling case for intervention is based on the belief that without intervention, recovery may take an unconscionably long time and that there are interventions which on balance can reduce the economy's fluctuations. As a practical matter, governments *must* intervene: political pressures will not allow them to sit idly by if the economy goes into a deep recession. In any case, the Fed must make decisions constantly about what to do. Even to keep the money supply constant, or to increase it at a fixed rate, requires decisions: forecasts about what the money supply would be in the absence of Fed action, and judgments about the consequences of particular actions.

The underlying assumption of the non-interventionists is that markets adjust quickly and so unemployment is, at most, a short-term affair. There have been periods in which this assumption seems unpersuasive: in the Great Depression, high unemployment persisted for many years. Unemployment rates in some European countries have exceeded 10 percent for more than a decade. Earlier chapters have explained both the reasons for, and consequences of, wage and price stickiness. As a practical matter, when unemployment rates are high, governments are under enormous pressures to reduce them.

Today, the leading school of thought of economists who believe that government can and should intervene to stabilize the economy is called **New Keynesianism.** They share Lord Keynes's view that unemployment may be persistent, and that though there may be market forces which restore the economy to full employment, those forces work so slowly that government action is required. The New Keynesian theories differ from older Keynesian analyses in their emphasis on microeconomics—they share, for instance, with many real business cycle and new classical economists, a view that the economy consists largely of profit-maximizing competitive firms, though they typically believe that markets often deviate significantly from the *perfectly* *competitive* ideal assumed by real business cycle and new classical theories. But they have identified a variety of reasons—such as costs of adjustment and imperfections of information—why markets do not adjust quickly to disturbances.

Moreover, they agree that while there are forces which enable the economy to dampen and absorb exogenous shocks, there are also endogenous forces which sometimes amplify shocks and make them more persistent. Noninterventionists emphasize the former forces. As firms cut back production in response to an inventory buildup, wages and prices fall. At these low prices and wages, firms decide it is a good time to buy new machines; households may decide it is a good time to buy durables and new houses. These decisions help raise aggregate demand, offsetting the dampening effect of the excess inventories.

By contrast, New Keynesian economists emphasize the forces within the economy which amplify fluctuations and help make those fluctuations persist. Thus, the fall in the price of oil in 1985 might have been viewed as a good thing for the economy—the reverse of the increase in the price of oil in 1973 and 1979. But the unanticipated fall in the price of oil led to massive disruptions and bankruptcies in oil-producing states; these in turn weakened the real estate market and banking system in those states, leading to an overall contraction of economic activity. The impacts were felt well beyond the oil industry, and in the process of being disseminated through the region, seemed to be amplified.

THE MULTIPLIER-ACCELERATOR

The most widely discussed of the systematic endogenous forces that amplify fluctuations is called the multiplier-accelerator. We already encountered the multiplier: an upturn in exports is amplified by the multiplier, so that the increase in GDP may be two or more times the increase in exports. But matters do not stop here: the increase in GDP leads firms to want to invest more to meet the increased demand for goods. Typically, it takes around $2 to $3 of capital to produce $1 of GDP. Thus, if firms expect output to increase by, say, $100 billion, they will want to increase their capital stock by $200 to $300 billion. This is called the **accelerator.** As firms increase their investment, GDP grows even more. Increased investment of $200 billion results in a further increase of GDP by $400 billion, if the multiplier is 2. But this increase in GDP may give rise to a further increase in the demand for investment. Thus, the multiplier and accelerator help to amplify and propagate what was initially an exogenous shock—an increase in exports.

Not only does the structure of the economy serve to amplify and propagate external shocks, it may also, on its own, convert an expansion into a downturn. To see how this occurs, consider what happens as the economy continues to expand. Eventually, it hits constraints. For example, shortages of labor may impose a limit on the expansion of the economy. Once these constraints are hit, the economy stops expanding, or at least stops expanding as fast. But when the economy expands at a slower rate, the demand for investment decreases. And because of the multiplier effects, this reduces aggregate demand. A downturn in the economy thus begins. As output declines, investment drops lower, further accentuating the decline. Investment comes to a standstill. But eventually the old machines wear out or become obsolete. Even to produce the low level of output associated with the recession, new investment is required. This new investment stimulates demand, which in turn stimulates investment; the economy turns up.

OTHER SOURCES OF AMPLIFICATION

There are other reasons that the internal structure of the economy may amplify fluctuations. For instance, firms rely heavily on profits as a source of funds for investment. They may face constraints on the amounts they can borrow and they may find it impossible to raise funds by issuing new shares, or feel that the cost of doing so is so unattractive, that they would prefer to rely on internally generated funds. As the economy goes into a downturn, profits fall; decreased profits lead to decreased investment, exacerbating the economic downturn.

While New Keynesians agree that adjustments in interest rates and prices may *partially* offset these destabilizing influences—lower interest rates providing greater impetus for firms to invest, for instance, in a recession—these adjustments are simply too weak to offset them fully.

SCHOOLS OF THOUGHT IN MACROECONOMIC POLICY

NONINTERVENTIONISTS

Real business cycle theorists believe fluctuations in economic activity are due to exogenous shocks and that markets respond quickly to economic disturbances. Government intervention is unnecessary.

New classical economists think that policies can have no long-run effect because the private sector anticipates the effects of policy and undoes them. Policies can only have a real effect in the short run, and then only if prices do not respond quickly.

Others believe that even though markets adjust slowly, discretionary macroeconomic policies make matters worse rather than better because of lags in determining the need for policy and then implementing it.

INTERVENTIONISTS

New Keynesians think markets respond slowly, so periods of unemployment can be extended. Discretionary macroeconomic policy can be effective.

Business cycles may be endogenous phenomena and forces exist that amplify fluctuations. Governments should both engage in discretionary macroeconomic policies and design built-in stabilizers that make the economy more stable.

POLICIES TO IMPROVE ECONOMIC PERFORMANCE

Interventionists claim not only that markets, by themselves, do not ensure full employment, but that government interventions can *and have* contributed to the stability of the economy. While there *are* instances in the past in which government actions may have exacerbated an economic downturn, they believe that by and large the government's record is a positive one, as evidenced, for instance, by Figure 35.1. In the period before World War II, government did not systematically try to stabilize the economy; it appears that the variability of output was higher—with many more episodes when not only did growth slow down, but output actually decreased.

While academic economists often debate *whether* government should intervene, most policy debates center around *when* and *how*. There are three sets of policies designed to improve the economy's economic performance.

First, government should attempt to change the structure of the economy to make it more stable. Automatic stabilizers (discussed in Chapter 32), which automatically lead to increased government expenditures when the economy goes into a downturn, are the most important example.

Second, it should use *discretionary* policy to stimulate the economy when output is low and unemployment high, and to dampen the economy when inflation is strong.

Third, it should attempt to lower the NAIRU, so that price stability (stable inflation) can be attained at a lower level of unemployment.

RULES VS. DISCRETION: AN INTERVENTIONIST PERSPECTIVE

Interventionists argue that discretionary macroeconomic policy can and has helped stabilize the economy. They also argue that the historical record shows why it is not possible to follow simple rules. Consider, for instance, the simple rule discussed earlier—that the money supply should simply increase at a constant rate, the rate of increase of *real* GDP. Since the monetary authorities do not directly control the money supply, this still entails some discretion: they must forecast what will be happening to the economy and, on the basis of that, make judgments concerning what policies to undertake so that the money supply will expand at the desired rate. While such policies enjoyed enormous popularity at the end of the 1970s and in the early 1980s, at least some of their consequences were viewed unfavorably. In the United States, under Fed chairman Paul Volcker, the seemingly single-minded pursuit of this policy led interest rates to soar—to over 17 percent—and to the worst recession in half a century. Furthermore, as we saw in Chapter 31, the marked changes in the relationship between the monetary aggregates (money supply) and output which have occurred during the past two decades removed the theoretical underpinnings of this approach. Inevitably, central banks must use discretion, if only to judge whether there has been a change in the structure of the economy.

INFLATION–UNEMPLOYMENT TRADE-OFFS

What should the government do when it intervenes actively? The analysis of Chapter 33 provides the analytic basis for these decisions. Clearly, we would like to have both low rates of inflation and low rates of unemployment. But is there a trade-off? Can we get, say, lower rates of unemployment only by allowing the inflation rate to increase?

In the years immediately following the discovery of the Phillips curve, most economists thought that there was a trade-off. Those economists who thought the costs of inflation were high argued for a high unemployment rate, while those who thought the benefits of low inflation paled in comparison with the costs of unemployment argued for somewhat lower unemployment rates. Thus disagreements about policy largely hinged upon disagreements about the *costs* of inflation and unemployment. Economists who focused on the hardship that unemployment imposed on workers advocated low unemployment policies; those who focused on the impact of inflation on investors (including retired individuals who depend on interest payments to live) advocated low inflation policies.

But in the 1970s, as the unemployment rate and inflation rate increased together and as economists became more aware of the importance of inflationary expectations and inflation inertia there developed an increasing consensus that the economy could not enjoy a sustained level of unemployment below the NAIRU, without ever-increasing inflation.

There still remained two elements of disagreement about the nature of the trade-off. First, while there was agreement that the long-run Phillips curve was (at least close to) vertical, some economists thought that in the short run—for a period of perhaps several years—the economy could experience lower unemployment while inflation increased only moderately. Others worried that with rational expectations, even short periods of low unemployment—unemployment below the NAIRU—could give rise to high levels of inflation. They saw the economy as standing on a precipice: leaning toward too low a level of unemployment quickly leads to soaring inflation.

The experience within the United States over the past fifteen years strongly suggests that those worries were unfounded. Slight deviations above or below the NAIRU seem to lead to slight increases or decreases in the rate of inflation. The economy does not stand on a precipice.

The second disagreement concerned the costs of "disinflation"—the name given to reducing the inflation rate. Assume policymakers made a mistake, and pushed the unemployment rate below the NAIRU. Inflation increased slightly. What would it take to reduce inflation? Clearly, the economy would have to operate for a while at a higher level of unemployment—at a level above the NAIRU. Those who advocated a cautious policy—making sure that

From 1992 to 1994 the economy recovered gradually from the 1991 recession. The unemployment rate fell slowly from 7.6 percent to 5.4 percent. As unemployment approached what was then viewed as the NAIRU of around 6 percent, the Fed became worried about an overheated economy. It started to raise interest rates. Beginning in 1994 it raised interest rates six times, for a total increase of 3 percent. The hope was for a "soft landing"—a smooth transition from recovery to sustained growth without an overshooting that would lead to inflation—which in turn would lead to higher interest rates, which in turn would lead to a new economic downturn. (See the figure below for a depiction of a soft landing versus the more typical overshooting pattern.)

Later, however, as the economy's unemployment rate gradually fell in 1996, to a low of 5.1 percent and growth increased, it appeared in retrospect that the Fed had achieved a landing, which if not perfect, was as smooth as any in recent decades. In fact, the Fed did not forecast correctly where the economy was going; indeed, because data became available with a lag, it did not even have an accurate picture of where the economy was at the time it acted. Critics argued vociferously against the interest rate hikes of December 1994 and February 1995, saying that they saw weaknesses in the economy down the road. The Fed ignored these warnings. Revised data issued in January 1996 showed that even as the Fed was increasing interest rates in February 1995, growth had stalled out—in the first quarter of 1995 it was less than one-half of one percent. As data came in through the spring of 1995 and worries about an economic slowdown mounted, the soft landing had been converted into a "bumpy soft landing."

the unemployment rate never fell below the NAIRU—worried that the costs of reducing inflation were very high. In particular, they looked to the experience of the 1970s and 1980s: to wring the inflationary expectations of the 1970s (when inflation hit double-digit levels) out of the economy, the United States had to go through a deep recession.

But the evidence from attempts to reduce more moderate inflation suggests that the costs are low. Indeed, the loss in output and employment from "killing" inflation are matched by the gains in output and employment during the period in which unemployment remained below the NAIRU.

CONTROVERSIES IN MACROECONOMIC POLICY

Evaluating the Costs of Inflation and Unemployment

How large are the costs of moderate inflation?

How large are the costs of unemployment?

Since the costs of inflation and the costs of unemployment are borne by different individuals, how do we "value" these different costs?

Trade-offs

How quickly will attempts to lower unemployment below the NAIRU lead to increases in prices and price expectations? How quickly will runaway inflation set in? Does the economy sit on a precipice?

Are there large costs associated with disinflation? What is the relationship between these costs and the benefits that the economy achieved in the period during which unemployment was lower than the NAIRU?

IMPLEMENTING POLICIES: TARGETS

So far, we have focused our discussion on *what are the trade-offs* and *what should be the objectives of macroeconomic policy.* But even when there is agreement about the objectives of macroeconomic policy, there may be disagreements about how best to achieve those objectives. For instance, the government might believe that the NAIRU is 5.6 percent, and might wish to keep the unemployment rate at that level, but it does not directly control the unemployment rate. The Fed might want to keep the inflation rate at 3 percent, but it does not directly control the inflation rate. Over the years, economists have come up with a variety of "targets"—intermediate variables, not necessarily of interest for their own sake, but which are easier to control than the variables of real interest, and which are (or were thought at the time to be) closely related to the variables of real concern. Thus, in the late 1970s and early 1980s, many central banks focused on the **monetary aggregates,** the statistics

Throughout the 1990s a central problem facing the Fed has been the uncertainty about the NAIRU. The Fed must assess the risks—the costs and benefits—associated with "overshooting" versus those of setting one's sights too low.

In 1994, for instance, some economists thought that the NAIRU was at 6.0 percent, while others thought that it had been lowered to around 5.6 percent. What if the Fed has assumed the NAIRU was 5.6 percent, when it was actually 6.0 percent? In Chapter 33, we learned that the sacrifice ratio gives the amount by which the unemployment rate has to be maintained above the NAIRU for one year to lower the inflation rate by 1 percentage point. It is conventionally estimated at around 2. Conversely, lowering the unemployment rate for a full year by .4 percentage points below the NAIRU increases the inflation rate by .2 percentage points. (If a 1 percent increase in inflation is associated with a 2 percentage point increase in unemployment, a 1 percentage point increase in unemployment will be associated with a .5 percentage point increase in inflation, and a .4 percentage point increase in unemployment will be associated with a .2 percentage point increase in inflation.) The cost of the Fed's error would be that inflation would have increased by .2 percentage points.

On the other hand, if the Fed assumed that the NAIRU had remained at 6.0 percent, when it had fallen to 5.6 percent, the economy would have suffered a higher level of unemployment than was necessary to maintain stable prices. What is the lost value of output—assuming that the Fed had persisted in maintaining the higher unemployment rate for a year? According to current estimates, Okun's law says that reducing unemployment by 1 percentage point increases output by 2 percent. Accordingly, maintaining the unemployment rate at a level that is .4 percent "too high" costs the economy .8 percent of GDP. In a $6 trillion economy, this translates into $48 billion per year—a fairly steep price to pay.

describing the money supply (M1, M2, etc.). Controlling these would, it was believed, stabilize the inflation rate. It was believed that there was a stable relationship between the money supply and nominal income. If the money supply increased by 3 percent, nominal income would increase by only 3 percent. And since most of the advocates of this theory believed that the economy normally operated at full employment, if the economy's full-employment output was growing at 3 percent, that would imply that there would be no inflation. (The rate of increase of nominal income is the rate of increase of real income plus the rate of increase of prices.) But just as the theory came to be widely believed, the empirical relationship fell apart, as we saw in Chapter 31. The ratio of the money supply (say M1) to nominal income appeared to vary in ways that were hard to predict. Thus, controlling the money supply was not a good target. At other times, central banks have focused on variables such as the real interest rate, the rate of inflation, or the unemployment rate. Today, in the United States, the Fed takes an eclectic approach, incorporating data about all of these variables (including the monetary aggregates) into its analysis.

STRUCTURAL POLICIES: REDUCING THE NAIRU

Discretionary monetary and fiscal policy, no matter how aggressively and well pursued, will never completely eliminate the economy's fluctuations. Governments therefore try to improve the structure of the economy, to dampen the fluctuations and to reduce the NAIRU, so that the economy can have lower unemployment rates without the threat of increasing inflation. The major set of policies aimed at dampening fluctuations are the automatic stabilizers, discussed in Chapter 32, which automatically reduce taxes and increase expenditures as the economy slows down. Here, we focus on policies aimed at lowering the NAIRU.

Government has tried to lower the NAIRU in several ways: by increasing labor mobility, increasing the competitiveness of the economy, controlling directly the increase in wages and prices, and moral suasion.

INCREASING LABOR MOBILITY

By reducing the time that it takes for people to move from job to job the government can reduce frictional unemployment and thus lower the NAIRU. Policies that facilitate labor mobility include one-stop job centers, which not only enable individuals to ascertain quickly vacancies for which they might be suited, but also provide information about training opportunities. A central part of Sweden's active labor policies are training programs that provide those who have lost their jobs the skills required for the new jobs being created. In December 1994, President Clinton proposed a broad program of "skill grants"—vouchers that those who have lost their jobs could use to obtain training at the school of their choice.

Some government policies, particularly in Europe, have probably reduced labor mobility—and thus increased the NAIRU. There is concern that legislation intended to increase workers' job security (by making it more difficult for employers to fire them) has had the side effect of making employers more reluctant to hire new workers, and thus has impeded the process of job transition. Changing these laws may lower the NAIRU.

MAKING THE ECONOMY MORE COMPETITIVE

A second approach, which received considerable attention in the late 1970s and early 1980s, entails shifting the aggregate supply curve down and to the right, as illustrated in Figure 35.5. This increases output, and thus reduces inflationary pressure. One way of shifting the aggregate supply curve down and to the right is by reducing regulations that inhibit competition.

These and other measures making the economy more competitive may lower the NAIRU: a more competitive economy—particularly one that is more open to international competition—will have less pressure to increase prices and wages, even when the unemployment rate is low. Workers worry, for instance, that if they demand significant wage increases, the products they produce will not be able to compete with foreign imports, demand for what they produce will decrease, and they will face a risk of losing their jobs.

Figure 35.5 EFFECTS OF REDUCED INDUS-TRIAL REGULATION

Reduced regulation that restricts competition is represented as a shift down and to the right of the short-run aggregate supply curve, from AS_0 to AS_1. Output increases and inflationary pressures are reduced.

WAGE AND PRICE CONTROLS AND MORAL SUASION

In the 1950s and 1960s, many believed that competition—market forces—were insufficient to control price and wage increases. Large unions could demand—and get—large wage increases, regardless of the unemployment rate; and industries, like steel, which were dominated by a few large producers could—and would—raise their prices, even when there was large excess capacity. In a number of instances, governments tried to reduce the inflationary pressures—at any level of unemployment—by imposing direct controls on wages and prices. Such controls, by interfering with how the price system serves to allocate resources, impose high costs on the economy and tend to be effective only for short periods of time. When the price controls are removed, prices increase rapidly, largely undoing any benefits from the lower rates of price increases while controls were in place. Today, few economists advocate price and wage controls as a way of lowering the NAIRU.

A less intrusive way that some governments have tried is "moral suasion" or jawboning, in which they try to *persuade* firms and workers not to raise prices and wages. The government sets wage and price guidelines, with which it hopes workers and firms will voluntarily comply. The government often has considerable leverage beyond its appeal to moral rectitude, because it can threaten not to buy from firms that violate its suggestions. There have been some dramatic episodes where such jawboning appears to have worked. President Kennedy, concerned that a proposed increase in prices by U.S. Steel would set off an inflationary spiral, successfully jawboned the company into rolling back the price increases. Today, however, most economists are skeptical about the power of moral suasion to have any long-term effect on price setting.

A BRIEF HISTORY OF MACROECONOMIC POLICY

The historical record, illustrated in Figure 35.1, shows clearly that fiscal and monetary policy has not been able to eliminate the economy's fluctuations. But fluctuations appear smaller today than before World War II, and government policy may have played a role. In the following sections, we review briefly the major policy debates of the past thirty years.

THE HEYDAY OF DISCRETIONARY FISCAL POLICY: THE 1960S

The heyday of discretionary fiscal policy occurred during the Kennedy and Johnson administrations. In 1963, with a weak economy, Kennedy's economic advisers—all dedicated Keynesians—argued for a tax cut to stimulate the economy. The tax cut was enacted, and worked just in the manner predicted. Later, in 1968, as the Vietnam War expenditures led to an overheating of the economy, President Johnson's advisers recommended the imposition of a surtax, to dampen slightly the economy.

THE ERA OF INFLATION AND ANTI-INFLATIONARY POLICY

As inflation increased markedly in the 1970s, macroeconomics increasingly became focused on reducing inflation. The fact that inflation and unemployment both increased—an effect that became known as stagflation—cast doubt on the traditional concept of the Phillips curve, with a stable trade-off between inflation and unemployment. As we have seen, new classical economists focused attention on the role of expectations, which could change quickly. This meant that bad economic policy could quickly give rise to inflation, but it also meant that good economic policy could quickly bring inflation under control.

The failure of government policy to provide a stable macroeconomic environment provided renewed interest in rules-based policy. Adopting rules-based policies would bring an immediate reward: the *expectation* that inflation would thereby be controlled would immediately bring down the inflation rate. In particular, monetarism, which sought to bring inflation under control by fixing the rate of growth of the money supply, enjoyed a brief moment of popularity in many industrialized economies—before becoming discredited as the relationship between money supply and national income became unstable. In the United States, tight monetary policy succeeded in bringing inflation down dramatically, from 12 percent per year in 1979 to 3 in 1983—but at a high cost, with unemployment soaring to over 10 percent at the depth of the recession. Economists still debate whether a more gradual policy would have succeeded in reducing inflation—with less drastic costs.

With rapid inflation, the problem did not seem to be lack of aggregate demand. Economists, who naturally think about markets in terms of demand and supply, thus turned more of their attention to aggregate supply. Indeed, a major cause of the inflationary episode were supply shocks, especially the increases in oil prices in 1973 and 1979. President Reagan wanted to reduce taxes *and* reduce inflation. Reducing taxes shifts the aggregate demand curve to the right, as consumers' disposable income rises. Reducing taxes may also shift the aggregate supply curve to the right, *if* as a result individuals are willing to work harder and firms invest more. In addition to these tax changes, President Reagan continued the process of *deregulation*, reducing the regulations which restricted competition in industries like airlines and natural gas, which President Carter had initiated. These reductions in taxes and regulations give rise to *supply-side* effects. If the supply-side effects exceed the demand-side effects, then inflation would be reduced; if demand-side effects dominate, a tax cut is inflationary. Some of President Reagan's economic advisers believed that the supply-side effects would dominate. Most economists were skeptical about the *magnitude* of the effects: in the short run, the shifts in the supply curve would not be large. The evidence appeared to confirm these predictions. Inflation was brought under control because of monetary policy; increased interest rates (soaring to 17 percent) more than offset the expansionary fiscal policy, shifting the aggregate demand curve far to the right.

POLICY IN THE 1990S

The tax reduction of 1981, unaccompanied by corresponding expenditure cuts, left a major legacy: huge deficits. The national debt quadrupled in twelve years and the deficit-GDP ratio reached more than 5 percent.

MACROECONOMIC POLICY IN A HIGH DEFICIT ENVIRONMENT

A consensus emerged in the early 1990s that the deficit had to be reduced. This had an important implication for macroeconomic policy: it virtually eliminated the scope for discretionary fiscal policy. When President Clinton took office in January 1993, he faced a dilemma. Although he was elected on a commitment to reduce unemployment, the necessity of reducing the deficit, would, in traditional macroeconomic theory, have imposed a huge drag on the economy, as the aggregate demand curve shifted to the left. But between 1992 and 1996 the deficit was reduced from $290 billion to $107 billion, and yet the economy expanded, with unemployment falling from over 7 percent to below 5.5 percent. There was a simple answer to this puzzle: reduced deficits lead to reduced interest rates. It was *as if* monetary and fiscal authorities had coordinated their policies, with monetary expansion more than offsetting fiscal contraction. Moreover, because bond markets seemed to believe that the deficit reduction was credible, long-term interest rates fell—even before the deficit reduction was fully implemented. This gave a big boost to interest-sensitive sectors, such as housing. Administration advocates argued that, as important as the deficit reduction was in allowing interest rates to fall, equally important was an economic environment that was conducive to business. This included efforts to make the product sector more competitive by aggressively pursuing antitrust policies, by opening up markets at home and abroad to international competition (see Chapter 38), and by reforming regulations, especially in telecommunications (where a new law passed in 1996 replaced the sixty-year-old regulatory regime which had ruled the industry).

MONETARY POLICY AND UNCERTAINTY OVER NAIRU

The major debate of the 1990s focused on *how* expansionary monetary policy should be. This debate hinges on uncertainty over NAIRU and the risks of aggressive versus conservative policies. In the early 1990s, the prevalent view was that the NAIRU was around 6 percent. As the unemployment rate reached 5.4 percent in 1995, and there was no evidence of inflationary pressures, many economists became convinced that the NAIRU was lower, and that interest rates should remain low to encourage the continuation of the expansion. Others worried that there were long lags—the evidence of incipient inflation would only turn up months later. The Fed, aware that it took six months or more before its policies had full effect, and worried that the economy would become overheated, gradually increased interest rates from 3 percent to nearly 6 percent between 1994 and 1995. The economy continued to expand (though at a more moderate pace), with unemployment continuing to fall until it reached 5.4 percent—with still no evidence of increasing inflation. The debate over whether there should be continued monetary easing continued through 1995 and 1996. Monetary conservatives, while lowering their estimate of the NAIRU, were convinced that further decreases in the unemployment rate would ignite inflation. Some argued that as long as the bond market believed that inflation would ignite, the Fed could not do much to lower the unemployment rate; even if it left short-run interest rates unchanged, long-term rates would rise, dampening the economy. Others advocated a gradual exploration of lower unemployment rates, to see whether the economy might operate at 5.3, 5.2, or even 5.1 percent—or lower—without starting inflation. All parties recognized that there was uncertainty about the NAIRU. The critical issues were the costs and benefits of conservative policies—temporarily missing the opportunity for more rapid growth and higher output until more evidence mounted, versus the risk of temporarily higher inflation should it turn out that the NAIRU was in fact 5.5 percent or higher.

ECONOMIC SECURITY

While the overall macroeconomic performance of the economy in the mid-1990s was strong (the sum of the unemployment and inflation rates, known as the misery index, was the lowest it had been in three decades), there were many individuals whose enthusiasm over the economy did not match the economic statistics. Many workers felt insecure. Economists traced this sense of insecurity to two trends.

First, in the face of competitive pressures, many American industries had been forced to restructure and to "downsize." One widely noted instance came in early 1996, when AT&T announced that it was letting 40,000 of its employees go. While there was no strong evidence that the overall rate of job dislocation—the chance that a worker who had been employed at a job for three or more years would lose it—had increased substantially, the rate for white-collar and older workers—groups which previously had been relatively secure in their jobs—was up dramatically.

Second, beginning in 1973, there had been a marked increase in wage inequality. Not only did the ratio of the wages at the bottom to those at the top fall, but the *real wage* of those at the bottom—the lower 40 percent—fell. Though by the mid-1990s there was evidence that the *trend* had slowed or slightly reversed itself, real wages at the bottom remained lower than they had been two decades earlier. This increased inequality meant that those who lost their jobs saw a real threat to their standard of living; even if they got another job, it was not as good. On average, dislocated workers who found a full-time job had their wages reduced by 10 percent; and even three years after having lost their jobs, a quarter had not regained employment. (Of these, half simply left the labor force.)

Joseph Schumpeter, a famous economist of the early twentieth century who emphasized the role of innovation, described the market economy as a process of creative destruction: jobs were always being destroyed at the same time that new jobs were being created. The AT&T layoffs referred to above illustrate this: while employment at AT&T was reduced, overall employment in the telecommunications sector was increased as a result of the vast array of new products that came about from enhanced competition in the sector. While the economy as a whole may benefit, particular individuals—those who lose their jobs—are worse off.

Those economists referred to earlier as "interventionists" believe not only that government should actively try to reduce the magnitude of economic fluctuations, but also that it should reduce the costs of unemployment and transitions. While non-interventionists argue that unemployment is at most a temporary phenomenon, and that individuals should cope with it on their own (for instance, by putting aside savings), interventionists believe that the government-run unemployment insurance program has made an important contribution in enhancing economic security. (This is true even if it may have, at the same time, led to higher unemployment rates because it reduced individuals' incentives to search for a new job.)

A variety of policies have been proposed to address the recent concerns about economic insecurity. Most important, low levels of unemployment imply that a worker who loses a job has a better chance of finding another. And a good "safety net"—including good unemployment insurance benefits—helps reduce the risks borne by workers. One of the main anxieties facing workers who lose their jobs is loss of health insurance. In their 1996 budget, the Clinton administration proposed extending unemployment benefits to include health insurance, but to date, the proposal has not been passed by Congress.

Three sets of proposals have been put forward to facilitate transitions from

POLICY PERSPECTIVE: THE McJOBS DEBATE

The success of the United States in creating new jobs in recent years contrasted markedly with that of Europe, as the following chart illustrates. Almost all of the eight million jobs created in the G-7 (the seven major industrialized countries) from 1994 to 1996 were in the United States—and over 90 percent of those created in the United States were in the private sector. In April 1996, the economic leaders of the G-7 nations met in Lille, France, to discuss the employment situation. President Chirac of France, aware of the dismal jobs performance of Europe, but concerned about the quality of the jobs created in America—labeled McJobs, in reference to hamburger flippers—called for a "third way." The Americans pointed out that this portrait of job creation in the United States was simply wrong. To be sure, a large number of the newly created jobs were in the service sector; after all, America was undergoing a transition from an economy based on manufacturing to one based on services, just as it had transformed from an agricultural economy into a manufacturing economy in the

nineteenth and early twentieth centuries. But the service sector included high-technology and high-paying sectors, including finance and computer services. A more refined analysis showed that the majority (more than 60 percent) of new jobs were in industries and occupations with median salaries exceeding the median for the economy as a whole.

Moreover, the number of individuals who were working part time because they could not find full-time employment had been consistently declining, while the number of individuals who held multiple jobs had remained roughly unchanged at around 6 percent. While some of these variations are part of cyclical patterns (typically in an economic recovery, more individuals decide to hold multiple jobs, simply because they are easier to obtain), the overall pattern did not support the charge that America had failed to create good-quality full-time jobs.

Source: Bureau of Labor Statistics, Department of Labor.

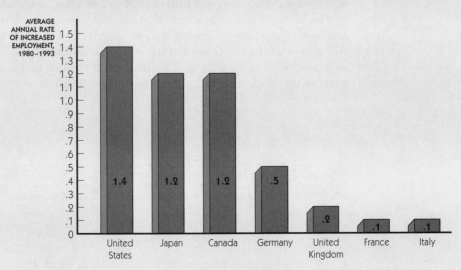

one job to another. Since educated workers make transitions more easily, concern about transitions has provided another rationale for strong support of education. The active labor market policies discussed earlier in the chapter are aimed at providing the training and information required to move workers from one job to another. To signify the importance of these efforts, Secretary of Labor Robert Reich proposed renaming the unemployment insurance system the "reemployment system."

The final set of proposals were concerned with pensions and health insurance. Many insurance policies had provisions that excluded coverage for conditions that members of the family had before the new job began. Proposals were put forward enhancing the "portability" of health insurance and pensions. In July 1996, Congress passed major legislation enchancing health insurance portability.

While these are examples of the kinds of proposals intended to address concerns about economic anxiety, there is far less agreement about what to do about the increased disparity in wages and incomes. Again, since low-skilled individuals are those that suffer most from an economic slowdown, maintaining a high level of employment is not only good macroeconomic policy; it is also good distribution policy.

ECONOMIC CHALLENGES OF THE TWENTY-FIRST CENTURY

As we have seen, every period has its own economic problems. Just as it is difficult to predict the performance of the economy a year or two from now, it is hard to predict the central problems and controversies that will be facing the economy in five or ten years. It is probable that the challenges we have discussed in this chapter—maintaining full employment with stable prices and addressing the concerns of dislocated and low-wage unskilled workers—will still be there. It is also probable that the two issues to which we turn in the next two chapters—enhancing the rate of growth and reducing the deficit—will also be at the forefront. But whatever the problems, the kinds of analytic tools and ways of thinking that we have taught in this and the preceding two parts of the book will be a central part of the framework that policymakers use as they address those problems.

REVIEW AND PRACTICE

SUMMARY

1. Those who bear the cost of inflation tend to be different from those who bear the cost of unemployment. The latter costs tend to be concentrated especially among the unskilled.

2. The economy is constantly subjected to fluctuations. The fluctuations are partially generated exogenously, by disturbances from the outside, and partially endogenously, by the structure of the economy. The structure of the economy may also amplify exogenous shocks, resulting in effects which persist long after the initial disturbance. Economic expansions have varied greatly in their duration, and contractions in their depth. Still, there are marked similarities among fluctuations in the manner in which different variables (like output, employment, and hours) move together.

3. Those who criticize active intervention argue that markets adjust quickly, so that unemployment is only short-lived. Attempts by government to intervene are not only unnecessary, but are largely ineffective, since they are offset by actions of the private sector. And to the extent that they do have effects, such policies often exacerbate fluctuations, because of the long lags and limited information of government and because political pressures result in its overheating the economy before elections.

4. Most governments believe that they should intervene to help stabilize the economy. Without government intervention, there may be long periods of high and persistent unemployment. While policymakers recognize that there are often long lags, and that policy is made with imperfect information (so that at times, policy may be ill-timed or counterproductive) on average, policy can be and has been stabilizing.

5. Critics of discretionary policy believe governments should tie their hands, using fixed rules. But critics of fixed rules argue not only that this represents giving up on an important set of instruments, but that fixed rules never work well, because they fail to respond to the ever-changing structure of the economy.

6. Current policy discussions recognize that the economy cannot be kept at unemployment rates below the NAIRU for long. The debate is over: (a) What is the level of the NAIRU and have changes in the structure of the economy lowered it? (b) What are the risks and rewards of aggressive policies trying to keep the unemployment rate right at the NAIRU, versus more cautious policies, which lower the unemployment rate only after more evidence that the NAIRU is lower has mounted?

7. Those who argue for aggressive policies believe that the costs in lost output and economic insecurity from the failure to keep unemployment as low as possible without giving rise to large inflationary risks are significant, while the real costs of low inflation are small, especially when there is indexing. They also believe that it is not too costly to correct "mistakes," that is, by pushing the unemployment rate below the NAIRU for a short period of time. Those who argue for more cautious policies worry that once started, inflationary episodes are hard to bring under control, typically requiring extended periods of high unemployment. They think not only that the costs of inflation are high, but also that the short-run benefits of reduced unemployment are more than offset by the risks of higher unemployment, should inflation be ignited and the Fed "forced" to disinflate.

8. Governments can pursue policies both to stabilize the economy (automatic stabilizers) and to lower the NAIRU (by improving labor mobility, increasing competitiveness of markets, and moral suasion).

9. Each period in our economy's history has had its own economic problems, such as avoiding overheating the economy in the years of the Vietnam War, controlling inflation and avoiding stagflation in the 1970s, recovering from the deep recession of 1981–83 or the far shallower recession of 1991–92. In the mid-1990s, with inflation under control, unemployment rates low, and the fiscal deficit reduced, concerns focused on stimulating economic growth, reducing wage inequality—or at least increasing real wages at the bottom—enhancing economic security, and reducing the deficit further.

KEY TERMS

exogenous	monetarists	monetary
endogenous	dynamic consistency	aggregates
real business cycle	New Keynesianism	

REVIEW QUESTIONS

1. How do inflation and unemployment affect different groups differently, and how do these differences affect views concerning macroeconomic policy?

2. What are the alternative explanations of the sources of the economy's fluctuations? What is the relationship between views about the nature of these fluctuations and views about the role of government?

3. What are some of the controversies today in macroeconomic policy? What are some of the disagreements concerning the risks asociated with pursuing an aggressive policy, maintaining the economy at a rate of unemployment as close to NAIRU as possible?

4. Why do some economists believe that active government intervention in an attempt to stabilize the economy is either unnecessary or undesirable? What are the counterarguments?

5. Describe the rules versus discretion debate.

6. What steps may the government take to lower the NAIRU?

7. How was it possible for the government to increase taxes and reduce expenditures in 1993, and yet stimulate the economy, helping bring it out of a recession?

8. Describe the principal macroeconomic problems of the past four decades.

9. What are some of the major macroeconomic challenges currently facing the country?

PROBLEMS

1. Describe the actions of the private sector that might offset the following actions of government. In which cases do you think the actions will *fully* offset the government actions?

(a) The government increases the money supply.

(b) The government attempts to increase aggregate demand by increasing government expenditures without increasing taxes.

(c) The government increases Social Security payments to the elderly in an attempt to make them better off. (Assume that the elderly currently receive some financial support from their children; or that the individuals save for their retirement needs, with the level of savings determined in order to attain a certain standard of living in retirement.)

(d) The government attempts to reduce inequality by taxing inheritances.

2. In parliamentary governments, such as the United Kingdom, the prime minister can announce a change in taxation or expenditure, and implement the change almost immediately. (A failure to ratify the proposal of the government would constitute a vote of no-confidence, and bring down the government.) How might this fact affect the balance between the use of monetary and fiscal policy?

3. Some critics of indexed bonds have argued that indexation will reduce government's resolve to fight inflation. Compare the *real* costs to government of an increase in inflation when the government has used, say, long-term indexed bonds and when it has used conventional long term bonds to finance indebtedness. Compare the real costs to bondholders of an increase in inflation in the two circumstances. Do you think that indexation will increase or decrease the resolve to fight inflation?

Other critics of indexed bonds have argued that indexation imposes a huge risk on the government, because if inflation increases, the government will have to pay more interest. Proponents suggest that indexation reduces the risk faced by the government, because there is less variability in the *real* payments made by government. Assume the rate of inflation in the future may be either 5 percent or 15 percent (with equal probability). Compare the risks associated with an indexed bond paying 2 percent real interest and a nominal bond paying 12 percent. Which form of bond do you think is less risky from the government's perspective?

4. If the economy is in a boom, why might a multiplier-accelerator model predict that it will eventually slow down? If the economy is in a recession, why might the multiplier-accelerator model predict that it will eventually speed up?

5. In the traditional multiplier-accelerator model, an increase in GDP of $100 billion gives rise to an increased demand for additional capital. If the desired ratio of capital to output is 2, and if the $100 billion increase in output is believed to be permanent, what is the increase in the desired level of capital? Assume firms try to fill this gap in one year. What then is the increase in desired investment? If prices of capital goods rise in booms and fall in economic downturns, why might increases in output give rise to smaller increases in the demand for investment in booms and larger increases in economic downturns? What happens to the demand for investment if firms believe that the economic expansion will not be sustained?

6. A decision tree outlines the consequences of each decision depending on how some uncertainty is resolved. Below is a decision tree for the Fed's decision to pursue an aggressive or a cautious unemployment/inflation policy. The NAIRU is either 5 percent or 6 percent, but the Fed is uncertain about the real value of the NAIRU. Under the aggressive strategy, the Fed will set the unemployment rate at 5 percent; under the cautious strategy, unemployment is set at 6 percent. Each strategy has different consequences, depending on the real value of the NAIRU. These are outlined in the decision tree.

Agressive Strategy: —————— NAIRU = 6 percent ——— Outcome?
set unemployment at
5 percent —————— NAIRU = 5 percent ——— Outcome?

Cautious Strategy: —————— NAIRU = 6 percent ——— Outcome?
set unemployment
at 6 percent —————— NAIRU = 5 percent ——— Outcome?

Fill in the outcomes for each branch of the decision tree under the following assumptions: (a) it takes two years to discover the true NAIRU (if the Fed chooses the aggressive strategy when the NAIRU is actually 6 percent, higher inflation will occur in two years, indicating the real value of the NAIRU); (b) keeping the unemployment rate 1 percentage point below (above) the NAIRU for one year increases (decreases) the inflation rate by 1 percentage point; (c) decreasing (increasing) the unemployment rate by 1 percentage point increases (decreases) output by 2 percent; (d) GDP is initially at $10 trillion; (e) after the real NAIRU is discovered, the Fed changes the unemployment rate so as to return the inflation rate to its original level over a two-year period; and (f) ignore any indirect effect of inflation on output. What happens to output and inflation during the four-year period for each policy option? Evaluate the trade-offs between the aggressive and cautious policies.

PART EIGHT

ISSUES IN MACROECONOMIC POLICY

Unemployment and inflation, the subjects of Parts Six and Seven, are not the only economic concerns that make the news. Deficits in the United States, starvation in Ethiopia, the economic crises in the formerly Communist countries of the Soviet Union and Eastern Europe, are among other events that have grabbed headlines in the past decade. In this part of the book, we use the principles and insights developed in the preceding chapters to take a look at these and other current public policy issues.

Chapter 36 discusses a major problem facing the United States: the slowdown in its rate of economic growth. The country is growing neither as fast as it did in earlier decades nor as fast as some of its major economic rivals. We ask, what causes economic growth, and what can be done to stimulate it?

Chapter 37 focuses on the fiscal deficit, which has been at the center of public concern now for more than a decade. We learn how the deficit impacts the economy, and what can be done about it.

U.S. economic policy emerges within an international context, which is why we consider so many international topics throughout this book. In Chapter 38, we focus on international trade policy, including barriers to trade, fair trade laws, and international trade agreements such as GATT and NAFTA.

The collapse of the Soviet empire is undoubtedly one of the biggest events of the twentieth century, just as its rise was. In the aftermath of World War I, the Soviets established an alternative economic system that they believed would eventually dominate capitalism. In Chapter 39, we look at what the system's basic tenets were, why it failed, and the problems these countries face today in making a transition to capitalism.

Most of the world lives in countries where incomes are but a fraction of those in the United States, Western Europe, Japan, and the other developed countries. By the standards in these less developed countries, referred to as the Third World, most people who consider themselves poor in the more developed countries are indeed well off. In Chapter 40, we learn some of the major differences between the developed and less developed countries. We also ask, what are some of the major issues facing these poorer countries as they struggle to grow and raise themselves out of the mire of poverty in which they have remained for centuries?

36

GROWTH AND PRODUCTIVITY

T he changes that have taken place in the U.S. standard of living during the past century are hard to comprehend. In 1900, Americans' level of consumption was little higher than the average citizen's in Mexico or the Philippines today. Life expectancy was low, in part because diseases like smallpox, diphtheria, typhoid fever, and whooping cough were still common. You were fifteen times more likely to catch measles in 1900 than you would be today. The abundance of land meant that relatively few Americans were starving, but luxuries were scarce. People worked as long as they could, and when they could no longer work, they became the responsibility of their children; there was no easy retirement.

During the nineteenth century, the standard of living in England and a few other European countries was perhaps slightly higher than that of the United States. These countries' standard of living was the highest in the world, but even within Europe, there were famines. In the most famous of these, the Irish potato famine of 1845–48, more than a tenth of the population died, and more than another tenth migrated to the United States. For those living in Asia, Africa, and Latin America, as the vast majority of people did then and do now, life was even harder.

KEY QUESTIONS

1. What are the principal determinants of growth in the economy?

2. What factors might account for the slowdown of growth in the United States? What, for instance, might explain the low savings rate or the low investment rate?

3. Are there policies available to the government that might stimulate economic growth?

Higher standards of living are reflected not only in higher incomes and longer life expectancies, but also in shorter working hours and higher levels of education. Improved education is both a benefit and a cause of higher living standards. Table 36.1 compares the United States in 1900 and 1995, indicating stark contrasts in standards of living. Underlying all these differences is an increase in the output for each hour worked, what Chapter 24 identified as productivity. One major goal of this chapter is to understand what causes productivity to increase. A second is to understand the slowdown in growth that has taken place during the last two decades.

The rate of growth of the economy depends on two factors: the rate of increase in the number of hours worked, and the rate of increase in the output per hour worked, the *productivity* of the labor force.

Table 36.1 **THE UNITED STATES IN 1900 AND 1995**

	1900	1995
Population	76 million	263 million
Life expectancy	47 years	77 years
GNP (in 1995 dollars)	$420 billion	$7,250 billion
GNP per capita (in 1995 dollars)	$5,500	$27,500
Average hours worked each week in manufacturing industry	59 hours	42 hours
Average hourly pay in manufacturing industry (in 1995 dollars)	$4.40	$12.35
Total telephones in country	1.3 million	>200 million
Percentage of those age 5–19 enrolled in school	51 percent	93 percent

Sources: Economic Report of the President (1996); Statistical Abstract of the United States (1995).

Rate of growth of economy = rate of increase in the number of hours worked + the rate of increase in the output per hour worked:

$g_Q = g_H + g_P$

where

g_Q = rate of growth of output

g_H = rate of increase in number of hours worked

g_P = rate of increase in productivity (output per hour)

During the 1990s, both of these have been markedly lower than they were in the 1960s. To understand why, we need to understand better the underlying forces giving rise to increases in the labor force and productivity.

EXPLAINING PRODUCTIVITY

For almost a century, the United States has been at the center of the technological advances that have changed the world. The telegraph, telephone, laser, transistor, airplane, assembly line, jet engine, atomic energy . . . the list of U.S. technological achievements goes on and on. Beyond these path-breaking developments are countless smaller improvements: new as well as better products, less expensive ways of making old products. The country has reaped a huge reward. Levels of productivity and living standards increased continually and rapidly. Today, productivity and standards of living in the United States are higher than in any other major country.

Figure 36.1 shows, however, that the rate of growth of productivity—per capita income—slowed considerably in the seventies and early eighties, and has remained low. (Productivity tends to vary markedly with business fluctuations. As the economy recovers from a recession, output increases faster than employment, and productivity soars; when the economy goes into an economic downturn, output decreases faster than employment, and productivity falls. Consequently, economists measure long-run productivity growth from one business cycle peak to the next [points where resources are being fully used] or over sufficiently long periods of time that the cyclical fluctuations become small relative to the long-term trends. Figure 36.1 takes this approach, measuring productivity growth over the previous decade. Cyclical effects are apparent: the low productivity growth for 1982 is in part attributable to the severe recession of that year.)

Does it make much difference if the average rate of productivity growth falls from about 2 percent to 1 percent? What's so important about a difference of

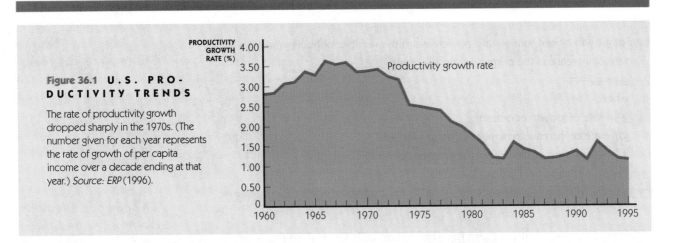

Figure 36.1 U.S. PRODUCTIVITY TRENDS

The rate of productivity growth dropped sharply in the 1970s. (The number given for each year represents the rate of growth of per capita income over a decade ending at that year.) *Source: ERP* (1996).

1 percentage point? In fact, it makes a great deal of difference, because the differences compound over time. Consider this simple calculation. Two countries start out equally wealthy, but one grows at 1 percent a year while the other grows at 2 percent a year. The difference in productivity would be barely perceptible for a few years. But after thirty years, the slower-growing country would be only three-quarters as wealthy as the faster-growing one. America's lower growth compared with the growth of other developed countries in the last two decades explains why many countries have almost caught up to the United States, as shown in Figure 36.2.

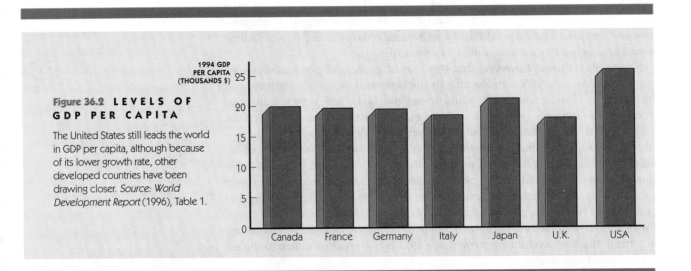

Figure 36.2 LEVELS OF GDP PER CAPITA

The United States still leads the world in GDP per capita, although because of its lower growth rate, other developed countries have been drawing closer. *Source: World Development Report* (1996), Table 1.

Lower growth in productivity means lower growth in standards of living. On average, people will have less of everything—from smaller houses, to poorer health care, to less travel, and fewer government services than otherwise. Many families have been able to sustain increases in their income, but only with both spouses working—and the reduced leisure puts strains on the families and represents a lowering of living standards.

To understand what may have contributed to the productivity slowdown, we need to understand what causes increases in output per hour in the first place. There are four key factors: savings and investment; education and the quality of the labor force; reallocating resources from low- to high-productivity sectors; and research and development. The next sections discuss these factors in turn.

SAVINGS AND INVESTMENT

Workers today are more productive than they were twenty or one hundred years ago because they have more and better machines. An American textile worker can produce far more than a textile worker in India, partly because of differences in the equipment they use. Many textile workers in India still use handlooms, similar to those used in America two hundred years ago.

Higher levels of investment relative to GDP result in more capital per worker. Economists call this **capital deepening.** As capital per worker increases, output per worker increases. Suppose an economy has an investment rate of 10 percent of GDP, and a low level of capital per worker. Increasing its investment rate to 15 percent will raise the level of capital per worker, and thus productivity. This is illustrated in Figure 36.3. Increasing capital per worker from k_0 to k_1, raises output per worker from y_0 to y_1.

In Chapters 25 and 26 we discussed the relationship between savings and investment. In a closed economy, savings equal investment, as illustrated in Figure 36.4. In the figure, we assume that savings do not depend on the interest rate. A reduction in savings leads to higher interest rates, and higher interest rates lead to lower investment.

In an open economy, matters are more complicated. Domestic savings need not equal investment, because the country can finance investment from abroad. (If this is done, gross national product (GNP)—the measure of output that nets out payments of interest and dividends to foreigners—will increase less than GDP, which is simply the amount produced within a country; citizens of the country will have to share the benefits of higher productivity with foreigners. But even though the U.S. economy is open, U.S. savings and investment tend to move together, with a reduction in national savings of $100 leading to a reduction of investment of between $35 and $50.

Figure 36.5 compares the savings rates in developed countries. Both in relation to other countries and historically, U.S. savings rates in recent years have been low. For example, the U.S. savings rate has been less than one-seventh that of Japan. Because of its adverse effects on investment, the low savings rate may underlie some of the slowdown in productivity.

Figure 36.3 INVESTMENT AND PRODUCTIVITY

An increase in the investment rate (the ratio of investment to GDP) results in capital deepening. As capital per worker increases, output per worker increases.

Figure 36.4 SAVINGS AND INVESTMENT

Lower savings rates lead to higher interest rates and lower levels of investment.

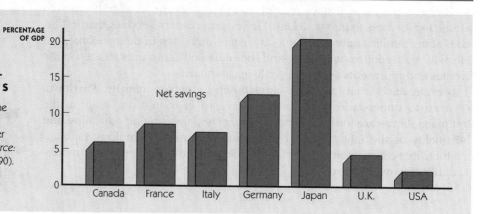

Figure 36.5 SAVINGS RATES IN DEVELOPED ECONOMIES

During the 1980s and 1990s, the United States savings rate was dramatically lower than in other industrialized economies. *Source: OECD, Economic Outlook* (1990).

WHY ARE U.S. SAVINGS SO LOW?

To see why U.S. savings are so low, it is useful to break down savings into three components: personal (or household) savings, business savings, and government savings (the fiscal surplus, when the government has one). Figure 36.6 shows how each of these as well as total savings has changed over time. The figure makes clear that the low level can largely be attributed to the huge gov-

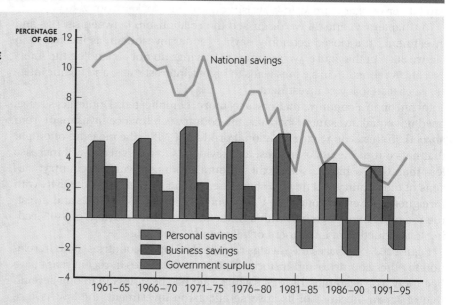

Figure 36.6 THE DECLINE IN U.S. SAVINGS

Savings can come from households, business, or government. During the 1980s, total national savings were exceptionally low. Though all three components were low, the most significant decline arose from government savings, and the second most significant from household savings. The federal deficit worsened in 1991 and 1992, but following the passage of the 1993 deficit reduction act and the economic recovery, the federal deficit improved markedly. *Source: ERP* (1996), Table B-28.

ernment deficits and a low level of household savings. Beginning in 1993, the federal government succeeded in reducing the deficit, from almost 5 percent of GDP in 1992 to under 2 percent in 1996. But at the same time, personal savings decreased slightly, moderating the overall increase in national savings. Here, we focus on household savings; Chapters 26 and 37 address government deficits.

We can use the basic framework for consumer choice introduced earlier to analyze the determinants of savings (see Chapters 8 and 9). Prices (here, the interest rate) and preferences affect the desire for consumption in the future versus consumption today. People save for future needs—for retirement (life-cycle savings); to buy a home, pay for their children's college education, or to meet certain other needs (target savings); for emergencies, for periods in which their incomes may be low, say because they are laid off from their job or in which their needs are high, or because they require medical attention (precautionary savings); and people save to leave something to their children (bequest savings).

During the past two decades, virtually all of the motives and incentives for saving changed in a way to discourage saving. Improved Social Security (particularly during the 1970s) reduced the need for private savings for retirement; improved capital markets and insurance—provided by both government and employers—meant that people did not have to save as much for emergencies; improved capital markets also meant that people did not have to save as much for a down payment on a house; and improved government student-loan programs meant that parents did not have to save as much for their children's education.

But one change should have stimulated savings: an increase in the real after-tax return. In the 1980s, taxes on the return to capital, particularly for upper-income levels, plummeted—from 70 percent in 1980 to 28 percent in 1986—and real before-tax returns soared. Nevertheless, savings fell. This should not come as too much of a surprise: we also learned in Chapter 5 that the effect of changes in real after-tax interest rates on savings, while positive, is probably small.[1]

But the changes discussed so far, by themselves, do not seem to account fully for the low levels of savings. Accordingly, economists have looked elsewhere for an explanation.

The **life-cycle theory of savings** emphasizes that savings will differ in different parts of an individual's life cycle. The 45–65 age group are typically high savers; no longer facing the burden of children, they recognize the necessity of setting aside money for their retirement. The percentage of the population in this group has been low since the mid-1970s, but has begun to increase in the 1990s. This should provide an impetus for an increased personal savings rate.

Some economists argued that the huge increase in real estate prices in the 1980s meant that more individuals were saving in the form of home equity; these savings were not recorded in the national income accounts. Though the

---

[1] There, we saw that while the *substitution* effect leads to increased savings, the *income* effect results in reduced savings. While on theoretical grounds the *net* effect is ambiguous, the evidence supports a small positive effect.

explanation seemed plausible at the time, it suggested that when real estate prices leveled out, or fell, as they did in the late 1980s and early 1990s, savings rates would increase. They did not.

Finally, some economists attribute the decline in savings rates to a change in values: the "Now" generation wants its consumption now, and puts less money aside for its children.

Whatever the explanation for low savings, those who believe that increasing savings is necessary to stimulate productivity feel stymied: microeconomic instruments to stimulate household savings, such as tax preferences, are likely to have at most small effects. Thus, economists have increasingly seen macroeconomic policies—particularly the reduction in the deficit—as the main way by which the government can enhance investment: by borrowing less, interest rates will be reduced and investment stimulated. Reducing the deficit increases national savings. This was the strategy for increasing national savings adopted by the Clinton administration in 1993. (At the same time, *how* the deficit is reduced matters. If high-return public investments, such as in infrastructure, education, and research, are reduced, overall investment may fall, and productivity growth may be slowed. We will look at these factors shortly.)

EXPLANATIONS OF LOW SAVINGS

Improved Social Security

Improved insurance markets

Improved capital markets

Change in values: less future-oriented behavior

INFRASTRUCTURE

Most discussions of the low level of investment in the United States focus on low *private* investment. But government investment is also important. These investments include roads, bridges, airports, and harbors, called **infrastructure.** Without adequate infrastructure, the private sector cannot perform effectively. During the 1980s, not only did the deficit soar, but infrastructure investment declined. In many cases, even maintenance activities were forgone, so that by 1992, the nation's infrastructure was in worse shape than it was a decade earlier. While the public capital stock amounted to 50 percent of GDP in 1970, by 1990, it amounted to only about 40 percent. This declining public capital stock has exerted a drag on the economy's productivity, though there are no precise estimates of the magnitude.

POLICIES TO STIMULATE SAVINGS AND INVESTMENT

Government has only limited tools to stimulate savings and investment. Reducing the fiscal deficit increases national savings, and in a closed (or not perfectly open) economy, this leads to increased investment. Reducing the deficit by cutting back on infrastructure investment (or other forms of investments such as in education) may, however, be counterproductive; overall investment (public plus private) may decline, and the public investment may yield as high or higher returns than the induced private investment.

When the economy is at full employment, in a closed economy investment subsidies have little or no effect on aggregate investment. With given government expenditures and consumption, the Fed simply has to raise interest rates to ensure that aggregate demand equals the full-employment level of output. Since savings is relatively insensitive to interest rates, investment (equal full-employment savings) will be relatively unaffected. In an open economy, investment subsidies induce more investment and more borrowing from abroad. If the subsidies lower the before-subsidy marginal return to investment to the point where it is below the cost of capital from abroad, the country (at the margin) is actually worse off as a result of the additional investment. GDP—what is produced in the United States—increases, but GNP—netting out what has to be paid to foreigners (so what Americans can actually spend)—actually decreases.

GDP can be increased if savings can be increased (and consumption reduced). The apparent unresponsiveness of savings to the real interest rate has made most economists skeptical about the potential use of tax policy to encourage savings. There is some evidence that IRAs (individual retirement accounts) have had some effect, largely because banks and other financial institutions have used them as the basis of advertising campaigns to obtain deposits.

WHY LOWER SAVINGS AND INVESTMENT IS NOT THE WHOLE STORY

As important as the low savings and investment rates are in explaining the low rates of growth of productivity, they are not the whole story. As we have seen, capital accumulation leads to increases in output per worker—in productivity. However, this effect is limited to the short run. After an increase in the rate of savings and investment, the economy eventually reaches a new ratio of capital to worker. This is capital deepening. At the new level of capital to worker, the economy is indeed operating at a higher level of productivity, but the productivity *increase* has run its course. This is illustrated in Figure 36.7, which uses a hypothetical time series for real output to display the economy's growth path. Three segments of the growth path are evident. The first segment (*AB*) represents the economy's growth before the increase in the rate of savings and investment. The steep segment that follows (*BC*) represents the period of capital accumulation arising from the increase in the rate of savings and investment; as capital per worker increases, so does productivity and the growth rate of the economy. But once the new, higher level of capital per worker is reached, the economy resumes its original growth rate, represented by the third segment (*CD*).

Figure 36.7 SHORT-RUN AND LONG-RUN EFFECTS OF CAPITAL DEEPENING

Capital deepening increases output per worker (productivity), and therefore economic growth, but the effects on the rate of growth of productivity (as opposed to the level of productivity) are limited to the short run. The graph shows three segments of a hypothetical growth path. *AB* represents the economy's growth before an increase in savings and investment. *BC*, the steep segment, represents the period of capital accumulation arising from an increase in savings and investment. Once the new, higher level of capital per worker is reached, the economy resumes its original growth rate, represented by the third segment, *CD*.

Figure 36.8 DIMINISHING RETURNS TO CAPITAL

With a given production function, the increase in capital goods per worker from k_2 to k_3 would result in a smaller increase in productivity than the corresponding increase from k_1 to k_2.

Figure 36.9 LONG-RUN U.S. PRODUCTIVITY GROWTH

Productivity growth increased sharply during the first part of the twentieth century, a period of rapid capital goods accumulation, before declining in the last few decades. *Source: Angus Maddison, Dynamic Forces in Capitalist Development*, 1991.

This analysis may suggest that repeated increases in the rate of savings and investment, generating continuous capital deepening, will result in a long-run increase in the rate of productivity increase and therefore a long-run increase in the rate of economic growth. This is *not* the case because of the law of diminishing returns, which says that as the amount of capital goods per worker continues to increase, successive increments of capital increase output per worker by less and less. Eventually, further increases in capital per worker will yield almost no increase in output per worker. Figure 36.8 shows that as the economy increases capital per worker from k_2 to k_3, the increase in output per worker is much smaller than when the economy increases capital per worker by a similar amount from k_1 to k_2.

Yet in fact, productivity growth did not diminish during periods of rapid capital accumulation. Figure 36.9 shows productivity growth in the United States in twenty-year periods since 1880. Productivity growth actually increased from 1900 to 1970 during a period of enormous accumulation of capital goods. Similar patterns have been observed elsewhere. Japan, for example, has had steadily increasing productivity growth along with large increases in capital goods per worker for the past quarter century.

The reason that productivity growth can continue over long periods is that capital deepening is not the only, or even the primary, source of productivity increases. If we are to understand why the rate of productivity growth has decreased, we need to look at the other sources, to which we now turn.

HIGHER QUALITY OF THE LABOR FORCE

A second major source of productivity growth, which today is even more important than increased capital per worker, is a higher-quality labor force. Running a modern industrial economy requires a well-educated labor force. In addition, an economy on the cutting edge of technological change needs trained engineers and scientists to discover and shape those innovations.

Spending money on education and training improves workers' skills and productivity. These expenditures are investments—just like investments in machines and buildings. And just as expenditures on plant and equipment result in physical capital, we say that expenditures on education result in **human capital.** Thus, increases in human capital are one of the major sources of economic growth.

One nationally representative survey found that establishments with more educated work forces had significantly higher productivity: increasing years of education by 10 percent increased productivity by 8.6 percent. Indeed, returns to education have increased markedly—even as the number of educated has increased: by 1994 the median full-time worker with at least a bachelor's degree earned 74 percent more per week than one with only a high school diploma—up from 36 percent in 1979. Though some of this difference may be attributed to the fact that those who graduate from college are more able (and hence would have earned higher incomes even if they had not gone on to college), even accounting for factors such as family background or high school performance, the returns to education appear significant. Just a year of college has been estimated to increase earnings by 5 to 10 percent, or more.

THE STRENGTHS OF THE U.S. EDUCATIONAL SYSTEM

In recent years, there have been significant increases at least in the "quantity" of education in the United States. More students are finishing high school. The drop-out rate fell from 14.1 to 11 percent between 1973 and 1993. More high school students are attending and completing college. The percent of high school graduates enrolling in college after graduation increased from 49 percent in 1980 to 62 percent in 1993. As the new, more highly educated workers have replaced older workers, the share of the work force with a college degree has nearly doubled, from 16 percent in 1973 to 29 percent in 1993. And enrollment in graduate schools has increased even more than undergraduate enrollment.

A particular strength of America's educational system has been its egalitarianism. While other countries have made decisions on whether a particular child is suitable for a college education at early ages (sometimes as young as eleven), in the United States such decisions are made much later, and students typically get repeated chances. Early sorting, based on test scores, gives a distinct advantage to children with more educated parents.

Another great strength is the U.S. system of junior colleges and state universities, many of which provide a high-quality education to those who could not afford to go to private schools or who may not have performed well in high school. In many countries, such students would have been precluded from further education. (Ironically, while in many respects the American educational system is more egalitarian than those of other developed countries, in one respect it is less so. Most European countries charge virtually no tuition to students who are admitted to their universities, and some actually pay all or part of students' living costs.)

Still another strength is America's universities, which number among the greatest in the world. Students from virtually every other country come to the United States to study, as both undergraduates and graduate students. The discoveries and innovations flowing out of the universities' research laboratories have been an important basis of America's technological superiority.

SYMPTOMS OF A U.S. HUMAN CAPITAL PROBLEM

While there is thus great strength within the U.S. educational system, there are symptoms of some problems that may be contributing to the slowdown of U.S. productivity. The concern is that while on quantitative measures the U.S. looks good, with high levels of expenditure and high levels of enrollment, the quality of U.S. education is low. On a number of standardized tests particularly in areas of science and mathematics, American students perform below students from many other countries—even countries which have until recently been classified as less developed, such as Korea and Taiwan (see Figure 36.10). Of course, standardized tests are imperfect and limited; one of the many problems with them is that they do not measure creativity. But the tests do measure success in certain objectives of education, such as mastery over basic skills. The poor performance of American students is thus disturbing.

Similarly, while America remains unique in the large fraction of its youth that goes to college, a smaller proportion of U.S. college students choose to study science and engineering, in comparison to students from some other countries, such as Japan and Korea. Evidence suggests that the fraction of the work force that are engineers and scientists is a major determinant of rapid economic growth.

Finally, a significant fraction of America's population is deprived of the opportunity to realize their full potential. The role of family background in determining educational achievement has increasingly been recognized. Children who grow up in poverty are less likely to attain an education commensurate with their ability. Yet the number of children in poverty has in-

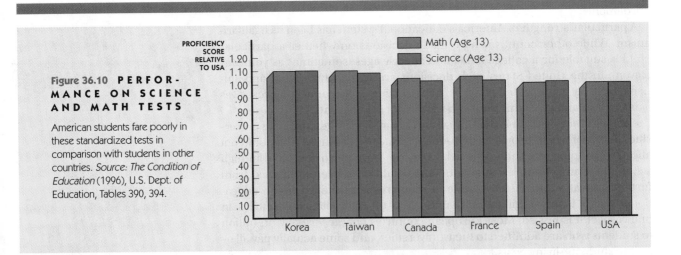

Figure 36.10 PERFORMANCE ON SCIENCE AND MATH TESTS

American students fare poorly in these standardized tests in comparison with students in other countries. *Source: The Condition of Education* (1996), U.S. Dept. of Education, Tables 390, 394.

creased markedly in recent decades, from 15 percent in 1970 to 21 percent in 1992. With the flight to the suburbs that began in the 1950s, and with increasing violence and drugs in inner city high schools, those left in inner cities are less likely to get a quality education. Moreover, a college education has become less affordable for children from poor families. Tuitions at public and private colleges and universities have increased at rates far exceeding increases in the cost of living; real incomes of poorer families have fallen; and the real value of government grant and loan programs (such as Pell grants) has declined. Not surprisingly, the gap between the fraction of children from poor families and rich families going on to higher education has increased.

REALLOCATING RESOURCES FROM LOW- TO HIGH-PRODUCTIVITY SECTORS

During the past century, the United States has evolved from an agricultural economy to an industrial economy to a service economy. Figure 36.11 shows this dramatic structural change. The service sector, broadly defined, includes not only traditional services such as haircuts and restaurant meals but also the more sophisticated services provided by doctors and lawyers, educational institutions, and computer programmers, among others. The medical sector alone has grown to the point where today it accounts for more than 14 percent of GDP.

The movement out of agriculture and into industry explains some of the productivity increase in the early part of the century. While the level of productivity in agriculture was increasing rapidly, it remained lower than in industry. Thus, as workers shifted out of low-productivity jobs in agriculture into high-productivity jobs in manufacturing, average productivity in the economy increased. With almost all labor now out of agriculture—and with agricultural productivity increased to the point where incomes in that sector are comparable to those in the rest of the economy—this kind of shift can no longer be a source of overall productivity growth. But there remain other opportunities. Productivity in the telecommunications and export sectors is substantially higher than in other parts of the economy. Telecommunications deregulation will facilitate the movement of resources into that sector. And recent international trade agreements (see Chapter 38) will open up new opportunities for export growth. Both should contribute to the overall increase in productivity.

TECHNOLOGICAL CHANGE

This final source of productivity growth may be the most important. Indeed, prior to 1973, as much as two-thirds of all increases in productivity were due to technological progress. One of the major differences between the economy today and in 1900 is the routine nature of change in the modern economy. The prototype of the nineteenth- and early twentieth-century inventors were people like Thomas Edison and Alexander Graham Bell—lone individuals,

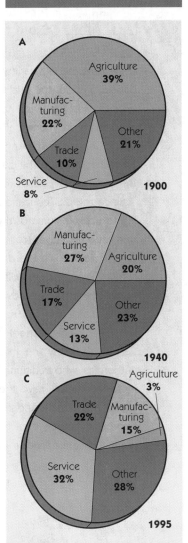

Figure 36.11 SECTORAL SHIFTS

Employment in the U.S. economy shifted from agriculture to manufacturing industries in the first half of this century and from manufacturing to services in the second half. *Sources: Historical Statistics of the United States (1975); ERP (1996), Table B-42.*

POLICY PERSPECTIVE: IMPROVING THE U.S. EDUCATION SYSTEM

There have been a variety of policy responses to concerns about the quality of the U.S. education system. Most of these have not entailed simply spending more money: already, the United States spends on a per student basis more than almost any other country. The question is, how to make the dollars spent more productive.

Since the U.S. educational system is clearly failing to achieve some of the goals expected of it, one set of initiatives (called Goals 2000) attempts to articulate goals and define performance measures. Given the mobility of Americans, there would be significant advantages to defining national standards—so that an employer would know what a high school diploma in Mississippi or California or New York meant. But state and local authorities, who traditionally have had responsibility for education, have strongly resisted establishing such national standards. Thus, federal legislation has encouraged each state to set up its own goals and performance measures.

There are also numerous proposals for reforming the ways in which elementary and high school education is organized. Most of these entail greater decentralization, that is, giving more autonomy to the school, as opposed to the school district. Voucher proposals—in which parents are given a certain amount of money to spend on the education of their children, and they can choose which school to attend—have been advocated by those who believe that vouchers would induce greater competition, and hence quality, in education. But critics have worried that such proposals would lead to the end of the public schools, would increase social segregation in education, and would be ineffective in improving quality, particularly in communities with less educated parents, who will be less able to make informed choices and less effective in influencing school policies than parents in communities with more highly educated parents.

Some of the programs that help the disadvan-

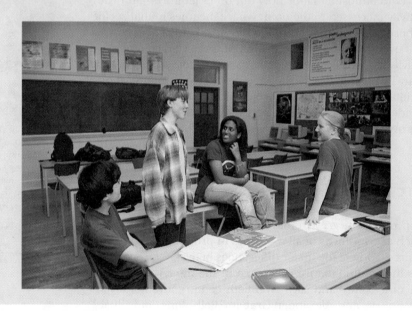

working by themselves or with a small number of collaborators. Small entrepreneurs and innovators continue to play a role in developing new products, particularly in the computer industry. But the prototype of a modern research effort, like the U.S. program to put an astronaut on the moon, has thousands of scientists working together to accomplish in a few short years what would have been almost unimaginable earlier. Technological change in the modern economy is a large-scale, systematic effort. Modern research is centered in huge laboratories, employing thousands of people. While some of these laboratories are run by the government—such as the Brookhaven, Argonne, and Lawrence laboratories, which carry out research in basic physics—many are private, like Bell Labs (part of AT&T), where the transistor and laser were developed. Indeed, most major firms spend about 3 percent of their gross revenues on research and development.

The current level of technological progress has become so expected that it is hard to believe how different the view of reputable economists was in the early 1800s. Real wages of workers were little higher than they had been five hundred years earlier, when the bubonic plague destroyed a large part of the population of Europe and thereby created a great scarcity of labor. After half a millennium of at best slow progress, Thomas Malthus, one of the greatest economists of that time, saw population expanding more rapidly than the capacity of the economy to support it. What was missing from his dismal forecast was technological change.

EXPENDITURES ON R & D

A major determinant of the pace of technological progress is the level of expenditures on R & D. These expenditures are a form of investment—expenditures today yield returns in the future.

While overall expenditures on R & D, as a percentage of GDP, are relatively high in the United States—only Japan and Germany are higher—much of this has been for defense purposes, as illustrated in Figure 36.12. Government nondefense R & D in the United States plays a relatively small role. Figure 36.13 shows how government and private R & D expenditures, as a percentage of GDP, have changed over the last twenty years. Federal expenditures on nondefense R & D have actually fallen. As Japanese and German scientists and engineers devote their efforts to building better consumer products, a disproportionate

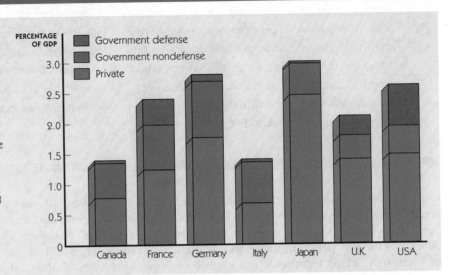

Figure 36.12 INTERNATIONAL COMPARISON OF R & D EXPENDITURES

While total U.S. R & D expenditures are comparatively high, a larger proportion of U.S. expenditures goes to defense. *Source:* National Science Foundation, "Science and Engineering Indicators" (1993), Tables 4-3, 5-39.

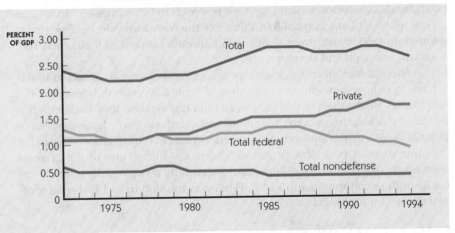

Figure 36.13 U.S. R & D EXPENDITURES AS A PERCENTAGE OF GDP

Total U.S. R & D expenditures have increased slightly since 1972, though in recent years there has been a slight decline. Overall increases in private R & D expenditures have offset the drop in total federal R & D expenditures. Federal nondefense R & D expenditures have remained low, dropping from .6 percent of GDP in 1972 to .4 percent of GDP in 1994. *Source: Statistical Abstract of the United States* (1995), Table 979.

fraction of America's scientists and engineers devote their efforts to building better bombs, missiles, and other weapons.

This underinvestment in R & D is reflected in the U.S. record on patents. Figure 36.14 shows that today, relative to the size of the population, the United States is performing more poorly (by this indicator) than Japan, the United Kingdom, and Germany.

The high rates of return on R & D expenditures support the view that there is underinvestment in research: some estimates put the private returns at over 25 percent, and since many of the returns accrue to firms other than

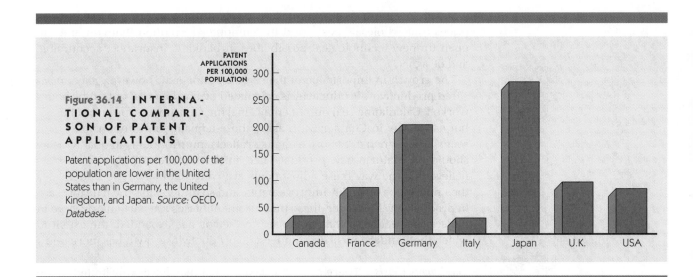

Figure 36.14 INTERNATIONAL COMPARISON OF PATENT APPLICATIONS

Patent applications per 100,000 of the population are lower in the United States than in Germany, the United Kingdom, and Japan. *Source:* OECD, *Database.*

those undertaking the research, social returns are estimated to be even higher. High risk, combined with limitations on the ability to borrow to finance R & D, provide part of the explanation for the seeming underinvestment in R & D.

Some economists, however, even while agreeing with the evidence concerning underinvestment in R & D, have raised questions about the importance of R & D in explaining the *current* productivity slowdown. It normally takes years for the effects of R & D to show up in productivity statistics. To the extent that the productivity slowdown in the 1970s was due to decreased expenditures on research, it would have been due to a decrease in expenditures in the 1950s and 1960s. But the 1960s in particular was a period of high spending on research.

OTHER POSSIBLE FACTORS

There may be other factors contributing to the slowdown in the pace of technological progress. Two that have received prominence in recent years relate the productivity slowdown to the increased importance of the service sector and the unexpected increase in energy prices in the 1970s.

Service Sector   Some economists, such as William Baumol of New York and Princeton Universities, contend that the decline in heavy industry—in steel, automobiles, and manufacturing in general—and growth in the service sector help explain the recent slowdown in productivity growth. In fact, in recent years, productivity growth in manufacturing has been quite robust, even higher than in the 1960s. Those worried about the potential for technological change in services cite such examples as haircutting: the only major innovation in the field in the past hundred years has been the electric hair clipper. But other economists are more hopeful. They cite the development by McDonald's of more efficient ways of delivering "fast food," improvements by many of the country's major retailers that have reduced the markup of retail prices over wholesale costs, and the computer revolution that continues to open up new technological possibilities in banking, insurance, accounting, and design.

The growth in importance of the service sector may, however, affect *measured* productivity. Productivity is calculated by dividing *real* output by hours worked. Calculating real output entails making adjustments for price change; but as we saw in Chapter 24, making those adjustments is not as easy as it seems. How much of the price change reflects improvements in quality? How should we evaluate new products, like automatic tellers? Many economists believe that the way these adjustments are conventionally done understates the importance of quality improvements, and so understates the true increase in productivity. Moreover, these measurement biases are particularly large in the service sector, so that as the service sector has expanded, the extent to which the standard measures understate productivity growth has increased.

The Energy Crisis   There are other factors that may have contributed to the slowdown of technological change. Some economists focus on the fact that the slowdown seems to have occurred around 1973, when oil prices soared. Much of the existing capital was designed for a world of cheap energy, and much of the investment in the subsequent years went not to capital deepening, but to replacing the old capital with more energy efficient machines and buildings. In this perspective, the standard procedures overestimate net investment since 1973. Moreover, firms diverted more of their research budgets to looking for ways of saving on energy, again at the expense of research that might have increased overall productivity. Other economists question the importance of the run-up in energy prices, since the real price had declined to earlier levels by the mid-1980s. In any case, energy constitutes a small percentage of GDP.

THE POLICY DEBATES OF THE 1990S

Policy discussions have focused on both corporate and public R & D expenditures. Because of the importance of spillovers or externalities—those undertaking research reap only a fraction of the total returns—there is widespread agreement that government should support R & D through preferential tax treatment (such as the incremental R & D tax credit, under which government in effect pays 25 percent of the increase in R & D expenditures).

Far more controversial, however, have been direct government expenditures to develop new technologies or to subsidize corporations doing so. Critics label such subsidies as *industrial policies*—an attempt by government to intervene in the markets' allocation of resources. They claim government is notoriously bad at picking winners, that is, areas with a high likelihood of success. In their view, firms driven by the profit motive are more likely to make good decisions than the government.

Technology advocates contend that there are important spillovers from technological research, that there is clear evidence of underinvestment in advanced technology (as one would expect, given the spillovers, and limitations of firms' ability to obtain funds to finance risky research), and that the govern-

CLOSE-UP: ENDOGENOUS GROWTH THEORY

Technological change is the primary cause of increases in standards of living. Recent theories of economic growth, with major contributions by Karl Shell of Cornell University and Paul Romer of University of California, Berkeley, have emphasized that the pace of technological change is at least partly endogenous, that is, a consequence of investment expenditures by private firms and government in R & D. To be sure, there is a certain unpredictable aspect to innovations: science fiction writers may speculate about the discoveries of the next century, but who at the beginning of the nineteenth century could have predicted the transistor, the laser, superconductivity, atomic energy, and the myriad of other breakthroughs that have lead to improvements in productivity? Still, by and large, if more money is spent on research, there will be more discoveries. Research is like drilling for oil: you can't be sure where you will find oil, but with a well-designed exploration strategy, there is a high likelihood that the more you spend on exploration, the more oil you will find. At least for a long while, increased expenditures on R & D can sustain increased rates of growth in productivity.

ment has had a credible record of picking winners—including, in recent years, the development of computers, the Internet, and the support of the computer chip industry. Furthermore, recent technology programs have introduced reforms to enhance the likelihood of success, including requiring recipients to put up a considerable amount of their own capital and subjecting applicants to a stiff competitive process in which independent experts are used to judge the likely significance of any spillovers.

Flat panel displays are the kinds of screens used in laptop computers. There are compact and have a myriad of uses, both civilian and military. In 1994 the Department of Defense announced its first major dual-use technology initiative, the support of production and research in flat panel displays in the United States. At the time, almost all such displays were imported from Japan. The Department of Defense worried that without a domestic source of these important high-technology components, the U.S. defense industry could be at a disadvantage. But while an important component in military computers, they also have obvious civilian uses. It made no sense simply to support the technology for the military.

Needless to say, the initiative received a mixed reception. Critics worried that it opened the door to a more aggressive industrial policy. Since much of modern technology had military uses, did this mean that the U.S. government was opening the door to support of any segment of the industry that failed the test of international competition? Advocates welcomed the explicit recognition that defense and civilian technologies are closely related, and that the most cost-effective way of providing for the military may be by providing broader-based civilian support.

Indeed, advocates of technology expenditures argue that the government has long had a policy of supporting technology—in effect an industrial policy—under the guise of the Defense Department. The issue, from their perspective, is whether, with the end of the Cold War, there should be a redeployment of expenditures toward research with more explicit nondefense benefits.

Another major policy debate has centered around the extent to which R & D should be cut, either to finance deficit reduction or tax cuts. Advocates say that deficit reduction and tax cuts will spur economic growth, while critics say that such policies are likely to be counterproductive, given the high returns to R & D and its crucial role in economic advances.

FACTORS CONTRIBUTING TO PRODUCTIVITY GROWTH

Savings and Investment (capital accumulation)

Improved quality of labor force

Reallocation of labor from low-productivity sectors to high-productivity sectors

Technological progress

TOTAL FACTOR PRODUCTIVITY

Low and declining rates of savings and investment, low and declining quality of U.S. education, and low and declining levels of government investment in civilian R & D may have all contributed to the low and declining rates of productivity growth in the United States. Economists have asked, can we quantify the roles of different factors? To do this, they have used a methodology called **total factor productivity analysis,** in which they ask, if there had been no technological change, based on what we know about the returns to and increases in the supply of capital (human and physical) and labor, how much would productivity have increased?

Suppose the share of capital in output—the amount of output attributable to capital (the total returns to capital divided by GDP)—is 20 percent, and the growth of capital is 10 percent. The share of capital in output (20 percent) multiplied by capital growth (10 percent) gives us the amount that capital growth contributes to the growth of output (2 percent).[2] The same logic applies to

---

[2]To see this, consider the change in output, ΔQ, "attributable" to an increase in capital by an amount ΔK, if r is the return to capital,

$$\Delta Q = r\Delta K.$$

The percentage increase in Q is just

$$\frac{\Delta Q}{Q} = \frac{r\Delta K}{Q}.$$

Multiplying the numerator and the denominator of the expression on the right-hand side by K, we obtain

$$\frac{\Delta Q}{Q} = \frac{rK}{Q}\frac{\Delta K}{K}.$$

labor. But capital and labor do not account for all of growth. The part of growth which cannot be explained by increases in capital and labor is called the increase in total factor productivity. The rate of total factor productivity increase is calculated as follows:

$$\text{TFP} = g_Q - (S_K \times g_K) - (S_L \times g_L)$$

where

S_K = share of capital in GDP
S_L = share of labor in GDP
g_Q = rate of growth of output
g_K = rate of growth of capital
g_L = rate of growth of labor.

The increase in total factor productivity reflects the increasing efficiency with which an economy's resources are used. Some of this is the result of research and development, but at least prior to 1973, much of the increase in total factor productivity could not be easily explained. The part that could not be explained was referred to as the **residual**—the part of growth that was "left over" after all the systematic sources of growth were taken into account. The spread of new production techniques, such as replaceable parts in the nineteenth century, the assembly line in the early twentieth century, and just-in-time inventory management techniques in recent years, are all examples of technological advances that bear little relationship to R & D expenditures, and thus form part of this "residual."

Figure 36.15 uses the methodology described earlier to analyze the sources of increase in productivity for three different time periods—1960 to 1973, 1973 to 1990, and 1990 to 1994.

Several conclusions emerge from the chart. First, the overall rate of productivity growth was much higher before 1973 than after—the slowdown in productivity growth to which we referred earlier. Second, since 1973 almost all productivity growth can be explained by increases in inputs (including research and development), while before 1973, there was a large residual. It is the decrease in the residual that appears to account for most of the slowdown in productivity. Third, since 1973, increases in capital have contributed less to economic growth, but increases in human capital (education and experience) have contributed more.

These results—and especially the fact that the unusually high rate of productivity growth in the 1950s and 1960s cannot be easily explained—pose major problems for those involved in long-term forecasting. Was the rapid growth of productivity in the 1950s and 1960s an aberration, a result of almost two decades of depression and war, with the consequent postponement of the introduction of new innovations into the economy? Or are the 1970s and

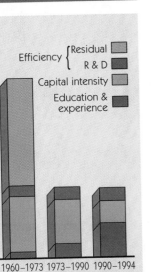

Figure 36.15 GROWTH ACCOUNTING

Over half of the decline in productivity growth since 1973 is left unexplained after accounting for changes in the education and experience of the work force, capital stock, and investments in R & D.

---

rK/Q is just the share of capital in GDP (rK is the total return to capital, and Q is output). Hence the percentage increase in output attributable to the increase in K is the percentage increase in capital times the share of capital.

1980s an aberration—a period of adjustment as fundamentally new technologies, such as computers, became more widely used, their full benefits only to be reaped in future decades?

GROWTH OF THE LABOR FORCE

Earlier in the chapter, we noted that the total growth rate of the economy equaled the growth in hours worked plus the growth in output per hour worked (productivity).

Slow growth in the mid-1990s was partially attributable to the slow pace of productivity, but it was also partially attributable to the slow growth of hours worked. In 1995, for instance, while the unemployment rate hovered around a relatively low 5.5 percent, hours worked increased by only around 1 percent, as compared to an average of 2.3 percent in the 1960s.

Growth in the labor force is driven by two factors: demographics and participation rates. In the Depression, birthrates declined, and then soared immediately after World War II (the baby boomer generation). Thus, as the baby boomers reached working age in the late 1960s and 1970s, the labor force increased markedly. At various times in the United States, immigration has also contributed substantially to the increase in labor force.

The decision whether to work—labor force participation—is affected by a variety of economic and noneconomic factors. There has been a marked increase in female labor force participation over the past quarter century, partially offset by a decrease in male labor force participation. Changes in attitudes

Figure 36.16 WOMEN'S LABOR FORCE PARTICIPATION RATE, CHILD DEPENDENCY RATIO, AND THE BIRTHRATE

The growth of female labor force participation has tapered in the 1990s, following rapid growth in the 1970s and 1980s. This trend appears to be associated with the leveling off of the child dependency ratio for women. By the 1990s, the affect of the reduced dependency ratio on labor force participation may have run its course. *Source: ERP* (1996), Chart 2-4.

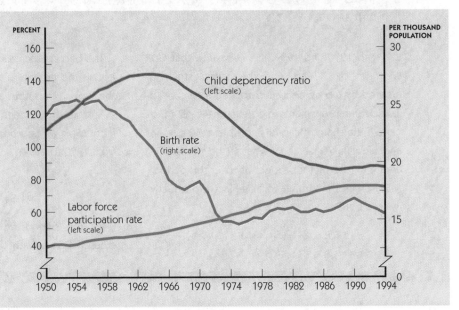

toward women working, especially when they have children, as well as changes in desired family sizes, reduced discrimination, and increased educational opportunities for women have all contributed to increased female participation. Improved Social Security and pension benefits have, on the other hand, led many men to retire earlier.

The lower than expected rate of growth of the U.S. labor force in the 1990s has been attributed largely to a slowing down of the rate of growth of female labor force participation. (See Figure 36.16.) One factor that may help explain this is changes in the number of dependents. As women postponed having children until they were older and as they chose to have smaller families, the number of dependents per working age woman declined. This decline appears to be associated with an increase in female participation. Now, this "dependency ratio" has leveled off, and so too has the increase in labor force participation.

Slower growth in the labor force caused by slower growth of the population has a markedly different effect than slower growth caused by lower productivity. The latter is associated with slower increases in standards of living. By contrast, faster population growth may give rise to congestion and place higher demands on the environment. On the other hand, some economists believe that the rapid expansion of the economy as it seeks to adapt to the increased labor force gives rise to a dynamism which generates increased productivity: increased labor force growth (at least to a point) helps cause increased productivity growth. But the causation also works in reverse: economic slowdowns, such as the Great Depression, lead to low birthrates.

THE COSTS OF ECONOMIC GROWTH

Faith in the virtues of economic progress is widespread. Few openly embrace the alternative of economic stagnation and lower standards of living. Yet not everyone benefits from changes in technology. In the early 1800s, English workmen destroyed labor-saving machinery rather than see it take over their jobs. They were referred to as **Luddites,** after their leader Ned Ludd, whose role may have been largely mythical. Concerns about workers thrown out of their jobs as a result of some innovation are no less real today.

What needs to be kept in mind, and has already been stressed earlier in the book, is that technological progress creates jobs as it destroys them. Of course, it can be hard to teach an old dog new tricks, so a middle-aged or older worker who loses her job may have real difficulty in getting another that is even nearly as good.

Not surprisingly, technical progress frequently meets with resistance. While there is growing acceptance that such resistance is futile—change will eventually come—and that the benefits of progress exceed the costs, there is also increasing recognition of the role of government in assisting individuals who are displaced by technological change in their transition to alternative employment. Such assistance can be thought of as a form of insurance. Most workers face the possibility that their jobs will be made technologically obsolete. Knowing that if they are thrown out of work for this reason they will be at least partially protected adds to a sense of security, something most workers value highly.

More generally, we saw in Part Five that in the long run, with flexible wages, the economy will create enough jobs to match the supply. In Part Six, we saw that in the short run, wage and price rigidity may lead to significant unemployment, but that there are government policies that can help ensure that the economy remains close to full employment. To the extent that government employs such policies, there will be fewer worries about jobs. There will be less resistance to new technologies that lead to job loss, as workers become more confident that the economy will at the same time generate new job opportunities.

ARE THERE LIMITS TO ECONOMIC GROWTH?

In the early 1800s, the famous British economist Thomas Malthus envisioned the future as one in which the ever-increasing labor force would push wages down to the subsistence level, or even lower. Any technological progress that occurred would, in his view, raise wages only temporarily. As the labor supply increased, wages would eventually fall back to the subsistence level.

Over the past century, there has been a decrease in the rate of population growth, a phenomenon perhaps as remarkable as the increase in the rate of technological progress. One might have expected improved medicine and health conditions to cause a population explosion, but the spread of birth control and family planning has had the opposite effect, at least in the more developed countries. Today family size has decreased to the point where in many countries population growth (apart from migration) has almost halted. Those who worry about the limits to growth today believe that *exhaustible* natural resources—like oil, natural gas, phosphorus, or potassium—may pose a limit to economic growth as they are used up in the ordinary course of production.

Most economists do not share this fear, believing that markets do provide incentives for wise use of most resources—that as any good becomes more scarce and its price rises, the search for substitutes will be stimulated. Thus, the rise in the price of oil led to smaller, more efficient cars, cooler but better insulated houses, and a search for alternative sources of energy like geothermal and synthetic fuels, all of which resulted in a decline in the consumption of oil.

Still, there is one area in which the price system does not work well—the area of externalities. Without government intervention, for example, producers have no incentive to worry about air and water pollution. And in our globally connected world, what one country does results in externalities for others. Cutting down the rain forest in Brazil, for example, may have worldwide climatic consequences. The less developed countries feel that they can ill afford the costs of pollution control, when they can barely pay the price of any industrialization. Most economists do not believe that we face an either/or choice. We do not have to abandon growth to preserve our environment. Nevertheless, a sensitivity to the quality of our environment may affect how we go about growing. This sensitivity is building a new consensus in favor of **sustainable development,** that is, growth not based simply on the exploitation of natural resources and the environment in a way that cannot be sustained. In many cases, policies can be devised that improve economic efficiency, and thus promote economic growth, at the same time that they decrease adverse environmental effects. These include elimination of energy subsidies and certain agricultural subsidies that induce farmers to use excessive amounts of fertilizers and pesticides.

THE PROGNOSIS

Though this century has been marked by large increases in productivity, the rate of productivity growth has not been steady. There have been periods of relative stagnation as well as periods in which the economy has burst forth with energy and growth. Is the decline in productivity growth in the United

States just a passing phase? Or were the high rates of productivity growth during the 1950s and 1960s the aberration?

The analysis of this chapter suggests grounds for both pessimism and optimism. There is no quick or easy reversal of many of the factors hampering productivity growth, such as the low rate of private savings. But some of the factors hampering productivity growth are more easily altered. These include the failure of government to improve the economy's infrastructure, the large fiscal deficit, and the low level of expenditures on research and development, at least expenditures directed at improving the economy's productivity rather than increasing military prowess.

Most economists think it unlikely that the United States will ever again be in the position of technological dominance it held for so long. But there is widespread optimism that the U.S. economy can return to a higher level of productivity growth, provided the right government policies are pursued.

REVIEW AND PRACTICE

SUMMARY

1. The United States experienced a marked slowdown in the rate of productivity growth in the early 1970s, compared with the preceding two decades. Even seemingly small declines in the rate of increase in productivity will have a powerful adverse effect on the standard of living over a generation or two.

2. There are four major sources of productivity growth: increases in the accumulation of capital goods (investment); a higher quality of the labor force; greater efficiency in allocating resources; and technological change. Since 1973 almost all of the increase in productivity can be attributed to increases in capital, improvements in human capital, and expenditures on research and development. In recent years, the relative role of human capital has increased and the role of physical capital has decreased.

3. The rate of savings in the United States has declined in recent years. Some of the reasons are improved government retirement programs, more extensive insurance coverage and greater ease in borrowing, and changes in social attitudes.

4. Because private savings does not respond much to after-tax rates of return (the interest elasticity is low), it is difficult to increase savings by providing tax incentives. Reducing the government deficit—such as occurred beginning in 1993—may be more effective.

5. Increases in human capital—improved education—are a major source of productivity increases. There are large returns to investments in education. While the U.S. educational system has important strengths,

there are serious concerns about the quality of education American students are receiving in preparation for the labor force and about the number of scientists and engineers being trained.

6. The twentieth century has been marked by shifts in the U.S. economy from an agricultural base to an industrial base and more recently to a service base. Some economists think that the potential for technological progress is less in the service sector than in the industrial sector, and this accounts for part of the productivity slowdown.

7. Improvements in technology, partly as a result of expenditures on research and development (R & D) are a major source of increases in productivity. Government supports R & D through both direct spending and tax incentives, though direct support for R & D that is not defense-related has actually declined during the past quarter century.

8. Some of the changes in the rate of growth of the economy are a result of changes in the rate of growth of the labor force. This is partly a result of demographics—changes in the number of children born in different years—and partly a result of decisions to participate in the labor force. There has been an overall trend for decreased labor force participation by men and increased labor force participation by women.

9. There has long been concern that certain natural resources (like oil) will someday run out, causing economic growth to halt. However, most economists would argue that the price of resources will increase as they become more scarce, and this will encourage both greater conservation and a search for substitutes.

10. Sustainable development requires growth strategies that use resources and the environment in ways that do not jeopardize future potential growth.

KEY TERMS

capital deepening	total factor	Luddites
life-cycle theory of	productivity	sustainable
savings	analysis	development
infrastructure		

REVIEW QUESTIONS

1. True or false: "Since growth-oriented policies might have an effect of only a percent or two per year, they are not worth worrying much about." Explain.

2. What are the four possible sources of productivity growth?

3. What are the various explanations of the slowdown of the rate of increase in productivity?

4. What are the components of overall U.S. savings, and how did they change in the 1980s?

5. What are some reasons for the decrease in the savings rate in recent years?

6. Will government policies to raise the rate of return on savings, such as exempting interest from taxes, necessarily lead to much increased savings?

7. What is the link between changes in savings and changes in investment in a closed economy, in a small open economy, and in a large open economy like the United States? What is the link between changes in the capital stock (investment) and the rate of growth of productivity in the short run? What is the link between changes in the capital stock and the *level* of productivity (output per worker) in the long run? What is meant by capital deepening?

8. What policies might the government use to increase investment in R & D?

9. What is total factor productivity and how is it measured?

10. What are some costs of economic growth? Short of seeking to restrain growth, how might government deal with these costs?

11. What are some of the concerns about limits to economic growth? How have they been overcome in the past?

PROBLEMS

1. Will the following changes increase or decrease the rate of household savings?
   (a) The proportion of people in the 45–64 age bracket increases.
   (b) Government programs provide secure retirement benefits.
   (c) Credit cards become much more prevalent.
   (d) The proportion of people in the 21–45 age bracket increases.
   (e) Government programs to guarantee student loans are enacted.

2. Explain how the following factors would increase or decrease the average productivity of labor:
   (a) successful reforms of the educational system;
   (b) the entry of new workers into the economy;
   (c) earlier retirement;
   (d) high unemployment rates during a recession.

3. Suppose a firm is considering spending $1 million on R & D projects, which it believes will translate into patents that it will be able to sell for $2.5 million in ten years. Assume that the firm ignores risk. If the interest rate is 10 percent, is the firm likely to attempt these R & D projects? If the government offers a 20 percent R & D tax credit, how does the firm's calculation change?

4. Explain why a rapid influx of workers might result in a lower output per worker (a reduction in productivity). Would the effect on productivity depend on the skill level of the new workers?

5. Explain, using supply and demand diagrams, how a technological change such as computerization could lead to lower wages of unskilled workers and higher wages of skilled workers.

6. Using the model of Chapter 25, discuss the effect on the level of investment for an open economy of (a) an increased government deficit; (b) an increased government expenditure, financed by taxes on households that reduce their disposable income; (c) an investment tax credit. How will such policies affect future living standards of those living in the country?

DEFICITS AND DEFICIT REDUCTION

We saw in Chapter 26 that beginning in 1981, the United States began to run high fiscal deficits. The increased deficits led to increasing debt, and an increasing burden on the government simply to pay interest on the debt. Beginning in 1993 the deficit was finally reduced not only as a percentage of GDP but in absolute terms—with the debt/GDP ratio leveling off and finally beginning to decline—and in 1995 there emerged a bipartisan consensus on working toward a balanced budget. Still there remained debates about how deficit reduction should be accomplished, and whether even the most aggressive proposed actions addressed the long-term problems of the country.

This chapter reviews the origins of the deficit problem and the debate about the consequences of deficits and how the deficit problem should be addressed. The final section addresses the long-term problems facing the United States and most other industrialized countries.

KEY QUESTIONS

1. What gave rise to the fiscal deficit? And why is it so difficult to reduce?

2. What are the central economic issues in the debate about how deficits should be reduced?

3. What are the procedural reforms that have been proposed to ensure that deficits do not emerge in the fu-

ture, and what are the problems with these reforms?

4. What are the long-term problems facing the United States and other industrialized countries that if not adequately addressed are likely to result in a deficit problem emerging in the future, even if the deficit is reduced now?

THE SOURCES OF THE CURRENT U.S. DEFICIT PROBLEM

The current U.S. deficit problem began around 1981. As we saw in Chapter 26, federal budget deficits soared in the 1980s and early 1990s, with the real deficit peaking at more than $290 billion in 1992. Figure 37.1 tells the same story in terms of the ratio of the deficit to GDP. The deficit as a percentage of GDP rose to a peacetime record of 6.3 percent in 1983, hovering between 3 and 5 percent for most of the remainder of the decade, and gradually decreasing from 4.9 percent in 1992 to around 2 percent by the mid-1990s.

A good way to pose the question of what caused the soaring budget deficit is to ask: What changed between the 1970s (and earlier decades) and the 1980s? There are five main answers to this question.

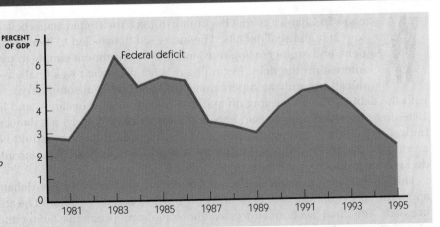

Figure 37.1 THE FEDERAL DEFICIT AS A PERCENTAGE OF GDP (1980–95)

The federal deficit as a percent of GDP reached a peacetime high in 1983 of 6.3 percent. It has since fallen gradually, reaching 2.3 percent in 1995. *Source: ERP* (1996), Table B-75.

Reduced Federal Taxes   During the 1970s, federal taxes usually collected between 18 and 19 percent of GDP. In 1980 and 1981 that percentage climbed to over 20 percent. (Remember, 1 percent of a multitrillion-dollar economy will be tens of billions of dollars.) Tax cuts enacted early in the Reagan presidency pushed the federal tax take back down to its historical range of 18–19 percent of GDP. The slight increase in taxes in 1993 has not altered this basic picture.

Higher Defense Spending   Federal defense spending fell during the 1970s, as the Vietnam War came to an end, from 8.4 percent of GDP in 1970 to 4.9 percent of GDP in 1979. In 1979, though, the Soviet Union invaded Afghanistan, and President Carter called for a large defense buildup. After Ronald Reagan was elected president in 1980, he followed through on these plans. From 1983 to 1988, defense spending exceeded 6 percent of GDP. With the end of the Cold War, there has been a reduction in defense spending to under 4 percent of GDP. Though the threat of small wars in various parts of the world has kept the "peace dividend" smaller than many had hoped, the reduction in defense spending as a percentage of GDP played an important part in the deficit reductions after 1993.

Higher Social Spending on the Elderly   As the elderly population in the United States has grown, not only absolutely but as a proportion of the population, federal expenditures on programs like Social Security and Medicare (providing health care to the aged) have expanded dramatically. These programs averaged 5.0 percent of GDP in the 1970s, but increased to over 6 percent of GDP by 1980 and close to 7 percent by 1982. By the mid-1990s they constitute 7 percent of GDP.

Increasing Health Care Expenditures   Through Medicare and Medicaid (the government program providing health care to the poor), the government has assumed an increasing share of total health care expenditures, to the point where today, the federal government alone pays 30 percent of all health care expenditures. Health care expenditures themselves have soared. Through the 1980s and early 1990s these expenditures were increasing at close to 12 percent per year, doubling every six years. A number of initiatives undertaken during the Bush and Clinton administrations have brought the rate of increase down to between 8 percent and 10 percent, a number still far higher than the rate of income growth.

Higher Interest Payments   Like other borrowers, the federal government pays interest. During the 1970s, federal interest payments were about 1.5 percent of GDP. But from 1983 to 1990 they exceeded 3 percent of GDP. The main reason was the increasing deficit. If the debt in 1995 were the same as it had been at the start of the Reagan era in 1981 (after adjusting for inflation), the government would be running a balanced budget, rather than a deficit of $160 billion. Deficits, through interest payments, feed on themselves.

Factors Not Contributing to the Deficit Problem   In a sense, any expenditure can be thought of as contributing to the deficit problem—if that expenditure were reduced, other things equal, the deficit would be reduced. But some factors

CLOSE-UP: MEASURING THE BUDGET DEFICIT—WHAT'S LARGE, WHAT'S REAL, AND WHAT'S RIGHT?

The deficits of the 1980s and 1990s have been huge. At its peak in 1992 the dollar figure was $290 billion. By 1996 it had been brought down to $117 billion. But are dollar amounts the right way to measure the size and importance of deficits? Shouldn't we take into consideration the effects of inflation and the growth of the overall economy?

Robert Eisner of Northwestern University argues for focusing on the overall increase in the *real* debt—that is, the debt adjusted for changes in the price level. With total debt outstanding to the public of approximately $3.6 trillion, an inflation rate of 3 percent implies a reduction of the real value of the debt of $108 billion per year. This decrease in the real value of the outstanding debt, in Eisner's view, should be subtracted from any increase in debt due to the deficit. In fiscal 1996, this inflation-adjusted deficit was only $9 billion, compared to the measured deficit of $117 billion.

According to this definition, the Carter administration actually ran an inflation-adjusted surplus due to the effects of inflation on the value of the debt. By contrast, the relatively low rates of inflation during the Reagan and Bush administrations were not enough to offset the large deficits due to expenditures far exceeding revenues.

The full-employment or structural deficit takes into account the level of economic activity in the economy, as we saw in Chapter 13. It asks, what would the deficit have been had the economy been operating at full employment? For instance, in 1991, as the economy was in recession, the deficit was officially $269 billion—the largest in history up to that point—but the structural deficit was $191 billion, still large by any standards, but $78 billion less than the actual deficit. But the Reagan years look particularly bad from this perspective, since, except during wars, the economy had never previously run large structural deficits.

In recent years, as well as in the years immediately following World Wars I and II, the U.S. government was saddled with a huge debt. The interest payments on this inherited debt make it particularly difficult to attain a balanced budget. The primary deficit asks what the deficit would have been had there been no inherited debt; that is, it subtracts interest payments from the deficit. If the government is running a primary surplus, it means that revenues more than cover current expenditures. The government ran a primary surplus for only the second time since 1979 in 1995 (see figure above).

Source: ERP (1996), Table B-76.

commonly given credit for the deficit problem do not deserve the blame they receive. For instance, polls suggest that many Americans believe welfare payments and foreign assistance are at fault. Yet, general welfare payments, such as aid to families with dependent children (AFDC) and food stamps, are less than 4 percent of the federal budget, and their share of the federal budget has decreased in recent decades. Under the AFDC program, benefits per family fell by 55 percent from 1970 to 1993. Similarly foreign assistance is minuscule—about 1 percent of the federal budget. Reducing welfare payments and foreign assistance would still leave a substantial deficit.

FACTORS CONTRIBUTING TO THE DEFICIT PROBLEM

Reduced taxation
Increased defense spending
Higher social spending on elderly
Increased public health costs
Higher interest payments

CONSEQUENCES OF GOVERNMENT DEFICITS

When the government runs a deficit, it must borrow to pay the difference between its expenditures and its revenues. When it runs a deficit year after year, it must borrow year after year. The cumulated value of these borrowings is the *federal debt*—what the government owes. Figure 37.2 shows the soaring federal debt. The immediate consequence of the soaring federal debt is that

Figure 37.2 **THE FEDERAL DEBT**

The debt represents the accumulation of previous deficits. Panel A shows the federal debt (in real dollars) soaring enormously in the 1980s; by the early 1990s it had far exceeded the previous record set in World War II. Panel B shows the debt as a percentage of GDP. While the real debt continued to increase in the mid-1990s, as a percentage of GDP it had finally begun to stabilize.

the government has to pay out more and more in interest—one of the factors that we identified earlier as contributing itself to the deficit.

Economists have traditionally argued that government borrowing, just like individual borrowing, makes sense or does not make sense according to the purpose for which the money is used. It makes sense to borrow to buy a house that you will live in for many years or a car that you will drive for several years. In that way, you spread out paying for the item as you use it. It makes economic sense to borrow money for an educational degree that will lead to a higher-paying job in the future. But if you are paying this year for the vacation from two years ago, maybe you should chop up your credit cards!

Countries are in a similar situation. Borrowing to finance a road, school, or industrial project that will be used for many years may be quite appropriate. Borrowing to pay for projects that are never completed (or perhaps are never even started) or borrowing to finance this year's government salaries poses real problems. Many governments have taken on more debt than they could comfortably pay off, forcing them to raise taxes sharply and reduce living standards. Others have simply failed to repay, jeopardizing their ability to borrow in the future.

Financing government expenditures by borrowing rather than by raising taxes results in higher levels of consumption in the short run (since disposable income is higher). When the economy is at full employment, higher consumption implies there is less room for investment. To maintain the economy at full employment without inflation, the Federal Reserve Board has to increase interest rates. Deficit financing leads to lower investment, and thus, in the long run, to lower output and consumption.

Reducing the deficit has the opposite effect: it allows interest rates to fall, stimulating investment, and thus promoting economic growth and better future living standards.

HOW FUTURE GENERATIONS ARE AFFECTED BY THE DEFICITS

By borrowing, the government places the burden of reduced consumption on future generations. The U.S. government partly financed World War II by borrowing rather than raising taxes. Suppose that the bonds it issued were purchased by forty-year-old workers. Then thirty years later, as these forty-year-olds enter retirement, the government decides to pay off the bonds by raising taxes on those who are then in the labor force. In effect, the government is transferring funds from these younger workers to those who *were* the workers during the war, who are now seventy and retired. Thus, part of the cost of the war is borne by the generation who entered the work force *after* the war. The lifetime consumption of those who were forty during the war is little affected. They might otherwise have put their savings into stocks or bonds issued by firms; the war (to the extent it is financed by debt, or bonds) affects the form of their savings, but not the total amount they have to spend over their lifetime.

ALTERNATIVE PERSPECTIVES ON THE BURDEN OF THE DEBT

Though the discussion so far represents the current dominant views, some believe that these views overstate the burden of the debt. Two different reasons are given.

THE "DEBT DOES NOT MATTER BECAUSE WE OWE IT TO OURSELVES" ARGUMENT

It used to be argued in the United States that the fiscal deficit does not matter because we simply owe the money to ourselves. The budget deficit was compared to the effect of one brother borrowing from another on the total welfare of the family. One member of the family may be better off, another worse off, but the indebtedness does not really matter much to the family as a whole. Financing government expenditures by debt, it was argued, could lead to a transfer of resources between generations, but this transfer would still keep all the buying power in the hands of U.S. citizens.

We now recognize that this argument is wrong on three counts. First, even if we owe the money to ourselves, the debt affects investment and thus future wages and productivity, as noted. And second, today we do not in fact owe the money to ourselves. The United States is borrowing abroad and becoming indebted to foreigners. The consequences of the country spending beyond its means are no different from those of a family spending beyond its means. Eventually it has to pay the price of the consumption binge. In the case of a national consumption binge, it is future generations that have to pay the price.

Third, simply to pay interest on the debt requires high levels of taxes, and taxes introduce distortions into the economy, discouraging work and savings. (There is some disagreement among economists about the *quantitative* significance of this effect.)

RICARDIAN EQUIVALENCE

There is a more recent argument that, in the face of increased deficits, individuals save more. Robert Barro of Harvard University—developing an argument made (and later rejected) by David Ricardo, one of the nineteenth century's greatest economists—believes that individuals care so much about their children that they increase their bequests when they see their offspring faced with future indebtedness caused by government deficits. To be able to be more generous in their bequests, they increase their household savings by exactly the amount of the increase in the deficit: national savings does not change. The increased government dissaving is fully offset. This view is called **Ricardian equivalence** because it contends that taxation and deficits are *equivalent* means of financing expenditures.

The evidence does not support Barro's theoretical contention. Increased government deficits may lead to slightly higher household savings, but far too little to offset fully those deficit increases. In the late 1980s and early 1990s, when the deficit was running at more than 5 percent of GDP, the household savings rate was only 3 to 4 percent. If Barro's theory were correct, then in the absence of the government deficit, household savings rates would have been an implausibly low number between minus 1 and minus 2 percent.

CONSEQUENCES OF GOVERNMENT DEFICITS

1. Some of the burden of current expenditures is shifted to future generations directly.
2. Issuing bonds may decrease investment and thus make future generations worse off indirectly.
3. Foreign indebtedness may increase, reducing future standards of living.
4. Government dissaving has not been offset by private savings.

ADDRESSING THE DEFICIT PROBLEM

At one level of analysis, reducing the deficit is a simple matter: either increase taxes or reduce expenditures. Currently, there appears limited public taste for tax increases, even on the wealthy. Thus discussions have focused on improving the efficiency of government or cutting back on government programs.

All through the years that the deficit was rising, politicians were arguing that both of these should be done; and yet remarkably little progress was made until 1993. The question is why?

CUTTING BACK ON GOVERNMENT PROGRAMS

Understanding how government spends money helps explain why reducing expenditures proved so difficult during the 1980s. There are two basic types of government expenditures: **discretionary** and **nondiscretionary.** Discretionary expenditures—which include expenditures on military, government operation, and most education and training programs—are decided on an annual basis. Each year, Congress and the president have the *discretion* to change their levels. By contrast, nondiscretionary spending is made up of interest payments on the national debt and **entitlements,** where the law specifies certain benefits—such as Social Security, Medicare, and food stamps—to which individuals who meet certain criteria are *entitled*, and expenditure is then determined simply by the cost of those entitlements.

THE FAILURES OF THE 1980s

President Reagan had made a commitment not to cut Social Security and to increase expenditures on defense. With these commitments, to eliminate the deficit would have required drastic—and seemingly unacceptable—cutbacks in other programs. The total of all nonmilitary discretionary expenditures was less than $300 billion, so that it was essentially impossible to eliminate a $200 billion deficit—which by 1992 had increased to close to $300 billion— simply by cutting back on these programs.

The challenge of reducing the deficit and keeping it low remains much the same today: as Figure 37.3 shows, nondefense discretionary expenditures represent a relatively small fraction of total government expenditures. Entitlement expenditures, especially those directed at the aged—Social Security, Medicare, and large parts of the Medicaid program—are large and anticipated to increase markedly as the baby boomers reach retirement. Unless these programs are reformed, there will be continuing pressures on other parts of the budget. If it is assumed that taxes cannot be increased and defense expenditures cannot be decreased, then the burden of adjustment falls on nondefense discretionary expenditures.

**Figure 37.3 THE CHAL-
LENGE OF REDUCING
FEDERAL SPENDING**

A large proportion of federal
spending is devoted to three areas:
defense, entitlement programs, and
interest payments. To reduce federal
spending, large cuts must be made in
at least some of these categories,
since other areas of spending are
simply not large enough to make much
difference. *Sources: ERP* (1995), Chart
2-12; *ERP* (1996), Table B-77.

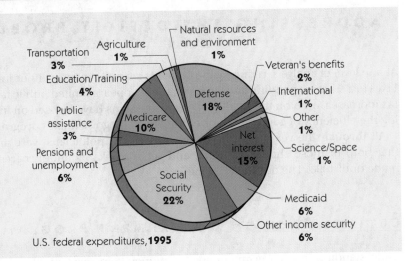

U.S. federal expenditures, **1995**

ONGOING ISSUES IN DEFICIT REDUCTION

By late 1995, a bipartisan consensus had been reached that the deficit should
be eliminated within a few years. Between 1992 and 1996, the deficit was in
fact reduced by 60 percent, and in real terms, and as a percentage of GDP, the
reduction was even more dramatic. The deficit reduction debate really became a debate over the size of government. One side argued that expenditures and taxes should be reduced; reduced taxes, especially on capital gains,
would stimulate economic growth. The other argued that these further cuts
in expenditures would jeopardize investments in human capital and technology, which had high returns, and accordingly would be counterproductive—
growth might actually be retarded. They argued further that while it was clear
that the benefits of capital gains tax reduction went disproportionately to the
wealthy—who had already received most of the benefits from economic
growth over the past two decades—it was not clear that there would be significant growth benefits. There was little evidence linking variations in a capital
gains tax to either savings, investment, or economic growth.[1] Indeed, because
some forms of investment would, with a capital gains tax reduction, receive
preferential tax treatment, the allocation of resources would be distorted and
economic efficiency, and possibly growth, impaired.

While there was a wide consensus on the desirability of deficit reduction,
there remained some who argued that tax reduction was more important
than deficit reduction. Thus, even if one could not reduce expenditures, the
beneficial effects of lower taxes (increased incentives to work and save)
exceeded the detrimental effects of the resulting increased deficits. Most

---

[1]Earlier discussions noted that the savings rate was not very sensitive to returns.

economists remained skeptical of these so-called **supply siders**, who emphasized the increased inputs of capital and labor from lower taxes. Critics of the supply-siders argued that there was little statistical evidence in support of such large supply responses, and that the "Reagan" experiment of lowering tax rates (the top tax rate was brought down from 70 percent to 50 percent in 1981, and then to 31 percent in 1986) had proven itself a failure, leading to huge deficits.

IMPROVING THE BUDGETARY PROCESS

The persistence of the deficit led many to argue that there should be a change in the way budgets are adopted. In this section, we consider two such changes. One of these has already been implemented; the other remains under discussion.

BUDGET ENFORCEMENT ACT AND SCORING

In 1990 Congress passed the Budget Enforcement Act, designed to reduce the likelihood of runaway deficits. Whenever Congress passes a new program, it is required to provide new taxes to pay for it, or to find offsetting expenditure

The Congressional Budget Office (CBO) has had a long reputation for being nonpartisan. The director of the CBO at the time that Clinton was introducing his managed health care reforms was Bob Reischauer, a Democrat; yet because he said that the evidence on the extent to which managed care would reduce health care costs was not clear, he refused to credit the programs with much savings. The nonpartisan nature of the CBO was reaffirmed when, under the new director, June O'Neill, appointed when the Republicans gained control of the House and Senate, the CBO refused to credit the Republican managed health care reforms with as much savings as they would have liked.

On other issues, however, critics worried whether the CBO was departing from its traditional nonpartisan view. Consider the question: How much would interest rates fall as a result of deficit reduction? Presumably, as government expenditures decreased, interest rates would fall, as the Fed took actions to ensure that the economy remained at full employment. To be sure, how much interest rates would fall was problematic, since it depended on the interest elasticity of investment (the percentage increase in investment resulting from a 1 percent decrease in the interest rate), of which economists had markedly different estimates. Still, she concluded that interest rates would fall by approximately 1.7 percentage points. But, the CBO refused to give the Clinton deficit reduction package *any* credit for interest rate reduction, since in their estimates, the Clinton budget deficit reduction package did not *fully* achieve a balanced budget. Critics of the CBO argued that, while they might disagree with the CBO assessment of the magnitude of the expenditure cuts, the cuts were sufficiently severe that there should have been *some* interest rate reductions—roughly in proportion to the reductions in the expenditures.

Other critics pointed out that even the CBO's estimate of the magnitude of the deficit (apart from interest rate reductions) was problematic, since these estimates were more conservative than not only those of the Clinton administration, but also of the consensus of business forecasters; and that its estimate of the rate of increase of health care costs failed to incorporate recent changes in trends in those variables, and was higher than those of the career actuaries who had for years collected the data and provided the estimates. But supporters of the CBO pointed out that in using those numbers, the CBO was simply continuing to use numbers similar to those that it had used under Democratic leadership. If there was a fault, it was not with partisan leadership, but with the longstanding methods of the CBO.

cuts. The Congressional Budget Office (CBO)—ostensibly a nonpartisan group of professionals—"scores" the program—that is, calculates how much it will cost. Inevitably, there are issues of judgment involved. Thus, in recent debates on health care reform, the CBO argued that managed care would, in the short run, result in only limited savings. Had they scored managed care as generating large savings, it might have been far easier to adopt health care reforms.

CAPITAL BUDGETS

Businesses emphasize the distinction between expenditures to buy machines—capital expenditures—and other expenditures. Investments enhance the firm's ability to produce in the future. We argued earlier that there was a marked difference between borrowing to make an investment and borrowing to buy a vacation. Government accounting systems do not make a distinction, though businesses do. Not only do businesses distinguish between the kinds of expenditure in their annual reports, but they maintain capital accounts which show their assets (including machines) and liabilities.

Some have argued that government should have a capital budget, which would identify expenditures on investments. While some countries have done so, the United States has not, partially because of the political problems of defining investments. Most capital budgets only include investments in physical objects, like roads; and education advocates have worried that such a capital budget would divert resources away from human capital formation, from education and research. Similarly, health advocates argue that providing good health care for children is an investment in their future, raising their productivity and lowering future expenditures on medical care.

OTHER STRATEGIES

Two other suggestions for improving the budgetary process have been widely discussed. One, the **line item veto,** gives the president the right to veto particular expenditures within a budget bill. It went into effect in January 1997. Previously, he could only accept or reject the entire bill. He was loathe to veto a large bill for, say, national defense, simply because of some small wasteful expenditure that goes to benefit the constituents of some Congressman. (See Policy Perspective box.) The other is a constitutional amendment, called the **balanced budget amendment,** requiring Congress to adopt a balanced budget. We discussed this earlier, in Chapter 32. Such an amendment has come within a few votes of passing several times. Advocates say it would (by definition) force fiscal responsibility; the government would have to come up with a balanced budget. Critics point out the severe problems of implementation: What happens if Congress fails to comply, for instance because revenues fall short because of an economic recession? Balancing the budget on the basis of prospective expenditures and revenues requires someone to make estimates. Who should do that, and how can one ensure that it is done in a nonpolitical way? Many economists criticize the balanced budget amendment because it takes away one of the main tools of economic stabilization; it will make it more difficult to maintain the economy at full employment, putting almost all of the responsibility on monetary policy. Those who are less confident of the ability of monetary policy to counter quickly a severe recession are particularly worried about such amendments. Some of the proposals—though not the ones that have come close to passage by Congress—have included escape clauses in the event of a recession.

Another proposal designed to reduce expenditures is the line-item veto, giving the president the right to veto particular expenditure items within the appropriations bills sent to him by Congress. Members of Congress frequently put into such bills "pork" provisions—such as new courthouses in their districts—and the line item veto is designed to allow the president to ferret out such expenditures.

Several states have such provisions. The evidence suggests that expenditures in states with the line item veto are no less than in states without it. One reason may be that governors are then brought into the "deals" which are inevitably put together to enable legislation to get passed.

While many members of Congress promised to support the line item veto, they have been worried that doing so would increase the president's power. In 1996, Congress passed and the president signed into law the line item veto.

THE LONG-TERM PROBLEM: ENTITLEMENTS AND THE AGED

Even if the United States is able to eliminate its deficit over the next few years, the long-term problem will persist: entitlement expenditures for Medicare and Social Security are likely to soar in the coming decades. The reasons are twofold. First, the number of elderly in the U.S. population will increase dramatically, vastly increasing the number of eligible recipients for Social Security and Medicare. Second, health care costs for the elderly may continue to increase.

THE GROWING U.S. ELDERLY POPULATION

The twenty years following World War II saw a huge increase in births in the United States, giving rise to the generation commonly known as the baby boomers. During the early decades of the twenty-first century, the baby boomers will reach retirement age. At the same time, life expectancy will also be skyrocketing. In 1935, when the Social Security system was adopted, life expectancy at age sixty-five was only 12.6 years; by 1995, it had increased by almost 50 percent to 17.2 years; by 2040, it is expected to increase to 19.1 years, with some calculations predicting an even greater increase to 21 years. These population trends will have dramatic consequences. The number of elderly

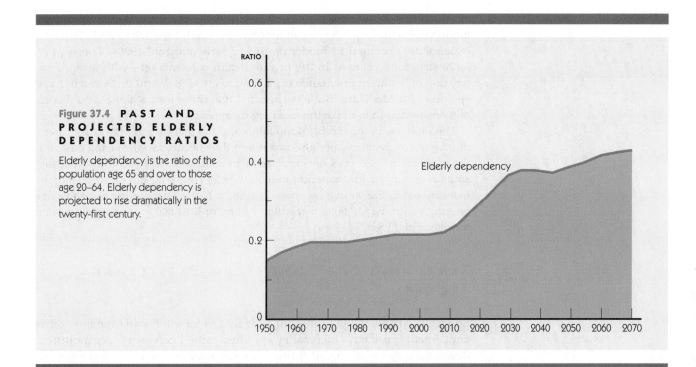

Figure 37.4 PAST AND PROJECTED ELDERLY DEPENDENCY RATIOS

Elderly dependency is the ratio of the population age 65 and over to those age 20–64. Elderly dependency is projected to rise dramatically in the twenty-first century.

will increase by 38 to 44 million by 2040, and there will be more Social Security beneficiaries to be supported by each working-age member of the population, as illustrated in Figure 37.4.

The increase in the number of beneficiaries has, of course, been anticipated. Social Security and Medicare tax rates have been set so that revenues today exceed expenditures, and the difference has been put in a government trust fund, to be used as the baby boomers reach retirement age. The problem is that the amount set aside has not been large enough. As of 1996, projections were that the Medicare trust fund would run out of funds in 6 years. In the case of Social Security, expenditures would exceed revenues in 2020, starting the depletion of the trust fund; it would be fully depleted in 2030.

INCREASING HEALTH CARE COSTS FOR THE ELDERLY

Trends in the costs of health care only exacerbate the problem. In the 1980s and early 1990s health care prices have increased at a pace far in excess of the increase in the cost of living. During the same time, health care costs for each elderly person have increased even more, with Medicare expenditures increasing at a rate of more than 10 percent per year. Looking ahead to the next century, such spending increases appear unsustainable.

The evolution of increasing health care costs has attracted some debate among policymakers. The rate of increase in health care prices and Medicare expenditures seemed to moderate in the early and mid-1990s. There were large structural reforms in the private health care market—with a rapid expansion of health maintenance organizations (HMOs)—and these might have spillovers for Medicare. But few expected that these forces alone would contain costs enough to make the problem disappear.

The increase in the elderly population and the increase in Medicare expenditures for each elderly person meant that the country faced soaring costs for the elderly, far in excess of Social Security and Medicare revenues. Already, some critics argue that expenditures on the elderly are far out of proportion to investments in the young: by one accounting, federal expenditures per capita amount to almost $16,000 for the elderly, and only $1,200 for each child under the age of eighteen.

REMEDYING THE LONG-TERM ENTITLEMENT PROBLEM

Budgetary arithmetic provides only two means for addressing the long-term entitlement problem: increasing revenues and decreasing expenditures. Revenues may be increased through higher tax rates or increased incomes (resulting from greater productivity). Expenditures are reduced when government programs are eliminated or downsized, and when the number of beneficiaries for entitlements are reduced. The recent political climate offers little optimism for those who propose higher tax rates, even though the magnitude of the tax increases required to bring the Social Security fund into balance are relatively modest—an increase in the payroll tax rate of less than 3 percent would probably do the trick.

Another line of attack is to change the benefit structure of entitlements in ways which reduce expenditures. For instance, increased life expectancy, along with a decline in the relative importance of physical labor in the workplace and improved health of the elderly, provides a rationale for restructuring Social Security. Many sixty-five-year-olds could continue to work. Indeed, the Social Security reforms of 1983 increased the normal retirement age to sixty-seven, and there have been proposals to link the normal retirement age to longevity—as life span increases, so would the retirement age.

There have also been proposals to invest portions of the Social Security trust fund in equities. Historically, equities have yielded a far higher return than government bonds (in which trust funds are currently invested). If equities continue to yield the same high returns, then the solvency of the trust fund can be extended, possibly even permanently, without reducing benefits or increasing taxes. Critics worry about the variability of the returns to the stock market, arguing that there is a chance that matters would be made even worse than they are today. They worry too that with the Social Security system buying fewer government bonds, the government would have to pay higher interest rates to finance its debt, exacerbating the deficit problem. At this point, there is no agreement about the likely magnitude of the increase in interest rates, and therefore about the quantitative significance of this concern.

The increases in public health care costs for the aged represent a more serious problem, and there is consensus that somehow these costs need to be brought under control. A seemingly easy way is simply to reduce the reimbursement rate for hospitals and doctors. However, critics of such proposals argue that there is a limit to this strategy—below some point, providers will either not provide services or there will be a decrease in the quality of services provided—and we may be near that point. Another way to control public health care costs is to force the aged to pay a larger fraction of their costs, but besides being politically unpopular, putting much of an additional burden on the elderly would force many of them into poverty. Introducing more means testing—making those who can afford it pay more—while helpful in reducing the deficit, would not address the more fundamental structural problems.

Structural reforms have focused on two strategies: improved consumers' incentives, and improved management of care. Most individuals have most of their serious health care costs paid for by insurance, and thus have no incentive to economize. Those who focus on incentives argue for more extensive use of deductibles, encouraging major medical and catastrophic insurance policies, which cover individuals for large bills only. Proposals for medical savings accounts would allow individuals to set aside money in a tax-exempt account to meet the expenses that they would then have to bear. Critics point out that most of the explosion of health care costs is associated precisely with these major medical expenses, and hence these reforms would not address the central issue. Moreover, medical savings accounts would do little to decrease government's costs, since individuals would opt for the catastrophic and major medical policies when they are healthy, but transfer to standard programs when they become sick—which is when most of the costs are incurred anyway.

Other structural reforms focus on **managed care.** These reforms recognize that most decisions about health care utilization are effectively made by doctors. The problem is to provide doctors with appropriate incentives. The fee-for-service system, in which doctors are paid for every service they perform, has incentives for doctors to provide more services than needed (especially since typically, insurance firms and government bear the costs, not the patient). Under managed care, the health care provider (typically an HMO) receives a fixed fee per year per patient. It thus has an incentive to ensure that they receive, for instance, cost-effective preventive care. Medicare reforms in 1983 resulted in hospitals receiving a fixed fee for each incidence of illness they treated; earlier they had been reimbursed on the basis of services performed. The new arrangement provided incentives for them to lower treatment costs. Unfortunately, it also provided an incentive for hospitals to get patients out of the hospital as soon as possible. Not surprisingly, post-hospital care costs ballooned. One widely discussed structural reform would make hospitals responsible for hospital and post-hospital care, providing them an incentive to manage overall costs, not only costs within the hospital.

Some critics of all of these proposals say that America will not be able to solve its health care cost problem until it faces up to the underlying cause: rapid changes in technology, which have enhanced the ability to extend life span, but at a high cost. The changes in technology, themselves, are a result of misdirected incentives: since life-prolonging innovations will get adopted, almost regardless of costs, researchers have little incentive to focus on costs (unlike other areas, in which costs are crucial). Research needs to be more cost conscious, and more of it needs to be redirected to reducing costs of health care.

Finally, society needs to ask fundamental questions: how much of its resources should be devoted to prolonging life, and how much should be spent on other uses, such as increasing the productivity of the young? Is a $20,000 hip replacement for a ninety-year-old with a life expectancy of a few years the most valuable use of society's resources? These are difficult and unpleasant questions, but as long as society as a whole bears the brunt of these costs, through its Medicare and Medicaid programs, there is no way of avoiding them.

REVIEW AND PRACTICE

SUMMARY

1. The early 1980s were marked by a surge in the size of federal budget deficits. There are five main causes for the increase: lower taxes, higher defense spending, higher spending on support for the elderly, higher health care expenditures, and higher interest payments.

2. Government borrowing can be an economic burden for future generations in several ways. First, future generations may have to bear the burden of paying off the borrowing; there is a transfer from one generation to another. Second, government borrowing can crowd out investment, which will reduce future output and wages. Third, when the money is borrowed from foreign investors, then Americans as a whole must pay some of their national income each year to foreigners just for interest, resulting in lower standards of living.

3. Government dissavings (deficits) have not been offset by private savings, as Ricardian equivalence would have suggested; and it is not true that "the debt does not matter, because we only owe it to ourselves."

4. Growing entitlement expenditures, growing interest expenditures from increasing federal indebtedness, and continuing commitments to defense all make reducing the deficit, or keeping it under control, difficult. Discretionary nondefense expenditures represent a relatively small fraction of all government expenditures. Without cutbacks in entitlements or defense, attaining and maintaining a zero deficit will entail huge cutbacks in these expenditures.

5. Current debates focus on the size of government, with some arguing for tax cuts financed by further expenditure cuts, while others argue that if high-return public investments in education, research, and infrastructure are reduced, growth will be impaired. Supply siders argue that tax cuts, even if unaccompanied by expenditure cuts, will stimulate the economy; and that their beneficial effects outweigh the costs of any increased deficit.

6. Earlier attempts to reform the budgetary process have met with only limited success. Requiring new expenditures to be paid for by new taxes or reduced expenditures has (apart from the ongoing increase in the cost of entitlements) curtailed the growth of the deficit, but not reduced it. Other proposals for reforming the budgetary process include the balanced budget amendment, capital budgeting, and the line-item veto.

7. Entitlements—such as increased Social Security and public health care expenditures—represent a major long-run deficit problem. Factors contributing to the entitlement problem are the aging population, increased life spans, earlier retirement ages, and soaring health care costs.

8. Among the proposals for containing the growth of government health care costs are those which provide increased incentives for consumers to economize in their use of health care services and those which provide improved incentives and responsibilities for doctors to manage care more efficiently.

KEY TERMS

Ricardian equivalence	nondiscretionary spending	line item veto
discretionary spending	entitlements	balanced budget amendment
	supply siders	managed care

REVIEW QUESTIONS

1. What happened to the size of the budget deficits in the 1980s? Had there ever been such large deficits in peacetime?

2. Name five fiscal changes that contributed to the large budget deficits of the 1980s.

3. What is the relationship between the deficits and the U.S. government debt?

4. What are the consequences of an increased deficit in a closed economy? in an open economy? How can borrowing from abroad affect future generations for the better? How can it affect future generations for the worse?

5. What is the argument that "the debt doesn't matter, since we owe it to ourselves"? What is wrong with this argument?

6. Since it is politically difficult to cut defense spending, entitlement programs, and interest payments, why can't federal spending be cut substantially by focusing on all the other federal programs?

7. How has the budgetary process been changed in order to control the deficit? Has it been successful? What further changes have been proposed? What are the problems with these proposals?

8. What role do entitlements play in the growth of the deficit? What accounts for the growth of entitlement spending? What can be done about it?

PROBLEMS

1. True or false: "Government borrowing can transfer resources from future generations to the present, but it cannot affect the overall wealth of the country." Discuss.

2. Explain how reducing the budget deficit would contribute to long-term growth in a closed economy, using the savings-investment identity. Use the savings-investment diagram introduced earlier to contrast the effects in an open and closed economy.

3. Suppose a certain country has private savings of 6 percent of GDP, foreign borrowing of 1 percent of GDP, and a balanced budget. What is its level of investment? If the budget deficit is 1.5 percent of GDP, how does your answer change?

4. The real value of the debt (in 1995 dollars) in 1995 was $3.6 trillion and in 1980 was $1.3 trillion. Assume that 50 percent of this buildup in the debt would have gone into investment, so that the capital stock would have been $1.15 trillion larger in 1995. Assume that the capital stock in 1995 was $15 trillion. By how much lower was GDP in 1995 as a result of the displaced investment, if the share of capital is .2? (Hint: use the results of Chapter 36, relating increases in outputs to increases in inputs.)

5. One proposal to contain the deficits is a balanced budget amendment to the constitution, that would require the government to maintain a balanced budget every year.
   (a) Explain why if the economy goes into a downturn, this would either force the government to raise taxes or reduce expenditures.
   (b) What would be the consequences of raising taxes or reducing expenditures under these circumstances?
   (c) How might you design a balanced budget amendment that would not force the government to cut back expenditures or raise taxes in an economic downturn?
   (d) Explain why if interest rates are increased to dampen the economy the balanced budget amendment might force the government to

cut back other expenditures (or raise taxes). More generally, describe the interaction between monetary and fiscal policy under a balanced budget amendment.

6. Should expenditures on health care for children be considered an "investment" in a capital budget? What other expenditures might legitimately be classified as "investment"?

7. Assume the government sells some of the land it currently rents out for grazing. Should the revenues received be counted as reducing the deficit? How would the transaction be treated under a capital budget?

8. "The resources that were spent fighting World War II were spent during the period 1940–1945. Hence, the generations that were alive and paying taxes during that period are the generations that bore the burden of the cost of the war, regardless of how it was financed." Discuss.

9. Why does the way government achieves deficit reduction make a difference for economic growth?

(a) Assuming the government raises taxes on interest income, what is the total impact on national savings, taking into account both deficit reduction and changes in private savings? What is the impact on investment? (Hint: how does your answer depend on the interest elasticity of savings?)

(b) Assuming the government raises taxes on wage income, what is the impact on GDP in the short run? (Hint: how does your answer depend on the elasticity of labor supply?) What is the impact on the deficit and on investment?

(c) Assume the government reduces expenditures on investments in technology and education, which yield a return of 15 percent, while the marginal return on private investment is 7 percent.

CHAPTER 38

TRADE POLICY

G o into any Gap or other clothing store and look at the labels: while some items are made in the U.S.A., others come from Hong Kong, Malaysia, China, Taiwan, the Philippines, or India. Today, Americans enjoy products produced around the world, and those in other countries travel in American jets, take American medicines, and watch American-made movies. In Chapter 3, we saw that there are gains for all countries when they produce and trade according to their comparative advantage.

In spite of the gains from trade, countries have imposed a variety of barriers to trade. Over the past fifty years, the United States has worked with other countries to lower these barriers to trade. This chapter explores both the barriers to trade and the major initiatives to remove these barriers.

1. Why and how do countries erect barriers to trade?

2. What is meant by fair trade laws? What is dumping, and why are economists often critical of antidumping laws?

3. Why are government subsidies to industries considered a barrier to trade? To what extent do countervailing duties correct this problem?

4. Why is protection so popular? Who are the winners and losers from free trade?

5. What are some of the institutions and agreements through which trade barriers have been reduced?

COMMERCIAL POLICY

Countries that have *no* barriers to trade are said to practice **free trade,** but most countries engage in some form of **protectionism,** that is, in one way or another they restrict the importation of goods. Policies directed at affecting either imports or exports are referred to as **commercial policies.** This and the next section take up the forms trade barriers take, their economic costs, and their economic and political rationale; the next section explores international attempts to reduce these trade barriers.

There are four major categories of trade barriers—tariffs, quotas, voluntary export restraints and other **nontariff barriers,** and a set of laws called "fair trade laws" that, by and large, actually serve to impede trade rather than promote fair trade.

TARIFFS

Tariffs are simply a tax on imports. Since a tariff is a tax that is imposed only on foreign goods, it puts the foreign goods at a disadvantage. It discourages imports.

Figure 38.1 shows the effect of a tariff. The figure shows a downward-sloping demand curve for the product, and an upward-sloping domestic supply curve. For simplicity, we consider the case of a country sufficiently small that the price it pays for a good on the international market does not depend on the quantity purchased. In the absence of a tariff, the domestic price is equal to this international price, p^*. The country produces Q_s, consumes Q_c, and imports the difference, $Q_c - Q_s$. With a tariff, the price consumers have to pay is increased from p^* to $p^* + t$, where t is the tariff. Domestic production is increased (to Q_s')—producers are better off as a result. But consumers are

Figure 38.1 EFFECT OF TARIFFS

A small country faces a horizontal supply curve for a good at the international price, p^*. In the absence of tariffs, the price in the country will be p^*. The country will produce Q_s (the quantity along the supply curve corresponding to p^*), consume Q_c (the quantity along the demand curve corresponding to p^*), and import $Q_c - Q_s$. A tariff at the rate t increases the price in the country to $p^* + t$, lowers aggregate consumption to Q_c' (the quantity along the demand curve corresponding to $p^* + t$), and increases domestic production to Q_s' (the quantity along the supply curve corresponding to $p^* + t$). Domestic producers are better off, but consumers are worse off.

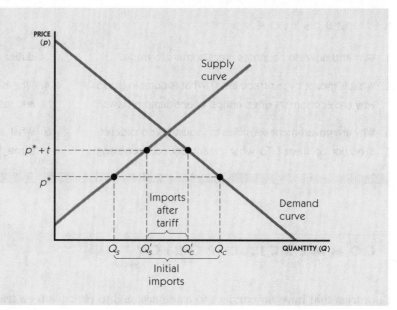

worse off, as the price they pay is increased. Their consumption is reduced to Q_c'. Since production is increased and consumption reduced, imports are reduced: the domestic industry has been protected against foreign imports.

QUOTAS

Rather than setting tariffs, many countries impose **quotas**—limits on the amount of foreign goods that can be imported. For instance, in the 1950s, the United States imposed a quota on the amount of oil that could be imported, and strict quotas still control the import of textiles.

Producers often prefer quotas. With limitations on the quantity imported, the domestic price increases above the international price. With quotas, domestic producers know precisely the magnitude of the foreign supply. If foreigners become more efficient or if exchange rates change in favor of foreigners, they still cannot sell any more. In that sense, quotas provide domestic producers with greater certainty than do tariffs, insulating them from the worst threats of competition.

Quotas and tariffs both succeed in raising the domestic price above the price at which the good could be obtained abroad. Both thus protect domestic producers. There is, however, one important difference: with quotas, those who are given permits to import get a profit by buying goods at the international price abroad and selling at the higher domestic price. The government is, in effect, giving away its tariff revenues. These profits are referred to as **quota rents.**

We can quantify the net loss to society from imposing tariffs. The difference between the amount consumers are willing to pay and what they have to pay is called consumer surplus. For the last unit consumed, the marginal benefit exactly equals the price paid, and so there is no consumer surplus. But for the first units consumed, individuals typically would be willing to pay far more—reflected in the fact that the demand curve is downward sloping in the figure below. In the initial situation, the consumer surplus is given by the triangle ABC, the area between the demand curve and the price line, p^*. After the price increase, it is given by the triangle ADE. The net loss is the trapezoid $BCED$.

But of this loss, the rectangle $BDHF$ represents increased payments to producers (the increased price, BD, times the quantity that they produce), and $HFGE$ is the tariff revenue of the government (imports, HE, × the tariff). Of the increased payments to domestic producers, some is the cost of expanding production. The rest represents a difference between price and the marginal cost of production—increased profits. This is the area $BIHD$. Thus, the societal loss is represented by two triangles, EGC and HFI. The triangle EGC is similar to the loss to consumers arising from a monopolist's raising his price. The triangle HFI is the waste of resources resulting from the fact that as the economy expands production because of the tariff, the cost of domestic production exceeds the costs of purchasing the good abroad.

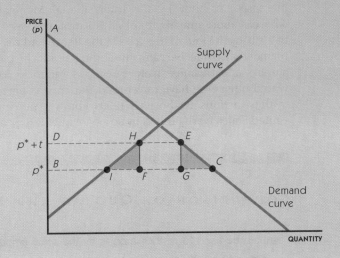

VOLUNTARY EXPORT RESTRAINTS

In recent years, international agreements have reduced the level of tariffs, and restricted the use of quotas. Accordingly, countries have sought to protect themselves from the onslaught of foreign competition by other means. One that became popular in the 1980s was **voluntary export restraints** (VERs). Rather than limiting imports of automobiles, for example, the United States persuaded Japan to limit its exports.

There are two interpretations of why Japan might have been willing to go along with this VER. One is that they worried the United States might take stronger actions, like imposing quotas. From Japan's perspective, VERs are clearly preferable to quotas, because with VERs, the quota rents accrue to Japanese firms. A second interpretation is that VERs enabled Japanese car producers to act collusively. It might have been in their self-interest to collude to reduce production and raise prices, but such collusion would have been illegal under antitrust laws. The VER "imposed" on the Japanese car producers output reductions they would have chosen themselves if they had been permitted to under the law. No wonder, then, that they agreed to go along! The cost to the American consumer of the Japanese VER was enormous. American consumers paid more than $100,000 in higher prices for every job created.

VERs and quotas are the clearest nontariff barriers. But today they are probably not the most important. A host of regulations have the same effect of imposing barriers to trade. For instance, health-related regulations have been abused in ways that restrict trade. When, in 1996, Russia threatened to halt U.S. exports of chickens for failure to satisfy health regulations, U.S. chicken exporters were faced with a nontariff barrier. Various types of regulations have been used to establish nontariff barriers.

During the 1980s, as tariff barriers were being reduced, nontariff barriers increased. A study by the International Monetary Fund concluded that, whereas about one-eighth of all U.S. imports were affected by protectionism in 1980, by the end of the decade the figure had risen to one-quarter. It is estimated that trade barriers (including nontariff barriers) may prevent consumers and business from buying as much as $50 billion in imports they would otherwise have purchased. Japan was particularly adversely affected by these actions. By the early 1990s, about 40 percent of Japan's exports to the United States were limited by some form of U.S. protectionism.

COMPARISON OF QUOTAS AND TARIFFS

Both can be used to restrict imports by the same amount, with the same effect on consumers and domestic producers.

With quotas, the difference between domestic price and international price accrues to the importer, who enjoys a quota rent.

With tariffs, the difference accrues to government as tariff revenues.

VERs (voluntary export restraints) are equivalent to quotas, except that the quota rents are given to foreign producers.

"FAIR TRADE" LAWS

Most people believe in competition. But most people believe that competition should be fair. When someone can undersell them, they suspect foul play. The government has imposed a variety of laws to ensure that there is effective and fair competition domestically. Laws have also been enacted by most countries to ensure "fair competition" in international trade. But most economists believe that in practice they are protectionist measures, reducing competition and restricting imports. To ensure fair competition, economists argue that the same laws which apply domestically should be extended internationally—that is, there should not be two standards of fairness, one applying domestically, one internationally. New Zealand and Australia, in their trade relations, have applied the same laws to trade between themselves that they do domestically. But elsewhere, progress has been limited.

There are three important "fair trade" laws, applying to dumping, countervailing duties, and market surges.

ANTIDUMPING LAWS

Dumping refers to the sale of products overseas at prices that are below cost and lower than those in the home country. Normally, consumers greet discounted sales with enthusiasm. If Russia is willing to sell aluminum to the United States at low prices, why should we complain? One reason that might be of concern is predatory pricing. By selling below cost, the foreign companies hope to drive the American firms out of business. Once they have established a monopoly position, they can raise prices. In such a case, American consumers gain only in the short run. In competitive markets, however, predation simply cannot occur, for in such markets, firms have no power to raise prices. In almost all of the cases where dumping has been found, markets are sufficiently competitive that predation is not of concern.

As administered, the antidumping laws are more frequently used as a protectionist tool. If dumping is discovered, a duty (tariff) is levied equal to the difference between the (calculated) cost of production and the price. Under the criteria employed, most American firms could be charged with dumping. Critics of the dumping laws worry that other countries will imitate American practices. If so, just as the international community has eliminated tariff barriers, a whole new set of trade barriers will have been erected.

SUBSIDIES AND COUNTERVAILING DUTIES

A second trade practice widely viewed as unfair is for governments to subsidize domestic firms' production or exports. For example, the government may give certain domestic industries tax breaks or pay a portion of the firms' costs. These subsidies give companies receiving them an unfair advantage. Trade is

Question: How, if Canada did not produce golf carts, could the cost of Canadian golf carts be used to accuse Poland of dumping? Answer: The United States sometimes achieves wonders when its markets are at stake.

The standard criterion for judging whether a country is dumping is whether it is selling commodities on the U.S. market at prices below those for which it sells them at home or elsewhere, or at prices below the costs of production. For nonmarket economies, the Department of Commerce formulated a special criterion—below what it would have cost to product the good in a "comparable" (or "surrogate") country.

The case of the Canadian golf cart and Poland is a real case. Poland was accused of dumping golf carts on the U.S. market at a time when Canada was not even making comparable golf carts. Commerce asked the question: What would it have cost for Canada to produce these golf carts, had it chosen to do so? Not surprisingly, the resulting cost estimate was higher than the price the real golf carts were being sold for in the United States, and Poland was found guilty of dumping. Similar charges have been made on similar grounds against Russian sales of natural resources.

For years, Western countries had preached to the Soviet Union and the other socialist countries the virtues of the market. Beginning in 1989, with the demise of communism, former iron-curtain countries sought to transform their economies into market economies. Under the old regime, these countries had traded mainly with themselves, and generally engaged in barter. In the new era, they sought to enter international markets, like any other market economy.

Though the design and production quality of many of its manufactured goods made them unsuitable for Western markets, Russia had a wealth of natural resources—including uranium, aluminum, and other products—that it could produce on a competitive basis. Moreover, with the reduction of defense expenditures—good news from virtually every perspective—Russia's demand for many of these raw materials was greatly reduced. It sought to enter international markets for these commodities at an unfortunate time, however, since the recession in Western economies

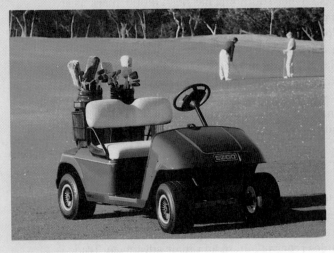

had resulted in low demand, and hence low prices, for these commodities. The increase in supply from Russia exacerbated these problems.

American producers attempted to discourage Russian exports by filing, or threatening to file, dumping charges. Though Russia was probably not selling these commodities at prices below those prevailing at home or elsewhere, or at prices below costs of production, the "surrogate" country criterion made the dumping charges a very real threat. Russia agreed to a cutback in aluminum production in 1994, to be matched by cutbacks in other countries.

To the Commerce and State Departments, this may have seemed a reasonable way to avoid trade conflict. But consumers paid a hidden high price, in terms of higher prices for aluminum and products using aluminum. In April of 1994, the Justice Department announced an investigation to see if the agreement and actions violated antitrust laws.

Meanwhile, since it was clear that the old dumping laws did not deal adequately with the problems of economies in transition, at summit meetings between Presidents Clinton and Yeltsin during 1993 and 1994, Clinton promised reform. A proposal was submitted to Congress, but failed to pass. Until such legislation is adopted, market access by these countries will continue to be a source of tension. They rightly claim that market economies fail to practice what they preach—the virtues of free markets.

determined not on the basis of comparative advantage, but of relative subsidy levels.

The usual logic of economics seems to be reversed. If some foreign government wants to subsidize American consumers, why should they complain? Presumably, only if the subsidies are part of a policy of predation—if the subsidies are used to drive American firms out of business and establish a monopoly position, after which prices will be raised. Most foreign subsidies do not fall into this category.

Opposition to these subsidies arises from the companies who see their businesses hurt. While the gains to consumers outweigh the losses to businesses, the gain to each consumer is small, and consumers are not well organized. Producers, being far more organized, are able and willing to bring their case to Washington. In response, Congress has passed laws allowing the U.S. government to impose **countervailing duties,** that is, taxes that offset any advantage provided by these subsidies.

While governments preach against other countries providing subsidies, however, they engage in the practice themselves, most commonly with export subsidies. At various times, the U.S government has subsidized the export of wheat, pork, peaches, and a host of other commodities.

MARKET SURGES

The final category of "fair trade" law is not really concerned with *unfair* trade, but with the consequences of rapid economic changes—in particular **surges** of imports—which may have strong adverse effects on particular industries.

Economic relations between Japan and the United States (as well as many other countries) have been tense for years. Underlying the tension is Japan's huge trade surplus (see figure below) and a variety of practices which have the effect of reducing access to the Japanese market. In response to these concerns, in early 1993 Japan and the United States signed an agreement, a so-called framework for addressing problems of market access. Discussions focused on several major areas, including procurement, insurance, and automobiles.

Underlying the discussions were several major differences in viewpoints. First, Japan emphasized that the trade surplus was largely a macroeconomic phenomenon, a result of its high savings rate. We saw in Chapter 7 that

$$X - M = S_d - I$$

that is, the trade surplus is just equal to the differ-ence between domestic savings (including government savings) and investment. Japan's trade surplus would only be reduced if it increased its investment or reduced its savings. Since Japan's interest rates were already low—by 1995, they were less than 1 percent per year—it could not do much in that way to stimulate investment, and it did not want to discourage savings.

The United States argued that the Japanese government should direct actions to stimulate imports: fiscal actions to stimulate its economy—increased expenditures and reduced taxes—would result in increased imports. They also argued for reduced nontariff barriers—such as regulations which kept out U.S. parts from the automobile market and anticompetitive practices which limited Japanese firms' purchases from foreign competitors.

To ensure that Japan actually reduced these impediments to imports, the United States argued for quantitative targets. In previous negotiations, Japan had promised to reduce trade barriers, but nothing had happened. The United States was concerned that without quantitative measures of progress, nothing would happen. Japan, for its part, argued that setting quantitative targets was equivalent to managing trade—and that violated basic principles of free trade. A compromise eventually was reached whereby a range of quantitative indicators measuring progress would be looked at, but no strict quotas for trade would be set.

A third set of issues revolved around the responsibility of government for lack of market access. Each side had a wealth of anecdotes. U.S. cars had made little headway in Japan, simply because American car manufacturers only made cars with steering wheels on the left-hand side. This was symptomatic of failing to pay attention to the realities of the marketplace.

But the Americans cited a host of government regulations—and the manner in which they were applied—which served as barriers to market access. When U.S. financial companies wanted to introduce new financial instruments into the Japanese market, for example, they were precluded from doing so—allegedly because Japanese regulators had to look at their "safety." During the delay, Japanese firms positioned themselves to enter the market. Thus, American firms lost the competitive advantage they would have had with earlier entry.

There is, in fact, a grain of truth in both sides' contentions: the basic trade imbalances are a result of macroeconomic imbalances, the surplus of savings over investment in Japan and of investment over savings in the United States. On the other hand, nontariff barriers impede access of foreigners to Japanese markets, keeping consumer prices there high, and probably discouraging Japanese consumption of imports. Even if eliminating these nontariff barriers did not redress the trade imbalance, it would at least make clear that the reason for these trade imbalances was not "unfair" trade practices.

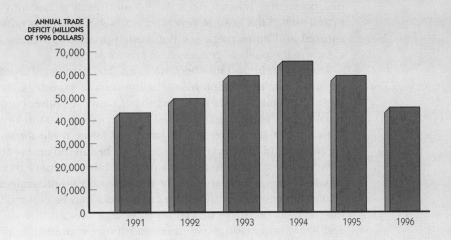

THE U.S. TRADE DEFICIT WITH JAPAN

The United States has had a huge trade deficit with Japan. In 1995, it began to decline. The trade deficit for 1996 is projected from data for the first nine months of the year. *Source:* Department of Commerce, Report FT-900.

The market surge laws are intended to provide temporary protection to give the industry time to adjust. In practice, the protection provided by antidumping laws is so much more effective that little reliance is placed on the market surge laws.

UNFAIR TRADE LAWS

Dumping
Countervailing duties
Market surges

POLITICAL AND ECONOMIC RATIONALE FOR PROTECTION

Chapter 3 showed how free trade, by allowing each country to concentrate production where it has a comparative advantage, can make all countries better off. Why, in spite of this, is protection so popular? The basic reason is simple: protection raises prices. While the losses to consumers from higher prices exceed the gains to producers in higher profits, producers are well organized and consumers are not; hence producers' voices are heard more clearly in the political process than are consumers'.

There is an important check on firms' ability to use the political process to advance their special interests: the interests of exporters, who realize that if the United States closes off its markets to imports, other countries will reciprocate. Thus, exporting firms like Boeing have been at the forefront of advancing an international regime of freer and fairer trade through international agreements, of the kind that will be described in the next section.

But before turning to a review of these international agreements, we need to take a closer look at some of the other economic aspects of protection. While with free trade, the country as a whole may be better off, certain groups may actually be worse off. Those especially affected include displaced firms and workers, low-wage workers, and those in industries in which without free trade, competition is limited.

DISPLACED FIRMS AND WORKERS

China has a comparative advantage in inexpensive textiles while the United States has a comparative advantage in manufacturing complex goods, like advanced telephone exchanges. If the United States starts to import textiles from

China, U.S. textile manufacturers may be driven out of business, and their workers will have to find work elsewhere. More than offsetting these losses are the gains to the export industries. In principle, the gainers in those industries could more than compensate the losers, but such compensation is seldom made: hence the opposition of the losers to opening trade.

Typically, economists shed few tears for the lost profits of the businesses who are hurt by opening trade. After all, that is just one of the risks that businesses face, and for which they are typically well compensated. New innovations destroy old businesses: the introduction of the automobile hurt the carriage trade. But barring the door to new technologies—or cheaper products from abroad—is bad economics—and bad economic policy.

There is, however, often more sympathy toward workers affected by trade—though there is no reason why there should be greater concern for workers displaced by opening trade than by new innovations. When the economy is running at close to full employment, workers who lose their jobs typically do find new employment. But they often go through a transition period of unemployment, and when they eventually do find a new job, there is a good chance that their wages will be lower (in the United States, in recent years, a worker who is successful in finding full-time employment experiences on average a 10 percent wage decline). While these particular laborers are worse off, workers as a whole are better off, because those who get newly created jobs in the export industries are paid far more (on average 13 to 15 percent more) than the average for the economy. Concern about the transitional costs borne by displaced workers has motivated Congress to pass laws for special assistance for these workers to help them find new jobs and obtain the requisite training.

Sensitivity to the problems of displaced workers is particularly strong when unemployment is high because those who lose a job cannot easily find alternative employment. Auto workers in Michigan who see their jobs lost as a result of imports of Japanese cars view the Japanese as "stealing" their jobs. Indeed, in such situations, trade is *blamed* for the high unemployment rate. If we restrict imports, it is argued, we will keep jobs in America.

BEGGAR-THY-NEIGHBOR POLICIES

In Chapter 27 we saw that output may be limited by aggregate demand. Aggregate demand depends on consumption, investment, government expenditures, and net exports. Net exports equal exports minus imports. Increasing imports thus reduces net exports—reducing aggregate demand, national output, and employment. Policies that attempt to increase national output by reducing imports are called **beggar-thy-neighbor policies,** because the jobs gained in one country are at the expense of jobs lost in another. If America imports less, foreigners export less. Restricting imports into the United States may *initially* have a positive effect on U.S. output. But the gains are typically a mirage. Other countries will import from us only if they can sell goods to us. Even without retaliatory measures by other countries, if the United States restricts imports, typically exports fall in tandem. Without exports to the United States, other countries' income falls, and with the fall in income, they import

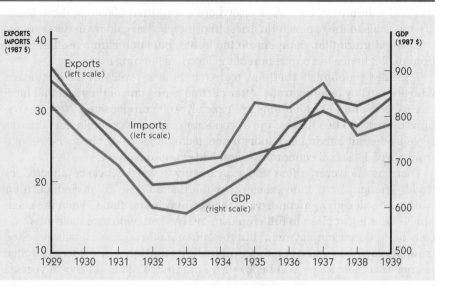

Figure 38.2 THE DECLINE IN INTERNATIONAL TRADE AND THE GREAT DEPRESSION

U.S. exports and imports fell dramatically during the Great Depression. One contributing factor to the decline in trade was the Hawley-Smoot Tariff Act introduced in 1930.

less, including from the United States. Moreover, when other countries see reduced exports as a result of active policies by other countries to restrict imports, they tend to respond by retaliating, by playing tit-for-tat.

The worst instance of these beggar-thy-neighbor policies occurred at the onset of the Great Depression, when, in 1930, the United States passed the Hawley-Smoot Tariff Act, raising tariffs on many products to a level which effectively prohibited many imports. Other countries retaliated. As U.S. imports declined, incomes in Europe and elsewhere in the world declined. As incomes declined and as these countries imposed retaliatory tariffs, they bought less from the United States. U.S. exports plummeted, contributing further to the economic downturn in the United States. With incomes in the United States plummeting further, U.S. imports declined even more, contributing still further to the decline abroad, which then fed further into the decline in U.S. exports. The downturn in international trade that was set off by the Hawley-Smoot Tariff Act, charted in Figure 38.2, is often pointed to as a major contributing factor in making the Great Depression as deep and severe as it was.

INTERNATIONAL TRADE AND JOBS

Opposition to imports is strongest when the economy is in a recession, but restricting imports as a way of creating jobs tends to be counterproductive.

WAGES IN IMPACTED SECTORS

Beyond these short-run problems of transition and unemployment, there may be long-run problems facing workers in impacted sectors. The United States has a comparative advantage in producing goods such as airplanes and high-tech products which require highly skilled workers. As the United States exports more of these goods, the demand for these skilled workers increases in the United States, driving up the wage of skilled workers. Similarly, the United States has a comparative disadvantage in producing goods which require a high ratio of unskilled labor, such as lower quality textiles. As imports compete against these U.S. industries and their production decreases, the demand for unskilled labor decreases. This drives down the wages of unskilled workers.

These decreased wages for unskilled workers are often blamed on imports from third world countries like China, where wages are but a fraction of those in the United States. The consensus among economists who have looked closely at the matter is that international trade explains a relatively small part of the decline in wages—perhaps 20 percent. Nonetheless, those who see their meager livelihood being threatened are among the most ardent advocates of trade restrictions. Again, economists argue that the appropriate response is not to restrict trade, but to increase skills: not only are the workers receiving the skills better off, as their wages rise commensurate with the increase in their productivity; but as more workers become skilled, the remaining supply of unskilled workers is reduced; and with a smaller supply of unskilled workers, the real wages of the remaining unskilled workers increases, offsetting the adverse effects of trade.

INCREASED COMPETITION

International trade also has other adverse effects in industries where competition is limited. With limited competition, firms enjoy monopoly or oligopoly profits. Some of these extra profits are often passed on to workers. Particularly when those industries are unionized, workers may receive wages far higher than workers of comparable skill working elsewhere in the economy.

EFFECTS OF TRADE ON WAGES

International trade may lower wages of unskilled U.S. labor and those working in industries where competition is limited.

International trade raises wages of skilled U.S. workers.

International trade introduces more competition; with the increased competition, monopoly and oligopoly profits get competed away. Firms are forced to pay competitive wages—that is, the lowest wage that they can for workers with the given skill.

THE INFANT INDUSTRY ARGUMENT

While job loss and decreased wages and profits from international competition provide much of the political motivation behind protection, economists have asked, are there any *legitimate* arguments for protection. That is, are there circumstances where protection may be in the *national* interest, and not just in the interests of those being protected? Two arguments have been put forward.

The first is the **infant industry argument.** Costs in new industries are often high, coming down as experience is gained. The infant industry argument is that, particularly in less developed countries, firms will never be able to get the experience required to produce efficiently unless they are protected from foreign competition.

Economists have traditionally responded to this argument skeptically. If it pays to enter the industry, eventually there will be profits. Thus, the firm should be willing to charge today a price below cost to gain the experience, because today's losses will be more than offset by the future profits. But more recently, the infant industry argument has found more favor. Firms can only operate at a loss if they can borrow funds. If capital markets do not work well, firms may not be able to borrow even if their eventual prospects are reasonable. This is a particular danger in less developed countries.

This may be a legitimate argument. But it is not an argument for protection. It is an argument for assistance, which can take the form of loans or direct subsidies. Economists argue for direct assistance rather than protection because the assistance is transparent. Everyone can see that it is a subsidy to producers. Economists criticize protection because it is a hidden tax on consumers, with the proceeds transferred to producers. The lack of transparency encourages what is referred to as rent seeking[1]: industries spend resources to persuade government to impose these hidden taxes which benefit themselves.

STRATEGIC TRADE THEORY

Another argument for protection is that protection can give a country a strategic trade advantage over rivals by helping reduce domestic costs. There may be economies of scale: the larger the level of production, the lower the mar-

---

[1]Rents refer to payments to a factor of production that are in excess of what is required to elicit the supply of that factor. In the absence of entry, protection would result in higher prices, yielding returns to the industry that are above their competitive levels; these higher returns are rents. The irony is that typically, the higher returns do attract entry, and the additional entry dissipates the rents—though prices remain high.

ginal costs. Protection ensures a large domestic sales base, and therefore a low marginal cost. The instances in which **strategic trade theory** might provide a rationale for protection appear relatively rare. Even then, they tend to be effective only when foreign governments do not retaliate by taking similar actions.

INTERNATIONAL COOPERATION

Recognizing both the temptation of shortsighted trade policy and the gains from trade, nations large and small have since World War II engaged in a variety of efforts to reduce trade barriers. At the global level, the prominent effort is known as the **General Agreement on Tariffs and Trade (GATT).** On a slightly smaller scale, regional trading blocs have also been developed.

GATT AND THE WTO

After World War II, the countries of the world realized that there was much to be gained from establishing an international economic order in which barriers to trade were reduced. They established the GATT. In 1995, this was replaced by the **World Trade Organization (WTO).**

GATT was founded on three guiding principles. The first was *reciprocity:* if one country lowered its tariffs, it could expect other countries in GATT to lower theirs. The second was *nondiscrimination:* no member of GATT could offer a special trade deal that favored only one or a few other countries. The third was *transparency:* import quotas and other nontariff barriers to trade should be converted into tariffs, so their effective impact could be ascertained.

GATT has proceeded in a number of stages, called **rounds** (the Kennedy Round, completed in 1967, the Tokyo Round, completed in 1979, and most recently, the Uruguay Round, completed in 1993). Collectively, the rounds have reduced tariffs on industrial goods markedly. The average tariff on manufactured goods was 40 percent in 1947. By 1992, they had been reduced to 5 percent, and the Uruguay Round reduced them still further.

The Uruguay Round was remarkable for two achievements. It began the process of extending the principles of free and fair trade to a number of much more difficult areas. There were, for instance, agreements to reduce agriculture subsidies, particularly export subsidies, and to ensure that intellectual property rights—patents and copyrights—were respected. Secondly, it created the WTO to help enforce the trade agreements. Previously, a country that believed that it was suffering from an "unfair trade" practice could bring a case to a GATT panel that would examine the evidence. Even if the panel was unanimous, however, in finding that an unfair trade practice had occurred, there was little in the way of effective enforcement. Under the WTO, a country injured by an unfair trade practice will be authorized to engage in retaliatory actions.

REGIONAL TRADING BLOCS

GATT and WTO have made some progress in reducing trade barriers among all countries. But the difficulties of reaching agreements involving so many parties have made progress slow. In the meantime, many countries have formed **trading blocs,** agreeing with their more immediate neighbors not only to eliminate trade barriers, but also to facilitate the flow of capital and labor. Perhaps the most important of these is the **European Union,** the successor to the **Common Market,** which now embraces most of Europe. The **North American Free Trade Agreement, NAFTA,** will result eventually in a free trade zone within North America—that is, an area within which goods and services trade freely, without tariffs or other import restrictions. There are also many smaller free trade zones, such as those between New Zealand and Australia, and among groups of countries in Latin America and in Central America.

While the gains from internationally coordinated reductions in trade barriers are clear, the gains from regional trading blocs are more controversial. Reducing trade barriers within a region encourages trade by members of the trading bloc. Lowering barriers among the countries involved results, of course, in **trade creation.** But it also results in **trade diversion.** Trade is diverted away from countries that are not members of the bloc, who might, in fact, have a comparative advantage in the particular commodity. Under these conditions, the global net benefits will be positive if the trade creation exceeds the trade diversion. Typically, when trade blocs are formed, tariffs against outsiders are harmonized. If the external trade barriers are harmonized at the lowest common level (rather than at the average or highest levels) at the same time that internal trade barriers are lowered, it is more likely that the trade creation effects exceed the trade diversion effects.

Expanding regional trading blocs to cover investment flows raises particular anxieties, especially when the bloc includes countries with very different standards of living. In the NAFTA debate, Ross Perot used the metaphor of a giant sucking sound: Mexico would suck up huge amounts of investment that otherwise would have occurred in the United States. The accusation was not just that goods produced today in Mexico would cost Americans jobs. It was also that American firms would move down to Mexico, to take advantage of low-wage labor, and the capital that flowed down to Mexico would not be available for investment in the United States.

Such arguments are based on an important misconception. They fail to take account of the fact that capital markets are already global. The United States is not limited in its investment to savings in the United States. Capital will flow to good investment opportunities wherever they are. If there are good investment opportunities in the United States, capital will flow there, regardless of how much Americans invest in Mexico. Investment barriers impede this flow of capital to its highest productive use, thus lowering world economic efficiency.

The "Perot" argument is based on a "zero sum" view of the world—that what

Mexico gains must come at the expense of the United States. Perot's argument is similar to the one that says when a country imports, it loses jobs: the gains to foreigners from their exports are at the expense of domestic firms, which otherwise would be creating these jobs. In Chapter 3, we saw what was wrong with this argument: the theory of comparative advantage says that when countries specialize in what they produce best, *both* countries are better off. Workers gain higher wages when they move into those sectors where their productivity is highest; and consumers gain from the lower prices. So too with investment. When investment flows to where its return is highest, world output is increased. Since the return to capital is increased when it is efficiently allocated, savings rates may also increase, so that the overall supply of funds will be higher. Higher savings rates and more efficient use of available savings will combine to give a higher world economic growth rate.

But just as not everyone necessarily gains from trade according to comparative advantage, so too not everyone will necessarily gain from the flow of capital to Mexico. There will be some investment diversion from other countries to Mexico, as Mexico becomes more attractive to investors throughout the world because of its improved access to the huge American market. Most economists believe that the net effect on investment in the United States will be negligible, and could even be positive. Industries within the United States that see their opportunities expand by selling more to Mexico will invest more, more than offsetting the reduced investment from firms that decline in the face of competition from Mexican imports.

In fact, investment flows augment the gains from trade which would occur in their absence because there are important trade-investment links. American companies producing abroad tend to use more parts from America, just as French companies producing abroad tend to use more French parts. Thus, flows of investment often serve as a precursor to exports.

TRADE-OFFS BETWEEN REGIONAL AND INTERNATIONAL AGREEMENTS

The potential economic trade-off between increased trade within the region and the expense of reduced trade outside the region has led some economists, such as Jagdish Bhagwati of Columbia University, to oppose regional trade agreements. There is also concern about political trade-offs. Should the U.S. government spend the limited political resources it has to overcome protectionist antitrade sentiment focusing on regional or worldwide agreements? Recent U.S. governments have pursued a pragmatic policy. Their ultimate objective is to eliminate economic barriers everywhere, by means of international approaches coordinated through the WTO. At the same time, they are aggressively pursuing regional trade agreements involving broad removal of barriers within the Western Hemisphere and between the United States and the countries of the Pacific Rim. They view this as the most practical way to achieve economic integration. Agreements may be easier to obtain among a limited set of often similar partners than among all the countries of the world.

CLOSE-UP: MERCANTILISM—OLD AND NEW

Mercantilism is the name of the school of thought that was prevalent in Europe between about 1500 and 1800 and focused on building up the power and wealth of the state through aggressive pursuit of exports. They also discouraged imports and thought that a country's strength was related to its store of gold and silver. Josiah Child, one of the better-known mercantilists, wrote in 1693: "Foreign trade produces riches, riches power; power preserves our trade and religion."

To have lots of products left over to export, the nation had to produce more than it consumed, so citizens were exhorted to work hard for low wages.

Adam Smith, the father of modern economics, recognized the fallacies in mercantilism. A country's wealth, he argued, was not measured by its gold and silver, but by the productivity of its resources. Smith pointed out that even from the standpoint of national power, a nation's army does not run on gold and silver, but on physical products like ships, food, clothing, and weapons.

The world has changed dramatically in the more than two centuries since Adam Smith formulated his attack on mercantilism. But the mercantilist spirit remains alive—and the criticisms of the new mercantilist arguments are direct descendants of Smith's analysis.

Modern mercantilists view exports as desirable today, not because they lead to the accumulation of gold, but because they lead to job creation. By the same token, imports are viewed poorly, both because they lead to job loss and dependency on foreigners.

Some countries, such as Japan and Korea, have successfully pursued strong export-oriented policies; and most economists believe that these policies have contributed to their economic success. But the reason is quite different from that of the older mercantilist theories that focused on the accumulation of riches. Japan and Korea did accumulate capital rapidly, but this was because of their extraordinarily high savings rates. Their export-oriented policies were important because to be successful in international markets, their industries had to be efficient and adopt high standards of production. Their export-oriented policies helped their industries become more competitive and adopt advanced technologies.

Today, in the United States, we recognize that trade is important, not because it creates jobs—if the Federal Reserve Board does its job, the economy will operate at or close to full employment most of the time—but because it leads to higher standards of living, as Americans can specialize in producing those goods in which it has a comparative advantage, and because competition from abroad forces American firms to become more efficient. These are essentially the same reasons that Smith put forward for why, though protection may benefit businessmen, free trade would be beneficial for society as a whole.

This is especially true in relation to complicated issues such as investment and regulations. The U.S. government also believes that a successful regional strategy will bring to bear pressures which will hasten fully international agreements.

AREAS OF INTERNATIONAL COOPERATION

Multilateral trade agreements—WTO

 Based on principles of reciprocity, nondiscrimination, and transparency

 Uruguay Round extended trade liberalization to services and agricultural commodities and helped establish intellectual property rights

Regional trade agreements—NAFTA, European Union

 Risk of trade diversion rather than trade creation

 But may be better able to address complicated issues, such as those involving investment

REVIEW AND PRACTICE

SUMMARY

1. Countries protect themselves in a variety of ways besides imposing tariffs. These nontariff barriers include quotas, voluntary export restraints, and regulatory barriers. Quotas and voluntary export restraints are now banned by international agreement. While in recent decades there have been huge reductions in tariff barriers, there has been some increase in nontariff barriers.

2. While all countries benefit from free trade, some groups within a country may be adversely affected. In the United States, unskilled workers and those in industries where, without trade, there is limited competition, may see their wages fall. Some workers may lose their jobs, and may require assistance to find new ones.

3. Laws nominally intended to ensure fair trade—the dumping, countervailing duty, and market surge laws—often are used as protectionist measures.

4. Concern about imports is particularly strong when unemployment is high. But beggar-thy-neighbor policies, which attempt to protect jobs by limiting imports, tend to be counterproductive.

5. The World Trade Organization, which replaced the GATT, provides a framework within which trade barriers can be reduced. It is based on reciprocity, nondiscrimination, and transparency. The Uruguay Round of

the GATT extended trade liberalization to new areas, including agriculture and intellectual property, and established the World Trade Organization.

6. Difficulties at arriving at trade agreements involving all of the nations of the world have resulted in broader regional agreements, including NAFTA. There is a risk that these regional agreements may give rise to trade diversion offsetting the benefits from trade creation.

KEY TERMS

protectionism	beggar-thy-neighbor	World Trade Organi-
nontariff barriers	policies	zation (WTO)
quotas	infant industry	North American
voluntary export re-	argument	Free Trade Agree-
straints	strategic trade	ment (NAFTA)
dumping	theory	trade creation
countervailing	General Agreement	trade diversion
duties	on Tariffs and	
market surges	Trade (GATT)	

REVIEW QUESTIONS

1. What are the various ways in which countries seek to protect their industries against foreign imports?

2. How do tariffs and quotas differ?

3. Why are consumers worse off as a result of the imposition of a tariff?

4. What are the laws designed to ensure fair international trade? How have they worked in practice?

5. What are nontariff barriers to international trade?

6. How is it possible that while there are gains to free trade, some groups are adversely affected? Which are the groups in the United States that are most adversely affected?

7. What are beggar-thy-neighbor policies? What are their consequences?

8. What do GATT and the WTO do? What are their basic underlying principles? What have been GATT's achievements? What further advances were accomplished under the Uruguay Round?

9. What is NAFTA? What are the advantages of regional free trade agreements?

10. What is meant by trade diversion versus trade creation?

PROBLEMS

1. Suppose that Japanese products go out of fashion in the United States. How would this affect Japan's exports? What would happen to the exchange rate? What would happen to national income in Japan, on the assumption that the Japanese government did not undertake offsetting actions? What effect would this, in turn, have on U.S. exports? On U.S. national income, again with the assumption that the U.S. government did not undertake offsetting actions? Use the diagrammatic techniques learned in earlier chapters to answer these questions.

2. Explain why the balance of trade between Japan and the United States would worsen as Japan goes into a recession, if at the same time, the United States is recovering from a recession.

3. Explain why, if the United States succeeded in getting Japan to remove some of its trade barriers, the exchange rate between the yen and the dollar might change, but the trade balance might not be affected much. Why would the removal of these trade barriers still be beneficial for the United States?

4. During 1993, the price of aluminum fell, partly because of the worldwide recession, which affected raw materials like aluminum particularly adversely, partly because new techniques allowed aluminum cans to be produced using about 10 percent less aluminum, and partly because Russia, no longer using the aluminum to make airplanes, began exporting it. The U.S. aluminum companies threatened to file dumping charges against Russia, although Russia was selling the aluminum at world prices. What do you think might have been the consequences if the dumping charges had actually been filed? (Some background facts that might be relevant: Japan is a major importer of aluminum; some U.S. aluminum companies are major owners of non-U.S. producers.)

5. If you were a government intent on discouraging imports, how might you use regulatory policies to further your objective?

6. If Mexican workers receive a third of the wages that U.S. workers do, why don't all American firms move down to Mexico?

7. If Mexico becomes a more attractive place to invest, is the United States helped or hurt?

8. Should the U.S. treat foreign-owned firms producing cars in the United States (like Mazda) differently from American firms? Should Ford, Chrysler, and GM be allowed to form a research consortium, excluding these producers? Should the U.S. government give money to a research consortium that excludes these firms? Should they be eligible for research funds themselves on a equal basis?

9. How should the government prioritize its efforts on opening markets to U.S. firms? By the impact on U.S. workers? Impact on U.S. companies?

Impact on U.S. investors? How would you prioritize the following four examples: (a) opening up the Japanese market to allow Toys-R-Us to open retail stores in Tokyo, selling toys made in China; (b) opening up the Japanese securities markets to ensure that Goldman Sachs and other U.S. investment firms can sell securities to Japanese pension funds; (c) opening up the Japanese car market to enhance the ability of GM, Ford, and Chrysler to sell U.S. cars in Japan; and (d) opening up the Chinese car market to enhance the ability of Toyota and Mazda to sell American-made cars to China?

CHAPTER 39

ALTERNATIVE ECONOMIC SYSTEMS

The Soviet Union has dissolved, and formerly Communist countries all over Eastern Europe and the Baltic areas are overhauling their economic systems, making them more market based. Even the most populous country in the world, China—though retaining communism as its *political* system—has committed itself to using markets in its economic life. Such an enormous change makes it difficult to remember the days of rivalry between the Soviet Union's Communist economy and the mixed capitalist economies of Western Europe and the United States. As recently as the 1970s, many Western observers, including reputable economists, considered it only a matter of time before the Soviet Union would draw even and eventually win the economic race.

Today the formerly Communist countries look to their Western European neighbors and see much higher living standards. This chapter contrasts Soviet-style economies with those of Western countries, highlighting the major differences that might account for their divergent growth paths and standards of living. Toward the end of the chapter, we will learn about the two major versions of socialism that differed from that of the former Soviet Union: the workers' cooperatives of the former Yugoslavia and the attempts by Hungary and China to incorporate elements of a market into socialism.

Studying these alternative economic systems is not only important in providing insights into the major economic and political conflict of the twentieth century. Understanding why socialism and communism have failed provides us insights into what makes markets work.

KEY QUESTIONS

1. What were the economic conditions that gave rise to the socialist idea?

2. What were the central characteristics of Soviet-style socialism? How did it differ from the market system in the way it allocated resources?

3. Why did it fail?

4. What are some of the principal reforms of Soviet-style socialism that have been tried, and how did they fared?

5. What problems do the former socialist economies face in making the transition to a market economy?

TERMINOLOGY

Several terms are useful in describing alternative economic systems. Under **socialism,** the government owns and operates the basic means of production—the factories that make cars and steel, the mines, the railroads, the telephone system, and so on. Under **communism,** the government essentially owns all property—not only the factories, but also the houses and the land. In practice, no government has abolished all private property. People still own the clothes they wear and durable consumption goods like cars and television sets.

The term "communism" is used to describe the economic system in countries that came under the domination of the Soviet Union and China in the years after World War II. These countries shared an economic system that involved not only state ownership of assets but also considerable central control of economic decisions. Because of the important role played by central planning, these economies are referred to as **planned economies.** These countries also had a political system that did not allow free elections, free speech, or a multitude of other rights found in democracies.

The economies of the United States and Western Europe, in contrast, are commonly referred to as capitalist economies, because of the important role played by private capital. They are also called mixed economies, since government plays a large role, and market economies, because of their heavy reliance on firms and households interacting in markets. Table 39.1 compares living standards in the Soviet-style economies just before the revolutionary events of 1989–91 with those in the rest of the world.

Table 39.1 **COMPARISON OF LIVING STANDARDS BETWEEN PLANNED AND MARKET ECONOMIES**

	GNP per capita (1988 $)	Annual GNP growth rate (%) 1965–1988	Life expectancy at birth	Adult illiteracy (%)
Soviet-style economies:				
USSR	2,660	4.0	70	<5
China	330	5.4	70	31
Hungary	2,460	5.1	71	<5
Market economies:				
U.S.A.	19,840	1.6	76	<5
India	340	1.8	58	57
Italy	13,330	3.0	77	<5
Egypt	660	3.6	63	56
Sweden	19,300	1.8	77	<5

THE ORIGINS OF SOCIALISM AND COMMUNISM

The eighteenth and nineteenth centuries produced the industrial revolution, and with it a dramatic change in the structures of the economies and societies it touched. New technologies resulted in development of the factory system and increased movement of workers from rural to urban areas. In the fast-growing cities, workers often lived in squalid conditions. In order for families to eke out a living, children went alongside their parents to work in the factories, where they worked long hours in unhealthy conditions. Periodically economies faced a recession or depression. Workers were thrown out of their jobs and forced to beg, steal, or starve. Life for the unlanded peasants in the rural sectors was hardly more idyllic. In Ireland in the 1840s, for instance, a fifth of the population (half a million people) starved to death.

While the vast majority of people thus lived on the edge of survival, a few had considerable wealth, often inherited. Between the very wealthy and the poor was a small but growing middle class, mainly commercial and professional. (By contrast, today in Europe and America, it is the middle class, consisting of professionals, businesspeople, and high-wage workers, that is dominant.)

Were these conditions inevitable? Could they be changed? If so, how? These questions preoccupied numerous social thinkers from the late eighteenth century on. Many saw the capitalist economic system as the culprit. The most influential critic of the capitalist system was a German man living in England named Karl Marx.

Marx believed that the force of history had led the economy inevitably to evolve from medieval feudalism to capitalism, and that the economy, just as inevitably, would evolve from capitalism to socialism and eventually to communism. Not only would there be no private property, the state would make all allocation decisions. "From each according to his ability," wrote Marx, "and to each according to his needs."[1] Clearly Marx's vision of socialism provided different answers from the market economy to the basic economic questions of what to produce and in what quantities, how to produce it, for whom it should be produced, and who makes the decisions. The state, *not* the market, would decide what, how, and for whom.[2]

Among those who found Marx's ideas particularly attractive was a Russian revolutionary, Vladimir Ilyich Lenin. In October 1917, the Bolsheviks—the party of Lenin, with Marxism as its official ideology—seized the government. The first "Communist" government was established. Translating Marx's ideology into a program for running a populous, poor, and largely undeveloped and rural country was no easy task. It was ironic that Russia, hardly touched by capitalism at the time of the revolution, became the first to try to implement Marx's ideas. Since Marx had predicted that countries would have to pass through the capitalist phase *on the way* to socialism, he had expected socialism to arise first in countries such as Britain or France.

Indeed, the economic system that we know today as communism is as much due to how Lenin and his successor, Joseph Stalin, adapted Marx's ideas to the situation they found in Russia as it is to Marx's original ideas. What Marx's reaction would be to what evolved there one can only guess, but a hint is provided by his comment on the ideas of the French Marxists: "As for me, I am not a Marxist."

DISILLUSIONMENT WITH MARKETS

In the United States and other developed countries today, there is widespread confidence in markets and in the efficiency with which they allocate resources. To be sure, there are market failures, periods of unemployment, and pockets of poverty. But we have seen in this book how markets by and large allocate resources efficiently. We have seen as well how selective government interventions can remedy the market failures and, if there is the political will, at least partially address the problem of the inequality of income generated by the market.

But this confidence has not always been present; neither is it universal now. When the United States went into the Great Depression in 1929, not to recover

---

[1] *Critique of the Gotha Program* (1875).

[2] In Marx's view, socialism and communism were transitional stages to an eventual time when the state would wither away. How production would be organized—how the basic decisions of what to produce, how to produce it, and for whom it should be produced would be made—in this eventual period was left unclear.

CLOSE-UP: MARXIST ECONOMICS

Of the many writers in the nineteenth century who advocated socialism, none was more influential than Karl Marx. His ideas not only influenced how socialism developed within the Soviet Union, they gave rise to the Marxist school of economics. Like any major school, ideas evolve, as do disagreements among its members. Following are a few of the major ideas.

One important idea concerns what determines, or should determine, prices. The answer given by the basic economic model is the law of supply and demand. Marx, by contrast, made use of what was called the labor theory of value, a set of ideas developed earlier by the British economist David Ricardo. The labor theory of value argued that the value of any good should be attributed to the workers who made it. A good that required more labor should be valued more highly, and vice versa. Marx considered the difference between what a good was sold for and the labor costs that went into making the good—the profits of the firm and the return to capital—as exploitation of workers. By contrast, in market economies profits are viewed as providing firms with incentives, and capital is seen as a scarce factor—like any other scarce factor, such as land or labor—that will be efficiently allocated only when it fetches a return.

Another important strand in Marxist thought is that the economic system affects human nature. This book has taken the preferences of individuals as given. The demand curves for candy and CDs, for example, have been based on the trade-offs that people are willing to make. And we have not asked why workers may shirk if they are not provided incentives.

Many Marxists believe that under a different so-cial system, people would be less materialistic, more concerned about helping one another, more committed to their jobs. During wartime, we often see changes in attitudes and behavior. Whether human nature is sufficiently mutable that *some* social system might achieve these idealistic goals over long periods of time remains debatable. What is clear is that none of the Soviet-style economies succeeded.

A third strand of Marxist thought emphasizes the link between politics and economics. Marxists claim that the answer to the question of "for whom" is provided by power—the economic power of monopolies and the political power of the wealthy. The wealthy use government to gain for themselves what they cannot achieve in the marketplace. Marxists cite instances of governments spending hundreds of billions of dollars to fight a war to preserve business interests, while claiming insufficient money to finance the rebuilding of urban ghettos or to provide free college education to the poor. The debate on the validity of these claims, as always with moral issues and other value judgments, takes us beyond the boundaries of economics.

Marx may have been correct in his emphasis on the importance of economic factors in determining the evolution of society. In an ironic twist of history, though, economic forces appear to have injured socialism more than capitalism. It is the economic successes of the capitalist systems of the industrialized world, combined with the economic failures of the Soviet-style socialist economies, that led to the reaction against socialism in Eastern Europe and the Soviet Union.

fully until World War II, millions of Americans were thrown out of jobs. The capitalist economic system did not seem to be functioning well. Today, to the billions of people still living in abject poverty in India, elsewhere in Asia, and in Africa and South America, markets have failed to meet their rising aspirations. And even within the industrialized countries, there are many who have not partaken of the general prosperity. For them the market system does not seem to have worked well.

It is not surprising, then, that many have sought an alternative economic system, which would generate faster sustained economic growth at the same time as it promoted greater equality. Throughout much of the twentieth century, many saw socialism as the answer. They believed that if the government controlled the economy, not only would recessions be eliminated, so too would what they saw as the chaos of the marketplace, for instance the excess expansion of capacity in one industry accompanied by shortages in another industry.

HOW SOVIET-STYLE SOCIALIST ECONOMIES WORK

Private property, prices, and the profit incentive play a central role in market economies. If these are abandoned in a Soviet-style socialist economy, what replaces them? Three major components are central planning, force, and political controls and rewards.

In Soviet-style economies, decision making, including coordination of economic activity, was to be done by government ministries, through central planning. Five-year plans were drawn up, with detailed targets—how much steel production was to be increased, how much food production, and so on. Individual plant managers were told not only what they were to produce, but how they were to produce it.

Market incentive schemes were also sometimes replaced by force. We saw in earlier chapters that some incentive schemes take the form of the carrot, some of the stick. The Soviet Union under Joseph Stalin preferred the stick. Those who did not meet their targets were rewarded with a sojourn in Siberia.

Political controls and rewards also helped replace the lack of economic incentives. Key positions in the economy went to faithful members of the Communist party. In the early days of the revolution, these included many who really believed in socialism as an alternative, superior form of economic organization. Given their ideological commitment, economic incentives to work hard to meet the goals were relatively unimportant. And to the extent that incentives were important, they were provided by the potential for promotion. But as the years went by, membership in the party came to be seen as the vehicle for getting ahead, not as a matter of belief. Under Leonid Brezhnev, who was the first secretary of the Communist party from 1964 to 1982, (a term used to describe the actual head of the party), this cynical attitude spread. The party faithful not only received good jobs but enjoyed other benefits, including access to special stores at which goods not generally available could be acquired.

A basic aspect of market economies, competition, was shunned. Just as the Communist party had a monopoly in the political sphere, no competition with government enterprises was allowed, and the government enterprises did not compete with one another. They did not, of course, eliminate all competition: there was still competition to be promoted to top positions and thus receive higher incomes and access to desirable goods. But success in this competition was not based on how efficiently you produced the goods that consumers wanted, or how innovative you were in devising new products. Rather, success was measured by how well you complied with the bureaucratic targets and requirements and how well you performed in the politics of the bureaucracy and party.

The planned economy or central planning failed miserably in replacing markets. The central planners simply did not have the requisite information. Workers, for instance, were often mismatched with jobs. They were given job security, but this reduced their economic incentives. Pay, and even promotion, were generally not related to performance, and thus the incentives were undermined. Without economic incentives, workers often exerted the minimal level of effort that they could get away with.

Similarly, firms had no incentive to produce beyond the quotas assigned to them. Indeed, they had an incentive not to do so. If they showed that they could produce more with fewer inputs, in subsequent years their quotas would be increased. In the absence of a price system, shortages often developed, not only of consumer goods, but also of inputs into production. Hence, firms squirreled away any extra raw materials they could get their hands on.

The absence of prices and profits had further debilitating effects. In market economies, returns to investment are the signals that determine how capital should be allocated. The quest for profits provides the incentive for entrepreneurs; equally important, losses are a signal for firms to close down. In socialist economies, with the state owning all firms and therefore all profits, profits provide little incentive. And losses are seldom used as a basis for shutting down establishments. If a firm makes a loss, the government meets the deficit. János Kornai, a Hungarian economist who teaches both in his native land and at Harvard, refers to this phenomenon as **soft budget constraints,** to contrast them with the harsh reality of budget constraints facing firms in a market economy. For the firm in a socialist system, there is no penalty for making losses, and no incentive to conserve on resources or to innovate.

In a way, it made sense for the Soviet government not to pay too much attention to profits, since the prices firms received for what they produced and the prices they paid for the inputs they used (including labor and capital) were not market-clearing prices. They did not represent the scarcity value of the resources used or of the goods produced. Thus, the profits were not a good measure of the benefits or costs of the firm's production. By the same token, since prices were not set at market-clearing levels, they did not reflect true scarcity. Hence returns to investment—measured in rubles—were not a sound guide for allocating investments. Prices and wages provided little guidance for whether firms should try to economize more on labor or capital or other inputs.

Figure 39.1 RAPID INDUSTRIALIZATION: MOVEMENTS ALONG THE PRODUCTION POSSIBILITIES CURVE

Soviet-style socialists believed that rapid growth of heavy industry was desirable, so they increased investment. But as the production possibilities curve shows, this can only be done at the expense of consumption. Central planners tried to move the economy toward a point such as E_1, with a high output of investment goods and a low output of consumption goods.

It is perhaps no accident that the fields in which the Soviet Union achieved its greatest success—military research, space technology, and mathematics and physics—were all fields in which markets play a limited role even in capitalist economies. In the absence of prices and interest rates to guide investment, decisions were made on beliefs about the "correct" path of development. Stalin had two basic ideas. First, he recognized that resources that were not allocated to consumption could be given to investment. In terms of the production possibilities curve depicted in Figure 39.1, his first objective was to reduce consumption and move the economy from a point such as E_0 to E_1. One of the aims of the collectivization of agriculture was to do just that, to squeeze the farmers as much as possible. But urban workers' wages were also kept low. By keeping wages low and the supply of consumer goods limited, the Soviet planners in effect "forced" the economy to have high savings.

His second idea was to focus investment on heavy industry. Stalin considered huge factories, such as steel mills, the central symbol of modern economies, which distinguished them from less developed, agrarian economies. He therefore invested primarily in heavy industry, providing little support for agriculture, consumer goods, or housing. The two ideas were in a sense intertwined. With low wages and low consumption, there was little need to invest in industries to provide consumption goods.

SOVIET-STYLE SOCIALISM AND INEQUALITY

The Soviet government, through its planning ministry, not only decided what was to be produced and how. It also provided the answer to the "for whom" question. In answering this question, three aspects of Soviet ideology played an important role. First, Soviet-style economies were committed to heavy industrialization and a de-emphasis on agriculture. Not surprisingly, then, a large part of the burden of the costs was borne by agriculture. Forced collectivization in agriculture kept agriculture wages low. In effect, there were high taxes on agriculture.

Second, the program of high savings and low consumption could be interpreted as putting an emphasis on consumption of future generations at the expense of consumption of the current generation.

Third, an attempt was made to reduce the inequality in society, at least according to the rhetoric of the leaders. The government determined everyone's wages. It decided how much more a skilled worker got than an unskilled worker. Some goods it allocated directly, such as markets for housing and medical care.

Whether or to what extent Soviet-style socialist systems were successful in reducing inequality remains debated. On the one hand, after confiscating all land and other property, there were no longer any very rich people. Also, free medicine and highly subsidized food and apartments provided a "safety net" for the poor. Moreover, one of the major sources of poverty—unemployment—was eliminated. But on the other hand, differences in life-style between the worst-off members of society and high party officials remained enormous. Whole families of ordinary citizens lived crowded together in one room. And though no one starved, they spent long hours in lines to obtain the barest necessities of life. By contrast, high party officials enjoyed vacations along the beaches of the Black Sea, could buy goods unavailable elsewhere at stores reserved for party members, and had chauffeur-driven cars and other powers and perquisites enjoyed by relatively few within the capitalist world. Large wage differentials, commensurate with those observed in capitalist economies, also existed, though they may have translated into smaller differences in living standards, given the many things provided cheaply by the state.

Even the most vaunted achievement of socialism, prevention of the abject extremes of poverty, has in recent years been thrown into doubt. In the period of 1960–61 in China, for example, demographers now estimate that as many as 20 million Chinese starved to death. In the democracies, a free press would have presumably ensured that a calamity like this could not have occurred. Something would have been done. In China, it went almost unnoticed.

THE BASIC ECONOMIC QUESTIONS UNDER SOVIET-STYLE SOCIALISM

1. What is produced?

   Heavy industrial goods

   Other goods as the state sees fit

2. How are goods produced?

   With technologies and inputs decided upon by the state (often capital-intensive technologies)

3. For whom are they produced?

   For future generations (high forced savings rates)

   For present generations according to the wages set by government (high "taxes" on agriculture)

   For government officials, who get high rewards

4. Who makes the decisions?

   Central planning authorities

FAILURE OF SOCIALISM

For several decades, Stalin's program appeared successful. He was able to force net investment rates up to almost unprecedented levels, more than 23 percent of net national product in 1937, for example. Many factories were built. The official statistics suggested a path of rapid industrialization and growth. There is growing doubt about the reliability of the statistics, but there is little doubt that any gains were accompanied by political repression. The USSR's economic progress was interrupted by World War II, in which 20 million Russians are believed to have died, and the economy was greatly disrupted.

The period after World War II saw the spread of Soviet-style socialism to Eastern Europe—Poland, Czechoslovakia, East Germany, Hungary, Romania, Bulgaria, Yugoslavia, and Albania—and, in 1949, to China.[3] In the case of the Eastern European countries, at least, the spread was hardly voluntary. It was the price they paid for being liberated from the Germans by Soviet troops at the end of the war. Before the war, some Eastern European countries had enjoyed reasonably high standards of living. Others, such as Albania, had been extremely poor and backward.

The ensuing decades witnessed several changes in attitudes toward the Soviet-style socialist experiment. At first, the "efficiency" virtues of the system were lauded. The planning mechanism replaced the perceived chaos of the marketplace. Investment could be directed in a rational way. Resources could be quickly mobilized. Moreover, the government could force the high levels of savings required for a successful development program. Textbooks as well as popular writings talked about a trade-off between growth and development on the one hand and freedom on the other. Strong central control was thought to be necessary for rapid growth. Moreover, it was thought that Soviet-style socialism could raise the quality of life to a level the market economy had not been able to attain. Basic human services like health and education could be brought to the masses.

But as economies like Czechoslovakia and Hungary, which had been prosperous before the war, fell behind other European countries, concerns about the efficiency of the system were raised. Such systems could force their citizens to save more because they could repress consumption, but could they allocate resources efficiently? It became increasingly clear that the countries were not growing as fast as one would have thought. The higher savings rates did little more than offset the higher levels of inefficiency.

By the mid-1970s, inklings of an impending economic crisis became more and more apparent. While agricultural productivity in the United States and Western Europe had boomed, in the Soviet-style socialist countries it had stagnated. Nikita Khrushchev, who led Russia from the death of Stalin until he was replaced by Brezhnev in 1964, recognized the problems in agriculture and directed more of the country's investment there. But in 1973, the Soviet Union began buying massive amounts of wheat from the United States and other Western countries to feed its people.

As Mikhail Gorbachev came to power in 1985 the magnitude of the problems the country faced became even clearer. It became evident that many of the statistics on industrial production had been more exaggerated than even

---

[3]Mongolia had adopted Soviet-style socialism much earlier, in 1924. Cuba adopted a variant much later, under Castro in 1959. North Korea and North Vietnam both adopted Soviet-style socialism as soon as their governments were established.

CLOSE-UP: ENVIRONMENTAL DAMAGE IN THE SOVIET UNION

One of the alleged advantages of centrally controlled economies was that unlike ruthless capitalists, socialist firms would take into account the costs and benefits to all members of society. In the area of environmental protection, that promise was not kept. In fact, in the words of one recent study, "When historians finally conduct an autopsy on the Soviet Union and Soviet Communism, they may reach the verdict of death by ecocide."

Market economies often have difficulty dealing with pollution externalities. But in attempting to grow faster, Soviet central planners often made pollution problems worse. For example, oil and energy prices were held deliberately low, as a form of assistance to manufacturers who used oil as an input. But lower prices encouraged wasteful use of energy. When combined with a lack of antipollution measures, this produced literally sickening air pollution. Today in the industrial center of what

was called Magniogorsk, nine out of ten children become ill with pollution-related diseases like bronchitis, asthma, and cancer.

Highly intensive farming, in a situation where no one had a property right to the land and an incentive to protect it, led to massive pesticide use and soil erosion. Three-quarters of the surface water in what used to be the Soviet Union is now badly polluted, either from industrial or agricultural sources.

Perhaps the most publicized result of all was the explosion at the Chernobyl nuclear power station in 1986, which exposed perhaps 20 million Soviet citizens to excessive radiation. If that nuclear power plant had been forced to use safety equipment to avoid that externality, it might well have been shut down years earlier.

Rather than correcting the market failures that led to pollution, Soviet central planners had magnified them into ecological disasters.

Sources: "Rubbishing of a Superpower," *The Economist,* April 25, 1992, pp. 99–100; M. Feshbach and A. Friendly, *Ecocide in the USSR* (New York: Basic Books, 1992).

Figure 39.2 THE RUSSIAN STANDARD OF LIVING

Today, after decades of socialism, the average standard of living in Russia is close to that of Brazil, Argentina, and other less developed nations. *Source: World Development Report* (1996), Table 1.

many skeptics had thought. Indicators of well-being, such as infant mortality statistics, had similarly been distorted.

In most economists' judgment, the Soviet-style socialist experiment was a failure. Today, more than seventy years after the Soviet-style socialist experiment began in Russia, income per capita is a tenth of what it is in the United States. Russia finds its standard of living close to that of Brazil, Argentina, and other countries considered to be underdeveloped, as illustrated in Figure 39.2. The Soviet-style socialist experiment had remarkable achievements, like the Sputnik satellite, but a productive and growing economy was not among them.

REASONS FOR THE FAILURE

The continued success of the capitalist system and the failure of Soviet-style socialist economies can be attributed to incentives and markets, or the lack of them.

The socialists failed to recognize the importance of incentives. Workers, both in collective farms and in manufacturing firms, had no incentive to do more than was required. Managers similarly had no incentives. Firms could not keep any profits they made, and managerial pay in any case did not depend on the profitability of the enterprise. There was no competition, and the soft budget constraints—the fact that losses would be made up by the government—further attenuated managerial incentives.

Equally important, there was no incentive for innovation and growth. The increases in productivity of the labor force in capitalist economies over the past century, with the concomitant increases in wages, are in no small measure the result of the innovative efforts of entrepreneurs. These entrepreneurs almost surely did not succeed out of the desire to enhance the welfare of their workers; they were motivated by the lust for profits and the desire for returns to their savings. But as Adam Smith said, such motives provide a far surer guide to the enhancement of a nation's wealth than any other.

Socialists wanted to replace the market mechanism for allocating resources with central planning. But they encountered two further problems. First, the bureaucrats did not have the requisite information to know how to allocate resources efficiently. Managers of firms had no incentive to tell the central planners what the minimum inputs required to meet their production goals were. Rather, they had every incentive to claim they needed more than they really did. This made their job easier. And they had no incentive to exceed their goals; for if they did, the planners would raise their targets for the next year.

Second, planners could not perfectly monitor the various firms in the economy, to ensure that resources were used in the way intended. And firms had only limited incentives to comply with the planners' directives. They were not rewarded, and they knew they were only imperfectly monitored. Sometimes the managers could divert resources meant for the firm to their own private use. Their disdain for the planners was enhanced by the fact that the planners often put impossible demands on them, such as asking them to produce outputs without providing them the requisite inputs. To fulfill their quota, firms had to acquire the inputs from a "gray" market outside the planning system.

The socialists did not understand the importance of capital markets, interest rates, and profits. As this text has emphasized, capital is a scarce resource. It must be allocated efficiently. Prices provide the signals that make this possible. Because the Soviet-stlye socialist economies set prices by command rather than through markets, prices did not provide the necessary signals. Try as they might to use the planning mechanism to replace the market mechanism, socialist government planning boards simply did not have the requisite information to allocate investment efficiently.

Given the scarcity of capital, the Soviet strategy of heavy industrialization probably did not make much sense. It would have made more sense to focus attention on industries that require less capital.

The failure of worker incentives, the failure of planners to allocate resources efficiently, and the failure of firms to use resources efficiently largely accounted for the inefficiency of the system. But there were other factors as well. The drabness of life, the lack of opportunity afforded by the system, the long hours spent in lines trying to get rotten vegetables or a small portion of meat, all contributed to social malaise, evidenced by a high incidence of alcoholism, which impaired worker productivity. The worker under Soviet-style socialism seemed truly alienated from his work.

CAUSES OF THE FAILURE OF SOVIET-STYLE SOCIALISM

1. Failure to provide adequate incentives to workers and managers

    Lack of competition, soft budget constraints, and lack of incentives to stimulate innovation and growth were major factors.

2. Failure of planning mechanism to replace markets

    Planners lacked the requisite information to allocate resources efficiently.

    Planners lacked the ability to monitor firms and make sure resources were used in the ways intended.

REFORMS IN THE SOVIET-STYLE SOCIALIST ECONOMIES

As the failures of Soviet-style socialism became more evident, a variety of reforms were discussed. Three courses of action were possible: try harder to make the socialist system work; give up on socialism and move to a market-based system;

or find a third way, which would be neither capitalism nor socialism. For three decades, beginning with Khrushchev, the Soviet Union tried the first strategy. Workers were exhorted to work harder. Money poured into agriculture but left little traces of enhanced productivity. Campaigns—including one against vodka—were launched to increase worker productivity.

During 1990 and 1991, there was much debate over whether or not the first strategy should be abandoned. In October of 1990, Gorbachev announced that the Soviet Union would be converted to capitalism in five hundred days. He soon dropped this program, whereupon the economists who had been advising him on the market strategy resigned. It appeared as if there would be another attempt to make socialism work. But then, following the attempted coup in August 1991 and the dissolution of the Soviet Union, directions were changed again: most of the newly created republics seemed committed to adopting some form of market system.

People looking for a third solution sought ways of combining what they saw as the strengths of capitalism with those of socialism. Hungary made some attempt to do this. But perhaps the most successful experiment was in China, where the so-called responsibility system in agriculture essentially allowed farmers to sell most of what they produced in markets and to keep the proceeds. As a result, agricultural production skyrocketed during the late 1970s and early 1980s. The annual growth rate of grain production in the six years after the responsibility system was adopted (1978–1984) was 5 percent, compared with 3.5 percent in the thirteen years before the new system (1965–1978).

MARKET SOCIALISM

An important idea behind several of the reform movements was market socialism, which argued that an economy could combine the advantages of market mechanisms with public ownership of the means of production. Oskar Lange—who was a professor of economics at the University of Chicago before returning to Poland after World War II, eventually to become a vice-president of that country's Communist government—was a leading advocate.

Under market socialism, prices would serve the same allocative role that they do in capitalist economies. Prices would be set so that demand equaled supply. Firms would act like competitive price takers. They would maximize their profits at the prices they faced. They would produce up to the point where price equaled marginal cost. They would hire labor up to the point where the value of the marginal product of labor was equal to the wage. But since government owned all machines and buildings, it would take responsibility for all investment decisions. These decisions would be made according to a national plan, which defined the nation's priorities. The planning process would entail close interaction between the government planners and the firms, with the firms informing the planners of what was required to meet various production goals.

In the 1930s, there was a great debate between the advocates of market socialism, including Oskar Lange, and a group of Austrian economists, including Ludwig von Mises and Nobel laureate Friedrich von Hayek. The Austrians did not believe that government could have the information required to efficiently allocate investment. They thought the task of allocating resources, or even setting market-clearing prices, was simply too complicated to be done by a government bureau. (As it turned out, they were largely correct.) And they did not believe government-owned firms would act like private firms. In their view, market socialism was doomed to failure. The advocates of market socialism emphasized the fact that there were, in modern terms, pervasive market failures. Capital and risk markets were imperfect. There were externalities. Competition was imperfect. The market gave rise to great inequality. And capitalist economies seemed prone to periodic chronic illnesses—to recessions and depressions. Pointing out these failures, of course, does not prove that market socialism can do any better, or even as well as capitalism.

PROBLEMS WITH MARKET SOCIALISM

Market socialism faces two key problems: obtaining the requisite information to set prices and providing managers with incentives.

Information to Set Prices In order to set prices at market-clearing levels, planners have to know, in effect, both demand and supply curves. They have to know an enormous amount about what consumers want as well as firms' capabilities. But they seldom have this information, partly, as noted, because firms have no incentive to tell planners their capabilities. Even with good information, it is extraordinarily difficult for a government bureaucracy to set prices at market-clearing levels. In Lange's time it was still plausible to hope, as he did, that faster computers would solve the problem. But as better and better computers have been developed, it has become increasingly clear that the problems of setting simultaneously the prices of the millions of goods produced in a modern market economy cannot be solved by a computer, however advanced.

Indeed, it has become clear that while prices play a central role in how the market economy functions, they are only part of the market's incentive systems. Customers also care about the *quality* of the goods they purchase. For instance, for firms, having inputs delivered on time is essential. Consider producing nails in a socialist economy. Given a directive to produce so many nails, the nail factory produces short, stubby nails. When the directive is modified to include a specification for a longer nail, the factory responds by producing a nail with the cheapest steel it can get hold of; the result is that the nail splits when hit too hard. When told that the steel should not be too brittle, the firm finds a kind of steel that bends too easily to make it useful for many purposes.

In market economies, firms will not produce at the market price unless they know they can sell the goods. In a socialist economy, the producer simply delivers the goods to another government enterprise, whose problem it is to sell the good. When China set too high a price for fans, for example, the factories produced more fans than could be sold. Meanwhile, there were huge shortages of most other consumer goods.

While setting prices wrong for consumer goods causes inconvenience, setting prices wrong for producer goods impairs the entire production process. If a firm producing an intermediate good cannot get some input it needs, it will not be able to provide its product to the firms that need it. A shortage at one critical point can have reverberations through other parts of the economy.

Incentives Under market socialism, managers often lack incentives. When the enterprise makes a profit, they cannot keep the profit. And when the enterprise makes a loss, the government makes up the deficit. Market socialism therefore does not resolve the problem of soft budget constraints. Furthermore, competition, which lies at the heart of the market's incentive system, is absent, and this lack of competition is reflected in all aspects of behavior, including the incentive to produce goods that reflect what customers want.

Some aspects of the experiments with market socialism have been successful, at least as compared with Soviet-style socialism. As was noted, the responsibility system of agriculture in China has resulted in huge increases in agricultural productivity. But overall, the success of most of the experiments is more debatable. To some, market socialism lacks the best features of both capitalism and socialism: it lacks the market's incentive structure and traditional socialism's other mechanisms of economic control. Within Hungary, for example, which had gone the farthest along the road to market socialism before 1989, a consensus developed against market socialism.

In 1992, China embarked on further reforms, in which prices and investment were increasingly placed in the hands of individual enterprises. What distinguished this form of market socialism from capitalism was the ownership of enterprises. Most were either state owned, or owned by villages and townships, or were cooperatives. The system, which had evolved gradually since 1979, had produced remarkable results—growth rates which averaged in excess of 10 percent for almost two decades.

WORKERS' COOPERATIVES IN YUGOSLAVIA

Yet another type of socialist experiment occurred in Yugoslavia. Marshal Tito, a communist who led the fight against the Nazis in Yugoslavia and became the country's leader after World War II, broke with Stalin in 1948. In the ensuing years, decentralization and decision making by firms became an important part of the Yugoslavian economy. Ownership of firms was turned over to the workers, who were responsible for choosing their own managers. (In practice, the Communist party exercised considerable influence both in the choice of managers and in the decisions made.)

The idea of worker-owned and -managed firms—cooperatives—has a long history throughout Europe and in the United States. Even today in the United States, there are some enormously successful worker-owned firms—Amana, which makes refrigerators; Avis, the country's second largest car rental company; and W. W. Norton, the publisher of this book. Ulgar, a successful household appliances firm, began as a worker cooperative in Mondragón, Spain.

Today, with thousands of workers located in many separate plants, it is still run as a cooperative.

A major argument for cooperatives is that because the worker is also part owner, she has a greater commitment to the firm and more incentive to work hard. While this argument seems valid for cooperatives involving relatively few workers, it does not apply as well to large enterprises. And this proved to be a problem in Yugoslavia. Managers elected by a vote of the workers may be as remote as managers chosen by a board of directors. In cooperatives with thousands of workers, each worker gets back a negligible amount of any extra profits that result from anything he does. The most successful cooperatives thus are often the smaller ones.

In Yugoslavia, the cooperatives encountered another problem—lack of incentive to hire new workers. If new workers have the same rights as old workers, the profits of the enterprise must be divided more ways. Whether for this or other reasons, Yugoslavia was plagued with high unemployment rates.

Investment posed still a third problem. When Yugoslavian workers left their cooperative, they received nothing. There was therefore little interest in investing, at least in the long term, or otherwise increasing the market value of the enterprise. Workers did not have an incentive to make investments that yielded returns beyond the date of their retirement.[4]

Some of these problems are not *inherent* in cooperatives. For instance, in cooperatives in the United States and Europe, when a person retires or leaves the cooperative for any other reason, he takes his capital out. He is viewed as a part owner of the enterprise; the share he owns depends on the rules of the cooperative, typically how long he has been with the cooperative and in what positions he has served. By the same token, when a worker joins a cooperative, she has in effect to buy a share. (The company may loan her the money, so her take-home pay may be reduced until she has contributed her capital share.) The better the cooperative does, the more she will be able to receive when she leaves. This provides an obvious incentive for the cooperative to make good investment decisions.

TRANSITION TO MARKET ECONOMIES

Many former socialist countries, including Hungary, the Czech Republic, and Poland, are today committed to becoming market economies. Others, such as Bulgaria, Romania, and Albania, want *some* market reforms, but how many and how fast remains uncertain. The following discussion describes key problems facing countries as they move toward a market economy.

---

[4]This list of problems that Yugoslavia faced is not meant to be exhaustive. There were others: lack of competition among people who purchased farmers' produce, for instance, meant that farmers received lower prices for their goods, and this discouraged farmers' production.

These problems of transition are exacerbated by the economic chaos in the former Soviet Union—the main trading partner of the Eastern European countries. As these countries face the problems of transition, they face the additional burden of finding new markets to replace sales to the Soviet Union, which have plummeted. To make matters worse, the kinds of goods they produced for the Soviet Union are not the high-quality goods consumers in Western Europe, Japan, and the United States want. Not only must they find new markets. They must also reorient their production.

MACROECONOMIC PROBLEMS

The first transition hurdle Eastern European economies face is a period of disruption in which living standards, at least for some, fall below even the low level that they had been under socialism.

A central problem with socialism was that resources were inefficiently allocated. If the economy is to move from a point inside its production possibilities curve (such as A in Figure 39.3) to a point on the curve, resources will have to be reallocated. Factories will have to be shut down. Workers will have to be let go. These disruptions will be reflected in high transitional unemployment. Transitional unemployment is like frictional unemployment—the unemployment that occurs as workers move between jobs—magnified many times over. Poland, the first country to attempt the transition, experienced unemployment rates estimated at 25–35 percent. In Romania, miners, seeing their real wages cut by a third, rioted and succeeded in bringing down the market-oriented prime minister. The new prime minister, however, was an economist even more committed to market reforms.

Unemployment is particularly serious in Eastern European countries, because they do not have the same kinds of safety nets that protect people forced out of jobs in Western Europe and the United States. This is not surprising, since under the previous regime unemployment was not a problem. Firms retained workers even when they were no longer needed; they had no profit motive, no budget constraint. But now, in the transition, firms do face budget constraints. Moreover, since capital markets are not yet working well, new firms are not being created and old firms are not expanding production to absorb the workers who have been laid off.

Inflation receives considerable attention in Eastern Europe these days, partly because it is felt by everyone, partly because typically wages do not keep pace with prices (so that living standards fall). But the fall in living standards is not really caused by the inflation. It is caused by the economic disruption of the transition process, which simultaneously reduces output, leads to inflation, and lowers living standards. In Russia inflation was not brought under control until 1994—and even then it proceeded at the rate of 18 percent per year.

The reason inflation always seems to arise in the transition is easy to see. The Soviet-style economies were run with prices below market-clearing levels. In Russia, indeed, the price of bread was kept so low that farmers found it cheaper to buy bread to feed their pigs than grain. Shortages were endemic. Hence, once prices were freed, price increases were inevitable. A onetime

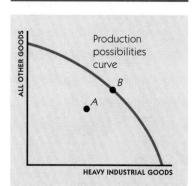

Figure 39.3 INEFFICIENCIES UNDER SOCIALISM

The Soviet-style socialist economies seemed to use their resources inefficiently, so that they operated substantially below the production possibilities curve, such as at point A. Moving the economy from A to a point like B, on the production possibilities curve, will entail substantial improvements in efficiency.

price increase is not the fundamental worry, however. The danger is that it will lead to inflationary expectations which, once established, perpetuate inflation.

Huge government deficits contribute to inflationary pressures. As the government's control over the economy weakens, its revenue sources often diminish. Under socialism, it could simply seize corporate profits. If it wanted to increase profits and thus its revenues, government could just increase the prices charged or reduce the wages paid. As government abandoned its role in wage and price setting, it lost its ability to raise revenues in this way. But cutting back on expenditures seems no easier in Eastern Europe than elsewhere. Food subsidies are a major drain on the budget, but government threats to reduce them have met with stiff opposition. As profits shrank, and, for huge numbers of enterprises, turned into losses, the economies in transition faced a dilemma. They could subsidize those enterprises making losses, or shut them down. With limited revenues, subsidies required deficit financing; and the debt contributed to inflationary pressures. If they were shut down, unemployment increased. Poland chose unemployment. Throughout much of the early 1990s, Russia seemed to choose inflation, with the unemployment rate remaining relatively low. Some countries got a large dose of both.

PRIVATIZATION AND COMPETITION

Private property and competition are at the center of the market economy. *Allowing* competition is easy. The government can simply say that anyone who wants to set up a firm and has the necessary resources can do so. Generating and sustaining competition are more difficult.

One important way for Eastern European countries to promote competition is through trade liberalization—opening up the economy to competition from abroad. But while most economists believe that trade liberalization will enhance economic efficiency in the long run, some are concerned about those who lose out in the competition, including people who lose their jobs. They give a variant of the infant industry argument, which goes like this. Enterprises in the former socialist economies have been insulated from competition for decades. It is unfair to suddenly subject them to competition and make their survival depend on this market test. They need time to learn how to compete.

Another way to promote competition is to sell off different parts of existing state enterprises to private entrepreneurs. There are few problems in selling off small businesses—barbershops, retail stores, restaurants. The real difficulties come in selling large enterprises like automobile or cement factories. Selling them to foreigners raises a host of thorny problems. No country likes to see its factories owned by foreigners. And if a country sells the factories to buyers abroad at too low a price, it is as if the country is giving away its hard-earned savings to foreigners. In Eastern Europe, there is a further problem. People with the most money include former party bosses. There is a bitter irony in seeing those who exploited the system under the

Communist government for their own advantage retain their advantageous position, this time as capitalist bosses.

Different countries have approached the problem of privatization differently. The Czech Republic first privatized stores, restricted purchases of the stores to citizens (and prohibited their resale to foreigners for two years), and accepted the grim fact that many of the hated Communist bosses would now become capitalist bosses. Economic efficiency, in the minds of Czech reformers, was more important than revenge. The country distributed vouchers to all citizens, which the citizens used to bid for shares in the larger, privatizing firms. Thus, in one stroke, the Czech Republic hoped both to privatize and to establish a viable stock market. With the widely distributed ownership of firms, they hoped to establish a people's capitalism. The next problem the Czechs face is that with no shareholders having a large stake in a firm, managers will run the firm with little outside check on their behavior. There have been proposals to deal with this problem, such as the establishment of holding companies or investment banks, but no consensus has emerged.

Hungary, by contrast, has taken the view that the advantages of foreign ownership—in particular, the advantage of foreigners' expertise—outweigh the disadvantages. Government officials point out that almost 40 percent of Belgian firms are foreign owned with no adverse effects. They envisage a similar role for foreign ownership within their own economy.

Russia, like the Czech Republic, used vouchers, but a large fraction of the shares were distributed to the workers and managers of each enterprise, raising questions about the extent to which managers will be subject to outside control.

SPEED OF TRANSITION

The pace of privatization has also varied greatly across countries and sectors. In Russia, by 1995, 55 percent of the large enterprises (outside of certain key sectors, such as energy) had been privatized. In the Czech Republic, 70 percent had been privatized. But in Romania and Bulgaria, privatization is proceeding at a very slow pace.

The former Soviet-style socialist economies face a difficult problem in deciding how fast to make the transition to capitalism. One approach is "cold turkey" or shock therapy. Make the plunge, live through a short nightmarish period, and then enjoy a future prosperity. The other approach calls for a more gradual transition and considers political as well as economic issues. For instance, will the pain caused by cold turkey be so great that support for the market will erode?

Poland tried the cold turkey approach, at least with respect to its macroeconomic adjustment. Inflation was brought under control, but at the expense of a drastic drop in output and employment, and the defeat of the government that undertook the plan. And even after the macroadjustments are made, the microeconomic problems—for instance, making factories more efficient, reallocating labor and capital—remain. Most of the other countries have moved more cautiously.

The debate about the speed of transition has been heated—both inside the countries and from foreign commentators. Those advocating a quick transition have cited the famous aphorism, "You can't jump across a chasm in two steps." Advocates of a slower transition pointed out that "It takes nine months even to produce a baby," to which the advocates of fast transition replied, "But you can't be half pregnant."

What is at issue involves both economics and politics. If a fast transition results in high levels of unemployment, political disillusionment can set in, and political pressures may halt the reform process. When the reformers lost the Russian elections in December 1993, Strobe Talbott, who headed U.S. Russian policy (he subsequently became Deputy Secretary of State) criticized the "shock therapy" of rapid transition by saying there was too much shock and too little therapy. He seemed to be suggesting that he thought that the transition had proceeded too rapidly, without sufficient attention to those hurt by it.

There was a quick response from market reformers, who argued that the problem was too slow, not too rapid, transition. In a sense, both were correct. The slow transition was evidenced in low unemployment rates and low rates of privatization. But the rapid rates of inflation had left many older people (whose pensions did not increase with inflation) with a rapidly decreasing standard of living. In the rush to engage in economic reforms, too little attention may have been placed on the safety net.

Even those countries that managed to arrest and reverse the decline in GDP during transition faced a problem of increasing inequality.

The problem is that the success of market economies depends on a host of long-established institutions, not just on the abstract concept of markets. And all these institutions have to be functioning reasonably well if the economy is to prosper. There must be credit institutions to sort out potential loan applicants, to monitor the loans, and to see that funds go where they are most productive and are used in the way promised. There must be a legal structure that ensures contracts will be enforced and determines what happens when one party cannot fulfill its contract (bankruptcy). There must be an antitrust policy that ensures firms compete against one another.

Beyond that, the more advanced countries have developed a set of safety nets to help certain segments of society, such as the unemployed. Since unemployment was not a problem in socialist economies, these societies do not have such safety nets. There may be a huge human toll if the transition, with its attendant unemployment, proceeds before the safety nets are in place. Yet the budgetary problems facing all of these governments make it hard to institute such programs quickly.

Those who advocate a more gradual transition to market economies believe that the long-run success of these economies will be enhanced by thinking through each of the components, trying to design the best possible institutions, adapting to the particular situations in which they find themselves, and borrowing where appropriate from the United States, Western Europe, and Japan.

Today, almost all the countries of the former Soviet empire pay lip service to a commitment toward market reform. In some, the pace is so gradual as to be, to date, almost imperceptible. In Ukraine, market reforms were resisted as long as possible. But as inflation rates soared to over 100 percent per month and as the economy became unable to pay for its imports of energy— leading to factories threatened with closure, homes unheated, and farms unable even to get oil to run their tractors—a set of reforms was put into place in 1994. In other countries, such as the Czech Republic, the reforms have been rapid.

Even with rapid reforms, for most of the countries in transition it will take years, perhaps decades, to overcome the problems bequeathed by their Communist systems.

REVIEW AND PRACTICE

SUMMARY

1. Socialism grew out of the grave economic problems that characterized nineteenth-century industrial economies—severe recessions and depressions, unemployment, and bad working and living conditions.

2. Soviet-style socialism used central planning, under which government bureaucrats made all major decisions about what would be produced, how it would be produced, and for whom it would be produced. Competition was banned. Prices, set by the government, often did not reflect relative scarcities. Private property was restricted.

3. In socialist economies, firms and workers lacked incentives. Firms had little incentive to make profits since profits went to the state, and little incentive to avoid losses since the government would meet any deficits. Firms thus faced soft budget constraints. Similarly, socialism protected workers against layoffs. The trade-off was that this greater security created a lesser incentive for efficiency and hard work.

4. In Soviet-style economies, the government used force to impose high savings rates (which meant low consumption) and decided where investment funds went, pushing heavy industrialization. Government often lacked the requisite information to make informed decisions concerning how to allocate resources. Central planning was not able to replace markets.

5. The Soviet-style socialist experiment is today considered a failure by most economists. Russia's standard of living is no higher now than that of many underdeveloped countries.

6. Three possible reforms have been proposed for Soviet-style socialist economies: try harder to make socialism work; give up on socialism and

move to a market-based system; find a third alternative between socialism and markets. Today the focus is on the latter two strategies.

7. Among the problems faced by countries in their transition to a market economy are unemployment and inflation. These countries also do not have in place a safety net to protect those hurt in the transition process.

8. Privatizing state-controlled firms has proved difficult in many countries, given the reluctance of governments to sell factories to foreigners or former party bosses, who are often the only ones with sufficient resources to buy the enterprises. Still, in many countries, there has been substantial progress in privatization, expecially where voucher schemes have been employed.

Key Terms

socialism
communism
planned economies

soft budget
constraints

Review Questions

1. What were some of the problems that motivated Karl Marx's criticism of capitalism?

2. What are some of the central characteristics of Soviet-style socialism?

3. How is the rate of national savings determined in a socialist economy, as opposed to a capitalist economy? How is the allocation of capital determined in a socialist economy, as opposed to a capitalist economy? Who determines what goods are produced in a socialist economy?

4. Why are budget constraints "soft" in socialist countries and "hard" in market economies?

5. What is market socialism? What did its advocates claim? What are the main problems it faces?

6. What are workers' cooperatives? What did its advocates claim for them? What were the problems of workers' cooperatives in Yugoslavia?

7. What are the central problems facing countries trying to move from Soviet-style socialism to market economies? Why are inflationary pressures common in a socialist country that is moving toward a market economy? Why is rising unemployment common?

8. What benefits do socialist economies hope to gain from privatization? What are some of the problems facing privatization programs?

9. What are the advantages and disadvantages of the "cold turkey" approach for a socialist economy in transition?

PROBLEMS

1. Explain how each of the following incentives is different in a socialist and a market economy:
   (a) the incentive of a manager to make wise decisions;
   (b) the incentive of workers to exert their best effort;
   (c) the incentive of a bank manager to screen prospective borrowers carefully.

2. Queues (lines) form when there is a shortage of goods. Use a supply and demand diagram to explain why socialist price controls tend to lead to queues.

3. Are the problems of soft budget constraints unique to socialist economies?

4. Why did the Soviet-style socialist economies have almost no safety nets of unemployment and welfare benefits?

5. In the Soviet-style socialist economies, housing was very scarce, and much of it was controlled by firms. What consequences might this have for labor mobility?

6. If you were a top official in a country that practiced Soviet-style socialism, would you rather have a very high income or access to a special store where all items are guaranteed to be in stock? Why?

7. Imagine that you are sixty years old and you work for a workers' cooperative in Yugoslavia. If you consider only your own self-interest, are you likely to support hiring more workers? Would you support long-term investments in capital?

40

DEVELOPMENT

T hree-quarters of the world's population live in **less developed countries,** or **LDCs.** In the United States, one of the world's wealthier nations, the idea of "less developed" is often applied to rural areas, or to urban areas where houses and businesses are run down. Life in the LDCs poses far more serious problems. It is not that houses are run down, but that a large percentage of the population have no housing at all; not that people's diet is limited, but that they are starving to death; not that medical care is far off or costly, but that it is simply unavailable. The contrast between life in some LDCs and life in the United States is significantly greater than the contrast between life in America today and two centuries ago.

The LDCs pose some of the most poignant problems in economics. There are no simple answers, no easy formulas that, if followed, will ensure successful solutions. Still, as this chapter explains, economists have learned a lot during recent decades about the process of economic development.

KEY QUESTIONS

1. In what ways, besides their grinding poverty, do the developing countries differ from the United States, Japan, and the countries of Western Europe?

2. What are the impediments to growth in developing countries?

3. What policies can these countries pursue to improve their standards of living?

BACKGROUND

Statistics cannot convey the full measure of what it means to live in a less developed country, but they can provide a start. In the United States, life expectancy at birth is about 77 years. In Peru, it is 65 years; in India, 61 years; in Nigeria, 52 years. In the United States, 8 infants die for every 1,000 live births; in Brazil, 57; in Pakistan, 95; in Ethiopia, 122. The average American completes 12 years of schooling, while the average African gets only 5 years. India, with a population three and a half times larger than that of the United States, has a GDP roughly one-fifth that of the United States. This means that per capita income in India is about 5 percent of that in the United States.

The statistics connect to one another in a vicious cycle. Little or no education, malnutrition, and poor health care reduce productivity and thus incomes. With low incomes, people in the LDCs cannot afford better education, more food, or better health care. Life is hard in LDCs. In many African countries, whose standards of living were already low, population has been growing faster than national income, so that per capita income is falling. Life is getting worse, not better.

The United Nations and the World Bank (a bank established by the major industrialized countries after World War II that provides loans to LDCs) group countries into three categories: low-income countries, with GNP per capita of $725 or less in 1994; high-income countries, with GNP per capita above $8,955; and middle-income countries, with GNP per capita in between. The low-income countries are the LDCs. The high-income countries are referred to as **developed countries.** Because the basis of their higher level of income is their higher level of industrialization, they are also referred to as the **industrialized countries.** Figure 40.1 shows countries in the various income categories. In the Western Hemisphere, hardly 200 miles apart, lie one of the richest countries, the United States, with a per capita income of $25,880 in 1994, and one of the poorest, Haiti, with a per capita income of $230.

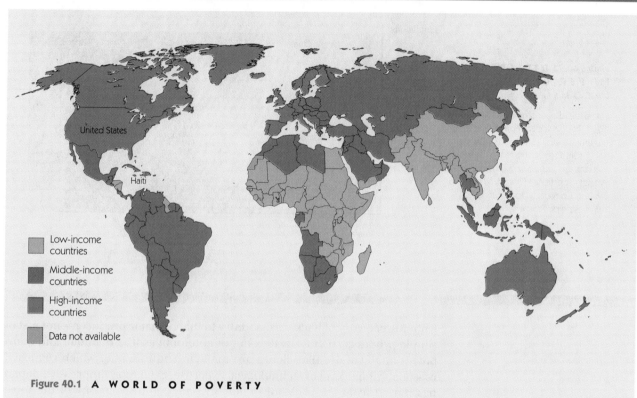

Figure 40.1 A WORLD OF POVERTY

This map shows the less developed countries (LDCs), here labeled "low-income countries," as well as the middle-income and developed countries. Most of the world lives in low-income countries. The developed countries consist mainly of those in Western Europe, the former colonies of Great Britain (Canada, Australia, New Zealand), the United States, and Japan. *Source: World Development Report* (1996).

The income gap among the high-income countries, including the countries of Western Europe, the United States, Canada, Japan, Australia, and New Zealand, has narrowed considerably over the past hundred years, but the gap between the high-income countries and the low-income countries has not. Figure 40.2 shows per capita income in several LDCs, ranging from $100 in Ethiopia to $720 in Egypt. Note that U.S. per capita income in 1994 was $25,880, compared to Ethiopia and Egypt that is 250 and 35 times as large, respectively. However, there are signs that change is possible. Some countries have made notable progress in recent years.

First, several countries have moved from the circle of LDCs to the ranks of middle-income countries. These are referred to collectively as **newly industrialized countries,** or **NICs** for short. These success stories include the "gang of four": South Korea, Taiwan, Singapore, and Hong Kong. Just thirty years after the devastating Korean War, for instance, South Korea has moved

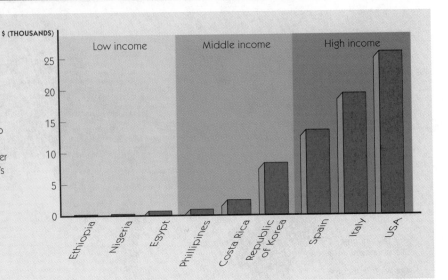

Figure 40.2 DIFFERENCES IN PER CAPITA INCOME

Some middle-income countries such as Costa Rica have per capita incomes up to ten times that of the world's poorest nations and yet are up to ten times smaller than the per capita income of the world's wealthiest nations. *Source: WDR (1996),* Table 1. Conversion to dollars uses purchasing power parity.

from the category of backward country to that of major producer—not just of simple products such as textiles but of automobiles (the Hyundai) and computers (many of the IBM clones are made in South Korea), which require a reasonably high level of technological expertise. Even more impressive, Japan has moved from the ranks of middle-income countries to one of the most prosperous in the world.

Second, there have been pockets of remarkable progress *within* the less developed countries. In the early 1960s, agricultural research centers around the world (funded largely by the Rockefeller Foundation) developed new kinds of seeds, which under correct conditions increase the yields per acre enormously. The introduction and dissemination of these new seeds, accompanied by enormous improvements in agricultural practices—known as the **green revolution**—led to huge increases in output. India, for example, finally managed to produce enough food to feed its burgeoning population, and now sometimes exports wheat to other countries.

Third, even the grim statistics for life expectancy—57 in Bangladesh and 52 in sub-Saharan Africa (compared to 77 in the United States)—represent improvements for many countries. But these improvements have a darker side in some countries—a population explosion reminiscent of the Malthusian nightmare. Malthus envisioned a world in which population growth outpaced increases in the food supply. In Kenya during the early 1980s, for instance, improved health conditions enabled the population to grow at the remarkable rate of 4.1 percent a year, implying a doubling of the population every eighteen years, while output increased only at the rate of 1.9 percent a year. Output increases do nothing to improve per capita income when the population grows even faster.

The 1980s was a particularly hard decade for some of the poorest countries,

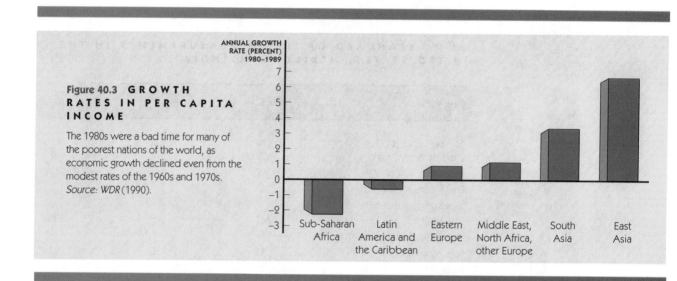

Figure 40.3 GROWTH RATES IN PER CAPITA INCOME

The 1980s were a bad time for many of the poorest nations of the world, as economic growth declined even from the modest rates of the 1960s and 1970s. *Source: WDR (1990).*

ANNUAL GROWTH RATE (PERCENT) 1980–1989

as Figure 40.3 shows. Sub-Saharan Africa[1] had basically stagnated for the previous quarter century. But during the 1980s per capita income actually fell by 2.4 percent per year. Latin America had grown at a little more than 2 percent a year in per capita income for the previous quarter century. During the 1980s per capita income there fell by .7 percent a year.

LIFE IN AN LDC

Just as there are large differences between the LDCs and the industrialized countries, so too are there large differences among the LDCs. The largest LDC of all, China, has a Communist government. The second largest, India, has an avowedly socialist government, but also functions as the world's largest democracy. Literacy standards in Costa Rica rank with those of the industrialized countries. But more than half of the adult population in sub-Saharan Africa is illiterate. One must be careful in generalizing about LDCs. Still, certain observations are true for *most* of them.

Table 40.1 summarizes some of the most important dimensions of living standards—contrasting the United States, a high-income country; Mexico (its nearest neighbor to the south), a middle-income country; and India, a low-income country. Incomes and life expectancies in most LDCs are low. A large fraction of the population lives in the rural sector and is engaged in agriculture. Lacking modern equipment like tractors, they work on small plots (an acre or two, compared to more than a hundred acres in the United States). In many cases, they even lack the resources to buy productivity-increasing inputs like fertilizer and pesticides—averaging less than half the fertilizer per acre used in more developed countries. In many countries, most farmers are

[1]All of Africa south of the Sahara except South Africa.

Table 40.1 **STANDARD OF LIVING MEASUREMENTS IN THE UNITED STATES, MEXICO, AND INDIA**

Category	U.S.	Mexico	India
GNP per capita ($)	25,880	4,180	320
Life expectancy (years)	77	71	62
Agriculture as % of GDP	2	8	32
Energy consumption per capita (kilograms of oil equivalent)	7,662	1,525	235
Food as % of total household consumption	13	35	52
Medical care as % of total household consumption	14	5	3
Average annual inflation (GDP deflator): 1984–94	3.3	40.0	9.7
Average annual growth of population (%): 1980–94	1.0	2.0	2.0
Infant mortality rate (per 1,000 live births)	8	35	70
Population per physician	420	1,242	2,460
Population in cities of 1 million or more as % of total population	43	28	9

Source: World Development Report (1991–1996). Data are for the most recent year available, in most cases 1994.

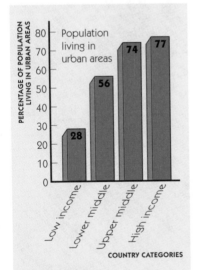

Figure 40.4 RATES OF URBANIZATION

The percentage of the population living in urban areas tends to be higher in developed countries than in LDCs.
Source: WDR (1996), Table 9.

landless, tilling the landlord's land under **sharecropping** arrangements, in which the landlord gets half the output. In several countries, **land reform** has redistributed land to the peasants. Such land reforms were a precursor to the remarkable growth in Taiwan and Japan. In other countries, such as the Philippines and Peru, the land reforms have been only partially successful.

Over the past fifty years, most LDCs have experienced gradual urbanization (see Figure 40.4). Those who live in the cities have a much higher standard of living, including access to better education and health facilities. The marked differences between the cities and rural areas have led some to refer to these economies as **dual economies.** While there are large income disparities between rural and urban sectors, there are equally large disparities within the urban sectors, with government workers and those few lucky enough to get jobs in manufacturing earning many times average wages. These high wages attract migrants from the rural sector, often resulting in high urban unemployment. Rates in some cities exceed 20 percent.

IMPORTANT DIFFERENCES BETWEEN DEVELOPED AND LESS DEVELOPED COUNTRIES

	DEVELOPED COUNTRIES	LDCs
Per capita income	Over $9,000	Less than $725 per year
Production/Employment	Less than 10% of the work force is in agriculture	More than 70% of the work force is in agriculture
Urbanization	Less than 30% live in rural areas	More than 60% live in rural areas
Population growth rate	Less than 1.0%	Often more than 3.0%

EXPLANATIONS OF UNDERDEVELOPMENT

Part of LDC poverty arises from lack of resources. They have less physical capital per capita and less human capital, with high illiteracy rates and low average years of schooling. The lower levels of physical capital per capita are not the result of low savings rates—in fact savings rates of most are considerably higher than that of the United States (see Figure 40.5). Their high population growth rates mean that they have to save a lot just to stand still.

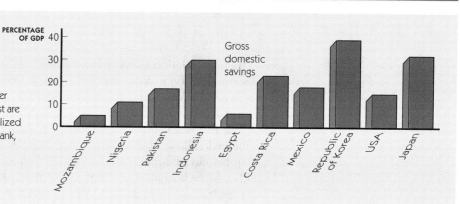

Figure 40.5 SAVINGS RATES

Savings rates in LDCs tend to be higher than in the United States, though most are not as high as in some other industrialized countries like Japan. *Source:* World Bank, WDR (1996).

USING ECONOMICS: THE MAGIC OF COMPOUNDING

The central challenge facing less developed countries is to increase living standards, or income per capita. There are two parts of a strategy to do this: faster growth in GDP and slower growth in population. Often policies seem to have a small effect: the rate of growth of GDP might be increased from 2 percent to 4 percent, and the rate of growth of population might be slowed from 3 percent to 1.5 percent. But because of the magic of compounding these slight differences can have cumulatively large effects over a span of a few decades.

For instance, with a 4 percent growth rate, output doubles every 18 years, while with a 2 percent growth rate, output doubles every 36 years. This means that in the relatively short horizon of 72 years, if two countries initially had the same output, the country with the higher growth rate has an output *four times* as great. In 144 years, a little less than a century and a half, the difference has magnified to sixteen times. (To derive these results, you can use what is sometimes called the rule of 72: something growing at the rate of g doubles in a period of time equal to 72 divided by the growth rate, g.*)

By the same token, a country with a population growth rate of 3 percent doubles its population every 24 years, while with a 1.5 percent growth rate, the population doubles in 48 years. If two countries had initially the same population, in 144 years, the faster growing country would have a population 8 times as large.

If the faster growing economy also had the slower growing population, output per capita would be 128 times as large.

Of course, there really is no magic in compounding: a faster growth rate today means that the economy is larger tomorrow, so that *base* from which further growth takes place is that much larger. The power of compounding is, however, real: fifty years ago, Korea had a slightly lower per capita income than India. Through growing slightly faster, year after year, today Korea has a per capita income that is eight times that of India.

*Formally, if GDP grows at the rate of g percent per year, GDP in t years will have grown by a factor e^{gt}. $e^{.72} = 2$, so GDP will have doubled when $gt = .72$. If $g = .02$, $t = .72/.02 = 36$. If $g = .04$, $t = .72/.04 = 18$.

High population growth rates have another effect. They have increased enormously the proportion of the young—who are dependent on others for their income. And they have made the task of improving educational levels even harder.

There is a vicious circle here. Typically, more educated women have smaller families. This is partly because they are more likely to be informed about family planning, but it is also partly because the opportunity cost of having children is higher for them—they must forgo more income.

Low education levels and lack of capital means that these economies cannot avail themselves of much of the most advanced technologies. With important exceptions,[2] they specialize in low-skill *labor-intensive* industries (products which require much labor relative to the amount of equipment they employ), like textiles.

IMPORTANCE OF CAPITAL

How much of the difference between developed and less developed countries can actually be attributed to lack of capital as opposed to inefficient use of capital? If a shortage of capital in LDCs were the major difference between the developed and less developed countries, the law of diminishing returns would predict that the return to capital in the industrialized countries would be much lower than the return in LDCs. The more capital a country has relative to its population, the lower is the output per machine and the lower the marginal return to capital. In other words, the shortage of capital in LDCs should make the return to capital greater. This difference in returns would naturally result in a movement of capital from the more developed to the less developed countries, as business firms searched out profitable investment opportunities.

The evidence shows some differences in the return to capital. But these differences are too small to demonstrate that a capital shortage is the major problem faced by the LDCs. Moreover, if a capital shortage were the major problem, the LDCs would use what capital they have very intensively. But this does not typically happen. For example, factories run extra daily shifts more often in developed countries than in LDCs.

A much more important impediment to growth in many less developed countries is the lack of efficiency in how scarce funds are used. In Venezuela, which tried to invest its oil dollars as fast as they came in during the 1970s, output increased by 10 cents for every dollar invested in capital equipment. In contrast, in the United States and other developed countries, each extra dollar of investment results on average in an output increase of between 30 and 50 cents—three to five times higher. In many LDCs, greater investment simply does not lead to much increased output.

There are a number of reasons for this. Some economists, such as Walter Rostow of the University of Texas, have argued that at any moment a country has only a limited absorptive capacity for more capital. LDCs lack the human capital, the experience, and technological know-how to pursue many projects simultaneously. The absorptive capacity is most limited in the poorest countries. When investments are pushed beyond absorptive capacity, they yield very low returns.

Many economists, however, believe that there are two more fundamental reasons for the low returns to capital: lack of developed capital markets to allocate capital efficiently, and well-intentioned government interventions which nonetheless support low-return projects. At least in the past, many

---

[2]There is, for instance, a large highly educated elite in India, which has become a center for the development of computer software.

CLOSE-UP: TRANSNATIONAL CORPORATIONS AS A SOURCE OF CAPITAL

Less developed countries lack capital, both to get the machines needed for greater production and to increase the human capital of their population. But where is that capital to come from?

LDCs can, through savings, provide some capital themselves. Countries like Mexico, Brazil, and South Korea have shown a capacity to save more than 20 percent of GDP per year. By world standards, those countries are fairly well off. The poorest countries, like many in Africa or Asia, save only about 7 percent of GDP.

The other alternatives all involve investment capital coming in from abroad, whether through foreign aid, private bank loans, or direct foreign investment. The problem with depending on foreign aid is that there is not enough. For example, in one recent year the total foreign aid received by all LDCs was perhaps 1 percent of their combined GDP.

Another possibility is private financial capital, commonly in the form of bank loans. This was tried with a vengeance in the 1970s. But after the experience of countries like Brazil, Argentina, and Mexico not being able to repay their loans on time in the 1980s, U.S. banks are not eager to plunge into a

massive new round of lending. They put their toes in the water again in the early 1990s, only to be burned again with the Mexican peso crisis of 1995.

The final possibility is direct foreign investment, more commonly known as investment by multinational or transnational corporations. This method has some obvious advantages. The transnational company has an interest in looking after its investment and managing it carefully, which means that the money is less likely to be spent inefficiently. The company, not the country, takes the risk. Moreover, the company doing the investment will often send new technology to the LDC and train workers there.

The main disadvantage of direct investment is political. The governments of LDCs often prefer loans or grants that they can spend as they wish over investment controlled by foreign business executives. In the past, LDCs often passed laws that discouraged foreign companies from investing. But as the options for obtaining capital from other sources dwindled, transnational corporations looked better as an alternative. The current level of direct foreign investment in LDCs is only about $10 billion. How-

countries thought that a symbol of development was having a steel mill or
some other big factory, even if such a factory was unsuitable for the economic
conditions of the country.

INEQUALITY

Many LDCs are also marked by high levels of inequality. Thousands of homeless people sleep in the streets along which the wealthy travel in expensive
cars. Some of this inequality is simply due to the law of supply and demand.
There is an abundance of unskilled labor and a scarcity of skilled labor and
entrepreneurs, so that unskilled wages are low and those who have skills do
well.

Indeed, earlier theories suggested that inequality contributed to economic
growth. Sir Arthur Lewis, who received the Nobel Prize for his work on development economics, argued that what he called the **surplus of labor** kept
wages low and profits high. Workers earning subsistence wages could not
save, but capitalists could, so that the higher profits contributed to a higher
savings rate. In this view, there was a trade-off between growth and equality.

Today, many economists believe that growth and equality are really complementary, as evidenced by the East Asia miracle discussed later in the chapter.

FACTORS CONTRIBUTING TO UNDERDEVELOP-
MENT

Lack of physical capital

Lack of education

Lack of technology

Lack of developed capital markets

Government interventions that impair efficient resource allocation

Extreme income inequality

Borrowing from abroad can make sound economic sense. For instance, much of the development of the American railroad network in the nineteenth century was financed by bonds issued in Europe. Over the past two decades, many firms and governments of less developed countries have borrowed billions of dollars from banks in the United States and other developed countries, as the table here shows. But while the nineteenth-century U.S. railroad companies were able to repay investments, it became apparent in the 1980s that some of the countries that had borrowed heavily—particularly Brazil, Argentina, and Mexico—could not repay what they owed. The resulting crisis threatened the economic prospects of the LDCs and the financial viability of many American banks.

The immediate cause of the problem was simple. In the 1970s, real interest rates were low, and banks were flush with "petro dollars"—dollars that oil producers, particularly in the Middle East, had earned from selling their oil at the high prices that prevailed beginning in 1973—and wanted to invest or deposit them abroad. Both borrowers and lenders were optimistic that the loans would create economic growth, and repayment would be easy.

Then three things happened. First, nominal and real interest rates soared in the late 1970s. The interest payments rose far beyond any level that the borrowers had imagined. Second, the world entered a recession in the early 1980s, and the worldwide slowdown in growth made it even more difficult for the LDCs to pay back what they owed. Third, oil prices fell in the early 1980s. Some of the largest borrowers had been oil producers, like Mexico and Indonesia, and they had

intended to repay their loans by selling oil.

But bad luck is not the only culprit. The banks are also to blame for failing to take into account the risks associated with the loans they were making. They should have realized, for instance, that prices for goods like oil are volatile. The banks also placed too much trust in the assurance of foreign governments that the loans would be invested productively. Much of the money was invested in projects that were probably not economically viable from the start. By contrast, some better-managed countries like the Republic of Korea borrowed heavily but invested the money wisely and have been able to repay it.

Massive defaults on loans were avoided only by debt rescheduling. As a payment came due, the banks lent the country more money, in effect postponing the date at which repayment was to occur. As a condition for this rescheduling, the lenders insisted that the borrowers "put their houses in order"—cutting back, for instance, on their huge budget deficits. But this strategy of squeezing the LDCs to pay had its own problems. The only way the countries could repay was for them to grow more. But growth required additional capital, which foreign lenders were reluctant to provide. The only way out was to forgive some of the debt and then count on the rest being repaid.

Debt forgiveness, which amounts to a gift to the debtor countries, also has its problems. For example, will forgiveness encourage countries to borrow more in the future than they have the capacity to repay? Is Brazil more deserving of such a multibillion-dollar gift than many poorer countries in Latin America or Africa, just because it borrowed more?

	Public or publicly guaranteed external debt in	
Country	1989	1994
Brazil	$84 billion	$151 billion
Mexico	$76	128
India	$54	99
Argentina	$51	77
Indonesia	$41	97
Egypt	$40	33
China	$37	101
Poland	$35	42
Turkey	$35	66
Nigeria	$32	34
Venezuela	$25	37
Algeria	$24	30
Philippines	$23	39
Morocco	$19	23
Korea	$17	55

Source: World Development Report (1996).

FAILED GOVERNMENT POLICIES

Most of the countries of Asia and Africa were colonies of the European powers until World War II. As they got their independence in the aftermath of the war, the new governments took upon themselves the responsibility of promoting economic development. Almost all believed that strong government action would be required, with some, such as India, taking an avowedly socialist strategy. These ideas were partly in revulsion to what they saw as the exploitive capitalism of their colonial masters, partly a reflection of the seeming success of the Soviet Union's rapid industrialization.

PLANNING

In many LDCs, the government attempted to direct the overall course of the economy by planning. A "Ministry of Planning" would draw up a detailed plan, typically for five years, specifying how much each sector of the economy would grow, how much investment would occur in each sector, where the output of each sector would go, and where each sector would receive its inputs. The Ministry of Planning had enormous powers, among them allocating investment funds and the foreign exchange required to import raw materials from abroad.

In many LDCs, the government undertook some of the investments itself, but it also gave powerful inducements to private firms to conform to the dictates of the government's plan—for example, by restricting access to needed foreign exchange only to approved investment projects or by making credit more readily available for approved investment projects.

In the last decade, there has been considerable disillusionment with planning—a disillusionment that set in even before the failures of the Soviet-style system became evident. Planned economies like India have done worse than unplanned economies like Hong Kong. There are good reasons for this. The 1960s' views on the need for planning ignored the extensive planning that goes on in all economies. For example, when U.S. Steel decided to build a steel mill on the southern shores of Lake Michigan in the early twentieth century, it made sure that there were sources of inputs and the transportation facilities to deliver these inputs—limestone from southern Indiana, coal and coke from Illinois, and iron ore from Minnesota. It also made sure there was a source of demand. The issue is not whether planning is needed—it surely is—but whether the most effective place to do the planning is in a government centralized bureau or at the level of the firm. Today most economists are skeptical about the ability of a centralized bureau to do effective planning.

One of the main arguments for centralized planning was its presumed greater ability to coordinate. But the experience of the past quarter century has shown that centralized planning offices generally do not do a good job at coordination. One reason is that they often lack the requisite information. Another is that firms can more easily deal with the details of investment projects—deciding what kind of plant to construct, how to construct it, making sure that it is constructed in an efficient way, and so on—than can government bureaucrats. And these details, more than anything else, determine the success of the projects.

TILTING THE ECONOMY

The purpose of planning, of course, was to do more than just substitute for the markets' role in coordinating economic activity. It was also at least to tilt the economy in ways that would enhance growth.

Some ideas on how this might be done were borrowed from the Soviet Union, such as an emphasis on capital-intensive industries like steel. Many countries pursued a policy known as **import substitution,** stressing the substitution of domestically produced goods for goods previously imported. In this view, the hallmark of a developed country is modern industry. Rather than importing steel, automobiles, TV sets, computers, and other such products, a nation should produce them itself in order to develop the skills necessary for modernization. It should produce, in other words, all the goods it had previously imported from the industrialized economies. This is the road to development that most of the larger LDCs, including India, China, and Brazil, undertook in the years after World War II. At times, each of these countries has taken import substitution to extremes, insisting, for example, on domestically produced computers even when they might not be able to perform the functions of imported computers.

India, like many other LDCs, has also placed a heavy emphasis on domestically owned businesses. At least 50 percent of each company must be owned by citizens of India. When Coca-Cola refused to disclose the secret of its closely guarded formula to its Indian-controlled subsidiary, the government shut down Coca-Cola. At times, it seemed as if "Indian-made cola for Indians" would become a rallying point for Indian nationalism, just as "Buy American" campaigns have been a rallying point for protectionism in America.

But the import substitution approach has disadvantages of its own. Trade barriers set up to protect domestic firms can end up protecting inefficient producers. The absence of foreign competition means that there is an insufficient spur to innovation and efficiency. The profits to which trade barriers frequently give rise provide a source of government corruption. And the trade barriers remain years after they are introduced.

In some cases, the value added of the protected industry is actually negative. Consider an LDC car producer. Many of the car parts have to be imported. The value added of the car manufacturer is not the total value of the car, but only the difference between the value of the car and the value of the imported components. Assume that because of sloppy manufacturing, a significant fraction of the imported parts are damaged. It might be cheaper for the country to import the entire car than import the components and assemble the car. Of course, with protection, the LDC car manufacturer may still be making profits. Consumers suffer, because they have to pay higher prices.

The problems are even worse when the protected industry is one like steel, whose product is used in other industries. An LDC car manufacturer might be profitable if it could only purchase steel at international prices. But if it is forced to pay inflated prices to buy domestically produced steel, it cannot compete with foreign producers. The government might try to offset this by subsidizing the car manufacturers. A subsidy or trade protection in one sector thus grows into a complex of subsidies and trade protection in other sectors.

Although trade protection to stimulate import substitution generally leads to massive inefficiencies, it has proved successful for a time in some countries—such as Brazil, which enjoyed several decades of rapid growth before the debt crisis of the 1980s tainted that picture. Also, supporters of import substitution note that many of the most rapid bursts of growth of the current developed countries occurred in wartimes, when the economy was inwardly directed, not export oriented. These same supporters, looking at the experience of Japan, argue that at least for industrial goods, import substitution—the development of a domestic market—must precede exports. Before Japan was able successfully to sell cars abroad, it first had to develop a market for Japanese cars at home.

WHEN GOVERNMENT BECOMES THE PROBLEM

Sometimes government has actually impeded the development process. It has done this both by allocating inefficiently those resources over which it has direct control and by interfering in the function of markets so that *they* could not efficiently allocate resources. Countries following the Soviet model attempted to imitate not only its reliance on planning but also its pattern of development, with heavy emphasis on industries such as steel—whether such a pattern of industrialization was appropriate for those countries or not.

Mao Tse-tung, perhaps because he saw that wheat was the predominant grain consumed in the more developed countries, directed that vast areas of China be converted from rice to wheat. This land was not suited for wheat, and agricultural productivity suffered. The conversion to wheat fields actually depleted the land of its fertility, so that when it was eventually returned to growing rice, productivity was lower.

There are flops in the private sector as well, like the Edsel or the nicotine-free cigarette—mistakes that cost the companies making them hundreds of millions of dollars. But the firm (its owners) bears the costs of these mistakes, and has a strong incentive to avoid making them. A company that makes a mistake cannot finance itself indefinitely. When the Ford Motor Company discovered that the Edsel was a mistake, it quickly discontinued production, cutting its losses. It knew, and acted upon, the basic lesson that such costs should be treated as bygones.

The government, by contrast, can support an unprofitable firm for many years. Also, the scale of mistakes governments make sets them apart from the mistakes of private firms. If a single farmer mistakenly decides to grow wheat rather than rice, the costs he faces are not comparable to the costs borne by China when Mao made his mistake.

Mao's mistake was an honest mistake of judgment, not a consequence of his pursuit of private interests. But some problems facing the LDCs arise from governmental corruption, and here private interests conflict with public ones. Corruption is often associated with the large role government plays in an LDC, particularly in restricting foreign trade. When the government imposes a high tariff or otherwise protects an industry, the protected firms can raise their prices and increase their profits. If there are only one or two such firms, they will be tempted to share some of the resulting profits with the government official responsible for the protection. And the government official, knowing this, has a strong incentive to ask the private firms to share some of the profits.

These problems arise in all countries. The building inspectors in New York have periodically been charged with accepting bribes to speed approvals, for instance. However, these problems are more likely to arise in countries where government salaries are low relative to the size of the bribes being offered, where institutions like a free press that might closely monitor this kind of corruption do not exist, and where government regulations are more pervasive.

Between honest mistakes and corruption lies a third category: rent-seeking activities. If government has the power to confer special benefits, people will seek those benefits for themselves. Firms will try to persuade government that they deserve protection from foreign competition, knowing that such protection will increase their profits. They may give outright bribes, or they may simply spend funds to help elect officials who are sympathetic to their views.

Critics of an activist role for government in development—such as Anne Krueger of Stanford University, formerly vice-president of the World Bank—see these problems as casting serious doubt on the wisdom of government planning. We might *imagine* a government's improving on the market, they argue, but if we look more closely at how governments actually behave, and take into account the natural incentives for counterproductive behavior on the part of government bureaucrats (as opposed to the incentives for efficiency on the part of private firms), we see that government activity can and often does impede development.

THE EAST ASIA MIRACLE

As the development strategies based on planning, import substitution, and heavy industrialization were failing, the countries of East Asia had been pursuing a different set of strategies and achieving growth rates of 7 percent or more year after year. At these growth rates, GDP doubles every ten years.

Several ingredients were essential to their success. Governments in these countries also took an active role. But they pursued market-oriented policies which encouraged development of the private sector. They sought to augment and "govern" the market, not to replace it. A key policy was to ensure the macroeconomic stability of the economy, avoiding for the most part high inflation. As part of this strategy, governments maintained a high level of fiscal responsibility, eschewing the huge budget deficits that characterize many LDCs.

They sought to augment all the ingredients to growth, including fostering high savings rates—often in excess of 25 percent. (See Figure 40.5.) In Japan, more than a third of these savings went into accounts at the postal savings banks established by the government. These provided a secure and easy way, particularly for those in the rural sector, to save. In Singapore, the government established a provident fund, to which all workers were required to contribute 40 percent of their income. The money went not only to finance their retirement, but also to purchase homes. More than 70 percent of all Singaporeans now own their own homes—in a country which, at independence in 1959, had an unemployment rate of more than 30 percent and negligible home ownership.

Many of the countries in East Asia began their growth spurt with a high level of literacy. But they pushed it even further, enhancing the opportunities particularly for women. These countries realized that if they were to become developed, they had to bridge the technological gap. Many countries, including Taiwan and Korea, sent thousands to the United States to study science and engineering. And they devoted huge resources to establishing quality universities within their own countries.

These governments also influenced the allocation of capital in a myriad of ways. Banks were discouraged from making real estate loans and loans for durable consumption goods. This helped to increase private savings rates and discouraged real estate speculation, which often serves to destabilize the economy. As a result, more funds were available for investment in growth-oriented activities, like new equipment.

In addition, governments established development banks, to promote long-term investment in activities like shipbuilding, steel mills, and the chemical industry. These interventions have been more controversial and their success has been mixed. The steel firms in Taiwan and Korea are among the most efficient in the world. But soon after the chemical industry was established in Korea, the price of oil, an essential ingredient, soared, and the industry suffered losses for almost two decades. With the decline in oil prices, it is now doing better. Proponents of these initiatives argue that they have technological benefits for other sectors and are necessary as part of a long-run growth strategy.

The Japanese government took a variety of other initiatives to promote certain industries. Among its most noted successes were its entry into the computer chip market. By the early 1980s, Japan looked as if it would completely dominate that market, before Intel and other American producers reasserted American leadership. The dangers of government intervention are often symbolized by the Japanese government's failed attempt to discourage Honda (a manufacturer of motorcycles) from entering the auto market, arguing that there were already too many producers.

EXPORT-LED GROWTH

One factor that distinguished the countries of East Asia from less successful LDCs was their emphasis on exports. A growth strategy focusing on exports is called **export-led growth,** in contrast to the import substitution policy described earlier. Firms were encouraged to export in a variety of ways, including being given increased access to credit, often at subsidized rates.

In export-led growth, firms produce according to their long-term comparative advantage. This is not current comparative advantage, based on current resources and knowledge. It is dynamic comparative advantage, based on acquired skills and technology, and recognition of the importance of learning by doing—of the improvement in skills and productivity that comes from production experience. With exports, demand for the goods produced by an LDC is not limited by the low income of its citizens. The world is its market.

Advocates of export-led growth also believe that the competition provided by the export market is an important stimulus to efficiency and modernization. The only way a firm can succeed in the face of keen international competition is to produce what consumers want, at the quality they want, and at the lowest possible costs. This keen competition forces specialization in areas where low-wage, less developed countries have a comparative advantage, such as labor-intensive products. It also forces firms to look for the best ways of producing. International firms often take a role in helping to enhance efficiency. For instance, the clothing store chain Benetton has developed production techniques that combine large production runs with rapid adaptability in style and color. In this way, the firm has been able to take advantage of low-wage LDCs by producing most of what it sells in these countries.

Finally, export-led growth has facilitated the transfer of advanced technology. Producers exporting to developed countries not only come into contact with efficient producers within those countries, they also learn to adopt their standards and production techniques. They come to understand better, for instance, why timeliness and quality in production are important.

FOSTERING EQUALITY

Another distinctive aspect of East Asia's development strategy is its emphasis on equality. We have already noted several aspects of these egalitarian policies: Singapore's home ownership program; the almost universal provision of elementary and secondary education, which includes women; and the land redistribution programs that were the precursor of growth in several of the countries, including Taiwan and Japan. In many of these countries, government has also tried to curb excessive wage inequality and to discourage conspicuous consumption by the rich.

Their experience has shown that one can have high savings rates without either the oppressiveness of Soviet-style governments or vast inequalities. The equality measures actually have promoted economic growth. The land reforms have resulted in increased agricultural production—the sharecropping system previously in place had had the effect of a 50 percent tax on output. The high education levels have increased productivity directly and facilitated the transfer and adoption of more advanced technology. And more education for women, as we have noted, is associated with declining rates of population growth.

But the greatest boon of equality for development may be through its political effects. Inequality frequently gives rise to political instability, and political instability has strong adverse effects on the economic climate. In such an atmosphere, both domestic and foreign firms will be reluctant to invest. The countries of East Asia not only managed to have remarkable political stability, but as their incomes grew, there was a strong trend toward democratization.

One of the policies these countries did *not* engage in was large-scale food subsidies. These are often justified as promoting equality, but in fact their effect is more problematic. This is because the food subsidies typically benefit mainly those in the urban sector, and are often paid for out of taxes (or suppressed prices) in the agricultural sector. Since those in the urban sector are on average far better off than those in the rural sector, this type of redistribution takes from the very poor to give to the poor. Food subsidies also can be a major budgetary drain on the government, reducing funds for growth-oriented investments.

REDEFINING THE ROLE OF GOVERNMENT

The central question many LDCs are asking today is, what can we learn from the success of the East Asian countries and the failures elsewhere? What can governments do, or refrain from doing, to effectively facilitate economic growth? Today, there is widespread consensus on the main elements of a successful development strategy.

Macroeconomic Stability   Governments need not only maintain macroeconomic stability, but constrain expenditures in line with their revenues.

Positive Investment Climate   A favorable climate for investment, including foreign investment, enhances growth not only by increasing the stock of capital, but also by facilitating the transfer of valuable technology.

Population Policy   High rates of growth of population put a strain on almost any economy, but especially poor economies. Savings must be devoted to housing the growing population and providing capital to the new entrants to the labor force, leaving little for capital deepening, which would enhance productivity. Today, knowledge about contraception is widespread; but knowledge about the means to control population is not enough. People have to want to reduce family size. In the absence of a social insurance system, parents often rely on large families to ensure that there is someone to take care of them in their old age. The benefits of having children are of course more than economic. The evidence suggests that one of the most reliable ways of controlling population is to increase the cost—the opportunity cost—of having children; educating women does exactly that. That is why female education not only has a direct benefit, in increased productivity, but an indirect benefit, in reduced population growth.

Provide More and Better Education   Education increases the productivity of the labor force and enables the economy to adopt more advanced technologies.

Provide an Institutional Infrastructure   Some examples of this type of infrastructure are an effective legal system, strong competition laws, and a regulatory system supporting a safe and sound financial system.

Provide a Physical Infrastructure   In this area, the direct role of government versus the private sector has been evolving. Many countries have discovered that parts of the infrastructure—like toll roads—can be provided privately, relieving the government of both fiscal and managerial burdens.

Avoid Protectionism   Avoid policies, such as protectionism, which reduce competition, leading to increased costs and prices.

While there is widespread consensus on these elements of a development strategy, some elements are more contentious. Most of the countries of East Asia actively promoted exports and the transfer and adaptation of modern technology. And most analysts of the East Asia experience give these policies considerable credit for their economic success. Yet critics worry that in other countries, these attempts by government to "direct" the development of the economy have been singularly unsuccessful; the programs have been captured by special interests, and used to enhance the profits of these special interests rather than to promote economic growth.

THE ROLE OF THE ADVANCED COUNTRIES

What can the advanced countries do to help? Direct foreign assistance, especially from the United States, has been declining in importance. In 1995, U.S. assistance as a percentage of GDP was lower than any other major industrialized country, and even in absolute dollars, was surpassed by France, Germany, and Japan. Even this does not tell the full story, since a disproportionate part of U.S. aid goes to Israel and Egypt.

Today, international capital markets are far better developed than they were fifty years ago, with funds investing in "emerging markets" becoming hot-ticket items on Wall Street. Countries, like China and Thailand, that provide an investment-friendly atmosphere have little trouble attracting funds. Still, for the poorest countries, especially in Africa, there is a huge need for development assistance. And for all of the developing countries, there is a need for technical assistance and help in areas like education and health in which the private sector is not particularly interested.

There is an ongoing debate about how effective such assistance has been. There have been huge successes, some supported by private foundations as well as by government. The development of high-yielding crops with the support of the Rockefeller Foundation and the dissemination of the seeds and new technologies throughout the developing world has resulted in a "green revolution." Countries like India have become self-sufficient in food. But there have also been failures. Food aid sometimes depresses local prices, hurting farmers and discouraging domestic production. Some large projects have been criticized for damaging the environment and resulting in increases in crop yields that were insufficient even to pay the interest on the loans.

Today, an increasing fraction of aid is distributed through multilateral development banks—the World Bank, the regional banks in Asia, Africa, and Latin America, and the EBRD, the European Bank for Reconstruction and Development, which focuses on the economies of Eastern Europe and the former Soviet Union.

Although support for foreign aid in the United States has been waning, many economists continue to emphasize the importance of trade for LDCs and developed countries alike. Giving less developed economies access to the

POLICY PERSPECTIVE: THE MEXICAN PESO CRISIS

In January 1995, the Mexican peso crashed, losing a quarter of its value (relative to the dollar) in a single day, and in the span of a couple weeks, more than 40 percent of its value. The U.S. government, other governments, and the International Monetary Fund (IMF) were called to the rescue. While the IMF pledged $7.7 billion in credits, the United States lent more than $20 billion to Mexico.

To the media and much of the public, the crash of the peso seemed like a shock. But many economists, such as Rudiger Dornbush of M.I.T., had anticipated the crisis. The Mexican government had made extremely impressive economic reforms under President Salinas, and the signing of NAFTA was a positive step for Mexico's economic future. But the Mexican government's macropolicies had been less sound. They had run moderate deficits over a number of years, which they had financed with short-term borrowing denominated in dollars. They had also worked hard to sustain the value of the peso—despite the much higher rate of inflation in Mexico than elsewhere. Thus, by late 1994, the peso was overvalued by at least 25 percent. Economists within the Mexican government realized this, but the government was unwilling to allow the peso to depreciate before the presidential election. The new Mexican government took only three weeks to recognize that it could not sustain the value of the peso. But it could not engineer a smooth reduction.

Many lost millions as a result of the decrease in the value of the peso. Still more millions were lost as the Mexican stock market crashed. Finally, those who had invested in Mexican bonds worried that the government would not be able to pay off bondholders when the debt became due. The U.S. government worried that the emerging turmoil would spread to other emerging markets, disrupting their growth plans. It also worried that an economic downturn in Mexico could lead to a flood of immigrants to the United States. These were among the reasons cited in favor of the Mexican bailout.

Critics of the bailout argued that the main beneficiaries were investors, who should have realized the risks they faced. The devalued peso would be good for the Mexican economy, as it promoted exports and discouraged imports. In fact, the Mexican trade deficit which had swelled over the past few years was reversed to a trade surplus in the first months of 1995.

The subsequent events did not fully resolve the question of whether the bailout should have

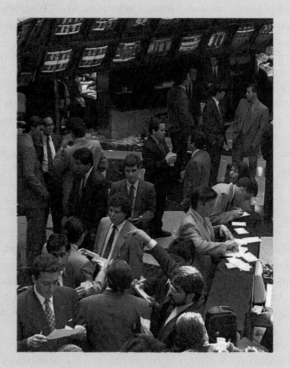

taken place. Mexico went through a deep economic downturn, with unemployment and interest rates soaring. By the middle of 1996, the economy had shown signs of a slow recovery, though the banking system remained fragile; still, Mexico was able to repay half of its loans from the U.S. government.

Even with the bailout, other countries like Argentina were hit hard by the "contagion" effect, resulting from the loss of investor confidence. It is difficult to ascertain how much harder these countries would have been hit had there not been a bailout.

But both within the United States and abroad, a consensus emerged that the Mexico experience should not be repeated. In a meeting of the leaders of the industrialized countries held in June 1995 in Halifax, Nova Scotia, they set in motion reforms which would increase the surveillance by the International Monetary Fund of the economies of the world, so that markets would be better informed concerning the risks that they face, and which would increase the funds available for lending in the event of a crisis. And discussions were begun on the development of "work-out arrangements" for countries, analogous to those available to firms in the event of bankruptcy. Whether these initiatives will suffice to avoid a similar crisis remains to be seen.

U.S. markets is a "win-win" policy. American consumers win by having a greater variety of goods at lower prices. The less developed country benefits by having a huge market for its goods. The United States has a system of preferential treatment for poor countries, called GSP (general system of preferences). Of course, as always with trade, some U.S. producers and their workers complain about the loss of jobs to these low-cost competitors. As argued in Chapter 3, the total benefits to trade generally outweigh the losses to certain groups.

THE PROSPECTS

The enhanced means of production that resulted from the industrial and scientific revolutions of the past two centuries have meant ever-rising living standards for most of those lucky enough to live in the developed countries of Europe and North America. And the past fifty years have extended the benefits of development to an increasing number of countries—in full measure to Japan, and more moderately to middle-income countries such as Singapore, South Korea, and Taiwan.

There are pockets of success elsewhere as well. The area around São Paulo in Brazil has the look and feel of prosperity. India, as noted above, has become self-sufficient with regard to food. Thailand has been having a boom. Success often seems precarious; for instance, for many of these countries, the debt crisis of the 1980s was a major setback, with growth stalling, and in some cases, incomes actually declining. Still, the outstanding lesson of recent decades is that success is possible. There is the real prospect that more and more of these countries, if they pursue wise policies and enjoy political stability, will be able to pull themselves out of the cycle of poverty in which they have lived for centuries.

But for the most unfortunate countries, such as sub-Saharan Africa—which lack human and physical resources and have burgeoning populations that consume much of whatever gains they are able to obtain—the prospects are less optimistic. Lack of hope contributes to political instability, making economic progress all the more difficult.

AN AGENDA FOR DEVELOPMENT

How the developed countries can help
- Reduce trade barriers
- Increase foreign aid
- Facilitate foreign investment

Growth-oriented policies for LDCs
- Reduce population growth
- Increase quantity and quality of education
- Provide a basic infrastructure (roads, ports, a legal system)
- Provide a favorable climate for investment, including foreign investment
- Facilitate development of capital markets (financial intermediaries)
- Spend more government revenues on investment rather than consumption, such as food subsidies
- Develop a competitive export sector

Policies that may inhibit growth
- Trade protection
- Regulations, licensing

REVIEW AND PRACTICE

SUMMARY

1. In less developed countries, or LDCs, life expectancies are usually shorter, infant mortality is higher, and people are less educated than in developed countries. Also, a larger fraction of the population lives in the rural sector, and population growth rates are higher.

2. In recent years, newly industrialized countries (NICs) such as South Korea, Singapore, Hong Kong, and Taiwan have managed to improve their economic status dramatically. Other LDCs, like India, have expanded food production considerably. But the standard of living in some of the poorest LDCs, such as many African nations, has actually been declining, as population growth has outstripped economic growth.

3. Among the factors contributing to underdevelopment are lack of physical capital, lack of education, lack of technology, and lack of developed capital markets. The factors interact: low education levels impede the transfer of advanced technology; low incomes make it difficult to invest heavily in education.

4. Central planning has not been effective in LDCs. Governments lack the requisite information and often misdirect resources.

5. Import substitution policies have often been implemented through protectionist policies, which have raised domestic prices, often give rise to inefficiencies, and, when applied to intermediate goods like steel, have adverse effects on those industries that use the input.

6. The success of the countries of East Asia is based on activist government policies, which include helping develop and using markets rather than replacing them; promoting high levels of investment and savings, and strong support for education; improving capital markets, which facilitate an efficient allocation of scarce capital; promoting exports; and fostering equality.

7. Effective development policies include maintaining macroeconomic stability (including sound fiscal policies), creating a positive investment climate (including for foreign investors), controlling population, providing more and better education, providing an institutional infrastructure (including an effective legal system, competition laws, and a sound financial system), and ensuring that there is the necessary infrastructure (roads, electricity), which may be provided either publicly or privately.

8. Advanced countries can help LDCs through the provision of aid (capital assistance), technical assistance, and opening markets to trade.

KEY TERMS

less developed countries (LDCs)	newly industrialized countries (NICs)	dual economies
developed or industrialized countries	green revolution	import substitution
		export-led growth

REVIEW QUESTIONS

1. List some important ways in which LDCs differ from more developed countries.

2. What are the most important factors inhibiting growth in the LDCs? Why is capital shortage *alone* not the most important factor? What can be done to help overcome the problem of capital shortage? How do some of the factors interact with each other?

3. How does rapid population growth make it more difficult to increase a country's standard of living?

4. Why has centralized government planning failed? Does planning occur in market economies?

5. How and why have governments sometimes tried to tilt the economy, interfering with how markets by themselves would allocate resources? Compare import substitution and export promotion strategies. Why have export promotion strategies, by and large, been more successful than import substitution strategies?

6. What are some of the factors that contributed to the East Asia miracle?

7. Why might fostering equality promote economic growth?

8. What are some of the roles that government can play in promoting economic development and growth?

9. What are some of the roles that the advanced countries can play in promoting economic development among the LDCs?

PROBLEMS

1. In the United States, the economy grew by 2.6 percent per year (in real terms) during the 1980s. In India, the economy grew by 5.3 percent during the 1980s. However, population growth in the United States was .8 percent annually, while population growth in India was 2.1 percent annually. Which country increased its standard of living faster for the average citizen? By how much?

2. Nominal GNP in Kenya was 9 billion shillings in 1967 and 135 billion shillings in 1987. The price level in Kenya (using 1980 as a base year) rose from 40 in 1967 to 200 in 1987. And the population of Kenya increased from 10 million to 22 million in those twenty years. What was the total percentage change in real GNP per capita in Kenya from 1967 to 1987?

3. True or false: "LDCs do not have much capital because their rates of saving are low. If they saved more or received more foreign aid, they could rapidly expand their economic growth." Discuss.

4. How might each of the following hinder entrepreneurs in LDCs?
   (a) lack of functioning capital markets;
   (b) pervasive government control of the economy;
   (c) lack of companies that offer business services;
   (d) a tradition of substantial foreign control of large enterprises.

5. What is the economist's case for having the government be responsible for providing infrastructure? (Hint: You may wish to review the concept of a public good.)

6. If many LDCs simultaneously attempted to pursue export-led growth, what would be the effect in world markets on the quantities and prices of products mainly sold by LDCs, like minerals, agricultural goods, and textiles? What effect might these quantities and prices have on the success of such export-led growth policies?

7. Explain how the idea of import substitution conflicts in the short run with the idea of comparative advantage. Need the two ideas conflict in the long run? Why or why not?

8. Why might a family in an LDC feel economic pressure to have more children than a family in a developed country?

GLOSSARY

absolute advantage: a country has an absolute advantage over another country in the production of a good if it can produce that good more efficiently (with fewer inputs)

accelerated depreciation: a provision of the tax code which allows for deductions from income for purposes of calculating tax liability for the depreciation of machines (that is, for their wearing out and obsolescence) which are in excess of the true decrease in value. This may entail, for instance, the use of a shorter life span than the actual life span of the machine or building

accelerator: the effect on GDP of the increase in investment that results from an increase in output. For instance, the greater output leads a firm to believe the demand for its products will rise in the future; the resulting increase in investment leads to growth in output and still further increases in investment, accelerating the expansion of the economy

accommodative monetary policies: monetary policies which accommodate changes in fiscal policy (or other changes in the economic environment) in ways which maintain the economy's macroeconomic performance

acquired endowments: resources a country builds for itself, like a network of roads or an educated population

adaptive: expectations are adaptive when events of the recent past are extrapolated into the future

adaptive expectations: expectations based on the extrapolation of events in the recent past into the future

adverse selection: the phenomenon that as an insurance company raises its price, the best risks (those least likely to make a claim) drop out, so the mix of applicants changes adversely; now used more generally to refer to effects on the mix of workers, borrowers, products being sold, and so forth resulting from a change in wages (interest rates, prices) or other variables

affirmative action: actions by employers to seek out actively minorities and women for jobs, and to provide them with training and other opportunities for job promotion

aggregate consumption function: the relationship between aggregate consumption and aggregate income

aggregate demand curve: a curve relating the total demand for the economy's goods and services at each price level, given the level of wages

aggregate expenditures schedule: a curve that traces out the relationship between expenditures—the sum of consumption, investment, government expenditures, and net exports—and national income, at a fixed price level

aggregate savings: the sum of the savings of all individuals in society

aggregate savings rate: the fraction of national income

that is saved; it is calculated by dividing aggregate savings by national income

aggregate supply: the amount of goods that firms would be willing to supply, given their plant and equipment, assuming wages and prices are flexible and adjust so that the labor force is fully employed

aggregate supply curve: a curve relating the total supply of the economy's goods and services at each price level, given the level of wages

antitrust laws: laws that discourage monopoly and restrictive practices and encourage greater competition

antitrust policy: policies designed to promote competition and to restrict anti-competitive practices

appreciation: a change in the exchange rate that enables a unit of currency to buy more units of foreign currencies

arbitrage: the process by which assets with comparable risk, liquidity, and tax treatment are priced to yield comparable expected returns

asset: any item that is long-lived, purchased for the service it renders over its life and for what one will receive when one sells it

assistance in kind: public assistance that provides particular goods and services, like food or medical care, rather than cash

asymmetric information: a situation in which the parties to a transaction have different information, as when the seller of a used car has more information about its quality than the buyer

automatic stabilizers: expenditures that automatically increase or taxes that automatically decrease when economic conditions worsen, and which therefore tend to stabilize the economy automatically

autonomous consumption: that part of consumption that does not depend on income

average costs: the total costs divided by the total output

average productivity: the total quantity of output divided by the total quantity of input

average tax rate: the ratio of taxes to taxable income

average variable costs: the total variable costs divided by the total output

balanced budget amendment: a proposed amendment to the Constitution which would require that the federal government have a balanced budget (that is, that prohibits deficits)

balanced budget multiplier: the increase in GDP from a dollar increase in government expenditures matched by a dollar increase in taxes

balance sheet: the accounting framework that shows a firms assets, liabilities, and net worth

bank run: a rush on a bank by its depositors to withdraw their funds, as they lose confidence in the bank's finances

barriers to entry: factors that prevent firms from entering a market, such as government rules or patents

barter: trade that occurs without the use of money

basic competitive model: the model of the economy that pulls together the assumptions of self-interested consumers, profit-maximizing firms, and perfectly competitive markets

basic research: fundamental research; it often produces a wide range of applications, but the output of basic research itself usually is not of direct commercial value; the output is knowledge, rather than a product; the output of basic research typically cannot be patented

beggar-thy-neighbor policies: restrictions on imports designed to increase a country's national output, so-called because they increase that country's output at the same time that they hurt the output of other countries

benefit tax: a tax that is levied on a particular product, the revenues of which go for benefits to those who purchase the product

bequest savings motive: people save so that they can leave an inheritance to their children

Bertrand competition: an oligopoly in which each firm believes that its rivals are committed to keeping their prices fixed and that customers can be lured away by offering lower prices

bilateral trade: trade between two parties

black market: an illegal market in which proscribed trades occur. For instance, in war time, when coupons are required to buy certain basic commodities, it may be illegal to buy and sell coupons; black markets typically develop in which these coupons are in fact traded

bloc granting: providing grants to states and localities without restrictions

boom: a period of time when resources are being fully used and GDP is growing steadily

breach: an individual is said to be in breach of a contract if he violates the agreement

budget constraint: the limitations on consumption of different goods imposed by the fact that households have only a limited amount of money to spend (their budget). The budget constraint *defines* the opportunity set of individuals, when the only constraint that they face is money

business cycle: the fluctuations in the level of economic activity in the economy. At one time, it was thought that these fluctuations were extremely regular; today, the term is used to refer to fluctuations even when they have no regular periodicity

capital: funds used for investment; the term is also used for the value of an individual's investment or a firm's capital stock

capital deepening: an increase in capital per worker

capital gain: the increase in the value of an asset between the time it is purchased and the time it is sold

capital goods: machines and buildings used to produce goods

capital goods investment: investments in machines and buildings (to be distinguished from investments in inventory, in research and development, or in training (human capital)

capital goods markets: the markets in which capital goods are traded

capital inflow: the inflow of capital (money) from abroad, to buy investments, to be deposited in U.S. banks, to buy U.S. government bonds, or to be lent in America for any reason

capital loss: a capital loss occurs when an asset is sold at a price below the price at which it was purchased; the difference is the magnitude of the capital loss

capital market: the various institutions concerned with raising funds and sharing and insuring risks; it includes banks, insurance markets, bond markets, and the stock market

capital outflows: the outflow of capital (money) to abroad

capital requirements: the capital that the government requires of banks (defined as a certain ratio of net worth to deposits) to ensure their financial viability

cartel: a group of producers with an agreement to collude in setting prices and output

categorical assistance: public assistance aimed at a particular category of people, like the elderly or the disabled

causation: the relationship that results when a change in one variable is not only correlated with but actually causes a change in another variable; the change in the second variable is a consequence of the change in the first variable, rather than both changes being a consequence of a change in a third variable

central bank: the bank that oversees and monitors the rest of the banking system and serves as the bankers' bank

centralization: organizational structure in which decision making is concentrated at the top

centrally planned economy: an economy in which most decisions about resource allocation are made by the central government

central planning: the system in which central government bureaucrats (as opposed to private entrepreneurs or even local government bureaucrats) determine what will be produced and how it will be produced

certificate of deposit (CD): an account in which money is deposited for a preset length of time, that yields a slightly higher return to compensate for the reduced liquidity

chain-weighted real GDP: the method of calculating real GDP in which the percentage increase in output from each year to the next is calculated by comparing the value of output of both years in the earlier year's prices

circular flow: the way in which funds move through the capital, labor, and product markets between households, firms, the government, and the foreign sector

classical economists: economists prevalent before the Great Depression who believed that the basic competitive model provided a good description of the economy and that if short periods of unemployment did occur, market forces would quickly restore the economy to full employment

classical unemployment: unemployment that occurs as a result of too-high real wages; it occurs in the supply-constrained equilibrium, so that rightward shifts in aggregate supply reduce the level of unemployment

closed economy: an economy that neither exports nor imports

Coase's theorem: the assertion that if property rights are properly defined, then people will be forced to pay for any negative externalities they impose on others, and market transactions will produce efficient outcomes

collude: when firms act jointly (more nearly as they would if there were a monopolist) to increase overall profits

command-and-control approach: the approach to controlling environmental externalities in which the government provides detailed regulations about what firms can and cannot do, including what technologies they can employ

commercial policies: policies directed at affecting either imports or exports

Common Market: the predecessor of the European Union

communism: an economic system in which the government owns all property and in which it is responsible for most economic decision making

comparative advantage: a country has a comparative advantage over another country in one good as opposed to another good if its *relative* efficiency in the production of the first good is higher than the other country's

compensating wage differentials: differences in wages that can be traced to nonpecuniary attributes of a job, such as the degree of autonomy and risk

competitive equilibrium price: the price at which the quantity supplied and the quantity demanded are equal to each other

competitive model: the basic model of the economy, in which profit-maximizing firms interact with rational, self-interested consumers in competitive markets, in which all participants are price takers (that is, assume that prices are unaffected by their actions)

complement: two goods are complements if the demand for one (at a given price) decreases as the price of the other increases

compound interest: interest paid on interest; a savings account pays compound interest when, say, interest is credited to the account every day, so that on subsequent days, interest is earned not only on the original principal, but also on the credited interest

constant returns: a production function has constant returns when increases in an input (keeping all other inputs fixed) increase output proportionately

constant returns to scale: a production function has constant returns to scale when equiproportionate increases in all inputs increase output proportionately

consumer price index: a price index in which the basket of goods is defined by what a typical consumer purchases

consumer protection legislation: laws aimed at protecting consumers, for instance by assuring that consumers have more complete information about items they are considering buying

consumer surplus: the difference between what a person would be willing to pay and what he actually has to pay to buy a certain amount of a good

consumption function: the relationship between disposable income and consumption

contestable markets: markets in which there is strong potential (or actual) competition; the theory of contestable markets predicts that even in a market with only one firm, that firm will make zero profits, so long as there is strong potential competition (which will be the case if sunk costs are low)

contingency clauses: statements within a contract that make the level of payment or the work to be performed conditional upon various factors

corporate finance: the branch of economics concerned with how firms raise capital and the consequences of alternative methods of raising capital

corporate income tax: a tax based on the income, or profit, received by a corporation

corporation: a firm with limited liability, owned by shareholders, who elect a board of directors that chooses the top executives

correlation: the relationship that results when a change in one variable is consistently associated with a change in another variable

cost-push inflation: inflation whose initial cause is a rise in production costs

countervailing duties: duties (tariffs) that are imposed by a country to counteract subsidies provided to a foreign producer

coupon rationing: a system of rationing (often used in wartime) in which, in order to buy some commodity, such as a pound of sugar, a coupon is required in addition to the dollar price. Each individual or household is issued so many coupons for certain essential commodities each month

Cournot competition: an oligopoly in which each firm believes that its rivals are committed to a certain level of production and that rivals will reduce their prices as needed to sell that amount

credentials competition: the trend in which prospective workers acquire higher educational credentials, not so much because of anything they actually learn in the process but to convince potential employers to hire them by signaling that they will be more productive employees than those with weaker credentials

credit constraint effect: when prices fall, firms' revenues also fall, but the money they owe creditors remains unchanged; as a result, firms have fewer funds of their own to invest. Because of credit rationing, firms cannot make up the difference; accordingly, investment decreases

credit rationing: credit is rationed when no lender is willing to make a loan to a borrower or the amount lenders are willing to lend to borrowers is limited, even if the borrower is willing to pay more than other borrowers of comparable risk who are getting loans

cross subsidization: the practice of charging higher prices to one group of consumers in order to subsidize lower prices for another group

crowding out: a decrease in private investment resulting from an increase in government expenditures

cyclical unemployment: the increase in unemployment that occurs as the economy goes into a slowdown or recession

dead-weight loss: the difference between what producers gain and (the monetary value of) what consumers lose, when output is restricted under imperfect competition; also, the difference between what the government gains and what consumers lose, when taxes are imposed

debt: capital, such as bonds and bank loans, supplied to a firm by lenders; the firm promises to repay the amount borrowed plus interest

decentralization: organizational structure in which many individuals or subunits can make decisions

decision tree: a device for structured decision making that spells out the choices and possible consequences of alternative actions

deficit: see **fiscal deficit**

deficit spending: the situation that exists when government expenditures are greater than revenues

deflation: a persistent decrease in the general level of prices

demand-constrained equilibrium: the equilibrium that occurs when prices are stuck at a level above that

at which aggregate demand equals aggregate supply; output is equal to aggregate demand

demand curve: the relationship between the quantity demanded of a good and the price, whether for an individual or for the market (all individuals) as a whole

demand deposits: deposits that can be drawn upon instantly, like checking accounts

demand-pull inflation: inflation whose initial cause is aggregate demand exceeding aggregate supply at the current price level

demand shocks: unexpected shifts in the aggregate demand curve

demographic effects: effects that arise from changes in characteristics of the population such as age, birthrates, and location

depreciation: (a) the decrease in the value of an asset; in particular, the amount that capital goods decrease in value as they are used and become old; (b) a change in the exchange rate that enables a unit of one currency to buy fewer units of foreign currencies

depreciation allowance: the provision of the tax code which allows for deductions from income for purposes of calculating tax liability for the depreciation of machines (that is, for their wearing out and obsolescence)

deregulation: the lifting of government regulations to allow the market to function more freely

devaluation: a reduction in the rate of exchange between one currency and other currencies under a fixed exchange rate system

developed or industrialized countries: the wealthiest nations in the world, including Western Europe, the United States, Canada, Japan, Australia, and New Zealand

diminishing marginal rate of substitution: the principle that as the individual gets more and more of one good, less and less of the other good is required to compensate her for a one unit decrease in consumption of the first good; since the marginal rate of substitution is the slope of the indifference curve, the principle of diminishing marginal rate of substitution is equivalent to the slope of the indifference curve becoming flatter as the quantity on the horizontal axis increases

diminishing marginal rate of technical substitution: the principle that as the firm uses more and more of one input, less and less of the other input is required to compensate it for a one unit decrease in the first input; since the marginal rate of technical substitution is the slope of the indifference curve, the principle of diminishing marginal rate of technical substitution is equivalent to the slope of the isoquant curve becoming flatter as the quantity of input on the horizontal axis increases

diminishing marginal utility: the principle that says that as an individual consumes more and more of a good, each successive unit increases her utility, or enjoyment, less and less

diminishing returns: the principle that says that as one input increases, with other inputs fixed, the resulting increase in output tends to be smaller and smaller

discount: assets which sell at a price below that which might be expected, given their expected returns, are said to sell at a discount; the term is also used to refer more specifically to assets which sell at a price below that which might be expected, given their observable attributes. Because the price of such assets is low, the return per dollar invested is high; the higher return is said to reflect a *risk premium*

discount rate: the interest rate charged to banks when they wish to borrow from the central bank

discouraged workers: workers who would be willing to work but have given up looking for jobs, and thus are not officially counted as unemployed

discretionary expenditures: government expenditures which are decided on an annual basis

disposable income: income after paying taxes

dissaving: negative savings; an individual is dissaving when consumption exceeds income

diversification: spreading one's wealth among a large number of different assets

dividends: that portion of corporate profits paid out to shareholders

division of labor: dividing a production process into a series of jobs, with each worker focusing on a limited set of tasks; the advantage of division of labor is that each worker can practice and perfect a particular set of skills

double coincidence of wants: one individual has what the other individual wants; required in order for barter to work

downward rigidity of wages: the situation that exists when wages do not fall quickly in response to a shift in the demand or supply curve for labor, resulting in an excess supply of labor

dual economy: the separation in many LDCs between an impoverished rural sector and an urban sector that has higher wages and more advanced technology

dual-use technologies: technologies that have both a civilian and a military use

due process: procedures designed to protect the public against arbitrary use of government power

dumping: the practice of selling a good abroad at a lower price than at home, or below costs of production

duopoly: an industry with only two firms

durable goods: goods that produce a service over a number of years, such as cars, major appliances, and furniture

dynamically efficient: an economy that appropriately balances short-run concerns (static efficiency) with long-run concerns (focusing on encouraging R & D)

dynamic consistency: a government promise (or plan) is dynamically consistent if the government actually carries out the proposed course of action

earned income tax credit: a reduction in taxes provided to low income workers based on the amount of income they earn and the size of their family

econometrics: the branch of statistics developed to analyze the particular kinds of problems that arise in economics

economic rents: payments made to a factor of production that are in excess of what is required to elicit the supply of that factor

economics: the social science that studies how individuals, firms, governments, and other organizations make choices, and how those choices determine the way the resources of society are used

economies of scope: the situation that exists when it is less expensive to produce two products together than it would be to produce each one separately

efficiency wage: the wage at which total labor costs are minimized

efficiency wage theory: the theory that paying higher wages (up to a point) lowers total production costs, for instance by leading to a more productive labor force

efficient market theory: the theory that all available information is reflected in the current price of an asset

elastic: see **relatively elastic**

elasticity of labor supply: the percentage change in

labor supplied resulting from a 1 percent change in wages

elasticity of supply: see **price elasticity of supply**

eminent domain: the right of government to seize private property for public use, provided it compensates the owner fairly

endogenous factors: properties of the economy itself, such as a tendency of the economy to become overconfident in expansions, which tend to generate or exacerbate economic fluctuations; more generally, an endogenous variable in a model is any variable that is determined within the model itself

entitlements: programs that provide benefits automatically to individuals meeting certain criteria (such as age)

entrepreneurs: people who create new businesses, bring new products to market, and develop new processes of production

entry-deterring practices: practices of incumbent firms designed to deter the entry of rivals into the market

equation of exchange: the equation relating velocity, the value of output, and the money supply ($MV = PY$)

equilibrium: a condition in which there are no forces (reasons) for change

equilibrium price: the price at which demand equals supply

equilibrium quantity: the quantity demanded (which equals the quantity supplied) at the equilibrium price, where demand equals supply

equity, shares, stock: terms that indicate part ownership of a firm; the firm sells these in order to raise money, or capital

equity capital: capital, such as shares (or stock), supplied to a firm by shareholders; the returns received by the shareholders are not guaranteed but depend on how well the firm does

estate tax: a tax on the estate (wealth) that an individual leaves to his heirs

European Union: the agreement among most of the countries of Western Europe not only to remove trade barriers but also to allow the free flow of labor and capital; it succeeded the Common Market

excess capacity: capacity in excess of that currently needed, sometimes used by an incumbent firm to discourage new entrants

excess demand: the situation in which the quantity demanded at a given price exceeds the quantity supplied

excess or **free reserves:** reserves that banks hold in excess of what are required

excess supply: the situation in which the quantity supplied at a given price exceeds the quantity demanded

exchange efficiency: the condition in which whatever the economy produces is distributed among people in such a way that there are no gains to further trade

exchange rate: the rate at which one currency (such as dollars) can be exchanged for another (such as marks, yen, or pounds)

excise tax: a tax on a particular good or service

exclusive dealing: a restrictive practice in which a producer insists that any firm selling its products not sell those of its rivals

exclusive territories: a vertical restriction in which a producer gives a wholesaler or retailer the exclusive right to sell a good within a certain region

exit the market: a consumer exits the market when he decides that at that price, he would prefer to consume none of it

exogenous shocks: disturbances to the economy originating outside the economy (such as wars or floods)

expectations-augmented Phillips curve: a Phillips curve relationship (that is, a relationship between inflation and unemployment) which takes into account the impact of inflationary expectations; as inflationary expectations increase, the inflation associated with any level of unemployment increases

expected return: the average return—a single number that combines the various possible returns per dollar invested with the chances that each of these returns will actually be paid

experimental economics: the branch of economics which analyzes certain aspects of economic behavior in a controlled, laboratory setting

export-led growth: the strategy that government should encourage exports in which the country has a comparative advantage to stimulate growth

exports: goods produced domestically but sold abroad

externality: a phenomenon that arises when an individual or firm takes an action but does not bear all the costs (negative externality) or receive all the benefits (positive externality)

facilitating practices: practices used by members of an oligopoly to make collusion easier

factor demand: the amount of an input demanded by a firm, given the price of the input and the quantity of output being produced; in a competitive market, an input will be demanded up to the point where the value of the marginal product of that input equals the price of the input

factors of production: the inputs that are used in the production process

federal debt: the cumulative amount that the federal government owes

federal governmental structure: a system in which government activity takes place at several levels—national, state, county, city, and others

Federal Open Market Committee (FOMC): the committee of the Federal Reserve System which sets monetary policy

Federal Reserve banks: banks that belong to the Federal Reserve system

Federal Reserve Board (Fed): the government agency responsible for controlling the money supply and interest rates

Federal Reserve system: the major banking system of the United States, consisting of the Federal Reserve Board, the regional Federal Reserve banks, and the member banks

fiat money: money that has value only because the government says it has value and because people are willing to accept it in exchange for goods

final goods approach to measuring GDP: the approach to measuring GDP which adds up the total dollar value of goods and services produced, categorized by their ultimate users/purchasers (consumption by households, investment by firms, investment by government, and net exports)

financial intermediaries: institutions that form the link between savers who have extra funds and borrowers who desire extra funds

financial investments: investments in stocks, bonds, or other financial instruments; these investments provide the funds that allow investments in *capital goods* (physical investments)

financial system: that part of the economy which includes all the institutions involved in moving savings from savers (households and firms) to borrowers, and in transferring, sharing, and insuring risks; it includes banks, insurance markets, bond markets, and the stock market

firm wealth effect: lower prices or lower demand cause firms' profits and net worth to fall, and this makes them less willing to undertake the risks involved with investment

fiscal deficit: the gap between government expenditures and its revenues from sources other than additional borrowing

fiscal policies: policies that affect the level of government expenditures and taxes

fiscal stimulus: an attempt by the government to stimulate the economy (increase aggregate demand) through fiscal policy, that is, a reduction in taxes or an increase in expenditures

fixed costs: the costs resulting from fixed inputs, sometimes called **overhead costs**

fixed exchange rate system: an exchange rate system in which the value of each currency is fixed in relationship to other currencies

fixed or **overhead inputs:** (a) inputs that do not change depending on the quantity of output, (b) fixed inputs also sometimes refer to inputs that are fixed in the short run—that is, they do not depend on *current* output—but may depend on output in the long run

flexible or **floating exchange rate system:** a system in which exchange rates are determined by market forces, the law of supply and demand, without government interference

flows: variables such as the output of the economy *per year*; stocks are in contrast to flows; flows measure the changes in stocks over a given period of time

flow statistics: measurements of a certain rate or quantity per period of time, such as GDP, which measures output per year

four-firm concentration ratio: the fraction of output produced by the top four firms in an industry

fractional reserve system: the system of banking in which banks hold a fraction of the amount on deposit in reserves

free-market economists: economists who believe that free markets are the best way by which the economy can achieve economic efficiency; typically, they believe that the basic competitive model provides a good description of most markets most of the time

free reserves: see **excess reserves**

free-rider: someone who enjoys the benefit of a (public) good without paying for it; because it is difficult to preclude anyone from using a pure public good, those who benefit from the goods have an incentive to avoid paying for them, that is, to be a free rider

free trade: trade among countries which occurs freely, without barriers such as tariffs or quotas

frictional unemployment: unemployment arising from the "friction" associated with people moving from one job to another, or moving into the labor force

full-employment deficit: the budget deficit that would have prevailed if the economy were at full employment, thus with higher tax revenues and lower public assistance expenditures

full-employment level of output: the level of output that the economy can produce under normal circumstances with a given stock of plant and equipment and a given supply of labor

full-employment or **potential output:** the level of output that would prevail if labor were fully employed (output may exceed that level if workers work more than the normal level of overtime)

gains from trade: the benefit s that each side enjoys from a trade

GDP deflator: a weighted average of the prices of different goods and services, where the weights represent the importance of each of the goods and services in GDP

GDP per capita: the value of all goods and services produced in the economy divided by the population

General Agreement on Tariffs and Trade (GATT): the agreement among the major trading countries of the world that created the framework for lowering barriers to trade and resolving trade disputes; established after World War II, it has now been succeeded by the World Trade Organization (WTO)

general equilibrium: the full equilibrium of the economy, when all markets clear simultaneously

general equilibrium analysis: a simultaneous analysis of all capital, product, and labor markets throughout the economy; it shows, for instance, the impact on all prices and quantities of immigration or a change in taxes

gift and estate tax: a tax imposed on the transfers of wealth from one generation to another

Gini coefficient: a measure of inequality (equal to twice the area between the 45-degree line and the Lorenz curve)

green GDP: a measurement of national output which attempts to take into account effects on the environment and natural resources

greenmail: a practice in which takeover artists buy shares in a firm and threaten a takeover unless they are compensated by the firm repurchasing their shares at an inflated price

green revolution: the invention and dissemination of new seeds and agricultural practices that led to vast increases in agricultural output in less developed countries during the 1960s and 1970s

gross domestic product (GDP): the total money value of the goods and services produced by the residents of a nation during a specified period

gross national product (GNP): a measure of the incomes of residents of a country, including income they receive from abroad but subtracting similar payments made to those abroad

highly leveraged: a firm is highly leveraged if it has a high ratio of debt to equity; it has, through borrowing, "highly leveraged" its equity

horizontal equity: the principle that says that those who are in identical or similar circumstances should pay identical or similar amounts in taxes

horizontal integration: the integration of a firm with other firms producing the same product (at the same level of production)

horizontal merger: a merger between two firms that produce the same goods

horizontal restrictions: restrictions (such as an agreement not to compete in price or to enter each others' markets) by competing firms (at the same level of production, for instance, among producers, or among wholesalers, or among retailers)

hostile takeover: when one management team (one firm) takes over the control of another, against the will of the second firm

human capital: the stock of accumulated skills and experience that make workers more productive

imperfect competition: any market structure in which there is some competition but firms face downward-sloping demand curves

imperfect information: a situation in which market participants lack information (such as information about prices or characteristics of goods and services) important for their decision making

imperfect market economists: economists who see significant discrepancies between the basic competitive model and the conditions observed in market economies

imperfect markets: markets that do not satisfy the assumptions of the basic competitive model, such as when competition is less than perfect, information is less than complete, or when there are externalities or markets are missing

imperfect substitutes: goods that can substitute for each other, but imperfectly so

implicit contract: an unwritten understanding between two groups involved in an exchange, such as an understanding between employer and employees that employees will receive a stable wage throughout fluctuating economic conditions

import function: the relationship between imports and national income

imports: goods produced abroad but bought domestically

import substitution: the strategy that focuses on the substitution of domestic goods for goods that were previously imported

incentive-equality trade-off: in general, the greater the incentives, the greater the resulting inequality

income approach to measuring GDP: the approach to calculating GDP that involves measuring the income generated to all of the participants in the economy

income effect: the reduced consumption of a good whose price has increased that is due to the reduction in a person's buying power, or "real" income; when a person's real income is lower, normally she will consume less of all goods, including the higher-priced good

income elasticity of demand: the percentage change in quantity demanded of a good as the result of a 1 percent change in income (the percentage change in quantity demanded divided by the percentage change in income)

income-expenditure analysis: the analysis that determines equilibrium output by relating aggregate expenditures to income

income-tested transfer: transfers to particular groups of individuals (such as the aged) based on their income

incomplete markets: situations in which no market may exist for some good or for some risk, or in which some individuals cannot borrow for some purposes

increasing returns: a production function has increasing returns when increases in an input (keeping all other inputs fixed) increase output more than proportionately

increasing, constant, or diminishing returns to scale: when all inputs are increased by a certain proportion, output increases by a greater, equal, or smaller proportion, respectively; increasing returns to scale are also called **economies of scale**

indexed funds: mutual funds that simply buy a fixed portfolio of stocks, usually linked to a market index, such as Standard & Poor's 500 Index. An S & P 500 indexed fund buys shares in the S & P index (in the proportion that they are within the index), or attempts to emulate the behavior of the S & P 500 closely

indexing: the formal linking of any payment to a price index

indifference curves: indifference curves give the combinations of goods among which an individual feels for equally (that is, which yield the same level of utility)

individual income tax: a tax based on the income received by an individual or household

industrial policies: government policies designed to promote particular sectors of the economy

industry: the collection of firms making the same product is called an industry

inelastic: see relatively inelastic

infant industry argument for protection: the argument that industries must be protected from foreign competition while they are young, until they have a chance to acquire the skills to enable them to compete on equal terms

inferior good: a good the consumption of which falls as income rises

infinite elasticity of demand: the situation that exists when any amount will be demanded at a particular price, but nothing will be demanded if the price increases even a small amount

infinite elasticity of supply: the situation that exists when any amount will be supplied at a particular price, but nothing will be supplied if the price declines even a small amount

inflation: the rate of increase of the general level of prices

inflationary spiral: a self-perpetuating system in which price increases lead to higher wages, which lead to further price increases

inflation inertia: the tendency of inflation to persist

inflation tax: the decrease in buying power (wealth) that inflation imposes on those who hold currency (and other assets, like bonds, the payments for which are fixed in terms of dollars)

information-based differential: a wage differential that results from imperfect information, for instance, the fact that a worker does not know the wage being offered by other employers, and that it would be costly for him to search to find out

informative advertising: advertising designed to provide consumers with information about the price of a good, where it may be acquired, or what its characteristics are

infrastructure: the roads, ports, bridges, and legal system that provide the necessary basis for a working economy

inputs: the various material, labor, and other factors used in production

insider-outsider theory: the theory that firms are reluctant to pay new workers (outsiders) a lower wage than current workers (insiders), because current workers will fear being replaced by the new, low-wage workers and will not participate in cooperating with and training them

inside traders: individuals who buy and sell shares of companies for which they work, making use of the inside information that they are thereby able to glean

intellectual property: proprietary knowledge, such as that protected by patents and copyright

interest: the return a saver receives in addition to the original amount she deposited (loaned), and the amount a borrower must pay in addition to the original amount he borrowed

interest elasticity of savings: the percentage increase in savings resulting from a one percent change in the interest rate

interest rate effect: the situation that exists when lower interest rates (resulting from an increase in the money supply or a fall in the price level) induce firms to invest more

intertemporal trades: trades that occur *between* two periods of time

investment: from the national perspective, an increase in the stock of capital goods or any other expenditure designed to increase future output; from the perspective of the individual, any expenditure designed to increase an individual's future wealth, such as the purchase of a share in a company. (Since some other individual is likely selling the share, that person is disinvesting, and the net investment for the economy is zero.)

investment function: the relationship between the level of real investment and the value of the real interest rate; also called the *investment schedule*

investment schedule: the relationship between the level of investment and the (real) rate of interest

investment tax credit (ITC): a provision of the tax code in which the government reduces a company's tax bill by an amount equal to a percentage of its spending on investment

investors: those who supply capital to the capital market (including individuals who buy shares of stock in a firm or lend money to a business)

involuntary unemployment: the situation that occurs when the supply of those willing to work at the going market wage exceeds the demand for labor

isocost: different combinations of inputs that cost the same

isoquants: different combinations of inputs that produce the same quantity of output

job discrimination: discrimination in which disadvantaged groups have less access to better paying jobs

joint products: products that are naturally produced together, such as wool and mutton

junk bonds: bonds which are especially risky, that is, have a high probability of default

Keynesian monetary theory: see **traditional monetary theory**

Keynesian unemployment: unemployment that occurs as a result of insufficient aggregate demand; it arises in the demand-constrained equilibrium (where aggregate demand is less than aggregate supply), so that rightward shifts in aggregate demand reduce the level of unemployment

kinked demand curve: the demand curve perceived by an oligopolist who believes that rivals will match any price cuts but will not match price increases

labor force participation decision: the decision by an individual to actively seek work, that is, to participate in the labor market

labor force participation rate: the fraction of the working-age population that is employed or seeking employment

labor hoarding: a situation where (in an economic downturn) firms keep workers on the job, though they do not fully utilize them

labor market: the market in which labor services are bought and sold

labor turnover rate: the rate at which workers leave jobs

lags: the difference in time between two events, such as between the time the government recognizes a problem and takes action, and between the time the action occurs and its macroeconomic effects are fully realized

land reform: the redistribution of land by the government to those who actually work the land

law of supply and demand: the law in economics that holds that *in equilibrium* prices are determined so that demand equals supply. Changes in prices thus reflect shifts in the demand or supply curves

leakages: income generated in one round of production that is not used to buy more goods produced within the country

learning by doing: the increase in productivity that occurs as a firm gains experience from producing, and that results in a decrease in the firm's production costs

learning curve: the curve describing how costs of production decline as cumulative output increases over time

legal entitlement: a right (or entitlement) granted by law; for instance, rent control laws may grant current occupants the right to continue to occupy an apartment for life at a pre-specified rent

less developed countries (LDCs): the poorest nations of the world, including much of Africa, Latin America, and Asia

liabilities: what a firm owes to others

life-cycle savings: savings that is motivated by a desire to smooth consumption over an individual's lifetime and to meet special needs that arise in various times of life; saving for retirement is the most important aspect of life-cycle savings

life-cycle savings motive: people save during their working lives so that they can consume more during retirement

life-cycle theory of savings: the theory of savings which emphasizes the importance of life-cycle savings, and that savings will differ in different parts of an individual's life cycle

limited liability: corporations have limited liability; with limited liability, the amount an investor in a corporation can lose is limited to the amount that he has invested in the firm

limit pricing: the practice of charging a lower price than the level at which marginal revenue equals marginal cost, as a way of deterring entry by persuading potential competitors that their profits from entering are likely to be limited

linear demand curve: a demand curve that is a straight line, that is, in which demand is a linear function of price

line item veto: the right of the president (or a governor) to veto a particular item (line) within a bill, without vetoing the entire bill

lines of credit: an agreement by a bank to lend a business automatically (up to some limit), as it is needed

liquidity: the ease with which an asset can be sold

local public goods: public goods that benefit only residents of a particular local area

long-run aggregate supply curve: the aggregate supply curve that applies in the long run, when wages and prices can adjust fully to ensure full employment

long-term bonds: bonds with a maturity of more than ten years

Lorenz curve: a curve that shows the cumulative proportion of income that goes to each cumulative proportion of the population, starting with the lowest income group

lottery: a process, such as picking a name from a hat, through which goods are allocated randomly

Luddites: early nineteenth-century workmen who destroyed labor-savings machinery rather than see it take over their jobs

luxury tax: an excise tax imposed on luxuries, goods typically consumed disproportionately by the wealthy

M1, M2, M3: measures of the money supply: M1 includes currency and checking accounts; M2 includes M1 plus savings deposits, CDs, and money market funds; M3 includes M2 plus large-denomination savings deposits and institutional money-market mutual funds

macroeconomics: the top-down view of the economy, focusing on aggregate characteristics

managed care: a health care system in which the health care provider, in return for a fixed fee per year, manages the care of the individual, including decisions about whether a specialist is required

managerial slack: the lack of managerial efficiency (for instance, in cutting costs) that occurs when firms are insulated from competition

marginal benefit: the extra benefits resulting, for instance, from the increased consumption of a commodity

marginal cost: the additional cost corresponding to an additional unit of output produced

marginal costs and benefits: the extra costs and benefits that result from choosing a little bit more of one thing

marginal product: the amount output increases with the addition of one unit of an input

marginal propensity to consume: the amount by which consumption increases when disposable income increases by a dollar

marginal propensity to import: the amount by which imports increase when disposable income increases by a dollar

marginal propensity to save: the amount by which savings increase when disposable income increases by a dollar

marginal rate of substitution: the slope of an indifference curve; the marginal rate of substitution tells how much of one good an individual is willing to give up in return for one more unit of another

marginal rate of technical substitution: the slope of an isoquant; the marginal rate of technical substitution tells how much of one input a firm can give up in return for one more unit of another, and still leave output unchanged

marginal rate of transformation: the slope of the production possibilities schedule; the extra output of one commodity resulting from a decrease in output of another commodity in an economy in which all resources are fully and efficiently used

marginal revenue: the extra revenue received by a firm for selling one additional unit of a good

marginal tax rate: the rate of tax at the margin; the extra tax that will have to be paid as a result of an additional dollar of income

marginal utility: the extra utility, or enjoyment, a person receives from the consumption of one additional unit of a good

marketable permits: a permit issued by the government which can be bought and sold that allows a firm to emit a certain amount of pollution

market clearing: the situation that exists when supply equals demand, so there is neither excess supply nor excess demand

market demand: the total amount of a particular good or service demanded in the economy

market demand curve: the total amount of a particular good or service demanded in the economy at each price; it is calculated by "adding horizontally" the individual demand curves, that is, at any given price, it is the sum of the individual demands

market economy: an economy that allocates resources primarily through the interaction of individuals (households) and private firms

market failure: the situation in which a market economy fails to attain economic efficiency

market failures approach: the argument that government may have an economic role to play when markets fail to produce efficient outcomes

market for risk: the market (the institutions and arrangements) in which risks are transferred (exchanged), transformed, and shared

market labor supply curve: the relationship between the wage paid and the amount of labor willingly supplied, found by adding up the labor supply curves of all the individuals in the economy

marketplace: the place where, in traditional societies, goods were bought and sold. In today's economy, only in the case of a few goods and services is there a well-defined marketplace

market power: a firm is said to have market power if it can significantly affect price through its actions (such as sales)

market risks: risks that arise from variations in market conditions, such as changes in prices or demand for a firm's product

markets: places where goods or services (including labor) are bought, sold, and traded. The term is used today metaphorically; there is no single marketplace where any particular good is bought and sold; the collection of all the places where exchanges take place is thought of as "the market." See also **capital market**

market structure: term used to describe the organization of the market, such as whether there is a high degree of competition, a monopoly, an oligopoly, or monopolistic competition

market supply: the total amount of a particular good or service that all the firms in the economy supply

market supply curve: the total amount of a particular good or service that all the firms in the economy together would like to supply at each price; it is calculated by "adding horizontally" the individual firm's supply curves, that is, it is the sum of the amounts each firm is willing to supply at any given price

market surplus: there is a market surplus (or surplus) if at the going price, the amount firms are willing to produce exceeds the amount households demand

maturity: the length of time before a loan or bond is due to be paid in full; a bond with a maturity of ten years will be paid off in full in ten years

median voter: the voter such that half the population have preferences on one side of this voter (for instance, they want higher government expenditures and taxes), while the other half of the population have preferences on the other side of this voter (they want lower taxes and expenditures)

medium of exchange: an item that can be commonly exchanged for goods and services throughout the economy

menu costs: the costs to firms of changing their prices

merit goods and bads: goods that are determined by government to be good or bad for people, regardless of whether people desire them for themselves or not

microeconomics: the bottom-up view of the economy, focusing on individual households and firms

middle-class entitlement program: programs that provide benefits automatically to individuals meeting certain criteria (such as age), irrespective of their income, most of the benefits of which accrue to middle-class individuals

missing market: when there is a good or service which individuals would like to purchase (at a price at which that good could be profitably produced) but which is not available in the market, the market for that good or service is said to be missing. More generally, when there is no market in which a good or service can be bought or sold, the market is said to be missing

mixed economy: an economy that allocates resources through a mixture of public (governmental) and private decision making

model: a set of assumptions and data used by economists to study an aspect of the economy and make predictions about the future or about the consequences of various policy changes

Modigliani-Miller theorem: the theorem that says that under a simplified set of conditions, the manner in which a firm finances itself does not matter

monetarists: economists who emphasize the importance of money in the economy; they tend to believe that an appropriate monetary policy is all the economy needs from government, and market forces will otherwise solve any macroeconomic problems

monetary aggregates: the statistics which describe the various measures of the money supply (M_1, M_2, and so forth)

monetary policies: policies that affect the supply of money and credit and the terms on which credit is available to borrowers

money: any item that serves as a medium of exchange, a store of value, and a unit of account

money multiplier: the amount by which a new deposit into the banking system (from the outside) is multiplied as it is loaned out, redeposited, reloaned, etc., by banks

monopolist: the single firm in a monopoly, that is, in an industry in which there is a single firm

monopolistic competition: the form of imperfect competition in which the market has sufficiently few firms that each one faces a downward-sloping demand curve, but enough that each can ignore the reactions of rivals to what it does

monopoly: a market consisting of only one firm

monopoly rents: the profits that accrue to a monopolist (as a result of its reducing its output from the competitive level to the monopoly level)

monopsonist: the single buyer of a good or service

moral hazard: the principle that says that those who

purchase insurance have a reduced incentive to avoid what they are insured against

multilateral trade: trade between more than two parties

multiplier: the factor by which a change in a component of aggregate demand, like investment or government spending, is multiplied to lead to a larger change in equilibrium national output

multiplier-accelerator model: a model that relates business cycles to the internal working of the economy, showing how changes in investment and output reinforce each other; the central ingredients of the model are the multiplier and the accelerator

mutual fund: a fund that gathers money from different investors and purchases a range of assets; each investor then owns a portion of the entire fund

myopic expectations: expectations are myopic when they are "short sighted," for instance, simply assuming that today's prices will continue into the future

nationalization: the process whereby a private industry is taken over by the government, whether by buying it or simply seizing it

natural endowments: a country's natural resources, such as good climate, fertile land, or minerals

natural monopoly: a monopoly that exists because average costs of production are declining beyond the level of output demanded in the market, thus making entry unprofitable and making it efficient for there to be a single firm

natural rate of unemployment: the rate of unemployment at which the rate of inflation is zero

negative public savings: a fiscal deficit, where expenditures exceeds revenues

negative sloped curve: a curve in which as the variable measured along the horizontal axis is increased, the variable measured along the vertical axis decreases

net capital inflows: total capital inflows minus total capital outflows

net domestic product (NDP): GDP minus the value of the depreciation of the country's capital goods

net export function: a curve that gives the level of net exports at each level of income

net exports: total exports minus total imports

neutrality of money: a situation where an increase in the money supply simply increases prices proportionately, and has no real effects on the economy

new classical economists: economists who, beginning in the 1970s, built on the tradition of classical economists and believed that by and large, market forces; if left to themselves, would solve the problems of unemployment and recessions

new growth economists: economists who, beginning in the 1980s, sought to understand better the basic forces that led the economy to grow fast at one time and slower at another, or some countries to grow faster than others

new Keynesian economists: economists who, beginning in the 1980s, built on the tradition of Keynesian economists and focused attention on unemployment; they sought explanations for the failure of wages and prices to adjust to make labor markets and possibly other markets clear

newly industrialized countries (NICs): nations that have recently moved from being quite poor to being middle-income countries, including South Korea, Taiwan, Singapore, and Hong Kong

nominal GDP: the value of gross domestic product in a particular year measured in that year's prices

nominal interest rate: the percentage return on a deposit, loan, or bond; the nominal interest rate does not take into account the effects of inflation

nonaccelerating inflation rate of unemployment (NAIRU): the level of unemployment at which actual (realized) inflation equals inflationary expectations; below this rate of unemployment, the rate of inflation increases; above it, it decreases

nondiscretionary: expenditures that are determined automatically, such as interest payments and expenditures on entitlements

nonexcludability: it costs a great deal to exclude any individual from enjoying the benefits of a pure public good; in the extreme, it may be impossible to exclude

nonpecuniary: aspects of a job other than the wage it pays

nonrivalrous: the property possessed by pure public goods that the consumption or enjoyment of the good by one individual does not subtract from that of other individuals

nontariff barriers: barriers to trade that take forms

other than tariffs (such as regulations which disadvantage foreign firms)

normal good: a good the consumption of which rises as income rises

normative economics: economics in which judgments about the desirability of various policies are made; the conclusions rest on value judgments as well as facts and theories

North American Free Trade Agreement (NAFTA): the agreement between Canada, the United States, and Mexico that lowered trade and other barriers among the countries

Okun's law: the observation that as the economy pulls out of a recession, output increases more than proportionately to increases in employment

oligopoly: the form of imperfect competition in which the market has several firms, sufficiently few that each one must take into account the reactions of rivals to what it does

open economy: an economy that is actively engaged in international trade

open market operations: central banks' purchase or sale of government bonds in the open market

opportunity cost: the cost of a resource, measured by the value of the next-best, alternative use of that resource

opportunity sets: a summary of the choices available to individuals, as defined by budget constraints and time constraints

output per capita: a nation's output divided by the number of individuals in the country

outputs: the outcomes of a production process

overhead costs: the costs a firm must pay just to remain in operation. They do not depend on the scale of production

Pareto efficient: a resource allocation is said to be Pareto efficient if there is no rearrangement that can make anyone better off without making someone else worse off

partial equilibrium analysis: an analysis that focuses on only one or a few markets at a time

partnership: a business owned by two or more individuals, who share the profits and are jointly liable for any losses

patent: a government decree giving an inventor the exclusive right to produce, use, or sell an invention for a period of time

paternalism: the making of judgments by government about what is good for people to have, rather than letting people choose on their own

payroll tax: a tax based on payroll (wages) that is used to finance the Social Security and Medicare programs

peak: the top of a boom

perfect competition: a situation in which each firm is a price taker—it cannot influence the market price; at the market price, the firm can sell as much as it wishes, but if it raises its price, it loses all sales

perfect information: a state in which market participants have full information about the goods being bought and sold (including the prices at which they are available at every location and all of the relevant characteristics)

perfectly elastic: infinite elasticity; a demand or supply curve is perfectly elastic if it is horizontal

perfectly inelastic: zero elasticity; a demand or supply curve is perfectly inelastic if it is vertical, so the demand or supply is completely insensitive to price

perfectly mobile capital: capital that responds quickly to changes in returns in different countries

permanent home hypothesis: the theory that individuals base their current consumption levels on their permanent (long-run average) income

permanent-income savings motive: people save in good years to tide them over in bad years; they choose their pattern of saving and spending year by year to average, or smooth, their consumption over good years and bad

persuasive advertising: advertising designed to make consumers feel good about the products that are being sold and more inclined to purchase them; it does not inform them about price or any characteristic of the product

Phillips curve: the trade-off between unemployment and inflation such that a lower level of unemployment is associated with a higher level of inflation

physical capital: investments in plant and equipment; the term is used to distinguish these investments from investments in people, called human capital

piece-rate system: a compensation system in which

workers are paid specifically for each item produced

planned economy: economies in which the government takes central responsibility for economic decision making, including developing plans for economic growth

planned and unplanned inventories: planned inventories are those firms choose to have on hand because they make business more efficient; unplanned inventories result when firms cannot sell what they produce

policy ineffectiveness proposition: the proposition that government policies are ineffective—policies aimed at stimulating aggregate demand at most change the price level

portfolio: an investor's entire collection of assets and liabilities

portfolio theories of monetary policy: theories that argue that monetary policy affects output through its effect on prices of various assets, in particular the prices of stocks

positive economics: economics that describes how the economy behaves and predicts how it might change—for instance, in response to some policy change

positively sloped curve: a curve in which as the variable measured along the horizontal axis is increased, the variable measured along the vertical axis increases

potential competition: competitive pressures that arise from the potential of firms to enter a market

potential GDP: a measure of what the value of GDP would be if the economy's resources were fully employed

precautionary savings motive: people save so that they will be able to meet the costs of an unexpected illness, accident, or other emergency

predatory pricing: the practice of cutting prices below the marginal cost of production to drive out a new firm (or to deter future entry), at which point prices can be raised again

premium: assets that sell at a price above that which might be expected, given their expected returns, are said to sell at a premium; the term is also used to refer more specifically to the higher price that an asset might sell at, above that which might be expected, given its observable attributes

present discounted value: how much an amount of money to be received in the future is worth right now

price: the price of a good or service is what must be given in exchange for the good

price ceiling: a maximum price above which market prices are not legally allowed to rise

price discrimination: the practice of a firm charging different prices to different customers or in different markets

price dispersion: a situation that occurs when the same item is sold for different prices by different firms

price elasticity of demand: the percentage change in quantity demanded of a good as the result of a 1 percent change in price (the percentage change in quantity demanded divided by the percentage change in price)

price elasticity of supply: the percentage change in quantity supplied of a good as the result of a 1 percent change in price (the percentage change in quantity supplied divided by the percentage change in price)

price floor: a minimum price below which market prices are not legally allowed to fall

price index: a measure of the level of prices found by comparing the cost of a certain basket of goods in one year with the cost in a base year

price leader: in some oligopolies, a particular firm, called the price leader, sets the price, with other firms quickly following suit

price level: some measure of the average prices in the economy; when analyzing the product market as a whole, the equilibrium *price level* is given by the intersection of the aggregate demand curve and the aggregate supply curve

price makers: firms that affect, or make, the price as a result of their actions, especially as a consequence of their level of production

price system: the economic system in which prices are used to allocate scarce resources

price takers: firms that take the price for the good or service they sell as given; the price is unaffected by their level of production

principal: the original amount a saver deposits in a bank (lends) or a borrower borrows

principal-agent problem: any situation in which one party (the principal) needs to delegate actions to another party (the agent), and thus wishes to provide the agent with incentives to work hard and make decisions about risk that reflect the interests of the principal

principle of consumer sovereignty: the principle that holds that each individual is the best judge of what makes him better off

principle of substitution: the principle that holds that in general there are large possibilities for substitution, both by consumers and by firms, so that an increase in the price of say an input will lead the firm to substitute other inputs in its place

Prisoner's Dilemma: a situation in which the noncooperative pursuit of self-interest by two parties makes them both worse off

private marginal cost: the marginal cost of production borne by the producer of a good; when there is a negative externality, such as air pollution, private marginal cost is less than social marginal cost

private property: ownership of property (or other assets) by individuals or corporations; under a system of private property, owners have certain property rights, but there may also be legal restrictions on the use of property

privatization: the process whereby functions that were formerly undertaken by government are delegated instead to the private sector

producer price index: a price index that measures the average level of producers' prices

product differentiation: the fact that similar products (like breakfast cereals or soft drinks) are perceived to differ from one another and thus are imperfect substitutes

production efficiency: the condition in which firms cannot produce more of some goods without producing less of other goods; the economy is on its production possibilities curve

production-facilitating function of inventories: the role of inventories in facilitating production, for instance, by avoiding costly stoppage of production as a result of an interruption of supplies

production function: the relationship between the inputs used in production and the level of output

production possibilities: the combination of outputs of different goods that an economy can produce with given resources

production possibilities curve: a curve that defines the opportunity set for a firm or an entire economy and gives the possible combinations of goods (outputs) that can be produced from a given level of inputs

production-smoothing function of inventories: the role of inventories in allowing production to continue at a steady level, in the face of fluctuations in demand

productivity, or GDP per hour worked: how much an average worker produces per hour, calculated by dividing real GDP by hours worked in the economy

productivity wage differential: wage differentials among individuals arising from differences in productivity

product liability: the obligation of a producer to compensate victims of a defective product that has injured them

product market: the market in which goods and services are bought and sold

product-mix efficiency: the condition in which the mix of goods produced by the economy reflects the preferences of consumers

profits: total revenues minus total costs

progressive tax: a tax in which the rich pay a larger fraction of their income than the poor

property rights: the rights of an owner of private property; these typically include the right to use the property as she sees fit (subject to certain restrictions, such as zoning) and the right to sell it when and to whom she sees fit

property tax: a tax based on the value of property

proprietorship: a business owned by a single person, usually a small business

protectionism: the policy of protecting domestic industries from the competition of foreign-made goods

public good: a good, such as national defense, that costs little or nothing for an extra individual to enjoy, and the costs of preventing any individual from the enjoyment of which are high; public goods have the properties of nonrivalrous consumption and nonexcludability

pure profit or **monopoly rents:** the profit earned by a monopolist that results from its reducing output and increasing the price from the level at which price equals marginal cost

pure public good: a good which possesses the property of nonexcludability (in which it is *impossible* to exclude any individual from enjoying the benefits of the good) and nonrivalrousness (the consumption or enjoyment of the good by one individual does not subtract at all from that of other individuals)

quantity theory of money: the theory that velocity is constant, so that changes in the money supply lead to proportionale changes in nominal income (which also equals the value of output)

quota rents: profits that accrue to firms which are allocated the rights to import a good subject to quotas that result from the artificially created scarcity

quotas: limits on the amount of foreign goods that can be imported

random walk: a term used to describe the way the prices of stocks move; the next movement cannot be predicted on the basis of previous movements

rational choice: a choice process in which individuals weigh the costs and benefits of each possibility, and in which the choices made are those within the opportunity set that maximize net benefits

rational expectations: expectations are rational when people make full use of all relevant available past data in their formation of expectations

rationed goods: when individuals get less of a good than they would like at the terms being offered, the good is said to be rationed

rationing by queues: allocating scarce resources on the basis of who is most willing and able to wait in line the longest

rationing system: any system of allocating scarce resources, applied particularly to systems other than the price system. Rationing systems include rationing by coupons and rationing by queues

reaction function: in the analysis of oligopolies, the reaction function gives the level of output of one firm, given the level of output of other firms (in Cournot competition) or the level of price of one firm, given the prices of other firms (in Bertrand competition)

real balance effect: as prices fall, the real value of people's money holdings increases, and they consume more

real business-cycle theorists: a school of economists who contend that the economy's fluctuations have nothing to do with monetary policy but are determined by real forces

real exchange rates: exchange rate adjusted for changes in the relative price levels in different countries

real GDP: the real value of all final goods and services produced in the economy, measured in dollars adjusted for inflation

real income: income measured by what it can actually buy, rather than by the amount of money

real interest rate: the real return to saving, equal to the nominal interest rate minus the rate of inflation

real product wage: the wage divided by the price of the good being produced

real wage: the nominal wage divided by the (consumer) price level

recession: two consecutive quarters of a year during which GDP falls

regressive tax: a tax in which the poor pay a larger fraction of their income than the rich

regulatory capture: a term used to describe a situation in which regulators serve the interests of the regulated rather than the interests of consumers

relatively elastic: a good is said to be relatively elastic when the price elasticity of its demand is greater than unity

relatively inelastic: a good is said to be relatively inelastic when the price elasticity of its demand is less than unity

relative performance compensation: pay based on performance on the job relative to others who have similar responsibilities and authority

relative price: the ratio of any two prices; the relative price of apples and oranges is just the ratio of their prices

rent: see **economic rent**

rent control: limitations on the level or rate of increase of rents which landlords can charge

rent seeking: the name given to behavior that seeks to obtain benefits from favorable government decisions, such as protection from foreign competition

reputation: the "good will" of a firm resulting from its past performance; maintaining one's reputation provides an incentive to maintain quality

resale price maintenance: a restrictive practice in which a producer insists that any retailer selling his product sell it at the "list price"

reservation wage: the wage below which an individual chooses not to participate in the labor market

reserve: money kept on hand by a bank in the event that those who have made deposits wish to withdraw their money

reserve requirements: the minimum level of reserves that the central bank requires be kept on hand or deposited with the central bank

residual: that part of the growth of the economy that cannot be explained by increases in inputs

restrictive practices: practices of oligopolists designed to restrict competition, including vertical restrictions like exclusive territories

retained earnings: that part of the net earnings of the firm that are not paid out to shareholders, but retained by the firm

revenue curve: the relationship between a firm's total output and its revenues

revenues: the amount a firm receives for selling its products, equal to the price received multiplied by the quantity sold

right-to-work laws: laws that prevent union membership from being a condition of employment

rigid prices: prices that do not adjust when demand differs from supply

risk averse, risk loving, risk neutral: given equal expected returns and different risks, risk-averse people will choose assets with lower risk, risk-loving people will choose assets with higher risk, and risk-neutral individuals will not care about differences in risk

risk premium: the additional interest required by lenders as compensation for the risk that a borrower may default; more generally, the extra return required to compensate an investor for bearing risk

sacrifice ratio: the amount by which the unemployment rate must be kept above the NAIRU for one year to bring down inflation by 1 percentage point

sales tax: a tax imposed on the purchase of goods and services

scarcity: term used to describe the limited availability of resources, so that if no price were charged for a good or service, the demand for it would exceed its supply

screening: the process of differentiating among job candidates, when there is incomplete information, to determine who will be the most productive

search: the process by which consumers gather information about what is available in the market, including prices, or by which workers gather information about the jobs that are available, including wages

seasonal unemployment: unemployment that varies with the seasons, such as that associated with the decline in construction in winter

shadow price: the true social value of a resource

sharecropping: an arrangement, prevalent in many less-developed countries, in which a worker works land, giving the landowner a fixed share of the output

shortage: a situation in which demand exceeds supply at the current price

short-run aggregate supply curve: the relationship between aggregate supply (what firms are willing to produce) and the price level that prevails in the short run; in particular, it is not assumed that wages adjust fully to ensure full employment (see long-run aggregate supply curve)

short-run production function: the relationship between output and employment in the short run, that is, with a given set of machines and buildings

short-term bonds: bonds that mature within a few years

signaling: conveying information, for example a prospective worker's earning a college degree to persuade an employer that he has desirable characteristics that will enhance his productivity

simple interest: a savings account pays simple (rather than compound) interest when interest is paid only against the original principal (deposit)

sin tax: an excise tax on alcohol and tobacco

slope: the amount by which the value along the vertical axis increases as the result of a change in one unit along the horizontal axis; the slope is calculated by dividing the change in the vertical axis (the "rise") by the change in horizontal axis (the "run")

Smith's "invisible hand": the idea that if people act in their own self-interest, they will often also be acting in a broader social interest, as if they had been directed by an "invisible hand"

smoothing consumption: consuming similar amounts in the present and future, rather than letting year-to-year income dictate consumption

social benefit: the benefits which accrue to society as a whole; the social benefit of an innovation includes not only the profits of the innovator, but the benefits that accrue to others, either as a result of the knowledge produced in the innovative process or because the new product is available at a price below that which the individual would be willing to pay

social insurance: insurance provided by the government to individuals, for instance, against disabilities, unemployment, or health problems (for the aged)

socialism: an economic system in which the means of production are controlled by the state

social marginal cost: the marginal cost of production, including the cost of any negative externality, such as air pollution, borne by individuals in the economy other than the producer

social science: a branch of science which studies human social behavior; the social sciences include economics, political science, anthropology, sociology, and psychology

soft budget constraints: budget constraints facing public enterprises, which can always turn to government for assistance in the event of a loss

stagflation: a situation in which high inflation is combined with low growth and high unemployment

static efficiency: the efficiency of the economy with given technology; taxes used to finance basic research and monopoly power resulting from patents result in a loss in static efficiency

static expectations: the belief of individuals that today's prices and wages are likely to continue into the future

statistical discrimination: differential treatment of individuals of different gender or race that is based on the use of observed correlations (statistics) between performance and some observable characteristics; it may even *result* from the use of variables like education in which there is a *causal* link to performance

sticky prices: prices that do not adjust or adjust only slowly toward a new equilibrium

sticky wages: wages that are slow to adjust in response to a change in labor market conditions

stock option: an option to buy a share of a stock at a particular price (usually within a particular period of time); if the value of the share increases (above that price), the value of the option increases; stock options are often used to reward corporate executives

stocks: variables like the capital stock or the money supply stock, that describe the state of the economy (such as its wealth) at a point of time; they are contrasted by flows

stock statistics: measurements of the quantity of a certain item at a certain point in time, such as capital stock, the total value of buildings and machines

store of value: something that can be accepted as payment in the present and exchanged for items of value in the future

strategic trade theory: the theory that holds that protection can give a country a strategic advantage over rivals, for instance by helping reduce domestic costs as a result of economies of scale

strike: the collective withdrawal of labor (usually organized by a union)

structural unemployment: long-term unemployment that results from structural factors in the economy, such as a mismatch between the skills required by newly created jobs and the skills possessed by those who have lost their jobs in declining industries

substitute: two goods are substitutes if the demand for one increases when the price of the other increases

substitution effect: the reduced consumption of a good whose price has increased that is due to the changed trade-off, the fact that one has to give up more of other goods to get one more unit of the high-priced good; the substitution effect is associated with a change in the slope of the budget constraint

sunk cost: a cost that has been incurred and cannot be recovered

supply-constrained equilibrium: the equilibrium that occurs when prices are stuck at a level below that at which aggregate demand equals aggregate supply; in a supply-constrained equilibrium, output is equal to aggregate supply but less than aggregate demand

supply curve: the relationship between the quantity supplied of a good and the price, whether for a single firm or the market (all firms) as a whole

supply shocks: unexpected shifts in the aggregate supply curve, such as an increase in the international price of oil or a major earthquake that destroys a substantial fraction of a country's capital stock

supply siders: economists who emphasize the importance of aggregate supply, in particular the responsiveness of supply to lower taxes and regulations; some argue that lowering tax rates leads to such large increases in inputs of capital and labor that total tax revenues may actually increase

surges: unexpected large increases in imports

surplus: the magnitude of the gain from trade, the difference between what an individual would have been willing to pay for a good and what she has to pay. See also **market surplus**

surplus labor: a great deal of unemployed or underemployed labor, readily available to potential employers

sustainable development: development that is based on sustainable principles; sustainable development pays particular concern to environmental degradation and the exploitation of natural resources

tacit collusion: collusive behavior among the firms of an oligpoly based on an implicit understanding that it is in each firm's best interest not to compete too vigourously; they tacitly understand that it is undesirable to undercut each others' prices, but there is no open discussion about price fixing

takeover: when one management team (one firm) takes over the control of another

target savings motive: people save for a particular target, for example to make a down payment on a house or to pay college tuition

tax expenditures: the revenue lost from a tax subsidy

tax-favored assets: the return on these assets receives favorable tax treatment, such as tax-exempt municipal bonds

tax subsidies: subsidies provided through the tax system to particular industries or to particular expenditures, in the form of favorable tax treatment

technological risks: risks facing a firm associated with technology, such as whether a new technology will work or be reliable

theorem: a logical proposition that follows from basic definitions and assumptions

theory: a set of assumptions and the conclusions derived from those assumptions put forward as an explanation for some phenomena

thin markets: markets with relatively few buyers and sellers

tie-ins: a restrictive practice in which a customer who buys one product must buy another

time constraints: the limitations on consumption of different goods imposed by the fact that households have only a limited amount of time to spend (twenty-four hours a day). The time constraint defines the opportunity set of individuals if the only constraint that they face is time

time value of money: the fact that a dollar today is worth more than a dollar in the future is called the time value of money

total costs: the sum of all fixed costs and variable costs

total factor productivity analysis: the analysis of the relationship between output and the aggregate of all inputs; total factor productivity growth is calculated as the difference between the rate of growth of output and the weighted average rate of growth of inputs, where the weight associated with each input is its share in GDP

trade creation: new trade that is generated as a result of lowered tariff barriers

trade deficit: the excess of imports over exports

trade diversion: trade that is diverted away from outside countries as a result of lowering tariffs between the members of a trading bloc

trade-offs: the amount of one good (or one desirable objective) that must be given up to get more of another good (or to attain more of another desirable objective)

trade secret: an innovation or knowledge of a production process that a firm does not disclose to others

trading blocs: groups of countries that agree to lower trade and other economic barriers among themselves

traditional monetary theory: the theory (first developed by John Maynard Keynes, and therefore sometimes referred to as Keynesian monetary theory) that the nominal interest rate is the opportunity cost of holding money, that the demand for money decreases as the interest rate rises, and that the interest rate is determined to equate the demand and supply of money

transactions costs: the extra costs (beyond the price of the purchase) of conducting a transaction, whether those costs are money, time, or inconvenience

transactions demand for money: the demand for money arising from its use in buying goods and services

transfer programs: programs directly concerned with redistribution, such as AFDC and Medicaid, that move money from one group in society to another

transplants: plants constructed in one country by firms based in another. U.S. factories producing Mazdas and Toyotas are Japanese transplants

Treasury bills (T-bills): bills the government sells in return for a promise to pay a certain amount in a short period, usually less than 180 days

trough: the bottom of a recession

trusts: organizations that attempted to control certain markets in the late nineteenth century; they were designed to allow an individual or group owning a small fraction of the total industry to exercise control

two-tier wage system: wage systems in which newly hired workers are paid lower wages than established workers are paid

unemployment rate: the fraction of the labor force (those unemployed *plus* those seeking jobs) who are seeking jobs but are unable to find them

union shops: unionized firms in which all workers are required to join the union as a condition of employment

unitary price elasticity: a demand curve has unitary price elasticity if the demand for the commodity decreases by one percent when the price increases by one percent. If demand has unitary elasticity, then expenditures on the good do not depend at all on price. A supply curve has unitary price elasticity if the supply of the commodity increases by one percent when the price increases by one percent

unit of account: something that provides a way of measuring and comparing the relative values of different goods

utility: the level of enjoyment an individual attains from choosing a certain combination of goods

utility possibilities curve: a curve showing the maximum level of utility that one individual can attain, given the level of utility attained by others

value-added: the value added in each stage of production is the difference between the value of the output and the value of the inputs purchased from other firms

value-added approach to measuring national output: in the value added approach to measuring national output, the value-added of each of the firms in the economy are added up

value of the marginal product of labor: the value of the extra output produced by an extra unit of labor; it is calculated by multiplying the marginal product of labor times the price of the good which is being produced

variable: anything that can be measured and that changes; examples of variables are prices, wages, interest rates, quantities bought and sold

variable costs: the costs resulting from variable inputs

variable inputs: inputs that rise and fall with the quantity of output

velocity: the speed with which money circulates in the economy, defined as the ratio of income to the money supply

vertical equity: the principle that says that people who are better off should pay more taxes

vertical integration: the integration of a firm with its supplier or customer

vertical merger: a merger between two firms, one of which is a supplier or distributor for the other

vertical restrictions: restrictions imposed by a producer on wholesalers and retailers who distribute its products; more generally, restrictions imposed by a firm on those to whom it sells its products

voluntary export restraints (VERs): restraints on exports that are "voluntarily" imposed by an exporting country, though often in response to a threat that if such constraints are not imposed, the importing country will impose import quotas

voluntary unemployment: a situation in which workers voluntarily drop out of the labor force when the wage level falls

voting paradox: the fact that under some circumstances there may be no determinate outcome with majority voting: choice A wins a majority over B, B wins over C, and C wins over A

wage discrimination: paying lower wages to women or minorities

wage-productivity curve: the curve that depicts the relationship between wages and productivity

wholesale price index: a price index that measures the average level of wholesale prices

work sharing: reducing all employees' hours by equal amounts rather than firing some workers

World Trade Organization (WTO): the organization established in 1995, as a result of the Uruguay round of trade negotiations, replacing GATT, designed to remove trade barriers and settle trade disputes

zero elasticity: a demand (or supply) curve has zero elasticity if the quantity demanded (or supplied) does not change at all if price changes; the demand (supply) curve is vertical

CREDITS

INDEX